W9-CBD-603

Court—Martial Procedure

Third Edition

Francis A. Gilligan

Office of the Prosecution
Office of Military Commission

Frederic I. Lederer

Chancellor Professor of Law & Director
Center for Legal and Court Technology
William & Mary Law School

Volume 2

 LexisNexis

QUESTIONS ABOUT THIS PUBLICATION?

For questions about the **Editorial Content** appearing in these volumes or reprint permission, please call:

Mark S. Peplowski at .... 1-800-424-4200 ext. 3667
Outside the United States and Canada please call .... (973) 820-2000

For assistance with replacement pages, shipments, billing or other customer service matters, please call:

Customer Services Department at .... (800) 833-9844
Outside the United States and Canada, please call   .... (518) 487-3000
Fax number .... (518) 487-3584
Customer Service Website .... http://www.lexisnexis.com/custserv/

For information on other Matthew Bender Publications, please call
Your account manager or .... (800) 223-1940
Outside the United States and Canada, please call .... (518) 487-3000

Editorial Offices
744 Broad Street, Newark, NJ 07102 (973) 820-2000
201 Mission St., San Francisco, CA 94105-1831 (415) 908-3200
www.lexis.com

MATTHEW◆BENDER

(Pub.62410)

Statement on Fair Use

Matthew Bender recognizes the balance that must be achieved between the operation of the fair use doctrine, whose basis is to avoid the rigid application of the copyright statute, and the protection of the creative rights and economic interests of authors, publishers and other copyright holders.

We are also aware of the countervailing forces that exist between the ever greater technological advances for making both print and electronic copies and the reduction in the value of copyrighted works that must result from a consistent and pervasive reliance on these new copying technologies. It is Matthew Bender's position that if the "progress of science and useful arts" is promoted by granting copyright protection to authors, such progress may well be impeded if copyright protection is diminished in the name of fair use. (See *Nimmer on Copyright* §13.05[E][1].) This holds true whether the parameters of the fair use doctrine are considered in either the print or the electronic environment as it is the integrity of the copyright that is at issue, not the media under which the protected work may become available. Therefore, the fair use guidelines we propose apply equally to our print and electronic information, and apply, within §§107 and 108 of the Copyright Act, regardless of the professional status of the user.

Our draft guidelines would allow for the copying of limited materials, which would include synopses and tables of contents, primary source and government materials that may have a minimal amount of editorial enhancements, individual forms to aid in the drafting of applications and pleadings, and miscellaneous pages from any of our newsletters, treatises and practice guides. This copying would be permitted provided it is performed for internal use and solely for the purpose of facilitating individual research or for creating documents produced in the course of the user's professional practice, and the original from which the copy is made has been purchased or licensed as part of the user's existing in-house collection.

Matthew Bender fully supports educational awareness programs designed to increase the public's recognition of its fair use rights. We also support the operation of collective licensing organizations with regard to our print and electronic information.

(Pub.62410)

DEDICATIONS

Dedicated to Colonel Cheryl A. Gilligan and Lieutenant Colonel Paul Bontrager and the other outstanding service members defending our country.

AND

In memory of Lieutenant Colonel Seymour G. Lederer, QM, AUS, and in honor of Calvin M. Lederer, Deputy Judge Advocate General, United States Coast Guard, and Colonel, JAGC, USA (retired). So long as our country has souls like these the Constitution and the nation shall endure.

Justice ought to bear rule everywhere, and especially in armies; it is the only means to settle order there, and there it ought to be executed with as much exactness as in the best governed cities of the kingdom, if it be intended that the soldiers should be kept in their duty and obedience.

ACKNOWLEDGMENTS

It is impossible to note and thank adequately the many people who have contributed over the years to this treatise, and we would rather make a general acknowledgment of our deep appreciation than run the risk of accidentally omitting someone. We would like to thank especially, however, Mrs. Della Harris, Director of the William & Mary Law School Faculty and Academic Support Center, without whose extraordinary hard work and infallible good humor this treatise would not exist.

The epigraph of this book, taken from the Art of War (1678) by Louis de Gaya, was reprinted as the title page in Clode, *Administration of Justice Under Military and Martial Law* (1892) and reprinted in turn in 2 Fredric I. Lederer, *Cases and Materials on the Military Criminal Legal System ii* (2d ed. 1975) and in later editions of the same work.

The views expressed in this book are those of the authors and do not reflect the official policy or position of the United States Court of Appeals for the Armed Forces, the Department of the Army, Department of Defense, or the United States Government.

Foreword by Judge Susan J. Crawford of the United States Court of Appeals for the Armed Forces

Our armed forces are spread throughout the world with the critical mission of defending the United States and our allies. The military criminal legal system directly impacts not only their lives but also their family members and friends. It affects armed forces readiness and thus the civilian citizens of the nation our personnel so ably protect. All have a substantial interest in the nature of the military justice legal system.

Disciplined personnel are necessary to defeat our enemies. Yet, nothing less than impartial justice will suffice when a member of the armed forces is charged with a criminal offense. Our personnel fight to defend the Constitution, and they merit its protections.

Whether you like hard copy or electronic texts, this scholarly third edition will be invaluable to expert and novice alike. This work has as its theme the ethical requirement that every client be represented zealously and competently. The treatise addresses in a comprehensive fashion the military criminal legal system and does so in both a scholarly and highly pragmatic manner. It should be of value to every practitioner.

As I observed in the earlier edition of this treatise:

[J]ustice requires careful procedures with an exact weighing of facts and laws. The military personnel of the United States are not and cannot be mere unthinking robots. They are courageous, thinking, creative individuals, and they must be treated as such. They deserve to be treated with respect and with justice. No soldier, airman, sailor, marine, or coast guardsman, male or female, will object to the swift and proper punishment of an offender. They ask only that the procedures used be fair; that those charged with misconduct have a proper hearing and be afforded the same basic rights fundamental as all American citizens. Recognizing the unique nature of military life and operations, they do not require every element of customary civilian procedure. They do demand candor, fairness, and justice. Nothing less is due them.

SUSAN J. CRAWFORD
Chief Judge – October 1, 1999 – September 30, 2004
Judge – November 19, 1991 – September 30, 1999;
October 1, 2004 – September 30, 2006

TABLE OF CONTENTS

Chapter 15 THE COURT MEMBERS

§ 15-10.00 INTRODUCTION
  § 15-11.00 In General
  § 15-12.00 Members Without a Military Judge
§ 15-20.00 NECESSARY QUALIFICATIONS FOR COURT MEMBERS
  § 15-21.00 In General
  § 15-22.00 Military Status
  § 15-23.00 Armed Force and Unit of Assignment
  § 15-24.00 Senior to the Accused
  § 15-25.00 Enlisted Personnel
  § 15-26.00 Disqualified Personnel
    § 15-26.10 — Codal Disqualifications
    § 15-26.20 — Regulatory Unavailability
§ 15-30.00 SELECTION OF COURT MEMBERS
  § 15-31.00 Selection by the Convening Authority Generally
  § 15-32.00 Procedure
  § 15-33.00 Criteria Involving Rank, Sex, Race, Religion, et al.
  § 15-34.00 Excusals
  § 15-35.00 Challenge to Entire Panel
§ 15-40.00 CONSTITUTIONAL CHALLENGES
§ 15-50.00 VOIR DIRE AND CHALLENGE
  § 15-51.00 In General
  § 15-52.00 Sources of Information for Challenges Other than Voir Dire
    § 15-52.10 — Pretrial Investigation of Court Members
    § 15-52.20 — Disclosure by the Members
    § 15-52.30 — Disclosure by the Government
  § 15-53.00 Voir Dire
  § 15-54.00 Individual Challenges for Cause
    § 15-54.10 — In General
      § 15-54.11 — — Procedures
    § 15-54.20 — Freedom from Substantial Doubt as to Legality,
          Fairness and Impartiality
      § 15-54.21 — — In General
      § 15-54.22 — — Sentencing Considerations
        § 15-54.22(a) — — Rigid Notion as to Punishment
        § 15-54.22(b) — — View of Capital Punishment
      § 15-54.23 — — Racial, Religious, Sexual, or Ethnic
            Prejudice
      § 15-54.24 — — Crime Victim
      § 15-54.25 — — Consults Legal Authority
      § 15-54.26 — — Relationships
      § 15-54.27 — — Law Enforcement Duty
      § 15-54.28 — — Sleeping Court Members
      § 15-54.29 — — Court Member Misconduct
    § 15-54.30 — Pretrial Publicity

Table of Contents

§ 15-55.00 Peremptory Challenges
  § 15-55.10 — In General
  § 15-55.20 — Additional Peremptory Challenges
  § 15-55.30 — Discriminatory Peremptory Challenges — *Batson v. Kentucky*
    § 15-55.31 — — In General
    § 15-55.32 — — Defendant's Burden
    § 15-55.33 — — Neutral Reasons
    § 15-55.34 — — Procedural Matters
    § 15-55.35 — — Systemic Impact of *Batson*
  § 15-56.00 Procedure for Exercising and Evaluating Challenges
  § 15-57.00 Waiver
  § 15-58.00 Tactical Considerations — The "Numbers Game"
§ 15-60.00 TRIAL BY MEMBERS: THE ACCUSED'S DECISION
§ 15-70.00 THE MEMBERS' FUNCTION
  § 15-71.00 In General
  § 15-72.00 "Jury Nullification"
§ 15-80.00 COMMAND INFLUENCE
§ 15-90.00 APPELLATE REMEDY

Chapter 16 COMMUNICATIONS PRIVILEGES FOR CONFIDENTIAL RELATIONS

§ 16-10.00 ARRAIGNMENT IN GENERAL
§ 16-20.00 TRIAL IN ABSENTIA
  § 16-21.00 Constitutional Law
  § 16-22.00 Military Law

Chapter 17 THE RIGHT TO A SPEEDY TRIAL

§ 17-10.00 INTRODUCTION
§ 17-20.00 SOURCES OF THE RIGHT
§ 17-30.00 CONSTITUTIONAL LAW
  § 17-31.00 "Pre-Accusation" Delay
  § 17-32.00 "Post-Accusation" Delay
  § 17-33.00 Effect of Dismissal of Charges
§ 17-40.00 MILITARY STATUTORY LAW AND ITS INTERPRETATION
  § 17-41.00 Article 10
    § 17-41.10 — Inception of Article 10 Accountability
      § 17-41.11 — — In General
      § 17-41.12 — — Civilian Confinement
    § 17-41.20 Speedy Trial Standard
  § 17-42.00 Article 33
  § 17-43.00 Article 98
§ 17-50.00 THE *BURTON* RULE
  § 17-51.00 The 90-Day Rule in General
  § 17-52.00 Prerequisites for the 90-Day Rule

Table of Contents

§ 17-52.10 — Inception of Government Accountability
§ 17-52.20 — Termination of Governmental Accountability
§ 17-53.00 Defense Requests for Delay
§ 17-54.00 Circumstances Justifying Delay
§ 17-54.10 — Extraordinary Circumstances
§ 17-54.20 — Other Circumstances Justifying Delay
§ 17-54.30 — Circumstances Not Justifying Delay
§ 17-55.00 Governmental Accountability upon the Commission or Discovery of Additional Misconduct
§ 17-56.00 The *Burton* Demand-for-Trial Rule
§ 17-57.00 The Overruling of *Burton*
§ 17-60.00 LOCAL RULES
§ 17-70.00 RULE FOR COURTS-MARTIAL 707
§ 17-71.00 The Two Rules
§ 17-71.10 — In General
§ 17-72.00 The 120-Day Rule
§ 17-72.10 — In General
§ 17-72.20 — Inception of Government Accountability
§ 17-72.21 — — Preferral of Charges
§ 17-72.22 — — Imposition of Restraint
§ 17-72.30 — Restarting the Time Period
§ 17-72.40 — Termination of Government Accountability
§ 17-73.00 Exclusions
§ 17-73.10 — In General
§ 17-73.20 — Possible Civilian Disposition; Department of Justice Involvement
§ 17-74.00 The 90-Day Rule
§ 17-80.00 WAIVER
§ 17-81.00 Failure to Demand Trial
§ 17-82.00 Failure to Raise the Issue at Trial
§ 17-83.00 Effect of a Guilty Plea
§ 17-84.00 Plea Bargains
§ 17-90.00 CONSEQUENCES OF VIOLATING THE SPEEDY TRIAL RIGHT
§ 17-100.00 LITIGATION OF SPEEDY TRIAL MOTIONS
§ 17-101.00 Preparation for Litigation
§ 17-102.00 Litigation
§ 17-110.00 APPEAL
§ 17-111.00 In General
§ 17-112.00 Government Appeal
§ 17-120.00 REHEARINGS

Chapter 18 MOTIONS

§ 18-10.00 INTRODUCTION
§ 18-11.00 Definition and Form

Table of Contents

§ 18-12.00 Types of Motions

§ 18-13.00 Timing

§ 18-14.00 Litigation of Motions

    § 18-14.10 — The Burdens of Production and Proof

        § 18-14.11 — — Burden of Production

        § 18-14.12 — — Burden of Proof

    § 18-14.20 — Litigation

    § 18-14.30 — Ruling

        § 18-14.31 — — Timing

        § 18-14.32 — — Essential Findings of Fact

        § 18-14.33 — — Resolution by the Fact Finder

        § 18-14.40 — Reconsideration and Appeal

§ 18-20.00 MOTIONS TO DISMISS

    § 18-21.00 In General

        § 18-21.10 — Definition

        § 18-21.20 — Effects of Granted Motions to Dismiss

        § 18-21.30 — Specific Motions in the Rules for Courts-Martial

    § 18-22.00 Lack of Jurisdiction

    § 18-23.00 Failure to Allege an Offense

    § 18-24.00 Speedy Trial

    § 18-25.00 Running of the Statute of Limitations

    § 18-26.00 Double Jeopardy, Collateral Estoppel, Multiplicity, and Prior Nonjudicial Punishment

    § 18-27.00 Immunity

    § 18-28.00 Command Influence

    § 18-29.00 Other Constitutionally Based Motions

        § 18-29.10 — Due Process

        § 18-29.20 — Vindictive Prosecution

        § 18-29.30 — Prosecutorial Misconduct

§ 18-30.00 MOTIONS FOR APPROPRIATE RELIEF

    § 18-31.00 In General

    § 18-32.00 Continuances

    § 18-33.00 Correction or Clarification of the Charges or Specifications

        § 18-33.10 — Amendment

        § 18-33.20 — Severance of a Duplicitous Specification

        § 18-33.30 — Bill of Particulars

    § 18-34.00 Change of Venue

    § 18-35.00 Motion in Limine

    § 18-36.00 Requests for Investigative and Expert Assistance

    § 18-37.00 Exclusion of Witnesses

    § 18-38.00 Severance of Co-Accused

    § 18-39.00 Severance of Offenses

§ 18-40.00 SUPPRESSION MOTIONS

    § 18-41.00 In General

Table of Contents

§ 18-42.00 The Disclosure Requirement
§ 18-43.00 Timing
§ 18-44.00 The Need for Specificity
§ 18-45.00 Litigation
§ 18-46.00 Rulings
§ 18-50.00 MOTIONS FOR FINDINGS OF NOT GUILTY

Chapter 19 PLEAS AND PROVIDENCY INQUIRIES

§ 19-10.00 PLEAS
    § 19-11.00 In General
    § 19-12.00 Not-Guilty Pleas
    § 19-13.00 Guilty Pleas
        § 19-13.10 — In General
        § 19-13.20 — Effects of Guilty Pleas
        § 19-13.30 — Guilty Pleas with Exceptions and Substitutions
    § 19-14.00 Standing Mute
    § 19-15.00 Confessional Stipulations
    § 19-16.00 Conditional Pleas
§ 19-20.00 GUILTY PLEA PROVIDENCY INQUIRY
    § 19-21.00 In General
    § 19-22.00 The *"Care"* Inquiry
        § 19-22.10 — *United States v. Care*
        § 19-22.20 — *Care* Codified
    § 19-23.00 Inquiry into a Pretrial Agreement
        § 19-23.10 — In General
        § 19-23.20 — Full Disclosure
        § 19-23.30 — Inquiry into Conditions
        § 19-23.40 — Sentence Limitations
    § 19-24.00 Rejection of an Improvident Plea and Its Consequences
        § 19-24.10 — In General
        § 19-24.20 — Evidentiary Consequences of Rejection of
            Improvident Pleas
        § 19-24.30 — Recusal of the Military Judge
    § 19-25.00 Noncompliance with Providency-Inquiry Requirements
    § 19-26.00 Appraisal of the Providency Inquiry
§ 19-30.00 ACCEPTANCE OF PLEAS AND SUBSEQUENT ATTACK
§ 19-40.00 WITHDRAWAL OF PLEA
§ 19-50.00 REVISION PROCEEDINGS AND OTHER CORRECTIVE
       DEVICES

Chapter 20 PROCUREMENT AND PRESENTATION OF EVIDENCE; COMPULSORY PROCESS AND CONFRONTATION

§ 20-10.00 INTRODUCTION
    § 20-11.00 In General
    § 20-12.00 The Burdens of Proof and Production

Table of Contents

§ 20-20.00 PROCUREMENT OF EVIDENCE
§ 20-21.00 In General
§ 20-22.00 The Decision to Obtain Evidence
§ 20-22.10 — In General
§ 20-22.11 — — General Procedures
§ 20-22.12 — — Expert Witnesses
§ 20-22.12(a) — — In General
§ 20-22.12(b) — — Expert Assistance Pretrial
§ 20-22.12(c) — — Obtaining Civilian Expert Assistance
§ 20-22.20 — Form of the Rule 703(c) Request
§ 20-22.30 — Timeliness
§ 20-22.40 — Materiality
§ 20-22.50 — Cumulative Testimony
§ 20-22.60 — Alternatives to a Witness' Personal Attendance at Trial
§ 20-22.70 — Defense Objections to Rule for Courts-Martial 703
§ 20-22.71 — — The Recipient of the Request
§ 20-22.72 — — Defense Disclosure of Tactics and Strategy
§ 20-22.73 — — Lack of Reciprocity in General
§ 20-22.80 — Revision of Rule for Courts-Martial 703
§ 20-23.00 The Power to Obtain Witnesses and Other Evidence
§ 20-23.10 — Evidence in the Custody or Control of Military Authorities
§ 20-23.20 — Evidence Not in Military Control
§ 20-23.21 — — Subpoenas
§ 20-23.22 — — The Warrant of Attachment
§ 20-23.22(a) — — In General
§ 20-23.22(b) — — Execution of Warrant
§ 20-23.22(c) — — Constitutionality of the Military Warrant of Attachment
§ 20-23.30 — Immunity
§ 20-23.31 — — In General
§ 20-23.32 — — The Nature of the Immunity Required
§ 20-23.32(a) — — In General
§ 20-23.32(b) — — Threat of Prosecution in a Foreign Jurisdiction
§ 20-23.33 — — Consequences of Granting Immunity
§ 20-23.33(a) — — At Trial
§ 20-23.33(b) — — To the Immunized Witness
§ 20-23.33(c) — — Post-trial
§ 20-30.00 CONFRONTATION AND COMPULSORY PROCESS
§ 20-31.00 In General
§ 20-32.00 The Right of Confrontation
§ 20-32.10 — In General

Table of Contents

§ 20-32.20 — The Right to Compel the Government to Produce Witnesses Whose Statements Are Used at Trial

§ 20-32.21 — — In General

§ 20-32.22 — — Witnesses Present in Court

§ 20-32.23 — — Hearsay From Declarants Not Present in Court

§ 20-32.23(a) — — In General

§ 20-32.23(b) — — Unavailability

§ 20-32.24 — — "Firmly Rooted" Hearsay Exceptions & Particularized Gaurantees of Trustworthiness

§ 20-32.25 — — "Particularized Guarantees"

§ 20-32.25(a) — — The Residual Hearsay Exception

§ 20-32.30 — The Right to Cross-Examine the Government's Witnesses at Trial

§ 20-32.31 — — In General

§ 20-32.32 — — The Rape-Shield Rule

§ 20-32.32(a) — — In General

§ 20-32.32(b) — — Potential Confrontation and Compulsory Process Problems

§ 20-32.33 — — Restrictions Due to Classified Material

§ 20-32.34 — — Cross-Examination During Suppression Hearings

§ 20-33.00 The Right of Compulsory Process

§ 20-33.10 — The Right to Compel the Attendance of Available Witnesses at Trial

§ 20-33.11 — — In General

§ 20-33.12 — — Requiring the Government to Grant Immunity to Prospective Defense Witnesses

§ 20-33.13 — — Improper Joinder

§ 20-33.20 — The Right to be Present for the Testimony of Defense Witnesses at Trial

§ 20.33.30 — The Right to Examine Defense Witnesses at Trial and to Present Defense Evidence

§ 20-33.31 — — General Constitutional Standards

§ 20-33.32 — — Competency of Witnesses

§ 20-33.33 — — Admissibility of Evidence

§ 20-33.33(a) — — In General

§ 20-33.33(b) — — Scientific Evidence

§ 20-33.33(c) — — Polygraph Evidence

§ 20-33.34 — — Preventing Defense Witnesses from Testifying

§ 20-33.35 — — Laboratory Reports

§ 20-40.00 DEPOSITIONS AND INTERROGATORIES

Chapter 21 TRIAL ON THE MERITS

§ 21-10.00 INTRODUCTION

Table of Contents

§ 21-11.00 In General

§ 21-12.00 Basic Procedure

§ 21-13.00 Mental State of the Accused

§ 21-14.00 Burdens of Proof

　§ 21-14.10 — In General

　§ 21-14.20 — Failure to Meet the Burden of Proof; Reopening of Prosecution's Case

§ 21-20.00 EVIDENTIARY MATTERS

§ 21-21.00 The Military Rules of Evidence Generally

§ 21-22.00 Admissibility Determinations

§ 21-23.00 Substitutes for Evidence

　§ 21-23.10 — Stipulations and Concessions

　§ 21-23.20 — Judicial Notice

　§ 21-23.30 — Presumptions

§ 21-30.00 EXAMINATION OF WITNESSES

§ 21-31.00 In General

§ 21-32.00 Mode and Scope of Examination

Chapter 22 SUMMATIONS, INSTRUCTIONS, DELIBERATIONS AND FINDINGS

§ 22-10.00 INTRODUCTION

§ 22-20.00 SUMMATIONS

§ 22-21.00 In General

§ 22-22.00 Content

§ 22-23.00 Limits on Final Arguments

　§ 22-23.10 — Inflammatory Arguments

　§ 22-23.20 — Arguing Facts Not in Evidence

　§ 22-23.30 — Personal Opinion and Personal Attack

　§ 22-23.40 — Comment on the Accused's Failure to Testify

　§ 22-23.50 — Law

　§ 22-23.60 — "Jury Nullification"

§ 22-24.00 Concession of Guilt

§ 22-25.00 Waiving Summation

§ 22-26.00 Error During Summation

　§ 22-26.10 — In General

　§ 22-26.20 — Waiver

§ 22-30.00 FINDINGS INSTRUCTIONS

§ 22-31.00 In General

§ 22-32.00 Content

　§ 22-32.10 — In General

　§ 22-32.20 — Summary of Evidence

§ 22-33.00 Additional Instructions

§ 22-34.00 Waiver of Error

§ 22-35.00 Trial by Judge Alone

§ 22-40.00 DELIBERATIONS

Table of Contents

§ 22-41.00 In General
§ 22-42.00 Voting
§ 22-50.00 FINDINGS
§ 22-51.00 In General
§ 22-52.00 Special Findings
§ 22-53.00 Reconsideration
§ 22-54.00 Impeachment of Verdict

Chapter 23 SENTENCING

§ 23-10.00 INTRODUCTION
§ 23-11.00 Sentencing in Brief
§ 23-12.00 Sentencing Philosophy
§ 23-13.00 Disparate Sentencing
§ 23-20.00 CONSTITUTIONAL LIMITATIONS
§ 23-21.00 In General
§ 23-22.00 Cruel and Unusual Punishment
§ 23-30.00 PERMISSIBLE SANCTIONS
§ 23-31.00 In General
§ 23-32.00 Specific Sanctions
§ 23-32.10 — The Death Penalty
§ 23-32.20 — Separation from the Armed Forces
§ 23-32.21 — — In General
§ 23-32.22 — — Dismissal
§ 23-32.23 — — Dishonorable Discharge
§ 23-32.24 — — Bad-Conduct Discharge
§ 23-33.00 Deprivation of Liberty
§ 23-33.10 — In General
§ 23-33.20 — Confinement
§ 23-33.30 — Hard Labor without Confinement
§ 23-33.40 — Confinement on Bread and Water
§ 23-33.50 — Restriction
§ 23-34.00 Financial Sanctions
§ 23-34.10 — Deprivations of Pay
§ 23-34.20 — Fines
§ 23-35.00 Reduction in Grade
§ 23-36.00 Reprimand
§ 23-40.00 SENTENCING EVIDENCE
§ 23-41.00 In General
§ 23-42.00 Evidence Admitted During Trial on the Merits
§ 23-43.00 Evidence Resulting from a Guilty Plea
§ 23-43.10 — In General
§ 23-43.20 — Providence Inquiry
§ 23-43.30 — Stipulation of Fact
§ 23-44.00 Prosecutorial Sentencing Evidence
§ 23-44.10 — In General

Table of Contents

§ 23-44.20 — Data from the Charge Sheet
§ 23-44.30 — Personnel Records
    § 23-44.31 — — In General
    § 23-44.32 — — Nonjudicial Punishment Records
    § 23-44.33 — — Written Reprimands
§ 23-44.40 — Previous Convictions
§ 23-44.50 — Evidence in Aggravation
    § 23-44.51 — — In General
    § 23-44.52 — — Impact on Victim or Family
    § 23-44.53 — — Effect and Amount of Drugs
    § 23-44.54 — — Financial Matters
    § 23-44.55 — — Impact on Discipline and Mission
    § 23-44.56 — — Future Dangerousness
§ 23-44.60 — Rehabilitative Potential
§ 23-44.70 — Capital Cases
§ 23-45.00 Defense Sentencing Evidence: Extenuation and Mitigation
§ 23-45.10 — In General
§ 23-45.20 — Extenuation and Mitigation Evidence
    § 23-45.21 — — Testimony by the Accused
       § 23-45.21(a) — — In General
       § 23-45.21(b) — — Unsworn Statements
    § 23-45.22 — — Defense Witnesses
    § 23-45.23 — — Command Influence
§ 23-45.30 — Capital Cases
§ 23-46.00 Prosecution Rebuttal
§ 23-50.00 SENTENCING FACTORS
§ 23-51.00 In General
§ 23-52.00 Maximum Imposable Sentence
    § 23-52.10 — In General
    § 23-52.20 — The "Escalator Clauses"
    § 23-52.30 — Rehearings
§ 23-53.00 Sentencing Factors in Noncapital Cases
    § 23-53.10 — The Accused's Plea
    § 23-53.20 — Cooperation with the Authorities
    § 23-53.30 — The Accused's False Testimony on the Merits
    § 23-53.40 — Time Spent in Pretrial Confinement
    § 23-53.50 — The Accused's Absence from Trial
    § 23-53.60 — Administrative Consequences of a Sentence
    § 23-53.70 — Recalcitrance
§ 23-60.00 SENTENCING ARGUMENT
§ 23-61.00 In General
§ 23-62.00 Defense Arguments *for* Serious Punishments
§ 23-70.00 INSTRUCTIONS
§ 23-80.00 DELIBERATIONS AND SENTENCE

Table of Contents

§ 23-81.00 Sentence Worksheet

§ 23-82.00 Procedure

§ 23-83.00 Reconsideration of Sentence

§ 23-84.00 Defective Sentences

§ 23-85.00 Suspension of Sentence

§ 23-86.00 Vacation Proceedings

Chapter 24 POST-TRIAL RESPONSIBILITIES AND ACTIONS

§ 24-10.00 INTRODUCTION

§ 24-20.00 POST-TRIAL DEFENSE DUTIES

   § 24-21.00 In General

   § 24-22.00 The Identity of the Post-Trial Defense Counsel

      § 24-22.10 — In General

      § 24-22.20 — For Service of the Post-Trial Recommendation

§ 24-30.00 DEFERMENT OF CONFINEMENT

   § 24-31.00 — In General

   § 24-32.00 — Alternative Restraint

   § 24-33.00 — Rescission of Deferment

§ 24-40.00 DEFENSE-SUBMITTED INFORMATION UNDER RULE 1105

   § 24-41.00 — In General

   § 24-42.00 — Timing

   § 24-43.00 — Waiver

   § 24-44.00 — Special and Summary Courts-Martial

§ 24-50.00 THE RECORD OF TRIAL

   § 24-51.00 The Requirement of a Verbatim Record

      § 24-51.10 — In General

      § 24-51.20 — Recording Failure; Incomplete Record

   § 24-52.00 Authentication

   § 24-53.00 Certificate of Corrections

   § 24-54.00 Service of the Record of Trial

§ 24-60.00 THE POST-TRIAL RECOMMENDATION

   § 24-61.00 In General

   § 24-62.00 The Staff Judge Advocate

      § 24-62.10 — In General

      § 24-62.20 — Disqualification of Staff Judge Advocate

   § 24-63.00 Content of Recommendation

   § 24-64.00 Defense Response

      § 24-64.10 — In General

      § 24-64.20 — Timeliness and Waiver

   § 24-65.00 The Staff Judge Advocate's "Addendum"

      § 24-65.10 — In General

      § 24-65.20 — New Matter

§ 24-70.00 ACTION BY THE CONVENING AUTHORITY

   § 24-71.00 In General

Table of Contents

§ 24-72.00 Disqualification of the Convening Authority

§ 24-73.00 Response to Matters Outside the Record

    § 24-73.10 — Postponement of Confinement — Effect of Civilian Sentence

§ 24-74.00 Sentence Conversions

§ 24-75.00 Restraint Pending Appeal

§ 24-76.00 Rehearings and DuBay Hearings

§ 24-80.00   POST-TRIAL DELAY

§ 24-90.00   APPELLATE REMEDIES

Chapter 25 APPEALS, EXTRAORDINARY RELIEF, AND EXECUTION OF SENTENCE

§ 25-10.00   INTRODUCTION

    § 25-11.00 In General

    § 25-12.00 The Appellate Process in Brief

        § 25-12.10 — In General

        § 25-12.20 — *DuBay* Hearings

    § 25-13.00   Deferral of Confinement Pending Appeal; "Excess Leave"

        § 25-13.10 — Release Pending Appeal; Deferral

        § 25-13.20 — Confinement Completion Prior to Appellate Completion; Excess Leave

§ 25-20.00   JURISDICTIONAL PREREQUISITES FOR JUDICIAL APPEAL; INFERIOR TRIBUNALS AND SENTENCES

§ 25-30.00   AUTOMATIC APPEAL AND ITS WAIVER

§ 25-40.00   THE RIGHT TO COUNSEL ON APPEAL

    § 25-41.00 In General

    § 25-42.00 Frivolous Appeals

§ 25-50.00   THE COURTS OF CRIMINAL APPEALS (THE COURTS OF MILITARY REVIEW)

    § 25-51.00 In General

    § 25-52.00 Jurisdiction

    § 25-53.00 Scope of Review

        § 25-53.10 — In General

        § 25-53.20 — Fact-Finding Powers

        § 25-53.30 — Sentencing

    § 25-54.00 Reconsideration

    § 25-55.00 Effect of Reversal of Conviction

§ 25-60.00   THE COURT OF APPEALS FOR THE ARMED FORCES

    § 25-61.00 In General

    § 25-62.00 Jurisdiction

    § 25-63.00 Issues Not Asserted Below

    § 25-64.00 Abatement Due to Death of the Accused

§ 25-70.00   REVIEW BY THE SUPREME COURT

§ 25-80.00   INTERLOCUTORY GOVERNMENT APPEALS

    § 25-81.00 In General

Table of Contents

§ 25-82.00 Appealable Orders
§ 25-82.10 — In General
§ 25-82.20 — Specific Types of Orders
§ 25-83.00 Scope of Review
§ 25-84.00 Procedure
§ 25-90.00   EXTRAORDINARY WRITS
§ 25-91.00 In General
§ 25-92.00 Relief in Aid of Jurisdiction
§ 25-93.00 "Agreeable to the Usages and Principles of Law"
§ 25-94.00 Legislative Review Appropriate
§ 25-100.00   EXECUTION OF SENTENCE
§ 25-110.00   RESTORATION; NEW TRIAL
§ 25-120.00   UNLAWFUL POST-TRIAL CONFINEMENT

Chapter 26 CIVILIAN COLLATERAL RELIEF

§ 26-10.00   INTRODUCTION
§ 26-11.00 In General
§ 26-12.00 The Historical Evolution of Civilian Collateral Attack
§ 26-20.00   THE CLAIMS COURT
§ 26-30.00   HABEAS CORPUS
§ 26-31.00 In General
§ 26-32.00 Custody
§ 26-32.10 — Generally
§ 26-32.20 — What Constitutes Custody
§ 26-32.30 — Who Is a Custodian
§ 26-32.40 — Prematurity
§ 26-32.50 — Concurrent-Sentence Doctrine
§ 26-32.60 — Mootness
§ 26-33.00 Exhaustion of Military Remedies
§ 26-33.10 — Generally
§ 26-33.20 — Meeting the Exhaustion Requirement
§ 26-33.30 — Presentation of Claims
§ 26-33.31 — Fair Identification of Claims
§ 26-33.32 — Fair Presentation of Claims
§ 26-34.00 Waiver
§ 26-35.00 "New" Rules

CHAPTER 15

THE COURT MEMBERS

§ 15-10.00 INTRODUCTION
  § 15-11.00   In General
  § 15-12.00   Members Without a Military Judge
§ 15-20.00 NECESSARY QUALIFICATIONS FOR COURT MEMBERS
  § 15-21.00   In General
  § 15-22.00   Military Status
  § 15-23.00   Armed Force and Unit of Assignment
  § 15-24.00   Senior to the Accused
  § 15-25.00   Enlisted Personnel
  § 15-26.00   Disqualified Personnel
     § 15-26.10 — Codal Disqualifications
     § 15-26.20 — Regulatory Unavailability
§ 15-30.00 SELECTION OF COURT MEMBERS
  § 15-31.00   Selection by the Convening Authority Generally
  § 15-32.00   Procedure
  § 15-33.00   Criteria Involving Rank, Sex, Race, Religion, et al.
  § 15-34.00   Excusals
  § 15-35.00   Challenge to Entire Panel
§ 15-40.00 CONSTITUTIONAL CHALLENGES
§ 15-50.00 VOIR DIRE AND CHALLENGE
  § 15-51.00   In General
  § 15-52.00   Sources of Information for Challenges Other than Voir Dire
     § 15-52.10 — Pretrial Investigation of Court Members
     § 15-52.20 — Disclosure by the Members
     § 15-52.30 — Disclosure by the Government
  § 15-53.00   Voir Dire
  § 15-54.00   Individual Challenges for Cause
     § 15-54.10 — In General
       § 15-54.11 — — Procedures
     § 15-54.20 — Freedom from Substantial Doubt as to Legality, Fairness and
           Impartiality
       § 15-54.21 — — In General
       § 15-54.22 — — Sentencing Considerations
         § 15-54.22(a) — — Rigid Notion as to Punishment
         § 15-54.22(b) — — View of Capital Punishment
       § 15-54.23 — — Racial, Religious, Sexual, or Ethnic Prejudice
       § 15-54.24 — — Crime Victim

(Rel.3—1/07 Pub.62410)

§ 15-54.25 — — Consults Legal Authority
§ 15-54.26 — — Relationships
§ 15-54.27 — — Law Enforcement Duty
§ 15-54.28 — — Sleeping Court Members
§ 15-54.29 — — Court Member Misconduct
§ 15-54.30 — Pretrial Publicity
§ 15-55.00 Peremptory Challenges
§ 15-55.10 — In General
§ 15-55.20 — Additional Peremptory Challenges
§ 15-55.30 — Discriminatory Peremptory Challenges — *Batson v. Kentucky*
§ 15-55.31 — — In General
§ 15-55.32 — — Defendant's Burden
§ 15-55.33 — — Neutral Reasons
§ 15-55.34 — — Procedural Matters
§ 15-55.35 — — Systemic Impact of *Batson*
§ 15-56.00 Procedure for Exercising and Evaluating Challenges
§ 15-57.00 Waiver
§ 15-58.00 Tactical Considerations — The "Numbers Game"
§ 15-60.00 TRIAL BY MEMBERS: THE ACCUSED'S DECISION
§ 15-70.00 THE MEMBERS' FUNCTION
§ 15-71.00 In General
§ 15-72.00 "Jury Nullification"
§ 15-80.00 COMMAND INFLUENCE
§ 15-90.00 APPELLATE REMEDY

§ 15-10.00 INTRODUCTION

§ 15-11.00 In General

Although the Constitution, in accord with our English roots,[1] guarantees a trial by jury in civilian criminal trials,[2] this fundamental right is inapplicable to members of the armed forces.[3] Instead, courts-martial use a military analogue

---

[1] *See generally* W. Forsyth, *History of Trial By Jury* (1852).

[2] U.S. Const. art. III, § 2, amend. VI; Duncan v. Louisiana, 391 U.S. 145 (1968) (right applicable to the states).

[3] *See, e.g.*, United States v. Witham, 47 M.J. 297, 301 (C.A.A.F. 1997) ("Again, we note that a military accused has no right to a trial by jury under the Sixth Amendment. . . . He does, however, have right to due process of law under the Fifth Amendment . . . and Congress has provided for trial by members at a court-martial."); Mendrano v. Smith, 797 F.2d 1538 (10th Cir. 1986), *citing* O'Callahan v. Parker, 395 U.S. 258, 261 (1969) (dictum); Whelchel v. McDonald, 340 U.S. 122, 127 (1950) (dictum); *Ex parte* Quirin, 317 U.S. 1, 40 (1942) (dictum); Kahn v. Anderson, 255 U.S. 1, 8 (1921); Betonie v. Sizemore, 496 F.2d 1001, 1007 (5th Cir. 1974); Branford v. United States, 356 F.2d 876, 877 (7th Cir. 1966); Daigle v. Warner, 490 F.2d 358, 364 (9th Cir. 1974) (dictum). *See also* United States v. McClain, 22 M.J. 124, 128 (C.M.A. 1986) ("courts-martial

(Rel.3—1/07 Pub.62410)

— the court members. Unlike civilian juries, courts-martial use nonunanimous two-thirds verdicts[4] of a panel that may be as small as three members.[5] Notwithstanding this unique aspect,[6] perhaps the most unusual and distinct aspect of the contemporary court-martial is the nature and selection of the court members. The Uniform Code of Military Justice provides in Article 25 (d)(2):

> When convening a court-martial, the convening authority shall detail as members thereof such members of the armed forces as, in his opinion, are best qualified for the duty by reason of age, education, training, experience, length of service, and judicial temperament. No member of an armed force is eligible to serve as a member of a general or special court-martial when he is the accuser or a witness for the prosecution or has acted as investigating officer or as counsel in the same case.

Perhaps the most unique feature of Article 25 is its insistence on the appointment of the court members by the convening authority — the officer whose responsibilities include clear prosecutorial duties.[7] The institution of the court members, however, finds its origin in the very nature of courts-martial. In its most basic sense, a court-martial originally was a group of officers appointed by the commander to hear evidence and recommend a finding to him. The court members were not just the primary component of the court-martial; for most purposes, they were the only component. They called and questioned the witnesses; heard the evidence; determined the law to apply; and determined guilt

---

have never been considered subject to the jury-trial demands of the Constitution") (*citing cf. Ex parte* Milligan, 71 U.S. (4 Wall.) 2 (1866)). *See generally* Henderson, *Courts-Martial and the Constitution: The Original Understanding*, 71 Harv. L. Rev. 1 (1957); Wiener, *Courts-Martial and the Bill of Rights: The Original Practice I*, 72 Harv. L. Rev. 1 (1958); Wiener, *Courts-Martial and the Bill of Rights: The Original Practice II*, 72 Harv. L. Rev. 266 (1958). The Fifth Amendment's express exemption of the armed forces from the federal right of grand jury indictment is thought to illustrate the framers' intent not to apply the right to trial by jury to the armed forces.

[4] U.C.M.J. art. 52(a)(2). Capital cases require a unanimous verdict. U.C.M.J. art. 52(a)(1).

[5] Special courts-martial require only three members (U.C.M.J. art. 16(2)) while general courts-martial require at least five. U.C.M.J. art. 16(1). Capital cases require "not less than 12" members, unless members are "not reasonably available" for reasons set forth in Article 25a. Former Chief Judge Sullivan has expressed the view that capital cases should have 12 members. United States v. Loving, 41 M.J. 213, 310 (1994), *quoting* United States v. Curtis, 32 M.J. at 271. *See also* § 15-40.00. The National Defense Authorization Act for Fiscal Year 2002, Pub. L. No. 107-107 (Dec. 28, 2001) amended the Uniform Code of Military Justice effective December 31, 2002, to create Article 25a. requiring "not less than 12" members for capital cases, unless members are "not reasonably available" for reasons set forth in the Article.

[6] Nonunanimous verdicts of less than twelve-member juries are constitutional when used by the states. Apodaca v. Oregon, 406 U.S. 404 (1972); Johnson v. Louisiana, 406 U.S. 356 (1972). However, civilian verdicts with less than six jurors concurring are unconstitutional. Ballew v. Georgia, 435 U.S. 223 (1978).

[7] Such as deciding on the disposition of charges. *See generally* Chapters 3 and 8. Strom Thurmond National Defense Authorization Act for Fiscal Year 1999 § 552 (1998) requires report on selection of court members.

(Rel.3—1/07 Pub.62410)

and sentence, subject to the decision of the convening authority.[8] Although the history of courts-martial in the modern era of the Uniform Code of Military Justice is largely the history of their legalization and civilianization, arguably, it has only been since 1948 that courts-martial have been subject to the control of military judges.[9] However, the pace of change since the Uniform Code of Military Justice has been swift, and at present it is fair to say that the military judge has fully replaced the court members as the primary aspect of a court-martial.[10] As a consequence, as long as a military judge is present,[11] court members are merely military jurors lacking any powers that would be considered unique in the civilian world.[12]

§ 15-12.00   Members Without a Military Judge

There is one significant caveat that must be added to this epitaph for the all-powerful court members. Although both general and special courts-martial use military judges,[13] the Uniform Code of Military Justice does not *require* judges at special courts-martial; rather, it permits their use.[14] It is service regulations that compel such use.[15] Should a special court-martial take place without a military judge,[16] the pre-1969[17] judgeless court will reappear with the senior officer of the court, the president, ruling finally on questions of law and, subject

----

[8] *See generally* Sections 1-40.00 *et seq.*

[9] *See* Section 14-10.00 (in 1948 the Army "law member" was given increased power over inter-locutory rulings).

[10] *See* Section 14-10.00.

[11] *See generally* Section 15-12.00.

[12] Although in the military, court members sentence the accused, a small minority of states have also placed sentencing power in their jurors.

[13] Summary courts-martial have no members; they are single officer courts with limited jurisdiction for generally minor offenses. *See generally* Section 8-31.30.

[14] U.C.M.J. art. 26(a).

[15] *See, e.g.,* Army Reg. No. 27-10, Miltary Justice ¶ 8-1c. (1) (16 November 2005):

A military judge will be detailed to each SPCM [special court-martial], unless a
military judge can not be obtained because of physical conditions or military
exigencies. . . . Mere inconvenience will not be a reason for failure to detail a military
judge.

See also Air Force Instruction 51-201, Law, Administration of Military Justice ¶ 5.1.2 (26 November 2003) ("The Chief Trial Judge . . . details military judges to SPCMs and GCM,") (query whether the regulation merely prescribes who will detail or also requires the detailing); [m]ilitary judges shall be detailed"); Coast Guard Military Justice Manual, Comdtinst M5810.1DC, Art. 3-H.1.bA-1 (17 August 2000) ("The Chief Trial Judge shall detail military judges to general and special courts-martial. A special court-martial must have a military judge detailed").

[16] A most unlikely event absent extraordinary combat exigencies.

[17] The Uniform Code was amended in 1968, effective 1969, to permit detailing of judges to special courts-martial.

(Rel.3—1/07 Pub.62410)

to objection by other members of the court, on any "interlocutory question of fact."[18]

§ 15-20.00   NECESSARY QUALIFICATIONS FOR COURT MEMBERS

§ 15-21.00   In General

In 1986, The Court of Military Appeals summarized, in *United States v. McClain,*[19] the development of the present prerequisites for duty as a court member:

> [Q]ualifications for service on courts-martial have been prescribed by Congress in the exercise of its power under Article I, § 8, cl. 14 of the Constitution.
>
> The chief qualification for court-martial service under the Articles of War as they existed at the time of World War I was status as an officer. Article of War (A.W.) 4 authorized "[a]ll officers in the military service of the United States, and officers of the Marine Corps when detached for service with the Army by order of the President . . . to serve on courts-martial." However, an officer was ineligible to sit when he was "the accuser or a witness for the prosecution." *See* A.W. 8. According to Manual for Courts-Martial, U.S. Army, 1917, "chaplains, veterinarians, dental surgeons, and second lieutenants in the Quartermaster Corps are not in practice detailed as members of courts-martial." Para. 6(b).
>
> In 1920, this sentence was added to Article of War 4:
>
> When appointing courts-martial the appointing authority shall obtain as members thereof those officers of the command who, in his opinion, are

---

[18] MCM, 1969 ¶ 57a. R.C.M. 502(b); 801(e)(2). R.C.M. 801(e)(2) declares:

(2) Rulings by the president of a special court-martial without a military judge.

(A) *Questions of law.* Any ruling by the president of a special court-martial without a military judge on any question of law other than a motion for a finding of not guilty is final.

(B) *Questions of fact.* Any ruling by the president of a special court-martial without a military judge on any interlocutory question of fact, including a factual issue of mental capacity of the accused, or on a motion for a finding of not guilty, is final unless objected to by a member.

(C) *Changing a ruling.* The president of a special court-martial without a military judge may change a ruling made by that or another president in the case except a previously granted motion for a finding of not guilty, at any time during the trial.

(D) *Presence of members.* Except as provided in R.C.M. 505 and 912, all members will be present at all sessions of a special court-martial without a military judge, including sessions at which questions of law or interlocutory questions are litigated. However, the president of a special court-martial without a military judge may examine an offered item of real or documentary evidence before ruling on its admissibility without exposing it to other members.

R.C.M. 801(e)(3) provides the procedures to be used when a member objects to a ruling by the president.

[19] 22 M.J. 124, 128–29 (C.M.A. 1986).

(Rel.3—1/07 Pub.62410)

best qualified for the duty by reason of age, training, experience, and judicial temperament; and officers having less than two years service shall not, if it can be avoided without manifest injury to the service, be appointed as members of courts-martial in excess of the minority membership thereof.[20]

. . . .

After World War II, the Elston Act[21] made further amendments to the Articles of War. Article of War 4 was revised to authorize the appointment of enlisted persons to serve as members of general and special courts-martial if the accused was an enlisted person and requested enlisted membership on the court. In connection with this change, enlisted persons were also made subject to the provision that court members should not have "less than two years' service . . . if it can be avoided without manifest injury to the service."

Article 25(d)(2) of the Uniform Code is similar to Article of War 4[22] in its direction that "[w]hen convening a court-martial, the convening authority shall detail as members thereof such members of the armed forces as, in his opinion, are best qualified for the duty by reason of age, education, training, experience, length of service, and judicial temperament." Under this codal provision length of service was to be considered by the convening authority; but Congress did not seek to prescribe any minimum for such service. For the first time "education" was specified as a criterion for appointment to courts-martial.

As this Court noted in *United States v. Greene*,[23] Article 25(d)(2) "should not be read in a vacuum, however, for the Congress of the United States, has by virtue of the passage of Article 25(a) and (b), Code, *above*, made eligible for membership on courts-martial '[a]ny commissioned officer on active duty' and '[a]ny warrant officer on active duty' if, in the latter instance, the accused is of a lesser grade than that of commissioned officer." Moreover, all enlisted members are eligible to serve, except for those in "the same unit as the accused."[24] Besides the statutory preference for members senior to the accused,[25] "[n]ot a single condition is inserted with regard to . . . [members'] rank or position within the military community, except those very general and personal factors which are to be considered by the convening authority in the exercise of his discretion."[26]

---

[20] 22 M.J. at 128 (*citing* App. 1, A.W. 4, *Manual for Courts-Martial*, U.S. Army, 1928). *See generally* Rigby, *Military Penal Law: A Brief Survey of the 1920 Revision of the Articles of War*, 12 J. Crim. L. & Criminology 84 (1922).

[21] Pub. L. No. 759, 62 Stat. 604 (1948).

[22] 22 M.J. at 129 n.2 ("The Articles for the government of the Navy did not prescribe in similar detail the qualifications for court member").

[23] 43 C.M.R. 72, 76-77 (C.M.A. 1970).

[24] *Citing* U.C.M.J. art. 25(c)(1).

[25] *Citing* U.C.M.J. art. 25(d)(1).

[26] *Quoting* United States v. Greene, 43 C.M.R. 72, 78 (C.M.A. 1970).

(Rel.3—1/07 Pub.62410)

In 2002, the Court dealt with a highly unusual case in which the President of the Court was the commanding officer of six other members. Reversing the conviction, the Court opined that:

> Where a panel member has a supervisory position over six of the other members, and the resulting seven members make up the two-thirds majority sufficient to convict, we are placing an intolerable strain on public perception of the military justice system. This is a contextual judgment. The President anticipated in the preamble to the Manual for Courts-Martial that judges would need to carefully balance national security with individual rights in applying the UCMJ. That preamble states: "The purpose of military law is to promote justice, to assist in maintaining good order and discipline in the armed forces, to promote efficiency and effectiveness in the military establishment, and thereby to strengthen the national security of the United States." What is reasonable and fair from the public's perception, as well as this Court's judgment as to what is reasonable and fair, would be different in the case of national security exigency or operational necessity. [27]

In short, fundamental issues of fairness are also of importance.

Notwithstanding the occasional presence of far more sophisticated legal issues, the most basic requirement for service as a court member is appointment in the convening orders by the convening authority. [28]

§ 15-22.00   Military Status

Article 25 of the Uniform Code requires that court members be "on active duty." [29] Because only members of the armed forces may serve on active duty,

---

[27] United States v. Wiesen, 56 M.J. 172, 175–176 (C.A.A.F. 2001).

See generally §§ 13-13.00, 13-14.00, *above.* On rare occasions, a convening order may be ambiguous in its appointments. In United States v. Gebhart, 34 M.J. 189, 193 (C.M.A. 1992), the court held that where a court member was both detailed and relieved in the same amending order and was treated by judge and counsel as a proper sitting member, "construction of the convening orders by the participants . . . is controlling." *See also* United States v. Sargent, 47 M.J. 367 (1997) (unexplained absence of detailed member was not jurisdictional); United States v. Turner, 47 M.J. 348 (1997) (non-jurisdictional error not to have written request or oral request on the record as required by Article 16(1) and R.C.M. 903(b)(2) but error did not materially prejudice accused, *citing* United States v. Mayfield, 45 M.J. 176 (1996)).

[28] *See generally* §§ 13-13.00, 13-14.00, *above.* On rare occasions, a convening order may be ambiguous in its appointments. In United States v. Gebhart, 34 M.J. 189, 193 (C.M.A. 1992), the court held that where a court member was both detailed and relieved in the same amending order and was treated by judge and counsel as a proper sitting member, "construction of the convening orders by the participants . . . is controlling." *See also* United States v. Sargent, 47 M.J. 367 (C.A.A.F. 1997) (unexplained absence of detailed member was not jurisdictional); United States v. Turner, 47 M.J. 348 (C.A.A.F. 1997) (non-jurisdictional error not to have written request or oral request on the record as required by Article 16(1) and R.C.M. 903(b)(2) but error did not materially prejudice accused, *citing* United States v. Mayfield, 45 M.J. 176 (C.A.A.F. 1996)).

[29] U.C.M.J. arts. 25(a), (b), (c)(1). *See also* R.C.M. 502(a)(1). The Discussion to R.C.M. 103(22) states:

(Rel.3—1/07   Pub.62410)

civilians are necessarily excluded from service as members of the court even if the accused is a civilian. The only "exception" to this general rule is that members of the National Oceanic and Atmospheric Administration and the Public Health Service are qualified to serve as court members while they are assigned to, and serving with, an armed force.[30]

Commissioned officers qualify as court members for the trial of an accused of any category,[31] while warrant officers qualify as court members for the trial of other warrant officers and enlisted members.[32] An enlisted member is not qualified to serve as a court member in the trial of a commissioned or warrant officer.[33]

§ 15-23.00   Armed Force and Unit of Assignment

A court member need not be a member of the same armed force[34] as the accused. In such a case, the member is still qualified, but "[w]hen a court-martial composed of members of different armed forces is selected, at least a majority of the members should be of the same armed force as the accused unless exigent circumstances make it impractical to do so without manifest injury to the service."[35]

Similarly, a court member need not be a member of the same command[36] as the accused. If the court member is not a member of the convening authority's command, however, the member's own commander must consent to such service on the court.[37]

Enlisted personnel should not be from the same unit as the accused.[38]

§ 15-24.00   Senior to the Accused

Article 25(d)(1) states, "When it can be avoided, no member of an armed force may be tried by a court-martial any member of which is junior to him in rank

---

"Active duty" means full-time duty in the active military service of the United States. It includes full-time training duty, annual training duty, and attendance while in the active military service, at a school designated a service school by law or by the Secretary of the military department concerned.

[30] R.C.M. 502(a) Discussion. Under such circumstances, these two agencies qualify as uniformed services.

[31] R.C.M. 502(a)(1)(A).

[32] R.C.M. 502(a)(1)(B).

[33] R.C.M. 502(a)(1)(C).

[34] R.C.M. 502(a)(1)(C).

[35] R.C.M. 502(a)(1)(C). Discussion.

[36] R.C.M. 503(a)(3).

[37] R.C.M. 503(a)(3). Such concurrence "may be oral and need not be shown by the record of trial." R.C.M. 503(a)(3). Discussion.

[38] See Section 15-25.00.

(Rel.3—1/07 Pub.62410)

or grade."[39] If a member who is junior in rank to the accused does sit, however, the error is not jurisdictional.[40] Although the seniority requirement sometimes helps to ensure added experience or maturity on the part of court members, the primary reason for its existence is historical. When promotion was slow and the armed forces small, promotion was often dependent upon the existence of personnel vacancies. The seniority requirement removed any temptation on the part of the members to convict the accused and thus perhaps create an opportunity for personal promotion.

§ 15-25.00 Enlisted Personnel

The right of enlisted personnel to have other enlisted personnel sit as court members stems from the 1948 Elston Act revision of the Articles of War.[41] Although the basic entitlement was continued in the Uniform Code of Military Justice, it was not without controversy.[42] Interestingly, some opposed it because of fear that enlisted members would be too command-oriented.

Systematic elimination of various grades of personnel from potential selection as court members is likely to be wrongful. The Court of Appeals for the Armed Forces declared in *United States v. Kirkland*[43] that:

> Whether a court-martial panel was selected free from systematic exclusion is a question of law which we review de novo. . . . The defense shoulders the burden of establishing the improper exclusion of qualified personnel from the selection process. . . . Once the defense establishes such exclusion, the Government must show by competent evidence that no impropriety occurred when selecting appellant's court-martial members.[44]

Applying that standard, the Court held that the military judge had erred by denying the defense request for a new court-martial panel that did not *per se* exclude enlisted members below the grade of E-7. In *Kirkland*, the exclusion

---

[39] *See also* R.C.M. 503(a)(1) Discussion.

[40] United States v. Schneider, 38 M.J. 387, 392 (C.M.A. 1993) (although the Court of Review held that failure to challenge a member junior to the accused waived the challenge issue, when the accused knew or through due diligence should have known of the member's status, the Court of Military Appeals, per Ryan, J., holds that the error was non-jurisdictional and, noting the reasons for the rule requiring that members be senior to the accused and citing this treatise, held that there was no possibility that the error could have prejudiced the accused, as the member didn't know that she was junior to the accused). United States v. McGee, 15 M.J. 1004 (N.M.C.M.R. 1983) (error waived by a failure to object).

[41] *See above* note 21 and accompanying text.

[42] *See, e.g., Hearings on S. 857 and H.R. 4080 Before a Subcomm. of the Senate Armed Services Comm.*, 81st Cong. 1st Sess. 56, 92–3, 142, 183 (1949).

[43] 53 M.J. 22 (C.A.A.F. 2000) (*distinguishing* United States v. Roland, 50 M.J. 66 (C.A.A.F. 1999)).

[44] 53 M.J. at 24 (citations omitted).

(Rel.3—1/07 Pub.62410)

was the result of an administrative method of asking for court member nominations in which the nomination forms listed and had room only for the grades of E-7 and below.

Interestingly, the special committee on military justice of the Association of the Bar of the City of New York wrote in 1949:

> There has been considerable discussion concerning the presence of enlisted men on military courts. Your committee believes that the public attention given to this aspect of the bill far outweighs its importance. The presence of enlisted men on courts is of doubtful value to the accused, since, in all likelihood, those appointed would be career soldiers, more severe than officers or their subordinates. If, however, the provision tends to give the enlisted man more confidence in the courts and a greater feeling that justice will be done, we see no objection to the experiment.[45]

Enlisted personnel often believe that, should enlisted members be requested, convening authorities will place the oldest, most senior noncommissioned or petty officers on the court. It is apparent that that fear is based upon fact, insofar as the first two decades following the Uniform Code's enactment are concerned:

> Statistics on the rank of enlisted personnel who have served as court members are fragmentary, but a study made by military defense counsel in *United States v. Crawford*[46] . . . is most revealing. The study showed that from 1959 through 1963 no enlisted man lower than grade E-4 served on an army court-martial. During the period from 1959 to 1962, 89.4 per cent of enlisted court members were in the three highest non-commissioned officer grades (E-7 through E-9), while at the same time fewer that six per cent of the men tried were in these same grades. Estimates by the Office of the Judge Advocate General of the Navy show that in recent years fewer than one per cent of the cases tried had enlisted members on the juries and that "the majority of such enlisted members are in pay grade E-7 or above." Similarly, the Office of the Judge Advocate General of the Air Force once indicated that "few if any enlisted men below the grade of E-5 have served" on courts-martial reviewed by that office.[47]

---

[45] *Hearings on S. 857 and H.R. 4080 Before a Subcomm. of the Senate Armed Services Comm.*, 81st Cong. 1st Sess. 183 (1949). *See also* Remcho, Military Juries: Constitutional Analysis and the Need for Reform, 47 Ind. L. J. 193, 196 (1972) (*citing* Schiesser, *Trial by Peers: Enlisted Members on Courts-Martial*, 15 Cath. U. L. Rev. 171, 195–97 (1966) ("[S]enior NCO's are more likely to view the actions of the accused in relation to the objectives of the military in enforcing discipline and ensuring compliance with the chain of authority").

[46] 35 C.M.R. 3 (C.M.A. 1964).

[47] Remcho, *Military Juries: Constitutional Analysis and the Need for Reform*, 47 Ind. L.J. 193, 196 (1972) (footnotes omitted); United States v. Roland, 50 M.J. 66 (C.A.A.F. 1999) (absent direct or circumstantial evidence of bad faith, nominations of E-5 and above for trial of private was not improper); United States v. White, 48 M.J. 251 (C.A.A.F. 1998) (preference for commanders was permissible as long as there was not an improper agenda — lower ranking members were not improperly excluded); United States v. Upshaw, 49 M.J. 111 (C.A.A.F. 1998) (It was not jurisdictional error to exclude all grades below E-7 when there was a mistaken belief that appellant was an E-6. The court held no showing of prejudice).

(Rel.3—1/07 Pub.62410)

Contemporary anecdotal evidence suggests that it appears far more likely in the present that midgrade enlisted personnel will be appointed.[48] What does seem to be almost universally true is that new or very junior enlisted personnel are almost never appointed. Although Article 25 contains neither a minimum grade nor an experience level, there is general belief that court members should have some degree of military experience before serving. Although it also cannot be demonstrated empirically, there does not appear to be any great likelihood that enlisted personnel are either more command-oriented or more conviction-prone than officers. In many cases, however, they do have relevant personal experience, that may cut in either direction, depending upon the facts of a case.

Article 25(c)(1) provides:

> Any enlisted member of an armed force on active duty who is not a member of the same unit as the accused is eligible to serve on general and special courts-martial for the trial of any enlisted member of an armed force who may lawfully be brought before such courts for trial, but he shall serve as a member of a court only if, before the conclusion of a session called by the military judge under section 839(a) of this title (article 39(a)) prior to trial or, in the absence of such a session, before the court is assembled for the trial of the accused, the accused personally has requested orally on the record or in writing that enlisted members serve on it. After such a request, the accused may not be tried by a general or special court-martial the membership of which does not include enlisted members in a number comprising at least one-third of the total membership of the court, unless eligible enlisted members cannot be obtained on account of physical conditions or military exigencies. If such members cannot be obtained, the court may be assembled and the trial held without them, but the convening authority shall make a detailed written statement, to be appended to the record, stating why they could not be obtained.[49]

---

[48] *But see* United States v. Nixon, 30 M.J. 1210 (A.C.M.R. 1990) (en banc), *aff'd*, 33 M.J. 433 (C.M.A. 1991) (eleven E-9's and two E-8's selected from group of E-4's to E-9's with one E-1); United States v. McClain, 22 M.J. 124 (C.M.A. 1986) *quoted at* Section 15-33.00.

[49] When the U.C.M.J. was originally enacted in 1950, an accused had to request enlisted personnel in writing; otherwise a jurisdictional defect occurred if such personnel were placed on the court. The U.C.M.J. was amended to permit oral requests to eliminate the ridiculous result of reversing a case in which the accused received his or her election but failed to request it properly. However, absent the accused's personal request, oral or written, for enlisted members, trial with enlisted members is jurisdictionally void; acquiescence is insufficient. United States v. Brookins, 33 M.J. 793, 795 (A.C.M.R. 1991). There must be absent evidence in the record of the request that the accused personally requested enlisted personnel. Trial with enlisted personnel is devoid of jurisdiction. United States v. Hood, 37 M.J. 784, 786 (A.C.M.R. 1993). In *United States v. Townes*, 52 M.J. 275, 277 (C.A.A.F. 2000), however, the Court held that the failure to obtain an express request for enlisted personnel was non-jurisdictional "because there is sufficient indication by appellee orally and on the record that he personally requested enlisted members." In large part, that "indication" appears to have been defense counsel's announcement of the accused's election in the presence of the accused and the lack of objection by the accused at any point during trial.

Article 25 also details the timing for a request for enlisted personnel. Rule for Courts-Martial echoes the codal requirement, R.C.M. 903(a)(1), and otherwise refers only to a "timely request."

(Rel.3—1/07 Pub.62410)

Although Article 25 mandates that a court consist of at least one-third enlisted personnel after a proper request,[50] no maximum limit is specified. Panels can consist of all or mostly enlisted personnel.[51] If the case is referred to a court containing enlisted members and the accused has not requested them, any error is harmless if the accused's intent has been to proceed by judge alone.[52]

As is the usual case, an enlisted member should be senior to the accused.[53]

The right to enlisted personnel is qualified by the requirement that an enlisted member must not be "a member of the same unit as the accused."[54] This aids neutrality by diminishing the probability of favoritism or risk of retaliation as well as exposure to pretrial "publicity." Article 25(c)(2) defines a unit: "In this article, 'unit' means any regularly organized body as defined by the Secretary convened, but in no case may it be a body larger than a company, squadron, ship's crew, or body corresponding to one of them."

An organization constitutes a "unit" regardless of size if it is within the codal definition.[55]

In a case in which a "company's" assigned strength was almost 1,000 men,[56] the Army Board of Review stated:

---

[50] *See generally* § 13-14.00 *above. See also* United States v. Morgan, 57 M.J. 119 (C.A.A.F. 2002) (record established the selection of enlisted members was accused's choice when counsel faxed the choice and there was no objection to the panel); United States v. Townes, 52 M.J. 275 (C.A.A.F. 2000) (failure to have personal request by the accused on the record as required by Article 25(c)(1) was nonjurisdictional, harmless error). R.C.M. 903(c)(1). Local imposition of a requirement demanding that a request be filed earlier than required by Article 25 is likely to yield reversible error if enlisted personnel are precluded as a sanction for non-compliance. *Cf.* United States v. Summerset, 37 M.J. 695 (A.C.M.R. 1993) (judge abused his discretion in denying accused's request for enlisted members four days prior to trial when no reasons set forth for denial). Although the court in *Summerset* used an abuse of discretion standard, as Judge Johnston, concurring in the result, noted, under the Code the judge had no discretion whatsoever and could not lawfully deny the request. 37 M.J. 699 (A.C.M.R. 1993).

[51] *E.g.,* United States v. Donley, 33 M.J. 44, 47 (C.M.A. 1991) (homicide case with one officer and four enlisted members).

[52] United States v. Berlingeri, 35 M.J. 794, 797 (N.M.C.M.R. 1992) (case reviews the evolution of law involving erroneous service of enlisted members).

[53] U.C.M.J. art. 25(d)(1).

[54] U.C.M.J. art. 25(c)(1). *See, e.g.,* United States v. Milam, 33 M.J. 1020 (A.C.M.R. 1991) (fact that two enlisted members were assigned to accused's company-sized unit of attachment required judge to grant causal challenges; although the defect was non-jurisdictional, the accused's challenges precluded waiver and reversal was required). *See also* United States v. Gray, 51 M.J. 1, 49–50 (C.A.A.F. 1999) (court rejected argument that the exclusion of enlisted members from the accused's unit is an improper criterium for selecting enlisted members).

[55] United States v. Wilson, 16 M.J. 678 (A.C.M.R. 1983); United States v. Scott, 25 C.M.R. 636 (A.B.R. 1958).

[56] Usually, an average "company" would not exceed about 200.

(Rel.3—1/07 Pub.62410)

[A]s the size of Army units is no longer regulated by statute, we do not attribute to the Congress an intention to apply the terms "unit" or "company" to military bodies of any particular strength or composition. . . . [C]ompanies as now organized may vary widely in their authorized strengths, and their actual strength can fluctuate from less than that considered normal for a squad or platoon to more than battalion size.[57]

The issue sometimes arises as to *who* is a member of the "same unit." One military text[58] reports that before the Uniform Code's enactment, the Articles of War referred to enlisted members "assigned" to the accused's unit.[59] Construing this language, one Board of Review held that only persons "formally" assigned to the same unit as the accused were within the proscription.[60] The Code, however, is more expansive in referring to "a member of the same unit,"[61] suggesting that both enlisted members "attached" as well as "assigned"[62] to the accused's unit are disqualified.[63] Unit disqualification is nonjurisdictional and can be waived if not raised.[64]

A more difficult matter is ascertaining the critical time under the law for determining whether the accused and the enlisted court member are members of the same unit. In 1954, the Naval Board of Review stated that "Article (25) provides at least that membership in the same unit at the time of trial is not permitted."[65] Construing Article 25 with an eye to its likely purpose, an enlisted

---

[57] Dep't of Army Pam. 27-173, Trial Procedure 20 (20 April 1990) (*quoting* United States v. Scott, 25 C.M.R. 636, 640 (A.B.R. 1958)). *See also* United States v. Timmons, 49 C.M.R. 94 (N.C.M.R. 1974).

[58] Dep't of Army Pam. 27-173, Trial Procedure 20–21 (20 April 1990).

[59] United States v. Quimbo, No. 335865, 2 B.R.J.C. (1949).

[60] No. 335865, 2 B.R.J.C. (1949).

[61] U.C.M.J. art. 25(c)(1).

[62] Personnel accountability is normally a matter of administrative law. In general terms, "attached" personnel belong to a different unit but have been temporarily loaned to the unit of attachment for specific purposes or duration.

[63] The twin purposes of the disqualification are to ensure the selection of members without any previous bias against the accused and to prevent ill feelings from developing among the members of the same unit. Enlisted soldiers attached to a unit are as exposed to prejudicial information circulating within the unit as assigned members. Ill will between an assigned and attached member of a unit can be just as disruptive as ill will between two assigned members of the unit. It would serve the legislative purposes to construe the disqualification as extending to at least members attached to the accused's unit.

[64] United States v. Wilson, 21 M.J. 193 (C.M.A. 1986). *See also* United States v. Kimball, 13 M.J. 659 (N.M.C.M.R. 1982); United States v. Tagert, 11 M.J. 677 (N.M.C.M.R. 1981); United States v. Martinez-Salazar, 146 F.3d 653 (9th Cir. 1998) (reversal required when defendant forced to use peremptory when challenge for cause improperly denied even if the defendant did not ask for additional peremptory).

[65] United States v. Cook, 16 C.M.R. 404, 406 (N.B.R. 1954); United States v. Zengel, 32 M.J. 642, 643 (C.G.C.M.R. 1991) (dictum).

(Rel.3—1/07 Pub.62410)

member should be disqualified if in the same unit as the accused at either the time of the offense *or* the trial.[66]

§ 15-26.00 Disqualified Personnel

§ 15-26.10 Codal Disqualifications

Article 25(d)(2) provides that accusers, prosecution witnesses, investigating officers, and counsel in the same case are ineligible to sit as court members.[67] A problem occasionally arises when a court member has certified or authenticated a prosecution exhibit, such as a personnel record. Even though the member may have done so without any personal knowledge of the case, he or she has been deemed a prosecution witness and, hence, disqualified.[68]

The Army's Trial Procedure text[69] reported:

> In one case, in which the court member authenticated the accused's service record but the accused had plead [sic] guilty, the Navy Board of Review refused to find error.[70] Reaching a contrary result, however, an Air Force Board of Review argued that "we are dealing with the question of the competency of a member of a court, which question is independent of and completely disassociated from the accused's plea. Obviously, the qualifications of a member of a court are not contingent upon nor affected by the accused's plea."[71]

Neither the Uniform Code nor the Rules for Courts-Martial prohibit categories of personnel from serving as court members, whether they be medical personnel,[72] lawyers,[73] or law enforcement personnel.[74]

§ 15-26.20 Regulatory Unavailability

Although Article 25(a) seems plain on its face by declaring, for example, "[a]ny commissioned officer on active duty is eligible to serve on all courts-martial,"[75]

---

[66] *Accord* Dep't of Army Pam. 27-173, Trial Procedure 21 (20 April 1990) ("A purposive construction would be that both times are critical").

[67] U.C.M.J. art. 25.

[68] United States v. Smith, 16 C.M.R. 453 (C.G.B.R. 1954) (record of prior convictions); United States v. McDermott, 14 C.M.R. 473 (N.B.R. 1953) (service record); United States v. Hurst, 11 C.M.R. 649 (C.G.B.R. 1953); United States v. Beeks, 9 C.M.R. 743 (A.F.B.R. 1953); United States v. Wells, 4 C.M.R. 501 (C.G.B.R. 1952).

[69] Dep't of Army Pam. 27-173, Trial Procedure 21 (20 April 1990).

[70] United States v. Forehand, 8 C.M.R. 564 (N.B.R. 1953).

[71] United States v. Morris, 9 C.M.R. 786, 788 (A.F.B.R. 1953).

[72] *But see* § 15-26.20.

[73] *But see* United States v. Sears, 20 C.M.R. 377 (C.M.A. 1956) (appointment of legal officers discouraged).

[74] United States v. Hedges, 29 C.M.R. 458 (C.M.A. 1960); United States v. Swagger, 16 M.J. 759, 760 (A.C.M.R. 1983) (discouraging such appointment). *See also* § 15-54.27.

[75] *See also* R.C.M. 502(a)(1).

(Rel.3—1/07　Pub.62410)

at least in the Army, service regulations prohibit or limit service as court members to chaplains, Medical Corps officers, Medical Specialist Corps officers, Dental Corps officers, Veterinary Corps officers, Army Nurse Corps officers, and Inspectors General.[76] One can argue that such limitations on the ability of a convening authority to appoint members does not contravene Article 25, in that the Article only declares who is potentially qualified. Such reasoning seems shallow, however. Although there are valid personnel reasons for wishing to conserve scarce personnel resources, given the plain meaning of Article 25, it would appear that a convening authority ought to be able to determine personally whom to appoint to a court-martial without a general restriction by category.

§ 15-30.00 SELECTION OF COURT MEMBERS

§ 15-31.00 Selection by the Convening Authority Generally

Arguably, the most critical and least necessary vestige of the historical origins of the military criminal legal system is the personal appointment of the members by the convening authority.[77] The Court of Military Appeals held that Article 25 requires that the convening authority personally appoint the court members.[78]

Even though the system seldom is used to "rig the court" with biased jurors, there can be little doubt that many personnel think that it is so used. Further, it *can* be used that way, despite the statutory prohibitions against it.[79] Judge Cox has wisely commented that "[t]he Government has the functional equivalent of an unlimited number of peremptory challenges."[80]

The present selection system stems from at least three philosophical assumptions: the desire for an experienced and knowledgeable panel; the acute need

---

[76] *See* Army Reg. No. 27-10 Military Justice ch. 7 (16 November 2005) (containing an informational reference of such restrictions).

[77] *See generally* Glazier, *He Called for His Pipe, and He Called for His Bowl, and He Called for His Members Three — Selection of Military Juries by the Sovereign: Impediment to Military Justice,* 157 Mil. L. Rev. 1 (1998); Lamb, *The Court-Martial Panel Selection Process: A Critical Analysis,* 137 Mil. L. Rev. 103 (1992) (recommending a fixed number of members, six for general courts and three for special courts; random selection of members from a specified nominee pool that would exclude generals, O-1's, W-1's, and E1-E3's but nominate equal numbers of each rank; and repeal of the current rule that the accused be tried by persons senior to the accused).

[78] United States v. Ryan, 5 M.J. 97 (C.M.A. 1978). *See also* United States v. Benedict, 55 M.J. 451, 454–55 (C.A.A.F. 2001); United States v. Kroop, 34 M.J. 628 (A.F.C.M.R. 1992), *aff'd,* 38 M.J. 470 (C.M.A. 1993) (collateral investigation of convening authority for similar conduct does not cloud election of members, but disqualifies the convening authority from taking action), *pet. denied,* 37 M.J. 256 (C.M.A. 1993).

[79] U.C.M.J. art. 37.

[80] United States v. Smith, 27 M.J. 242, 252 (C.M.A. 1988) (*citing* United States v. Carter, 25 M.J. 471, 479 (C.M.A. 1988)).

(Rel.3—1/07 Pub.62410)

to prevent unnecessary operational interference with critical personnel; and a preference to ensure trial by the best qualified panel possible.

The obvious alternative to the present system is some form of random selection — a controversial topic, although it has been debated and espoused by many.[81] There is no legitimate reason why random selection cannot be implemented within the armed forces. Retention of the present law's requirement for commissioned officers (absent an enlisted accused's request for enlisted personnel) would preserve the "blue ribbon" jury approach, if needed, while giving the accused the option to include enlisted personnel. Exclusion of enlisted personnel with less than a fixed period of service, perhaps two years, would protect against a juror unfamiliar with military life. Similarly, permitting the convening authority to excuse members for operational needs ought to meet personnel needs. Random selection would necessarily mean that the convening authority would no longer have assurance that each court member met with command approval. Because command approval is more likely to mean that the members hold views akin to those of the convening authority rather than being the best potential members available, it is hard to see why this justification should be given weight.

Random selection has been tried in the Army. Although the limited nature of the experiment cannot be given undue emphasis, it appears to have been successful.[82] In 1988, the Court of Military Appeals endorsed random selection as a mechanism for assuring representativeness in court-martial panels.[83]

---

[81] See, e.g., Joint Hearings on S. 745–762, S. 2906 and 2097, Before the Subcomm. on Constitutional Rights of the Senate Judiciary Comm. and Senate Armed Services Comm., 89th Cong., 2d Sess. 93–94 (1966); H.R. 95, 94th Cong., 1st Sess. ¶ 825 (1975); S. 987, 93d Cong., 1st Sess. ¶ 825 (1973); Brookshire, Juror Selection Under the Uniform Code of Military Justice: Fact and Fiction, 58 Mil. L. Rev. 71, 94–107 (1972); Remcho, Military Juries: Constitutional Analysis and the Need for Reform, 47 Ind. L. J. 193, 224–31 (1972). United States v. Benedict, 55 M.J. 451, 454–55 (C.A.A.F. 2001); Page 15, n. 77. See also National Institute of Military Justice, Report of the Commission on the 50th Anniversary of the Uniform Code of Military Justice (recommends that the selection of the members be removed from the convening authority). See www. NIMJ.org. The DOD Joint Service Committee on the Method of Selection of Members of the Armed Forces to Serve on Courts-Martial (1999) concluded the current practice best applies the criteria for selection of court members.

[82] Memorandum from the SJA Fort Riley, Kansas and then Major Rex Brookshire, Project Officer to HQDA (DAJA-MJ), Implementation of the Random Juror Selection Pilot Program (3 December 1973-31 December 1974) (10 March 1975) reprinted at 2A F. Lederer, Cases and Materials on the Analysis of the Military Criminal Legal System 865 (2d ed. 1975). Potential "negative" results included a slight increase in "jury trials" and "a reluctance on the part of court-martial members to adjudge a severe sentence when the only misconduct involved relates strictly to military offenses." 2A F. Lederer, Cases and Materials on the Analysis of the Military Criminal Legal System 868–69 (Memo at 4–5) (2d ed. 1975).

[83] United States v. Smith, 27 M.J. 242, 249 (C.M.A. 1988) (but noting that the convening authority would have to personally appoint those who were randomly selected).

(Rel.3—1/07   Pub.62410)

If only to eliminate an unnecessary anachronism that distorts the military and civilian perception of an otherwise model system, Congress should amend Article 25 to provide for some form of random selection as soon as possible.[84]

§ 15-32.00 Procedure

The convening authority or his or her successor in command[85] must personally exercise the nondelegable power of selecting the participants.[86] The normal procedure in the Army, for example, is that the staff judge advocate (SJA) will bring to the convening authority the relevant personnel listing of the command and a recommended list of those whom the SJA believes should sit on the court-martial panel, based on duty, experience, prior participation, and division of work among staff sections. The SJA will normally recommend the number to be appointed in light of the Uniform Code's statutory minimum.[87] The convening authority will then select the members of the court martial. These members will normally sit for a period of time, likely six months, but some time later, likely at the end of three months, the convening authority will select a new half of a new panel.

In most jurisdictions, the convening authority will select one panel for the specified time, and each case will be referred to it. In busy jurisdictions, additional panels will be selected and appointed. During the Vietnam War, some commands operated three separate, concurrent courts-martial. At the time of referral,[88] the convening authority must personally select the panel to hear the case.[89]

The convening authority may request recommendations for appropriate court members from staff elements or subordinate units, or both, so long as the request

---

[84] Strom Thurmond National Defense Authorization Act for Fiscal Year 1999 § 552 (1998) required report on selection of court members. *See* n.81.

[85] United States v. Richardson, 5 M.J. 627 (A.C.M.R. 1978) (successor in command can appoint or adopt the appointment of members previously selected by a successor in command). *See also* United States v. Alvarez, 5 M.J. 762 (A.C.M.R. 1978).

[86] United States v. Ryan, 5 M.J. 97 (C.M.A. 1978); United States v. Newcomb, 5 M.J. 4 (C.M.A. 1978). *Compare* United States v. Ryan, 5 M.J. 97 (C.M.A. 1978) (personnel in the office of the staff judge advocate determining the panel and then selecting the enlisted personnel from a list previously selected by the convening authority was jurisdictional error) *with* United States v. Sands, 6 M.J. 666, CM 437166 (A.C.M.R., November 9, 1978) (staff judge advocate personnel merely selecting panel and not enlisted members for panel was not error of jurisdictional nature). A convening authority can adopt court members selected by a predecessor commander *when the command itself has changed.* United States v. Allgood, 41 M.J. 492 (C.A.A.F. 1995); Runkle v. United States, 122 U.S. 543 (1887) (President Hayes could correct invalid court-martial order issued by predecessor, President Grant).

[87] Five members for a general court-martial and three for a special court-martial.

[88] *See generally* Chapter 10.

[89] United States v. Simpson, 36 C.M.R. 293 (C.M.A. 1966) (nonjurisdictional error). Permitting staff personnel to select the panel would be an improper delegation of authority. However, there is nothing to prevent the staff from recommending a panel.

(Rel.3—1/07   Pub.62410)

does not arbitrarily exclude persons of particular grades.[90] Recommendations may not come from the trial counsel or the chief of military justice.[91] Under present law, however, the trial counsel or Chief of Criminal Law may ascertain the availability of alternative court members already approved by the convening authority and report that availability to the convening authority.[92] The Court of Appeals for the Armed Forces has sustained a methodology by which the convening authority effectively rubber stamps subordinate choices, hewing to the literal language of Article 25.[93] So long as the convening authority personally concurs in the names of the members, the requirements of the Code are met. In a well written dissent, Judge Effron has noted that when a convening authority is handed a "fait accompli," and does not personally select the members, the convening authority deprives the accused of the Article 25 right granted by Congress to have the convening authority select the "best qualified" members.[94] The armed forces constitute the last United States jurisdiction known to use a "blue ribbon jury system." If for reasons of convenience or efficiency they abandon the arguably special benefits of Article 25 selection, the attraction of random selection becomes more compelling.

In 2004, the Court condemned but sustained the use of an extraordinary selection procedure whereby the command's assistant staff judge advocate nominated members to the convening authority from a list of volunteers obtained from the command.[95] Ultimately, the nine member panel as selected by the convening authority, who was not part of this novel process, contained seven volunteers. The Court declared that "we reject and condemn the impermissible screening of potential members with this irrelevant variable," but held that "it

---

[90] United States v. Greene, 43 C.M.R. 72 (C.M.A. 1970). All officers are eligible for appointment to courts-martial. In *Greene*, a subordinate who was to furnish names was impermissibly misled into believing that only lieutenant colonels and colonels should be appointed. *See also* United States v. Daigle, 1 M.J. 139 (C.M.A. 1975) (impermissibly excluded warrant officers by asking for only second lieutenants to colonel). *But see* United States v. Credit, 2 M.J. 631 (A.F.C.M.R. 1976), *rev'd on other grounds*, 4 M.J. 118 (C.M.A. 1977) (permissible to ask for only second lieutenants through colonel in Air Force because of the limited number of warrant officers due to the grade being eliminated except for the few remaining on active duty). *See generally* § 15-33.00. *See also* United States v. Pugh, 2002 CCA LEXIS 103 (A.F. Crim. App. Apr. 9, 2002) (recommendation of an assistant staff judge advocate did not override personal selection by convening authority), *pet. denied*, 57 M.J. 448 (C.A.A.F. 2002).

[91] United States v. Cherry, 14 M.J. 251 (C.M.A. 1982); United States v. McCall, 26 M.J. 804 (A.C.M.R. 1988) (improper for people in Criminal Law Division to take names off one order and put them on the accused's court-martial panel); United States v. Crumb, 10 M.J. 520 (A.C.M.R. 1980).

[92] United States v. Marsh, 21 M.J. 445, 447–48 (C.M.A.), *cert. denied*, 479 U.S. 1016 (1986).

[93] *E.g.* United States v. Benedict, 55 M.J. 451, 454–455 (C.A.A.F. 2001).

[94] 55 M.J. at 458–459.

[95] United States v. Dowty, 60 M.J. 163 (C.A.A.F. 2004).

(Rel.3—1/07 Pub.62410)

did not taint the proceedings or prejudice Appellant."[96] It should be apparent that selecting members from volunteers has the potential for distorting the neutrality of the panel in an entirely unacceptable fashion.

If the accused requests enlisted personnel, normally the staff judge advocate will make recommendations in a letter to the convening authority. This letter will also include as an enclosure the list of enlisted members in the command. From that list, the convening authority will select the enlisted personnel, together with any personnel he or she wishes to excuse from the officer panel because of the new members.

It is unclear whether the staff judge advocate should continue to play a role in assisting the convening authority with selection of court members. Although that role has been taken for granted, the advent of independent defense services in the Air Force and Army[97] make the staff judge advocate in those services more than ever the chief prosecutor. Consequently, it is questionable whether this is sound now.[98] A better practice would be for the convening authority to rely upon a neutral staff member involved in personnel matters.

§ 15-33.00 Criteria Involving Rank, Sex, Race, Religion, et al.[99]

Article 25 would appear to grant the convening authority unlimited discretion in selection of court members. The Court of Military Appeals, however, held that limits do exist. In a 1986 decision, *United States v. McClain,*[100] Chief Judge Everett, in considering the impact of appointment of enlisted personnel from the top three grades on the SJA's recommendation, summarized the court's prior holdings concerning selection of members by military grade:

> This Court decided in *Greene*[101] that a court-martial panel had been improperly selected when its membership consisted of three colonels and six lieutenant colonels. The Court reasoned that, in view of the codal provisions for eligibility to court membership and the standards for selection of court members, a convening authority violated the Code by appointing only very senior officers to the court-martial. . . .
>
> Later, in *United States v. Daigle,*[102] . . . Judge Cook, writing for a unanimous Court, held improper the convening authority's fixed policy

---

[96] 60 M.J. at 165 (C.A.A.F. 2004).

[97] The Coast Guard and Navy military law centers separate the staff judge advocate's duties from the prosecution. Thus, the functions of the staff judge advocate or district legal officer in those services are, at least arguably, somewhat different from those of their counterparts in the Army and Air Force.

[98] *Cf.* United States v. Kemp, 46 C.M.R. 152 (C.M.A. 1973). *But see* United States v. Marsh, 21 M.J. 445, 448 (C.M.A. 1986).

[99] *See also* Section 15-35.00.

[100] 22 M.J. 124, 129 (C.M.A. 1986).

[101] 43 C.M.R. 72 (C.M.A. 1970).

[102] 1 M.J. 139 (C.M.A. 1975).

(Rel.3—1/07 Pub.62410)

of excluding lieutenants and warrant officers from the membership of courts-martial. He emphasized:

> Discrimination in the selection of court members on the basis of improper criteria threatens the integrity of the military justice system and violates the Uniform Code. Except for the statutory preference for exclusion of persons in a rank lower than the accused, all ranks are eligible to serve on a court-martial. [Citations omitted.] When rank is used as a device for deliberate and systematic exclusion of qualified persons, it becomes an irrelevant and impermissible basis for selection.[103]

In *United States v. Yager*,[104] Judge Cook explained:

> In *Daigle*, the Court was confronted with a situation where a group of otherwise qualified individuals was excluded from membership on a court-martial solely on the basis of rank. There was no demonstrable relationship between the excluded ranks and Article 25(d)(2), which requires a convening authority to detail those "best qualified for the duty by reason of age, education, training, experience, length of service, and judicial temperament."

He did not find *Daigle* inconsistent with a system of appointing enlisting members which excluded grades E-1 to E-3 because he concurred with the court below in that case that their disqualification "is an embodiment of the application of the statutory criteria."[105] His rationale parallels to some extent that used by Chief Judge Quinn [in 1964] upholding the procedures then used in the Army for selecting enlisted members, even though statistics in that service revealed that no one in a grade below E-4 had ever served as a court-martial member and that almost 90% of the enlisted members had been selected from grades of E-7, E-8, or E-9.[106] He [Judge Quinn] wrote:

> Here, the only purpose in looking to the senior noncommissioned ranks was to obtain persons possessed of proper qualifications to judge and sentence an accused. There was no desire or intention to exclude any group or class on irrelevant, irrational, or prohibited grounds. In short, the evidence leaves no room to doubt that the selection process was designed only to find enlisted men qualified for court service. The senior noncommissioned ranks provided a convenient and logically probable source for eligibles. To refer first to those ranks for prospective members is not an impermissible choice.[107]

In the present case, the method of selection used by the convening authority resulted in the nomination of 54 enlisted persons — none of whom was below the grade of E-4. However, appellant was an E-3, so the exclusion of the lower

---

[103] 1 M.J. at 140–41 (footnote omitted).

[104] 7 M.J. 171, 172 (C.M.A. 1979).

[105] 7 M.J. at 172.

[106] United States v. Crawford, 35 C.M.R. 3 (C.M.A. 1964).

[107] 35 C.M.R. at 12.

(Rel.3—1/07 Pub.62410)

three enlisted grades was permissible under Article 25(d)(1) — which directs that, "[w]hen it can be avoided," court members should not be "junior to . . . [the accused] in rank or grade." On the other hand, the appointment to the court-martial only of persons in the upper three grades was not proper.

In some situations, the legality of an action depends on its impact — regardless of the intent with which the act is performed. . . . In other situations, legality hinges on the presence or absence of a specific intent. . . .

Here, the findings made by the military judge make clear that the staff judge advocate intended to exclude junior members because he believed they were more likely to adjudge light sentences. He intended to utilize the statutory criteria set forth in Article 25(d)(2) of the Code — especially length of service — to obtain court membership that he believed would adjudge heavier sentences. However, the history of that statutory provision makes clear that Congress never intended for the statutory criteria for appointing court members to be manipulated in this way.[108]

Concurring in the result, Judge Cox opined:

> I disagree with any language . . . which appears to *per se* prohibit the appointment of a court-martial panel consisting entirely of senior officers or enlisted servicemembers. . . .
>
> The deliberate selection or exclusion of a certain class of service persons for the purpose of increasing the severity of the sentence is wrong. A proper concern, however, is the selection of servicepersons who will adjudge a sentence that is fair and just, considering the circumstances of the particular case.
>
> Because of the keen sensitivity shown by the convening authority, we normally would apply the presumption of regularity and assume that the convening authority was aware of his responsibilities and performed them properly.[109] We cannot do that here.[110]

In 1990, the Army Court of Military Review, en banc, sustained the convening authority's selection of only E-8's and E-9's from a much broader enlisted panel on the grounds that the convening authority's testimony that he had tried to pick those personnel who "would assure the accused the fairest trial" was proper under Article 25.[111] In 1993, however, the same court held unlawful a convening

---

[108] 22 M.J. at 129–31. *Cf.* United States v. Roland, 50 M.J. 66 (C.A.A.F. 1999).

[109] *Citing* United States v. Moschella, 43 C.M.R. 383 (C.M.A. 1971).

[110] 22 M.J. at 133.

[111] United States v. Nixon, 30 M.J. 1210 (A.C.M.R. 1990) (en banc), *aff'd*, 33 M.J. 433 (C.M.A. 1991). *But see* the dissent, stating that the convening authority had applied "a virtually irrebuttable presumption that enlisted personnel below the grade of those he selected . . . lack the ability to make findings and adjudge sentences in accordance with the instructions of the military judge." 30 M.J. at 1214 (A.C.M.R. 1990).

(Rel.3—1/07 Pub.62410)

authority's direction to simply obtain NCO's by number and grade (limited to E-7 and E-8).[112] And in 2000, the Court of Appeals for the Armed Forces reversed a case in which enlisted personnel had effectively been limited to E-7 and above.[113]

A variation of selection of members by rank is selection by command status. In *United States v. Hilow*,[114] the court dealt with the intentional selection by the Division Deputy Adjutant General on behalf of the convening authority of panel nominees "who were commanders and supporters of a command policy of hard discipline." Holding that "the deliberate stacking of the pool of potential members . . . violated Article 37 [prohibiting command influence on member selection]," the court continued to hold that even the convening authority's unknowing selection of members failed "to purge this error of prejudice."[115] The court reversed the accused's conviction despite his decision to be tried by judge alone. Although *Hilow* does not condemn the selection of only commanders *per se* as members, it explicitly condemns selection of "persons who are partial towards the prosecution or irrevocably support local command policies without regard to higher authority or inflexibly embrace a draconian punishment philosophy . . . ."[116] To the extent that a convening authority selects subordinate commanders as members with the expectation that they will implement his or her will, that selection is flawed.

In *United States v. Smith*,[117] the court turned to sex and, indirectly, to race and religion, when it considered whether a convening authority could intentionally appoint female officers to the court primarily or solely because they were women. The court held:

---

[112] United States v. Smith, 37 M.J. 773 (A.C.M.R. 1993) (the error deprived the court of jurisdiction).

[113] United States v. Kirkland, 53 M.J. 22 (C.A.A.F. 2000). *See generally* § 13-14.00 *above. See also* United States v. Morgan, 57 M.J. 119 (C.A.A.F. 2002) (record established the selection of enlisted members was accused's choice when counsel faxed the choice and there was no objection to the panel); United States v. Townes, 52 M.J. 275 (C.A.A.F. 2000) (failure to have personal request by the accused on the record as required by Article 25(c)(1) was nonjurisdictional harmless error).

[114] 32 M.J. 439 (C.M.A. 1991).

[115] 32 M.J. at 440 (C.M.A. 1991). Dissenting in part, Judge Cox wondered whether the case suggests the abandonment of the court's harmless error rule for cases like this. 32 M.J. at 444 (C.M.A. 1991). *See also* United States v. Roland, 50 M.J. 66 (C.A.A.F. 1999) (absent direct or circumstantial evidence of bad faith, nominations of E-5 and above for trial of private was not improper); United States v. Upshaw, 49 M.J. 111 (C.A.A.F. 1998) (it was nonjurisdictional error to exclude all grades below E-7 when there was a mistaken belief that appellant was an E-6. The court held there was no showing of prejudice).

[116] 32 M.J. at 441–42 (C.M.A. 1991).

[117] 27 M.J. 242 (C.M.A. 1988) (opinion by Everett, C.J. with Cox J. concurring and Sullivan, J. concurring in the result).

(Rel.3—1/07 Pub.62410)

[W]e infer . . . that a convening authority is not precluded by Article 25 from appointing court-martial members in a way that will best assure that the court-martial panel constitutes a representative cross-sample of the military community. . . .

Thus, a commander is free to require representativeness in his court-martial panels and to insist that no important segment of the military community — such as blacks, Hispanics, or women — be excluded from service on court-martial panels. [118]

Although female officers could thus be appointed to ensure that women were represented on the panel as such, they could not, however, be appointed only in cases involving sex offenses, as was the practice at Fort Ord in *Smith*. Such appointment "indicated that the female members were named to help assure a particular outcome" and required reversal. [119]

In 1992 the Coast Guard Court of Military Review contributed an interesting gloss to the selection question when, in the trial of an officer charged with offenses relating to the grounding and loss of his vessel, it sustained the convening authority's decision to limit selection of members to officers with significant sea-going experience. [120]

Although the law concerning appointment of members seems reasonably clear, it is not clear whether the same rules apply to discontinuance of a panel. Because courts-martial panels customarily sit for a period of months hearing a number of cases, it is unclear whether a convening authority may prematurely discontinue a panel in hopes that he or she will get a more pleasing result from a new panel. Certainly such an intent would run afoul of the *McClain* and *Smith* decisions. Yet, it may be minimally acceptable if the new panel is selected properly without intent to obtain more convictions or larger sentences. [121]

Court members may be appointed to ensure more severe sentences, stack the panel with a certain profile, or exclude certain grades. They may also be appointed as a result of an administrative mistake. The court might treat the later situation differently. However, do the other situations involve issues of unlawful command influence that may be waived if known and not raised? [122]

§ 15-34.00 Excusals

Prior to the Military Justice Act of 1983, only the convening authority could excuse members. [123] This proved unworkable, because an excusal request may

---

[118] 27 M.J. at 249 (C.M.A. 1988).

[119] 27 M.J. at 250 (C.M.A. 1988).

[120] United States v. Lynch, 35 M.J. 579, 587 (C.G.C.M.R. 1992).

[121] And presumably not under circumstances in which the new court members are aware of the reason for their selection.

[122] *Cf.* United States v. Wealser, 43 M.J. 15 (C.A.A.F. 1995).

[123] MCM, 1969 ¶ 37.

(Rel.3—1/07 Pub.62410)

arise at the last minute when the convening authority cannot be immediately reached. It also required that the convening authority be contacted as to every excusal. Under current law, the convening authority [124] may change the members of the court-martial before assembly of the court without showing good cause. [125] The convening authority's delegatee may excuse no more than one third before assembly. [126] A violation of this rule is nonjurisdictional. After assembly, no member may be excused except by the convening authority on good cause shown on the record, [127] by the judge for good cause shown on the record, [128] or as a result of challenge. [129] Good cause includes physical disability, military exigencies, and other extraordinary circumstances, [130] but does not include temporary inconveniences normal to military life. [131]

§ 15-35.00   Challenge to Entire Panel

When a convening authority systematically excludes a group of otherwise qualified servicemembers for an irrational or inappropriate reason, such as to obtain more severe sentences, the selection process is improper, [132] and the panel may be challenged. "[T]he moving party shall be entitled to present evidence, including any written materials considered by the convening authority in selecting the members. Any other party may also present evidence on the matter." [133]

The Army Court of Military Review held:

> Initially, we note that there is a presumption of regularity which attaches to the official acts of the convening authority. . . .

---

[124] The change also may be made by the convening authority's delegee under service regulations (R.C.M. 505(c)(1)(B)(i)) so long as not more than one-third of the total number of members detailed to the court are affected. R.C.M. 505(c)(1)(B)(ii).

[125] R.C.M. 505(c)(1). The critical point for substitution without showing good cause is before trial on the merits has commenced. United States v. Hawkins, 24 M.J. 257 (C.M.A. 1987).

[126] R.C.M. 505(c)(1)(B)(ii).

[127] R.C.M. 505(c)(2)(A)(i).

[128] R.C.M. 505(c)(2)(A)(ii).

[129] Pursuant to R.C.M. 912. R.C.M. 505(c)(2)(A)(iii).

[130] R.C.M. 505(f).

[131] R.C.M. 505(f).

[132] United States v. McClain, 22 M.J. 124 (C.M.A. 1986); United States v. Daigle, 1 M.J. 139 (C.M.A. 1975) (improper to automatically exclude lieutenants and warrant officers); United States v. Greene, 43 C.M.R. 72 (C.M.A. 1970) (convening authority considered only lieutenant colonels and colonels for membership). See also United States v. Lewis, 46 M.J. 338 (C.A.A.F. 1997) (appellant had not met burden to show court packing). See generally § 15-33.00.

[133] R.C.M. 912(b)(2). R.C.M. 912(b)(1) provides:

> Before the examination of members under subsection (d) of this rule begins, or at the next session after a party discovered or could have discovered by the exercise of diligence, the grounds therefor, whichever is earlier, that party may move to stay the proceedings on the ground that members were selected improperly.

(Rel.3—1/07 Pub.62410)

This presumption can only be overcome by clear and convincing evidence that there was a policy violative of Article 25, UCMJ. . . . We hold that, in keeping with established precedent, without some showing of impropriety, there is no requirement that every economic, racial or ethnic class or persons of all military grades be appointed as members of courts-martial.[134]

It will be a rare case in which the defense has direct information that the convening authority chose the court members because of their sentences or the number of acquittals. The burden of proof is on the defense to show improper selection by the convening authority.[135] The defense might carry this burden by showing changes that are made in the nominating, screening, or selection process following significant court "undesirable" results such as a particularly lenient sentence.

Under the Rules for Courts-Martial, failure to challenge the panel waives the issue unless the panel is defective within the sense of Article 25's statutory qualifications for members.[136]

§ 15-40.00 CONSTITUTIONAL CHALLENGES

Although the Sixth Amendment right to a jury trial does not apply in the armed forces,[137] the due process rationale of the Supreme Court in *Ballew v. Georgia*[138] might reasonably do so. In *Ballew*, the Court found that the quality of group deliberation decreases in proportion to the size of the jury involved, and when the jury verdict is reduced to the point where it can be delivered by less than six jurors, it is constitutionally suspect and unacceptable.[139] Inasmuch as Article 16 of the Uniform Code provides that except in capital cases general courts-martial shall consist of not less than five members[140] and special courts-martial not less than three members,[141] and that panels frequently convict without six concurring members, it is apparent that *Ballew*'s result is inconsistent with both military law and practice.

---

[134] United States v. McLaughlin, 27 M.J. 685, 687 (A.C.M.R. 1988).

[135] United States v. McClain, 22 M.J. 124 (C.M.A. 1986); United States v. James, 24 M.J. 894 (A.C.M.R. 1987). When the accused alleges that the court members were selected solely on rank, with the exclusion of junior members, the burden of proof to establish improper selection is on the accused. *See also* United States v. Cunningham, 21 M.J. 585 (A.C.M.R. 1985); United States v. Carman, 19 M.J. 933 (A.C.M.R. 1985).

[136] R.C.M. 912(b)(3). *But see* United States v. Beehler, 35 M.J. 502 (A.F.C.M.R. 1992) (refused to apply waiver for failure to raise institutional bias until after plea).

[137] *See above* note 3.

[138] 435 U.S. 223 (1978). *See also* Burch v. Louisiana, 441 U.S. 130 (1979).

[139] 435 U.S. 223 (1978).

[140] U.C.M.J. art. 16(1).

[141] U.C.M.J. art. 16(2).

(Rel.3—1/07 Pub.62410)

Given that the framers did not have access to contemporary scientific research, it is difficult to ascribe an intent to permit court-martial verdicts that might be unreliable.[142] The rationale of *Ballew* might apply either as a result of military due process, or the due process clause of the Fifth Amendment. The 2002 addition to the Uniform Code of Military Justice of Article 25a, ordinarily requiring a 12 member panel for capital cases,[143] will moot any attack against a capital case, leaving the military criminal legal system open, however, to *Ballew* for other cases.

Arguably, the *Ballew* conclusion is inapplicable in light of the unique nature of the armed forces.[144] The military courts have been unwilling to apply the empirical data referred to in *Ballew*, since the material was compiled from juries randomly selected in civilian communities.[145] In the absence of evidence impeaching the quality of military verdicts, the courts have not as yet been willing to apply *Ballew* to the military.[146]

---

[142] Although the framers surely knew or should have known that the court-martial verdicts of their day lacked the safeguards applicable to civilian criminal trials.

[143] The National Defense Authorization Act for Fiscal Year 2002, Pub. L. No. 107-107 (Dec. 28, 2001), amending the Uniform Code of Military Justice effective December 31, 2002.

[144] The court members are selected from a more homogeneous group and are more attuned to what is necessary to the nature of their society than civilian jurors are likely to be.

[145] United States v. Wolff, 5 M.J. 923 (N.C.M.R. 1978).

[146] *See, e.g.,* Mendrano v. Smith, 797 F.2d 1538, 1546–47 (10th Cir. 1986). Having first held that the right to a jury is inapplicable to the armed forces, the court in *Mendrano* held that due process did not require application of *Ballew* to the military:

> The two-thirds rule, as implemented by the Manual For Courts-Martial, lessens the problem of the hung jury with the votes of only two-thirds of the voting panel members being required to convict. Furthermore, there is a significant recompense to the defendant, in that failure of two-thirds to vote for conviction results in acquittal. This balancing does not seem constitutionally impermissible. We are mindful that, in the context of civil jury trials, in *Burch* the Court rejected a time-saving argument as speculative on that record and, more importantly, because the State there had reduced the jury size to the minimum number of six (the same number as on petitioner's court-martial panel), threatening the constitutional principles that led to the establishment of the size threshold. . . . Nevertheless, we feel that in the military context the obvious policy preference by Congress for lessening the hung-jury problem in courts-martial should be given deference. . . .
>
> While this appeal presents close and troubling questions, after considering the critical constitutional protections involved, as well as the congressional judgment expressed in the adoption of the two-thirds rule for the military tribunals, the compensating factor of the rule for acquittal where a conviction is not approved, and the lack of any claim or showing of empirical data here that the two-thirds rule impairs the quality of court-martial results so as to amount to a constitutional infringement, we conclude that the balance that has been struck does not violate the Due Process Clause or other constitutional principles relied on by the petitioner.

(Rel.3—1/07 Pub.62410)

§ 15-50.00   VOIR DIRE AND CHALLENGE

§ 15-51.00   In General

It is imperative that court members be impartial. To ensure this, military law provides that both parties may challenge members for cause.[147] Recognizing that a party may strongly distrust a member and yet be unable to articulate a proper causal challenge, each party is also given a peremptory challenge.[148] Although there is no limit to the number of causal challenges that may be made, each party ordinarily only receives one peremptory challenge.[149] To effectuate the right to challenge, the military judge routinely advises the members in the preliminary instruction of the need for their impartiality and of the nature of the *Manual's* disqualifications.[150] The members are then asked whether they are "aware of any matters which might raise a substantial question concerning your participation in this trial as a court member?"[151] Each party may then conduct a voir dire of the members.

If a member is excused pursuant to challenge, neither party has a right to have the excused member replaced so long as the quorum requirement is met.[152]

§ 15-52.00   Sources of Information for Challenges Other than Voir Dire

§ 15-52.10   Pretrial Investigation of Court Members

Although voir dire may be a useful tool for inquiring into the beliefs and experience of court members, it is time consuming and, absent proper preparation, often wide of the mark. Adequate pretrial preparation is of great value in preparing a proper voir dire or establishing a challenge. The Rules for Courts-Martial authorize the use of pretrial questionnaires to obtain information about prospective court members.[153] Such questionnaires may be used at the discretion of the trial counsel; they must be used if the defense counsel so requests.[154]

---

[147] *See* Section 15-54.00.

[148] *See* Section 15-55.00.

[149] *But see* Section 15-55.20.

[150] Dep't of Army Pam. 27-9, Military Judges' Benchbook 2, Section V (15 September 2002).

[151] Dep't of Army Pam. 27-9, Military Judges' Benchbook 45 (15 September 2002).

[152] United States v. Anderson, 36 M.J. 963, 975 (A.F.C.M.R. 1993).

[153] Such questionnaires are often becoming important civilian tools. *See generally* Cox, *Delving Into the Jurors' Minds*, Nat'l L. J., January 21, 1991, at 1. They may be subject to media inspection. *Compare* Lesher Communications v. Superior Court, 224 Cal. App. 3d 774, 274 Cal. Rptr. 154 (1990) *with* Copley Press v. Superior Court, 223 Cal. App. 3d 994, 273 Cal. Rptr. 22 (1990).

[154] R.C.M. 912(a)(1). *See also* United States v. Slubowski, 5 M.J. 862, 886 n.2 (N.C.M.R. 1978) ("We note with approval the practice of submitting form questionnaires concerning the background of members in order to expedite voir dire examination. Such questionnaires must be appended to the record as appellate exhibits.").

(Rel.3—1/07 Pub.62410)

Data that may be obtained from court members by questionnaire include: date of birth; sex; race; marital status; number, age, and sex of family members; home of record; civilian and military education; current unit of assignment; past duty assignments; awards and decorations; date of rank; and whether the member has acted in any disqualifying capacity, such as forwarding the case with recommendation as to disposition or acting as accuser or investigating officer. Counsel may also request additional information with the approval of the military judge.[155]

Upon request, any party will be provided a copy of any written materials considered by the convening authority in selecting the court members detailed to the court.[156] Use of pretrial questionnaires is a valuable tool that saves time and improves the quality of voir dire at trial.[157]

No mechanism exists in the armed forces for the type of personal investigation of individual jurors sometimes engaged in in civilian practice. On the other hand, the comparatively small size of most military installations usually makes it easy for counsel to make informal inquiries about members. As is often the case with hearsay or reputation, information gained in such a manner may be unreliable.

§ 15-52.20   Disclosure by the Members

The members are advised by the military judge in his or her preliminary instructions of the need for impartiality and requested to advise the judge of any known grounds for challenge.[158]

§ 15-52.30   Disclosure by the Government

In *United States v. Glenn,*[159] the court held, with a fair degree of exasperation, that where a court member was the sister-in-law of the deputy staff judge advocate who was involved in the case, the deputy had an "affirmative duty to inform the staff judge advocate, trial counsel, and defense counsel" that he was related to the member. Having so held, the court reversed the conviction, even though the member had completed an affidavit swearing that she had no prior knowledge of the case and had been unaffected by the relationship. At the least, the *Glenn*

---

[155] R.C.M. 912(a)(1). *See, e.g.,* United States v. Credit, 2 M.J. 631 (A.F.C.M.R. 1976), *rev'd on other grounds,* 4 M.J. 118 (C.M.A. 1977).

[156] R.C.M. 912(a)(2).

[157] U.S. Dep't of Army Pam. 27-10, Trial Counsel and Defense Counsel Handbook 3-138 to 3-142 (C1, 1 March 1983).

[158] Dep't of Army Pam. 27-9, Military Judges' Benchbook 41 (30 September 2002). *See also* United States v. Lake, 36 M.J. 317 (C.M.A. 1993) (no evidence of willful concealment or deliberate disregard of judge's instructions).

[159] 25 M.J. 278, 280 (C.M.A. 1987); United States v. Schuller, 17 C.M.R. 101 (C.M.A. 1954) (holding that accused could not waive issue when trial counsel and law officer failed to disclose to accused that law officer had previous participation in appellant's case as SJA to the convening authority).

(Rel.3—1/07   Pub.62410)

case requires notice by the government lawyers involved of any relationship with a member. It may be that in future years the case will serve as a broader precedent.[160]

§ 15-53.00 Voir Dire

"Voir dire," or the examination of court members to determine their fitness to sit, is an ancient phrase that means "to speak the truth."[161] Voir dire is ordinarily conducted before challenges to obtain sufficient information to make appropriate challenges. However, inasmuch as a challenge for cause may be made at any time in the trial should circumstances warrant,[162] limited voir dire may take place after assembly.

"If the members have not already been placed under oath for the purpose of voir dire, they should be sworn before they are questioned."[163]

Voir dire may be used to determine whether a court member is statutorily qualified to sit, whether the member is and will remain impartial, and whether the member's actions or belief is such that his or her service as a court member would give rise to an appearance of unfairness. In addition, and critically, because court members will sentence a convicted accused, counsel may properly use voir dire to explore the member's views of sentencing. Although voir dire can be used for many other purposes, such as highlighting various issues, educating the court members, or building rapport between counsel members, such uses are improper unless done in the otherwise proper process of voir dire.[164] Using voir dire for purposes such as arguing one's case or exposing the members to inadmissible evidence is unethical and improper, and likely to elicit a mistrial motion, if not a contempt citation.

---

[160] *But see* United States v. Modesto, 43 M.J. 315 (C.A.A.F. 1995) (in cross-dressing prosecution, failure of trial counsel and member to disclose that member had cross-dressed at Halloween party was not a violation of R.C.M. 912(c)).

[161] Black's Law Dictionary 1412 (5th ed. 1979).

[162] R.C.M. 912(f)(2)(B). *See, e.g.*, United States v. Cleveland, 6 M.J. 939 (A.C.M.R. 1979) (court member was sending notes to other members contrary to instructions of judge); United States v. Thompson, 5 M.J. 28 (C.M.A. 1978) (a court member's comment that absent witness "can't be much of a witness or he would be present" did not reflect so deep-seated a prejudice against the witness that it would not yield to the judge's explanation). Under some circumstances peremptory challenges may be exercised after a trial on the merits. R.C.M. 912(g)(2).

[163] Discussion to R.C.M. 912(d) making reference to R.C.M. 807(b)(2) Discussion (B). *See* United States v. Clemons, 35 M.J. 767 (A.C.M.R. 1992) (error in failing to swear court members was waived by failure to object).

[164] This is not to deny that voir dire may play a legitimate tactical role. Few questions can be asked in an entirely neutral fashion, and to require neutrality might well defeat the very purpose of voir dire. Accordingly, voir dire may be tied to opening statements, the presentation of evidence, closing arguments, and judicial instructions. The key, however, is that questions may not be asked for other purposes; they must have independent legitimacy as a proper part of the process of voir dire and challenge.

(Rel.3—1/07 Pub.62410)

In a very basic way, voir dire is examination or interrogation of the court members. Jurors normally come to court prepared to hear the examination of witnesses and not themselves. In the armed forces, the routine practice is for the military judge to instruct the members during the preliminary instructions as to the purpose and nature of voir dire. [165]

In civilian practice, most federal judges conduct most or all of the voir dire personally, limiting counsel to submitting proposed questions. [166] Most state judges, however, have permitted almost unlimited voir dire by counsel, with limited, if any, questions on their own part. [167] Traditional military practice has followed the state approach. Although both trial and defense counsel have the same right of voir dire, often the voir dire has been conducted only by the defense counsel, with the trial counsel limiting himself or herself primarily to rehabilitation questions. The judge may have asked some clarifying questions, but was usually silent otherwise. Traditional practice may change, however, as a result of Rule for Courts-Martial 912(d). Following Federal Rule of Criminal Procedure 24(a), Rule 912(d) states:

> The military judge may permit the parties to conduct the examination of members or may personally conduct the examination. In the latter event the military judge shall permit the parties to supplement the examination by such further inquiry as the military judge deems proper or the military judge shall submit to the members such additional questions by the parties as the military judge deems proper. A member may be questioned outside the presence of other members when the military judge so directs.

---

[165] Dep't of Army Pam. 27-9, Military Judges' Benchbook 2, sections V and VI (15 September 2002). It may be that more specific judicial instructions would be appropriate when voir dire necessarily involves sophisticated legal issues such as the affirmative defenses of mental responsibility or self-defense; it would be wise for the judge to give a preliminary instruction to the court members.

[166] One study of the federal courts indicated that three-fourths of the district judges conducted voir dire examinations without oral participation by counsel. G. Bermant, *Conduct of the Voir Dire Examination: Practices and Opinions of Federal District Judges* 6 (1977). The judges involved in the Second Circuit Court of Appeals experiment, which allowed each counsel to conduct a ten-minute examination, reacted positively to the experiment, and some indicated they would continue it in the future. Even so, the judges thought it was fair to assume that the questioning of the court members solely by the judges is more expeditious. Given the option, civilian federal judges prefer to conduct the voir dire. Sand and Reiss, *A Report on Seven Experiments Conducted by District Court Judges in the Second Circuit*, 60 N.Y.U. L. Rev. 423 (1985). Empirical studies comparing the length of voir dires in which counsel participate indicate that they are less time consuming than commonly thought. Levit, Nelson, Ball & Chernick, *Expediting Voir Dire: An Empirical Study*, 44 S. Cal. L. Rev. 916, 949 (1971). Notwithstanding this, it is apparent that in some "horror story" cases, voir dire can go on for weeks or months.

[167] Almost without exception, lawyers prefer to conduct their own voir dire. Judges, however, prefer the alternative to avoid wasting time and possible exposure of the jurors to inadmissible evidence. It is interesting to note that periodic attempts are made to change the Federal Rules of Criminal Procedure to permit lawyer voir dire as a matter of right. *See, e.g.*, Note, *A Right to Voir Dire?*, 73 A.B.A. J. 31 (1987).

(Rel.3—1/07   Pub.62410)

Some military judges are now taking advantage of the opportunity to personally conduct voir dire.[168]

Counsel may voir dire the entire panel, portions of the panel, and individual members. Ordinarily, counsel will begin with the panel and move to individuals. The Court of Appeals for the Armed Forces has observed, however, that "this Court [has] intimated that the parties must show that individual *voir dire* is necessary because certain areas could not be covered in group questioning,"[169] suggesting a bias in favor of constraining individual voir dire; indeed, the court has affirmatively stated that there is no right to individual voir dire by counsel.[170] With the judge's consent, members may be questioned outside the presence of the other members, something that may be essential to prevent tainting the remaining members with inappropriate views or information.[171]

The scope of voir dire, civilian or military, is a matter within the discretion of the trial judge,[172] and in practice that discretion is extraordinarily broad. The

---

[168] *See generally* United States v. Jefferson, 44 M.J. 312, 318–19 (C.A.A.F. 1996) (discussing history of judge-conducted voir dire). The judge might also personally inquire into possible predisposition, the members' willingness to comply with the presumption of innocence, and possible bias in favor of the credibility of commanders and law enforcement officials when testifying as witnesses. *See also* United States v. Dewrell, 55 M.J. 131, 137 (C.A.A.F. 2001) ("We hold that the questions asked by the military judge were clearly adequate to cover the statutory qualification of the members. Thus, there was no abuse of discretion by the military judge.")

[169] United States v. Belflower, 50 M.J. 306, 309 (C.A.A.F. 1999) (judge did not abuse his discretion in refusing to permit individual voir dire, *citing* United States v. Jefferson, 44 M.J. 312, 320–21 (C.A.A.F. 1996), discussed *below*.

[170] United States v. Fulton, 55 M.J. 88 (C.A.A.F. 2001) (parties do not have right to individually voir dire the members); *cf.* United States v. Lambert, 55 M.J. 293, 296 (C.A.A.F. 2001) (defense counsel has no right to individually voir dire members even during an inquiry into member misconduct during deliberations).

[171] *Cf.* United States v. Awan, 966 F.2d 1415, 1431–33 (11th Cir. 1992) (Sixth Amendment not violated by jurors' exposure to juror's verification of the evidence).

[172] R.C.M. 912(d) Discussion. *But see* United States v. Jefferson, 44 M.J. 312, 322 (C.A.A.F. 1996). In *Jefferson*, the court addressed various procedural issues involved with voir dire: "tag teams," individual versus group voir dire, and reopening of voir dire. The court in *Jefferson* upheld the discretion of the judge-controlled voir dire but held that the judge abused his discretion when he denied defense counsel the opportunity to reopen voir dire to explore forgotten areas concerning past criminal victimization of prospective members' family and friends. The Constitution mandates very little in the area of voir dire. *See* Mu'min v. Virginia, 500 U.S. 415 (1991) (judge not required to ask jurors about the contents of news reports they had read about the case); Rosales-Lopez v. United States, 451 U.S. 182 (1981); Ham v. South Carolina, 409 U.S. 524, 527–28 (1973) (judge has broad discretion to decide whether to ask questions suggested by counsel); United States v. Smith, 27 M.J. 25 (C.M.A. 1988). *See also* United States v. Barnes, ACMR 8702529 (A.C.M.R. Oct. 28, 1988) (proper for the military judge to prevent the defense counsel from asking members whether they would be more comfortable as trial or defense counsel and to prevent a hypothetical question as to whether the court president would be comfortable with a court member trying his son if they thought as the president did). *See also* Davis v. State, 611 A.2d 1008 (Md. App. 1992)

(Rel.3—1/07 Pub.62410)

Court of Military Appeals strongly urged granting counsel great latitude during voir dire; however,

> [w]hen a member is examined with a view to challenge, it is to be remembered that he may be asked any pertinent question tending to establish a disqualification for duty on the court. Statutory disqualifications, implied bias, actual bias, or other matters which have some substantial and direct bearing on an accused's right to an impartial court, are all proper subjects of inquiry. *The accused should be allowed considerable latitude in examining members so as to be in a position intelligently and wisely to exercise a challenge for cause or a peremptory challenge.* Accordingly, when there is a fair doubt as to the propriety of any question, it is better to allow it be answered. While materiality and relevancy must always be considered to keep the examination within bounds, they should be interpreted in a light favorable to the accused. If there is doubt in the mind of the . . . [military judge] as to the propriety and good faith of the questions, he can and should require the examiner to disclose the relevancy of the examination, rather than merely forbid the inquiry. [173]

Effective voir dire depends on honest and accurate answers by the court members. In *United States v. Mack*, [174] the Court of Military Appeals for the Armed Forces adopted the Supreme Court's test for determining the effect of a juror's non-disclosure during voir dire: "[A] party must first demonstrate that a juror failed to answer honestly a material question on voir dire, and then further show that correct response would have provided a valid basis for a challenge for cause." [175] Because the trial record is usually inadequate to resolve appellate allegations of court member nondisclosure, a *DuBay* evidentiary hearing is often necessary. [176]

The judge is free to exclude questions that are intended to embarrass a member, pry into personal matters not necessary to the voir dire, or that are for an improper purpose. The judge is also able to restrict the examination of the court members within reasonable bounds so as to expedite the trial. In the armed forces, however, "jury sentencing" makes a much more probing voir dire both necessary and lawful than would be acceptable in most civilian courts. Appellate courts may be

---

(forcefully reasserting the trial judge's wide discretion). *But see* United States v. Adams, 36 M.J. 1201, 1205 (N.M.C.M.R. 1993) (judge conducted initial voir dire and collapsed numerous questions concerning members' knowledge and opinions about urinalysis program into one general question; inappropriate limitation of voir dire was an abuse of discretion and required reversal).

[173] United States v. Smith, 27 M.J. 25, 27 (C.M.A. 1988) (*quoting* from United States v. Parker, 19 C.M.R. 400, 405 (C.M.A. 1955) but adding emphasis).

[174] 41 M.J. 51 (C.M.A. 1994).

[175] 41 M.J. at 55 (C.M.A. 1994). United States v. Humpherys, 57 M.J. 83, 96 (C.A.A.F. 2002); United States v. Taylor, 44 M.J. 254 (C.A.A.F. 1996) (no showing that court member who was later prosecuted failed to answer any question falsely); United States v. Modesto, 43 M.J. 315 (C.A.A.F. 1995) (defense never asked any member whether he had cross-dressed). Failure to give true feelings could lead to challenges for cause.

[176] 41 M.J. at 55.

(Rel.3—1/07 Pub.62410)

particularly concerned when dealing with a trial judge's refusal to permit voir dire into possible racial prejudice.[177] Both counsel and judge should keep in mind that voir dire often probes matters of personal concern to the members and if not clearly relevant can be readily considered as an unwarranted privacy violation.[178]

Because a proper voir dire should be tied to the unique facts of each case, no real guidance can be given as to construction of a desirable voir dire. There are any number of trial practice books containing illustrative questions. The key to their use is a careful tailoring of relevant sample questions to the facts at hand.[179] In a case involving pretrial publicity,[180] voir dire into that area would be essential, as may be inquiry into the willingness of members to comply with the judge's instructions when special facts or issues apply. Surely, inquiry into the member's outlook on sentencing is essential, most especially in capital cases, where the death penalty may affect findings as well.[181] If there is reason to believe that the members may have been affected by unlawful command influence,[182] voir dire of the members would be crucial in establishing the members' disability.

Voir dire is not unlimited. In a case with a mandatory sentence of life imprisonment, voir dire may be restricted to prevent the members from learning of the statutory penalty prior to sentencing.[183] The Court of Military Appeals also rejected "jury nullification" as a justification for voir dire.[184]

---

[177] *Compare* Ham v. South Carolina, 409 U.S. 524 (1973) *with* Turner v. Murray, 476 U.S. 28 (1986). The Supreme Court has held "that absent 'special circumstances' that create a particularly compelling need to inquire into racial prejudice, the Constitution leaves the conduct of voir dire to the sound discretion of state trial judges." *Turner*, 476 U.S. at 37, n.12 (holding it unconstitutional for a state judge to prohibit defense voir dire on the issue of racial bias in an interracial capital case).

[178] *See generally* Karen Monsen, *Privacy for Prospective Jurors at What Price? Distinguishing Privacy Rights from Privacy Interests; Rethinking Procedures to Protect Privacy in Civil and Criminal Cases*, 21 Rev. of Litigation 285 (2002).

[179] The classic example is the civilian defense counsel who asks the jurors whether they would be more likely to believe a police officer than another witness solely because of the officer's status as a law enforcement officer. The question is both routine and potentially useful. It is, however, embarrassing when no police officers will testify.

[180] *See, e.g.,* Murphy v. Florida, 421 U.S. 794 (1975); United States v. Garwood, 20 M.J. 148 (C.M.A.), *cert. denied*, 474 U.S. 1005 (1985).

[181] *E.g.,* Morgan v. Illinois, 504 U.S. 719 (1992) (in a state system in which the jury decides whether to adjudge the death penalty, a capital defendant has a due process right to have the potential jurors asked whether they would automatically vote to impose the death sentence; any such juror may be challenged for cause). *See* Section 15-54.22.

[182] *See, e.g.,* United States v. Miller, 19 M.J. 159 (C.M.A. 1985).

[183] United States v. Smith, 27 M.J. 25 (C.M.A. 1988); *but see* 27 M.J. 29 (C.M.A. 1988) (Everett, C.J. concurring and holding the case to its facts while *citing* United States v. Jefferson, 22 M.J. 315, 329 (C.M.A. 1986).

[184] 27 M.J. at 29 (*citing* United States v. Jefferson, 22 M.J. 315, 329 (C.M.A. 1986)).

(Rel.3—1/07 Pub.62410)

Although the Court of Military Appeals emphasized the importance of wide ranging voir dire, the standard for appellate review is more limited:

> But one of the well-recognized rules of criminal jurisprudence is that wide discretion is vested in trial judges as to questions which must be answered by jurors on voir dire. Appellate courts should reverse only when a clear abuse of discretion, prejudicial to a defendant, is shown. Conceding that the purposes of voir dire are to determine whether individual jurors can fairly and impartially try the issues, and to lay a foundation so that peremptory challenges can be wisely exercised, those purposes do not permit the examination to range through fields as wide as the imagination of counsel. Because bias and prejudice can be conjured up from many imaginary sources and because peremptory challenges are uncontrolled except as to number, the areas in which counsel seek to question must be subject to close supervision by the . . . [military judge].[185]

Even on appeal, however, the Court of Appeals for the Armed Forces has indicated that it will not always bow to the military judge's discretion. In *United States v. Richardson*,[186] for example, the Court held that the military judge had erred by not permitting defense counsel additional voir dire of officer members who had previously received legal advice from the trial counsel in their official duties.

Voir dire is a fundamental part of a criminal trial. It is important enough that the Supreme Court has held that it may not, per se, be closed to the public.[187] Counsel would be wise to keep in mind, however, that voir dire should not be conducted for its own sake; it is a means to an end and not an end in itself. The difficulty inherent in voir dire is the same difficulty that is inherent in challenges. Although counsel would like to select members likely to be favorable to their positions,[188] absent clear evidence that a member ought not to sit, most counsel can only guess when exercising their challenges.[189]

---

[185] United States v. Smith, 27 M.J. 25, 28 (C.M.A. 1988) (quoting from United States v. Parker, 19 C.M.R. 400, 406 (C.M.A. 1955)). *See also* Patton v. Yount, 467 U.S. 1025, 1039 (1984); United States v. Jones, 722 F.2d 528 (9th Cir. 1983); United States v. Primrose, 718 F.2d 1484 (10th Cir. 1983), *cert. denied*, 466 U.S. 974 (1984); United States v. Moran, 1999 CCA Lexis 89 (A.F. Crim. App. Mar. 8, 1999), *pet. denied*, 52 M.J. 416 (C.A.A.F. 1999) (no abuse of discretion to preclude voir dire regarding fact that administrative separation would be "available regardless of your decision").

[186] 61 M.J. 113 (C.A.A.F. 2005).

[187] Press-Enterprise Co. v. Superior Court, 464 U.S. 501 (1984).

[188] *See, e.g.*, J. Frank, *Courts on Trial* 121–23 (1949) (citing sources); Fahringer, *In the Valley of the Blind: A Primer on Jury Selection in a Criminal Case*, 43 Law & Contemp. Probs. 116, 117 (1980); Kuhn, *Jury Discrimination: The Next Phase*, 41 S. Cal. L. Rev. 235, 286 (1968). Although the defense may ethically attempt to obtain a favorable jury, one can argue easily that the prosecutor may ethically seek only a neutral and impartial jury.

[189] The myths rife among the civilian and military bars as to the types of jurors who should be challenged are incredible. "How to" books from various periods often present unbelievable pieces of advice that include the starkest possible racial, religious, ethnic, sexual, and gender stereotypes and slurs possible.

(Rel.3—1/07 Pub.62410)

In the event of inappropriately terminated voir dire or possible non-disclosure of important information by a member, when appropriate the appellate courts may order a *DuBay*[190] fact-finding hearing.[191]

§ 15-54.00 Individual Challenges for Cause

§ 15-54.10 In General[192]

Unlike the few statutory grounds for challenge for cause in the federal system,[193] Rule for Courts-Martial 912(f)[194] lists numerous specific grounds for challenge to assist the judge.[195] Inasmuch as the protections of the Bill of Rights apply only to the defendant,[196] the *Manual*'s requirements could be viewed as having special value to the prosecution, particularly the Rule 912(f)(1)(N) requirement that "[a] member shall be excused for cause whenever it appears that the member. . . . [s]hould not sit as a member in the interest of having the court-martial free from substantial doubt as to legality, fairness, and impartiality."

Rule for Courts-Martial 912(f)(1) provides:

A member shall be excused for cause whenever it appears that the member:

(A) Is not competent to serve as a member under Article 25(a), (b), or (c);[197]

(B) Has not been properly detailed as a member of the court-martial;[198]

(C) Is an accuser as to any offense charged;

---

[190] United States v. DuBay, 37 C.M.R. 411 (C.M.A. 1967).

[191] *E.g.,* United States v. Sonego, 61 M.J. 1 (C.A.A.F. 2005); United States v. Mack, 41 M.J. 51, 55–56 (C.A.A.F. 1994).

[192] *See also* Section 14-40.00 (disqualification of the military judge).

[193] 28 U.S.C. § 1865(b).

[194] U.C.M.J. art. 25(d)(2) states only that "[n]o member of an armed force is eligible to serve as a member of a general or special court-martial when he is the accuser or a witness for the prosecution or has acted as investigating officer or as counsel in the same case."

[195] Enumeration of the grounds for challenge is important as the Supreme Court has never sought to define impartiality. *See* United States v. Wood, 299 U.S. 123, 145–46 (1936).

[196] The Framers recognized that the government would have sufficient power to protect its own interests.

[197] Lack of statutory qualification is a ground for challenge for cause and is nonwaivable. R.C.M. 912(f)(4). The requirement that enlisted members belong to different units from the accused, however, (*see* Section 15-24.00) is nonjurisdictional and may be waived unless specific prejudice is shown. *See* United States v. Wilson, 21 M.J. 193 (C.M.A. 1986).

[198] Court members must be personally selected by the convening authority. United States v. Ryan, 5 M.J. 97 (C.M.A. 1978). *See* Section 15-31.00.

(Rel.3—1/07 Pub.62410)

(D) Will be a witness in the court-martial;[199]

(E) Has acted as counsel for any party as to any offense charged;[200]

(F) Has been an investigating officer as to any offense charged;[201]

(G) Has acted in the same case as convening authority[202] or as the legal officer or staff judge advocate[203] to the convening authority;

(H) Will act in the same case as reviewing authority or as the legal officer or staff judge advocate to the reviewing authority;

(I) Has forwarded charges in the case with a personal recommendation as to disposition;[204]

(J) Upon a rehearing or new or other trial of the case was a member of the court-martial which heard the case before;

(K) Is junior to the accused in grade or rank, unless it is established that this could not be avoided;

(L) Is in arrest or confinement;

(M) Has informed or expressed a definite opinion as to the guilt or innocence of the accused as to any offense charged;[205] or

---

[199] United States v. Mansell, 23 C.M.R. 377 (C.M.A. 1957) (witness for prosecution after excusal); United States v. Bell, 3 M.J. 1010 (A.C.M.R. 1977) (not abuse of discretion to grant challenge for cause against director of regional personnel center who lifted two of three "flagging" actions against accused). The "witness" disqualification extends to a member who has expertise in a relevant area, or who has personal knowledge of facts relevant to the case, even though he or she does not actually take the witness stand, and even though no challenge is made. *See* United States v. Conley, 4 M.J. 327 (C.M.A. 1978); United States v. Ivey, 37 C.M.R. 626 (A.B.R. 1967).

[200] Including the situation where the court member, or military judge, by his or her questioning of witnesses, departs from an impartial role and becomes an advocate for either side. United States v. Lamela, 7 M.J. 277 (C.M.A. 1979). *See also* United States v. Hampton, 50 C.M.R. 233 (A.C.M.R. 1975) (member serving temporarily in prosecutor's office should have been excused).

[201] *See, e.g.,* United States v. Burkhalter, 38 C.M.R. 64 (1967) (public affairs officer responsible for investigating an incident in order to prepare and issue press releases is subject to challenge); United States v. Edwards, 15 C.M.R. 299 (C.M.A. 1957) (provost marshal who forwarded autopsy report on victim not investigating officer). *See also* § 15-54.27.

[202] The prohibition applies even when the officer appointed himself or herself while serving as an acting commander and is no longer the convening authority at the time of trial.

[203] *Cf.* United States v. Roberts, 22 C.M.R. 112 (C.M.A. 1956); United States v. Crunk, 15 C.M.R. 290 (C.M.A. 1954).

[204] *See* United States v. Strawbridge, 21 C.M.R. 482 (A.B.R. 1955) (member who forwarded charges in closely related case held disqualified). *Cf.* United States v. Lake, 36 M.J. 317 (C.M.A. 1993) (receiving charges for summary court-martial, convening authority did not disqualify member when she did not remember such action and the information should reasonably have been known by counsel).

[205] *See* United States v. Ovanda-Moran, 48 M.J. 300 (C.A.A.F. 1998) (Held even though a court member stated it would be unnatural if an accused did not testify, no abuse of discretion to deny challenge since member stated he would follow the judge's instructions and would not use the

(Rel.3—1/07　Pub.62410)

(N) Should not sit as a member in the interest of having the court-martial free from substantial doubt as to legality, fairness, and impartiality.[206]

The military criminal legal system has long had a tradition that military judges should be liberal in granting challenges,[207] and the judge may excuse a member for cause sua sponte.[208] At the same time, some judges have tended to deny causal challenges to ensure prompt case disposition.[209] In the past, Judge Cox "would, almost always, defer to the discretion of the military judge" when reviewing denials of causal challenges.[210]

Although causal challenges should[211] be granted liberally, on review the judge is given "great deference" because of demeanor evidence; the trial judge's causal challenge decision will be overturned only for clear abuse of discretion.[212]

---

accused's silence as an indication of guilt); United States v. Miller, 19 M.J. 159 (C.M.A. 1985) (former member of court who expressed opinion that accused was guilty tainted other members); United States v. Lane, 18 M.J. 586 (A.C.M.R. 1984) (member believed accused must prove innocence). *Compare* United States v. Coffin, 25 M.J. 32 (C.M.A. 1987) (fact that member knew that the accused, who was charged with drug offenses, had undergone an urinalysis was sufficient for him not to have sat on the case) *with* United States v. Towers, 24 M.J. 143 (C.M.A. 1987) (previous experience as a social services counselor who investigated child-abuse cases did not, *per se*, disqualify her in a child-abuse case).

[206] *See generally* United States v. White, 36 M.J. 284, 288 (C.M.A. 1993) ("Technical expertise is not automatically disqualifying"; a reporting relationship between members is not *per se* disqualifying 36 M.J. 288 (C.M.A. 1993); United States v. Lake, 36 M.J. 317 (C.M.A. 1993) ("Insubstantial participation in a case, . . . innocuous prior knowledge of the facts of a case . . . or official acquaintance with government witnesses are not *per se* disqualifying," noting that defense counsel could have reasonably discovered the grounds for challenge); United States v. Bannwarth, 36 M.J. 265, 266 (C.M.A. 1993) (member's friendship with accuser is not an automatic disqualification); United States v. Ingham, 36 M.J. 990, 994 (A.C.M.R. 1993) (member could sit despite professional relationship with TC absent showing of actual or implied bias), *aff'd*, 42 M.J. 218 (C.A.A.F. 1995); United States v. Perez, 36 M.J. 1198 (N.M.C.M.R. 1993) (prospective witnesses should be excused from the court on causal challenge). *See* § 15-54.21, *below*.

[207] MCM, 1969 (Rev. ed.) ¶ 62h(2) (not included in the Rules for Courts-Martial, but its omission was not intended to change the policy); United States v. Jobson, 31 M.J. 117, 122 (C.M.A. 1990) (Sullivan, concurring); United States v. Smart, 21 M.J. 15, 18 n.1 (C.M.A. 1985). *See also* United States v. Kelley, 40 M.J. 515, 518 (A.C.M.R. 1994) (denial of causal challenge after equivocal statement of member on voir dire in rape case implying bias required reversal; judge should have made further inquiry). *See generally Smart*, 21 M.J. at 21.

[208] United States v. Strand, 59 M.J. 455 (C.A.A.F. 2004) (*citing* R.C.M. 912(f)(4)).

[209] *Smart*, 21 M.J. at 21.

[210] 21 M.J. at 21 (Cox, J. concurring).

[211] United States v. Jobson, 31 M.J. 117, 122 (C.M.A. 1990) (Sullivan, J. concurring).

[212] United States v. White, 36 M.J. 284, 287 (C.M.A. 1993). Judge Sullivan, concurring, opines that, as implied bias under R.C.M. 912(f)(1)(N) is judged on an objective standpoint, to deny a challenge "solely" because of a judge's credibility determination would be an abuse of discretion. 36 M.J. 288 (C.M.A. 1993). *See also* Patton v. Yount, 467 U.S. 1025, 1038 (1984) ("As we have said on numerous occasions, the trial court's resolution of [juror bias] questions is entitled, even on direct appeal, to 'special deference'"); United States v. Quintero-Barraza, 78 F.3d 1344, 1349 n.5 (9th Cir. 1995).

(Rel.3—1/07 Pub.62410)

Causal challenges may be made at any time during trial, and it may well be that counsel will not learn critical information until after voir dire and challenge. Questions by members during trial, for example, may justify challenge. In *United States v. Hill*,[213] the court noted:

> We have observed that, "under certain conditions, the sheer number of questions by a court member may highlight his bias against an accused or be an important factor in determining the existence of partiality in a member as to a particular issue in dispute." . . . At the same time, we have made clear that, while this may be a factor in evaluation, the real inquiry is a more holistic one — whether "the overall questioning by these members creates an impression or a substantial doubt that [they] had departed from [their] required character as . . . unbiased member[s] of the court . . ."[214]

Casual challenges during member deliberations are both few and difficult, and likely to come about primarily through information volunteered by other members. Although recent civilian cases have opined, for example, that it is proper for the court to dismiss a juror unwilling or unable to follow the law, the courts have been highly reluctant to determine that such removal was in fact necessary.[215]

§ 15-54.11   Procedures

In *United States v. Jefferson*,[216] the court addressed various procedural issues involved with voir dire: "tag teams," (Two defense counsel conducting voir dire) individual[217] versus group voir dire and reopening voir dire. The court held that the military judge has the discretion to control voir dire, including its procedure.[218] However, the judge's discretion is not unlimited. In *Jefferson*, after completion of voir dire and following a recess, the defense asked for permission to reopen the voir dire to explore forgotten areas concerning friends and family members being victims of crimes. Holding that the military judge erred in refusing permission, the Court opined:

> We recognize that judges are sometimes required to "ride" a circuit and often have crowded dockets. But when co-counsel reminds counsel conducting the *voir dire* that further inquiry was omitted on a critical issue, judges should be patient and allow that inquiry to be conducted . . . .[219]

---

[213] 45 M.J. 245 (C.A.A.F. 1996).

[214] 45 M.J. at 249 (C.A.A.F. 1996).

[215] United States v. Symington, 195 F.3d 1080, 1087 (9th Cir. 1999) ("We hold that if the record evidence discloses any *reasonable* possibility that the impetus for a juror's dismissal stems from the juror's views on the merits of the case, the court must not dismiss the juror."); United States v. Thomas, 116 F.3d 606 (2d Cir. 1997) (removal not adequately justified).

[216] 44 M.J. 312 (C.A.A.F. 1996).

[217] 44 M.J. at 316–17, 320–22 (C.A.A.F. 1996).

[218] United States v. DeNoyer, 44 M.J. 619 (A. Crim. App. 1996).

[219] 44 M.J. at 322.

(Rel.3—1/07   Pub.62410)

§ 15-54.20 Freedom From Substantial Doubt as to Legality, Fairness and Impartiality

§ 15-54.21 In General

Perhaps the single most important ground for causal challenge is Rule 912(f)(1)(N), which provides that a "member shall be excused for cause whenever it appears that the member. . . . [s]hould not sit as a member in the interest of having the court-martial free from substantial doubt as to legality, fairness, and impartiality." This is a critical "catch-all." Chief Judge Everett has expressed his concern that the "exhortation" to be liberal in granting challenges in this area "often has been ignored."[220] The Court of Appeals explained the liberal grant mandate:

> A trial court's standard is to grant challenges for cause liberally. An appellate court's standard is to overturn a military judge's ruling on a challenge for cause only for a clear abuse of discretion. This means that military judges must follow the liberal-grant mandate in ruling on challenges for cause, but we will not overturn the military judge's determination not to grant a challenge except for a clear abuse of discretion in applying the liberal-grant mandate.[221]

This means "great deference" to the trial judge.[222] But this same deference does not apply when the challenge is based on implied bias.[223] Judge Everett speculated that the failure to grant a challenge may be caused by fears of reducing the number of members below statutory minimums and because the court members may view their excusal as an "insult to their fairness and integrity."[224]

Court members are human beings with varied backgrounds and experiences. An accused does not have a right to a "virgin" jury, civilian or military.[225]

---

[220] United States v. Mason, 16 M.J. 455, 457 (C.M.A. 1983) (Everett, C.J., dissenting in a case dealing with the predecessor *Manual* provision).

[221] United States v. White, 36 M.J. 284, 287 (C.M.A. 1993). Senior-subordinate reporting relationships between members have been troublesome as some might infer that the subordinate would not feel free to reach a conclusion independent of the senior. *E.g.*, United States v. Wiesen, 56 M.J. 172 (C.A.A.F. 2001). A proposed change to R.C.M. 912(f)(1)(N) provides "The existence of a command or supervisory relationship between two or more members of a court-martial panel (even where such members constitute a majority sufficient to reach a finding of guilty) shall not constitute grounds for removal for cause." Professor Lederer believes that such an amendment would be unwise given the traditional desire to keep court-martial verdicts free of the suspicion of command influence.

[222] R.C.M. 912(f)(1)(N).

[223] United States v. Minyard, 46 M.J. 229, 231 (C.A.A.F. 1997). *See also* United States v. New, 55 M.J. 95, 99 (C.A.A.F. 2000) (R.C.M. 912(f)(1)(N) " 'codifies a general ground for challenge' which includes both actual and implied bias," *citing* United States v. Minyard, 46 M.J. 229, 231 (C.A.A.F. 1997); United States v. Armstrong, 54 M.J. 51 (C.A.A.F. 2000).

[224] United States v. Mason, 16 M.J. 455, 457 (C.M.A. 1983) (Everett, C.J., dissenting in a case dealing with the predecessor *Manual* provision).

[225] *See, e.g.*, United States v. Jobson, 31 M.J. 117, 121–22 (C.M.A. 1990).

(Rel.3—1/07 Pub.62410)

Whether it is pretrial publicity,[226] knowledge of some of the facts of the case,[227] or some preconceived notions of the law or appropriate sentence, the critical question is whether the member can set those aside and fairly and impartially try the accused pursuant to the judge's instructions.[228] At the same time, the doctrine of implied bias[229] may require excusal of members for reasons of public policy rather than actual bias. In *United States v. Wiesen,*[230] the Court applied an implied bias rationale to hold that the President of the Court who commanded six other members, should have been excused; "Where a panel member has a supervisory position over six of the other members, and the resulting seven members make up the two-thirds majority sufficient to convict, we are placing an intolerable strain on public perception of the military justice system."[231]

[226] *See generally* Sections 13-35.00 *et seq.*

[227] *See, e.g.,* United States v. Jobson, 31 M.J. 117 (C.M.A. 1990) (awareness of pretrial agreement not *per se* disqualification); United States v. Tompkins, 30 M.J. 1090, 1092 (N.M.C.M.R. 1989) (fact that member saw some correspondence related to the case did not require granting causal challenge). Accidental *ex parte* contact with witnesses is a risk. *See, e.g.,* United States v. Elmore, 31 M.J. 678, 689 (N.M.C.M.R. 1990) (*citing* United States v. Adamiak, 15 C.M.R. 412, 417 (C.M.A. 1959), *aff'd,* 33 M.J. 387, 394 (C.M.A. 1991) (prosecution expert witness' unintentional pretrial dinner and breakfast with members did not require their excusal when the trial judge determined that no prejudice or taint existed). *See also* United States v. White, 36 M.J. 284, 288 (C.M.A. 1993) ("Although contact between witnesses and court members, even if innocent or inadvertent, gives rise to perceptions of unfairness, it is not automatically disqualifying"). *Ex parte* communications require reversal unless there is a " 'clear and positive showing' that the improper communication . . . did not and could not operate in any way to influence the decision." 31 M.J. 689 (N.M.C.M.R. 1990) (*quoting* Adamiak, 15 C.M.R. at 418).

[228] *See, e.g.,* United States v. Rockwood, 52 M.J. 98, 105–06 (C.A.A.F. 1999); United States v. Schlamer, 52 M.J. 80, 93 (1999) (judge did not abuse discretion in not granting challenge for cause against member who, without legal training, answered questionnaire by stating that accused should have the opportunity to be heard but would not draw any adverse inferences if the accused did not testify); United States v. Coppock, 37 M.J. 145 (C.M.A. 1993) (court members exposed to pretrial publicity were not disqualified when they stated that they would have an open mind and act on the evidence received); United States v. Armstrong, 30 M.J. 769, 771 (A.C.M.R. 1990) (indecent liberties with a child case; judge did not abuse discretion in rejecting a causal challenge of member who said she would keep an open mind but opined that children were not as likely to lie as adults); United States v. Sloan, 30 M.J. 741 (A.F.C.M.R. 1990) (drug case; denial of causal challenges did not constitute an abuse of discretion when based only on the members having heard rumors about the case and having expressed distaste about drug offenses). In the unusual case of United States v. Taylor, 41 M.J. 701, 704 (A.F. Crim. App. 1995), the court held that absent false material answers on voir dire or a showing of prejudice, the mere fact that the president of the court had previously committed other criminal acts, for which he was subsequently convicted, did not justify relief.

[229] *See* note 223 *above.*

[230] 56 M.J. 172 (C.A.A.F. 2001). *See* note 241 *below.*

[231] 56 M.J. at 175–176. This decision could be overturned by rule amendment. *See* n.221 *above.*

§ 15-54.22   Sentencing Considerations

§ 15-54.22(a)   Rigid Notion as to Punishment

Although a mere distaste for criminal conduct or a particular offense is not enough to disqualify a member, an inflexible attitude concerning a particular offense that will not be changed by either the evidence or the military judge's instructions substantiates a causal challenge.[232] A member who initially indicates a preconceived notion concerning penalty may remain on the case if he or she credibly states that he or she can consider and decide the case upon the evidence and the judge's instructions. Such a disclaimer must be delivered in a manner indicative of truthfulness without any equivocation, and there must be no other evidence of record controverting the disclaimer or questioning its sincerity.[233]

In *United States v. Heriot*,[234] the court addressed the issue of sentencing predisposition. The accused was charged with violation of Navy regulations prohibiting unlawful possession, transfer, or sale of marijuana. On voir dire, one member stated that if the accused were convicted his sentence should at least include a reduction of one grade. He also stated that the accused should not remain as a noncommissioned officer. He did not believe, however, that a sentence should necessarily include either confinement or a bad-conduct discharge. In an opinion by Chief Judge Everett, the court indicated that it was sympathetic to the plight of court members being questioned on voir dire with hypothetical questions.[235] On the one hand, the court wished to encourage candor from the members; on the other, it was

> reluctant to hold that a prospective member who is not evasive and admits to harboring an opinion that many others would share — such as that a convicted drug dealer should not remain a noncommissioned officer or should be separated from the Armed Service — must automatically be excluded if challenged for cause.[236]

However, a court member who indicates that under no circumstances will he or she ever consider adjudging some type of lenient sentence is

> by implication, affirming that he will disregard the evidence in extenuation and mitigation and the arguments that counsel and that he will not listen

---

[232] R.C.M. 912(f)(1)(N) Discussion; United States v. Heriot, 21 M.J. 11 (C.M.A. 1985); United States v. Tippit, 9 M.J. 106 (C.M.A. 1980); United States v. Karnes, 1 M.J. 92 (C.M.A. 1975).

[233] United States v. Smart, 21 M.J. 15, 18–20 (C.M.A. 1985) (captain indicated that he would not consider a no-punishment option).

[234] 21 M.J. 11 (C.M.A. 1985).

[235] 21 M.J. at 13 (C.M.A. 1985).

[236] 21 M.J. at 13 (C.M.A. 1985).

to contrary views that may be expressed by other court members when the court closes to deliberate on the sentence. [237]

Judge Everett suggested that when this issue arises, the military judge "may wish to give the member additional instructions and ask him some clarifying questions." [238] The court ultimately found that the judge erred in failing to excuse the member but that under the circumstances it was nonprejudicial. [239] The Court of Appeals for the Armed Forces summarized the law in this area thusly: "An inflexible member is disqualified; a tough member is not." [240]

The critical question in all causal challenge issues is whether the trial judge abused his or her discretion in denying or granting the challenge. [241] In *United States v. Reynolds*, [242] for example, the court indicated that a member is not automatically disqualified if he admits an unfavorable inclination towards a particular offense. In *Reynolds*, a theft case, the court member indicated a highly qualified preference for a punitive discharge based on counsel's hypothetical voir dire question. Although prior case law would have sustained a challenge, the court held that the trial judge, faced with judging the credibility and demeanor of the court members, had not abused his discretion in rejecting it. [243]

---

[237] 21 M.J. at 13 (C.M.A. 1985). *See, e.g.,* United States v. Rolle, 53 M.J. 187, 191 (C.A.A.F. 2000) (test for inelastic attitude is "whether member's attitude is of such a nature that he will not yield to the evidence presented and the judge's instructions," *quoting* United States v. McGowan, 7 M.J. 205, 206 (C.M.A. 1979); United States v. Giles, 48 M.J. 60, 63 (C.A.A.F. 1998) (member demonstrated inelastic attitude).

[238] 21 M.J. at 13. Rather than doing this after the questions have already been asked, it would be better for the judge to precede voir dire with instructions on predisposition, credibility of witnesses, and the reasonable-doubt standard. Otherwise, counsel will abandon predisposition as a way of challenging senior members and move to the other two areas. Recent cases indicate this trend. *See* United States v. Carter, 25 M.J. 471 (C.M.A. 1988) (colonel); United States v. Towers, 24 M.J. 143 (C.M.A. 1987) (lieutenant; previous experience as social services counselor); United States v. Reynolds, 23 M.J. 292 (C.M.A. 1987) (colonel); United States v. Davenport, 17 M.J. 242 (C.M.A. 1984) (lieutenant colonel); United States v. Mason, 16 M.J. 455 (C.M.A. 1983) (lieutenant colonel); United States v. Harris, 13 M.J. 288 (C.M.A. 1982) (colonel).

[239] 21 M.J. at 14.

[240] United States v. Schlamer, 52 M.J. 80, 93 (C.A.A.F. 1999).

[241] *See, e.g.,* United States v. White, 36 M.J. 284 (C.M.A. 1993); United States v. Paige, 23 M.J. 512, 513 (A.F.C.M.R. 1986) ("[H]is ruling denying a challenge for cause will be reversed on appeal only if there is a clear abuse of discretion.") (*quoting* United States v. Hawks, 19 M.J. 736 (A.F.C.M.R. 1984)). *See also* United States v. Harris, 13 M.J. 288, 293 (C.M.A. 1982) (Cook, J. concurring in the result) (*citing* United States v. Boyd, 7 M.J. 282 (C.M.A. 1979)); United States v. Deain, 17 C.M.R. 44, 49 (C.M.A. 1954); United States v. Sloan, 30 M.J. 741 (A.F.C.M.R. 1990).

[242] 23 M.J. 292 (C.M.A. 1987).

[243] 23 M.J. at 294 (C.M.A. 1987). United States v. McLaren, 38 M.J. 112, 118 (C.M.A. 1993) ("unfavorable inclination toward an offense is not automatically disqualifying"); United States v. Bannwarth, 36 M.J. 265 (C.M.A. 1993) (same).

(Rel.3—1/07　Pub.62410)

§ 15-54.22(b)   View of Capital Punishment

The proper test under the Sixth and Fourteenth Amendments for determining when a prospective juror may be excluded for cause because of his or her views on capital punishment is whether the juror's views would prevent or substantially impair performance of his or her duties as a juror in accordance with his or her instructions and oath.[244] This test does not require the conclusion that the juror would "automatically" vote against capital punishment or that the juror's bias be "unmistakably clear."[245] This is a factual determination, and a judge's decision to exclude a juror is entitled to a presumption of correctness. In *Wainwright v. Witt*,[246] the Court suggested possible voir dire questions for counsel.[247] If the prosecution is successful with these questions, the defense should seek to rehabilitate the juror by showing that, in some cases, the juror could impose the death penalty.

The exclusion of jurors because they cannot vote for capital punishment under any circumstances does not violate the Sixth or Fourteenth Amendment.[248] Despite data to the contrary, the Supreme Court has rejected the contention that

---

[244] Wainwright v. Witt, 469 U.S. 412, 423–25 (1985). *See* United States v. Gray, 51 M.J. 1, 31–32 (C.A.A.F. 1999), *affirming*, (applying Supreme Court precedents; "would a member's views prevent or substantially impair the performance of his duties as a juror . . . ."). *See generally* John H. Blume, Sheri Lynn Johnson & A. Brian Threlkeld, *Symposium: Probing, Life Qualifications Through Expanded Voir Dire*, 29 Hofstra L. Rev. 1209 (2001).

[245] 469 U.S. at 423–25. *See also* Adams v. Texas, 448 U.S. 38 (1980) (improper to exclude potential jurors who indicated that they would be more emotionally involved or would view their tasks with greater seriousness knowing that a potential punishment might be the death penalty); Lockett v. Ohio, 438 U.S. 586 (1978) (permissible to exclude potential juror who made it "unmistakably clear" that he could not be trusted to "abide by existing law" and conscientiously follow the instructions of the judge); United States v. Loving, 41 M.J. 213, 294 (C.A.A.F. 1994) (appointment of members by convening authority does not prohibit peremptory challenges by the prosecution against members who are not death qualified).

[246] 469 U.S. 412 (1985).

[247] 469 U.S. at 432 n.12. Other suggested questions:

Would you automatically vote against the imposition of capital punishment without regard to any evidence that might develop at the trial of the case before you?

Would your attitude toward the death penalty prevent you from making an impartial decision as to the defendant's guilt?

Are you a religious person?

Does your religion hold that capital punishment is morally wrong?

Do you have any qualms about capital punishment?

If the evidence warrants it, are you willing to condemn a man to die?

Can you envision any case in which the death penalty might be warranted?

Can you in good conscience take an oath or is your conviction so strong knowing that capital punishment is an option that you cannot take an oath to abide by the law?

[248] Lockhart v. McCree, 476 U.S. 162 (1986).

(Rel.3—1/07 Pub.62410)

a "death qualified" jury is more likely to convict than one that includes jurors with objections to the death penalty.[249] In *Morgan v. Illinois*,[250] the Court held that when a state jury is responsible for adjudging the death penalty, a juror who would automatically vote to impose the death sentence may be challenged for cause. The same result should follow in military law.

The 11th Circuit has held that the Constitution does not prohibit a death sentence adjudged by a jury that did not believe that a sentence of death would ever be carried out.[251]

In *Gray v. Mississippi*,[252] the Court, in a five-to-four opinion, held that the improper exclusion of a juror from a capital jury required reversal of the death sentence because it prejudiced an accused's right to an impartial jury. The Court refused to apply the harmless-error test, even though the prosecution had one peremptory challenge left. Justice Powell concurred in part and concurred in the judgment. He refused to concur in the part of the opinion that indicated that an erroneous exclusion of a scrupled, yet eligible, court member may be an isolated incident that would have no prejudicial effect in the case.[253] He seemed to indicate that in some isolated instances the exclusion will not result in reversal, but can result in harmless error.[254]

§ 15-54.23　Racial, Religious, Sexual, or Ethnic Prejudice

Racial or religious prejudice is ordinarily a proper ground for challenge.[255] The Air Force Court of Military Review opined that membership in a specific religion is not a ground in and of itself for challenge, but that a "member's religious beliefs are an appropriate subject of inquiry, but only to the extent to which they cast light on his *personal* fairness and impartiality."[256] Presumably

---

[249] 476 U.S. 162 (1986).

[250] 504 U.S. 719 (1992).

[251] Ingram v. Zant, 26 F.3d 1047, 1050 (11th Cir. 1994), *cert. denied*, 513 U.S. 1167, 115 S. Ct. 1137 (1995).

[252] 481 U.S. 648 (1987).

[253] 481 U.S. at 670 & n.2. (1987).

[254] 481 U.S. at 670 & n.2. (1987).

[255] *Cf.* Turner v. Murray, 476 U.S. 28 (1986); Ham v. South Carolina, 409 U.S. 524 (1973). *See* United States v. Credit, 2 M.J. 631, 646 (A.F.C.M.R. 1976), *rev'd*, 4 M.J. 118 (C.M.A. 1977); United States v. Grittman, 16 C.M.R. 328 (A.B.R. 1954).

[256] United States v. Credit, 2 M.J. 631, 646 (A.F.C.M.R. 1976) (emphasis in original). *Cf.* Mil. R. Evid. 610. Inquiry into a member's religion without specific justification is questionable. *See, e.g.*, United States v. Barnes, 604 F.2d 121, 141 (2d Cir. 1979), *cert. denied*, 446 U.S. 907 (1980); Yarborough v. United States, 230 F.2d 56, 63 (4th Cir.), *cert. denied*, 351 U.S. 969 (1956). *See also* United States v. DeJesus, 347 F.3d 500, 510 (3d Cir. 2003) (government assertion that struck jurors' "unusual amount of religious activity suggested strong religious beliefs, which could prevent them from convicting the defendant" constituted a proper reason for their excusal).

(Rel.3—1/07　Pub.62410)

bias involving sex, sexual preference, national origin, ethnic group or any other "class" prejudice of potential impact on the trial also would justify challenging a member who apparently holds such a prejudice.

§ 15-54.24 Crime Victim

The mere fact that a court member has been a victim of crime is not enough for a causal challenge, but repeated victimization or some other special characteristic may be sufficient. [287]

§ 15-54.25 Consults Legal Authority

A member who improperly obtains legal advice from the *Manual for Courts-Martial* shall be excused for cause unless voir dire indicates the member will forego this advice or reading. [288]

§ 15-54.26 Relationships

Professional acquaintance with counsel[289] for either side, or casual or

---

[287] *E.g.*, United States v. Miles, 58 M.J. 192 (C.A.A.F. 2003) (judge erred in not granting challenge for cause against member in cocaine case who wrote an article on the impact of cocaine based on his nephew's death as a result of his mother's use of cocaine during her pregnancy); United States v. Henley, 53 M.J. 488, 492 (C.A.A.F. 2000) (Court held that the judge did not abuse her discretion in granting a challenge for cause against a member who had two friends who were victims of sexual abuse and the member believed that someone "with an extensive collection of pornography probably had a 'fixation or something of that nature.' "); United States v. Velez, 48 M.J. 220 (C.A.A.F. 1998) (held that the court member was not disqualified because two of his friends were raped in the past year and he had some concern for his own daughter, when member said this would not impact on his decision); United States v. Jefferson, 44 M.J. 312, 322 (C.A.A.F. 1996) (judge abused his discretion when he denied defense counsel the opportunity to reopen voir dire to explore forgotten areas concerning past criminal victimization of prospective members' family members and friends); United States v. Daulton, 45 M.J. 212 (C.A.A.F. 1996) (error not to grant challenge for cause when member's sisters were abused by grandfather); United States v. Fulton, 44 M.J. 100 (C.A.A.F. 1996) (judge did not abuse discretion in refusing to grant challenge for cause against member because one was the victim of a crime 20 years ago); United States v. Brown, 34 M.J. 105 (C.M.A. 1992) (judge's denial of causal challenge in a sodomy case in which a court member had a son who had been a victim of a homosexual assault was proper, given judge's questioning of member and his responses); United States v. Smart, 21 M.J. 15, 18–20 (C.M.A. 1985) (despite sincere, honest expression of impartiality by court member in robbery trial, fact that member had been victim of "six or seven" robberies supported finding of implied bias); United States v. Porter, 17 M.J. 377, 379 (C.M.A. 1984); United States v. Harris, 13 M.J. 288 (C.M.A. 1982) (disclaimer insufficient where member worked with two victims of the accused). *See also* United States v. Campbell, 26 M.J. 970 (A.C.M.R. 1988) (error not to grant challenge of court member who was the victim of four barracks larcenies); United States v. Smith, 25 M.J. 785 (A.C.M.R.), *pet. denied*, 27 M.J. 18 1988) (no error in not granting challenge where members admitted being victims of unrelated crime and testified that their being a victim would not affect their ability to determine a fair sentence).

[288] United States v. Hawks, 19 M.J. 736 (A.F.C.M.R. 1984).

[289] United States v. Downing, 56 M.J. 419 (C.A.A.F. 2002) (when there is a question of the

(Rel.3—1/07 Pub.62410)

professional acquaintance with the victim's father,[260] is not, per se, a ground for challenge. In a most unusual case, the Court of Appeals for the Armed Fores has even sustained a conviction in which the convening authority's son sat as president of the court.[261]

A rating relationship in which one member is responsible for rendering a routine fitness report on another does not, per se, disqualify a member from sitting,[262] because the members are instructed that the influence of rank or

relationship between the trial counsel and one of the potential members, the issue should be explored on the record by the judge; here the accused did not meet the burden necessary to establish an improper relationship even though the member dealt professionally with counsel); United States v. Ali, 49 M.J. 1 (C.A.A.F. 1998) (working relationship between officer and an enlisted member lasting less than one year does not suggest predisposition as to witness's credibility); United States v. Dubar, 48 M.J. 288 (C.A.A.F. 1998) (defense counsel waived any error concerning the trial counsel's failure to disclose that the member was an expert witness for the prosecution. The court specifically did not address the issue of whether the trial counsel should have disclosed the prior professional relationship. It would be wiser for counsel to do so because the "trial counsel [is not] the arbiter of the merits of a challenge" for cause); United States v. Napoleon, 46 M.J. 279 (C.A.A.F. 1997) (professional relationship is not per se disqualifying); United States v. Hamilton, 41 M.J. 22, 25 (C.M.A. 1994) (judge did not abuse discretion in refusing to grant causal challenges of three members who had past completed legal-assistance client relationships with the assistant trial counsel). United States v. Porter, 17 M.J. 377 (C.M.A. 1984). A social relationship between a company commander who will testify in sentencing and a court member is not a ground for challenge for cause. United States v. Guthrie, 25 M.J. 808 (A.C.M.R. 1988). But the appearance is such that the member should be excused. See also United States v. Lake, 36 M.J. 317 (C.M.A. 1993) (coordinating interview between member of command and federal law enforcement agent about appellant was not disqualifying when raised by affidavit for the first time on appeal); United States v. Bannwarth, 36 M.J. 265 (C.M.A. 1993) ("Friendship with the accuser is not automatically disqualifying"). Cf. United States v. Kennedy-Axsom, 48 M.J. 846, 848 (A.F. Crim. App. 1998) (being a spouse of a former prosecutor does not disqualify member).

[260] United States v. Velez, 48 M.J. 220 (C.A.A.F. 1998) (post-empanelment disclosure of professional relationship with a rebuttal witness was not a basis of challenge for cause); United States v. Huitt, 25 M.J. 136 (C.M.A. 1987) (judge did not abuse discretion in failing to grant a challenge for cause against two members who were casual professional and social acquaintances of the father of one of four victims of sexual abuse).

[261] United States v. Strand, 59 M.J. 455 (C.A.A.F. 2004). Arguably, this is actually a waiver case. Defense counsel was clearly competent, voir dired the members, including the officer in question, exercised challenges for other members, and apparently discussed the officer's relationship with his client, and did not challenge the member. The Court determined that on the facts of the case the military judge did not abuse his discretion in not sua sponte removing the convening authority's son from the panel. Although the Court's decision is defensible on waiver theory, one can only wonder how the highest court in the military legal system, a court charged with protecting both the appearance as well as the reality of fairness, could tolerate such an absurd situation. It appears to mock the doctrine of implied bias and to elevate legal form over substance.

[262] United States v. Chollet, 30 M.J. 1079, 1081–82 (C.G.C.M.R. 1990) (failure to grant challenge of member who was directly rated by convening authority and a rater of another member was not an abuse of discretion but may not have been wise); United States v. Garcia, 26 M.J. 844 (A.C.M.R. 1988). See also United States v. Murphy, 26 M.J. 454 (C.M.A. 1988). But see

(Rel.3—1/07 Pub.62410)

position may not be used during deliberations. An allegation of use of rank permits an inquiry into the existence of such an act and its impact on the verdict.[263]

Although rare, it is certainly possible for a member to be related to a party, counsel, judge, or convening authority,[264] to name but a few possibilities. Indeed this may be more possible today given the increased use of reserve personnel and the historical tendency of some National Guard units to have multiple family members. Whether a challenge will lie clearly depends upon the specific facts of a case, but ordinarily a family relationship existing between a member and another person of consequence to the case would appear to call for at least a rebuttable presumption that excusal is appropriate. At the same time, the accused should preserve the issue by affirmatively mounting a challenge lest waiver take place.

§ 15-54.27 Law Enforcement Duty

While military courts have long frowned on the practice of appointing to the court personnel who hold law enforcement assignments, such individuals are ordinarily not disqualified from duty as court members solely for that reason.[265]

United States v. Abdelkader, 34 M.J. 605 (A.F.C.M.R. 1992) (judge abused his discretion in rejecting a causal challenge to the vice wing commander who would review performance reports of seven other members and who had been briefed on the case facts; peremptory challenge to the member preserved the issue under R.C.M. 912(f)(4)). *See* notes 223, 231–32 and § 15-54.29.

[263] Mil. R. Evid. 606(b). *See, e.g.,* United States v. Loving, 41 M.J. 213, 238 (C.A.A.F. 1995) (consideration of affidavits permitted to determine if unlawful command influence was exercised in deliberations). *Cf.* United States v. Cleveland, 128 F.3d 267 (5th Cir. 1997) (proper for judge to issue order forbidding the news media or anyone else from interviewing the jurors concerning their deliberations without the judge's permission).

[264] United States v. Strand, 59 M.J. 455 (C.A.A.F. 2004) (president and sole officer on the court was the son of the acting convening authority).

[265] *See generally* United States v. Berry, 34 M.J. 83, 87–88 (C.M.A. 1992) (judge abused his discretion in rejecting causal challenge to law enforcement agent with close professional relationship to prosecution witness; note, however, Judge Cox's concurrence stating that there is no *per se* rule against present or past law enforcement personnel serving as members. 34 M.J. at 88 (C.M.A. 1992)); United States v. Dale, 39 M.J. 503, 505 (A.F.C.M.R. 1993), *rev'd*, 42. M.J. 384 (C.A.A.F. 1995). The difficulty inherent in applying this perhaps overly simplistic statement is apparent from *Dale.* In *Dale,* as Judge Pearson's dissent reflects, 39 M.J. at 507 (A.F.C.M.R. 1993), the member, Deputy Chief of Security Police, sat in at the base "Cops and Robbers meetings" with base legal personnel and OSI. Although he intentionally missed the meeting discussing the instant case, his normal presence at these law and order meetings and occasional duties were such as to cause at least a substantial appearance of evil. *Compare Berry, above, with* United States v. Fulton, 44 M.J. 100 (C.A.A.F. 1996) (judge did not abuse discretion in refusing to grant challenge for cause against member because he was Chief of Security Police officer for the command, but with minimal involvement with local security police for crimes similar to those the accused was alleged to have committed); Harris v. State, 572 A.2d 573 (Md. App. 1990) (in drug prosecution former state trooper was not *per se* disqualified); Borman v. State, 229 A.2d 440 (Md. App. 1967) (declined to disqualify three jurors married to members of police department).

(Rel.3—1/07 Pub.62410)

In *United States v. Swagger,*[266] however, the Army Court of Military Review held that to ask a major installation's principal law enforcement officer "to exercise an objective and unbiased mental process to determine the guilt or innocence of an accused, places a burden upon an individual that is greater than most can or should bear. We are convinced that at least is the common perception."[267]

Daulton, Fulton, and *Dale* represent the proposition that challenges for cause should be granted against individuals when they are the embodiment of law enforcement on post.

§ 15-54.28　Sleeping Court Members

The problem of the sleepy court-member is recurrent. In *United States v. West,*[268] the judge sua sponte raised the issue of an apparently sleeping member. Commending the judges's actions, the court opined:

> The problem of the sleeping court member or juror is not unique. . . . Indeed, over the vigorous dissent of Judge Cook, this Court held that reversal is required where a court member in sworn testimony averred that while he did not think he was totally asleep, he was "a little lethargic"; "fighting sleep"; "heavy eyelidded . . . trying to pay attention to what . . . the military judge was saying." *United States v. Brown,* 3 M.J. 368 (C.M.A. 1977).
>
> The rule was predicated upon the court member's "obligation . . . to be both attentive and dignified." *United States v. Groce,* 3 M.J. 369, 370 (C.M.A. 1977) (footnote omitted). The existing rule also provides that the error is not waived by "defense counsel's failure . . . to . . . move for mistrial, challenge the inattentive member, or request a reiteration of the instructions." 3 M.J. at 371 (C.M.A. 1977).
>
> Although a more modern view might compel us to reject this *per se* approach of reversing the conviction without testing for prejudice, we need not reach that question here. *United States v. Fisher,* 21 M.J. 327, 328 (C.M.A. 1986) ("[a] *per se* approach to plain-error review is flawed") (quoting *United States v. Young,* 470 U.S. 1, 16 n.14 . . . (1985)).
>
> We also need not reach the questions concerning impeachment of jury verdicts raised by the recent Supreme Court decision of *Tanner v. United States,*. . . 107 S. Ct. 2739 (1987) . . ., which suggests that the question of the inattentive juror is "internal" and does not give rise to an attack upon the jury verdict. "Courts wisely have treated allegations of a juror's inability to hear or comprehend at trial as an internal matter." *Id.* at 2746 (citations omitted).

---

[266] 16 M.J. 759 (A.C.M.R. 1983). *Cf.* United States v. Kennedy-Axsom, 48 M.J. 846, 849 (A.F. Crim. App. 1998) (being acquainted with prosecutor does not automatically disqualify witnesses — numerous cases cited).

[267] 16 M.J. at 760. In *Swagger,* the member was also the president of the court.

[268] 27 M.J. 223 (C.M.A. 1988).

(Rel.3—1/07　Pub.62410)

We reaffirm the principle that court members have an obligation to remain attentive, and the military judge has the responsibility to ensure that they do so. Here, the military judge was sensitive to this responsibility, investigated the situation, and found as a matter of fact that the court member "was not asleep" during the trial, was "fighting sleep," but "was not asleep or inattentive," and was "alert." Based upon his findings, he denied appellant's motion for a mistrial.

The question whether the court member was asleep or inattentive is clearly a question of fact. A military judge's findings of fact, supported by competent evidence in the record, will not be disturbed on appeal. *United States v. Burris*, 21 M.J. 140 (C.M.A. 1985).[269]

§ 15-54.29 Court Member Misconduct

Court member misconduct may include *ex parte* communications with counsel[270] or judge, seeking advice from outside experts,[271] consulting legal authority, bringing prejudicial materials into member sessions,[272] or personally inspecting the scene of the crime. In *Smith v. Phillips*,[273] the Supreme Court rejected an assertion of implied bias based upon the failure of the prosecutor to disclose that a juror had applied for employment with the prosecutor.[274] Justice O'Connor suggested "extreme situations that would justify a finding of implied bias," such as the juror being an "actual employee of prosecuting agency . . . close relative of . . . participant . . . or that the juror was a witness . . . [to] transaction".[275] However,

> [Our] cases demonstrate that due process does not require a new trial every time a juror has been placed in a potentially compromising situation. Were

---

[269] 27 M.J. at 224 (footnote omitted). *See also* United States v. Norment, 34 M.J. 224, 227 (C.M.A. 1992) (when inattentive court members are seen, the issue should be raised so it may be appropriately disposed of by challenges, mistrial, etc.) (Crawford, J., concurring in result); United States v. Boswell, 36 M.J. 807, 812 (A.C.M.R. 1993) (judge did not abuse his discretion in excusing sleeping member rather than rehabilitating the member by reading back portions of the testimony); United States v. Louketis, 1992 WESTLAW 396238 (A.F.C.M.R. Dec. 18, 1992) (based on counter affidavits, internal evidence in record and waiver, court rejected allegation that members were sleeping); United States v. Signs, ACMR 8903808 (A.C.M.R. May 31, 1991) (after precautionary instruction, the failure by defense to raise issue of court member sleeping constitutes waiver); United States v. Frierson, 24 M.J. 647 (A.C.M.R.), *pet. denied*, 25 M.J. 241 (C.M.A. 1987) (issue of inattentive or sleeping court member waived).

[270] *E.g.*, United States v. Reynolds, 40 M.J. 198 (C.M.A. 1994).

[271] United States v. Mosqueda, 43 M.J. 491 (C.A.A.F. 1996).

[272] *Cf.* United States v. Lambert, 55 M.J. 293 (C.A.A.F. 2001) (a member had a book *Guilty as Sin* with her during some sessions leading the judge to voir dire the members to ensure lack of prejudice).

[273] 455 U.S. 209, 216 (1982).

[274] The state court below had found no influence on the jury panel.

[275] 455 U.S. at 222.

(Rel.3—1/07 Pub.62410)

that the rule, few trials would be constitutionally acceptable. The safe-guards of juror impartiality, such as *voir dire* and protective instructions from the trial judge, are not infallible; it is virtually impossible to shield jurors from every contact or influence that might theoretically affect their votes. Due process means a jury capable and willing to decide the case solely on the evidence before it, and a trial judge ever watchful to prevent prejudicial occurrences and to determine the effect of such occurrences when they happen.[276]

Accordingly, application of the harmless error test may be appropriate in some cases.[277]

An oft expressed concern by Chief Judge Cox was that as the convening authority selects the members the government effectively has an unlimited number of peremptory challenges.[278] The traditional response to such a criticism is that the convening authority is limited by the Constitution and Code.[279] The court, concerned with the public perception of challenges, has adopted an implied bias doctrine in some cases, including one case in which there was no evidence but argument that one member's spouse was an investigator (even though he did not testify at the trial or the Article 32 investigation).[280] It is difficult to apply this new test. The Court of Appeals for the Armed Forces did not apply implied bias, for example, when someone rummaged through the court members' purses and stole money even though the defendant was charged with larceny.[281] The court distinguished this case from the arguably similar civilian case of *Hunley v. Godinez*[282] citing among other factors that the two members who had money

---

[276] 455 U.S. at 217. *Cf.* United States v. Calamita, 48 M.J. 917, 923 (A.F. Crim. App. 1998) (failure to raise implied bias at trial constitutes waiver).

[277] *Compare* Rushen v. Spain, 464 U.S. 114, 119–20 (1983) (*ex parte* communication between judge and juror held harmless) *with* United States v. Mosqueda, 43 M.J. 491, 494 (C.A.A.F. 1996) (found actual prejudice: "The information potentially gleaned from the outside contact [in violation of instruction] was crucial to the trial").

[278] United States v. Carter, 25 M.J. 471, 478 (C.M.A. 1988) (Cox, J., concurring). United States v. Witham, 47 M.J. 297, 304 (C.A.A.F. 1997) (Cox, C.J., concurring, "open to suggestions . . . for a clearer way to define this phenomena").

[279] United States v. Smith, 27 M.J. 242, 250 (C.M.A. 1988) (improper to detail female members to achieve guilty verdict).

[280] United States v. Minyard, 46 M.J. 230 (C.A.A.F. 1997). *See also* United States v. Young-blood, 47 M.J. 338 (C.A.A.F. 1997) (some members attended commander's briefing about discipline); United States v. Daulton, 45 M.J. 212 (C.A.A.F. 1996) (erred in not excusing member whose sister was abused by their grandfather and his rehabilitative answers were not "resounding"); United States v. Fulton, 44 M.J. 100 (1996); United States v. Dale, 42 M.J. 384 (C.A.A.F. 1995).

[281] United States v. Lavender, 46 M.J. 485 (C.A.A.F. 1997).

[282] 784 F. Supp. 522 (N.D. Ill.), *aff'd*, 975 F.2d 316 (7th Cir. 1992).

(Rel.3—1/07 Pub.62410)

stolen were removed.[283] The Second Circuit has opined that implied bias should be limited to "truly 'exceptional' " cases.[284]

The standard of review for rulings on actual bias is whether the judge has abused his or her discretion.[285] The military judge does not enjoy the same degree of deference on rulings involving implied bias. Issues of implied bias are determined by an objective standard viewed through the eyes of the public rather than the eye of a military member.[286]

United States v. Youngblood,[287] court members had attended a staff meeting in which the Wing Commander had addressed discipline issues and had noted unfavorable personnel actions he had taken when he was disappointed in the discipline or leadership actions taken by subordinate officers who had not been severe enough in dealing with apparent offenders. Reversing the sentence, the majority noted: "The remarks [by the general] were recent and fresh in the minds of the court members. The threat was not hypothetical but was specific and reinforced by a recent example."[288]

The court has taken the view that it can judge the perception of bais as well as the trial judge. Thus, a trial judge's decision does not deserve the same deference as it would in an actual bias case.

§ 15-54.30 Pretrial Publicity

In unusual cases pretrial publication may so permeate the proceedings as to prevent a fair trial. The "constitutional standard," however, is " 'not whether the community remembered the case, but whether the jurors . . . had such fixed opinions that they could not judge impartially the guilt of the defendant' . . . 'It is not required . . . that the jurors be totally ignorant of the facts and issues involved.' "[289] Through voir dire, the defendant should establish the prejudicial impact on the members.

There are two types of prejudice that might impact on the right to a fair trial: presumed and actual. There is a presumption of prejudice when the appellant establishes that the pretrial publicity is prejudicial and inflammatory and has

---

[283] *Lavender,* 46 M.J. at 489. In United States v. Rome, 47 M.J. 467, 469 (C.A.A.F. 1998), the court cited *Lavender* for the proposition that "implied bias should be invoked rarely."

[284] United States v. Torres, 128 F.3d 38 (2d Cir. 1997).

[285] United States v. Armstrong, 54 M.J. 51, 53 (C.A.A.F. 2000); United States v. White, 36 M.J. 284 (C.M.A. 1993).

[286] United States v. Dale, 42 M.J. 384, 386 (C.A.A.F. 1995).

[287] 47 M.J. 338 (C.A.A.F. 1997).

[288] 47 M.J. at 342 (C.A.A.F. 1997). *See also* United States v. Gray, 51 M.J. 1, 27–29 (C.A.A.F. 1999) (defendant did not establish actual prejudice on panel).

[289] Mu'Min v. Virginia, 500 U.S. 415, 430 (1991).

(Rel.3—1/07 Pub.62410)

saturated the community. To establish saturation, "there must be evidence of the amount of pretrial publicity and the number of individuals exposed to it."[290]

As to actual prejudice, exposure to "highly significant information" or incriminating matters is not by itself a basis for challenge.[291]

§ 15-55.00   Peremptory Challenges

§ 15-55.10   In General

Peremptory challenges are the military equivalent of civilian "strikes." Under ordinary circumstances, each party has one peremptory challenge,[292] which may be exercised freely and without explanation.[293] Peremptory challenges were adopted by the Army in 1920,[294] and by the Navy only via the Uniform Code of Military Justice.[295]

Peremptory challenges are made after the voir dire examination and after the determination of any challenges for cause.[296] Ordinarily, the trial counsel will make his or her peremptory challenge before the defense.[297]

Chief Judge Cox oft expressed concern over what he considered the government's equivalent of an unlimited number of peremptory challenges -the right to select members.[298] Given not just the ability but the Article 25 obligation of the convening authority to hand select members, Judge Cox's analysis is at least persuasive — especially if one functionally assigns the convening authority a prosecutorial function. Of course, the convening authority's ability to select members is limited by law, custom, and practicality, making Judge Cox's equivalency with the prosecution at least suspect — for most cases. The court's consistent approach to the potential power disparity in the area is to encourage judges to grant causal challenges liberally.[299] At the same time, the court has

---

[290] United States v. Curtis, 44 M.J. 106, 139 (C.A.A.F. 1996). *See also* United States v. Simpson, 58 M.J. 368 (C.A.A.F. 2003) (relying on *United States v. Curtis*).

[291] 44 M.J. at 139. *See also* Wainwright v. Witt, 469 U.S. 412 (1985); Chandler v. Florida, 449 U.S. 560 (1981).

[292] U.C.M.J. art. 41(b).

[293] R.C.M. 912(g)(1); *but see* Section 55.30, dealing with Batson v. Kentucky, 476 U.S. 79 (1986).

[294] *Hearings on H.R. 2498 before Subcomm. of the House Armed Services Comm.*, 81st Cong., 1st Sess. 1027 (1949). *See also Hearings on S. 64 before Subcomm. of the Comm. on Military Affairs*, U.S. Senate, 66th Cong., 1st Sess. 591, 1169, 1373 (1919).

[295] U.S. Senate, 66th Cong., 1st Sess. 591, 1169, 1373 (1919).

[296] R.C.M. 912(g)(1).

[297] R.C.M. 912(g)(1).

[298] *See, e.g.*, United States v. Carter, 25 M.J. 471, 478 (C.M.A. 1988) (Cox, J., concurring); United States v. Witham, 47 M.J. 297, 304 (C.A.A.F. 1997) (Cox, C.J., concurring, "open to suggestions . . . for a clearer way to define this phenomena").

[299] *E.g.*, United States v. White, 36 M.J. 284, 287 (C.M.A. 1993).

(Rel.3—1/07 Pub.62410)

also applied the doctrine of "implied bias," an objective standard that would require excusal of a potential member despite the member's assertion of lack of actual bias.[300]

§ 15-55.20   Additional Peremptory Challenges

Perhaps the greatest advantage of limiting the number of peremptory challenges to one per party is that it greatly speeds jury selection. The real question, however, is whether peremptories are of value to the parties. Although virtually every lawyer is convinced that he or she can intelligently use a peremptory challenge to help obtain a court more to his or her client's interest, there is no reliable evidence to substantiate this.[301]

Moreover, systemically, there is a valid difference between ensuring a neutral jury and helping counsel obtain a favorable panel. Notwithstanding this, periodically the suggestion is made that the number of peremptories be increased. Although proposals to amend the Uniform Code or the *Manual for Courts-Martial* have been unsuccessful, the Court of Military Appeals altered the situation judicially.

In *United States v. Carter*,[302] a majority of the court held that when the government used its peremptory challenge to reduce the panel below the minimum statutory quorum, upon defense request the trial judge could, as a discretionary matter, grant additional challenges.[303] Reviewing the history of both Article 41 of the Uniform Code and the nature and powers of the military judge, Chief Judge Everett opined that the judge "has a *duty* to grant additional peremptory challenges if he determines that this is necessary to assure a fair trial."[304] Insofar as the procedural posture before the court was concerned, Chief Judge Everett noted that, when the court sinks below the statutory minimum, it is the convening authority who adds new members, rather than the random selection process common to civilian courts.[305] Concurring, Judge Cox agreed with Chief Judge Everett's legal analysis,[306] but held that the judge's liberal

---

[300] *E.g.*, United States v. Dinatale, 44 M.J. 325, 328 (C.A.A.F. 1996); United States v. White, 36 M.J. 284, 287–288 (C.M.A. 1993) (Sullivan, C.J. concurring); §§ 15-54.21, 15-54.29, 15-55.10. *But see Dinatale, above*, 44 M.J. at 329 (Cox, C.J. concurring, questioning the existence of "implied bias").

[301] One can argue that the primary use of a peremptory challenge is to excuse a member whose bias or disqualification is apparent but not severe enough in the opinion of the trial judge to justify granting a causal challenge.

[302] 25 M.J. 471 (C.M.A. 1988).

[303] This is the minimum holding. *Carter*, which overruled United States v. Holley, 17 M.J. 361 (C.M.A. 1984) and was given only prospective effect, is far broader in its language. *Cf.* R.C.M. 912(g)(2).

[304] 25 M.J. at 476 (footnote omitted) (emphasis in original).

[305] 25 M.J. at 475.

[306] Noting that the convening authority effectively has unlimited peremptory challenges because he or she appoints the members. 25 M.J. at 478.

(Rel.3—1/07   Pub.62410)

use of challenges led him to conclude that, on the facts of the case, the judge had not erred in denying an additional peremptory. Judge Sullivan, in effect, dissented.[307] The court in *Carter* did not indicate whether an additional challenge must be used only against new members or may be used against those original members still sitting.

In 1990, Congress amended Article 41 to provide:

(b)(1)Each accused and the trial counsel are entitled initially to one peremptory challenge of members of the court. The military judge may not be challenged except for cause.

(2) If exercise of a peremptory challenge reduces the court below the minimum number of members required by section 816 of this title (article 16), the parties shall (notwithstanding section 829 of this title (article 29)) either exercise or waive any remaining peremptory challenge (not previously waived) against the remaining members of the court before additional members are detailed to the court.

(c) Whenever additional members are detailed to the court, and after any challenges for cause against such additional members are presented and decided, each accused and the trial counsel are entitled to one peremptory challenge against members not previously subject to peremptory challenge.[308]

This amendment resolves the issue of the propriety of additional peremptories when the court falls below quorum. It may leave open the question of increased peremptories under other circumstances, although the revision of Article 41 could be read as expressing congressional intent not to permit an increase outside the narrow area permitted.[309] The issue might best be posed by a sudden post-challenge discovery of new information about a court member that did not quite rise to the level of a causal challenge. After the presentation of evidence on the merits, it is discretionary with the judge to permit additonal peremptory challenges.[310]

§ 15-55.30   Discriminatory Peremptory Challenges — *Batson v. Kentucky*

§ 15-55.31   In General

In *Batson v. Kentucky*,[311] the Supreme Court held that prosecutors must justify peremptory jury challenges that appear to be motivated solely by racial

---

[307] Because the court gave the new rule prospective effect, he concurred in the result.

[308] National Defense Authorization Act for Fiscal Years 1991 and 1992, Pub. L. 101-510 § 541, 104 Stat. 1565 (1990). Article 41(a)(1) was also amended to permit additional peremptories when the court falls below quorum.

[309] *Cf.* United States v. White, 22 C.M.R. 897, 901 n.3 (A.F.C.M.R. 1956).

[310] R.C.M. 912(g)(2). But this would not preclude a challenge for cause. R.C.M. 912(f)(2)(B). *Cf.* Art.41(b)(1) states that the accused is "entitled initially to one peremptory challenge."

[311] 476 U.S. 79 (1986).

(Rel.3—1/07　Pub.62410)

considerations. The defense makes out a prima facie case of a *Batson* violation simply by establishing a prosecutorial peremptory challenge against a member of the same cognizable racial group as the accused. [312] Once the defendant makes a prima facie showing, the burden shifts to the prosecution to provide a neutral explanation for challenging the member. Although the Court emphasized that the explanation need not rise to the same level as justifying a challenge for cause, the prosecutor cannot justify the peremptory only on the basis of intuitive judgment.

Reasoning that *Batson* was an equal protection decision applicable to the armed forces via the Fifth Amendment, the Court of Military Appeals held *Batson* applicable to the armed forces in *United States v. Santiago-Davila*. [313] Concurring, Judge Cox suggested adoption of the decision of the Army Court of Military Review in *United States v. Moore*, [314] that the government ought not to exercise a peremptory challenge against a member of the accused's race unless a challenge for cause has been previously denied against that member. [315] Subsequently, the court adopted *Moore*. [316] Despite argument by Judge Wiss that *Batson* should be applied to the selection of court members by the convening authority, the Court of Appeals for the Armed Forces has thus far held *Batson* to its procedural posture — challenges by counsel. [317]

The Supreme Court revisited the *Batson* scenario, albeit with a twist, in the 1990 case of *Holland v. Illinois*. [318] In *Holland*, a white defendant challenged under the Sixth Amendment the prosecution's use of peremptory challenges to remove all blacks from the jury. Expressly reserving judgement on the possible application of the equal protection clause on the facts, [319] the Court, per Justice Scalia, held:

---

[312] *Batson*, 476 U.S. at 95–98. *See generally* Major John I. Winn, *A Practitioner's Guide to Race and Gender Neutrality in the Military Courtroom*, Army Law, May, 1995, at 32. In Commonwealth v. Carson, 741 A.2d 686, 696 (Pa. 1999), *cert. denied*, 530 U.S. 1216 (2000), the Court held that a judge did not violate the defendant's rights by raising the *Batson* issue sua sponte.

[313] 26 M.J. 380 (C.M.A. 1988). Chief Judge Everett opined that in light of the fact that the armed services "have been a leader in eradicating racial discrimination," even if *Batson* was not directly applicable, the court was sure that Congress "never intended to condone the use of a government peremptory challenge for the purpose of excluding a 'cognizable racial group.' " 26 M.J. 390 (C.M.A. 1988)

[314] 26 M.J. 692 (A.C.M.R. 1988) (en banc), *rev'd*, 28 M.J. 366 (C.M.A. 1989).

[315] United States v. Santiago-Davila, 26 M.J. 380, 393 (C.M.A. 1988), stating that "[i]f the grounds for the challenge for cause are on the record, *Batson* . . . will most likely be satisfied."

[316] United States v. Moore, 28 M.J. 366 (C.M.A. 1989).

[317] United States v. Loving, 41 M.J. 213, 315–25 (C.A.A.F. 1994) (Wiss, J., dissenting). *See also* Loving v. Hart, 47 M.J. 438, 455 (C.A.A.F. 1998) (J. Wiss' view echoed by J. Effron).

[318] 493 U.S. 474 (1990).

[319] A matter the Court held had not been raised. 493 U.S. 487, n.3 (1990).

(Rel.3—1/07 Pub.62410)

We reject petitioner's fundamental thesis that a prosecutor's use of peremptory challenges to eliminate a distinctive group in the community deprives the defendant of a Sixth Amendment right to the "fair possibility" of a representative jury. [320]

In so holding, the Court strongly supported the institution of the peremptory challenge. [321]

In 1991, in *Powers v. Ohio*, [322] the Court held that under the equal protection clause, "a criminal defendant may object to race-based exclusions of jurors effected through peremptory challenge whether or not the defendant and the excluded juror share the same race." [323]

In 1992, in *Georgia v. McCollum*, [324] the Court extended *Batson* to defense peremptories. Reasoning that "if a court allows jurors to be excluded because of group bias, 'it is [a] willing participant in a scheme that could only undermine the very foundation of our system of justice — our citizens' [sic] confidence in it,'" [325] the Court held that racially discriminatory defense challenges constituted state action and violated the equal protection clause. "Accordingly, if the State demonstrates a prima facie case of racial discrimination by the defendants, the defendants must articulate a racially neutral explanation for peremptory challenges." [326] Accordingly, the discussion of *Batson* that follows must now be read to apply to the defense counsel as well as the prosecutor. *McCollum* necessarily raises, but does not resolve, the question of whether *Batson* extends to challenges of other cognizable groups, especially women. In 1994, the Court in a 6-3 vote in *J.E.B. v. Alabama ex rel. T.B.*, [327] held that the equal protection clause requires the extension of *Batson* to gender-based peremptories. [328] Justice O'Connor concurred but opined that only the government should be prohibited from using gender in challenges; Justices Scalia, Rehnquist and Thomas dissented. *J.E.B. v. Alabama ex rel. T.B.* with its requirement to justify the excusal of women increases the probability that peremptory challenges, now increasingly subject to detailed explanation, may someday be eliminated as more troublesome than they are worth. Perhaps recognizing this, however, the Court may have significantly retreated in its peculiar 1995 per curiam decision of *Purkett v.*

---

[320] 493 U.S. at 478 (1990).

[321] 493 U.S. at 479–84 (1990).

[322] 499 U.S. 400 (1991).

[323] 499 U.S. at 402 (1991). *See also* 499 U.S. 410 (1991).

[324] 505 U.S. 40, 42 (1992).

[325] 505 U.S. at 49–50 (1992).

[326] 505 U.S. at 59 (1992).

[327] 511 U.S. 127 (1994).

[328] The extension of *Batson* to gender raises interesting issues. Is it a *Batson* violation to strike a member of a profession that is substantially, but not entirely characterized by women? *Cf.* United States v. Chaney, 53 M.J. 383, 385 (C.A.A.F. 2000) (nurse).

(Rel.3—1/07 Pub.62410)

Elem.[329] *In Purkett,* a racial challenge case, the Court initially noted that *Batson* requires a three-step adjudication process: first, a decision as to whether an opponent has made out a prima facie case of racial discrimination; second, whether the challenger has made a race-neutral explanation; and third, if such an explanation is given, whether the opponent has proven purposeful racial discrimination. The Court then held that when counsel furnishes a race-neutral explanation for peremptory challenges, the explanation need be neither "persuasive, or even plausible."[330] Dissenting, Justices Stevens and Breyer opined that the Court had invalidated an important part of *Batson* by not requiring that the race-neutral explanation be related to the instant case. In *Johnson v. California,*[331] the Court clarified the defendant's burden under *Batson.* The Court rejected California's approach under which the defendant was required to show that it was more likely than not that "the other party's peremptory challenges, if unexplained, were based on impermissible group bias".[332] Instead, the Court re-emphasized *Batson's* original language, "a prima facie case of discrimination can be made out by offering a wide variety of evidence, so long as the sum of the proffered facts gives 'rise to an inference of discriminatory purpose.'"[333]

At present, *Batson* does not extend to challenges based on a member's religion or group memberships.[334]

In light of *Batson,* there are three primary questions to address:

(1) When does the defense make out a prima facie discriminatory challenge by the prosecution?

(2) What constitutes neutral reasons by a prosecutor that will justify a challenge?

(3) What procedural rules apply?

§ 15-55.32 Defendant's Burden

Before *Powers v. Ohio,*[335] the court stated in *Batson* that to establish discriminatory jury selection,

---

[329] 514 U.S. 765 (1995). Counsel's explanation for one juror was that the juror had long unkempt hair, a mustache, and a goatee.

[330] 514 U.S. at 768 (1995).

[331] 125 S. Ct. 2410 (2005).

[332] 125 S. Ct. at 2413 (2005).

[333] 125 S. Ct. at 2416 (2005), *citing* 476 U.S. at 93–94 (*citing* in turn, Washington v. Davis, 426 U.S. 229, 239–42 (1976)).

[334] United States v. Williams, 44 M.J. 482, 485 (C.A.A.F. 1996); Casarez v. State, 913 S.W.2d 468 (Tex. Crim. App. 1994) (striking for religious affiliation did not violate *Batson*). *But see* Jordan v. Lefevre, 206 F.3d 196 (2d Cir. 2000) (trial judge must determine if prosecutor had discriminatory intent).

[335] 499 U.S. 400 (1991).

(Rel.3—1/07 Pub.62410)

the defendant first must show that he is a member of a cognizable racial group . . . and that the prosecutor has exercised peremptory challenges to remove from the venire members of the defendant's race. Second, the defendant is entitled to rely on the fact . . . that peremptory challenges constitutes a jury selection practice that permits "those to discriminate who are of a mind to discriminate." Finally, the defendant must show that these facts and any other relevant circumstances raise an inference that the prosecutor used that practice to exclude the venireman from the petit jury on account of their race. [336]

Although civilian courts had differed on when *Batson* was "triggered," [337] the Court of Military Appeals, in *United States v. Moore*, [338] extended *Batson* by creating a *per se* rule that "every peremptory challenge by the Government of a member of the accused's race, upon objection, must be explained by trial counsel." [339] Despite the expansion of *Batson* to members of other races, [340] it remains necessary to define "race" for *Batson* purposes.

In *United States v. Santiago-Davila*, the court defined Puerto Ricans as a cognizable racial group and hinted that it might examine service regulations and other governmental programs to determine who is a member of a "cognizable group" in the future. [341] Military courts have subsequently accepted Blacks [342] and Hispanics [343] as such groups. [344]

§ 15-55.33 Neutral Reasons

Once *Batson* has been timely and adequately raised, the burden shifts to the prosecution to establish that its peremptory challenge was not racially motivated.

Nor may the prosecutor rebut the defendant's case merely by denying that he had a discriminatory motive or "affirm[ing] [his] good faith in making individual selections." . . . If these general assertions were accepted as rebutting a defendant's prima facie case, the Equal Protection Clause

---

[336] Batson v. Kentucky, 476 U.S. 79, 96 (1986) (citations omitted).

[337] Some have required minimum percentages before *Batson* applies. United States v. Vaccaro, 816 F.2d 443, 457 (9th Cir. 1987). Still others have rejected a mathematical formula. United States v. Clemons, 843 F.2d 741 (3d Cir. 1988).

[338] 28 M.J. 366 (C.M.A. 1989).

[339] 28 M.J. at 368 (C.M.A. 1989).

[340] Powers v. Ohio, 499 U.S. 400 (1991).

[341] *Santiago-Davila*, 26 M.J. at 390–91. *See also* State v. Allen, 53 Crim. L. Rep. (BNA) 1093 (Fla., Apr. 8, 1993); Mejia v. State, 328 Md. 522, 616 A.2d 356 (1992) (if there is a dispute about a juror's race or origin, it should be raised before the trial judge outside the jury's presence).

[342] United States v. Cooper, 30 M.J. 201 (C.M.A. 1990); United States v. Moore, 28 M.J. 366 (C.M.A. 1989).

[343] United States v. Chan, 30 M.J. 1028 (A.F.C.M.R. 1990).

[344] *See, e.g.*, United States v. De Gross, 913 F.2d 1417 (9th Cir. 1990); People v. Irizarry, 560 N.Y.S.2d 279 (N.Y. App. 1990).

(Rel.3—1/07 Pub.62410)

"would be but a vain and illusory requirement." . . . The prosecutor therefore must articulate a neutral explanation related to the particular case to be tried. The trial court then will have the duty to determine if the defendant has established purposeful discrimination.[345]

This *Batson* language would lead one to conclude that it is not enough for the prosecutor to justify a peremptory challenge by asserting "[n]o particular reason"[346] or to attempt some facile conclusionary justification.[347] This statement of law is now in doubt, however, because the Court in *Purkett v. Elem*[348] held that when counsel furnishes a race-neutral explanation for peremptory challenges, the explanation need not be either "persuasive, or even plausible."[349] It may be that the Court's statement in *Purkett* is of little importance, given that the Court also noted that the trial judge might then find purposeful discrimination despite the racially neutral explanation. On appeal, the issue will be whether the judge abused his or her discretion in resolving the propriety of the justification.[350] The nature of the necessary justification is still developing. In *United States v. Cooper*,[351] the court, noting that the case on appeal had been tried prior to military decisions implementing *Batson*, held minimally sufficient at that time a "marginal" conclusionary explanation based on familiarity with the member's prior duty experience and current duty position, and a review of her personnel records.[352] In *United States v. Lawrence*,[353] a pre-*Purkett* case, the Air Force

---

[345] *Batson*, 476 U.S. at 98 (citations and footnotes omitted).

[346] United States v. Chan, 30 M.J. 1028 (A.F.C.M.R. 1990).

[347] Slappy v. State, 503 So. 2d 350 (Fla. 1987) (need not accept peremptory challenge at face value), *aff'd*, 522 So. 2d 18 (Fla.), *cert. denied*, 487 U.S. 1219 (1988). A racially neutral justification may not be race-neutral when its implications are taken into consideration. *E.g.*, United States v. Bishop, 959 F.2d 820 (9th Cir. 1992) (a challenge to a black eligibility worker living in South Central Los Angeles on the grounds that she is likely to believe the police pick on black people and is likely to take the side of those having a "tough time" isn't race-neutral; her locality is being used as a substitute for race).

[348] 514 U.S. 765 (1995) (per curiam). Counsel's explanation for one juror was that the juror had long unkempt hair, a mustache, and a goatee.

[349] 514 U.S. at 767 (1995); People v. Jamison, 50 Cal. Rptr. 2d 679 (Cal. App. 1996) (rejecting *Purkett v. Elem*, held avoidance of eye contact insufficient to justify peremptory challenge); State v. Mickie, 549 N.W.2d 793 (Wis. 1996) ("look of violence" justified challenge).

[350] United States v. Curtis, 33 M.J. 101, 105 (C.M.A. 1991) (judge's acceptance of trial counsel's explanation that he was concerned that the challenged member spoke in terms of trial being an educational experience wasn't clearly erroneous). United States v. Cooper, 30 M.J. 201, 202 (C.M.A. 1990).

[351] 30 M.J. 201 (C.M.A. 1990).

[352] 30 M.J. at 203 (C.M.A. 1990). Counsel stated at trial, "what we're really relying on is what all [sic] know about her current duty position [company commander] past experience in the Army, *i.e.* [sic], her worldly experience." 30 M.J. at 203 (C.M.A. 1990). *See also* United States v. St. Fort, 26 M.J. 764 (A.C.M.R. 1988) (*Batson* was satisfied by explaining that a challenge of the most junior officer member was based on the member's empathy with the accused's wife and that the member had been too sympathetic in past); United States v. Shelby, 26 M.J. 921 (N.M.C.M.R.

(Rel.3—1/07   Pub.62410)

Court of Military Review held sufficient trial counsel's justification, substantiated by counsel's notes, that counsel's peremptory challenge was motivated only by the member's criminology background.

Critically, the United States Court of Appeals for the Armed Forces rejected *Purkett* in *United States v. Tulloch,* [354] reasoning that the unique nature of court-martial member selection precluded trial counsel from so easily removing a member selected by the convening authority.

Although not strictly necessary, it may be useful for the trial court to state on the record the judge's opinion of counsel's sincerity, knowledge of trial techniques, and observations of the manner in which the prosecutor has examined the members on voir dire. The judge also may be able to consider the race of the victim and the primary witnesses. [355]

The trial judge must determine whether trial counsel's otherwise acceptable explanation is legitimate. In determining whether the explanation is a pretext for a racially motivated challenge, the judge may consider:

(1) any bias shown during the voir dire;

(2) a perfunctory examination of the challenged juror;

(3) questions of the juror that seemed to provoke a hostile or unfavorable response;

(4) a reason for challenge unrelated to the case; [356]

(5) a reason not applied equally to other jurors;

(6) the nature of the crime; and

(7) the race of accused and victim. [357]

In *United States v. Hurn,* [358] the Court held inadequate trial counsel's explanation that he was trying to protect the "quorum" by ensuring that a defense challenge would not reduce the percentage of enlisted members below one-third

---

1988) (court interpreted challenge of most junior member as a challenge of the member with the least experience of the officer and enlisted members remaining on panel).

[353] 30 M.J. 1140, 1141 (A.F.C.M.R. 1990).

[354] 47 M.J. 283 (C.A.A.F. 1997).

[355] Hatten v. State, 628 So. 2d 294 (Miss. 1993) (judge must set forth factual findings on the record); State v. Butler, 731 S.W.2d 265 (Mo. Ct. App. 1987).

[356] *See, e.g.,* United States v. Chaney, 53 M.J. 383, 385 (C.A.A.F. 2000) (member challenged as nurse and not as a woman); United States v. Norfleet, 53 M.J. 262, 271–272 (C.A.A.F. 2000) (dispute between member and legal office constitutes a reasonable; gender neutral basis for peremptory); United States v. Thomas, 40 M.J. 726 (N.M.C.M.R. 1995) (member's participation in prior acquittal).

[357] *See, e.g.,* Slappy v. State, 503 So. 2d 350 (Fla. 1987), *aff'd,* 522 So. 2d 18 (Fla.), *cert. denied,* 487 U.S. 1219 (1988).

[358] 55 M.J. 446 (C.A.A.F. 2001).

(Rel.3—1/07 Pub.62410)

when counsel challenged the only Caucasian. Reasoning that counsel could have challenged any other member to achieve the same result, the Court of Appeals held the explanation not to be "race neutral."[389] The Seventh Circuit has opined that in determining motivation the court must compared those challenged with those retained.[360]

In its 2005 decision in *Miller-El v. Dretke*,[361] a habeas case, the Supreme Court conducted an extraordinarily detailed analysis of the voir dire and challenge conducted in a death penalty case. Evaluating the number and percentage of potential black jurors struck, the reasons for the challenges, as compared with those given for white jurors, procedural tactics employed by the prosecution, and the history of racially motivated juror selection in the Texas jurisdiction, the Court concluded by clear and convincing evidence that jurors had been struck for impermisisble racial reasons. Although the case is clearly fact-dependent, it makes it apparent that judges are certainly not bound by counsel's explanations for member challenges.

A key question that remains unanswered is whether the Court of Military Appeals will permit a prosecution challenge based solely on the prosecutor's legitimate hunch and past experience, something that *Batson*, read strictly, would appear to permit.[362] That question was answered clearly in *United States v. Tulloch*,[363] in which a majority of the court, relying on the critical structural differences between civilian juries and military courts, rejected *Purkett v. Elem.*

---

[389] In an affidavit filed more than two years after the incident, counsel explained that the member had had a busy schedule and that counsel was trying to do him a favor by the challenge. The Court of Appeals for the Armed Forces rejected the affidavit as undercutting the court's procedure. 55 M.J. at 449. The Court subsequently sustained the conviction, relying in part on an affidavit of the member in question. United States v. Hurn, 58 M.J. 199 (C.A.A.F. 2003).

[360] Henderson v. Walls, 296 F.3d 541, 548–550 (7th Cir. 2002).

[361] 125 S. Ct. 2317 (2005). Interestingly, Justice Breyer, concurring, appears to be prepared to abandon *Batson* as unworkable and to hold peremptory challenges unconstitutional. *See* 125 S. Ct. at 2340–2344.

[362] In *Santiago-Davila*, 26 M.J. at 393, n.15, Judge Cox, concurring, expressed concern that he did not "know what impact it will have on the Hound Dog Rule." Although Judge Cox may have been somewhat facetious, the issue is nonetheless real. The "Hound Dog Rule" refers to counsel's initial reaction to the jurors when they first enter the courtroom. They may snap, snarl or glance approvingly, just as two hound dogs react when passing each other in the street. But does this behavior serve as a basis for challenge? Courts have sustained challenges based on a potential juror's mannerisms, conduct, attitude, and demeanor. *See, e.g.*, United States v. Clemons, 941 F.2d 321 (5th Cir. 1991) ("disinterested demeanor" and "inattentiveness" valid reasons); United States v. Moreno, 878 F.2d 817 (5th Cir. 1989) ("gut reaction" that commercial artist would be lenient was valid reason); United States v. Forbes, 816 F.2d 1006, 1010–11 (5th Cir. 1987) ("posture and demeanor"); United States v. Vaccaro, 816 F.2d 443, 457 (9th Cir. 1987) (poor attitude and demeanor). *See* Purkett v. Elem, 131 L. Ed. 2d 834 (1995) (per curiam); Casarez v. State, 913 S.W.2d 468 (Tex. Crim. App. 1995) (striking for religious affiliation did not violate *Batson*).

[363] 47 M.J. 283 (C.A.A.F. 1997).

(Rel.3—1/07 Pub.62410)

Reasoning that under Article 25 convening authorities are required to select as members their best qualified officers, the court determined that trial counsel were not permitted to vitiate a member's selection without adequate cause. Accordingly, the court held that trial counsel may not strike a member "on the basis of a proffered reason . . . that is unreasonable, implausible, or that otherwise makes no sense."[364]

Although some courts have been troubled by dual motivation problems — justification for a challenge that contains both a proper and improper motive[365] — the Court of Military Appeals required that no part of the justification violate *Batson.*[366]

Because of the structural differences between civilian juries and court panels, soft data, such as tone of voice, body language, or blinking, may not justify a peremptory challenge.[367] "[T]he considerations that led us in *Tulloch* to impose specific procedural requirements on the Government's representative in responding to *Batson* challenges are not applicable to peremptory challenges made by the defense."[368]

One must ask if these differences do exist, should *Batson* have been applied in the first instance?

§ 15-55.34 Procedural Matters

Ordinarily, defense counsel raises *Batson*. Whether the military judge should do so sua sponte is unclear.[369] The trial judge determines, as a matter of discretion, whether the prosecution explanation for a *Batson* peremptory suffices. Clearly, defense counsel may oppose the prosecution justification. The procedure should follow that of a motion argument. Under ordinary circumstances, an adversary hearing would be inappropriate.[370] Should a hearing be necessary,

---

[364] 47 M.J. at 287. (C.A.A.F. 1997).

[365] *E.g.,* Wallace v. Morrison, 87 F.3d 1271 (11th Cir. 1996) (if dual motivation, one reason must be valid); Howard v. Senkowski, 986 F.2d 24 (2d Cir. 1993); Lingo v. State, 437 S.E.2d 463 (Ga. 1993) (inconsistent explanations do not undermine reason for peremptory challenge).

[366] United States v. Greene, 36 M.J. 274, 280 (C.M.A. 1993) (reasons cannot be considered disjunctively); Wallace v. Morrison, 87 F.3d 1271 (11th Cir. 1996) (if dual motivation one reason must be valid). As for the civilian federal courts, a number of circuits have adopted the dual motivation analysis. *See, e.g.,* United States v. Tokars, 95 F.3d 1520, 1533 (11th Cir. 1996).

[367] United States v. Tulloch, 47 M.J. 283 (C.A.A.F. 1997).

[368] United States v. Witham, 47 M.J. 297, 304 (C.A.A.F. 1997) (Effron, J., concurring).

[369] *See* Commonwealth v. Carson, 741 A.2d 686, 696 (Pa. 1999), *cert. denied,* 530 U.S. 1216 (2000) (holding judge did not violate the defendant's rights by raising the *Batson* issue sua sponte). *See also* United States v. Walker, 50 M.J. 749, 750 (N.M. Crim. App. 1999) (observing that military judge raised *Batson* sua sponte).

[370] *But see* United States v. Thompson, 827 F.2d 1254 (9th Cir. 1987) (adversary hearing). *Cf.* United States v. Davis, 809 F.2d 1194 (6th Cir.), *cert. denied,* 483 U.S. 1007 (1987).

(Rel.3—1/07 Pub.62410)

every effort should be made to protect against invasion of work product and trial tactics.

A *Batson* violation should be waived absent a timely objection.[371]

An apparent *Batson* violation may be cured post-trial on appeal via affidavit[372] or a limited post-trial *DuBay* hearing.[373]

§ 15-55.35 Systemic Impact of *Batson*

If the *Batson* burden is to be given weight,[374] it will likely be difficult, if not impossible, to fully justify a *Batson* peremptory challenge. After all, peremptory challenges were intended for situations in which counsel could not adequately articulate a causal challenge. The attempt to comply with *Batson* should either significantly limit prosecution peremptories or waste a fair amount of trial and appellate court time in reviewing *Batson* litigation. This would be particularly true if the courts use a liberal definition of "cognizable group."

It would not be unreasonable at this stage in American jurisprudence to follow the advice of Justice Marshall in *Batson* and eliminate the peremptory challenge.[375] Given the single challenge provided each party in the armed forces,

---

[371] *But see* United States v. Shelby, 26 M.J. 921 (N.M.C.M.R. 1988). United States v. Walker, 50 M.J. 749 (N.M. Crim. App. 1999) (waiver of *Batson* by failure to raise issue at trial), *pet. denied,* 52 M.J. 473 (C.A.A.F. 1999).

[372] United States v. Hurn, 58 M.J. 199 (C.A.A.F. 2003) (although Court of Criminal Appeals required testimony of trial counsel it accepted, without objection, affidavit of member); United States v. Moore, 26 M.J. 692 (A.C.M.R.), *rev'd,* 28 M.J. 366 (C.M.A. 1989) (insufficient affidavits); United States v. Cox, 23 M.J. 808 (N.M.C.M.R. 1986). The affidavit process may be inadequate to resolve the issue in any given case, requiring *DuBay* fact finding. *E.g.,* United States v. Hurn, 55 M.J. 446 (C.A.A.F. 2001) (fact finding powers of the courts of criminal appeals insufficient to resolve affidavit problem).

[373] Santiago-Davila, 26 M.J. at 393. *See also above* note 362.

[374] As one would hope, if the case is to afford meaningful protection.

[375] *Batson,* 476 U.S. at 107. *See also Hearings on S. 64, Subcomm. of the Senate Comm. on Military Affairs,* 66th Cong., 1st Sess. General Chamberlain said: "The accused should not be given the right to peremptory challenge. Care should be taken that each member of the court is free from bias and prejudice and that he has not formed an opinion in the case." *Id.* at 724. Professor Morgan testified that the accused should have a peremptory challenge. *Id.* at 1374 (1919). *See* Colonel (Ret.) Norman G. Cooper and Major Eugene R. Milhizer, *Should Peremptory Challenges Be Retained in the Military Justice System in Light of Batson v. Kentucky and Its Progeny?* Army Law, October, 1992 at 10. Although also concluding that peremptories are likely to be eliminated, Lieutenant Colonel James Young suggests that so long as they are retained in the armed forces, the unique military method of court member appointment would discourage the convening authority from appointing minority group members to the court. Young, *The Continued Viability of Peremptory Challenges in Courts-Martial,* Army Law, January 1992, at 20, 23–24. Interestingly, in *United States v. Loving,* 41 M.J. 213, 294–95 (C.M.A. 1994), the court rejected a systemic challenge to peremptories in capital cases. *See also* Akil Reed Amar, *Reinventing Juries: Ten Suggested Reforms,* 28 U. C. Davis L. Rev. 1169, 1181 (1995); Nancy S. Marder, *Beyond Gender: Peremptory Challenges and the Roles of the Jury,* 73 Tex. L. Rev. 1041, 1045 (1995) (peremptories remove a wide range of values and perspectives).

(Rel.3—1/07 Pub.62410)

the loss might not be significant. At the least, as Judge Cox has pointed out,[376] so long as the convening authority picks the court members, the prosecution would not seem in great need of peremptories.

§ 15-56.00 Procedure for Exercising and Evaluating Challenges

The normal procedural sequence for voir dire and challenge is:

1. Reading of the preliminary instructions by the military judge;

2. Ascertainment of any known grounds for challenge by the court members;

3. Voir dire by the trial counsel;[377]

4. Exercise of causal challenges by the trial counsel followed by judicial ruling upon them;

5. Exercise of peremptory challenges by the trial counsel;[378]

6. Voir dire by the defense counsel;

7. Exercise of causal challenges by the defense counsel followed by judicial ruling upon them;

8. Exercise of peremptory challenges by the defense counsel;

9. Addition of new members if the court falls below quorum;[379] and

10. Reseating of the members in order of seniority.[380]

The better procedure, however, is for all voir dire to be completed before challenges are exercised. This gives both counsel the advantage of information obtained from the other counsel's voir dire. To the extent possible, challenges should be made out of the presence of the court members so that the party making the challenge may avoid, as much as may be possible, any animosity on the part of the remaining members. Rule 912(f)(3) specifies:

> Each party shall be permitted to make challenges outside the presence of the members. The party making a challenge shall state the grounds for it. Ordinarily the trial counsel shall enter any challenges for cause before the defense counsel. The military judge shall rule finally on each challenge. When a challenge for cause is granted, the member concerned shall be

---

[376] United States v. Carter, 25 M.J. 471, 478 (C.M.A. 1988).

[377] Ordinarily, when first seated the members will take an oath to answer all questions truthfully and to faithfully and impartially try the case. Failure to administer the oath before voir dire is not an absolute requirement so long as the oath is administered. United States v. Clemons, 35 M.J. 767, 769 (A.C.M.R. 1992) (dictum as no objection and no prejudice).

[378] R.C.M. 912(g)(1); United States v. Newson, 29 M.J. 17 (C.M.A. 1989).

[379] Which permits their voir dire and causal challenge. Even if peremptories have all been exercised, it may be that an additional peremptory will be granted on request. *See* Section 15-55.20.

[380] Court members are seated with the senior member, the president, in the center, with the remaining members seated to the right and left of the president in descending alternating order of seniority.

(Rel.3—1/07 Pub.62410)

excused. The burden of establishing that grounds for a challenge exist is upon the party making the challenge. A member successfully challenged shall be excused.

The Court of Military Appeals held that, in unusual circumstances, the military judge may change the sequence of peremptory challenges:

> Indeed, there is no impediment to such a departure where a judge makes adequate findings on an adequate record. The term "ordinary" is sufficient to limit changes to "extraordinary" or "uncommon" circumstances. [381]

When resolving causal challenges, the key issue is whether the court members will keep an open mind and decide the case on the evidence. A jury without some preconceived ideas is not required — only that they can set aside any such matters and hear the case impartially. [382] This leads to possible rehabilitation of a member who would appear subject to causal challenge. Should a member thus admit during defense voir dire, for example, that he or she has been exposed to some information relevant to the case or has some ideas concerning the accused's guilt or deserved punishment, the judge may attempt to rehabilitate the member. This is usually done by explaining the requirement for neutrality and asking whether the member can set aside the troubling data or views. Should the member agree that he or she can and will do so, they usually will be able to sit. [383] Although such a result may be correct in many cases, in some it is clearly inappropriate and compels the use of a peremptory challenge to cure the judge's action. The Air Force Court of Military Review indicated that on appeal the court will apply an abuse of discretion test when the defense challenges the trial judge's denial of a causal challenge. [384]

Although it is nontraditional, should there be any likelihood of the court dropping below the statutory minimum, the convening authority should appoint alternate members who would be available in the event of a challenge. [385]

---

[381] United States v. Newson, 29 M.J. 17, 20 (C.M.A. 1989) (footnote omitted).

[382] See, e.g., United States v. Paige, 23 M.J. 512, 513 (A.F.C.M.R. 1986). In *Paige*, the court added: "The willingness of the government to accept the possibility of a reversal based on the trial judge's ruling denying the challenge is not an acceptable criteria." 23 M.J. 512, 513 (A.F.C.M.R. 1986). See also United States v. Chollet, 30 M.J. 1079, 1081 (C.G.C.M.R. 1990).

[383] See, e.g., United States v. Carns, 27 M.J. 820 (A.C.M.R. 1988). See also United States v. Mason, 16 M.J. 455 (C.M.A. 1983).

[384] United States v. Stewart, 33 M.J. 519, 521 (A.F.C.M.R. 1991) (dictum), citing United States v. Sloan, 30 M.J. 741 (A.F.C.M.R.), pet. denied, 32 M.J. 41 (C.M.A. 1990).

[385] United States v. Mason, 16 M.J. 455, 458 (C.M.A. 1983) (Everett, C.J. dissenting); Lyons v. United States, 683 A.2d 1066 (D.C. App. 1996) (limitation of peremptory not "structural" error). But see Tankleff v. Senkowski, 135 F.3d 235 (2d Cir. 1998) (Batson error is structural defect citing numerous cases).

(Rel.3—1/07 Pub.62410)

§ 15-57.00   Waiver

Unless a member is not qualified to sit under Article 25(a)–(c) of the Uniform Code, failure to make a timely challenge waives the challenge,[386] although the military judge may sua sponte excuse a member for cause.[387] Until 1990, the courts were divided as to whether the erroneous refusal of a judge to grant a defense causal challenge is cured by the exercise of a peremptory challenge against that member. Rule for Courts-Martial 912(f)(4) provides:

> When a challenge for cause has been denied, failure by the challenging party to exercise a peremptory challenge against any member shall constitute waiver of further consideration of the challenge upon later review. However, when a challenge for cause is denied, a peremptory challenge by the challenging party against any member shall preserve the issue for later review, provided that when the member who was unsuccessfully challenged for cause is peremptorily challenged by the same party, that party must state that it would have exercised its peremptory challenge against another member if the challenge for cause had been granted.

The authors of the Rule recognized that the issue it dealt with "has been a subject of some controversy."[388] They explained that "[t]he requirement that a party peremptorily challenging a member it has unsuccessfully challenged for cause state that it would have peremptorily challenged another member is designed to prevent a 'windfall' to a party which had no intent to exercise its peremptory challenge against any other member."[389] In *United States v. Jobson,*[390] the Court of Military Appeals bolstered the Rule:

> We reject the opinion of the United States Air Force Court of Military Review herein that, if an accused elects to remove the objectional member from the panel, the error can be tested for harmlessness. . . . To so hold

---

[386] R.C.M. 912(f)(4). The Rule states: "except that membership of enlisted members in the same unit as the accused may be waived. Membership of enlisted members in the same unit as the accused and any other ground for challenge is waived if the party knew of or could have discovered by the exercise of diligence the ground for challenge and failed to raise it in a timely manner." R.C.M. 912(f)(4). United States v. Bannwarth, 36 M.J. 265 (C.M.A. 1993) (failure to challenge member based on friendship with accuser waived any error — found no cumulative error).

[387] R.C.M. 912(f).

[388] Analysis of the Rules for Courts-Martial, MCM, 20051998, A21-6159 (*citing* United States v. Harris, 13 M.J. 288 (C.M.A. 1982) (per Fletcher, J., with Cook, J., concurring in result); United States v. Russell, 43 C.M.R. 807 (A.C.M.R. 1971), "and cases cited therein"). *See also* United States v. Martinez-Salazar, 146 F.3d 653 (9th Cir. 1998) (reversal required when defendant forced to use peremptory when challenge for cause improperly denied even if defendant did not request additional peremptory).

[389] Analysis of the Rules for Courts-Martial, MCM, 20051998, A21-6159. *See also* United States v. Eby, 44 M.J. 425 (C.A.A.F. 1996) (to preserve issue, must state who would have been challenged — known as "but for" rule. But for the denial of the challenge for cause, counsel would have peremptorily challenged another member).

[390] 31 M.J. 117, 120–21 (C.M.A. 1990).

would render the language of RCM 912(f)(4) meaningless and, in every case, would require an accused, *at his peril*, to leave the objectional member on the panel in order to obtain review of the military judge's ruling on his challenge for cause.[391]

The Supreme Court subsequently held in *United States v. Martinez-Salazar*,[392] a case arising under the Federal Rules of Criminal Procedure, that

We reject the Government's contention that under federal law, a defendant is obliged to use a peremptory challenge to cure the judge's error. We hold, however, that if the defendant elects to cure such an error by exercising a peremptory challenge, and is subsequently convicted by a jury on which no biased juror sat, he has not been deprived of any rule-based or constitutional right.[393]

Resting its decision on the fact that military trials are governed by the Rule for Courts-Martial, rather than the Federal Rules of Criminal Procedure, the Court of Appeals for the Armed Forces has declined to follow *Martinez-Salazar* in favor of Rule 912(f)(4).[394]

In 2005, the President changed Rule 912(f)(4) to provide that when a challenge for cause has been denied, the successful use of a peremptory challenge by either party, excusing the challenged member from further participation in the court-martial now precludes appellate review of the challenge of that excused member.[395]

§ 15-58.00 Tactical Considerations — The "Numbers Game"

Quite obviously, counsel will wish to challenge members who may vote against their party.[396] Absent either express comment or conduct on the part of a member or the type of competent scientific sampling and analysis rarely available,[397]

---

[391] 31 M.J. 121 (C.M.A. 1990) (emphasis in original) (following United States v. Moyar, 24 M.J. 635 (A.C.M.R. 1987)); United States v. Anderson, 23 M.J. 894 (A.C.M.R. 1987). *See, e.g.,* United States v. Abdelkader, 34 M.J. 605 (A.F.C.M.R. 1992) (peremptory challenge to the member who should have been excused for cause preserved the issue under R.C.M. 912(f)(4)). *See also* United States v. Miles, 58 M.J. 192, 195 (C.A.A.F. 2003) (majority refused to apply a harmless error test when member no longer sat); United States v. Armstrong, 54 M.J. 51 2000). United States v. Jobson, 31 M.J. 117 (C.M.A. 1990) is not overruled by United States v. Martinez-Salazar, 528 U.S. 304 (2000) because Jobson grants more rights). *See generally* William T. Pizzi & Morris B. Hoffman, *Jury Selection Errors on Appeal*, 38 Am. Crim. L. Rev. 1391, 1392 N.7 (2001) (Even Before Martinez-Salazar, Many Federal and State Courts Apply Harmless Error Standard to Loss of Peremptory Challenge).

[392] 528 U.S. 304 (2000).

[393] 528 U.S. at 307 (2000).

[394] United States v. Armstrong, 54 M.J. 51 (C.A.A.F. 2000).

[395] 70 Fed. Reg. 60697 (October 18, 2005). *See also* § 1-52.00.

[396] *See generally* Dwight H. Sullivan, *Playing the Numbers: Court-Martial Panel Size and the Military Death Penalty,* 158 Mil. L. Rev. 1 (1998).

[397] And, we believe, largely untested in the armed forces.

(Rel.3—1/07 Pub.62410)

challenges are almost always inherently speculative. Notwithstanding this, many counsel have been playing the "numbers game" for years. The numbers game stems from the requirement that if an accused is not convicted by a two-third majority of the members, he or she is instantly acquitted. Accordingly, the prosecution and defense have differing numerical goals for every initial panel of members. Given a five-or six-member court, for example, the prosecution need only convince four for a conviction; [398] the defense needs reasonable doubt in two or three members. Five would thus be a better number for the defense, and six for the prosecution. The problem with playing the numbers game, of course, is that often counsel have no real idea whether the member they challenge peremptorily to play it is the ideal member counsel should have retained.

§ 15-60.00   TRIAL BY MEMBERS: THE ACCUSED'S DECISION

As in civilian life, a jury trial is the norm in the armed forces. If the accused does not request, and receive, a trial by judge alone, [399] the accused will receive a trial with members. If an enlisted accused does not request trial with enlisted personnel, trial will be by an officer panel.

The accused may defer the decision as to the fact finder until before assembly. [400] An accused may attempt to request trial by judge alone at any time before the end of the Article 39(a) session, or, in the absence of such a session, before assembly. [401] Whether to grant an untimely request is within the discretion of the trial judge. [402] The *Manual* implies the military judge does not have the discretion to approve an untimely request made after the introduction of evidence. [403]

The chart below displays the number of member trials by type of court-martial against the total number of trials in that category. [404] Unfortunately, the data are not particularly illuminating, as they do not differentiate between guilty pleas and contested cases.

---

[398] Any fraction of a member rounds the required number up to the next whole member.

[399] Which is potentially available in all noncapital cases. *See generally* Section 14-64.20.

[400] R.C.M. 903(a)(2).

[401] R.C.M. 903(d); R.C.M. 903(a).

[402] R.C.M. 903(e); United States v. Kauffman, 3 M.J. 794 (A.C.M.R. 1977).

[403] R.C.M. 903(e). ("However, the military judge may until the beginning of the introduction of evidence on the merits, as a matter of discretion, approve an untimely request or withdrawal of a request").

[404] The difference between the two numbers yields the number of trials by judge alone.

(Rel.3—1/07   Pub.62410)

FISCAL YEAR 2005 MEMBER TRIALS COMPARED TO ALL TRIALS OF THAT CATEGORY*
ARMY AIR FORCE NAVY/ MARINE COAST GUARD

	Army	Air Force	Navy/Marine
General Courts	173/825	160/432	81/359
Special Courts	76/700	155/517	98/1610

*Compiled from the Reports of the Judge Advocates General for October 1, 2004 to September 30, 2005.

**Published Air Force and Navy-Marine individual figures reflecting judge alone and member trials do not equal the total number of trials by type reported by those services.[405]

Counsel have long preferred jury trials when the factual issues look appealing to the members and judge alone trials when the case might turn on the law. Military practitioners often report the belief that court members make a particular effort to follow the military judge's instructions and may elevate the burden of proof to an absolute certainty standard.[406] Experimentation at the College of William and Mary[407] suggests that college students, from whom most officers come,[408] when faced with comprehensible instructions, particularly a burden of proof instruction, give them great weight and attempt to comply with them. Counsel may thus be too quick to abandon members trials when faced with difficult facts, but possibly desirable law.

§ 15-70.00   THE MEMBERS' FUNCTION

§ 15-71.00   In General

Absent a special court-martial without a military judge,[409] the court members perform two functions: fact finding and sentencing. It is their function to evaluate the evidence and to apply to the facts that they determine to have occurred the law as given to them by the military judge. In the normal case, if at least two-thirds of the members do not find the accused guilty[410] beyond a reasonable

---

[405] www.armfor.uscourts.gov/annual/FY05/FY05AnnualReport.pdf.

[406] There is no necessary correlation between such a defense-oriented interpretation and sentencing philosophy.

[407] Conducted by Ms. Vicki Hellgeston in satisfaction of a Masters Degree in Law and Psychology.

[408] Concededly, this is an inadequate connection; commissioned officers may be such a distinct group as to have an entirely different reaction. However, the results match the empirical experience of the authors.

[409] *See* Section 15-12.00.

[410] The two-thirds verdict has disturbed numerous commentators. *See, e.g.*, Cohen, *The Two Thirds Verdict: A Surviving Anachronism in an Age of Court-Martial Evolution*, 20 Cal. W. L. Rev. 9

(Rel.3—1/07 Pub.62410)

doubt as to a given specification or charge, they must acquit the accused of that specification or charge. Generally, there cannot be a "hung jury" on findings in the military. [411]

It is also the members' duty to sentence the accused [412] should they convict. A sentence requires agreement by two-thirds, [413] three-quarters, [414] or all, [415] depending upon the offense. [416] If the accused pleads guilty, the trial judge will determine the providency [417] of the plea outside the presence of the members, [418] and the members will then sentence the accused.

There have been periodic calls to eliminate at least the non-capital sentencing function of the court members in favor of judge sentencing. [419] Such a change

---

(1983); Note, *The Military Justice System and the Right to Trial By Jury: Size and Voting Requirements of the General Courts-Martial For Service-Connected Civilian Offenses*, 8 Hast. Const. L.Q. 617 (1981). Given that acquittal follows instantly if the members cannot agree on a conviction, one wonders how many accused might elect a different requirement. Note that a capital case requires a unanimous finding. R.C.M. 921(c)(2)(A).

[411] There have been persistent recommendations that member sentencing in the armed forces be abolished in favor of judge sentencing. *See, e.g.*, Lovejoy, *Abolition of Court Member Sentencing in the Military*, Mil. L. Rev. 1 (1994). Non-capital case jury sentencing is now rare in the United States; approximately eight states retain it in one form or another. Mil. L. Rev. 1 (1994) at 24, n.147 *citing* Reese, *Jury Sentencing in Texas: Time for a Change?* 31 S. Tex. L.J. 331, 328–29 [sic] (1990). Within the military the issue is substantially more complicated than in civilian life. Unlike civilian juries, courts-martial, by definition "blue-ribbon juries," often hear multiple cases. Further, the members come from a unique society, which the judge shares, but not entirely from the same perspective. The current system protects the accused against excessive sentencing to some degree because when one sentencing agency becomes unduly severe, defense counsel recommend requesting trail by the other. On the other hand, there is nothing in the system today that protects against unduly lenient sentencing, and absent the Courts of Criminal Appeals, which can sharply moderate intemperate sentencing, sentencing disparity can more easily occur with member sentencing.

[412] Of course, if trial is by judge alone, the judge will sentence.

[413] R.C.M. 1006(d)(4)(4)(C).

[414] For sentences in excess of ten years' confinement, including life. R.C.M. 1006(d)(4)(4)(B).

[415] For the death sentence. R.C.M. 1006(d)(4)(4)(A).

[416] *See generally* Chapter 23.

[417] *I.e.*, the legal adequacy.

[418] *See generally* Chapter 19.

[419] *See, e.g.*, Colonel James A. Young III, *Revising the Court Member Selection Process*, 163 Mil. L. Rev. 91 (2000); Lovejoy, *Abolition of Court Member Sentencing in the Military*, Mil. L. Rev. 1 (1994). Non-capital case jury sentencing is now rare in the United States; approximately eight states retain it in one form or another. Mil. L. Rev. 1 (1994) at 24, n.147 *citing* Reese, *Jury Sentencing in Texas: Time for a Change?* 31 S. Tex. L.J. 331, 328–29 [sic] (1990). Within the military the issue is substantially more complicated than in civilian life. Unlike civilian juries, courts-martial, by definition "blue-ribbon juries," often hear multiple cases. Further, the members come from a unique society, which the judge shares, but not entirely from the same perspective. The current system protects the accused against excessive sentencing to some degree because when

(Rel.3—1/07 Pub.62410)

would clearly improve efficiency. However, member sentencing supplies a valuable and irreplaceable pragmatic evaluation of offenders and their conduct by those most likely to be able to realistically evaluate them. Further, member sentencing provides a check against overly severe judicial sentences.

In order to accomplish their duty, the members have potentially broad powers. Subject to the Rules of Evidence, they may call witnesses[420] and, via written questions submitted to the judges, question witnesses.[421]

Whether counsel should be permitted to interview court members post-trial is a controversial topic.[422] In *United States v. Thomas*,[423] Judge Lawrence, with the endorsement of Judge Reed, opined in dictum that, "Under existing military law, such post-trial contact was not unethical or unlawful, but it should be."[424] Although this issue is necessarily complex, it is apparent that judges and counsel receive some form of authoritative guidance and, should it be constitutional, standardized rule-making is highly desirable.[425]

§ 15-72.00 "Jury Nullification"

The military judge instructs the members on the law they are to apply. It is their duty to follow that law. Notwithstanding this, the members, like a civilian jury, have the power to acquit against the weight of the evidence. Many defense

---

one sentencing agency becomes unduly severe, defense counsel recommend requesting trail by the other. On the other hand, there is nothing in the system today that protects against unduly lenient sentencing, and absent the Courts of Criminal Appeals, which can sharply moderate intemperate sentencing, sentencing disparity can more easily occur with member sentencing.

[420] R.C.M. 801(c). *See, e.g.*, United States v. Lampan, 14 M.J. 22, 26 (C.M.A. 1982); United States v. Lents, 32 M.J. 636, 638 (A.C.M.R. 1991). Failure of counsel to request cross-examination of witnesses called by the members will waive the right to examination; however, given a request for cross by the defense, failure of the judge to permit cross-examination could compel reversal of any resulting conviction. United States v. Campbell, 37 M.J. 1049 (N.M.C.M.R. 1993) (finding no prejudice on the facts of the case).

[421] Mil. R. Evid. 614. *See also* United States v. Carter, 40 M.J. 102, 104 (C.M.A. 1994) (Judge's refusal to allow members to ask written questions after closing arguments and findings instructions didn't constitute an abuse of discretion). *See also* United States v. Gray, 51 M.J. 1, 50 (C.A.A.F. 1999) (appellant was not denied his right to an impartial jury because the members were allowed to ask questions). Civilian jurisdictions often question the desirability of jury questions. *See, e.g.*, State v. Costello, 646 N.W.2d 204 (Minn. 2002) (prohibiting juror question); *Thomas Lundy, Jury Instruction Corner,* The Champion 48 (December 2002) (discussing juror questioning). Neither of the authors, both former military judges, have observed significant difficulties with military practice.

[422] *See generally* Stone, USAF, *Post-trial Contact with Court Members: A Critical Analysis*, 38 A.F. L. Rev. 179 (1994).

[423] 39 M.J. 626 (N.M.C.M.R. 1993), *rev'd on other grounds*, 46 M.J. 311 (C.A.A.F. 1997).

[424] 39 M.J. at 640 (N.M.C.M.R. 1993).

[425] 39 M.J. at 643, n.3 (N.M.C.M.R. 1993) (Jones, J., dissenting).

(Rel.3—1/07 Pub.62410)

counsels, military and civilian, have longed for the right to explicitly[426] advise jurors of this power of "jury nullification." In 1988, the Court of Military Appeals wrote in *United States v. Smith*:[427]

> The final matter we will address in this case is the practice of "jury nullification." . . . The Court of Military Review stated in its opinion that defense counsel mentioned this practice as a reason justifying his request to advise the members prior to findings of the mandatory life sentence for premeditated murder. . . . More importantly, we do not equate express concern for serious and thoughtful consideration of guilt or innocence with implied advocacy of deliberate disregard of the law. In any event, we conclude that this justification for these proposed questions is totally unacceptable and inconsistent with the earlier decision of this Court in *United States v. Jefferson*.[428] There, this Court relied on a state court decision[429] which expressly rejected advice as to the sentence for this irregular purpose. . . .

With the exception of Maryland[430] and Indiana,[431] every jurisdiction in the United States has rejected a jury nullification instruction,[432] and there is surely no reason for the armed forces to deviate from the general rule.

§ 15-80.00 COMMAND INFLUENCE

Unlawful command influence[433] is the ultimate threat to the impartiality of military criminal law. The history of military justice prior to the Uniform Code of Military Justice is filled with examples of court members attempting to comply with the real or perceived desires of the convening authority (their commander) as to findings or sentence or both. During World War II, it was customary in many commands to sentence the convicted accused to the maximum to permit the convening authority to do as he wished with the offender. Both via the enactment of the Uniform Code of Military Justice generally, and via the statutory

---

[426] Defense counsel routinely hint at this via emphasis and discussion of the application of the prosecution's burden of proof.

[427] 27 M.J. 25, 28–29 (C.M.A. 1988). *See also* United States v. Hardy, 46 M.J. 67, 71–72 (C.A.A.F. 1997) (implicit rejection of the right to nullification instruction).

[428] *Citing* 22 M.J. 315, 329 (C.M.A. 1986).

[429] State v. Walters, 294 N.C. 311, 240 S.E.2d 628, 630 (1978).

[430] In which instructions are "advisory." *See generally* Wyley v. Warden, 372 F.2d 742 (4th Cir.), *cert. denied,* 389 U.S. 863 (1967).

[431] Korroch & Davidson, *Jury Nullification: A Call for Justice Or An Invitation To Anarchy?,* 139 Mil. L. Rev. 131 (1993) (*citing* at note 58, V. Hans & N. Vidmar, *Judging the Jury* 157 (1968) for the proposition that Maryland and Indiana permit nullification instructions).

[432] *See, e.g.,* Sparf v. United States, 156 U.S. 51, 102 (1895); United States v. Dougherty, 473 F.2d 1113 (D.C. Cir. 1972).

[433] *See generally* West, *A History of Command Influence on the Military Judicial System,* 18 U.C.L.A. L. Rev. 1 (1970).

(Rel.3—1/07 Pub.62410)

prohibition of such influence in Article 37 specifically, Congress attempted to prohibit command from affecting the results of trial.[434] Unfortunately, unlawful command influence continued after the Uniform Code became effective in 1951.[435]

In its original form, command influence usually meant command efforts to directly or indirectly affect the members.[436] For example, in a classic 1953 case, *United States v. Littrice*,[437] the Court of Military Appeals condemned the act of an executive officer who briefed the members before trial as to their duties.

> [H]e informed the members . . . that they should not usurp the prerogatives of the reviewing authority; that it had been his experience that court-martial records received a thorough review in the Seventh Army; that he read excerpts from a letter from Headquarters . . . on the subject of retention of thieves in the Army . . . .[438]

The letter complained of inadequate sentences and noted that proper performance as court members should be recognized on their efficiency reports.[439] In an often quoted passage, the court wrote:

> Thus, confronted with the necessity of maintaining a delicate balance between justice and discipline, Congress liberalized the military judicial system but also permitted commanding officers to retain many of the powers held by them under prior laws. While it struck a compromise, Congress expressed an intent to free courts-martial members from any improper and undue influence by commanders which might affect an honest and conscientious consideration of the guilt or innocence of an accused.[440]

More recently, the court has observed that "[c]ommand influence is the mortal enemy of military justice."[441]

Blatant attempts to influence the members are now rare,[442] although they do

---

[434] *See generally* United States v. Cruz, 20 M.J. 873, 878–82 (A.C.M.R. 1985) (en banc).

[435] 20 M.J. 873, 884–93 (A.C.M.R. 1985).

[436] Although this is still possible, today it is more likely to take the form of perceived command interest in the disposition of charges, dissuasion of potential defense witnesses (*see, e.g.*, United States v. Thomas, 22 M.J. 388 (C.M.A. 1986), *cert. denied*, 479 U.S. 1085 (1987)), or interference with military judges by other military lawyers.

[437] 13 C.M.R. 43 (C.M.A. 1953).

[438] 13 C.M.R. at 46 (C.M.A. 1953).

[439] 13 C.M.R. at 50 (C.M.A. 1953).

[440] 13 C.M.R. at 47 (C.M.A. 1953).

[441] United States v. Thomas, 22 M.J. 388, 393 (C.M.A. 1986).

[442] To the extent that such a thing can be comical, some cases can be amusing in a droll sense. In the 1960s, 93 general courts-martial were affected at Fort Leonard Wood by the actions of the convening authority. Among other matters, the convening authority gave the "cold shoulder" to court members who disappointed him and warm receptions to those who pleased him; his most unique effort was to engage in a brief building contest in which he elevated the seat of the president

(Rel.3—1/07 Pub.62410)

take place.[443] Instead, commanders may try to obtain their goals through manipulation of the Codal system. In *United States v. Redman*,[444] for example, the convening authority appointed new members because of dissatisfaction with the original panel's results. The Army Court of Military Review opined that such an action, albeit within the literal authority granted by Article 25, was "inconsistent with the spirit of impartiality of Article 25 and the limitation on command influence contained in Article 37 of the Code."[445]

Far more probable than attempts to directly influence members are attempts to resolve discipline problems involving criminal conduct that "spill over" into the trial arena. Such attempts usually involve either a commander's good-faith effort to encourage personnel to avoid misconduct and those who commit it,[446] or policy letters attempting to supply command guidance on the same subject.[447] One commentator has observed:[448]

> Influencing court-martial members through policy directives is a recurring problem because such directives originate at senior levels and necessarily address disciplinary issues. Promulgating policy directives does not, however, automatically result in unlawful command influence. Appellate courts have recognized the "propriety and necessity of the 'determination and promulgation of general service or command policies and pronouncements which are a proper exercise of the command function.' "[449] Such directives will not result in unlawful command influence unless they tend to control the judicial process rather than merely attempt to "improve the discipline of the command."

of the court over the judge's bench, while the judge replied in kind. To cope with the situation, the Court of Military Appeals remanded the affected cases for trial-level hearings, creating the now well-known *DuBay* procedure. United States v. DuBay, 37 C.M.R. 411 (C.M.A. 1967).

[443] *See, e.g.*, United States v. Stephens, 21 M.J. 784, 786 (A.C.M.R. 1986) (evidence was sufficient to permit a "reasonable person" to conclude that NCO member was told by his battalion sergeant major, based on his perception of what the general wanted, to sentence an NCO convicted of drug offenses to at least 30 years). *See generally* Bower, *Unlawful Command Influence: Preserving the Delicate Balance*, 28 A.F. L. Rev. 65 (1988).

[444] 33 M.J. 679 (A.C.M.R. 1991). The convening authority in *Redman* was selected subsequently for a third star. 140 Cong. Rec. S9119 (15 July 1994).

[445] 33 M.J. at 683 (A.C.M.R. 1991) (dictum), *citing* United States v. McClain, 22 M.J. 124 (C.M.A. 1986).

[446] *See, e.g.*, United States v. Cruz, 25 M.J. 326, 328 (C.M.A. 1987) (an extreme case involving a mass apprehension and formation of a "peyote platoon"). *See also* United States v. Biagase, 50 M.J. 143 (C.A.A.F. 1999) (reading confession at unit formations). *See* § 23-53.60 as to impropriety of arguing command policy.

[447] *See, e.g.*, United States v. Hawthorne, 22 C.M.R. 83 (C.M.A. 1956) (the seminal case). *See also* United States v. Toon, 48 C.M.R. 139 (A.C.M.R. 1973).

[448] Harty, *Unlawful Command Influence and Modern Military Justice*, 36 Naval L. Rev. 231, 234 (1986).

[449] *Citing* United States v. Eland, 17 M.J. 596, 599 (N.M.C.M.R. 1983) (*quoting* United States v. Grady, 15 M.J. 275, 276 (C.M.A. 1983)).

(Rel.3—1/07 Pub.62410)

Such letters and directives, however, are like mine fields — far more likely to cause harm to oneself than to injure the enemy. Their irony is that, to be effective, they must necessarily deal with specific matters that are likely to affect future court members.

Likening command influence to a violation of an accused's constitutional rights,[450] the Court of Military Appeals held:

> Consequently, in cases where unlawful command influence has been exercised, no reviewing court may properly affirm findings and sentence unless it is persuaded beyond a reasonable doubt that the findings and sentence have not been affected by the command influence.[451]

The armed forces have made major efforts to eliminate command influence. The Office of the Judge Advocate General of the Army, for example, at one point advised all staff judge advocates to arrange to review "all speeches and policy statements of the commander" to avoid suggestions of command influence.[452] These requirements will be reviewed at Article 6 (UCMJ) inspections. That command influence is still a problem despite efforts like this suggests the possibility of the need for systematic restructuring.[453]

---

[450] Opining that it "tends to deprive servicemembers of their constitutional rights." United States v. Thomas, 22 M.J. 388, 393 (C.M.A. 1986).

[451] 22 M.J. at 394 (C.M.A. 1986).

[452] Message from B.G. Hansen for S.J.A., J.A., Legal Counsel, Unlawful Command Influence (Jan. 1991).

[453] Message from B.G. Hansen for S.J.A., J.A., Legal Counsel, Unlawful Command Influence (Jan. 1991). Particularly troubling are the occasional efforts to affect trial results through dissuading witness testimony. *E.g.*, United States v. Jameson, 33 M.J. 669 (N.M.C.M.R. 1991) (reprisals were taken against defense extenuation and mitigation witnesses after their testimony). *See generally* § 23-45.23, *below*. United States v. Gleason, 39 M.J. 776, 780–81 (A.C.M.R. 1994) is an unusual case. The Special Forces battalion commander told his officers that the trial counsel prosecuting the Battalion Sergeant Major was their "friend," and that the defense counsel was the "enemy." Subsequently, the staff judge advocate caused a retraction, characterized as "ineffective." The trial counsel's mistaken belief that a defense witness should have told the prosecution about the witness' testimony, which the CID knew of, led to the battalion commander preventing the assignment of the witness as company first sergeant. Command influence "is a malignancy that eats away at the fairness of our military justice system." 39 M.J. at 782 (A.C.M.R. 1994). Here it was a "command climate or atmosphere," 39 M.J. at 782 (A.C.M.R. 1994) — "a pervasive atmosphere that bordered on paranoia," 39 M.J. at 782 (A.C.M.R. 1994), according to trial Judge Cole's findings. In a discouraging note, the Court of Military Review opined that lawyers and judges did everything possible to correct the situation, but that a command problem existed that required a different command atmosphere. Interestingly, apparently the commander was relieved and the SJA removed from O-6 promotion list, although no other corrective command action was taken. 39 M.J. at 783, n.7. (A.C.M.R. 1994). Finding no prejudice on the merits, the Court affirmed the findings but sharply reassessed the sentence to reach a result that would have occurred without command influence. *Rev'd*, 43 M.J. 69 (C.A.A.F. 1995).

Jameson and *Gleason* and other like scenarios suggest that trial of the offending officers may be the only feasible method of coping with such conduct.

(Rel.3—1/07   Pub.62410)

§ 15-90.00   APPELLATE REMEDY

When voir dire has been cut off[454] or there has been non-disclosure,[455] the appellate court may order a hearing under *United States v. DuBay.*[456] *United States v. Reichardt*[457] does not require a different result.

---

[454] United States v. Mack, 41 M.J. 51 (C.A.A.F. 1994).

[455] United States v. Sonego, 61 M.J. 1 (C.A.A.F. 2005); United States v. Jefferson, 44 M.J. 312 (C.A.A.F. 1996). *See also* Ross v. Oklahoma, 487 U.S. 81 (1988); United States v. Prati, 861 F.2d 82, 87 (5th Cir. 1988).

[456] 37 C.M.R. 411 (C.M.A. 1967).

[457] 28 M.J. 113 (C.M.A. 1989). *But see* United States v. McMillion, 16 M.J. 658 (A.C.M.R. 1983).

(Rel.3—1/07   Pub.62410)

CHAPTER 16

ARRAIGNMENT

§ 16-10.00 ARRAIGNMENT IN GENERAL
§ 16-20.00 TRIAL IN ABSENTIA
  § 16-21.00 Constitutional Law
  § 16-22.00 Military Law

§ 16-10.00 ARRAIGNMENT IN GENERAL

Under Rule for Courts-Martial 904, "[a]rraignment . . . shall consist of reading the charges and specifications to the accused and calling on the accused to plead."[1] Absent waiver, arraignment is improper, although probably nonprejudicial, if the charges are not read.[2] "However, waiver can be implied where the parties proceeded as if there were an arraignment, a formal plea was entered, and there was no objection to the defective arraignment at trial."[3]

The actual submission of the plea is not part of the arraignment.[4] For historical reasons,[5] the *Manual for Courts-Martial* contemplates that arraignment will be held in the presence of the court members following their assembly and any voir dire and challenge.[6] However, the *Manual*, pursuant to the Uniform Code of Military Justice,[7] also authorizes the military judge, when so authorized by the

---

[1] The accused may, and usually does, waive the reading of the charges and specifications (*see* R.C.M. 904) unless there is reason to doubt their exact nature, which may occur if the charges have been amended. Even with the consent of the accused, absent a change to the Code an arraignment may not be conducted on speaker telephones. United States v. Reynolds, 49 M.J. 260 (C.A.A.F. 1998).

Video-teleconferencing authorized: Section 556 of the National Defense Authorization Act (NDAA) for fiscal year 2006 (Pub. L. No. 109-163, 119 Stat. 3136 (Jan. 7, 2006)) amends Article 39 to permit administrative sessions of a court-martial (those held outside the presence of the members/jury) to be conducted using audiovisual technology. Under this amendment, video-teleconferencing of such sessions is authorized as long as at least one defense counsel is physically in the presence of the accused and authorized by service regulation.

[2] United States v. Napier, 43 C.M.R. 262 (C.M.A. 1971).

[3] United States v. Lichtsinn, 32 M.J. 898, 899 (A.F.C.M.R. 1991) ("The parties clearly proceeded as if there had been an arraignment, a formal plea was entered, and there was no objection . . ."). United States v. Stevens, 25 M.J. 805, 807 (A.C.M.R. 1988), (*citing* Garland v. Washington, 232 U.S. 642 (1914) (but holding "that, even absent waiver, appellant was not prejudiced by a flawed arraignment process")).

[4] R.C.M. 904 Discussion.

[5] *See generally* Chapters 1 and 15.

[6] R.C.M. 804; 904 and Discussion; MCM, 2005 App. 8-12.

[7] U.C.M.J. art. 39(a)(3).

(Rel.3—1/07 Pub.62410)

regulations of the Secretary concerned, to hold the arraignment at an Article 39(a) session out of the presence of the court members,[8] and this is now the customary procedure[9] when a judge presides over the trial.[10]

The actual arraignment is normally phrased:

> [name of the accused], how do you plead? Before receiving your pleas, I advise you that any motions to dismiss any charge or to grant other relief should be made at this time.[11]

Thus, as a matter of practice only, arraignment includes the formal call for motions, and pretrial motions will be heard prior to the submission of pleas. Consequently, it will be an unusual case in which the accused will be arraigned before court members. Indeed, to save the time of members, arraignment and motion practice is often scheduled one or more days in advance of the actual trial. A failure to raise many types of motions[12] prior to the submission of the plea will constitute waiver; however, some motions that would otherwise be waived may be made after the plea, if good cause is shown.[13]

After arraignment, "no additional charges may be referred to the same trial without consent of the accused."[14] At least of equal importance: the voluntary post-arraignment absence of the accused from trial permits trial in absentia.

Many states have long used videoconferencing regularly for first appearances and arraignments and even pretrial hearings,[15] e.g., and remote first appearance and arraignment are permissible under the Federal Rules of Criminal procedure when the accused consents to it. The armed forces might be well advised to consider expressly permitting the remote arraignments.

---

[8] R.C.M. 803. An "Article 39(a)" session is simply a court hearing held without the court members (the military jury). The session takes its name directly from the enabling provision of the Uniform Code of Military Justice, Article 39(a).

[9] See R.C.M. 904 Discussion; Dep't Army Pam. 27-9, Military Judges' Benchbook 13 (15 September 2002).

[10] It is legally possible to have a special court-martial without a military judge. See generally Section 15-12.00. To the best of the authors' knowledge, there have only been three special courts-martial without judges since approximately 1977, and those cases (Navy), conceded to be aberrations, took place before 1980. Summary courts-martial, of course, do not have judges and are governed by R.C.M. 1304(b)(2)(B) for arraignments.

[11] MCM, 2005 App. A8-4; Dep't Army Pam. 27-9, Military Judges' Benchbook 13 (15 September 2002).

[12] See, e.g., Mil. R. Evid. 304(d)(2)(A), 311(d)(2)(A), 321(c)(2)(A), R.C.M. 905(e). See generally Chapters 18 and 19.

[13] Mil. R. Evid. 304(d)(2)(A), 311(d)(2)(A), 321(c)(2)(A), R.C.M. 905(e).

[14] R.C.M. 601(d)(2).

[15] E.g., People v. Lindsey, 201 Ill.2d 45, 772 N.E.2d 1268 (2002).

(Rel.3—1/07 Pub.62410)

§ 16-20.00   TRIAL IN ABSENTIA

§ 16-21.00   Constitutional Law

The Supreme Court has long held that the voluntary post-arraignment absence of a defendant from trial will permit trial to proceed notwithstanding the accused's absence.[16] Thus, in *Taylor v. United States*,[17] the Court held that the unexplained failure of the defendant to appear at trial, first after the lunch recess and then on the morning of the second day of trial, permitted the trial to proceed in his absence. The Court stated that the defendant did not have to be personally advised as "it is demonstrated that he knew or had been expressly warned by the trial court not only that he had a right to be present but also that the trial would continue in his absence."[18]

§ 16-22.00   Military Law

The *Manual for Courts-Martial* takes advantage of constitutional precedent by declaring:

> The further progress of the trial to and including the return of the findings and, if necessary, determination of a sentence shall not be prevented and the accused shall be considered to have waived the right to be present whenever an accused, initially present:
>
> (1) Is voluntarily absent after arraignment (whether or not informed by the military judge of the obligation to remain during the trial). . . .[19]

Prior to the promulgation of the Rules for Courts-Martial, the *Manual* prohibited trial in absentia unless the accused had voluntarily and improperly absented himself "after the trial has commenced in his presence and he has been arraigned."[20] This provision required defining "commenced." The present rule is similar to Federal Rule of Criminal Procedure 43(b) (c)(1)(A)&(B), but is critically different in one respect: it substitutes for the civilian rule's "trial has begun" prerequisite a simple arraignment trigger-point. The drafters observed:

> This is a clearer demarcation of the point after which the accused's voluntary absence will not preclude continuation of the proceedings. Since there are several procedural steps, such as service of charges, which, while associated with the trial process, do not involve a session, the arraignment

---

[16] *See, e.g.,* Diaz v. United States, 223 U.S. 442 (1912).

[17] 414 U.S. 17 (1973).

[18] 414 U.S. at 19 (1973).

[19] R.C.M. 804(b)(1).

[20] MCM, 1969 (rev. ed.) 11c.

(Rel.3—1/07 Pub.62410)

is a more appropriate point of reference. This is consistent with the previous military rule.[21]

The change eliminates any argument that an accused can only be tried in absentia in a trial with members if the accused absents himself or herself after jury selection begins.[22]

Assuming that the accused has been present at arraignment, the focus must then turn to "voluntary absence." The Discussion to Rule 804(b) states:

> "Voluntary absence" means voluntary absence from trial. For an absence from court-martial proceedings to be voluntary, the accused must have known of the scheduled proceedings and intentionally missed them. For example, although an accused servicemember might voluntarily be absent without authority, this would not justify proceedings with a court-martial in the accused's absence unless the accused was aware that the court-martial would be held during the period of the absence.

An accused who is in military custody or otherwise subject to military control at the time of trial or other proceeding may not properly be absent from the trial or proceeding without securing the permission of the military judge on the record.

The prosecution has the burden to establish by a preponderance of the evidence that the accused's absence from trial is voluntary. Voluntariness may not be presumed, but it may be inferred, depending on the circumstances. For example, it may be inferred, in the absence of evidence to the contrary, that an accused who was present when the trial recessed and who knew when the proceedings were scheduled to resume, but who nonetheless is not present when court reconvenes at the designated time, is absent voluntarily.

Where there is some evidence that an accused who is absent for a hearing or trial may lack mental capacity to stand trial, capacity to voluntarily waive the right to be present for trial must be shown. *See* R.C.M. 909.

---

[21] Analysis of the Rules for Courts-Martial, Rule 804(b), MCM, 2005, A21-45. The drafters were correct that the new rule is consistent with the prior practice and *Manual* interpretation. It may not be consistent with reasonable alternative interpretations of the old *Manual* rule. United States v. Bass, 40 M.J. 220, 223 (C.M.A. 1994). Note that Federal Rule of Criminal Procedure 43 has been amended since the promulgation of the Rules for Courts-Martial.

[22] Virgin Islands v. George, 680 F.2d 13 (3d Cir. 1982); United States v. Miller, 463 F.2d 600 (1st Cir.), *cert. denied*, 409 U.S. 956 (1972). Because of the critical language difference between the military rule and the then Federal Rule of Criminal Procedure ("arraignment" vs. "commenced"; now "arraignment" vs. "trial has begun"), the Supreme Court's recent decision in *Crosby v. United States*, 506 U.S. 255 (1993), holding that a civilian federal defendant must be present when trial actually "commences," is inapplicable to the armed forces. Under military law, the critical initial question is whether the accused was present at the arraignment. *Cf.* United States v. Price, 48 M.J. 181 (C.A.A.F. 1998) (R.C.M. 804(b) permits a trial in absentia after the accused is asked "How do you plead?").

United States v. Lane, 48 M.J. 851 (A.F. Crim. App. 1998) (waiver of trial in absentia by counsel permissible after the judge granted two continuances).

(Rel.3—1/07   Pub.62410)

The Discussion concern with a "voluntary" absence is rooted in case law. Although military courts have followed the principle that a voluntary absence of the accused from trial constitutes a waiver of the accused's right to be present at trial,[23] there has been concern that the absence truly have been voluntary. Thus, in *United States v. Cook*,[24] for example, the court held that mere absence was insufficient to constitute waiver when there was evidence that the accused was suffering from a mental disorder that could have caused his absence, and in *United States v. Peebles*,[25] the court held that the failure of the accused to receive actual notice of the trial date, some eight months after the case had been continued for an unknown period, did not justify trial in absentia.

Notably, in *Peebles*, Judge Cook held that notice to the *defense counsel* of the trial date was insufficient to constitute notice to the accused "where the appellant has not specifically granted his counsel the authority to waive his right to be present."[26] Interestingly, Judge Cook may have accepted the theory that a lawful instruction to the accused to keep authorities notified of his current residence would justify trial in absentia after arraignment if the accused failed to comply with that order.[27] Opining that although "notice of the exact date of trial and warning of the consequences of action are highly desirable" they are "not prerequisites," the Navy-Marine Court of Military Review sustained trial in absentia after the military judge advised the accused that the Government anticipated trial would be "some time next week" and warned the accused that the case could be tried if the accused voluntarily were absent from court.[28] In dictum, the Army Court of Military Review stated that "Absent extraordinary circumstances, an accused is deemed to have been advised of a trial date once it is communicated to his lawyer."[29] The court has also held that lack of advice to an accused that the accused could be tried in his or her absence doesn't preclude a finding of voluntary absence.[30] In 1993 the Court of Military Appeals clarified matters by holding in *United States v. Sharp*,[31] not only that notice to the accused of the exact trial date is not required for trial in absentia, but also that it agreed

---

[23] *See, e.g.*, United States v. Bystrzycki, 8 M.J. 540 (N.C.M.R. 1979); United States v. Allison, 47 C.M.R. 968 (A.C.M.R. 1973). In a somewhat unusual variation on the usual flight situation, in 1992 the Air Force Court of Military Review found that an accused who had voluntarily taken an overdose of sleeping pills had thus waived his right to be present at the rest of the trial. United States v. Thrower, 36 M.J. 613, 615 (A.F.C.M.R. 1992).

[24] 43 C.M.R. 344 (C.M.A. 1971).

[25] 3 M.J. 177 (C.M.A. 1977).

[26] 3 M.J. at 180 (C.M.A. 1977).

[27] 3 M.J. at 180 (C.M.A. 1977).

[28] United States v. Jones, 34 M.J. 899, 910–912 (N.M.C.M.R. 1992).

[29] United States v. Yarn, 32 M.J. 736, 739 (A.C.M.R. 1991).

[30] United States v. Smith, 37 M.J. 523, 525 (A.C.M.R. 1993).

[31] 38 M.J. 33, 35 (C.M.A. 1993).

(Rel.3—1/07 Pub.62410)

with the civilian position "that the defense has the burden of going forward and offering evidence to rebut the inference that the absence was voluntary."[32]

An accused need not be aware that he or she can be tried in absentia to be so tried. So long as the accused knows of the need to attend trial and intentionally absents himself or herself after arraignment, trial in absentia is lawful. Voluntary absence within the meaning of Rule for Courts-Martial 804(b) doesn't require that the judge or commander warn the accused of the consequences of absence from trial.[33]

In *United States v. Sanders*,[34] the Navy-Marine Court of Military Review held that the attorney client privilege does not prohibit the defense counsel from testifying to having advised his client of the scheduled trial date. The court also held that mere averments of notice are insufficient to permit trial in absentia; rather, sworn testimony is required. Note that so long as the accused knew the date that trial was scheduled for, he or she need not know the actual date the case took place when trial was delayed.[35]

The Court of Military Appeals expressly failed in *Peebles* to address the question of whether an accused must be tried in absentia by the same court that arraigned the defendant, or whether trial may be held by a different court. The issue remains unresolved.

Trials in absentia are not mandated; rather, they are lawfully possible, given the prerequisites.[36] Although often every step is taken to avoid trials in absentia, such trials are held within the armed forces — particularly in the Navy in past years. Such a trial often presents numerous small problems for participating counsel, because defense counsel may not waive, without the express authorization of the accused, any matter that would normally require the accused's consent. Thus, trial in absentia is usually a fully contested case in every possible fashion, regardless of the issue or question involved.

---

[32] 38 M.J. at 37 (C.M.A. 1993), *quoting* United States v. Abilar, 14 M.J. 733, 735 (A.F.C.M.R. 1982), *pet. denied*, 15 M.J. 324 (C.M.A. 1983).

[33] United States v. Bass, 40 M.J. 220, 223 (C.M.A. 1994), holds that the civilian "commencement of trial" is arraignment in the military.

[34] 31 M.J. 834 (N.M.C.M.R. 1990).

[35] United States v. Yarn, 32 M.J. 736, 737 (A.C.M.R. 1991).

[36] R.C.M. 804(b)(1) Discussion states, for example, that:

Subsection (1) authorizes but does not require trial to proceed in the absence of the accused upon the accused's voluntary absence. When an accused is absent from trial after arraignment, a continuance or a recess may be appropriate, depending on all the circumstances.

(Rel.3—1/07 Pub.62410)

CHAPTER 17

THE RIGHT TO A SPEEDY TRIAL

§ 17-10.00 INTRODUCTION
§ 17-20.00 SOURCES OF THE RIGHT
§ 17-30.00 CONSTITUTIONAL LAW
   § 17-31.00   "Pre-Accusation" Delay
   § 17-32.00   "Post-Accusation" Delay
   § 17-33.00   Effect of Dismissal of Charges
§ 17-40.00 MILITARY STATUTORY LAW AND ITS INTERPRETATION
   § 17-41.00   Article 10
      § 17-41.10 — Inception of Article 10 Accountability
         § 17-41.11 — — In General
         § 17-41.12 — — Civilian Confinement
      § 17-41.20 Speedy Trial Standard
   § 17-42.00   Article 33
   § 17-43.00   Article 98
§ 17-50.00 THE *BURTON* RULE
   § 17-51.00   The 90-Day Rule in General
   § 17-52.00   Prerequisites for the 90-Day Rule
      § 17-52.10 — Inception of Government Accountability
      § 17-52.20 — Termination of Governmental Accountability
   § 17-53.00   Defense Requests for Delay
   § 17-54.00   Circumstances Justifying Delay
      § 17-54.10 — Extraordinary Circumstances
      § 17-54.20 — Other Circumstances Justifying Delay
      § 17-54.30 — Circumstances Not Justifying Delay
   § 17-55.00   Governmental Accountability upon the Commission or Discovery of Additional Misconduct
   § 17-56.00   The *Burton* Demand-for-Trial Rule
   § 17-57.00   The Overruling of *Burton*
§ 17-60.00 LOCAL RULES
§ 17-70.00 RULE FOR COURTS-MARTIAL 707
   § 17-71.00   The Two Rules
      § 17-71.10 — In General
   § 17-72.00   The 120-Day Rule
      § 17-72.10 — In General
      § 17-72.20 — Inception of Government Accountability
         § 17-72.21 — — Preferral of Charges
         § 17-72.22 — — Imposition of Restraint

(Rel.3—1/07   Pub.62410)

　　　§ 17-72.30 — **Restarting the Time Period**
　　　§ 17-72.40 — **Termination of Government Accountability**
　§ 17-73.00　**Exclusions**
　　　§ 17-73.10 — **In General**
　　　§ 17-73.20 — **Possible Civilian Disposition; Department of Justice Involvement**
　§ 17-74.00　**The 90-Day Rule**
§　17-80.00 **WAIVER**
　§ 17-81.00　**Failure to Demand Trial**
　§ 17-82.00　**Failure to Raise the Issue at Trial**
　§ 17-83.00　**Effect of a Guilty Plea**
　§ 17-84.00　**Plea Bargains**
§　17-90.00　**CONSEQUENCES OF VIOLATING THE SPEEDY TRIAL RIGHT**
§　17-100.00 **LITIGATION OF SPEEDY TRIAL MOTIONS**
　§ 17-101.00　**Preparation for Litigation**
　§ 17-102.00　**Litigation**
§　17-110.00 **APPEAL**
　§ 17-111.00　**In General**
　§ 17-112.00　**Government Appeal**
§　17-120.00 **REHEARINGS**

§ 17-10.00　INTRODUCTION

Pragmatically, the right to a speedy trial is a somewhat contradictory phrase, for many, if not most, defendants would rather postpone trial as long as possible in hope of either obtaining additional tactical advantage (*e.g.*, faded memories of prosecution witnesses) or simply avoiding the inevitable adjudication.[1] Furthermore, a too speedy trial may itself be unlawful, as it might well deprive the accused of the time necessary to prepare a defense.[2] The usual problem, however, is not a too speedy trial, but rather inordinate delay in bringing an accused to trial — delay that not only may be prejudicial to an accused,[3] but

---

[1] *See, e.g.*, Strunk v. United States, 412 U.S. 434, 439 n.2 (1973).

[2] This concern is dealt with in part by Article 35 of the Uniform Code of Military Justice, which provides that an accused may not be involuntarily brought to trial "in a general court-martial case within a period of five days after the service of charges upon him or in a special court-martial within a period of three days after the service of charges upon him." Trial that complies with Article 35 may, however, be too rapid for adequate defense preparation, in which case a due process objection under the Fifth Amendment will lie. *Cf.* United States v. McFarlane, 23 C.M.R. 320, 323 (C.M.A. 1957); United States v. Parker, 19 C.M.R. 201 (C.M.A. 1955). When multiple offenses are involved, some of which have not been timely served pursuant to Article 35, in the ordinary case (in which there is good reason for trial to proceed) properly served charges may be severed from those for which the period has not yet run. United States v. Oakley, 33 M.J. 27, 36 (C.M.A. 1991). The preference for trial of all known charges, R.C.M. 906(b)(10) Discussion, is not a right. 33 M.J. 27, 36 (C.M.A. 1991).

[3] *Cf., e.g.*, Strunk v. United States, 412 U.S. 434, 439 (1973) and cases cited therein (emotional stress caused by delay and attendant uncertainties).

(Rel.3—1/07 Pub.62410)

also adverse to the general military interest in resolving criminal cases as rapidly as possible.[4] Consequently, any discussion of the right to a speedy trial must address not only when an individual is entitled to a speedy trial, but the related question of when relief will be granted because of violation of that right.

Like his or her civilian counterpart, the armed forces member is guaranteed a speedy trial under the Sixth Amendment.[5] That right, however, given its present Supreme Court interpretation, is mostly illusory.[6] Consequently, the military member is particularly fortunate in that the constitutional right is significantly buttressed by additional protections stemming primarily from Article 10 of the Uniform Code of Military Justice and the Rules for Courts-Martial. Those protections, which take the form of judicial interpretation and implementation of the statute as well as executive order, have the effect of supplying the soldier, sailor, airman, marine, or coast guardsman with a highly effective and unparalleled[7] guarantee of speedy trial. Indeed, no member of the armed forces is to

[4] Speedy trial is important for unique reasons in the armed forces. Unlike civilian society, which is relatively static, military personnel must be instantly mobile for operational reasons. Trial delays can delay the reassignment or replacement of the accused and may well interfere with the assignment or duty performance of witnesses and court members who may be vitally needed to command or perform duty in combat or support units.

[5] Cf. United States v. Burton, 44 C.M.R. 166, 171 (C.M.A. 1971) [hereinafter cited as Burton].

[6] Although lengthy delay, especially delay spent in pretrial confinement, will justify dismissal of charges, the courts have been loathe to find violations of the constitutional right to a speedy trial, and lengthy delays have been commonplace. The Supreme Court has held that a seven-year delay is violative of the speedy trial right, (Dickey v. Florida, 398 U.S. 30 (1970)), while a five-year delay is not, (Barker v. Wingo, 407 U.S. 514 (1972)), although each case must be decided on its facts. Barker v. Wingo, 407 U.S. at 521. Recent statistics are more acceptable in light of the Federal Speedy Trial Act of 1974.

	Total	Dismissed	Guilty Plea	Bench Trial	Jury Trial
Number	63,148	6,607	51,918	899	3,724
Median (months)	5.8	5.0	5.7	1.1	10.5

Median time intervals from filing to disposition of criminal defendants disposed of by United States District Courts, October 1, 20011996 to September 30, 20021997, from Lloyd L.. Wienbreg Criminal Process 799814 (76th ed. 20041998) (citing Table D-6, Annual Report of the Director of the Administrative Office of the United States Courts, 20021997).

[7] Compare, e.g., R.C.M. 707 (requiring dismissal of charges after 120 days of notice of referral, arrest or confinement) with The Federal Speedy Trial Act of 1974, as amended, 18 U.S.C. §§ 3161–64 (which requires trial of persons held in pretrial confinement within 90 days following the beginning of detention (18 U.S.C. § 3164) and trial of other persons within 100 days of arrest (18 U.S.C. § 3161)). The Speedy Trial Act contains numerous exceptions. See, e.g., 18 U.S.C. § 3161(h)(8)(A), which exempts "[a]ny period of delay resulting from a continuance granted by any judge . . . if the judge granted such continuance on the basis of his findings that the ends of justice served by taking such action outweigh the best interest of the public and the defendant in a speedy trial." 18 U.S.C. § 3161(h)(8)(A). Nonexclusive criteria to be used in determining when to grant such a continuance are specified in 18 U.S.C. § 3161(h)(8)(B).

(Rel.3—1/07 Pub.62410)

be held, absent extraordinary circumstances, in pretrial confinement for a period, excluding defense delays, in excess of 120 days.[8] Because the sole remedy for an individual whose speedy trial rights have been violated is dismissal of charges,[9] the government pays a heavy price should an individual be denied these rights.

A request for speedy trial, whether coupled with a request for release from pretrial restraint or not, is properly addressed to the appropriate convening authority prior to referral of charges, and to the military judge appointed to hear the accused's case after referral. If the accused's right to a speedy trial was violated, the defense should move for dismissal of charges. When the defense has adequately raised the issue at trial, the burden is on the prosecution to prove by a preponderance of evidence that the accused's right to a speedy trial was not violated,[10] and if the prosecution fails to carry its burden, charges must be dismissed.[11]

A proper analysis of the right to a speedy trial and the remedy for its violation requires a detailed review of the sources of the right and their application to the armed forces member.

§ 17-20.00   SOURCES OF THE RIGHT

The accused's right to a speedy trial is based primarily upon five sources:

1. The explicit Sixth Amendment speedy trial guarantee;[12]
2. The Fifth Amendment due process clause;[13]
3. Article 10 of the Uniform Code of Military Justice;[14]
4. Article 33 of the Uniform Code of Military Justice;
5. Rule for Courts-Martial 707;[15] and
6. Case law.

The military accused receives the benefit of all of these disparate sources. However, because the Rules for Courts-Martial both implement and attempt to

---

[8] *Burton,* 44 C.M.R. 166, 171 (C.M.A. 1971); R.C.M. 707 (d); *see generally* Sections 17-50.00 and 17-74.00.

[9] Strunk v. United States, 412 U.S. 434 (1973); United States v. Hubbard, 44 C.M.R. 185 (C.M.A. 1971). *But see* Section 17-43.00.

[10] R.C.M. 905(c)(1).

[11] *See above* note 9.

[12] U.S. Const. amend VI: "In all criminal prosecutions, the accused shall enjoy the right to a speedy and public trial . . . ." *See* Section 17-30.00.

[13] U.S. Const. amend V. *See* Section 17-31.00.

[14] U.C.M.J. art. 10. *See* Section 17-41.00.

[15] R.C.M. 707; Section 17-100.00.

(Rel.3—1/07   Pub.62410)

modify case law that itself implements the statute, some confusion is unavoidable, depending upon the source of the rule being examined.

Case law is particularly important in this area, and of all military speedy trial cases, *United States v. Burton*[16] was the most important. Until overruled in 1993, *Burton* required the dismissal of all charges if the accused had been in pretrial confinement for more than 90 days after subtracting any applicable defense delays.

The federal Speedy Trial Act[17] is inapplicable to the armed forces.

§ 17-30.00 CONSTITUTIONAL LAW

Any examination of the right to a speedy trial within the armed forces must perforce begin with the United States Constitution, which guarantees in the Sixth Amendment that "[i]n all criminal prosecutions, the accused shall enjoy the right to a speedy and public trial."[18] Technically, the application of that amendment to the armed forces is, however, uncertain. Commentators have been unable to agree as to whether the framers of the Bill of Rights intended them to apply generally to the armed forces.[19] The Supreme Court has stated, notwithstanding dicta in *Ex Parte Quirin*[20] to the effect that " 'cases, arising in the land or naval forces' . . . are expressly excepted from the Fifth Amendment, and are deemed excepted by implication from the Sixth,"[21] that the related question of whether the constitutional right to counsel applies to the armed forces "has been much debated and never squarely resolved."[22] Despite the Supreme Court's hesitancy, the Court of Military Appeals has held that "it is apparent that the protections in the Bill of Rights, except those which are expressly or by necessary implication inapplicable, are available to members of our armed forces."[23] Insofar as the

---

[16] 44 C.M.R. 166 (C.M.A. 1971).

[17] 18 U.S.C. §§ 3161–64.

[18] U.S. Const. amend VI.

[19] *Compare* Henderson, *Courts-Martial and the Constitution: The Original Understanding*, 71 Harv. L. Rev. 293 (1957) *with* Wiener, *Courts-Martial and the Bill of Rights: The Original Practice (pts. 1–2)*, 72 Harv. L. Rev. 1, 266 (1958). In addition to finding the Sixth Amendment generally inapplicable to the armed forces, Colonel Wiener states that, with one exception that occurred in 1815, no one in 1855 or earlier rested the desirable dispatch of military and naval trials on any constitutional requirement. 72 Harv. L. Rev. 266, 281 (1958). *See generally* Section 1-52.00.

[20] 317 U.S. 1 (1942).

[21] 317 U.S. 40 (1942).

[22] Middendorf v. Henry, 425 U.S. 25, 33 (1976) (footnote omitted). Of course, the original intent of the framers is not necessarily dispositive of the constitutional question. *See, e.g.*, Justice Marshall's dissenting opinion in *Middendorf*, in which he states that even if his view that the intent of the framers was to make the Sixth Amendment right to counsel applicable to the armed forces was erroneous, the original intent would not "be determinative of the contemporary scope of the Sixth Amendment." 425 U.S. 53 (1976).

[23] United States v. Jacoby, 29 C.M.R. 244, 246–47 (C.M.A. 1960) (holding the Sixth Amend-

speedy trial right is concerned, the Court of Military Appeals both stated that the military statutory right to speedy trial, Article 10,[24] "reiterates" the Sixth Amendment right[25] and assumed in its opinions that the right applies to courts-martial.[26] Accordingly, it is essential to examine the constitutional precedents in this area.

§ 17-31.00 "Pre-Accusation" Delay

The Supreme Court held in *United States v. Marion*[27] that "it is either a formal indictment or information or else the actual restraints imposed by arrest and holding to answer a criminal charge that engage the particular protections of the speedy trial provision of the Sixth Amendment,"[28] and in *Dillingham v. United States,*[29] the Court expressly held that the speedy trial right applies upon arrest.[30] Thus, absent such indictment, information, or restraint, the Sixth Amendment protection is inapplicable.[31]

---

ment right of confrontation applicable to the armed forces). *See also* United States v. Stuckey, 10 M.J. 347, 349 (C.M.A. 1981) (Fourth Amendment shields members of the armed forces) (Everett, C.J.; Fletcher, J., concurring in the result; Cook, J. concurring and dissenting); United States v. Tempia, 37 C.M.R. 249 (C.M.A. 1967) (holding Miranda applicable to the armed forces). Prior to *Jacoby*, the Court of Military Appeals utilized what was customarily termed the "military due process" test, which was based solely on the Uniform Code of Military Justice and, potentially, other congressionally granted rights. *See, e.g.*, United States v. Sutton, 11 C.M.R. 220, 222–23 (C.M.A. 1953). *See generally*, H. Moyer, Justice and the Military § 2-105 (1972); Wurfel, "*Military Due Process": What Is It?*, 6 Vand. L. Rev. 251 (1953).

[24] *See generally* Section 17-41.00.

[25] United States v. Hounshell, 21 C.M.R. 129, 132 (1956).

[26] *See, e.g.*, United States v. Burton, 44 C.M.R. 166, 171 (C.M.A. 1971) where the court stated: "An obvious question is whether the Sixth Amendment requires a more prompt trial than does Article 10 . . . We assume for present purposes that the requirements of Articles 10 are more rigorous." *See also* United States v. Powell, 2 M.J. 6, 8 (C.M.A. 1976) in which the court may have indicated a firmer position on the issue.

[27] 404 U.S. 307 (1971) [hereinafter *Marion*].

[28] 404 U.S. 320 (1971).

[29] 423 U.S. 64 (1975) (per curiam).

[30] 423 U.S. 65 (1975). The term "arrest" is used by the Court in its civilian meaning and presumably is identical with either "apprehension" or "arrest." U.C.M.J. arts. 7(a) and 9(a). It is possible that an apprehension can be distinguished from a civilian arrest because it often does not have the same consequences as would arrest for a civilian. *See, e.g.*, Dillingham v. United States, 423 U.S. at 65, (*citing* United States v. Marion, 404 U.S. 307, 320–21 (1971)). Pay, for example, continues in the military, and an individual's freedom may only be temporarily interrupted. However, the "public obloquy" and "anxiety" referred to in *Marion*, 404 U.S. at 320, are present during and after an "apprehension" as well as an "arrest."

[31] *See, e.g.*, Pharm v. Hatcher, 984 F.2d 783 (7th Cir. 1993) (right doesn't accrue just because the accused was incarcerated via a detainer filed to obtain the incarcerated accused from another state).

(Rel.3—1/07 Pub.62410)

Within the armed forces there is no clear analog to indictment or information, because the Uniform Code of Military Justice utilizes neither procedural step.[32] If one views indictment or information as the point at which the civilian defendant is virtually guaranteed prosecution; that is, the point at which the true prosecutorial decision has been made or the point at which the defendant has been formally "accused," the functional equivalent in the armed forces can be said to be either the preferral[33] or referral[34] of charges, or the imposition of pretrial restraint,[35] whichever comes first.[36] When dealing with another Sixth Amendment application question, the authors of the Military Rules of Evidence determined that the civilian procedural stages of arraignment or indictment had to be viewed as the functional equivalent of the initiation of the formal military criminal process and utilized the preferral of charges or the imposition of pretrial arrest, restriction, or confinement as their equivalent.[37] In view of the President's use of their decision,[38] it would seem appropriate to defer to it for speedy trial purposes as well. Thus, the Sixth Amendment right to a speedy trial should be applicable upon preferral of charges or the imposition of pretrial apprehension,[39] arrest, restriction, or confinement, whichever is the earliest. This, incidentally, incorporates the remainder of the *Marion* test inasmuch as it defines the "actual restraints imposed by arrest and holding to answer a criminal charge" which also

---

[32] *See* United States v. Vogan, 35 M.J. 32, 33 (C.M.A. 1992) ("There is no clear analog to the 'formal indictment or information' in the Armed Forces, however, preferral or referral of charges or pretrial restraint approach being analogous").

[33] Preferral of charges is analogous to the signing of a criminal complaint in civilian procedure. *See generally* R.C.M. 307(a); Chapter 8.

[34] Referral is the act of ordering charges to trial and is roughly equivalent in effect to an information or indictment in civilian procedure. *See generally* U.C.M.J. art. 34; Chapter 10.

[35] Such restraint clearly includes "restriction." *See, e.g.*, United States v. Smith, 38 C.M.R. 225 (C.M.A. 1968).

[36] Viewing the military criminal legal system as it actually works, the preferral of charges is much closer in effect to a prosecutor's information than a mere complaint, as preferral is customarily made by the accused's commanding officer. Although senior commanders must make an independent decision on the disposition of those charges (*see generally* Chapter 8) and trial does not always result, it is apparent that in most cases trial does result with the only significant question being the nature of the forum of disposition. Pretrial confinement requires a magisterial determination of probable cause and is primarily or solely designed to ensure presence at trial. Consequently, pretrial confinement itself is a good indication of the government's intent to try the accused.

[37] Mil. R. Evid. 305(d)(1)(B). *See also* Analysis of the Military Rules of Evidence 1980 Amendments to the *Manual for Courts-Martial*, MCM, 20051984, A22-153.

[38] The Military Rules of Evidence constitute Part III of the 2005 *Manual for Courts-Martial* and were promulgated by Executive Order 12198 Prescribing Amendments to the *Manual for Courts-Martial, United States*, 1969 (Revised Edition) 45 Fed. Reg. 16, 932 (1980).

[39] Mil. R. Evid. 305(d)(1)(B), however, does not apply upon simple apprehension. *See, e.g.*, Analysis of the Military Rules of Evidence 1980 Amendments to the *Manual for Courts-Martial*, MCM, 20051984, A22-153.

trigger the right to a speedy trial.[40] The initiation of administrative action incidental to possible prosecution (*i.e.*, a "flagging action"[41] or "legal hold")[42] does not by itself trigger application of the Sixth Amendment right.

Although the Sixth Amendment right to a speedy trial will thus be inapplicable to even substantial periods of "pre-accusation"[43] delay, in any specific case, the Fifth Amendment due process clause may be applicable to protect an accused against egregious delay. In *United States v. Lovasco*,[44] the Supreme Court held that a preindictment delay of some eighteen months did not violate the due process clause, even though the defense claimed that the death of two material witnesses[45] had occurred during the delay, thus prejudicing the defense. In so holding, the Court did concede, however, that pre-accusation delay could result in a due process violation,[46] and cited *Marion*[47] for the proposition that "proof of prejudice is generally a necessary but not sufficient element of a due process claim, and that the due process inquiry must consider the reasons for the delay as well as the prejudice to the accused."[48] It then accepted as adequate the government's explanation that its delay in *Lovasco* had been intended to discover

---

[40] 404 U.S. 307, 320 (1971).

[41] A "flagging action" is an administrative direction that an individual be basically held in a status quo position until resolution of pending criminal charges. Reassignments, promotions, and favorable personnel actions may all be deferred. The expression is an Army one and might not be used in the other services. "Legal hold" might connote the same or a similar administrative status for the Navy.

[42] United States v. Amundson, 49 C.M.R. 598 (C.M.A. 1975).

[43] "Pre-accusation delay" refers to the period prior to preferral of charges or the initiation of pretrial restraint, including apprehension. Although most cases may begin with an apprehension at or soon after the offense, or with a preferral of charges soon after the offense, the government may choose, for investigative purposes among other reasons, to defer either apprehension or preferral of charges.

[44] 431 U.S. 783 (1977) [hereinafter *Lovasco*].

[45] 431 U.S. 796 (1977). It seems apparent that the Court doubted the probative value of the defense's claimed "material witnesses," although that was not articulated as part of the Court's rationale.

[46] 431 U.S. 789 (1977). *See also* United States v. MacDonald, 456 U.S. 1, at 67 (1982). "Although delay prior to arrest or indictment may give rise to a due process claim under the Fifth Amendment . . . or to a claim under any applicable statutes of limitations, no Sixth Amendment right to a speedy trial arises until charges are pending." The Court of Military Appeals has stated:

> [I]ndeed, Sixth Amendment considerations might well be overcome by Fifth
> Amendment due-process considerations in an aggravated case. Here, the length of delay,
> while extensive, was balanced by the explanations for the delay and the relative absence
> of prejudice to the accused. However, in another case, improper reasons and/or the
> showing of specific prejudice to the accused might well trigger a Fifth Amendment
> violation.

United States v. Johnson, 17 M.J. 255, 261 n.5 (C.M.A. 1984).

[47] *Above* note 27.

[48] 431 U.S. at 790 (1977).

(Rel.3—1/07   Pub.62410)

others who might have been involved in the crime. The Court expressly left to the lower courts "the task of applying the settled principles of due process that we have discussed to the particular circumstances of individual cases."[49] In refusing to supply any specific guidance, the Court did, however, cite the government's concession that a "tactical" delay or a delay "incurred in reckless disregard of circumstances, known to the prosecution, suggesting that there existed an appreciable risk that delay would impair the ability to mount an effective defense" would amount to a due process violation.[50]

In *United States v. Reed*,[51] the court stated:

> Most of the federal courts, relying on *Lovasco* and *Marion*, have held that the defendant has the burden of proof to show an egregious or intentional tactical delay and actual prejudice.

Speculation by the defendant is not sufficient . . . . The defense may establish prejudice by showing: (1) the actual loss of a witness, as well as "the substance of their testimony and the efforts made to locate them"; . . . or (2) the loss of physical evidence.

§ 17-32.00 "Post-Accusation" Delay

The constitutional right to a speedy trial does apply upon the formal initiation of prosecution.[52] Unfortunately, the Supreme Court has not set forth any specific test to utilize in determining when the right has been violated.

In 1972, the Supreme Court expressly adopted a balancing test and identified four illustrative factors that should be assessed in determining whether there is a denial of the right to a speedy trial: "Length of delay, the reason for the delay, the defendant's assertion of his right, and prejudice to the defendant."[53] Although the Court conceded that the right to a speedy trial could not be violated until "there is some delay which is presumptively prejudicial," the necessary magnitude of such delay was viewed as dependent upon the "peculiar circumstances of the case,"[54] and the Court suggested that "the delay that can be tolerated for an ordinary street crime is considerably less than that for a serious, complex

---

[49] 431 U.S. at 797 (1977).

[50] 431 U.S. at 795, n.17 (1977).

[51] 41 M.J. 449, 452 (C.A.A.F. 1995).

[52] United States v. Marion, 404 U.S. 307, 320 (1971). *See* § 17-31.00, *above*. The Sixth Amendment right doesn't apply to persons in post-trial confinement for another offense. United States v. Vogan, 35 M.J. 32, 33 (C.M.A. 1992) (in addition, R.C.M. 707(a)(2) doesn't apply to a person in administrative segregation who is already in confinement by reason of prior conviction. 35 M.J. 34 (C.M.A. 1992)). However, Fifth Amendment due process relief could apply depending upon the circumstances. 35 M.J. 34 (C.M.A. 1992).

[53] Barker v. Wingo, 407 U.S. 514, 530 (1972) (footnote omitted).

[54] 407 U.S. 530, 531 (1972).

(Rel.3—1/07 Pub.62410)

conspiracy charge."[55] Similarly, the Court expressed the view that the government's reason for delay must be weighed, and a "deliberate attempt to delay the trial in order to hamper the defense should be weighed heavily against the government."[56] While the Court intentionally chose not to require that the defendant demand a speedy trial as a condition precedent to complaining of a speedy trial violation, the Court clearly would weigh heavily against the defendant a knowing acquiescence in delay.[57] In dealing with the prejudice factor, the Court recognized that delay itself can be prejudicial in the sense that a defendant will, at the least, likely experience anxiety awaiting trial. On the other hand, if the defendant were not aware of the pending charges, such lack of knowledge would tend to negate a showing of prejudice.[58] The Court was more concerned, however, with any specific prejudice that could hinder impairment of the defense case and noted specifically the possibility of the death or disappearance of a witness or the loss of memory of a witness.[59] Thus, although delay itself may be argued to be prejudicial, particularly delay that occurs during the pretrial incarceration of a defendant,[60] it is likely that only evidence of specific prejudice will be weighed heavily.[61]

In *Doggett v. United States*,[62] the Supreme Court held that an eight and one half-year delay between indictment and arrest, including six years of government negligence, violated the Sixth Amendment right to a speedy trial and required

---

[55] 407 U.S. 531 (1972).

[56] 407 U.S. 531 (1972) (footnote omitted).

[57] 407 U.S. 529 (1972). *See also* United States v. Grom, 21 M.J. 53 (C.M.A. 1985) (applied *Barker* factors).

[58] *See, e.g.*, United States v. Hawes, 40 C.M.R. 176 (C.M.A. 1969). Although it would thus be desirable to know whether the accused were in fact aware of the charges, it would be a violation of the accused's right against self-incrimination under Article 31 and the Fifth Amendment for the judge to ask the accused at trial whether he or she were aware of the charges, United States v. Turnipseed, 42 C.M.R. 329 (C.M.A. 1970).

[59] 407 U.S. at 532.

[60] It is clear that pretrial confinement makes delay of particularly great concern. In *Barker v. Wingo*, 407 U.S. 514 (1972), the Supreme Court observed that "[l]engthy exposure to these [jail] conditions 'has a destructive effect on human character and makes the rehabilitation of the individual offender much more difficult.' " 407 U.S. 520 (1972). The special emphasis placed on limiting pretrial confinement is well demonstrated by the speedy trial rule in *United States v. Burton*, 44 C.M.R. 166 (C.M.A. 1971). In addition to announcing the *Burton* rule, the court also stated that "[i]n some situations the length and circumstances of pretrial confinement can be prejudicial in themselves." 44 C.M.R. 171 (C.M.A. 1971) (*citing* United States v. Keton, 40 C.M.R. 176 (C.M.A. 1969)). *See also* 18 U.S.C. § 3164.

[61] *See generally* Nagle, *Demonstrating Prejudice in Speedy Trial Cases*, 13 The Advocate 89, 97–104 (1981). *See also*, Note, *Whatever Happened to Speedy Trial?*, 2 The Advocate 2 (No. 9, Nov. 1970).

[62] 505 U.S. 647, 112 S. Ct. 2686, 120 L. Ed. 520 (1992).

(Rel.3—1/07　Pub.62410)

reversal, despite the accused's inability to show specific prejudice. The Court noted:

> Depending on the nature of the charges, the lower courts have generally found post accusation delay "presumptively prejudicial" at least as it approaches one year . . . . We note that, as the term is used in this threshold context, "presumptive prejudice" does not necessarily indicate a statistical probability of prejudice; it simply marks the point at which courts deem the delay unreasonable enough to trigger the *Barker* enquiry.[63]

> . . . [W]e generally have to recognize that excessive delay presumptively compromises the reliability of a trial in ways that neither party can prove or, for that matter, identify. While such presumptive prejudice cannot alone carry a Sixth Amendment claim without regard to the other *Barker* criteria,

> . . . it is part of the mix of relevant facts, and its importance increases with the length of delay.[64]

Although the Court had requested briefs on the subject, the majority did not deal with whether the Sixth Amendment protects an accused from prejudice in the form of post-offense life disruption.[65] Interestingly, noting that the speedy trial right doesn't apply until arrest or accusation, the dissent in *Doggett* argued that the right protects against only delay-related liberty and not delay-related trial prejudice.[66]

§ 17-33.00   Effect of Dismissal of Charges

Reasoning that upon dismissal of charges, the accused occupies a position no worse than that held by any person subject to criminal investigation, the Supreme Court held in 1982 that "[o]nce charges are dismissed, the speedy trial guarantee is no longer applicable" even though prosecution is later resumed.[67] The Court, however, did expressly note that it was not considering a case in which dismissal was used in order to circumvent the speedy trial guarantee,[68] thus suggesting strongly that dismissal of charges cannot be used to stop the period of speedy trial accountability from running. In 1986, however, the Court may have signaled a different perspective when it held that under the Sixth Amendment the government was not responsible for the period after dismissal of charges, even though the government was appealing that dismissal.[69]

---

[63] 505 U.S. 647, 652 n.1, 112 S. Ct. 2686, 120 L. Ed. 520 (1992).

[64] 505 U.S. 647, 655–56, 112 S. Ct. 2686, 120 L. Ed. 520 (1992). *See also* United States v. Cardona, 302 F.3d 494, 498–499 (5th Cir. 2002) (five year delay creates presumption of prejudice).

[65] 505 U.S. 647, 655–656, 112 S. Ct. 2686, 120 L. Ed. 520 (1992).

[66] 505 U.S. 647, 659, 112 S. Ct. 2686, 120 L. Ed. 520 (1992) (Thomas, J., dissenting).

[67] United States v. MacDonald, 456 U.S. 1, 8 (footnote omitted).

[68] 456 U.S. 10 n.12.

[69] United States v. Loud Hawk, 474 U.S. 302 (1986) (5-4 decision).

(Rel.3—1/07 Pub.62410)

§ 17-40.00   MILITARY STATUTORY LAW AND ITS INTERPRETATION

§ 17-41.00   Article 10

Article 10 of the Uniform Code of Military Justice provides that "when a person is placed in arrest or confinement prior to trial, immediate steps shall be taken to inform him of the specific wrongs of which he is accused and to try him or to dismiss the charges." Although the Court of Military Appeals did has not relyied solely on Article 10 to grant relief upon a denial of the right to a speedy trial, it has indicated that its requirements are presumed to be more stringent than those of the Sixth Amendment.[70]

Court of Military Appeals cases interpreting Article 10 that were decided prior to the 1984 promulgation of the Rules for Courts-Martial are somewhat suspect in light of the Rules' codification of speedy trial law. Although the President clearly has the power under Article 36(a) of the Uniform Code to prescribe "pretrial, trial, and post-trial procedures" for courts-martial, that Article, by its own language, does not permit the President to contradict or supersede another article of the Code. Thus, although the President may prescribe more generous speedy trial rules and remedies than those guaranteed by Article 10, the President may not limit the statutory right. Notwithstanding this, because virtually all pre-1984 military speedy trial law is common law, growing out of Article 10, there is nothing to prevent the courts from reinterpreting the statutory right in light of the Rules for Courts-Martial.[71] Should that occur, pre-1984 cases will be of dubious vitality.

§ 17-41.10   Inception of Article 10 Accountability

§ 17-41.11   In General

In determining whether Article 10 is applicable to delay, one must first determine whether the period of delay involved is controlled by Article 10. Although case law holds the government responsible upon imposition of restraint[72] upon the accused, the express language of the statute makes it applicable only when the accused has been placed in "arrest or confinement." "Arrest," as defined by Article 9 of the Uniform Code,[73] "is the restraint of a person by an order . . . directing him to remain within certain specified limits." Consequently,

---

[70] United States v. Burton, 44 C.M.R. 166, 171 (C.M.A. 1971). For a review of the law of speedy trial before *Burton, see* Tichenor, *The Accused's Right to a Speedy Trial in Military Law*, 52 Mil. L. Rev. 1 (1971).

[71] *See generally* Section 17-71.20.

[72] *See, e.g.,* United States v. Amundson, 49 C.M.R. 598, 600 (C.M.A. 1975).

[73] U.C.M.J. art. 9(a).

(Rel.3—1/07   Pub.62410)

"arrest" includes what is customarily termed "restriction";[74] the *Manual for Courts-Martial* defines "restriction in lieu of arrest" as "the restraint of a person by oral or written orders directing the person to remain within specified limits. . . ."[75] It differs from arrest as a matter of law only insofar as an arrested individual cannot be required to perform his full military duty[76] while a restricted person may be required to participate in all military duties and activities while under the restriction.[77] "Arrest" may also suggest, in terms of its actual use, a much more limited sphere of movement (*e.g.*, arrest in quarters) than that customarily provided by "restriction." Although the *1969 Manual for Courts-Martial* stated that restriction can be imposed "without imposing arrest,"[78] a statement omitted from the present *Manual*, it is clear that, at least in most cases, restriction will be treated as "arrest" for purposes of Article 10.[79]

---

[74] *See, e.g.*, United States v. Smith, 38 C.M.R. 225 (C.M.R. 1968) (restriction to post); United States v. Williams, 37 C.M.R. 209 (C.M.A. 1967) (rigorous restriction to unit).

[75] R.C.M. 304(a)(2). The Rule continues: "a restricted person shall, unless otherwise directed, perform full military duties while restricted."

Whether given limits on an individual constitute "restriction" has often proved difficult to ascertain. In the past, for example, the Court of Military Appeals has indicated some ambiguity as to how to treat the removal of the pass privileges of an accused. Although the court treated such a removal, which had the result of prohibiting the accused from leaving the installation, as a restriction in *United States v. Powell*, 2 M.J. 6 (C.M.A. 1976), the court subsequently declared that it rejected the implication "that a withdrawal of a pass alone is an arrest within the meaning of Article 10, U.C.M.J." United States v. Walls, 9 M.J. 88, 90 (C.M.A. 1980). *See also* United States v. Burrell, 13 M.J. 437, 439 (C.M.A. 1982). The court's holding in *Walls* can be justified by the fact that the accused had not in fact requested a pass and had been off the installation a number of times to see counsel and to perform duty. 9 M.J. at 89. Yet, the court's holding appears erroneous. Although the right to leave the military installation has traditionally been considered a "privilege," more recently for most of the last decade it has generally been considered a right. *Cf.* United States v. Powell, 2 M.J. 6, 7 (C.M.A. 1976). Consequently, "lifting pass privileges" constitutes a significant infringement on the servicemember's liberty, even though he or she may obtain permission to leave the installation on a case-by-case basis. In summary, unless the armed forces choose to make departure from the installation truly a privilege, *Walls* seems clearly erroneous, and the court's earlier decision in Powell accurate.

In 1986, "conditions on liberty," R.C.M. 304(a)(1), was deleted as one of the factors that trigger the R.C.M. 707(a) 120-day speedy trial rule. *See* § 17-72.22.

[76] R.C.M. 304(a)(3).

[77] R.C.M. 304(a)(2).

[78] MCM, 1969 ¶ 20b. This would appear to have been an attempt to create a status of restraint similar to arrest but lacking its rigor and disqualification from performing duty. Given Article 9, it is possible to argue that "restriction" is illegal in view of the congressional intent expressed in Article 9. Of course, restriction has been used under the U.C.M.J. since the *1951 Manual for Courts-Martial*, and it is improbable that the Court of Military Appeals would nullify it.

[79] Although Judge Cook rejected this position, stating that "[r]estriction is a lesser form of restraint than arrest" (United States v. Nelson, 5 M.J. 189, 191 (C.M.A. 1978); *see also* United States v. Walls, 9 M.J. 88, 90 (C.M.A. 1980)), it is apparent that the Court of Military Appeals has treated restriction as the equivalent of arrest for purposes of inception of Article 10 accountability. *See,*

(Rel.3—1/07 Pub.62410)

Determining whether Article 10 applies upon the mere apprehension of an individual is more complicated. Both the Uniform Code and the *Manual* distinguish between "arrest" and "apprehension," with "apprehension" being defined as "the taking of a person into custody."[80] Yet, the *Manual* declares, for purposes of proving the offense of escape from custody,[81] that "once there has been a submission to apprehension or a forcible taking into custody, it [custody] may consist of control exercised in the presence of the prisoner by official acts or orders."[82] Thus, "apprehension" is potentially identical with "arrest," as it does not require actual restraint. On the other hand, the Uniform Code sharply distinguishes between those persons who may apprehend[83] and those who may arrest, with the latter group being limited to commissioned officers.[84] Further, an apprehension is usually transitory, while arrest may be of significant duration. Accordingly, a strict reading of the Uniform Code would lead to the conclusion that Article 10 was not intended to extend to mere apprehensions — notwithstanding that the definition of "apprehension" overlaps that of "arrest." This conclusion is likely erroneous, however, insofar as the present ambit of Article 10 is concerned. The Court of Military Appeals has repeatedly stated that the government is accountable for delay upon "restraint" of the accused,[85] and apprehension is clearly restraint, albeit of exceedingly short term. Of more importance is the fact that the court has presumed that the requirements of Article 10 are more stringent than those of the Sixth Amendment.[86] Should it formally hold this to be the case, the Supreme Court's holding in *Dillingham v. United States*[87] that civilian arrest begins the Sixth Amendment period of accountability will be fully applicable to the armed forces. On balance, the Supreme Court's rationale in *Dillingham* is persuasive, and in the absence

---

e.g., United States v. Burrell, 13 M.J. 437, 430 (C.M.A. 1982); United States v. Walls, 9 M.J. 88, 90 (C.M.A. 1980); United States v. Nelson, 5 M.J. 189, 190–91 (C.M.A. 1978); United States v. Powell, 2 M.J. 6 (C.M.A. 1976). The issue of whether restriction is to be equated with arrest for Article 10 purposes is often confused with the unrelated questions of whether a given action constitutes a restriction (*e.g.*, United States v. Walls, 9 M.J. 88 (C.M.A. 1980) (whether removal of pass privileges constituted restriction)) or whether a given restriction is such as to be the equivalent of confinement. *E.g.*, United States v. Schilf, 1 M.J. 251 (C.M.A. 1976).

[80] U.C.M.J. art. 7(a); R.C.M. 302(a)(1).

[81] U.C.M.J. art. 95.

[82] MCM, 20051984, Part IV ¶ 19(c)(43)(a)A).

[83] U.C.M.J. art. 7(b).

[84] U.C.M.J. arts. 9(b), (c). Note that although both Articles 7 and 9 require probable cause, they express it differently; *compare* Articles 7(b) *and* 9(d).

[85] *See, e.g.*, United States v. Amundson, 49 C.M.R. 598, 600 (C.M.A. 1975).

[86] United States v. Hatfield, 44 M.J. 22 (C.A.A.F. 1996). The court has held, however, that the *Barker* factors should be taken into account in determining whether an Article 10 violation has taken place. United States v. Cooper, 58 M.J. 54 (C.A.A.F. 2003).

[87] 423 U.S. 64 (1975) [hereinafter *Dillingham*].

(Rel.3—1/07 Pub.62410)

of express legislative intent should be incorporated into the interpretation of Article 10 — particularly inasmuch as the definitions of apprehension and arrest are so similar in fact and theory.

By its terms, Article 10 does not apply if an individual has not been placed in arrest or confinement, even though charges have been preferred. Notwithstanding this, numerous decisions of the Court of Military Appeals and the subordinate courts state that the period of accountability for speedy trial is usually "the day formal charges are preferred or the day restraint is imposed upon the accused, whichever first occurs."[88] There appears to be no authority for the conclusion that Article 10 accountability, as originally intended, had anything at all to do with the date that charges are preferred. Indeed, the legislative history of Article 10 strongly suggests that it was intended only to remedy delay that involved pretrial restraint.[89] A historical review of the origins of the assertion that preferral of charges is involved indicates that it may have begun life in *United States v. Williams*,[90] when the court, in considering how to treat a period of civilian confinement for speedy trial purposes, stated: "For present purposes, we may presume that confinement, or the formal presentment of charges, whichever first occurs, determines the beginning [of accountability] of the period." This was clear dictum, as the court determined that the appropriate period began with the date that Williams was confined, a date prior to the date charges were preferred. To the extent that the expression was more than pure obiter dictum, it may be that it was a recognition that formal presentment of charges begins the period of accountability for Sixth Amendment speedy trial and Fifth Amendment due process purposes. Most subsequent cases that have glibly recited the standard of accountability have also dealt with actual pretrial restraint, but at least one, *United States v. Amundson*,[91] has actually utilized the date of preferral, albeit to find that no Article 10 violation existed. Consequently, it may well be that the initial date for Article 10 accountability is now broader than Congress initially intended. This is particularly likely in view of the incorporation of Sixth

---

[88] United States v. Amundson, 49 C.M.R. 598, 600 (C.M.A. 1975) and cases cited therein. In *United States v. Nelson*, 5 M.J. 189, 190 (C.M.A. 1978), the Court of Military Appeals, per Judge Perry, declared that "Congress intended that an accused be in arrest or confinement for a period of some significant duration before the Government runs the risk of activating Article 10." Notwithstanding the court's language, it appears that the court was trying to determine whether Article 10 had been violated; that is, whether the accused had been denied a speedy trial, rather than determining whether a period of accountability had ever begun.

[89] *Uniform Code of Military Justice: Hearings on H.R. 2498 Before a Subcomm. of the House Comm. on Armed Services*, 81st Cong., 1st Sess. 905-12 (1949). Although members of the subcommittee, its professional staff, and Mr. Felix Larkin, Assistant General Counsel, Department of Defense, discussed Article 10 extensively, Article 10 was apparently viewed solely as a tool to terminate lengthy pretrial confinement by compelling speedy trial or dismissal.

[90] 30 C.M.R. 81, 82 (C.M.A. 1961).

[91] 49 C.M.R. 598, 600 (C.M.A. 1975).

(Rel.3—1/07 Pub.62410)

Amendment speedy trial standards into Article 10 by the Court of Military Appeals.[92]

In 2003, the Court of Appeals for the Armed Forces held that Article 10's speedy trial protection does not stop upon arraignment and continues through trial:[93]

> Having said that, however, we hasten to emphasize that by the time an accused is arraigned, a change in the speedy-trial landscape has taken place. This is because after arraignment, "the power of the military judge to process the case increases, and the power of the [Government] to affect the case decreases."[94] . . . As a result, once an accused is arraigned, significant responsibility for ensuring the accused's court-martial proceeds with reasonable dispatch rests with the military judge. The military judge has the power and responsibility to force the Government to proceed with its case if justice so requires.[95]

§ 17-41.12   Civilian Confinement

A military accused may either coincidentally or otherwise spend time in pretrial civilian confinement. Civilian confinement of an accused because of an alleged civil offense is not attributable to military authorities for speedy trial purposes whether the accused was initially confined by civilian authorities,[96] apprehended by the armed forces and released to civilian authorities,[97] or confined in a civilian facility with a military detainer pending.[98] The Air Force Court of Review has held that civilian confinement will not be accountable, even if the accused would have been released earlier absent a military offense.[99]

However, when the defendant, because of surrender or arrest, is in civilian confinement being held for the military, the government is responsible for the period of time after it has been notified of such confinement.[100] It may be that, in the absence of notification, the government will also be responsible from the time when reasonable inquiry would have established the defendant's civilian confinement.[101] Consequently, the trial counsel should contact civilian authorities and make efforts to secure the individual's release from pretrial confinement

---

[92] *See above* notes 25 and 26. Article 10 is distinct from the Rules for Courts-Martial. *See* note 305 and accompanying text.

[93] United States v. Cooper, 58 M.J. 54, 60 (C.A.A.F. 2003).

[94] *Doty*, 51 M.J. at 465–66.

[95] 58 M.J. at 60 (citations omitted).

[96] United States v. Williams, 30 C.M.R. 81 (C.M.A. 1961).

[97] United States v. Reed, 2 M.J. 64, 67 (C.M.A. 1976).

[98] United States v. Asbury, 28 M.J. 595 (N.M.C.M.R. 1989).

[99] United States v. Bragg, 30 M.J. 1147 (A.F.C.M.R. 1990).

[100] United States v. Keaton, 40 C.M.R. 212 (C.M.A. 1969).

[101] *See* Note, 77 Yale L.J. 767, 777 (1968).

(Rel.3—1/07 Pub.62410)

when counsel becomes aware of it,[102] even if the accused does not affirmatively demand release.[103]

§ 17-41.20 Speedy Trial Standard

Prior to *United States v. Burton*[104] and again, after its 1993 overruling, most decisions of the United States Court of Military Appeals and its subordinate courts dealt with, and in the current context of the Court of Appeals for the Armed Forces and its subordinate courts, now again deal with, pretrial delay in the context of defendants held in pretrial confinement or its equivalent. Like the Supreme Court's decision in *Barker v. Wingo*,[105] the Court of Military Appeals utilized a balancing test when applying Article 10 and its constitutional analogs, and has considered the same factors assessed in *Barker*.[106] However, it has generally done so in cases involving sharply shorter delays than are customary in civilian litigation and has thus indicated that far shorter delay would be considered tolerable within the armed forces.

The general test to be applied to pretrial delay governed by Article 10 is the reasonable diligence test: "It suffices to note that the touch stone for measurement of compliance . . . is not constant motion, but reasonable diligence in bringing the charges to trial,"[107] and that "[b]rief periods of inactivity in an otherwise active prosecution are not unreasonable or oppressive."[108]

In determining whether reasonable diligence has been exercised, the Court of Military Appeals for the Armed Forces has has utilized a balancing test that generally employs the same factors addressed by the Supreme Court,[109] first looking to the period of delay, being less tolerant of it than would civilian courts. Next, the court will look to the nature of the delay to determine if it was

---

[102] *See* Smith v. Hooey, 393 U.S. 374 (1969).

[103] ABA Standards for Criminal Justice, Standard 12-2.3(e) (2d ed. 1980) declares that for speedy trial purposes "[a] defendant should be considered unavailable [and thus the time involved should not be held against the government] whenever the defendant's whereabouts are known but his or her presence for trial cannot be obtained or whenever the defendant resists being returned to the state for trial." This suggests that, when an accused who wishes to be returned to military custody and whose release could be obtained is involved, the delay should be attributed to the government.

[104] 44 C.M.R. 166 (C.M.A. 1971), *overruled*, United States v. Kossman, 38 M.J. 258, 261 (C.M.A. 1993).

[105] 407 U.S. 514 (1972).

[106] § 17-41.00.

[107] United States v. Tibbs, 35 C.M.R. 322, 325 (C.M.A. 1965) (citations omitted). *See also* United States v. Powell, 2 M.J. 6 (C.M.A. 1976).

[108] United States v. Tibbs, 35 C.M.A. 322, 325 (C.M.A. 1965) (*citing* United States v. Williams, 30 C.M.R. 81, 88 (C.M.A. 1961)).

[109] *E.g.*, United States v. Cooper, 58 M.J. 54 (C.A.A.F. 2003); United States v. Birge, 52 M.J. 209 (C.A.A.F. 1999).

(Rel.3—1/07 Pub.62410)

oppressive or unreasonable. Pretrial confinement is weighed heavily, but lesser forms of restraint may also be significant. In *United States v. Hester*,[110] for example, the Army Board of Reviewcourt found that a five-month restriction to a military intelligence unit in Korea, located in a facility built much like a maximum security prison, was vexatious and oppressive, resulting in a denial of the right to a speedy trial.

An otherwise reasonable period of delay may be unreasonable if the accused has suffered specific prejudice,[111] such as the loss of material witnesses[112] or the failure to be advised of his or her right to counsel during lengthy pretrial confinement.[113] Normal administrative consequences collateral to awaiting trial do not constitute prejudice, however.[114] Although specific prejudice to the accused is not a prerequisite to finding a violation of the right to a speedy trial,[115] it is clearly helpful. Although pretrial confinement has long been considered per se "prejudice," for speedy trial purposes—albeit not necessarily sufficiently prejudicial to grant relief absent sufficient delay, in its increasing emphasis on the *Barker* factors, the Court of Appeals for the Armed Forces has held that evaluation of "prejudice" requires more than just the existence of pretrial confinement.[116]

An additional factor to be considered is whether the accused demanded a speedy trial. The weight to be attached to a demand for trial should depend on the "frequency and force of the objections as opposed to attaching significant weight to a purely pro forma objection."[117] The trial judge must also consider the cause for a failure to demand trial. A decision on the part of defense counsel not to object to the delay for tactical reasons should be treated differently from a delay that resulted because no counsel was appointed.

In 2005 the Court of Appeals for the Armed Forces further clarified the Article 10 speedy trial standard when it opined that:

---

[110] 37 C.M.R. 652 (A.B.R. 1967).

[111] Barker v. Wingo, 407 U.S. 514 (1972). A delay that is beneficial to the accused may be considered in denying a speedy trial motion raised for the first time on appeal. United States v. Pierce, 41 C.M.R. 225 (C.M.A. 1970). The timeliness of the pretrial proceedings should not be tested by a measured period of time, but rather by a general rule that entails a "functional analysis" of the facts in each case to determine whether the government proceeded with reasonable diligence and without deliberate oppression of the accused. United States v. Amundson, 48 C.M.R. 914 (N.C.M.R. 1974), *aff'd*, 49 C.M.R. 598 (C.M.A. 1975).

[112] *See, e.g.*, United States v. Parish, 38 C.M.R. 209 (C.M.A. 1968); United States v. Dupree, 42 C.M.R. 681 (A.C.M.R. 1970).

[113] United States v. Przybycien, 41 C.M.R. 120 (C.M.A. 1969).

[114] *See, e.g.*, United States v. Black, 50 C.M.R. 369 (N.C.M.R. 1975).

[115] *See, e.g.*, Moore v. Arizona, 414 U.S. 25 (1973).

[116] United States v. Cooper, 58 M.J. 54 56–57 (C.A.A.F. 2003), *citing* United States v. Birge, 52 M.J. 209 (C.A.A.F. 1999).

[117] Barker v. Wingo, 407 U.S. 514, 529 (1972).

the military judge erred in determining that he was required to find gross negligence to support an Article 10 violation in the absence of Government spite or bad faith. An Article 10 violation rests in the failure of the Government to proceed with reasonable diligence. A conclusion of unreasonable diligence may arise from a number of different causes and need not rise to the level of gross neglect to support a violation . . . . Finally, the military judge erred by limiting his consideration of the Barker v. Wingo factors to a Sixth Amendment speedy trial analysis. We have held that "it is 'appropriate' to consider those factors 'in determining whether a particular set of circumstances violates a servicemember's speedy trial rights under Article 10.[118]

The court also observed that "Article 10 and R.C.M. 707 are distinct, each providing its own speedy trial protection. The fact that a prosecution meets the 120-day rule of R.C.M. 707 does not directly 'or indirectly' demonstrate that the Government moved to trial with reasonable diligence as required by Article 10."[119]

Because *Burton* was overruled, many of the prior decisions may retain some precedental value in related areas such as the definition of pretrial confinement and its functional equivalent and those circumstances justifying pretrial delay. Although non-constitutional speedy trial issues are now based upon Article 10 and the Rules for Courts-Martial, the wise advocate should not entirely ignore pre-*Burton*-related precedents.

§ 17-42.00 Article 33

Article 33 of the Uniform Code of Military Justice requires:

When a person is held for trial by general court-martial the commanding officer shall, within eight days after the accused is ordered into arrest or confinement, if practicable, forward the charges, together with the investigation and allied papers to the officer exercising general court-martial jurisdiction. If that is not practicable, he shall report in writing to that officer the reasons for delay.[120]

The eight-day rule set forth in Article 33 evidences a congressional expectation that the Article 32 pretrial investigation[121] and actions associated with it normally should be accomplished within eight days with an escape clause if the complicated nature of the investigation makes such speed impractical.[122]

---

[118] United States v. Mizgala, 61 M.J. 122, 129 (C.A.A.F. 2005).

[119] 61 M.J. 128 (C.A.A.F. 2005).

[120] U.C.M.J. art. 33. *See generally Article 33, A New Life for Speedy Trial,* 8 The Advocate 3 (March-April 1976).

[121] *See generally* Chapter 9.

[122] *See, e.g.,* United States v. Marshall, 47 C.M.R. 409, 412 (C.M.A. 1973); United States v. Mason, 45 C.M.R. 163 (C.M.A. 1972). *See generally Article 33 — A Different Approach,* 8 The Advocate 8 (March-April 1976). The author of this article argues that because Article 33 was

(Rel.3—1/07 Pub.62410)

Non-compliance weighs against the government in showing the requisite due diligence required by Article 10,[123] but, to date, has not been enough in itself to justify dismissal of charges in the absence of prejudice.[124] In one case in which the confined accused was pending trial by special court-martial, but additional charges made trial by general court-martial more appropriate, the commander was held to have complied with the eight-day rule by forwarding a report to the general court-martial-convening authority within eight days of the receipt of the Article 32 investigating officer's recommendation of trial by general court-martial.[125]

§ 17-43.00   Article 98

Article 98 of the Uniform Code of Military Justice declares:

Any person subject to this chapter who — (1) is responsible for unnecessary delay in the disposition of any case of a person accused of an offense under this chapter; or (2) knowingly and intentionally fails to enforce or comply with any provision of this chapter regulating the proceedings before, during, or after trial of an accused; shall be punished as a court-martial may direct.[126]

The President has prescribed a maximum punishment of a bad-conduct discharge and six months' confinement at hard labor as the penalty for a violation of Article 98(1).[127]

Although Congress intended that this Article, in conjunction with Article 10, would ensure speedy trials,[128] it has proven to be of little utility. The authors believe that two prosecutions have been commenced under the Article since it became effective in 1951; however, neither case involved a sufficiently serious sentence so as to result in a recorded appellate opinion. Notwithstanding this, the Court of Military Appeals has cited Article 98 a number of times,[129] and it remains a potential tool to ensure speedy trials within the armed forces.

---

intended to give rise to a speedy Article 32 investigation, the remedy for its violation should not be dismissal but rather a prohibition on trying the case as a general court-martial. This conclusion follows from the fact that a general court-martial should not take place, absent waiver, without an Article 32 investigation, although failure to comply with Article 32 is nonjurisdictional.

[123] *See, e.g.*, United States v. Fernandaz, 48 C.M.R. 460 (N.C.M.R. 1974).

[124] United States v. Gatson, 48 C.M.R. 440 (N.C.M.R. 1974).

[125] United States v. Mladjen, 41 C.M.R. 159 (C.M.A. 1969).

[126] U.C.M.J. art. 98. *See generally* Thorne, *Article 98 and Speedy Trials — A Nexus Revived?*, Army Law. 8 (July, 1976).

[127] MCM, 2005, App. 12.

[128] *Uniform Code of Military Justice: Hearings on H.R. 2498 Before a Subcomm. of the House Comm. on Armed Services*, 81st Cong., 1st Sess. 907–08, 982 (1949).

[129] *See, e.g.*, United States v. Powell, 2 M.J. 6, 8 (C.M.A. 1976); United States v. Timmons, 46 C.M.R. 226 (C.M.A. 1973).

(Rel.3—1/07 Pub.62410)

§ 17-50.00 THE *BURTON* RULE

Established by *United States v. Burton*, the military's 90-day speedy trial rule was overruled in 1993 by *United States v. Kossman*.[130] Accordingly, most of this section's content may be only of historical interest as a record of the only American jurisdiction that actually delivered on the promise of speedy trial and its travails in doing so. However, many of the decisions interpreting and implementing *Burton* may retain some precedental value in related areas such as the definition of pretrial confinement and its functional equivalent and those circumstances justifying pretrial delay. Further, one might note that *Burton* itself was born of judicial despair with the prosecution's inability or refusal to comply with Article 10's speedy trial right and commandment. Should the same problems that gave rise to *Burton* reappear, as an experienced cynic might well suggest is probable, the Court of Appeals for the Armed Forces 3-2 majority of *Kossman* might shift and, with all due respect for systemic stability and precedent, might revive *Burton*. An early 21st Century perspective suggests that there is sufficient pretrial delay that retention of this section of the treatise is justified.

§ 17-51.00 The 90-Day Rule in General

Pursuant to *United States v. Burton*,[131] in the absence of a defense request for a delay or extraordinary circumstances, a presumption of a violation of Article 10 exists when the pretrial confinement or arrest of the defendant for the offense charged exceeds ninety days. In addition to this 90-day rule and the "presumption" applicable to it, the court in *Burton* also stated that when the defense requests speedy disposition of the charge, the government must respond to the request and proceed immediately or show adequate cause for further delay.[132] The *Burton* "demand prong" was overruled in 1988.[133]

---

[130] 38 M.J. 258, 261 (C.M.A. 1993). *See generally* § 17-57.00.

[131] 44 C.M.R. 166 (C.M.A. 1971). The Burton presumption is applicable only to offenses committed on or after December 17, 1971. United States v. Gray, 47 C.M.R. 484 (C.M.A. 1973). When the offenses of absence without leave and desertion are involved, it is the inception date of the offense that is used to determine the date the offense was "committed." *See, e.g.*, United States v. Harmash, 48 C.M.R. 809 (A.C.M.R. 1974); United States v. James, 48 C.M.R. 698 (A.C.M.R. 1974); United States v. Georgio, 48 C.M.R. 620 (N.C.M.R. 1973). When multiple offenses are involved, Burton applied only to those offense occurring after December 17, 1971. *See, e.g.*, United States v. Ellis, 48 C.M.R. 904 (N.C.M.R. 1974).

[132] Technically speaking, the *Burton* "presumption" is really a rule of substantive law rather than a proper evidentiary presumption; similar to all other "irrebuttable" or "conclusive" presumptions, it cannot be rebutted by the government once it is applicable.

[133] United States v. McCallister, 27 M.J. 138 (C.M.A. 1988).

§ 17-52.00   Prerequisites for the 90-Day Rule

§ 17-52.10   Inception of Government Accountability

The court's decision in *Burton*, although based in part upon Article 10,[134] is not congruent with it. Although Article 10 applies upon arrest or confinement, *Burton* is applicable only to pretrial confinement[135] or its functional equivalent.[136] Accordingly, *Burton* was much narrower in scope than Article 10 and is primarily intended to deter or remedy pretrial confinement.[137]

Retention beyond an individual's term of service is not tantamount to confinement.[138] Whether any given restriction was the functional equivalent of confinement depended on the degree of restraint inherent in the restriction.[139] In *United*

---

[134] Article 10 has a fairly broad application and may extend to post apprehension delay. *See* Section 17-41.10.

[135] 44 C.M.R. at 172.

[136] *Compare* United States v. Schilf, 1 M.J. 251 (C.M.A. 1976).

[137] Interestingly, the Court of Military Appeals implied in *Burton* that a dismissal under Article 10 might not be identical with a dismissal under the Sixth Amendment, thus suggesting that prosecution might eventually take place notwithstanding a *Burton* dismissal. 44 C.M.R. at 172 n.1. To date, however, *Burton* has been interpreted to prohibit retrial after dismissal. *See, e.g.,* United States v. Marshall, 47 C.M.R. 409, 412–13 (1973).

[138] *See, e.g.,* United States v. Grom, 21 M.J. 53, 55 (C.M.A. 1985) (where accused's life and daily routine were largely unaffected, involuntary retention and service beyond his normal date of separation from active duty did not constitute the equivalent of pretrial confinement); United States v. Rachels, 6 M.J. 232 (C.M.A. 1979); United States v. Amundson, 49 C.M.R. 598 (C.M.A. 1975).

[139] *See, e.g.,* United States v. Burrell, 13 M.J. 437, 440 (C.M.A. 1982) ("The conditions of accused's 'restriction' to the hospital were not such as to constitute the equivalent of arrest or confinement. . . . [The] accused was not limited either in time or place when he chose to leave the hospital, the only condition being that he be escorted — a fact which, in part, was designed for his own protection"); United States v. Schilf, 1 M.J. 251 (C.M.A. 1976) (accused's restriction to the confines of his squadron area, with hourly sign-in procedure, was the equivalent of confinement); United States v. Amundson, 49 C.M.R. 598 (C.M.A. 1975) (although the accused allegedly was placed on "legal hold" status, denied commissary privileges, leave, and assignment to off-base details, and separated from his family, he was not held in "confinement, arrest or restriction" within the meaning of the Code); United States v. Peoples, 6 M.J. 904 (A.C.M.R. 1979) (excluding individual from the living and recreational areas assigned to another unit is neither restriction or arrest). *See also* United States v. McDowell, 19 M.J. 937 (A.C.M.R. 1985) (the court held that restriction of the accused was the equivalent of confinement. Under the terms of the restriction order, the accused was restricted to his barracks; could not go anywhere without an escort; could not leave the post; was only allowed outside his immediate area twice a week; when given a pass could only go to movie theaters and post exchange; was required to sign in and out when he went to chapel; was only given $20 of his pay each week; and was given a number of menial tasks); United States v. Stokes, 8 M.J. 694 (A.F.C.M.R. 1979), *aff'd*, 12 M.J. 229 (C.M.A. 1982) (the accused's restriction to post, pursuant to a treaty agreement with Spain, which effectively separated the accused from his family, did not constitute confinement).

(Rel.3—1/07   Pub.62410)

States v. Powell,[140] for example, Judge Cook referred to a withdrawal of privileges because of misconduct as having the substantive effect of restriction, but did not consider it the functional equivalent of confinement. Notwithstanding the inapplicability of *Burton,* however, the court held in *Powell* that the right to a speedy trial had been violated because of the inaction of the government while the accused was restricted for 100 of 161 days prior to trial. On the surface, this would appear to be nothing more than a dismissal under Article 10 for failure to move with "due diligence."[141] However, some two years later, in *United States v. Nelson,*[142] Judge Perry declared in dicta that he interpreted *Powell* as treating restriction for 110 of 161 days prior to trial as arrest within the meaning of Article 10, thereby triggering *Burton.* This in itself would be an expansion of *Burton,* since the latter referred only to "confinement," although Article 10 covers both confinement and arrest.

Generally, for *Burton* purposes, confinement must relate to the charge to which the speedy trial motion is directed.[143] This does not mean, however, that where the accused is otherwise in confinement the government is in a position to proceed in leisurely fashion until charges in the instant offense are either preferred or forwarded. The period of time for which the government is accountable "should commence when the Government had in its possession substantial information on which to base the preference of charges."[144] Confinement within the meaning of *Burton* does not include confinement on a previously adjudged sentence,[145] and may not include confinement at the request of a foreign nation.[146]

Civilian restraint that effectively restricts military prosecution is not confinement within the *Burton* standard.[147] Similarly, confinement at the request of a foreign country does not count towards determining government accountability to bring the accused to trial for military charges that have also been preferred.[148]

---

[140] 2 M.J. 6, 7 (C.M.A. 1976). The court's treatment of the removal of pass privileges in *Powell* was implicitly overruled by *United States v. Walls,* 9 M.J. 88, 90 (C.M.A. 1980).

[141] *See* Section 17-41.20.

[142] 5 M.J. 189, 191 (C.M.A. 1978).

[143] *See, e.g.,* United States v. Nash, 5 M.J. 37 (C.M.A. 1978); United States v. Johnson, 48 C.M.R. 599 (C.M.A. 1974). *See also* Section 17-55.00.

[144] United States v. Johnson, 48 C.M.R. 599, 601 (C.M.A. 1974).

[145] United States v. Gettz, 49 C.M.R. 79 (N.C.M.R. 1974); United States v. Georgio, 48 C.M.R. 620 (N.C.M.R. 1973).

[146] United States v. Thomas, 49 M.J. 200 (C.A.A.F. 1998); United States v. Murphy, 18 M.J. 220, 227 (C.M.A. 1984) (Everett, C.J. and Fletcher, J. concurring in the result). *See also* United States v. Youngberg, 48 M.J. 123 (C.A.A.F. 1998).

[147] United States v. Harris, 50 C.M.R. 225 (A.C.M.R. 1975); United States v. Steverson, 45 C.M.R. 649 (A.F.C.M.R. 1972).

[148] United States v. Thomas, 49 M.J. 200, 207 (C.A.A.F. 1998); United States v. Murphy, 18 M.J. 220 (C.M.A. 1984). *See also* United States v. Youngberg, 48 M.J. 123 (C.A.A.F. 1998).

(Rel.3—1/07 Pub.62410)

Where the servicemember has absented himself or herself from the installation, surrenders at another installation, is confined there, and is then returned to the home station, the burden is on the government "to persuade [the judge] factually why some date other than the [original] commencement of confinement ought to be the commencement of the *Burton* period."[149]

Burton was held inapplicable if the accused was in confinement pending a rehearing, even if the original trial was defective.[150]

§ 17-52.20   Termination of Governmental Accountability

In normal circumstances, governmental accountability terminated with the Article 39(a) session of a trial. This presupposed, however, the beginning of actual trial.[151] The Court of Military Appeals indicated in dictum that an Article 39(a) session called to dispose of motions would not terminate the 90-day period when the government is not ready to proceed with the case-in-chief.[152] Similarly, the release of the defendant from confinement at the last hour should not have terminated the ninety days, because the purpose of *Burton* is to guarantee speedy trial, not mitigate pretrial confinements.[153]

---

[149] United States v. Howell, 49 C.M.R. 394, 395 (A.C.M.R. 1974).

[150] United States v. Gonda, 27 M.J. 636, 637 (A.C.M.R. 1988). *See* United States v. Howard, 35 M.J. 763, 768 (A.C.M.R. 1992) (speedy trial clock for rehearing starts when convening authority decides to disapprove sentence at original trial).

[151] An "Article 39(a) session" is a court hearing held out of the presence of the court members (*i.e.*, the military jurors) and takes its name from Uniform Code Article 39(a) which authorizes it. Most trials begin with a brief Article 39(a) session, at which the accused is advised of his or her rights to counsel, to trial by judge alone, and to a court with enlisted personnel when applicable. The accused is then arraigned and tried. However, an Article 39(a) session may be held for any appropriate purpose, including hearing requests for continuances, discovery or other motions. It is not unknown for the government to request an Article 39(a) session in order to complete proceedings through arraignment, only to then request a lengthy continuance — the whole purpose of the proceeding being to avoid *Burton*.

[152] United States v. Cole, 3 M.J. 220 1225 n.4 (C.M.A. 1977) (Perry, J., with Fletcher, C.J., concurring and Cook, J., concurring in the result). *Citing* United States v. Beach, 1 M.J. 118 (C.M.A. 1975), the court in *Cole* stated that the Article 39(a) session does not toll the running of the *Burton* period. *But see* United States v. Glahn, 49 C.M.R. 47 (A.C.M.R. 1974), holding that an Article 39(a) session tolls the running of the 45-day rule period, even though the session was initiated in bad faith. *Glahn* is questionable precedent, however, in light of *Cole*.

[153] *But see* United States v. Ledbetter, 2 M.J. 37 (C.M.A. 1976) (accused's release on 88th day of post-trial confinement tolled the running of the 90-day *Burton* period). *See also* United States v. Amerine, 17 M.J. 947, 950 (A.F.C.M.R. 1984) (Removing the accused from pretrial confinement and withdrawing the charges tolled the speedy trial rules. "At no time during the proceedings did the trial defense counsel suggest that the withdrawal of the initial charges was accomplished for an improper purpose."); United States v. Hagler, 7 M.J. 944 (N.C.M.R. 1979) (accused's 75 days in pretrial confinement did not trigger *Burton* presumption). It is unclear whether a dismissal of charges, followed by a release from pretrial confinement, with a subsequent reinstitution of the prosecution via new charges and a new period of pretrial restraint, would be treated as one

(Rel.3—1/07   Pub.62410)

§ 17-53.00 Defense Requests for Delay

Defense requests for delay [154] may have reduced the period of time for which the government is accountable. The Court of Military Appeals has stated that "[c]ontinuances or delays granted only because of a request of the defense and for its convenience are excluded from the 3-month period." [155] In 1990, the court, by footnote, stated:

> Where the defense affirmatively seeks a delay or where it consents to a delay or where it requests government action which necessarily requires reasonable time for accomplishment, then the defense waives government speedy trial accountability for those periods of time. [156]

Technically, this seems to be dictum. [157] Accordingly, the prior rule appears to remain valid — that defense-requested delay will not be excluded if the government was not able to proceed during all or part of the time and was not adversely affected by the delay in the proceedings. [158] Thus, to escape accountability for a given period, the government must show that the government was ready to proceed or was adversely affected (*e.g.*, it obtained an overseas witness) in addition to showing a defense request for delay. [159] When an accused has been released from pretrial confinement during a delay requested by the defense, only that part of the period that was actually spent in confinement is deductible. [160] Absence or misconduct of the defendant that has the effect of adversely affecting the processing of the charges is considered as either tolling the period or giving

prosecution with one period of pretrial confinement for *Burton* purposes. Under Sixth Amendment standards, absent bad faith, the periods would not be added. United States v. MacDonald, 456 U.S. 1 (1982).

[154] What constitutes a "request" for delay has not been formally specified. *See* United States v. Givens, 30 M.J. 294, 300 (C.M.A. 1990) (Everett, C.J., concurring) (delay request may be made informally in a phone call or via consent given by gesture).

[155] United States v. Driver, 49 C.M.R. 376, 378 (C.M.A. 1974). Note that in the absence of specific evidence, a record that a delay was the shared responsibility of counsel may be held a defense request for delay. United States v. Talavera, 8 M.J. 14, 18 (C.M.A. 1979). Defense actions other than requests for continuance may constitute defense delay. *See, e.g.*, United States v. Buskirk, 49 C.M.R. 788 (A.C.M.R. 1975), in which the defense and prosecution entered into a formal agreement under which the accused would be released from pretrial confinement to operate as a law enforcement informant with the ultimate goal of entering into a favorable plea bargain. The agreement was considered a defense delay. *See also* §§ 17-52.20; 17-70.00.

[156] United States v. King, 30 M.J. 59, 66 n.7 (C.M.A. 1990) (Cox, J.).

[157] 30 M.J. 71 (C.M.A. 1990) (Sullivan, J., concurring).

[158] *See* United States v. Jones, 6 M.J. 770 (A.C.M.R. 1978) (any defense-requested delay is deductible provided that the government would otherwise have been prepared to proceed with the processing of charges or trial of the case).

[159] 6 M.J. 770 (A.C.M.R. 1978). *See also* United States v. Cole, 3 M.J. 220 (C.M.A. 1977).

[160] United States v. O'Neal, 48 C.M.R. 89 (A.C.M.R. 1973).

(Rel.3—1/07 Pub.62410)

rise to deductible time. The parties may also stipulate that a given period should not be considered in determining whether the 90-day rule is applicable.[161]

Pretrial psychiatric examinations conducted at the defense's request give rise to defense delays under *Burton*.[162] Presumably, a psychiatric examination ordered at the government's request[163] would be allocated to the prosecution. The fact that the defense officially requested certain delays may not be conclusive in the event of government wrongdoing. Thus, in *United States v. Schilf*, the Court of Military Appeals affirmed the finding of the Air Force Court of Military Review in which it "aptly held early periods of delay purportedly pursuant to defense requests to be fully accountable to the Government because they were procured by the trickery of the . . . chief of military justice and were not based on genuine defense desires or needs."[164] In *Schilf*, the chief of military justice had agreed to release the accused from pretrial confinement "on the condition that appellant's counsel cover the anticipated delays in bringing his client to trial."[165] Reversing the conviction in *Schilf*, the Court of Military Appeals soundly condemned the government's conduct.

There are a number of circumstances that may have constituted either a delay chargeable to the government or a defense delay, depending upon the exact nature of the matters giving rise to the delay. Thus, mere acquiescence by the defense in a new trial date would not be treated as defense delay even if the defense benefits from it (although a specific request for delay will, of course, be considered a defense delay).[166] Similarly, a request for an administrative discharge in lieu of trial by court-martial[167] would not be considered as giving

---

[161] United States v. Montague, 47 C.M.R. 796 (C.M.A. 1973).

[162] United States v. Bone, 11 M.J. 776 (A.F.C.M.R. 1981); United States v. Hensley, 50 C.M.R. 677 (A.C.M.R. 1975). *See also* United States v. Colon-Angueira, 16 M.J. 20 (C.M.A. 1983); United States v. Rogers, 7 M.J. 274, 275 n.1 (C.M.A. 1979); United States v. McClain, 1 M.J. 60 (C.M.A. 1975); United States v. Freeman, 23 M.J. 531, 535 (A.C.M.R. 1986). *But see* United States v. McDowell, 19 M.J. 937 (A.C.M.R. 1985) (government bears some responsibility for completion of examination).

[163] Mil. R. Evid. 302.

[164] 1 M.J. 251, 253 (C.M.A. 1976) (footnote omitted).

[165] 1 M.J. 253 n.5 (C.M.A. 1976).

[166] *See, e.g.*, United States v. Wolzok, 50 C.M.R. 572, 574 (C.M.A. 1975); United States v. Reitz, 48 C.M.R. 178 (C.M.A. 1974). If more than a mere acquiescence on the part of the defense is present, the change in trial date may be held to be defense delay. *Compare, e.g.*, United States v. Ellison, 48 C.M.R. 858, 860 (A.C.M.R. 1974) *with* United States v. O'Neal, 48 C.M.R. 89, 92 (A.C.M.R. 1973). *O'Neal* may be erroneous. It may be that delays would not be deductible unless approved by the military judge or convening authority. United States v. Cook, 27 M.J. 212 (C.M.A. 1988); United States v. Carlisle, 25 M.J. 426 (C.M.A. 1988). The practical effect will be that the prosecution must bring to the attention of the staff judge advocate or judge informal arrangements that in the past have lead to many misinterpretations.

[167] This type of discharge, termed a "Chapter 10" in the Army and an "OTH" (other than honor-

(Rel.3—1/07 Pub.62410)

rise to defense delay unless the defense requested that trial be delayed pending resolution of the discharge request,[168] and, absent a request for delay, plea bargaining would normally not give rise to a defense delay unless the government showed that the ne-gotiations affected its ability to proceed to trial.[169] When the defense withdrew an earlier waiver of Article 32 investigation, the defense would be charged with a delay for reprocessing the charges.[170] A defense counsel's leave would not normally give rise to defense delay unless the government showed that it was prepared to go to trial during the leave and thus was forced to defer trial.[171] Where the leave would clearly have the effect of postponing trial (*e.g.*, as when a military judge extends a trial date at a docketing session so as to accommodate the counsel's leave),[172] the leave would be held to constitute a defense delay. In short, in the absence of a defense requested delay, one must generally determine whether the incident in question clearly gave rise to delay. If not, the delay would not be allocated to the defense.[173]

When an accused exercised one of the rights enumerated in the Uniform Code of Military Justice, the resulting delay was generally considered part of the procedural process necessary to bring the case to trial and did not constitute defense delay under *Burton*. Thus, exercise by the accused of the right to the

---

able) discharge in the Navy, allows the accused to avoid trial via administrative discharge. Depending upon the accused's background and the convening authority's decision, the accused may be given an honorable, general, or other than honorable discharge. *See generally* Chapter 3. Although usually the purpose of the request for discharge is to avoid trial, the request can be approved during or after trial, in which case the proceedings are a nullity. Thus, a request does not inherently require that trial be delayed, although the parties normally prefer this.

[168] *See, e.g.*, United States v. Shavers, 50 C.M.R. 298, 301 n.8 (A.C.M.R. 1975), holding that delay caused by a request for an administrative discharge would not be considered defense delay when the record was "silent as to whether the accused specifically sought a delay in the proceedings, pending action on his request," at least when "the request for discharge did not impede the progress of the case in any way." *Compare Shavers with* United States v. Bush, 49 C.M.R. 97, 100–101 (N.C.M.R. 1974), in which the court found that delay was inherent in the request and thus was defense delay. One must question this rationale. *See above* note 166-67 and *below* note 292.

[169] *See, e.g.*, United States v. Perkins, 1 M.J. 571 (A.C.M.R. 1975), in which the court held that submission of an offer to plead guilty one day prior to the scheduled trial date necessarily required trial to be postponed. *See also* United States v. Batton, C.M. 429786 (A.C.M.R. Dec. 10, 1975) (unpublished).

[170] United States v. Herron, 4 M.J. 30 (C.M.A. 1977).

[171] United States v. Perkins, 1 M.J. 571, 573 (A.C.M.R. 1975).

[172] United States v. Lyons, 50 C.M.R. 804 (A.C.M.R. 1975); *but see* United States v. Henderson, 1 M.J. 421, 423 (C.M.A. 1976), stating that "the [*Burton*] standard contemplates and provides for the normal delays which might be expected during this process occasioned, among other causes, by personnel shortages, docketing conditions, and leave of counsel."

[173] *See, e.g.*, United States v. Ward, 50 C.M.R. 273, 274–75 (C.M.A. 1975), in which the defense requested that the accused be tried on all known charges at one trial, but did not contemplate delay, leaving the decision to the government. *See also* United States v. Smith, 2 M.J. 394, 395 n. 1 (A.C.M.R. 1975) (delay caused by request for new counsel was defense delay).

(Rel.3—1/07 Pub.62410)

minimum waiting period between service of charges and trial prescribed by the Code[174] was generally not be considered defense delay. This general proposition was not, however, accepted by the courts,[175] which generally looked only to whether the defense took an action that clearly would result in delay rather than to ask why the accused took such action.

Because of the nature of the armed forces, it is apparent that some delays involving the defense were not considered defense delays under *Burton*. Thus, the absence of a defense counsel due to official temporary duty elsewhere will not constitute defense delay unless it was shown that the travel was performed for defense or personal reasons.[176] Given that defense counsel represent defendants in the military as their military duty, one pondered whether a delay in one case caused by duties in another case can be held against the first accused. It is clear that under present law, the time necessary to obtain individual counsel constitutes defense delay.[177]

§ 17-54.00   Circumstances Justifying Delay

Early in the Court of Military Appeals' elaboration of the *Burton* speedy trial rule, it declared that delay caused by extraordinary circumstances would not be held against the government[178] and stated that to escape liability for delay, "[w]hen a *Burton* violation has been raised by the defense, the Government must demonstrate that really extraordinary circumstances beyond such normal problems as mistakes in drafting, manpower shortages, illnesses, and leave contributed to the delay."[179]

§ 17-54.10   Extraordinary Circumstances

Examples of such extraordinary circumstances include:

(1) A case arising in a combat environment;[180]

---

[174] The accused is entitled to five days between service of charges and trial by general court-martial and three days between service of charges and trial by special court-martial. U.C.M.J. art. 35.

[175] United States v. Cherok, 22 M.J. 438 (C.M.A. 1986) (requesting delay solely for speedy trial issue will be considered defense-requested delay). *But compare Cherok with* United States v. Lazausblas 62 M.J. 39, 42 (C.A.A.F. 2005); United States v. Longhofer, 29 M.J. 22 (C.M.A. 1989).

[176] United States v. Lyons, 50 C.M.R. 804, 805–806 (A.C.M.R. 1975). *But see* United States v. Montanino, 40 M.J. 364, 366–67 (C.M.A. 1994) (Wiss, J., dissenting from decision that accused expressly waived delay due to counsel's Sinai Desert deployment).

[177] *See below* note 187. *See, e.g.,* United States v. Badger, 7 M.J. 838 (A.C.M.R. 1979.

[178] United States v. Marshall, 47 C.M.R. 409, 412 (C.M.A. 1973).

[179] 47 C.M.R. at 413 (C.M.A. 1973). United States v. Facey, 26 M.J. 421 (C.M.A. 1988) (delayed accused's trial to await the outcome of co-accused's trial); United States v. Grom, 21 M.J. 53, 57 (C.M.A. 1985) (implied that it was justifiable delay to wait until after trial of co-conspirator).

[180] *Marshall,* 47 C.M.R. at 412.

(Rel.3—1/07   Pub.62410)

(2) A case arising in a foreign country, if the government can show specific problems caused by the location (*e.g.*, investigation by foreign police, difficulties in obtaining foreign national witnesses, travel problems, or contested jurisdictional issues).[181] Mere foreign location is insufficient;[182]

(3) The case is either serious or complex;[183]

(4) Operational demands;[184]

(5) The unauthorized absence of an essential prosecution witness;[185]

(6) The diversion of investigative or legal personnel to investigate apparent sabotage of an important operational unit fleet;[186]

(7) Psychological examination ordered by the investigating officer;[187] and

(8) The accused's additional misconduct, under some circumstances.[188]

The unavailability of a military judge on the proposed date was held not to be an "extraordinary circumstance" beyond the control of the government.[189]

§ 17-54.20 Other Circumstances Justifying Delay

Although the *Burton* standard "included allowances for the several necessary pretrial stages through which a proceeding may progress,"[190] the Court of

---

[181] United States v. Stevenson, 47 C.M.R. 495 (C.M.A. 1973); United States v. Marshall, 47 C.M.R. 409 (C.M.A. 1973); United States v. O'Neal, 48 C.M.R. 89 (A.C.M.R. 1973).

[182] United States v. Henderson, 1 M.J. 421 (C.M.A. 1976) (mere foreign location is insufficient to excuse delay).

[183] *See, e.g.*, United States v. Cole, 3 M.J. 220, 226–27 (C.M.A. 1977). This justification is fairly limited in scope and does not give rise to carte blanche. "[A] riot involving a horde of individuals in an open community at night where complicity may be difficult to establish . . . may be [a complex case]," but a riot occurring in daylight in a confinement facility with many witnesses is not. United States v. Presley, 48 C.M.R. 464, 467 (A.C.M.R. 1974). The issue of "complexity should not be confused with uncertainty." United States v. Mitchel, C.M. 429740 (A.C.M.R. Jan.27, 1974) (unpublished opinion); *but see* United States v. Toliver, 48 C.M.R. 949 (C.M.A. 1974). Although the "seriousness" of an offense allegedly is a factor to be considered, it appears to be of little or no value as an extraordinary factor and should not be relied upon alone. *See, e.g.*, United States v. Henderson, 1 M.J. 421 (C.M.A. 1976), in which charges were dismissed in a murder-for hire case due to violation of the accused's right to a speedy trial (accused was held in pretrial confinement for 132 days in Okinawa).

[184] United States v. Marshall, 47 C.M.R. 409 (C.M.A. 1973).

[185] United States v. Johnson, 48 C.M.R. 599 (C.M.A. 1974). The government, however, must proceed to effect the witness' return to duty.

[186] United States v. Johnson, 48 C.M.R. 599 (C.M.A. 1974).

[187] United States v. McClain, 1 M.J. 60 (C.M.A. 1975).

[188] United States v. Turk, 24 M.J. 277 (C.M.A. 1987); United States v. Johnson, 1 M.J. 101, 105 (C.M.A. 1975).

[189] *See, e.g.*, United States v. Johnson, 49 C.M.R. 13 (A.C.M.R. 1974); United States v. Sawyer, 47 C.M.R. 857 (N.C.M.R. 1973).

[190] United States v. Marshall, 47 C.M.R. 409, 412 (C.M.A. 1973).

Military Appeals stated that, in effect, delay would not be charged against the government when "for reasons beyond the control of the prosecution the processing was necessarily delayed."[191] Such periods included:

(1) Delay occasioned by defense repudiation of a prior waiver of an Article 32 investigation;[192]

(2) Delay resulting from a notice required to obtain a witness in a foreign country;[193] and

(3) reasonable period of time to obtain individual defense counsel.[194]

§ 17-54.30 Circumstances Not Justifying Delay

What the court has termed a "normal incident of military practice" would not be treated as a circumstance justifying a delay under the *Burton* rule.[195] Some examples of such incidents included:

(1) Shortage of personnel;[196]

(2) Illness, injury, or absence of the convening authority, staff judge advocate, or deputy staff judge advocate;[197]

(3) Backlogs resulting from shortage of personnel;[198]

(4) Inexperienced personnel;[199]

---

[191] 47 C.M.R. 409, 412 (C.M.A. 1973). *See also* United States v. Talavera, 8 M.J. 14, 18 (C.M.A. 1979) and cases cited therein.

[192] *See* United States v. Herron, 4 M.J. 30 (C.M.A. 1977). When the investigating officer delays the investigation to pursue a witness that neither side requests, the time should not be chargeable to either side for purposes of R.C.M. 707. *Cf.* United States v. Brodin, 25 M.J. 580 (A.C.M.R. 1987) (time chargeable to government; charges dismissed).

[193] United States v. Talavera, 8 M.J. 14, 18 (C.M.A. 1979) (per Cook, J., with Fletcher, C.J., concurring in the result only). *Cf.* United States v. Cook, 27 M.J. 212 (C.M.A. 1988) (request by defense that the government produce an essential witness is not a defense request for delay — delay will be chargeable to the government unless approval for delay by convening authority or judge).

[194] *See, e.g.,* United States v. Badger, 7 M.J. 838 (A.C.M.R. 1979), holding that one day is a reasonable time in which to contact a unit in Korea from a unit in Georgia. Presumably, the government is not liable for the time it takes an independent defense command to process a request for individual military counsel when the requested counsel is a member of the command.

[195] *See generally* United States v. Marshall, 47 C.M.R. 409, 412 (C.M.A. 1973). *See also* Section 17-53.00.

[196] United States v. Stevenson, 47 C.M.R. 495 (C.M.A. 1973).

[197] United States v. Marshall, 47 C.M.R. 409 (C.M.A. 1973).

[198] United States v. O'Neal, 48 C.M.R. 89 (A.C.M.R. 1973).

[199] United States v. Stevenson, 47 C.M.R. 495 (C.M.A. 1973).

(Rel.3—1/07 Pub.62410)

(5) Heavy caseload of the prosecution, defense counsel, or military judge;[200] and

(6) Resolution of foreign jurisdiction.[201]

§ 17-55.00 Governmental Accountability upon the Commission or Discovery of Additional Misconduct

The Court of Military Appeals indicated that governmental accountability for pretrial delay will be individual and separate for multiple offenses[202] and has specifically rejected the argument that the period of accountability starts anew as the result of subsequent or subsequently discovered offenses.[203] To permit this would have relieved the government from accountability for the original charge regardless of the government's ability to proceed. Whether the additional offense will constitute an extraordinary circumstance depends on balancing the right to a speedy trial, the combination of all known charges, and the efficient administration of justice.

When an individual who had been placed in confinement committed another serious offense, as distinguished from a very minor action, the government would be allowed reasonable processing time if it elected to try both offenses together — so long as it proceeded diligently on the original charges. Absent this rule, the government would be placed in the intolerable position of being required to have separate trials for each separate offense.[204] The government, however, could use the subsequently discovered offense as a reason for not proceeding diligently in the first instance. A practical solution to the problem of subsequent misconduct would have been to require the defendant to elect either separate trials or a single trial of all known charges.

The defendant's misconduct also came into play when he or she was released from pretrial confinement prior to the expiration of the 90-day period and at some point during the release committed another offense — other than absence from

---

[200] *See, e.g.,* United States v. Pyburn, 48 C.M.R. 795 (C.M.A. 1974); United States v. Johnson, 49 C.M.R. 13 (A.C.M.R. 1974) (unavailability of judge not beyond control of the government); United States v. Sawyer, 47 C.M.R. 857 (N.C.M.R. 1973) (no showing that another judge could not be obtained); *but see* United States v. Slaughter, C.M. 429715 (A.C.M.R. March 29, 1974) (unpublished opinion holding that unavailability of the judge is neither government nor defense delay). *Slaughter* was distinguished in United States v. Eaton, 49 C.M.R. 426 (A.C.M.R. 1974), and is of limited authority.

[201] United States v. Young, 1 M.J. 71 (C.M.A. 1975).

[202] United States v. Johnson, 1 M.J. 101 (C.M.A. 1975).

[203] *See, e.g.,* United States v. Ward, 50 C.M.R. 273, 275 (C.M.A. 1975).

[204] Indicating the usual policy, the *1969 Manual for Courts-Martial* declared that all charges "ordinarily should be tried at a single trial." MCM, 1969 ¶¶ 30g; 33h. *Cf.* R.C.M. 307(c)(4); R.C.M. 401(c). Although this requirement was not retained in the Rules for Courts-Martial, it remains the normal and desirable practice.

(Rel.3—1/07 Pub.62410)

his or her unit — and, as a result of the second offense, was placed in pretrial confinement. The Court of Military Appeals indicated that under these circumstances a new 90-day period would not start when the accused was again placed in confinement. The question would be whether the government had proceeded reasonably on both the original charge and the additional charges. [205] In resolving this question, one of the key factors would be to what extent the defendant's second offense affected the government's ability to proceed on both the original and additional charges. [206] When the additional offense after release from initial confinement is absence without leave for a substantial period of time, a new 90-day period may have resulted or the segmented periods of confinement may have been combined. [207]

§ 17-56.00   The *Burton* Demand-for-Trial Rule

In addition to the 90-day rule, the Court of Military Appeals announced in *Burton* that

> when the defense requests a speedy disposition of the charges, the Government must respond to the request and either proceed immediately or show adequate cause for any further delay. A failure to respond to a request for a prompt trial or to order such a trial may justify extraordinary relief. [208]

The demand-for-trial rule set forth in *Burton* was thus an independent rule, not dependent upon the expiration of ninety days in confinement. In *United States v. Schilf*, [209] the court stated:

> We believe that many of the problems involved in attributing pretrial delays will be ameliorated if all such requests for delay, together with the reasons therefor, were acted upon by the convening authority prior to referral of charges to a court-martial, or by the trial judge after such referral, rather than for them to be the subject of negotiation and agreement between opposing counsel. [210]

The government could establish that the demand for trial was met by either proceeding immediately with the trial or by immediately releasing the accused from pretrial confinement. [211] A third possibility, not recommended, was to

---

[205] United States v. Nash, 5 M.J. 37 (C.M.A. 1978) (where the accused was reconfined on charges unrelated to those for which he had been originally confined and then released, the period of confinement allocated to the first offense for *Burton* purposes did not include the entire period of confinement).

[206] *See, e.g.,* United States v. Brooks, 48 C.M.R. 257 (C.M.A. 1974).

[207] *See, e.g.,* United States v. Bush, 49 C.M.R. 97 (N.C.M.R. 1974).

[208] 44 C.M.R. at 172.

[209] 1 M.J. 251 (C.M.A. 1976).

[210] 1 M.J. at 253 (C.M.A. 1976). *Cf. above* note 166.

[211] *See, e.g.,* United States v. Mock, 49 C.M.R. 160 (A.C.M.R. 1974); United States v. Stevens, CM 430296 (A.C.M.R. May 9, 1974) (unpublished).

(Rel.3—1/07 Pub.62410)

docket the accused's case for trial.[212] Charges could also be dismissed, of course.[213]

Although the Court of Military Appeals did not specify in *Burton* the remedy appropriate for a failure to comply with the demand rule, it affirmed a dismissal of charges based upon a 29-day delay between demand and trial when the government failed to show an adequate cause for delay.[214]

In *United States v. McCallister*,[215] the court held that the demand rule of *Burton* "no longer serves a useful function" and prospectively overruled it. The court reasoned that the 90-day dismissal rule, coupled with the Sixth Amendment and Rule for Courts-Martial 707, sufficed to protect the military accused.[216]

§ 17-57.00 The Overruling of *Burton*

When the Court of Military Appeals overruled the *Burton* "demand prong" in 1988, it justified its decision as follows:

> When this Court announced its decision in *Burton*, it did so in response to the urging of appellate defense counsel that we "promulgate new guidance for determining compliance with the speedy trial provisions of the Sixth Amendment and Articles 10, 30(b), and 33, . . ." respectively. . . . 44 C.M.R. at 171. Both the "3-month" rule and the "demand prong" of *Burton* were products of an environment in which virtually no guidance was available to assist military judges in applying the Uniform Code's speedy trial guarantees.

> Accordingly, the Court determined that a confined accused can and must be brought to trial within 3 months from his incarceration — a period subsequently clarified to mean 90 days. . . . Additionally, in recognition that not all cases need even that long to reach trial, the Court also required that, if an accused "requests a speedy disposition of the charges, the

---

[212] *Compare* United States v. Stevens, CM 430296 (A.C.M.R. May 9, 1974) ("the docketing of the case . . . was a sufficient response") *and* United States v. Williams, 12 M.J. 894 (A.C.M.R. 1982) (appointment of Article 32 officer as an appropriate response) *with* United States v. Mitchel, CM 429740 (A.C.M.R. January 29, 1974) ("We doubt that an Article 39(a) session for arraignment purposes only will be sufficient of itself to satisfy the mandate to 'proceed immediately' ").

[213] If the initial charges were dropped, governmental accountability for later charges would depend on the relationship between the original and final charges. *See generally* Section 17-55.00.

[214] United States v. Johnson, 1 M.J. 101, 105–06 (C.M.A. 1975); *but see* United States v. Gordon, 2 M.J. 517 (A.C.M.R. 1976) (unexplained delay of 44 days did not warrant dismissal). It should be noted that the dismissal of charges in *Johnson* was the result of the unique circumstances of the case, including the fact that the accused had spent 59 days in confinement after the commission of the given offense and before the demand for trial. Although the court sustained the dismissal, it clearly did not require dismissal as the sole or even favored remedy for failure to comply with the demand rule. United States v. Morrow, 16 M.J. 328 (C.M.A. 1983) (reassessment not appropriate remedy).

[215] 27 M.J. 138 (C.M.A. 1988).

[216] 27 M.J. at 140 (C.M.A. 1988). *See* Section 17-57.00.

(Rel.3—1/07 Pub.62410)

Government must respond to the request and either proceed immediately or show adequate cause for any further delay." . . . 44 C.M.R. at 172.

Since our decision in *Burton*, the President has promulgated a comprehensive set of rules designed to promptly process all cases for trial — regardless whether the accused is confined — and, at the same time, to acknowledge certain practical impediments to that process which may, from time to time, excuse some delay. *See* R.C.M. 707. At the same time, this Court has continued to enforce the 90-day rule for accused in pretrial confinement or its equivalent and the "demand prong" of *Burton* as well.[217] . . .

We are now of the view that the "demand prong" for *Burton* no longer serves a useful function as a distinct means to the end of a speedy trial. An incarcerated accused must, with extraordinary exceptions, be brought to trial within 90 days of his imprisonment (*Burton*); all accused, whether incarcerated or not, must, consistent with R.C.M. 707 and with specific exceptions, be brought to trial within 120 days from "notice to the accused of preferral of charges" or from "imposition of restraint," *see* R.C.M. 707(a); and any claim of denial of a Sixth Amendment speedy trial will be examined under the four-part analysis set forth in *Barker v. Wingo, above* — one element of which includes an accused's demand for speedy trial. This Court's experience since the promulgation of R.C.M. 707 satisfies us that any purpose sought to be served originally by the "demand prong" of *Burton* now is fully met by the three sets of protection just mentioned.[218]

McCallister was ultimately followed by *United States v. Kossman*,[219] which by a 3-2 vote overruled and abrogated *Burton*[220] in favor of Rule for Court-Martial 707. Writing for a majority that included Judges Crawford and Gierke, Judge Cox found significant the following post-*Burton* procedural developments:

- The credit of pretrial confinement against any confinement sentence

- The promulgation of Rule for Court-Martial 707, providing for a 120-day rule[221]

Noting that the President may, under Article 36 of the Uniform Code of Military Justice, prescribe rules so long as they do not conflict with the Code

---

[217] Continuing at 27 M.J. at 140, n.4, the court said "[w]e note that R.C.M. 707(d) . . . incorporates the 90-day rule. *See* Drafters' Analysis, R.C.M. 707(d) at A21–38 (Change 3), and no case has been made for a longer period."

[218] 27 M.J. at 140-41.

[219] 38 M.J. 258, 261 (C.M.A. 1993).

[220] This discussion of *Kossman* is substantially taken from Fredric Lederer, *Speedy-trial: A Strategic Advance To the Past*, a lecture delivered to The 1994 Judicial Conference of the United States Court of Military Appeals. *See also* Fredric Lederer, *Funeral Oration in Honor of United States v. Burton*, Army Law., July 1994, at 40.

[221] 38 M.J. at 260 (matters of little help, however, to an accused who serves pretrial confinement and who is either acquitted or receives a sentence without confinement).

(Rel.3—1/07 Pub.62410)

or the court's interpretation of it, Judge Cox stated that with respect to Rule for Court-Martial 707 the President "has acted responsibly."[222] The court then declared the *Tibbs* standard of "reasonable diligence" the appropriate standard for interpreting Article 10.[223]

Justifying his position, Judge Cox specifically noted that the *Burton* test had the effect of insulating delays of less than 90 days of pretrial confinement and

> [three] months is a long time to languish in a brig . . . . Four months is even longer. We see nothing in Article 10 that suggests that speedy trial motions could not succeed where a period under 90 — or 120 — days is involved.[224]

Judges Sullivan and Wiss dissented in two separate, well-written opinions.[225]

The immediate result of *Kossman* was the abolition of the 90 day automatic dismissal rule leaving Rule 707 as the only implementation of Article 10's speedy trial requirement. Because Rule for Courts-Martial 707 provides an unfettered authorization for the convening authority and military judge to authorize delays, the Rule provides no significant protection for an accused, especially a confined accused. Further, the court per Judge Cox, made it clear that although Rule 707 "does provide good guidance to both the Bench and Bar," Rule 707 should not be relied upon exclusively.[226] Having thus provided a firm foundation for military judges to declare Rule 707's 120-day safe-haven rule excessive and invalid on the facts of any given case, Judge Cox also emphasized that even longer periods of delay could well be reasonable, mentioning such matters of logistical challenges, operational requirements and "ordinary judicial impediments, such as crowded dockets, unavailability of judges, and attorney caseloads, must be realistically balanced." Notably, Judge Cox's inclusion of "unavailability of judges, and attorney caseloads," if incorporated into Rule 707 common law, would justify delays, including those affecting those confined pretrial, simply because of inadequate legal staffing. This would be a far cry from *Burton's* demanding standard.

Unless all of the prior *Burton* case law is read into the *Kossman/Tibbs/*Rule 707 standard, counsel, SJAs, and judges have no guidance at all as to what constitutes a "speedy trial." Arguably, as Chief Judge Sullivan, dissenting, noted in *Kossman*, "The result is chaos." The situation was further complicated insofar as speedy trial *dismissals* are concerned because in Article 62 interlocutory appeals the appellate review standard permits overturning the trial judge's speedy

---

[222] 38 M.J. at 261.

[223] *See* § 17.41-20, *above.*

[224] 38 M.J. at 261.

[225] 38 M.J. at 262. *See also* 38 M.J. at 267–68 (Wiss, J., dissenting).

[226] 38 M.J. at 364 n.3.

trial decision only for "abuse of discretion."[227] Chaos did not reign after *Kossman,* although one may argue whether the current regime is superior to that of *Burton.*

From a practical perspective, it is unclear that the *Kossman* majority has assisted either the accused or the government. *Prosecutors* and their superiors have always been hostile to speedy trial limits because they imperil prosecutions and place great burdens on what in the past were often overworked and understrength legal offices.[228] Although *Kossman* may be helpful to prosecutors, it is not helpful to personnel availability. One of the primary reasons for the military speedy trial rule is the need for rapid case disposition in order to interfere as little as possible with the availability of personnel for deployment and other assignments. Prosecution is now largely the responsibility of lawyers, and the lack of the *Burton* rule will insulates prosecution delay from command oversight, to say nothing of unforeseen effects on other commands. Ironically, the demise of *Burton* may also make it more difficult to resist further cuts in lawyer staffing because those non-lawyers charged with personnel adjustments in our new world are likely to be concerned only with immediate needs rather than long term systemic effect. If inadequate legal resources justify case delay, the accurate and traditional justification for maintaining lawyer strength in a time of military "downsizing" is undercut, perhaps fatally.

In the first Court of Appeals for the Armed Forces case after *Kossman,* the court in *United States v. Hatfield*[229] affirmed the trial judge's dismissal for lack of a speedy trial. Identifying 48 days of delay, the trial judge (and appellate court) found a number of major deficiencies in case processing.[230] Reversing the Navy Marine Court of Criminal Appeals, the court re-emphasized its language in *Kossman: "If our decision today vests military judges with a degree of discretion, so be it."*[231] *Hatfield* suggests that the abolition of the 90-day rule may sometimes be of assistance to the accused as well as the government.

§ 17-60.00 LOCAL RULES

In *United States v. Walker,*[232] the court, in dictum, stated that when a government agency promulgates a rule or regulation to guide its action, the agency will be bound by the rule even though the rule is not constitutionally

---

[227] 38 M.J. at 361–62.

[228] 38 M.J. at 362.

[229] 44 M.J. 22 (C.A.A.F. 1996).

[230] Noting, for example, that it took "NEARLY A MONTH" for the defense counsel to be identified. 44 M.J. at 24 (capitalization in original).

[231] 44 M.J. at 24, *quoting from* 38 M.J. at 262 (emphasis in original).

[232] 47 C.M.R. 288, 290 (A.C.M.R. 1973); *see also* United States v. Caceres, 440 U.S. 741, 751 n.14 (1979).

(Rel.3—1/07 Pub.62410)

required. Following this rationale, in 1978 military trial judges dismissed charges against defendants in two Air Force cases [233] on the grounds that the delay in the cases violated Air Force regulations. [234] The primary example of such a nonconstitutional, nonstatutory rule, however, was found in the Army's "45-Day Rule" in Europe. That rule perhaps best shows the extent to which a regulation or directive can create an additional protective "overlay" that expands an underlying right.

Now rescinded, the European supplement to Army Regulation No. 27-10, Military Justice, imposed the following rule:

> Unless charges referred to a summary or a special court-martial (excepting a special court-martial empowered to adjudge a bad-conduct discharge) are brought to trial within 45 days from the date pretrial confinement, arrest, or restriction is imposed or the date charges are preferred, whichever is earlier, the charges will be dismissed by the general court-martial convening authority upon written application of the accused submitted prior to his being "brought to trial" when either the court or an Article 39(a) session is called to order. [235]

Although the regulation required that a request for dismissal had to be addressed to the convening authority, a military judge could review the convening authority's actions. [236] The 45-day rule period was tolled when an Article 39(a) session was called to order, even if the session was called only for the purpose of tolling the rule. [237]

For a trial period, the 45-day rule was limited only to summary and special courts-martial not empowered to adjudge a bad-conduct discharge. The strictures of the rule could consequently be avoided by referring a case to a BCD special court-martial, although dismissal was an appropriate remedy when it could be shown that a case was referred for this purpose.

---

[233] Dettinger v. United States, 7 M.J. 216 (C.M.A. 1979).

[234] Air Force Manual 111-1, Military Justice Guide ¶¶ 1-3a; 1-3a(2); 1-3b (2 July 1973). The regulation did not require dismissal as a remedy for its violation. United States v. McGraner, 13 M.J. 408 (C.M.A. 1982).

[235] U.S. Army Europe Supplement 1 to Army Regulation No. 27-10 ¶ 2-4.1a (Interim change 4-1, December 22, 1980). Since rescinded.

[236] United States v. Dunks, 50 C.M.R. 312, 313 (A.C.M.R. 1975), *reversed on other grounds*, 1 M.J. 254 (C.M.A. 1976). *Compare* United States v. Walker, 47 C.M.R. 288, 291 (A.C.M.R. 1973), *with* United States v. Cruz, 47 C.M.R. 299 (A.C.M.R. 1973).

[237] United States v. Glahn, 49 C.M.R. 47 (A.C.M.R. 1974).

(Rel.3—1/07 Pub.62410)

§ 17-70.00   RULE FOR COURTS-MARTIAL 707

§ 17-71.00   The Two Rules

§ 17-71.10   In General

As originally promulgated, Rule 707 of the Rules for Courts-Martial contained two distinct rules: the "120 day rule" and the "90 day rule." The former was the broader rule, normally requiring that an accused be brought to trial within 120 days after notice of preferral of charges, imposition of restraint, or entry on active duty for trial of a reservist.[238] The latter rule normally required the accused to be tried within 90 days after pretrial arrest or confinement.[239] Violation of either rule required dismissal of the "affected charges."[240] The 120-day rule was by far the more complex.

In June, 1991, the President amended the *Manual for Courts-Martial*, replacing Rule 707 with a significantly modified speedy trial rule. Among other changes, the new rule omits the 90-day rule.

Note that "Article 10 and R.C.M. 707 are distinct, each providing its own speedy trial protection. The fact that a prosecution meets the 120-day rule of R.C.M. 707 does not directly 'or indirectly' demonstrate that the Government moved to trial with reasonable diligence as required by Article 10."[241]

§ 17-72.00   The 120-Day Rule

§ 17-72.10   In General

Rule 707(a) specifies that:

The accused shall be brought to trial within 120 days after the earlier of:

(1) Preferral of charges;

(2) The imposition of restraint under R.C.M. 304(a)(2)–(4); or

(3) Entry on active duty under R.C.M. 204.

The Rule is subject to the exceptions of Rule 707(b), which includes release "from pretrial restraint for a significant period . . . ."

§ 17-72.20   Inception of Government Accountability

The 120-day rule is triggered by "preferral of charges," imposition of restraint, or entry on active duty under R.C.M. 204 of a reservist pending trial, whichever is earlier. Paralleling the constitutional rule, the Discussion provides: "Delay from

---

[238] R.C.M. 707(a).

[239] R.C.M. 707(d).

[240] R.C.M. 707(e).

[241] United States v. Mizgala, 61 M.J. 122, 129 (C.A.A.F. 2005).

(Rel.3—1/07 Pub.62410)

the time of an offense to preferral of charges or the imposition of pretrial restraint is not considered for speedy trial purposes."[242]

The Court of Military Appeals addressed the issue of an accused outside the reach of prosecution in *United States v. Powell*:[243]

[W]here an accused has placed himself outside the reach of the Government during all relevant times under RCM 707 so that, by his own misconduct, it is physically impossible for the Government to bring him to trial, the speedy trial clock of RCM 707(a), which is fully wound and ready to run . . . does not begin to tick until the date on which the accused returns to government control.[244]

§ 17-72.21 Preferral of Charges

The original 120-day rule ran from *notice* of the preferral of charges even if the accused was not subject to restraint. By its terms, preferral alone did not initiate accountability. The notice requirement imposed unnecessary complexity. "Notice" has formal attributes; mere knowledge by the accused is insufficient.[245] The government could not use the "notice" requirement as a subterfuge, because significant delay between preferral and notice could result in dismissal.[246] The June 1991 amendment of Rule 707(a) simplified matters as it deleted the "notice of" preferral in favor of just "preferral". The date of preferral is now decisive.

In calculating the number of days involved, "[t]he date of preferral of charges . . . shall not count for purposes of computing time under subsection (a) of this rule,"[247] and "[w]hen charges are preferred at different times, the accountability for each charge shall be determined from the appropriate date under subsection

---

[242] R.C.M. 707(a) Discussion. *See also* Section 17-31.00. For multiple charges tried separately, *see* United States v. Garner, 39 M.J. 721, 725 (N.M.C.M.R. 1993) (following United States v. Duncan, 38 M.J. 476 (C.M.A. 1993), the accused was informed of the basis for both the initial pretrial confinement and reconfinement; R.C.M. 707(d) was fully complied with). Whether Rule 707 applies at all to a post-trial confinee subject to trial for offenses committed in confinement is unclear. United States v. Vogan, 32 M.J. 959, 960–61 (A.C.M.R. 1991), *aff'd*, 35 M.J. 32 (C.M.A. 1992).

[243] 38 M.J. 153 (C.M.A. 1993).

[244] 38 M.J. at 155 (C.M.A. 1993). *See also* United State v. Thomas, 49 M.J. 200 (C.A.A.F. 1998) (applying *Powell*, clock didn't run while the accused was in German custody).

[245] United States v. Maresca, 26 M.J. 910, 917 (N.M.C.M.R. 1988), *aff'd on other grounds*, 28 M.J. 328 (C.M.A. 1989) (informally giving copy of charges does not trigger 120-day rule. "Counsel are warned, however, that delays between preferral and notification of charges for the purpose of manipulating the speedy trial provisions cannot and will not be tolerated . . . . [S]uch deliberate delaying tactics fall comfortably within the scope of Article 98").

[246] Thomas v. Eddington, 26 M.J. 95 (C.M.A. 1988) (charges dismissed because the notice of preferral was delayed for months). *See also* United States v. Leamer, 29 M.J. 616 (C.G.C.M.R. 1989).

[247] R.C.M. 707(b)(1).

(Rel.3—1/07 Pub.62410)

(a).[248] The accused's right to a speedy trial is evaluated for each charge;[249] the right to a speedy trial may be violated as to one charge and not another.[250]

Repreferral of essentially the same offenses should not restart the 120-day rule, because "[a]llowing the Government to restart the 'speedy trial clock' under such circumstances would grant a license for improper manipulation which could rob R.C.M. 707(a) of its effectiveness."[251]

§ 17-72.22   Imposition of Restraint

The 120-day rule also begins upon the "imposition of restraint under R.C.M. 304(a)(2)–(4)."[252] Accordingly, accountability begins upon imposition of restriction in lieu of arrest or confinement. Originally, the Rule was also "triggered" by imposition of "conditions on liberty."[253] However, this was thought to be too amorphous a standard, as well as something that sometimes happens without the prosecution's knowledge.[254] As a result, Rule 707(a) was amended in 1986,[255] and, as of March, 1987, "conditions on liberty" as such were are irrelevant to the Rule.

The ongoing problem is usually to determine whether conditions placed on the accused's liberty constitute "restriction."[256] This is generally a highly fact specific determination. It appears, however, that the courts tend to not interpret limitations as "restriction." Often this flies in the face of contemporary military reality. For example, although for many years personnel had to have permission to leave the installation (*i.e.*, on "pass"), in today's military, such permission usually is automatic. Yet, the Army Court of Military Review held that limiting an individual to post by denying "pass privileges" is not a "restriction."[257]

---

[248] R.C.M. 707(b)(2).

[249] It may be that this would better be phrased each "specification" as it is possible to add specifications to a charge. However, the use of the technical term "charge" may be decisive.

[250] United States v. Robinson, 28 M.J. 481, 483 (C.M.A. 1989) (R.C.M. 707(a)(2) "sometimes" permits different speedy trial clocks even though offenses have been preferred at the same time).

[251] United States v. Kuelker, 20 M.J. 715, 716 (N.M.C.M.R. 1985).

[252] R.C.M. 707(a)(2).

[253] R.C.M. 304(a)(1).

[254] *See generally*, Finnegan, *Pretrial Restraint and Pretrial Confinement*, Army Law, Mar. 1985, at 15.

[255] Executive Order No. 12550 (Feb. 19, 1986).

[256] *See generally* Section 17-41.10. *See also* United States v. Facey, 26 M.J. 421 (C.M.A. 1988) (limit to 100-mile radius of installation for all unit personnel not "restriction"); United States v. Wilkinson, 27 M.J. 645 (A.C.M.R. 1988), *pet. denied*, 28 M.J. 230 (C.M.A. 1989) (denial of "pass" privileges does not equate to a restriction).

[257] United States v. Wilkinson, 27 M.J. 645 (A.C.M.R. 1988), *pet. denied*, 28 M.J. 230 (C.M.A. 1989). *See also* United States v. Wagner, 39 M.J. 832, 833–34 (C.M.A. 1994) (difference between "pulling pass privileges" and restriction in lieu of arrest for R.C.M. 707 distinguishing between married serviceman assigned overseas with off-post quarters and single soldier in barracks).

A number of cases exist that hold various restraints on liberty to be "administrative restraint" rather than "restriction."[258] Such restraint is a limitation "imposed for operational or other military purposes independent of military justice, including administrative hold or medical reasons."[259] In *United States v. Bradford*,[260] the Court of Military Appeals held that in determining the purpose of restraint, it is the *primary* purpose of the restraint that is determinative:

> We recognize that an administrative restriction under R.C.M. 304(h) must not become a subterfuge whereby a commander may avoid a successful claim that speedy trial has been denied. However, we believe the test is whether the primary purpose in imposing conditions on liberty is to restrain an accused prior to trial in order to assure his presence at trial or to avoid interference with the trial process. In applying this standard, we may inquire whether the same conditions would have been imposed, even if no trial by court-martial were in prospect.[261]

Confinement imposed by a prior sentence should not constitute "restraint" for purposes of Rule 707.[262]

"The date on which pretrial restraint . . . is imposed . . . shall not count for purposes of computing time under subsection (a) of this rule."[263]

§ 17-72.30 Restarting the Time Period

Under Rule 707(b)(2) as originally promulgated:

> If charges are dismissed, if a mistrial is granted, or — when no charges are pending — if the accused is released from pretrial restraint for a significant period, the time under this rule shall run only from the date on which charges or restraint are reinstituted.

The June 1991 amendment of Rule 707 clarifies the effect of mistrial, dismissal, or release from restraint as follows:

> (b)(3) *Events which affect time periods.*
>
> (A) *Dismissal or mistrial.* If charges are dismissed or if a mistrial is granted, a new 120-day time period under this rule shall begin on the date of dismissal or mistrial for cases in which there is no repreferral and cases in which the accused is in pretrial restraint. In all other cases, a new 120-day time period under this rule shall begin on the earlier of

---

[258] United States v. Bradford, 25 M.J. 181 (C.M.A. 1987) (denial of port liberty); United States v. Wilkes, 27 M.J. 571 (N.M.C.M.R. 1988) (liberty-risk candidate); United States v. Miller, 26 M.J. 959 (A.C.M.R. 1988), *pet. denied*, 28 M.J. 164 (C.M.A. 1989) (post-suicide attempt hospitalization).

[259] R.C.M. 304(h).

[260] 25 M.J. 181 (C.M.A. 1987).

[261] 25 M.J. at 186 (C.M.A. 1987). *See also* United States v. Wilkes, 27 M.J. 571 (N.M.C.M.R. 1988).

[262] United States v. Vogan, 32 M.J. 959 (A.C.M.R. 1991), *aff'd*, 35 M.J. 32 (C.M.A. 1992).

[263] R.C.M. 707(b)(1).

(i) the date of repreferral;

(ii) the date of imposition of restraint under R.C.M. 304(a)(2)–(4). [264]

(B) *Release from restraint.* If the accused is released from pretrial restraint for a significant period, the 120-day time period under this rule shall begin on the earlier of

(i) the date of preferral of charges;

(ii) the date on which restraint under R.C.M. 304(a)(2)–(4) is reimposed; or

(iii) the date of entry on active duty under R.C.M. 204. [265]

(C) *Government appeals.* If notice of appeal under R.C.M. 908 is filed, a new 120 day time period under this rule shall begin, for all charges neither proceeded on nor severed under R.C.M. 908(b)(4), on the date of notice to the parties under R.C.M. 908(b)(48) or 908(c)(3), unless it is determined that the appeal was filed solely for the purpose of delay with the knowledge that it was totally frivolous and without merit. After the decision of the Court of Criminal Appeals Military Review under R.C.M. 908, if there is a further appeal to the Court of Military Appeals for the Armed Forces or, subsequently, to the Supreme Court, a new 120-day time period under this rule shall begin on the date the parties are notified of the final decision of such court. [266]

(D) *Rehearings.* If a rehearing is ordered or authorized by an appellate court, a new 120 day time period under this rule shall begin on the date that the responsible convening authority receives the record of trial and the opinion authorizing or directing a rehearing. [267]

Pragmatically, the rule can be divided into two situations: dismissal or mistrial and release for "a significant period" when charges are not pending.

Although the meaning of a "mistrial" is clear, the definition of dismissal has proven somewhat troublesome. In *United States v. Britton,* [268] the Court of Military Appeals distinguished withdrawal of charges from "dismissal" and held that dismissal requires an affirmative act of the convening authority. In the court's mind, "Dismissal . . . contemplate[s] that the accused no longer faces charges, that conditions on liberty and pretrial restraint are lifted, and that he is returned

---

[264] United States v. Anderson, 50 M.J. 447 (C.A.A.F. 1999) (dismissal of charges, absent a subterfuge, restarts the speedy trial clock).

[265] United States v. Ruffin, 46 M.J. 657 (N.M. Crim. App. 1997) (When accused released from confinement for significant period of time, speedy trial clock starts at time of new trigger event, charges preferred the following day), *aff'd,* 48 M.J. 211 (C.A.A.F. 1998).

[266] *See* United States v. Reap, 41 M.J. 340 (C.A.A.F. 1995).

[267] Executive Order 12767, Amendments to the *Manual for Courts-Martial, United States,* 1984 (June 27, 1991).

[268] 26 M.J. 24, 26 (C.M.A. 1988).

to full-time duty with full rights as accorded to all other servicemembers."[269] Accordingly, a withdrawal and repreferral do not constitute a "dismissal."[270]

Far more ambiguous than "dismissal" is Rule 707(b)(3)(B)'s provision permitting the period to run anew when no charges are preferred and the accused is released from pretrial restraint for "a significant period." Despite this inherent ambiguity, the cases thus far support the proposition that five or more days is sufficiently "significant."[271] Whether a period of less than five days is enough waits to be seen. Presumably, a release intended to circumvent the speedy trial rules would be a "subterfuge" and of no avail.[272]

Speedy trial accountability after a prior release is "triggered" by the imposition of new restraint if charges are not pending. Otherwise — absent dismissal or mistrial — the period runs from preferral, or if charges have already been preferred and dismissed, or mistried, to the date of dismissal or mistrial. The old rule was unclear. In 1988, in *United States v. Gray*,[273] the three judges of the Court of Military Appeals filed three differing opinions and could not agree on whether accountability began upon preferral, notice of preferral, or imposition of restraint. In *United States v. Facey*,[274] the court unanimously, but without reference to *Gray*, held that when no additional pretrial restraint was imposed after release, accountability began upon the date when new charges are preferred.[275] And in *United States v. Campbell*,[276] the Army Court of Military

---

[269] 26 M.J. 26 (C.M.A. 1988). For differing views of "dismissal," *compare* United States v. Bolado, 34 M.J. 732, 736–38 (N.M.C.M.R. 1991), *with* United States v. Mickla, 29 M.J. 749 (A.F.C.M.R. 1989).

[270] 26 M.J. at 26; *see also* United States v. Hayes, 37 M.J. 769 (A.C.M.R. 1993) (dismissal of charges pending lengthy DNA testing that would have violated 120-day rule stopped the clock even though new charges were contemplated and actually preferred after testing. R.C.M. 707(b)(3)(A) permits dismissal with intent to reprefer, at least when there is a proper reason to delay); United States v. Bolado, 34 M.J. 732 (N.M.C.M.R. 1991) (contrary to *Mickla, below*, dismissal will restart the clock even though intent was to reinstitute charge); United States v. Mickla, 29 M.J. 749 (A.F.C.M.R. 1989); United States v. Mucthison, 28 M.J. 1113 (N.M.C.M.R. 1989).

[271] United States v. Wilkinson, 27 M.J. 645 (A.C.M.R. 1988), *pet. denied*, 28 M.J. 230 (C.M.A. 1989) (50 days); United States v. Miller, 26 M.J. 959 (A.C.M.R. 1988), *pet. denied*, 28 M.J. 164 (C.M.A. 1989) (five days); United States v. Gray, 21 M.J. 1020 (N.M.C.M.R. 1986) (47 days), *aff'd*, 26 M.J. 16 (C.M.A. 1988) (three opinions); United States v. Hulsey, 21 M.J. 717 (A.F.C.M.R. 1985) (five days). *See also* United States v. Smith, 32 M.J. 586 (A.C.M.R. 1990) (two days AWOL).

[272] United States v. Robinson, 47 M.J. 506 (N.M. Crim. App. 1997) (when the dismissal is a subterfuge, it will not restart the speedy trial clock). *Cf.* United States v. Hulsey, 21 M.J. 717 (A.F.C.M.R. 1985).

[273] 26 M.J. 16 (C.M.A. 1988).

[274] 26 M.J. 421 (C.M.A. 1988). *See also* United States v. Ruffin, 46 M.J. 657 (N.M. Crim. App. 1997) (When accused released from confinement for significant period of time, speedy trial clock starts at time of new trigger event.), *aff'd*, 48 M.J. 211 (C.A.A.F. 1998).

[275] 26 M.J. 424 (C.M.A. 1988). In United States v. Callinan, 32 M.J. 701, 703 (A.F.C.M.R. 1991),

(Rel.3—1/07   Pub.62410)

Review held misconduct unrelated to the specification involved in a speedy trial motion "will restart the speedy trial clock, not just toll its running."[277]

The Army Court of Military Review has opined in dictum that withdrawal of charges for referral to a higher court doesn't restart the Rule 707 speedy trial clock,[278] and added that the trial judge retained jurisdiction for speedy trial accountability purposes even after withdrawal of the charges.[279]

§ 17-72.40   Termination of Government Accountability

Government accountability terminates when the accused is "brought to trial."[280] Under the old rule, he or she is brought to trial when a "plea of guilty is entered to an offense"[281] or evidence on the merits was presented to the fact finder.[282] The original drafters seem to have accepted earlier case law that an Article 39(a) session alone would not terminate government accountability.

The new Rule 707 defines "brought to trial" as arraignment of the accused.[283] Whether this will permit arraignments solely to terminate speedy trial accountability remains to be seen. The Court of Appeals for the Armed Forces has held, however, that Article 10's speedy trial protection does not stop upon arraignment.[284]

---

the court noted that because conditions on liberty no longer "trigger" speedy trial right under Rule 707, continued imposition of such conditions does not prevent a finding of release for "a significant period."

[276] 32 M.J. 564 (A.C.M.R. 1991).

[277] 32 M.J. at 566 (A.C.M.R. 1991). *Cf.* United States v. Anderson, 50 M.J. 447 (C.A.A.F. 1999), *cert. denied*, 528 U.S. 1054 (1999).

[278] United States v. Weatherspoon, 39 M.J. 762, 766 (A.C.M.R. 1994) (technically dictum).

[279] 39 M.J. at 767, n.4 (A.C.M.R. 1994).

[280] R.C.M. 707(a), 707(b)(3) (pre-1991 amendment). The new rule does not have a specific termination provision.

[281] R.C.M. 707(b)(3)(A) (pre-1991 amendment).

[282] R.C.M. 707(c)(3)(B) (pre-1991 amendment).

[283] Executive Order 12767, Amendments to the *Manual for Courts-Martial, United States*, 1984 Rule 707 (b)(1) (June 27, 1991). *See, e.g.*, United States v. Stokes, 39 M.J. 771, 773 (A.C.M.R. 1994). For the impact of the amendment of Rule 707 on cases pending at the time of it effective date, *see* United States v. Powell, 38 M.J. 153, 154–55 (C.M.A. 1993), United States v. Patterson, 39 M.J. 678, 681 (N.M.C.M.R. 1993). *Cf.* United States v. Doty, No. 51 M.J. 464 (C.A.A.F. 1999) (speedy trial clock stops on arraignment even though government not ready to proceed).

[284] United States v. Cooper, 58 M.J. 54 (C.A.A.F. 2003). The Court opined, however:

Having said that, however, we hasten to emphasize that by the time an accused is arraigned, a change in the speedy-trial landscape has taken place. This is because after arraignment, "the power of the military judge to process the case increases, and the power of the [Government] to affect the case decreases." . . . *Doty*, 51 M.J. at 465–66. As a result, once an accused is arraigned, significant responsibility for ensuring the accused's court-martial proceeds with reasonable dispatch rests with the military judge.

(Rel.3—1/07   Pub.62410)

§ 17-73.00 Exclusions

§ 17-73.10 In General

It is apparent that in some circumstances the government should be relieved from responsibility for delay in bringing a case to trial. Perhaps the most obvious is a defense request for a continuance unmotivated by government misconduct. As a result, Rule 707(c) contained explicit categories of circumstances in which delay would not be the responsibility of the government for speedy trial motions. Notwithstanding these express exceptions, the Court of Military Appeals held that exceptions 707(c)(1)–(8) "contemplate that the length of time excluded will be *reasonable*." [285] *Factual* findings of reasonableness were thus necessary. [286]

The following periods were excluded from the speedy trial rules of the original Rule 707:

(1) Any periods of delay resulting from other proceedings in the case, including: [287]

(A) Any examination into the mental capacity or responsibility of the accused; [288]

(B) Any hearing on the capacity of the accused to stand trial and any time during which the accused lacks capacity to stand trial;

(C) Any session on pretrial motions; [289]

(D) Any appeal filed under R.C.M. 908 unless it is determined that the appeal was filed solely for the purpose of delay with the knowledge that it was totally frivolous and without merit; [290] and

(E) Any petition for extraordinary relief by either party. [291]

The military judge has the power and responsibility to force the Government to proceed with its case if justice so requires.

58 M.J. at 60.

[285] United States v. Longhofer, 29 M.J. 22, 27 (C.M.A. 1989) (emphasis in original).

[286] 29 M.J. 22, 27 (C.M.A. 1989).

[287] *See* United States v. Porter, 36 M.J. 812, 818–19 (A.C.M.R. 1993) (court held that the government was not liable for time involved in the accused's suit in the Panamanian court system, brought to contest United States jurisdiction; the list of "other proceedings" in former Rule 707(c)(1) was not exclusive) (alternative holding).

[288] Section 17-53.00. *See* United States v. Mahoney, 28 M.J. 865 (A.F.C.M.R. 1989) (68-day period for exam was "reasonable," which is the test); United States v. Hirsch, 26 M.J. 800 (A.C.M.R. 1988), *pet. denied*, 27 M.J. 404 (C.M.A. 1988) (102-day delay reasonable). *Cf.* United States v. Burris, 20 M.J. 707 (A.C.M.R. 1985).

[289] *See, e.g.*, United States v. Pettaway, 24 M.J. 589 (N.M.C.M.R. 1987) (12 days in between sessions excluded).

[290] *See, e.g.*, United States v. Ramsey, 28 M.J. 370, 373 (C.M.A. 1989).

[291] 28 M.J. 370, 373 (C.M.A. 1989). *See also* Porter v. Eggers, 32 M.J. 583 (A.C.M.R. 1990) (delay to obtain foreign waiver of jurisdiction).

(Rel.3—1/07 Pub.62410)

(2) Any period of delay resulting from unavailability of a military judge when the unavailability results from extraordinary circumstances.

(3) Any period of delay resulting from a delay in a proceeding or a continuance in the court-martial granted at the request or with the consent of the defense.[292]

(4) Any period of delay resulting from a failure of the defense to provide notice, make a request, or submit any matter in a timely manner as otherwise required by this *Manual*.[293]

(5) Any period of delay resulting from a delay in the Article 32 hearing or a continuance in the court-martial at the request of the prosecution if:

(A) The delay or continuance is granted because of unavailability of substantial evidence relevant and necessary to the prosecution's case when the Government has exercised due diligence to obtain such evidence and there exists at the time of the delay grounds to believe that such evidence would be available within a reasonable time;[294] or

(B) The continuance is granted to allow the trial counsel additional time to prepare the prosecution's case and additional time is justified because of the exceptional circumstances of the case.

---

[292] *See, e.g.*, United States v. McKnight, 30 M.J. 205 (C.M.A. 1990); United States v. Jackson, 30 M.J. 687 (A.C.M.R. 1990). Delays will not be deductible unless approved by the convening authority or the military judge. United States v. Lamer, 32 M.J. 63 (C.M.A. 1990) (three months for government to obtain defense expert held attributable to the defense since delay not approved by the trial judge). United States v. Cook, 27 M.J. 212 (C.M.A. 1988); United States v. Carlisle, 25 M.J. 426 (C.M.A. 1988); United States v. Kohl, 26 M.J. 919 (N.M.C.M.R. 1988).

A request for delay should not ordinarily be inferred; it should be express. United States v. Givens, 28 M.J. 888 (A.F.C.M.R. 1989); United States v. Raichle, 28 M.J. 876 (A.F.C.M.R. 1989). In 1989, the Court of Military Appeals wrote:

If the delay is occasioned by a specific request from an accused, in writing or on the record, and such a delay is granted by either the convening authority, the Article 32 investigating officer, or a military judge, the Government shall be relieved of accountability. RCM 707(c)(3).

United States v. Longhofer, 29 M.J. 22, 28 (C.M.A. 1989).

As to the consequences of a delay request, in *McKnight* the court declared: "Defense counsel has no affirmative obligation to move the case to trial. However, when trial or some earlier proceeding is delayed for his convenience or needs, he does have some obligation to cooperate reasonably in rescheduling the proceedings." 30 M.J. at 208.

[293] *See, e.g.*, United States v. Arnold, 28 M.J. 963 (A.C.M.R. 1989).

[294] *See, e.g.*, United States v. Byard, 29 M.J. 803 (A.C.M.R. 1989) (government must use due diligence to obtain evidence). *Cf.* United States v. Tebsherany, 32 M.J. 351, 355 (C.M.A. 1991) ("[I]t would follow that time requested by counsel to examine material not disclosed until the pretrial investigation might, under facts showing bad faith, be charged to the United States in accounting for the pretrial delay").

(6) Any period of delay resulting from the absence or unavailability of the accused. [295]

(7) Any reasonable period of delay when the accused is joined for trial with a coaccused as to whom the time for trial has not yet run and there is good cause for not granting a severance. [296]

(8) Any period of delay, not exceeding 60 days, occasioned in processing and implementing a request pursuant to R.C.M. 204 to order a member of a reserve component to active duty for disciplinary action.

(9) Any other period of delay for good cause, including unusual operational requirements and military exigencies. [297]

---

[295] *See, e.g.*, United States v. Brown, 30 M.J. 839 (N.M.C.M.R. 1990) (following United States v. Lilly, 22 M.J. 620, 624 (N.M.C.M.R. 1986)). In United States v. Turk, 24 M.J. 277 (C.M.A. 1987), the court, in an unanimous opinion, held that the reasonable period of time required to return the defendant to his ship will be excludable for speedy trial purposes. As to civilian confinement, *see* Section 17-41.12. In United States v. Porter, 36 M.J. 812, 818–19 (A.C.M.R. 1993), the court held that the government was not liable for time involved in the accused's suit in the Panamanian court system, brought to contest United States jurisdiction).

[296] *Cf.* United States v. Facey, 26 M.J. 421 (C.M.A. 1988). Rule 707(c)(7) is taken from the dictum in United States v. Johnson, 1 M.J. 294, 296 n.4 (C.M.A. 1976):

> In instances of multiple accused in which the Government elects to join the
> proceedings, the question of unlawful pretrial delays must be examined as to each
> accused separately, and only those delays attributable to an individual accused for his
> "convenience and benefit," as opposed to some nebulous concept of "the defense," may
> be charged against him.

Pursuant to this dictum, the burden seems to be on the government. Under R.C.M. 707(c)(7), the defense seems to be required to show good cause for granting a severance. Of course, the "good cause" would be pretrial confinement for a significant period of time awaiting the government to perfect its case against the co-accused. As a practical matter, the parties can obtain a severance by asking for a different fact finder.

[297] *See, e.g.*, United States v. Longhofer, 29 M.J. 22, 28 (C.M.A. 1989) (security clearance). *See generally* Section 17-32.20.

The Court of Military Appeals drew a distinction between the 120-day rule and the *Burton* Rule, distinguishing earlier (*Burton*) cases that hold that delay incident to a request for discharge in lieu of court-martial while the accused was in confinement are not deductible from government accountability. *Compare* United States v. Higgins, 27 M.J. 150 (C.M.A. 1988), *cert. denied*, 489 U.S. 1015 (1989) *with* United States v. O'Brien, 48 C.M.R. 42 (C.M.A. 1973). The court held in *United States v. Higgins*, 27 M.J. 150 (C.M.A. 1988), that the delay in processing a resignation in lieu of court-martial outside of the command under an Air Force regulation that requires that the trial be delayed until the resignation is processed is deductible from government accountability pursuant to R.C.M. 707(c)(9) (R.C.M. 707(c)(8) prior to the March 1987 amendment). Exec. Order No. 12, 586 (1987). It seems strange to call the processing of a discharge at the service headquarters for 45 days a circumstance justifying delay for "good cause" (the Army can process these in three working days after receipt).

In the second portion of the exclusion, emphasis should be placed on "operational" rather than "unusual." *See, e.g.*, United States v. Ruhling, 28 M.J. 586, 593 (N.M.C.M.R. 1988) ("It would

(Rel.3—1/07 Pub.62410)

The 1991 amendment to Rule 707 completely replaces the old Rule 707(c) with the following:

(c) *Excludable delays.* All periods of time during which appellate courts have issued stays in the proceedings, or the accused is hospitalized due to incompetence, or is other wise in the custody of the Attorney General, shall be excluded. . . . All other pretrial delays approved by a military judge or the convening authority shall be similarly excluded.[298]

> (1) *Procedure.* Prior to referral, all requests for pretrial delay, together with supporting reasons, will be submitted to the convening authority or, if authorized under regulations prescribed by the Secretary concerned, to a military judge for resolution. After referral, such requests for pretrial delay will be submitted to the military judge for resolution.[299]

Although this amendment has the great virtue of requiring predelay approval,[300] it is at the extreme cost of eliminating the present enunciated exceptions. The grant of discretion intended is made clear by the Discussion:

> The decision to grant or deny a reasonable delay is a matter within the sole discretion of the convening authority or a military judge. This decision should be based on the facts and circumstances then and there existing. Reasons to grant a delay might, for example, include: time to enable counsel to prepare for trial in complex cases; time to allow examination into the mental capacity of the accused; time to process a member of the reserve component to active duty for disciplinary action; time to complete other proceedings related to the case; time requested by the defense; time to secure the availability of the accused, substantial witnesses, or other evidence; time to obtain appropriate security clearances for access to classified information or time to declassify evidence; or any other period of delay for good cause.[301]

---

be difficult to imagine a better example of peacetime military exigency or unusual operational requirement than a combatant ship facing an advanced and compressed schedule with its imminent deployment to a tense theater of operations . . .").

[298] An accused who is absent without leave tolls the government's duty to bring the accused to trial. United States v. Dies, 45 M.J. 376, 378 (C.A.A.F. 1996)

> [W]e held that an accused who is an unauthorized absentee is stopped from asserting a denial of speedy trial during the period of his absence, at a minimum. This is to say that he has waived — by conduct — his right to a speedy trial as to that interim at least. We will not require the Government to undertake futile efforts to proceed to trial while an accused is so absent.

[299] Executive Order 12767, Amendments to the *Manual for Courts-Martial, United States*, 1984 (June 27, 1991). In what some might term a surprise holding, in 1997 the Court of Appeals for the Armed Forces held that Rule 707(c)(1) permits the convening authority to approve delays *after the fact.* United States v. Thompson, 46 M.J. 472 (C.A.A.F. 1997).

[300] And authorizing the judge to grant it even before referral.

[301] Discussion accompanying Executive Order 12767, Amendments to the *Manual for Courts-Martial, United States*, 1984 (June 27, 1991).

(Rel.3—1/07 Pub.62410)

Either the common law resulting from this amendment will simply restate the old Rule and its interpretation, or it will justify its departure. Given the service's traditional hostility to an effective speedy trial right and the Discussion's attempt to grant "sole discretion" to the convening authority or judge, the amendment may make a mockery of the Rule.

In one sense the prior Rule 707(c)(9) "escape clause" may shed light on the new discretionary delay provision. Prior Rule 707(c)(9) was a broad catch-all excusing as it did "[a]ny other period of delay for good cause, including unusual operational requirements and military exigencies." The courts emphasized its discretionary nature and its intent to deal with "unique situations."[302]

The Court of Military Appeals held that the exception required "a causal connection" between the event and the delay sought to be excluded, or a "nexus."[303] The court spelled out the procedure for applying the exception:

> If the delay is occasioned by a specific request for a delay "for good cause" made in writing or on the record by the Government and the delay is granted by either the convening authority, the Article 32 investigating officer, or the military judge, such delay shall be excluded; provided, however, the grant for delay made by the convening authority or Article 32 investigating officer is subject to de novo review by a military judge upon motion of the defense.[304] These exclusions are subject to review both for abuse of discretion and reasonableness. . . . The primary purpose for written requests for delay or for motions on the record of the Article 32 investigation or Article 39(a), . . . court sessions is to memorialize and litigate questions of delay contemporaneous with the event and to avoid the salvage operation required of military judges and appellate courts faced with trying to allocate periods of delay long after the event occurred.

> If "good cause, including unusual operational requirements and military exigencies" exists, even though not previously litigated or no delay was granted, the Government shall be relieved of accountability, subject to the test of reasonableness. RCM 707(c)(9). The military judge has to find that the unusual event being relied upon actually caused a delay in the Government's preparation of its case and that it was reasonable for the delay to result. Once the causal connection between the event and the delay is established, the time may be subtracted from the 120-day time limit. The Government need not establish, however, that this delay "proximately caused" the trial not to take place within the total time period. How can one ever say that some unforeseen delay which may take place in the early days following notification was indeed the straw that broke the camel's back?[305]

---

[302] United States v. Longhofer, 29 M.J. 22, 27 (C.M.A. 1989) (*quoting* United States v. Durr, 21 M.J. 576, 578 (A.C.M.R. 1985)).

[303] 29 M.J. at 27 (C.M.A. 1989).

[304] *Citing* United States v. Carlisle, 25 M.J. at 428.

[305] 29 M.J. at 28–29 (C.M.A. 1989) (footnotes omitted).

(Rel.3—1/07 Pub.62410)

Note, however, that current Rule 707(c) does not require "good cause" although the courts may choose to read that into the rule in order to protect Article 10 speedy trial rights. In 1994 the Army Court of Military Review, citing this treatise for the proposition that the new rule is similar to the old good cause rule, held that four days for the convening authority to decide whether to proceed or to withdraw and refer charges didn't abuse the judge's discretion.[306]

Interpreting Rule 707(c), the Air Force Court of Criminal Appeals has held that when a party requests a delay, the delay runs not from the date of the request but from the date of the approved event.[307]

The 1991 *Manual* changed the termination of government accountability. Contrary to prior rules, arraignment under R.C.M. 904 stops the 120-day clock.[308] The 120-day clock is restarted when charges are dismissed,[309] the accused is released from restraint for significant period of time,[310] the government appeals under R.C.M. 908,[311] a rehearing is ordered,[312] or the accused is committed for competency examination.[313] It appears the Court of Appeals will apply the "plain meaning" to these rules absent the President exceeding his authority or a rule being unconsitutional.[314]

§ 17-73.20   Possible Civilian Disposition; Department of Justice Involvement

In *United States v. Duncan*,[315] the Army Court of Military Review was faced with the trial of the supervisor of an Army covert intelligence support group. Because of the nature of the case, both the FBI and the Department of Justice were heavily involved. During the subsequent Rule 707 speedy trial motion, the military judge held the prosecution unaccountable for that part of the delay caused by DOJ action to establish prosecutorial primacy, ruling that the Army had to

---

[306] United States v. Weatherspoon, 39 M.J. 762, 766 (A.C.M.R. 1994).

[307] United States v. Nichols, 42 M.J. 715 (A.F. Crim. App. 1995).

[308] R.C.M. 707(b)(1). United States v. Doty, 51 M.J. 464 (C.A.A.F. 1999) (speedy trial clock stops on arraignment even though government not ready to proceed).

[309] R.C.M. 707(b)(3)(A). United States v. Anderson, 50 M.J. 447 (C.A.A.F. 1999) (dismissal of charges stopped speedy trial clock when defense did not object even though new charges encompassed some of originanl conduct). Note that the Article 10 speedy trial right continues after arraignment. United States v. Cooper, 58 M.J. 54 (C.A.A.F. 2003).

[310] R.C.M. 707(b)(3)(B); United States v. Ruffin, 48 M.J. 211 (C.A.A.F. 1998) (clock stopped even though charges preferred one day after accused's release from confinement and there was no additional restraint).

[311] R.C.M. 707(b)(3)(C).

[312] R.C.M. 707(b)(3)(D).

[313] R.C.M. 707(b)(3)(E).

[314] United States v. Ruffin, 48 M.J. 211 (C.A.A.F. 1998).

[315] 34 M.J. 1232 (A.C.M.R. 1992).

(Rel.3—1/07   Pub.62410)

comply with the directions of the Attorney General.[316] On appeal, the Court of Review reversed, holding that the Attorney General and her or his subordinates have no legal authority to order a stay of a court-martial and no control over military prosecution,[317] and that accordingly, the prosecution was responsible for the delay. The Court of Military Appeals affirmed the decision of the Court of Military Review.[318] Senior Judge Everett, with Judges Sullivan and Wiss, concurring, added, however:

> [W]e realize that often it will be desirable to defer proceedings in one court while related proceedings are completed in another court . . . . We are convinced, however that — absent extraordinary circumstances not present here — a delay for this reason is excludible on grounds of "good cause" only when the accused is informed at the time of the purported reason and given some opportunity to contest the decision.[319]

§ 17-74.00   The 90-Day Rule

As promulgated Rule 707(d) required that:

> When the accused is in pretrial arrest or confinement under R.C.M. 304 or 305, immediate steps shall be taken to bring the accused to trial. No accused shall be held in pretrial arrest or confinement in excess of 90 days for the same or related charges. Except for any periods under subsection (c)(7) of this rule, the periods described in subsection (c) of this rule shall be excluded for the purpose of computing when 90 days has run. The military judge may, upon a showing of extraordinary circumstances, extend the period by 10 days.

It is immediately apparent that although this Rule restated the basic 90-day rule of *United States v. Burton*,[320] it was more lenient both in terms of duration[321] and its exceptions[322] until its abolition in 1991.

The Rule 707, 90-day rule applied in addition to, rather than in lieu of, *United States v. Burton*.[323] Accordingly, delay in excess of ninety days, after subtracting applicable delays, while the accused is in confinement, yielded dismissal under the rule[324] or *Burton*.

---

[316] 34 M.J. at 1237 (A.C.M.R. 1992).

[317] 34 M.J. at 1239 (A.C.M.R. 1992).

[318] 38 M.J. 476 (C.M.A. 1993).

[319] 38 M.J. at 479-80 (C.M.A. 1993). Judges Gierke and Cox concurred in this part of the opinion. Critically, Judge Crawford did not participate in the case. Accordingly, it is not clear whether the court would apply this dictum as holding in a similar case. *See* Major Kevan F. Jacobson, *United States v. Duncan: The United States Court of Military Appeals Frowns on "Retroactive" Pretrial Delays*, Army Law., May 1994, at 48.

[320] Section 17-50.00.

[321] The time may be extended to 100 days.

[322] All of the Rule 707(c) exceptions apply except for that applicable to joint trial.

[323] *See* Section 17-51.00.

[324] *See, e.g.*, United States v. Durr, 21 M.J. 576 (A.C.M.R. 1985).

(Rel.3—1/07   Pub.62410)

/91 amendment to Rule 707 eliminated the 90-day rule entirely.[325] It
that this change was adverse to the government's interests. The old rule
d Burton; the new one forces the courts to either abandon *Burton*
ale or continue it "lock, stock, and barrel."

-80.00 WAIVER

7-81.00 Failure to Demand Trial

Although some civilian courts have applied a demand-waiver doctrine under
which the failure to demand a speedy trial constitutes a waiver, the Supreme
Court has stated, in *Barker v. Wingo*,[326] that "presuming waiver of a fundamental
right from inaction, is inconsistent with this Court's pronouncements on waiver
of constitutional rights."[327] The Court thus has indicated that waivers should
be intentional relinquishments or abandonments of rights that should not be
presumed because of inaction or acquiescence.[328] The fact that a delay in trial
may work to the benefit of the defendant rather than to his or her detriment "does
not argue for placing the burden of protecting the right solely on defendants."[329]
Because society has an interest, especially in the military community, in swift
prosecution, it is the prosecution who should attempt to obtain a speedy trial
and thereby also protect the accused's right to a speedy trial.[330] The Court of
Appeals for the Armed Forces has held, however, that an Article 10 waiver does
not require an affirmative waiver on the record, thus permitting the court to infer
a waiver.[331] In 2005, the court opined that "a litigated speedy trial motion under
Article 10 is not waived by a subsequent unconditional guilty plea."[332]

§ 17-82.00 Failure to Raise the Issue at Trial

The issue of whether failure to raise a speedy trial issue at trial precludes raising
the matter on appeal technically remains unsettled as a general question. In *United*

---

[325] Executive Order 12767, Amendments to the *Manual for Courts-Martial, United States*, 1984
(June 27, 1991).

[326] 407 U.S. 514 (1972).

[327] 407 U.S. at 525 (1972). *Cf.* R.C.M. 907(b)(2)(A).

[328] 407 U.S. at 525–26 and cases cited therein. Failure to demand trial is a factor that should
be taken into account in determining whether the right to a speedy trial has been violated. *See
also* Section 17-41.20. In *State v. Austin*, 731 A.2d 678, 684 (R.I. 1999) the Court observed,
"[W]hen assessing a defendant's assertion of his right to a speedy trial, this Court looks for actions
sufficiently aggressive to constitute the equivalent of a 'banging on the courthouse doors.' ".

[329] 407 U.S. at 527.

[330] 407 U.S. at 527.

[331] United States v. Birge, 52 M.J. 209 (C.A.A.F. 1999).

[332] United States v. Mizgala, 61 M.J. 122, 127 (C.A.A.F. 2005). Although the court wrote, "we
hold," the quoted language technically is dictum as the court also concluded that no Article 10
error took place.

States v. Schalck, [333] the Court of Military Appeals permitted a speedy trial issue to be raised for the first time on appeal, accepting as correct the government's concession that "deprivation of due process of law is not waived by failure to assert it prior to trial" [334] and stating that the "issues of speedy trial and denial of the due process are frequently inextricably bound together and the line of demarcation is not always clear." [335] Although *Schalck* could have been inter- preted as permitting waiver of a speedy trial claim not made at trial when that claim did not involve additional due process elements, [336] it gave rise to a line of cases holding that failure to raise a speedy trial claim at trial does not result in waiver of the issue. [337] A significant exception was the decision of the Court of Military Appeals in *United States v. Pierce,* [338] in which the court held that failure to raise a speedy trial motion at trial resulted in its waiver notwithstanding *Schalck.* [339] The court's holding in *Pierce,* however, seems to have been a clear result of the court's conclusion that from the facts of the case *Pierce* was not only not prejudiced by the delay, most of which was not spent in a confined status, but may have actually benefited from it due to civilian resolution of charges in the interim.

Two possible readings of *Pierce* thus result: when "an accused suffers little pretrial confinement" [340] and has apparently not suffered specific prejudice, failure to raise the speedy trial issue at trial waives it; or when the sole issue is one of speedy trial rather than a combined matter of speedy trial and failure to comply with Article 33 [341] or of speedy trial and due process, waiver will not take place. The resolution of the issue may have occurred in *United States*

---

[333] 34 C.M.R. 151 (1964).

[334] 34 C.M.R. at 153 (1964).

[335] 34 C.M.R. at 153 (1964).

[336] *Schalck's* due process claim was based upon the fact that he was in pretrial confinement for 96 days without charges being preferred. Thus, the claim was based jointly upon Articles 10 and 33 of the Code with the alleged violation of Article 33 requiring that charges be forwarded within eight days after arrest or confinement (or a written explanation be given for noncompliance) occupying a particularly important role.

[337] *See, e.g.,* United States v. White, 38 C.M.R. 260 (C.M.A. 1968); United States v. Jennings, 37 C.M.R. 378 (C.M.A. 1967); *but see* United States v. Pierce, 41 C.M.R. 225 (C.M.A. 1970), discussed *below.*

[338] 41 C.M.R. 225 (C.M.A. 1970).

[339] 41 C.M.R. at 227 (C.M.A. 1970).

[340] 41 C.M.R. at 227 (C.M.A. 1970). Note that the court may have reached its holding because of concern that in cases like *Pierce* the government would have no reason to anticipate the later raising of a speedy trial issue and would thus not present evidence on the issue at trial requiring a remand at the appellate level when the issue was first raised. 41 C.M.R. at 227 (C.M.A. 1970).

[341] *See* Section 17-42.00. In *Pierce,* the court stated that "here we are concerned only with the operative effect of Article 10," and distinguished by citation two cases that also dealt with Article 33. 41 C.M.R. at 227 and cases cited therein.

(Rel.3—1/07 Pub.62410)

v. Sloan,[342] when the Court of Military Appeals held that for *Burton*[343] purposes, "absent evidence indicating a denial of military due process or manifest injustice, an accused who does not object at the time of trial to a delay in excess of three months in bringing him to trial will be precluded from raising the issue at the appellate level."[344]

Given the court's opinion in *Sloan*, it seems clear that it will apply the same rule to all speedy trial cases regardless of the nature of the delay.[345] This legal conclusion is bolstered by the fact that delay is a common defense tactic that may very well work to the advantage of the accused because witnesses may become unavailable, forgetful, or intimidated by a third party. For this reason, and the fact that judicial economy would argue against the government being required, absent a defense motion, to set forth the reasons why the defendant was not denied a speedy trial, the failure to raise the issue at trial should be considered a defense waiver.[346]

This result is bolstered by the ethical duty of the defense counsel to object at trial to a perceived violation of the defendant's rights. In practice, failure to object is far more likely to stem from counsel's determination that any delay can be satisfactorily established in the form of extraordinary circumstances, defense request for delay, or misconduct by the defendant than from inadequacy of counsel.

The Court of Military Appeals appeared inclined toward this view of defense waiver in *United States v. Britton*,[347] when, having first held that for purposes of appeal "Whether a speedy trial has been waived is a mixed question of law and fact,"[348] it opined that "while it is the general rule that failure to make a timely motion at trial *may* estop one from raising the issue on appeal, failure to raise the issue does not preclude the Court of Military Review in the exercise of its powers from granting relief."[349]

In 1990, the court held in *United States v. Reinecke*,[350] that defense's failure to object to government delay while it occurred waived any objection to the

---

[342] 48 C.M.R. 211 (C.M.A. 1974).

[343] 44 C.M.R. 166 (1971). *See generally* Section 17.50 *et seq.*

[344] 48 C.M.R. 211, 214. *Cf.* R.C.M. 907(b)(2)(A); United States v. Huffman, 40 M.J. 225 (C.M.A. 1994) (refused to apply waiver to alleged Article 13 violation).

[345] 48 C.M.R. at 213. *See also* United States v. Hounshell, 21 C.M.R. 129, 132 (C.M.A. 1956) (dicta) cited in *Sloan*, 48 C.M.R. at 213.

[346] United States v. Birge, 52 M.J. 209 (C.A.A.F. 1999).

[347] 26 M.J. 24, 27 (C.M.A. 1988).

[348] 26 M.J. 24, 27 (C.M.A. 1988) (*citing cf.* United States v. Fisher, 21 M.J. 327 (C.M.A. 1986)).

[349] 26 M.J. 24, 27 (C.M.A. 1988) (emphasis in original).

[350] 32 M.J. 63 (C.M.A. 1990).

(Rel.3—1/07 Pub.62410)

delay.[351] In *United States v. Vendivel*,[352] the Air Force Court of Military Review held that absent plain error, failure to raise a Rule 707 speedy trial issue at trial waives the issue. In 1999, in *United States v. Birge*,[353] the court opined in dictum[354] that *Sloan* had held that failure to raise the issue constituted waiver of an Article 10 protest, and that "[c]ivilian law does not support a requirement for an affirmative and fully developed waiver."[355]

§ 17-83.00 Effect of a Guilty Plea

Past case law indicated that the mere fact that an accused pleads guilty at trial does not prohibit raising a speedy trial issue on appeal.[356] What was unclear was when such an issue could be raised. In *United States v. Sloan*,[357] the Court of Military Appeals focused not on the fact that the accused had pled guilty, but rather on whether the issue had been first raised at trial prior to the plea, and if not, whether the failure to raise the issue could be excused.[358] Consequently, the court appeared to follow the rule that whenever a speedy trial issue had been raised at trial, the issue could be raised on appeal notwithstanding a plea of guilty. The failure to raise such a claim at trial would be excused in a case involving a plea of not guilty.[359] This result seems correct, since a guilty finding, whether pursuant to a plea or not, has nothing to do with the speedy trial issue.[360] Notwithstanding this, as amended in June, 1991, Rule 707(e) provides that absent a conditional plea, a successful guilty plea "waives any speedy trial issue as to that offense."[361] Although such a provision is clearly lawful insofar as Rule 707 protections are concerned, whether a guilty plea waives

---

[351] 32 M.J. 64 (C.M.A. 1990).

[352] 37 M.J. 854, 857 (A.F.C.M.R. 1993) (finding plain error where delay, due to accused's multi-year AWOL, was lengthy, but repreferral would be barred by statute of limitations. 37 M.J. at 859 (A.F.C.M.R. 1993)).

[353] 52 M.J. 209 (C.A.A.F. 1999).

[354] Applying the Supreme Court's *Barker v. Wingo*, 407 U.S. 514 (1972) factors, the Court concluded that no speedy trial violation had taken place and decided that the case did not "present an appropriate vehicle form resolving the relationship between the rule and the statute." 52 M.J. at 212.

[355] 52 M.J. at 211.

[356] *See, e.g.*, United States v. Sloan, 48 C.M.R. 211, 213 (C.M.A. 1974) and cases cited therein.

[357] 48 C.M.R. 211, 213 (C.M.A. 1974).

[358] 48 C.M.R. at 213–14 (C.M.A. 1974).

[359] *See* Section 17-82.00.

[360] It is true that a guilty plea presumably negates a claim that specific prejudice has been suffered of a nature that would affect the ability to defend, if one determines that the outcome rather than the process is determinative. However, the right to a speedy trial quite clearly is concerned with factors other than avoiding the wrongful conviction of the innocent.

[361] *See* United States v. Pruitt, 41 M.J. 739 (N.M. Crim. App. 1994), *citing* United States v. Cornelius, 37 M.J. 622 (A.C.M.R. 1993).

(Rel.3—1/07 Pub.62410)

Article 10 protections is another matter. In *United States v. Mizgala*, [362] the Court of Appeals for the Armed Forces noted that its "cases involving waiver and unconditional guilty pleas have vacillated." Conceding that a guilty plea waived speedy trial claims under Rule 707 and the Sixth Amendment, the court then opined that: that "a *litigated* speedy trial motion under Article 10 is not waived by a subsequent unconditional guilty plea." [363] The court found dispositive "the legislative importance given to a speedy trial under the UCMJ and the unique nature of the protections of Article 10." [364] Given the express language of the court, the effect of a guilty plea without a prior speedy trial motion remains unclear.

Statutory and constitutional efficacy are different matters, and in 1999, in *United States v. Birge*, [365] the Court of Appeals for the Armed Forces went to some effort to avoid deciding whether a guilty plea waives an Article 10 violation.

§ 17-84.00 Plea Bargains

Under current precedent, the convening authority cannot require the defendant to waive the right to a speedy trial or agree not to raise the issue at trial as part of a negotiated agreement with a convening authority. [366] Such an agreement is "contrary to public policy and void." [367] Given the changing perspective of the Court of Appeals as to the scope of military plea bargaining, it may well be that soon this too will be negotiable. [368]

§ 17-90.00 CONSEQUENCES OF VIOLATING THE SPEEDY TRIAL RIGHT

The only remedy for a violation of the right to a speedy trial, whether constitutional, statutory, or under the Rules for Courts-Martial, is dismissal. [369] There is no requirement for the defense to establish prejudice in order to have the charges dismissed for a violation of the rule. [370]

---

[362] 61 M.J. 122, 126 (C.A.A.F. 2005).

[363] 61 M.J. at 127 (C.A.A.F. 2005) (emphasis added). Although the court wrote, "we hold," the quoted language technically is dictum as the court also concluded that no Article 10 error took place.

[364] 61 M.J. at 126.

[365] 52 M.J. at 212.

[366] United States v. Cummings, 38 C.M.R. 174 (C.M.A. 1968).

[367] 38 C.M.R. at 177 (C.M.A. 1968).

[368] *See* Section 12-25.00 *et seq.*

[369] Strunk v. United States, 412 U.S. 434 (1973); United States v. Burton, 44 C.M.R. 166 (C.M.A. 1971); R.C.M. 707(d).

[370] United States v. Kuelker, 20 M.J. 715 (N.M.C.M.R. 1985).

The 1991 amendment of Rule 707 created a dismissal without prejudice:

(d) *Remedy.* A failure to comply with the right to a speedy trial will result in dismissal of the affected charges. This dismissal will be with or without prejudice to the government's right to reinstitute court-martial proceedings against the accused for the same offense at a later date. The charges must be dismissed with prejudice where the accused has been deprived of his or her constitutional right to a speedy trial. In determining whether to dismiss charges with or without prejudice, the court shall consider among others, each of the following factors: the seriousness of the offense; the facts and circumstances of the case that lead to dismissal; the impact of a reprosecution on the administration of justice; and the prejudice to the accused. [371]

When determining whether a decision to dismiss without prejudice is error, an abuse of discretion standard will be applied. [372]

Rule 707(d) attempts to create a dismissal without prejudice even for violations of Article 10 of the Uniform Code. This was a significant departure from prior case law. Should the *Burton 90-day rule be reinstated,* [373] for example, a dismissal is mandated if the accused is held in pretrial confinement for more than ninety days after subtracting ninety days notwithstanding this proposed change. In any event, it is unclear what purpose is served by introducing the civilian concept of a dismissal without prejudice.

§ 17-100.00 LITIGATION OF SPEEDY TRIAL MOTIONS

§ 17-101.00 Preparation for Litigation

Although it is apparent that it is impossible to prepare for all of the vicissitudes of litigation, counsel can, to a large extent, prepare for the litigation of speedy trial motions. At a minimum, careful records should be kept of any matter that might affect the issue and its date, [374] and possible agreements or requirements

---

[371] Executive Order 12767, Amendments to the *Manual for Courts-Martial, United States,* 1984 (June 27, 1991).

[372] United States v. Greig, 44 M.J. 356 (C.A.A.F. 1996) (would not address dismissal without prejudice for untried charges); United States v. Edmond, 41 M.J. 419, 420–22 (C.A.A.F. 1995) (applying civilian precedent and commenting that in *United States v. Taylor,* 487 U.S. 326, 338–39 (1988), the court noted that it would examine the following factors: "truly neglectful" government "attitudes"; intentional versus "isolated unwitting violation[s]; excuses for the delay; and responsibility for the delay . . . ." The court also observed that "The Federal Courts have looked at similar factors, such as 'intentional dilatory conduct,' . . .; a 'pattern of neglect,' . . .; and simple inadvertence." Applying these factors, the court held there was no abuse of discretion in refusing to dismiss the charges with prejudice); United States v. Crouch, 84 F.3d 1497 (5th Cir. 1996) (en banc) (due process violation requires showing a of "actual, substantial prejudice").

[373] *See* Section 17-50.00.

[374] *See* Section 17-102.00.

(Rel.3—1/07   Pub.62410)

that might affect the trial date should be recorded in writing. The defense should, of course, demand trial in writing as early as possible. The Court of Military Appeals has stated:

> It is heartening to see the practice develop where the trial counsel feels obliged and the trial judge feels empowered to have the Government offer its grounds for delay *before* the delay is taken, in the form of a motion for continuance, thereby involving judicial authority and judicial discretion properly at an early stage. [375]

Rule 707(c) now mandates formal action to obtain delays.

§ 17-102.00   Litigation

The speedy trial issue may be raised initially either by serving a request for dismissal on the convening authority or by a motion to dismiss [376] at trial. In addition, the military judge may, upon examining the charge sheet as to the date of the offense or the date of pretrial restraint, raise the issue sua sponte. This may be desirable because a failure to assert a speedy trial motion at trial may not necessarily constitute waiver when a violation of due process is raised. [377] At trial, the issue is litigated at an Article 39(a) session prior to the plea. For ease of submission to the trial judge, counsel ordinarily should stipulate to a chronology of those landmark dates that are uncontested, [378] while contesting the others. Some of the common dates that should be included in such a chronology are:

> Date of offense or discovery of offense; Start of law enforcement or command investigation; Date and nature of pretrial restraint; Appointment of defense counsel or request for counsel; Completion of police investigation; Preferral of charges; Reading of charges to the accused; Appointment of Article 32 investigating officer; First available hearing date for defense counsel; Defense request for delay in the Article 32 hearing; Completion of Article 32 investigation; Article 32 investigation received by summary court-martial-convening authority; Receipt in office of staff judge advocate; Referral; Date government ready to proceed after referral; Date the case was docketed.

Other possible dates include:

> Apprehension of defendant; Request for psychiatric examination; Request for overseas witnesses; Demand from defense for speedy trial and any response thereto; Submission of request for administrative discharge if delay requested pending outcome; Other misconduct committed by the accused; Deposition of unavailable witness; Identification of informant if

---

[375] United States v. Johnson, 3 M.J. 143, 149–50 n.21 (C.M.A. 1977) (emphasis in original).

[376] R.C.M. 905(a).

[377] *See* Section 17-82.00.

[378] *See* United States v. Cole, 3 M.J. 220 (C.M.A. 1977) for an excellent example of a chronology; this one by then Major, now Colonel, Howard Eggers.

(Rel.3—1/07   Pub.62410)

requested by defense; Operational demands (e.g., date of vessel deployment); Diversion of investigative personnel; Employment of civilian counsel; Release from pretrial restraint; Request for trial on all known charges; Date of subpoena of foreign witnesses.

It is not enough for the prosecution to present a chronology at the trial level. It must also be established that the alleged circumstances *"contributed to or caused the delay."*[379]

As with many motions, once the issue is raised by the defense counsel, or by the military judge sua sponte, the government has the burden[380] to establish by a preponderance of the evidence[381] that the accused's right to a speedy trial was not violated. When litigating a speedy trial motion, the defense should ensure that it has indicated with some specificity the legal grounds upon which the motion is based. Otherwise, the motion may be resolved without adequate attention to the particular legal basis counsel intended to rely upon.

§ 17-110.00 APPEAL

§ 17-111.00 In General

If the issue has been raised at trial, the defense may appeal the denial of a speedy trial motion on the same basis as any other claimed trial error.[382] To assist the appellate courts, the military judge should set forth the reasoning for the ruling.[383] The standard of appellate review is de novo for both Article 10[384] and Rule 707[385] issues.

Refusing to hold that the trial judge erred as a matter of law by holding the government accountable for a period of time under Rule 707, the Court of Military Appeals, in *United States v. Burris*,[386] indicated that, unless the ruling dismissing charges was unsupported by the evidence of record or was clearly erroneous, it would not reverse the trial judge on appeal.[387]

---

[379] United States v. Johnson, 3 M.J. 143, 149 (C.M.A. 1977) (emphasis in the original). *See also* United States v. Henderson, 1 M.J. 421, 424–25 (C.M.A. 1976).

[380] R.C.M. 905(c). United States v. Brown, 28 C.M.R. 64, 69 (C.M.A. 1959).

[381] 28 C.M.R. 64, 69 (C.M.A. 1959).

[382] *See* § 17-80.00 for the waiver effect of not raising a speedy trial issue at trial with or without a subsequent guilty plea.

[383] 28 C.M.R. 64, 69 (C.M.A. 1959).

[384] United States v. Cooper, 58 M.J. 54, 59 (C.A.A.F. 2003).

[385] United States v. Doty, 51 M.J. 464, 465 (C.A.A.F. 1999).

[386] 21 M.J. 140 (C.M.A. 1985).

[387] 21 M.J. at 144 (C.M.A. 1985).

(Rel.3—1/07 Pub.62410)

In the ordinary case, extraordinary relief would not lie, because the normal appellate process would be considered sufficient.[388]

§ 17-112.00   Government Appeal

In determining whether relief was available to the government[389] to reverse a trial judge's grant of such a motion with its resulting dismissal, the Court of Military Appeals held in 1981 that:

> A decision adverse to the government [dismissing charges] is not open to review and reversal by superior judicial authority. . . . Neither is the ruling open to review and reversal on a petition for extraordinary relief when it has such arguable support in the evidence as not to appear capricious or whimsical . . . [E]xtraordinary relief . . . will not lie because from "the facts of record, another judge, might perhaps, reach a different conclusion as to the unreasonableness of the delay."[390]

In 1987, however, the court held that on the facts presented, the military judge had failed to rely on *any* evidence of record to support his findings, and that, accordingly, a government appeal under Article 62 of the Uniform Code[391] was possible.[392] As amended in 1991,[393] Rule 707(b)(3)(C) expressly contemplates government appeals, thus apparently mooting most disputes.

§ 17-120.00   REHEARINGS

Pursuant to Rule for Courts-Martial 707(b)(3)(D) when "a rehearing is ordered or authorized by an appellate court, a new 120-day time period . . . shall begin on the date that the responsible convening authority receives the record of trial and the opinion authorizing or directing a rehearing." In *United States v.*

---

[388] *Cf.* United States v. MacDonald, 435 U.S. 850 (1978). Pascascio v. Fischer, 34 M.J. 996, 1002 (A.C.M.R. 1992) (*citing* United States v. MacDonald, *above*, and rejecting the theory that speedy trial involves a right not to be tried, the court held that a writ of mandamus, the functional military equivalent of a civilian interlocutory appeal, isn't available for denial of a speedy trial motion; extraordinary relief may be proper for cases involving a motion denial that "constitutes a usurpation of judicial power or amounts to a recurring legal error . . ."). Mandamus is appropriate for a speedy trial case "in instances where the lower court ignored precedent clearly on point or failed to correctly apply the Rules for Courts-Martial to a clear case of government negligence." Evans v. Kilroy, 33 M.J. 730, 733 (A.F.C.M.R. 1991).

[389] Dettinger v. United States, 7 M.J. 216 (C.M.A. 1979). Although the court in *Dettinger* recognized the possibility of such relief to the government, it found the facts insufficient to grant it.

[390] United States v. Strow, 11 M.J. 75 (C.M.A. 1981) (Misc. Docket) (citations omitted but *quoting* United States v. Dettinger, *above* note 233, 7 M.J. at 224).

[391] *See also* R.C.M. 908.

[392] United States v. Bradford, 25 M.J. 181, 184–85 (C.M.A. 1987). It would seem that ordinarily a speedy trial resolution must be a mixed question of law and fact.

[393] Executive Order 12767, Amendments to the *Manual for Courts-Martial, United States* 1984 (June 27, 1991).

(Rel.3—1/07 Pub.62410)

Becker, [394] the majority held that the Rule applies to "sentence-only" rehearings, as well as to complete ones. However, the usual remedy for a speedy trial violation, dismissal, is inapplicable. Instead a rehearing violation requires only sentence relief. [395]

[394] 53 M.J. 229 (C.A.A.F. 2000).

[395] 53 M.J. at 232.

CHAPTER 18

MOTIONS

§ **18-10.00 INTRODUCTION**
  § 18-11.00   **Definition and Form**
  § 18-12.00   **Types of Motions**
  § 18-13.00   **Timing**
  § 18-14.00   **Litigation of Motions**
      § 18-14.10 — The Burdens of Production and Proof
          § 18-14.11 — — Burden of Production
          § 18-14.12 — — Burden of Proof
      § 18-14.20 — Litigation
      § 18-14.30 — Ruling
          § 18-14.31 — — Timing
          § 18-14.32 — — Essential Findings of Fact
          § 18-14.33 — — Resolution by the Fact Finder
      § 18-14.40 — Reconsideration and Appeal
§ **18-20.00 MOTIONS TO DISMISS**
  § 18-21.00   **In General**
      § 18-21.10 — Definition
      § 18-21.20 — Effects of Granted Motions to Dismiss
      § 18-21.30 — Specific Motions in the Rules for Courts-Martial
  § 18-22.00   **Lack of Jurisdiction**
  § 18-23.00   **Failure to Allege an Offense**
  § 18-24.00   **Speedy Trial**
  § 18-25.00   **Running of the Statute of Limitations**
  § 18-26.00   **Double Jeopardy, Collateral Estoppel, Multiplicity, and Prior Nonjudicial Punishment**
  § 18-27.00   **Immunity**
  § 18-28.00   **Command Influence**
  § 18-29.00   **Other Constitutionally Based Motions**
      § 18-29.10 — Due Process
      § 18-29.20 — Vindictive Prosecution
      § 18-29.30 — Prosecutorial Misconduct
§ **18-30.00 MOTIONS FOR APPROPRIATE RELIEF**
  § 18-31.00   **In General**
  § 18-32.00   **Continuances**
  § 18-33.00   **Correction or Clarification of the Charges or Specifications**
      § 18-33.10 — Amendment
      § 18-33.20 — Severance of a Duplicitous Specification

(Rel.3—1/07 Pub.62410)

§ 18-33.30 — Bill of Particulars

§ 18-34.00   Change of Venue

§ 18-35.00   Motion in Limine

§ 18-36.00   Requests for Investigative and Expert Assistance

§ 18-37.00   Exclusion of Witnesses

§ 18-38.00   Severance of Co-Accused

§ 18-39.00   Severance of Offenses

§   18-40.00 SUPPRESSION MOTIONS

§ 18-41.00   In General

§ 18-42.00   The Disclosure Requirement

§ 18-43.00   Timing

§ 18-44.00   The Need for Specificity

§ 18-45.00   Litigation

§ 18-46.00   Rulings

§   18-50.00 MOTIONS FOR FINDINGS OF NOT GUILTY

§ 18-10.00   INTRODUCTION

§ 18-11.00   Definition and Form

A motion is nothing more or less than an application to the court for specified relief.[1] Because the convening authority is a judicial figure in military law, motions may be directed to both the convening authority and the military judge.[2] The Rules for Courts-Martial provide that a motion "may be oral or, at the discretion of the military judge, written" and "shall state the grounds upon which

---

[1] R.C.M. 905(a).

[2] R.C.M. 905(j) provides:

Except as otherwise provided in this Manual, any matters which may be resolved without trial of the general issue of guilt may be submitted by a party to the convening authority before trial for decision. Submission of such matter to the convening authority is not, except as otherwise provided in this Manual, required, and is, in any event without prejudice to the renewal of the issue by timely motion before the military judge.

Speedy trial motions (Chapter 17), discovery (Chapter 11), and witness requests (Chapter 20) are frequently addressed to the convening authority as are requests for a mental examination of the accused. R.C.M. 706(b). Under R.C.M. 906(b)(1), a motion for a continuance may only be made to the military judge. It should be noted that R.C.M. 905(j) gives the convening authority and the military judge concurrent authority to dispose of motions after referral of charges. *See* Commentary to R.C.M. 905(j). Prior to referral, the military judge customarily will lack jurisdiction to rule on motions. *See generally* Chapter 15.

Those provisions of the R.C.M. that deal with the form of motions (R.C.M. 905(a), (h)) apply only to submissions to the military judge. Accordingly, motions to the convening authority may be either written or oral. However, as a matter of practicality, such motions usually should be written, if only to preserve them for the record.

(Rel.3—1/07 Pub.62410)

it is made and . . . the ruling or relief sought."[3] Unlike Federal Rule of Criminal Procedure 12(b) (now Rule 47(b), from which part of Rule 905(a) was taken),[4] Rule 905 clearly makes oral motions the norm, with written motions being subject to the judge's discretion.[5] Pursuant to Rule for Courts-Martial 905(h), written motions may, when appropriate, "be supported by affidavits, with service and opportunity to reply to the opposing party."

§ 18-12.00 Types of Motions

Although the divisions are not necessarily formal ones, motions are customarily divided[6] into:

Motions to dismiss[7]

Motions for appropriate relief[8]

Suppression motions, and[9]

Motions for findings of not guilty[10]

§ 18-13.00 Timing

Motions to the trial court[11] are governed by Rule for Courts-Martial 905(b), which states:

---

[3] R.C.M. 905(a).

[4] The Analysis of R.C.M. 905(a) states that this portion of the Rule "is based on the second sentence of paragraph 67c of MCM, 1969 (rev.), although to be consistent with Federal practice . . . express authority for the military judge to exercise discretion over the form of motions has been added." Analysis of the Rules for Courts-Martial, MCM, 2005, A21-53.

[5] *Compare* R.C.M. 905(a) ("Motions may be oral or, at the discretion of the military judge, written.") *with* MCM, 1969 para. 67c. It may be that this result was not intended, especially in light of R.C.M. 905(h), which states that "[w]ritten motions may be submitted to the military judge after referral." However, both the text of the Rule and a comparison with Fed. R. Crim. P. 12(b) as it existed when the Rules for Courts-Martial were written yield this result. The civilian federal rule states that "[m]otions may be written or oral at the discretion of the trial judge," expressing no preference, while the military rule appears to permit written motions only when the judge, in his or her discretion, permits them. If this conclusion is accurate, the result is unfortunate. Although judicial efficiency is to be encouraged, especially in the armed forces where unnecessary delay might affect operational readiness, the preference for oral motions appears unnecessary and may encourage sloppy practice. Additionally, it may be employed to limit the administrative support available to counsel. Rule 47(b) of the current Federal Rules of Criminal Procedure provides that "A motion—except when made during a trial or hearing—must be in writing, unless the court permits the party to make the motion by other means."

[6] *See, e.g.,* Discussion to R.C.M. 905(a).

[7] *See* Section 18-20.00.

[8] *See* Section 18-30.00.

[9] *See* Section 18-40.00.

[10] *See* Section 18-50.00.

[11] *See above* note 2 for motions made to the convening authority.

(Rel.3—1/07 Pub.62410)

Any defense, objection, or request which is capable of determination without the trial of the general issue of guilt may be raised before trial. The following must be raised before a plea is entered:

(1) Defenses or objections based on defects (other than jurisdictional defects) in the preferral, forwarding, investigation, or referral of charges;[12]

(2) Defenses or objections based on defects in the charges and specifications (other than failure to show jurisdiction or to charge an offense, which objections shall be resolved by the military judge at any time during the pendency of the proceedings);

(3) Motions to suppress evidence;[13]

(4) Motions for discovery under Rule for Courts-Martial 701 or for production of witnesses;

(5) Motions for severance of charges or accused; or

(6) Objection based on denial of request for individual military counsel or for retention of detailed defense counsel when individual military counsel has been granted.

An untimely motion results in waiver,[14] but military appellate courts can be hostile to what they may view as unnecessary refusals to hear motions solely

---

[12] *E.g.*, United States v. Straight, 42 M.J. 244, 247 (C.A.A.F. 1995) (waiver of any error in capital referral for rape).

[13] Actually this is an overstatement. The Analysis of the Rule states that this subsection "is consistent with Mil. R. Evid. 304(d)(2)(A); 311(d)(2)(A); 321(c)(2)(A)." Those Rules, however, require that suppression motions be made before plea only when the evidence upon which they are being made was previously disclosed by the prosecution under Mil. R. Evid. 304(d)(1); 311(d)(1); 321(c)(1). Given the intent expressed in the Commentary to R.C.M. 905(b), the Rule obviously applies only to those circumstances in which disclosure has been made.

[14] R.C.M. 905(e) provides:

Failure by a party to raise defenses or objections or to make motions or requests which must be made before pleas are entered under subsection (b) of this rule shall constitute waiver. The military judge for good cause shown may grant relief from the waiver.

Other motions, requests, defenses, or objections, except lack of jurisdiction or failure of a charge to allege an offense, must be raised before the court-martial is adjourned for that case and, unless otherwise provided in this *Manual*, failure to do so shall constitute waiver.

R.C.M. 905(e) was amended in 1990 to insert "motions" in the first sentence "to clarify that 'requests' and 'objections' include 'motions.' " Changes to the Analysis accompanying Executive Order No. 12708, Amendments to the Manual for Courts-Martial, United States, 1998. *See, e.g.*, United States v. Allen, 59 M.J. 478, 483 (C.A.A.F. 2004) ("Under Rule for Courts-Martial 907(b)(2)(D)(ii), an allegation of improper use of immunized testimony in the prosecutorial decision constitutes a waivable basis for a motion to dismiss.") (reviewed for plain error); United States v. Richter, 51 M.J. 213, 223-24 (C.A.A.F. 1999) (failure to allege at trial possible command coercion in preferral of charges by commander was waived); United States v. Abrams, 50 M.J. 361 (C.A.A.F. 1999) (failure to attach and seal military records of key government witness required reversal to augment record-failure to request attachment at the time of authentication or at the Court of Criminal

(Rel.3—1/07 Pub.62410)

for reasons of untimeliness.[15] However, jurisdictional motions may be made at any time,[16] as may motions attacking the pleadings for failure to allege an offense.[17] Motions are normally disposed of either at an Article 39(a) session called for that purpose or immediately after arraignment.[18]

§ 18-14.00 Litigation of Motions

§ 18-14.10 The Burdens of Production and Proof

§ 18-14.11 Burden of Production

The general rule is that the burden of production[19] is on the party desirous of raising an issue.[20] As to the burden of proof,[21] the Rules for Courts-Martial

---

Appeals does not waive issue); United States v. Fahey, 33 M.J. 920 (A.C.M.R. 1991) (waiver of motion to sever). Local rules of court "cannot establish additional requirements that override rules prescribed by the President in the *Manual for Courts-Martial*. United States v. Norman, 42 M.J. 501, 503 (A. Crim. App. 1995) (technically dictum as error was harmless) (trial judge erred by refusing to hear Rule 304 suppression motion because defense failed to serve motion within the five-day local court rule requirement).

[15] United States v. Rozier, 41 M.J. 707 (C.A.A.F. 1995) (Refusing to hear an Article 13 commingling with sentenced prisoners motion on timeliness grounds was an abuse of discretion). This makes sense given the military courts' special concern that defense counsel supply competent representation. It makes little sense to sustain a judge's refusal to hear a motion due to counsel's error only to then reverse the conviction for counsel's inadequacy.

[16] United States v. Henderson, 59 M.J. 350 (C.A.A.F. 2004) (failure to object to fatal jurisdictional defect due to referral of capital offense by special court-martial convening authority of no consequence).

[17] R.C.M. 905(e), *above* note 14; R.C.M. 907(b)(1).

[18] Arraignment consists of the request for a plea. *See generally* Chapter 16. The Analysis of R.C.M. 905(c) indicates that then Fed. R. Crim. P. 12(c) (generally providing that the court "may, at arraignment or . . . thereafter . . . set a time for the making of pretrial motions or requests. . . .") was not adopted because, unlike civilian practice, arraignment in courts-martial "usually occurs only a short time before trial and in many cases it occurs the same day as trial." Ordinarily, motions will be litigated prior to plea. *See* R.C.M. 905(d).

[19] This is also known as the burden of going forward. It is the responsibility of a party to raise an issue in order for it to be litigated.

[20] *E.g.,* United States v. Lewis, 46 M.J. 338, 342 (C.A.A.F. 1997) (burden on defense to show "court stacking"). This is usually a matter of common sense. It is not a necessary rule, however. Until the advent of the Military Rule of Evidence, for example, the prosecution had both the burden of production and the burden of proof to show that an admission made by the accused had been voluntarily obtained by the government. If the government did not go forward with that evidence *sua sponte*, the evidence was inadmissible. This rule survives in part in those Military Rules of Evidence governing suppression motions, inasmuch as they expressly permit the military judge in certain circumstances to authorize the accused to enter a "general motion to suppress or general objection." *See, e.g.*, Mil. R. Evid. 304(d)(3). In such a case, the defense need only make the motion, and the burden of proof immediately shifts to the prosecution.

[21] This is also known as the burden of persuasion.

(Rel.3—1/07 Pub.62410)

specify: "Except as otherwise provided in this *Manual* the burden of persuasion on any factual issue the resolution of which is necessary to decide a motion shall be on the moving party."[22] The exceptions provided in the *Manual* are suppression motions[23] and motions alleging "lack of jurisdiction, denial of the right to speedy trial under Rule for Courts-Martial 707, or the running of the statute of limitations," in which case the burden of proof is on the government.[24] In addition, once raised, the prosecution has the burden of proving that the accused is competent to stand trial[25] and the burden of negating unlawful command influence.[26]

§ 18-14.12   Burden of Proof

Rule for Courts-Martial 905(c)(1) provides that: "Unless otherwise provided in this Manual, the burden of proof on any factual issue the resolution of which is necessary to decide a motion shall be by a preponderance of the evidence."

The primary exceptions to this burden of proof are three categories of suppression motions in which the government must prove legality by clear and convincing evidence.[27] In addition, once adequately raised by "some evidence,"[28] the government must negate the possibility of unlawful command influence by proof beyond a reasonable doubt.[29]

§ 18-14.20   Litigation

The Rules for Courts-Martial inherently provide for two different procedures for the litigation of motions. Rule for Courts-Martial 905(h) permits counsel to submit written motions[30] accompanied by affidavits. The Rule expressly states that written "motions may be disposed of before arraignment and without a

---

[22] R.C.M. 905(c)(2)(A).

[23] Mil. R. Evid. 304(e), 311(e), 321(d) place the burden of proof on the government once the defense has raised the issue.

[24] R.C.M. 905(c)(2)(B).

[25] R.C.M. 908(b)(2).

[26] *Cf.* United States v. Thomas, 22 M.J. 388, 394 (C.M.A. 1986), *cert. denied*, 479 U.S. 1085 (1987). *See generally* Section 18-28.00.

[27] Mil. R. Evid. 313(b) (certain inspections); 314(e)(5) (consent searches); 321(d)(2) (allegedly unreliable identification).

[28] United States v. Ayers, 54 M.J. 85, 95 (C.A.A.F. 2000).

[29] United States v. Ayala, 43 M.J. 296, 300 (C.A.A.F. 1995) (trial standard); *Cf.* United States v. Wallace, 39 M.J. 284 (C.A.A.F. 1994) (no unlawful command influence where superior commander suggested that subordinate reconsider recommendation in light of additional information); United States v. Thomas, 22 M.J. 388, 394 (C.M.A. 1986), *cert. denied*, 479 U.S. 1085 (1987) (appellate standard). *See also* United States v. Ayers, 54 M.J. 85 (C.A.A.F. 2000) (appellant failed to establish command influence by senior leadership in Aberdeen cases).

[30] *But see above* note 5 and accompanying text.

(Rel.3—1/07   Pub.62410)

session." Accordingly, the military judge may, with the consent of counsel,[31] resolve motions out of court. Presumably, this is not likely to happen often for matters of importance[32] and then only if there is no significant issue of fact. Absent this procedure, which places a premium on written briefs, the normal procedure for motion litigation will be for counsel to present and respond to motions in open court at an Article 39(a) session.

Although the specific procedure to be followed in motion litigation is not mandated by the Rules for Courts-Martial, it is apparent that after the moving party has made the motion, the military judge should determine whether the opposing party disagrees with the moving party's view of the facts. If not, the motion should be resolved purely on the law, unless the judge *sua sponte* decides that an evidentiary presentation is necessary. If a factual difference of consequence exists, however, an evidentiary hearing must be held. Unless the party holding the burden of production[33] can raise the issue solely by a recitation of the alleged facts, rather than by the presentation of evidence,[34] the moving party should then present evidence on the issue, with the opposing party's presentation, if any, following. As noted above,[35] the party holding the burden of production normally has the burden of proof or persuasion as well. When that is not the case, the moving party may prefer to present just enough evidence to raise the issue properly and shift the burden of proof to the opposition.

The rules of evidence, including the hearsay rule, will normally apply to motion litigation. However, "the military judge is not bound by the rules of evidence except those with respect to privileges" when the judge resolves "[p]reliminary questions concerning the qualification of a person to be a witness, the existence of a privilege, the admissibility of evidence, an application for a continuance, or the availability of a witness."[36]

Although the military judge has the discretion to control the sequence and number of arguments, customarily counsel for the party with the burden of proof will open, and counsel for the opposing party will respond.

---

[31] The remainder of R.C.M. 905(h) gives counsel the right to an Article 39(a) session. As a result, the judge cannot determine motions out of court if counsel desire to prevent such a procedure.

[32] It is a rare counsel who is prepared to forego oral argument.

[33] *See* Section 18-14.11.

[34] This is the case for suppression motions. Analysis of Mil. R. Evid. 304(d)(3), Manual for Courts-Martial, 2005, A22-11 and A22-12.

[35] *See* Section 18-14.10.

[36] Mil. R. Evid. 104(a).

§ 18-14.30   Ruling

§ 18-14.31   Timing

Rule for Courts-Martial 905(d) provides in part:

> A motion made before pleas are entered shall be determined before pleas are entered unless, if not otherwise prohibited by this Manual, the military judge for good cause orders that determination be deferred until trial of the general issue or after findings, but no such determination shall be deferred if a party's right to review or appeal is adversely affected.

Based upon then Federal Rule of Criminal Procedure 12(e),[37] this provision parallels similar requirements for suppression motions expressly set forth in the Military Rules of Evidence.[38] Although neither the Rules for Courts-Martial nor their Discussion or Commentary define "good cause" or explain when the "party's right to . . . appeal is adversely affected," it is clear that a ruling may not be deferred until after plea when the plea would waive the motion.[39] Accordingly, the military judge may not defer ruling on any motion that would be waived by a guilty plea unless the accused has advised the judge that a not-guilty plea will be entered regardless of the motion's result.

§ 18-14.32   Essential Findings of Fact[40]

Rule for Courts-Martial 905(d) requires the military judge to *sua sponte* "state the essential findings on the record" when "factual issues are involved," and failure to make essential findings can be reversible error.[41] Accordingly, counsel would be well advised to submit prepared findings of fact for the judge to adopt. The military judge need not, of course, accept such a proffer.

Because essential findings are tied to motion resolution, normally they must be made before pleas are entered:[42]

> One of the purposes of the requirement for essential findings is to preserve the government's right to appeal under Article 62(a)(1). Note that unlike

---

[37] R.C.M. 905(d) Analysis.

[38] Mil. R. Evid. 304(d)(4); 311(d)(4); 321(f).

[39] *See, e.g.*, Analysis of the 1980 Amendments to the *Manual for Courts-Martial*, Analysis of Rule 304(d)(4), now available at MCM, 2005 A22-12. Accordingly, a judge may not defer ruling in the hope that the accused, faced with a choice between pleading guilty and retaining a plea bargain or pleading not guilty and giving up such a bargain but obtaining a ruling, will be compelled to plead guilty. As to "good cause" in the context of motions in limine, *see* United States v. Itelweg, 32 M.J. 129, 133 (C.M.A. 1991) (questioning whether there is a meaningful distinction between "good cause" and judicial discretion).

[40] *generally* Section 14-64.30.

[41] United States v. Butterbaugh, 21 M.J. 1019 (N.M.C.M.R. 1985) (mere general resolution of speedy-trial motion by trial judge without essential findings required reversal).

[42] R.C.M. 905(d).

normal practice, under Article 62 the Courts of Military Review [now the Courts of Criminal Appeals] can hear only questions of law; they are bound by the trial court's factual determinations. As appealable motions concern matters that can terminate trial before presentation of evidence on the merits (*e.g.*, major suppression motions, speedy trial motions, double jeopardy motions), normally the motion must be resolved prior to entrance of plea. R.C.M. 905(d) declares that a motion "determination shall not be deferred if a party's right to review or appeal is adversely affected.[43]

The minimum content of essential findings is uncertain. In 1985, the Navy-Marine Court of Military Review wrote:

[A] military judge must, whether the motion be granted or denied, set forth: (1) the specific facts found based on the totality of the evidence introduced, which are relevant to and support his legal decision — not merely recite the evidence presented or state that the facts are not in dispute; (2) the legal basis for his decision; and (3) any other statement which would serve to clarify his reason(s) for decision in order that an appellate court may determine whether he applied — or misapplied — appropriate legal standards and/or presumptions and whether his decision amounts to an abuse of discretion. Additionally, it is of no moment that the evidence adduced at trial on the motion is not in dispute, for it is the importance of the specific facts found to support the ruling and the use made of those facts which is at the core of requiring a military judge to set forth his reasons for decision.[44]

Such a broad content may be desirable, but it is not probable that it is actually required.[45]

§ 18-14.33 Resolution by the Fact Finder

Like the other motion rules, Rule for Courts-Martial 905(d) requires the military judge to determine and rule upon all motions.[46] A number of circumstances exist in which the judge's responsibility to so rule either duplicates or is merged into the general responsibility of the fact finder to determine the guilt or innocence of the accused. When the accused claims that conviction for a lesser-included offense is barred by the statute of limitations, for example, the resolution of the motion must await the decision of the fact finder as to the guilt of the

---

[43] Fredric Lederer, *Special, Essential and Similar Findings,* (32d Military Judge Course TJAGSA, 5 June 1989) (based in part on similar materials by then Major David Schlueter).

[44] United States v. Postle, 20 M.J. 632, 640 (N.M.C.M.R. 1985). The Air Force appears to follow *Postle.* United States v. Reinecke, 30 M.J. 1010, 1015 (A.F.C.M.R.), *rev'd on other grounds sub nom* United States v. Stozier, 31 M.J. 283 (C.M.A. 1990). *See also* United States v. Reinecke, 31 M.J. 507, 509 n.* (A.F.C.M.R. 1990), *rev'd on other grounds,* 32 M.J. 63 (C.M.A. 1990).

[45] United States v. Ruhling, 28 M.J. 586, 592–93 (N.N.C.M.R. 1988) (as long as the record shows the correct application of law to the facts demonstrated in the record, the conviction should be upheld).

[46] R.C.M. 905(d). United States v. Bell, 25 M.J. 676 (A.C.M.R. 1987) (failure of judge to rule on a motion is an implied denial of the motion).

(Rel.3—1/07 Pub.62410)

accused of the lesser-included offense rather than the greater offense expressly charged.[47] A somewhat related problem is posed by a jurisdictional motion in which the salient factor is a fact that must be determined ultimately by the fact finder. If in personam jurisdiction is dependent upon the date the alleged offense was committed, for instance, resolution of the date of the offense would seem to be the responsibility of both the military judge for purposes of the motion, and the court members for purposes of the resolution of guilt.

The procedure to be used when such a motion is raised is unclear. It would appear improper for the military judge to abdicate in favor of the members when trial is with members. However, the issue should not be taken from the members either. Accordingly, the best solution would appear to be a compromise. When the motion to dismiss is dependent on facts to be established in the trial of the general issue, both the judge and the members should determine the facts in question, with the accused prevailing should either judge or members rule in his or her behalf. Procedurally, this could mean two separate hearings on the same issue. In the alternative, this would seem to be a proper situation for the judge to defer ruling, in which case the judge could consider the evidence introduced on the merits, receive the verdict of the members, and then enter a determination on the motion if the issue had not been rendered moot by the verdict.[48]

§ 18-14.40 Reconsideration and Appeal

In any motion determination, one party is apt to be a loser and desirous of obtaining a different result — not just because of the instant case, but also because the result may apply to subsequent trials.[49] Prior to the 1983 Military Justice Act, the only avenues available to secure relief, other than the usual defense appeal, were reconsideration or extraordinary relief.

Pursuant to Article 62(a) of the Uniform Code, Rule for Courts-Martial 905(f) provides that "the military judge may reconsider any ruling, other than one amounting to a finding of not guilty," *sua sponte*, or upon the request of any party. The convening authority may direct reconsideration when the military judge has dismissed a specification, but the final determination on such ruling is solely for the military judge.[50]

The government may file an interlocutory appeal from an adverse ruling by the military judge[51] on a motion that effectively terminates the proceedings with

---

[47] *See generally* Section 18-25.00.

[48] United States v. Griffith, 27 M.J. 42 (C.M.A. 1988) (judge may grant finding of not guilty after the court members return with finding of guilty). *See also* Section 18-50.00.

[49] *See generally* Section 18-26.00; R.C.M. 905(f).

[50] *See* United States v. Ware, 1 M.J. 282 (C.M.A. 1976). Reconsideration is thus not a substitute for a government appeal.

[51] R.C.M. 908. An adverse pretrial ruling by the convening authority normally may be renewed before the military judge. R.C.M. 905(j). *See generally* Chapter 25.

(Rel.3—1/07 Pub.62410)

respect to a charge or specification. The defense may be able to obtain the functional equivalent of an appeal by filing a petition for extraordinary relief with the Court of Criminal Appeals or the Court of Appeals if "good cause" is shown.[52] Extraordinary relief is not, however, a general substitute for an appeal and ordinarily will not be granted solely because the military judge erred.[53]

§ 18-20.00   MOTIONS TO DISMISS

§ 18-21.00   In General

§ 18-21.10   Definition

Rule for Courts-Martial 907(a) defines a motion to dismiss as "a request to terminate further proceedings as to one or more charges and specifications on grounds capable of resolution without trial of the general issue of guilt." Although accurate, this definition may be somewhat misleading. Some motions, especially those dealing with subject matter jurisdiction and the statute of limitations, may inherently require resolution of the same issues inherent in a determination of guilt or innocence.

§ 18-21.20   Effects of Granted Motions to Dismiss

Traditionally, military law has not distinguished between motions to dismiss granted with prejudice and those granted without prejudice. Given the nature of military law in general and the present Rules for Courts-Martial in particular, it would seem that with few, if any, exceptions, all dismissals, except one form of speedy trial dismissal, are ordered with prejudice,[54] although that terminology

---

[52] Court of Appeals R. 4(b)(1); R.C.M. 1204(a) Discussion. *See, e.g.,* Cooke v. Orser, 12 M.J. 335 (C.M.A. 1982) (writ of mandamus issued compelling the trial judge to dismiss charges against the accused because of a government promise of immunity); Dettinger v. United States, 7 M.J. 216 (C.M.A. 1979) (where the military judge granted a defense speedy-trial motion, the court, albeit denying relief, held that the court had jurisdiction to entertain and issue a writ of mandamus to the trial judge to, in effect, reverse a ruling). *See generally* Chapter 25.

[53] Dew v. United States, 48 M.J. 639 (A. Crim. App. 1998). *See generally* Chapter 25.

[54] This is not to say that a dismissal without prejudice is impossible — at least without reference to the Rules for Courts-Martial. *See, e.g.,* United States v. Doss, 15 M.J. 409, 412 n.6 (C.M.A. 1983). Arguably, the same result has been obtained via the withdrawal of charges from one court-martial with their later referral to a different tribunal. *See, e.g.,* United States v. Cook, 12 M.J. 448, 453–54 (C.M.A. 1982). Under R.C.M. 905(g), the question is likely to be: "What matter has been placed in issue and finally determined?" In United States v. Jackson, 15 M.J. 988 (N.M.C.M.R. 1983), *aff'd,* 20 M.J. 83 (C.M.A. 1985), for instance, the court dealt with a case in which the military judge at trial one had held that the statute of limitations required dismissal of charges while at trial two, utilizing a different and timely charge sheet, the judge held the prior ruling not binding. In *Jackson,* the appellate court held that the first determination had dealt solely with the effect of the statute of limitations based on the first charge sheet. Consequently, the determination had no effect on the second trial, which utilized a different charge sheet. The court

(Rel.3—1/07 Pub.62410)

is not used. Rule 707, Speedy Trial, is written in such a way as to authorize dismissals with and without prejudice.[55]

Rule for Courts-Martial 905(g) provides in relevant part that:

> Any matter put in issue and finally determined by a court-martial . . . may not be disputed by the United States in any other court-martial of the same accused, except that, when the offense(s) charged at one court-martial did not arise out of the same transaction as those charged at the court-martial at which the determination was made, a determination of law and the application of law to the facts may be disputed by the United States.

Thus, a dismissal remains the law of the case not only for a successor trial, but also in any other case involving the accused, so long as it arises "out of the same transaction." Military law does not permit a trial to be terminated by a dismissal only to be begun anew at a later time.[56]

§ 18-21.30 Specific Motions in the Rules for Courts-Martial

The specific types of motions to dismiss set forth in Rule for Courts-Martial 907(b), which are listed below, are illustrative only and are not exhaustive. Motions to dismiss include motions based upon:

> Lack of jurisdiction, Failure to allege an offense, Violation of the right to a speedy trial, Violation of the prohibition against double jeopardy, Violation of the prohibition against multiplicity for findings, Violation of the prohibition against former punishment, Violation of the prohibition against trial following transactional immunity, Violation of the prohibition against trial following a pardon,[57] Constructive condonation of desertion,[58] A defective specification,[59] Command influence, Violation of due process, Vindictive prohibition.

---

also could have looked to the specification rather than the charge sheet, in which case a different result would have followed. Although certainly unclear, Example (1) in the Discussion of R.C.M. 905(g) appears to look to the specification involved to determine the effect of a statute of limitations ruling.

[55] See Section 17-90.00.

[56] Once a specification is dismissed, for example, because it fails to allege an offense or because it suffers some procedural irregularity which renders it legally insufficient, it may not later be referred for trial in a corrected form R.C.M. 905(g) and Discussion. A different result may take place, depending upon the nature of the matter actually at issue and depending upon whether the specification has been withdrawn by the convening authority rather than dismissed.

[57] Rule for Courts-Martial 907(b)(2)(D)(1) requires that a charge or specification be dismissed on motion when "Prosecution is barred by . . . [a] pardon issued by the President."

[58] Rule for Courts-Martial 907(b)(2)(D)(iii) requires that the charge or specification be dismissed on motion when "constructive condonation of desertion [is] established by unconditional restoration to duty without trial of a deserter by a general court-martial convening authority who knew of the desertion." The Rule's predecessor provision, MCM, 1969 (rev. ed.) ¶ 68 *f*, added that:

> "If an officer exercising general court-martial jurisdiction has directed that a deserter be restored to duty but that he remain subject to trial for the offense, such a restoration is not a constructive condonation of desertion."

(Rel.3—1/07 Pub.62410)

§ 18-22.00   Lack of Jurisdiction[60]

Rule for Courts-Martial 907(b)(1) declares that "a charge or specification shall be dismissed at any stage of the proceedings" if "[t]he court-martial lacks jurisdiction to try the accused for the offense."[61] Consequently, a motion to dismiss lies if the government lacks either in personam[62] or subject-matter jurisdiction.[63] A motion to dismiss for lack of jurisdiction may also be made, alleging "that the court is not properly constituted because it was not convened by an official empowered to convene it"[64] or that it otherwise lacks jurisdiction over the accused[65] or offense.[66] A jurisdictional motion is not waivable and may be made at any time.[67]

§ 18-23.00   Failure to Allege an Offense

A motion to dismiss lies if the specification does not state an offense.[68] The motion is nonwaivable and may be made at any time.[69]

§ 18-24.00   Speedy Trial[70]

A motion to dismiss lies if the accused's right to a speedy trial under the Rules for Courts-Martial,[71] the Uniform Code of Military Justice,[72] or the Sixth

---

[59] Rule for Courts-Martial 907(b)(3) provides:

A specification may be dismissed upon timely motion by the accused if . . . the specification is so defective that it substantially misled the accused, and the military judge finds that, in the interest of justice, trial should proceed on [the] remaining charges and specifications without undue delay. . . .

[60] *See generally* Chapter 2.

[61] Analysis of R.C.M. 907(b).

[62] *See* Section 2-20.00.

[63] *See* Section 2-30.00.

[64] MCM, 1969 (rev. ed.) ¶ 68*b* (2). R.C.M. 907(b)(1)(A) is based on ¶ 68*b*, Analysis of R.C.M. 907(b)(1)(A). For the authority to convene different tribunals and their jurisdiction, *see* Chapters 8 and 13.

[65] A summary court-martial may not, for example, try an officer. U.C.M.J. art. 20. *See generally* Chapter 8.

[66] Neither a summary nor a special court-martial may try an accused for a capital offense. U.C.M.J. arts. 19, 20; United States v. Henderson, 59 M.J. 350 (C.A.A.F. 2004). *See generally* Chapter 8.

[67] R.C.M. 907(b)(1). *See also* Nancy Jean King, *Priceless Process: Nonnegotiable Features of Criminal Litigation*, 47 U.C.L.A. L. Rev. 113, 143-147 (1999) (many courts permit waiver of jurisdiction).

[68] R.C.M. 907(b)(1)(B). *See generally* Chapter 6.

[69] R.C.M. 907(b)(1). *See also* Nancy Jean King, *Priceless Process: Nonnegotiable Features of Criminal Litigation*, 47 U.C.L.A. L. Rev. 113, 176-178 (1999) (many courts permit waiver of error that indictment is facially unconstitutional).

[70] *See generally* Chapter 17.

[71] R.C.M. 707.

(Rel.3—1/07 Pub.62410)

Amendment has been violated.[73] Under the Rules for Courts-Martial, a speedy trial motion is ordinarily waived if not made prior to "the final adjournment of the court-martial in that a case."[74]

§ 18-25.00 Running of the Statute of Limitations[75]

Article 43 of the Uniform Code of Military Justice sets forth the differing time limits for the military statute of limitations.[76] A motion to dismiss on the grounds that the statute has run is expressly authorized by Rule for Courts-Martial 907(b)(2)(B) and must be made prior to conclusion of proceedings.[77] Unlike other matters subject to motions to dismiss, the Rules for Courts-Martial expressly require that "if it appears that the accused is unaware of the right to assert the statute of limitations in bar of trial, the military judge shall inform the accused of this right."[78] A knowing accused may waive the protection of the statute.[79]

The statute of limitations is tolled when properly sworn charges and specifications are received by the summary court-martial-convening authority.[80] The charges must be properly sworn; there is no good-faith exception.[81] When

---

[72] U.C.M.J. art. 10.

[73] R.C.M. 907(b)(2)(A). The Rule states that dismissal upon motion will occur if "[d]ismissal is required under R.C.M. 707." Although R.C.M. 707 is intended to embody the requirements of U.C.M.J. art. 10 and the Sixth Amendment, those requirements are technically independent of R.C.M. 707, and a motion to dismiss will lie under them even if such would not be justified by the Rule. United States v. Mizgala, 61 M.J. 122 (C.A.A.F. 2005). For the law of speedy trial, *see generally* Chapter 17.

[74] R.C.M. 907(b)(2). *See* Section 17-82.00.

[75] *See generally* Sections 6-40.00 and 12-25.14.

[76] U.C.M.J. art. 43.

[77] R.C.M. 907(b)(2)(B); United States v. Salter, 20 M.J. 116 (C.M.A. 1985).

[78] 20 M.J. 116 (C.M.A. 1985); United States v. Tunnell, 23 M.J. 110 (C.M.A. 1986); United States v. Jackson, 20 M.J. 83 (C.M.A. 1985); United States v. Troxell, 30 C.M.R. 6 (C.M.A. 1960). The accused in *Troxell* pled guilty to absence without leave notwithstanding the application of the statute of limitations to that offense because he had entered into a pretrial agreement with the convening authority that required him to plead guilty to that offense in lieu of standing trial for desertion, a more serious offense.

[79] R.C.M. 907(b)(2)(B); 910(e) Discussion. *See also* United States v. Thompson, 59 M.J. 432, 440 (C.A.A.F. 2004) ("It is possible that Appellant, had he been advised properly by the military judge, might have decided to waive the statute of limitations for tactical reasons.").

[80] Frage v. Moriarty, 27 M.J. 341 (C.M.A. 1988). *See also* United States v. Waller, 24 M.J. 266 (C.M.A. 1987) (timing will focus on the receipt of the original specifications and not the amendment). In *United States v. Miller*, 38 M.J. 121, 124 (C.M.A. 1993), *overruling* United States v. Rodgers, 24 C.M.R. 36 (C.M.A. 1957), the court altered long-established military practice in this area by holding that so long as the given offenses were properly referred and received by the summary court-martial convening authority within the requisite time, the fact that the accused is brought to trial on new charge sheets, *i.e.*, not the original paperwork, is of no importance. The key aspect for statute of limitations purposes is whether the original charges are involved.

[81] 27 M.J. at 343.

(Rel.3—1/07 Pub.62410)

charges are dismissed as defective or insufficient and the statute of limitations has not barred these offenses, the statute of limitations is extended for 180 days, during which time the revised charges and specifications must be received by the summary court-martial-convening authority.[82]

The statute of limitations is also tolled by war for absence without leave, missing movement, capital offenses, and a number of specified offenses.[83] Because the military statute of limitations, prior to the 1986 amendment, provided different periods for different offenses,[84] a statute-of-limitations motion could present an unusual problem, in that its resolution could require determination of the fundamental issue of guilt or innocence. For example, the statute of limitations for desertion[85] was three years, while the statute of limitations for absence without leave,[86] a lesser-included offense of desertion, was two years.[87] If the statute of limitations was tolled at twenty-six months, for example, an accused charged with desertion would have been protected by the statute if convicted of absence without leave, but not if convicted of desertion. Prior to the Rules for Courts-Martial, the *Manual for Courts-Martial* stated:

> If . . . an accused is found guilty of an included offense to which he has not entered a plea of guilty, and against which it appears that the statute of limitations . . . has run, the military judge . . . will, as soon as such a finding is announced, advise him in open session of his right to avail himself of the statute. If an accused interposes the statute, the issue will be determined in substantially the same manner as a motion to dismiss on the grounds of the statute of limitation.[88]

Although these express directions have not been included in the Rules for Courts-Martial, the Discussion to Rule 907(b)(2)(B) restates the general substance of the prior *Manual* provision. Accordingly, a motion to dismiss because the statute of limitations has run may be dependent upon the express or implicit findings of fact made by the members during findings.[89] Because in time of war

---

[82] U.C.M.J. art. 43(g). This amendment was added by the Military Justice Amendments of 1986, Pub. L. No. 99-661, 100 Stat. 3906 (1986) and does not affect offenses prior to November 14, 1986.

[83] U.C.M.J. art. 43(a) and (f). *See* United States v. Dowty, 48 M.J. 102 (C.A.A.F. 1998) (statute limitation is tolled by the Right to Financial Privacy Act, 12 U.S.C. § 3419); United States v. Anderson, 38 C.M.R. 110 (C.M.A. 1957); United States v. Taylor, 11 C.M.R. 428 (A.B.R. 1953). Although some federal criminal statutes may toll the statute of limitations, *e.g.*, *Dowty, above*, not all do. *E.g.*, United States v. McElhaney, 54 M.J. 120 (C.A.A.F. 2000).

[84] Although this is still true to a limited degree, the variance has been greatly reduced.

[85] U.C.M.J. art. 85.

[86] U.C.M.J. art. 86.

[87] U.C.M.J. arts. 43(b) and (c).

[88] MCM, 1969 para. 74*h*.

[89] As a result, should the defense move to dismiss because the statute of limitations has run on

(Rel.3—1/07 Pub.62410)

the statute of limitations may be extended by the service Secretary concerned for those offenses that are considered "detrimental to the prosecution of the war or inimical to the national security,"[90] this problem could recur.

This problem continues when an accused is charged for example, with a "capital" offense such as rape, for which there is no statute of limitations, but is convicted of a lesser-included offense which may be time-barred.[91]

§ 18-26.00　Double Jeopardy, Collateral Estoppel, Multiplicity, and Prior Nonjudicial Punishment

The accused may move to dismiss a specification because it subjects the accused to double jeopardy[92] or is unnecessarily multiplicitous for findings.[93] The accused may also raise a defense of collateral estoppel by asserting that a critical factual element of the offense was previously established in his or her behalf at a prior trial.[94] Although not amounting to double jeopardy or collateral estoppel, the accused may move to dismiss an offense if he or she has already been punished for that offense "if that offense is minor."[95]

§ 18-27.00　Immunity[96]

The military accused is protected by both the constitutional privilege against self-incrimination and the statutory privilege found in Article 31 of the Uniform Code of Military Justice. Rule for Courts-Martial 907(b)(2)(D)(ii) indicates that a charge or specification shall be dismissed on motion when "[p]rosecution is barred by . . . [i]mmunity from prosecution granted by a person authorized to do so." The Rule is somewhat misleading inasmuch as it implies that immunity

---

an offense, the crux of that motion will be decided by the fact-finder and not by the military judge. The military judge must instruct on the elements of all lesser-included offenses raised by the evidence only if the accused waives the bar of the statute of limitations. R.C.M. 920(e)(2) (overruling United States v. Wiedemann, 36 C.M.R. 521 (C.M.A. 1966)). This February 1986 amendment is consistent with Spaziano v. Florida, 468 U.S. 447 (1984).

[90] U.C.M.J. art. 43(e).

[91] *E.g.*, United States v. Thompson, 59 M.J. 432 (C.A.A.F. 2004).

[92] U.S. Const. amend. VI; R.C.M. 907(b)(2)(C). *See generally* Chapter 7. Note that the accused may also raise a defense of collateral estoppel. *See* R.C.M. 905(g); Ashe v. Swenson, 397 U.S. 436 (1970). Because of the dual sovereignty doctrine, *see* § 7-50.00, *above*, the accused does not have a right to have the court-martial abated pending dismissal of similar state charges. United States v. Anderson, 36 M.J. 963, 968, n. 8 (A.F.C.M.R. 1993).

[93] R.C.M. 907(b)(3)(B). *See generally* Section 6-34.20.

[94] *See* Section 7-60.00.

[95] R.C.M. 907(b)(2)(D)(iv). The Rule states that such a motion lies if "[p]rosecution is barred by . . . [p]rior punishment under Articles 13 or 15 for the same offense, if that offense was minor." *See generally* Section 8-29.10.

[96] *See generally* Chapter 20.

(Rel.3—1/07　Pub.62410)

may never be pled in bar if not expressly authorized by an appropriate official.[97] In *Cooke v. Orser*,[98] the court held that the staff judge advocate, by his own words, created a reasonable expectation in petitioner that if he satisfactorily cooperated with the command in the matters concerning national security, there would be no court-martial by military authorities. . . . More importantly, with notice of possible confusion as to the terms of this understanding, he failed to clarify the situation. As a result, he repeatedly reenforced petitioner's and the OSI agents' view of the agreement and continued to accept the benefit of petitioner's ongoing performance.[99]

As a result, the court concluded that the accused had been deprived of due process of law[100] and ordered that the charges against him be dismissed.[101]

Military law recognizes both transactional and testimonial immunity as being sufficient to overcome the constitutional and statutory privileges against self-incrimination.[102] Although military law recognizes "de facto" immunity, which can arise by adverse reliance upon official promise, it is especially difficult to claim successfully.[103] Rule for Courts-Martial 704 provides a limited opportunity

---

[97] It is, however, clarified in the Discussion to R.C.M. 704(b). *See also* Analysis to R.C.M. 704(b).

[98] 12 M.J. 335 (C.M.A. 1982).

[99] 12 M.J. at 342–43 (C.M.A. 1982). *See also* United States v. Jones, 52 M.J. 60 (C.A.A.F. 1999) (discussion of "informal immunity"); Samples v. Vest, 38 M.J. 482 (C.M.A. 1994) (dictum recognizing de facto immunity); United States v. Kimble, 33 M.J. 284 (C.M.A. 1991) (special court-martial convening authority's decision that any trial would be by civilian authorities held binding when transmitted to and relied upon by the accused); United States v. Wagner, 35 M.J. 721 (A.F.C.M.R. 1992) (applying *Cooke*).

[100] 12 M.J. at 343 (C.M.A. 1982). Chief Judge Everett concurred in Judge Fletcher's opinion 12 M.J. 355–58 (C.M.A. 1982), but also held that although the staff judge advocate ordinarily lacked the power to grant immunity, the promise of immunity by the staff judge advocate was sufficient under MCM, 1969 para. 68h, to bind the convening authority on whose behalf the staff judge advocate acted. 12 M.J. at 353–54 (C.M.A. 1982). Judge Cook dissented as to both rationales.

[101] 12 M.J. at 346. *See also* United States v. Kimble, 30 M.J. 892, 895 (A.F.C.M.R. 1990) (Air Force made representations about nonprosecution under mistaken belief that only two acts of child sexual abuse had happened, not a continuing course of action, but the Air Force was not a party to any agreement between accused and state authorities); United States v. Spence, 29 M.J. 630, 637 (A.F.C.M.R. 1989) (citing cases).

[102] R.C.M. 704(a); United States v. McKeal, 63 M.J. 81 (C.A.A.F. 2006); United States v. Jones, 52 M.J. 60 (C.A.A.F. 1999); United States v. Villines, 13 M.J. 46 (C.M.A. 1982); United States v. Churnovic, 22 M.J. 401 (C.M.A. 1986) (court might enforce a promise of immunity made by a noncommissioned officer expressly given that authority by the unit's executive officer); United States v. Brown, 13 M.J. 253 (C.M.A. 1982) (court enforced an informal agreement by the staff judge advocate that had been authorized by the convening authority). *See generally* Chapter 20.

[103] *See, e.g.*, § 20-23.31; United States v. Conklan, 41 M.J. 800, 803 (A. Crim. App. 1995) (statements and actions of accused's battalion commander and tacit approval of general court-martial convening authority didn't constitute defacto transactional immunity absent fulfillment by accused of any condition set by superior authority; reenlistment was insufficient).

(Rel.3—1/07 Pub.62410)

for the accused to obtain immunity for defense witnesses. Absent discriminatory use of immunity by the government, or governmental overreaching, the decision to grant or withhold defense immunity is that of the general court-martial convening authority.[104]

§ 18-28.00   Command Influence

Command influence is the improper use, or perception of use, of superior authority to interfere with the court-martial process.[105] It may consist of interference with the disposition of charges,[106] with judicial independence,[107] with the obtaining or presentation of evidence,[108] or with the independence and neutrality of court members.[109] The military judge has wide discretion in granting relief for command influence — relief that ranges from a dismissal to a change of venue.

When the issue of command influence is raised, the courts will examine a number of factors to determine if there was prejudicial error, including:

(1) the nature of the act or statement;[110]

(2) the proximity in time of the act or statement to the trial;[111]

---

[104] *See generally* United States v. Ivey, 55 M.J. 251, 254–257 (C.A.A.F. 2001).

[105] *See generally* U.C.M.J. art. 37; R.C.M. 104; Gaydos & Warren, *Commanders Need to Know About Unlawful Command Control*, Army Law, October 1986, at 9.

[106] *See* Section 8-16.00.

[107] *See* Section 14-80.00.

[108] *See* Section 8-16.00. *See also* United States v. Dykes, 38 M.J. 270 (C.M.A. 1993) (evidentiary hearing required in light of affidavits claiming command interference with six personnel — but not opinion of the court); United States v. Jones, 30 M.J. 849 (N.M.C.M.R. 1990) (relief of two drill instructors after pro defense testimony).

[109] *E.g.*, United States v. Baldwin, 54 M.J. 308 (C.A.A.F. 2001) (alleged classes that included criticism of lenient sentences required further inquiry). *See* Section 15-90.00. *Cf.* United States v. Rockwood, 52 M.J. 98 (C.A.A.F. 1999) (appellant's criticism of the command was not sufficient to show that the trial was infected with command influence); United States v. Jones, 15 M.J. 967 (A.C.M.R. 1983) (improper for judge to admonish court members about lenient sentences).

[110] *See, e.g.*, United States v. Ayers, 54 M.J. 85 (C.A.A.F. 2000) (strong statement about cleaning up sexual harassment in the military as the result of Aberdeen cases did not constitute command influence); United States v. Jones, 52 M.J. 60 (C.A.A.F. 1999) (a threat to prosecute for failure to comply with a pretrial agreement does not constitute command influence-it is statement of intent to enforce agreement); United States v. Cole, 38 C.M.R. 94 (C.M.A. 1967) (memorandum indicating that commander was determined to pursue all the means at his disposal to deter and punish thieves); United States v. Hawthorne, 22 C.M.R. 83 (C.M.A. 1956) (raised for the first time on appeal the question of a policy directive on the elimination of regular Army repeat offenders); United States v. Littrice, 13 C.M.R. 43 (C.M.A. 1953) (court members charged with knowledge of directive because members were judicially required to know of contents).

[111] *Compare* United States v. Wright, 37 C.M.R. 374 (C.M.A. 1967) (impropriety of staff judge advocate's lecture to court members immediately prior to the trial) *with* United States v. Danzine, 30 C.M.R. 350 (C.M.A. 1961) (lecture one month prior to trial not unlawful command influence).

(Rel.3—1/07   Pub.62410)

(3) the rank and position of the person acting or making the statement;[112]

(4) the specificity of the act's or statement's reference to the trial;[113]

(5) type of plea;[114]

(6) the extent to which the act or statement was addressed to personnel participating in the trial.[115]

Because of the usual appellate posture, most appellate holdings dealing with command influence take an appellate stance. Thus, the Court of Military Appeals held:

> Consequently, in cases where unlawful command influence has been exercised, no reviewing court may properly affirm findings and sentence unless it is persuaded beyond a reasonable doubt that the findings and sentence have not been affected by the command influence.[116]

Because allegations of command influence are especially likely to be fact-dependent, many such cases ultimately require additional fact-finding in the form of post-trial DuBay hearings ordered by the appellate courts.[117] In 1990, the Navy-Marine Court of Military Review attempted to elucidate the various burdens involved:[118]

> A presumption, although a rebuttable one, of prejudice exists where there is an appearance of unlawful command influence.[119]

> The accused bears the burden of raising the issue of unlawful command influence. He does so by establishing the existence of at least the appearance of unlawful command influence. . . . Mere assertions or speculation without some supporting evidence are not sufficient to raise the issue. Although we find no case that directly states what amount or type of

---

[112] See, e.g., United States v. Allen, 43 C.M.R. 157 (C.M.A. 1971) (reading of Secretary of the Navy's directive was prejudicial during sentencing despite instruction to disregard).

[113] See, e.g., United States v. Olson, 29 C.M.R. 102 (C.M.A. 1960) (president of court in bad check case was convening authority's deputy chief-of-staff and was responsible for the formulation of policy directives).

[114] United States v. Kitts, 23 M.J. 105 (C.M.A. 1986); United States v. Thomas, 22 M.J. 388 (C.M.A. 1986).

[115] See, e.g., United States v. Watkins, 46 C.M.R. 270 (C.M.A. 1973) (staff judge advocate furnished court members with excerpts of Manual prior to the trial); United States v. Wright, 37 C.M.R. 374 (C.M.A. 1967) (not raised at trial level; impropriety of staff judge advocate's lecture to court members immediately prior to the trial).

[116] United States v. Thomas, 22 M.J. 388, 394 (C.M.A. 1986).

[117] E.g., United States v. Dugan, 58 M.J. 253, 260 (C.A.A.F. 2003) (possible impact of convening authority's commander's call on sentencing views of members).

[118] United States v. Allen, 31 M.J. 572 (N.M.C.M.R. 1990).

[119] 31 M.J. 590 (N.M.C.M.R. 1990) (citing United States v. Crawley, 6 M.J. 811 (A.F.C.M.R. 1978)). As to the distinction between "actual" and "apparent" command influence, see Allen, 31 M.J. at 589–90.

(Rel.3—1/07 Pub.62410)

evidence is sufficient to raise the issue, our review of precedent reveals that in each reported case the defense had some specific direct or circumstantial evidence — something other than coincidence — that some specific incident occurred that directly involved the appellant's own trial. . . and, in light of Judge Cox's concurring opinion in *United States v. Levite*, 25 M.J. 334, 341 (C.M.A.1987), that the accused's burden includes (1) "asserting the facts of his allegation with sufficient particularity and substantiation so that if true, any reasonable person can only conclude that unlawful influence existed"; (2) declaring that the proceedings were unfair; and (3) showing that the unlawful command influence was the proximate cause of that unfairness. *Levite*, 25 M.J. at 341. But, under current judicial precedent, the accused is still not required to show specific prejudice. 25 M.J. at 341. The accused need only show sufficient evidence that raises a presumption of the existence of unlawful command influence. . . . Once it bears that burden, the presumption is ripe for rebuttal and the burden shifts to the Government to demonstrate that unlawful command influence does not exist or did not prejudice the accused. Similarly, the Government must produce more than mere assertions of impartiality by the person alleged to have been influenced. . . . In fact, statements made by subordinates that they were not influenced are "inherently suspect, not because of the credibility of the witness but because of the difficulty of the subordinates in ascertaining for himself the effect of any attempted command influence."[120] . . . If the evidence supports a factual basis for the allegation, the Government must rebut the existence of unlawful command influence by clear and convincing evidence.[121]

More recently, the Court of Appeals for the Armed Forces has opined:

Implicit in our decisions involving unlawful command influence is the recognition that two distinct issues are involved after the burden shifts to the Government: (1) what must be proven? and (2) what is the quantum of proof required? With respect to the first, we now expressly reaffirm and amplify what we said in *[United States v.] Gerlich*, [45 M.J. 309 (C.A.A.F. 1996)]. The Government may carry its burden (1) by disproving the predicate facts on which the allegation of unlawful command influence is based; (2) by persuading the military judge or the appellate court that the facts do not constitute unlawful command influence; (3) if at trial, by producing evidence proving that the unlawful command influence will not affect the proceedings; or (4), if on appeal, by persuading the appellate court that the unlawful command influence had no prejudicial impact on the court-martial.[122]

The Army Court of Military Review held that "waiver may be applied in an appropriate case."[123] In *United States v. Villareal*,[124] the Court of Appeals for

---

[120] *Allen*, 31 M.J. at 591 (quoting United States v. Rosser, 6 M.J. 267, 272 (C.M.A. 1979)).

[121] 31 M.J. at 591. United States v. Ayala, 43 M.J. 296 (C.A.A.F. 1995); United States v. Stombaugh, 40 M.J. 208 (C.M.A. 1994); United States v. Jones, 30 M.J. 849, 854 (N.M.C.M.R. 1990).

[122] United States v. Biagase, 50 M.J. 143, 151 (C.A.A.F. 1999).

[123] United States v. Redman, 33 M.J. 679, 683 (A.C.M.R. 1991) (satisfaction with the remedy for an unsuccessful attempt to manipulate the court members constituted waiver).

[124] 52 M.J. 27 (C.A.A.F. 1999).

(Rel.3—1/07 Pub.62410)

the Armed Forces held that at least the perception of command influence could be cured by transfer of the case to a new and separate convening authority.

The remedy at trial for command influence need not be dismissal. In *United States v. Clemons,*[125] faced with evidence that defense witnesses may have been dissuaded from testifying, the judge permitted the accused to testify to what he believed the witnesses would have said, prohibited government aggravation and credibility witnesses, and instructed the members to consider the accused's version of what the nontestifying witnesses would have said.[126]

§ 18-29.00 Other Constitutionally Based Motions

§ 18-29.10 Due Process

A motion to dismiss for a violation of due process may be granted when the conduct is so outrageous that it would be fundamentally "unfair or shocking to a universal sense of conscience which generally includes: coercion, violence or brutality to the person."[127] In other words, "when the conduct of law enforcement

---

[125] 35 M.J. 767 (A.C.M.R. 1992).

[126] Measures to offset command influence are case specific. However, some steps that the judge may take to ameliorate command influence include: providing more expansive challenges, United States v. Biagase, 50 M.J. 143 (C.A.A.F. 1999), banning an offending person from courtroom; United States v. Rivers, 49 M.J. 434 (C.A.A.F. 1998), direct questioning of potential witnesses to determine if they could and would testify freely or ordering the production of otherwise unwilling witnesses, directing a command retraction of improper remarks, precluding attack or impeachment of defense witnesses or of aggravating government witnesses; United States v. Clemons, 35 M.J. 767 (A.C.M.R. 1992), and transfer of the case to another jurisdiction, *e.g.,* United States v. Villareal, 52 M.J. 27 (C.A.A.F. 1999); alteration of the rating chain, *e.g.,* United States v. Biagase, 50 M.J. 143 (C.A.A.F. 1999); retraction of inappropriate policy letters, memoranda, or remarks, *e.g.,* United States v. Rivers, 49 M.J. 434 (C.A.A.F. 1998); and permitting defense testimony as to improper command conduct), United States v. Southers, 18 M.J. 795 (A.C.M.R. 1984).

[127] United States v. Patterson, 25 M.J. 650, 651 (A.F.C.M.R. 1987) (violation of the Fourth Amendment is not a violation of due process when the evidence is not admitted at the trial). *See* United States v. Marshank, 777 F. Supp. 1507 (N.D. Cal. 1991) (use of lawyer against client required reversal); United States v. Argo, 46 M.J. 454 (C.A.A.F. 1997) (appellant had not met burden to establish selective prosecution); United States v. Wilson, 44 M.J. 223, 225 (C.A.A.F. 1996) (conduct of government was not outrageous as there was no evidence that defendant who was prey for law enforcement was enrolled in drug treatment program); United States v. Cooper, 33 M.J. 356 (C.M.A. 1991), *adhered to,* 35 M.J. 417 (C.M.A. 1992), *cert. denied,* 507 U.S. 985 (1993) (no violation of due process for government agents to solicit accused's involvement in drugs when the agents did not know the accused was enrolled in drug treatment program; scathing dissent by Senior Judge Everett). *But see* United States v. White, 950 F.2d 426 431 (7th Cir. 1991) ("We have previously noted that there is doubt as to the validity of the outrageous governmental conduct doctrine. . . . In any event we have never reversed a conviction on this ground."). *See also* Rochin v. California, 342 U.S. 165 (1952). For appellate treatment of government misconduct, see, *e.g.,* United States v. McCoy, 31 M.J. 323 (C.M.A. 1990). *See also* United States v. Harris, 41 M.J. 433 (C.A.A.F. 1995) (distinguishing *Cooper, above*).

(Rel.3—1/07 Pub.62410)

agents is so outrageous that due process principles would absolutely bar the government from invoking judicial processes to obtain a conviction."[128] The burden is upon the accused to establish such a violation.[129]

The seminal cases dealing with a violation of due process because of outrageous government conduct are *Rochin v. California*[130] and *Irvine v. California*.[131] *Rochin* involved police officers breaking into the defendant's bedroom, attempting to pull capsules from his throat, and finally pumping his stomach to retrieve the capsules. The Supreme Court found this to be outrageous: "too close to the rack and the screw to permit of constitutional differentiation."[132] In *Irvine*, the police had repeated illegal entries into the defendant's home for the purpose of installing secret microphones, including one in his bedroom from which they listened for over a month. The plurality distinguished *Rochin* as a case involving coercion, violence and brutality to the person, rather than a trespass to property. A review of the decisions finding outrageous Government conduct suggests a necessity for brutal physical or psychological coercion. Courts should resist applying the due process standard in a subjective manner "draw[ing] on our merely personal and private notions and disregard[ing] the limits that bind judges in their judicial function."[133] In *United States v. Tucker*,[134] the court opined

---

[128] United States v. Russell, 411 U.S. 423, 431–32 (1973). *See also* United States v. LeMasters, 40 M.J. 178 (C.M.A. 1994) (stating "It is reprehensible to believe that agents of the OSI would condone the adulterous sodomous criminal behavior of this agent in order to make a simple-possession-of-cocaine charge," but not deciding whether conduct was outrageous); United States v. Payne, 962 F.2d 1228, 1231–32 (6th Cir. 1992) (four factors to examine in determining if conduct was outrageous); United States v. Hart, 963 F.2d 1278 (9th Cir. 1992) (befriending accused during emotional turmoil did not constitute outrageous government conduct); United States v. Winslow, 962 F.2d 845, 849 (9th Cir. 1992) (furnishing bomb components not outrageous conduct). *See also* United States v. Pinson, 56 M.J. 489, 493 (C.A.A.F. 2002) ("appellant has not carried his burden to show intentional or outrageous government misconduct"); United States v. Beckley, 55 M.J. 15 (C.A.A.F. 2001) (to succeed because of potential ethical violations, the defense must show that the conduct was so outrageous to violate due process).

[129] United States v. Patterson, 25 M.J. 650 (A.F.C.M.R. 1987). *See also* United States v. Cuellar, 96 F.3d 1179 (9th Cir. 1996) (informant's contingent fee arrangement, not based on conviction but on percentage of laundered funds and the number of resulting cases, was not outrageous conduct); United States v. Harris, 997 F.2d 812 (10th Cir. 1993) (supplying drugs to known drug addict as middleman was not outrageous); Hauser v. United States, 990 F.2d 1262 (9th Cir. 1993), *cert. denied*, 114 S. Ct. 392 510 U.S. 948 (1993) (informer was not automatically presumed to be a government agent, to hold government responsible for conduct); United States v. Simpson, 813 F.2d 1462 (9th Cir.), *cert. denied*, 484 U.S. 898 (1987) (employing female prostitute who engaged in sex with the accused not outrageous); United States v. McCarty, 25 M.J. 667 (A.F.C.M.R. 1987) (employing female OSI undercover agent not outrageous); People v. Auld, 815 P.2d 956 (Colo. App. 1991) (undercover agent posed as defendant).

[130] 342 U.S. 165 (1952).

[131] 347 U.S. 128 (1954).

[132] 342 U.S. at 172.

[133] *Rochin*, 342 U.S. at 170.

(Rel.3—1/07   Pub.62410)

that of the United States Courts of Appeal only the Third Circuit had actually dismissed a case because of outrageous government conduct and that the circuit had subsequently "disavowed" that decision.

Courts have occasionally dealt with complaints that government agents have intentionally used either sexual conduct[135] or drugs[136] to obtain a defendant's co-operation. In *United States v. Cuervelo,*[137] the court stated that to obtain a post-trial hearing on the grounds of improper sexual conduct, the defendant must show at a minimum:

(1) that the government consciously set out to use sex as a weapon in its investigatory arsenal, or acquiesced in such conduct for its own purposes upon learning that such relationship existed;

(2) that the government agent initiated a sexual relationship, or allowed it to continue to exist, to achieve governmental ends; and

(3) that the sexual relationship took place during or close to the period covered by the indictment and was entwined with the events charged therein.

§ 18-29.20   Vindictive Prosecution[138]

Vindictive prosecution may serve as the basis for a motion to dismiss. "For the Government to make distinctions does not violate equal protection guarantees unless constitutionally suspect classifications like race, religion, or national origin are utilized or unless there is an encroachment on fundamental constitutional rights like freedom of speech or of peaceful assembly."[139]

To establish discriminatory prosecution, it must be shown that other violators similarly situated are generally not prosecuted for the type of conduct forming the basis of the charge against the accused and that the government's selection of the accused has been based on bad faith; that is, impermissibly selected based

---

[134] 28 F.3d 1420 (6th Cir. 1994); United States v. Pipes, 87 F.3d 840 (6th Cir. 1996) (failure to follow state regulation did not amount to "egregious governmental conduct" requiring dismissal of charges); Note, *In Defense of the Outrageous Government Conduct Defense in the Federal Courts,* 84 Ky. L.J. 415 (1995).

[135] *E.g.,* United States v. Simpson, 813 F.2d 1462 (9th Cir. 1987) (FBI continued to use addict as a government informant even after the FBI learned that she had become sexually involved with the defendant and was involved with drugs).

[136] *E.g.,* United States v. Santana, 6 F.3d 1 (1st Cir. 1993) (supplying large amount of drugs was not outrageous when done to earn trust of large drug dealer); United States v. Godshalk, 44 M.J. 487 (C.A.A.F. 1996) (Trying to prevent client suicide, even though prompted by the government, does not constitute outrageous conduct).

[137] 949 F.2d 559, 567 (2d Cir. 1991).

[138] *See* Section 3-52.40.

[139] United States v. Means, 10 M.J. 162, 165 (C.M.A. 1981). *See also* United States v. Torquato, 602 F.2d 564 (3d Cir. 1979), *cert. denied,* 444 U.S. 941 (1979).

(Rel.3—1/07 Pub.62410)

on race, religion, or desire to prevent the exercise of his or her constitutional rights.[140] There is a presumption of good faith, so the accused bears a heavy burden of proof.[141] The Air Force Court of Military Review opined in dictum that absent a showing that the exercise of due diligence would not have discovered the alleged selective prosecution, failure to raise the issue at trial results in waiver.[142]

Once plea bargaining has begun, it is not unconstitutional for the government to threaten to bring more serious charges against the accused should he or she refuse to plead guilty.[143] However, increasing the severity of the prosecution because of the assertion by the accused of his or her rights may be unlawful.[144]

§ 18-29.30 Prosecutorial Misconduct

Prosecutorial misconduct may include interference with defense counsel or the accused's relationship with defense counsel, improper failure to disclose evidence, interference with witnesses, selective prosecution, and the like. The defense carries a heavy burden[145] to establish that such conduct prejudiced the substantial rights of the defendant. To date, the Court of Appeals has refused to adopt a per se reversal or a less demanding standard for invasion of the right to counsel or interference with witnesses.[146]

---

[140] United States v. Garwood, 20 M.J. 148, 154 (C.M.A. 1985) (citing United States v. Berrios, 501 F.2d 1207, 1211 (2d Cir. 1974)). *See also* United States v. Henry, 42 M.J. 231 (C.A.A.F. 1995) (combination of possible conflict of interest and selective prosecution requires rehearing); United States v. Bradley, 27 M.J. 872 (A.F.C.M.R. 1989). It is not enough for the defendant to show that he was statistically treated differently. He must show that the decision maker in his case acted with a discriminatory purpose. The Court in McCleskey v. Kemp, 481 U.S. 279, 281 (1987), indicated that discretion "is essential to the criminal justice process." The Court demands "exceptionally clear proof" before they will interfere with exercise of discretion. This rationale will apply to statistical studies as to pretrial agreements and the major charges. United States v. Bourgeois, 964 F.2d 935 (9th Cir. 1992) (excellent discussion of discriminatory prosecution).

[141] United States v. Bourgeois, 964 F.2d 935 (9th Cir. 1992). *See also* United States v. Arias, 575 F.2d 253, 255 (9th Cir. 1978) (defendant has heavy burden when claiming malicious prosecution); Nixon v. United States, 703 F. Supp. 538, 570 (S.D. Miss. 1988).

[142] United States v. El-Amin, 38 M.J. 563, 564 (A.F.C.M.R. 1993).

[143] Bordenkircher v. Hayes, 434 U.S. 357 (1978).

[144] *Compare* Blackledge v. Perry, 417 U.S. 21 (1974) *and* United States v. Goodwin, 457 U.S. 368 (1982). *See also* United States v. Meyer, 810 F.2d 1242 (D.C. Cir. 1987); United States v. Davis, 18 M.J. 820 (A.F.C.M.R. 1984); Stayton v. Westbrook, 18 M.J. 520 (A.F.C.M.R. 1984); United States v. Blanchette, 17 M.J. 512 (A.F.C.M.R. 1983); United States v. Bass, 11 M.J. 545 (A.C.M.R. 1981).

[145] United States v. Argo, 46 M.J. 454, 461–63 (C.A.A.F. 1997). *See also* R.C.M. 905(c)(2)(A).

[146] United States v. Meek, 44 M.J. 1 (C.A.A.F. 1996).

(Rel.3—1/07 Pub.62410)

§ 18-30.00   MOTIONS FOR APPROPRIATE RELIEF

§ 18-31.00   In General

A motion for appropriate relief has been defined as "a request for a ruling to cure a defect which deprives a party of a right or hinders a party from preparing for trial or presenting its case." [147] The specific motions for appropriate relief set forth in the Rules for Courts-Martial are illustrative and are nonexclusive. [148]

Motions for appropriate relief include, but are not limited to, motions:

For continuances To record a denial of counsel; [149] To correct defects in the article 32 investigation or pretrial advice; [150] To correct or clarify the charges and specifications for discovery; [151] For procurement and

---

[147] R.C.M. 906(a). The present definition differs somewhat from MCM, 1969 (rev. ed.) 69a from which it was taken. Analysis of the Rule for Courts-Martial, Rule 906(a), MCM, 2005, A21-54. ¶ 69a defined a motion for appropriate relief as "one made to cure a defect of form or substance which impedes the accused in properly preparing for trial or conducting his defense." The Analysis to R.C.M. 906(a) states:

> The phrase concerning deprivation of rights is new; it applies to such pretrial matters as defects in the pretrial advice and the legality of pretrial confinement. Paragraph 69a of MCM, 1969 (Rev.) provided only for the accused to make motions for appropriate relief. This rule is not so restricted because the prosecution may also request relief.

[148] R.C.M. 906(b). *See, e.g.,* United States v. Anderson, 36 M.J. 963, 973 (A.F.C.M.R. 1993) (request for daily transcript rejected).

[149] R.C.M. 906(b)(2) provides that on motion of the accused "the military judge shall ensure that a record" shall be made of the "denial of individual military counsel or of [the] denial of [a] request to retain detailed counsel." The Rule expressly prohibits the military judge from dismissing the charges against the accused in the event of an erroneous decision to supply the requested counsel, although it permits the judge to grant reasonable continuances when delay is necessary to process a counsel request or to resolve the problem. The Rule is based on United States v. Redding, 11 M.J. 100 (C.M.A. 1981). Analysis to R.C.M. 906(b)(2). *See generally* Section 5-23.50.

[150] Before a case may be referred to a general court-martial, the Uniform Code of Military Justice requires that a pretrial investigation be conducted (U.C.M.J. art. 32; *see also* R.C.M. 405; *see generally* Chapter 9) and a pretrial advice be rendered by the convening authority's staff judge advocate or legal advisor. U.C.M.J. art. 34; R.C.M. 406; *see generally* Chapter 10. R.C.M. 906(b)(3) allows the accused to move for the correction of a defective investigation or advice. The Rule's Discussion notes: "If the motion is granted, the military judge should ordinarily grant a continuance so the defect may be corrected." The Rule and its Discussion stem in part (Analysis to R.C.M. 906(b)(3)) from United States v. Johnson, 7 M.J. 396 (C.M.A. 1979), in which the court held: "We conclude that a defect in the pretrial investigation does not deprive the court-martial of jurisdiction. Rather, the trial must be postponed until the convening authority determines whether to order a continuance of the proceedings or to dismiss the charges." 7 M.J. at 398 (C.M.A. 1979) (footnote omitted). The Rule is also based upon MCM, 1969 (rev. ed.) ¶ 69c, which stated: "Such a motion should be granted only if the accused shows that the defect in the conduct of the investigation has in fact prevented him from properly preparing for trial or has otherwise injuriously affected his substantial rights."

[151] *See* Chapter 11.

(Rel.3—1/07   Pub.62410)

production of evidence, including witnesses;[152] For severance of charges;[153] or their joinder;[154] For severance of co-accused;[155] For change of venue; To limit sentence due to multiplicity;[156] In limine; To strike testimony;[157] For mistrial;[158] Relating to the mental capacity or responsibility of the accused;[159] Exclusion of spectators;[160] Exclusion of

[152] *See* Chapter 20.

[153] *See* Section 6-35.10. R.C.M. 601(e)(2) provides that the convening authority may send even unrelated charges to trial. R.C.M. 906(b)(10) permits severance of offenses "but only to prevent manifest injustice." *See generally* United States v. Curry, 31 M.J. 359, 372–75 (C.M.A. 1990). The lack of procedural guidelines in Rule 906 also creates a risk that it may violate the Uniform Code of Military Justice. The powers to convene court-martial and to refer charges are solely vested in the convening authority. R.C.M. 906(b)(10) in effect gives the military judge the power to refer the severed charge or specification. To the extent that the Rule may contemplate trial by the same court-martial to which the specification was originally referred, it may not run afoul of the Code. Should the severed charge be tried by another court-martial without the express authority of the convening authority, it would appear to be clearly illegal, notwithstanding the President's authority to prescribe rules regulating trial procedure. U.C.M.J. art. 36(a).

[154] *See generally* Chapter 6, *above*; R.C.M. 601(e)(2); R.C.M. 906(b)(10) Discussion. Although military law has a preference for the concurrent trial of all known charges, *see* United States v. Oakley, 33 M.J. 27, 36 (C.M.A. 1991), that preference is not a binding rule. *E.g.*, Oakley, *above* (Article 35 may justify proceeding only on those charges served in a timely fashion); United States v. Fahey, 33 M.J. 920, 921 (A.C.M.R. 1991) (absent plain error, failure to move for joinder of all known charges before plea waives issue).

[155] *See* Section 6-35.20.

[156] R.C.M. 906(b)(12); *see* Section 6-34.30. The Discussion of the Rule notes that ordinarily resolution of this motion should await findings. When a not-guilty plea will be entered and a contested case heard is a matter of common sense, because an acquittal of one or more of the specifications may render the issue moot. However, this should not be possible if a guilty plea may be entered. Rule for Courts-Martial 905(d) prohibits deferral of ruling on a pre-plea motion unless determination is deferred for good cause. Such cause may not be present if the accused is considering a guilty plea and must know whether the specifications are multiplicitous to decide upon the plea. Inasmuch as the providency inquiry will require the military judge to advise the accused of the maximum sentence imposable (R.C.M. 909(c)(1)), this matter would have to be determined in any event if the accused pleads guilty.

[157] When inadmissible evidence has been adduced, a motion to strike that testimony is appropriate. *See, e.g.*, Mil. R. Evid. 301(f)(2) (motion to strike direct testimony when the witness exercises the right against self-incrimination on cross-examination). *See also* United States v. Gray, 74 F.3d 304 (1st Cir. 1996) (striking a defense witness's testimony is a drastic remedy and should only be granted when invocation of the self-incrimination privilege frustrates cross-examination); United States v. Rivas, 3 M.J. 282 (C.M.A. 1977). *See also* Combs v. Commonwealth, 74 S.W.3d 738, 742-746 (Ky. 2002) (assertion of privilege by witness could have been sufficiently accommodated to permit testimony) (citing cases). When the motion is granted, the military judge should instruct the members to disregard the struck evidence. United States v. Moore, 36 M.J. 329, 334-35 (C.M.A. 1993) (Court noted in dictum that Mil. R. Evid. 301(f)(2) "only empowers — it does not require — a military judge to strike [the] testimony . . . . [S]triking . . . testimony is not permitted . . . if the refusal to answer questions relates only to matters that 'are purely collateral' ").

[158] *See* Section 7-22.00.

[159] *See generally* R.C.M. 706, 908; Mil. R. Evid. 302.

[160] *See generally* Section 13-35.20 *et seq.*

(Rel.3—1/07 Pub.62410)

witnesses; and Request for immunity of defense witnesses.thority grant testimonial immunity, or that the proceedings be abated until the privilege being claimed by the witness is lost, or until the immunity is granted. R.C.M. 704(e). If the judge determines that the witness' testimony would be "central" to the defense case, and that the witness plans to invoke rights under the self-incrimination clause, the judge may require the convening authority to grant testimonial immunity or, as to the affected specification, abate that portion of the proceedings until such relief is granted. R.C.M. 704(e). *See also* United States v. Zayas, 24 M.J. 132 (C.M.A. 1987). *See generally* Chapter 20.

§ 18-32.00 Continuances

The Rules for Courts-Martial expressly deal with continuances only by declaring that a "continuance may be granted only by the military judge."[162] The Discussion to the Rule fleshes it out somewhat by declaring:

> The military judge should, upon a showing of reasonable cause, grant a continuance to any party for as long, and as often as may appear to be just. Article 40. Whether a request for a continuance should be granted is a matter within the discretion of the military judge. Reasons for a continuance may include: insufficient opportunity to prepare for trial; unavailability of an essential witness; the interest of Government in the order of trial of related cases; and illness of an accused, counsel, military judge, or member.

A continuance should be granted upon the showing of reasonable cause.[163] Proper reasons for a continuance are too numerous to mention, but they include: the opportunity to prepare for trial,[164] unavailability of an essential witness,[165] nondisclosure to a party as required by the rules,[166] request for counsel,[167] the

---

[162] R.C.M. 906(b)(1). The Analysis to the Rule states that the power previously vested in the convening authority by MCM, 1969 para. 58a, to postpone trials was deleted as "inconsistent with the authority of the military judge to schedule proceedings and control the docket." (*Citing* United States v. Wolzok, 1 M.J. 125 (C.M.A. 1975)).

[163] R.C.M. 906(b)(1) Discussion.

[164] United States v. Cokeley, 22 M.J. 225, 229–30 (C.M.A. 1986) ("[I]t was an abuse of discretion for the military judge to admit the deposition over defense objection without granting a further continuance to obtain a medical update so it could be determined whether the witness would be available to testify in court within a reasonable period. This constitutes prejudicial error and requires further proceedings.").

[165] United States v. Powell, 49 M.J. 220 (C.A.A.F. 1998); United States v. Royster, 42 M.J. 488 (C.A.A.F. 1995) (appropriate to deny continuance mid-trial because of unavailability of witness — also permissible to have members read transcript rather than having it read to them); United States v. Burns, 27 M.J. 92, 98 n.5 (C.M.A. 1988); United States v. Vanderwier, 25 M.J. 263 (C.M.A. 1987) (witness who was on board ship still in training was available within the meaning of the Military Rules of Evidence — no accommodations had been made in setting the trial date so that the witness could testify before the fact finder).

[166] R.C.M. 701(g)(3)(B).

(Rel.3—1/07   Pub.62410)

statutory waiting period,[168] illness of a party to the trial, disruption of the trial for natural or unnatural causes, and the prevention of the impact of prejudicial pre-trial publicity.[169]

Whether to grant a continuance is solely[170] within the discretion of the military judge, whose decision will only be reversed for an abuse of discretion.[171] The extent of the trial judge's discretion was demonstrated in the Supreme Court's decision in *Morris v. Slappy*.[172] The Court held that the failure to grant a six-week continuance to allow the accused to be defended by a public defender who had represented him at a preliminary hearing and had supervised an extensive investigation did not violate the Sixth Amendment. Shortly before trial, the accused's attorney had been hospitalized for emergency surgery, and another trial attorney in the public defender's office had been assigned to the accused. At the opening of the trial, the accused's motion for a continuance was denied. On federal collateral attack, the Ninth Circuit Court of Appeals reversed the conviction for violation of the Sixth Amendment because the trial court failed to inquire about the probable length of the public defender's absence and failed to weigh the accused's interest in continued representation by this attorney against the state's interest in continuing with the scheduled trial. The Supreme Court reversed, finding no Sixth Amendment violation and no abuse of discretion.

---

[167] United States v. Gipson, 25 M.J. 781 (A.C.M.R. 1988) (four delays at Article 32 investigation and two granted by judge; a third was refused). *See, e.g.,* United States v. Cook, 487 F.2d 963 (9th Cir. 1973) (not an abuse of discretion to deny request for continuance to obtain counsel the day of trial). *See also* United States v. Kinard, 45 C.M.R. 74 (C.M.A. 1972) (At two prior sessions, counsel was directed to help the accused obtain civilian counsel. At the third session some two months later, the government presented evidence that it had done all it could to assist the accused. The trial judge offered a continuance if there was an assurance of obtained civilian counsel. The accused would not give this assurance. Defense counsel indicated that he was prepared to proceed. The denial of a continuance under the circumstances was held not to be a denial of the right to counsel). *See also* United States v. Miller, 47 M.J. 352 (C.A.A.F. 1998) (error in not granting continuance to obtain newly hired civilian counsel at post-trial Article 39(a) session).

[168] United States v. Cruz-Maldonado, 20 M.J. 831 (A.C.M.R. 1985) (absent a request for a continuance or an objection, it is not error to continue within the statutory waiting period); United States v. Garcia, 10 M.J. 631 (A.C.M.R. 1980).

[169] Patton v. Yount, 467 U.S. 1025, 1035 (1984) ("But it is clear that the passage of time between a first and a second trial can be a highly relevant fact. In the circumstances of this case, we hold that it clearly rebuts any presumption of partiality or prejudice that existed at the time of the initial trial"); Sheppard v. Maxwell, 384 U.S. 333 (1966).

[170] R.C.M. 906(b)(1).

[171] *See, e.g.,* United States v. Andrews, 36 M.J. 922, 924 (A.F.C.M.R. 1993) (citing cases and holding that denial of first defense request for 10–14 days of additional investigation and preparation was reasonable given, among other matters, grant of investigative assistance, prior government delay of 30 days approved over defense objection, and lack of specific reason for government objection); United States v. Thomas, 22 M.J. 57 (C.M.A. 1986).

[172] 461 U.S. 1 (1983).

(Rel.3—1/07   Pub.62410)

Whether the judge has abused his or her discretion in granting a continuance depends on a number of factors,[173] including: surprise,[174] nature of any evidence involved,[175] timeliness of the request,[176] substitute testimony or evidence,[177] availability of witness or evidence requested,[178] length of continuance,[179]

---

[173] United States v. Wiest, 59 M.J. 276, 279 (C.A.A.F. 2004) ("surprise, nature of any evidence involved, timeliness of the request, substitute testimony or evidence, availability of witness or evidence requested, length of continuance, prejudice to opponent, moving party received prior continuances, good faith of moving party, use of reasonable diligence by moving party, possible impact on verdict, and prior notice," *quoting* United States v. Miller, 47 M.J. 352, 358 (C.A.A.F. 1997)).

[174] *See* Williams v. Florida, 399 U.S. 78, 85–86 (1970) (prosecution entitled to continuance when surprised by alibi witness); Fed. R. Evid. 403, Advisory Committee Note ("While it can scarcely be doubted that claims of unfair surprise may still be justified despite procedural requirements of notice and instrumentalities of discovery, the granting of a continuance is a more appropriate remedy than exclusion of the evidence.").

[175] *See* United States v. Hawkins, 19 C.M.R. 261, 268 (C.M.A. 1955). In *Hawkins*, even though the defense request was made on the date of trial, the failure to produce a witness to show entrapment was an abuse of discretion. The witness was located at the stockade on the date and place of trial and would not have interrupted the schedule of the prosecution. The court said:

> The necessity for having a witness present often does not arise until the trial has proceeded well along toward finality and the touchstone for untimeliness should be whether the request is delayed unnecessarily until such a time as to interfere with the orderly prosecution of the case. Even then, if good cause is shown for the delay, a continuance should be granted to permit the evidence to be produced.

See also United States v. Johnson, 33 M.J. 855 (A.C.M.R. 1991) (abuse of discretion to reject defense continuance to obtain psychiatric expert witness even though the defense counsel did not request the witness through the trial counsel).

[176] *See* Morris v. Slappy, 461 U.S. 1 (1983); Ungar v. Sarafite, 376 U.S. 575, 590–91 (1964); United States v. Jones, 730 F.2d 593, 596 (10th Cir. 1984). United States v. Sullivan, 26 M.J. 442 (C.M.A. 1988) (failure to grant continuance on the day of trial when the defense had been granted a 45-day continuance, declined a 24-hour recess, and made no representation that additional evidence could be gathered during continuance).

[177] United States v. Price, 41 M.J. 403 (C.A.A.F. 1995) (after two sanity boards, defense not entitled to continuance for third board). United States v. Nichols, 6 C.M.R. 27, 35 (C.M.A. 1952) (failure to grant a continuance to permit psychiatric examination and evidence as to mental strain on the accused was not error when such evidence would have been cumulative with lay testimony; court said "expert [testimony] might conceivably result in a lesser sentence, but any such assumption must necessarily develop out of speculation and conjecture").

[178] *See* United States v. Barreto, 57 M.J. 127 (C.A.A.F. 2002) (judge did not abuse his discretion in refusing to delay trial until appellant's amnesia improved); United States v. Cokeley, 22 M.J. 225 (C.M.A. 1986) (abuse of discretion for the military judge not to grant a continuance to determine if the victim would be available to testify in person within a reasonable period of time); United States v. Hawkins, 19 C.M.R. 261 (C.M.A. 1955) (in some instances, no abuse of discretion to deny a continuance to obtain witness).

[179] Hutchins v. Garrison, 724 F.2d 1425, 1433–34 (4th Cir. 1983), *cert. denied*, 464 U.S. 1065 (1984) (counsel had 11 days to review requested material prior to request for continuance); Alford v. United States, 709 F.2d 418, 424 (5th Cir. 1983) (denial improper when only three weeks to prepare).

(Rel.3—1/07   Pub.62410)

prejudice to opponent,[180] moving party received prior continuances,[181] good faith of moving party,[182] use of reasonable diligence by moving party,[183] need for the continuance by the defense team,[184] possible impact on verdict, and prior notice.[185] The failure to grant a continuance should not be reversible error unless it was prejudicial to the moving party.[186]

To alleviate some of the problems concerning motions for continuances, when local rules are proper,[187] a court may require that a motion for continuance be

---

[180] *See* United States v. Bright, 9 M.J. 789 (A.C.M.R. 1980) (The accused was charged with various offenses of possession, sale, and transfer of a controlled substance on three different dates. According to the government evidence, the witness for which the accused requested the continuance was "independently and singularly" involved with the offenses on two dates and also "involved" with the offense on the third date. The failure to grant a continuance under such circumstances was error.).

[181] United States v. Bright, 9 M.J. 789 (A.C.M.R. 1980).

[182] *See, e.g.,* United States v. Phillips, 37 M.J. 532 (A.C.M.R. 1993) (denial of continuance made at last minute by newly retained civil counsel was not an abuse of discretion given that the previous session had been continued despite presence of at least eight witnesses from outside the state, the number of prior sessions, and the judge's factual finding that the accused was trying to manipulate the system); United States v. Jones, 730 F.2d 593, 596 (10th Cir. 1984); Gaspar v. Kassm, 493 F.2d 964 (3d Cir. 1974); United States v. Hampton, 7 M.J. 284 (C.M.A. 1979) (failure to grant a continuance to interview 14 witnesses not error when there was no serious question as to the relevancy of the witnesses). *See also* United States v. James, 34 C.M.R. 27 (C.M.A. 1963) (no abuse of discretion to deny a two-day continuance where the witness' identification of evidence was known on the first day of trial when the defense counsel was given a chance to interview witness to determine the witness' credibility, and defense counsel refused this offer).

[183] *See* Winston v. Prudential Lines, Inc., 415 F.2d 619 (2d Cir. 1969), *cert. denied*, 397 U.S. 918 (1970); United States v. Clark, 35 M.J. 98 (C.M.A. 1992) (no abuse of discretion when continuance requested at last minute in order to obtain testimony of accused's wife and daughter when the accused had previously refused to inform the government of their location).

[184] *See, e.g.,* United States v. Davis, 36 M.J. 702, 706 (A.C.M.R. 1992) (refusal to grant continuance for detailed counsel to prepare after withdrawal of civilian counsel was not an abuse of discretion when detailed counsel had substantial prior preparation).

[185] United States v. James, 34 C.M.R. 27 (C.M.A. 1963).

[186] *E.g.,* United States v. Wellington, 58 M.J. 420 (C.A.A.F. 2003) (need not decide if judge abused discretion in not granting continuance when there was no showing of prejudice); United States v. Brownfield, 52 M.J. 40, 44 (C.A.A.F. 1999) (even if the judge erred in not granting continuance, there was no prejudice to the accused); United States v. Weisbeck, 50 M.J. 461 (C.A.A.F. 1999) (numerous factors cited in finding abuse of discretion in not granting continuance); United States v. Thomas, 33 M.J. 694, 702–03 (A.C.M.R. 1991) (denial of unopposed second continuance motion by defense counsel was an abuse of discretion and necessitated reversal where the denial deprived the accused of civilian counsel and an expert extenuation and mitigation psychiatric witness and affected the accused's right to detailed counsel). *Compare* United States v. Wirsing, 719 F.2d 859, 866 (6th Cir. 1983) (actual prejudice from failure to sever offenses and grant more preparation time in complex case) *with* Skillern v. Estelle, 720 F.2d 839, 852 (5th Cir. 1983), *reh'g denied*, 469 U.S. 1067 (1984) (failure to grant additional preparation time not prejudicial).

[187] *See* Section 14-62.10.

(Rel.3—1/07 Pub.62410)

in writing and that it set forth the grounds for continuance, including, when relevant, why the witness or evidence needed is not available and that due diligence has been used in attempting to procure the evidence or witness, and a proposed stipulation of the facts to be proven and the period of time requested. Such a motion should be submitted within a specified time period prior to trial or as soon as practical.

While the denial of a defense request for continuance may be reviewed on appeal, it is unclear whether the denial of a government continuance request to obtain essential witnesses is appealable. If the government motion is not appealable, the military judge's ruling is not reviewable. Certainly, such an interlocutory appeal is possible only when the the judge's action would effectively terminate the proceeding.[188] The converse is also true.[189] "Admittedly, this interpretation leaves the defense with some advantages, because denial of a defense-requested continuance may be challenged on appeal as a violation of the accused's sixth-amendment right to produce evidence, and the Government has no corresponding constitutional right."[190] As Judge Cox noted in *United States v. Browers*:[191] "A mere weakening of the Government's case is not sufficient"[192] to allow the government to appeal the judge's ruling under Article 62. He continued:

> If it is apparent that the trial will not succeed because a witness is unavailable or for failure of proof and the military judge refuses to grant a continuance, the convening authority certainly can consider withdrawing the charges and rethinking alternative courses of action which are open to him, e.g., preferring new charges.[193]

§ 18-33.00 Correction or Clarification of the Charges or Specifications

§ 18-33.10 Amendment[194]

Rule for Courts-Martial 906(b)(4) permits the prosecution to move to amend a charge or specification. The Rule limits the motion by providing that: "A charge

---

[188] United States v. Browers, 20 M.J. 356, 359–60 (C.M.A. 1985).

[189] United States v. Robinson, 593 F.2d 573 (4th Cir. 1979). Denial of government request for continuance after suppression of crucial evidence held to be abuse of discretion. Appealable under 18 U.S.C. § 3731 (1986).

[190] United States v. Browers, 20 M.J. 356, 360 (C.M.A. 1985).

[191] 20 M.J. 356, 360 (C.M.A. 1985).

[192] 20 M.J. 356, 360 (C.M.A. 1985).

[193] 20 M.J. at 361 (C.M.A. 1985). He went on to emphasize the power of the military judge and indicated that "[t]he appellate courts of our system must zealously defend the military trial judge's authority to manage the proceedings over which he presides." 20 M.J. at 361 (C.M.A. 1985).

[194] *See* Section 6-50.00.

or specification may not be amended over the accused's objection unless the amendment is minor within the meaning of Rule for Courts-Martial 603(a)."[195]

The Discussion to the Rule amplifies it:

> An amendment may be appropriate when a specification is unclear, redundant, inartfully drafted, misnames an accused, or is laid under the wrong article. A specification may be amended by striking surplusage . . . or substituting or adding new language. . . . When a specification is amended after the accused has entered a plea to it, the accused should be asked to plead anew to the amended specification. A bill of particulars . . . may also be used when a specification is indefinite or ambiguous. [196]

§ 18-33.20　Severance of a Duplicitous Specification[197]

Rule for Courts-Martial 906(b)(5) provides for the "[s]everance of a duplicitous specification[198] into two or more specifications" on motion. The nonbinding Discussion of the Rule states:

> The sole remedy for a duplicitous specification is severance of the specification into two or more specifications, each of which alleges a separate offense contained in the duplicitous specification. However, if the duplicitousness is combined with or results in other defects, such as misleading the accused, other remedies may be appropriate.

Although the Discussion may be accurate, its conclusion that severance is the only remedy in the normal case is suspect and is not supported by the cases cited in the Analysis to the Rule. Matter reviewed as surplusage may, for example, be struck on motion. [199]

§ 18-33.30　Bill of Particulars

Rule for Courts-Martial 906(b)(6) provides the first explicit authority for the defense to move for a bill of particulars,[200] an instrument of potentially great use to the defense given the notice pleading used in military law. When the accused does not ask for a bill of particulars, the accused cannot later complain should he or she be found guilty of a lesser-included offense. [201]

---

[195] R.C.M. 603(a) defines "minor changes" thusly: "Minor changes in charges and specifications are any except those which add a party, offense, or substantial matter not fairly included in those previously preferred, or which will likely mislead the accused as to the offenses charged." *See also* Discussion to R.C.M. 603(a).

[196] R.C.M. 906(b)(4). *See generally* Chapter 6. *Compare* United States v. Arbic, 36 C.M.R. 448 (C.M.A. 1966) *with* United States v. Krutsinger, 35 C.M.R. 207 (C.M.A. 1965).

[197] *See* Section 6-33.00.

[198] *See generally* Chapter 6.

[199] R.C.M. 906(b)(6). As the Analysis to the Rule notes, however, the use of bills of particulars have been recognized in military law for some years. *See, e.g.,* United States v. Means, 30 C.M.R. 290 (C.M.A. 1961).

[200] *See generally* Chapter 6.

[201] United States. v. Harris, 25 M.J. 281 (C.M.A. 1987).

(Rel.3—1/07　Pub.62410)

Although the Rule does not further define or clarify a "bill of particulars," the Discussion states:

> The purposes of a bill of particulars are to inform the accused of the nature of the charge with sufficient precision to enable the accused to prepare for trial, to avoid or minimize the danger of surprise at the time of trial, and to enable the accused to plead the acquittal or conviction in bar of another prosecution for the same offense when the specification itself is too vague, and indefinite for such purposes.

Although a bill of particulars expands upon a specification and thus functions to some degree in practice as a discovery device, it may not be used as a general discovery tool.[202] Additionally, the nature of the bill of particulars makes it an inadequate substitute for sworn charges. Accordingly, it may not be used to remedy an otherwise legally deficient specification.[203]

§ 18-34.00   Change of Venue

Rule for Courts-Martial 906(b)(11) provides that: "The place of trial may be changed when necessary to prevent prejudice to the rights of the accused or for the convenience of the Government if the rights of the accused are not prejudiced thereby." The Analysis to the Rule states that it is based upon the prior *Manual* provision[204] and (then) Federal Rule of Criminal Procedure 21. Federal Rule of Criminal Procedure 21(b) provides that when prejudice to the accused is not involved, the court may transfer the case, in whole or in part, upon motion of the defendant when it is for "the convenience of parties and witnesses and in the interests of justice."

Rule 906(b)(11) permits transfer for the convenience of the government only and changes prior law.[205] The reason for this difference is unexplained, and it appears unjustifiable. The difference is clearly in violation of the mandate of

---

[202] R.C.M. 906(b)(6). Clearly, a bill of particulars may only be obtained when the specification is inadequate in some fashion to supply sufficient detail. Accordingly, its discovery function is greatly limited. *See generally* United States v. Williams, 40 M.J. 379, 381 nn. 2–4 (C.M.A. 1994) (extensive dictum on bill of particulars).

[203] Discussion of R.C.M. 906(b)(6). As that Discussion points out, "[a] bill of particulars need not be sworn because it is not part of the specification."

[204] MCM, 1969 (rev. ed) ¶ 69e provided: "If the accused demonstrates that there exists at the place of trial . . . so great a general atmosphere of prejudice against him that he cannot obtain a fair and impartial trial in that place, he is entitled, upon a motion for a change of venue, to be tried at some other place."

[205] United States v. Nivens, 45 C.M.R. 194 (C.M.A. 1972). In *Nivens*, the court held that the list of motions for appropriate relief in the *1969 Manual for Courts-Martial* was illustrative only and did not bar a venue change for the convenience of the defense. 45 C.M.R. at 196–97 (C.M.A. 1972). This approach is unlikely to be accurate under the Rules for Courts-Martial, inasmuch as R.C.M. 906(b)(11) expressly permits a change of location for the government, somewhat clearly prohibiting a transfer for defense's convenience.

(Rel.3—1/07 Pub.62410)

Article 36(a) of the Uniform Code of Military Justice, which requires the President's regulations to "apply the principles of law . . . generally recognized in the trial of criminal cases in the United States district Courts" insofar "as he considers practicable." If a trial may reasonably be transferred for the government's convenience, the government can hardly argue that transfer for the defendant's convenience is "impracticable."

A motion to change venue is likely to be associated with a defense claim of prejudicial pretrial publicity.[206] Proof of extensive media coverage of a case, however, is not, itself, grounds for changing the situs of trial, even if the members have heard or read about the case.[207] Rather, in the usual case, the members should be questioned via the voir dire procedure first[208] to determine whether they would be adversely affected by the media exposure.[209] Under the Constitution, "[i]t is not required . . . that the jurors be totally ignorant of the facts and issues involved. . . . It is sufficient if the juror can lay aside his impression or opinion and render a verdict based on the evidence presented in court."[210] When the publicity is both extensive and likely to prejudice the accused, a change of venue may be required, even if the members indicate that they have not formed an opinion in the case.[211]

A venue change may also be ordered when "necessary to permit adequate defense trial preparation" — specifically to accord "an accused his right to a thorough pretrial investigation and the discovery of favorable witnesses."[212]

A motion to change venue is an interlocutory matter and not subject to review,[213] except via extraordinary relief or on appeal of a resulting conviction.

---

[206] See generally Section 13-35.00.

[207] E.g., United States v. Loving, 34 M.J. 956, 964–65 (A.C.M.R. 1992) (given that the judge took proper measures to ensure that the members were free from possible outside influence, even though the case was capital a venue change was not needed in the absence of an "atmosphere of hostility").

[208] See generally Chapter 15.

[209] United States v. Hurt, 27 C.M.R. 3 (C.M.A. 1958); United States v. Smith, 1 M.J. 1204 (N.C.M.R. 1977).

[210] Irvin v. Dowd, 366 U.S. 717, 722–23 (1961).

[211] Rideau v. Louisiana, 373 U.S. 723 (1963).

[212] United States v. Carey, 1 M.J. 761, 765 (A.F.C.M.R. 1975). This appears to remain accurate under the terms of R.C.M. 906(b)(11) when it permits change of situs "to prevent prejudice to the rights of the accused." In ruling on such a motion, the judge may consider the existence or lack thereof of any pretrial efforts to obtain a situs change. United States v. Hurt, 27 C.M.R. 3 (C.M.A. 1958); United States v. Carter, 25 C.M.R. 370 (C.M.A. 1958).

[213] U.C.M.J. art. 51(b); R.C.M. 905(f). See also Chenoweth v. Van Arsdall, 46 C.M.R. 183 (C.M.A. 1973); United States v. Nivens, 45 C.M.R. 194 (C.M.A. 1972); United States v. Carey, 1 M.J. 761 (A.F.C.M.R. 1975).

(Rel.3—1/07   Pub.62410)

On appeal, the trial judge's decision will stand unless the judge abused his or her discretion.[214]

§ 18-35.00 Motion in Limine

Rule for Courts-Martial 906(b)(13) authorizes either party to request a "[p]reliminary ruling on admissibility of evidence."[215] The Discussion of the Rule notes that whether to rule is a matter within the discretion of the military judge.[216] In acknowledging the difficulties inherent in considering motions in limine, which serve pragmatically as advance advisory rulings, the Court of Military Appeals stated in *United States v. Cofield*:[217]

> Of course, in deciding whether to defer [ruling on a motion in limine], the judge should consider the risk that a mistrial may ensue if the prosecution attempts to impeach an accused by use of a prior conviction or other evidence which is then held to be inadmissible. Likewise, the judge may properly consider the loss of time for busy — sometimes impatient — court members who must wait during trial while he rules in an out-of-court hearing. Furthermore, the judge should have some reasonable assurance that the ruling will be decisive as to the accused's choice whether to take the stand. In that connection, he may seek to be advised as to the probable scope and content of the accused's proposed testimony.

Other than a motion to exclude evidence,[218] a party may make a motion in limine to permit the introduction of uncharged instances of conduct, to permit bolstering of the key witness, or to impeach the opponent's key witness.[219] This motion permits a ruling in advance of trial. Additionally, counsel may seek to determine the admissibility of various hearsay statements under Article VIII of the Military Rules of Evidence.

The hearing on the motion as to the admission or exclusion of the evidence is held out of the presence of the fact finder at a time convenient for the parties. A motion in limine is critical in determining trial strategy as to voir dire, opening statement, order of witnesses, and the scope of examination. Where the evidence is sought to be admitted by the prosecution, a defense motion in limine would be advisable. However, the prosecution may have the right to appeal an adverse

---

[214] United States v. Carter, 25 C.M.R. 370 (C.M.A. 1958); United States v. Hurt, 27 C.M.R. 3 (C.M.A. 1958); United States v. Anderson, 36 M.J. 963, 969 (A.F.C.M.R. 1993); United States v. Carey, 1 M.J. 761 (A.F.C.M.R. 1975).

[215] R.C.M. 906(b)(13).

[216] R.C.M. 906(d)(13) Discussion.

[217] 11 M.J. 422, 430–31 (C.M.A. 1981).

[218] Usually potential impeachment evidence.

[219] Professor Lederer terms this a "reverse motion in limine" or a "motion to clarify or declare admissibility." *See* Imwinkelried, *The Pretrial Important and Adaptation of the "Trial" Evidence Rules*, 25 Loy. L.A. L. Rev. 965 (1992).

(Rel.3—1/07 Pub.62410)

ruling by the judge on a motion in limine. [220] Otherwise, if the defense waits until the point in trial when the prosecution seeks to introduce the evidence, the prosecution will have no right of appeal. Rather than appealing a motion granted in limine, an adverse ruling may force the prosecution to gather more evidence linking the defendant to the charged or uncharged act. Additionally, it will allow relitigation of the issue based upon the new evidence at the trial itself. With this caveat in mind, it is wise for the parties to use the motion in limine as to various evidentiary matters. When a motion in limine is made, the judge may defer ruling, grant a tentative ruling, or make a final decision, subject to new evidence being presented by the parties. [221]

From the points of view of judicial economy and trial strategy, the judge would like to make the ruling as early as possible. [222] The judge, however, does have other valid concerns. Foremost, the procedure for deciding admissibility is normally made on offers of proof, although it may be made by hearing the witnesses during the session out of the hearing of the fact finder. In any event, what is done during the pretrial stage, especially via offers of proof, may differ greatly from what is actually presented at trial. Second, the proponent may not introduce the evidence where the admissibility of the evidence is questionable or the case is stronger than anticipated. In many instances, a balancing test, for example under Military Rules of Evidence 403, 404(b), 412, 608, and 609, may be employed by the judge. Several factors employed in applying the balancing test, such as necessity of the testimony or the criticality of the credibility of the accused, cannot be adequately evaluated absent the factual content. Thus, the judge would actually not save time by having a pretrial hearing.

The Supreme Court recognized the difficulty inherent in limine motions in *Luce v. United States*, [223] holding that an accused who did not testify at trial

---

[220] *See, e.g.*, United States v. Day, 591 F.2d 861 (D.C. Cir. 1978); United States v. Peterson, 20 M.J. 806 (N.M.C.M.R. 1985).

[221] For the judge's evidentiary responsibilities in resolving the motion in limine, see United States v. Hamilton, 36 M.J. 927, 928, 930 (A.F.C.M.R. 1993).

[222] Judge Cox indicated in United States v. Rivera, 24 M.J. 156, 159 (C.M.A. 1987), that a motion in limine is primarily a defense motion to litigate suppression motions and to block the government's use of witnesses or evidence that is reasonably believed to be inadmissible. He declared his "grave reservations" about the government's use of a motion in limine (termed a "preemptive strike" by Judges Cox and Everett) to oppose evidence likely to be offered by the defense as part of the defense case in-chief. 24 M.J. 159 (C.M.A. 1987). The government's use of motions in limine are more administrative in nature, such as not producing a witness, limiting cross-examination of a government witness, or relieving the government of certain administrative responsibility. One court has pointed out that the most efficient procedure for determining admissibility under this approach is an in-limine hearing, at which time the trial court may consider offers of proof, affidavits, stipulations, or learned treatises. United States v. Downing, 753 F.2d 1224, 1241 (3d Cir. 1985).

[223] 469 U.S. 38 (1984). *See also* United States v. Cannon, 30 M.J. 886 (A.F.C.M.R. 1990) (proper

(Rel.3—1/07   Pub.62410)

may not challenge on appeal an in-limine ruling admitting a prior conviction for impeachment under Federal Rule of Evidence 609(a). Luce's attorney had made a motion in limine to preclude the government from impeaching his client if he testified. Counsel made no commitment that the accused would testify nor did he make a proffer to the court so as to outline the nature of the testimony. In denying the motion, the trial judge did note that the ruling could vary, depending upon the nature and scope of Luce's trial testimony, and explained that the prior conviction could not be used for impeachment if the accused limited his testimony to explain his attempt to flee from the arresting officer. The Court indicated that the in-limine ruling was not reviewable unless the accused testified. Without such testimony, the record is incomplete, and a "reviewing court is handicapped in any effort to rule on subtle evidentiary questions outside a factual context." [224] In addition, when the accused does not testify, the reviewing court "has no way of knowing whether the Government would have sought to impeach with the prior conviction. If, for example, the Government's case is strong, and the defendant is subject to impeachment by other means, a prosecutor might elect not to use an arguably inadmissible prior conviction." [225] If the accused does not testify, there is little evidence for the appellate courts to determine if there was harmless error. "Were in limine rulings under Rule 609(a) reviewable on appeal, almost any error would result in the windfall of automatic reversal." [226] The Court also noted that its ruling would prevent defense counsel from making motions in limine solely for appellate reasons. [227]

---

to defer ruling on in limine motion when future events are unclear); United States v. Jefferson, 22 M.J. 315 (C.M.A. 1986) (indicating it was too speculative to say that the accused did not testify because a letter written by him was admitted into evidence; *citing Luce*).

[224] 469 U.S. at 41 (1984).

[225] 469 U.S. at 42 (1984).

[226] 469 U.S. at 42 (1984).

[227] 469 U.S. at 42 (1984). Justice Brennan, with whom Justice Marshall joined, sought to limit the case to its holding: "I understand it [the Court] to hold only that a defendant who does not testify at trial may not challenge on appeal an in limine ruling respecting admission of a prior conviction for purposes of impeachment under Rule 609(a) of the Federal Rules of Evidence." 469 U.S. at 43 (1984). Justice Brennan noted two reasons. First, the weighing of probative value or prejudicial effect can only be done in the "specific factual context of a trial as it has unfolded." 469 U.S. at 43 (1984). Second, if the accused does not testify, the "reviewing court is handicapped in making the required harmless-error determination." 469 U.S. 43 (1984). This reasoning would not apply when the "determinative question turns on legal and not factual considerations, a requirement that the defendant actually testify at trial to preserve the admissibility issue for appeal might not necessarily be appropriate." 469 U.S. at 44 (1984).

While the concurring justices sought to limit the ruling, they were ambivalent at best. They recognized that when the issue is not solely a legal one but one that will turn on the factual context of the case, the motion in limine should not be reviewable unless the accused testifies. Thus, the rationale of the case applies to impeachment by specific instances of conduct, specific contradiction of the accused, inconsistent acts by the accused, and prior inconsistent statements by the accused.

Attempting to hold *Luce* to its facts, the Court of Military Appeals, in *United States v. Gamble,* [228] held that the denial of a defense motion to prohibit admission of evidence offered against the accused under Military Rule of Evidence 404(b) was final and reviewable. The court added that "court-martial practice need not follow every aspect of Federal criminal practice." [229] To clarify what it termed the "mixed signals" it had been sending, the court then held, on September 8, 1990, "that the reviewability of *in limine* rulings in courts-martial tried after the date of this opinion will be controlled by *Luce* and by future decisions of the Supreme Court." [230] In *United States v. Gee,* [231] the Court of Military Appeals held that *Luce* was not limited to Rule 609(a) motions and that when defense counsel sought a ruling prohibiting prosecution impeachment of defense character witnesses, failure to call those witnesses forestalled appellate review of the judge's failure to grant the motion. In 1996, the Court adopted the 10th Circuit's approach which requires that: "First we ask whether the matter was adequately presented to the . . . [trial] court . . . . Second we determine whether the issue is of the type that can be finally decided in a pretrial hearing. . . . [Finally] the . . . court's ruling must be definitive." [232]

Under current law the military judge has considerable discretion in deciding whether and when to rule on motions in limine. [233]

When the judge fails to grant a motion in limine, it places the defense counsel on notice to renew the objection when the evidence is offered; the failure to so move will be considered a waiver. [234] The Supreme Court held in 2000 in *Ohler*

Moreover, in light of the concurring opinion of Justice Brennan, unrebutted by the *Luce* majority opinion, it is unclear whether *Luce* applies only to reviewability of *in limine* rulings as to admissibility of prior convictions under Fed. R. Evid. 609(a) or applies more generally.

United States v. Sutton, 31 M.J. 11, 17, n.4 (C.M.A. 1990). Subsequently, *Luce* was largely nullified by the December 1, 2000, change to Federal Rule of Evidence 103.

[228] 27 M.J. 298, 307 (C.M.A. 1988).

[229] 27 M.J. 298, 307 (C.M.A. 1988).

[230] United States v. Sutton, 31 M.J. 11, 17–18 (C.M.A. 1990). Judge Sullivan, concurring, commented that he "would hold that it [*Luce*] should apply as in civilian courts to impeachment evidence." Judge Cox, concurring, added that he "would not go so far as to say I would *never* review a trial judge's refusal to suppress evidence unless the accused takes the stand." (emphasis in the original).

[231] 39 M.J. 311 (C.M.A. 1994).

[232] United States v. Dollente, 45 M.J. 234, 240 (C.A.A.F. 1996), *quoting* United States v. Mejia-Alarcon, 995 F.2d 982, 986-87 (10th Cir. 1993). *See* United States v. Cardreon, 52 M.J. 213 (C.A.A.F. 1999).

[233] United States v. Toohey, 2006 CAAF LEXIS 995 (C.A.A.F. August 9, 2006). United States v. Cannon, 33 M.J. 376, 381–82 (C.M.A. 1991), citing United States v. Sutton, 31 M.J. 11 (C.M.A. 1990).

[234] United States v. Thomas, 11 M.J. 388, 392 (C.M.A. 1981). *See also* United States v. Brannan, 18 M.J. 181, 185 (C.M.A. 1984) (court relied on the fact that the defense counsel did not renew his objection, even though the trial judge again stated he would rule on any objection at the time of the witness testimony).

(Rel.3—1/07   Pub.62410)

v. United States,[235] that the action of a defense counsel in impeaching the accused with a prior conviction that counsel previously sought to prohibit the use of, waives appeal.

§ 18-36.00   Requests for Investigative and Expert Assistance

In the normal case, the accused is on notice of the offenses with which he or she is charged and can adequately defend against them — especially with the discovery procedures promulgated in the Rules for Courts-Martial.[236] In the abnormal case, this may not be true. In *Halfacre v. Chambers,*[237] for example, the accused was charged with purchasing opium while on shore leave in Pakistan. Trial was to take place in Japan, and the accused's defense counsel asked the military judge to order the government to supply him with transportation to Pakistan to gather evidence. When the judge denied the transportation request, but granted a continuance for counsel to travel at his own expense and during leave, the accused petitioned the Court of Military Appeals for relief. In response, the court ordered that the proceedings be stayed and transportation be supplied to the defense counsel at government expense.[238]

The defense may also wish to seek the appointment of law-enforcement members or other personnel as defense investigators or seek funds to privately retain such investigators. Under normal circumstances, this motion should be denied, as the defense normally has adequate assistance via the discovery rules in the Rules for Courts-Martial and the Article 32 investigation. However, in special cases the defense may be able to make a convincing showing of a need for special assistance,[239] especially where the prosecution has been given special aid. In 1970, the Court of Military Appeals held, in *Hutson v. United States,*[240]

---

[235] 529 U.S. 753 (2000).

[236] *See, e.g.,* R.C.M. 701. *See also* R.C.M. 703(c), (d).

[237] U.S.C.M.A. Misc. Docket No. 76-29 (unpublished journal entry, July 13, 1976).

[238] U.S.C.M.A. Misc. Docket No. 76-29. The stay was later vacated. 2 M.J. 188 (C.M.A. 1976).

[239] There are many instances when the defense may want expert assistance. Some past examples include a government requirement that the defense stipulate as part of a pretrial agreement that imprisonment prevents recidivism of sexual offenders (*cf.* United States v. Harrod, 20 M.J. 777 (A.C.M.R. 1985)); prosecution evidence as of rape trauma syndrome (*cf.* United States v. Cameron, 21 M.J. 59 (C.M.A. 1985)); and sophisticated pathology reports in homicide cases. *See generally* Margolin & Wagner, *The Indigent Criminal Defendant and Defense Services: A Search for Constitutional Standards,* 24 Hastings L.J. 647, 663 (1973). Many times a government pathologist will have a series of slides that cannot be interpreted by counsel without training in that area. Counsel would be unlikely to spot possible errors or omissions, thus an expert may be critical in the case. This might also be true in blood-pathology and plant-identification cases. 20 M.J. 777 (A.C.M.R. 1985).

United States v. Rouse, 100 F.3d 560 (8th Cir. 1996) (defense psychiatrist may be able to examine child victims under some circumstances).

[240] 42 C.M.R. 39 (C.M.A. 1970).

(Rel.3—1/07 Pub.62410)

that assistance available to the defense in civilian federal cases [241] was inapplicable to members of the armed forces and stated in dictum that the accused's only assistance was the Article 32 investigation. Although *Hutson* is still good law, there is no reason to believe that it would be dispositive should the defense make a compelling showing of an overriding need for such assistance to have a fair trial.

In *Ake v. Oklahoma*,[242] Justice Marshall, writing for seven members of the Supreme Court, held that when a defendant in a capital case demonstrates that mental responsibility will be a significant factor at the trial, the due process clause requires that the state assure the accused access to a competent psychiatrist to conduct an appropriate examination and assist in the evaluation, preparation, and presentation of the defense. The Court indicated that this does not give the indigent defendant a constitutional right to consult a psychiatrist of his choice or to receive funds for his own hire.[243] The rationale of the majority that psychiatrists gather facts through professional examination, interviews, and reports, and analyze these for the court members would apply to a number of expert witnesses.[244] The expert is also needed to assist counsel in preparing the cross-examination of the state's witnesses to ensure an accurate resolution of the issue in the case.[245] How far this holding will be extended remains to be seen. Chief

---

[241] 18 U.S.C. § 3006A.

[242] 470 U.S. 68 (1985); White v. Johnson, 153 F.3d 197 (5th Cir. 1998) (failure to appoint expert under *Ake* could be harmless error); Brewer v. Reynolds, 51 F.3d 1519 (10th Cir. 1995) (agreed with *Starr v. Lockhart*, 23 F.3d 1280, 1291–92 (8th Cir. 1994) that harmless error may be applied to *Ake* violations).

[243] 470 U.S. at 83. ("This is not to say . . . that the indigent defendant has a constitutional right to choose a psychiatrist of his personal liking or to receive funds to hire his own."). *See also* Burger v. Zant, 984 F.2d 1129 (11th Cir. 1993) (government complies with *Ake* by providing a capital defendant his choice of psychiatrist).

[244] 470 U.S. at 80. The Court stated:

In this role, psychiatrists gather facts, both through professional examination, interviews, and elsewhere, that they will share with the judge or jury; they analyze the information gathered and from it draw plausible conclusions about the defendant's mental condition, and about the effects of any disorder on behavior; and they offer opinions about how the defendant's mental condition might have affected his behavior at the time in question. They know the probative questions to ask of the opposing party's psychiatrists and how to interpret their answers.

[245] 470 U.S. at 81–82 (footnotes omitted). The Court stated:

By organizing a defendant's mental history, examination results and behavior, and other information, interpreting it in light of their expertise, and then laying out their investigative and analytic process to the jury, the psychiatrists for each party enable the jury to make its most accurate determination of the truth on the issue before them. It is for this reason that States rely on psychiatrists as examiners, consultants and witnesses, and that private individuals do as well, when they can afford to so do. In so saying we neither approve nor disapprove the widespread reliance on psychiatrists but instead recognize the unfairness of a contrary holding in light of the evolving practice.

(Rel.3—1/07 Pub.62410)

Justice Burger concurred in the judgment, indicating that he thought the case was limited to the facts and the question presented.[246] Justice Rehnquist dissented, indicating that the rule was limited to capital cases and emphasizing that the accused was not entitled to an independent psychiatrist or consultant.[247]

Ake may be the basis for furnishing expert assistance to the accused.[248] The sources of the right might be the equal protection clause,[249] due process clause,[250] right to counsel,[251] or compulsory process.[252] To establish the right to expert assistance, the judge must examine three factors: The accused's interest, the government's interest, and that the probable value of the assistance will outweigh the risk of an erroneous result.[253]

While the Supreme Court may limit *Ake* to a psychologist in a capital case involving the issue of mental responsibility, the Court of Military Appeals indicated in dictum that military due process is more expansive.[254]

The foregoing leads inexorably to the conclusion that, without the assistance of a psychiatrist to conduct a professional examination on issues relevant to the defense, to help determine whether the insanity defense is viable, to present testimony, and to assist in preparing the cross-examination of a State's psychiatric witnesses, the risk of an inaccurate resolution of sanity issues is extremely high.

[246] 470 U.S. at 87. "This is a capital case in which the Court is asked to decide whether a State may refuse an indigent defendant 'any opportunity whatsoever' to obtain psychiatric evidence for the preparation and presentation of a claim of insanity by way of defense when the defendant's legal sanity at the time of the offense was 'seriously in issue.' The facts of the case and the question presented confine the actual holding of the Court."

[247] 470 U.S. at 87. ("I would limit the rule to capital cases, and make clear that the entitlement is to an independent psychiatric evaluation, not to a defense consultant.")

[248] *E.g.*, People v. Lawson, 163 Ill. 2d 187, 644 N.E.2d 1172 (1994) (Dictum that *Ake* partial authority for decision that defense is entitled to funds for shoe print expert). The Solicitor General argued in *United States v. Short*, 50 M.J. 370 (C.A.A.F. 1999), *cert. denied*, 528 U.S. 1105 (2000) that the federal cases "do not stand for the more general proposition asserted by petitioner of a right to a government-funded expert assistant of the defendant's choice without a showing of necessity." Brief at 7-8.

[249] *See, e.g.*, Britt v. North Carolina, 404 U.S. 226, 227 (1971) ("*Griffin v. Illinois* and its progeny established the principle that the State must, as a matter of equal protection, provide indigent prisoners with the basic tools of an adequate defense or appeal, when those tools are available for a price to other prisoners.").

[250] *See, e.g.*, Ake v. Oklahoma, 470 U.S. 68 (1985); Caldwell v. Mississippi, 472 U.S. 320, 324 n.1 (1985) (Court refused to reverse trial court's determination that the defendant was not entitled to an expert because the defendant had "offered little more than undeveloped assertions that the requested assistance would be beneficial").

[251] *See generally* Paul C. Giannelli & Edward J. Imwinkelried, *Scientific Evidence* § 4-6(A) at 242 (3d ed. 1999).

[252] Paul C. Giannelli & Edward J. Imwinkelried, Scientific Evidence § 4-6(A) at 242 (3d ed. 1999).

[253] Ake v. Oklahoma, 470 U.S. 68, 77–91 (1985).

[254] United States v. Garries, 22 M.J. 288 (C.M.A. 1986). The Navy Court of Military Review

(Rel.3—1/07   Pub.62410)

Servicemembers are entitled to investigative or expert assistance when necessary for an adequate defense.[255] But again, it is for the defense to establish what the expert will do, why a government expert might not suffice, and if they have the assistance available within their office, why that would not be adequate.[256]

The defense has the burden of establishing that the expert testimony is relevant, necessary, and pertains to a significant factor. Certainly, where the defense refused to make a showing of necessity or where the government offers the defense counsel the service of a government expert who would work under an order of confidentiality, the defense has not met this burden.[257] "[C]ounsel are

held that the "paragraph 121" inquiry satisfies the due process requirements and the obligation set forth in *Ake*. United States v. Davis, 22 M.J. 829 (N.M.C.M.R. 1986), *aff'd*, 24 M.J. 222 (C.M.A. 1987).

[255] *See generally* United States v. McAllister, 55 M.J. 270 (C.A.A.F. 2001) (failure to provide requested expert required reversal). *McAllister* which involved a request by the defense to change DNA-related experts after the convening authority had authorized the expert initially requested by the defense, suggests a liberal perspective when DNA testing is concerned.

[256] Preutt v. Thompson, 996 F.2d 1560, 1573 (4th Cir. 1993) (defendant cannot complain about lack of expert assistance when he was allowed to consult expert he selected); United States v. Garries, 22 M.J. 288 (C.M.A. 1986); United States v. Burnette, 29 M.J. 473 (C.M.A. 1990) (defense entitled to an expert other than government witness); United States v. Turner, 28 M.J. 487, 488 (C.M.A. 1989) ("To assure that indigent defendants will not be at a disadvantage in trials where expert testimony is central to the outcome, the Supreme Court has ruled that a defendant must be furnished expert assistance in preparing his defense . . . . For trial by court-martial the same requirement could be inferred from Article 46 . . . even if it were not constitutionally mandated"); United States v. Toledo, 25 M.J. 270 (C.M.A. 1987) (accused has no right to pick a specific government expert and then declare a privilege; the court did set forth a procedure to have the communications with the government expert subject to the attorney-client privilege); United States v. Hagen, 25 M.J. 78 (C.M.A. 1987) (the accused has no right to expert of choice); United States v. Fontenot, 26 M.J. 559 (A.C.M.R. 1988), *rev'd on other grounds*, 29 M.J. 253 (C.M.A. 1989) (The accused was examined by a sanity board. The court held that the accused's motion for examination by a civilian psychiatrist was properly denied because there was no showing that the sanity board was inadequate, nor was there any request for a second sanity board, nor did the defense make an offer of proof of what additional information the civilian psychiatrist would furnish). *See also* United States v. Thomas, 33 M.J. 644 (N.M.C.M.R. 1991) (court refused to appoint expert to conduct post-trial psychological evaluation of the accused). In *United States v. Robinson*, 39 M.J. 88 (C.M.A. 1994), the accused requested a secretor test. Ruling that there was no evidence to establish its possible application the trial court rejected the request. Although the Court of Military Appeals upheld the judge's ruling on the grounds that the accused had failed to demonstrate the necessity for the test, Judge Cox, dissenting, having first noted that "He who has the gold, rules," urged that the simple test was the accused's *only* defense and complained, "Shame on you, Air Force, for denying him that simple test!" 39 M.J. at 90 (C.M.A. 1994).

Air Force Instruction 51-201, Law, Administration of Military Justice ¶ 6.5.2.1 (26 November 2003), provides that in urinalysis cases parties must ascertain the availability of seek government experts before requesting civilian experts. *Cf.* United States v. Warner, 62 M.J. 114 (C.A.A.F. 2005).

[257] *Cf.* United States v. Ford, 51 M.J. 445, 455–56 (C.A.A.F. 1999) (defense failed to carry its

(Rel.3—1/07　Pub.62410)

expected to educate themselves to attain competence in defending an issue presented in a particular case," employing "a number of primary and secondary material."[258] Nor will the defense meet the burden when there is a viable alternative available, such as an independent investigator who will work under an order of confidentiality.

The procedure to apply for expert assistance is set forth in Rule for Courts-Martial 703(d). The defense must serve notice on the prosecution that it intends to submit a request to the convening authority for authorization to employ an expert.[259] This request shall include a complete statement of the reasons why the expert is necessary and the estimated cost of employment.[260] If the request is denied by the convening authority, it may be resubmitted to the military judge.[261] If the military judge grants the motion for employment of the expert or finds the government is required to provide a substitute, the proceeding shall be abated if the government fails to comply with the ruling.[262] It may be that the review to the military judge will be an *ex parte* proceeding in order to avoid giving the prosecution an unfair advantage.[263] Also, the defense may not submit a request to the convening authority for the same reason.

In light of the separate defense services in the Army and Air Force, budget funds might best be allocated to them for expert or investigative assistance. This would eliminate most issues concerning assistance.

§ 18-37.00 Exclusion of Witnesses

Military Rule of Evidence 615 provides:

> At the request of the prosecution or defense the military judge shall order witnesses excluded so that they cannot hear the testimony of other

---

burden for a defense explosives expert after prosecution made its experts available and defense failed to show an appropriate expert existed); United States v. Gonzalez, 39 M.J. 459, 461 (C.M.A. 1994) (court adopted a three prong test); United States v. Garries, 22 M.J. 288, 291 (C.M.A. 1986). *See also* Cartwright v. Maynard, 802 F.2d 1203, 1211 (10th Cir. 1986); Volson v. Blackburn, 794 F.2d 173, 175 (5th Cir. 1986); Vassar v. Solem, 763 F.2d 975 (8th Cir. 1985).

[258] United States v. Kelly, 39 M.J. 235, 238 (C.M.A. 1994). *See also* United States v. Short, 50 M.J. 370, 373 (C.A.A.F. 1999) (*citing Kelly, above*).

[259] R.C.M. 703(d).

[260] R.C.M. 703(d).

[261] R.C.M. 703(d).

[262] R.C.M. 703(d).

[263] United States v. Garries, 22 M.J. 288, 291 (C.M.A. 1986). *See also* State v. Ballard, 333 N.C. 515, 428 S.E.2d 178 (1993) (defense entitled to *ex parte* hearing to protect Fifth and Sixth Amendment privilege when attempting to make threshold showing of necessity for psychiatric expert); *Ex parte* Moody, 684 So. 2d 114 (Ala. 1996) (when seeking expert, defendant entitled to *ex parte* hearing to determine whether there will be encroachment on the right not to incriminate oneself).

(Rel.3—1/07 Pub.62410)

witnesses, and the military judge may make the order *sua sponte*. This rule does not authorize exclusion of (1) the accused, or (2) a member of an armed service or an employee of the United States designated as representative of the United States by the trial counsel, or (3) a person whose presence is shown by a party to be essential to the presentation of the party's case or (4) a person authorized by statute to be present at courts-martial, or (5) any victim of an offense from the trial of an accused for that offense because such victim may testify or present any information in relation to the sentence or that offense during the presentencing proceedings.

This rule was taken from Federal Rule of Evidence 615 with only minor changes of terminology to conform with military practice but prior to the addition of subsections (4) and (5). [264] Under the rule, the military judge lacks any discretion to exclude potential witnesses who come within its scope unless the accused's constitutional protections dictate otherwise. The courts are continuing to interpret the scope of Rule 615. [265] In the armed forces, for example, the Rule does not apply to unknown rebuttal witnesses. [266]

The Fourth Circuit Court of Appeals, in *United States v. Farnham*, [267] indicated that the court should narrowly construe the civilian version of Rule 615(2), at

---

[264] Analysis of the Rules for Courts-Martial, MCM, 2005, A22-48-49. The change to the Federal Rules was based on the "Victim of Crime Bill of Rights," 42 U.S.C. § 10606. In dicta in *United States v. McVeigh*, 6 F.3d 325, 336 (10th Cir. 1997), the court opined that Fed. R. Evid. 615 was not superseded by the Victims Rights Act. The impact on the military prior to the change of the Military Rules of Evidence was explored in *United States v. Spann*, 48 M.J. 586 (N.M. Crim. App. 1998), *aff'd*, 51 M.J. 89 (C.A.A.F. 1999). Military Rule of Evidence 415 was amended by operation of law, Fed. R. Evid. 1102, on June 1, 2000, adopting Federal Rule of Evidence 615(4) to prohibit exclusion of "a person authorized by statute to be present." The pragmatic effect of this change is to implement 18 U.S.C § 3510(a) which in turn prohibits exclusion from trial of any victim "because such victim may, during the sentencing hearing, make a statement or present any information in relation to the sentence." *See also* United States v. Spann, 51 M.J. 89 (C.A.A.F. 1999). The 2002 Amendment to the Manual made the adoption of the Federal Rule language explicit. *See also* United States v. Langston, 53 M.J. 335 (C.A.A.F. 2000)(Rule 615 applies during providence inquiry in a mixed plea case).

[265] *See* United States v. Gammon, 961 F.2d 103, 105 (7th Cir. 1992) (no requirement to exclude witness' testimony for violation of Rule 615 when no evidence of collusion); United States v. Mohney, 949 F.2d 1397, 1405 (6th Cir. 1991) (under Rule 615(3) the judge may allow two witnesses to remain in the courtroom); United States v. Michael, 33 M.J. 900, 903 (A.F.C.M.R. 1991) (this rule should not be extended to prohibit pretrial communications between the witnesses absent extraordinary circumstances).

[266] United States v. Gittens, 39 M.J. 325 (C.M.A. 1994).

[267] 85-5209 (4th Cir. May 27, 1986); United States v. Jackson, 60 F.3d 128 (2d Cir. 1995) (judge has discretion to exempt more than one witness from sequestration order); United States v. Miller, 48 M.J. 49 (C.A.A.F. 1998) (Court held that under Mil. R. Evid. 615, once the prosecutor designates an individual as the government representative, "the military judge had little discretion to exclude him." The defense counsel did not ask for the representation to testify first).

(Rel.3—1/07 Pub.62410)

least when that provision is used to permit a law-enforcement officer to remain in the courtroom prior to his or her testimony in the same case.[268]

Neither Military nor Federal Rule of Evidence 615 deprives a judge entirely of methods of coping with appointment of a law-enforcement witness as a "government representative." Despite the language of Rule 615 and the Federal Advisory Committee Notes that authority to exclude a witness under Rule 615(1)-(3) is not within the discretion of the trial judge, the courts have indicated that it is within the discretion of the trial judge to exempt an expert witness from hearing the testimony of other witnesses[269] unless the expert witness is essential to the management of the case.[270] Military Rule of Evidence 615 does not limit the discretion of the judge under Military Rule of Evidence 611[271] to order a witness who will be present during the trial to testify early in the proceedings to avoid the tailoring of testimony or the perception of unfairness.[272]

In *United States v. Ayala*,[273] the court indicated that requiring the government representative to testify first in the case substantially limited the chance of the witness tailoring testimony. The possibility of fabrication remains, however. Notwithstanding this, the test is likely to remain that of the sound discretion of the trial judge.[274]

---

[268] Where the defendant's conviction turned on the relative credibility of the defendant and the agents regarding a conversation, letting a second agent remain in the courtroom while the first agent testified was reversible error. Chief Judge Winter pointed out that the framers designed Rule 615 to aid the truth-seeking process. It would be nearly impossible to prove that the witness' testimony would have been different if he had not been present in the courtroom. *See also* United States v. Jackson, 60 F.3d 128 (2d Cir. 1995) (judge has discretion to exempt more than one witness from sequestration order). *But see* United States v. Miller, 48 M.J. 49, 58 (C.A.A.F. 1998) (Court held that under Mil. R. Evid. 615, once the prosecutor designated an individual as the government representative, "the military judge had little discretion to exclude him." The defense counsel did not ask for the representative to testify first).

[269] Morvant v. Construction Aggregates Corp., 570 F.2d 626 (6th Cir. 1978).

[270] The trial court must accept any reasonable representation to this effect by counsel. United States v. Phillips, 515 F. Supp. 758 (E.D. Ky. 1981).

[271] Military Rule of Evidence 611(a) provides, "The military judge shall exercise reasonable control over the mode and order of interrogating witnesses and presenting evidence so as to (1) make the interrogation and presentation effective for the ascertainment of the truth, (2) avoid needless consumption of time, (3) protect witnesses from harassment or undue embarrassment."

[272] Mil. R. Evid. 611. Wills v. Russell, 100 U.S. 621, 626 (1879).

[273] 22 M.J. 777 (A.C.M.R. 1986).

[274] *See, e.g.,* United States v. Scott, 13 M.J. 874 (N.M.C.M.R. 1982), *rev'd on other grounds,* 16 M.J. 449 (C.M.A. 1983, *on remand,* 17 M.J. 724 (N.M.C.M.R. 191983), *aff'd,* 22 M.J. 297 (C.M.A. 1986), *cert. denied,* 480 U.S. 931 (1987) (no abuse of discretion in denying a request that the government representative testify first, especially since the agent's testimony was not offered to corroborate testimony of prior witnesses). *See also* United States v. Rivera, 971 F.2d 876, 891–92 (2d Cir. 1992) (may exempt two witnesses).

(Rel.3—1/07 Pub.62410)

The better rule would be to eliminate Rule 615(2) and to give the trial court judge the authority to exempt a witness, particularly an expert witness, from being sequestered upon a showing of adequate necessity, as granted by Rule 615(3).

§ 18-38.00　Severance of Co-Accused

Although Rule for Courts-Martial 601(e)(3) permits joint trials of co-accused who participated in "the same act or transaction or in the same series of acts or transactions," Rule 906(b)(9) permits severance of "multiple accused, if it appears that an accused or the Government is prejudiced by a joint or common trial." The Rule continues to mandate that in a common trial "a severance shall be granted whenever any accused, other than the moving accused, faces charges unrelated to those charged against the moving accused." Severance motions are to be liberally construed[275] and the judge's decision on such a motion is reviewed on an abuse of discretion standard.[276]

§ 18-39.00　Severance of Offenses

Rule for Courts-Martial 906(b)(10) permits severance of offenses, "but only to prevent manifest injustice." Although the Discussion to the Rule suggests that severance may be appropriate to avoid a violation of an accused's speedy trial rights, severance may be more necessary to permit improper "overflow" effects from uncharged misconduct. The admissibility of uncharged conduct, however, does "not become the primary test for severance";[277] that remains the manifest injustice standard.

§ 18-40.00　SUPPRESSION MOTIONS

§ 18-41.00　In General

Motions to suppress are governed by the Military Rules of Evidence, originally promulgated by the President in 1980.[278] The Rules govern motions to suppress unlawful admissions and confessions,[279] evidence allegedly obtained from unlawful searches and seizures,[280] and evidence allegedly obtained from

---

[275] United States v. Mayhugh, 41 M.J. 657, 659 (N.M. Crim. App. 1995), aff'd, 44 M.J. 363 (C.A.A.F. 1996), citing Discussion to R.C.M. 906(b)(9).

[276] 41 M.J. at 659–60 (N.M. Crim. App. 1995).

[277] United States v. Foster, 40 M.J. 140, 147 (C.M.A. 1994) (citing United States v. Curry, 31 M.J. 359, 375 (C.M.A. 1990)).

[278] Exec. Order No. 12198, March 12, 1980. The Military Rules of Evidence are unique in the United States because they codify in Section III the law of confessions and admissions, search and seizure, and eye-witness identification.

[279] Mil. R. Evid. 304.

[280] Mil. R. Evid. 311.

(Rel.3—1/07　Pub.62410)

unlawful identifications.[281] Although different rules address each individual subject, with one minor exception,[282] the procedural aspects of the three rules are identical.[283] As a consequence, this examination will focus on Military Rule of Evidence 304, Confessions and Admissions.

§ 18-42.00 The Disclosure Requirement[284]

Military Rule of Evidence 304(d)(1) provides: "Prior to arraignment, the prosecution shall disclose to the defense the contents of all statements, oral or written, made by the accused that are relevant to the case, known to the trial counsel, and within the control of the armed forces."[285] The disclosure requirement may function as a discovery device, but its primary intent is to supply the defense with sufficient information on which to prepare a suppression motion.[286]

Under normal circumstances, the sole evidentiary consequence of a prosecution failure to disclose is to permit the defense to make a suppression motion after submission of a plea[287] in conjunction with a recess or continuance as appropriate. As the Air Force Court of Military Review observed in *United States v. Reynolds*,[288] however:

> If . . . the failure to make a timely disclosure is inadvertent and unintentional, a continuance to discover the circumstances surrounding the [undisclosed] statement is appropriate. On the other hand, if the failure is deliberate and done in order to attain an unfair advantage, the trial judge can take whatever action which is appropriate which might include the exclusion of the statement.[289]

Disclosure is mandatory even if no evidentiary sanction will result. Customarily, disclosure should be made in writing and formally served on the opposing

---

[281] Mil. R. Evid. 321.

[282] Military Rule of Evidence 304 requires disclosure regardless of whether the prosecution intends to introduce the evidence.

[283] *See* Mil. R. Evid. 304(d); 311(d); 321(c).

[284] *See* Sections 11-23.00 and 11-24.00.

[285] The equivalent rules for search and seizure (Mil. R. Evid. 311(d)(1)) and eye witness identifications (Mil. R. Evid. 321(c)(2)) are identical, except that the government need disclose only that evidence obtained from a search or seizure or identification that it plans to offer against the accused at trial. Military Rule of Evidence 304(d)(1) is unique in that it requires all known statements. *But see* United States v. Callara, 21 M.J. 259 (C.M.A. 1986). The author of the Rule believed that admissions by the accused were more likely to yield derivative evidence subject to suppression than other forms of evidence.

[286] Analysis of the 1980 Amendments to the *Manual for Courts-Martial*, Analysis of Mil. R. Evid. 304(d)(1), MCM, 1984, A22-20.

[287] Mil. R. Evid. 304(d)(2)(B).

[288] 15 M.J. 1021 (A.F.C.M.R. 1983).

[289] 15 M.J. at 1023 (A.F.C.M.R. 1983) (*citing generally* S. Saltzburg, L. Schinasi, & D. Schlueter, *Military Rules of Evidence* 79 (1981)).

party.[290] Such disclosure should include the entire text of any statement involved or an accurate description of any physical evidence seized.

Derivative evidence is not subject to mandatory disclosure under the rules,[291] although such disclosure is to be strongly encouraged. If derivative evidence is disclosed, the defense must move to suppress it prior to plea or waive the issue.[292]

§ 18-43.00   Timing

If the evidence in question has been disclosed by the prosecution, the defense must move to suppress it prior to entering a plea or the defense may not raise the issue at a later time except as permitted by the military judge for good cause shown. Failure to so move or object constitutes a waiver of objection.[293] If the evidence was not disclosed prior to arraignment, "the prosecution shall provide timely notice to the military judge and to counsel for the accused. The defense may enter an objection at that time and the military judge may make such orders as are required in the interests of justice."[294]

Unless a conditional guilty plea is permitted,[295] a guilty plea waives all suppression motions.[296]

§ 18-44.00   The Need for Specificity

Prior to the Military Rules of Evidence, the defense moved to suppress evidence[297] simply by so moving or objecting. The defense was not generally required to carry any specific burden of production, and the burden of proof was

---

[290] Analysis of the Military Rules of Evidence 1980 Amendments to the *Manual for Courts-Martial*, Analysis of Mil. R. Evid. 304(d)(1), MCM, 2005 A22-11.

[291] Mil. R. Evid. 304(d)(2)(C). Derivative evidence was treated differently from primary evidence because of the difficulty in determining what is truly derivative of any given piece of evidence. Inasmuch as the disclosure requirement is a binding one, it was thought unwise to put a burden on the prosecution that it, in good faith, might not be able to fulfill. It was the expectation that evidence that was clearly derivative would be automatically disclosed.

[292] Mil. R. Evid. 304(d)(2)(C).

[293] Mil. R. Evid. 304(d)(2)(A).

[294] Mil. R. Evid. 304(d)(2)(B). *See also* Section 18-43.00.

[295] R.C.M. 910(a)(2).

[296] Mil. R. Evid. 304(d)(5); 311(i); 321(g).

[297] Technically speaking, suppression motions did not exist. Rather, the accused was entitled to object to the evidence when offered. With the permission of the military judge, however, counsel could object prior to plea in the form of a motion to suppress. In the area of confessions and admissions, matters were technically different, because the *Manual for Courts-Martial* required the prosecution to prove the voluntariness of any statement made by the accused before entering it into evidence. Notwithstanding this affirmative burden of production (as well as proof), the defense normally raised the issue first as indicated above.

(Rel.3—1/07 Pub.62410)

shifted to the prosecution immediately upon making the motion or objection. The Military Rules of Evidence altered this:

> The military judge may require the defense to specify the grounds upon which the defense moves to suppress or object to evidence. If defense counsel, despite the exercise of due diligence, has been unable to interview adequately those persons involved in the taking of a statement, the military judge may make any order required in the interests of justice, including authorization for the defense to make a general motion to suppress or general objection. [298]

Although the Rule leaves the decision as to specificity to the judge's discretion, it is presumed that judges customarily will require specificity. The defense meets its burden of production by making an offer of proof — reciting the relevant facts of the case as the defense sees it — and then presenting its interpretation of the law as applied to those facts. The defense cannot be required to present evidence to raise the issue. [299] The defense motion must be sufficiently specific to give the judge and opposing counsel notice as to the exact illegality complained of. Although this is somewhat more difficult in the area of search and seizure than in confessions, the Rule contemplates more than a general allegation of illegality. Examples would include:

> The accused was the subject of an alleged inspection that was not a lawful inspection because its primary purpose was the prosecution of offenders.

> The accused invoked her right to counsel but was interrogated anyway.

> The accused was the subject of a lineup after the imposition of charges, but was not advised of his right to counsel. [300]

The defense need not make a specific objection if counsel, "despite the exercise of due diligence, has been unable to interview adequately those persons involved in the taking of a statement." [301] The Analysis to the Rules clarifies this provision thusly:

> In view of the waiver that results in the event of failure to object, defense counsel must have sufficient information in order to decide whether to object to the admissibility of a statement by the accused. Although

---

[298] Mil. R. Evid. 304(d)(3); 311(d)(3); 321(c)(3).

[299] Analysis of the Military Rules of Evidence 1980 Amendments to the *Manual for Courts-Martial*, Analysis of Mil. R. Evid. 304(d)(3), MCM, 2005 A22-11-12. The defense was not required to present actual evidence, because it was viewed as too onerous a burden given the state of discovery at that time. Further, actual production of evidence is likely to be unnecessarily time consuming when the facts can basically be established by comparison between the defense and prosecution factual positions, with only the differences being resolved by presentation of evidence.

[300] *See* Analysis of the Military Rules of Evidence 1980 Amendments to the *Manual for Courts-Martial*, Analysis of Mil. R. Evid. 304(d)(3), MCM, 2005, A22-11-12, for a list of examples of specific objections in the area of confessions and admissions.

[301] Mil. R. Evid. 304(d)(3). *See also* Mil. R. Evid. 311(d)(3); 321(c)(3).

(Rel.3—1/07 Pub.62410)

telephone or other long distance communication may be sufficient to allow a counsel to make an informed decision, counsel may consider a personal interview to be essential in this area and in such a case counsel is entitled to personally interview the witnesses . . . before specificity can be required. When such an interview is desired but despite due diligence counsel has been unable to interview adequately those persons . . . the military judge has authority to resolve the situation. Normally this would include the granting of a continuance for interviews or other appropriate relief. If an adequate opportunity to interview is absent, even if this results solely from the witness' unwillingness to speak to the defense, then the specificity requirement does not apply. Lacking adequate opportunity to interview, the defense may be authorized to enter a general objection to the evidence.[302]

This rule stems from the difficulty inherent in interviewing people long distance. Not only must counsel often have in-person contact to overcome the psychological reluctance common to many witnesses when asked to supply information, but also counsel must have a first-hand opportunity to appraise the potential courtroom demeanor of the potential witness.

When counsel cannot adequately interview the necessary witnesses, he or she may be entitled to make a general motion or objection. Such a procedure instantaneously shifts the burden of proof of legality to the prosecution simply by the making of the motion or objection. When the witnesses are available, the preferred remedy is granting a continuance and directing the witnesses to cooperate with defense interviews.[303]

§ 18-45.00 Litigation

After the defense has presented its position via an offer of proof, the prosecution should then be required to state both its view of the facts and its legal position. Only if there is a difference in the factual interpretations should evidence be required, and then only as to those matters about which there is dispute. Once the defense has carried its burden of production by raising, via its offer of proof, matters which, if uncontradicted, would justify relief, the burden of proof shifts to the prosecution, which normally must establish by a preponderance of the evidence[304] that the evidence in question was lawfully obtained.

---

[302] Analysis of the Military Rules of Evidence 1980 Amendments to the *Manual for Courts-Martial*, Analysis of Mil. R. Evid. 304(d)(3), MCM, 2005, A22-11.

[303] When the witness is a servicemember, this is a lawful order. Whether civilian or military, this would appear to be within the subpoena power and the court's inherent authority.

[304] Mil. R. Evid. 304(e)(1); 311(e)(1); 321(d). Clear and convincing evidence is necessary when trying to establish a lawful consent to a search or seizure (Mil. R. Evid. 314(e)(5)) or trying to prove that a later identification was not the result of an earlier unnecessarily suggestive identification. Mil. R. Evid. 321(d)(2). Mil. R. Evid. 304(d)(3); 311(d)(3) ("persons involved in the search or seizure"); 321(c)(3) ("persons involved in the lineup or other identification process").

(Rel.3—1/07 Pub.62410)

The accused may testify on the suppression motion and "may be cross-examined only as to the matter on which he or she testifies. Nothing said by the accused on either direct or cross-examination may be used against the accused for any purpose other than impeachment, or for a prosecution for perjury, false swearing, or the making of a false official statement."[305]

§ 18-46.00   Rulings

Ordinarily, suppression motions must be ruled upon by the military judge prior to the accused's plea.[306] They cannot be reconsidered by the court members, although the procedure by which an accused's statement was obtained may be shown to the members for whatever impact it may have on the weight to be given to the statement.[307] When ruling, the military judge must "state essential findings of fact on the record."[308]

§ 18-50.00   MOTIONS FOR FINDINGS OF NOT GUILTY

Rule for Courts-Martial 917(a) provides:

> The military judge, on motion by the accused or *sua sponte*, shall enter a finding of not guilty of one or more offenses charged after the evidence on either side is closed and before findings on the general issue of guilt are announced if the evidence is insufficient to sustain a conviction of the offense affected. If a motion for a finding of not guilty at the close of the prosecution's case is denied, the defense may offer evidence on that offense without having reserved the right to do so.

As the Analysis of the Rule confirms, the Rule prohibits the military judge from deferring ruling on a motion for a finding of not guilty until after findings.[309]

This motion is analogous to a motion for judgment for acquittal in civilian law.[310] Both require a determination of whether there is sufficient evidence to sustain a conviction of the charge. The military standard for making such a determination is whether there exists "any substantial evidence before the court which, together with all justifiable inferences to be drawn therefrom, reasonably

---

[305] Mil. R. Evid. 304(f); 311(f); 321(e).

[306] Mil. R. Evid. 304(d)(4); 311(d)(4); 321(f). *See generally* Sections 18-14.31 and 18-40.00. *But see cf.* United States v. Helweg, 32 M.J. 129 (C.M.A. 1991).

[307] Mil. R. Evid. 304(e)(2).

[308] Mil. R. Evid. 304(d)(4); 311(d)(4); 321(f). *See generally* Sections 14-64.00 and 18-14-32.

[309] Given the difficulty inherent in taking an offense from the "jury," the inability to defer (justified in part by the rationale that it would be "awkward to proceed to sentencing with the same members" after setting aside some findings as "irrational") is unfortunate.

[310] Fed. R. Crim. P. 29. United States v. Perez, 40 M.J. 373, 376 (C.M.A. 1994).

(Rel.3—1/07   Pub.62410)

tends to establish every essential element of these offenses.[311] If so, the motion should not be granted.

Relying on congressional intent,[312] the Court of Military Appeals has held that the military judge has the authority to grant a motion for a finding of not guilty after sentence if the evidence is legally insufficient.[313] This is a practical result that gives the military judge virtually the same authority as an Article III judge.[314] Limiting such post-trial relief to "legal insufficiency," rather than permitting a grant when the finding is "contrary to the weight of the evidence," differs from the Article III rule,[315] but such civilian grants are exceedingly rare.

A motion for a finding of not guilty is considered an interlocutory question. As such, the ruling of a military judge is final.[316]

Before deciding on the motion, the military judge may require defense counsel to specifically indicate how the evidence is insufficient.[317] In addition, the

------

[311] United States v. Tobin, 38 C.M.R. 423, 426–27 (C.M.A. 1968); R.C.M. 917(d); United States v. Spearman, 48 C.M.R. 405, 406–07 (C.M.A. 1974) (the court held that an accused is not entitled to the granting of a motion for finding of not guilty if there is a prima facie case with respect to a lesser-included offense, but in such instance "the accused may well be entitled to a motion for appropriate relief and seek to have the Military Judge instruct the factfinders that no evidence has been introduced as to the offense charged and that their consideration of the issue of guilt or innocence is limited to the lesser included degree"). *See* R.C.M. 917(e).

[312] United States v. Griffith, 27 M.J. 42, 45 (C.M.A. 1988). In justifying its conclusion, the court in *Griffith* may have overstated its authority. Its reference to language in the legislative history that "the law officer now becomes more nearly an impartial judge in the manner of civilian courts" was taken from the context that the judge would not enter the deliberation room with the court members. *Hearings on H.R. 2498 Before a Subcomm. of the House Armed Services Comm.*, 81st Cong., 1st Sess. 602, 603, 609, 772, 774–75, 777, 1152 (1949). *See also Hearings on S. 857 and H.R. 4080 Before a Subcomm. of the Senate Armed Services Comm.*, 81st Cong., 1st Sess. 40–41, 126, 157, 160, 257 (1949).

The judge's authority ends with authentication of the record unless the convening authority refers the case to the judge. United States v. Toy, 32 M.J. 753 (A.C.M.R. 1991).

[313] United States v. Griffith, 27 M.J. 42 (C.M.A. 1988). The Joint Service Committee on Military Justice refused to consider this proposal at a meeting on 21 September 1988.

[314] 27 M.J. 48 (C.M.A. 1988).

[315] Fed. R. Crim. P. 33.

[316] U.C.M.J. art. 51(b). *See also* R.C.M. 917(f). The ruling of the president of the court-martial, however, is not. His ruling must instead be made subject to the objections of the court. United States v. McCants, 27 C.M.R. 420 (C.M.A. 1959). Before calling for objections, the president should instruct the court members as to the elements of the offense and the standard for ruling on such a motion. U.C.M.J. art. 51(b). If any member of the court objects to the president's ruling, the court shall be closed and the question decided by the members of the court by voice vote. R.C.M. 917(b). "The motion shall specifically indicate wherein the evidence is insufficient." Article 52(c) provides that voice votes on such questions are determined by majority vote and that, in the event of a tie vote, the question is resolved against the accused.

[317] R.C.M. 917(b).

(Rel.3—1/07 Pub.62410)

military judge may, at his discretion, defer any action on the motion to allow the trial counsel to reopen and produce any available evidence he or she has on the motion.[318] Thus, the defense counsel should think carefully about making such a motion when the evidence is easily remedied by trial counsel.

A determination by the court, either by the judge or the court members, sustaining the motion amounts to a finding of not guilty and, therefore, an acquittal on that specification. Upon such a determination, the court members should be instructed that they need not make findings as to that specification and also that that specification should not be considered for any purpose. Failure to so instruct, which results in prejudice to the accused, will necessitate a reversal.[319] Once a finding of not guilty has been entered, the guarantees of protection against double jeopardy prohibit the withdrawal of the acquittal regardless of how wrong or mistaken the finding may have been.[320] Thus, the propriety of the ruling cannot later be reconsidered.[321] The judge may grant a motion in such a way as to yield an acquittal on the charged offense, but leaving a lesser included offense.[322] When doing so, the judge should properly instruct the members, rather than create a new specification embodying only the lesser included offense.[323]

When an offense with a lesser-included offense is included, denial of the motion is not necessarily fatal to the accused. If, after the motion is denied, the government later fails to introduce sufficient evidence on the pleaded charge, the accused may make a motion for appropriate relief and request that the military judge instruct the fact finders that no evidence has been introduced as to the offense charged and that their consideration is limited to the issue of guilt or innocence of the lesser-included offenses.[324] In addition, an accused may appeal the denial of his motion; however, if at the time of the appeal, sufficient evidence exists to sustain the conviction, the conviction will not be reversed because of an erroneous denial of the motion at trial.

---

[318] *Cf.* United States v. Phare, 45 C.M.R. 18 (C.M.A. 1972).

[319] Sanabria v. United States, 437 U.S. 54 (1978); Fong Foo v. United States, 369 U.S. 141 (1962).

[320] United States v. Edwards, 39 C.M.R. 952 (A.F.B.R. 1968).

[321] United States v. Wilson, 6 M.J. 214 (C.M.A. 1979); R.C.M. 917(e).

[322] R.C.M. 917(e).

[323] United States v. Ureta, 41 M.J. 571, 580 (A.F. Crim. App. 1995), *aff'd*, 44 M.J. 290 (C.A.A.F. 1996).

[324] R.C.M. 917(g); United States v. Burroughs, 12 M.J. 380 (C.M.A. 1982).

CHAPTER 19

PLEAS AND PROVIDENCY INQUIRIES

§ 19-10.00 PLEAS
  § 19-11.00   In General
  § 19-12.00   Not-Guilty Pleas
  § 19-13.00   Guilty Pleas
      § 19-13.10 — In General
      § 19-13.20 — Effects of Guilty Pleas
      § 19-13.30 — Guilty Pleas with Exceptions and Substitutions
  § 19-14.00   Standing Mute
  § 19-15.00   Confessional Stipulations
  § 19-16.00   Conditional Pleas
§ 19-20.00 GUILTY PLEA PROVIDENCY INQUIRY
  § 19-21.00   In General
  § 19-22.00   The *"Care"* Inquiry
      § 19-22.10 — *United States v. Care*
      § 19-22.20 — *Care* Codified
  § 19-23.00   Inquiry into a Pretrial Agreement
      § 19-23.10 — In General
      § 19-23.20 — Full Disclosure
      § 19-23.30 — Inquiry into Conditions
      § 19-23.40 — Sentence Limitations
  § 19-24.00   Rejection of an Improvident Plea and Its Consequences
      § 19-24.10 — In General
      § 19-24.20 — Evidentiary Consequences of Rejection of Improvident Pleas
      § 19-24.30 — Recusal of the Military Judge
  § 19-25.00   Noncompliance with Providency-Inquiry Requirements
  § 19-26.00   Appraisal of the Providency Inquiry
§ 19-30.00 ACCEPTANCE OF PLEAS AND SUBSEQUENT ATTACK
§ 19-40.00 WITHDRAWAL OF PLEA
§ 19-50.00 REVISION PROCEEDINGS AND OTHER CORRECTIVE DEVICES
§ 19-60.00 POST-TRIAL MODIFICATIONS OF PRETRIAL AGREEMENTS
§ 19-70.00 FAILURE OF THE GOVERNMENT TO COMPLY WITH TERMS OF A
              PRETRIAL AGREEMENT

(Rel.3—1/07 Pub.62410)

§ 19-10.00   PLEAS

§ 19-11.00   In General

Pursuant to the *Manual for Courts-Martial*, permissible pleas include not-guilty and guilty pleas, and pleas of guilty to a lesser-included offense.[1] For reasons of military legal history, pleas are entered to both a charge and the specification(s) under it,[2] although a charge without a specification should have no legal utility if objected to on grounds of vagueness. Each type of plea has different legal consequences, and an accused may, of course, enter different pleas to different specifications and charges. The mere submission of a plea, regardless of type, may make some motions, such as suppression motions,[3] untimely.[4]

---

[1] R.C.M. 910(a). A conditional guilty plea is also authorized under certain circumstances. R.C.M. 910(a)(2). *See* Section 19-16.00.

[2] The "charge" refers to the Article of the Uniform Code of Military Justice allegedly violated (*i.e.*, Charge I, Violation of Article 86) while the "specification" is the specific allegation of criminal misconduct. *See generally* Section 6-10.00.

[3] If the disclosure rules of the Military Rules of Evidence are complied with (Mil. R. Evid. 304(d)(1); 321(c)(2)(A)), "any motion to suppress . . . shall be made by the defense prior to submission of a plea. In the absence of such a motion or objection, the defense may not raise the issue at a later time except as permitted by the military judge for good cause shown. Failure to so move or object constitutes a waiver of the motion or objection." R.C.M. 905(e), Mil. R. Evid. 304(d)(2)(A); 311(d)(2)(A); 321(c)(2)(A).

[4] Matters generally waived if not raised prior to plea include:

Objections to amendment of specification. *See, e.g.*, R.C.M. 905(e)(1), United States v. Rodman, 41 C.M.R. 102 (C.M.A. 1969); United States v. Clark, 49 C.M.R. 192 (A.C.M.R. 1974).

Objection to unsworn charges. *See, e.g.*, R.C.M. 905(e)(1); United States v. Taylor, 36 C.M.A. 63 (C.M.A. 1965).

Objection to a denial of a request for individual military defense counsel for retention of detailed counsel when individual military counsel has been granted. *See, e.g.*, R.C.M. 905(e)(6); United States v. Cutting, 34 C.M.R. 127 (C.M.A. 1964).

Speedy trial motions under R.C.M. 707 and United States v. Burton, 44 C.M.R. 166 (C.M.A. 1971) unless compelling circumstances are present. United States v. Sloan 48 C.M.R. 211 (C.M.A. 1974). *Cf.* R.C.M. 907(b)(2)(A) (no exception set forth in waiver rule). *See generally* Section 17-80.00.

As to self-incrimination, *see* United States v. Hilton, 27 M.J. 323, 324–25 (C.M.A. 1989).

Waiver of various objections may occur even prior to arraignment or plea. Thus, any objection to the absence of a court member, for example, is waived if not asserted prior to assembly of the court (United States v. Cross, 50 C.M.R. 501 (A.C.M.R. 1975); *cf.* R.C.M. 912(g)(2) (silent)), and any objection to the referral of charges to trial is waived if not made "prior to plea or prior to the conclusion of any Article 39(a) session held prior to assembly [of the court-martial] whichever occurs earlier." United States v. Platt, 44 C.M.R. 70, 73 (C.M.A. 1971) (citing MCM, 1969 (rev. ed) ¶ 67*b* (now R.C.M. 905(e)). In *Platt*, Judge Quinn held that the defense had waived any objection to the lack of a new referral to trial following a mistrial; Judge Darden concurred in the result and Judge Ferguson dissented. *See also* R.C.M. 905(e).

In addition to the Manual waiver rules the Court of Appeals has applied the "invited error"

(Rel.3—1/07 Pub.62410)

If the judge fails to take the accused's plea and continues trial as if a not-guilty plea had been entered, reversible error will not be found.[5]

A plea of guilty may not be submitted in a case in which the death penalty may be adjudged.[6]

Ethically, the decision to plead guilty or not guilty to an offense is one for the *accused* to make, not counsel,[7] after receiving the defense counsel's professional advice. Because an innocent accused may not lawfully plead guilty in the armed forces,[8] counsel's advice to plead guilty normally will be based upon tactical reasons.

A primary concern to be addressed by counsel when deciding how to advise the client is whether the accused could or should take the stand at trial should a not-guilty plea be entered. In determining the advisability of such action, counsel must consider the possibility of impeachment of the accused with prior silence,[9] illegally obtained evidence,[10] prior instances of bad acts,[11] or prior convictions,[12] among others. Counsel should be particularly concerned about the possibility of the defendant committing perjury or appearing to commit perjury on the stand. Not only may counsel not aid or assist perjurious testimony,[13] the

doctrine. *See, e.g.*, United States v. Raya, 45 M.J. 251, 254 (C.A.A.F. 1996); United States v. Dixon, 45 M.J. 104, 107 (C.A.A.F. 1996); United States v. Crigler, 27 C.M.R. 337, 339 (C.M.A. 1959).

[5] United States v. Taft, 44 C.M.R. 122 (C.M.A. 1971); *but see* Ferguson, J. dissenting. 44 C.M.R. 124 (C.M.A. 1971).

[6] U.C.M.J. art. 45(b); R.C.M. 910(a). *See* United States v. Dock, 28 M.J. 117 (C.M.A. 1989). Although Article 45(b) prohibits a guilty plea to a capital offense, an accused will not be heard to complain about a plea agreement under which an accepted plea of guilty results in non-capital referral while a rejected plea leaves the case capital. United States v. Snodgrass, 37 M.J. 844, 847 (A.F.C.M.R. 1993). The constitutionality of the military death penalty was upheld in *Loving v. United States*, 517 U.S. 748 116 S. Ct. 1737 (1996).

[7] ABA Model Rules Of Professional Conduct, Rule 1.2(a) (1998); ABA Standards For Criminal Justice § 4-5.2(a)(i)(3d ed. 1993).

[8] *See generally* Section 19-13.01.

[9] Silence may constitute an admission when it does not constitute a reliance on the privilege against self-incrimination or related rights. MCM, 1984 App. 22-18-19 (citing Mil. R. Evid. 301(f)(3)). *See also* Mil. R. Evid. 304(h)(3). *Compare* Doyle v. Ohio, 426 U.S. 610 (1976) *and* United States v. Hale, 422 U.S. 171 (1975) *with* Jenkins v. Anderson, 447 U.S. 231 (1980) *and* Anderson v. Charles, 447 U.S. 404 (1980). *See also* United States v. Noel, 3 M.J. 328 (C.M.A. 1977) (dicta); § 14-63.10.

[10] Mil. R. Evid. 311(b)(1); Walder v. United States, 347 U.S. 62 (1954); United States v. Havens, 446 U.S. 620 (1980). Insofar as illegally obtained statements are concerned, see Mil. R. Evid. 304(b)(1).

[11] Mil. R. Evid. 608(b).

[12] Mil. R. Evid. 609.

[13] American Bar Association Model Code Of Professional Responsibility And Code Of Judicial Conduct (1976), EC 705, EC 7-26. *See generally* Section 5-56.00.

(Rel.3—1/07   Pub.62410)

judge may take the accused's perceived perjury into account on sentencing, if the perjury appears to be a "complete fabrication without the slightest merit whatsoever."[14] Similarly, the court members may be instructed, when they serve as a sentencing agency, that, during the findings portion of trial, they may take the accused's perjury into account on sentencing if they find that the accused committed perjury beyond a reasonable doubt.[15]

Although there is no constitutional right to plead guilty,[16] the judge may not invite or compel the accused to plead not guilty simply to avoid the often lengthy and cumbersome guilty-plea providency inquiry.[17]

§ 19-12.00   Not-Guilty Pleas

A not-guilty plea to a specification places all relevant matters in issue and requires the prosecution to prove the guilt of the accused of the offense charged in the specification beyond a reasonable doubt.

§ 19-13.00   Guilty Pleas

§ 19-13.10   In General

In contemporary law, the guilty plea can be viewed in two alternative fashions: as a confession of factual guilt, or as "a waiver of the right to trial on the issue of innocence or guilt by a court."[18] By holding in *North Carolina v. Alford*[19] that a defendant may constitutionally plead guilty while expressly maintaining his innocence of the charges to which he is pleading guilty, the Supreme Court has accepted the latter view.[20] Military law, on the other hand, rejects the *Alford*

---

[14] R.C.M. 1001(b)(4)(5); United States v. Grayson, 438 U.S. 41, 44 (1978). *See also* United States v. Warren, 13 M.J. 278 (C.M.A. 1982); United States v. Wallace, SPCM 18075 (A.C.M.R. Dec. 7, 1979) (unpublished opinion).

[15] *See* § 23-53.30.

[16] Corbitt v. New Jersey, 439 U.S. 212, 223 (1978). *Cf.* United States v. Johnson, 12 M.J. 673 (A.C.M.R. 1981) (Judge may not reject plea because accused would not name his supplier).

[17] *See, e.g.,* United States v. Williams, 43 C.M.A. 579 (A.C.M.R. 1970). *See generally* Moriarty, *The Providence Inquiry: A Guilty Plea Gauntlet?*, 13 The Advocate 251 (1981).

[18] Tesler, *The Guilty Plea is Innocent: Effects of North Carolina v. Alford in Pleading Under the U.C.M.J.*, 26 JAG J. 15, 21 (1971) [hereinafter cited as Tesler]. *Compare* United States v. Jackson, 390 U.S. 570 (1968) *with* Brady v. United States, 397 U.S. 742 (1970); Parker v. North Carolina, 397 U.S. 790 (1970); McMann v. Richardson, 397 U.S. 759 (1970); North Carolina v. Alford, 400 U.S. 25 (1970). *See generally* Vickery, *The Providency of Guilty Please: Does the Military Really Care?*, 58 Mil. L. Review. 209 (1972) [hereinafter cited as Vickery]. Moriarty, *The Providence Inquiry: A Guilty Plea Gauntlet?*, 13 The Advocate 251 (1981) [hereinafter cited as Moriarty].

[19] 400 U.S. 25 (1970) [hereinafter cited as *Alford*].

[20] The Federal Rules of Criminal Procedure now accept the *Alford* result. Fed. R. Crim. P. 11(d); (f).

(Rel.3—1/07   Pub.62410)

approach[21] in favor of requiring that, if the accused chooses to plead guilty, he or she must explicitly admit factual guilt in open court.[22] Indeed, if the trial judge's providency inquiry[23] reveals even a potential defense, the judge must reject the plea[24] and submit the case to trial[25] even though the act of declaring the tendered plea improvident may nullify a carefully negotiated plea-bargain.

This rejection of *Alford* is compelled by Article 45 of the Uniform Code of Military Justice.[26] as well as by its legislative history, both of which require the rejection of a guilty plea "unless the accused admits doing the acts charged."[27] Although it has been said that this requirement is the result of "Congressional paternalism and a desire to avoid the appearance of any impropriety in the military justice system,"[28] the original requirement can also be viewed as codifying the then generally accepted functional definition of a guilty plea.[29] Given that *Alford* permits rather than requires[30] the taking of a guilty plea

---

[21] U.C.M.J. art. 45; R.C.M. 910(e); Shepardson v. Roberts, 14 M.J. 354, 358 (C.M.A. 1983); United States v. Logan, 47 C.M.A. 1, 2 (C.M.A. 1973); United States v. Care, 40 C.M.R. 247 (C.M.A. 1969).

[22] The sole exception to this rule occurs when the accused is unable to recall the details of the offense but, having ascertained their circumstances, chooses to plead guilty. R.C.M. 910(e) Discussion; United States v. Butler, 43 C.M.R. 87 (C.M.A. 1971) (loss of memory); United States v. Luebs, 43 C.M.R. 315 (C.M.A. 1971) (lack of memory due to intoxication). *See also* United States v. Roane, 43 M.J. 93, 98 (C.A.A.F. 1995) ("[M]ilitary practice differs from that in other federal courts that permit the accused to plead guilty even though the defendant personally professes innocence-a so-called 'Alford plea.'").

[23] *See generally* Section 19-20.00.

[24] U.C.M.J. art. 45. A military judge may not arbitrarily reject a plea of guilty. If the plea is pursuant to a pretrial agreement and is arbitrarily rejected, especially if done at the insistence of the prosecutor, the agreement will still be binding on the convening authority. United States v. Penister, 25 M.J. 148 (C.M.A. 1987) (citing United States v. Johnson, 12 M.J. 673 (A.C.M.R. 1981), *pet. denied*, 13 M.J. 239 (1982); United States v. Williams, 43 C.M.R. 579, 582 (A.C.M.R. 1970).

[25] When a plea is declared to be improvident, neither the attempted plea nor anything said in conjunction with it is later admissible against the accused. Mil. R. Evid. 410. *But see* United States v. Mezzanatto, 513 U.S. 196 (1995) (accused can waive Rule 410 protections).

[26] U.C.M.J. art. 45(a). "If an accused after arraignment . . . after a plea of guilty sets up matters inconsistent with the plea . . . the court shall proceed as though he had pleaded not guilty."

[27] *Hearings on Sen. Rep. 486 Before the Comm. on Armed Services, Establishing a Uniform Code of Military Justice*, 81st Cong., 1st Sess. 20 (1949).

[28] Moriarty, *The Providence Inquiry: A Guilty Plea Gauntlet?*, 13 The Advocate 251, 253 n.12 (1981) (citing Vickery, *above* note 18 at [sic] 58–59 and related text).

[29] This is not to suggest that the desire to avoid the appearance of evil was not a significant factor in the drafting of the U.C.M.J. As then Captain Vickery recognized (Vickery, *above* note 18 at 230), Congress "was keenly aware of the necessity of keeping military justice beyond reproach." The Uniform Code of Military Justice was itself a reaction to the public's outrage at the real and perceived abuses in military justice that occurred during the Second World War.

[30] North Carolina v. Alford, 400 U.S. 25, 38 n.11 (1970). *See also* United States v. Brooks, 43 C.M.R. 945, 952 (A.F.C.M.R.), *pet. denied*, 43 C.M.R. 413 (C.M.A. 1971).

(Rel.3—1/07 Pub.62410)

accompanied by a protestation of innocence, the propriety of the military's insistence upon an admission of factual guilt is subject to debate. Critics have suggested that the requirement does not serve the accused's interests, as it requires an innocent accused who desires to accept a favorable pretrial agreement either to lie during providency to preserve the bargain or reject the offer, risking in the process a larger sentence than would have resulted had the deal been taken.[31] Some also believe that the military rule was justified at the time of the enactment of the Uniform Code of Military Justice because of the limited right to counsel then available, but is now obsolete because of the expansive right to counsel in the armed forces.[32]

In large part, it seems that the position one takes in this debate depends upon whether one views the situation from the perspective of the individual defendant or that of the system in general. Those who support the present system, including the authors, argue that a judicial system that permits *Alford* pleas ultimately casts doubts upon its own fairness and justice, as it explicitly recognizes and assists an individual who may be innocent to plead guilty and be subjected to punishment.[33] Those who support this position will concede that, in any specific case, such a position may be detrimental to a given defendant, but they argue that taken to its ultimate position, *Alford*, in conjunction with the Supreme Court's decisions on plea bargaining,[34] would permit the innocent to be tempted or coerced into pleading guilty on a regular basis. As should be apparent, the heart of the debate in the military is the plea-bargaining system. Were it not for pretrial agreements, it would be unlikely for a military accused to plead guilty while claiming innocence.[35]

---

[31] *See, e.g.*, Tesler, *above* note 18 at 40–41. Interestingly, there is significant interest on the part of the defense that military judges not reject guilty pleas (for fear of the loss of the benefits of any negotiated plea bargain). *See, e.g.*, Moriarty, *above* note 18 at 261–64.

[32] *See, e.g.*, Moriarty, *above* note 18 at 253 n.12. To the extent that one should remain concerned about the appearance of justice as well as with its actuality, Captain Moriarty's conclusion that the current provision for counsel renders the military's present position on guilty pleas "archaic" seems clearly erroneous. Counsel in courts-martial are usually military lawyers who could be viewed by both their clients and outside observers as being interested in their own career advancement, a perception that would not be helped were *Alford* to be adopted. Further, the right to counsel at special courts-martial is legally a conditional one, with no right to counsel applying to summary courts-martial at all. *See* Sections 5-12.20 and 5-12.30.

[33] Notably, the prosecution in *Alford* actually presented evidence to prove Alford's guilt, and *Alford*, taken alone, could have been viewed as a unique case of no precedential value because of that presentation of evidence.

[34] *See, e.g.*, Bordenkircher v. Hayes, 434 U.S. 357 (1978) (permitting the prosecution to charge the defendant with a more serious offense if he refuses to plead guilty to the instant offense).

[35] *Alford* and related cases dealing with the voluntariness of guilty pleas have often grown out of state statutory systems in which a defendant who pleads not guilty and who is then convicted could receive a larger sentence (usually death) than he could if he pled guilty. *See above* note 18. No such possibility exists under the U.C.M.J. Consequently, one is concerned in the military only with plea bargaining.

(Rel.3—1/07   Pub.62410)

§ 19-13.20   Effects of Guilty Pleas

A guilty plea to a specification amounts to a judicial confession of every element of the offense charged and permits a finding of guilty without any proof by the prosecution.[36] It thus constitutes waiver by the accused of the right against self-incrimination, the right to confront adverse witnesses, and the right to have the trier of fact determine the accused's guilt or innocence after the presentation of evidence by the prosecution. Generally, a provident guilty plea waives all nonjurisdictional defects, whether raised at trial or not, that do not violate the accused's right to due process.[37] Among the matters that are waived are:

> Defects in the Article 32 investigation;[38] Defects in pretrial advice;[39] Minor defects in the specifications;[40] Confession, search and seizure, and other evidentiary objections;[41] The right against self-incrimination[42] Motions for discovery;[43] Motions of severance of charges or accused;[44] Denial of request for individual or detailed counsel.[45]

---

[36] *See, e.g.,* United States v. James, 10 M.J. 646 (N.C.M.R. 1980); R.C.M. 910(g). With the judge's permission, however, evidence could still be introduced under the *1969 Manual. See* MCM, 1969 ¶ 70a. This was because of a belief that aggravating evidence could not be introduced after acceptance of guilty plea. *But see* R.C.M. 1001(b)(4); Chapter 23.

[37] *See generally,* Note, *Issues Waived by Provident Guilty Plea,* 13 The Advocate 354 (1981); Vitaris, *The Guilty Plea's Impact on Appellate Review,* 13 The Advocate 236 (1981). *See also* Blackledge v. Perry, 417 U.S. 21 (1974) (holding that the defendant could challenge the state's action in indicting him on felony charges as a result of his appeal of a misdemeanor conviction, notwithstanding his plea of guilty to the felony charge, because the very indictment denied him due process). *Compare* Blackledge v. Perry *with* Menna v. New York, 423 U.S. 61 (1975) (per curiam).

[38] R.C.M. 905(e); United States v. Lopez, 42 C.M.R. 268 (C.M.A. 1970); United States v. Packer, 8 M.J. 785 (N.C.M.R. 1980); United States v. Pounds, 50 C.M.R. 441 (A.F.C.M.R. 1975).

[39] R.C.M. 905(e). But "the military judge for good cause shown may grant relief from the waiver." R.C.M. 905(e).

[40] R.C.M. 905(e). *Cf.* United States v. McMillian, 33 M.J. 257 (C.M.A. 1991) (guilty plea does not prevent raising multiplicity motion prior to sentencing if there is no prejudice to the government and the judge treats them as multiplicitous for sentencing).

[41] 33 M.J. 257 (C.M.A. 1991); Mil. R. Evid. 304(d)(5), 311(i), 321(g); United States v. Dusenberry, 49 C.M.R. 536 (C.M.A. 1975); United States v. Blakney, 2 M.J. 1135 (C.G.C.M.R. 1976). There is an exception for conditional pleas. R.C.M. 910(a)(2).

[42] United States v. Spivey, 10 M.J. 7 (C.M.A. 1980); United States v. Lopez, 42 C.M.R. 268 (C.M.A. 1970). *See also* United States v. Martin, 4 M.J. 852 (A.C.M.R. 1978). Note, however, Chief Judge Everett's opinion in *Spivey, above* (concurring in the result only) in which he distinguishes between cases with accepted guilty pleas and those without. *Cf.* R.C.M. 910(a)(2).

[43] R.C.M. 905(e).

[44] R.C.M. 905(e).

[45] R.C.M. 905(e).

Failure of the charges and specifications to state an offense is never waived.[46] The Army Court of Criminal Appeals has held that a claim of transactional immunity survives a guilty plea.[47]

It should be noted that although a guilty plea certainly constitutes a waiver of the privilege against self-incrimination insofar as the findings of guilty of the given offense are concerned, it does not constitute a waiver of the privilege insofar as it applies to sentencing. Relying on the Supreme Court's application of the Fifth Amendment privilege to the sentencing portion of capital cases,[48] the Court of Military Appeals held that the Fifth Amendment privilege survives a guilty finding and applies to sentencing.[49] In so doing, the court determined that the Supreme Court's holding applied equally to noncapital cases.[50]

A particularly difficult question is presented when an accused pleads guilty to one offense and not guilty to another, and the government desires to use the defendant's guilty plea in the case involving the other offense. It has long been held in military law that "admissions implicit in a plea of guilty to one offense cannot be used as evidence to support the findings of guilty of an essential element of a separate and different offense,"[51] although a guilty plea to a

---

[46] See, e.g., United States v. Lumagui, 31 M.J. 789, 790 (A.F.C.M.R. 1990) (failure to state offense includes an offense based on "an unconstitutional statute or regulation").

[47] United States v. Conklan, 41 M.J. 800, 803–804 (A. Crim. App. 1995).

[48] Estelle v. Smith, 451 U.S. 454 (1981).

[49] United States v. Sauer, 15 M.J. 113 (C.M.A. 1983).

[50] Estelle v. Smith, 451 U.S. 454 (1981), was decided in the context of a capital case using a bifurcated sentencing procedure in which the burden of proof was on the government. Although the Court carefully noted that it did "not hold that the same Fifth Amendment concerns are necessarily presented by all types of interviews and examinations that might be ordered or relied upon to inform a sentencing determination" (451 U.S. at 469 n.13), it forthrightly declared that "[w]e can discern no basis to distinguish between the guilt and penalty phases of respondent's capital murder trial so far as the protection of the Fifth Amendment privilege is concerned." 451 U.S. at 462–63 (footnote omitted). Even taking into consideration the Court's concerns about the death penalty, especially in the context of the use of psychiatric evidence to establish future "dangerousness," the Texas procedure that gave rise to Estelle v. Smith seems so analogous to the military sentencing procedure as to make the case fully applicable to the military. Because Estelle v. Smith involved a not-guilty plea and trial on the merits, however, its impact on this specific issue is not clear.

[51] See, e.g., United States v. Grijalva, 55 M.J. 223 (C.A.A.F. 2001); United States v. Caszatt, 29 C.M.R. 521, 522 (C.M.A. 1960). See also United States v. Wahnon, 1 M.J. 144 (C.M.A. 1975) (guilty plea to absence without leave may not be admitted in evidence to establish the elements of a separate charge of "missing movement through design" to which the accused pled not guilty). Although sustaining the rule, the Court of Military Appeals conceded in 1986 that it might merit reexamination. United States v. Rivera, 23 M.J. 89 (C.M.A. 1986). Compare Caszatt, above, with United States v. Ramelb, 44 M.J. 625 (A. Crim. App. 1996) (prior to United States v. Figura, 44 M.J. 308 (C.A.A.F. 1996), the court held that judicial policy prohibited the accused's statement during a plea being admitted on merits on contested charge); United States v. Thomas, 39 M.J. 1094, 1095–96 (A.C.M.R. 1994) (one offense contained within the other, making admission usable). This issue was left unresolved. United States v. Nelson, 51 M.J. 399 (C.A.A.F. 1999).

(Rel.3—1/07   Pub.62410)

lesser-included offense relieves the prosecution of the need to prove those elements of a greater offense that it shares with the lesser-included offense.[52] In view of its status as a judicial confession, this limitation upon the use of a guilty plea is of questionable accuracy. The historical justifications for the rule appear to be threefold:

(1) It is required by the *Manual for Courts-Martial*;[53]

(2) It prevents affirmative res judicata;[54] and

(3) It prohibits the admission of irrelevant evidence.[55]

Although at least one court held[56] that ¶ 70b of the *1951 Manual for Courts-Martial*[57] mandated the rule because of its requirement that the accused be advised that "the plea [of guilty] . . . authorizes conviction of the offense to which the plea relates," the *Manual*'s definition of a guilty plea certainly carries no limitation on the use of a plea with it. Use of a guilty plea— a judicial confession— as proof does not amount to affirmative res judicata or collateral estoppel, any more than does an out-of-court admission later used in court to prove elements of two or more offenses. Further, Military Rule of Evidence 803(22) now expressly contemplates the use in evidence against the accused of convictions based upon pleas of guilty.[58] The last concern is one of relevancy.

The court has sustained use of admissions made during plea to sustain on appeal the conviction of the accused based upon admission of elements of a technically different but virtually identical offense in lieu of the charged offense. *E.g.*, United States v. Brown, 45 M.J. 389 (C.A.A.F. 1996) (in contested trial the majority struck down the anti-union statute but upheld conviction for closely related offense under Article 134); United States v. Epps, 25 M.J. 319 (C.M.A. 1987) (upheld guilty plea for closely related offense). The rational of *Epps* is supported by the legislative history. "The Board of Review shall affirm a finding of guilty or a lesser included offense (see Art. 59) if the evidence is sufficient." Senate Comm. on Armed Services, Establishing a Uniform Code of Military Justice, S. Rep. No. 81-486, at 28; House Comm. on Armed Services, Uniform Code of Military Justice, H.R. Rep. No. 81-491, at 31-32 (1949).

[52] *See, e.g.*, United States v. Grijalva, 55 M.J. 223 (C.A.A.F. 2001); United States v. Owens, 28 C.M.R. 312 (C.M.A. 1959).

[53] United States v. Dorrell, 18 C.M.R. 424, 425 (N.B.R. 1954).

[54] United States v. Caszatt, 29 C.M.R. 521, 523 (C.M.A. 1960).

[55] 29 C.M.R. 521, 523 (C.M.A. 1960).

[56] United States v. Dorrell, 18 C.M.R. 424, 425 (N.B.R. 1954).

[57] MCM, 1969 ¶ 70b contained a similar provision. Later *Manuals* do not have such a provision.

[58] This conclusion follows logically and is justified in large part by the unusual reliability factor inherent in a voluntary, counseled, plea. The final result may be affected, however, by Military Rule of Evidence 803(22). In relevant part, the Rule declares as a hearsay exception:

Evidence of a final judgment, entered after a trial or upon a plea of guilty . . . adjudging a person guilty of a crime punishable by death, dishonorable discharge or imprisonment in excess of one year, to prove any fact essential to sustain the judgment . . . . The pendency of an appeal may be shown but does not affect admissibility.

Although phrased as a hearsay objection, Rule 803(22) permits use of the judgment despite the

(Rel.3—1/07   Pub.62410)

It is apparent that in any given case a guilty plea to one offense does not necessarily bear on the commission of another offense,[59] but to state that evidence may be irrelevant in any specific case is not usually a justification for outright prohibition of that type of evidence.[60] In summary, a guilty plea should be treated as an admission when the plea has been accepted by the military judge, following a providency inquiry, and will be used at the same trial.[61] Interestingly,

hearsay rule. Mil. R. Evid. 801(c). A confession is an admission and not hearsay under Mil. R. Evid. 801(d)(2)(A). It is clear that Rule 803(22) expressly countenances use of convictions as affirmative evidence of those facts "essential to sustain the judgment," thus supporting the conclusion that guilty pleas are admissible for the same purpose.

Although the Rule speaks of a "final judgment, entered . . . upon a plea of guilty," it appears probable that, in military practice, this is equated with acceptance of the plea rather than completion of the bifurcated trial. Although not necessarily fully settled, it would appear that a guilty plea normally constitutes a conviction in the civilian courts. However, a bifurcated trial structure may affect that conclusion— at least when a plea of not guilty has been entered. Given that Mil. R. Evid. 803(22) has been taken from Fed. R. Evid. 803(22) without significant change, and that the Court of Appeals has accepted that the right against self-incrimination is waived upon the acceptance of a guilty plea, the acceptance of the plea should be enough to permit use of a guilty plea to the extent that Mil. R. Evid. 803(22) is involved.

The Rule, however, does apparently limit the use of guilty pleas, inasmuch as only crimes of sufficiently serious magnitude, those "punishable by death, dishonorable discharge or imprisonment in excess of one year," qualify. This limitation is logically unnecessary and was made part of the Federal Rule of Evidence to ensure that the accused would feel sufficiently threatened to fully defend against the charges, so as to ensure reliability of the judgment when it was offered at a later, probably civil, trial. Such concern is misplaced when viewed in the context of use of a guilty plea given at the same proceeding. However, despite the fact that Rule 803(22) is technically only a hearsay exception, to permit use of guilty pleas to offenses not within the ambit of Rule 803(22) would yield an inappropriate disparity of result. Consequently, as a matter of policy, the better view would be to permit use of guilty pleas to prove aspects of other offenses allegedly committed by the same defendant when those pleas are to offenses sufficiently serious to come within Rule 803(22).

[59] See, e.g., United States v. Vasquez, 9 M.J. 517 (A.F.C.M.R. 1980).

[60] Use of a relevant plea of guilty as an admission might well prove unduly prejudicial to an accused in which case use of the plea could be excluded under Mil. R. Evid. 403. It is clear that certain types of evidence have been declared to be inadmissible because of concern about the probability of misuse. See, e.g., Mil. R. Evid. 407, 408, 411, 412. However, such decisions usually have been made because the evidence is also highly unlikely to be probative and thus would be logically irrelevant under Mil. R. Evid. 401 in any event. Important evidence that could be both relevant and probative has usually been permitted, albeit with cautionary language (e.g., Mil. R. Evid. 404(b) (admissibility of evidence of other crimes, wrongs, and acts)), unless other reasons of social policy dictate their exclusion. See, e.g., Mil. R. Evid. 410, 412. Evidence of a plea of guilty to another offense could be declared inadmissible in a case involving another offense if the courts determine not only that the evidence was generally likely to be irrelevant and misused, but also desire to encourage pleas of guilty even though such pleas would not be necessarily determinative of entire cases. See generally McCormick, Evidence § 318 (4th ed. 1992).

[61] Professor Lederer, one of the principal authors of the Military Rules of Evidence, was strongly opposed to the adoption of Mil. R. Evid. 803(22) (see above note 58), because it permitted a

(Rel.3—1/07 Pub.62410)

construing the consequences of a guilty plea made under the Federal Rules of Criminal Procedure, the Supreme Court observed "once the plea has been accepted, statements or admissions made during the preceding plea colloquy are later admissible against the defendant, as is the plea itself."[62]

As a matter of law, a guilty plea is "a mitigating factor" insofar as sentencing is concerned.[63]

§ 19-13.30   Guilty Pleas with Exceptions and Substitutions

Traditionally, an accused could choose to plead guilty with "exceptions." In such a case, the defense counsel, following the form prescribed in the *Manual for Courts-Martial*,[64] would submit the accused's guilty plea "excepting the words, to the excepted words not guilty, and to the remainder of the specification and charge, guilty." Such a plea can be used to reduce an offense to a lesser-included offense or in some cases to limit the maximum sentence. Thus, in an absence-without-leave case charging a forty-five-day absence, the defense might plead guilty to the inception or beginning date of the absence, but not to the termination date. In such a case, the prosecution has the option of either proving the excepted language beyond a reasonable doubt or abandoning the attempt. In the absence case, abandoning the attempt would reduce the maximum sentence to thirty days confinement at hard labor from a potential period of imprisonment (when tried before a general court-martial) of one year.[65]

An accused may choose to enter a guilty plea that excepts certain language and substitutes new language for the excepted matter. This customarily will be done to correct an erroneous specification (*e.g.*, by substituting a new termination date in an absence offense) or to reduce an offense to a lesser-included offense. In making such a plea, the defense implicitly waives any objection it might have to unsworn charges. In the event of a plea by exceptions and substitutions, the

judgment in one case to be used against the same defendant at another trial. He viewed this as having the same effect as affirmative res judicata or collateral estoppel, notwithstanding that the evidence would not have conclusive effect as a matter of law. His opposition focused on the subsequent use of a conviction at another trial— a trial that might well not have been foreseen at the time the first trial occurred, and he was primarily concerned about a conviction, not yet final, that followed a plea of not guilty. His opposition to the rule, expressed often during the worldwide preparatory instruction in the Military Rules of Evidence, did not extend to the admission in evidence of a guilty plea (i.e., a complete confession) made at the same trial in which that plea is to be offered in evidence to prove a different offense than the plea concerned.

[62] Mitchell v. United States, 526 U.S. 314, 324 (1999)(holding that a guilty plea under the Federal Rules of Criminal Procedure did not constitute a waiver of the privilege against self-incrimination at senetencing).

[63] R.C.M. 1001(f)(1).

[64] *See* MCM, 2005,. Appendix A10-1, which retains the form for findings.

[65] MCM, 2005, Pt. IV ¶ 10e(1).

prosecution remains free to prove the originally charged offense beyond a reasonable doubt or to choose not to present evidence on the issue.

The 1993 change to the *Manual for Courts-Martial*, amending Rules for Courts-Martial 910(a)(1) and 918(a)(1), eliminated the need for archaic military pleading procedure in this area by permitting pleading to a lesser included offense without giving exceptions and substitutions. Exceptions and substitutions remain possible, and useful.

§ 19-14.00   Standing Mute

When an accused stands mute and refuses to enter a plea, a plea of not guilty will be entered, and trial will proceed on that basis. Standing mute is unusual and often takes the prosecution by complete surprise. Because of this, standing mute occasionally has been used as a tactical device by the defense. Under military law, when the accused has been charged with a military offense, the trial counsel must affirmatively prove jurisdiction over the accused beyond a reasonable doubt.[66] When the accused stands mute, there may be insufficient evidence to satisfy the jurisdictional requirement absent submission of evidence by the prosecution on that specific issue. This is especially likely to occur when the prosecution intends to prove its case solely or primarily via documentary evidence, as is usually the case in an absence-without-leave case. In this respect, note that ¶ 70*a* of the *1969 Manual for Courts-Martial* stated:

> A plea of not guilty or guilty will, in the absence of a motion to grant appropriate relief, be regarded as a waiver of any objection which must be raised by such a motion before plea, including any objection based on a misnomer of the accused. . . . By standing mute, an accused does not waive any objection otherwise waived by a plea.

The present *Manual* lacks a similar prohibition. Absent a waiver of the jurisdictional issue, should the prosecution fail to supply enough evidence to establish in personam jurisdiction over the accused, the defense is entitled to an acquittal.

§ 19-15.00   Confessional Stipulations

Because a plea of guilty waives many objections that might be made at trial,[67] prior to the advent of a conditional guilty plea[68] it was thought that the only way for the defense to preserve these objections was to go to trial. This was adverse to defense interests, and it cost the government the time and effort of a full trial.

---

[66] *See* Section 2-52.10.

[67] *See above* note 4.

[68] *See* Section 9-16.00; R.C.M. 910(a)(2). Conditional pleas were held to be improper under the prior *Manual*. United States v. Higa, 12 M.J. 1008 (A.C.M.R. 1982).

(Rel.3—1/07 Pub.62410)

To preserve the issues that the defense thought might be successful on appeal, and at the same time give the client some security by limiting the sentence, defense counsel devised a procedure by which the defense could enter a plea of not guilty and enter into a confessional stipulation. There was benefit to both parties as it avoided the necessity to go to trial for the sole purpose of preserving pretrial objections. The Court of Military Appeals declared that a "confessional stipulation" is a stipulation which practically amounts to a confession. We believe that a stipulation can be said to amount "practically" to a judicial confession when, for all facts purposes, it constitutes a de facto plea of guilty, *i.e.*, it is the equivalent of entering a plea of guilty to the charge.[69]

In 1980, the *Manual for Courts-Martial* was amended to recommend that these types of stipulations "should" not be received in evidence.[70] The military judge was required to treat such a stipulation much as a guilty plea,[71] but its waiver effect was significantly less. The effect of these stipulations was to encourage appellate litigation, raise issues of factual sufficiency, diminish the finality of the criminal process, reduce the effectiveness of appellate review because of the lack of a full record, and eliminate invoking the harmless-error doctrine on constitutional questions.

The *2005 Manual* permits a confessional stipulation, but indicates that one should not be accepted unless the judge ascertains:

> (A) from the accused that the accused understands the right not to stipulate and that the stipulation will not be accepted without the accused's consent; that the accused understands the contents and effect of the stipulation; that a factual basis exists for the stipulation; and that the accused, after consulting with counsel, consents to the stipulation; and (B) from the accused and counsel for each party whether there are any agreements between the parties in connection with the stipulation, and, if so, what the terms of such agreements are.[72]

---

[69] United States v. Bertelson, 3 M.J. 314, 315 n.2 (C.M.A. 1977). *See also* R.C.M. 811(c) Discussion. *See also* United States v. Dixon, 45 M.J. 104, 107 (C.A.A.F. 1996) ("[A] stipulation practically amounts to a confession for purposes of *Bertelson* only 'when it establishes directly or by reasonable inference, *every* element of a charged offense and when the defense does not present evidence to contest any potential remaining issue on the merits.' ").

[70] MCM, 1969 ¶ 54f(1) (C3 March 12, 1980).

[71] United States v. Aiello, 7 M.J. 99, 100 (C.M.A. 1979).

[72] R.C.M. 811(c) Discussion. *See also* United States v. Bertelson, 3 M.J. 314, 315 n.2 (C.M.A. 1977). Under *Bertelson*, when a confessional stipulation is made, the court requires that the judge must personally apprise the accused that the stipulation may not be accepted as evidence without his consent; that the judge must inform the accused "that the Government has the burden of proving beyond a reasonable doubt every element of the offense(s) charged and that by stipulating to the material elements of the offense(s), the accused alleviates that burden." 3 M.J. 316 (C.M.A. 1977). Finally, the military judge is also required to conduct an inquiry similar to a guilty-plea providency inquiry. *See also* United States v. Watruba, 35 M.J. 488 (C.M.A. 1992) (apparent split on application of *Bertelson*— detailed discussion of its establishment, comparison with guilty plea providency

(Rel.3—1/07 Pub.62410)

If the confessional stipulation is made pursuant to a pretrial agreement, the judge must inquire into that agreement. [73]

Under [74] contemporary practice, a conditional plea of guilty is likely to be more useful and efficient than a confessional stipulation. However, if the military judge will not accept such a plea, [75] and the convening authority is willing to accept a stipulation in return for a pretrial agreement, such a stipulation may have utility and importance.

In *United States v. Lawrence*, [76] the court held that a confessional stipulation may not be employed to preserve an issue for appeal. Instead, a conditional plea in accordance with R.C.M. 910(a)(2) should be used. This position is complicated, however, when a service, as did the Air Force, limits conditional guilty pleas. [77]

§ 19-16.00   Conditional Pleas

The *2005 Manual for Courts-Martial* permits conditional guilty pleas. Rule for Courts-Martial 910(a)(2) specifies:

> With the approval of the military judge and the consent of the Government, an accused may enter a conditional plea of guilty, reserving in writing the right, on further review or appeal, to review of the adverse determination of any specified pretrial motion. If the accused prevails on further review or appeal, the accused shall be allowed to withdraw the plea of guilty. The Secretary concerned may prescribe who may consent for the Government; unless prescribed by the Secretary concerned, the trial counsel may consent on behalf of the Government.

The conditional plea of guilty permits the accused to preserve unsuccessful pretrial motions for appeal while still pleading guilty. [78] When such a plea is

---

inquiry, and with federal requirement; note Judge Crawford's dissent for the view that *Bertelson* should be overruled. 35 M.J. 492 (C.M.A. 1992). *But see* United States v. Craig, 48 M.J. 77 (C.A.A.F. 1998) (Court seemed to be overruling *United States v. Watruba*, 35 M.J. 488 (C.M.A. 1992)— in holding that the failure to properly advice the defendant was harmless error); United States v. Enlow, 26 M.J. 940 (A.C.M.R. 1988).

[73] R.C.M. 910(f). *See generally* Section § 9-23.00.

[74] *E.g.*, Adams v. Peterson, 988 F.2d 835 (9th Cir. 1992) (en banc).

[75] R.C.M. 910(b).

[76] 43 M.J. 677 (A.F. Crim. App. 1995).

[77] Air Force Instruction 51-201, Law Administration of Military Justice ¶ 8.2 (3 October 1997); Memorandum for All Staff Judge Advocates and Chief Circuit Judges (July 3, 1995), *but see* United States v. Phillips, 32 M.J. 955 (A.F.C.M.R. 1991). The current Air Force regulation limits conditional guilty pleas, directing that they should be accepted only when the issue preserved for appeal is case dispositive." Air Force Instruction 51-201, Law Administration of Military Justice ¶ 8.2 (26 November 2003).

[78] And thus protecting any pretrial agreement.

(Rel.3—1/07 Pub.62410)

permitted,[79] the Rule relieves the accused of having to choose between pleading guilty, which would protect a plea bargain but (because of its waiver impact) prohibit appeal of most pretrial motions,[80] or plead not guilty to permit appeal of denied pretrial motions, at the possible cost of a plea bargain. Forcing the defense to elect trial to appeal what is usually a denied suppression motion is often not in the government's interest. Accordingly, the Rule permits a conditional plea, but requires the consent of both the judge and prosecution.

"Since the purpose of a conditional guilty plea is the conservation of judicial and governmental resources, the discretion allowed the trial judge and the government is not subject to challenge by an accused."[81]

The Rule does not specify when the military judge must decide whether to consent to a proposed conditional plea.[82] It would be wise, however, for the judge to defer decision until after resolution of all pretrial matters.

The Air Force Court of Military Review expressed its serious concern that the record in a conditional plea case may fail to "disclose why the controverted evidence was important— or even relevant."[83] It behooves the military judge in a conditional plea case to ensure that the record includes a sufficient offer of proof making plain the government's theory of relevance and admissibility.

A military judge should be reluctant to accept a conditional plea because of the impact it will have on an accused who is sentenced to confinement. Prisoners who have made a conditional plea may believe that they will succeed in their appeal and resist confinement. Conditional pleas should be permitted only when a great deal is to be gained from avoiding trial.

§ 19-20.00 GUILTY PLEA PROVIDENCY INQUIRY

§ 19-21.00 In General

Military law places great emphasis on ensuring that guilty pleas and their functional equivalents, confessional stipulations, are made intelligently and voluntarily. To accomplish this aim, the military judge is required to conduct

---

[79] The current Air Force regulation limits conditional guilty pleas, directing that they should be accepted only when the issue preserved for appeal is case dispositive." Air Force Instruction 51-201, Law Administration of Military Justice ¶ 8.2 (26 November 2003).

[80] Including suppression motions.

[81] United States v. Forbes, 19 M.J. 953, 954 (A.F.C.M.R. 1985). See also United States v. Johnson, 12 M.J. 673 (A.C.M.R. 1981) (military judge was held to have erroneously rejected the accused's plea because he would not name his drug supplier). The Federal Rule is similar. United States v. Bell, 966 F.2d 914 (5th Cir. 1992) (conditional plea may be rejected for any or no reason).

[82] The real question is whether the issues preserved by the plea are case or offense dispositive. United States v. Phillips, 32 M.J. 955 (A.F.C.M.R. 19912). See also United States v. Pond, 36 M.J. 1050, 1060 (A.F.C.M.R. 1993).

[83] United States v. Phillips, 32 M.J. 955, 956 (A.F.C.M.R. 1991).

a detailed inquiry into the proposed plea prior to accepting it. The inquiry, known as a providency inquiry, takes place at an Article 39(a) session out of the presence of any court members and requires substantial interchange between judge and accused with mere representations on the part of counsel being considered legally insufficient.[84] During the inquiry the military judge must advise the accused of the effects of a guilty plea, ensure that the accused understands both the right to plead not guilty and the effects of pleading guilty, and ascertain the facts of the alleged offense from the accused to be sure that the plea is in fact justified and voluntary. When a pretrial agreement is involved, the providency inquiry extends to the agreement and its consequences. Subsequent to the inquiry, the judge decides, as an interlocutory matter, whether to accept the plea. Should the military judge fail to comply with the providency inquiry requirements, reversal of the conviction normally will be required. Full compliance with the requirements now appears likely to insulate to some extent the plea of guilty, and thus the conviction, from subsequent allegations of improprieties.

Under present procedure, the accused is placed under oath during the providency inquiry.[85] As a result, a statement made by the accused during a providency inquiry may later be used as the basis for a charge of perjury against the accused or as a matter in aggravation during sentencing.[86] Because the military accused cannot plead guilty while maintaining innocence, it has been suggested that such a procedure, now apparently discretionary in the federal district courts,[87] would simply permit the government, already able to at least tempt an innocent accused to plead guilty with an unusually lenient plea bargain, to prosecute defendants whose only real crime was to succumb to the generally condemned attractions of plea bargaining.

---

[84] The refusal to accept counsel's representations, although often aggravating to counsel, is reasonable inasmuch as the intent of the providency inquiry is to ensure that the accused understands his or her rights and the effects of the plea, and is voluntarily pleading guilty. To permit counsel to respond in lieu of the accused would make the inquiry an empty ritual. While the accused often complicates the inquiry with incomplete or "erroneous" answers, that very happenstance justifies the present nature of the inquiry, for if an accused has problems with the judge's inquiry, the accused may well not fully comprehend what he or she is doing.

[85] R.C.M. 910(e); cf. Mil. R. Evid. 410. Failure to place the accused under oath is error, but reversal is inappropriate absent prejudice. United States v. Riley, 35 M.J. 547 (A.C.M.R. 1992).

[86] R.C.M. 910(c)(5); United States v. Holt, 27 M.J. 57 (C.M.A. 1988) (sentencing). See Chapter 23. The Court of Appeals for the Armed Forces has observed, "Guilty pleas and accompanying statements in one jurisdiction are generally admissible in other jurisdictions to prove the element of other crimes." United States v. Gray, 51 M.J. 1, 25 (C.A.A.F. 1999).

[87] Fed. R. Crim. P. 11(bc)(15) ("the defendant may be placed under oath. . . .").

§ 19-22.00   The *"Care"* Inquiry

§ 19-22.10   *United States v. Care*

The present military providency inquiry was mandated by the Court of Military Appeals in *United States v. Care*,[88] as a result of its concern that the providency inquiry then used[89] was inadequate to meet both systemic needs and evolving civilian federal law.[90] Subsequently written into the *Manual for Courts-Martial*,[91] *Care* required that the military judge personally advise the accused on the record of:

(1) The elements of the offense;[92]

(2) That his or her plea admits every element, act, or omission contained in the offense;

(3) That the plea authorizes conviction without further proof;

---

[88] 40 C.M.R. 247 (C.M.A. 1969) [hereinafter cited as *Care*]. *See generally* United States v. Sweet, 38 M.J. 583, 587–90 (N.M.C.M.R. 1993) (background of the *Care* inquiry).

[89] MCM, 1951 ¶ 70*b* required that the judge explain the meaning and effect of a plea of guilty "unless it affirmatively appears that the accused understands the meaning and effect thereof." The explanation required was limited in scope. United States v. Martinez, 27 M.J. 730 (A.C.M.R. 1988) (when accused has already been advised of his rights, the written-rights advisement on DD Form 1722 is sufficient).

[90] The Court in *Care* analyzed the Supreme Court's guilty plea decisions (most importantly McCarthy v. United States, 394 U.S. 459 (1969)) and then Fed. R. Crim. P. 11, 40 C.M.R. 247, 250–52 (C.M.A. 1969), determined that its own prior recommendation to improve the providency inquiry (United States v. Chancelor, 36 C.M.R. 453 (C.M.A. 1966)) had been ignored (40 C.M.R. 247, 253), and determined that only by promulgated requirements for a providency inquiry could the providency inquiry be properly strengthened. *See* Elling, *Guilty Plea Inquiries: Do We Care Too Much?*, 134 Mil. L. Rev. 173 (1991).

[91] MCM, 1969 ¶ 70b(2), as amended by Exec Order 11835 (1975). At least in practice, Tthe military providency inquiry is now significantly more demanding than that of Fed. R. Crim. P. 11. R.C.M. 910(c) *follows* Fed. R. Crim. P. 11(c).

[92] This requirement can be demanding. *See, e.g.*, United States v. Bullman, 56 M.J. 377 (C.A.A.F. 2002) (plea improvident because judge did not define "dishonorable" for dishonorable failure to pay debt despite definition of "dishonorable" with respect to dishonored checks); United States v. Roeseler, 55 M.J. 286 (C.A.A.F. 2001) (judge's explanation was sufficient to cover attempted conspiracy in case in which the plans victims of a murder for hire were fictitious); United States v. Geary, 30 M.J. 855, 858 (N.M.C.M.R. 1990) ("when a FACA [Federal Assimilated Crimes Act, 18 U.S.C. § 13] offense is alleged, the jurisdictional basis for the assimilation of the state statute becomes an element of the offense which . . . must be explained to an accused during the providency inquiry into a guilty plea"). In 2003, the Court of Appeals for the Armed Forces reversed an accused's conviction of a specification for which the judge failed to adequately explain the elements of the offense. United States v. Redlinski, 58 M.J. 117 (C.A.A.F. 2003). Dissenting, Chief Judge Crawford noted that the record "contained a stipulation of fact, factual admission, a factual inquiry, and assurance from defense counsel that Appellant committed the offense" and opined that in conformity with civilian federal precedent this should be enough. 58 M.J. at 123.

(Rel.3—1/07 Pub.62410)

(4) The maximum sentence;[93]

(5) That if the judge accepts the plea, the maximum punishment can be imposed;

(6) That a plea of guilty waives the right against self-incrimination,[94] the right to trial by court-martial on the merits, and the right to confrontation.

Under *Care*, the trial judge is required make a factual inquiry into the offense to which the plea was made. The inquiry must be sufficiently detailed so that on appeal it can be determined whether a substantial conflict exists between the actual facts and the plea.[95] The inquiry must include a significant interchange directly with the accused.[96] When the accused has entered into a stipulation of fact describing the commission of the offense, as is customary incident to a pretrial agreement, the judge may and should use the stipulation in the factual inquiry.[97]

---

[93] *See* United States v. Hardcastle, 53 M.J. 299 (C.A.A.F. 2000) (all parties and the judge were unaware that administrative regulations prohibited receipt of pay and allowances, which prohibition effectively increased the sentence and nullified part of the pretrial agreement); United States v. Williams, 53 M.J. 293 (C.A.A.F. 2000) (same); United States v. Walker, 34 M.J. 264 (C.M.A. 1992) (where punishment was approximately one-half of that believed possible by the accused (51/2 yrs. vs. 10 1/2 yrs.), the accused's plea, based on a five-year pretrial agreement, was improvident). Although courts generally agree that an accused need not be advised of "collateral" consequences of convictions, they do not agree as to which consequences can be said to be merely collateral. *Compare* United States v. Littlejohn, 224 F.3d 960 (9th Cir. 2000) *with* United States v. Morse, 36 F.3d 1070 (11th Cir. 1994) (ineligibility for federal benefits). *See also* Major Jeff Walker. *The Practical Consequences of a Court-Martial Conviction*, The Army Lawyer, December, 2001 at 1; Gabriel J. Chin & Richard W. Holmes, Jr., *Effective Assistance of Counsel and the Consequences of Guilty Pleas*, 87 Cornell L. Rev. 697 (2002) (Failure to advise the defendant of the collateral consequences as required by ABA Standards for Criminal Justice: Pleas of Guilty, Standard 14-3.2(f) (1999) may constitute ineffectiveness of counsel.).

[94] *E.g.*, United States v. Hansen, 59 M.J. 410 (C.A.A.F. 2004).

[95] United States v. Jemmings, 1 M.J. 414 (C.M.A. 1976). *See generally* United States v. Dunning, 40 M.J. 641, 645 (N.M.C.M.R. 1994). An individual who is innocent cannot plead guilty, because Article 45 of the Uniform Code of Military Justice requires a plea of guilty to be in accord with the actual facts. However, the factual inquiry does not preclude a guilty plea if the accused cannot remember the facts. *See above* note 22. *See also* Section 19-13.10.

[96] *See, e.g.*, United States v. Williams, 27 M.J. 671 (A.C.M.R. 1988) (judge may not rely on statements of counsel that an affirmative defense is not available). As to whether the trial counsel can rebut the accused's providency inquiry statements, see United States v. Peck, 36 M.J. 900, 902, n.5 (A.F.C.M.R. 1993).

[97] *See* United States v. Sweet, 38 M.J. 583, 592 (N.M.C.M.R. 1993), *aff'd*, 42 M.J. 183 (C.A.A.F. 1995) (upheld plea inquiry based stipulation and yes and no answers to judge's inquiry—encouraging use of such stipulations); United States v. Abdullah, 37 M.J. 692, 694 (A.C.M.R. 1993) (By the terms of the pretrial agreement, a stipulation of fact is used to support the guilty plea and may not be used in trial of an offense to which the accused has pled not guilty.).

(Rel.3—1/07 Pub.62410)

Personal awareness of guilt is not a prerequisite to entry of a plea of guilty, and it is sufficient that the accused is convinced of his or her own guilt.[98] When the factual inquiry reveals a potential defense, the guilty plea is set aside[99] and a plea of not guilty entered. The mere possibility of a defense, however, does not warrant setting a plea aside.[100] Even if the plea is initially accepted as provident, if subsequent evidence offered during sentencing reveals a defense that is inconsistent with the plea, the trial judge must inquire into the discrepancy and, if it cannot be explained adequately, set aside the plea of guilty.[101] The Court of Appeals for the Armed Forces may be broadening the judge's responsibility insofar as the providence inquiry is concerned. In *United States v. Jordan*,[102] a majority of the Court set aside a guilty plea to an Article 134 offense on the grounds that the accused's simple "yes" to the judge's question of whether the accused's conduct had been prejudicial to the good order and discipline or service discrediting were merely "legal conclusions" without factual admissions to support them.

When advising the accused, the judge must explain any legal terms that a lay person might not understand.[103] A failure to expressly list the elements of the offense, however, is harmless error if the military judge has described the elements in an extensive factual discussion with the accused.[104] Similarly, failing to advise the accused of one of the elements of the offense is not reversible error if the judge discusses the factual basis for that element[105] with the accused.

---

[98] The accused's assessment of guilt may be based upon the weight of the government's evidence. United States v. Moglia, 3 M.J. 216 (C.M.A. 1977).

[99] Declared improvident, or, in the vernacular, "blew providency." It appears that even an accused's later unsworn statement during sentencing can call the plea into question if the statement is inconsistent with guilt. *See* United States v. Vega, 39 M.J. 79 (C.M.A. 1994) (court will examine stipulation to determine if an unsworn statement constitutes some evidence in "substantial conflict" with guilty plea).

[100] United States v. Shackelford, 2 M.J. 17 (C.M.A. 1976); United States v. Logan, 47 C.M.R. 1, 3 (C.M.A. 1973).

[101] *See, e.g.*, United States v. Timmins, 45 C.M.R. 249 (C.M.A. 1972).

[102] 57 M.J. 236 (C.A.A.F. 2002).

[103] United States v. Craney, 1 M.J. 142 (C.M.A. 1975) (difference between principal and aider and abettor); United States v. Thomas, 6 M.J. 573 (A.C.M.R. 1978) (definition and effect of stipulation of fact); United States v. Arrington, 5 M.J. 756 (A.C.M.R. 1978) (thorough discussion of the elements of each offense). Although simple military offenses do not require an explanation of the offense's elements, in the event of more complex cases such as conspiracy, failure to explain the elements will result in reversal. United States v. Nystrom, 39 M.J. 698, 701–02 (N.M.C.M.R. 1993) citing United States v. Pretlow, 13 M.J. 85 (C.M.A. 1982). In an accessory after the fact offense where the accused actually knows of the commission of the offense by the principal, failure, as in this case, to explain the elements of the underlying offense of murder, is error. *Nystrom*, 39 M.J. at 702.

[104] United States v. Kilgore, 44 C.M.R. 89 (C.M.A. 1971). *See also* United States v. Williams, 6 M.J. 884 (A.C.M.R. 1979).

[105] United States v. Otterbeck, 50 C.M.R. 7 (N.C.M.R. 1974).

(Rel.3—1/07 Pub.62410)

A guilty plea must be set aside on appeal if the accused substantially misunderstood the maximum potential sentence.[106] This has occurred most often when, on appeal, certain offenses are determined to have been multiplicitous for sentencing purposes.[107] It may also happen when, on appeal, the plea to one of the specifications is found to have been improvident, unless the accused indicated at trial an intent to plead guilty regardless of the minimum or maximum sentence.[108]

The procedure for ensuring a knowing and voluntary guilty plea in the armed forces is thus detailed and painstaking. Although highly commendable as a matter of public policy it inherently poses difficulties. Not only are some accused confused by the judge's probing questions, defense counsel may be confronted by inconsistent ethical imperatives. A judicial error in the inquiry may amount to reversible error even in the absence of defense objection.[109] Given counsel's ethical duty to the client, remaining silent may be tactically advantageous.[110] Yet at the same time, counsel is an "officer of the Court," and the plea inquiry is designed to ensure that the accused's rights are protected and that justice is seen to be done.

§ 19-22.20   *Care* Codified

The requirements of *United States v. Care* have been codified in Rule for Court-Martial 910, which provides:

---

[106] There is no mathematical formula to determine whether a substantial misunderstanding existed. Some of the factors that might be considered are set forth in *United States v. Walls*, 3 M.J. 882, 885 (A.C.M.R. 1977), *aff'd*, 9 M.J. 88 (C.M.A. 1980). *See also* United States v. Castrillon-Moreno, 7 M.J. 414 (C.M.A. 1979) (where accused was advised that maximum punishment was ten years' confinement rather than two years', the misunderstanding was substantial); United States v. Muir, 7 M.J. 448 (C.M.A. 1979) (where accused was advised that maximum punishment was two years rather than one year, the mistake was not substantial). There are recent cases in which the plea of guilty was declared improvident because it was predicated upon a substantial misunderstanding on the accused's part of the maximum punishment. United States v. Wirth, 24 M.J. 536 (A.C.M.R. 1987); United States v. Poole, 24 M.J. 539 (A.C.M.R. 1987)., *aff'd*, 27 M.J. 272 (C.M.A. 1988).

[107] *See generally* Section 6-34.30.

[108] *Cf.* United States v. Frangoules, 1 M.J. 467 (C.M.A. 1976) (the accused's guilty plea was provident when made with the knowledge that some of the offenses may have been multiplicitous and regardless of the ultimate decision as to the maximum legal sentence). *See also* United States v. Castrillon-Moreno, 7 M.J. 414, 415 (C.M.A. 1979).

[109] *Compare* military practice with *United States v. Vonn*, 535 U.S. 55 (2002) (defendant who fails to object to a possible Rule 11 violation (guilty plea inquiry) waives the issue absent plain error).

[110] *See* Victor Kelley, 3 National Military Justice Group 6 (Winter 2004) ("I know of no fiduciary loyalty that the defense owes to the military judge. It may well be that the judge incorrectly advises the accused or omits an element of the offense. Should this occur, and should the prosecutor miss it, the defense has an instant appellate issue."). Of course, counsel cannot "plant" error.

(Rel.3—1/07 Pub.62410)

(c) *Advice to accused.* Before accepting a plea of guilty, the military judge shall address the accused personally and inform the accused of, and determine that the accused understands the following:

(1) The nature of the offense to which the plea is offered, the mandatory minimum penalty, if any, provided by law, and the maximum possible penalty provided by law;

(2) In a general or special court-martial, if the accused is not represented by counsel, that the accused has the right to be represented by counsel at every stage of the proceedings;

(3) That the accused has the right to plead not guilty or to persist in that plea if already made, and that the accused has the right to be tried by a court-martial, and that at such trial the accused has the right to confront and cross-examine witnesses against the accused, and the right against self-incrimination;

(4) That if the accused pleads guilty, there will not be a trial of any kind as to those offenses to which the accused has so pleaded, so that by pleading guilty the accused waives the rights described in subsection (c)(3) of this rule; and

(5) That if the accused pleads guilty, the military judge will question the accused about the offenses to which the accused has pleaded guilty, and, if the accused answers these questions under oath, on the record, and in the presence of counsel, the accused's answers may later be used against the accused in a prosecution for perjury or false statement.

(d) *Ensuring that the plea is voluntary.* The military judge shall not accept a plea of guilty without first, by addressing the accused personally, determining that the plea is voluntary [111] and not the result of force or threats or of promises apart from a plea agreement under R.C.M. 705. The military judge shall also inquire whether the accused's willingness to plead guilty results from prior discussions between the convening authority, a representative of the convening authority, or trial counsel, and the accused or defense counsel.

(e) *Determining accuracy of plea.* The military judge shall not accept a plea of guilty without making such inquiry of the accused as shall satisfy the military judge that there is a factual basis for the plea. The accused shall be questioned under oath about the offenses.

Rule 910 provides a more flexible approach than that mandated by the common law based on *Care.* Whether it will result in a significant change in military practice remains to be seen. The Court of Appeals for the Armed Forces has expressly refused to adopt a test requiring rote recitation of the *Care* requirements. Instead, the Court has opined that "the issue is not whether there is 'exemplary compliance with what we had in mind in *Care*,' but rather whether

---

[111] "Voluntary" does not require that the accused be fully aware of all the details surrounding the case. *E.g.,* United States v. Seybold, 979 F.2d 582, 586–88 (7th Cir. 1992) (guilty plea voluntary even though defendant did not know all of government evidence).

(Rel.3—1/07 Pub.62410)

'the combination of all the circumstances' leads the court to conclude that the accused's plea was informed and voluntary."[112]

Customary practice often extends beyond the minimum Rule 910/*Care* requirements. Failure to comply with such local practices ought not to be error. For example, although the normal process is to do so, the failure of the judge to inform the accused during the providence inquiry that until imposition of sentence the accused may, subject to the judge's discretion, withdraw his or her plea is not error.[113]

§ 19-23.00 Inquiry into a Pretrial Agreement

§ 19-23.10 In General

Plea bargains present special problems. Military law requires voluntary guilty pleas, but plea bargains provide explicit incentives to plead guilty. To ensure the voluntariness of the plea and to prevent improper terms from being imposed in pretrial agreements, the Court of Military Appeals, in *United States v. Green*,[114] required the trial judge, as part of the providency inquiry, to carefully inquire into the terms of any applicable pretrial agreement.[115] Under *Green*, the judge must:

(1) Ensure that the agreement encompasses all the understandings of all parties;

(2) Examine each specific condition to determine both that the accused understands it, and that it does not violate public policy;

(3) Ascertain if there is a sentence limitation;

(4) Discover and resolve any ambiguities in the agreement; and

(5) Ensure that his or her interpretation of the agreement conforms to that of counsel for both sides.[116]

---

[112] United States v. Hansen, 59 M.J. 410, 412 (C.A.A.F. 2004), *quoting* United States v. Harris, 26 M.J. 729, 732 (A.C.M.R. 1988), in turn *quoting* United States v. Burton, 44 C.M.R. 166 (C.M.A. 1971).

[113] United States v. Silver, 40 M.J. 351, 352–53 (C.M.A. 1994).

[114] 1 M.J. 453 (C.M.A. 1976) [hereinafter cited as *Green*]. *See also* United States v. King, 3 M.J. 458 (C.M.A. 1977).

[115] *Green* arguably deals with a different form of voluntariness from that dealt with by *Care*. Although the providency inquiry in general is intended to ensure that the accused understands his or her rights and opinions, the *Green* inquiry primarily guarantees that the accused truly understands the nature of the plea bargain entered into. Consequently, *Green* is intended to protect the accused by inquiring into and approving the contract entered into between the accused and the government. *Green* thus assumes that the plea will be voluntary so long as the accused receives what he or she believes has been promised.

[116] United States v. Kitts, 23 M.J. 105, 108 (C.M.A. 1986). The Judicial Conference of the United States has recommended that in plea bargain cases, civilian federal trial judges should be required

(Rel.3—1/07 Pub.62410)

The pretrial agreement must be in writing to avoid any uncertainty as to the substance of the agreement.[117] Although an accused's plea must be knowing and voluntary, and a military accused must understand and concur in a pretrial agreement for it to be accepted by the military judge, the Supreme Court has held that the Constitution does not require the government to disclose exculpatory material before plea.[118] Accordingly, it least in a civilian case the defendant's decision to accept a plea bargain need not be a fully informed one.

The *Green* requirements were simplified and codified in Rule for Courts-Martial 910(f). Rule 910(f)(4) requires the judge to make an inquiry to ensure: "(A) That the accused understands the agreement; and (B) That the parties agree to the terms of the agreement." The Discussion notes that: "If the plea agreement contains any unclear or ambiguous terms, the military judge should obtain clarification from the parties. If there is doubt about the accused's understanding or any terms in the agreement, the military judge should explain those terms to the accused."[119]

The authority of the judge to modify pretrial agreements when the parties do not concur in their understanding of the agreement's terms remains in question. The obligation is upon the judge to clarify any ambiguities in the agreement and to ensure that both parties understand it. Certainly, the accused can reject the agreement after such clarification. But may the government? Rule 910(h)(3) indicates that both parties have to consent to the agreement after ambiguities are resolved, and probably both parties must consent to the agreement after the judge rejects conditions that he or she believes do not comply with Rule for Courts-Martial 705.

In 2003, the Court of Appeals for the Armed Forces held that appellate courts cannot "impose alternative relief on an unwilling appellant to rectify a mutual misunderstanding of a material term in a pretrial agreement."[120]

---

to ensure that the defendant understands the terms of the plea bargain. *Letter from the Chair of the Advisory Committee on Federal Rules of Criminal Procedure to the Chair of the Standing Committee* (May 15, 1998), 65 Crim. L. Rptr. (BNA) 140 (May 5, 1999).

[117] R.C.M. 705(d)(3). In this respect, Air Force Instruction 51-201, Law, Administration of Military Justice ¶ 6.8 (26 November 20053 October 1997) provides that pretrial agreements will be in writing and signed by the accused and counsel.

[118] United States v. Ruiz, 536 U.S. 622 2002 U.S. LEXIS 4650 (June 24, 2002). *Cf.* United States v. Garlich, 61 M.J. 346 (C.A.A.F. 2005)(applicability of *Ruiz* not addressed).

[119] R.C.M. 910(f)(4)(B) Discussion.

[120] United States v. Perron, 58 M.J. 78, 84 (C.A.A.F. 2003).

§ 19-23.20   Full Disclosure

Because one of the main reasons for the *Green* decision was to prevent unwritten *sub rosa* agreements that would violate public policy,[121] the trial judge should ask counsel *and* the accused if the agreement encompasses all of the parties' understandings.[122] Merely asking the accused would not ensure the absence of such agreements,[123] if only because the accused may not understand the nature and consequences of such an agreement. If the accused responds that there are no *sub rosa* agreements, silence by counsel "may be considered acquiescence in the representation of the accused and tantamount to a verbal response."[124] When there is an assertion by counsel that there are no *sub rosa* agreements, the appellate courts "will not consider inconsistent post-trial assertions."[125] Notwithstanding this general rule, the Court of Appeals for the Armed Forces has departed from it on at least one occasion when the accused alleged that the parties had effectively made a sub rosa agreement pursuant to which the defense would not raise motions alleging improper pretrial confinement and command influence.[126]

In addition to the inquiry by the judge when appropriate, the pretrial agreement might contain a statement that the pretrial agreement originated with the accused and counsel.[127]

---

[121] *See, e.g.*, United States v. Holland, 1 M.J. 58 (C.M.A. 1975). *See* Chapter 12. *See also* United States v. Bartley, 47 M.J. 182 (C.A.A.F. 1997) (unlike *Weasler*, fatal to fail to disclose pretrial agreement to waive potential command influence issue).

[122] R.C.M. 910(f)(3).

[123] *See, e.g.*, United States v. Troglin, 44 C.M.R. 237 (C.M.A. 1972).

[124] United States v. Cain, 5 M.J. 698, 700 (N.C.M.R. 1978). *Cf.* R.C.M. 910(f)(2) Discussion ("Even if the military judge fails to so inquire or the accused answers incorrectly, counsel have an obligation to bring any agreements or understandings in connection with the plea to the attention of the military judge"). In *United States v. Corriere*, 24 M.J. 701 (A.C.M.R. 1987), the court indicated that quibbling about the contents of a pretrial agreement may raise questions about competency. 5 M.J. 708 n.7 (N.C.M.R. 1978). The court also condemned the lack of integrity before a trial judge. It indicated that false statements to a court may raise ethical issues under a recent ruling of the ABA. 5 M.J. 708 n.7 (N.C.M.R. 1978).

[125] United States v. Muller, 21 M.J. 205, 207 (C.M.A. 1986). *See also* United States v. Miles, 12 M.J. 377 (C.M.A. 1982) (will not consider post-trial affidavits submitted long after the fact).

[126] United States v. Sherman, 51 M.J. 73 (C.A.A.F. 1999). It may be that the Court was especially concerned in this case about the claims of command influence about which the Court is always sensitive.

[127] On appeal, the court may receive affidavits to clarify which party originated the agreement. United States v. Zelenski, 24 M.J. 1, 2 (C.M.A. 1987). In the alternative a *DuBay* factfinding period could be ordered.

(Rel.3—1/07 Pub.62410)

Although the Rules for Court-Martial no longer require that a retrial agreement originate with the accused, when the accused does initiate an agreement that fact should be set forth to further bolster the voluntariness of the agreement.[128]

§ 19-23.30 Inquiry into Conditions

The judge must ensure that the accused is aware of[129] and understands each condition in the agreement and that none of the conditions violate public policy.[130] Conditions that are against public policy should be struck from the agreement with the consent of the parties,[131] and the agreement should be considered without those conditions.

§ 19-23.40 Sentence Limitations

In reviewing a pretrial agreement, the judge must review any agreement as to sentence. If trial is before a court with members, the judge must ensure at

---

[128] Executive Order 12767, Amendments to the *Manual for Courts-Martial, United States*, 1984 (June 27, 1991) amended R.C.M. 705(d)(1) to permit the government to initiate plea bargaining. To the extent that the accused has initiated an agreement and that fact is not clear, it would be helpful to have it recited in the actual agreement. *See, e.g.*, United States v. Reed, 26 M.J. 891 (A.F.C.M.R. 1988).

[129] *E.g.*, United States v. Morales-Santana, 32 M.J. 557 (A.C.M.R. 1990) (fine may not be approved as part of pretrial agreement when not mentioned in agreement and there was no inquiry by the judge on the possibility of a fine).

[130] *See* Section 12-25.20. *Cf.* United States v. Baumgart, 23 M.J. 888, 889 n.2 (A.C.M.R. 1987), in which the court was concerned about the waiver of various rights:

An aggressive staff judge advocate, considering the preeminent bargaining position he occupies as the convening authority's principal legal advisor, probably will be able to convince the defense counsel in a given general court-martial jurisdiction that their clients will receive more favorable "deals" by waiving their right to a trial by members. Over a period of time, the continuous use of this tactic could effectively dampen, if not as a practical matter destroy, an appellant's statutory option to a trial by members and yet, meet the subtle requirements for "voluntariness" of a negotiated plea. For other views concerning this practice, *see generally United States v. Giordano*, NMCM 860981 (N.M.C.M.R. 8 Sep. 1986) (unpub.). Compare the majority opinion of Chief Judge Gormley in *Giordano*, condoning the practice of submitting pretrial agreements with provisions waiving a trial by members, with the opinion of Judge Grant concurring in result. Judge Grant traces the legislative history of Article 16, Uniform Code of Military Justice, and concludes that, because the practice of the command was to require a provision for trial by judge alone "as a condition precedent to favorably considering the agreement . . . the influence of the convening authority in the forum selection process was equally prevalent" and resulted in the "contravention of Article 16." We believe, however, that currently military law requires that we uphold the use of the practice, at least under the particular facts of this case.

See also United States v. McFayden, 51 M.J. 289 (C.A.A.F. 1999) (waiver of Article 13 violations not impermissible); United States v. Zelenski, 24 M.J. 1 (C.M.A. 1987); United States v. Jones, 23 M.J. 305, 307 n.4 (C.M.A. 1987).

[131] Otherwise, the agreement will be voided, a result that neither party normally desires. R.C.M. 910(f)(1) states that a "pretrial agreement may not be accepted if it does not comply with R.C.M. 705" (emphasis added). *See also* § 12-25.00 et. seq.

an Article 39(a) session that his or her interpretation of the sentence is consistent with the accused's understanding of the agreement. If the trial is by judge alone, examination of the sentencing portion of the agreement must ordinarily be delayed until sentence is announced.[132] Failure to do so, however, is not likely to result in reversal absent some form of specific prejudice.[133] Service members frequently bargain to limit the financial consequences of their convictions, ordinarily seeking to constrain the amount of forfeitures or fines that may be adjudged. In a surprising number of cases, accused have found their agreements in this area to be meaningless because administratively they are no longer subject to pay. Most often this is because they are beyond their contractual period of service; they have passed their "ETS" date. Finding that they are payless, they attack the providence of their pleas, claiming either that they lacked a proper understanding of the maximum sentence or that they have failed to receive the benefit of their bargained for pretrial agreement. Although entitlement to pay ordinarily is a "collateral" matter, a pretrial agreement entered into under the erroneous understanding that the accused will have access to pay for matters such as family support can vitiate the plea.[134]

§ 19-24.00   Rejection of an Improvident Plea and Its Consequences

§ 19-24.10   In General

The *Care* and *Green* decisions manifest a determination on the part of the Court of Military Appeals that guilty pleas should not be received in the armed forces unless they are truly voluntary and based upon an intelligent understanding of the plea's meaning and effect. With the plea-bargaining system that exists in some of the armed forces, this necessarily includes a determination of the nature and extent of any plea bargain entered into, because a misunderstanding on the part of the accused as to the nature of a pretrial agreement makes the plea, at least in one sense, involuntary.[135]

---

[132] R.C.M. 910(f)(3). United States v. Green, 1 M.J. 453, 456 (C.M.A. 1976). However, examination of the quantum portion in a judge alone trial "is not absolutely prohibited. The judge must merely be cautious about obtaining foreknowledge of sentence provisions to avoid prejudicial error." United States v. Diaz, 30 M.J. 957, 959 (C.G.C.M.R. 1990) (defense counsel disclosed the terms).

[133] *See, e.g.,* United States v. Diaz, 30 M.J. 957, 959 (C.G.C.M.R. 1990). *Cf.* United States v. Green, 1 M.J. 453, 456 (C.M.A. 1976). *See also* United States v. Williams, 6 M.J. 884 (A.C.M.R. 1979) (court disapproved the practice of making a prefindings examination of the quantum in every guilty plea case tried by judge alone, but failed to find prejudicial error where trial judge viewed the quantum portion of the pretrial agreement prior to adjudging sentence).

[134] *See generally* United States v. Perron, 58 M.J. 78 (C.A.A.F. 2003); United States v. Smith, 56 M.J. 271 (C.A.A.F. 2002) (Court remanded the case in the hope that appropriate relief might be available; otherwise the plea was to be vacated).

[135] Since one must presume that in the usual case the misled accused would have pled guilty with a clear understanding of what had actually been promised.

(Rel.3—1/07 Pub.62410)

Given *Care* and *Green* and their philosophical underpinnings, a military judge should lack any discretion whatsoever to accept or reject a plea. Either the plea is provident, in which case it should be accepted, or it is improvident and must be rejected. In actual practice, however, the issue is by no means so clear. Many accused lack the ability to articulate their responses fully, notwithstanding substantial pretrial preparation by their defense counsel. Given an apparent claim of innocence or a statement inconsistent with guilt, for example, a military judge could simply reject the plea, or could, in the alternative, discuss the matter at greater length and perhaps grant a recess for the accused to consult with counsel. The judge's decision in such a case is discretionary. A judge may also have discretion, at least pragmatically, to interpret ambiguities in the accused's responses— especially inasmuch as demeanor may play a significant part in the judge's determination as to the accused's comprehension and intent. Given the degree of discretion available to the judge in determining providency, it is surprising that no military authority exists as yet to determine the actual nature of that discretion,[136] and any resolution must await the development of case law. It is clear, however, that even though the accused does not have a right to plead guilty,[137] rejection of a plea may substantially injure an accused,[138] and rejection of a plea should only take place after a reasonable attempt to determine that the plea is in fact improvident.[139]

One commentator has suggested that the proper solution to an equivocal statement by the accused would be to have "the government present its evidence to demonstrate the accused's 'factual guilt'"[140] while the defense counsel explains why the statement fails to raise more than "a mere possibility of evidence."[141] While such a procedure might be appropriate in some cases, in

---

[136] *See generally* Moriarty, *above* for an outstanding discussion of the discretion problem.

[137] *See above* note 16.

[138] When an accused has a pretrial agreement, it is conditioned upon a successful guilty plea. While equitable considerations might suggest that an accused who makes a good-faith effort to plead guilty, only to have the judge reject the plea, should be given the benefit of the bargain, the government has lost what it sought to gain by the agreement and is not required to comply with it. The accused without a pretrial agreement is not quite as troubling, but may have had reasonable cause to plead guilty (*e.g.*, to avoid the stress of a contested case or to avoid involving some specific person as a witness) and should not have his or her election summarily set aside.

[139] *See, e.g.*, United States v. Ammidown, 497 F.2d 615 (D.C. Cir. 1973) (trial judge abused discretion in rejecting plea). Then Captain Moriarty (*above* note 18 at 263) states: "An inevitable result of the accused's natural proclivity to rationalize his conduct, equivocal statements are the price paid for free and open discourse with the military judge. Deeming a plea improvident on the basis of these equivocal statements would only encourage 'canned answers' to 'canned questions." [footnotes omitted].

[140] Moriarty, *above* note 18 at 266.

[141] Moriarty, *above* note 18 at 267. *Cf.* United States v. Loya, 49 M.J. 104 (C.A.A.F. 1998) (Reversible error not to allow the defense to introduce during sentencing that good treatment could have

(Rel.3—1/07 Pub.62410)

general it would appear inappropriate both because the equivocal response would suggest that the accused was not necessarily convinced of his or her guilt— the minimum requirement of *Care*— and also because the government, in the presentation of evidence in a pretrial agreement case, would have lost much of what it bargained for. Given an unsought declaration of improvidence, it has been suggested that the defense attempt to preserve the plea on the record and, if trial continues before a new judge,[142] again attempt to plead guilty lest the accused be held to have waived objection to the declaration of improvidence.[143] Another commentator has suggested that when the defense faced with such declaration has a pretrial agreement, it should attempt, via a motion for appropriate relief, to limit the maximum sentence to that in the agreement.[144]

§ 19-24.20 Evidentiary Consequences of Rejection of Improvident Pleas

Military Rule of Evidence 410[145] provides, in relevant part, that neither "a plea of guilty which was later withdrawn" nor "any statement made in the course of any judicial inquiry regarding" such plea is admissible against the accused who made the plea. When a plea is rejected as improvident, it should occupy the same status as a withdrawn plea. Consequently, absent waiver,[146] the accused whose plea is rejected as improvident is secure against use of any statements made during the providency inquiry.[147] When a stipulation of fact has been made, it should be withdrawn along with the guilty plea.[148]

---

helped the victim. The judge did not admit the evidence, probably thinking it would make the plea improvident. The judge should have rejected the plea or asked defense counsel and the accused to waive the possibility of a defense.).

[142] *See* Section 19-24.30.

[143] Moriarty, *above* note 18 at 265 n.53 (citing United States v. Reese, SPCM 15453 (A.C.M.R. Mar. 20, 1981) (unpublished)) (stating in dicta that waiver could result if counsel failed to "renew the pleas" or make "an appropriate motion").

[144] Tesler, *above* note 18 at 27 n.42.

[145] *As amended by* Executive Order 12306, 46 Fed. Reg. 29693 (June 3, 1981).

[146] *Cf.* United States v. Mezzanatto, 513 U.S. 196 (1995) (accused may waive Rule 410 protections covering pretrial plea discussions).

[147] Mil. R. Evid. 410 also declares that "a statement is admissible (i) in any proceeding wherein another statement made in the course of the same plea or plea discussions has been introduced and the statement ought in fairness to be considered contemporaneous with it." Consequently, the accused may open the door to any statements made as part of the providency inquiry. *See* Section 23-60.00. An accused who is not pleading guilty to all charged offenses may be reluctant to plead guilty because statements made during the inquiry may be admissible against the accused in the trial of those offenses. Pre-plea objections to such use will be waived if the accused pleads not guilty. United States v. Nelson, 51 M.J. 399 (C.A.A.F. 1999) (by failing to plead guilty, accused failed to preserve issue of whether statements made during providency inquiry could be introduced on other charges).

[148] United States v. Daniels, 28 C.M.R. 276 (C.M.A. 1959).

(Rel.3—1/07 Pub.62410)

§ 19-24.30   Recusal of the Military Judge

When a military judge rejects a guilty plea as improvident, trial on the merits must follow. In such a case, the trial judge would preside knowing that the accused has attempted to plead guilty and may be further burdened by seriously damaging statements made by the accused during the providency inquiry or as part of a stipulation of fact. Thus, the trial judge may be aware of inadmissible information so substantial in quantum and so damaging to the accused as to make it difficult for the judge to continue to sit. Indeed, the Court of Military Appeals cited with approval a statement made by the United States Court of Appeals for the D.C. Circuit that "[t]he disciplined judicial mind should not be subjected to any unnecessary strain; even the most austere intellect has a subconscious."[149] Recusal should only take place, however, when necessary, and military law does not require recusal solely because a judge has declared a plea improvident.[150]

§ 19-25.00   Noncompliance with Providency-Inquiry Requirements

The history of compliance with the *Care* and *Green* providency inquiry requirements has been a rocky one, with significant resistance on the part of what were then the service Courts of Military Review— particularly to strict compliance with the *King/Green* requirements.[151] Rule for Courts-Martial 910 was intended to limit such strict requirements. Since Rule for Courts-Martial 910 is based on an executive order, and *Care* and *Green* were exercises of judicial supervisory power, the Court of Appeals for the Armed Forces may show some flexibility in determining whether departures from strict compliance will require reversal.

Some examples of flexibility have occurred. Thus, when a military judge who accepted a guilty plea by an accused on the theory that the accused was an aider and abettor to larceny failed to specifically inquire about the accused's intent to act as an aider and abettor, reversal was not required when the accused's

---

[149] United States v. Bradley, 7 M.J. 332, 334 (C.M.A. 1979) (citing United States v. Walker, 473 F.2d 136, 138 (D.C. Cir. 1972)).

[150] *See, e.g.*, United States v. Winter, 35 M.J. 93, 95 (C.M.A. 1993) (judge who rejects plea and proceeds to try the accused is not per se disqualified; however, the facts of any given case may require recusal). *See generally* § 14-40.0 *et seq.*

[151] *See generally* Lukjanowicz, *The Providency Inquiry: An Examination of Judicial Responsibilities*, 13 The Advocate 333 (1981) [hereinafter cited as Lukjanowicz] for an outstanding historical review of the appellate treatment of noncompliance by the trial judiciary with the *King/Green* requirements. It took substantial time for the trial judiciary to fully comply with the *Care* and *King/Green* requirements, and even now the complexity of some inquiries, especially in the area of pretrial agreements, makes strict compliance pragmatically difficult. Thus, staff judge advocates on review and the appellate courts are often faced with technically defective providency inquiries in cases in which it is reasonably clear that the accused knowingly and voluntarily pled guilty. Their resistance to reversal and potential retrial is understandable, although systemically unfortunate.

"factual account of the incident established his role as at least an aider and abettor."[152] In so holding, the court declared:

> He [the appellant] submits, however, that the military judge's failure to specifically inquire about his intent requires reversal. We disagree. We have always rejected such a structured, formalistic interpretation of *United States v. Care*, ... Rather the Court has examined the entire inquiry to ascertain if the appellant was adequately advised.[153]

Although the court has not accepted a theory of "substantial compliance" with *Care*, it has perhaps altered in part the *Care* requirements in order to emphasize the intent behind *Care*, rather than to dwell on the mechanism normally to be used to secure it. In the area of inquiry into pretrial agreements— the *King/Green* inquiry — the Court of Military Appeals was on record as requiring strict compliance with its requirements,[154] but it clearly created an exception to that standard in the area of the "comportment question"[155] by holding that the judge's failure to ask counsel whether their understanding of the pretrial agreement comported with the judge's does not require reversal in absence of evidence of disagreement.[156] One commentator has suggested that this constitutes a sub silentio overruling of the strict compliance standards of *King* and *Green*.[157] While this may be true,[158] a conservative reading of the cases would simply suggest that a limited exception in the area of the comportment question has been made. When a question has arisen concerning proper compliance with the providence inquiry, it may be appropriate for an appellate court to order a limited *DuBay*[159] hearing to ascertain whether an issue actually does exist (*e.g.*, whether

---

[152] United States v. Crouch, 11 M.J. 128, 129 (C.M.A. 1981).

[153] 11 M.J. 129–30 (C.M.A. 1981).

[154] United States v. Crowley, 7 M.J. 336 (C.M.A. 1979); United States v. King, 3 M.J. 458 (C.M.A. 1977). *Cf.* R.C.M. 910(f) and Discussion.

[155] *See generally* Section 19-23.02.

[156] United States v. Dinkel, 13 M.J. 400 (C.M.A. 1982); United States v. Passini, 10 M.J. 108 (C.M.A. 1980) (agreement susceptible to only one interpretation and if counsels' agreement had differed with the judge's they would have so stated); United States v. Hinton, 10 M.J. 136 (C.M.A. 1981); United States v. Lott, 9 M.J. 70 (C.M.A. 1980). *See also* United States v. Lay, 10 M.J. 678 (A.C.M.R.), *pet. denied*, 11 M.J. 347 (C.M.A. 1981); United States v. Harvey, 6 M.J. 545 (N.C.M.R. 1978); United States v. Jefferson, 5 M.J. 715 (A.C.M.R. 1978); United States v. Milum, 5 M.J. 672 (A.C.M.R. 1978). Interestingly, in *Passini*, the court stated: "This inference [that counsel understanding of the agreement was the same as the judge's] is all the stronger since counsel were under a duty to reveal in open court any discrepancy between the pretrial agreement and their understanding thereof." 10 M.J. at 109.

[157] Lukjanowski, *above* note 140 at 345.

[158] *See, e.g.*, United States v. Cruz, 10 M.J. 32, 33 n.1 (C.M.A. 1980) stating that:

> Whether strict or substantial compliance with the *King/Green* mandate is necessary need not delay us here, since all terms of the pretrial agreement were mutually understood.

[159] United States v. DuBay, 37 C.M.R. 411 (C.M.A. 1967). *See, e.g.*, United States v. Sherman,

(Rel.3—1/07 Pub.62410)

there is disagreement as to the terms of a pretrial agreement) rather than simply reversing the conviction.[160] In this respect, it should be noted that an issue may be resolved simply by finding it to be moot.[161]

§ 19-26.00 Appraisal of the Providency Inquiry

There should be little doubt that the providency inquiry mandated in courts-martial has been generally successful in achieving its aims of ensuring intelligent and voluntary pleas and supervising the practice of plea bargaining. The procedures used also may be justly faulted as often over-technical and as containing within them the ability to interfere with the attorney-client relationship.[162] No solution may exist, however. Many of the safeguards that exist in the military criminal legal system are intended not only to ensure justice per se, but also to dispel the continual inherent distrust of the system held by most of its accuseds and many of its observers.[163] The providency inquiry makes the most suspect portion of any American judicial system— plea bargaining— open and subject to regulation. Indeed, it has in most respects made the military justice system a national model. A decrease in the scrutiny of the providency inquiry would necessarily suggest both the actuality and appearance of a pressure to plead guilty. Reversals for "technical" violations are a more difficult matter. While some of the pretrial agreement inquiry, such as the comportment question,[164] could be altered in favor of placing the responsibility on counsel to raise potential

---

51 M.J. 73, 74 (C.A.A.F. 1999) (ordered DuBay hearing "to determine whether there was a sub rosa agreement between the parties not to raise issues of unlawful command influence and the legality of appellant's pretrial confinement.").

[160] *Cf.* United States v. Victor, 10 M.J. 69 (C.M.A. 1980); United States v. Killebrew, 9 M.J. 154 (C.M.A. 1980). *But see* United States v. Williamson, 42 M.J. 613, 626 (N.M. Crim. App. 1995) (should be an alternative other than a "rehearing," such as supplement of record).

[161] Examples of mootness include an ambiguous pretrial agreement, the effect of which is rendered moot by a sentence less severe than either interpretation, or a pretrial agreement condition allegedly in violation of public policy (*e.g.*, a provision providing for cancellation of the agreement upon further misconduct of the accused when that condition has not and will not come into play because of expiration of the relevant time period).

[162] The probing-plea inquiry used in the armed forces often has the unfortunate side effect of suggesting to the accused that he or she is misguided in pleading guilty, and that the judge personally wants a plea of not guilty. Not only is it difficult for many defendants to continue in their pleas, but the inquiry seems to divide client from counsel and suggest that the attorney has given inadequate advice.

[163] This is not to suggest that the civilian criminal justice system is necessarily held in great repute. The military justice system labors under a unique disadvantage insofar as public perception is concerned, because all of its participants and components are members of a disciplined organization, the existence of which normally depends upon following the orders of superiors. It is often difficult for an accused to recognize that counsel, judge, and members are independent of command.

[164] *See* Section 19-23.20.

(Rel.3—1/07 Pub.62410)

concerns,[165] any significant change would be undesirable. A shift to "substantial compliance" as a standard for appellate affirmance would be appropriate, except that history shows that given such a guidepost, many members of the judiciary would seize upon the change to justify even greater departures from the standard. The present system has at least the virtue of a degree of certainty when viewed in light of the opinions of the Court of Appeals for the Armed Forces.

The primary, if not sole, purpose of the providency inquiry is to ensure that the accused's plea is provident. It is not to obtain information for sentencing[166] or for use in other investigations or prosecutions.[167] Should the judge attempt an unnecessarily probing inquiry, the accused may balk and a previously negotiated agreement may unravel.

§ 19-30.00   ACCEPTANCE OF PLEAS AND SUBSEQUENT ATTACK

If the plea is found provident, findings based on the plea will be entered, unless such action is prohibited by service regulations or the plea is to a lesser included offense.[168]

The courts have been careful to ensure satisfaction of the *Care/Green* and R.C.M. 910 inquiry. They have been loath to permit a battle of affidavits to impeach the providence of the plea. "In determining the providence of a guilty plea, the scope of review is limited to the record of the trial."[169] The courts will disregard post-trial assertions to impeach a plea that is provident on its face.

Rule for Courts-Martial 913(a) provides that "If mixed pleas have been entered, the military judge should ordinarily defer informing the members of the offenses to which the accused pleaded guilty until after the findings on the remaining contested offenses have been entered." Advising the members of the existence of a guilty plea after a contested trial that may have resulted in acquittal on the

---

[165] *See above* note 130.

[166] Although any information given may be so used. United States v. Holt, 27 M.J. 57 (C.M.A. 1988) (the government may introduce, in aggravation on sentencing, statements made under oath during providency that are otherwise admissible and do not run afoul of the Military Rules of Evidence). See also § 23-43.20.

[167] *See* United States v. Miller, 23 M.J. 553 (C.G.C.M.R. 1986), *reaffirmed after reconsideration*, 23 M.J. 837 (C.G.C.M.R. 1987) (judge should not have asked accused to identify drug supplier); United States v. Kelly, A.C.M.R. 8600707 (A.C.M.R. Dec. 21, 1987) (as part of inquiry, judge may not compel the accused to reveal the name of his confederates or suppliers); United States v. Ortega, C.M. 446846 (A.C.M.R. Mar. 7, 1986).

[168] R.C.M. 910(g).

[169] United States v. Roane, 43 M.J. 93, 99 (C.A.A.F. 1995); United States v. Lawson, 40 M.J. 475, 476 (C.M.A. 1994); United States v. Muller, 21 M.J. 205, 207 (C.M.A. 1986) ("Because the military judge properly inquired and received assurance from appellant that no *sub rosa* agreement existed, we will not consider inconsistent post-trial assertions."); United States v. Miles, 12 M.J. 377, 379 (C.M.A. 1982). *See also* United States v. Torres, 53 M.J. 211 (C.A.A.F. 2000).

(Rel.3—1/07 Pub.62410)

other charges requires care on the part of the judge who should emphasize that the procedure is prescribed by law.[170]

It has long been held in military law that "admissions implicit in a plea of guilty to one offense cannot be used as evidence to support a finding of guilty of an essential element of a separate and different offense."[171] The Court of Military Appeals stated that admissions in a plea of guilty inquiry to an offense can be considered only when the plea relates to a lesser included offense within the same specification and charge.[172]

§ 19-40.00 WITHDRAWAL OF PLEA

Prior to announcement of sentence, an accused may request permission of the military judge to withdraw an accepted plea of guilty and substitute either a plea of not guilty or a plea of guilty to a lesser-included offense, and the judge may, within his or discretion, permit such withdrawal.[173] To date, there are no guidelines to be used in determining when the judge should utilize the court's discretion, although it is clear that the *Manual for Courts-Martial* does not contemplate withdrawal of the plea as a matter of right.[174]

In their original formulation, the American Bar Association's Standards Relating to Pleas of Guilty[175] were only slightly more helpful when they declared

---

[170] For an example of how not to advise the members, *see United States v. Childress*, 33 M.J. 602, 604 (A.C.M.R. 1991), in which the judge explained that he had committed "what may be considered . . . a fraud on you."

[171] United States v. Abdullah, 37 M.J. 692, 693 (A.C.M.R. 1993), *quoting* United States v. Caszatt, 29 C.M.R. 521, 522 (C.M.A. 1960).

[172] *Abdullah*, 37 M.J. at 693, *citing* United States v. Rivera, 23 M.J. 89, 85 (C.M.A. 1986).

[173] R.C.M. 910(h). *See also* United States v. Young, 2 M.J. 472 (A.C.M.R. 1975); United States v. Politano, 34 C.M.R. 298 (C.M.A. 1964).

[174] United States v. Young, 2 M.J. 472, 476 (A.C.M.R. 1975). Where MCM, 1951 ¶ 70b stated "[w]henever a plea of guilty has been received, [and] the accused asks to be allowed to withdraw it . . . he should be permitted to do so," MCM, 1969 ¶ 70b stated "[i]f before sentence is announced . . . the accused asks permission to withdraw a plea of guilty . . . the military judge . . . may, as a matter of discretion, permit him to do so." R.C.M. 910(h)(1) has similar language. In *United States v. Silver*, 40 M.J. 351 (C.M.A. 1994), the court stated that there is no requirement to advise the accused of the right to withdraw from pretrial agreement "absen[t] any indication" that he or she wanted to withdraw. Procedurally, Air Force Instruction 51-201, Law, Administration of Military Justice 6.9.2 (26 November 2003), provides that withdrawal from a pretrial agreement will be in writing and signed by the convening authority. *Cf.* United States v. Hyde, 520 U.S. 670 117 S. Ct. 1630 (1997) (federal defendant may not withdraw from pretrial agreement without setting forth a "fair and just reason" under Fed. R. Crim. P. 11(e)(4)).

[175] ABA Standards for Criminal Justice, Standards Relating to Pleas of Guilty § 2.1(a) (approved draft 1968). The current Standard retains withdrawal "for any fair and just reason" and adds that "In determining whether a fair and just reason exists, the court should also weigh any prejudice to the prosecution caused by reliance on the defendant's plea." ABA Standards for Criminal Justice: Pleas of Guilty Standard 14-2.1(a) (3d ed. 1999).

(Rel.3—1/07 Pub.62410)

that: "Before sentence, the court in its discretion may allow the defendant to withdraw his plea for any fair and just reason unless the prosecution has been substantially prejudiced by reliance upon the defendant's plea."[176] Although the somewhat vague standard of "good cause" might thus be appropriate in the armed forces, what would constitute an abuse of discretion in this area is unclear. The ABA Standards may be of some assistance in this particular, as they provide for withdrawal as a matter of right when the defendant "proves that withdrawal is necessary to correct a manifest injustice"[177] and the motion for withdrawal "is timely" and "made with due diligence, considering the nature of the allegations therein."[178] Manifest injustice exist when the accused prove that:

(A) the defendant was denied effective assistance of counsel as guaranteed by the Constitution, statute, or rule;

(B) the plea was not authorized or ratified by the defendant or by a person authorized to so act in the defendant's behalf;

(C) the plea was involuntary or was entered without knowledge of the charge or that the sentence actually imposed could be imposed;

(D) the defendant did not receive the charge or sentence concessions contemplated by the plea agreement and the prosecuting attorney failed to seek or not to oppose the concessions as promised in the plea agreement; or

(E) the defendant did not receive the charge or sentence concessions contemplated by the plea agreement, which was either tentatively or fully concurred in by the court, and the defendant did not affirm the plea after being advised that the court no longer concurred and after being called upon to either affirm or withdraw the plea; or

(F) the guilty plea was entered upon the express condition, approved by the judge, that the plea could be withdrawn if the charge or sentence concessions were subsequently rejected by the court.[179]

---

[176] ABA Standaards Relating to Pleas of Guilty § 2.1(a) (approved draft 1968). The Third Edition softens this to provide, "In determining whether a fair and just reason exists, the court should also weigh any prejudice to the prosecution caused by reliance on the defendant's plea." ABA Standards for Criminal Justice: Pleas of Guilty Standard 14-2.1(a) (3d ed. 1999).

[177] ABA Standards for Criminal Justice: Pleas of Guilty Standard 14-2.1(b)(i) (3d ed. 1999).

[178] ABA Standards for Criminal Justice: Pleas of Guilty Standard 14-2.1(b)(i) (3d ed. 1999).

[179] ABA Standard 2.1(a)(ii). The Second Edition of the Standards are virtually identical, but add two additional justifications: that the defendant may withdraw the plea if the judge previously concurred in charge or sentence concessions and no longer concurs, or the plea was conditioned upon concessions now negated by the court. ABA Standards for Criminal Justice: Pleas of Guilty Standard 14-2.1(b) (3d ed. 1999). See also United States v. Johnson, 977 F.2d 1297 (8th Cir. 1992) (other factors to consider).

(Rel.3—1/07 Pub.62410)

In one unusual civilian case, the court held that a failure to supply constitutionally required exculpatory material led directly to the defendant's guilty plea and granted his post-conviction motion to withdraw the plea.[180]

When the trial judge fails to carry out an adequate providency inquiry, revision proceedings may be ordered.[181] The Navy-Marine Court of Military Review viewed such a revision proceeding as returning the trial to the point at which the accused initially pled guilty, and has thus stated that in such a case the accused has an absolute right to withdraw the prior guilty plea and to, in effect, plead anew.[182] It is, however, by no means clear that a revision proceeding actually has such an effect, and the Navy-Marine Court of Military Review may have been in error.[183]

§ 19-50.00 REVISION PROCEEDINGS AND OTHER CORRECTIVE DEVICES

Article 60(e)(2) of the Uniform Code provides that:

A proceeding in revision may be ordered if there is an apparent error or omission in the record or if the record shows improper or inconsistent action by a court-martial with respect to the findings or sentence that can be rectified without material prejudice to the substantial rights of the accused. In no case, however, may a proceeding in revision—

(A) reconsider a finding of not guilty of any specification or a ruling which amounts to a finding of not guilty;

(B) reconsider a finding of not guilty of any charge, unless there has been a finding of guilty under a specification laid under that charge, which sufficiently alleges a violation of some article of this chapter; or

(C) increase the severity of some article of the sentence unless the sentence prescribed for the offense is mandatory.[184]

If this provision is read liberally, revision proceedings might be authorized when there has been a defective *Care* or *Green* inquiry. Nevertheless, the courts are split on the availability of revision when the *Green* inquiry is faulty. The

---

[180] State v. Sturgeon, 605 N.W.2d 589 (Wis. App. 1999). *See also* John G. Douglass, *Fatal Attraction? The Uneasy Courtship of Brady and Plea Bargaining,* 50 Emory L.J. 437 (2001).

[181] *See* Section 19-50.00. *See also* R.C.M. 910(f) Discussion; United States v. Bray, 12 M.J. 553 (A.F.C.M.R. 1981) (revision preceding is sufficient to remedy any deficiency in making confessional stipulation inquiry).

[182] United States v. Newkirk, 8 M.J. 684 (N.C.M.R. 1980). *Cf.* R.C.M. 910(h)(3).

[183] The dicta in *Newkirk, above* note 170, is based upon United States v. Politano, 34 C.M.R. 298 (C.M.A. 1964), which was, in turn, based upon MCM, 1951 ¶ 70*b*, which has since been amended. *Compare* MCM, 1951 ¶ 70*b with* MCM, 1969 ¶ 70*b.* Both *Manual* provisions were intended to follow the Federal Rules of Criminal Procedure, which do not require a rehearing to begin with the prefindings stage. *See also* R.C.M. 910(f) Discussion.

[184] U.C.M.J. art 60(e)(2).

(Rel.3—1/07 Pub.62410)

Army and Air Force Courts of Military Review permitted revision to determine if the judge's understanding of the agreement is consistent with that of counsel.[185] The Navy-Marine Court of Military Review, on the other hand, did not allow revision unless the accused is given a chance to replead.[186] Absent a showing of prejudice to the accused, revision should be allowed whenever a *Care* inquiry is defective.[187] In addition to a revision hearing, a *DuBay* hearing may be held when it is determined that the accused's plea may be improvident.[188]

§ 19-60.00   POST-TRIAL MODIFICATIONS OF PRETRIAL AGREEMENTS

Although apparently still infrequent, it is apparent that after trial some accused have gone to the convening authority and proposed after-the-fact modifications of their pretrial agreements.[189] In *United States v. Pilkington*,[190] for example, the accused, without the assistance of counsel, offered to trade a prohibition on approval of a punitive discharge for a smaller amount of confinement. Thus far, the Court of Appeals for the Armed Forces has permitted this practice. The Court has emphasized its concern that the accused must be making a "fully informed and considered decision" that is not a product of coercion.[191] Yet, as Judges Sullivan and Effron have complained, the practice deprives the accused (and inherently the military legal system) of judicial scrutiny.[192] Appellate scrutiny is late, imperfect, and a questionable use of judicial resources. Given the enormous trial court effort focused on review of plea bargaining, this post-trial practice appears at least aberrational from a systemic perspective.

---

[185] United States v. Smith, 5 M.J. 842 (A.C.M.R. 1978); United States v. Seberg, 5 M.J. 589 (A.F.C.M.R. 1978).

[186] United States v. Newkirk, 8 M.J. 684 (N.C.M.R. 1980) and cases cited therein.

[187] *Compare* United States v. Kaetzel, 48 C.M.R. 58 (A.F.C.M.R. 1973) *with* United States v. Berkley, 47 C.M.R. 30 (A.C.M.R. 1973). A revision proceeding would appear to be the most efficient technique for resolving a providency inquiry, as the military judge may then ascertain whether any difficulties actually exist and may advise the accused of any omitted material. Experience indicates that most alleged providency inquiry errors are in fact technical in nature and do not involve errors actually affecting the accused. Consequently, the interests of both the accused and the government would best be served by use of this comparatively speedy device.

[188] United States v. Wirth, 25 M.J. 863 (A.C.M.R. 1988).

[189] 51 M.J. 415 (1999).

[190] United States v. Pilkington, 51 M.J. 415 (1999); United States v. Dawson, 51 M.J. 411 (C.A.A.F. 1999).

[191] 51 M.J. at 416.

[192] 51 M.J. at 417.

(Rel.3—1/07   Pub.62410)

§ 19-70.00 FAILURE OF THE GOVERNMENT TO COMPLY WITH TERMS OF A PRETRIAL AGREEMENT

Pretrial agreements acts as contracts between the accused and the government. In *Santabello v. New York*,[193] the Supreme Court opined that in the event of the failure of a material term of a plea bargain, the defendant should have the right to either specific performance or to withdraw the plea. Professors LaFave, Israel, and King observe that "although federal courts finding a *Santobello* violation on habeas corpus by a state prisoner ordinarily give the state court the opportunity to decide which remedy is more appropriate, federal courts ruling on claims by federal prisoners and state courts ruling on claims of state defendants rather regularly opt for the remedy of specific performance."[194] Dealing with the situation in which specific performance is impossible, the Court of Appeals for the Armed Forces, has rejected the argument that the courts of criminal appeals can create satisfactory alternative forms of specific performance.[195] The Court observed:

> We therefore hold that imposing alternative relief on an unwilling appellant to rectify a mutual misunderstanding of a material term in a pretrial agreement violates the appellant's Fifth Amendment right to due process. An appellate court may determine that alternatives to specific performance or withdrawal of a plea could provide an appellant with the benefit of his or her bargain—and may remand the case to the convening authority to determine whether doing so is advisable—but it cannot impose such a remedy on an appellant in the absence of the appellant's acceptance of that remedy.[196]

> In such a case the parties may voluntarily enter into a new, post trial agreement, to preserve the plea.[197] In the alternative, the consideration for the original plea having failed, the pretrial agreement based on it also fails.

---

[193] 404 U.S. 257, 263 (1971).

[194] Wayne R. LaFave, *et al* Criminal Procedure 977-978 (4th ed. 2004).

[195] United States v. Perron, 58 M.J. 78 (C.A.A.F. 2003).

[196] 58 M.J. at 86 (footnotes omitted).

[197] 58 M.J. 86 at n.7.

CHAPTER 20

PROCUREMENT AND PRESENTATION OF EVIDENCE; COMPULSORY PROCESS AND CONFRONTATION

§ 20-10.00 INTRODUCTION
  § 20-11.00   In General
  § 20-12.00   The Burdens of Proof and Production
§ 20-20.00 PROCUREMENT OF EVIDENCE
  § 20-21.00   In General
  § 20-22.00   The Decision to Obtain Evidence
    § 20-22.10 — In General
      § 20-22.11 — — General Procedures
      § 20-22.12 — — Expert Witnesses
        § 20-22.12(a) — — In General
        § 20-22.12(b) — — Expert Assistance Pretrial
        § 20-22.12(c) — — Obtaining Civilian Expert Assistance
    § 20-22.20 — Form of the Rule 703(c) Request
    § 20-22.30 — Timeliness
    § 20-22.40 — Materiality
    § 20-22.50 — Cumulative Testimony
    § 20-22.60 — Alternatives to a Witness' Personal Attendance at Trial
    § 20-22.70 — Defense Objections to Rule for Courts-Martial 703
      § 20-22.71 — — The Recipient of the Request
      § 20-22.72 — — Defense Disclosure of Tactics and Strategy
      § 20-22.73 — — Lack of Reciprocity in General
    § 20-22.80 — Revision of Rule for Courts-Martial 703
  § 20-23.00   The Power to Obtain Witnesses and Other Evidence
    § 20-23.10 — Evidence in the Custody or Control of Military Authorities
    § 20-23.20 — Evidence Not in Military Control
      § 20-23.21 — — Subpoenas
      § 20-23.22 — — The Warrant of Attachment
        § 20-23.22(a) — — In General
        § 20-23.22(b) — — Execution of Warrant
        § 20-23.22(c) — — Constitutionality of the Military Warrant of Attachment
    § 20-23.30 — Immunity
      § 20-23.31 — — In General

§ 20-23.32 — — The Nature of the Immunity Required

§ 20-23.32(a) — — In General

§ 20-23.32(b) — — Threat of Prosecution in a Foreign Jurisdiction

§ 20-23.33 — — Consequences of Granting Immunity

§ 20-23.33(a) — — At Trial

§ 20-23.33(b) — — To the Immunized Witness

§ 20-23.33(c) — — Post-trial

§ 20-30.00 CONFRONTATION AND COMPULSORY PROCESS

§ 20-31.00 In General

§ 20-32.00 The Right of Confrontation

§ 20-32.10 — In General

§ 20-32.20 — The Right to Compel the Government to Produce Witnesses Whose Statements Are Used at Trial

§ 20-32.21 — — In General

§ 20-32.22 — — Witnesses Present in Court

§ 20-32.23 — — Hearsay From Declarants Not Present in Court

§ 20-32.23(a) — — In General

§ 20-32.23(b) — — Unavailability

§ 20-32.24 — — "Firmly Rooted" Hearsay Exceptions & Particularized Gaurantees of Trustworthiness

§ 20-32.25 — — "Particularized Guarantees"

§ 20-32.25(a) — — The Residual Hearsay Exception

§ 20-32.30 — The Right to Cross-Examine the Government's Witnesses at Trial

§ 20-32.31 — — In General

§ 20-32.32 — — The Rape-Shield Rule

§ 20-32.32(a) — — In General

§ 20-32.32(b) — — Potential Confrontation and Compulsory Process Problems

§ 20-32.33 — — Restrictions Due to Classified Material

§ 20-32.34 — — Cross-Examination During Suppression Hearings

§ 20-33.00 The Right of Compulsory Process

§ 20-33.10 — The Right to Compel the Attendance of Available Witnesses at Trial

§ 20-33.11 — — In General

§ 20-33.12 — — Requiring the Government to Grant Immunity to Prospective Defense Witnesses

§ 20-33.13 — — Improper Joinder

§ 20-33.20 — The Right to be Present for the Testimony of Defense Witnesses at Trial

§ 20.33.30 — The Right to Examine Defense Witnesses at Trial and to Present Defense Evidence

§ 20-33.31 — — General Constitutional Standards

§ 20-33.32 — — Competency of Witnesses

(Rel.3—1/07 Pub.62410)

§ 20-33.33 — — Admissibility of Evidence
  § 20-33.33(a) — — In General
  § 20-33.33(b) — — Scientific Evidence
  § 20-33.33(c) — — Polygraph Evidence
§ 20-33.34 — — Preventing Defense Witnesses from Testifying
§ 20-33.35 — — Laboratory Reports
§ 20-40.00 DEPOSITIONS AND INTERROGATORIES

§ 20-10.00 INTRODUCTION

§ 20-11.00 In General

Although pretrial litigation often seems to render trial on the merits something of an anticlimax, adversarial adjudication remains the focus of the criminal justice system, military or civilian.[2] Once trial on the merits has begun, trial and defense counsel naturally utilize the rules of evidence in the fashion most likely to make the most of the evidence available to them. Yet, as all military lawyers are aware, the period since the enactment of the Uniform Code of Military Justice has brought sweeping changes, not only in military criminal law, but also in the "constitutionalization" of the law of evidence. Increasingly, considerations of compulsory process and confrontation play important roles in determining what evidence can be obtained and used at trial. Accordingly, this chapter undertakes to review the law applicable to the procurement and admission of evidence on the merits[3] in the armed forces in light of the Sixth Amendment rights to compulsory process and confrontation.[4] Such a review necessarily entails a consideration of matters that are generally considered procedural, primarily the law applicable to witness procurement, as well as matters clearly evidentiary in nature.

§ 20-12.00 The Burdens of Proof and Production

Because burdens of proof and production, like presumptions,[5] are substitutes for evidence and dictate which party must address and prove an issue, no

---

[2] Ironically, the large number of guilty pleas in both civilian and military law often renders trial on the merits the rarity rather than the usual rule. Notwithstanding this, the entire criminal justice system is oriented around the contested trial, which thus supplies a normative standard.

[3] Although the rules of evidence do apply to sentencing proceedings in the armed forces (Mil. R. Evid. 1101), this chapter will deal only with trial on the merits.

[4] This chapter will not, therefore, generally address the innumerable questions inherent in the Military Rules of Evidence.

[5] Although the Supreme Court has clearly permitted various forms of presumptions in criminal cases, whether statutory or common law in origin (Barnes v. United States, 412 U.S. 837 (1973)), it has yet to expressly indicate the necessary relationship between the basic fact and the presumed fact. 412 U.S. 837 at 845 (1973) (stating that the court need not choose between the different tests of "more likely than not" or "beyond a reasonable doubt" as possession of stolen property

discussion of the law relating to the procurement and admission of evidence can be undertaken without consideration of these burdens.[6] In *In re Winship*,[7] the Supreme Court held that "the Due Process Clause protects the accused against conviction except upon proof beyond a reasonable doubt of every fact necessary to constitute the crime with which he is charged."[8] The defense can clearly be given the burden of raising and proving traditional affirmative defenses as they are outside the legislative definition of the offense. *Winship, however,* left open what facts were necessary "to constitute the crime." The Court appears to have clarified its intent in *Patterson v. New York*[9] by holding that the legislature may constitutionally define a crime in whatever fashion it deems desirable and may then require a defendant, proven to have committed the unlawful conduct, to carry the burden of proving the application of any exception to the statute that the legislation chooses to recognize.[10] Because this could permit the perverse

---

gave rise to the presumed fact of guilty knowledge beyond a reasonable doubt); Turner v. United States, 396 U.S. 398, 416 (1970) (suggesting need for a beyond-a-reasonable-doubt standard); Leary v. United States, 395 U.S. 6, 36 (1969) (statutory presumption must be more likely than not given the underlying fact); Tot v. United States, 319 U.S. 463, 467 (1943) (presumption is invalid if there is no rational connection between the basic and presumed facts). Mandatory presumptions "violate the Due Process Clause if they relieve the State of the burden of persuasion on an element of the offense." Francis v. Franklin, 471 U.S. 307, 314 (1985). *See generally* Edward J. Imwinkelried, Paul C. Giannelli, Francis A. Gilligan & Fredric I. Lederer, Courtroom Criminal Evidence Ch. 29 (4th ed. 2006). The topic of presumptions is complex. *See generally* Allen, *Structuring Jury Decisionmaking in Criminal Cases: A Unified Constitutional Approach to Evidentiary Devices,* 94 Harv. L. Rev. 321 (1980).

[6] *See, e.g.,* United States v. Phillips, 42 M.J. 346, 349 (C.A.A.F. 1995) (No violation of Article 13 because of no "intent to punish or stigmatize a person waiting disciplinary disposition." Judge Wiss, concurring in result, would shift the burden. "Look for evidence of an intent to punish — and unlawful, negative purpose for the condition; in the absence of such evidence, shift the focus and look for evidence that the condition serves 'a legitimate nonpunitive governmental objective' — a lawful, positive purpose; and in the absence of the latter, a court may *infer* an intent to punish, even though actual evidence of such intent is not discernible." 42 M.J. at 352.); United States v. Gardner, 35 M.J. 300, 303 (C.M.A. 1992) (Crawford, J., concurring) (discussion of burdens).

[7] 397 U.S. 358 (1970).

[8] 397 U.S. at 364 (1970). *See also* Jackson v. Virginia, 443 U.S. 307, 318 (1979) (on appeal the question is whether the evidence of record could reasonably support a finding of guilt beyond a reasonable doubt). Although the Court in *Winship* refers to every fact necessary to constitute the crime, it is clear that the language means that every element of the offense must be proven beyond a reasonable doubt. *See* Mullaney v. Wilbur, 421 U.S. 684, 698 (1975) (use of the word element). Just as the prosecution may not be relieved of its duty of proof via a change of burdens, it may not be given the benefit of an evidentiary presumption that yields the same result. Francis v. Franklin, 471 U.S. 307, 313–14 (1985); Sandstrom v. Montana, 442 U.S. 510, 520–24 (1979).

[9] 432 U.S. 197 (1977). *Compare* Patterson v. New York *with* Mullaney v. Wilbur, 421 U.S. 684 (1975). *Patterson* was relied upon in Martin v. Ohio, 480 U.S. 228 (1987).

[10] 432 U.S. at 210. *Patterson* necessarily limits *Mullaney v. Wilbur,* 421 U.S. 684 (1974). *Compare Patterson,* 432 U.S. at 210–16 *with Mullaney,* 421 U.S. at 698–99.

(Rel.3—1/07   Pub.62410)

result of a legislature defining a crime so broadly that the defendant effectively had the burden to prove innocence, *e.g.*, *"All persons within 100 yards of an individual killed by force or violence shall be guilty of murder; it shall be an affirmative defense that the person did not commit the homicide,* [11] there must be some form of limit to such a rule. In *Schad v. Arizona,* [12] a plurality of the Court suggested that common law and history would act as a constraint, opining that:

> The use here of due process as a measurement of the sense of appropriate specificity assumes the importance of history and widely shared practice as concrete indicators of what fundamental fairness and rationality require. In turning to these sources we again follow the example set in the burden-shifting cases where we have often found it useful to refer both to history and to the current practice of other States in determining whether a State has exceeded its discretion in defining offenses. . . . [A] freakish definition of the elements of a crime that finds no analogue in history or in the criminal law of other jurisdictions will lighten the defendant's burdens. [13]

Subsequently, in *Medina v. California,* [14] the Court declared that its *Patterson* rule stands unless the burden shifting "'offends some principle of justice so rooted in the traditions and conscience of our people as to be ranked as fundamental.'" [15]

As a result, matters such as insanity, which excuse the offense but which are not part of the statutory definition, need not constitutionally be proven beyond a reasonable doubt; indeed the burden of proof for these affirmative or special defenses may constitutionally be placed on the defense. [16] Because Article 92 of the Uniform Code of Military Justice permits commanders to promulgate regulations and prosecute offenders for their violation, Supreme Court precedent would potentially permit the government to shift burdens to the defense in many areas. With the exception of the "insanity defense," [17] within the armed forces,

---

[11] Fredric I. Lederer, *Fundamental Criminal Procedure* 418 (1999). In *Martin v. Ohio*, 480 U.S. 228, 240 (1987), Justice Powell, dissenting, wrote: "Today's decision could be read to say that virtually all state attempts to shift the burden of proof for affirmative defenses will be upheld, regardless of the relationship between the elements of the defense and the elements of the crime." *See also* Hicks v. Feiock, 485 U.S. 624, 629 (1988) (whether forcing defendant to prove inability to comply with support-payment order violated due process depended in part on whether inability was an element of the offense or an affirmative defense).

[12] 501 U.S. 624 (1991).

[13] 501 U.S. at 640 (1991).

[14] 505 U.S. 437 (1992).

[15] 505 U.S. at 446 (1992) *quoting Patterson v. New York*, 432 U.S. at 202.

[16] Leland v. Oregon, 343 U.S. 790 (1952) (defendant could be required to prove insanity beyond a reasonable doubt); State v. Herrera, 895 P.2d 359 (Utah 1995) (due process does not require an insanity defense).

[17] R.C.M. 920(e)(2)(D)("the burden of proving the defense of lack of mental responsibility by clear and convincing evidence is upon the accused."). *See also* R.C.M. 921(c)(4).

(Rel.3—1/07   Pub.62410)

however, at present the *Manual for Courts-Martial*, which is subject to relatively easy amendment, places the burden on the government to establish the accused's guilt beyond a reasonable doubt, both with respect to the elements of the offense[18] and with respect to special defenses[19] that are placed in issue by some evidence.[20]

The burden of proof, sometimes referred to as the burden of persuasion, must be distinguished from the burden of production, sometimes referred to as the burden of going forward. The party with the burden of production has the burden of producing evidence sufficient to raise the issue. This burden may be distinct from the burden of proof. As already indicated, the *Manual for Courts-Martial*, for example, places the burden of production for affirmative or special defenses primarily on the defense, but, once such a defense is raised, places the burden of disproving such a defense beyond a reasonable doubt on the government.

In the military context, the difference between the burdens of proof and production can be of particular importance because the *Manual for Courts-Martial* appears to restrict the government from placing the burden of proof on the defense.[21] No such limitation exists with respect to the burden of production, and, consequently, the defense may lawfully be required to assert, for example, exceptions to criminality recognized in punitive regulations. Thus, in *United States v. Cuffee*,[22] the Court of Military Appeals held that, when a regulation prohibited possession of a hypodermic syringe with a hypodermic needle unless possessed in the course of "official duty or pursuant to valid prescription," the defense had the burden of production in that it had to raise the exceptions via evidence.[23] Once raised, the burden of proof or persuasion shifts to the government, which must disprove the claim to the exception beyond a reasonable doubt. This division of responsibility, which the court explicitly held constitutional,[24] appears clearly appropriate, in that it is difficult if not impossible for the government to negate all possibilities of an exception while such information

---

[18] R.C.M. 920(e)(2)(D).

[19] R.C.M. 916(b).

[20] R.C.M. 916(b). The *Manual* actually places the burden of proof to negate the defense on the government whenever the defense is raised by some evidence. Thus, the government's or the court-martial's evidence may itself raise a special defense. R.C.M. 916(b) Discussion. *Cf.* U.C.M.J. art. 50a; Ellis v. Jacob, 26 M.J. 90 (C.M.A. 1988).

[21] Other than lack of mental responsibility. *See above note* 11. Given the nature of the Uniform Code of Military Justice, the *Manual*'s primary present effect is to prohibit the armed forces from creating punitive regulations (under U.C.M.J. art. 92) which place the burden of proof on the defense. As an executive order, the *Manual* is, of course, subject to revision.

[22] 10 M.J. 381 (C.M.A. 1981) (clarifying United States v. Verdi, 5 M.J. 330 (C.M.A. 1978)). *See also* United States v. Lavine, 13 M.J. 150 (C.M.A. 1982).

[23] 10 M.J. at 381.

[24] 10 M.J. at 383–84 (citing at 384, Sandstrom v. Montana, 442 U.S. 510, 518 (1979)).

(Rel.3—1/07 Pub.62410)

is peculiarly in the possession of the defense. [25] However, once the issue is joined and specific, there is no reason not to put the government to its burden. The result of this allocation of burdens is to require the defense in such a case to obtain and present evidence sufficient to raise the issue. [26]

§ 20-20.00 PROCUREMENT OF EVIDENCE

§ 20-21.00 In General

Although closely related, one may reasonably distinguish, albeit somewhat artificially, between discovery and the procurement of evidence. Discovery [27] primarily concerns itself with learning details of the opponent's case (*i.e.*, of the *existence* of evidence), while the procurement of evidence concerns the ability to *obtain* evidence.

Congress has declared:

> The trial counsel, the defense counsel, and the court-martial shall have equal opportunity to obtain witnesses and other evidence in accordance with such regulations as the President may prescribe. Process issued in court-martial cases to compel witnesses to appear and testify and to compel the production of other evidence shall be similar to that which courts of the United States have criminal jurisdiction may lawfully issue. . . . [28]

In response, the President has directed through the *Manual for Courts-Martial* that process be issued by the *trial counsel* on behalf of *both* the defense and prosecution, [29] and that defense requests for witnesses be submitted to the trial counsel with any disagreements between defense and trial counsel about calling the witnesses to be resolved by the military judge. [30] The present system

---

[25] *See also* Part IV, ¶ 37(c)(5), MCM, 2005, which requires the accused to go forward with any evidence raising an exception to the inferred wrongfulness of drug offenses. Once an exception is raised, however, the government must prove beyond a reasonable doubt that the acts were wrongful.

[26] This is not, incidentally, the rule for litigating suppression motions. Under Mil. R. Evid. 304 (confessions and admissions), 311 (search and seizure), and 321 (eye-witness identification), the defense is required to raise its issues by an offer of proof rather than the actual presentation of evidence. *See, e.g.*, Analysis of the Military Rules of Evidence, 1980 Amendments to the Manual for Courts-Martial, Analysis of Rule 304(d)(3), *reprinted at* MCM, 2005, A22-11.

[27] *See generally* Chapter 11.

[28] U.C.M.J. art. 46. *See, e.g.*, United States v. Mustafa, 22 M.J. 165, 168 (C.M.A. 1986) (citing Article 46, the court stated: "There can be no question that a military accused is entitled to have equal opportunity with the Government to obtain witnesses to assist him in his defense"). Article 46 implements the accused's Sixth Amendment right to compulsory process. United States v. Davison, 4 M.J. 702, 704 (A.C.M.R. 1977).

[29] R.C.M. 703(c).

[30] R.C.M. 703(c)(2)(D). The trial counsel should inform the convening authority, however, when significant or unusual costs would be involved in obtaining a witness so the convening authority can elect to dispose of the matter by other means. R.C.M. 703(c)(2) Discussion.

necessarily raises two distinct questions: when will the trial counsel attempt to obtain evidence, and what means are available to the trial counsel to do so.

§ 20-22.00   The Decision to Obtain Evidence

§ 20-22.10   In General

§ 20-22.11   General Procedures

Insofar as witnesses are concerned,[31] the *Manual for Court-Martial* vests in the trial counsel the decision and authority to obtain witnesses whose testimony is relevant and necessary for the prosecution.[32] The trial counsel also acts as the official through whom the defense ordinarily procures witnesses. The defense counsel must submit a written list of witnesses to the trial counsel.[33] The defense request must also contain the telephone number, if known, address or location of the witness, and a sufficient synopsis of the expected testimony sufficient to show its relevance and necessity.[34] If the trial counsel contends production is not required under the rule, the matter is submitted to the military judge. "A matter is not in issue when it is stipulated as a fact."[35] Accordingly, a witness would be unnecessary if he or she were to be called solely to establish a fact already established by agreement between the parties.

Under Rule 703, the individual trial counsel's affirmative decision to obtain a witness is not subject to review. In actual practice, the prosecution's decision is subject to the review of the trial counsel's superiors, usually the staff judge advocate and convening authority, who may direct the trial counsel not to subpoena or otherwise obtain a witness for a variety of reasons,[36] including financial ones.

The defense's attempt to obtain witnesses is, however, subject to definite review. Although the defense could obtain its own witnesses and call them at trial,[37] it lacks the power to subpoena them or to pay witness fees or travel costs

---

[31] Documentary and other evidence is generally dealt with in the same manner as witnesses. *See generally* R.C.M. 703(f).

[32] R.C.M. 703(c)(1).

[33] R.C.M. 703(c)(2)(A).

[34] R.C.M. 703(c)(2)(B). For witnesses on sentencing, the defense must make an additional showing why the witness' personal appearance is necessary under R.C.M. 1001(e). R.C.M. 703(c)(2)(B)(ii).

[35] R.C.M. 703(b)(1) Discussion. *Cf.* Section 20-22.60.

[36] Such reasons could include a desire not to interfere with the activities of the witness, particularly likely when the witness is a highly placed civilian or military officer, a possibility of revealing classified information, or simply a desire to avoid delaying the trial.

[37] United States v. Breeding, 44 M.J. 345, 351–52 (C.A.A.F. 1996) ("Even where witnesses are going to appear voluntarily, the judge" still determines admissibility of the evidence).

(Rel.3—1/07   Pub.62410)

unless it complies with Rule for Courts-Martial 703. Consequently, if the defense desires to escape the constraints of Rule 703, it is in practice limited in most cases to local volunteer witnesses. Even then, a failure to comply with Rule 703 means that the trial counsel is legally blameless if the witness fails to appear, depriving the defense of a potentially useful weapon at trial.[38]

Subject to the potential availability of extraordinary relief,[39] the decision of the military judge as to the materiality and procurement of a witness is not subject to interlocutory review. The Court of Military Appeals held that "once materiality has been shown the Government must either produce the witness or abate the proceedings."[40] Thus, military operations, expense, or inconvenience can only delay the trial rather than justifying proceeding without an otherwise material witness.[41] A witness who cannot be located, however, obviously cannot be produced, and trial need not be affected. If a witness' location is known but the witness is unavailable, the judge could but need not order a continuance or an abatement of the proceedings[42] unless the unavailability was the fault of, or could have been prevented by, the requesting party.[43]

---

[38] In a highly unusual case, the defense might be able to show that it has a substantial interest outweighing the government's interest in knowing the identity of the defense witnesses. Under these circumstances, the defense should make an *ex parte* application to the military judge, with the record of the application remaining sealed until trial.

If the prosecution has failed to obtain a defense witness without cause, the military judge may take corrective action to include granting a continuance or giving special instructions to the members. *Cf.* United States v. Kilby, 3 M.J. 938, 944-45 (N.C.M.R. 1977). Such a result is less likely if the defense fails to comply with Rule 703.

[39] *Cf.* Dettinger v. United States, 7 M.J. 216 (C.M.A. 1979). § 25-90.00.

[40] United States v. Carpenter, 1 M.J. 384, 385-86 (C.M.A. 1976). *Accord* United States v. Willis, 3 M.J. 94 (C.M.A. 1977); United States v. Eiland, 39 M.J. 566, 569 (N.M.C.M.R. 1993) (abating proceedings pending the unlikely obtaining of two favorable Spanish witnesses is proper under R.C.M. 703(b)(3), is not an abuse of discretion, and the decision to reject a government offer to stipulate to the substance of the testimony as an adequate substitute wasn't erroneous). The quoted language has been disclaimed by Judge Cook as being overbroad. 3 M.J. 96-100 (C.M.A. 1977) (Cook, J., dissenting). The court has held, however, that there is no right to cumulative evidence. United States v. Williams, 3 M.J. 239, 243 (C.M.A. 1977). *See generally* section § 20-22.50.

[41] In limited circumstances, substitutes for live testimony, such as stipulations, may be acceptable. *See generally* Section 20-22.60.

[42] *Cf.* United States v. Barreto, 57 M.J. 127 (C.A.A.F. 2002) (judge did not abuse his discretion in refusing to abate proceedings until unknown witness might have appeared as a result of newspaper ads).

[43] R.C.M. 703(b)(3).

§ 20-22.12   Expert Witnesses

§ 20-22.12(a)   In General

Because many trials depend upon the use of expert testimony, procurement of expert witnesses may clearly be critical to a case. The Court of Military Appeals indicated:

> [A]s a matter of military due process, servicemembers are entitled to investigative or other expert assistance when necessary for an adequate defense, without regard to indigency. . . . Unlike the civilian defendant, however, the military accused has the resources of the Government at his disposal. . . . In the usual case, the investigative, medical, and other expert services in the military are sufficient to permit the defense to adequately prepare for trial.[44]

§ 20-22.12(b)   Expert Assistance Pretrial

Dealing with an espionage case in which the accused requested an expert assistant to deal with classified material, the Navy-Marine Court of Military Review elaborated:

> The right to present evidence necessarily includes the right to prepare. Military due process entitles a servicemember to the assistance of an expert when necessary to the preparation of an adequate defense. . . . "Necessity" has been defined by the [civilian] Federal courts as "reasonably necessary." . . . "Adequate defense" has been defined as including "preparation for cross-examination of a government expert as well as presentation of an expert defense witness.". . . The standard for evaluating the necessity for the defense to have expert assistance has been more liberally interpreted by the [civilian] Federal courts than has the standard for the production of an expert witness. . . .
>
> The servicemember bears the burden of demonstrating the necessity for the expert assistance he requests. . . . There are three aspects to showing necessity. First, why the expert assistance is needed. Second, what would the expert assistance accomplish for the accused. Third, why is the defense counsel unable to gather and present the evidence that the expert assistant would be able to develop. . . . In particular, the defense must show what it expects to find, . . . how and why the defense counsel and staff cannot do it, . . . how cross-examination will be less effective. . ., how the alleged information would affect the Government's ability to prove guilt . . .; what the nature of the prosecution's case is, including the nature of the crime, and the evidence linking him to the crime, and how the requested expert would otherwise be useful.
>
> Based upon all of the evidence presented, the military judge then must determine whether the defense has borne its burden by applying the standard of whether a reasonable probability exists that the expert services

---

[44] United States v. Garries, 22 M.J. 288, 290–91 (C.M.A.), *cert. denied*, 479 U.S. 985 (1986) (citations omitted).

requested would be of assistance and that denial of that assistance would result in a fundamentally unfair trial.[45]

The Court of Military Appeals strongly endorsed the defense right to expert pretrial assistance "upon a proper showing of necessity."[46] The defense is entitled to a "defense expert with professional qualifications reasonably comparable to those of the Government's expert."[47] Accordingly, in the average case the defense may neither demand a specific expert nor reject all governmental employees.[48] It need not, however, accept a potential government witness.[49]

§ 20-22.12(c) Obtaining Civilian Expert Assistance

Presumably because of availability and lack of cost,[50] most counsel use government-employed experts, despite fear of lack of neutrality or of information leakage. The *Manual for Courts-Martial* does contemplate, however, the possible employment of other experts:

> When the employment at government expense of an expert is considered necessary by a party, the party shall, in advance of employment of the expert, and with notice to the opposing party submit a request to the convening authority to authorize the employment and to fix the compensation for the expert. The request shall include a complete statement of reasons why employment of the expert is necessary and the estimated cost of employment. A request denied by the convening authority may be renewed before the military judge who shall determine whether the testimony of the expert is relevant and necessary, and, if so, whether the Government has provided or will provide an adequate substitute. If the military judge grants a motion for employment of an expert or finds that the Government is required to provide a substitute, the proceedings shall be abated if the Government fails to comply with the ruling. In the absence of advance authorization, an expert witness may not be paid fees other than those to which entitled under subsection (e)(2)(D) of this rule.[51]

---

[45] United States v. Allen, 31 M.J. 572, 623–24 (N.M.C.M.R. 1990) (citations and footnotes omitted).

[46] United States v. Burnette, 29 M.J. 473, 475 (C.M.A. 1990). *See also* United States v. Short, 50 M.J. 370 (C.A.A.F. 1999) (counsel must take reasonable steps to educate themselves); United States v. Campbell, 50 M.J. 154 (C.A.A.F. 1999); United States v. Gonzalez, 42 M.J. 469 (C.A.A.F. 1995); United States v. Kelly, 39 M.J. 235 (C.M.A. 1994); United States v. Robinson, 39 M.J. 88 (C.M.A. 1994).

[47] United States v. Warner, 62 M.J. 114, 118 (C.A.A.F. 2005).

[48] 29 M.J. at 476.

[49] 29 M.J. at 476. *See also* United States v. Warner, 62 M.J. 114, 120 (C.A.A.F. 2005).

[50] The prosecution will be concerned with expenditure of government funds, while the defense will be limited to the funds available to the accused unless the government can be required to pay an expert's fee under R.C.M. 703(b).

[51] R.C.M. 703(d).

(Rel.3—1/07 Pub.62410)

In the past, requests for employment of civilian experts under Rule for Courts-Martial 703(d) and its predecessor provision were rarely successful.[52] It may be that contemporary efforts are slightly more likely to succeed.[53] However, denials are frequent, although the denial of any specific request may raise significant questions of the rights to compulsory process and fair trial under the Constitution.[54]

It is clear that an accused has no right to select the expert of his choice and bind the government to pay for him. The Navy-Marine Court opined that to obtain a expert other than a local governmental employee, [D]efense counsel, at a minimum must demonstrate to the convening authority that (1) working through their own resources, they have exhausted the possibilities for Government assistance within their particular geographical location, (2) established that their further communication with a potential Government expert assistant would necessarily compromise client confidences, and (3) formally request of the convening authority, with the proper showing of necessity and relevance, that the expert assistance provided be rendered under an order of confidentiality. Once charges have been referred to trial, application for expert assistance may be made to the military judge, followed by a defense-requested continuance to prepare for trial with that assistance.[55]

"Fairness counts," as Chief Judge Everett, concurring in *United States v. Van Horn*,[56] wrote: "where there are divergent scientific views, the Government cannot select a witness whose views are very favorable to its position and then claim that this same witness is 'an adequate substitute' for a defense-requested expert of a different viewpoint."[57]

---

[52] *See, e.g.,* United States v. Johnson, 47 C.M.R. 402, 404–06 (C.M.A. 1973) (holding that the defense failed to demonstrate necessity for employment of a civilian psychiatrist). Such a request, however, may spur offers of governmental assistance. *See, e.g.,* United States v. Garries, 22 M.J. 288, 291 (C.M.A. 1986) (offer of "an Air Force investigator who would work under an order of confidentiality").

[53] United States v. McAllister, 55 M.J. 270 (C.A.A.F. 2001) (convening authority had authorized a civilian expert; failure of judge to permit accused to use an alternative and more appropriate DNA expert required reversal). *Cf.* United States v. Hagen, 25 M.J. 78, 83 (C.M.A. 1987) (trial judge ordered production of civilian psychiatrist, but dispute over fees ultimately resulted in nonproduction). United States v. Kelly, 39 M.J. 235, 237 (C.M.A. 1994) ("Unlike other jurisdictions, the military criminal justice system has not limited *Ake* to psychiatric assistance . . . or to capital cases").

[54] Ake v. Oklahoma, 470 U.S. 53 (1985). *See generally* Section 20-30.00. For a thorough analysis of the scope and adequacy of R.C.M. 703(d), see Hahn, *Voluntary and Involuntary Expert Testimony in Courts-Martial*, 106 Mil. R. Evid. 77 (1984).

[55] United States v. Huerta, 31 M.J. 640, 643 n.1. (N.M.C.M.R. 1990).

[56] 26 M.J. 434, 439 (C.M.A. 1988).

[57] *See also* United States v. Guitard, 28 M.J. 952, 954 (N.M.C.M.R. 1989).

(Rel.3—1/07　Pub.62410)

One of the difficulties that faces defense counsel seeking employment of a civilian expert is the need to justify the employment. Should counsel's need be dictated by confidential or privileged information, counsel may wish to ask for an *ex parte* court hearing. In *United States v. Garries,*[58] however, the court said:

> Although appellant has provided no authority for the use of *ex parte* proceedings in the military, we recognize inherent authority in the military judge to permit such a procedure in the unusual circumstance where it is necessary to insure a fair trial. By its very nature, however, an *ex parte* proceeding may provide undue advantage to one party. . . . Use of an *ex parte* hearing to obtain expert services would rarely be appropriate in the military context because funding must be provided by the convening authority and such a procedure would deprive the Government of the opportunity to consider and arrange alternatives for the requested expert services.[59]

It is important to note that nothing in the Uniform Code of Military Justice or the *Manual of Courts-Martial* requires payment of special fees to obtain the testimony of an expert who happens to be an ordinary witness. Thus, a medical doctor who has previously treated the accused could be subpoenaed and paid normal witness fees if he or she were to be questioned about that treatment. The *Manual* would appear to require some form of expert fee if the expert were to be asked to make special preparations for testimony.[60]

In *United States v. Thomas,*[61] the Navy-Marine Court of Military Review held that it had the authority to determine whether the accused on appeal was entitled to specifically requested expert assistance in order to prepare his appeal, although it did not reach the issue of whether it had the authority to compel funding for such a request if other authorities failed to do so after a judicial finding of necessity. Appellant defense counsel had requested funds to hire an expert to conduct "a psychosocial evaluation of the appellant" to assist appellant counsel in raising allegation of ineffective assistance of trial defense counsel. When those funds were denied, the accused filed an extraordinary writ in the nature of coram nobis. In this context, the court held:

> [T]o prevail in his request for government funding of a psychosocial background investigation, appellant must at least identify some psychosocial factors in his background which, if his defense counsel had discovered

---

[58] 22 M.J. 288 (C.M.A.), *cert. denied*, 479 U.S. 985 (1986).

[59] 22 M.J. at 291 (C.M.A.) (citations omitted).

[60] R.C.M. 703(d) speaks of employment of expert witnesses. Accordingly, requiring an expert to perform tests in advance of trial or to make other pretrial preparation would require an expert fee. The weight of nonmilitary authority, however, would not require payment of expert fees if preparation by the expert was not required. *See generally*, Hahn, *Voluntary and Involuntary Expert Testimony in Courts-Martial*, 106 Mil. R. Evid. 101 (1984).

[61] 33 M.J. 644 (N.M.C.M.R. 1991). *See also* United States v. Gray 51 M.J. 1 (C.A.A.F. 1999).

(Rel.3—1/07 Pub.62410)

them and presented evidence of them to the court, the outcome on sentencing might reasonably have been different.[62]

§ 20-22.20 Form of the Rule 703(c) Request

The *Manual for Courts-Martial* requires that a request for a defense witness be in writing and contain a synopsis of the expected testimony of the witness.[63] In certain circumstances, however, the government will be held responsible for knowledge within its possession, so that an otherwise deficient Rule 703 request will be held sufficient.[64]

Rule 703 necessarily presumes that the defense will be able to adequately interview[65] the witness in order to set forth an adequate synopsis, and the courts

---

[62] 33 M.J. at 648 (N.M.C.M.R. 1991). *See also* United States v. Short, 50 M.J. 370 (C.A.A.F. 1999) (counsel must take reasonable steps to educate themselves); United States v. Campbell, 50 M.J. 154 (C.A.A.F. 1999); United States v. Gonzalez, 42 M.J. 469 (C.A.A.F. 1995); United States v. Kelly, 39 M.J. 235 (C.M.A. 1994); United States v. Robinson, 39 M.J. 88 (C.M.A. 1994). R.C.M. 703(c)(2)(B)(i).

[63] *See, e.g.*, United States v. Wagner, 5 M.J. 461, 469 (C.M.A. 1978); United States v. Lucas, 5 M.J. 167, 172 (C.M.A. 1978). The procedure is recounted in numerous cases. *E.g.*, United States v. Jouan, 3 M.J. 136 (C.M.A. 1977); United States v. Iturralde-Aponte, 1 M.J. 196 (C.M.A. 1975); United States v. Manos, 37 C.M.R. 274, 280–81 (C.M.A. 1967) (Quinn, C.J., concurring in part, dissenting part) (request should include synopsis of expected testimony, logical and legal relevance of evidence); United States v. Powell, 4 M.J. 551 (A.F.C.M.R. 1977); United States v. Courts, 4 M.J. 518 (C.G.C.M.R. 1977), *aff'd*, 9 M.J. 285 (C.M.A. 1980); United States v. Green, 2 M.J. 823 (A.C.M.R. 1976); United States v. Corley, 1 M.J. 584 (A.C.M.R. 1975). A diminished standard of materiality appears to apply to experts who have prepared government laboratory reports offered against the accused at trial. United States v. Vietor, 10 M.J. 69 (C.M.A. 1980).

[64] *E.g.*, United States v. Lucas, 5 M.J. 167, 172 (C.M.A. 1978) (staff judge advocate charged with knowledge of the content of a pretrial statement made by the witness at the pretrial investigation).

[65] Chief Judge Everett appeared to believe that some form of contact is generally necessary, but that contact need not be an in-person interview. United States v. Vietor, 10 M.J. 69, 78 (C.M.A. 1980) (Everett, C.J., concurring in the result). *Cf.* United States v. Jefferson, 13 M.J. 1, 7–8 (C.M.A. 1982) (Everett, C.J., dissenting) (failure to interview witness was ineffective assistance). The drafters of the Military Rules of Evidence, on the other hand, concluded that the defense counsel must be afforded the right to an in-person interview of potential witnesses before counsel could be required to raise a suppression motion with specificity. 1980 Amendments to the Manual for Courts-Martial, Analysis of Rule 304(d)(3), reprinted at MCM, 2005, A22-11-12. Inas-much as the procurement of a witness on the merits may be more essential to due process than the procurement of a witness for a suppression motion, the Military Rules of Evidence necessarily suggest that the defense must be afforded the right to an in-person interview before a request for a witness under Rule 703 can be held insufficiently justified. While the defense's right to access to the witnesses is clear, a witness does not have to cooperate with and talk to counsel. United States v. Killebrew, 9 M.J. 154, 161 (C.M.A. 1980); United States v. Doyle, 17 C.M.R. 615, 640 (A.F.B.R. 1954). *Cf.* United States v. Enloe, 35 C.M.R. 228 (C.M.A. 1965) (regulation requiring third party to be present for defense-counsel interviews of OSI agents invalid). For those circumstances in which the accused may be limited by official authority in contacting witnesses *see* § 11-50.00, *above*. *See, e.g.*, United States v. Nieves, 44 M.J. 96 (C.A.A.F. 1996); United States v. Meek, 44 M.J. 1 (C.A.A.F. 1996) (unlawful to dissuade defense witness from testifying).

(Rel.3—1/07 Pub.62410)

may be expected to be particularly hostile to a witness request made without any contact with the given witness.[66] Chief Judge Everett of the Court of Military Appeals recognized that in some cases, such as those in which the witness is hostile, the synopsis requirement cannot be met, and "a rigid application of these requirements would produce a conflict with an accused's statutory and constitutional right to compulsory process."[67] Consequently, when defense counsel cannot contact a witness who is believed to have material testimony, that fact should be set forth with an explanation.[68] When a defense request for a witness is heard by the military judge, the judge must determine the issue "on the basis of the matters presented to the judge . . . not just those contained in the written request."[69]

§ 20-22.30 Timeliness

Although Rule for Courts-Martial 703(c)(2)(C) provides only that witness lists shall be submitted within a reasonable time, the military judge may set a specific date by which witness lists must be produced.[70]

Members of the Court of Military Appeals clearly indicated their willingness to consider the timeliness of a defense request,[71] and the Courts of Military

---

[66] *See, e.g.,* United States v. Rockwood, 52 M.J. 98, 104 (C.A.A.F. 1999) (counsel had not even tried to speak with convening authority who was requested as witness); United States v. Corley, 1 M.J. 584, 586 (A.C.M.R. 1975) (counsel's representations that two witnesses would give alibi testimony held insufficient when not corroborated or verified in any way); United States v. Carey, 1 M.J. 761, 766–67 (A.F.C.M.R. 1975).

[67] United States v. Vietor, 10 M.J. 69, 77 (C.M.A. 1980) (Everett, C.J., concurring in the result).

[68] *Cf.* United States v. Carey, 1 M.J. 761, 767 (A.F.C.M.R. 1975).

[69] United States v. Corley, 1 M.J. 584, 586 (A.C.M.R. 1975) (citing United States v. Jones, 44 C.M.R. 269 (C.M.A. 1972)). *See* United States v. Harvey, 2006 CAAF LEXIS 1202 ** 37 (C.A.A.F. 2006) (dissent) ("We have never held that a statement by an attorney constitutes evidence or an accepted proffer. In essence, the majority seems to convert the statement by the trial defense counsel to the status of unrebutted evidence. n1 . . . To convert statements by counsel and a military judge to findings of fact is not only new, but also unprecedented."); United States v. Courts, 4 M.J. 518, 525–26 (C.G.C.M.R. 1977) (Lynch, J., concurring in part, dissenting in part); United States v. Green, 2 M.J. 823, 826 (A.C.M.R. 1976). *Jones,* however, does not necessarily stand for this proposition, since the court in *Jones* determined the propriety of the trial judge's ruling on the basis of all the information given to the judge because he "presumably . . . considered it in his ruling." 44 C.M.R. at 271.

[70] R.C.M. 703(c)(2)(C).

[71] *See, e.g.,* United States v. Vietor, 10 M.J. 69, 72, 78 (C.M.A. 1980) (Cook, J., and Everett, C.J., individually concurring in the result with separate opinions); United States v. Stocker, 7 M.J. 373, 374 (C.M.A. 1979) (summary disposition) (Cook, J., dissenting on the grounds that defense request for witness was untimely). *See also* United States v. McElhaney, 54 M.J. 120, 127 2000) (timeliness of request is one factor to examine as to production of witness).

(Rel.3—1/07   Pub.62410)

Review utilized untimeliness in holding that the defense lacked a right to witnesses.[72] The Army Court of Military Review held:

> Although untimeliness is not *per se* grounds for denying a request for a witness, timeliness of a defense request for a witness may be considered. . . . The "touchstone" for untimeliness should be whether the request is delayed unnecessarily until such a time as to interfere with the orderly prosecution of the case. . . . The rules do not set out a specific timetable for submission of witness requests; however, the discussion in R.C.M. 703(e)(1) does suggest that "a request . . . should be made so that the witness will have at least 48 hours notice before starting to travel. . . .[73]

As reflected above, untimeliness has been defined as "whether the request is delayed unnecessarily until such a time as to interfere with the orderly prosecution of the case."[74] The Court of Military Appeals stated in dicta, however, that "while a defense counsel, for tactical reasons, may properly delay a request for witnesses until after the charges are referred to trial, he thereby assumes the risk that . . . in the interval the witness may become unavailable to testify at trial."[75] Thus, by awaiting referral of charges, counsel may not have an untimely submission, but may be unable to obtain the requested witness. An unnecessary delay in filing a request risks having the request treated as untimely, especially when the delay results in the transfer of a witness known to the defense to be pending reassignment.[76] In most cases, given the brevity of most courts-martial, a request for the procurement of a witness made at trial, untimely or otherwise, effectively constitutes a motion for a continuance. When the request is untimely, the decision is discretionary with the military judge.[77] Nonetheless, if the defense shows that

---

[72] *See, e.g.*, United States v. Onstad, 4 M.J. 661, 664 (A.C.M.R. 1977) (dicta). A theory of waiver may be applicable. *Cf.* United States v. Briers, 7 M.J. 776 (A.C.M.R. 1979) (failure to request lab analyst when judge gave defense right to do so constitutes waiver); United States v. Mackey, 7 M.J. 649, 654 (A.C.M.R. 1979) (same).

[73] United States v. Brown, 28 M.J. 644, 647 (A.C.M.R. 1989).

[74] United States v. Hawkins, 19 C.M.R. 261, 268 (C.M.A. 1955) (error to fail to produce witness located in stockade at trial situs where request made day before trial); United States v. Brown, 28 M.J. 644, 647 (A.C.M.R. 1989). *Cf.* United States v. Mitchell, 11 M.J. 907 (A.C.M.R. 1981) (proper to deny request for material witness where defense knew of witness before trial but delayed request until government rested its case).

[75] United States v. Cottle, 14 M.J. 260, 263 (C.M.A. 1982). The lack of a pretrial request is not conclusively untimely. *See, e.g.*, United States v. Johnson, 3 M.J. 772, 773 (A.C.M.R. 1977); United States v. Phillippy, 2 M.J. 297, 300 (A.F.C.M.R. 1976).

[76] *E.g.*, United States v. Onstad, 4 M.J. 661, 664 (A.C.M.R. 1977) (dicta) (overseas witness). *See also* United States v. Credit, 2 M.J. 631, 646 (A.F.C.M.R. 1976), *rev'd on other grounds*, 4 M.J. 118 (C.M.A. 1977), *aff'd on remand*, 6 M.J. 719 (A.F.C.M.R. 1978), *aff'd*, 8 M.J. 190 (C.M.A. 1980) (defense request reviewed during trial implicitly held to be untimely when request had been withdrawn and lab technician discharged in interim).

[77] *See, e.g.*, United States v. McElhaney, 54 M.J. 120, 127 (C.A.A.F. 2000) (timeliness of request is one factor to examine as to production of witness); United States v. Reveles, 41 M.J. 388, 394 (C.A.A.F. 1995) (untimeliness of the defense request one of a number of factors relied upon in

(Rel.3—1/07 Pub.62410)

the witness is material and necessary, the judge should, in the interests of justice, grant the request.[78] To do otherwise would penalize the accused for the counsel's conduct and would raise a strong probability of ultimate reversal for inadequacy of counsel.

§ 20-22.40 Materiality

The *1969 Manual* required that a defense request for a witness give "full reasons which necessitate the personal appearance of the witness, and . . . any other matter showing that the expected testimony is necessary to the ends of justice."[79] Perhaps because the prosecution was not to procure a prosecution witness on its own motion unless "satisfied that the testimony of the witness is material and necessary,"[80] the courts had consistently viewed paragraph 115 as requiring that the defense demonstrate the "materiality" of its requested witnesses.[81] The exact meaning of "materiality" was unclear. In its evidentiary sense, "materiality" requires at least that the evidence involved be relevant.[82]

---

holding that the trial judge didn't abuse his discretion in denying expert witness request); United States v. Stocker, 7 M.J. 373, 374 (C.M.A. 1979) (summary disposition) (Cook, J., dissenting).

[78] *See, e.g.,* United States v. Jouan, 3 M.J. 136, 137 (C.M.A. 1977); United States v. Brown, 28 M.J. 644, 647 (A.C.M.R. 1989) (The judge abused discretion in not calling three witnesses from the accused's unit, a three-hour drive from the site of the trial. The defense counsel made an oral request on Friday afternoon six days prior to trial and made a complete written request two days prior to trial. The judge did not note any prior untimely requests by the same counsel); United States v. Green, 2 M.J. 823, 826 (A.C.M.R. 1976); United States v. Onstad, 4 M.J. 661, 664 (A.C.M.R. 1977).

[79] MCM, 1969 (rev. ed.) ¶ 115a.

[80] MCM, 1969 (rev. ed.) ¶ 115a.

[81] *See, e.g.,* United States v. Hampton, 7 M.J. 284, 285 (C.M.A. 1979); United States v. Wagner, 5 M.J. 461 (C.M.A. 1978); United States v. Lucas, 5 M.J. 167 (C.M.A. 1978); United States v. Iturralde-Aponte, 1 M.J. 196 (C.M.A. 1975); United States v. Marshall, 3 M.J. 1047 (A.F.C.M.R. 1777). *Cf.* United States v. Valenzuela-Bernal, 458 U.S. 858 (1982) (noting, however (at note 9), that the Court expressed no opinion on the showing that a criminal defendant must make to obtain compulsory process for securing the attendance of witness within the United States).

[82] *See, e.g.,* United States v. Courts, 4 M.J. 518, 522–23 (C.G.C.M.R. 1977). Mil. R. Evid. 401 defines what is often termed logical relevance or the requirement that the evidence involved has a tendency to make the existence of any fact of consequence to the determination of the action more probable or less probable than it would be without the evidence. Phrased differently, in the case of determining witness availability, the evidence must tend to negate the prosecution's case or tend to support the defense's. United States v. Iturralde-Aponte, 1 M.J. 196, 197–98 (C.M.A. 1975). Relevance has additional scope, however, inasmuch as evidentiary rules that exclude evidence because of doubt of its probative value, prejudicial impact on the members, or for other reasons for social policy are often termed rules of legal relevance. *See, e.g.,* Edward J. Imwinkelried, Paul C. Giannelli, Francis A. Gilligan & Fredric I. Lederer, *Courtroom Criminal Evidence* ch. 3 (4th ed. 2006). Mil. R. Evid. 403–05; 407–12 are rules of legal relevance as are the rules of privilege, Mil. R. Evid. 501–09, and testimony that is inadmissible under them should not ordinarily be material for purposes of obtaining witnesses. *But see* Chambers v. Mississippi, 410 U.S. 284 (1973); Section 20-33.30.

(Rel.3—1/07 Pub.62410)

In its alternative common law evidentiary connotation, it also may mean that considering all of the factors unique to the case,[83] the evidence is important, a determination which might include the availability of substitute forms of evidence.[84] The Court of Military Appeals attempted to clarify the issue:

> The word "material" appears misused. Obviously a witness' testimony must be material to be admissible. . . . However, the terms may have been confused in earlier cases, the true test is essentiality. If a witness is essential for the presentation of the prosecution's case, he will be present or the case will fail. The defense has a similar right.[85]

The use of the word "essential" can hardly be considered as resolving this question, for the term is itself subject to ambiguity. What degree of probative value is necessary before a prospective witness' testimony will be "essential" In past cases, witnesses needed by the accused to establish affirmative defenses, such as lack of jurisdiction or self-defense, were usually considered to be material witnesses,[86] as were defense character witnesses[87] when the accused's character

---

[83] United States v. Tangpuz, 5 M.J. 426, 429 (C.M.A. 1978).

[84] A true materiality standard should not include this factor. To the extent that it plays a role in the question of making a witness available (see Section 20-22.40), it is because of the phrasing of ¶ 115a, which had a somewhat different emphasis.

[85] United States v. Bennett, 12 M.J. 463, 465 n.4 (C.M.A. 1982). In the past, in determining whether a failure to obtain a requested defense witness necessitated reversal, the court stated: "materiality . . . must embrace the 'reasonable likelihood' that the evidence could have affected the judgment of the military judge or court members." United States v. Hampton, 7 M.J. 284, 285 (C.M.A. 1979) (citing Giglio v. United States, 405 U.S. 150, 154 (1972); United States v. Lucas, 5 M.J. 167, 172–73 (C.M.A. 1978); United States v. Tippit, 7 M.J. 908 (A.F.C.M.R. 1979). See Westen, Compulsory Process II, 74 Mich. L. Rev. 191, 222–23 & n.108 (1975) [hereinafter Compulsory Process II].

[86] See, e.g., United States v. Hampton, 7 M.J. 284 (C.M.A. 1979) (lack of jurisdiction; witness immaterial when defense counsel had not interviewed him); United States v. Iturralde-Aponte, 1 M.J. 196 (C.M.A. 1975) (self-defense); United States v. Dawkins, 10 M.J. 620 (A.F.C.M.R. 1980) (insanity defense; witness immaterial when psychiatric interview with defendant is needed and witness does not interview defendant); United States v. Jones, 6 M.J. 770 (A.C.M.R. 1978) (insanity defense; witness immaterial when no indication he would retract earlier sanity board opinions); United States v. Christian, 6 M.J. 624 (A.C.M.R. 1978) (suppression motion: witness immaterial if no adequate showing that witness remembered incident); United States v. Krejce, 5 M.J. 701 (N.C.M.R. 1978) (lack of jurisdiction); United States v. Onstad, 4 M.J. 661 (A.C.M.R. 1977) (informant's perjury at Art.32 investigation, but inadequate showing of materiality on facts); United States v. Green, 2 M.J. 823 (A.C.M.R. 1976) (alibi); United States v. Staton, 48 C.M.R. 250 (A.C.M.R. 1974) (no intent to desert): United States v. Snead, 45 C.M.R. 382 (A.C.M.R. 1972) (entrapment).

[87] United States v. Williams, 3 M.J. 239 (C.M.A. 1977); United States v. Carpenter, 1 M.J. 384 (C.M.A. 1976); United States v. Giermek, 3 M.J. 1013 (C.G.C.M.R. 1977); United States v. Ambalada, 1 M.J. 1132 (N.C.M.R. 1977). See generally Mil. R. Evid. 404(a)(1), 405(a), (b). When the defendant's character for truthfulness is in issue, polygraph evidence may be material. Because such evidence has traditionally been viewed as being logically and legally irrelevant, however, there is no compulsory-process right to introduce such evidence. United States v. Scheffer, 523

was in issue.[88] While these cases may deal with "essential" evidence, it is unlikely that the defense could have or should have been restricted to witnesses presenting evidence of such ultimately critical value.

Interestingly, Rule 703(b)(1) created a potentially more useful standard: "Each party is entitled to the production of any witness whose testimony on a matter in issue on the merits or an interlocutory question would be relevant and necessary." The Discussion of the Rule states: "Relevant testimony is necessary when it is not cumulative and when it would contribute to a party's presentation of the case in some positive way on a matter in issue."[89] The Rule is qualified in Rule 703(b)(3), which provides that, notwithstanding Rule 703(b)(1), a party is not entitled to production of a witness who would be unavailable under Military Rule of Evidence 804(a) unless the witness' testimony "is of such central importance to an issue that it is essential to a fair trial. . . ." The Rule's caveat is not likely to be of importance except insofar as it incorporates, through Military Rule of Evidence 804(a)(6), Article 49(d)(2) of the Uniform Code which, in relevant part, makes a witness unavailable "by reason of . . . military necessity, . . . or other reasonable cause." Unless this exception is utilized in an improbably broad fashion, the Rule appears both more useful and more likely to obtain and present evidence than does the court's "essentiality" standard.[90]

The court clarified to some degree both procedural and evidentiary rules that apply to witness requests in *United States v. Breeding.*[91] The judges differed as to whether a voluntary defense witness should be given a subpoena to assure an employer that he or she will be a witness.[92]

U.S. 303 (1998). A witness who is more credible and articulate is material even though another witness has already testified to the events. United States v. Jouan, 3 M.J. 136 (C.M.A. 1977).

[88] Mil. R. Evid. 404(a) strictly limits use of character evidence, restricting it in most cases to "[e]vidence of a pertinent trait of the character of the accused." Mil. R. Evid. 404(a)(1). The Analysis of Rule 404 declares that the Rule makes evidence of good general character inadmissible although it would allow "evidence of good military character when that specific trait is pertinent . . . for example, in a prosecution for disobedience of orders." Analysis of the Military Rules of Evidence, 1980 Amendments to the *Manual for Courts-Martial*, Analysis of Rule 404(a), *reprinted at* MCM, 2005, A22–33.

[89] *See* United States v. Dorgan, 39 M.J. 827 (A.C.M.R. 1994) (denial of defense witness request for a "registered source" who was a material witness under Rule 703 prejudiced the accused and required reversal of the conviction).

[90] Whether the "essentiality test" of United States v. Bennett, 12 M.J. 463 (C.M.A. 1982) was meant to apply to trial-level determinations is questionable. It may be that essentiality is only a test for prejudice to be applied to a witness for whom process should have been issued, but who was unavailable. *See generally* R.C.M. 703(b)(3) Analysis.

[91] 44 M.J. 345, 349–50 (C.A.A.F. 1996).

[92] 44 M.J. at 352–54 (C.A.A.F. 1996).

(Rel.3—1/07   Pub.62410)

§ 20-22.50   Cumulative Testimony

Inherent in the right to compulsory process is the limitation of relevancy.[93] Military Rule of Evidence 403 allows evidence to be excluded, even if logically relevant,[94] "if its probative value is substantially outweighed . . . by considerations . . . of needless presentation of cumulative evidence." If evidence is cumulative under Rule 403, it is "legally irrelevant," and there is no right to introduce it.[95]

The issue of cumulative testimony often arises when character evidence is sought to be introduced.[96] To establish an adequate record for appeal, the defense should furnish to the judge the name and location of each character witness, how long each witness has known the defendant, the capacity in which the witness knew the defendant, and the characteristics to which the witness will testify.[97] The standard used in determining cumulativeness is not merely whether the evidence is repetitive. Instead, the military judge must "in his sound discretion decide whether, under the circumstances of the given case, there is anything to be gained from an additional witness saying the same thing other witnesses have said."[98] If testimony is declared to be cumulative, the judge should indicate how many of such witnesses will be subpoenaed at government expense. Only the defense, though, can decide which witnesses will be called to testify.[99]

---

[93] See § 20-22.40 above notes 82, 84.

[94] 44 M.J. 352–54 (C.A.A.F. 1996).

[95] United States v. Williams, 3 M.J. 239, 242 (C.M.A. 1977). See United States v. Staton, 48 C.M.R. 250, 254 (A.C.M.R. 1974); Mil. R. Evid. 402. See above note 82 for the definition of legal relevance. Clearly irrelevant evidence cannot be considered essential evidence under United States v. Bennett, 12 M.J. 463, 465 n.4 (C.M.A. 1982).

[96] E.g., United States v. Breeding, 44 M.J. 345, 351 (C.A.A.F. 1996) (set forth factors to examine in determining whether evidence is cumulative); United States v. Credit, 8 M.J. 190 (C.M.A. 1980); United States v. Tangpuz, 5 M.J. 426 (C.M.A. 1978); United States v. Williams, 3 M.J. 239 (C.M.A. 1977); United States v. Courts, 4 M.J. 518 (C.G.C.M.R. 1977), aff'd, 9 M.J. 285 (C.M.A. 1980); United States v. Elliott, 3 M.J. 1080 (A.C.M.R. 1977); United States v. Scott, 3 M.J. 1111 (N.C.M.R. 1977). Note that paragraph 115 of the Manual for Courts-Martial was amended in 1981 so as to generally eliminate limit live-witness testimony on sentencing. These provisions have been continued since the 1984 Manual, See R.C.M. 703(c)(2)(B)(ii).

[97] See United States v. Manos, 37 C.M.R. 274, 280–81 (C.M.A. 1967) (Quinn C.J., concurring in part, dissenting in part); Section 20-22.11. Note that, because the government determines whether to make witnesses available, the trial counsel need not be concerned with this procedure.

[98] United States v. Williams, 3 M.J. 239, 243 n.8 (C.M.A. 1977). Accord United States v. Scott, 3 M.J. 1111, 1113 (N.C.M.R. 1977).

[99] United States v. Williams, 3 M.J. 239, 243 n.9 (C.M.A. 1977) (Perry, J., Fletcher, C.J., concurring; Cook, J., dissenting). In an appropriate case, the judge would clearly be able to make that determination. United States v. Harmon, 40 M.J. 107, 108 (C.M.A. 1994) (failure to permit four character witnesses was not an abuse of discretion. "If the proponent of the witnesses seeks an advance ruling and the judge limits the number of witnesses as cumulative, the defense has the option of deciding which witnesses to call. . . . However, here, the defense proceeded to elicit

(Rel.3—1/07 Pub.62410)

§ 20-22.60 Alternatives to a Witness' Personal Attendance at Trial

The Court of Military Appeals stated that, even though a witness is material, personal attendance at trial may be obviated by other effective alternatives,[100] including depositions, interrogatories, and stipulations to the expected testimony of the witness.[101] If the government is willing to stipulate to the witness' expected testimony, there may be no need for the witness,[102] especially inasmuch as the defense may obtain more through a stipulation than it would through live testimony because the government loses the chance of rebuttal.[103] The decision to admit alternatives lies in the discretion of the judge.[104] The fundamental issue is whether "the effect of the form of the testimony under the particular facts and circumstances of the case will . . . diminish the fairness of the proceedings."[105] Because the circumstances of each individual case are extremely important, the judge should explicitly state the reasons for allowing alternative forms of testimony to ensure adequate review of each decision.[106]

Older cases allowed the judge to use a balancing test in deciding whether to allow alternatives to the witness' personal appearance.[107] However, a

---

testimony from its witnesses without seeking an advance ruling. . .," and thus the judge could properly preclude testimony of the fourth witness; in this circumstance the defense doesn't have a choice of witnesses). However, in the usual situation, the decision is for the defense.

[100] United States v. Scott, 5 M.J. 431, 432 (C.M.A. 1978); United States v. Willis, 3 M.J. 94, 98 (C.M.A. 1977) (Cook, J., dissenting). *See also* United States v. Campos, 42 M.J. 253, 262 (C.A.A.F. 1995) (alternative for testimony permitted on command influence issue); United States v. Courts, 9 M.J. 285, 292–93 (C.M.A. 1980).

[101] *E.g.*, United States v. Snead, 45 C.M.R. 382, 386 (A.C.M.R. 1972) (listing alternatives). *See also* R.C.M. 703(b)() and (3).

[102] This may be particularly true of some character witnesses. While character evidence given by the defendant's commanding officer occupies a unique and favored position in military judicial proceedings (United States v. Carpenter, 1 M.J. 384, 386 (C.M.A. 1976)), performance ratings, fitness reports, and efficiency reports may be acceptable substitutes. United States v. Tangpuz, 5 M.J. 426, 430 (C.M.A. 1978).

[103] For sentencing witnesses, the government may be required to stipulate to the facts to which the witness was expected to testify. United States v. Gonzalez, 16 M.J. 58 (C.M.A. 1983).

[104] United States v. Scott, 5 M.J. 431, 432 (C.M.A. 1978). It should be noted that most of the cases in which substitutes for live testimony were urged by the government were cases in which the testimony was offered for sentencing purposes by the defense. With the revision of the *Manual for Courts-Martial* to generally eliminate live testimony for sentencing (*see* MCM, 1969, para. 75, now R.C.M. 1001(e)), the number of appellate cases involving the use of substitutes for live testimony should diminish.

[105] *Scott*, 5 M.J. at 432. Thus, if a witness' credibility is important, live testimony should be required. United States v. Meadow, 14 M.J. 1002 (A.C.M.R. 1982) (reversible error to force stipulation of expected trustworthiness-opinion testimony of highly successful medical doctor on the merits in close larceny case).

[106] *Scott*, 5 M.J. at 432.

[107] United States v. Manos, 37 C.M.R. 274, 279 (C.M.A. 1967); United States v. Sweeney, 34 C.M.R. 379 (C.M.A. 1964).

(Rel.3—1/07 Pub.62410)

presumption existed that the defense request was to be granted if it would be "done without manifest injury to the service," [108] with military necessity or convenience often being cited as reasons for refusing to require the personal appearance of the witness. [109] The Court of Military Appeals, in *United States v. Carpenter* [110] and *United States v. Willis*, [111] overruled that approach. The current standard requires that a witness' personal appearance depends only on the materiality of the testimony; [112] reasons of military necessity should only affect the question of when a witness can testify. [113] Even though obtaining witnesses for the defense may be inconvenient and costly to the government, the defendant cannot be compelled to accept a substitute based on those reasons alone. [114]

§ 20-22.70　Defense Objections to Rule for Courts-Martial 703

Applying as it does to virtually all defense witnesses, Rule 703 produces two primary complaints: that the defense must "submit its request to a partisan advocate for a determination," [115] and that, in doing so, it necessarily reveals defense strategy and testimony to the government. [116] Inasmuch as the trial counsel is exempt from any similar situation, equal protection complaints are also raised. [117]

§ 20-22.71　The Recipient of the Request

As a matter of practice, the prosecution's decision to procure a witness is subject only to the review of those who have endorsed the prosecution of the accused, that is, the staff judge advocate and convening authority. [118] Although

---

[108] *Manos*, 37 C.M.R. at 279.

[109] *See, e.g., Sweeney*, 34 C.M.R. at 386.

[110] 1 M.J. 384 (C.M.A. 1976).

[111] 3 M.J. 94 (C.M.A. 1977).

[112] United States v. Carpenter, 1 M.J. 384, 386 (C.M.A. 1976).

[113] 1 M.J. 384, 386 (C.M.A. 1976).

[114] United States v. Willis, 3 M.J. 94, 96 (C.M.A. 1977).

[115] *Carpenter*, 1 M.J. at 386 n.8.

[116] Disclosure results not only from notice of who the defense wishes to call, but more importantly, from the requirement that the defense must show materiality in order to obtain the witness, a requirement that necessarily reveals defense strategy. *See* Sections 20-22.71 and 20-22.72.

[117] A trial counsel must, however, disclose all witnesses the government will call in its case-in-chief, as well as any sworn or signed statements relating to the charged offense that are in the trial counsel's possession. R.C.M. 701(a)(1)(C), (3)(A). Also, the trial counsel must give notice of any rebuttal witnesses if notified of the defense's intent to raise an alibi or mental responsibility defense. R.C.M. 701(a)(3)(B).

[118] In most of the armed forces, the prosecutor is rated by these officers, or their equivalents, and thus promotion is contingent on the prosecutor's compliance with their wishes.

(Rel.3—1/07　Pub.62410)

the law requires these officers to be neutral,[119] both common sense and experience suggest that an inherent conflict of interest exists when the defense requests that a given witness be obtained. Any given witness potentially represents the expenditure of funds[120] for a purpose contrary to what may be viewed as the best interest of the given officer or service. A number of commentators have recognized, for example, that the staff judge advocate is, in effect, the chief prosecutor for the convening authority,[121] and Rule for Courts-Martial 703 asks a great deal of such a person. Furthermore, as a matter of law, Rule 703(c)(2)(C) declares that the trial counsel will take action to provide a witness requested by the defense unless the trial counsel contends that the witness production is not required by the rule. In effect, the trial counsel has a substantial amount of leverage over the defense.[122] The Court of Military Appeals noted this objection to Rule for Courts-Martial 703 and stated in dicta that "the requirement appears to be inconsistent with Article 46."[123] Then Chief Judge Everett appears to have implicitly rejected this view by stating that "the Government is entitled to prescribe reasonable rules whereunder it will have adequate opportunity either to arrange for the presence of the witness or to explore any legally permissible alternative to the presence of the witness."[124]

The defense may be able to escape the need to advise the prosecution of its requested witnesses by directly requesting the witness from the military judge.

---

[119] And experience suggests that most of them make great efforts to carry out their legal duty.

[120] Budgeting the courts-martial varies within the armed forces, with not all services budgeting specifically for trials. When witness expenses come out of a ship's operating budget, for example, one can expect the ship's captain, who is the convening authority, to be particularly resistant to any expense.

[121] See, e.g., Hodson, *The Manual for Courts-Martial-1984*, 57 Mil. R. Evid. 1, 15 (1972), in which General Hodson, formerly The Judge Advocate General of the Army and then Chief Judge of the Army Court of Military Review, said: "I would favor recognizing the staff judge advocate and the commander for what they are. They are the Government." Indeed, he proposed reorganizing the military criminal legal system so that the staff judge advocates would resemble United States Attorneys. Hodson, *The Manual for Courts-Martial-1984*, 57 Mil. R. Evid. at 8 (1972).

[122] The Court of Military Appeals said that its application of Rule 703 leaves no doubt that an accused's right to secure the attendance of a material witness is free from substantive control by trial counsel. United States v. Arias, 3 M.J. 436, 438 (C.M.A. 1977). *But see* United States v. Cottle, 14 M.J. 260, 261 (C.M.A. 1982) (trial counsel denied the witness request). Trial counsels can and have rejected R.C.M. 703 requests as being procedurally deficient, however, using the rejection as a tactical ploy to discourage either the defense from requesting the witness or the judge from granting the request due to the lateness of the final request, or to encourage the defense counsel to plea bargain.

[123] United States v. Carpenter, 1 M.J. 384, 386 n.8 (C.M.A. 1976). *Accord* United States v. Williams, 3 M.J. 239, 240 n.2 (C.M.A. 1977).

[124] United States v. Vietor, 10 M.J. 69, 77–78 (C.M.A. 1980). Chief Judge Everett concurred in the result of *Vietor* only, while Judge Fletcher, also concurring in the result alone, found Judge Everett's analysis unacceptable. 10 M.J. at 78 (C.M.A. 1980).

(Rel.3—1/07 Pub.62410)

Under present law, this solution would appear appropriate only when the defense has a substantial interest in not advising the government of the identity of the witness, an interest that clearly outweighs the government's interest in knowing their identity. Inasmuch as this procedure would require the judge to use novel procedures to ensure that the necessary witness fee could be paid and a subpoena served on a noncooperative witness, the most probable circumstance justifying this procedure would be a defense showing that the prosecution would be likely to tamper with the witness. In such a unique circumstance, the military judge should seal the record of the witness request until the conclusion of the witness' testimony.

§ 20-22.72   Defense Disclosure of Tactics and Strategy

The defense objection that Rule for Courts-Martial 703 necessarily reveals defense tactics and strategy can be divided into two components: the disclosure itself and the lack of reciprocity. Proper compliance with Rule 703 will result in a disclosure to the government of all defense witnesses and a synopsis of their individual testimonies. Although counsel may well believe that they are required to disclose more than the law actually requires,[125] there is no doubt but that the quantum actually required, as well as the quantum occasionally demanded by prosecutors, is enough to be very revealing. The prosecution has no equivalent requirement,[126] and the broad discovery available to the defense as a matter of practice can hardly be equated with the template of the defense case required under Rule 703. Any Fifth Amendment objection[127] to Rule for Courts-Martial 703 appears to be foreclosed by the Supreme Court's decision in *Williams v. Florida*.[128] In *Williams*, the Court sustained Florida's notice-of-alibi rule against constitutional self-incrimination objections on the grounds that the defense was only divulging information that it would have to reveal at trial.[129] Although

---

[125] *See, e.g.*, United States v. Dixon, 8 M.J. 858, 865 (N.C.M.R. 1980). *See also* § 11-12.00.

[126] R.C.M. 701(a)(3)(A) requires the prosecution to notify the defense, without a defense request, of witnesses it intends to call in its case-in-chief. R.C.M. 701(a)(1)(C) requires the prosecution to provide the defense, without a defense request, any sworn or signed statement relating to the offense that is in the trial counsel's possession.

[127] Although the Supreme Court's decisions may resolve the Fifth Amendment question, they leave untouched the parallel Article 31 (the military's statutory right against self-incrimination) question. The Article 31 argument now seems foreclosed by the Court of Military Appeal's position that Article 31 merely parallels the Fifth Amendment and does not provide additional protection. *See, e.g.*, United States v. Harden, 18 M.J. 81 (C.M.A. 1984).

[128] 399 U.S. 78 (1970).

[129] The view has been, in effect, that the information gained by the prosecution is de minimis and serves the interests of justice and judicial efficiency by avoiding surprise. *See generally* Van Kessel, *Prosecutorial Discovery and the Privilege Against Self-Incrimination: Accommodation or Capitulation*, 4 Hastings Const. L.Q. 855, 882–89 (1971). Inasmuch as the information obtained from the defense may lead the government to evidence otherwise undiscoverable, at least until the defense portion of the case, it can hardly be said that the defense material is de minimis. Rather, it may practically assist the government greatly in making out its case-in-chief.

(Rel.3—1/07   Pub.62410)

Williams appears to require a reciprocal duty on the part of the government,[130] that requirement is met simply by making discovery of the prosecution case available to the defense;[131] response in kind is not apparently required.

§ 20-22.73   Lack of Reciprocity in General

Defense counsel have contended that Rule for Courts-Martial 703 "improperly discriminates against an accused because it imposes burdens in the procurement of a defense witness that are not imposed upon the Government."[132] In effect, this is a claimed violation of Article 46 and a denial of equal protection. Chief Judge Everett may have addressed this when he stated that Rule for Courts-Martial 703 not only provides the government with an opportunity to explore any permissible alternative to the witness,[133] but also ensures that the defense counsel, who might be spurred as an advocate to request witnesses in the hope that the delay and expense would result in dismissal or an attractive plea bargain, have a good-faith belief that the testimony will benefit the accused.[134] The Courts of Military Review justified Rule for Courts-Martial 703 as permitting the trial court to avoid cumulative testimony[135] and ensuring "that government funds are not wasted in producing witnesses who are not absolutely necessary and material."[136] Although these purposes are praiseworthy, the present procedural mechanism is unnecessary to assure that they are well served.

§ 20-22.80   Revision of Rule for Courts-Martial 703

The primary defense objections to Rule for Courts-Martial 703 could be met by requiring both trial and defense counsel to submit witness requests to the military judge for resolution. Although this could be done in an *ex parte* fashion, thus shielding the defense case from the government, the interests of justice would best be served in the normal case by requiring service of witness requests on the opposing party with adversarial litigation before the trial judge. This would permit the stipulations and concessions that may hasten the process. Further, it would equalize the parties' information and permit either side to argue against a given witness request. Such a system would moot virtually all of the present

---

[130] Wardius v. Oregon, 412 U.S. 470 (1973).

[131] 412 U.S. 470 (1973). *See also* United States v. Dixon, 8 M.J. 858, 865 (N.C.M.R. 1980) (discovery afforded defense via Article 32 proceedings more than balances government's discovery from Rule 703).

[132] United States v. Arias, 3 M.J. 436, 438 (C.M.A. 1977).

[133] United States v. Vietor, 10 M.J. 69, 77–78 (C.M.A. 1980).

[134] 10 M.J. 79 (C.M.A. 1980). *See also* United States v. Warner, 62 M.J. 114 (C.A.A.F. 2005). United States v. Kilby, 3 M.J. 938, 944–45 (N.C.M.R. 1977).

[135] United States v. Dixon, 8 M.J. 858, 865 (N.C.M.R. 1980).

[136] United States v. Christian, 6 M.J. 624, 627 (A.C.M.R. 1987) (Deford, J. concurring). *Accord* United States v. Williams, 3 M.J. 239 (C.M.A. 1977).

(Rel.3—1/07   Pub.62410)

objections to Rule 703. Opponents would most likely argue that it would remove fiscal control from the convening authority and further extend the power and number of military judges. As to the former, a revised Rule 703 could leave the government with the option of funding the witnesses or dismissing charges — a reasonable, although unpalatable, choice.[137]

§ 20-23.00   The Power to Obtain Witnesses and Other Evidence

§ 20-23.10   Evidence in the Custody or Control of Military Authorities

In addition to a comprehensive body of discovery rules,[138] the *Manual for Courts-Martial* fully treats *production* of evidence.[139] Production of evidence under Rule for Courts-Martial 703(f)[140] parallels production of witnesses under

---

[137] *Cf.* R.C.M. 703(d) (employment of experts).

[138] *See generally* Chapter 11.

[139] Within this category, one might distinguish between obtaining evidence that already exists and obtaining assistance to develop evidence that does not yet exist. United States v. Metcalf, 34 M.J. 1056, 1059 (A.F.C.M.R. 1992) (court order to prosecution to test accused's urine for cocaine metabolites benzoylecgonine and ecgoninemethylester was the equivalent of asking for defense investigative assistance, 34 M.J. 1060 (A.F.C.M.R. 1992), and was not within R.C.M. 703(f)). It is not clear that this distinction is necessarily meaningful in the usual case. *E.g., Metcalf*, 34 M.J. at 1063–64 (Dixon, C.J., dissenting).

(f) *Right to evidence.*

(1) *In general.* Each party is entitled to the production of evidence which is relevant and necessary.

(2) *Unavailable evidence.* Notwithstanding subsection (f)(1) of this rule, a party is not entitled to the production of evidence which is destroyed, lost, or otherwise not subject to compulsory process. However, if such evidence is of such central importance to an issue that it is essential to a fair trial, and if there is no adequate substitute for such evidence, the military judge shall grant a continuance or other relief in order to attempt to produce the evidence or shall abate the proceedings, unless the unavailability of the evidence is the fault of or could have been prevented by the requesting party.

(3) *Determining what evidence will be produced.* The procedures in subsection (c) of this rule apply to a determination of what evidence will be produced, except that any defense request for the production of evidence shall list the items of evidence to be produced and shall include a description of each item sufficient to show its relevance and necessity, a statement where it can be obtained, and, if known, the name, address, and telephone number of the custodian of the evidence.

(4) *Procedures for production of evidence.*

(A) *Evidence under the control of the Government.* Evidence under the control of the Government may be obtained by notifying the custodian of the evidence of the time, place, and date the evidence is required and requesting the custodian to send or deliver the evidence.

(B) *Evidence not under the control of the Government.* Evidence not under the control of the Government may be obtained by subpoena issued in accordance with subsection (e)(2) of this rule.

(C) *Relief.* If the person having custody of evidence requests relief on grounds that

(Rel.3—1/07   Pub.62410)

Rule for Courts-Martial 703(a)-(e), insofar as entitlement,[141] procedure,[142] and remedy (if important evidence is lost, destroyed, or is not subject to compulsory process)[143] are concerned. Evidence under control of the military is obtained by notifying the custodian of the time, place, and date the evidence is required and requesting the custodian to send or deliver the evidence.[144]

When witnesses are involved, the *Manual* states that, customarily, the attendance of a witness stationed near enough to the trial location can be obtained through informal coordination with the witness and the commander. If informal coordination is inadequate, or attendance would involve travel at government expense,[145] the appropriate commander should be requested to issue the necessary orders.[146]

Notwithstanding its phrasing, the *Manual* does not appear to intend that the commanding officer of the accused will have any general discretion to reject the request. The decisions of the Court of Military Appeals treated the government in a unitary fashion, and when a material defense witness is not made available, trial must be abated until the witness is available.[147] The court has implicitly recognized that witnesses may not be instantly available and that, in normal practice, the reasonable needs of the individual and the service are to be accommodated.

In the event of noncompliance with the trial counsel's request for evidence under Rule for Courts-Martial 703(f) or a military judge's request for

compliance with the subpoena or order of production is unreasonable or oppressive, the convening authority or, after referral, the military judge may direct that the subpoena or order of production be withdrawn or modified. Subject to Mil. R. Evid. 505 and 506, the military judge may direct that the evidence be submitted to the military judge for an *in camera* inspection in order to determine whether such relief should be granted. R.C.M. 703(f).

[141] Under R.C.M. 703(f)(1), parties are entitled to relevant and necessary evidence. Unlike the standards for witness production, however, the standards for production of evidence on the merits and in sentencing are the same. For a discussion of "relevant and necessary," see United States v. Metcalf, 34 M.J. 1056, 1059, n.3 (A.F.C.M.R. 1992).

[142] R.C.M. 703(f)(3) requires the defense to submit a written list to the trial counsel with a description sufficient to show the evidence is relevant and necessary and its location.

[143] R.C.M. 703(f)(2).

[144] R.C.M. 703(f)(4)(A).

[145] R.C.M. 703(e)(1) Discussion.

[146] R.C.M. 703(e)(1) Discussion.

[147] United States v. Willis, 3 M.J. 94, 96 (C.M.A. 1977) (quoting United States v. Daniels, 48 C.M.R. 655 (C.M.A. 1974)); United States v. Carpenter, 1 M.J. 384 (C.M.A. 1976). In an appropriate case, dismissal of charges may be necessary.

(Rel.3—1/07 Pub.62410)

evidence,[148] the only meaningful sanction may be to abate the proceedings[149] and perhaps prefer criminal charges against those refusing to comply.[150]

§ 20-23.20   Evidence Not in Military Control

Although most civilian evidence is obtained through the voluntary cooperation of the appropriate individuals, recourse to process is occasionally necessary. Congress has provided:

> Process issued in court-martial cases to compel witnesses to appear and testify and to compel the production of other evidence shall be similar to that which courts of the United States having criminal jurisdiction may lawfully issue and shall run to any part of the United States, or the territories, Commonwealths, and possessions.[151]

At the outset, it is apparent that despite the ability of federal district courts to subpoena United States citizens residing abroad,[152] such process in courts-martial is unavailable.[153] The *Manual* states that "[i]n foreign territory, the attendance

---

[148] R.C.M. 703(e)(2)(C) gives the trial counsel subpoena power over civilians. Although the provision could be read as limiting the trial counsel's power of subpoena to civilians, it seems more likely that the *Manual*'s drafters took for granted government compliance with R.C.M. 703 and simply granted express power to deal with the case of civilians. However, to the extent that the *Manual* fails to grant subpoena power to compel military production of evidence, it seems clear that the *Manual* necessarily grants such power to the military judge. In *United States v. Toledo*, 15 M.J. 255, 256 (C.M.A. 1983), the court held that the trial judge erred by refusing to order the prosecution to obtain a transcript of a prosecution witness' prior federal district court testimony for impeachment use. Further support for the authority of the military judge to compel military production of evidence can be derived from the military judge's broad powers to call witnesses (Mil. R. Evid. 614), require additional evidence (R.C.M. 801(c)), regulate discovery (R.C.M. 701(g)(3)), and direct that evidence be submitted for an in-camera inspection (R.C.M. 703(f)(4)(C)).

[149] United States v. Willis, 3 M.J. 94 (C.M.A. 1977); United States v. Carpenter, 1 M.J. 384 (C.M.A. 1976).

[150] A refusal to supply evidence pursuant to either R.C.M. 703 or a court order may constitute a violation of Articles 98 or 134. *Cf.* United States v. Perry, 2 M.J. 113, 116 (C.M.A. 1977) (Fletcher, C. J., concurring) (violation of speedy-trial right); United States v. Powell, 2 M.J. 6, 8 (C.M.A. 1976) (unnecessary delay in completing Article 32 proceedings). Refusal to obey a court order may also constitute a disobedience under Articles 90 and 92.

[151] U.C.M.J. art. 46.

[152] 28 U.S.C. §§ 1783; 1784; Fed. R. Crim. P. 17(e)(2). *See* Blackmer v. United States, 284 U.S. 421 (1932). *See generally* Merin, *Walsh Act Sets Harsh Penalties for Ignoring Subpoenas Abroad*, Nat'l L.J., April 18, 1983, at 26, col. 1.

[153] Of course, the "territories, Commonwealths, and possessions" of the United States are not "abroad." Presumably, a court-martial could constitutionally be given the power to subpoena United States citizens outside the United States to trials taking place within the United States. Civilian federal courts have such power. *See above* note 148. The applicability of 28 U.S.C. § 1783 to courts-martial has not been judicially determined. *See* United States v. Harding, 63 M.J. 65, 67 (C.A.A.F. 2006); United States v. Bennett, 12 M.J. 463, 470 (C.M.A. 1982). Alternatively, a U.S. District Court may be empowered under 28 U.S.C. § 1783 to order a U.S. citizen outside the United

of civilian witnesses may be obtained in accordance with existing agreements or, in the absence thereof, within the principles of international laws."[154] Therefore, courts-martial lack the power to compel the attendance abroad of witnesses who could otherwise be compelled to attend courts-martial tried within the United States. Whether various federal statutes might permit the use of overseas subpoenas to obtain *documents* is unclear.[155]

Compulsory process is available in two forms: subpoena and warrant of attachment. The subpoena compels the attendance of a witness by the coercion of law, while a warrant of attachment results in the apprehension of the witness and coerced physical transportation to trial.

§ 20-23.21 Subpoenas

Pursuant to Article 46 of the Uniform Code of Military Justice, the *Manual for Courts-Martial* provides for the issuance of subpoenas by the trial counsel to compel the attendance of civilian witnesses.[156] The Manual provides a model subpoena form[157] and states that service should generally be made by mail.[158] The trial counsel is directed "to assure timely and appropriate service"[159] when formal service is necessary. A subpoena may be served by the person issuing it, a U.S. Marshal, or any person not less than age eighteen.[160] According to the *Manual*, personal service "should ordinarily be made by a person subject to the code."[161] In the event of noncompliance with the subpoena, the witness would be subject to criminal prosecution in a United States district court under the provisions of Article 47 of the Uniform Code of Military Justice.[162] Such

---

States to testify at a court-martial within the United States. The statute allows a U.S. District Court to order a witness to appear before it or before a person or body designated by it. The court-martial could be the person or body designated by the district court. *See* United States v. Daniels, 48 C.M.R. 655, 657 (C.M.A. 1974) (Quinn, J., concurring); United States v. Daneza, 528 F.2d 390 (2d Cir. 1975) (statute applied to grand jury). *See generally* Annot. A.L.R. Fed. 894 (1977).

[154] R.C.M. 703(e)(2)(E)(ii).

[155] *E.g.*, United States v. Wooten, 34 M.J. 141, 145–46 (C.M.A. 1992) (subpoena in United States of bank records for use in a court-martial in Germany). As witnesses cannot be compelled to travel overseas, authentication of such documents could be extraordinarily troublesome.

[156] A subpoena may also be issued by a summary court-martial. R.C.M. 703(e)(2)(C). United States v. Curtin, 44 M.J. 439 (C.A.A.F. 1996) (trial counsel's subpoena is a judicial subpoena within the meaning of the Right to Financial Act, 12 U.S.C. § 3410).

[157] MCM, 2005, A7-1.

[158] R.C.M. 703(e)(2)(D) Discussion.

[159] R.C.M. 703(e)(2)(D) Discussion.

[160] R.C.M. 703(e)(2)(D).

[161] R.C.M. 703(e)(2)(D) Discussion.

[162] Article 47 penalizes an individual not subject to court-martial jurisdiction who, having been properly subpoenaed, willfully neglects or refuses to appear, or refuses to qualify as a witness, or to testify, or to produce any evidence that that person may have been legally subpoenaed to

(Rel.3—1/07 Pub.62410)

a sanction is not particularly useful insofar as obtaining the testimony of the witness is concerned. Given a witness who refuses to comply, the trial counsel may request a United States district court to direct the attendance of the witness or, more directly, may issue a warrant of attachment.

§ 20-23.22   The Warrant of Attachment [163]

§ 20-23.22(a)   In General

The warrant of attachment, usually know as a bench warrant in civilian practice, directs the seizure of a witness who has refused to appear before a court-martial and orders the production of the witness [164] before the tribunal, the process of which has been disobeyed. The attachment prerogative has existed almost as long as the power of compulsory process [165] and may be regarded as inherent to compulsory process. [166] The express authority of courts-martial to attach civilian witnesses first appeared in Army general orders in 1868 [167] and, virtually unchanged since that date, was incorporated into the modern *Manual for Courts-Martial*. [168] The power to attach is not found expressly in the Uniform Code of Military Justice, but attachment is authorized by the *Manual for Courts-Martial*, which provides:

---

produce. U.C.M.J., art. 47(a)(3). The article provides for a maximum punishment of a fine of not more than $500, or imprisonment for not more than six months, or both. U.C.M.J., art. 47(b). A prerequisite condition for an Article 47 prosecution is that the witness has been duly paid or tendered the fees and mileage of a witness at the rates allowed to witnesses attending the courts of the United States. U.C.M.J., art. 47(a)(2). Interestingly, the Code appears to deprive the civilian prosecutor of any prosecutorial discretion. As Article 47(c) states: "The United States attorney . . . shall, upon the certification of the facts to him by the military court . . . file an information against and prosecute any person violating this article." This is not to say that the prosecution would necessarily comply with Article 47. *See, e.g.*, Lederer, *Warrants of Attachment — Forcibly Compelling the Attendance of Witnesses*, 98 Mil. R. Evid. 1, 4 n.9 (1982).

[163] Much of the following text and accompanying footnotes are taken from Calvin M. Lederer, *Warrants of Attachment — Forcibly Compelling the Attendance of Witnesses*, 98 Mil. R. Evid. 1 (1982), written by then Major Calvin M. Lederer, when he was a member of the faculty of The Judge Advocate General's School, U.S. Army. The authors gratefully acknowledge Colonel Lederer's permission to utilize his outstanding article so extensively. Those interested in this general topic are urged to read his comprehensive treatment of the topic.

[164] The *Manuals* since 1984 specifically authorize using the warrant attachment to compel production of documents.

[165] *See, e.g.*, 12 Op. Att'y Gen. 501 (1868).

[166] *See, e.g.*, Barry v. United States ex rel. Cunningham, 279 U.S. 597 (1929); United States v. Caldwell, 2 U.S. (2 Dall.) 333 (1795). *See also* 9 Op. Att'y Gen. 266 (1859).

[167] General Orders No. 93, Headquarters of the Army (Nov. 9, 1868). *See also* J. Winthrop, Military Law and Precedents 202 n.46 (1886, 1920 reprint); Digest of Opinions, The Judge Advocate General 490 (1988).

[168] R.C.M. 703(e)(2)(G).

(Rel.3—1/07   Pub.62410)

Neglect or refusal to appear

(i) *Issuance of warrant of attachment.* The military judge or, if there is no military judge, the convening authority may, in accordance with this rule, issue a warrant of attachment to compel the attendance of a witness or production of documents.

(ii) *Requirements.* A warrant of attachment may be issued only upon probable cause to believe that the witness was duly served with a subpoena, that the subpoena was issued in accordance with these rules, that appropriate fees and mileage were tendered to the witness, that the witness is material, that the witness refused or willfully neglected to appear at the time and place specified on the subpoena, and that no valid excuse reasonably appears for the witness' failure to appear.

(iii) *Form.* A warrant of attachment shall be written. All documents in support of the warrant of attachment shall be attached to the warrant, together with the charge sheet and convening orders.

(iv) *Execution.* A warrant of attachment may be executed by a United States marshal or such other person who is not less than 18 years of age as the authority issuing the warrant may direct. Only such non-deadly force as may be necessary to bring the witness before the court-martial or other proceeding may be used to execute the warrant. A witness attached under this rule shall be brought before the court-martial or proceeding without delay and shall testify as soon as practicable and be released.[169]

The *2005 Manual* places the full discretion and responsibility for issuance of a warrant of attachment with the military judge.[170] In the absence of a military judge, authority rests with the convening authority.[171] By placing authority in the military judge to issue the warrant, the *Manual* obviously contemplates that the warrant can only issue after referral of charges. The *Manual* authorizes issuance any time thereafter, even before the court actually convenes.

The *Manual* states that a warrant should issue only when the witness is material,[172] when there is probable cause to believe a properly issued subpoena was duly served,[173] and when the witness, without a valid excuse, refused or

---

[169] R.C.M. 703(e)(2)(G). *See also* United States v. Harding, 63 M.J. 65 (C.A.A.F. 2006). United States v. Cokeley, 22 M.J. 225 (C.M.A. 1986).

[170] R.C.M. 703(e)(2)(G)(i). In the pre-1984 previous *Manuals*, the trial counsel had discretion to issue the warrant. The military judge was given the authority in the *1984 Manual* to resolve Fourth Amendment issues regarding the neutrality and detachment of the issuing official. *See generally* Lederer, *above* note 163.

[171] The convening authority would issue the warrant only when there was a special courtmartial without a military judge or a summary court-martial. R.C.M. 703(e)(2)(G)(i).

[172] *See* Section 20-22.40.

[173] Refusal to accept a subpoena thus prohibits use of the warrant of attachment. United States v. Davis, 29 M.J. 357, 359 (C.M.A. 1990). This is an absurd result that should not be countenanced. Necessary amendments to relevant provisions should be made as quickly as possible.

(Rel.3—1/07 Pub.62410)

willfully neglected to appear.[174] The *Manual*'s criterion appears to be actual necessity — the witness must actually fail to appear at the time and place specified on the subpoena.[175]

Procedurally, the *Manual* does not prescribe the form of the warrant.[176] Although the *Manual* directs that supporting documents be attached,[177] that requirement is intended to support the government's position in the event of a habeas corpus petition[178] and does not appear to be a formal condition to be met before the warrant may issue.

§ 20-23.22(b) Execution of Warrant

The warrant may be executed by a United States marshal[179] or any person not less than the age of 18.[180] Discretion as to who executes the warrant lies with the issuing authority.[181] The *Manual* contemplates that force may be necessary for the successful execution of the warrant,[182] although no statute or other executive order expressly allows the use of force on, or permits the deprivation of liberty of, a civilian by military authority.[183]

§ 20-23.22(c) Constitutionality of the Military Warrant of Attachment

Clearly, the apprehension by military authorities of a civilian witness who is not the subject of criminal charges is troubling and raises a number of constitutional questions, among the most important of which are the following:

(1) Whether any innocent citizen may be arrested to obtain testimony?

---

[174] R.C.M. 703(e)(2)(G)(ii).

[175] Some civilian courts, however, utilize material-witness statutes to order arrest of witnesses who may not appear. Noncompliance with a subpoena is not a condition precedent for issuance of an arrest warrant. *See, e.g.*, Bacon v. United States, 449 F.2d 933 (9th Cir. 1971).

[176] The *Manual* prescribes no specific form for the warrant, although earlier *Manuals* did so. *See, e.g.*, MCM, 1921 at 655; MCM, 1928 at 88. The present form, DD Form 454, is prescribed by the Department of Defense.

[177] R.C.M. 703(e)(2)(G)(iii).

[178] *See generally* MCM, 1969 (rev. ed.) ¶ 115(d)(3).

[179] R.C.M. 703(e)(2)(G)(iv). The *1969 Manual* had expressed a preference that United States marshals execute the warrant when practicable. MCM, 1969, para. 115(d)(3).

[180] R.C.M. 703(e)(2)(G)(iv).

[181] R.C.M. 703(e)(2)(G)(iv).

[182] Only such nondeadly force as may be necessary to bring the witness before the courtmartial or proceeding may be used to execute the warrant. R.C.M. 703(e)(2)(G)(iv).

[183] Despite the introduction of several bills over a period of years, Congress has declined to enact legislation specifically giving military personnel arrest power over civilians by statute. One such bill was S. 727, 97th Cong., 1st Sess. (1981), which would have authorized the Secretary of Defense to "invest officers . . . of the Department of Defense . . . with the power to arrest individuals on military facilities and installations."

(Rel.3—1/07 Pub.62410)

(2) Whether military authorities may apprehend a civilian to obtain testimony at a court-martial?

(3) What quantum of proof is necessary before a warrant of attachment may issue?

(4) Who may issue a warrant of attachment?

The first of these questions must be considered resolved:at least twenty-seven states expressly utilize variations of the warrant of attachment[184] and all states subscribe to the Uniform Act to Secure the Attendance of Witnesses from Without a State in Criminal Proceedings.[185] The fundamental concept of the arrest of material witnesses is also accepted throughout the American judicial system.[186] Although it could be said that warrants of attachment directing the attachment of civilians might better be placed in the hands of civilian judicial authorities, the only court that has considered the issue to date[187] has clearly rejected that position.[188] The last two questions, however, raise issues of substantially greater legal import.

Although the Supreme Court has held that "a subpoena to appear before a grand jury is not a 'seizure' in the Fourth Amendment sense,"[189] it is apparent that the actual apprehension of an individual and his or her involuntary physical

---

[184] Lederer, *above* note 162.

[185] The Act provides that a host state must honor an order from another state directing that a given witness be taken into custody.

[186] *See above* note 165. *See also* Bacon v. United States, 449 F.2d 933 (9th Cir. 1971).

[187] United States v. Shibley, 112 F. Supp. 734 (S.D. Cal. 1953).

[188] The court in *Shibley* addressed the issue of whether a Marine Court of Inquiry had the same power to compel attendance as did a court-martial. In resolving that issue, it also addressed the issue of the warrant of attachment, as *Shibley* had been apprehended and brought before the court of inquiry. The court stated:

If the only method of making this provision (authorizing the summoning of witnesses) effective were resort to prosecution under (Article 47), the result would be ineffective and illusory. Punishment as an offense cannot compel disclosure to make an inquiry effective. And if boards of inquiry are to perform their functions . . . they can do so only if means exist to bring summarily recalcitrant witnesses before them. And the warrant of attachment traditionally provides such means. The suggestion has been made that only civil courts can compel appearance . . . after a civilian witness' refusal. . . . This remedy, if it existed, would be equally visionary. It would tie the military tribunals to the civil courts contrary to the spirit of military law. More, there is not in the (Uniform Code of Military Justice) a provision similar to (other statutes unrelated to the military which require resort to federal judges to enforce agency subpoenas). Its absence indicates that the means to compel attendance must exist in the court of inquiry itself. Otherwise, the courts are given the naked power to summon, but no power to use a summary method to compel attendance.

United States v. Shibley, 112 F. Supp. 734, 743 n.19 (S.D. Cal. 1953).

[189] United States v. Dionisio, 410 U.S. 1, 9 (1973).

(Rel.3—1/07 Pub.62410)

removal to testify[190] at a court-martial necessarily constitutes such a seizure.[191] Except for a limited number of exceptions, the Fourth Amendment commands that seizures be based upon probable cause, and at least one court has held that a seizure of a material witness must be based upon probable cause.[192] This conclusion seems correct and fully applicable to the military warrant of attachment. What is less clear, however, is what probable cause must establish. In the normal attachment case, the absence of the subpoenaed witness at trial is apparent and is more than enough to support the issuance of a warrant insofar as it is necessary to procure that person's attendance.[193] Yet, the *Manual for Courts-Martial* contemplates only the attachment of a witness who will give "material" testimony.[194] Accordingly, it would seem reasonable to require that the materiality of the witness be demonstrated prior to the issuance of the warrant, although it might be argued that a subpoena need not be based on probable cause[195] and will be considered valid until properly voided by the Court.[196] As a result, a supposed lack of materiality may only be raised by the prospective witness via a motion to quash the subpoena. Although the issue is a close one, as a matter of policy the better course is to demonstrate materiality of the witness on a preponderance basis beforehand when seeking a warrant of attachment. Firstly, it should be simple for counsel to demonstrate materiality in view of the fact that the *Manual* presently requires the defense to demonstrate materiality and the government to only call material witnesses.[197] Secondly, demonstration of materiality seems appropriate because of both the dislocation to the witness and the nature of the military intrusion into civil matters caused by the warrant.

The final question to be resolved is who should grant the warrant of attachment. The Supreme Court[198] and Court of Military Appeals[199] declared that issuing officers for search warrants must be neutral and detached. The *1984 Manual*

---

[190] In order to secure the necessary testimony, the witness may be required to travel and may necessarily be held in custody for at least a few days.

[191] *See, e.g.*, United States v. Dionisio, 410 U.S. 1, 8–12 (1973) (distinguishing the subpoena situation, in which the coercion is the force of law, from detention of the individual effected by the police); Bacon v. United States, 449 F.2d 933, 942 (9th Cir. 1971).

[192] 449 F.2d at 943.

[193] *See, e.g.*, United States v. Evans, 574 F.2d 352, 355 (6th Cir. 1978).

[194] *See* Section 20-22.40.

[195] United States v. Dionisio, 410 U.S. 1 (1973).

[196] *Cf.* Dolman v. United States, 439 U.S. 1395, 1395 (1978) (Rehnquist, Circuit Justice) (invalidity of an injunction may not ordinarily be raised as a defense in contempt proceedings for its violation); Walker v. City of Birmingham, 388 U.S. 305, 315–20 (1967); United States v. United Mine Workers, 330 U.S. 258, 293–94 (1947).

[197] *See* Sections 20-22.11 and 20-22.40.

[198] Coolidge v. New Hampshire, 403 U.S. 443 (1971).

[199] United States v. Ezell, 6 M.J. 307 (C.M.A. 1979).

(Rel.3—1/07   Pub.62410)

resolved most of the problems inherent in the *1969 Manual* that had made the trial counsel the authorizing official. Under the *1984* and *2005 Manuals*, the military judge, or if there is no military judge, [200] the convening authority, will issue the warrant. Under normal circumstances, the disqualification rules for military judges and convening authorities will ensure the requisite neutrality and detachment. [201] Only in the relatively rare situation where the summary court-martial-convening authority is also the accuser might the convening authority not be sufficiently neutral and detached. [202] Should this problem be foreseen before referral, however, the summary court-martial-convening authority can forward the charges to a superior competent authority with a recommendation to convene a summary court-martial. [203] Should the problem arise after referral, it may be possible to withdraw the charges without prejudice and forward them to a superior competent authority with a recommendation for referral to another summary court-martial. The superior competent authority then, as convening authority, could issue the warrant. [204]

§ 20-23.30   Immunity

§ 20-23.31   In General

The Supreme Court has long recognized that a valid claim to the privilege against self-incrimination may be overcome by a grant of immunity. [205] Accordingly, when the prosecution [206] seeks the testimony of a witness who will claim the constitutional or statutory privilege, it may compel the individual's testimony through a grant of immunity. [207] Although the armed forces have claimed the power to grant immunity since at least 1917, [208] no statute existed [209] or

---

[200] *See above* note 171.

[201] *See generally* R.C.M. 902, 504(c).

[202] An accuser is one who signs or swears to charges, directs that charges be nominally signed or sworn by another, or any person who has other than an official interest in the accused's prosecution. U.C.M.J., art. 1(9). The latter type of accuser will not normally be neutral and detached.

[203] R.C.M. 604(a).

[204] R.C.M. 604(b) provides that charges may be withdrawn after introduction of evidence on the general issue of guilt only if necessitated by urgent and unforeseen military necessity. See also § 8-15.00.

[205] *See, e.g.*, Kastigar v. United States, 406 U.S. 441 (1972); Brown v. Walker, 161 U.S. 591 (1896). *See generally*, Green, *Grants of Immunity of Military Law*, 53 Mil. R. Evid. 1, 3–16 (1971) [hereinafter cited as Green]. *See also* Green, *Grants of Immunity and Military Law*, 1971-1976, 73 Mil. R. Evid. 1 (1976).

[206] Insofar as the ability of the defense to obtain immunity for defense witnesses is concerned, see Section 20-33.12.

[207] U.C.M.J. art. 31. *See generally*, Lederer, *Rights Warnings in the Armed Services*, 72 Mil. R. Evid. 1 (1976). *See also* Mil. R. Evid. 301–05.

[208] Green, *above* note 205, at 17 (citing MCM, 1917); R.C.M. 907(d)(2)(D)(ii).

[209] Green, *above* note 205, at 17. *But see* the Organized Crime Control Act of 1970, discussed *below* note 217 and accompanying text, which has limited application.

(Rel.3—1/07 Pub.62410)

authorized the armed forces to grant immunity. Dealing with this issue in 1964 in *United States v. Kirsch*,[210] the Court of Military Appeals held that it perceived "a Congressional grant of power to provide immunity from prosecution in the provisions of the Uniform Code; and a valid delineation of a method by which to exercise the power in the *Manual for Courts-Martial*."[211] In *Kirsch*, the court reasoned that, inasmuch as the Uniform Code provides the convening authority with the power to overturn a conviction,[212] and thus through the right against double jeopardy, the power to absolutely protect an accused from criminal sanction, a convening authority need not actually try an accused and overturn a conviction to grant immunity to a servicemember.[213] The court also noted that Congress was well aware of the various *Manuals for Courts-Martial* and regulations providing for immunity and had failed to object to the military's interpretation of the law.[214]

Although expressly recognizing the power of a convening authority to grant immunity, the court made it clear that immunity could not be granted for offenses over which military courts lack jurisdiction,[215] and thus, implicitly, a convening authority cannot grant immunity to persons not subject to trial by court-martial.[216]

Although *Kirsch* remains the dispositive case in this area, enactment of the Organized Crime Control Act of 1970[217] complicated matters substantially. The Act centralized in the Attorney General the federal government's power to grant immunity and could be read to deprive the armed forces of any general power to grant immunity due to the absence of express reference to courts-martial. Although the military departments could, as federal agencies, obtain the Attorney General's permission to grant immunity to a witness,[218] one commentator, after a thorough examination of the legislative history of the Act, could find no reason

---

[210] 35 C.M.R. 56 (C.M.A. 1964).

[211] 35 C.M.R. at 62–63 (C.M.A. 1964).

[212] *See* U.C.M.J. art. 64.

[213] 35 C.M.R. at 64.

[214] 35 C.M.R. at 66. The present *Manual* provisions referring to immunity are R.C.M. 704 and Mil. R. Evid. 301(c)(1). Only a general court-martial convening authority may grant immunity within the armed forces. R.C.M. 704(c)(1); United States v. Villines, 13 M.J. 46, 53 (C.M.A. 1982); United States v. Joseph, 11 M.J. 333, 334 (C.M.A. 1981). *But see* United States v. Villines, 13 M.J. 46, 61– 62 (C.M.A. 1982) (Everett, C. J., dissenting). Immunity may be granted, of course, by the Attorney General pursuant to statute.

[215] 35 C.M.R. at 68.

[216] Immunity may be granted to such persons pursuant to the Organized Crime Control Act of 1970, 18 U.S.C. §§ 6001–05. *See, e.g.*, United States v. Andreas, 14 M.J. 483, 485–86 (C.M.A. 1983).

[217] 18 U.S.C. §§ 6001–05.

[218] 18 U.S.C. §§ 6001, 6004.

(Rel.3—1/07　Pub.62410)

to believe that the Act was intended to affect the armed forces in any other fashion.[219] Notwithstanding this, then Assistant Attorney General Rehnquist, Office of Legal Counsel, having opined that courts-martial constitute "proceedings before an agency" within the meaning of the Act, but that the Act had not repealed the armed forces' powers to grant immunity under *Kirsch*, stated that immunity could not be granted without the consent of the Attorney General in any case in which the Department of Justice might have an interest.[220] Although in accord with the Act's spirit, such a result hardly seems possible in view of the finding that the Act did not repeal the military's power to grant immunity and the absence in the legislative history of any intent to affect the armed forces.

At present, the assumption is that Congress has implicitly granted the armed forces the power to grant immunity to any servicemember who may be tried by court-martial for the offense about which the member will testify, but that the immunity must be obtained under the Organized Crime Control Act of 1970 whenever the case has Department of Justice interest. Given (later) Chief Justice Rehnquist's findings, the latter requirement, albeit an excellent policy decision, appears a legal nullity. The real question is whether the armed forces in fact have power to grant immunity.[221] Assuming that federal statute has not deprived the military of that power, one must reexamine *Kirsch*. Concededly, the court's holding in *Kirsch* is unusual and somewhat tortured, and the court need not have concluded as it did. The court could easily have held that, although a convening authority could in effect grant immunity, the Code did not authorize the issuance of such a grant absent trial.[222] The weight of legal history does support *Kirsch*, however, and, as the armed forces are part of the federal government, it would also appear reasonable to conclude that a grant of transactional immunity[223] properly issued by the armed forces is binding on the remainder of the federal government and the states.[224] Any future revision of the Uniform Code of

---

[219] Green, *above* note 205, at 29–31.

[220] Coast Guard Law Bulletin No. 413, setting forth the 22 September 1971 memorandum of the Assistant Attorney General, Office of Legal Counsel (William H. Rehnquist), *reprinted in part in* VI Criminal Law Materials 32–50 (The Judge Advocate General's School, U.S. Army 1981).

[221] *But see* United States v. Villines, 13 M.J. 46, 61 (C.M.A. 1982) (Everett, C. J., dissenting) (noting that the assumption that 18 U.S.C. §§ 6001–05 (1976) did not preempt the military's power to grant immunity is not indisputable).

[222] *See* Green, *above* note 205, at 26–27.

[223] *Kirsch* dealt with a grant of transactional immunity. Although not fully resolved it appears that the armed forces may use grants of testimonial immunity as well as grants of transactional immunity. *See* Section 20-23.32.

[224] U.C.M.J. art. 76. In relevant part, Article 76 declares that the "proceedings . . . of courtmartial as approved, reviewed, or affirmed as required by this chapter . . . are final and conclusive." This interpretation of Article 76 may be erroneous, in that the Article clearly is intended to deal with the finality and effects of convictions. Given that immunity in the armed forces is ultimately based upon the effects of Articles 64 and 76, and the constitutional prohibition against double

Military Justice should resolve this matter, however, by creating express statutory authority for the armed forces to grant immunity. At present, the military system is clearly vulnerable to challenge in the federal district courts.

The President, exercising his authority under Article 36 of the Code, has granted the general court-martial convening authority the power to grant immunity to any person subject to the Code. [225] The same convening authority may not grant immunity to a person subject to the Code who might be prosecuted in a United States district court, however, unless authorized to do so by the Attorney General or his designee. [226] The authority to grant immunity may not be further delegated, but this limitation does not appear to prevent a special court-martial convening authority from entering into a pretrial agreement with the accused setting forth a provision that the accused promises to testify in another courtmartial.

Implied immunity or "de facto" immunity may result if an agent of the convening authority promises that in return for certain disclosures the suspect will not be prosecuted. [227] The Court of Military Appeals did not hesitate to

---

jeopardy, however, Article 76 might reasonably be interpreted to reach this far. If not, a grant of immunity in the armed forces should act to bar the use of testimony, and the product thereof, by a state or the federal government. New Jersey v. Portash, 440 U.S. 450 (1979) (grand jury testimony given pursuant to a grant of immunity was involuntary and could not be used for impeachment of the declarant at his later trial); Murphy v. Waterfront Comm'n, 378 U.S. 52 (1964).

[225] R.C.M. 704(c)(1).

[226] R.C.M. 704(c)(1). The Discussion to the Rule notes:

When testimony or a statement for which a person subject to the code may be granted immunity may relate to an offense for which that person could be prosecuted in a United States district court, immunity should not be granted without prior coordination with the Department of Justice. Ordinarily coordination with the local United States Attorney is appropriate. Unless the Department of Justice indicates it has no interest in the case, authorization for the grant of immunity should be sought from the Attorney General. A request for such authorization should be forwarded through the office of the Judge Advocate General concerned. Service regulations may provide additional guidance. Even if the Department of Justice expresses no interest in the case, authorization by the Attorney General for the grant of immunity may be necessary to compel the person to testify or make a statement if such testimony or statement would make the person liable for a Federal civilian offense.

[227] See, e.g., United States v. Jones, 52 M.J. 60, 65-67 (C.A.A.F. 1999) (de facto immunity arises when there is an after-the-fact determination based on a promise by a government official not to prosecute the individual); United States v. Spence, 29 M.J. 630 (A.F.C.M.R. 1989) (each case is fact specific) "When competent Air Force officials appointed to deal with child abuse expressly or implicitly promise an individual for some eight months that he will be placed in therapy rather than prosecuted, we will enforce the promise. The Air Force cannot break its word." 29 M.J. 637 (A.F.C.M.R. 1989) (emphasis omitted). Compare Spence with United States v. Kimble, 30 M.J. 892, 895 (A.F.C.M.R. 1990) and United States v. Flemmi, 225 F.3d 78 (1st Cir. 2000) (FBI's agents promises of immunity are not binding).

(Rel.3—1/07   Pub.62410)

enforce such promises. [228] In *United States v. Churnovic*, [229] for example, Chief Judge Everett [230] opined that he would enforce a promise of immunity made to the accused by a senior noncommissioned officer (NCO) who was expressly given that authority by the ship's executive officer. [231] However, for a promise of immunity to be enforceable, Judge Everett wrote that the accused must have reasonably relied upon it to his detriment, and that in his opinion a sailor suspected of murder or some similar offense could not reasonably rely upon a promise by his captain that he would not be prosecuted in return for information. [232] Judge Everett decided, however, that a sailor can rely on a grant of immunity from a captain for offenses that the captain normally would have the power to dispose of, such as the ones at issue (introducing hashish, possession of hashish with the intent to distribute, and wrongfully using hashish).

Of course, an express or implied promise of immunity obtained by fraud would not be enforceable. [233] In *Churnovic*, the authority of the senior NCO who talked to the accused was unclear. Judge Everett indicated that the defense has the burden of establishing the existence of a binding promise of transactional immunity. [234]

---

[228] Cooke v. Orser, 12 M.J. 335 (C.M.A. 1982). The court enforced a promise of immunity made by a staff judge advocate. *See also* Samples v. Vest, 38 M.J. 482 (C.M.A. 1994) (in dictum recognized de facto immunity); United States v. Kimble, 33 M.J. 284 (C.M.A. 1991) (special courtmartial convening authority's decision that any trial would be held binding by civilian authorities when transmitted to and relied upon by the accused); United States v. Brown, 13 M.J. 253 (C.M.A. 1982) (The court enforced an informal agreement set forth by the staff judge advocate who had been instructed to do that by the convening authority). Whether a given government activity or program should result in immunity or its functional equivalent may require careful regulatory analysis. *See, e.g.*, United States v. Corcoran, 40 M.J. 478 (C.M.A. 1994) (DOD Family advocacy program did not provide immunity from prosecution).

[229] 22 M.J. 401 (C.M.A. 1986).

[230] Judge Sullivan did not participate, and Judge Cox concurred in the result.

[231] Judge Everett indicated that he could logically infer from the record that the executive officer gave the authority with the full knowledge of the convening authority, the ship's captain. *Compare Churnovic with* Cunningham v. Gilevich, 36 M.J. 94 (C.M.A. 1992) (denying writs of prohibition and mandamus). In *Cunningham*, the court, allegedly applying prior law, decided that petitioners did not carry their burden of showing that their commander "'unequivocally promised' with the implicit approval of his superiors, that they would not be prosecuted if they testified before . . . [investigating boards]." 36 M.J. at 101 (C.M.A. 1992). "Unlike [those cases] . . . petitioner's case involves a situation in which the superior did not suspect his subordinates of wrongdoing. Those cases involved an offer of immunity which presumed some culpability on the part of the offeree." 36 M.J. at 100 (C.M.A. 1992). However, command emphasis and continuing efforts to get them to testify violated Article 31, and under Article 31(d) no prosecution could take place based even in part on their board testimony or its derivative evidence.

[232] 22 M.J. at 405. Query: should this result follow when the captain is a senior officer, or when circumstances, such as a combat environment, might justify reliance?

[233] 22 M.J. at 407.

[234] 22 M.J. at 407.

(Rel.3—1/07 Pub.62410)

The remedy to be afforded an accused given de facto immunity has been disputed. Judge Cox, for example, urged that rather than prohibiting an entire prosecution, a fruit of the poisonous tree approach should be used, which would permit the prosecution but suppress any evidence obtained from the de facto immunity.[235] Although such an approach seems appropriate when only the pragmatic results to the accused are concerned, *i.e.*, the accused is in no worse shape than before the de facto "grant," in those few cases in which command channels are directly involved the government ought to be bound by its promise.[236]

§ 20-23.32   The Nature of the Immunity Required

§ 20-23.32(a)   In General

Following civilian precedent, military grants of immunity extended transactional immunity[237] until the Supreme Court's 1972 decision in *Kastigar v. United States*,[238] in which it held that only testimonial immunity is necessary to overcome the Fifth Amendment privilege. The ability of the armed forces to grant testimonial immunity since *Kastigar* is unclear. The promulgation of the Military Rules of Evidence expressly authorized the granting of testimonial immunity,[239] but the President's rulemaking power under Article 36 of the Code does not extend to violating a congressional statute.[240] Further, members of the armed forces have been granted a statutory right against self-incrimination which, for much of its history, had been held to be broader than the Fifth Amendment privilege.[241] The legislative history of the statutory privilege suggests that, in

---

[235] United States v. Kimble, 33 M.J. 284, 293–94 (C.M.A. 1991) (special court-martial convening authority's decision that any trial would be by civilian authorities held binding by majority when transmitted to and relied upon by the accused) (Cox, J. dissenting).

[236] *Compare Kimble, above* note 235, *with* United States v. Zupkofska, 34 M.J. 537 (A.F.C.M.R. 1991) (lack of promise by commander and judge's suppression of statements made by accused pursuant to agent's remarks significant in deciding not to recognize de facto immunity).

[237] Under transactional immunity, a witness is granted immunity from prosecution for any transaction or offense concerning which the witness testified.

[238] 406 U.S. 441 (1972).

[239] Mil. R. Evid. 301(c)(1). *See also* United States v. Villines, 13 M.J. 46, 60 (C.M.A. 1982) (Everett, C. J., dissenting).

[240] U.C.M.J. art 36(a) ("Pretrial, trial, and post-trial procedures . . . may be prescribed by the President by regulations which shall . . . not be contrary to or inconsistent with this chapter.").

[241] *See generally* Lederer, *Rights Warnings in the Armed Services*, 72 Mil. R. Evid. 1, 2–9 (1976). *But see* United States v. Armstrong, 9 M.J. 374 (C.M.A. 1980), in which Chief Judge Everett rejected earlier holdings, while Judges Cook and Fletcher stated that nothing in the case required the court to reexamine the settled construction of Article 31; that the Article "has a broader sweep than the Fifth Amendment." 9 M.J. at 384 (quoting United States v. Ruiz, 23 C.M.A. 181, 182, 48 C.M.R. 797, 798 (1974)). The court has clearly narrowed the scope of Article 31, however, United States v. Armstrong, 9 M.J. 374 (C.M.A. 1980); United States v. Lloyd, 10 M.J. 172 (C.M.A. 1982).

(Rel.3—1/07 Pub.62410)

relevant part, it was indeed intended merely to echo the Fifth Amendment privilege,[242] in which case the Court's holding in *Kastigar* would clearly apply to the armed forces. However, the holdings of the Court of Military Appeals create some uncertainty. Until fairly recently, the court repeatedly held that the statutory right was more protective than the constitutional one. Although the court has since either rejected or modified this position,[243] enough doubt exists that a reasonable argument can be mounted to the effect that the statutory right requires transactional immunity, especially since the present statutory right and all of its predecessors were enacted during the period in which transactional immunity was viewed as constitutionally necessary to overcome the Fifth Amendment privilege.[244] The issue may have been resolved, however, in *United States v. Villines*,[245] in which a fragmented Court of Military Appeals appears to have accepted the granting of testimonial immunity by a general court-martial-convening authority.[246] Rule for Courts-Martial 704(a) expressly accepts testimonial immunity.

§ 20-23.32(b) Threat of Prosecution in a Foreign Jurisdiction

For immunity to overcome the right against self-incrimination, it must, at minimum, successfully protect the witness against any use of the testimony given pursuant to the grant, including any derivative use thereof.[247] Even if a military grant of immunity is not binding on the states, either through Article 76 or the Supremacy Clause, the Supreme Court's decision in *Murphy v. Waterfront Commissioner of New York Harbor*[248] would protect the witness from use of the immunized testimony in a state court. The same result will follow if the witness is potentially subject to prosecution in a foreign nation.

The Supreme Court finally held in 1998 that "concern with foreign prosecution is beyond the scope of the Self-incrimination Clause."[249] The issue may not yet be entirely resolved, however. Five justices opined:

---

[242] Lederer, *Rights Warnings in the Armed Services, above* note 241, at 6–9. *See also Lloyd*, 10 M.J. 172; *Armstrong*, 9 M.J. 374.

[243] *See Lloyd*, 10 M.J. 172; 9 M.J. 374.

[244] *See generally* Edward J. Imwinkelried, Paul C. Giannelli, Franic A. Gilligan & Fredric I. Lederer, Courtroom Criminal Evidence § 1730–36 (4th ed. 2006). Some prosecutors may use "pocket immunity," the promise of the prosecutor rather than a proper grant. The Bank of Nova Scotia v. United States, 487 U.S. 250 (1988).

[245] 13 M.J. 46 (C.M.A. 1982). *See also* United States v. Newman, 14 M.J. 474, 481 (C.M.A. 1983) ("our Court has clearly authorized such immunity").

[246] 13 M.J. at 52–54 (Fletcher, J.); 13 M.J. at 56 (Cook, J., concurring in the result); 13 M.J. at 59 (Everett, C. J., dissenting). *See also* United States v. Rivera, 1 M.J. 107 (C.M.A. 1975) (failing to raise the testimonial immunity issue).

[247] Kastigar v. United States, 406 U.S. 441 (1972).

[248] 378 U.S. 52 (1964).

[249] United States v. Balsys, 524 U.S. 666, 669 (1998).

This is not to say that cooperative conduct between the United States and foreign nations could not develop to a point at which a claim could be made for recognizing fear of foreign prosecution under the Self-incrimination Clause as traditionally understood. If it could be said that the United States and its allies had enacted substantially similar criminal codes aimed at prosecuting offenses of international character, and if it could be shown that the United States was granting immunity from domestic prosecution for the purpose of obtaining evidence to be delivered to other nations as prosecutors of a crime common to both countries, then an argument could be made that the Fifth Amendment should apply based on fear of foreign prosecution simply because that prosecution was not fairly characterized as distinctly "foreign." The point would be that the prosecution was as much on behalf of the United States as of the prosecuting nation, so that the division of labor between evidence-gatherer and prosecutor made one nation the agent of the other, rendering fear of foreign prosecution tantamount to fear of a criminal case brought by the Government itself.

Whether such an argument should be sustained may be left at the least for another day, since its premises do not fit this case.[250]

With Justice Stevens concurring, and Justices Breyer and Ginsburg dissenting in favor of application of the right to risk of overseas prosecution, cooperative law enforcement abroad may well trigger the privilege.

The Supreme Court's result is consistent with the long standing interpretation of the scope of the statutory military right against self-incrimination, Article 31.[251]

The question of application of the right against self-incrimination to *military* personnel who fear foreign prosecution is not entirely foreclosed, however. Given the concerns of some of the justices about cooperative law enforcement abroad, the close working relationships that sometimes exist between American military authorities and host nations might trigger Fifth Amendment application.

To the extent that these holdings are correct as they relate to civilian life,[252] they hardly seem applicable to the armed forces. Testimony before military proceedings, including the functional equivalent of the grand jury — the Article 32 proceeding[253] — is almost never secret. Furthermore, servicemembers are

---

[250] 524 U.S. at 697-99 (1998).

[251] United States v. Murphy, 21 C.M.R. 158 (C.M.A. 1956).

[252] At the heart of the question is the probability of successful overseas prosecution. This necessarily requires one to determine not only foreign law but also the probability of overseas interest in prosecution and the probability that the jurisdiction can reach the American accused. In *Flanagan*, the witness held joint U.S. and Irish citizenship and was an unindicted co-conspirator in a plan to ship weapons to Ireland and Great Britain. The trial judge held that both Ireland and Northern Ireland enforced their laws, implicitly making prosecution likely.

[253] U.C.M.J. art. 32.

subject to involuntary transfer to virtually any nation in the world. Indeed, trial may be taking place in a country with an interest in trying the accused.[254] Consequently, the civilian law seems inapposite. In 1956, the Court of Military Appeals was faced with a threat of foreign prosecution[255] when an accused complained that a Korean civilian witness was erroneously forced to testify at his court-martial despite his fear of Japanese prosecution. In dicta, not joined by any other member of the court, Judge Latimer stated that both the constitutional and statutory[256] rights against self-incrimination extended "only to 'a reasonable fear or prosecution' under the law of the United States."[257]

The right against self-incrimination is a favored right under American law. Although the government does have a right to "every man's evidence," that right is contingent on the right to remain silent. Where potential foreign prosecution is possible, at least when that prosecution is a consequence of military service, the privileges against self-incrimination should apply absent immunity that is effective to prevent the use or derivative use of immunized testimony in a prosecution in any jurisdiction, domestic or foreign.

§ 20-23.33 Consequences of Granting Immunity

§ 20-23.33(a) At Trial

Pursuant to the Military Rules of Evidence:

> When a prosecution witness . . . has been granted immunity or leniency in exchange for testimony, the grant shall be reduced to writing and shall be served on the accused prior to arraignment or within a reasonable time before the witness testifies. If notification is not made as required by this rule, the military judge may grant a continuance until notification is made, prohibit or strike the testimony of the witness, or enter such other order as may be required.[258]

The rule thus ensures the defense a meaningful opportunity to cross-examine the immunized prosecution witness. The Rule is taken from the decision of the Court

---

[254] A foreign host nation clearly has an interest in trying an American servicemember who has violated its laws or injured its people. The United States has negotiated status of forces agreements or concluded executive agreements with many host nations that generally result in court-martial of nearly all such offenders. However, a foreign trial is a clear possibility and in some countries, for some types of offenses, a probability.

[255] United States v. Murphy, 21 C.M.R. 158 (C.M.A. 1956).

[256] U.C.M.J. art. 31.

[257] 21 C.M.R. at 163 (citing Slochower v. Board of Education, 350 U.S. 551 (1956)). Judge Latimer's reliance on *Slochower* was misplaced.

[258] Mil. R. Evid. 301(c)(2).

(Rel.3—1/07 Pub.62410)

of Military Appeals in *United States v. Webster,* [259] and its analysis states that disclosure should be made prior to arraignment. [260]

§ 20-23.33(b) To the Immunized Witness

When the witness has been granted transactional immunity, the witness may not be later prosecuted by the armed forces [261] for any offense included within the grant. [262] When the witness has been given testimonial immunity, [263] the witness may later be prosecuted, but only if the prosecution can adequately show in court, by evidence, [264] that the government has not relied on the immunized testimony or any product thereof. [265] It appears from the decision of the Court of Military Appeals in *United States v. Rivera* [266] that the Court of Appeals for the Armed Forces will strictly hold the government to this requirement, and probably would not allow the government to prosecute a previously immunized witness without being able to prove that the case preparation was complete prior to the witness' testimony pursuant to the grant. [267] Even then, the trial counsel

---

[259] 1 M.J. 216 (C.M.A. 1975).

[260] Analysis of the Military Rules of Evidence, 1980 Amendments to the *Manual for Courts-Martial,* 1969, Analysis of Rule 301(c)(2), *reprinted in* MCM, 2005, A22-6.

[261] It is unclear whether the accused could be prosecuted lawfully by a civilian jurisdiction. *See* Section 20-23.31.

[262] The accused may be prosecuted for committing perjury while testifying pursuant to the immunity grant. *See* United States v. Olivero, 39 M.J. at 250–51 (C.M.A. 1994) (but finding inadequate proof of perjury). For discussion of why transactional immunity wasn't given to a "Tailhook" accused, *see* Samples v. Vest, 38 M.J. 482 (C.M.A. 1994).

[263] Testimonial immunity protects the witness against subsequent use of the testimony and any product derivative of it with the possible exception of the discovery of a live witness as a result. *Cf.* United States v. Ceccolini, 435 U.S. 268 (1978). Testimonial immunity is sometimes known as "use plus fruits" immunity.

[264] The rules of evidence may not apply to this showing. Mil. R. Evid. 104(a). It is unclear, however, whether either Federal or Military Rule of Evidence 104(a) applies in determinations involving constitutional rights.

[265] Mil. R. Evid. 301(c)(1). *See* United States v. McGeeney, 44 M.J. 418 (C.A.A.F. 1996) (government met its heavy burden to establish non-use of immunized testimony; United States v. Rivera, 1 M.J. 107 (C.M.A. 1975) (seminal case). *See also* United States v. Pielago, 135 F.3d 703, 707 (11th Cir. 1998) (that some immunized testimony is employed to obtain an indictment does not require *per se* rule of dismissal); United States v. Allen, 59 M.J. 478 (C.A.A.F. 2004) (government used independently volunteered evidence). In *McGeeney, above,* Judge Crawford, concurring in the result, opined that an immunity grant "does not preclude the non-evidentiary use of immunized testimony." 44 M.J. at 424.

[266] 1 M.J. 107 (C.M.A. 1975). *See also* United States v. Boyd, 27 M.J. 82 (C.M.A. 1988) (government did not carry its burden by only having the staff judge advocate, assistant staff judge advocate, and investigator testify. No cocaine charges were brought against the accused until after he testified at Wills' trial and Wills agreed to testify against the accused); United States v. Whitehead, 5 M.J. 294 (C.M.A. 1978).

[267] As to the scope in the civilian federal courts of "nonevidentiary use" of immunized testi-

(Rel.3—1/07 Pub.62410)

must be shown to be unaware of the nature of the testimony given under the grant.[268] A subsequently prosecuted witness may raise a prior immunity grant on a motion to dismiss.[269] Given the government's responsibility to *prove*[270] nonuse of immunized testimony, in a substantial case it will likely be difficult for the government to successfully prosecute an accused who has previously given immunized testimony. Further, the Court of Military Appeals held that "the Government may not *prosecute* unless it can show, by a preponderance of the evidence, that the prosecutorial decision was untainted by the immunized testimony."[271]

The prosecution is not precluded from prosecuting an immunized witness when the government's criminal investigation is complete prior to the grant of immunity. Even if the investigation was not complete, if all of the evidence admitted by the prosecution was obtained independently, there is no violation of the Fifth Amendment. The government might meet its burden of proof by sealing the testimony that was immunized and allowing no access to the prosecutor. When the investigation is complete, the prosecution should seal the investigation until a motion is made at the time of trial. Additionally, the government might establish that the immunized testimony did not add to its case.

---

mony, including its use as investigatory leads and refreshment of witness memory, *see* United States v. North, 910 F.2d 843, 856–73 (D.C. Cir. 1990). This rule may not extend so far as to prevent use of a new witness discovered via the immunized testimony, *see* United States v. Ceccolini, 435 U.S. 268 (1978), although any logical analysis of the right against self-incrimination would result in exclusion of such evidence.

[268] Knowledge of the probable nature of a witness' response that permits highly useful trial preparation should be considered improper fruit of the immunized testimony. *See* United States v. Rivera, 1 M.J. 107 (C.M.A. 1975). *See also* United States v. Lucas, 25 M.J. 9 (C.M.A. 1987) (if judge becomes aware of the issue of the use of immunized testimony, judge should ask defense counsel if they want to raise the issue.); United States v. Garrett, 24 M.J. 413 (C.M.A. 1987) (trial counsels not essential witnesses as to independent basis for government's evidence at retrial when the parties stipulated to their expected testimony). *See also* United States v. North, 910 F.2d 843, 856–73 (D.C. Cir. 1990).

[269] R.C.M. 907(b)(2)(D)(ii); United States v. Hampton, 775 F.2d 1479, 1488 (11th Cir. 1985) (where testimony of an immunized witness enables the government to build a case against his coconspirator, who consequently strikes a plea bargain with prosecutors and agrees to testify against the immunized witness, the testimony of the co-conspirator must be deemed to have been indirectly derived from the testimony of the immunized witness in violation of *Kastigar*).

[270] *See, e.g.,* United States v. North, 910 F.2d 843, 856–73 (D.C. Cir.), *modified and reh'g denied,* 920 F.2d 940 (D.C. Cir. 1990) (en banc), *cert. denied,* 500 U.S. 59359 U.S.L.W. 3793 (U.S. May 28, 01991), discussing the necessary scope of *Kastigar* hearings. Prior to *North,* the military case law seemed the most beneficial to the accused in the nation. *Cf.* United States v. McGeeney, 44 M.J. 418 (C.A.A.F. 1996); Cunningham v. Gilevich, 36 M.J. 94 (C.M.A. 1992).

[271] United States v. Olivero, 39 M.J. 246, 249 (C.M.A. 1994), citing United States v. Kimble, 33 M.J. 284 (C.M.A. 1991). *See also* United States v. McGeeney, 44 M.J. 418 (C.A.A.F. 1996); United States v. Corcoran, 40 M.J. 478 (C.M.A. 1994) (DOD family advocacy program did not provide immunity from prosecution.).

(Rel.3—1/07   Pub.62410)

An accused's failure to affirmatively move to dismiss on the ground that the decision to prosecute resulted from an improper use of immunized testimony may constitute waiver.[272] In such a case, an appellate court will conduct a plain error evaluation;[273] only if plain error existed will the court grant relief.

If the government's burden is not made too onerous, the government may be more willing in the future to grant use immunity.[274] The gist of using or granting immunity is that the government must not obtain an unfair advantage over the accused or person who has been granted the immunized testimony. A previously immunized accused may not be impeached at trial with testimony given pursuant to the grant, as such testimony is deemed coerced and involuntary.[275]

Immunized material is inadmissible against the accused at a later trial (except for perjury while testifying under the grant), whether that evidence is offered on the merits or for impeachment of the formerly immunized accused.[276] The accused may waive an immunity grant's protection, however. In *United States v. Vith*,[277] the accused, pursuant to a grant of immunity, testified against a coactor. Vith was later prosecuted and convicted of his own offenses. He then submitted a request for clemency to the convening authority, a request that included a discussion of what Vith claimed he had done pursuant to the grant, including participation in a controlled drug buy. The staff judge advocate responded by submitting in rebuttal three pages of testimony from the co-actor's trial, including one page of Vith's immunized testimony. The court resolved Vith's complaint that the convening authority had lost his impartiality by exposure to the immunized testimony:

> We hold that the Fifth Amendment does not shield a person from a *legitimate response* to his adverse allegation concerning the *immunity process* or the *terms of the immunity grant* because these matters are collateral to a criminal trial.[278]

§ 20-23.33(c)   Post-trial

Within the armed forces, immunity may only be granted by the convening authority[279] or by the action of a convening authority.[280] From 1958 until 1983,

[272] United States v. Allen, 59 M.J. 478 (C.A.A.F. 2004), *citing* R.C.M. 907(b)(2)(D)(ii).

[273] 59 M.J. at 478.

[274] United States v. Gardner, 22 M.J. 28 (C.M.A. 1986).

[275] New Jersey v. Portash, 440 U.S. 450 (1979).

[276] New Jersey v. Portash, 440 U.S. 450, 459 (1979).

[277] 34 M.J. 277, 279 (C.M.A. 1992).

[278] 34 M.J. at 279 (C.M.A. 1992) (emphasis in original). Although the majority did not use waiver to reach its result, waiver seems applicable.

[279] The convening authority may grant immunity to any servicemember subject to referral of charges and trial by that convening authority. *See* Section 20-23.31.

(Rel.3—1/07 Pub.62410)

the Court of Military Appeals reasoned that it was unlikely that a convening authority would grant or obtain immunity for a witness who was not expected to testify truthfully. Consequently, it had consistently held that, by granting immunity, the convening authority[281] and staff judge advocate[282] involved in the grant were disqualified from taking post-trial actions. The Court repudiated this doctrine in its entirety in *United States v. Newman*,[283] reasoning that the advent of testimonial immunity coupled with the adoption of Military Rule of Evidence 607, which provides that a party may impeach his or her own witnesses, had eliminated any possibility that a convening authority or staff judge advocate could be viewed as having vouched for a witness' credibility by issuing a grant of immunity. The court did not, however, determine the effect of a grant of transactional immunity, declaring that the "key inquiry is whether [the convening authority's] actions before or during the trial create, or appear to create, a risk that he will be unable to evaluate objectively and impartially all the evidence in the record of trial."[284]

§ 20-30.00 CONFRONTATION AND COMPULSORY PROCESS

§ 20-31.00 In General

From the perspective of an accused, perhaps the most important constitutional protections are the Sixth Amendment rights to confrontation and compulsory process, the rights that, with the right against self-incrimination, epitomize the adversary system. Viewed in general terms, the right to confrontation gives the accused the right to be present at trial[285] and, under normal circumstances, to confront face-to-face[286] the witnesses offered by the prosecution. The right to

---

[280] When a convening authority lacks the power to immunize a witness because that person is not subject to court-martial, immunity may be obtained from the Department of Justice based upon the Organized Crime Control Act of 1970 (18 U.S.C. §§ 6001–05 (1976)). *See Criminal Law Items, Grants of Immunity*, ARMY LAW., Dec. 1973, at 22–25; *Criminal Law Items Addendum*, ARMY LAW., Feb. 1974, at 14.

[281] *See, e.g.*, United States v. Espiet-Betancourt, 1 M.J. 91 (C.M.A. 1975); United States v. Williams, 45 C.M.R. 66 (C.M.A. 1972). *But see* United States v. Griffin, 8 M.J. 66 (C.M.A. 1979) (disqualification is not required when a defense witness is immunized).

[282] *See, e.g.*, United States v. Johnson, 4 M.J. 8 (C.M.A. 1977); United States v. Diaz, 47 C.M.R. 50 (C.M.A. 1972).

[283] 14 M.J. 474 (C.M.A. 1983).

[284] 14 M.J. at 482 (C.M.A. 1983).

[285] Illinois v. Allen, 397 U.S. 337 (1970). *Compare with* Kentucky v. Stincer, 482 U.S. 730 (1987) (exclusion from witness competency hearing did not violate the confrontation clause, as it did not affect his right to effective cross-examination).

[286] Defendants do not have an absolute right to face-to-face confrontation, however. In *Maryland v. Craig*, 497 U.S. 836 (1990), a five-to-four majority of the Supreme Court concluded that the normal preference for face-to-face confrontation would sometimes have to "give way to consider-

(Rel.3—1/07   Pub.62410)

compulsory process gives the defense the right to obtain and present evidence on its behalf. Clearly, the two rights are interdependent and must be viewed together, although Professor Westen has correctly suggested that compulsory process is probably the more important of the two. The right to present defense evidence is likely more valuable than the ability to contest prosecution evidence inasmuch as the former may correct for mistakes in the latter.[287]

Were the Sixth Amendment rights to confrontation and compulsory process, both applicable to courts-martial,[288] to be interpreted in a literal and expansive fashion, it is apparent that present evidentiary and procedural standards would be greatly affected. At the very least, the confrontation right would constitutionalize the hearsay rule and render all hearsay inadmissible. Consequently, it is not surprising that most commentators have rejected such interpretation.[289] The Supreme Court, while also rejecting such literal interpretation,[290] has refused to fully acknowledge the dimensions of the two rights, preferring to deal with confrontation and compulsory process issues on a case-by-case basis, although its 2004 decision in *Crawford v. Washington*[291] may be a sea change. The

---

ations of public policy and the necessities of the case." *Craig*, 497 U.S. at 849 (citing Mattox v. United States, 156 U.S. 237, 243 (1895)). In *Craig*, the Court held that the use of one-way closed circuit television for the testimony of an alleged child-abuse victim who was subject to counsel's cross-examination out of the presence of the defendant did not violate the confrontation clause. In an innovative use of remote two-way testimony via satellite, the Supreme Court of Florida upheld a criminal conviction in which the complainants testified from Argentina, holding that under the federal Confrontation Clause "the procedure must (1) be justified, on a case-specific finding, based on important state interests, public policies, or necessities of the case and (2) must satisfy the other three elements of confrontation — oath, cross-examination, and observation of the witness's demeanor." Harrell v. State, 709 So. 2d 1364 (Fla. 1998), *cert. denied*, 525 U.S. 903 67 U.S.L.W. 3237 (U.S. 1998). *See also* Horn v. Dretke, 2005 U.S. Dist. LEXIS 27951 (E.D. Tex. November 8, 2005)(rejection by state court of defendant's claim that remote testimony of critically ill inmate violated the Confrontation Clause was not "an unreasonable application of clearly established federal law" for habeas purposes). *But see* United States v. Yates, 393 F.3d 1182 (11th Cir. 2004) (testimony of remote prosecution witnesses from Australia violated the Confrontation Clause), *vacated and rehearing en banc granted*, 404 F.3d 1291 (11th Cir. 2005).

[287] Westen, *The Compulsory Process Clause*, 73 Mich. L. Rev. 71, 183 (1974).

[288] The Court of Military Appeals held that the Bill of Rights applies to members of the armed forces unless expressly or implicitly excepted. *See, e.g.*, United States v. Jacoby, 29 C.M.R. 244, 246–47 (C.M.A. 1960). In addition, Article 46 of the Uniform Code of Military Justice provides for equal access to witnesses for the prosecution, defense, and court-martial while providing for compulsory process.

[289] *See, e.g.*, Graham, *The Right of Confrontation and the Hearsay Rule: Sir Walter Raleigh Loses Another One*, 8 Crim. L. Bull. 99 (1972).

[290] *E.g.*, Maryland v. Craig, 497 U.S. 836, 847–48 (1990); Ohio v. Roberts, 448 U.S. 56 (1980); Dutton v. Evans, 400 U.S. 74 (1970).

[291] 541 U.S. 36 (2004)(holding that government use of "testimonial" hearsay violates the Confrontation Clause when the declarant is not subject to cross-examination) and effectively overruling *Ohio v. Roberts*, 448 U.S. 56 (1980). Although the decision is sweeping, the Court failed to define 'testimonial', leaving the issue to subsequent cases. *See, e.g.*, Davis v. Washington, 126 S. Ct. 2266 (2006) (911 calls).

(Rel.3—1/07 Pub.62410)

pragmatic utility of the rights to the defense primarily stems from their unsettled nature. The adversary system that they protect has been incorporated into military criminal law by the Uniform Code of Military Justice [292] and case law. It is in the question of how they affect specific areas of the law, areas that are still unresolved, that they are pragmatically important and present the able defense counsel with significant opportunities. Accordingly, having examined the present procedural mechanisms for procuring evidence, it is appropriate to turn to an examination of the effects of the Sixth Amendment on the procurement and admissibility of evidence. Given that this entire area is a developing one, the focus of this examination is necessarily on the decisions of the Supreme Court rather than the Court of Appeals for the Armed Forces.

Counsel should heed an initial caveat, however. Although these constitutional rights are of great importance to the accused, they may be waived by the defense, [293] and their violation may constitute harmless error, [294] particularly when the defense has made an inadequate record.

§ 20-32.00 The Right of Confrontation

§ 20-32.10 In General

The Sixth Amendment declares: "In all criminal prosecutions, the accused shall enjoy the right . . . to be confronted with the witnesses against him." At a minimum, the right to confrontation gives the accused the right to be present at trial [295] to confront the evidence offered by the government on the issue of

---

[292] See, e.g., U.C.M.J. art. 46. Most of the usual features of the adversary system are arguably inherent in the Uniform Code's provisions for counsel (U.C.M.J. arts. 27, 38) and the right against self-incrimination found in Article 31.

[293] See, e.g., United States v. Dean, 31 M.J. 196, 203 (C.M.A. 1990).

[294] See, e.g., United States v. Ferdinand, 29 M.J. 164, 168 (C.M.A. 1989).

[295] The confrontation right does not extend to the accusation stage of proceedings (see Gerstein v. Pugh, 420 U.S. 103, 119–25 (1975) (implied); McCray v. Illinois, 386 U.S. 300 (1967); Cooper v. California, 386 U.S. 58, 62 n.2 (1967); but see Roviaro v. United States, 353 U.S. 53 (1957) or to the type of sentencing proceedings usually followed by civilian jurisdictions. See Williams v. New York, 337 U.S. 241 (1949). But cf. Gardner v. Florida, 430 U.S. 349 (1977) (plurality opinion) (in cases in which death penalty might be imposed, due process requires that defendant be allowed to inspect evidence used in sentencing); Specht v. Patterson, 386 U.S. 605 (1967) (when special sentencing procedures for specific crimes (e.g., sex offenses) exist, due process requires, inter alia, confrontation of witnesses). See also Fed. R. Crim. P. 32(c).

The peculiar nature of military sentencing (e.g., adversarial and an independent part of the trial) may require application of the right.

The confrontation clause also protects the accused against ex parte proceedings unauthorized under the jurisdiction's law. E.g., Parker v. Gladden, 385 U.S. 363 (1966); Lewis v. United States, 146 U.S. 370 (1892); United States v. Reynolds, 489 F.2d 4 (6th Cir. 1973) (harmless error on facts). However, the right to be present at trial does not merely incorporate the jurisdiction's law

(Rel.3—1/07 Pub.62410)

guilt or innocence [296] unless the accused has waived that right in some fashion. [297]

Defendants do not have an absolute right to confront adverse witnesses face-to-face. [298] In *Maryland v. Craig*, [299] a five-to-four majority of the Supreme Court concluded that the normal preference for face-to-face confrontation would sometimes have to "give way to considerations of public policy and the necessities of the case." [300] The Court held that the use of one-way closed-circuit television for the testimony of an alleged child-abuse victim who was subject to counsel's cross-examination out of the presence of the defendant did not violate the confrontation clause. *Craig* was followed by the Court of Military Appeals in *United States v. Thompson*, [301] in which two members of the court, sustaining

by reference, but stands as an independent standard of the validity of local statutes that allow trial in absentia. *See In re Oliver*, 333 U.S. 257 (1948); § 14-63.10.

Determinations involving the identity of informants are likely to involve *ex parte* hearings. *E.g.*, United States v. Straughter, 950 F.2d 1223, 1231–32 (6th Cir. 1991) (judge may conduct *in camera* hearing as to disclosure of informant's identity); United States v. Johns, 948 F.2d 599, 606 (9th Cir. 1991) (no right to be present at *in camera Franks* hearing when there is fear for informant's safety); People v. Castillo, 80 N.Y.2d 578, 607 N.E.2d 1050 (1992) (four-step process in judging the constitutionality of *in camera* hearing of informant on probable cause for search warrant issued by judge who personally examined the informant).

[296] *See* Snyder v. Massachusetts, 291 U.S. 97 (1934); Dowdell v. United States, 221 U.S. 325 (1911) (interpretation of the Philippines' Bill of Rights). *See also* United States v. Silverman, 976 F.2d 1502 (6th Cir. 1992) (en banc) (confrontation clause does not apply under federal sentencing guidelines); United States v. Wise, 976 F.2d 393 (8th Cir. 1992) (en banc) (same).

[297] Voluntary absence from trial after arraignment permits trial in absentia. Taylor v. United States, 414 U.S. 17 (1973) (per curiam); United States v. Tortora, 464 F.2d 1202 (2d Cir. 1972). *Compare* United States v. Peebles, 3 M.J. 177 (C.M.A. 1977) (absence held to be involuntary) *with* United States v. Condon, 3 M.J. 782 (A.C.M.R. 1977) (voluntary absence). In a trial in absentia, the judge might instruct court members that they can draw no inference of guilt from the defendant's absence. *See generally* Section 16-20.00. The conduct of the accused may also constitute an implicit waiver of the right to be present. Illinois v. Allen, 397 U.S. (1970); United States v. Cook, 43 C.M.R. 344 (C.M.A. 1971). *See generally* R.C.M. 804, Presence of the accused at trial proceedings.

[298] *See, e.g.*, Kentucky v. Stincer, 482 U.S. 730 (987).

[299] 496 U.S. 836 (1990); United States v. Longstreath, 45 M.J. 366 (C.A.A.F. 1996) (permitted one-way closed circuit TV when victim's testimony was audible and visible in courtroom); United States v. Daulton, 45 M.J. 2122 (C.A.A.F. 1996) (removing defendant from courtroom while not allowing continuous communication between counsel violated the defendant's assistance of counsel and right of confrontation and the error was not harmless beyond a reasonable doubt).

[300] 496 U.S. 681 (1990) (citing Mattox v. United States, 156 U.S. 237, 243 (1895)). *Compare Craig with* Coy v. Iowa, 47 U.S. 1012 (1988) (no individualized findings that witnesses needed special protections; Court declined to define any evidentiary prerequisites such as less restrictive alternatives). *See also* Harrell v. State, 709 So. 2d 1364 (Fla. 1998); *cert. denied*, 525 U.S. 903 67 U.S.L.W. 3237 (U.S. 1998), *above* note 277.

[301] 31 M.J. 168 (C.M.A. 1990). *See also* United States v. Williams, 37 M.J. 289 (C.M.A. 1993) (confrontation not violated when child seated so that a full side profile of the witness was visible to accused).

(Rel.3—1/07 Pub.62410)

a procedure by which minor witnesses testified with their backs to the accused, emphasized that the military judge had found that special procedures were necessary to protect the child witnesses.[302] Concurring, Chief Judge Everett interpreted *Craig* as permitting a change from the norm of face-to-face confrontation "only if literal confrontation will cause such emotional trauma that the child cannot reasonably communicate information to the trier of fact."[303] Other, similar, cases can be expected.[304] Both the Rules for Courts-Martial and the Military Rules of Evidence have now been amended to expressly permit remote child witness testimony.[305] The Court of Appeals for the Armed Forces has sustained a trial judge's finding that remote video was a necessary medium for the testimony of an 11 year-old rape victim.[306] Whether remote two-way testimony by government witnesses complies with the Confrontation Clause remains unclear.[307]

Presumably, the framers intended the confrontation right to have some greater import than merely the right of the accused to face those witnesses the government chooses to call at trial. Thus far, the Supreme Court has been unwilling to hold that the confrontation clause provides the accused with a pretrial right to obtain evidence for use at trial.[308] The question, then, is how far, if at all, the Sixth Amendment protects the accused at trial against admission of various forms of evidence.[309] Insofar as testimonial government hearsay is concerned,

---

[302] 31 M.J. 173 (C.M.A. 1990).

[303] 31 M.J. 173 (C.M.A. 1990).

[304] *See, e.g.,* United States v. States, 45 M.J. 366 (C.A.A.F. 1996); United States v. Daulton, 45 M.J. 212 (C.A.A.F. 1996); United States v. Helms, 39 M.J. 908, 911 (N.M.C.M.R. 1993) (dictum that two-way video link for child sexual abuse witness to testify from library across hall from courtroom was proper); United States v. Romey, 29 M.J. 795 (A.C.M.R. 1989), *aff'd,* 32 M.J. 180 (C.M.A. 1991) (child victim whispered answers to counsel's questions to mother who then "relayed" them); United States v. Bramel, 29 M.J. 958 (A.C.M.R. 1990) (permissible at Article 32 investigation to place partition between victim and accused). *See generally* Harrell v. State, 709 So. 2d 1364 (Fla. 1998), *cert .denied,* 525 U.S. 903 (1998).

[305] R.C.M. 914A and Mil. R. Evid. 611(d) as amended in the 1999 Change to the Manual for Courts-Martial.

[306] United States v. McCollum, 58 M.J. 323 (C.A.A.F. 2003) (as a consequence of the judge's ruling the accused voluntarily absented himself from the courtroom and observed the proceedings via one-way television).

[307] *See* note 277 *above; see generally* Fredric Lederer, *The Potential Use of Courtroom Technology in Major Terrorism Cases,* 12 WM & Mary Bill Rts. J. 887 906-25 (2004).

[308] Pennsylvania v. Ritchie, 480 U.S. 39 (1987) (four-member plurality held that confrontation is a *trial* right; compulsory process right is no greater than that afforded by due process).

[309] For an outstanding analysis of this matter in conjunction with the compulsory process clauses, see Westen, *Confrontation and Compulsory Process: A Unified Theory of Evidence for Criminal Cases,* 91 Harv. L. Rev. 567, 570 (1978) [hereinafter cited as *Confrontation and Compulsory Process*].

(Rel.3—1/07 Pub.62410)

the Supreme Court may have resolved the issue, at least for the present, by holding that the Confrontation Clause bars all such hearsay.[310]

§ 20-32.20   The Right to Compel the Government to Produce Witnesses Whose Statements Are Used at Trial

§ 20-32.21   In General

Construed narrowly, the right to be present at trial is of use to the defendant only because the accused is thus aware of the government's evidence and is thereby enabled to prepare and present a defense. If this were the limits of the Sixth Amendment, however, the government could subject the defendant to "trial by affidavit," as long as the defendant was faced with the evidence in court. Yet, it has been obvious since the earliest confrontation cases that the prohibition of trials by affidavit is a basic concept of confrontation.[311] Consequently, the Sixth Amendment must limit the government's ability to present its case in hearsay form to some degree.[312] Yet, having refused to find the confrontation right and the common-law hearsay rule co-extensive, the Court has also expressly permitted admission of some hearsay:[313]

> While a literal interpretation of the Confrontation Clause could bar the use of any out-of-court statement when the declarant is unavailable, this Court has rejected that view as "unintended and too extreme."[314] Rather, we

---

[310] Crawford v. Washington, 541 U.S. 36 (2004). *See generally Crawford and Hearsay: One Year Later*, 20 ABA Criminal Justice, Summer, 2005 (symposium edition); Section 20-32.23 *below*.

[311] *See* Crawford v. Washington, 541 U.S. 36 (2004); Mattox v. United States, 156 U.S. 237, 242 (1895). The confrontation right necessarily asks whether the government is estopped from introducing out-of-court statements by witnesses who are unavailable for courtroom examination. If confrontation includes such a rule, it would presuppose "that evidence in any form other than direct testimony is too unreliable ever to be used against the accused in a criminal proceeding." *Confrontation and Compulsory Process, above* note 296, at 583. Not only would confrontation contain procedural guarantees, but the concept would imply that a substantive constitutional standard governs admissibility of evidence.

[312] Idaho v. Wright, 497 U.S. 805, 814 (1990). Out-of-court statements not offered for their truth do not implicate the confrontation clause. *See, e.g.*, United States v. Bruner, 657 F.2d 1278 (D.C. Cir. 1981) (prescriptions admitted only to show that they were used to obtain drugs); De Benedictis v. Wainwright, 674 F.2d 841 (11th Cir. 1982) (contents of fraudulent telephone solicitations not offered for truth).

[313] In its early cases, the Supreme Court suggested that the state may use some out-of-court statements so long as the prosecution could not produce the evidence in a more reliable form. In *Mattox v. United States*, 156 U.S. 237 (1895), the Court allowed prior recorded testimony and a dying declaration to be used against the defendant after the prosecution showed that the declarant was dead and that the evidence was unavailable in more reliable form. *See also* Kirby v. United States, 174 U.S. 47, 61 (1899). Similarly, in California v. Green, 399 U.S. 149 (1970), the Court held that the state could use testimony given at a preliminary hearing once the prosecution had attempted and failed to obtain the testimony from the witness on direct examination.

[314] Bourjaily v. United States, 483 U.S. 171, 182 (1987).

(Rel.3—1/07 Pub.62410)

have attempted to harmonize the goal of the Clause — placing limits on the kind of evidence that may be received against a defendant — with a societal interest in accurate factfinding, which may require consideration of out-of-court statements. [315]

Although the Supreme Court has declared that "the Confrontation Clause reflects a *preference* for face-to-face confrontation at trial," [316] it has held some hearsay constitutionally admissible against the defendant, notably that hearsay evidence which has been deemed sufficiently reliable, using a variety of different tests. In 2004, in an abrupt departure from prior caselaw, the Supreme Court held in *Crawford v. Washington*, [317] that the Confrontation Clause bars all prosecution testimonial hearsay. In *Crawford*, the petitioner was tried for assault and attempted murder, and defended on the basis of self-defense. The state court admitted his wife's statement to the police at the station house the night of the incident as a declaration against interests because she refused to testify based on the marital privilege. In reaching its decision that the evidence was received in violation of the Confrontation Clause, the Supreme Court repudiated its prior holdings that permitted such use as long as it fell "within a firmly rooted hearsay exception" or held "particularized guarantees of trustworthiness." [318] *Crawford* thus makes constitutionally inadmissible prosecution testimonial hearsay whether the declarant is available or unavailable. To determine the impact of *Crawford* in any given case, one must first ask whether the declarant is present in court (or testifying via a deposition), in which circumstance no confrontation issue is likely present; and then one should ask whether hearsay evidence from an absent declarant is "testimonial."-The definition of "testimonial" remains uncertain, [319] and the Supreme Court must supply further guidance. At present, the implications of *Crawford* are highly uncertain. Although the Court has prohibited at least some forms of hearsay, presumably at least those in which a hearsay declarant made statements expecting them to be used against the defendant in a subsequent criminal prosecution, it may well prove that there are no Confrontation Clause restrictions on many forms of hearsay. Ultimately, the case may prove to be highly pro-prosecution. In 2005, however, the Court of Appeals for the Armed Forces declared that when a statement complies with Crawford's requirements for admissibility, the pre-*Crawford* rule then applies: "We agree with the conclusion of every published appellate court decision that has considered this

---

[315] Quoting Ohio v. Roberts, 448 U.S. 56, 63 (1980).

[316] Maryland v. Craig, 497 U.S. 836, 849 (1990) (quoting Ohio v. Roberts, 448 U.S. 56, 63 (1980)) (emphasis added in *Craig*).

[317] Crawford v. Washington, 541 U.S., 36 124 S. Ct. 1354 (2004). *See* note 315 and accompany text, *below*.

[318] Idaho v. Wright, 497 U.S. 805 (1990).

[319] *See, e.g.,* United States v. Scheurer, 62 M.J. 100 (C.A.A.F. 2005)(statement by appellant's wife to friend who secretly recorded it was not "testimonial"). *See generally Crawford and Hearsay: One Year Later*, 20 ABA Criminal Justice, Summer, 2005 (symposium edition).

(Rel.3—1/07 Pub.62410)

issue since *Crawford*: the Ohio v. Roberts [448 U.S. 56 (1980)] requirement for particularized guarantees of trustworthiness continues to govern confrontation analysis for nontestimonial" statements."[320] — Professor Lederer doubts the accuracy of this conclusion. Although it is conservative position with public policy merits behind it, if Confrontation prohibits "testimonial" hearsay, there would appear to be no historical reason for an intermediate position to apply to other forms of hearsay evidence.

§ 20-32.22   Witnesses Present in Court

At least to the extent that the accused is present in court and able to crossexamine adverse witnesses under oath, the confrontation clause is fully satisfied. Under traditional hearsay analysis, an out-of-court statement offered for its truth is hearsay even if the declarant is now testifying under oath to it.[321] This conclusion flows from the time-lag between the out-of-court statement and the accused's inability to contemporaneously cross-examine the declarant concerning it.[322] One could argue, therefore, that just because a declarant either is on the stand or could be called to the stand for cross-examination, the declarant is not "available" for confrontation purposes. Constitutionally, however, the critical constitutional question appears to be whether the accused has an opportunity to cross-examine the declarant.[323] As that opportunity does not appear to have to be "meaningful,"[324] it is unlikely that the confrontation clause would treat a declarant as unavailable if he or she were actually in court and either on the stand or subject to being called by the accused. Certainly, the Court of Military Appeals was untroubled by this rule.[325]

---

[320] United States v. Scheurer, 62 M.J. 100, 106 (C.A.A.F. 2005)(subsequently discussing United States v. Holmes, 406 U.S. 337, 347 (5th Cir. 2005).

[321] *See, e.g.*, Fed. R. Evid. 801(d)(1); Mil. R. Evid. 801(d)(1), which declare as nonhearsay statements:

     a. Those inconsistent with the declarant's testimony, and given under oath and subject to the penalties of perjury.

     b. Those consistent with the declarant's testimony and offered to rebut an express or implied charge against the declarant of recent fabrication or improper influence or motive.

     c. One of identification of a person made after perceiving the person.

[322] Under the Federal and Military Rules of Evidence only three categories of out-of-court statements offered for their truth constitute nonhearsay when the declarant is subject to cross-examination under oath. Fed. R. Evid. 801(d)(1); Mil. R. Evid. 801(d)(1).

[323] Idaho v. Wright, 497 U.S. 805 (1990); Delaware v. Fensterer, 474 U.S. 15, 22 (1985) (per curiam); United States v. McGrath, 39 M.J. 158 (C.M.A. 1994).

[324] Delaware v. Fensterer, 474 U.S. 15, 22 (1985) (per curiam).

[325] United States v. Morgan, 31 M.J. 43, 45 (C.M.A. 1990); United States v. Deland, 22 M.J. 70, 72 (C.M.A. 1986).

(Rel.3—1/07   Pub.62410)

§ 20-32.23   Hearsay From Declarants Not Present in Court

§ 20-32.23(a)   In General

The right to confrontation can be divided into three portions: the right to be present for the evidence of adverse witnesses,[326] the right to have the testimony of those witnesses taken under oath in open court in the presence of the accused, and the right to cross-examine those witnesses.[327] Hearsay testimony deprives the accused of each of these rights. From a policy perspective, apparently reliable out-of-court statements (hearsay) from unavailable witnesses are more compelling in terms of admissibility than are statements of witnesses who could be called. Notwithstanding this, a large number of common law and codified hearsay exceptions do not require unavailable declarants.[328]

Having declared that the confrontation clause is not identical with the hearsay rule,[329] the Supreme Court is compelled to determine whether hearsay that is admissible under normal evidentiary rules satisfies the clause. The Supreme Court in *Crawford v. Washington,*[330] effectively rejected over 20 years of critical caselaw by repudiating its earlier emphasis on hearsay reliability. Previously, the Court had focused on whether prosecutorial hearsay was reliable. If so, it was admissible except in the case of the former testimony exception which required the unavailability of the declarant. In *Crawford,* however, Justice Scalia, writing for seven justices and using an historical approach, held unconstitutional governmental "testimonial" hearsay:

> Where nontestimonial hearsay is at issue, it is wholly consistent with the Framers' design to afford the States flexibility in their development of hearsay law—as does [Ohio v.] Roberts, and as would an approach that exempted such statements from Confrontation Clause scrutiny altogether. Where testimonial evidence is at issue, however, the Sixth Amendment demands what the common law required: unavailability and a prior opportunity for cross-examination. We leave for another day any effort to spell out a comprehensive definition of "testimonial." Whatever else

---

[326] It is possible that a perjuring witness will be unable to face the accused in open court.

[327] It appears to be this aspect of confrontation that the Supreme Court is now stressing:

The central concern of the Confrontation Clause is to ensure the reliability of the evidence against a criminal defendant by subjecting it to rigorous testing in the context of an adversary proceeding before the trier of fact. . . . Although face-to-face confrontation forms the "core of the values furthered by the Confrontation Clause," . . . we have nevertheless recognized that it is not the sine qua non of the confrontation right.

Maryland v. Craig, 497 U.S. 836, 845–47 (1990) (citations omitted).

[328] *See, e.g.,* Fed. R. Evid. 803; Mil. R. Evid. 803 (23 enumerated exceptions and a residual general exception).

[329] *See above* note 311.

[330] Crawford v. Washington, 541 U.S. 36 (2004).

(Rel.3—1/07 Pub.62410)

the term covers, it applies at a minimum to prior testimony at a preliminary hearing, before a grand jury, or at a former trial; and to police interrogations. These are the modern practices with closest kinship to the abuses at which the Confrontation Clause was directed.[331]

Presumably, "cross-examination" means cross-examination under oath in some form of legal hearing, thus saving the hearsay exception for former testimony when the declarant is unavailable at trial. Whether non-testimonial hearsay is to be governed by the pre-*Crawford* confrontation clause or, more likely, only by a jurisdiction's evidentiary rules is unclear. we simply do not know the extent of *Crawford*.[332] — See generally. It *may* extend to a large variety of hearsay exceptions in which individuals make oral statements akin to in-court testimony. It may extend only to statements taken by the police and during legal proceedings. It is unlikely to extend to dying declarations.[333] Professor Lederer believes that it is unlikely to bar traditional business records. The truth is, however, that we do not know. Further Supreme Court caselaw is critically needed. In the meantime, what we do know is that *Crawford* has swept away a good deal of law and that. We await future case law developments to further clarify the situation.[334] Courts must cope with uncertainty, and some, including the Court of Appeals for the Armed Forces, have held that the pre-*Crawford* rules, notably the *Ohio v. Robert's* requirement that hearsay have "particularized guarantees of trustworthiness," still apply to non-testimonial hearsay.[335]

§ 20-32.23(b) Unavailability

Under military law, a declarant can be unavailable because of death, disappearance,[336] illness, amnesia or insanity,[337] exercise of a testimonial privilege,[338] or because of "imprisonment, military necessity,[339] nonamenability to

---

[331] 541 U.S. 68 (2004).

[332] *See generally Crawford and Hearsay: One Year Later*, 20 ABA Criminal Justice, Summer, 2005 (symposium edition).

[333] 541 U.S. at 68 n. 6.

[334] *See* Leonard Post, *Eyes on clarifying 'Crawford'; Thousands of cases hang in balance*, NAT'L L. J., October 24, 2005 at 1; Davis v. Washington, 154 Wn.2d 291, 111 P.3d 844, *cert. granted*, 126 S.Ct. 547 (2005); Hammon v. State, 829 N.E.2d 444 (Ind.), *cert. granted*, 126 S.Ct. 552 (2005).

[335] United States v. Scheurer, 62 M.J. 100, 106 (C.A.A.F. 2005).

[336] United States v. Thornton, 16 M.J. 1011 (A.C.M.R. 1983); United States v. Hubbard, 18 M.J. 678 (A.C.M.R. 1984), *aff'd in part and rev'd in part*, 28 M.J. 27 (C.M.A. 1989). *Cf.* United States v. Clark, 35 M.J. 98 (C.M.A. 1992) (witnesses unavailable because of the accused's refusal to cooperate in locating wife and child).

[337] Mil. R. Evid. 804(a)(3), (4). *See also* Ohio v. Roberts, 448 U.S. 56, 74 (1980).

[338] Mil. R. Evid. 804(a)(1), (2).

[339] *E.g.*, United States v. Boswell, 36 M.J. 807, 811 (A.C.M.R. 1993) (two military police officers deployed to Saudi Arabia who had returned witnesses to the United States and then went back to their units abroad were unavailable due to military necessity under Mil. R. Evid. 804(A)(6)).

(Rel.3—1/07   Pub.62410)

process,[340] or other reasonable cause."[341] The "requirements for establishing unavailability" for use of the hearsay exceptions in the Military Rules of Evidence "may not be so high as those imposed by the Sixth Amendment."[342] Similarly, other provisions of military law dealing with "unavailability" are not likely to be dispositive.[343]

The standard to be applied in determining constitutional unavailability is unclear. In Ohio v. Roberts,[344] the Court quoted Barber v. Page[345] for the proposition that a "witness is not 'unavailable' for purposes of . . . the exception to the confrontation requirement unless the prosecutorial authorities have made a goodfaith effort to obtain his presence at trial."[346] But having declared that the prosecution is not required to perform "a futile act" to locate the witness[347] when there is clearly no possibility of doing so successfully, such as in the event of death of the witness, the Court stated:

> But if there is a possibility, albeit remote, that affirmative measures might produce the declarant, the obligation of good faith may demand their

---

[340] *E.g.,* United States v. Hamilton, 36 M.J. 927, 932 (A.F.C.M.R. 1993) (no authority to compel a Philippine citizen to travel to United States to testify).

[341] U.C.M.J. art. 49(d)(2), *incorporated in* Mil. R. Evid. 804(a)(6). *See* Mil. R. Evid. 804(d)(5). It is unclear as to what would constitute adequate military necessity. When the provision was included in the Military Rules of Evidence, its general utility was considered questionable in view of the precedents dealing with depositions. *See, e.g.,* United States v. Davis, 41 C.M.R. 217, 223–24 (C.M.A. 1970).

[342] United States v. Cordero, 22 M.J. 216, 220 (C.M.A. 1986). *See also* United States v. Burns, 27 M.J. 92, 96 (C.M.A. 1988).

[343] *See, e.g.,* U.C.M.J. art. 49(d)(1) dealing with depositions. Even though distinguishable, decisions dealing with such provisions may be useful. In the area of depositions, actual unavailability must be established, and the prosecution must produce independent evidence of the witness' actual departure. United States v. Davis, 41 C.M.R. 217 (1970) ("100-mile rule" for depositions invalidated absent actual unavailability); United States v. Troutman, 42 C.M.R. 419 (A.C.M.R. 1970). *See* United States v. Johnson, 44 C.M.R. 414 (A.C.M.R. 1971). The same analysis applies when the witness is allegedly unwilling to appear. United States v. Obligacion, 37 C.M.R. 300 (C.M.A. 1967); United States v. Stringer, 17 C.M.R. 122 (C.M.A. 1954). *See also* United States v. Daniels, 48 C.M.R. 655 (C.M.A. 1974). *Compare* United States v. Gaines, 43 C.M.R. 397 (C.M.A. 1971) *and* United States v. Hodge, 20 C.M.A. 412, 43 C.M.R. 252 (1971) (dictum) (unavailability caused by the discharge of witness at government's convenience), *with* United States v. Dempsey, 2 M.J. 242 (A.F.C.M.R. 1976) (witness was expected to appear at trial; government did not cause unavailability). Unless the prosecution has made a good-faith effort to secure the witness, imprisonment does not make the witness unavailable. Barber v. Page, 390 U.S. 719 (1968).

[344] 448 U.S. 56, 74 (1980).

[345] 390 U.S. 719, 724, 725 (1968).

[346] 448 U.S. at 74 (quoting Barber v. Page, 390 U.S. at 724–25) (emphasis added in *Roberts*).

[347] Ohio v. Roberts, 448 U.S. at 74. *Compare* Mancusi v. Stubbs, 408 U.S. 204 (1972) *and* United States v. Daniels, 48 C.M.R. 655 (C.M.A. 1974) *with* Barber v. Page, 390 U.S. 719 (1968).

effectuation. The lengths to which the prosecution must go to produce a witness . . . is a question of reasonableness.[348]

In light of the Supreme Court's effective overruling of its prior line of cases dealing with the Confrontation Clause and hearsay,[349] the impact of those cases and even the need to discuss unavailability for constitutional reasons is unclear. However, unavailability may yet play a role in future Constitutional jurisprudence, and it is too soon to abandon it wholesale. Should it prove relevant,[350] Given that Justice Brennan dissented in Ohio v. Roberts on the ground that the government failed to make a bona fide search to find the missing hearsay declarant,[351] it is apparent that although a mere possibility of obtaining the declarant was not enough to prevent use of a hearsay declaration,[352] significant government efforts to locate the declarant may be necessary to establish unavailability. The essential standard is one of reasonableness.[353] Thus, a witness is unavailable when, for some reason, the witness is beyond the reach of the court-martial.[354] The Court of Military Appeals held:

---

[348] 448 U.S. at 74 (quoting California v. Green, 399 U.S. at 189 n.22) (concurring opinion citing Barber v. Page) (emphasis in original).

[349] Crawford v. Washington, 541 U.S. 36 (2004).

[350] Although improbable, the Court of Appeals for the Armed Force could hold that "military due process" requires application of the pre-Crawford case law to the armed forces even although no longer valid in the civilian community.

[351] 448 U.S. at 79–82.

[352] See United States v. Bright, 9 M.J. 789 (A.C.M.R. 1980); United States v. Hubbard, 18 M.J. 678 (A.C.M.R. 1984), aff'd in part and rev'd in part, 28 M.J. 27 (C.M.A. 1989). See also Mancusi v. Stubbs, 408 U.S. 204 (1972).

[353] Ohio v. Roberts, 448 U.S. at 74. Compare Mancusi, above note 344, with Barber v. Page, 390 U.S. 719 (1968). The government cannot rely merely on its regular procedures for producing witnesses and must make a good-faith effort to use all practical methods to produce the witness in person. See United States v. Ortiz, 35 M.J. 391 (C.M.A. 1992) (failure to grant continuance under the circumstances was an abuse of discretion). United States v. Vanderwier, 25 M.J. 263 (C.M.A. 1987) (no accommodations to adjust trial with witness's training schedule); United States v. Fisher, 24 M.J. 358 (C.M.A. 1987) (two witnesses who were at alleged marijuana party with the accused were essential witnesses); United States v. Cordero, 22 M.J. 216, 220 (C.M.A. 1986) (if availability depended only on payment for travel from Germany to post, witness would be considered to be available); United States v. Thornton, 16 M.J. 1011 (A.C.M.R. 1983) (sufficient good-faith effort to attempt compulsory process through German authorities and to locate witness through friends and family); United States v. Hubbard, 18 M.J. 678 (A.C.M.R. 1984) (sufficient good-faith effort where attempt was made to contact AWOL soldier witness through parents and police), aff'd, 28 M.J. 27 (C.M.A. 1989). Cf. United States v. Arnold, 18 M.J. 559 (A.C.M.R. 1984) (constitutional availability issue waived by failure to object), aff'd, 25 M.J. 129 (C.M.A. 1987).

[354] Although U.C.M.J. art. 49(d)(1), permits the use of depositions when the witness is outside the civil jurisdiction in which trial takes place or is more than 100 miles from the location of trial, the Court of Military Appeals has limited the Article to civilian witnesses. United States v. Davis, 41 C.M.R. 217 (C.M.A. 1970); United States v. Ciarletta, 23 C.M.R. 70, 78 (C.M.A. 1957).

(Rel.3—1/07 Pub.62410)

In interpreting *Roberts*, this Court has emphasized that a witness is not "unavailable" unless the Government has exhausted every reasonable means to secure his live testimony.[355] . . . Military orders provide a ready means for assuring the presence of service personnel to testify at a trial or investigation. . . . However, courts-martial also are empowered to obtain the presence of civilian witnesses.[356]

Accordingly, a witness should not be "unavailable" if a potentially successful warrant of attachment has not been issued. Indeed, the court has opined that "[a]ffirmative measures to protect an accused's Sixth Amendment right to confront and cross-examine witnesses . . . do not end simply with service of a subpoena."[357]

The Court of Military Appeals also suggested that "the indicia of reliability as to the former testimony of an absent witness might be taken into account in determining how far a prosecutor must go in his 'good faith' efforts to locate the witness."[358]

When a witness persists in a claim of privilege, proper or not, the witness ought to be considered unavailable if he or she refuses to comply with the judge's orders to testify.[359] Ordinarily, this problem arises in the context of an assertion

The court's reasoning in *Davis* to the effect that the jury must weigh the demeanor of the witness (41 C.M.R. at 220 (quoting Barber v. Page, 390 U.S. 719, 725 (1968))) suggests that the Article may be invalid as to civilians as well. *See also* United States v. Chatmon, 41 C.M.R. 807 (N.C.M.R. 1970). In United States v. Hinton, 21 M.J. 267, 271 (C.M.A. 1986), the Court stated:

Where civilian witnesses are involved, it is desirable for a warrant of attachment to be served by a Marshal or other civil officer in order to minimize possible friction or misunderstanding. However, if no civil officer is available, there still remains the lawful alternative of service of the warrant by a military officer.

[355] *Citing* United States v. Barror, 23 M.J. 370, 373 (C.M.A. 1987); United States v. Hines, 23 M.J. 125 (C.M.A. 1986); United States v. Cokeley, 22 M.J. 225 (C.M.A. 1986); *cf.* United States v. Hinton, 21 M.J. 267 (C.M.A. 1986).

[356] United States v. Burns, 27 M.J. 92, 97 (C.M.A. 1988). *See also* United States v. Ortiz, 35 M.J. 391 (C.M.A. 1992) (wife located in Berlin was subject to warrant of attachment; continuance to obtain her presence was necessary); United States v. Wind, 28 M.J. 381 (C.M.A. 1989) (trial counsel's efforts held reasonable).

[357] United States v. Ferdinand, 29 M.J. 164, 167 (C.M.A. 1989), *cert. denied*, 493 U.S. 1044110 S. Ct. 840 (1990) (mother refused to produce child sexual-abuse victim in court despite subpoena and judge's order; judge's erroneous admission of residual hearsay statement held harmless error). *See also* United States v. Ortiz, 35 M.J. 391 (C.M.A. 1992) (wife located in Berlin was subject to warrant of attachment; continuance to obtain her presence was necessary).

[358] 27 M.J. at 98 (citing United States v. Crockett, 21 M.J. 423 (C.M.A.), *cert. denied*, 479 U.S. 835 (1986)).

[359] In some cases, out-of-court statements have been excluded when the declarant, though physically present, asserted the right against self-incrimination. *See* Roberts v. Russell, 392 U.S. 293 (1968); Bruton v. United States, 391 U.S. 123 (1968); Douglas v. Alabama, 380 U.S. 415 (1965); United States v. Brice, 19 M.J. 170 (C.M.A. 1985) (dictum that it may be violation of the Sixth Amendment for prosecution to give witness Article 31 rights resulting in witness refusing to testify);

(Rel.3—1/07 Pub.62410)

of the right against self-incrimination. Interestingly, although the Court of Military Appeals held that an accused may not insist on transactional immunity as a condition for making herself available to testify,[360] "it is easier to contend that an offer of [testimonial] immunity is included within the term 'other reasonable means' for purposes of Mil. R. Evid. 804(a)(5) and within 'a good-faith effort' for purposes of the Sixth Amendment."[361] However, the courts have been extremely reluctant to compel the government to provide testimonial (or "use") immunity to a witness not yet tried. A grant of immunity has been required only when the prosecution intentionally disrupts the fact-finding process, when there is a violation of due process, when the prosecution acts on the basis of religion, race, or other discriminatory criteria, or when the potential testimony is clearly necessary and exculpatory.[362] In some situations, though, the government's interest in withholding immunity is minimal compared to the defendant's interest in obtaining the testimony. If the prosecution has already prepared its case against the witness, the government's burden to trace its evidence to independent sources ordinarily should be insufficient to justify refusal to grant testimonial immunity.

In such a case, the prosecution should be forced to choose between granting immunity or proceeding without the evidence.[363]

Child-abuse cases are continual problems, as quite frequently at least one parent or guardian prefers to keep the child out of court to avoid further discomfort or trauma on the part of the child.[364] Interestingly, the Court of Military Appeals stated in dicta:

United States v. Lawless, 13 M.J. 943 (A.F.C.M.R. 1982) (proper to exclude testimony of witness who invoked rights). *But see* Parker v. Randolph, 442 U.S. 62 (1979). Again, these cases suggest that prosecutorial conduct played a role and that the prosecution could have made the declarant available. When the challenged statements were made by co-defendants on trial with the accused, for example, severance of the trial might have obviated the self-incrimination issue. *Confrontation and Compulsory Process, above* note 296, at 585 n.43. Alternatively, the government could have tried the declarants before trying the defendant against whom the statements were to be used. 442 U.S. 62 (1979). Finally, if the declarants continued to claim their self-incrimination privilege, they could have been made available by a grant of testimonial immunity. *442 U.S. 62 (1979) at 581–82 n.38.*

[360] United States v. Cordero, 22 M.J. 216, 221 (C.M.A. 1986).

[361] 22 M.J. 216, 221 (C.M.A. 1986).

[362] United States v. Villines, 13 M.J. 46 (C.M.A. 1982); United States v. Barham, 625 F.2d 1221 (5th Cir. 1980); Government of the Virgin Islands v. Smith, 615 F.2d 964 (3d Cir. 1980); United States v. Morrison, 535 F.2d 223 (3d Cir. 1976); United States v. Alessio, 528 F.2d 1079 (9th Cir. 1976); United States v. Lowell, 490 F. Supp. 897 (D.N.J. 1980); United States v. De Palma, 476 F. Supp. 775 (S.D.N.Y. 1979).

[363] Even if there is no violation of the defendant's confrontation rights, rights under Article 47 may be violated. *Cf.* United States v. Gardner, 22 M.J. 28 (C.M.A. 1986).

[364] *See, e.g.,* United States v. Ferdinand, 29 M.J. 164, 165–66 (C.M.A.), *cert. denied,* 493 U.S. 1044110 S. Ct. 840 (1990).

(Rel.3—1/07 Pub.62410)

We are mindful, as are several state jurisdictions, that a child may be found to be unavailable to testify if a psychiatrist or psychologist has determined that participation in a trial would be too traumatic for the child.[365]

Such a determination must be reflected in the record, however.[366]

In determining when a witness is available,[367] the Court has rejected the argument that the government has no obligation to produce witnesses from beyond its territorial boundaries.[368] Presumably, a witness is not constitutionally "unavailable" when the prosecutor is responsible for the absence of the witness.[369]

Whether the government has met its obligation to produce a witness is a constitutional question, and the standard is a strict one.[370] Because the Sixth Amendment protects only the accused, the government has the burden of establishing unavailability when that is required.[371]

§ 20-32.24 "Firmly Rooted" Hearsay Exceptions & Particularized Guarantees of Trustworthiness & In General

Prior to the Supreme Court's 2004 decision in *Crawford v. Washington*,[372] hearsay evidence could be may be admitted against the accused only if it had "only if it bears "adequate 'indicia of reliability.' Reliability could can be inferred without more in a case where the evidence fellalls within a firmly rooted hearsay exception. In other cases, the evidence would must be excluded, at least absent

---

[365] 29 M.J. 167 (C.M.A.) (footnote omitted).

[366] 29 M.J. 167 (C.M.A.).

[367] *See, e.g.,* Mil. R. Evid. 804(a); United States v. Cokeley, 22 M.J. 225 (C.M.A. 1986). The court indicated that when a witness is suffering from a temporary disability, the confrontation clause requires some delay to permit the witness to recover. There can be no bright-line rule to anticipate every case of an incapacitated witness. There are some factors the court might consider in determining the availability of the witness: the importance of the testimony, the amount of delay necessary to obtain live testimony, the trustworthiness of the alternative to live testimony, the nature and extent of earlier cross-examination, the prompt administration of justice, and any special circumstances militating for or against the delay.

[368] Pointer v. Texas, 380 U.S. 400 (1965).

[369] *See, e.g.,* Berger v. California, 393 U.S. 314 (1969); Barber v. Page, 390 U.S. 719 (1968); Brookhart v. Janis, 384 U.S. 1 (1966); Pointer v. Texas, 380 U.S. 400 (1965); Motes v. United States, 178 U.S. 458 (1900); Kirby v. United States, 174 U.S. 47 (1899). For the analysis of these cases, see *Confrontation and Compulsory Process, above* note 296, at 584 n.43, suggesting an underlying due process violation.

[370] *See* United States v. Lynch, 449 F.2d 1011 (D.C. Cir. 1974). *Cf.* United States v. Arnold, 18 M.J. 559 (A.C.M.R. 1984) (constitutional availability issue waived by failure to object), *aff'd*, 25 M.J. 129 (C.M.A. 1987).

[371] *See, e.g.,* United States v. Cordero, 22 M.J. 216, 221 (C.M.A. 1986). Under the normal evidentiary rules the *proponent* of the hearsay must prove unavailability.

[372] 541 U.S. 36 (2004).

a showing of particularized guarantees of trustworthiness."[373] In light of the Court's abandonment in *Crawford* of its prior reliability rationale in favor of a ban on "testimonial" hearsay, an immense number of hearsay cases construing the Court's prior precedents are now of questionable value, although the Court of Appeals for the Armed Forces in 2005 assumed that the "firmly rooted" or having "particularized guarantees of trustworthiness" requirements are to be applied when a statement complies with *Crawford.*[374]

Whether the court is correct is questionable. However, under current caselaw, counsel who deal with non-testimonial hearsay offered against the accused may have to comply with the pre-Crawford caselaw.

Prior to *Crawford,* the Court had sustained as "firmly rooted" only the hearsay exceptions for former testimony,[375] co-conspirators' declarations,[376] and declarations against interest.[377] The Court had, however, indicated in dicta that business records and dying declarations were "firmly rooted."[378] Stemming as it does from its case-by-case treatment of the issue, the failure of the Court to "bless" other hearsay exceptions is not dispositive if the test survives *Crawford.* Even if other exceptions fail to meet the "firmly rooted" standard, they may be acceptable under the "particularized guarantees" rationale.[379]

Although most if not all of the traditional common-law hearsay exceptions may be "firmly rooted," the mere existence of a codified or common-law exception in a jurisdiction does not necessarily mean that the exception will qualify for confrontation-clause purposes.[380] One could argue, for example, that the "present sense impression" contained within the Federal and Military Rules of Evidence[381] is sufficiently distinct from the common-law spontaneous declaration to fail to qualify if one equated "firmly rooted" with "long-established" (albeit that such a conclusion appears erroneous).[382] One must be

---

[373] Idaho v. Wright, 497 U.S. 805, 814–15 (1990) (quoting Ohio v. Roberts, 448 U.S. 56, 65 (1980)). Actually the *Ohio v. Roberts* version of "firmly rooted" seemed to require a long-established hearsay exception in lieu . That interpretation, phriasing, which manadated an historical test, was transmuted to an interpretation that contemplates "firmly rooted" jurisdiction-counting in *Idaho v. Wright,* 497 U.S. 805 (1990).

[374] United States v. Scheurer, 62 M.J. 100 (C.A.A.F. 2005).

[375] *See, e.g., Ohio v. Roberts, 448 U.S. 56, 65 (1980). See generally Chapter 9.*

[376] Bourjaily v. United States, 483 U.S. 171, 182–84 (1987).

[377] Williamson v. United States, 512 U.S. 594 (1994).

[378] Ohio v. Roberts, 448 U.S. 56, 66 n.8 (1980).

[379] See, e.g., Idaho v. Wright, 497 U.S. 805, 820 (1990).

[380] Further, codified hearsay exceptions may function somewhat differently from their

[381] Fed. R. Evid. 803(1); Mil. R. Evid. 803(1).

[382] When codified, that exception was split into present-sense impressions (Fed. R. Evid. 803(1); Mil. R. Evid. 803(1)) and excited utterances. Fed. R. Evid. 803(2); Mil. R. Evid. 803(2)). Excited utterances may be close enough to the common-law rule to qualify, even if present-sense

(Rel.3—1/07 Pub.62410)

particularly alert for exceptions that include common-law exceptions but extend them, especially to a degree not shared by many contemporary jurisdictions and thus may not be "firmly rooted."

Under Military Rule of Evidence 803(6) for example, records of regularly conducted activity are admissible as exceptions to the hearsay rule. The essential requirement for the "business records" exception is that the record be made and kept "in the course of a regularly conducted business activity."[383]

Like its civilian equivalent, however, Rule 803(6) extends the exception to "opinions, or diagnoses,"[384] matters that may be outside the "long established" historical exception. Of greater importance are the uniquely military expansions found in the Military Rules of Evidence. Military Rule of Evidence 803(6) contains, for example, a long litany of records that are expressly declared to be within the exception. Those records include, however, not just noncontroversial matters, but also forensic laboratory reports. Although the admissibility of laboratory reports has plagued the military courts,[385] the Court of Military Appeals held that such reports are properly admitted under the business-record exception.[386] In the view of the court, a chemical analysis is inherently neutral;

---

impressions fail. In United States v. Arnold, 25 M.J. 129 (C.M.A. 1987), *affirming*, 18 M.J. 559 (A.C.M.R. 1984), a "child molestation case" in which the court was asked to rule upon the constitutionality of the admission of an alleged excited utterance, the court was unable to muster a majority. Judge Cox wrote the opinion with Judge Sullivan concurring in the result and Chief Judge Everett dissenting. Judge Cox opined that excited utterances constitute a "long established, well recognized" exception to the hearsay rule and thus are so "inherently reliable as to be admissible and, thus, conform to the constitutional guarantee of confrontation." 25 M.J. at 133. Apparently frustrated, Judge Cox continued:

"Let there be no doubt, however that this Court favors confrontation, and this case should be read very narrowly. . . . But, we recognize that '[t]here is a real world as well as a theoretical one.'" 25 M.J. at 133.

Although Judge Cox's opinion has no precedental impact, inasmuch as it was not joined by another judge, it raises two interesting questions in the area of confrontation: are we ignoring reality in a reliance on legal formalism, and to what degree do the shocking facts of many of these cases affect our objective reasoning?

[383] Fed. R. Evid. 803(1); Mil. R. Evid. 803(1).

[384] It is by no means clear that the Rule is intended to permit circumvention of the expert testimony rules, liberal though they are. *Cf.* United States v. Benedict, 27 M.J. 253, 260–61 (C.M.A. 1988) (sanity board reports). Although current civilian law is sparse and confused, there may be a trend to admit records of regularly conducted activity containing expert opinion and to leave to the trial judge the discretion to rule the evidence inadmissible when appropriate.

[385] *E.g.*, United States v. Vietor, 10 M.J. 69 (C.M.A. 1980); United States v. Strangstalien, 7 M.J. 225 (C.M.A. 1979); United States v. Miller, 49 C.M.R. 380 (C.M.A. 1974); United States v. Evans, 45 C.M.R. 353 (C.M.A. 1972). *Cf.* United States v. Harper, 22 M.J. 157, 160–61 (C.M.A. 1986).

[386] *See, e.g.*, United States v. Vietor, 10 M.J. 69 (C.M.A. 1980); United States v. Strangstalien, 7 M.J. 225 (C.M.A. 1979). *But see* United States v. Oates, 560 F.2d 45 (2d Cir. 1977); United States v. Ruffin, 575 F.2d 346 (2d Cir. 1978); State v. Henderson, 554 S.W.2d 117 (Tenn. 1977).

the chemist's job is to analyze the substance, not exercise prosecutorial discretion,[387] and there is no reason to suspect the chemist of bias. The court's conclusions are subject to dispute, particularly where, as is the usual case in the Army, the laboratory report is the product of a forensic laboratory operated by a law-enforcement agency.[388] Although the codified military hearsay exception for laboratory reports may comply with past decisions of the Court of Military Appeals, it seems highly unlikely that it could be considered a "firmly rooted" hearsay exception. Accordingly, given a proper confrontational challenge, such a report, even if "non-testimonial," should be inadmissible unless the exception fits the "particularized guarantees" prong of the confrontation test. This should be particularly true when, as is the usual case, a laboratory report may be used to present in summary form an expert opinion susceptible to disagreement.[389]

The fact that an exception is "firmly rooted" is not necessarily determinative of a given statement's admissibility under the confrontation clause. In *Ohio v. Roberts*,[390] the Court wrote: "The Court has applied this 'indicia of reliability' requirement principally by concluding that certain hearsay exceptions rest upon such solid foundations that admission of virtually any evidence comports with the 'substance of the constitutional protection.'"[391]

---

[387] United States v. Evans, 45 C.M.R. 353 (1972). *See also* United States v. Hernandez-Rojas, 617 F.2d 533 (9th Cir. 1980); United States v. Orozco, 590 F.2d 789 (9th Cir. 1979); United States v. Grady, 544 F.2d 598 (2d Cir. 1978); Saltzburg, Martin & Capra, *above* note 373, at 1746; English, *Should Laboratory Reports Be Admitted at Courts-Martial to Identify Illegal Drugs?*, Army Law., May 1978, at 25, 30.

[388] Recognizing that such reports are subject to attack on an individual basis, the court has allowed the defendant to attack the report's accuracy (United States v. Miller, 49 C.M.R. 380 (C.M.A. 1974); United States v. Evans, 45 C.M.R. 353 (C.M.A. 1972); United States v. Davis, 14 M.J. 847 (A.C.M.R. 1982)), both in terms of the analyst's competence and the regularity of the test procedures. As one writer has noted, the analyst's testimony will be of little use in most instances. English, *above* note 380, at 31. *See also* Dutton v. Evans, 400 U.S. 74, 95–96 (1970) (Harlan, J., concurring). Later cases have accepted this doctrine. *See, e.g.,* United States v. Vietor, 10 M.J. 69 (C.M.A. 1980); United States v. Strangstalien, 7 M.J. 225 (C.M.A. 1979). The prosecution can avoid the laboratory report issue by stipulating to the identity of the substance tested or to the analyst's testimony, or by deposing the chemist. In addition, the prosecution should inform the defense as soon as possible that the lab report will be offered into evidence and inquire if the defense desires the analyst's presence at trial. English, *above* note 380, at 33.

[389] *Cf.* United States v. Harper, 22 M.J. 157 (C.M.A. 1986). In *Harper*, the court said that it did not have to address a pure paper case, that is, the proof of wrongful use on the basis of laboratory reports itself. The court did indicate that the federal case law has recognized the efficiency of laboratory results of urinalysis to show marijuana use in the context of prison disciplinary proceedings and probation proceedings. 22 M.J. 162 n. 4 (C.M.A. 1986).

[390] 448 U.S. 56, 66 (1980) (emphasis added).

[391] Note that Fed. R. Evid. 803(6); Mil. R. Evid. 803(6) exclude statements from the exception when "the course of information or the method or circumstances or preparation indicate lack of trustworthiness." *See, e.g.,* United States v. Licavoli, 604 F.2d 613 (9th Cir. 1979).

(Rel.3—1/07 Pub.62410)

Before the prosecution may offer a hearsay statement, not "firmly rooted," made by an unavailable declarant against the accused at trial on the merits, under the pre-*Crawford* opinions, it must demonstrate that the statement has sufficient "indicia of reliability"[392] to effectively substitute for defense cross-examination of the witness.[393] In 1990, the Supreme Court put it thus: "[I]f the declarant's truthfulness is so clear from the surrounding circumstances that the test of cross-examination would be of marginal utility, then the hearsay rule does not bar admission of the statement at trial."[394]

Attempting to further define "particularized guarantees," the Court added:

We think the "particularized guarantees of trustworthiness" required for admission under the Confrontation Clause must likewise be drawn from the totality of circumstances that surround the making of the statement and that render the declarant particularly worthy of belief. . . . Because evidence possessing "particularized guarantees of trustworthiness" must be at least as reliable as evidence admitted under a firmly rooted hearsay exception, . . . we think that evidence admitted under the former requirement must similarly be so trustworthy that adversarial testing would add little to its reliability. . . . Thus, unless an affirmative reason, arising from the circumstances in which the statement was made, provides a basis for rebutting the presumption that a hearsay statement is not worthy of reliance at trial, the Confrontation Clause requires exclusion of the out-of-court statement.[395]

[W]e are unpersuaded by the State's contention that evidence corroborating the truth of a hearsay statement may properly support a finding that the statement bears "particularized guarantees of trustworthiness." To be admissible under the Confrontation Clause, hearsay evidence used to convict a defendant must possess indicia of reliability by virtue of its inherent trustworthiness, not by reference to other evidence at trial.[396]

---

[392] Dutton v. Evans, 400 U.S. 74, 89 (1970).

[393] *See* Ohio v. Roberts, 448 U.S. 56, 70–71 (1980). *See also* United States v. Connor, 27 M.J. 378 (C.M.A. 1989) (verbatim Article 32 testimony admissible if the accused had the opportunity to cross-examine. Defense counsel's statement of motive for cross-examination will not be controlling).

[394] Idaho v. Wright, 497 U.S. 805, 820 (1990). The Court discussed the underlying rationales for the hearsay exceptions for excited utterances, dying declarations, and statements for purposes of "medical treatment," explaining why those rationales made it unlikely for a declarant to lie. 497 U.S. 805, 820 (1990).

[395] 497 U.S. 820–21 (1990) (disapproving many factors previously relied upon).

[396] 497 U.S. 822 (1990). The Court later continued:

In short, the use of corroborating evidence to support a hearsay statement's "particularized guarantees of trustworthiness" would permit admission of a presumptively unreliable statement by bootstrapping on the trustworthiness of other evidence at trial, a result we think at odds with the requirement that hearsay evidence admitted under the Confrontation Clause be so trustworthy that cross-examination of the declarant would be of marginal utility.

Corroboration may be available at the appellate level when testing for harmless error.

(Rel.3—1/07 Pub.62410)

As a consequence, if post *Crawford* precedents require adherence to pre-*Crawford* confrontation law for non-testimonial prosecution hearsay, when a hearsay exception is not "firmly rooted," the judge should state on the record the special facts that indicate the high degree of trustworthiness that justifies the admission of the evidence.[397]

Note that in determining whether there are particularized guarantees, one matter that has been resolved is the use of corroborating evidence to establish reliability. The Court of Military Appeals often considered the presence of evidence corroborating a hearsay statement as an important factor in determining "particularized guarantees."[398] In 1990, however, the United States Supreme Court, in *Idaho v. Wright*,[399] held:

In short, the use of corroborating evidence to support a hearsay statement's "particularized guarantees of trustworthiness" would permit admission of a presumptively unreliable statement by bootstrapping on the trustworthiness of other evidence at trial, a result we think at odds with the requirement that hearsay evidence admitted under the Confrontation Clause be so trustworthy that cross-examination of the declarant would be of marginal utility.[400]

Although *Wright* is controlling in the military, its application need not bar admission of hearsay,[401] and the Court of Military Appeals so held in *United States v. McGrath*[402] in construing the scope of the residual hearsay rules when confrontation is not at issue.

Thus far, the Court has sustained as "firmly rooted" only the hearsay exceptions for former testimony,[403] co-conspirators' declarations,[404] and declarations against interest.[405] The Court has, however, indicated in dicta that business records and dying declarations are "firmly rooted."[406] Stemming as it does from its case-by-case treatment of the issue, the failure of the Court thus far to "bless" other hearsay exceptions is not dispositive. Even if other exceptions fail to meet

---

[397] United States v. Hines, 23 M.J. 125, 135 (C.M.A. 1986) (citing S. Rep. No. 1277, 93th Cong., 2d Session).

[398] *See, e.g.*, United States v. Hines, 23 M.J. 125, 136, 137–38 (C.M.A. 1986).

[399] 497 U.S. 805 (1990).

[400] The Court did observe, however, that "we think the presence of corroborating evidence more appropriately indicates that any error in admitting the statement might be harmless." 497 U.S. 823 (1990).

[401] United States v. Moreno, 31 M.J. 935, 939 (A.C.M.R. 1990) (videotaped disposition), *aff'd*, 36 M.J. 107 (C.M.A. 1992).

[402] 38 M.J. 158 (C.M.A. 1994).

[403] *See, e.g.*, Ohio v. Roberts, 448 U.S. 56, 65 (1980). *See generally* Chapter 9.

[404] Bourjaily v. United States, 483 U.S. 171, 182–84 (1987).

[405] Williamson v. United States, 512 U.S. 594 (1994).

[406] Ohio v. Roberts, 448 U.S. 56, 66 n.8 (1980).

(Rel.3—1/07　Pub.62410)

the "firmly rooted" standard, they may be acceptable under the "particularized guarantees" rationale.[407]

Although most if not all of the traditional common-law hearsay exceptions may be "firmly rooted," the mere existence of a codified or common-law exception in a jurisdiction does not necessarily mean that the exception will qualify for confrontation-clause purposes.[408] One could argue, for example, that the "present senseimpression" contained within the Federal and Military Rules of Evidence[409] is sufficiently distinct from the common-law spontaneous

---

[407] *See, e.g.,* Idaho v. Wright, 497 U.S. 805, 820 (1990). *See generally* Section 20-32.25.

[408] Further, codified hearsay exceptions may function somewhat differently from their common-law antecedents. As the drafters of the Military Rules of Evidence noted, the unique nature of Article 32 investigations raises the question of how the former testimony exception applies to Article 32 hearings. Analysis of the 1980 Amendments to the *Manual for Courts-Martial,* Analysis of Rule 804, *reprinted in* MCM, 1998, A22-54, A23-55. Article 32 hearings are designed "to function as discovery devices for the defense as well as to recommend an appropriate disposition of charges." MCM, 1998, A22-54, A23-55, (citing Hutson v. United States, 42 C.M.R. 39 (C.M.A. 1970); United States v. Samuels, 27 C.M.R. 280, 286 (C.M.A. 1959)). *See also* United States v. Obligacion, 37 C.M.R. 300, 302 (C.M.A. 1967). Merely having an opportunity to develop the witness' testimony is not enough; there must be a similar motive in each proceeding to do so. Mil. R. Evid. 804(b)(1). The similarmotive requirement exists to ensure sufficient identify of issues, thus creating an adequate interest in examining the witness. S. Saltzburg, M. Martin & D. Capra, Federal Rules Of Evidence Manual 1833 (7th ed. 1998) [hereinafter cited as Saltsburg, Martin & Capra]. But it is not enough for a defense counsel to state that counsel is only using the Article 32 hearing for discovery purposes and thus prohibit the use of the Article 32 testimony under this exception. United States v. Connor, 27 M.J. at 388–90 (C.M.A. 1989). The defense counsel's expression of intent during the Article 32 hearing is not subsequently binding on the military judge at trial. 27 M.J. at 388–90 (C.M.A. 1989).

The Court of Military Appeals rejected the dichotomy set forth by the drafters of the Military Rules of Evidence claiming that it is contrary to precedents of the court and is practically unworkable. 27 M.J. at 388 (C.M.A. 1989). When the defense counsel proceeds to cross-examine a witness, it could be for substantive evidence, discovery, rehabilitation, impeachment, or bolstering. Thus, the court stated, "[as] we interpret the requirement of 'similar motive,' if the defense counsel has been allowed to cross-examine the government witness without restriction on scope of cross-examination, then the provisions of Mil. R. Evid. 804(b)(1) . . . and of the Sixth Amendment are satisfied, even if that opportunity is not used." 27 M.J. at 389 (C.M.A. 1989). *But see* Lederer, *The Military Rules of Evidence: Origins and Judicial Implementation,* 130 Mil. R. Evid. 5, 24–26 (1990). The court held that the verbatim statement of a witness given at an Article 32 investigation was admissible even though the defense attorney for a co-accused conducting the cross-examination for all of the accused had stated he was only doing it for discovery purposes. The court noted that a verbatim statement otherwise admissible may be inadmissible if it is unreliable as a matter of law. *Connor* at 391 (citing United States v. Burns, 27 M.J. 92, 98 (C.M.A. 1988) (Cox, J., concurring in the result)). *See also* United States v. Spindle, 28 M.J. 35 (C.M.A. 1989); United States v. Hubbard, 28 M.J. 27 (C.M.A. 1989). To avoid this result, the defense counsel may waive the Article 32 investigation or at least object to a witness adopting a statement given to a commander or police prior to the investigation.

[409] Fed. R. Evid. 803(1); Mil. R. Evid. 803(1).

(Rel.3—1/07 Pub.62410)

declaration to fail to qualify.[410] One must be particularly alert for exceptions that include common-law exceptions but extend them.Under Military Rule of Evidence 803(6) for example, records of regularly conducted activity are admissible as exceptions to the hearsay rule. The essential requirement for the "business records" exception is that the record be made and kept "in the course of a regularly conducted business activity."[411] Like its civilian equivalent, however, Rule803(6) extends the exception to "opinions, or diagnoses,"[412] matters that may be outside the "firmly rooted" historical exception. Of greater importance are the uniquely military expansions found in the Military Rules of Evidence. Military Rule of Evidence 803(6) contains, for example, a long litany of records that are expressly declared to be within the exception. Those records

---

[410] When codified, that exception was split into present-sense impressions (Fed. R. Evid. 803(1); Mil. R. Evid. 803(1)) and excited utterances. Fed. R. Evid. 803(2); Mil. R. Evid. 803(2)). Excited utterances may be close enough to the common-law rule to qualify, even if present-sense impressions fail. In United States v. Arnold, 25 M.J. 129 (C.M.A. 1987), *affirming*, 18 M.J. 559 (A.C.M.R. 1984), a "child molestation case" in which the court was asked to rule upon the constitutionality of the admission of an alleged excited utterance, the court was unable to muster a majority. Judge Cox wrote the opinion with Judge Sullivan concurring in the result and Chief Judge Everett dissenting. Judge Cox opined that excited utterances constitute a "long established, well recognized" exception to the hearsay rule and thus are so "inherently reliable as to be admissible and, thus, conform to the constitutional guarantee of confrontation." 25 M.J. at 133. Apparently frustrated, Judge Cox continued:

"Let there be no doubt, however that this Court favors confrontation, and this case should be read very narrowly. . . . But, we recognize that '[t]here is a real world as well as a theoretical one.'" 25 M.J. at 133.

Although Judge Cox's opinion has no precedental impact, inasmuch as it was not joined by another judge, it raises two interesting questions in the area of confrontation: are we ignoring reality in a reliance on legal formalism, and to what degree do the shocking facts of many of these cases affect our objective reasoning?

[411] Mil. R. Evid. 803(6). *See also* Fed. R. Evid. 803(6), Adv. Comm. Notes, 56 F.R.D. 183, 308 (basis of exception). The specific list of records given in the rule are normally records of regularly conducted activity in the armed forces. Analysis of the 1980 Amendments to the *Manual for Courts-Martial*, Analysis of Mil. R. Evid. 803(6), *reprinted at* MCM, 1998, A22-51. *See also* United States v. Harper, 22 M.J. 157 (C.M.A. 1986) (The court expressly indicated that it did not have to address the issue of whether the accused could be found guilty of wrongful use of marijuana solely on the basis of the results of urinalysis); United States v. Evans, 45 C.M.R. 353, 354 (C.M.A. 1972). If the circumstances surrounding the making of the report indicate the lack of trustworthiness, the report can be excluded. Mil. R. Evid. 803(6). *See also* Palmer v. Hoffman, 318 U.S. 109 (1943); United States v. Manuel, 43 M.J. 282, 289 (C.A.A.F. 1995) (suppressed urinalysis test when there was a finding of gross negligence in failing to retain the accused's sample). *But cf.* United States v. Evans, 45 C.M.R. at 356 (when analyst is called to testify, issue is weight to be given to lab report, not initial admissibility).

[412] It is by no means clear that the Rule is intended to permit circumvention of the expert testimony rules, liberal though they are. *Cf.* United States v. Benedict, 27 M.J. 253, 260–61 (C.M.A. 1988) (sanity board reports). Although current civilian law is sparse and confused, there may be a trend to admit records of regularly conducted activity containing expert opinion and to leave to the trial judge the discretion to rule the evidence inadmissible when appropriate.

(Rel.3—1/07 Pub.62410)

include, however, not just noncontroversial matters, but also forensic laboratory reports. Although the admissibility of laboratory reports has plagued the military courts,[413] the Court of Military Appeals has held that such reports are properly admitted under the business-record exception.[414] In the view of the court, a chemical analysis is inherently neutral; the chemist's job is to analyze the substance, not exercise prosecutorial discretion,[415] and there is no reason to suspect the chemist of bias. The court's conclusions are subject to dispute, particularly where, as is the usual case in the Army, the laboratory report is the product of a forensic laboratory operated by a law-enforcement agency.[416] Although the codified military hearsay exception for laboratory reports may comply with past decisions of the Court of Military Appeals, it seems highly unlikely that it could be considered a "firmly rooted" hearsay exception. Accordingly, given a proper confrontational challenge, such a report should be inadmissible unless the exception fits the "particularized guarantees" prong of the confrontation test. This should be particularly true when, as is the usual case, a laboratory report may be used to present in summary form an expert opinion susceptible to disagreement.[417]

[413] *E.g.*, United States v. Vietor, 10 M.J. 69 (C.M.A. 1980); United States v. Strangstalien, 7 M.J. 225 (C.M.A. 1979); United States v. Miller, 49 C.M.R. 380 (C.M.A. 1974); United States v. Evans, 45 C.M.R. 353 (C.M.A. 1972). *Cf.* United States v. Harper, 22 M.J. 157, 160–61 (C.M.A. 1986).

[414] *See, e.g.*, United States v. Vietor, 10 M.J. 69 (C.M.A. 1980); United States v. Strangstalien, 7 M.J. 225 (C.M.A. 1979). *But see* United States v. Oates, 560 F.2d 45 (2d Cir. 1977); United States v. Ruffin, 575 F.2d 346 (2d Cir. 1978); State v. Henderson, 554 S.W.2d 117 (Tenn. 1977).

[415] United States v. Evans, 45 C.M.R. 353 (1972). *See also* United States v. Hernandez-Rojas, 617 F.2d 533 (9th Cir. 1980); United States v. Orozco, 590 F.2d 789 (9th Cir. 1979); United States v. Grady, 544 F.2d 598 (2d Cir. 1978); Saltzburg, Martin & Capra, *above* note 373, at 1746; English, *Should Laboratory Reports Be Admitted at Courts-Martial to Identify Illegal Drugs?*, Army Law., May 1978, at 25, 30.

[416] Recognizing that such reports are subject to attack on an individual basis, the court has allowed the defendant to attack the report's accuracy (United States v. Miller, 49 C.M.R. 380 (C.M.A. 1974); United States v. Evans, 45 C.M.R. 353 (C.M.A. 1972); United States v. Davis, 14 M.J. 847 (A.C.M.R. 1982)), both in terms of the analyst's competence and the regularity of the test procedures. As one writer has noted, the analyst's testimony will be of little use in most instances. English, *above* note 380, at 31. *See also* Dutton v. Evans, 400 U.S. 74, 95–96 (1970) (Harlan, J., concurring). Later cases have accepted this doctrine. *See, e.g.*, United States v. Vietor, 10 M.J. 69 (C.M.A. 1980); United States v. Strangstalien, 7 M.J. 225 (C.M.A. 1979). The prosecution can avoid the laboratory report issue by stipulating to the identity of the substance tested or to the analyst's testimony, or by deposing the chemist. In addition, the prosecution should inform the defense as soon as possible that the lab report will be offered into evidence and inquire if the defense desires the analyst's presence at trial. English, *above* note 380, at 33.

[417] *Cf.* United States v. Harper, 22 M.J. 157 (C.M.A. 1986). In *Harper*, the court said that it did not have to address a pure paper case, that is, the proof of wrongful use on the basis of laboratory reports itself. The court did indicate that the federal case law has recognized the efficiency of laboratory results of urinalysis to show marijuana use in the context of prison disciplinary proceedings and probation proceedings. 25 M.J. at 162 n.4.

(Rel.3—1/07 Pub.62410)

The fact that an exception is "firmly rooted" is not necessarily determinative of a given statement's admissibility under the confrontation clause. In Ohio v. Roberts,[418] the Court wrote: "The Court has applied this 'indicia of reliability' requirement principally by concluding that certain hearsay exceptions rest upon such solid foundations that admission of virtually any evidence comports with the 'substance of the constitutional protection.'"[419] Although we may be placing too much weight on such a slim reed, it seems probable that the Court has left open an "escape clause" for unreliable hearsay.[420]

All discussions of the admissibility of hearsay evidence under the confrontation clause are subject to a significant caveat. The Supreme Court has not ruled upon the application of the confrontation clause to the armed forces. As a result, it is at least conceivable that the Constitution permits a more permissive standard than is mandated for civilian trials.[421] This could permit even the use of "testimonial" hearsay against an accused. At the same time, the Court of Appeals for the Armed Forces could decide that unique military needs could justify retaining all or part of the Supreme Court's pre-*Crawford* case law as a further protection for the accused.

§ 20-32.25   "Particularized Guarantees" In General

Before the prosecution may offer a hearsay statement, not "firmly rooted," made by an unavailable declarant against the accused at trial on the merits, it must demonstrate that the statement has sufficient "indicia of reliability"[422] to effectively substitute for defense cross-examination of the witness.[423] In 1990, the Supreme Court put it thus: "[I]f the declarant's truthfulness is so clear from the surrounding circumstances that the test of cross-examination would be of marginal utility, then the hearsay rule does not bar admission of the statement at trial."[424]

---

[418] 448 U.S. 56, 66 (1980).

[419] 448 U.S. 56, 66 (1980)(emphasis added).

[420] Note that Fed. R. Evid. 803(6); Mil. R. Evid. 803(6) exclude statements from the exception when "the course of information or the method or circumstances or preparation indicate lack of trustworthiness." *See, e.g.*, United States v. Licavoli, 604 F.2d 613 (9th Cir. 1979); United States v. Oates, 560 F.2d 45 (2d Cir. 1977); *but see* Clark v. City of Los Angeles, 650 F.2d 1033 (9th Cir. 1981). Although there is no general provision to the codified hearsay exceptions (*but see* Mil. R. Evid. 403), perhaps the court's language implies a constitutional one.

[421] No public policy would justify this conclusion, however, short of long-term major conflict.

[422] Dutton v. Evans, 400 U.S. 74, 89 (1970).

[423] *See* Ohio v. Roberts, 448 U.S. 56, 70–71 (1980). *See also* United States v. Connor, 27 M.J. 378 (C.M.A. 1989) (verbatim Article 32 testimony admissible if the accused had the opportunity to cross-examine. Defense counsel's statement of motive for cross-examination will not be controlling).

[424] Idaho v. Wright, 497 U.S. 805, 820 (1990). The Court discussed the underlying rationales for the hearsay exceptions for excited utterances, dying declarations, and statements for purposes

Attempting to further define "particularized guarantees," the Court added:

> We think the "particularized guarantees of trustworthiness" required for admission under the Confrontation Clause must likewise be drawn from the totality of circumstances that surround the making of the statement and that render the declarant particularly worthy of belief. . . . Because evidence possessing "particularized guarantees of trustworthiness" must be at least as reliable as evidence admitted under a firmly rooted hearsay exception, . . . we think that evidence admitted under the former requirement must similarly be so trustworthy that adversarial testing would add little to its reliability. . . . Thus, unless an affirmative reason, arising from the circumstances in which the statement was made, provides a basis for rebutting the presumption that a hearsay statement isnot worthy of reliance at trial, the Confrontation Clause requires exclusion of the out-of-court statement.[425]

> [W]e are unpersuaded by the State's contention that evidence corroborating the truth of a hearsay statement may properly support a finding that the statement bears "particularized guarantees of trustworthiness." To be admissible under the Confrontation Clause, hearsay evidence used to convict a defendant must possess indicia of reliability by virtue of its inherent trustworthiness, not by reference to other evidence at trial.[426]

As a consequence, when a hearsay exception is not "firmly rooted," the judge should state on the record the special facts that indicate the high degree of trustworthiness that justifies the admission of the evidence.[427] Statements against interest, notably confessions in criminal cases, are admissible as exceptions to the hearsay rule.[428] Admissibility is premised on the fact that the statement would tend "to subject [the declarant] to civil or criminal liability" in such a fashion that a reasonable person would not make the statement unless he or she thought it to be true.[429] The assumption that people do not make disserving statements unless they are true underlies the exception,[430] and this assumption ordinarily

---

of "medical treatment," explaining why those rationales made it unlikely for a declarant to lie. 497 U.S. 805, 820 (1990).

[425] *Id.* at 820–21 (disapproving many factors previously relied upon).

[426] *Id.* at 822. The Court later continued:

> In short, the use of corroborating evidence to support a hearsay statement's "particularized guarantees of trustworthiness" would permit admission of a presumptively unreliable statement by bootstrapping on the trustworthiness of other evidence at trial, a result we think at odds with the requirement that hearsay evidence admitted under the Confrontation Clause be so trustworthy that cross-examination of the declarant would be of marginal utility.

Corroboration may be available at the appellate level when testing for harmless error.

[427] United States v. Hines, 23 M.J. 125, 135 (C.M.A. 1986) (citing S. Rep. No. 1277, 93th Cong., 2d Session).

[428] Mil. R. Evid. 804(b)(3). This assumes that Military Rules of Evidence 306 is not applicable.

[429] Mil. R. Evid. 804(b)(3).

[430] Fed. R. Evid. 804(b)(3), Adv. Comm. Notes, 56 F.R.D. 183, 327.

appears to establish "indicia of reliability" for confrontation purposes.[431] Particular concern for reliability is involved in the offer of a third party's confession to exculpate the defendant. To obviate the danger of fabrication, the Federal and Military Rules of Evidence require corroborating evidence to "clearly indicate the trustworthiness of the statement."[432] Perhaps more important, however, are statements against interest that implicate the accused. If the confession includes statements implicating the accused, under general principles the statements may be admissible as contextual statements.[433] Yet, there is some uneasiness in "identifying all third-party confessions implicating a defendant as legitimate declarations against penal interest."[434] The Courts of Military Review

---

[431] *See also* United States v. Alvarez, 584 F.2d 694 (5th Cir. 1978). In United States v. Nutter, 22 M.J. 727, 731 (A.C.M.R. 1986), the court observed: "The penal interest exception is regarded by many as a rule of recent origin rather than a "firmly rooted" hearsay exception; others argue that this is an historical anomaly and that this exception should be regarded as 'firmly rooted.' We believe that the latter view is correct." (rejecting the corroboration requirement imposed by Alvarez).

[432] Fed. R. Evid. 804(b)(3); Mil. R. Evid. 804(b)(3). *See* McCormick On Evidence §§ 317–18 (4th ed. Supp. 1992) [hereinafter McCormick]. The Courts of Military Review have also applied this requirement to third-party statements that inculpate the accused. United States v. Garrett, 16 M.J. 941 (N.M.C.M.R. 1983); United States v. Robinson, 16 M.J. 766 (A.C.M.R. 1983).

[433] McCormick, *above* note 432, § 319, at 343–48. *See also* United States v. Barrett, 539 F.2d 244 (1st Cir. 1976) (contextual statements admissible if neutral in interest and giving meaning to statement).

A declarant's inculpatory statement made to the authorities that implicates the accused may be the result of a desire to improve the declarant's position in plea bargaining or a similar motive. United States v. McConnico, 7 M.J. 302, 308 (C.M.A. 1979). *See* Westen, *Confrontation and Compulsory Process, above* note 296, at 570. The statement implicating the accused would then be self-serving and should be excluded as not against the declarant's interest (Fed. R. Evid. 804(b)(3), Adv. Comm. Notes, 56 F.R.D. at 328; *see also* Parker v. Randolph, 442 U.S. 62, 85–86 (1979) (Stevens, J., dissenting); Bruton v. United States, 391 U.S. 123, 141–42 (1968) (White, J., dissenting); United States v. Oliver, 626 F.2d 254 (2d Cir. 1980); United States v. Love, 592 F.2d 1022 (8th Cir. 1979); United States v. Lilley, 581 F.2d 182 (8th Cir. 1978); *but see McConnico*, 7 M.J. at 308 (no reason to exclude when confession offered solely to establish commission of crime by principal, confession was voluntary, and declarant refused to testify because of privilege against self-incrimination), a similar statement made to an accomplice could easily qualify as one falling under the hearsay exception. *See* McCormick, *above* note 432, § 318, at 340–43; Fed. R. Evid. 804(b), Adv. Comm. Notes, 56 F.R.D. at 328. *Cf.* Dutton v. Evans, 400 U.S. 74 (1970) (coconspirator exception). *But see, e.g.*, United States v. Pena, 527 F.2d 1356 (5th Cir. 1976) (no declaration when declarant may not have believed he was confessing to crime). Thus, any confrontation issue depends directly on the circumstances surrounding the declarant's confession. *See McConnico*, 7 M.J. at 309. Obviously, if the codefendant takes the stand, no problem exists, inasmuch as the exception is premised on the declarant's unavailability. *See* Nelson v. O'Neil, 402 U.S. 622 (1971); Mil. R. Evid. 306, 76 Dick. L. Rev. 354 (1972). *See also* United States v. Perner, 14 M.J. 181 (C.M.A. 1982).

[434] United States v. McConnico, 7 M.J. 302, 308 (C.M.A. 1979) (citing FED. R. EVID. 804(b), Adv. Comm. Notes, 56 F.R.D. 183, 328). *Accord* United States v. Sarmiento-Perez, 633 F.2d 1092 (5th Cir. 1981); United States v. White, 553 F.2d 310 (2d Cir. 1977).

(Rel.3—1/07   Pub.62410)

and Courts of Criminal Appeals have been extremely hostile to declarations against the penal interests of witnesses that also inculpate the accused,[435] and those hostilities echo the confrontation clause's reliability focus.[436] Following Williamson v. United States,[437] the court held that judges must admit statements that are "truly self-inculpatory."[438] The court also held, following the majority federal rule, that declarations against penal interest are "firmly-rooted hearsay exceptions."[439] Although the Court of Military Appeals indicated that it would treat declarations against penal interest as "well established" for confrontation purposes,[440] in the context of accomplice statements it has held: The criterion,

---

[435] United States v. Nutter, 22 M.J. 727 (A.C.M.R. 1986) (The court held that Hall, an inmate at the detention barracks, could recount a statement by McCray describing McCray's participation in an assault and homosexual rape perpetrated by McCray and two unnamed individuals. The judge did not allow Hall to recount that McCray had either mentioned or implicated the accused by name, but allowed Hall to testify as to the details of McCray's description of the offense, which tended to implicate the accused as one of two accomplices. In particular, Hall recounted McCray's statement that one of the fellow assailants had to be pulled away from the victim). In *Nutter*, a good resource case, the court noted that declarations against interest were firmly rooted exceptions to the hearsay rule. *But see* note 431 (court conceding that others hold a contrary view). *See also* United States v. Garrett, 16 M.J. 941 (N.M.C.M.R. 1983); United States v. Robinson, 16 M.J. 766 (A.C.M.R. 1983), *aff'd*, 24 M.J. 413 (C.M.A. 1987); United States v. Garrett, 17 M.J. 907 (A.F.C.M.R. 1984). *But see* United States v. Vazquez, 18 M.J. 668 (A.C.M.R. 1984). *See generally* Brown, *A Case for the Admissibility of the Inculpatory Statement Against Penal Interest: Overcoming the Judicial Reluctance to Change*, 105 Mil. R. Evid. 97 (1984).

[436] Arguably, the use of a codefendant's confession violates the rationale of Bruton v. United States, 391 U.S. 123 (1968). *See* Sections 35.20 and 20-33.13 for a more detailed discussion, which held that use at a joint trial of codefendant A's confession, which implicates codefendant B but is not admissible against B, violates B's confrontation right, and that limiting instructions are inadequate to protect B. Gray v. Maryland, 523 U.S. 185 (1998) (*Bruton* violation when the redaction might identify defendant). *But see* Parker v. Randolph, 442 U.S. 62 (1979) (*Bruton* not applicable to interlocking confessions of multiple defendants with proper limiting instructions).

The confession strengthens the government's case by evidence that the codefendant B cannot test by cross-examination, and the evidence is equally damaging whether it proves the fact of the commission of the crime or the identity of the defendant as perpetrator. *See McConnico*, 7 M.J. at 315–16 (C.M.A. 1979) (Perry, J., dissenting). *But see id.* at 309–10. *Cf.* Parker v. Randolph, 442 U.S. at 72–73 (codefendant confession less prejudicial when defendant has confessed also). The declarant's confession often will be as inconsistent with the defense, even if it does not explicitly refer to the defendant or of anyone else, as if it clearly named the defendant; the confession can factually contradict the defense's theory, or the facts can be such that both the declarant and the defendant are probably guilty, if either is. A. Amsterdam, Trial Manual For The Defense Of Criminal Cases 1-273, 359–60 (3d ed. 1975). The Court of Military Appeals avoided the issue in light of the differing opinions of the Supreme Court, preferring to decide the question by assuming a violation of the confrontation clause and then deciding the error was harmless. *McConnico*, 7 M.J. at 309–10. *See also* Section 6-35.20.

[437] 512 U.S. 594 (1994).

[438] United State v. Jacobs, 44 M.J. 301, 306 (C.A.A.F. 1996).

[439] *Id.*

[440] United States v. Wind, 28 M.J. 381, 385 (C.M.A. 1989); *see also* United States v. Greer, 33 M.J. 426, 431 n.3 (C.M.A. 1991).

(Rel.3—1/07 Pub.62410)

however, is not whether a declarant's statement might be admissible to help convict him if at some later time he were brought to trial but, instead, whether the declarant would himself have perceived at the time that his statement was against his penal interest.[441]

§ 20-32.25(a) The Residual Hearsay Exception

The drafters of the Federal Rules of Evidence initially proposed the virtual elimination of the hearsay rule. Congress preferred the traditional approach, however, and the present system of exclusion with numerous exceptions resulted. The primary remnants of the drafters' position were the two "open-ended" exceptions, the residual hearsay rules, Rule 803(24) and 804(b)(5), now relocated without change as Rule 807. In relevant part, Rule 807 provides for admissibility of the following: A statement not specifically covered by Rule 803 or 804 but having equivalent circumstantial guarantees of trustworthiness, if the court determines that (A) the statement is offered as evidence of a material fact; (B) the statement is more probative on the point for which it is offered than any other evidence which the proponent can procure through reasonable efforts; and (C) the general purposes of these rules and the interests of justice will best be served by admission of the statement into evidence. However, a statement may not be admitted under this exception unless the proponent of it makes known to the adverse party sufficiently in advance of the trial or hearing to provide the adverse party with a fair opportunity to prepare to meet it, the proponent's intention to offer the statement and the particulars of it, including the name and address of the declarant.Military Rule of Evidence 807 was taken without change from the Federal Rule of Evidence. The scope of the residual exception remains to be seen. The critical question, however, is the constitutionality of the exceptions in light of the confrontation clause.[442] It is apparent that the residual rule is not "firmly rooted."[443] Although the residual exception has seen use in a wide variety of circumstances, it often seems that the primary use of the exception in the armed forces is in child-abuse cases, particularly sexual abuse.[444] The courts' treatment of confrontation clause issues in these and other

---

[441] United States v. Greer, 33 M.J. 426, 430 (C.M.A. 1991) (citing cases) (holding that accomplice statements were not in fact against the declarant's penal interests and were inadmissible under Mil. R. Evid. 804(b)(3) and the confrontation clause).

[442] The Court of Military Appeals has held that the rules' requirement for "equivalent circumstantial guarantees of trustworthiness" can be equated to the confrontation clause's "indicia of reliability."United States v. Hines, 23 M.J. 125, 134 (C.M.A. 1986).

[443] Idaho v. Wright, 497 U.S. 805, 816 (1990).

[444] In discussing such cases, the Supreme Court has written:

The state and federal courts have identified a number of factors that we think properly relate to whether hearsay statements made by a child witness in child sexual abuse cases are reliable. *See, e.g.,* State v. Robinson, 153 Ariz. 191, 201, 735 P.2d 801, 811 (1987) (spontaneity and consistent repetition); Morgan v. Foretich, 846 F.2d 941,

(Rel.3—1/07 Pub.62410)

cases makes it clear that the courts will sometimes find the facts of a given hearsay statement sufficiently reliable, but that case-by-case consideration often yields few firm guidelines.[445] One matter that has been resolved is the use of

948 (Cir. 4th 1988) (mental state of the declarant); State v. Sorenson, 143 Wis. 2d 226, 246, 421 N.W.2d 77, 85 (1988) (use of terminology unexpected of a child of similar age); State v. Kuone, 243 Kan. 218, 221–222, 757 P.2d 289, 292–293 (1988) (lack of motive to fabricate). Although these cases (which we cite for the factors they discuss and not necessarily to approve the results that they reach) involve the application of various hearsay exceptions to statements of child declarants, we think the factors identified also apply to whether such statements bear "particularized guarantees of trustworthiness" under the Confrontation Clause. These factors are, of course, not exclusive, and courts therefore have considerable leeway in their consideration of appropriate factors. We therefore decline to endorse a mechanical test for determining "particularized guarantees of trustworthiness" under the Clause. Rather, the unifying principle is that these factors relate to whether the child declarant was particularly likely to be telling the truth when the statement was made.

Idaho v. Wright, 497 U.S. 805, 821–22 (1990).

[445] United States v. Hines, 23 M.J. 125 (C.M.A. 1986). The utility of the residual hearsay exception (formerly Mil. R. Evid. 803(24) and 804(b)(5)) is unclear under this test. Neither exception is a firmly rooted exception, yet both are contingent upon the proffered hearsay being material, probative, and having circumstantial guarantees of trustworthiness equivalent to the enumerated exceptions. *See* United States v. Hyder, 47 M.J. 46 (C.A.A.F. 1997) (citing *Yeager, below*, the court held that a statement of co-actor which implicates his soon-to-be fiancee had a number of guarantees of truthfulness); United States v. Ureta, 44 M.J. 290, 296–98 (C.A.A.F. 1996) (admitted victim's videotaped statement to investigators relying on *Wright* factors and "open-ended, non-leading questions; repeated emphasis on truthfulness; and declarations against declarant's interest"); United States v. Yeager, 27 M.J. 199 (C.M.A. 1988) (number of factors established reliability); United States v. Quick, 26 M.J. 460 (C.M.A. 1988) (statement of four-year-old girl to baby sitter, corroborated by accused's statement, was admissible); United States v. Smith, 26 M.J. 152 (C.M.A. 1988) (testimony of victim's boyfriend made at trial of co-accused was admissible since boyfriend could not testify because of defense delay); United States v. Dunlap, 39 M.J. 835 (A.C.M.R. 1994) (teacher's inquiry about molestation during class didn't qualify); United States v. Lyons, 33 M.J. 543, 546–48 (A.F.C.M.R. 1991) (videotape of deaf, mute, and retarded woman's reenactment of sexual assault qualified), *aff'd*, 36 M.J. 183 (C.M.A. 1992); United States v. Fink, 32 M.J. 987, 992 (A.C.M.R. 1991) (permitted when retarded child made spontaneous statements to teacher's aide about abuse by father); United States v. Ruffin 12 M.J. 952 (A.F.C.M.R. 1982) (hearsay statements by minors held admissible under Mil. R. Evid. 804(b)(5)); United States v. Whalen, 15 M.J. 872 (A.C.M.R. 1983) (retracted written and sworn confession sufficiently trustworthy under residual hearsay rule where witness, as well as CID agent who took confession, testified and were subjected to extensive cross-examination). *But see* United States v. Thornton, 16 M.J. 1011 (A.C.M.R. 1983) (statement to assistant SJA not sufficiently trustworthy under Residual Hearsay Rule and not sufficiently reliable under confrontation clause); United States v. White, 17 M.J. 953 (A.F.C.M.R. 1984) (statement of accused's mother unreliable in view of conflicting evidence on her mental condition); United States v. Crayton, 17 M.J. 932 (A.F.C.M.R. 1984) (earlier statements of child witness who later recanted untrustworthy); United States v. Guaglione, 27 M.J. 268 (C.M.A. 1988) (statement obtained by police faking a hometown news release was inadmissible — no corroboration); United States v. Williamson, 26 M.J. 115 (C.M.A. 1988) (statements of four-year-old was not admissible).

(Rel.3—1/07 Pub.62410)

corroborating evidence to establish reliability. The Court of Military Appeals often considered the presence of evidence corroborating a hearsay statement as an important factor in determining "particularized guarantees."[446] In 1990, however, the United States Supreme Court, in *Idaho v. Wright*,[447] held:

> "In short, the use of corroborating evidence to support a hearsay statement's 'particularized guarantees of trustworthiness' would permit admission of a presumptively unreliable statement by bootstrapping on the trustworthiness of other evidence at trial, a result we think at odds with the requirement that hearsay evidence admitted under the Confrontation Clause be so trustworthy that cross-examination of the declarant would be of marginal utility.[448]

Although *Wright* is controlling in the military, its application need not bar admission of hearsay,[449] and the Court of Military Appeals so held in *United States v. McGrath*[450] in construing the scope of the residual hearsay rules when confrontation is not at issue.

§ 20-32.30   The Right to Cross-Examine the Government's Witnesses at Trial

§ 20-32.31   In General

While the Sixth Amendment to some degree requires the state to disclose its evidence to the accused at trial and to present its evidence in the best available form,[451] it also protects the accused's interest in cross-examining opposing witnesses, a right of invaluable importance.[452] In *Smith v. Illinois*,[453] for example, the defendant was prevented from cross-examining a prosecution witness about his real name and address.[454] Reversing the conviction, the Supreme Court held that the permissible scope of defense cross-examination of a prosecution witness is measured by independent constitutional standards.[455]

---

[446] *See, e.g.*, United States v. Hines, 23 M.J. 125, 136, 137–38 (C.M.A. 1986).

[447] 497 U.S. 805 (1990).

[448] The Court did observe, however, that "we think the presence of corroborating evidence more appropriately indicates that any error in admitting the statement might be harmless." 497 U.S. at 823 (1990).

[449] United States v. Moreno, 31 M.J. 935, 939 (A.C.M.R. 1990) (videotaped disposition), *aff'd*, 36 M.J. 107 (C.M.A. 1992).

[450] 38 M.J. 158 (C.M.A. 1994).

[451] *See* Section 20-32.23(a). *Cf.* Pennsylvania v. Ritchie, 480 U.S. 39 (1987).

[452] *See, e.g.*, Harper v. Kelly, 916 F.2d 54 (2d Cir. 1990) (barring examination into victim's emotional state during robbery violated accused's right to confrontation in light of its relevancy to the victim's identification of the defendant).

[453] 390 U.S. 129 (1968).

[454] Apparently because the information was deemed irrelevant and thus beyond the scope of cross-examination.

[455] 390 U.S. at 132–33 (1968).

(Rel.3—1/07 Pub.62410)

Smith reflects the concept that, when applicable, the right to confrontation preempts the normal rules of evidence.[456] Far better known than *Smith* is *Davis v. Alaska*.[457] In *Davis*, an important state witness was a juvenile on juvenile court probation. Relying on a state law designed to protect the confidentiality of juvenile court records, the trial judge precluded defense cross-examination relating to the witness' juvenile record and his possible bias. Even though the state had an "important interest" in creating a privilege for juvenile records,[458] the Court held that the defendant's right to confrontation outweighed the state's interest in the privilege. *Davis* suggests that the defendant's right of cross-examination can be defeated, if at all, only for the most compelling reasons.[459]

The Court emphasized the importance of the defense's ability to show bias of a government witness in *Delaware v. Van Arsdall*,[460] holding that the complete denial of bias cross-examination violated the confrontation clause. The Court recognized some limitations on the right of cross-examination, however:

> It does not follow, of course, that the Confrontation Clause of the Sixth Amendment prevents a trial judge from imposing any limits on defense counsel's inquiry into the potential bias of a prosecution witness. On the contrary, trial judges retain wide latitude insofar as the Confrontation Clause is concerned to impose reasonable limits on such cross-examination based on concerns about, among other things, harassment, prejudice, confusion of the issues, the witness' safety, or interrogation that is repetitive or only marginally relevant.[461]

---

[456] *See* Alford v. United States, 282 U.S. 687 (1931); United States v. Jacoby, 29 C.M.R. 244, 248 (C.M.A. 1960); United States v. Speer, 2 M.J. 1244 (A.F.C.M.R. 1976).

[457] 415 U.S. 308 (1974).

[458] 415 U.S. at 319 (1974).

[459] *See* Westen, *Confrontation and Compulsory Process, above* note 309, at 581. *Davis* also implies that cross-examination for impeachment purposes is more favored in confrontation analysis. *See* United States v. Saylor, 6 M.J. 647 (N.C.M.R. 1978); United States v. Streeter, 22 C.M.R. 363 (A.B.R. 1956); Fed. R. Evid. 611(b); Mil. R. Evid. 611(b); McCormick, at § 29, at 58 (2d ed. 1972). When the witness refuses to answer on cross-examination, the accused's usual remedy for this denial of his right to confront an adverse witness is to have that witness' direct testimony stricken from the record. United States v. Rivas, 3 M.J. 282, 285 (C.M.A. 1977) (footnote omitted). *See also* Mil. R. Evid. 301(f)(2); United States v. Demchak, 545 F.2d 1029 (5th Cir. 1977); United States v. Vandermark, 14 M.J. 690 (N.M.C.M.R. 1982). The remedy must be requested by the defense and is invariably granted unless the refusal applies only to collateral matters. United States v. Hornbrook, 14 M.J. 663 (A.C.M.R. 1982); United States v. Lawless, 13 M.J. 943 (A.F.C.M.R. 1982), *aff'd*, 18 M.J. 255 (C.M.A. 1984). However, the military judge has no duty to strike, *sua sponte*, the direct testimony in order to einsure the basic fairness of the court-martial when the direct testimony is not inadmissible *per se*. Rivas, 4 M.J. at 286. *See also* United States v. Terrell, 4 M.J. 720 (A.F.C.M.R. 1977); United States v. Boone, 17 M.J. 567 (A.F.C.M.R. 1983); United States v. Weeks, 17 M.J. 613 (N.M.C.M.R. 1983). The harmless error rule does apply in this area. United States v. Moore, 36 M.J. 329 (C.M.A. 1993) (if any error, it was harmless).

[460] 475 U.S. 673 (1986) (holding that a confrontation-clause error can be tested for constitutional harmless error).

[461] 475 U.S. at 678 (1986).

(Rel.3—1/07 Pub.62410)

Although the Court's opinions in this area, strictly construed, indicate only that the defense must be permitted to show the bias of a hostile witness,[462] it is apparent that they also stand for the proposition that the accused must be permitted a meaningful cross-examination of a witness regardless of local rules of evidence.[463] This right does not extend to a meaningful cross-examination of a witness whose memory is inadequate.[464]

In *Delaware v. Fensterer,*[465] the Court considered a confrontation challenge involving the basis of expert testimony. The prosecution expert testified to his conclusion but was unable to remember which of three possible methods he had used to reach that conclusion. The Court held this inability nonviolative of the confrontation clause: "[I]t does not follow that the right to cross-examine is denied by the State whenever the witnesses' lapse of memory impedes one method of discrediting him."[466] Concurring in the judgment, Justice Stevens stated: "The question decided by the Court today concerns the admissibility of an earlier out of-court conclusion reached by a witness who disclaims any present recollection of the *basis* for that conclusion."[467]

Cross-examination serves three main functions: it sheds light on the credibility of the direct testimony; it brings out additional facts related to those elicited on

---

[462] Davis v. Alaska, 415 U.S. 308 (1974); Alford v. United States, 282 U.S. 687 (1931); United States v. Jones, 49 M.J. 85 (C.A.A.F. 1998) (error to exclude evidence as to victim's capacity to observe and remember).

[463] *See, e.g.,* Davis, 415 U.S. at 320, in which the Court held that the state's policy in protecting juvenile offenders' records cannot require yielding of so vital a constitutional right as the effective cross-examination for bias of an adverse witness.

[464] Delaware v. Fensterer, 474 U.S. 15 (1985) (per curiam).

[465] 474 U.S. 15 (1985). See also United States v. Owens, 484 U.S. 554 (1988). United States v. Lawson, 653 F.2d 302 (7th Cir. 1981), *cert. denied,* 454 U.S. 1150 (1982) (Expert had limited personal contact with the defendant and relied on hearing information in formulating his opinion on insanity. While an expert's testimony that was based entirely on hearsay reports might satisfy Federal Rule of Evidence 703, it would nevertheless violate a defendant's constitutional right to confront adverse witnesses. The government could not, for example, simply produce a witness who did nothing but summarize out-of-court statements by others.); State v. Towne, 142 Vt. 241, 246, 453 A.2d 1133, 1135 (1982) (expert testified that he had spoken by telephone with an author about the case and author agreed with his opinion). *See also* Carlson, *Collision Course in Expert Testimony: Limitations on Affirmative Introduction of Underlying Data,* 36 U. Fla. L. Rev. 234 (1984).

[466] *Fensterer,* 474 U.S. at 19.

[467] 474 U.S. at 24 (emphasis in original). *See also* United States v. Bridges, 55 M.J. 60, 65 (C.A.A.F. 2001) (although unwilling prosecution witness took the stand and answered some preliminary questions, she refused to testify further leading to a finding of unavailability and, after defense rejection of cross-examination, a defense waiver of the right to confrontation); United States v. McGrath, 39 M.J. 158, 163 (C.M.A. 1994); McCormick, *above,* note 432, § 21, at 47.

(Rel.3—1/07 Pub.62410)

direct examination; and in jurisdictions allowing "wide-open" cross-examination, it brings out any additional facts tending to elucidate any issue in the case.[468]

While the standard of relevancy applied to direct testimony can be logically applied to facts elicited on cross-examination for use on the merits,[469] the standard is markedly different for facts obtained to evaluate the credibility of evidence given during direct examination. In those instances, the test is "whether it will to a useful extent aids the court or jury in appraising the witness's credibility of the witness and assessing the probative value of the direct testimony."[470] Questioning for this purpose takes various forms, and the criteria of relevancy are vague. Close adherence to a fixed standard may limit the usefulness of the cross-examination, but the dangers of undue prejudice and excessive consumption of time clearly lurk in the background.[471] Clearly, evidence that is irrelevant cannot invoke the confrontation clause. However, it is probable that evidence that is technically relevant to impeachment might not have the degree of probative value of importance necessary to make the clause applicable.

Codifying the common law, Military Rule of Evidence 506(a) creates an informant's privilege that, when invoked by the prosecution, permits the government not to disclose the identity of an informant. Although Rule 506(c)(1) provides that there is no privilege if the informant appears as a witness, Rule 506 has the potential to limit defense cross-examination of other witnesses.[472] Under normal circumstances, this limitation on confrontation will be upheld.[473]

---

[468] John W. Strong, Kenneth Broun, George E. Dix, Edward J Imwinkelried, D.H. Kaye, Robert Mosteller & E.F. Roberts, *McCormick on Evidence, above* note 432, §§ 24; 26-27; 29 (5th ed. 1999). *See also* Edward J. Imwinkelried, Paul C. Giannelle; Francis A. Gilligan & Fredric I. Lederer, Criminal Courtroom Evidence §§ 106-109 (4th ed. 2006). The armed forces is not a wide-open jurisdiction, as cross-examination is restricted to the scope of the direct. Mil. R. Evid. 611(b).

[469] McCormick, *above* note 432, § 29, at 101.

[470] McCormick, *above*, note 432, at § 29, at 99.

[471] Thus, the trial judge has the power to control the extent of cross-examination. Fed. R. Evid. 611(a); Mil. R. Evid. 611(a).

[472] For other circumstances in which the privilege does not apply, see generally Rule 506(c).

[473] *E.g.*, United States v. Lonetree, 35 M.J. 396 (C.M.A. 1992) (Sentelle, D.C. Cir.) (judge prohibited defense from obtaining intelligence agent's name or background). *See also* United States v. Foster, 986 F.2d 541 (D.C. Cir. 1993) (in some cases the government may invoke the observation post privilege when the location secrecy is important to maintain future usefulness); United States v. Orozco, 982 F.2d 152 (5th Cir. 1992) (no disclosure required if informant was an eyewitness who played a minor role).

§ 20-32.32   The Rape-Shield Rule

§ 20-32.32(a)   In General

In one situation in particular, that of sexual assault cases, potentially relevant cross-examination has been restricted by the Military Rules of Evidence. When the issue of consent is raised in a forcible rape case, evidence of character traits of the victim has generally been considered relevant[474] notwithstanding its usual lack of probative value and the detrimental impact of its admission on victims and factfinders. In reaction to political pressure from women's rights organizations and law enforcement agencies,[475] however, the overwhelming majority of jurisdictions now limit the relevance of the past sexual behavior of a victim of a forcible sexual offense.[476] The military approach, codified in Military Rule of Evidence 412, substantially follows Federal Rule of Evidence 412.[477] As originally promulgated, Subdivision (a) expressly declared that, in any case in which the defendant is charged with a "sexual misconduct,"[478] the court-martial cannot admit into evidence reputation or opinion evidence concerning the past sexual behavior[479] of an alleged victim.[480] Subdivision (b)(1) precluded admission of the victim's past sexual behavior unless the evidence was constitutionally required or was offered to show:

> (A) evidence of specific instances of sexual behavior by the alleged victim offered to prove that a person other than the accused was the source of semen, injury, or other physical evidence; or

> (B) evidence of specific instances of sexual behavior by the alleged victim with respect to the person accused of sexual misconduct offered by the accused to prove consent or by the prosecution.[481]

---

[474] McCormick, *above* note 432, § 193, at 822–23.

[475] 23 C. Wright & K. Graham, Federal Practice & Procedure: Evidence § 5382, at 492–531 (1980) [hereinafter Wright & Graham].

[476] "[A]lmost every jurisdiction in this country has enacted some sort of rape shield law." R. Lempert & S. Saltzburg, A Modern Approach To Evidence 636 (2d ed. 1983).

[477] Analysis of the Military Rules of Evidence, 412, MCM, 2005, A22-35, 22-36. The original military rule was somewhat broader than the original civilian rule in that it applied to any nonconsensual sexual offense. Mil. R. Evid. 412(a). *See generally,* Fredric Lederer, *The Military Rules of Evidence: Origins and Judicial Implementation,* 130 Mil. R. Evid. 5, 20–23 (1990). The current civilian and military rules are much broader, applying as they do, to "alleged sexual misconduct."

[478] Illustrations of included offenses are listed in Mil. R. Evid. 412(e).

[479] Past sexual behavior is defined in Mil. R. Evid. 412(d). *See* Wright & Graham, *below* note 475, § 5384, at 538–48.

[480] Mil. R. Evid. 412(a). *Compare* Mil. R. Evid. 405(a) (when character evidence is used circumstantially, only reputation or opinion evidence is admissible). Rule 412 takes the opposite view, admitting only specific acts and limiting the circumstances in which that evidence is admissible.

[481] Mil. R. Evid. 412(b)(1). *See also* United States v. Elvine, 16 M.J. 14, 18 (C.M.A. 1983).

(Rel.3—1/07   Pub.62410)

Notably, unlike Rule 412(b), Rule 412(a) did not provide in its text for admission of evidence that is constitutionally required but otherwise prohibited by the Rule. The drafters of the Rule, however, declared in the Analysis that "evidence that is constitutionally required to be admitted on behalf of the defense remains admissible notwithstanding the absence of express authorization in Rule 412(a)."[482] Rule 412 was subsequently amended, and Rule 412(a) now declares inadmissible, subject to the above exceptions, "in any proceeding involving alleged sexual misconduct," "evidence offered to prove that any alleged victim engaged in other sexual behavior" or "evidence offered to prove any alleged victim's sexual predisposition."[483]

In light of the 1998 amendment of Rule 412, the Court of Appeals for the Armed Forces has interpreted the Rule's protections as extending to a "'victim of alleged sexual misconduct'" rather than when the accused is charged with a "nonconsual sexual offense".[484]

Unlike Federal Rule of Evidence 412, which requires fourteen days written notice of defense intent to offer evidence governed by the rape-shield rule, in order to speed trials Military Rule of Evidence 412 simply requires "at least 5 days" notice. What constitutes adequate notice has been left to case law as has been the consequence of noncompliance with the requirement.[485] In *Michigan v. Lucas*,[486] the Supreme Court held that preclusion of defense evidence for noncompliance with the state rape-shield rule's notice requirement was not per se unconstitutional. Given the permissive nature of the military rule, it seems improbable that preclusion would be ordered for noncompliance absent the most extraordinary circumstances.[487]

§ 20-32.32(b)   Potential Confrontation and Compulsory Process Problems

Rape-shield laws, including Military Rule of Evidence 412, generally have been upheld against claims that they violate the right of confrontation.[488]

---

[482] Analysis of the Military Rules of Evidence, Analysis of Mil. R. Evid. 412, MCM, 2005, A22-35. *See generally* Fredric Lederer, *The Military Rules of Evidence, Origin and Judicial Implementation,* 130 Mil. R. Evid. 5, 22 (1990). The analytical mode is set out most fully in United States v. Dorsey, 16 M.J. 1 (C.M.A. 1983). *See generally* Rose & Chapman, *The Military's Rape Shield Law: An Emerging Roadmap,* Army Law., May 1984, at 29.

[483] R.C.M. 412

[484] United States v. Banker, 60 M.J. 216, 220 (C.A.A.F. 2005).

[485] *Cf.* United States v. Sanchez, 44 M.J. 174 (C.A.A.F. 1996).

[486] 500 U.S. 145 (1991).

[487] *E.g.,* United States v. Whitaker, 34 M.J. 822, 829 (A.F.C.M.R. 1992).

[488] United States v. Hollimon, 16 M.J. 164 (C.M.A. 1983); United States v. Pickens, 17 M.J. 391 (C.M.A. 1984); United States v. Johnson, 17 M.J. 517 (A.F.C.M.R. 1983). *See generally* Annot., 1 A.L.R. 4th 283, 292–300 (1980); Wright & Graham, *above* note 424, § 5387, at 571

Nevertheless, the application of those laws in a particular case may violate the defendant's right to cross-examine a prosecution witness.[489] The rule may also violate the accused's right to present favorable defense evidence through means other than cross-examination.[490]

The remainder of subdivision (b) of Rule 412 expressly provides that evidence constitutionally required to be admitted shall be admitted despite the general prohibition on evidence of the sexual history of the victim. The Court of Military Appeals provided an analytical mode for determining whether any type of sexual misconduct evidence is constitutionally required. Relying primarily on compulsory process analysis, the court has stated that constitutionally required evidence must be relevant, material, and favorable to the accused.[491] Sexual misconduct evidence may be constitutionally required when the victim's sexual history is proffered to show a motive for fabricating a rape charge[492] or that the rape charge

---

n.53. United States v. Dorsey, 16 M.J. 1 (C.M.A. 1983); United States v. Colon-Angueira, 16 M.J. 20 (C.M.A. 1983); United States v. Ferguson, 14 M.J. 840 (A.C.M.R. 1982); State v. DeLawder, 28 Md. App. 212, 344 A.2d 446 (1975); State v. Jalo, 27 Or. App. 845, 557 P.2d 1359 (1976). In *Ferguson*, the Court of Review held that evidence of the victim's past sexual history, coupled with the testimony of a psychiatrist, should have been admitted to establish a motive for a false accusation of rape. The court's opinion reviews a number of cases dealing with the effect of the confrontation clause on rape-shield rules and represents a useful resource to counsel faced with this issue. *See also* United States v. Elvine, 16 M.J. 14 (C.M.A. 1983) (inadequate offer of proof).

[489] Davis v. Alaska, 415 U.S. 308 (1974); Chambers v. Mississippi, 410 U.S. 284 (1973).

[490] United States v. Colon-Angueira, 16 M.J. 20 (C.M.A. 1983) (accused prevented from questioning own witness about prosecutrix's own statements of her sexual misconduct). Wright & Graham, *above* note 475, § 5387, at 574 n.73. For other situations, *see also* United States v. Johnson, 17 M.J. 517 (A.F.C.M.R. 1983) (prior sexual activity of stepdaughters not relevant to show they had independent knowledge of sexual matters).

[491] The Court of Military Appeals, relying primarily on compulsory-process grounds, has stated the test to admit any type of sexual misconduct evidence is that it be relevant, material, and favorable to the accused. United States v. Hollimon, 16 M.J. 164, 165 (C.M.A. 1983). *See also* United States v. Pickens, 17 M.J. 391 (C.M.A. 1984).

[492] *See* United States v. Dorsey, 16 M.J. 1 (C.M.A. 1983); United States v. Colon-Angueira, 16 M.J. 20 (C.M.A. 1983); United States v. Ferguson, 14 M.J. 840 (A.C.M.R. 1982); Lewis v. State, 591 So. 2d 922 (Fla. 1991) (permissible to introduce sex with boyfriend to support defense that rape complaint was fabricated to explain results of gynecological examination); State v. De-Lawder, 28 Md. App. 212, 344 A.2d 446 (1975); State v. Jalo, 27 Or. App. 845, 557 P.2d 1359 (1976). In *Ferguson*, the Court of Review held that evidence of the victim's past sexual history, coupled with the testimony of a psychiatrist, should have been admitted to establish a motive for a false accusation of rape. The court's opinion discusses rape-shield rules, and represents a useful resource to counsel faced with this issue. *See also* United States v. Elvine, 16 M.J. 14 (C.M.A. 1983) (inadequate offer of proof).

As to evidence of second abusers, the court will examine similarity of abusers, similarity of acts, temporal and geographical facts, and expert testimony. *See, e.g.*, United States v. Pagel, 45 M.J. 64 (C.A.A.F. 1996) (not admissible); United States v. Buenventura, 44 M.J. 72 (C.A.A.F. 1996) (admissible); United States v. Gober, 43 M.J. 52 (C.A.A.F. 1995) (not admissible).

(Rel.3—1/07   Pub.62410)

might be used by the victim to explain her pregnancy,[493] injury[494] or, in the case of a minor, an all-night absence from home,[495] or to show that a person other than the accused was responsible for the offense.[496] Applying the Rule becomes more problematic in other contexts, such as impeachment by showing bias or specific contradiction. In a group-rape case, the accused might claim, for example, that the victim's testimony has been influenced because she had previously had sexual relations with one of the rapists.[497] Conversely, a witness who corroborates part of the victim's story might be biased because he or she is her lover or, at the least, has previously had sexual relations with the victim.[498] *Davis v. Alaska*[499] may be little help in such a case, as *Davis* could be read as allowing cross-examination to establish that the witness has a reason to accuse someone, but without showing that the witness has a particular bias for accusing the defendant.[500] In *United States v. Williams*,[501] the court held that evidence of the putative victim's extramarital affair with a person other than the accused at the time of the alleged rape was constitutionally required to be admitted. Applying *Olden v. Kentucky*[502] and *Delaware v. Van Arsdall*,[503] the court held that those "decisions encompass the test for 'constitutionally required' evidence

---

[493] State v. DeLawder, 28 Md. App. 212, 344 A.2d 446 (1975).

[494] In contrast to the Court of Military Appeals' decision in United States v. Welch, 25 M.J. 23 (C.M.A. 1987), the Eighth Circuit Court of Appeals, in United States v. Shaw, 824 F.2d 601 (8th Cir. 1987), held that testimony that an 11-year-old victim's hymen was not intact was not evidence of an injury within the meaning of Federal Rule of Evidence 412(b)2(A). This conclusion was based on expert testimony that the membrane tends to stretch rather than rupture as is commonly believed and that many activities other than sexual intercourse may cause such a condition. Under *Shaw*, evidence of physiological accommodation of the hymen, even if caused by sexual activity, falls short of establishing injury so as to trigger Rule 412. Some commentators have suggested that, when the government offers any evidence as to physical consequences that the act took place, the defendant should be allowed to introduce past sexual behavior. Wright & Graham, *above* note4note 42440, at 598 (1980). *See also* United States v. Azure, 845 F.2d 1503 (8th Cir. 1988) (even though the child's vagina was enlarged or the wall torn, courts found no abuse of discretion in not admitting evidence of prior acts after an *in camera* hearing); State v. Figueroa, 1990 Ohio App. LEXIS 5793 (December 27, 1990).

[495] Wright & Graham, *above* note 475, § 5387, at n.73.

[496] United States v. Buenaventura, 45 M.J. 72 (C.A.A.F. 1996).

[497] United States v. Jensen, 25 M.J. 284 (C.M.A. 1987). *See also* State v. Colbath, 540 A.2d 1212 (N.H. 1988) (several hours prior to the rape, the victim was provocative with several men in a bar, including the accused).

[498] Wright & Graham, *above* note 475, § 5387, at 576.

[499] 415 U.S. 308 (1974).

[500] Wright & Graham, *above* note 475, § 5387, at 577.

[501] 37 M.J. 352, 359–61 (C.M.A. 1993) (holding that the judge abused his discretion in refusing to hear post trial newly discovered evidence of the alleged victim's extramarital affair).

[502] 488 U.S. 227 (1988).

[503] 475 U.S. 673 (1986).

(Rel.3—1/07 Pub.62410)

used by this court in *United States v. Dorsey*."[504] The court then concluded "that the cross-examination of the victim about her extramarital affair would have been relevant, material and favorable to the defendant."[505] Concurring, Judge Gierke expressed concern that the various terms used by the author judges might mislead the judiciary and that the three judges might unintentionally be adopting the "conceivable benefit rule" previously rejected by the Supreme Court. He then emphasized that before evidence normally inadmissible under Rule 412 could be constitutionally admitted it need not only be relevant and favorable to the defense but that it also had to be "material" in the sense of "necessary."[506] Judges Crawford and Cox concurred in the result, expressing concern with the results of some of the court's earlier Rule 412 cases. Although unclear, it may be that in Williams the court was manifesting the intent to be somewhat more protective in the future of the sexual privacy of alleged sexual assault victims.

It has been assumed that the accused has the right to contradict evidence of sexual behavior elicited by the prosecution, such as evidence that the victim was a virgin prior to the incident.[507] This view assumes too much; Rule 412 bars such evidence whoever introduces it, and ordinarily the accused has no right to compound the error.[508] On the other hand, evidence of prior sexual behavior may be relevant to rebut testimony not inadmissible itself under Rule 412.[509] The Court of Military Appeals stated that sexual conduct evidence may be constitutionally required in rebuttal,[510] to impeach by contradiction,[511] or to

---

[504] 37 M.J. at 360, *referring to* United States v. Dorsey, 16 M.J. 1 (C.M.A. 1983).

[505] 37 M.J. at 360.

[506] 37 M.J. at 361.

[507] 37 M.J. at 361.

[508] 37 M.J. at 581. The commentators contradict themselves at this point, saying first that admission of impeachment or rebuttal evidence may be constitutionally required, and then that impeachment by specific contradiction need not be permitted under Rule 412(b)(1). *Compare* Wright & Graham, *above* note 475, § 5386, at 562–63, *with* Rule 412(b)(1) § 5387, at 576–77. Impeachment through bias appears to be allowed, however. Waiver may be inapplicable here because the Rule is intended, in part, to protect the victim who is not a party to the case. Doe v. United States, 666 F.2d 43, 46 (4th Cir. 1981).

[509] For example, to counter a claim that the rape has left the victim debilitated, evidence that she later engaged in strenuous sexual activity might be proffered. When the victim denies a bias against the accused, episodes of lesbian activities might be submitted as contradiction. Wright & Graham, *above* note 475, § 5387, at 577 n.90. 37 M.J. at 581. Clearly, the exception suggested here should be narrowly construed to prevent the exception from overwhelming the rule. *See generally* United States v. Wirth, 18 M.J. 214, 218 (C.M.A. 1984); United States v. Banker, 15 M.J. 207, 211 (C.M.A. 1983) (explains impeachment by contradiction).

[510] United States v. Elvine, 16 M.J. 14, 17 (C.M.A. 1983). The relevance of prosecution rebuttal evidence is determined in light of the evidence first introduced and issues initially raised by the defense.

[511] United States v. Hollimon, 16 M.J. 164, 166 (C.M.A. 1983).

(Rel.3—1/07 Pub.62410)

rebut testimony not admissible itself under Rule 412.[512]

The victim's credibility is also challengeable by showing some defect in her ability to perceive, recall, or narrate.[513] Such defects may implicitly involve proof of prior sexual behavior, such as mental defects caused by tertiary syphilis.[514] In some cases, admission of the evidence may be required under the confrontation clause.[515]

Impeaching the victim by introducing evidence of false accusations has not received much attention. Under the terms of Rule 412, this is not "past sexual behavior."[516] Admission would seem to be limited by Military Rule of Evidence 608, which limits impeachment by specific acts to inquiry on cross-examination and subjects it to the court's discretion.[517] Notwithstanding the strictures of Rule 608, an accused's constitutional right to cross-examine in this instance includes the right to introduce evidence of previous false accusations.[518]

---

[512] *See generally* United States v. Wirth, 18 M.J. 14, 17 (C.M.A. 1984); United States v. Banker, 15 M.J. 207, 211 (C.M.A. 1983) (explains impeachment by contradiction).

[513] McCormick, *above* note 432, § 44, at 160.

[514] Evidence of disease or physical condition, per se, are not rendered inadmissible by Mil. R. Evid. 412.

[515] Wright & Graham, *above* note 475, § 5387, at 577. *But see* People v. Nemie, 87 Cal. App. 3d 926, 151 Cal. Rptr. 32 (1978) (evidence of victim's prior sexual history excluded on issue of her ability to perceive penetration).

[516] Mil. R. Evid. 412(d). *See also* Wright & Graham, *above* note 475, § 5384, at 546–47. *Cf.* Miller v. State, 779 P.2d 87 (Nev. 1989).

[517] Mil. R. Evid. 608(b).

[518] Wright & Graham, *above* note 42440, § 5387, at 580. Olden v. Kentucky, 488 U.S. 227 (1988) (per curiam) (confrontation clause is violated when rape-case defendant is not permitted to cross-examine the rape victim concerning a motive to testify falsely); United States v. Sojfer, 47 M.J. 425 (C.A.A.F. 1998) (no error in excluding evidence of prior rape report of victim to establish that victim misinterpreted defendant's abdominal examination of victim); United States v. Sanchez, 44 M.J. 174 (C.A.A.F. 1996) (motive to fabricate a charge recognized as a basis for constitutionally compelling admission of evidence that otherwise would be excluded under Mil. R. Evid. 412); United States v. Owen, 24 M.J. 390 (C.M.A. 1987) (improper to prohibit defense from introducing evidence of prior false accusations of rape — no indication of preliminary determination); Stewart v. State, 531 N.E.2d 1146 (Ind. 1988) (witness to sex crime cannot be impeached by evidence of prior false accusations); State v. Barber, 13 Kan. App. 2d 224, 766 P.2d 1288 (1989) (evidence of false accusations is admissible if the trial judge has made a preliminary determination that there is a reasonable probability of falsehood); Commonwealth v. Wall, 606 A.2d 449 (Pa. Super. 1992) (exclusion of prior false claim violated the right to confrontation). A distinction should be made between accusations that are factually unfounded and cases that are dismissed; Clinebell v. Commonwealth, 235 Va. 319, 368 S.E.2d 263 (1988) (after initial preliminary determination of the same probability as in *Barber*, false accusations admissible). *Cf.* State v. Oliver, 158 Ariz. 22, 760 P.2d 1071 (1988) (when defense is fabrication by child of tender years, evidence of prior sexual acts is admissible to establish basis for detail of testimony); Summitt v. State, 101 Nev. 159, 697 P.2d 1374 (Nev. 1985) (same); State v. Howard, 121 N.H. 53, 426 A.2d 457 (N.H. 1981) (same). *See also* United States v. Avery, 52 M.J. 496, 499 (C.A.A.F. 2000) (Sullivan, J. concurring

(Rel.3—1/07   Pub.62410)

Finally, the accused might wish to impeach the victim with evidence of past convictions. While Rule 609 would appear to control the admission of convictions into evidence [519] to the extent to which the nature of an underlying conviction may be offered for impeachment purposes, the harder case arises when the impeachment is by convictions for past sex-related crimes, such as prostitution or obscenity. [520] Rule 412 does not by its express language exclude such evidence, for it is the fact of criminal conduct — the conviction — that is important. However, such evidence indirectly includes evidence of past sexual conduct. Though *Davis v. Alaska* [521] may appear to require admission of the convictions, it may not be controlling; some courts have concluded that *Davis* only allows use of juvenile convictions to show bias rather than for general impeachment. [522] Thus, a prostitution conviction might be used to show that the victim had a motive to accuse the defendant of rape, [523] but not merely to impeach the victim's veracity. This issue is not likely to arise, as these sexually related convictions are not likely to be probative of untruthfulness and thus would neither be admissible under Military Rules of Evidence 609(a) or 608(b) nor Davis.

Rule 412 requires the judge to hold an in camera hearing to determine whether evidence of a victim's past sexual behavior is admissible. [524] However, if counsel's offer of proof concerning such behavior fails on its face to contain evidence reasonably considered constitutionally required, no in camera hearing is necessary. [525] Procedurally, the Court of Appeals for the Armed Forces has

---

in part and in the result); Quinn v. Haynes, 234 F.3d 837, 846 (4th Cir. 2000) ("A true allegation of another sexual assault is completely irrelevant to credibility and offends the clear language of [the statels] rape shield law, which is why a threshold showing of falsity ultimately is required."); United States v. Velez, 48 M.J. 220, 227 (C.A.A.F. 1998) ("The mere filing of a complaint is not even probative of the truthfulness or untruthfulness of the complaint filed. . . . Thus, its relevance on the question of credibility of a different complaint in an unrelated case. . . . entirely escapes us."); Boggs v. Collins, 226 F.3d 728, 738 (6th Cir. 2000) (citing the Eighth and the Ninth Circuit holding cross-examination of prior false rape allegation was properly prohibited); Lopez v. State, 18 S.W.3d 220, 223 (Tex. Crim. App. 2000) ("Other states have held that the Confrontation Clause requires creating a special exception for sexual offense to allow *admission of [extrinsic evidence of]* prior false accusations abuse by the complainant despite evidentiary bars.").

[519] Mil. R. Evid. 609(a). The military judge's discretion to exclude the evidence is not applicable, since exclusion is warranted only if the probative value of the conviction is less than its prejudicial effect on the accused. Mil. R. Evid. 609(a)(1). Such evidence can hardly be prejudicial to the accused, but would only be of concern to the victim.

[520] United States v. Saipaia, 24 M.J. 172, 175 (C.M.A. 1987) (if accused had admitted sexual intercourse, victim's prior activities as a prostitute would have been especially relevant).

[521] 415 U.S. 308 (1974).

[522] *E.g.*, People v. Conyers, 86 Misc. 2d 754, 382 N.Y.S.2d 437 (1976); State v. Burr, 18 Or. App. 494, 525 P.2d 1067 (1974). *Contra* State v. Cox, 42 Ohio St. 2d 200, 327 N.E.2d 639 (1975).

[523] United States v. Saipaia, 24 M.J. 172 (C.M.A. 1987).

[524] United States v. Sanchez, 44 M.J. 174 (C.A.A.F. 1996).

[525] 44 M.J. 174 (C.A.A.F. 1996). United States v. Moulton, 47 M.J. 227 (C.A.A.F. 1997) (failed to make proffer as to how dating fit within an exception to Mil. R. Evid. 412).

(Rel.3—1/07   Pub.62410)

opined that "While evidence of a motive to fabricate an accusation is generally constitutionally required to be admitted, the alleged motive must itself be articulated to the military judge in order for him to properly assess the threshold requirement of relevance."[526]

§ 20-32.33 Restrictions Due to Classified Material

By the very nature of military service, trial by court-martial may unavoidably involve classified information.[527] In *United States v. Lonetree*,[528] the accused, a Marine security guard at the United States Embassy in Moscow, was charged, among other offenses, with supplying information to soviet agents. At trial, the accused was prohibited under Military Rule of Evidence 505 from cross-examining a government witness concerning his true name, background information, and specific information relating to whether the witness had been assisted by other covert agents at a given time.[529] The Navy-Marine Court of Review initially held that "even though an accused has the right under the Sixth Amendment to require disclosure of background information of a Government witness, such a right 'is not . . . absolute.'"[530] The court then determined that otherwise privileged information must yield to the accused's rights when that information is "relevant and necessary" as stated in Rule 505, but that standard incorporates a "balancing of needs" test that balances the accused's need for the examination against national security concerns:

> Accordingly, . . . we equate the "relevant and helpful" phrase of Roviaro[531] with the "relevant and material" standard in R.C.M. 505(i)(4)(B), and further, we conclude that "essential to a fair determination of a cause" is equivalent to the Manual's standard of "necessary to an element of the offense or a legally cognizable defense."[532]

It appears that, to the extent that the tests differ, the defense may solicit on cross-examination classified information if that information is either "essential to a fair determination of" the case or "necessary to an element of the offense or a legally cognizable defense."[533]

---

[526] United States v. Banker, 60 M.J. at 224 (C.A.A.F. 2004).

[527] *See, e.g.*, Mil. R. Evid. 505.

[528] 31 M.J. 849 (N.M.C.M.R. 1990), *aff'd*, 35 M.J. 396 (C.M.A. 1992).

[529] 31 M.J. at 856 (N.M.C.M.R. 1990).

[530] 31 M.J. at 859 (N.M.C.M.R. 1990) (citing McGrath v. Vinzant, 528 F.2d 681, 684 (1st Cir. 1976)). *See generally* United States v. Alston, 460 F.2d 48 (5th Cir. 1972).

[531] Roviaro v. United States, 353 U.S. 53 (1957) (informant's privilege, used by analogy).

[532] Lonetree, 31 M.J. at 861.

[533] 31 M.J. at 862.

(Rel.3—1/07 Pub.62410)

§ 20-32.34   Cross-Examination During Suppression Hearings

Although the accused's right to cross-examine is generally protected and can be abridged only for compelling reasons, a less stringent standard is used in suppression hearings. In *McCray v. Illinois*,[534] the Supreme Court held that the confrontation clause was not violated when the judge hearing the suppression motion refused to allow defense cross-examination directed toward obtaining the name and address of the informant alleged to have provided probable cause for the arrest. Lower courts have extended *McCray* to situations in which valid security interests necessitate receiving in camera government evidence proffered at the suppression hearing.[535] In such instances, however, a "least restrictive alternative" approach is used; confrontation is limited only to the extent necessary to protect the valid government interest.[536] While the court may restrict cross-examination to avoid "backdoor" discovery by the defense, it may not limit questioning that is clearly relevant to the defense claim.[537]

[534] 386 U.S. 300 (1967). *See also* Clark v. Ricketts, 958 F.2d 851 (9th Cir. 1991) (no right to name and address of John Doe witness when judge determined at *in camera* hearing there had been a threat to the life of the witness).

[535] *E.g.*, Pennsylvania v. Ritchie, 480 U.S. 39 (1987) (judge has discretion to hold *in camera* proceedings to determine whether privileged information should be given to one party without violating Sixth Amendment); United States v. Bell, 464 F.2d 667 (2d Cir. 1972) (when government introduced hijacker detection profile, defendant was excluded, but defense counsel was allowed to cross-examine); United States v. Rivers, 49 M.J. 434 (C.A.A.F. 1998) (judge did not abuse his discretion in reviewing *in camera* and not releasing three sworn statement and investigative notes when totally unconnected to trial); United States v. Reece, 25 M.J. 93 (C.M.A. 1987) (judge abused discretion in not ordering *in camera* inspection of material if victim had history of inpatient treatment for drug behavioral problems). *Cf.* Gannett Co. v. De Pasquale, 443 U.S. 368, 439 (1979) (Blackmun, J., concurring in part, dissenting in part) (exclusion of public); United States v. Grunden, 2 M.J. 116 (C.M.A. 1977) (same); United States v. Arroyo-Angulo, 580 F.2d 1137 (2d Cir. 1978) (some defendants and counsel excluded from selected pretrial proceedings upon request of other defendants who were informants). These incidents can also be analyzed in terms of the government's privilege to withhold classified or sensitive information or the identity of an informant. *See* Mil. R. Evid. 505(i), 506(i), 507(d) (*in camera* hearings to determine extent of disclosure). *See also* Wellington, *In Camera Hearings and the Informant Identity Privilege Under Military Rule of Evidence 507*, Army Law., Feb. 1983, at 9. *Cf.* Waller v. Georgia, 467 U.S. 39 (1984) (party seeking to close hearing on motion to suppress must advance an overriding interest that is likely to be prejudiced, and the closure must be no broader than necessary to protect that interest); Press Enterprise Co. v. Superior Court of California, 464 U.S. 501 (1984) (right to privacy of jurors insufficient reason to close voir dire).

[536] United States v. Clark, 475 F.2d 240 (2d Cir. 1973).

[537] Hill v. United States, 418 F.2d 449 (D.C. Cir. 1968).

§ 20-33.00   The Right of Compulsory Process

§ 20-33.10   The Right to Compel the Attendance of Available Witnesses at Trial

§ 20-33.11   In General

Implementing the defendant's right to compulsory process under the Sixth Amendment,[538] the Uniform Code of Military Justice provides that the accused has the same ability as the prosecution to secure "witnesses and other evidence."[539] At the very least, compulsory process means that the defendant is entitled to use the government's subpoena power to compel the attendance of witnesses on behalf of the defense. The clause does more than just incorporate whatever subpoena rights the defendant has under the statute; it creates as an independent constitutional standard.[540] As such, the defendant's compulsory process right extends beyond the subpoena power and includes not only writs of attachment and writs of habeas corpus ad testificandum,[541] but also noncoercive devices for requesting and inducing the appearance of witnesses.[542] Witnesses within and outside the jurisdiction are encompassed by the right.[543] The compulsory process clause, however, has importance beyond its basic ambit, for it would appear not only to provide the defense with its fundamental right to obtain defense witnesses, but also to provide the defense with the authority

---

[538] United States v. Davison, 4 M.J. 702, 704 (A.C.M.R. 1977).

[539] U.C.M.J. Art. 46.

[540] Wigmore believed otherwise. 8 J. Wigmore, Evidence § 2191 (J. McNaughton rev. ed. 1961). *See* State *ex rel.* Rudolph v. Ryan, 327 Mo. 728, 38 S.W.2d 717 1931); State *ex rel.* Gladden v. Lonergan, 201 Or. 163, 269 P.2d 491 (1954).

[541] *See, e.g.,* Barber v. Page, 390 U.S. 719, 724 (1968) (dictum); Johnson v. Johnson, 375 F. Supp. 872 (W.D. Mich. 1974); Curran v. United States, 332 F. Supp. 259 (D. Del. 1971) (denying petition on facts). *See also* 28 U.S.C. § 2241(c)(5) (1976) (authorizing writs of habeas corpus *ad testificandum* and *ad prosequentum*). For the nature of military compulsory process, *see* Sections 20-21.00 and 20-30.00.

[542] Such as the good-faith power of the prosecution and the convening authority to ask a person to return as a witness. *Compare* Barber v. Page, 390 U.S. 719 (1968) *with* Mancusi v. Stubbs, 408 U.S. 204 (1972). The results of the two cases can be seen as requiring the prosecution to use established procedures making it reasonably likely that the witness would be produced, but not requiring use of futile or improbable procedures. Westen, *Compulsory Process II*, 74 MICH. L. REV. 191, 286–88 (1975) [hereinafter *Compulsory Process II*]. *See also* United States v. Davison, 4 M.J. 702, 705 (A.C.M.R. 1977) (Jones, S.J., concurring).

[543] *Compulsory Process II, above* note 542, at 281–98. This is not to say, however, that a court necessarily will have the statutory or inherent power to compel the attendance of a witness. *See above* note 146 for the limitations on court-martial subpoena power when trial takes place in a foreign nation.

(Rel.3—1/07 Pub.62410)

to obtain and present important defense evidence notwithstanding usual procedural and evidentiary rules.[544]

Though the compulsory process right is extensive, it is not absolute. The government has no duty to search for witnesses whom it has no reasonable probability of discovering or producing.[545] Instead, as with the government's obligation to confront the accused with witnesses against him,[546] the government need only make a good-faith effort to locate and produce defense witnesses.[547] The similarity should not be surprising in light of the common purpose of the confrontation and the compulsory process clauses to secure "the attendance of witnesses in order to enhance the ability of a defendant to elicit and present testimony in his defense."[548] Further, the right to obtain witness testimony does not extend to being able to force a witness to submit to medical or other expert examination.[549]

The defense's right to witnesses extends only to "material witnesses."[550] Within the armed forces, the determination of materiality is not susceptible to gradation. The testimony of a given witness either is or is not material to the proceeding at hand,[551] and "once materiality has been shown the Government must either produce the witness or abate the proceeding."[552] Given the state of

---

[544] As to the potential conflict between the defense's need for evidence and the shielding effect of evidentiary privileges, see Westen, *The Compulsory Process Clause*, 73 Mich. L. Rev. 71, 159–77 (1974).

[545] Mancusi v. Stubbs, 408 U.S. 204 (1972). *Cf.* Ohio v. Roberts, 448 U.S. 56, 74 (1980); United States v. Killebrew, 9 M.J. 154, 161 (C.M.A. 1980).

[546] *See* Section 20-32.30.

[547] Mancusi v. Stubbs, 408 U.S. 204 (1972); United States v. Vietor, 10 M.J. 69, 72 (C.M.A. 1980) (Cook, J.); United States v. Davison, 4 M.J. 702, 705 (A.C.M.R. 1977) (Jones, S. J., concurring); United States v. Kilby, 3 M.J. 938, 944 (N.C.M.R. 1977). Once the witness is found, the government cannot lose him. *See* United States v. Potter, 1 M.J. 897 (A.F.C.M.R. 1976). Conversely, the defense must use reasonable diligence in obtaining evidence. *E.g.*, United States v. Jones, 6 M.J. 770 (A.C.M.R. 1978); United States v. Onstad, 4 M.J. 661 (A.C.M.R. 1977); United States v. Marshall, 3 M.J. 1047, 1049 n.2 (A.F.C.M.R. 1977); United States v. Carey, 1 M.J. 761 (A.F.C.M.R. 1975); United States v. Corley, 1 M.J. 584 (A.C.M.R. 1975); United States v. Young, 49 C.M.R. 133 (A.F.C.M.R. 1974).

[548] Westen, *Confrontation and Compulsory Process, above* note 542, at 589.

[549] United States v. Anderson, 55 M.J. 198, 202 (C.A.A.F. 2001), *citing* United States v. Owen, 24 M.J. 390, 395 (C.M.A. 1987). *Compare* People v. Lopez, 800 N.E.2d 1211 (Ill. 2003) (may not require the alleged victim to undergo physical examination) with Commonwealth v. Barroso, 122 S.W.3d 554 (Ky. 2003) (may force disclosure of psychotherapist records of the alleged victim under compulsory process clause).

[550] *Cf.* United States v. Valenzuela-Bernal, 458 U.S. 858 (1982). *See generally* Section 20-22.40.

[551] United States v. Willis, 3 M.J. 94, 95 (C.M.A. 1977).

[552] United States v. Carpenter, 1 M.J. 384, 385–86 (C.M.A. 1976). *Accord* United States v. Williams, 3 M.J. 239, 243 (C.M.A. 1977). There is no constitutional right to introduce irrelevant or immaterial evidence. Washington v. Texas, 388 U.S. 14, 23 (1967); Williams, 3 M.J. at 242.

(Rel.3—1/07 Pub.62410)

military criminal law, the only significant compulsory process problem is the requirement found in Rule for Courts-Martial 703 that a request for defense witnesses, with adequate justification, be submitted to the prosecution.[553]

§ 20-33.12 Requiring the Government to Grant Immunity to Prospective Defense Witnesses

Under current law, the defense has a constitutional right to obtain available material defense witnesses. A particular problem is posed when the only reason for the "unavailability" of a witness is his or her refusal to testify for fear of self-incrimination,[554] a refusal protected under the Fifth Amendment and Article 31 privileges against self-incrimination. When the prosecution faces this problem, it has the power to grant immunity to the witness,[555] which deprives the witness of any valid constitutional objection to testifying.[556] The defense, however, lacks the power to extend immunity. Although the prosecution could grant immunity to defense witnesses to enable them to testify, almost without fail it refuses to do so voluntarily.

Prosecutorial objection to granting immunity to defense witnesses is based on the following factors:

1. There is no way in which to adequately ensure in advance that the testimony of the defense witness would in fact be material;

2. Immunity complicates or makes impossible subsequent prosecution of the witness;[557]

3. Given the difficulties inherent in subsequent prosecutions, the government would run the risk of immunizing large "fish" in order to prosecute "small fry" and would thus seriously interfere with prosecutorial discretion.

All of these concerns are valid. They are not, however, dispositive. Normally, the materiality concern can be met via an adequate, detailed, defense offer of proof,[558] preferably made to a military judge.[559] In addition, a procedure may

---

[553] *See* Section 20-22.71.

[554] Insofar as the potential conflict between the defense's need for evidence and the shielding effect of evidentiary privileges see Westen, *Compulsory Process, above* note 542, at 159–77 (1974).

[555] *See also* Section 20-23.31.

[556] Kastigar v. United States, 406 U.S. 441, 453 (1972).

[557] The prosecution could grant the accused testimonial (or "use plus fruits") immunity, under which nothing the witness said, or any product thereof, could later be used against the witness. *Kastigar*; Mil. R. Evid. 301(c)(1). However, military law takes an unusually expansive view of the derivative evidence rule, and it would be very difficult for the prosecution to adequately prove in court that a case against an immunized witness was actually prepared and tried without use of the immunized testimony. United States v. Graves, 1 M.J. 50 (C.M.A. 1975). *See also* United States v. North, 910 F.2d 843, 856–73 (D.C. Cir. 1990).

[558] Perhaps counsel should be required to verify the offer of proof in a fashion similar to Fed. Rule Civ. P. 11.

(Rel.3—1/07 Pub.62410)

exist, at least in civilian practice, to cope with the situation in which the defense may demonstrate a reasonable belief that the witness has material testimony but is unable to actually demonstrate the existence of the testimony.

> Arguably a judge can grant the witness use immunity for purposes of an in camera hearing out of the presence of the prosecutor, in order to determine whether the witness possesses exculpatory evidence. If the testimony is material, the court can then force the prosecution to choose between allowing the witness to testify in open court under a grant of use immunity or withholding immunity and thus foregoing prosecution. If the witness' evidence is immaterial, the judge can then seal the in camera testimony, thereby protecting the witness from self-incrimination while sparing the prosecution the burden of attempting to trace any further evidence against the witness to independent sources.[560]

That immunity significantly complicates subsequent prosecution of the immunized witness cannot be gainsaid. The real question here is the government's choice of the accused. If the accused's right to a fair trial mandates the testimony of the witness and the grant of immunity will effectively prohibit the later prosecution of the witness, the government must be prepared to pay that price unless the government has chosen, unknowingly or knowingly, an accused less culpable than the witness. In such a case, the government should forego prosecution of the instant accused in order to prosecute the more culpable witness. In short, in an appropriate case, the defense's right to the testimony of a material witness should outweigh the government's interest in not bestowing testimonial immunity on the witness.[561]

---

[559] Under contemporary procedure, the authority to grant immunity normally is held by the convening authority.

[560] *Confrontation and Compulsory Process, above* note 542, at 581–82 n.38 (citing United States v. Melchor Moreno, 536 F.2d 1042, 1047 n.7 (5th Cir. 1976)). Professor Westen questioned the ability of the court to prevent disclosure to the prosecution. If evidence allegedly privileged against disclosure to the defense can be protected, though (*see* Mil. R. Evid. 505–07), there seems to be no reason why guarding against disclosure to the prosecution would be any more problematic. The issue is complicated by the fact that, at present, in the armed forces immunity usually is granted by the convening authority rather than the military judge. Thus, the intermediate use of immunity would normally need command cooperation. Further, it is not likely that a trial judge would threaten dismissal of charges if the convening authority failed to grant such immunity when the potential evidence is so speculative.

[561] *See* United States v. Heldt, 668 F.2d 1238, 1282–83 (D.C. Cir. 1981) (immunity need not be granted to defense witnesses who are actual or potential targets of the prosecution); Government of the Virgin Islands v. Smith, 615 F.2d 964 (3d Cir. 1980); United States v. Morrison, 535 F.2d 223 (3d Cir. 1976); State v. Broady, 41 Ohio App. 2d 17, 321 N.E.2d 890 (1974). The government's interest may be established if the witness is a potential target of prosecution. United States v. Turkish, 623 F.2d 769 (2d Cir. 1980). The granting of immunity to the witness need not be the only possible remedy, however. In an appropriate case, the case might be continued until the witness' status is clarified, such as by conviction. *But see* United States v. Villines, 13 M.J. 46 (C.M.A. 1982) (right against self-incrimination in contested case persists pending appeal); United

(Rel.3—1/07 Pub.62410)

Thus far, however, the courts have been extremely reluctant to compel the government to grant immunity to defense witnesses.[562] Within the armed forces, the ultimate resolution of this issue is unclear. Although in *United States v. Villines*,[563] a majority of the three-member court sustained a conviction in which a defense request that a defense witness be granted immunity was denied, the Court of Military Appeals was badly divided on the issue. The decision consisted of an opinion by Judge Fletcher with Judge Cook concurring in the result and Chief Judge Everett dissenting. A synthesis of the three opinions suggests that a majority of the court believed that immunity could be granted to enable defense witnesses to testify "when clearly exculpatory evidence is involved."[564] Furthermore, the decision on such a defense request must be made without utilizing "an unjustifiable standard [or improper consideration] such as race, religion, or

---

States v. Warren, No. 9501596 n.5 (A. Crim. App. Oct. 9, 1997) ("The majority federal rule holds that there is no overreaching by the government 'whenever the witness for whom immunity is sought is an actual or potential target of prosecution,' and that the judge summarily reject such claims for immunity." Citing *Turkish*, 623 F.2d at 778.). *See also* Flanaghan, *Compelled Immunity for Defense Witnesses: Hidden Costs and Questions*, 56 Notre Dame L. Rev. 447, 46–63 (1981) (immunity should not be granted to defense witnesses in multiculprit cases because of the impact on the prosecution).

[562] *See, e.g.*, United States v. Monroe, 42 M.J. 398 (C.A.A.F. 1995); Carter v. United States, 684 A.2d 331 (D.C. App. 1996) (en banc) (rejected analysis in Government of Virgin Islands v. Smith, *above* note 522); United States v. Medina, 992 F.2d 573, 586 (6th Cir. 1993); United States v. Schweihs, 971 F.2d 1302, 1315 (7th Cir. 1992) (courts do not have authority to grant immunity absent request from prosecutor); United States v. Jones, 13 M.J. 407 (C.M.A. 1982); United States v. Herman, 589 F.2d 1191 (3d Cir. 1978); United States v. Carmen, 577 F.2d 556 (9th Cir. 1978). For cases discussing an asserted duty to grant defense witnesses immunity, *see* United States v. Villines, 13 M.J. 46 (C.M.A. 1982); United States v. Westerdahl, 945 F.2d 1083, 1086 (9th Cir. 1991) ("A criminal defendant is not entitled to compel the government to grant immunity to a witness . . . . We have recognized an exception to this rule in cases where the fact-finding process is intentionally distorted by prosecutorial misconduct, and the defendant is thereby denied a fair trial . . ."); United States v. Barham, 625 F.2d 1221 (5th Cir. 1980); Government of the Virgin Islands v. Smith, 615 F.2d 964 (3d Cir. 1980); United States v. Morrison, 535 F.2d 233 (3d Cir. 1976); United States v. Alessio, 528 F.2d 1079 (9th Cir. 1976); United States v. Lowell, 490 F. Supp. 897 (D.N.J. 1980); United States v. De Palma, 476 F. Supp. 775 (S.D.N.Y. 1979). *See generally* Note, 81 GEO. L.J. 1267, 1384, n.2044 (1993) (survey of the circuits); Myhre, *Defense Witness Immunity and the Due Process Standard: A Proposed Amendment to the* Manual for Courts-Martial, 136 Mil. R. Evid. 69 (1992); Note, *The Case Against a Right to Defense Witness Immunity*, 83 Colum. L. Rev. 139 (1983). Though there may be no constitutional obligation on the prosecution to grant immunity to defense witnesses (*but see Confrontation and Compulsory Process, above* note 542, at 581 n.38), arguably, an obligation under Article 46 exists to effectuate the article's mandate of equal access to witnesses. *But cf.* United States v. Davison, 4 M.J. 702 (A.C.M.R. 1977) (Art. 46 only implements Sixth Amendment rights).

[563] 13 M.J. 46 (C.M.A. 1982).

[564] *See, e.g.*, United States v. Alston, 33 M.J. 370, 373–75 (C.M.A. 1991) (defense has no right to immunity grant of possible witness for interview purposes, especially as defense failed to meet the critical-importance standard).

(Rel.3—1/07 Pub.62410)

other arbitrary classification" and without the intent of making such a decision "with the deliberate intention of distorting the judicial fact finding process."[565] The court has also held it improper to deny immunity to a defense witness on the basis that no reasonable trier of fact would credit the testimony sought.[566] Rejecting the view of Chief Judge Everett that both the general court-martial convening authority and the military judge may grant immunity, Judges Fletcher and Cook appeared to hold that only the convening authority has that power.

As amended by the 1993 Change 6 to the Manual for Courts-Martial, Rule for Courts-Martial 704(e) provides that:

Unless limited by superior competent authority, the decision to grant immunity is a matter within the sole discretion of the appropriate general court-martial convening authority. If a defense request to immunize a witness has been denied, the military judge may, upon motion by the defense, grant appropriate relief directing that either an appropriate general court-martial convening authority grant testimonial immunity to a defense witness or, as to the affected charges and specifications, the proceedings against the accused be abated, upon findings that:

(1) The witness intends to invoke the right against self-incrimination to the extent permitted by law if called to testify; and

(2) The Government has engaged in discriminatory use of immunity to obtain a tactical advantage, or the Government, through its own over-reaching, has forced the witness to invoke the privilege against self-incrimination; and

(3) The witness' testimony is material, clearly exculpatory, not cumulative, not obtainable from any other source and does more than merely affect the credibility of other witnesses.[567]

While recognizing *Villnes* and *Zayas*, the court in *United States v. Monroe* saw no distinction between the Manual's "central importance" in R.C.M. 704(e) and the "clearly exculpatory" language from those cases.[568] It cited the difference in the federal courts without expressing a view.[569]

---

[565] 13 M.J. at 55 (C.M.A. 1982). One might argue that the dissenting view of Chief Judge Everett in *Villines* has now become the majority view of the Court of Military Appeals. United States v. Zayas, 24 M.J. 132 (C.M.A. 1987) (on remand the witness indicated the accused was driving the car). In United States v. Jones, 13 M.J. 407 (C.M.A. 1982), the court rejected a defense claim that it was entitled to have a defense witness immunized, stating that there was no reasonably foreseeable testimony beneficial to the defense.

[566] United States v. Thomas, 37 M.J. 302 (C.M.A. 1993).

[567] See United States v. Ivey, 55 M.J. 251, 254-257 (C.A.A.F. 2001) (immunity for military and civilian witnesses not granted); United States v. Richter, 51 M.J. 213, 223 (C.A.A.F. 1999) (Under R.C.M. 704(e) prosecution target awaiting trial need not have been granted immunity).

[568] United States v. Monroe, 42 M.J. 395 (C.A.A.F. 1995).

[569] 42 M.J. at 401–02 (C.A.A.F. 1995).

(Rel.3—1/07 Pub.62410)

§ 20-33.13 Improper Joinder

Although joinder of accuseds is allowed under Rule for Courts-Martial 601(c)(3),[570] such joinder may dissuade a co-accused from testifying for the accused.[571] Indeed, the Manual Discussion counsels that if "the testimony of an accomplice is necessary, he should not be tried jointly with those against whom he is expected to testify."[572] When an accused claims that he or she has been deprived of favorable testimony by joinder, the principal problem is determining the real cause of the co-accused's silence.[573] Such claims for severance are usually treated with skepticism, especially in civilian courts.[574] The Discussion to Rule 906(b)(9) declares, however, that in a common trial, a motion to sever "should be liberally considered"[575] and states that one of the grounds for this motion is that the "moving party desires to use the testimony of one or more of the co-accused. . . ."[576] In light of the prosecution's obligation to avoid harassing or discouraging defense witnesses from testifying[577] and the discussion of Rule 906(b)(9)'s liberal standard, the accused should not be required to show to a certainty that the co-accused has already given exculpatory testimony out-of-court and that joinder could silence the witness. On the contrary, the government should be required to show that joinder would have no such effect.[578] Severance

---

[570] The procedure creates several savings, notably time, expense, and prosecutorial effort. R.C.M. 307(c)(5) Discussion. *See also* Westen, *Compulsory Process, above* note 542 at 141.

[571] From the accused's perspective, joinder may deny the defense the benefit of favorable testimony from a co-accused, either because the testimony would improperly prejudice the co-accused (*e.g.*, Byrd v. Wainwright, 428 F.2d 1017 (5th Cir. 1970)) or because the co-accused refuses to testify. *E.g.*, United States v. Shuford, 454 F.2d 772 (4th Cir. 1971).

[572] R.C.M. 307(c)(5) Discussion.

[573] Westen, *Compulsory Process, above* note 542, at 142–43. *See also* Sections 6-60.00.

[574] *See* United States v. Boscia, 573 F.2d 827 (3d Cir. 1978); United States v. Bumatay, 480 F.2d 1012 (9th Cir. 1973); United States v. Pellon, 475 F. Supp. 467 (S.D.N.Y. 1979); United States v. Stitt, 380 F. Supp. 1172 (W.D. Pa. 1974), *aff'd mem.*, 510 F.2d 971 (3d Cir. 1975); United States v. Sweig, 316 F. Supp. 1148 (S.D.N.Y. 1970).

[575] R.C.M. 906(b)(9) Discussion. When there are multiple accused, there will be an automatic severance when they select different fact finders.

[576] R.C.M. 906(b)(9) Discussion.

[577] *See* Section 20-33.31.

[578] Westen, *Compulsory Process, above* note 542, at 143. *See* United States v. Duzac, 622 F.2d 911 (5th Cir. 1980); United States v. Starr, 584 F.2d 235 (8th Cir. 1978); United States v. Smolar, 557 F.2d 13 (1st Cir. 1977); United States v. Anthony, 565 F.2d 533 (8th Cir. 1977); United States v. Kozell, 468 F. Supp. 746 (E.D. Pa. 1979); United States v. Aloi, 449 F. Supp. 698 (E.D.N.Y. 1977); United States v. Iezzi, 451 F. Supp. 1027 (W.D. Pa. 1976); United States v. Boscia, 573 F.2d 827 (3d Cir. 1978); United States v. Buschmann, 386 F. Supp. 822 (E.D. Wis. 1975), *aff'd on other grounds*, 527 F.2d 1082 (7th Cir. 1976).

(Rel.3—1/07 Pub.62410)

should be ordered whenever it is more probable than not that the co-accused will testify for the accused at a separate trial.[579]

§ 20-33.20　The Right to be Present for the Testimony of Defense Witnesses at Trial

The right to be present at trial is normally discussed in the confrontation context.[580] There is little, if any, discussion in the case law on the extent of the accused's constitutional right to be present when defense witnesses testify, as the government is "not in the habit of requiring defense witnesses to testify outside the defendant's presence."[581] This issue could arise, nonetheless, in the context of the presentation of classified information.

It is likely that the average accused would not hold a security clearance, especially a top-secret or higher clearance. Should the defense desire to present classified evidence and the accused be unable to obtain a proper clearance, the prosecution would be likely to move to exclude the accused from trial. In such a case, the right to confrontation is inapplicable by definition. Yet, the confrontation clause's rationale applies with equal force in this context. During the prosecution's case-in-chief, the accused needs to know exactly what the government witnesses are saying in order to prepare the defense.[582] In the ordinary case, the accused needs to know exactly what the defense witnesses are saying so that he or she can better elicit testimony. In particular, the accused must guide counsel's inquiry based upon the accused's knowledge and should be prepared to respond to that testimony should the accused elect to take the stand.

As a result, the accused's interest in being present for the testimony of defense witnesses should be infringed only when the accused forfeits the right[583] or for a compelling government interest.[584]

---

[579] See United States v. Wofford, 562 F.2d 582 (8th Cir. 1977); United States v. Bumatay, 480 F.2d 1012 (9th Cir. 1973); MCM, 1969 (rev. ed.) ¶ 69d (citing this as one of the more common grounds for severance).

[580] See, e.g., Maryland v. Craig, 496 U.S. 836 (1990).

[581] Westen, *Confrontation and Compulsory Process, above* note 542, at 589.

[582] Preparation does not eliminate the possibility of surprise testimony; at best, preparation only gives an approximation of what a witness will say, and turncoat witnesses are not unknown. To evaluate the impact of a witness, the accused needs to know the exact substance of each witness' testimony. The cynic would ask then if the defendant will tell counsel. Cf. Yale. Kamisar, Wayne R. Lafave & Jerold H. Israel, Modern Criminal Procedure 1618–19 (5th ed. 1980) (unrealistic to expect attorney to consult with defendant on every trial decision). In the area of classified information, counsel's pretrial access to the witness and the information known to the witness may have been severely limited.

[583] See Westen, *Confrontation and Compulsory Process, above* note 542, at 573–75 n.18.

[584] Westen, *Confrontation and Compulsory Process,* note 542, at 589. See Section 13-35.24.

(Rel.3—1/07　Pub.62410)

§ 20-33.30   The Right to Examine Defense Witnesses at Trial and to Present Defense Evidence

§ 20-33.31   General Constitutional Standards

The "most important question" under the compulsory process clause[585] is whether the defendant's right to compel attendance of witnesses at trial includes the right to introduce their testimony into evidence.[586] Two theoretical possibilities exist: the Sixth Amendment merely incorporates by reference the government's definition of "witness" as contained in rules on competency, relevancy, materiality, and privilege, or the Sixth Amendment establishes an independent definition of "witness" based on its own standards of admission of defensive evidence. Obviously, arguments for both approaches exist, and there is always a risk of making every evidentiary question in a criminal case a constitutional one. Wigmore's view was that the constitutional rule overrode state law only to guarantee the right to compel attendance of witnesses, but that the states could establish rules to govern admissibility of the evidence.[587] On the other hand, if the government is free to determine who is a witness in the context of compulsory process, the purpose of the clause could be easily and completely frustrated.[588]

In *Washington v. Texas*,[589] the Supreme Court resolved the fundamental question by holding that compulsory process includes both the right to compel the attendance of defense witnesses and the right to introduce their testimony into evidence. The Court's decision consisted of two parts. First, the witnesses the defendant may subpoena must be congruent with those allowed to testify for the defendant.[590] Second, and of more significance, it is constitutional law alone that ultimately determines whether testimony is admissible on behalf of the defendant. The framers were not content to rely on rules of evidence

---

[585] Westen, *Confrontation and Compulsory Process, above* note 542, at 590.

[586] *See generally* Imwinkelried, *Recent Developments: Chambers v. Mississippi — The Constitutional Right to Present Defense Evidence*, 62 Mil. R. Evid. 225 (1973). In United States v. Mustafa, 22 M.J. 165, 168–69 (C.M.A. 1986), Judge Cox, in dictum, indicated that Article 46 *and Ake v. Oklahoma*, 470 U.S. 68 (1985), gave the accused the right to have access to a qualified psychiatrist or psychologist to present an insanity defense.

White v. Johnson, 153 F.3d 197 (5th Cir. 1998) (failure to appoint expert under *Ake* could be harmless error).

[587] 8 J. Wigmore, Evidence § 2191, at 68–69 (rev. ed. 1961).

[588] Westen, *Confrontation and Compulsory Process, above* note 542, at 591.

[589] 388 U.S. 14 (1967).

[590] Otherwise, the defendant would only have the right to subpoena witnesses who could not be put on the stand or the right to call witnesses who could not be subpoenaed; either right alone would be an empty one. 388 U.S. 23 (1967).

(Rel.3—1/07   Pub.62410)

governing admissibility, but intended to create a constitutional standard with which to judge those rules.[591]

Washington also established the content of the constitutional standard. The state rule of evidence at issue[592] was invalid, not because it was discriminatory or irrational,[593] but because the government interest was inadequate to justify restricting the defendant's right to present evidence in his defense.[594] More recently, the Supreme Court has held it a violation of the Sixth and Fourteenth Amendments to prohibit the accused from introducing testimony about the physical and psychological circumstances in which his or her confession was obtained.[595] "Indeed, stripped of the power to describe to the jury the circumstances that prompted his confession, the defendant is effectively disabled from answering the one question every rational juror needs answered: If the defendant is innocent, why did he previously admit his guilt?"[596]

There is some congruence between the Court's view of compulsory process expressed in *Washington* and its view of confrontation as stated in *Smith v. Illinois*[597] and *Davis v. Alaska.*[598] In both *Washington* and *Smith*, the defendant was prevented by a state rule of evidence from obtaining testimony from a witness who was present and ready to testify. Holding that the Sixth Amendment requires that the trier of fact be allowed to give the evidence whatever weight and credibility may be appropriate, the Court in both instances overturned the evidentiary rule. Similarly, the presence of a legitimate state interest was raised to justify exclusion of evidence in *Washington* and *Davis*. Neither denying the importance of the asserted state interests, nor challenging the value of the rules used to further those interests, the Court held in both cases that the defendant had a superior interest in presenting defense evidence. Implicit in *Washington* and *Davis* was the notion that a defendant's rights under the Sixth Amendment are not absolute. However, questions of admissibility due to competence,

---

[591] 388 U.S. at 20, 22 (1967).

[592] 388 U.S. at 16, 17 n.4 (1967) (Texas law made accomplices incompetent to testify for one another).

[593] 388 U.S. at 22–23 (1967) (rule disqualifying alleged accomplice from testifying for defendant is absurd in light of exceptions to rule and sheer common sense).

[594] Although the state had an interest in excluding evidence that probably was false and self-serving, because the trier of fact could be trusted to adequately evaluate the evidence, the state's interests were outweighed by the defendant's. *See also* Chambers v. Mississippi, 410 U.S. 284 (1973).

[595] Crane v. Kentucky, 476 U.S. 683 (1986). *See also* United States v. Leiker, 37 M.J. 418 (C.M.A. 1993) (accused has the right to ask about interrogation techniques).

[596] 476 U.S. 689 (1986). *See also* United States v. Woolheater, 40 M.J. 170 (C.M.A. 1994) (failure to admit evidence of another perpetrator violated the defendant's rights).

[597] 390 U.S. 129 (1968).

[598] 415 U.S. 308 (1974).

(Rel.3—1/07 Pub.62410)

materiality, or privilege concerns ultimately constitute federal questions determined by strict constitutional standards.[599]

§ 20-33.32   Competency of Witnesses

Both *Washington v. Texas*[600] and *Chambers v. Mississippi*[601] indicate that evidentiary competency rules may raise constitutional issues. Generally, though, the constitutional questions about competency have been reduced by the broad competency standard contained in Military Rule of Evidence 601; unless provided otherwise, any person is competent to testify.[602] The only restrictions on competency are those prohibiting the military judge and court members from testifying as witnesses.[603]

Under the military rule, a court member "may testify on the question whether extraneous prejudicial information was improperly brought to the attention of the members of the court-martial, whether any outside influence was improperly brought to bear upon any member, or whether there was unlawful command influence."[604] The Rule does not draw the line at the jury room door, but between the mental processes of court members and the presence of conditions or events designed to improperly influence court members in or out of the jury room. The Rule thus distinguishes between subjective and objective events and prohibits testimony about conduct that has no verifiable objective manifestations.[605]

[599] *See* Westen, *Compulsory Process, above* note 542, at 159–77; 194–231.

[600] 388 U.S. 14 (1967).

[601] 410 U.S. 284 (1973).

[602] The analysis of the Rule states that its plain meaning would eliminate any judicial discretion in the area of competence. Analysis of the Military Rules of Evidence1980 Amendments to the *Manual for Courts-Martial*, Analysis of Rule 601, *reprinted at* MCM, 2005, A22–44. Other traditional competency questions also were rendered obsolete by the *Manual* revision. Hearsay, for example, is no longer incompetent. Mil. R. Evid. 801.

[603] Mil. R. Evid. 605(a), 606(a).

[604] Mil. R. Evid. 606(b). *See* United States v. Dugan, 58 M.J. 253 (C.A.A.F. 2003) (effect of command influence on deliberations could be explored by limited voir dire of the members regarding what was said during deliberations "about the commander's comments," but not as to the effect on the members of anything said).

[605] *See* Mil. R. Evid. 606(b); United States v. Bishop, 11 M.J. 7 (C.M.A. 1981) (proper to consider personal familiarity of members with crime scene). *See also* Rushen v. Spain, 464 U.S. 114, 121 n.5 (1983) ("A juror may testify concerning any mental bias in matters unrelated to the specific issues that the juror was called upon to decide and whether extraneous prejudicial information was improperly brought to the juror's attention. . . . But a juror generally cannot testify about the mental process by which the verdict was arrived."); United States v. Brooks, 42 M.J. 484, 486 (C.A.A.F. 1995) (would not allow question of members two weeks after ambiguous verdict — but held "apparent irregularity in the voting procedures"); United States v. Straight, 42 M.J. 244, 249– 50 (C.A.A.F. 1995) (common knowledge about parole does not fit within the three exceptions in Mil. R. Evid. 606(b)); United States v. Langer, 41 M.J. 780 (A.F. Crim. App. 1995) (defense counsel's questionnaire for court members was highly improper).

(Rel.3—1/07 Pub.62410)

Civilian federal case law interpreting Federal Rule of Evidence 606(b) has permitted inquiries of members concerning allegedly false statements made on voir dire.[606]

The Court of Appeals for the Armed Forces has held that Military Rule of Evidence 606(b) does not apply to military judges.[607]

The basic interests furthered by the Rule are the protection of court members from defense probing[608] and the need for finality in criminal convictions. If a broad inquiry were allowed, the verdict would be subject to constant attack. Ironically, the compulsory-process clause guarantees the right of the accused to present evidence on the merits, but may not extend to the deliberation process.

If a court member's "misconduct becomes known to a party during the progress of a trial, he must call it to the attention of the court, and if he fails to do so he has waived that right and cannot later assert such error."[609]

§ 20-33.33   Admissibility of Evidence

§ 20-33.33(a)   In General

Even though a witness is competent to testify, his or her testimony may be excluded on evidentiary grounds. *Chambers v. Mississippi,*[610] a case susceptible to multiple interpretations, suggested that evidence rules cannot be applied to infringe the defendant's right to present a defense. In *Chambers*, the Supreme Court overturned a conviction because the defendant was not permitted to solicit

---

[606] *See, e.g.,* United States v. Henley, 238 F.3d 1111, 1121 (9th Cir. 2001); Hard v. Burlington Northern R.R., 812 F.2d 482, 485 (9th Cir. 1987).

[607] United States v. McNutt, 62 M.J. 16 (C.A.A.F. 2005).

[608] *See* Parker v. Gladden, 385 U.S. 363, 369 (1966) (Harlan, J., dissenting); Miller v. United States, 403 F.2d 77, 82 (2d Cir. 1968). Given the usual complexity of instructions, it would be easy to establish that the court members misunderstood or misapplied an instruction. If the inquiry was about a member's unlawful command influence over another, however, the misconduct would be a proper area for inquiry. United States v. Carr, 18 M.J. 297 (C.M.A. 1984).

United States v. Ovando-Moran, 48 M.J. 300 (C.A.A.F. 1998) (post-trial advocacy session invaded the deliberative process); United States v. Wallace, 28 M.J. 640 (A.F.C.M.R. 1989) (reversed sentence for failure to hold post-trial hearing when member called judge prior to authentication indicating that several members convinced the others that a punitive discharge can be easily upgraded to general discharge).

[609] United States v. Rhea, 29 M.J. 991, 997 (A.F.C.M.R. 1990). *See also* United States v. Thomas, 116 F.3d 606 (2d Cir. 1997); United States v. Norment, 34 M.J. 224, 227 (C.M.A. 1992) (Crawford, J., concurring).

[610] 410 U.S. 284 (1973). *Chambers* is an unusual case. Justice Powell, its author, expressly limited its holding to the facts and circumstances of the case. 410 U.S. at 303 (1973). However, it is impossible to ignore the broader import of the case, which seems clearly to be that the defense may present relevant and critical defense evidence notwithstanding state evidentiary rules to the contrary. *See* Imwinkelried, *above* note 586, for an outstanding examination of the case. As to the effect of evidentiary privileges, see text *above* note 359.

(Rel.3—1/07 Pub.62410)

declarations against penal interest — confessions to the crime made by a third party — because of state evidentiary law. The import of *Chambers* was, and remains, unclear. Some commentators have interpreted it as a unique case growing out of unusual facts and an unusual combination of state evidentiary principles. Others have interpreted it as a major, if not seminal, case providing the defense with a constitutional right to present important probative evidence notwithstanding normal evidentiary rules. Under this latter view, *Chambers* is both a confrontation and compulsory process case, and thus one of potentially great value. Although the Supreme Court has stated that the compulsory process clause includes the right to call "material and favorable" defense witnesses[611] and the right of the defendant to testify in his or her own behalf,[612] the Court has not as yet set forth the parameters of the clause. The ultimate interpretation of *Chambers* remains to be rendered.

The Court of Military Appeals followed a reasonably broad interpretation of *Chambers*,[613] to the extent that the defense evidence is reliable[614] and important.[615] Furthermore, the court appears to have placed some emphasis on the fact that the hearsay declarant in *Chambers* was available at trial,[616] suggesting that the court will limit *Chambers* to circumstances in which the declarant is present at trial although not subject to full cross-examination.

§ 20-33.33(b) Scientific Evidence

Although *Chambers* has great potential scope, mainly in the hearsay area, it may have particular value in the area of scientific evidence, particularly in circumstances in which the defense desires to offer evidence of an exculpatory polygraph examination.[617] Before scientific evidence is admitted, it must be shown to be relevant, that is, to make the existence of any fact "more probable

---

[611] United States v. Valenzuela-Bernal, 458 U.S. 858, 867 (1982).

[612] Rock v. Arkansas, 483 U.S. 44, 52 (1987).

[613] United States v. Johnson, 3 M.J. 143 (C.M.A. 1977).

[614] United States v. Burks, 36 M.J. 447 (C.M.A. 1993) (no right to admit anonymous letter confessing to crime); United States v. Hayes, 36 M.J. 361 (C.M.A. 1993) (evidence that children tested positive for sexually transmitted disease not relevant when there is no connection between dates of testing and dates of offenses); United States v. Perner, 14 M.J. 181, 184 (C.M.A. 1982). *Cf.* United States v. Richardson, 15 M.J. 41, 46 (C.M.A. 1983); United States v. Ferguson, 15 M.J. 12, 24, 25 (C.M.A. 1983) (Everett, C.J., concurring in the result).

[615] *Ferguson*, 15 M.J. 12, 16 (C.M.A. 1983). *See also Ferguson*, 15 M.J. at 24 (Everett, C.J., concurring in the result) (evidence should be pertinent to a material issue). As for the Courts of Military Review, see United States v. Combs, 35 M.J. 820, 827 (A.F.C.M.R. 1992) (exclusion of forensic psychiatrist's testimony as to accused's intent was error).

[616] *Perner*, 14 M.J. at 184 n.3. *See also Johnson*, 3 M.J. at 147–48 (declarant, who had refused to testify pursuant to the right against self-incrimination, was in the courtroom).

[617] United States v. Gipson, 24 M.J. 246 (C.M.A. 1987).

(Rel.3—1/07 Pub.62410)

or less probable than it would be without the evidence."[618] Traditionally, for scientific evidence, this meant that the proponent had to establish that

(1) the underlying scientific principle is valid;

(2) the technique properly applies the principle;

(3) the instruments used were in proper working order;

(4) proper procedures were used; and

(5) the people conducting the test and interpreting the results were qualified.[619]

"Traditionally," the proof of the validity of novel scientific evidence requires the proponent to show that the relevant scientific principle "is sufficiently established to have gained general acceptance in the particular field in which it belongs."[620] Pursuant to this test, the *Frye* test, if the idea behind a scientific technique is invalid, evidence obtained through that technique is irrelevant.[621] The difficulty with *Frye* is whether its "bean counting" general acceptance test is truly helpful in determining the validity of scientific principle or evidence, particularly when modern science crosses so many disciplines.

In 1993 the Supreme Court, construing the Federal Rules of Evidence in general and Rule 702 in particular, held in *Daubert v. Merrell Dow Pharmaceuticals*,[622] that *Frye* did not survive the adoption of the Federal Rules. The Court held, however, that Rule 702's "requirement that an expert's testimony pertain to 'scientific knowledge' establishes a standard of evidentiary reliability. This entails a preliminary assessment of whether the reasoning or methodology underlying the testimony is scientifically valid and of whether that reasoning or methodology properly can be applied to the facts in issue."[623] The Court held

---

[618] Mil. R. Evid. 401.

[619] *See* Frye v. United States, 293 F. 1013 (D.C. Cir. 1923); United States v. Houser, 36 M.J. 392 (C.M.A. 1993); United States v. Ford, 16 C.M.R. 185 (C.M.A. 1954).

[620] Frye v. United States, 293 F. 1013, 1014 (D.C. Cir. 1923). United States v. Houser, 36 M.J. 392 (C.M.A. 1993). The opponent of the evidence may use the protections available through voir dire, cross-examination and limiting instructions. *See generally* Edward J. Imwinkelried, Paul C. Giannelli, Francis A. Gilligan & Fredric I. Lederer, *Courtroom Criminal Evidence* §§ 605–11 (4th ed. 2006).

[621] *See* United States v. Hulen, 3 M.J. 275, 277 (C.M.A. 1977) (Perry, J., concurring); United States v. Helton, 10 M.J. 820, 823 (A.F.C.M.R. 1981); United States v. De Bentham, 348 F. Supp. 1377 (S.D. Cal. 1972), *aff'd*, 470 F.2d 1367 (9th Cir. 1972).

[622] 509 U.S. 579 (1993).

[623] *See* Daubert v. Merrell Dow Pharmaceuticals, Inc., 43 F.3d 1311, 1317 n.5 (9th Cir. 1995) (Two "principal ways" to interpret the new test in the *Daubert* context: show that the research was conducted independent of litigation; or, secondly, show that the research has been subject to peer review. "There are, of course, exceptions. Fingerprint analysis, voice recognition, DNA finger-printing. . . .").

(Rel.3—1/07 Pub.62410)

Daubert applicable to non-scientific expert testimony as well in *Kumho Tire Co. v. Carmichael.*[624]

Given *Daubert*, it is highly improbable that the Compulsory Process Clause would mandate admission of evidence that failed the Rule 702 test. Because Military Rule of Evidence 702 was adopted verbatim from the Federal Rules, as were many of the remaining Section 700 rules, *Daubert* should apply to the armed forces mooting compulsory process questions in the area of scientific evidence.

The Court of Appeals for the Armed Forces seemed divided as to whether *Daubert* created a new rule.[625] The court does apply, *Daubert,* however.[626]

Because the compulsory-process right to present evidence extends only to relevant evidence,[627] there is no violation of the defendant's constitutional or statutory[628] rights when evidence is not admitted if the minimal constitutional foundation requirements have not been met.

§ 20-33.33(c) Polygraph Evidence

Under the 1969 *Manual for Courts-Martial*, the results of polygraph tests and hypnotically induced interviews were explicitly declared to be inadmissible in the military.[629] The bar was omitted in 1980 from the Military Rules of Evidence, however, leaving admissibility of such evidence to the same rules that govern the civilian federal courts. In 1987 the Court of Military Appeals[630] joined the few jurisdictions that have held that the trial judge has the discretion to admit the results of polygraph examinations[631] by holding in three separate opinions

---

[624] 526 U.S. 137 (1999).

[625] *Compare* United States v. Youngberg, 43 M.J. 379 (C.A.A.F. 1995) *with* United States v. Nimmer, 43 M.J. 252 (C.A.A.F. 1995).

[626] E.g., United States v. Billings, 61 M.J. 163 (C.A.A.F. 2005)(*e.g.,* "Under Daubert, the proponent of expert testimony must be able to establish both the expert's qualifications and the reliability of the expert's basis for forming an opinion. "The proponent of evidence has the burden of showing that it is admissible." [citing United States v. Palmer, 55 M.J. 205, 208 (C.A.A.F. 2001)]. The Government did not carry that burden. Instead, it relied on the mere "ipse dixit of the expert." [citing Kumho Tire Co., 526 U.S. at 157.] 61 M.J. at 168 (C.A.A.F. 2005))

[627] *See* United States v. Williams, 3 M.J. 239, 242 (C.M.A. 1977); United States v. Carpenter, 1 M.J. 384 (C.M.A. 1976).

[628] U.C.M.J. art. 46.

[629] MCM, 1969 para. 142e.

[630] United States v. Gipson, 24 M.J. 246 (C.M.A. 1987).

[631] *See* E. Imwinkelried, P. Giannelli, F. Gilligan & F. Lederer, Courtroom Criminal Evidence § 618 (4th ed. 2005) (two jurisdictions have followed this rule).

that a judge had abused his discretion by not allowing the defense counsel to lay a foundation to admit such evidence.[632]

The 1991 amendment to the *Manual for Courts-Martial* created Military Rule of Evidence 707, prohibiting the admissibility of polygraph examination and restoring the armed forces to the 1969 Manual rule. Such a prohibition would seem to raise weighty compulsory process questions under *Chambers*. Although polygraph evidence presents significant reliability, evaluative,[633] and administrative problems,[634] it is unclear whether those difficulties would be constitutionally sufficient to sustain an absolute bar.[635] Indeed, in 1994, the Army Court of Military Review held Military Rule of Evidence 707 unconstitutional on the facts of the case before it.[636] However, in 1998 the Supreme Court declared Rule 707 constitutional in *United States v. Scheffer*.[637] The Court in an 8-1 decision

---

[632] Writing the lead opinion, Judge Cox did not rest admissibility on a constitutional basis, but on the ground that each side had the right to admit relevant and helpful evidence: "A few courts have experimented with the notion that an accused has an independent, constitutional right to present favorable polygraph evidence. We do not subscribe to this theory" (footnote omitted). *Gipson*, 24 M.J. at 252. Chief Judge Everett, concurring, said that he could not justify a rule that permitted a judge to exclude all polygraph evidence. 24 M.J. at 255. Judge Sullivan dissented on the basis that the judge did not exclude all evidence or adopt a per se rule, but ruled that neither side would be permitted to lay a foundation for the admission of such evidence. 24 M.J. at 255.

[633] *See generally* E. Imwinkelried, P. Giannelli, F. Gilligan, & F. Lederer, Courtroom Criminal Evidence § 618 (4th ed. 2005).

[634] The military environment may present special difficulties, notably lack of access to competent polygraph examiners. Although military examiners are presumably at least as competent as their civilian colleagues, operational deployments make access to the comparatively few examiners difficult if not impossible. Admission of polygraph evidence could yield a difficult policy choice: should the right depend on the accused's assignment and the availability of an examiner, leading to a grossly disparate access to potential defense evidence, or should polygraph evidence be totally prohibited? Note that the other obvious option — a basic right to polygraph evidence — must be assumed to be impossible to implement in a combat environment, if not in general.

Admission of polygraph evidence may lead to other difficulties, including substantial time delays inherent in qualifying and contesting the competence of the examiner and in inquiring into the specific testing and the underlying scientific and technological theory, design, and implementation. *See generally* Edward J. Imwinkelried, Paul C. Giannelli, Francis A. Gilligan, & Fredric I. Lederer, *Courtroom Criminal Evidence* §§ 620, 622 (4th ed. 2005).

[635] *Cf.* Rock v. Arkansas, 483 U.S. 44 (1987) (absolute bar on post-hypnosis testimony of defendant held unconstitutional). *See* Houston v. Lockhart, 958 F.2d 826 (8th Cir. 1992) (failure to admit polygraph because prosecutor reneged on oral agreement did not infringe constitutional protection); United States v. A & S Council Oil Co., 947 F.2d 1118, 1133–34 (4th Cir. 1991) (no constitutional right to introduce polygraph showing deception to impeach government witness — good survey of other cases); United States v. Bortnovsky, 879 F.2d 30, 35 (2d Cir. 1989) (no right to introduce polygraphs in Second Circuit — compiling cases). *See also* U.C.M.J. art. 46.

[636] United States v. Williams, 39 M.J. 555, 558 (A.C.M.R. 1994) (holding that the prohibition on polygraphs violated due process and right to present evidence, citing, among other cases, *Chambers*), *rev'd on other grounds*, 43 M.J. 348 (C.A.A.F. 1995).

[637] 523 U.S. 303 (1998).

held there was not a constitutional right to introduce exculpatory polygraph examinations. Four justices would not go as far to say that litigation over collateral matters or that polygraphs would undercut the jury. "I doubt, though, that the rule of per se [DNA] exclusion is wise, and some later case might present a more compelling case for the introduction of the testimony that this one does."

Can one find a more compelling case than Scheffer? Scheffer tested positive during a urinalysis test that was performed because he was serving as a police informant. The urinalysis test was performed by the police and the polygraph test was administered by the police using police equipment.

The Court of Appeals noted the tension between the Military Rules of Evidence 104 and 707 and suggested an amendment to the rules.[638]

§ 20-33.34   Preventing Defense Witnesses from Testifying

The defendant's right to present evidence may be frustrated not only by evidentiary rules, but also by the actions of the prosecutor or the judge.[639] The

---

[638] United States v. Light, 48 M.J. 187 (C.A.A.F. 1998).

[639] The constitutional principle was recognized by the Supreme Court in a due process decision, Webb v. Texas, 409 U.S. 95 (1972) (although relying on a compulsory process case, Washington v. Texas, 388 U.S. 14 (1967)). While acknowledging the state's interest in preventing perjury, the Court overturned the defendant's conviction on due process grounds because the trial judge had used "unnecessarily strong terms" to warn the only defense witness about perjury and "effectively drove that witness off the stand." 409 U.S. at 98. Webb thus establishes that a practice that effectively deters a material defense witness from testifying is invalid unless necessary to accomplish a legitimate state interest.

Webb only addressed the situation of judicial interference with the defendant's right to present evidence. Other cases support the proposition that the trial court has power to deal with the actions of counsel. See Taylor v. Illinois, 484 U.S. 400 (1988) (blatant violation of discovery rules permits judge to exclude testimony of undisclosed witness without violating right of compulsory process); United States v. Nobles, 422 U.S. 225 (1975) (Court upheld a trial judge's refusal to allow the testimony by a defense investigator because the defense would not produce a copy of the relevant portions of the investigator's report for use by the prosecution during cross-examination. As the Court explained, the Sixth Amendment does not confer the right to present testimony free from legitimate demands of the adversarial system; one cannot invoke the Sixth Amendment as a justification for presenting what might have been a half-truth). Clinton, *The Right to Present a Defense: An Emergent Constitutional Guarantee in Criminal Trials,* 9 Ind. L. Rev. 711, 848 (1976). *See also* United States v. Cool, 409 U.S. 100 (1972); United States v. Sears, 20 C.M.A. 380, 384, 43 C.M.R. 220, 224 (1971); United States v. Giermek, 3 M.J. 1013, 1016 (C.G.C.M.R. 1977); United States v. Staton, 48 C.M.R. 250, 254 (A.C.M.R. 1974); United States v. Snead, 45 C.M.R. 382, 385 (A.C.M.R. 1972). *See also* United States v. Phaneuf, 10 M.J. 831 (A.C.M.R. 1981); Commonwealth v. Sena, N.E.2d (Mass. May 19, 1999) (two defense discovery violations, one by the former defense counsel did not justify exclusion of defense evidence).

Other cases hold that harassment or other efforts designed to discourage defense witnesses also violate the defendant's rights. Such efforts have included perjury warnings and threats of prosecution or arrest. *See, e.g.,* United States v. Thomas, 488 F.2d 334 (6th Cir. 1973). *See also* United States v. Meek, 44 M.J. 1 (C.A.A.F. 1996) (trial counsel committed ethical violation in attempting to dissuade defense witness from testifying).

compulsory process clause prohibits the government from deliberately harassing or removing witnesses. Legitimate procedures may be employed, though, such as advising a witness of the penalty for perjury or of the privilege against self-incrimination,[640] thus suggesting that there is a fine line between proper and improper conduct. Some conduct, though, may be so flagrant as to violate the compulsory process clause.[641]

Although older military cases support the proposition that negligent discharge of a defense witness violates the government's duty to ensure the attendance of the witness at trial,[642] the Supreme Court's 1982 decision in *United States v. Valenzuela*[643] placed that general statement in doubt. Concerned with the deportation of a potential witness, the Court held in *Valenzuela* that the statutory policy of rapid deportation of illegal aliens requires that the defendant make "a plausible showing that the testimony of the deported witnesses would have been material and favorable to his defense, in ways not merely cumulative to the testimony of available witnesses."[644] Although the Court expressly stated in footnote 9 that it expressed no opinion "on the showing which a criminal defendant must make in order to obtain compulsory process for securing the attendance . . . of witnesses within the United States,"[645] and the holding may be limited to cases in which the desired witness has been deported, the case may be persuasive when the armed forces have properly discharged a service member, albeit with negligent timing.

One can reasonably argue that the elimination of unfit members of the armed forces is necessary to an effective armed force and that Congress has clearly recognized this via its knowledge and recognition of the discharge system. If this should prove accurate, no sanction would be assessed against the government unless the lost testimony fit the test pronounced in Valenzuela.

---

[640] Mil. R. Evid. 301(b)(2). Such an advice ought not to be given in open court by counsel in an attempt to freeze the testimony of an opposing witness. When given, it should be given by the military judge either *sua sponte* or upon request of counsel.

[641] *See, e.g.,* United States v. Edmond, 63 M.J. 343 (C.A.A.F. 2006); United States v. Giermek, 3 M.J. 1013, 1016 (C.G.C.M.R. 1977).

[642] *See* United States v. Potter, 1 M.J. 897 (A.F.C.M.R. 1976) (negligent discharge of defense witness violates government's duty to ensure witness' presence at trial). *See also* Singleton v. Lefkowitz, 583 F.2d 618 (2d Cir. 1978). The defendant must show that the alleged conduct did in fact cause the witness not to testify or to change his or her testimony. Once the defendant has made a prima facie case of harassment, the prosecution has the burden of demonstrating the contrary. United States v. Morrison, 535 F. 2d 223 (3d Cir. 1976); United States v. Thompson, 5 M.J. 28 (C.M.A. 1978); United States v. Kennedy, 24 C.M.R. 61 (C.M.A. 1957). *See also* United States v. Rhodes, 14 M.J. 919 (A.F.C.M.R. 1982).

[643] 458 U.S. 858 (1982).

[644] 458 U.S. at 873 (1982).

[645] 458 U.S. at 873 n.9. (1982).

(Rel.3—1/07   Pub.62410)

§ 20-33.35   Laboratory Reports

In the military, one of the most troublesome issues raised in a compulsory process analysis is the right to challenge the admission of laboratory reports. Reports are clearly admissible under the hearsay exception for records of regularly conducted activity,[646] but assuming a report is constitutionally admissible on such a basis, the critical question is whether the defense can present evidence to impeach the report. Commonly, this impeachment is directed toward the competency of the analyst involved and the procedures used in the test.[647] The Court of Military Appeals concluded that the defendant has the right "to call the analyst under appropriate circumstances" for this purpose.[648] While the right is uncontroverted, the mechanics involved cause considerable problems.

Generally, a defense request for the analyst must comply with the procedures established under Rule 703 of the Manual, including the implied prerequisites of timeliness and materiality.[649] There is no consensus, however, on the exact standards required in this situation. The problem stems from the peculiar nature of the testimony involved. The analyst's statements are used against the defendant at trial and the analyst is actually a witness for the government, even if he or she does not personally appear.[650] Thus, when the defense calls the analyst, defense counsel may have difficulties interviewing the witness.[651] If a pretrial interview cannot be accomplished, the defense may not have enough information with which to establish the materiality and necessity of the analyst's personal

---

[646] United States v. Vietor, 10 M.J. 69, 70 (C.M.A. 1980) (Cook, J.); United States v. Strangstalien, 7 M.J. 225, 229 (C.M.A. 1979); United States v. Evans, 45 C.M.R. 353, 355–56 (C.M.A. 1972); Mil. R. Evid. 803(6), (8)(B); Analysis of the Military Rules of Evidence 1980 Amendments to the *Manual for Courts-Martial*, Analysis of Rule 803(6), *reprinted at* MCM 2005, A22–53. *See* United States v. Licavoli, 604 F.2d 613, 622 (9th Cir. 1979) (Fed. R. Evid. 803(6)). *See also* United States v. Coleman, 631 F.2d 908, 910 (D.C. Cir. 1980); United States v. Hernandez-Rojas, 617 F.2d 533, 534 (9th Cir. 1980); United States v. Sawyer, 607 F.2d 1190, 1193 (7th Cir. 1979); United States v. Orozco, 590 F.2d 789, 793 (9th Cir. 1979). *Contra* United States v. Oates, 560 F.2d 45, 66–68 (2d Cir. 1977). As for the impact of the confrontation clause, *see generally* Imwinkelried, *The Constitutionality of Introducing Evaluative Laboratory Reports Against Criminal Defendants*, 30 Hastings L.J. 621 (1979).

[647] *See* Imwinkelried, *A New Era in the Evolution of Scientific Evidence, below* note 664, in which the author argued that the increasing rejection of the holding in *Frye v. United States*, 293 F. 1013 (D.C. Cir. 1923), makes it necessary to attack the weight of scientific evidence permitting the admission of a laboratory report.

[648] United States v. Vietor, 10 M.J. 69, 72 (C.M.A. 1980) (Cook, J.); United States v. Strangstalien, 7 M.J. 225, 229 (C.M.A. 1979) (Fletcher, C.J.).

[649] *See* Sections 20-22.30 and 20-22.40.

[650] *Vietor*, 10 M.J. at 81 (Fletcher, J., concurring in result) (citing Westen, *Confrontation and Compulsory Process, above* note 542, at 694 n.105).

[651] *See Vietor*, 10 M.J. at 77 (Everett, C.J., concurring in result) (implied in analysis of MCM 1969, para. 115a); Mil. R. Evid. 806.

testimony.[652] At this point, in interpreting Rule 703's predecessor provision, the judges on the Court of Military Appeals have applied different standards of materiality and, implicitly, have thus applied different standards of compliance with Rule 703.

Judge Fletcher would have required the government to show either unavailability or that there would be no utility for confrontation.[653] Apparently, no formal request would be needed, and the defense would not be required to expressly show materiality or necessity.[654] This view assumes that cross-examination of the analyst is always material and necessary because it detracts from the weight given to the evidence of the laboratory report.[655] Judge Cook, on the other hand, believed that compliance with the usual standards is appropriate. The government must produce a witness only upon the defendant's showing of materiality and necessity,[656] and this standard is no different for laboratory reports.[657] To hold that a mere unsupported request triggers the obligation to obtain the witness would nullify the purpose of the hearsay exception.[658] The accused's right to call the chemist is thus qualified by the normal standards of materiality.

It would appear that in Judge Cook's view, the defense counsel would have to attempt to contact the analyst before trial and submit a request as for any other witness.[659]

Chief Judge Everett appeared to take the middle ground. Recognizing that the substance of what is now Rule 703 serves legitimate government interests, he

---

[652] *Vietor*, 10 M.J. at 77–78 (Everett, C.J., concurring in result).

[653] United States v. Strangstalien, 7 M.J. 225, 229 (C.M.A. 1979). *See also Vietor*, 10 M.J. at 81 (Fletcher, J., concurring in result).

[654] *Vietor*, 10 M.J. at 80 (Fletcher, J., concurring in result).

[655] 10 M.J. at 82 (citing Westen, *Confrontation and Compulsory Process, above* note 542, at 619 n.143); Imwinkelried, *A New Era in the Evolution of Scientific Evidence, below* note 664.

[656] *See, e.g.*, United States v. Williams, 3 M.J. 239, 243 (C.M.A. 1977); United States v. Carpenter, 1 M.J. 384, 385–86 (C.M.A. 1976). In United States v. Davis, 14 M.J. 847 (A.C.M.R. 1982), the court held that failure to order a chemist to be produced was reversible error. In *Davis*, the court interpreted *Vietor* as requiring the defense to make some plausible showing of how the requested witness would be material and favorable to the defense. 14 M.J. at 847 (footnote omitted).

[657] *See* United States v. Strangstalien, 7 M.J. 225, 230 (C.M.A. 1979) (Cook, J., concurring in part, dissenting in part); United States v. Johnson, 3 M.J. 772, 775 (A.C.M.R. 1977) (DeFord, J., dissenting).

[658] Strangstalien, 7 M.J. at 230 (Cook, J., concurring in part, dissenting in part); United States v. Watkins, 5 M.J. 612, 614 (A.C.M.R. 1978); United States v. Credit, 2 M.J. 631, 647 (A.F.C.M.R. 1976); *rev'd on other grounds*, 4 M.J. 118 (C.M.A. 1977), *on remand*, 6 M.J. 719 (A.F.C.M.R. 1978), *aff'd*, 8 M.J. 190 (C.M.A. 1980).

[659] *See* United States v. Vietor, 10 M.J. 69, 71–72 (C.M.A. 1980) (Cook, J.) (counsel was remiss in not contacting the witness); *Strangstalien*, 7 M.J. at 230 (Cook, J., concurring in part, dissenting in part).

(Rel.3—1/07 Pub.62410)

would require the defense to follow the paragraph's procedure,[660] but "rigid application of these requirements would produce a conflict with an accused's statutory and constitutional right to compulsory process" in some cases.[661] Interviewing the analyst may be impossible in some instances, and strict compliance with Rule 703 should not be required. As under Judge Fletcher's approach, this assumes that the analyst's personal testimony is inherently material on the weight given to the laboratory report.[662]

While the views of each judge have merit, there is another approach that better reflects the issues involved. Instead of combining the questions of the analyst's qualifications and the test procedures actually used, the two questions should be considered separately. In the abstract, the analyst's qualification should seldom be at issue initially when the test involved is simple, as in the cases of counting sperm cells, blood typing, or drug analysis.[663] If the test is complicated, such as neutron activation analysis or human leukocyte antigen testing, then the analyst's ability to perform the test and interpret the results becomes important.[664] Depending on the complexity of the text, the requisite showing of materiality and necessity in support of a defense request for the analyst should vary. If the test is a simple one, the defense should be required to interview the analyst before trial about his or qualifications and to show that the analyst's qualifications are inadequate to perform the test. The underlying presumption is that any analyst is capable of performing simple tests.[665] When the test is

[660] *Vietor*, 10 M.J. 69, 77–78 (C.M.A. 1980). Judge Everett's conclusion finds support in other cases. *See* United States v. Williams, 3 M.J. 239 (C.M.A. 1977); United States v. Dixon, 8 M.J. 858 (N.C.M.R. 1980); United States v. Christian, 6 M.J. 624, 627 (A.C.M.R. 1978) (DeFord, J., concurring); United States v. Kilby, 3 M.J. 938, 944–45 (N.C.M.R. 1977).

[661] *Vietor*, 10 M.J. at 77 (Everett, C.J., concurring in result).

[662] *Vietor*, 10 M.J. at 76–77 (Everett, C.J., concurring in result), 82 (Fletcher, J., concurring in result) (citing Westen, *Confrontation and Compulsory Process, above* note 542, at 619 n.143.

[663] Qualification as an expert requires only that his or her testimony will help the trier of fact to understand the evidence or to determine a fact in issue. Mil. R. Evid. 702. The witness need not be the most expert or proficient in his or her field. United States v. Barker, 553 F.2d 1013, 1024 (6th Cir. 1977) (Fed. R. Evid. 702). Competency in this situation only involves the ability to perform the test.

[664] *See* Imwinkelried, *A New Era in the Evolution of Scientific Evidence — A Primer on Evaluating the Weight of Scientific Evidence*, 23 WM. & Mary L. Rev. 261, 278–83 (1981).

[665] *See* Mil. R. Evid. 702. There are other tests that require subjective evaluation, such as paper chromatography, which requires the analyst to subjectively analyze sometimes subtle identifications of the color streak on the filter paper. Paul C. Giannelli & E. Edward J. Imwinkelried, *Scientific Evidence* § 23-2 (3d ed. 1999); thin-layer chromatography; *id.* at 358-62 (In examining thin-layer chromatography, the analyst must identify a color to identify the unknown substance. Some companies that manufacture the equipment supply color charts for comparison, while others provide photographs of the plates to enable the trier of fact to make a better independent comparison at trial); gas chromatography; *id.* at 362, color-change tests, nonspecific tests used to identify drugs. *Id.* at § 23-2(B).

(Rel.3—1/07 Pub.62410)

more complex, the analyst's ability becomes more important; for example, not everyone can conduct neutron activation analysis. Because the test results then depend more on the analyst's ability to do the test and read the results, the presumption of competency is weaker, and the court should recognize that the analyst's qualifications are inherently material. As a result, although the defense request for the analyst should be as detailed as possible, the standard used in determining compliance with Rule 703 should be lower.

A different standard should be applied when the defense wants to examine the analyst about the test procedures actually used. Because the test procedures can affect the test results,[666] the defense should only have to meet a standard similar to that applied when the analyst's competency to perform or interpret a complex test is involved. Obviously, the defense should always try to determine before trial what the proper procedures are and whether they were used on that particular sample. But, in light of increasing evidence that forensic laboratories are incapable of accurately performing any but the simplest tests,[667] a court should not be too eager to presume that the test procedures were proper per se or that the proper procedures were actually used. If, in the request under Rule for Courts-Martial 703, the defense offers any evidence that the actual procedures were improper, the analyst should be required to testify.[668]>

Like many evidentiary rules, this approach is based on assumptions about how various scientific tests are performed and who performs them. The armed forces utilize "on-the-job training" to prepare many personnel to function within the armed forces. If a significant expansion in personnel forced hasty training of otherwise unqualified personnel, it would be appropriate for military judges to assume that the qualifications of a forensic chemist, for example, should be in doubt until shown otherwise by the government. In effect, this would nullify the "presumption" that any normal analyst is capable of performing routine tests.[668]

§ 20-40.00   Depositions And Interrogatories[669]

Article 49 of the Uniform Code of Military Justice expressly authorizes any party to take "oral or written depositions" unless prohibited from doing so by

---

[666] This includes: careless handling, storage, and preparation of the evidence; improper procedures actually used; and improper procedures in theory. *See* United States v. Davis, 14 M.J. 847 (A.C.M.R. 1982).

[667] *See* Imwinkelried, *below* note 664, at 267–69 (citing four surveys) *See* Paul Giannelli, *Ake v. Oklahoma: The Right to Expert Assistance in the Post Daubert, Post-DNA World*, 89 Cornell L. Rev. 1305 (2004). The Court of Military Appeals has presumed a regularity of handling and storage procedures in the chain of custody. United States v. Strangstalien, 7 M.J. 225, 229 (C.M.A. 1979). (Fletcher, C.J.).

[668] *See above* note 663.

[669] U.C.M.J. art. 49 uses the expression "written deposition" to refer to what R.C.M. 702(g)(2)(C) and customary civilian practice refer to as written interrogatories.

(Rel.3—1/07   Pub.62410)

the military judge or other proper officer.[670] Military Rule of Evidence 804 permits the use in evidence of depositions under certain conditions. It is apparent that the intent of Article 49 was to utilize depositions in lieu of live testimony.[671] According to the terms of Article 49(d), a deposition may be used only when "the witness resides or is beyond the State, Territory Commonwealth, or District of Columbia in which the court . . . is ordered to sit, or beyond 100 miles from the place of trial or hearing,"[672] or when the witness is actually unavailable[673] or cannot be located.[674]

The Court of Military Appeals held that the geographic provision for depositions are invalid insofar as it relates to service members[675] and has strongly suggested that constitutional standards dictate the same result insofar as civilians are concerned.[676] Thus, actual unavailability is necessary.[677] Whatever the

---

[670] U.C.M.J. art. 49(a). *See generally* McGovern, *The Military Oral Deposition and Modern Communications*, 45 Mil. R. Evid. 43 (1969); Everett, *The Role of the Deposition in Military Justice*, 7 Mil. R. Evid. 131 (1960). The codal provision permits taking depositions unless the proper officer forbids it for good cause. U.C.M.J. art. 49(a). R.C.M. 702 provides that any party may request to take oral depositions or, with approval of the other party, written depositions. Written depositions may be ordered without consent, however, for sentencing witnesses. R.C.M. 702(c)(3)(B). The request may be granted before or after referral by the convening authority or after referral by the military judge. R.C.M. 702(b). A request may be denied only for good cause. R.C.M. 702(c)(3). If the case is being tried as a capital case, only the defense may utilize depositions. U.C.M.J. art. 4(d)–(f).

[671] U.C.M.J. art. 49(d)(1). *See below* note 672.

[672] U.C.M.J. art. 49(d)(2) (permits depositions when "the witness by reason of death, age, sickness, bodily infirmity, imprisonment, military necessity, nonamenability to process, or other reasonable cause is unable or refuses to appear"). The current approach of the Court of Military Appeals to military necessity in the general area of witness procurement suggests that, absent declared war, it is improbable that depositions will be justified by military necessity.

[673] U.C.M.J. art. 49(b)(2).

[674] U.C.M.J. art. 49(b)(3).

[675] *See above* notes 354, 355. For depositions of foreign witnesses, *see generally* United States v. Hamilton, 36 M.J. 927 (A.F.C.M.R. 1993).

[676] 36 M.J. 927 (A.F.C.M.R. 1993). Although Mil. R. Evid. 804(a) is illustrative rather than limiting, its express enumeration of U.C.M.J. art. 49(d)(2) and silence as to Article 49(d)(2) suggest that a deposition obtained under Article 49(d)(1) may be inadmissible under the Military Rules of Evidence. *See also* United States v. Hamilton, 36 M.J. 927 (A.F.C.M.R. 1993) (deposition of civilian in the Philippines).

[677] This includes unavailability because of military necessity. *Cf.* United States v. Vanderwier, 25 M.J. 263, 266 (C.M.A. 1987).

That a court could be moved to the locus of the witness does not equate to a confrontation violation, as there is no requirement of absolute unavailability, only a requirement that the government make a good-faith effort to obtain the presence of the witness at trial. United States v. Crockett, 21 M.J. 423, 426–27 (C.M.A. 1986). It is interesting to note that the request for trial by judge alone in United States v. Crockett, 21 M.J. 423 (C.M.A. 1986), was made after a videotape deposition was taken in Florida. The court did not consider the request to be a significant factor

(Rel.3—1/07   Pub.62410)

Article's original intent, the primary use of depositions is now clearly limited to preservation of testimony.[678] It was the intent of Congress that no deposition take place unless the accused is given the opportunity to attend,[679] and military law gives the accused the right to attend the deposition with counsel.[680] Under these circumstances, the accused's core confrontation right is protected, since the accused is both present at a prosecution deposition and has the right through counsel to cross-examine the witness being deposed. What the accused loses is the ability to conduct the cross-examination before the members of the court. Accordingly, use of a deposition is analogous to the use of former testimony, and the Court of Military Appeals held that the "confrontation clause . . . requires the Government to demonstrate that the declarant is unavailable when it seeks to admit a deposition against an accused at a criminal trial in the place of live testimony."[681] This rule may cause acute problems in wartime given the need for rapid mobility.

Procedurally, the Code requires that reasonable written notice of the time and place of the deposition be given to those parties who have not requested the deposition[682] and that "depositions may be taken before and authenticated by any military or civil officer authorized . . . to administer oaths."[683] *The Manual for Courts-Martial* requires that oral depositions be recorded verbatim, normally by the officer taking the deposition.[684] Appropriate objections should be made during the deposition, but the deposing officer is not to rule upon them; they are merely to be recorded for later resolution.[685] Although, absent actual

---

in determining availability. "Even for a judge alone trial the two witnesses were 'unavailable' because the cost, expense, delay, and disruption resulting from a change of the trial location still would have been unreasonably great. Bringing a court-martial to a witness is more difficult than bringing a witness before a court-martial." *Crockett*, 21 M.J. at 427–28.

[678] *See, e.g.*, R.C.M. 702(a) Discussion (a deposition may be taken to preserve the testimony of a witness who is likely to be unavailable at the investigation under Article 32 or at the time of trial) (citations omitted). It is possible to use the coercive nature of depositions as a discovery device, except that it is not likely that such a deposition would be approved.

[679] *Uniform Code of Military Justice, Hearings Before a Subcomm. of the House Comm. on Armed Services on H.R. 2498*, 81st Cong., 1st Sess. 696 (1949) (statement of Rep. Elston).

[680] United States v. Jacoby, 11 C.M.A. 248, 253, 29 C.M.R. 244, 249 (C.M.A. 1960). *Jacoby* was codified in MCM, 1969 (rev. ed.) ¶ 117b(2), which declared that the right to counsel held by an accused at a deposition was the same as that prescribed for trial by the type of court-martial before which the deposition was to be used.

[681] United States v. Cokeley, 22 M.J. 225, 228 (C.M.A. 1986).

[682] U.C.M.J. art. 49(b); R.C.M. 702(e). *See also* United States v. Marsh, 35 M.J. 305 (A.F.C.M.R. 1992) (what is adequate notice).

[683] U.C.M.J. art. 49(b); R.C.M. 702(d)(1). *See also* United States v. Washington, 46 M.J. 477, 482–84 (C.A.A.F. 1997) (minimum requirements of fairness requires deposition officers to be disinterested).

[684] R.C.M. 702(f)(6), (8).

[685] R.C.M. 702(f)(7).

(Rel.3—1/07　Pub.62410)

unavailability, the defense generally has the right to prohibit the receipt into evidence of a deposition, trial tactics are often such that the defense has no particular reason to object to the use of depositions, provided that the testimony of the witness can carry sufficient persuasive effect. In 1983, Congress amended Article 49(d) to permit the recording of depositions on "audiotape, videotape or similar material" and the playing of these tapes to the fact finder at trial.[686] Given the widespread availability of videotape recorders in modern society and in the armed forces, both trial and defense counsel should make increasing use of videotaped depositions.[687] Such depositions can save substantial amounts of trial time, may be edited following the military judge's ruling on objections, and will convey the demeanor of the witness to the fact finder. Indeed, given mutual consent, whole portions of trial can be presented in this fashion.[688]

When it seeks to introduce a deposition, the Government has the "burden of demonstrating that a witness is unavailable."[689]

In determining whether to admit the deposition of a witness who is temporarily unable to be present for trial, the military judge should consider all circumstances of the case, includ[ing] the importance of the testimony, the amount of delay necessary to obtain the in-court testimony, the trustworthiness of the alternative to live testimony, the nature and extent of earlier cross-examination, the prompt

---

[686] U.C.M.J. art. 49(d). Military Justice Act of 1983, Pub. L. No. 98-209, 97 Stat. 1393. *See also* Section 13-35.24. This provision became effective on August 1, 1984. In United States v. Crockett, 21 M.J. 423, 425 (C.M.A. 1986), the court indicated that, even prior to the amendment to Article 49 of the code, it was permissible for the government to admit videotapes of witnesses who were not subject to a subpoena and would not attend the trial on the basis of invitational travel orders.

Under Military Rule of Evidence 101(b), military courts are to follow the rules in federal district courts unless they are inconsistent with the Manual or the Code. Mil. R. Evid. 101(b). Because the use of videotape depositions has become commonplace in civil and criminal trials in the federal courts, arguably the use of videotape would have been admissible, even prior to the amendment.

Presentation at trial of a videotaped deposition does not violate the Sixth Amendment, because the accused and his counsel are given the opportunity of seeing the witness face-to-face and of subjecting the witness to the ordeal of cross-examination. Further, it provides the fact finder with a better basis for perceiving a witness' demeanor and evaluating his credibility than does a written deposition. In fact, the playing of a videotape is such that fact finders would be better equipped to determine the trustworthiness of the absent witness than they would be if they were reading a transcript from a preliminary hearing where defense counsel had the full opportunity for cross-examination.

[687] *See* McGovern, *The Military Oral Deposition and Modern Communications, above* note 670, at 59-75.

[688] Entire civilian criminal trials were have been conducted in this fashion years ago by Judge McCrystal in Ohio. Numerous civil cases have also been so conducted. Because of the ability to present edited videotapes to juries, substantial amounts of juror and trial time have been saved.

[689] United States v. Cokeley, 22 M.J. 225, 229 (C.M.A. 1986).

administration of justice, and any special circumstances militating for or against delay. [690]

The military judge's determination of unavailability is subject to review for abuse of discretion. [691]

---

[690] United States v. Vanderwier, 25 M.J. 263, 266 (C.M.A. 1987) (quoting United States v. Cokeley, 22 M.J. 225, 229 (C.M.A. 1986)).

[691] United States v. Hampton, 33 M.J. 21 (C.M.A. 1991) (pregnant German national in United States who refused to travel to Germany held unavailable by trial judge, permitting use of videotaped deposition). United States v. Vanderwier, 25 M.J. 263, 266 (C.M.A. 1987). In *Vanderwier*, the court expressed a strong desire that the trial judge making such a decision "articulate any weighing of relevant considerations or explain his reasons for admitting the deposition." 25 M.J. 263, 266 (C.M.A. 1987). See also United States v. Baker, 33 M.J. 788, 790–91 (A.F.C.M.R. 1991) (abuse of discretion when judge held previously cooperative witness unavailable because she was in the Philippines and her husband had said she would not return to the United States).

CHAPTER 21

TRIAL ON THE MERITS

§ 21-10.00 INTRODUCTION
  § 21-11.00   In General
  § 21-12.00   Basic Procedure
  § 21-13.00   Mental State of the Accused
  § 21-14.00   Burdens of Proof
    § 21-14.10 — In General
    § 21-14.20 — Failure to Meet the Burden of Proof; Reopening of Prosecution's Case
§ 21-20.00 EVIDENTIARY MATTERS
  § 21-21.00   The Military Rules of Evidence Generally
  § 21-22.00   Admissibility Determinations
  § 21-23.00   Substitutes for Evidence
    § 21-23.10 — Stipulations and Concessions
    § 21-23.20 — Judicial Notice
    § 21-23.30 — Presumptions
§ 21-30.00 EXAMINATION OF WITNESSES
  § 21-31.00   In General
  § 21-32.00   Mode and Scope of Examination

§ 21-10.00   INTRODUCTION

§ 21-11.00   In General

Before trial on the merits may begin, the accused must be advised of his or her rights to counsel[1] and fact finder,[2] and must make all necessary elections. The accused must also make all necessary pretrial motions[3] and must be arraigned.[4] Should trial be with members, the appointed members are subject to voir dire and challenge.[5] Finally, after assembly,[6] trial on the merits may begin.

---

[1] *See generally* § 5-12.00.

[2] Except in a capital case, the accused may elect trial by military judge alone or with members. *See generally* Sections 14-64.20 and 15-10.00. If trial is with members, an enlisted accused may request trial with enlisted members. *See* Section 15-25.00.

[3] *See generally* Chapter 18.

[4] *See generally* Chapter 16.

[5] *See generally* Chapter 15.

[6] R.C.M. 911. Noncompliance with R.C.M. 813(a)'s requirement that the names and ranks of

Trial on the merits in the armed forces is functionally identical with trial on the merits in a civilian federal district court. Insofar as findings are concerned, unless trial proceeds without a military judge,[7] the only significant difference is the members' ability and likelihood to propound their own questions to witnesses.[8] The most important difference between civilian and military cases is that courts-martial are bifurcated proceedings; that is, upon conviction of the accused, an adversarial sentencing hearing takes place in a subsequent proceeding.[9]

There is no difference between trial by judge alone and trial with members except for the obvious lack of instructions or need for sidebar conferences in bench trials.

§ 21-12.00 Basic Procedure

Pursuant to Rule for Courts-Martial 913, the usual sequence for trial on the merits consists of

(1) Preliminary instructions[10]

(2) Opening statement by trial counsel

(3) Opening statement by defense counsel[11]

(4) Presentation of evidence for the prosecution

---

members be announced when the court is first called to order is nonjurisdictional. United States v. Fell, 33 M.J. 628, 633 (A.C.M.R. 1991). *Accord*, United States v. Kaopua, 33 M.J. 712, 713 (A.C.M.R. 1991).

[7] An almost inconceivable possibility. *See* Section 15-12.00.

[8] Although they may do so, they are also bound by the rules of evidence.

[9] Which customarily takes place immediately following announcement of findings. *See generally* Chapter 23.

[10] R.C.M. 913(a). *See* Dep't of Army Pam. 27-9, Military Judges' Benchbook 36–41 (15 September 2002). Of course, if trial is by judge alone, there are no instructions.

[11] The defense may defer opening until the beginning of the defense's case. R.C.M. 913(b) specifies:

Each party may make one opening statement to the court-martial before presentation of evidence has begun. The defense may elect to make its statement after the prosecution has rested, before the presentation of evidence for the defense. The military judge may, as a matter of discretion, permit the parties to address the court-martial at other times.

One of the ongoing questions is whether a defense opening alone can open the door to prosecution evidence. The Court of Military Appeals implied that it cannnot and that trial counsel can respond only via closing argument. United States v. Turner, 39 M.J. 259, 262 (C.M.A. 1994) (dictum; *see* Crawford, J., dissenting at 266, claiming that the majority rule in the federal circuits is to the contrary). *See also* United States v. Houser, 36 M.J. 392, 400 (C.M.A. 1993); United States v. Franklin, 35 M.J. 311, 317 (C.M.A. 1992); United States v. Karas, 950 F.2d 31, 37 (1st Cir. 1991) (dictum to effect that defense opening did not open the door to Fed. R. Evid. 404(b) evidence).

(Rel.3—1/07 Pub.62410)

(5) Presentation of evidence for the defense

(6) Presentation of prosecution evidence in rebuttal

(7) Presentation of defense evidence in surrebuttal

(8) Additional rebuttal evidence in the discretion of the military judge

(9) Presentation of evidence requested by the military judge or members[12]

(10) Closing argument by trial counsel[13]

(11) Closing argument by defense counsel[14]

(12) Rebuttal argument by trial counsel[15]

(13) Closing and substantive instructions[16]

(14) Deliberations and vote on verdict[17]

(15) Findings (verdict announcement)[18]

This sequence is the ordinary one. The military judge has the discretion to alter it as need arises.

On appeal, it is likely that the trial judge's decision on the issue of incompetency or incapacity will be reviewed for abuse of discretion.[19]

§ 21-13.00 Mental State of the Accused

Rule for Courts-Martial 909(a) declares:

No person may be brought to trial by court-martial if that person is presently suffering from a mental disease or defect rendering him or her mentally incompetent to the extent that he or she is unable to understand the nature of the proceedings against that person or to conduct or cooperate intelligently in the defense of the case.

Unlike the question of the accused's mental responsibility at the time of the offense,[20] the accused's capacity to participate in trial is an interlocutory matter for the trial judge.[21] In light of the presumption of mental capacity,[22] trial may

---

[12] R.C.M. 913(c) (subsection letters omitted).

[13] R.C.M. 919(a). *See generally* Chapter 22.

[14] R.C.M. 919(a).

[15] R.C.M. 919(a). Many judges discourage rebuttal argument by the trial counsel.

[16] *See* R.C.M. 920. Counsel should request instructions prior to final argument. *See* R.C.M. 920(c). *But see* United States v. Pendry, 29 M.J. 694, 695 n.2 (A.C.M.R. 1989).

[17] R.C.M. 921. *See generally* Chapter 22.

[18] R.C.M. 922. *See generally* Chapter 22.

[19] United States v. Proctor, 34 M.J.549, 553 (A.F.C.M.R. 1992), *aff'd*, 37 M.J. 330 (C.M.A. 1993) ("There is no indication that the judge abused his discretion . . . or that he was otherwise incorrect").

[20] *See* R.C.M. 916(k).

[21] R.C.M. 909(c)(1).

[22] R.C.M. 909(b).

(Rel.3—1/07 Pub.62410)

proceed unless lack of capacity is shown by a preponderance of the evidence.[23] Article 76b(a)(1) provides that:

> In the case of a person determined under this chapter to be presently suffering from a mental disease or defect rendering the person mentally incompetent to the extent that the person is unable to understand the nature of the proceedings against that person or to conduct or cooperate intelligently in the defense of the case, the general court-martial convening authority for that person shall commit the person to the custody of the Attorney General.

Rule for Courts-Martial 909(c) implements the statute:

> If an inquiry pursuant to R.C.M. 706 conducted before referral concludes that an accused is suffering from a mental disease or defect that renders him or her mentally incompetent to stand trial, the convening authority before whom the charges are pending for disposition may disagree with the conclusion and take any action authorized under R.C.M. 401, including referral of the charges to trial. If that convening authority concurs with the conclusion, he or she shall forward the charges to the general court-martial convening authority. If, upon receipt of the charges, the general court-martial convening authority similarly concurs, then he or she shall commit the accused to the custody of the Attorney General. If the general court-martial convening authority does not concur, that authority may take any action that he or she deems appropriate in accordance with R.C.M. 407, including referral of the charges to trial.

In *United States v. Salahuddin*,[24] the appellant had been found to have been incompetent to participate in his defense by a defense requested R.C.M 706 sanity board and had then been committed to the custody of the Attorney General who transferred him to the Federal Bureau of Prisons. Salahuddin sought a writ of mandamus requiring the government to first prove "by more than a preponderance of the evidence, not only that he is mentally incompetent, but that he 'requires hospitalization for his own welfare and protection of others.'" The Air Force Court of Criminal Appeals rejected the petition stating simply that "We, and every federal appellate court that has examined this issue, disagree. The purpose of any hearing, under Article 76b or the federal statute, 18 U.S.C. § 4241(d), is to determine the competency of an accused to stand trial, not to determine the propriety of commitment to the Attorney General."[25] Accordingly, when an accused is found to be incompetent to stand trial, commitment to the Attorney General is automatic.

The Navy-Marine Court of Military Review, in *Freeman v. Stuart*,[26] denied a challenge by an accused, previously found incompetent to stand trial, to forcible

---

[23] R.C.M. 909(c)(2). *See* Medina v. California, 505 U.S. 437 (1992) (state may require that a defendant who alleges incompetence to stand trial prove that by a preponderance of the evidence). As to amnesia, *see* United States v. Barreto, 57 M.J. 127 (C.A.A.F. 2002).

[24] 54 M.J. 918 (A.F. Crim. App. 2001), *pet. denied*, 54 M.J. 456 (C.A.A.F. 2001).

[25] 54 M.J. at 920.

[26] 33 M.J. 659 (N.M.C.M.R. 1991).

(Rel.3—1/07 Pub.62410)

treatment with antipsychotic medication that would likely render him competent to stand trial, because the decision was a medical one made with proper due process protections. Subsequently, however, the Supreme Court held that forced administration of antipsychotic drugs to a state defendant during trial violated the Sixth and Fourteenth Amendments absent at least "a finding of overriding justification and a determination of medical appropriateness."[27] In 2003, however, the Court in *Sell v. United States*[28] permitted forced medication for the purpose of rendering a defendant fit to stand trial, but with conditions:

> [T]he Constitution permits the Government involuntarily to administer antipsychotic drugs to a mentally ill defendant facing serious criminal charges in order to render that defendant competent to stand trial, but only if the treatment is medically appropriate, is substantially unlikely to have side effects that may undermine the fairness of the trial, and, taking account of less intrusive alternatives, is necessary significantly to further important governmental trial-related interests.

> This standard will permit involuntary administration of drugs solely for trial competence purposes in certain instances. But those instances may be rare. That is because the standard says or fairly implies the following:

> First, a court must find that *important* governmental interests are at stake. The Government's interest in bringing to trial an individual accused of a serious crime is important. That is so whether the offense is a serious crime against the person or a serious crime against property. In both instances the Government seeks to protect through application of the criminal law the basic human need for security.

> Courts, however, must consider the facts of the individual case in evaluating the Government's interest in prosecution. Special circumstances may lessen the importance of that interest. The defendant's failure to take drugs voluntarily, for example, may mean lengthy confinement in an institution for the mentally ill—and that would diminish the risks that ordinarily attach to freeing without punishment one who has committed a serious crime. We do not mean to suggest that civil commitment is a substitute for a criminal trial. The Government has a substantial interest in timely prosecution. And it may be difficult or impossible to try a defendant who regains competence after years of commitment during which memories may fade and evidence may be lost. The potential for future confinement affects, but does not totally undermine, the strength of the need for prosecution. The same is true of the possibility that the defendant has already been confined for a significant amount of time (for which he would receive credit toward any sentence ultimately imposed, . . . Moreover, the Government has a concomitant, constitutionally essential interest in assuring that the defendant's trial is a fair one.

> Second, the court must conclude that involuntary medication will *significantly further* those concomitant state interests. It must find that

---

[27] Riggins v. Nevada, 504 U.S. 127 (1992), *citing* Washington v. Harper, 494 U.S. 210 (1990).
[28] 539 U.S. 166 (2003).

(Rel.3—1/07 Pub.62410)

administration of the drugs is substantially likely to render the defendant competent to stand trial. At the same time, it must find that administration of the drugs is substantially unlikely to have side effects that will interfere significantly with the defendant's ability to assist counsel in conducting a trial defense, thereby rendering the trial unfair. . . .

Third, the court must conclude that involuntary medication is *necessary* to further those interests. The court must find that any alternative, less intrusive treatments are unlikely to achieve substantially the same results. . . . And the court must consider less intrusive means for administering the drugs, *e.g.,* a court order to the defendant backed by the contempt power, before considering more intrusive methods.

Fourth, as we have said, the court must conclude that administration of the drugs is *medically appropriate, i.e.,* in the patient's best medical interest in light of his medical condition. The specific kinds of drugs at issue may matter here as elsewhere. Different kinds of antipsychotic drugs may produce different side effects and enjoy different levels of success.

We emphasize that the court applying these standards is seeking to determine whether involuntary administration of drugs is necessary significantly to further a particular governmental interest, namely, the interest in rendering the defendant *competent to stand trial.* A court need not consider whether to allow forced medication for that kind of purpose, if forced medication is warranted for a *different* purpose . . . .[29]

Accordingly, subject to service regulations it would appear to be potentially lawful to involuntarily administer medication to restore an accused to competence for the purpoes of trial.

§ 21-14.00 Burdens of Proof

§ 21-14.10 In General

The government must prove the accused guilty beyond a reasonable doubt[30] or the accused will be acquitted. Insofar as defenses are concerned,

[e]xcept for the defense of lack of mental responsibility, once a defense under this rule is placed in issue by some evidence, the prosecution shall have the burden of proving beyond a reasonable doubt that the defense

---

[29] 539 U.S. 179–82 (2003).

[30] The Discussion to Rule 918(c) defines "reasonable doubt" as follows:

A reasonable doubt is a doubt based on reason and common sense. A reasonable doubt is not mere conjecture; it is an honest, conscientious doubt suggested by the evidence, or lack of it, in the case. An absolute or mathematical certainty is not required. The rule as to reasonable doubt extends to every element of the offense. It is not necessary that each particular fact advanced by the prosecution which is not an element be proved beyond a reasonable doubt.

See also Dep't of Army Pam. 27-9, Military Judges' Benchbook 52–53 (15 September 2002).

(Rel.3—1/07 Pub.62410)

did not exist. The accused has the burden of proving the defense of lack of mental responsibility by clear and convincing evidence.[31]

§ 21-14.20 Failure to Meet the Burden of Proof; Reopening of Prosecution's Case

Should the prosecution fail to meet its burden of proof as to any specification at the close of its case, the defense may make a motion for a finding of not guilty.[32] Under Rule for Courts-Martial 917, a motion for a finding of not guilty shall be granted only in the absence of some evidence which, together with all reasonable inferences and applicable presumptions, could reasonably tend to establish every essential element of an offense charged. The evidence shall be viewed in the light most favorable to the prosecution, without an evaluation of the credibility of witnesses.[33]

If the defense motion should identify a fatal omission in the evidence,[34] in lieu of accepting the acquittal the prosecution may request permission to reopen its case-in-chief. Most civilian jurisdictions have left the propriety of such a "second chance" to case law. Rule 913(c)(5), however, explicitly, states: "The military judge may, as a matter of discretion, permit a party to reopen its case after it has rested." Neither the Discussion of the Rule nor its Analysis[35] supply guidance as to how the judge should apply that discretion.[36]

The armed forces have a long history of applying the "sportsman's theory of justice" under which a party, particularly the government, is responsible for its mistakes. Under such an approach, a fatal error in the government's proof should be final; it ought not to be given a second chance to do it "right." Unfortunately, such an approach, despite its obvious attraction to the defense, cheats justice because of the unnecessary error of the trial counsel. Accordingly, the judge should permit reopening in every case unless reopening might result in some form of specific prejudice to the accused other than an adverse verdict.[37] This

---

[31] R.C.M. 916(b).

[32] R.C.M. 917. *See generally* Section 18-50.00. The defense may also make such a motion at the close of the defense's case. R.C.M. 917(a).

[33] R.C.M. 909(d).

[34] R.C.M. 917(b) requires that the motion "specifically indicate wherein the evidence is insufficient."

[35] Merely citing the origin of the Rule in MCM, 1969 (rev. ed.) ¶ 71a; Analysis of the Rules for Courts-Martial, MCM, 2005, A21-62.

[36] For one view as to how that discretion should be applied in the United States district courts, *see* United States v. Peay, 972 F.2d 71 (4th Cir. 1992).

[37] Reopening can be of significant value to the defense and may not only serve the interests of justice but may also obviate a request for a new trial. *See* United States v. Fisiorek, 43 M.J. 244 (C.A.A.F. 1995) (defense should have been permitted to reopen to present newly discovered evidence).

(Rel.3—1/07 Pub.62410)

clearly presents a tactical dilemma for the defense. Should counsel make a motion for a finding of not guilty at the close of the government's case, its very motion may identify the prosecution's error and permit it to rectify it. Should counsel fail to make the motion and proceed with a defense case-in-chief, it risks solving the evidentiary deficiency during its case. Tactically, it would appear that if the defense is sure that the prosecution has failed to carry its burden—and can repair the error—it would be wise to waive a defense case and argue the deficiency in closing argument. Rule 913(c)(5) is ambiguous in its reach. It may well be that trial counsel could request permission to reopen following a defense summation, but it seems unlikely that most judges would permit it.[38]

§ 21-20.00 EVIDENTIARY MATTERS

§ 21-21.00 The Military Rules of Evidence Generally

The rules of evidence in the armed forces are codified in the Military Rules of Evidence.[39] Originally effective in 1980,[40] the rules largely echo the Federal Rules of Evidence[41] except for two major topics:[42] they have a complete body of codified privilege rules,[43] and, in Section III,[44] they codify the law of interrogation and confessions, search and seizure, and eyewitness identification.

§ 21-22.00 Admissibility Determinations

With perhaps one major exception,[45] all evidentiary decisions are made by the military judge. "In making these determinations the military judge is not bound by the rules of evidence except those with respect to privileges."[46]

---

[38] Although this could be said to be due to the vestiges of the sportsman's theory of justice, at this stage of trial, it might better be said to be due to the need for an end to the trial. If the government can reopen at such a late date, there might never be an end to a case.

[39] MCM, 1998, Part III.

[40] *See generally* Lederer, *The Military Rules of Evidence, Origins and Judicial Implementation*, 130 Mil. L. Rev. 5 (1990); Lederer, *The Military Rules of Evidence: An Overview*, 12 The Advocate 113, 114 (1980).

[41] A number of important differences do exist, however. In the area of hearsay, for example, the hearsay exception for "business records" (Mil. R. Evid. 803(6)) is far broader than its civilian equivalent and includes an exception for forensic laboratory reports.

[42] The Military Rules do not include the Federal Rules' codification of presumptions, because the Federal Rules deal only with presumptions in civil cases.

[43] Mil. R. Evid. § V.

[44] The Military Rules of Evidence are organized by "section" rather than "article," as are the Federal Rules of Evidence. The framers of the Military Rules wished to eliminate possible confusion between the rules and the articles of the Uniform Code of Military Justice.

[45] Mil. R. Evid. 1008, Function of Military Judge and Members, dealing with the "best evidence rule."

[46] Mil. R. Evid. 104(a).

(Rel.3—1/07 Pub.62410)

Pursuant to Military Rule of Evidence 103(a), absent plain[47] or constitu-tional[48] error,

> [e]rror may not be predicated upon a ruling which admits or excludes evidence unless the ruling materially prejudices a substantial right of a party, and
>
> (1) *Objection.* In case the ruling is one admitting evidence, a timely objection or motion to strike appears of record, stating the specific ground of objection, if the specific ground was not apparent from the context; or
>
> (2) *Offer of proof.* In case the ruling is one excluding evidence, the substance of the evidence was made known to the military judge by offer or was apparent from the context within which questions were asked.[49]

The *Manual* does not specify the burden of proof applicable to evidentiary determinations, except that when admissibility is dependent upon the existence of a given fact,[50] the judge "shall admit it upon, or subject to, the introduction of *evidence sufficient to support a finding* of the fulfillment of the condition."[51] Similarly, the standard of admissibility for authentication is *"evidence sufficient to support a finding* that the matter in question is what its proponent claims,"[52] and it is likely that "evidence sufficient to support a finding" is adequate.

§ 21-23.00 Substitutes for Evidence

§ 21-23.10 Stipulations and Concessions

Stipulations are commonplace in courts-martial practice, and often greatly speed the trial by permitting counsel to dispense with witnesses or other evidence. Rule for Courts-Martial 811(a) states: "The parties may make an oral or written stipulation to any fact, the contents of a document, or the expected testimony of a witness." A stipulation is an express agreement between or among the parties[53] that a certain fact is true or that a witness, if present to testify under oath or affirmation, would testify in substance as related in the stipulation. Unless withdrawn, the stipulation is binding on the parties[54] for trial and its legal aftermath.

Stipulations of expected testimony or of the contents of a document merely reflect what a witness would be expected to testify or what the document contains.

---

[47] Mil. R. Evid. 103(d).

[48] Mil. R. Evid. 103(a).

[49] Mil. R. Evid. 103(a).

[50] "[T]he fulfillment of a condition of fact." Mil. R. Evid. 104(b).

[51] Mil. R. Evid. 104(b) (emphasis added).

[52] Mil. R. Evid. 901(a) (emphasis added).

[53] In routine practice, a stipulation is a written agreement with the signatures of trial and defense counsel and the accused. Customarily, it is marked by the judge as an exhibit.

[54] R.C.M. 811(b).

(Rel.3—1/07 Pub.62410)

Absent other agreement, the stipulation does not concede admissibility. Rule 811(e) states: "The contents of a stipulation of expected testimony or of a document's contents may be attacked, contradicted, or explained in the same way as if the witness had actually so testified or the document had been actually admitted." This permits counsel to enter into a stipulation but preserve evidentiary objections.

Under military law, the military judge is required to ensure that the parties have voluntarily entered into a stipulation.[55] Although the Rule is silent, its Discussion states: "Ordinarily, before accepting any stipulation the military judge should inquire to ensure that the accused understands the right not to stipulate, understands the stipulation, and consents to it." The remainder of the Discussion deals with confessional stipulations.[56]

In ordinary practice, most military judges engage in an extremely probing stipulation-providency inquiry similar to that used for guilty-plea providency inquiries.[57] Although both well-intentioned and praiseworthy, such warnings often suggest to the accused that something is amiss with the stipulation and may injure the attorney-client relationship.

Interestingly, the Rules for Courts-Martial are silent on the subject of concessions. At least theoretically, stipulations differ from concessions, in that stipulations are agreements among the parties while concessions are unilateral. Charged with homicide, an accused might, for example, concede the killing but argue self-defense. The distinction between stipulations and concessions may be illusionary, because the opposing party may be able to reject a concession.[58] However, to the extent that concessions are usable, they do not need consent of the other party and do not require that the judge inquire into the conceding party's willingness to concede.

Pragmatically, concessions may find their greatest use in the area of evidentiary admissibility. Opposing counsel will often explicitly concede admissibility of a piece of opposing counsel's evidence. Ironically, the term "concession" is misplaced. Often known as a "stipulation of admissibility" in civilian practice, this is really a failure to object. Under both the Federal and Military Rules of Evidence, failure to object to an evidentiary proffer ordinarily waives any such objection.[59] Accordingly, counsel need not "stipulate" or "concede" admissibility; they need only not oppose it.

---

[55] R.C.M. 811(c).

[56] *See generally* § 19-15.00.

[57] For discussion of the stipulation providency inquiry and when the inquiry is needed, *see generally* United States v. Ballew, 38 M.J. 560 (A.F.C.M.R. 1993).

[58] As in a concession of the qualifications of a witness to testify as an expert witness.

[59] Fed. R. Evid. 103; Mil. R. Evid. 103.

(Rel.3—1/07 Pub.62410)

§ 21-23.20 Judicial Notice

Judicial notice is governed primarily by Military Rule of Evidence 201 which, like its civilian counterpart, governs notice of adjudicative facts.[60] Judicial notice is mandatory when it is appropriate[61] and properly presented to the judge.[62] Because of the constitutional burden of proof in criminal cases, the court members may not be instructed to take the judicially noticed facts as conclusive.[63]

Unlike the Federal Rules of Evidence, the Military Rules contain Rule 201A, Judicial Notice of Law.[64] Law may be an adjudicative fact, as in a prosecution under the Assimilated Crimes Act,[65] as incorporated by Article 134 of the Uniform Code of Military Justice.[66] In such a case, the requirements of Military Rule of Evidence 201 apply.[67]

§ 21-23.30 Presumptions

Because Article III, Presumptions, of the Federal Rules of Evidence applies only to civil cases, and the constitutionality of criminal presumptions is uncertain, the Military Rules of Evidence do not codify presumptions. Consequently, presumptions are either governed by specific rules, such as the presumption of capacity to stand trial,[68] or by case law.

§ 21-30.00 EXAMINATION OF WITNESSES

§ 21-31.00 In General

In order to testify, a witness must either swear or affirm to tell the truth[69] and must have personal knowledge of what he or she will testify.[70] This latter rule is often misunderstood. It does not mean that the witness must have firsthand knowledge of the event about which the case is concerned. Rather, it requires only that the witness have firsthand knowledge of the material to which he or

---

[60] *I.e.*, those facts that counsel would otherwise have to prove via ordinary evidence.

[61] Mil. R. Evid. 201(b).

[62] Mil. R. Evid. 201(d) (when "supplied with the proper information"). Accordingly, if counsel want the judge to take notice of water depth based on tide tables, for example, the tables and accompanying chart would have to be handed up. The judge may take judicial notice *sua sponte*. Mil. R. Evid. 201(c).

[63] Mil. R. Evid. 201(g).

[64] In civilian law, this subject is dealt with by the Federal Rules of Criminal Procedure.

[65] 18 U.S.C. § 13.

[66] "Crimes and offenses not capital."

[67] Mil. R. Evid. 201A (a).

[68] R.C.M. 909(b).

[69] Mil. R. Evid. 603.

[70] Mil. R. Evid. 602.

she will testify. In other words, a hearsay witness need not know whether the hearsay is true, but must have heard or read the hearsay about which he or she will testify.

§ 21-32.00   Mode and Scope of Examination

The military judge "has reasonable control over the mode and order of interrogating witnesses and presenting evidence."[71] Counsel are foreclosed from using leading questions on direct examination "except as may be necessary to develop the testimony of the witness" or when the witness is "hostile" or "identified with an adverse party."[72] Literally, the Military Rules of Evidence declare that "[l]eading questions should not be used on the direct examination of a witness."[73] Although the Rule is thus not mandatory, its normal interpretation is to prevent leading questions on direct, when objected to, unless the questions either fall within the Rules' exceptions or the military judge has approved their use.

The Military Rules of Evidence follow the Federal Rules by limiting the scope of cross-examination "to the subject matter of the direct examination and matters affecting the credibility of the witness."[74] The limitation is, however, subject to the discretion of the military judge[75] who may thus permit it, particularly when to do so would be to avoid needless waste of time or confusion.

Both the military judge and the members may question and call witnesses.[76] The Military Rules of Evidence apply, however, and either party may object as appropriate.[77] Counsel may not complain that such questioning or the calling of a witness has injured or destroyed trial tactic or strategy.

---

[71] Mil. R. Evid. 611(a). *See also* § 14-63.00.

[72] Mil. R. Evid. 611(c).

[73] Mil. R. Evid. 611(a).

[74] Mil. R. Evid. 611(b).

[75] Mil. R. Evid. 611(b).

[76] Mil. R. Evid. 614. *See also* United States v. Gray, 51 M.J. 1, 50 (C.A.A.F. 1999) (appellant was not denied his right to an impartial jury because the members were allowed to ask questions).

[77] This clearly places counsel in a difficult position if the question has been asked by the military judge.

(Rel.3—1/07   Pub.62410)

CHAPTER 22

SUMMATIONS, INSTRUCTIONS, DELIBERATIONS AND FINDINGS

§ 22-10.00 INTRODUCTION

§ 22-20.00 SUMMATIONS

§ 22-21.00   In General

§ 22-22.00   Content

§ 22-23.00   Limits on Final Arguments

§ 22-23.10 — Inflammatory Arguments

§ 22-23.20 — Arguing Facts Not in Evidence

§ 22-23.30 — Personal Opinion and Personal Attack

§ 22-23.40 — Comment on the Accused's Failure to Testify

§ 22-23.50 — Law

§ 22-23.60 — "Jury Nullification"

§ 22-24.00   Concession of Guilt

§ 22-25.00   Waiving Summation

§ 22-26.00   Error During Summation

§ 22-26.10 — In General

§ 22-26.20 — Waiver

§ 22-30.00 FINDINGS INSTRUCTIONS

§ 22-31.00   In General

§ 22-32.00   Content

§ 22-32.10 — In General

§ 22-32.20 — Summary of Evidence

§ 22-33.00   Additional Instructions

§ 22-34.00   Waiver of Error

§ 22-35.00   Trial by Judge Alone

§ 22-40.00 DELIBERATIONS

§ 22-41.00   In General

§ 22-42.00   Voting

§ 22-50.00 FINDINGS

§ 22-51.00   In General

§ 22-52.00   Special Findings

§ 22-53.00   Reconsideration

§ 22-54.00   Impeachment of Verdict

(Rel.3—1/07   Pub.62410)

§ 22-10.00 INTRODUCTION

After the parties have completed presentation of evidence on the merits, counsel will make final argument; in a trial with members, the military judge will give his or her closing instructions; the judge or members will deliberate; and findings will be announced.[1] Should the accused stand convicted of one or more specifications, trial will proceed to the sentencing phase.[2]

To some extent, both this description and those of most trial practice texts are misleading. They tend to suggest the occurrence of a series of discrete, if not totally independent, events, when in actual fact they must be interrelated. For example, no competent counsel should make final argument — a summation — in a trial with members without having previously requested from the judge detailed "jury" instructions and a ruling on the content of the judge's final instructions.[3] Trial is indeed a "seamless web" when properly tried, and counsel must make every effort to remember that each aspect of the case is interrelated with all others, with the summation as the final focus and the verdict (findings) as the final result.

§ 22-20.00 SUMMATIONS

§ 22-21.00 In General

The procedural framework for summations is set forth simply by Rule for Courts-Martial 919(a):

> After the closing of evidence, trial counsel shall be permitted to open the argument. The defense counsel shall be permitted to reply. Trial counsel shall then be permitted to reply in rebuttal.[4]

Although rare, summations may continue past the rebuttal point for a "second round" of arguments.[5]

Whether termed a "summation," "final argument," or "closing argument," most counsel consider their opportunity to argue their case to the fact finder one of the most important moments of trial. The terminology chosen to reflect counsel's

---

[1] *See* Section 21-12.00; R.C.M. 919(a); Chapters 20, 21, 22.

[2] *See generally* Chapter 23.

[3] *See* Section 22-31.00.

[4] Judges, however, are prone to prohibit or discourage rebuttal argument, particularly in bench trials.

[5] The Discussion to R.C.M. 919(b) states:

The rebuttal argument of trial counsel is generally limited to matters argued by the defense. If trial counsel is permitted to introduce new matter in closing argument, the defense should be allowed to reply in rebuttal. However, this will not preclude trial counsel from presenting a final argument.

See also Mil. R. Evid. 611.

(Rel.3—1/07 Pub.62410)

last-findings advocacy does tend to emphasize different aspects of that advocacy. "Summation" is correct in that counsel should "sum up" the evidence and analyze its strengths and weaknesses. "Final argument" emphasizes counsel's ability and ethical duty to marshal the facts as an advocate and to attempt to persuade the fact finder to accept that party's legal position. As Professor Lederer has noted:

> Books and movies have long highlighted closing argument, often presenting it as trial's single most dramatic moment. This is because it is only at closing that a lawyer may unleash the full power of the lawyer's creativity and advocacy. The lawyer not only marshals the evidence, emphasizing strengths and minimizing weaknesses in counsel's case -while trying to lessen the impact of the other side's evidence -counsel tries to help the fact-finder find human reasons to reach a desirable verdict. Quotations from great books, reminders of common human experience, humorous anecdotes, even spell-binding oratory can be used during closing, all subject to somewhat amorphous rules of constraint that the judge may exercise as a matter of discretion. Lawyers may make limited reference to the law of the case, for example, but are frequently limited in jury arguments to referring to the law as expressed in the jury instructions: "As her honor will instruct you, proximate cause means . . . ."

> Modern trial technology permits lawyers to enrich closing arguments with visuals of documents, graphical summaries, and computer based slides, to mention only a few possibilities.[6]

§ 22-22.00   Content

Insofar as content is concerned, the Rules for Courts-Martial state only that "[a]rguments may properly include reasonable comment on the evidence in the case, including inferences to be drawn therefrom, in support of a party's theory of the case."[7] The Discussion is more expansive:

> Argument may include comment about the testimony, conduct, motives, interests, and biases of witnesses to the extent supported by the evidence. Counsel should not express a personal belief or opinion as to the truth or falsity of any testimony or evidence or the guilt or innocence of the accused, nor should counsel make arguments calculated to inflame passions or prejudices. In argument counsel may treat the testimony of witnesses as conclusively establishing the facts related by the witnesses. Counsel may not cite legal authorities or the facts of other cases when arguing to members on findings.

> Trial counsel may not comment on the accused's exercise of the right against self-incrimination or the right to counsel. . . . Trial counsel may not argue that the prosecution's evidence is unrebutted if the only rebuttal could come from the accused. When the accused is on trial for several offenses and testifies only as to some of the offenses, trial counsel may

---

[6] Frederic I. Lederer, *Excerpts from Basic Advocacy and Litigation in a Technological World* § 14-13.00 at 127 (2005 Draft Edition).

[7] R.C.M. 919(b).

not comment on the accused's failure to testify as to the others. When the accused testifies on the merits regarding an offense charged, trial counsel may comment on the accused's failure in that testimony to deny or explain specific incriminating facts that the evidence for the prosecution tends to establish regarding that offense.

Trial counsel may not comment on the failure of the defense to call witnesses or of the accused to testify at the Article 32 investigation or upon the probable effect of the court-martial's findings on relations between the military and civilian communities.[8]

Because the scope of final argument is so broad and its limits so vague,[9] it is often more useful to explore limits on argument. In doing so, it is helpful to recognize that, although both trial and defense counsel enjoy wide latitude in making final argument, pragmatically, trial counsel is more limited than is the defense, as prejudicial prosecution argument will justify or require reversal.[10]

§ 22-23.00   Limits on Final Arguments

§ 22-23.10   Inflammatory Arguments

Cases focusing on inflammatory argument necessarily deal with prosecutorial overreaching.[11] While trial counsel may comment earnestly and forcefully on the evidence, as well as on any reasonable inferences that may be drawn from it,[12] counsel may not inject inflammatory arguments that tend to inflame passions rather than provide a rational basis for a finding.[13] The Court of Military Appeals stated: Counsel "may strike hard blows, but he is not at liberty to strike foul blows."[14] As the Air Force Court of Military Review observed:

---

[8] Discussion to R.C.M. 919(b).

[9] *Citing* R.C.M. 801(a)(3), the Discussion to R.C.M. 919(b) states: "The military judge may exercise reasonable control over argument." *See also* Yarborough v. Gentry, 540 U.S. 1 (2003) (counsel's closing was not ineffective; counsel has tactical discretion in making argument).

[10] An acquittal cannot be reversed, of course. Recognition of the differing practical implications of improper argument by counsel should not be interpreted as acceptance of a double standard. Although the defense counsel need not worry about "justice," as must the trial counsel, defense counsel is limited not just by law when making an argument, but also by professional ethics. *See, e.g.*, United States v. Young, 470 U.S. 1, 9–10 (1985) (citing ABA Standards for Criminal Justice 4.97 (2d ed. 1980)).

[11] Improper defense argument ordinarily will be harmless in a single-defendant case.

[12] *See, e.g.*, United States v. Day, 9 C.M.R. 46 (C.M.A. 1953); United States v. Fields, 40 C.M.R. 396 (A.B.R. 1968); Haight, *Argument of Military Counsel on Findings, Sentence and Motions: Limitations and Abuses*, 16 Mil. R. Evid. 59 (1962).

[13] *See, e.g.*, ABA Standards for Criminal Justice, The Prosecution Function, § 3-5.8 (3d ed. 1993); United States v. Quarles, 25 M.J. 761 (N.M.C.M.R. 1987) (accused described as prurient sex fiend); United States v. Clifton, 15 M.J. 26 (C.M.A. 1983); United States v. Nelson, 1 M.J. 235 (C.M.A. 1975) (trial counsel compared defense witness tactics to those used by Hitler); United States v. Johnson, 1 M.J. 213 (C.M.A. 1975); United States v. Shamberger, 1 M.J. 377 (C.M.A. 1976); United States v. White, 3 M.J. 619 (N.C.M.R. 1977).

[14] United States v. Doctor, 21 C.M.R. 252 (C.M.A. 1956).

(Rel.3—1/07 Pub.62410)

In assessing the inflammatory nature of a closing argument, the presentation must be looked at in its entirety and not through isolated sentences or phrases. . . .

A criminal trial is not a tea dance, but an adversary proceeding to arrive at the truth. Both sides may forcefully urge their positions so long as they are supported by the evidence. Considering the trial counsel's closing argument *in toto*, it was within the bounds of fair comment considering the state of the evidence.[15]

Inflammatory remarks alone will not require reversal absent sufficient prejudice to the accused. The Supreme Court has, for example, held that for constitutional purposes "it is not enough that the prosecutors' remarks were undesirable, or even universally condemned, . . . [t]he relevant question is whether the prosecutors' comments 'so infected the trial with unfairness as to make the resulting conviction a denial of due process.'"[16]

Even if his or her remarks are not inflammatory per se, counsel should refrain from referring to class, race, religion, nationality, or social class unless it has a factual bearing on an issue.[17] The courts have condemned racist remarks in argument.[18] The Court of Appeals for the Armed Forces has expressed special concern about racial remarks. Although it has indicated that it will test for the prejudicial effect of such remarks, especially in the context of a bench trial, it has also made it clear that such conduct constitutes error:

In our view, unwarranted references to race or ethnicity have no place in either the military or civilian forum . . . . However, we see no reason not to adhere to the prevailing approach [of testing for prejudice] . . . . Our holding acknowledges the importance of a fair trial and the insidious impact that racial or ethnic bias, or stereotype, can have on justice. At the same time, our holding acknowledges that where, in fact, there is no prejudice to an accused, we should not forsake society's other interests in the timely and efficient administration of justice, the interests of victims, and in the military context, the potential impact on national security deployment.

---

[15] United States v. Rodriguez, 28 M.J. 1016, 1022–23 (A.F.C.M.R. 1989) (citing United States v. White, 23 M.J. 84 (C.M.A. 1986)).

[16] Darden v. Wainwright, 477 U.S. 168, 181 (1986) (quoting from the case below (699 F.2d at 1036) *and applying* Donnelly v. DeChristoforo, 416 U.S. 637 (1974)). *Darden* was a federal habeas corpus case. Racist argument, even accidentally made, likely will compel reversal. United States v. Thompson, 37 M.J. 1023 (A.C.M.R. 1993) (en banc).

[17] *See, e.g.*, United States v. Diffoot, 54 M.J. 149, 150 (C.A.A.F. 2000) (prejudicial error to refer to co-conspirators as "amigo" and "compadre" and press jury to find "guilt by association"); United States v. Begley, 38 C.M.R. 488 (A.B.R. 1967). On the grounds that it is a deliberate attempt to destroy objectivity, Pennsylvania has prohibited prosecutorial references to biblical or other religious writings to support imposition of the death penalty. Pennsylvania v. Chambers, 599 A.2d 630 (Pa. 1991), *cert. denied*, 112 S. Ct. 2290 (1992). *See also* United States v. Lawrence, 47 M.J. 572, 574 (N.M. Crim. App. 1997) (in context, plain error to refer to appellant and "his compatriots as 'Jamaican brothers' ").

[18] *E.g.* McCleskey v. Kemp, 481 U.S. 279, 310 (1987).

(Rel.3—1/07 Pub.62410)

Therefore, we agree with the [Court of Criminal Appeals]. Appellant did not suffer material prejudice to a substantial right. Trial counsel's statement was before a military judge alone. Military judges are presumed to know the law and to follow it absent clear evidence to the contrary . . . . Finally, there is no indication in the record that the statement affected the military judge or impacted Appellant's sentence. . . .

We caution, however, that such prejudice determinations are fact specific. In a given situation racial or ethnic remarks, including before a military judge, may deny an accused a fair trial. Race is different. . . . Therefore, it is the rare case indeed, involving the most tangential allusion, where the unwarranted reference to race or ethnicity will not be obvious error. Our concern with unwarranted statements about race and ethnicity are magnified when the trial is before members. This is true whether or not it is motivated by animus, as we cannot ultimately know what effect, if any, such statements may have on the fact finder or sentencing authority.[19]

United States v. Causey[20] dealt with a closing argument that although not classically inflammatory suffered from much the same defects. Responding to a defense of innocent ingestion in a marijuana case, trial counsel commented, "What you've heard today is the brownie defense. . . . Now if you buy [sic] here today, you're going to hear it a million times again back in your units." Ultimately concluding that the error was waived for failure to object, the court applied the ABA Standard for Criminal Justice — The Prosecution Function[21] and concluded that counsel's argument would inappropriately divert the members "from its duty to decide the case on the evidence, by injecting issues broader than the guilt or innocence of the accused under the controlling law, or by making predictions of the consequences of the jury's verdict."[22]

§ 22-23.20 Arguing Facts Not in Evidence

It is improper for counsel to argue facts not in evidence or to misstate the facts.[23] Such remarks invite the fact finder to consider evidence outside the

---

[19] *United States v. Rodriguez*, 60 M.J. 87, 89–90 (C.A.A.F. 2004) (reviewing *sentencing* argument in which trial counsel made a reference to the Latino accused's conduct not being "some sort of a Latin movie. . . ."]

[20] 37 M.J. 308, 310–11 (C.M.A. 1993).

[21] 3.87–3.88 (2d ed. 1986).

[22] 3.87–3.88 (2d ed. 1986) subsection (d).

[23] United States v. Mitchell, 1 F.3d 235 (4th Cir. 1993) (reference to prior conviction of co-conspirator plain error). United States v. Carroll, 678 F.2d 1208 (4th Cir. 1982) (prosecutor's improper argument alluding to evidence not before the court was reversible error despite limiting instructions), cited in United States v. Evans, 27 M.J. 34, 41 (C.M.A. 1988). *See also* United States v. Clifton, 15 M.J. 26 (C.M.A. 1983) (improper to argue practices and fantasies of rapists); United States v. Allen, 29 C.M.R. 355 (C.M.A. 1960) (trial counsel improperly referred to the book *Anatomy of a Murder* to insinuate that the defense counsel could fabricate an insanity defense);

(Rel.3—1/07 Pub.62410)

record. The prohibition extends to referring to uncalled witnesses.[24]

While counsel may not state facts not in evidence, counsel may comment on facts of contemporary history or matters of common knowledge.[25]

If counsel refers to inadmissible evidence during argument, opposing counsel may request a curative instruction from the military judge.[26]

§ 22-23.30 Personal Opinion and Personal Attack

It is improper for counsel to express a personal belief in the guilt or innocence of the accused or the credibility of a witness.[27] Such comments invade the province of the fact finder and imply that counsel for either side may have superior knowledge of the case, but was forbidden from telling the court all. Further, such comment would place the individual belief of counsel before the fact finder. Not only would that assert counsel's individual credibility and integrity, it would damage or destroy the current right to counsel. If defense counsel may be expected to allege the client's innocence and fails to do so, clearly the fact finder will determine that silence constitutes admission. The practical result of this limitation is the use of the "royal" plural during argument (counsel state "it is our position," "we maintain,") or identification by party ("it is the government's position that"). The personal opinion rule does not prohibit counsel from marshaling the evidence and arguing that, logically, only one result is possible; rather, the rule prohibits placing the counsel's individual belief and credibility on the line.

Similarly, counsel may not personally attack opposing counsel.[28]

United States v. Carr, 25 M.J. 637 (A.C.M.R. 1987) (improper to argue that trauma of rape victim could be considered in aggravation — not cured by instruction); United States v. Johnson, 24 M.J. 796 (A.C.M.R. 1987) (although improper to argue from testimony that "the eyes of the CID are upon this trial," court found waiver over judge's dissent); United States v. Moore, 6 M.J. 661 (A.F.C.M.R. 1978) (improper for trial counsel to argue about the impact of medic selling drugs in hospital when the only evidence was that he sold drugs to informant who did not work in hospital). *But see* United States v. Gatto, 995 F.2d 449 (3d Cir. 1993) (witness may testify about defendant's in-court behavior and it may be subject to argument); United States v. Webb, 38 M.J. 62 (C.M.A. 1993) (prosecutor could comment on defense's failure to fulfill promise of producing wife as alibi witness).

[24] United States v. Tackett, 36 C.M.R. 382 (C.M.A. 1966); United States v. Tawes, 49 C.M.R. 590 (A.C.M.R. 1974). R.C.M. 701(c) provides that it is proper to comment on opposing counsel's failure to call a witness on his or her witness list.

[25] *See, e.g.,* United States v. Garcia, 1 M.J. 26 (C.M.A. 1975); United States v. Ong, 38 C.M.R. 121 (C.M.A. 1967); United States v. Poteet, 50 C.M.R. 73 (N.C.M.R. 1975).

[26] United States v. Nelson, 1 M.J. 235, 240 n. 8 (C.M.A. 1975) (recommending that Donnelly v. Christoforo, 416 U.S. 637 (1974), be followed).

[27] R.C.M. 919(g) Discussion; ABA Standards, The Prosecution Function § 3-5.8(b) (32d ed. 199380); United States v. Knickerbocker, 2 M.J. 128 (C.M.A. 1977).

[28] *See, e.g.,* United States v. Young, 470 U.S. 1, 9–10 (1985) (citing ABA Standarads for Criminal Justice 4.99 (2d ed. 1980)).

(Rel.3—1/07 Pub.62410)

A statement of personal opinion or a personal attack during summation can best be dealt with by judicial instruction.[29] It does not justify a similar action by opposing counsel.[30]

§ 22-23.40 Comment on the Accused's Failure to Testify

The trial counsel may not comment, directly or indirectly, on the accused's exercise of the privilege against self-incrimination, whether at trial[31] or otherwise,[32] unless, of course, the defense opens the door to such comment.[33] The ways in which the prosecution surfaces the accused's silence appear to be almost infinite. A frequent attempt, however, is a prosecutorial assertion that the government's evidence is "uncontradicted" when the accused is the only person who could have contradicted the evidence.[34]

In addition:

> It is axiomatic that trial counsel is prohibited from commenting on or alluding to an accused's failure to produce witnesses in his behalf . . . .

[29] See, e.g., United States v. Knickerbocker, 2 M.J. 128, 129 (C.M.A. 1977).

[30] Cf. United States v. Young, 470 U.S. 1 (1985). In Young, the Court recognized the existence of the "invited response" doctrine 470 U.S. 1 (1985) at 12), but held that the issue was "not the prosecutor's license to make otherwise improper arguments, but whether the prosecutor's 'invited response,' taken in context, unfairly prejudiced the defendent." 470 U.S. 1 (1985). See also United States v. Rivera, 971 F.2d 876, 883–84 (2d Cir. 1992) (setting forth what may be proper reply).

[31] Griffin v. California, 380 U.S. 609 (1965). Cf. United States v. Stadler, 47 M.J. 206 (C.A.A.F. 1997) (Majority held it harmless for the prosecution to comment on the failure of defendant to identify woman he talked with on telephone who told him he could keep $1,000 extra per month for his overseas housing allowance. JJ. Gierke and Crawford would have held the argument proper); United States v. Hasting, 461 U.S. 499 (1983) (improper abuse of supervisory power to reverse a conviction to discipline prosecutors for continuing violations of Griffin, regardless of whether the prosecutor's arguments constituted harmless error). See also United States v. Cook, 48 M.J. 64 (C.A.A.F. 1998) (court noted in dictum a number of instances of admissibility and inadmissibility of nontestimonial acts); United States v. Bowen, 27 C.M.R. 148 (C.M.A. 1958); United States v. Grissom, 1 M.J. 525 (A.F.C.M.R. 1975). In 1999, the Supreme Court held that the privilege extended to post-guilty plea sentencing; the plea does not extinguish the privilege. Mitchell v. United States, 526 U.S. 314 (1999).

[32] United States v. Hale, 422 U.S. 171 (1975). An assertion of the right against self-incrimination must be distinguished from the mere silence of the accused.

> At common law, an individual who heard a remark to which an innocent person would normally respond could be impeached with his or her silence. . . . The Supreme Court has sustained impeachment of an accused with his or her silence so long as:. . . The silence doesn't follow rights warnings, and . . . the accused did not affirmatively assert the right against self-incrimination.

Fredric Lederer, An Introduction to Impeachment 4 (33d Military Judge Course, TJAGSA 23 May, 1990). See generally Jenkins v. Anderson, 447 U.S. 231 (1980).

[33] See, e.g., United States v. Gilley, 56 M.J. 113 (C.A.A.F. 2001).

[34] See, e.g., United States v. Harris, 14 M.J. 728 (A.F.C.M.R. 1982); cf. United States v. Saint John, 48 C.M.R. 312 (C.M.A. 1974).

(Rel.3—1/07   Pub.62410)

If made, such comments require the record to be tested for prejudice . . . .[35]

Although the trial counsel may not comment on the accused's assertion of the statutory or constitutional right to remain silent,[36] counsel may comment on a prior statement by the accused that did not include material first raised by the accused at trial.[37] The critical question is whether the privilege is involved.[38]

Comment by the trial counsel on the accused's exercise of the privilege may necessitate a mistrial when sufficiently serious. It is unclear whether reference to the accused's silence during defense argument justifies prosecution comment.[39]

In *Portuondo v. Agard*,[40] a 7-2 decision, Justice Scalia writing for the majority stated "[W]e see no reason to depart from the practice of treating testifying

---

[35] United States v. Carter, 61 M.J. 30 (C.A.A.F. 2005)(comment by trial counsel that testimony of the sexual assault complainant was "uncontradicted" and "uncontroverted" in conjunction with a reference to the accused's right not to incriminate himself was improper comment on the right against self-incrimination and, despite defense failure to object, constituted plain error, requiring reversal); United States v. Stadler, 47 M.J. 206 (C.A.A.F. 1997) (waiver of prosecution comments on defendant's failure to call witness known only to him); United States v. Cook, 48 M.J. 236 (C.A.A.F. 1998) (2-1-2 opinion) (argument on defendant's silence in face of accusation by friend); United States v. Cook, 48 M.J. 64 (Armed. F. 1998) (defense waived any error when prosecution argument focused on defendant's demeanor at trial); United States v. Taylor, 47 M.J. 322, 324, 328–329 (C.A.A.F. 1997) (applying "law of case," court divided on whether counsel may argue inferences when witnesses not called were available to only one side or equally available to both sides); United States v. Espronceda, 36 M.J. 535, 541 (A.F.C.M.R. 1992) (but such a comment may not be improper when made in response to defense argument), citing United States v. Mobley, 31 M.J. 273 (C.M.A. 1990); United States v. Swoape, 21 M.J. 414 (C.M.A. 1986).

[36] It is also improper for the trial counsel to argue that the co-accused pled guilty but the accused had not. United States v. Johnson, 1 M.J. 213 (C.M.A. 1975).

[37] United States v. Nelson, 1 M.J. 235, 237 (C.M.A. 1975) (prior exculpatory statement).

[38] *See, e.g.,* United States v. Carpenter, 51 M.J. 393 (C.A.A.F. 1999) (harmless error to argue that accused testified last so he could tailor his testimony); United States v. Fields, 15 M.J. 34 (C.M.A. 1983) (per curiam); United States v. Reiner, 15 M.J. 38 (C.M.A. 1983) (per curiam) (trial counsel's reference to Article 32 inquiry was made to show that the accused had prior knowledge of the government's evidence). A comment on the accused's conduct incident to the offense of which he is charged is not a violation of the right against self-incrimination. *See, e.g.,* United States v. Garren, 53 M.J. 142 (C.A.A.F. 2000) (false official statements).

It is not improper for the trial counsel to draw attention to the fact that the accused made an unsworn statement on sentencing rather than testifying under oath when the judge's instructions provide correct and clear instructions. United States v. Breese, 11 M.J. 17 (C.M.A. 1981).

[39] *See* United States v. Robinson, 485 U.S. 25, 32 (1988) ("where . . . the prosecutor's reference to the defendant's opportunity to testify is a fair response to a claim made by defendant or his counsel, we think there is no violation of the privilege"); State v. Poe, 717 S.W.2d 855 (Mo. App. 1986) (accused waived his Fifth Amendment right by giving closing argument that included his version of the incident). *See also* United States v. Frentz, 21 M.J. 813, 818 (N.M.C.M.R. 1985) (reference to invocation of rights during defense's opening).

[40] 528 U.S. 61 (2000).

defendants the same as other witnesses."[41] The Court allowed the prosecutor to argue that the accused, even though required to be present at trial under state law, by testifying last could tailor his testimony in the case. Justices Stevens and Breyer, concurring, opined, however, that the defendant's Sixth Amendment right "to be confronted with the witnesses against him" serves the truth-seeking function of the adversary process. Moreover, it also reflects respect for the defendant's individual dignity and reinforces the presumption of innocence that survives until a guilty verdict is returned. The prosecutor's argument in this case demeaned that process, violated that respect, and ignored that presumption. Clearly such comment should be discouraged rather than validated. The Court's final conclusion, which I join, that the argument survives constitutional scrutiny does not, of course, deprive States or trial judges of the power either to prevent such argument entirely or to provide juries with instructions that explain the necessity, and the justifications, for the defendant's attendance at trial.[42] Justices Ginsburg and Souter dissented because the majority "transform[ed] a defendant's presence at trial from a Sixth Amendment right into an automatic burden on his credibility"[43] and "undermines all defendants equally and therefore does not help answer the question that is the essence of a trial's search for truth: Is this particular defendant lying to cover his guilt or truthfully narrating his innocence?"[44] Whether the Court of Appeals for the Armed Forces will follow *Portuondo v. Agard* remains to be seen. It is clear that the decision stands only for the proposition that such comment is constitutional in the civilian courts.

§ 22-23.50   Law

The judge is responsible for the law to be applied by the fact finder. Ordinarily, counsel may not advise the members of the law.[45] Once advised by the military judge of the substance of the instructions to be given, however, counsel may refer to those instructions during argument. Somewhat ironically, counsel may argue the law so long as it is put "in the mouth" of the judge.

§ 22-23.60   "Jury Nullification"

Although the court members have the power to acquit an accused despite evidence sufficient for a conviction, defense counsel may not advise the members of that power and ask them to use it.[46]

---

[41] 528 U.S. at 73.

[42] 528 U.S. at 76.

[43] 528 U.S. at 76.

[44] 528 U.S. at 79.

[45] *See, e.g.*, United States v. McCauley, 25 C.M.R. 327 (C.M.A. 1958); *but see* United States v. Jefferson, 22 M.J. 315, 329 (C.M.A. 1986) (comment on maximum sentence for felony murder during findings argument "is not inappropriate").

[46] United States v. Hardy, 46 M.J. 67 (C.A.A.F. 1997); United States v. Smith, 27 M.J. 25, 29

(Rel.3—1/07   Pub.62410)

Jury nullification can take place in findings or sentence. One of the first instances in this country was the trial of William Penn, Pennsylvania's founder, who was charged with a breach of the peace by assembling about three hundred people to conduct worship services on the street. Despite overwhelming evidence, the jury acquitted him. The jury was fined and juror Bushell was jailed when he refused to pay the fine. Bushell was granted a writ of habeas corpus because he could not be fined or imprisoned for voting to acquit Penn.[47]

Various issues arise:

1. May jury nullification be argued?[48]

2. Should the judge instruct the jury *sua sponte*?

3. Should there be an instruction based on a defense request?

4. Should there be an instruction when the jury asks about its power?

5. May the jury be asked about nullification during voir dire?[49]

Nullification has become an increasingly popular tactic as numerous resister groups attempt to defy mainstream, governmental authority.

Commentators have argued the pros[50] and cons[51] of nullification.

Arguments supporting jury nullification as an explicit instruction include:

1. Failure to give it deceives the jurors;

(C.M.A. 1988) (citing United States v. Jefferson, 22 M.J. 315, 329 (C.M.A. 1986)). *See generally* Section 15-82.00; Adler, *Courtroom Putsch? Jurors Should Reject Laws They Don't Like, Activist Group Argues*, Wall. St. J., January 4, 1991, at 1, col. 1. *See generally* § 15.82.00, *above*. *See also* United States v. Thomas, 116 F.3d 606 (2d Cir. 1997) (Under certain circumstances, a juror who plans on jury nullification may be excused mid-trial.).

[47] Bushell's Case, 124 Eng. R. 1006 ((1670). *See also* Sparf v. United States, 156 U.S. 51, 119 (1895). *See generally* Clay S. Conrad, Jury Nullification, The Evolution of a Doctrine (1998).

[48] Pounders v. Watson, 117 S. Ct. 2359, 2363 (1997) (upholding contempt conviction of attorney after she asked witness in front of the jury about the witness' sentence in clear violation of the judge's instructions); United States v. Manning, 79 F.3d 212, 219 (1st Cir. 1996) (rejecting efforts by defense to inform jury of severity of punishment an attempt to invoke jury nullification); United States v. Calhoun, 49 F.3d 231, 236 n.6 (6th Cir. 1995) (upholding trial judge's refusal to inform the jury of sentence if defendant found guilty).

[49] Drew v. Collins, 964 F.2d 411, 416–17 (5th Cir. 1992) (upholding trial judge's decision to exclude juror who stated on several occasions that he would hold prosecution to burden higher than beyond a reasonable doubt); Commonwealth v. Chambers, 528 Pa. 558, 599 A.2d 630, 635 (1991) (same); Castillo v. State, 913 S.W.2d 529, 537 (Tex. Crim. App. 1995) (Mansfield, J., dissenting).

[50] Alan W. Scheflin & Jon M. Van Dyke, *Merciful Juries: The Resilience of Jury Nullification*, 48 Wash. & Lee L. Rev. 165 n.2 (1991).

[51] 48 Wash. & Lee L. Rev. 166 n.3 (1991).

(Rel.3—1/07 Pub.62410)

2. The jury should serve as the conscience of the community and protect it against unfair laws or oppressive prosecutorial practices;

3. The instruction is necessary because community values change faster than the laws;

4. Absent the instruction, the accidental presence of knowledgeable jurors may turn a jury trial into a lottery.

Arguments in opposition to an instruction include assertions that such an instruction:

1. Leads to chaos and lawlessness;

2. Undermines the very basis of equal justice, as individual jurors vote their biases;

3. Erodes the sense of responsibility of the individual jurors if they think that they will be subject to censure for unpopular but correct verdicts.

In *United States v. Hardy*,[52] the court asserted that, while court members have the power to ignore the instructions and render a general verdict, the judge is not required to give a defense-requested jury nullification instruction. The goals served by jury nullification are protected by such requirements as the general verdict, double jeopardy protection, and limitation on inquiring into the deliberative process of court members. To allow jury nullification would be especially antithetical to the military, which is based on the principle of obedience to orders. The Court of Military Appeals opined:

> While civilian juries and court-martial members always have had the power to disregard instructions on matters of law given them by the judge, generally it has been held that they need not be advised as to this power, even upon the request of the defense.[53]

> [S]ince the court members must vote on the sentence, they can engage in "jury nullification" and can adjudge a sentence of less than the minimum confinement prescribed by the Code. Of course, such action — which the military judge's instruction was intended to forestall — would be irresponsible as well as unlawful and certainly should not be encouraged.[54]

In addition, in *Shannon v. United States*,[55] the Supreme Court held that the jury should not be told of the sentencing options if it has no role in sentencing.

To inform jurors of the sentencing options would mean that the verdict likely would be dependent upon the sentencing options, which the Court thought was improper.

---

[52] 46 M.J. 67 (1997).

[53] United States v. Mead, 16 M.J. 270, 275 (C.M.A. 1983).

[54] United States v. Shroeder, 27 M.J. 87, 90 (C.M.A. 1988).

[55] 512 U.S. 573 (1994).

(Rel.3—1/07　Pub.62410)

§ 22-24.00   Concession of Guilt

In the normal contested case, there is no justification for defense counsel to concede the guilt of the accused unless it is to a lesser-included offense and is intended as a critical tactical move. The defense counsel must be very cautious when conceding guilt, as it may raise a charge of incompetency of counsel.[56] Should counsel concede guilt as to an offense to which the accused made an earlier, improvident plea,[57] the judge need not conduct a providence inquiry.[58]

§ 22-25.00   Waiving Summation

Either trial or defense counsel may waive closing argument. Should trial counsel waive argument and the defense follow suit, trial counsel will be estopped from using rebuttal argument, as there will be nothing to rebut.

Given the importance placed on closing argument, counsel should waive it only for the most compelling reasons. Should the defense waive argument, it would be advisable for the military judge to ascertain the reasons for the waiver during an Article 39(a) session. In light of the military judge's authority over the trial, the judge likely has the discretion to require one or both sides to sum up.

On occasion, judges, especially civilian judges, have attempted to persuade counsel to waive argument, especially in bench trials. Although a judge may be convinced that there is nothing that counsel may say that would be of value, judges, too, are human, and counsel ought to resist such an effort.

§ 22-26.00   Error During Summation

§ 22-26.10   In General

It has long been the custom of the legal profession to regard the needless interruption of an opponent's final argument as rude and discourteous. Ordinarily, counsel's response to error during an opponent's summation is an advocate's response during counsel's own summation. This may be inadequate, however, if the error is substantial or if an opportunity to respond may not exist.[59] In such circumstances, it is imperative that counsel make a timely objection lest waiver result.[60] The military judge may take action *sua sponte*, but absent plain error, such action is not required.

---

[56] Section 5-44.00. *See also* United States v. Burwell, 50 C.M.R. 192 (A.C.M.R. 1975).

[57] As, perhaps, in an attempt to preserve a plea bargain that was technically invalidated by the judge's rejection of the attempted plea of guilty.

[58] *See* United States v. Caldwell, 9 M.J. 534 (A.C.M.R. 1980).

[59] As when the error occurs during trial counsel's rebuttal.

[60] *See* Section 22-26.20.

(Rel.3—1/07 Pub.62410)

As then Captain Cuculic of The Judge Advocate General's School Criminal Law Division wrote,[61] remedies for improper argument include:

1. Stopping the argument;[62]

2. Curative judicial instructions;[63]

3. A judicially ordered retraction from counsel;[64]

4. A mistrial.[65]

Civilian law has recognized an "invited response" doctrine that permits counsel to make what would otherwise be an improper argument in order to respond to opposing counsel's impropriety. The Supreme Court rejected this approach, however, in *United States v. Young*,[66] noting that the effect of the response must be evaluated in the context of the initial impropriety.

In trials by judge alone, there is a presumption that the judge exercised proper discretion in distinguishing between proper and improper argument.[67]

§ 22-26.20   Waiver

Rule for Courts-Martial 919(c) provides that "[f]ailure to object to improper argument before the military judge begins to instruct the members on findings shall constitute waiver of the objection."[68] Rule 919(c) is based on Rule 29.1 of the Federal Rules of Criminal Procedure and is claimed to have been "generally consistent" with prior practice, although some of the cases cited supported *sua sponte* action by the trial judge.[69]

The waiver rule will not be applied in cases of "plain error."[70] Appellate courts will invoke the plain-error doctrine to rectify those errors that seriously affect

---

[61] Cuculic, Arguments (33d Military Judge Course, TJAGSA June, 1990).

[62] *Citing* United States v. Grady, 15 M.J. 275 (C.M.A. 1983); United States v. Nelson, 1 M.J. 235 (C.M.A. 1975).

[63] Citing United States v. Horn, 9 M.J. 429 (C.M.A. 1980); United States v. Carpenter, 29 C.M.R. 234 (C.M.A. 1960).

[64] Citing United States v. Lackey, 25 C.M.R. 222 (C.M.A. 1958).

[65] Citing United States v. O'Neal, 36 C.M.R. 189 (C.M.A. 1966); United States v. McPhaul, 22 M.J. 808 (A.C.M.R.), *pet. denied*, 23 M.J. 266 (C.M.A. 1986).

[66] 470 U.S. 1 (1985), *above* note 25. *See also* United States v. Grady, 15 M.J. 275 (C.M.A. 1983) (regardless of who initiated the argument as to command policies, the judge had the *sua sponte* duty to give a curative instruction).

[67] *See, e.g.*, United States v. O'Neal, 36 C.M.R. 189 (C.M.A. 1966); United States v. Shamlian, 25 C.M.R. 290 (C.M.A. 1958).

[68] *See, e.g.*, United States v. Toro, 37 M.J. 313 (C.M.A. 1993). A similar rule applies to arguments before sentencing. R.C.M. 1001(g).

[69] Analysis of the Rules for Courts-Martial, MCM, 1984, A21-60.

[70] *See, e.g..*, United States v. Fisher, 21 M.J. 327 (C.M.A. 1986); United States v. Thompson, 37 M.J. 1023 (A.C.M.R. 1993) (en banc) (defining and finding plain error); United States v. Williams, 23 M.J. 776 (A.C.M.R. 1987).

(Rel.3—1/07 Pub.62410)

the fairness, integrity, or public reputation of the judicial proceedings.[71] As the Supreme Court concluded in *Donnelly v. DeChristoforo*,[72] a due process violation occurs when the argument affects the fairness of the proceedings. In *United States v. Young*,[73] the Court emphasized that a conviction should be overturned on plain-error grounds when the error so undermines the fundamental fairness of the trial as to contribute to a miscarriage of justice.[74] The Court of Military Appeals, however, seemed to be placing greater emphasis on defense counsel's professional ability and obligation to object when appropriate. In *United States v. Edwards*,[75] the court, finding waiver in the absence of plain error, noted that a defense counsel is "not a potted plant."

A finding that defense counsel waived any objection to improper argument does not necessarily resolve the issue, as that failure might constitute inadequacy of counsel.[76]

Interestingly, in the current volume of their treatise, Professors LaFave, Israel, and King, have written:

> Appellate courts, while commonly finding a lack of prejudice flowing from improper summation by the prosecutor, have with mounting frustration expressed concern over the frequency with which such prosecutorial improprieties occur. Sometimes, courts have even suggested that they might well be required to reverse convictions without a showing of prejudice in order to deter such prosecutorial misconduct . . . .[77]

---

[71] *See, e.g.,* United States v. Williams, 23 M.J. 776 (A.C.M.R. 1987).

[72] 416 U.S. 637 (1974). *See also* Darden v. Wainwright, 477 U.S. 168 (1986).

[73] 470 U.S. 1 (1985).

[74] 470 U.S. 1 (1985). *See also* United States v. Hasting, 461 U.S. 499 (1983), *above* note 28. United States v. Moore, 36 M.J. 329 (C.M.A. 1993) (court found waiver when the prosecution argued acts of misconduct for impeachment as substantive evidence; the court did not comment on whether the judge had a duty to interrupt argument).

Because appellate courts seldom reverse a conviction because of improper arguments, Wayne R. LaFave & Jerrold H. Israel, Criminal Procedure § 23.5, at 36 (1984), some courts have suggested that they might reverse a conviction to prevent prosecutorial misconduct. Wayne R. LaFave & Jerrold H. Israel, Criminal Procedure § 23.5, at 36 (1984) (citing United States v. Farnkoff, 535 F.2d 661 (1st Cir. 1976)); United States v. Benter, 457 F.2d 1174 (2d Cir.), *cert. denied*, 409 U.S. 842 (1972); Harris v. United States, 402 F.2d 656 (D.C. Cir. 1968); *but see* United States v. Hasting, 461 U.S. 499, 506–07 (1983) (improper abuse of supervisory power to reverse a conviction to discipline prosecutors for continuing violations of *Griffin* regardless of whether the prosecutor's arguments constituted harmless error). Such a practice is ordinarily counterproductive. It would be more beneficial if trial or appellate judges cited counsel for professional misconduct and allowed the service disciplinary boards to decide if action should be taken against counsel, military or civilian.

[75] 35 M.J. 351, 354 (C.M.A. 1992) (claiming to have "purloined" the remark from Brendan Sullivan, Esquire).

[76] *Cf.* United States v. Kadlec, 22 M.J. 571 (A.C.M.R. 1986) (arguing for punitive discharge was not ineffective assistance of counsel).

[77] Wayne R. LaFave, Jerrold H. Israel & Nancy J. King, Criminal Procedure 1151 (4th ed. 2004).

§ 22-30.00   FINDINGS INSTRUCTIONS

§ 22-31.00   In General

In the American legal system, civilian or military, jurors determine the facts and apply the law to those facts to determine the legal result.[78] The applicable law is given to the jurors in the form of the judge's "instructions." Also known in the civilian federal courts as the judge's "charge," these instructions are a distilled summary of the law applicable to the case.[79] When done correctly, the instructions are carefully "tailored" to the case[80] — meaning that the law is presented in terms of the facts of the actual case[81] — and contain language that is comprehensible to the jurors. The duty of the trial judge to instruct the court washas been emphasized by the Court of Military Appeals.[82] This duty exists "irrespective of the desires of counsel."[83]

Judicial instructions play a major part in every trial with court members. Generally, the court members will be introduced to the trial by the judge's preliminary instructions.[84] Then throughout the trial the judge may instruct the court as to the reason that certain evidence has been introduced or inform the court to disregard specific evidence. Finally, at the end of both the prosecution and defense cases, including rebuttal, the judge will hold an Article 39(a) session to determine the closing instructions to be given on findings. In addition to basic procedural instructions, the closing instructions likely will address elements of the offenses, lesser-included offenses, defenses, evidentiary matters, presumptions, and the standard of proof.[85]

---

[78] *See, e.g.*, United States v. Noe, 22 C.M.R. 198, 200 (C.M.A. 1956).

[79] *See* Section 22-32.00.

[80] United States v. Harrison, 41 C.M.R. 179 (C.M.A. 1970). *See also* United States v. Pennington, 45 C.M.R. 235 (C.M.A. 1972); United States v. O'Hara, 33 C.M.R. 379, 381 (C.M.A. 1963).

[81] For example: "If you are not convinced beyond a reasonable doubt from her letter to Captain Caryn as well as the other evidence in the case that Private Jones intended at some moment during her three year absence to remain absent permanently from the Army, you cannot convict her of desertion."

[82] United States v. Graves, 1 M.J. 50 (C.M.A. 1975).

[83] 1 M.J. 53 (C.M.A. 1975). *See also* United States v. Hunter, 21 M.J. 240, 242 n.4 (C.M.A. 1986) (It is not improper for the judge to instruct the court on a defense, even though the defense counsel has waived that instruction. Conversely, if the judge does not give the instruction, the waiver is valid).

[84] R.C.M. 913(a). Preliminary instructions are discretionary with the trial judge. R.C.M. 913(a); Chapter 14. *See also* United States v. Waggoner, 6 M.J. 77 (C.M.A. 1978). These instructions may include other matter, such as a specific instruction on reasonable doubt and credibility of witnesses. United States v. Ryan, 21 M.J. 627 (A.C.M.R. 1985). Such instructions are desirable, however. United States v. Waggoner, 6 M.J. 77 (C.M.A. 1978).

[85] If there is a conviction, the judge must instruct the court on sentencing matters. *See generally Annual Review of Developments in Instructions*, Army Law, published annually; United States v. Poole, 47 M.J. 17 (C.A.A.F. 1997) (mere flight not element of offense of resisting apprehension or special defense requiring instruction).

(Rel.3—1/07   Pub.62410)

Although judges have the responsibility for giving proper instructions, counsel may request specific instructions, and, indeed, subject to ethical considerations, competent counsel should always seek to do so unless the applicable standard instruction is at least as favorable as any reasonable proposed instruction would be.

While counsel may request instructions from the military judge, the judge has substantial discretionary power in deciding on the instructions to give . . . . The test to determine if denial of a requested instruction constitutes error is whether (1) the charge is correct; (2) "it is not substantially covered in the main charge"; and (3) "it is on such a vital point in the case that the failure to give it deprived defendant of a defense or seriously impaired its effective presentation." . . . We review the military judge's refusal to give the defense — requested instruction . . . under an abuse-of-discretion standard of review.[86]

It is impossible to overstate the importance of the judge's closing instructions on findings. The law presumes that the members hear and apply each word.[87] Given that the law is frequently at least somewhat unclear as to the legal impact of given facts, enormous room exists for creativity. A large percentage of appellate cases address primarily or entirely the adequacy and accuracy of the judge's instructions. As common law is based primarily on court decisions, it becomes apparent that our law is largely based on the instructions given by trial judges. Although the armed forces use a "form book," the Military Judges' Benchbook,[88] the form instructions it contains should be used as the beginnings of tailored instructions.[89] Counsel should hand their proposed, written[90] instructions to the trial judge not later than the close of evidence,[91] with a copy served on opposing counsel to allow for examination and research.[92]

The judge should carefully consider counsels' proposed instructions, but is not bound by them. Subject to waiver by counsel,[93] the judge is solely responsible

---

[86] United States v. Damatta-Olivera, 37 M.J. 474, 478 (C.M.A. 1993).

[87] *See, e.g.,* United States v. Smith, 25 C.M.R. 86, 88–89 (C.M.A. 1958).

[88] Dep't of Army Pam. 27-9.

[89] Counsel are encouraged to tailor instructions for the case, but a "trial judge generally will not abuse his discretion by refusing a proposed instruction drawn in a partisan manner." Fletcher, *Instructions — An Under Utilized Opportunity for Advocacy,* 10 The Advocate 7, 8 (1978).

[90] R.C.M. 920(c); 1005(c) (written proposed instructions may be required).

[91] Many counsel and judges routinely use oral requests, however. Indeed, military practice is often far more casual than is normally necessary or appropriate in peacetime. Frequently, the entire pre-argument instruction discussion consists of a brief Article 39(a) session at which counsel orally request form instructions by number, with summary rulings by the trial judge.

[92] R.C.M. 108. The proposed instructions should be marked as appellate exhibits.

[93] *See* Section 22-34.00. *See, e.g.,* United States v. Simpson, 58 M.J. 368 (C.A.A.F. 2003) ("Any such deficiency [as to the instructions] is waived by defense counsels' failure to object unless the instructions were so incomplete as to constitute plain error," citing United States v. Glover, 50 M.J. 476, 478 (C.A.A.F. 1999)).

for the content of the instructions.[94] In many civilian trials, the court will begin preparation of draft instructions well before the close of evidence to ensure sufficient time for legal research and drafting. Military law permits such a process. The judge may even consult the case file before trial[95] in order to begin drafting.

An Article 39(a) session should be held prior to counsels' summations. At this session, counsel should present any necessary argument in support of their proposed instructions. The judge should then rule on the proposed instructions so that counsel will know what to include in their closing arguments.[96] "In the event the judge precludes an argument on requested instructions or merely denies them all, it is remiss of defense counsel not to request the judge to state the reasons for his or her refusal."[97] According to the Air Force Court of Military Review, [t]he applicable test for determining whether a denial of a requested instruction is error is well settled. The test is whether: (1) the requested instruction is itself a correct charge; (2) it is not substantially covered in a given instruction; and (3) it is on such a vital point in the case that the failure to give it deprived the accused of a defense or seriously impaired an effective presentation.[98]

Following counsel's final arguments,[99] the judge gives his or her instructions to the court members. Normally, the instructions are oral.[100] If written instructions are given, they may not be taken into closed session by the members over an objection.[101] The source of a given instruction[102] should not be disclosed.[103]

---

[94] On appeal, appellate defense counsel often argue that the judge should have given some instruction *sua sponte*. If the judge has given the essential instructions, such an appeal is not likely to succeed. *E.g.*, United States v. Smith, 34 M.J. 341 (C.M.A. 1992) (no *sua sponte* instruction required on character evidence).

[95] United States v. Paulin, 6 M.J. 38 (C.M.A. 1978). *Compare* United States v. Mitchell, 36 C.M.R. 14 (C.M.A. 1965) *with* United States v. Fry, 23 C.M.R. 146 (C.M.A. 1957), which it overruled.

[96] R.C.M. 920(c). This can be difficult when the judge agrees to give an instruction "similar in substance" to one requested by counsel. *See also* United States v. Sadler, 29 M.J. 370, 373 (C.M.A. 1990) ("Discussion of instructions should be conducted on the record, rather than in a conference under RCM 802. . .").

[97] Fletcher, *Instructions — An Under Utilized Opportunity for Advocacy*, 10 The Advocate 7, 10 (1978).

[98] United States v. Espronceda, 36 M.J. 535, 539 (A.F.C.M.R. 1992).

[99] Absent timely objection and specific predudice, giving instructions prior to, rather than after, closing arguments is not reversible error. United States v. Pendry, 29 M.J. 694 (A.C.M.R. 1989).

[100] R.C.M. 920(d). *See generally* United States v. Ginter, 35 M.J. 799, 801 (N.M.C.M.R. 1992) (submission of written instructions to the members is discretionary with the judge under R.C.M. 920(d); no case exists in which refusal to provide members with written instructions constituted an abuse of discretion).

[101] R.C.M. 920(d); 1005(d). *Cf.* Fed. R. Crim. P. 30(a) (requiring requests).

[102] *I.e.*, whether the source is trial counsel, defense counsel, or judge.

[103] Discussion to R.C.M. 920(c). *See* United States v. Wynn, 29 C.M.R. 11 (C.M.A. 1966).

(Rel.3—1/07 Pub.62410)

Even after the court members have closed for deliberation, the court may be reopened for additional instructions.[104]

§ 22-32.00   Content

§ 22-32.10   In General

Minimum requirements for closing instructions are set forth in both Article 51(c) of the Uniform Code of Military Justice[105] and Rule 920 of the Rules for Courts-Martial. Rule 920 is far more demanding than the Code provision.

Rule 920(a) requires that "[t]he military judge shall give the members appropriate instructions on findings." The Discussion adds:

Instructions consist of a statement of the issues in the case and an explanation of the legal standards and procedural requirements by which the members will determine findings. Instructions should be tailored to fit the circumstances of the case, and should fairly and adequately cover the issues presented.

Rule 920(e) mandates:

Instructions on findings shall include:

(1) A description of the elements of each offense charged, unless findings on such offenses are unnecessary because they have been entered pursuant to a plea of guilty;

(2) A description of the elements of each lesser included offense in issue, unless trial of a lesser included offense is barred by the statute of limitations (Article 43) and the accused refuses to waive the bar;

(3) A description of any special defense under R.C.M. 916 in issue;[106]

---

[104] United States v. Lampani, 14 M.J. 22 (C.M.A. 1982).

[105] Under Article 51(c) of the Uniform Code of Military Justice:

Before a vote is taken on the findings, the military judge or the president of a court-martial without a military judge shall, in the presence of the accused and counsel, instruct the members of the court as to the elements of the offense and charge them —

(1) that the accused must be presumed to be innocent until his guilt is established by legal and competent evidence beyond reasonable doubt;

(2) that in the case being considered, if there is a reasonable doubt as to the guilt of the accused, the doubt must be resolved in favor of the accused and he must be acquitted;

(3) that, if there is reasonable doubt as to the degree of guilt, the finding must be in a lower degree as to which there is no reasonable doubt; and

(4) that the burden of proof to establish the guilt of the accused beyond reasonable doubt is upon the United States.

These requirements are essential but insufficient absent other necessary instructions such as those on the elements of the offense and any applicable defenses.

[106] See, e.g., United States v. Franklin, 4 M.J. 635 (A.F.C.M.R. 1977). It matters not that the accused is the sole source of the evidence insofar as the reasonable character of the accused's

(4) A direction that only matters properly before the court-martial may be considered;

(5) A charge that—

(A) The accused must be presumed to be innocent until the accused's guilt is established by legal and competent evidence beyond reasonable doubt;[107]

(B) In the case being considered, if there is a reasonable doubt as to the guilt of the accused, the doubt must be resolved in favor of the accused and the accused must be acquitted;

(C) If, when a lesser included offense is in issue, there is a reasonable doubt as to the degree of guilt of the accused, the finding must be in a lower degree as to which there is not reasonable doubt;[108] and

---

explanation is for the jury to decide. United States v. Steward, 43 C.M.R. 140 (C.M.A. 1971). *See also* United States v. Barnes, 39 M.J. 230 (C.M.A. 1994) (judge had *sua sponte* responsibility to instruct on the affirmative defense of physical inability to report to work; error was prejudicial and required reversal of the conviction of that offense); United States v. Sellers, 33 M.J. 364, 368 (C.M.A. 1991) (judge's responsibility to *sua sponte* instruct on a defense; "borderline" case but court decided that mistake of fact was not reasonably raised by the evidence in the rape case). *See generally* United States v. Gillenwater, 43 M.J. 10, 13 n. 5 (C.A.A.F. 1995) (when to give an "affirmative defense" instruction).

[107] *See* United States v. Robinson, 38 M.J. 30 (C.M.A. 1993) (citing Cage v. Louisiana, 498 U.S. 39 (1990) in which the Court condemned a reasonable doubt instruction which expressly defined reasonable doubt as "grave uncertainty" and "actual substantial doubt" in conjunction with the words "moral certainty," the Court of Military Appeals held that the standard Military Judges' Benchbook reasonable doubt instruction was not erroneous because it did not contain the "grave uncertainty" or "actual substantial doubt" language denounced in *Cage*. Moreover, the military judge instructed the jury that "[p]roof beyond a reasonable doubt means *proof* to a moral certainty . . ."). Query as to consistency of court in comparing *Robinson*, which applied waiver, to *United States v. Demerse*, 37 M.J. 488 (C.M.A. 1993) (waiver not applied as to post-trial recommendation).

[108] *See* United States v. Jackson, 12 M.J. 163 (C.M.A. 1981). A lesser-included offense is "in issue" when "some evidence" has been presented, regardless of credibility or quantum "upon which members might rely if they choose." Discussion to R.C.M. 920(e). The meaning of "might rely" in the nonbinding Discussion is unclear. In United States v. Rodwell, 20 M.J. 264, 265 (C.M.A. 1985), the court, applying the pre-R.C.M. law, wrote that "the military judge has a duty to instruct *sua sponte* on all lesser-included offenses reasonably raised by the evidence." The "reasonably raised" standard appears more useful than "might rely."

Defense counsel may wish to avoid an instruction on a lesser-included offense in order to avoid a possible "jury" compromise. *See, e.g.*, United States v. McCray, 15 M.J. 1086 (A.C.M.R. 1983). Going for "all or nothing" is a viable, albeit dangerous, defense tactic. The judge has the discretion to accept or reject it. This appears to be the test used by the Court of Appeals for the Armed Forces:

When evidence is adduced during the trial which "reasonably raises" an affirmative defense or a lesser-included offense, the judge must instruct the court panel regarding that affirmative defense or lesser-included offense. . . . The test whether an affirmative defense is reasonably raised is whether the record contains some evidence to which the court members may attach credit if they so desire.

United States v. Davis, 53 M.J. 202, 205 (2000)(citations omitted).

(Rel.3—1/07 Pub.62410)

(D) The burden of proof to establish the guilt of the accused is upon the Government. [When the issue of lack of mental responsibility is raised, add:] However, the burden of proving the defense of lack of mental responsibility by clear and convincing evidence is upon the accused.

(6) Directions on the procedures under R.C.M. 921 for deliberations and voting;[109] and

(7) Such other explanations, descriptions, or directions as may be necessary and which are properly requested by a party or which the military judge determines, *sua sponte*, should be given.

The adequacy of an instruction will be evaluated in terms of both content and clarity. In *United States v. Smith*,[110] Chief Judge Quinn wrote for the court:

Certainly, grammatical nicety is not the Standard by which the law tests an instruction. It is not the number or the position of the commas, semicolons, or periods that counts, but whether the instruction as a whole provides meaningful legal principles for the court-martial's consideration. . . .[111]

The instructions as a whole must state the law with sufficient clarity to be understood by the members.[112] If the instruction contains mutually inconsistent

---

Note that under Rule for Courts-Martial 902(f) failure to object to an instruction waives the objection absent plain error. Although the content of the instructions is always a matter for the military judge, it is unclear as to whether an affirmative request by the accused that the judge *not* instruct on a lesser included offense necessarily permits the judge to withhold the instruction. The best known use of this defense tactic is the "all or nothing" approach by which the accused gambles that the evidence is insufficient for a conviction for the charged offense and wishes to withhold from the members the possibility of convicting on a lesser included offense. Jurisprudentially, this makes sense if the risk is that the members might compromise on a lesser included offense which may not be adequately substantiated by the evidence. It is questionable when the lesser included offense is realistic. Not instructing on the offense warps the nature of deliberation and can result in injustice. This tension gives rise to serious disagreement in the courts as to the propriety of the all or nothing approach. *See, e.g.* Commonwealth v. Roberts, 555 N.E.2d 588, 592 (Mass. 1990) (discretionary with judge); State v. Boeglin, 731 P.2d 943 (N.M. 1987) (the defendant may not complain if the court follows defendant's request and does not instruct on the lesser included) required). Note that some courts have held that inasmuch as the decision as to how to plead belongs solely to the defendant personally, only the defendant may decide whether to request a lesser included offense instruction. *E.g.*, People v. Brocksmith, 642 N.E.2d 1230 (Ill. 1994).

[109] *See* United States v. Truitt, 32 M.J. 1010 (A.C.M.R. 1991) (instruction that junior member shall collect and count the votes is important to avoid undue influence in rank — failure to give instruction is not prejudicial unless there is a showing of prejudice, for example by affidavit establishing improper use of superiority of rank); United States v. Llewellyn, 32 M.J. 803, 805 (A.C.M.R. 1991).

[110] 25 C.M.R. 86, 88 (C.M.A. 1958).

[111] 25 C.M.R. 86, 88 (C.M.A. 1958) (citing United States v. Noe, 22 C.M.R. 198 (C.M.A. 1956)).

[112] Interestingly, the Supreme Court has opined that "Nothing in *Boyde* precludes a state court from assuming that counsel's arguments clarified an ambiguous jury charge. This assumption is

(Rel.3—1/07 Pub.62410)

provisions, the "instruction as a whole" doctrine is inappropriate.[113] A judge who has given incorrect instructions may correct the error by clearly withdrawing the erroneous instructions and supplying correct ones.[114] On appeal, the court will review the propriety of the instructions on a de novo basis.[115]

§ 22-32.20 Summary of Evidence

Instructions must fully and fairly present the factual issues to be determined by the court members. . . . To achieve that purpose, the instructions may have to call attention to particular items of evidence so that court members can know and understand these specified rules of law. . . . How extensive the factual summary should be rests largely with the discretion of the [judge]. . . . Every summary of the evidence, however, must be fair, neither favoring one side nor discrediting the other.[116]

The military judge has the discretionary power to summarize and comment on the evidence.[117] The instructions should not assume as true, however, the existence or nonexistence of a material fact in issue as to which the evidence is conflicting, as to which there is a dispute, or which is not supported by the evidence.[118] Should the judge decide to summarize the evidence, it is important that he or she instruct the court members that they are to determine the weight of the evidence and the credit to be given to the witnesses, and that they are not bound by the judge's summary, but should rely on their own recollection of the evidence of the case.[119]

---

particularly apt when it is the prosecutor's argument that resolves an ambiguity in favor of the defendant." Middleton v. McNeil, 541 U.S. 433, 438, 1833 (2004) (referring to Boyde v. California, 494 U.S. 370, 378 (1990); emphasis in original).

[113] United States v. Pelletier, 36 C.M.R. 152 (C.M.A. 1966); United States v. Noe, 22 C.M.R. 198 (C.M.A. 1956).

[114] United States v. Quintanilla, 56 M.J. 37, 146–147 (C.A.A.F. 2001).

[115] 56 M.J. at 146, citing United States v. Maxwell, 45 M.J. 406, 424 (C.A.A.F. 1996).

[116] United States v. King, 37 C.M.R. 281, 285 (C.M.A. 1967) (citations omitted). See also R.C.M. 920(e) Discussion.

[117] This is in accord with the power held by civilian federal judges. Many states do not permit any judicial summation or comment. 1 J. Weinstein & M. Berger, Weinstein's Evidence ¶ 107.02, at 107–8 (2d ed. 2005).

[118] R.C.M. 920(e) Discussion.

[119] It would be well also for the judge to advise the court members that his or her instructions or comments during the trial should not be considered as evidencing his or her opinion, and that the determination as to guilt or innocence is left to the court members. Instructions are not a cure-all for improper conduct during trial. United States v. Clower, 48 C.M.R. 307, 310 (C.M.A. 1974) (such instruction will not cure questions by the trial judge akin to impeachment of the defendant). See also United States v. Mass, 49 C.M.R. 586 (A.C.M.R. 1974) (judge's questioning of defense character witness left court members with judge's view as to seriousness of offense).

(Rel.3—1/07 Pub.62410)

When the judge summarizes, counsel must be given the opportunity to object to the summary and to correct omissions or errors in the summary.[120] In the ideal case, the summary will be written and prepared early enough to permit counsel to comment on it prior to the instructions. Such a procedure is uncommon, however, in the armed forces.

If the summary is inaccurate, on appeal the appellate courts must determine if there was a fair risk of harm to the defendant.[121]

§ 22-33.00 Additional Instructions

Rule 920(e)(7) provides for "[s]uch other explanations, descriptions, or directions as may be necessary and which are properly requested by a party or which the military judge determines, *sua sponte*, should be given."[122] The provision recognizes that it is impossible to delimit all of the potentially necessary instructions. As trials are fact-dependent, required instructions will vary according to those facts. Instructions that are frequently necessary, however, may address:[123]

Uncharged misconduct[124]

Credibility of witnesses[125]

---

[120] This can be done easily by the judge asking counsel at the end of the instructions for "any corrections or objections" to the instructions.

[121] *See* R.C.M. 920(f). *See* United States v. Figura, 44 M.J. 308, 310 (C.A.A.F. 1996) (Judge Sullivan exhorted: "[J]udges — use your power under RCM 920 to give the jury a good, exhaustive, accurate, and fair view of the facts. . . .").

[122] United States v. Fleming, 38 M.J. 126, 129, n. * (C.M.A. 1993) (citing United States v. Grunden, 2 M.J. 116, 124, n.21 (C.M.A. 1977): "Members should be instructed any time any unusual trial procedure might suggest the guilt of the accused").

[123] *See also* Discussion to R.C.M. 920.

[124] Inadmissible evidence of uncharged misconduct must be struck completely. Evidence may, however, be admissible for one purpose while inadmissible for others. *See, e.g.*, Mil. R. Evid. 404(b). In such a case, a limiting instruction is necessary. Mil. R. Evid. 105. *See, e.g.*, United States v. McIntosh, 27 M.J. 204, 207 (C.M.A. 1988) (*sua sponte* instruction required to ensure limited use of evidence of possible debt pursuant to Mil. R. Evid. 404(b). Often the more pressing question is whether the defense may intentionally waive such an instruction. *Compare* United States v. Grunden, 2 M.J. 116 (C.M.A. 1977) (waiver not acceptable) *with* United States v. Wray, 9 M.J. 361 (C.M.A. 1980) *and* United States v. Fowler, 9 M.J. 149 (C.M.A. 1980) (retreating from the *Grunden* rule). *See* United States v. Figura, 44 M.J. 308, 310 (C.A.A.F. 1996) (Judge Sullivan exhorted: "[J]udges — use your power under RCM 920 to give the jury a good, exhaustive, accurate, and fair view of the facts. . . .").

[125] *See, e.g.*, United States v. Combest, 14 M.J. 927 (A.C.M.R. 1982) (request for instruction needed to preserve error). Accomplice testimony is of suspect reliability, and on request the judge must so instruct. *See, e.g.*, United States v. Bey, 16 C.M.R. 239 (C.M.A. 1954). *Sua sponte* instructions may be necessary in some cases. *See, e.g.*, United States v. Lee, 6 M.J. 96 (C.M.A. 1978) (when "critical" testimony is involved); United States v. DuBose, 19 M.J. 877 (A.F.C.M.R. 1985) ("pivotal" testimony). *See generally* United States v. Boswell, 30 M.J. 731 (A.F.C.M.R.

(Rel.3—1/07 Pub.62410)

Character of the accused[126]

Limited use of given evidence[127]

Failure of the accused to take the stand[128]

Reconsideration of verdict[129]

§ 22-34.00   Waiver of Error

Rule for Courts-Martial 920(f) provides:

Failure to object to an instruction or to omission of an instruction before the members close to deliberate constitutes waiver of the objection in the absence of plain error. The military judge may require the party objecting to specify of what respect the instructions given were improper. The parties shall be given the opportunity to be heard on any objection outside the presence of the members.[130]

"Plain error" exists when the mistake would result in a miscarriage of justice or affect the integrity and fairness of the judicial process.[131] A failure to give

---

1990). *E.g.*, United States v. Gillette, 35 M.J. 468 (C.M.A. 1992) (accomplice instruction should be given on request, but judge should label a witness an accomplice).

[126] *See* United States v. Philips, 11 C.M.R. 137 (C.M.A. 1953); Mil. R. Evid. 404(a). *See also* United States v. Pujana-Mena, 949 F.2d 24 (2d Cir. 1991) (Second Circuit joins seven other circuits in holding that a stand-alone defense character instruction is not mandatory).

[127] Mil. R. Evid. 105. *See also* Mil. R. Evid. 412 (rape-shield rule).

[128] Mil. R. Evid. 301(g). Under the unique military rule, if the defense requests that such an instruction not be given, the defense election should be complied with unless the instruction is necessary in the interests of justice. *See also* United States v. Charlette, 15 M.J. 197 (C.M.A. 1983).

[129] The court members may reconsider any finding or sentence before announcement in open court. R.C.M. 924(a); R.C.M. 1009. Most judges will not, in the first instance, instruct the court on voting for reconsideration. The judge will instruct the members to return if there is a question as to the procedures for reconsideration. *See* Dep't of Army Pam. 27-9, Military Judges' Benchbook ¶ 2 30. The judge may advise the court members that repeated requests for reconsideration of either the findings or sentence may not be used to obtain a hung court. United States v. Wilson, 8 M.J. 204 (C.M.A. 1984). *See generally* Section 22-53.00.

[130] *See, e.g.*, United States v. Simpson, 58 M.J. 368 (C.A.A.F. 2003) ("Any such deficiency [as to the instructions] is waived by defense counsels' failure to object unless the instructions were so incomplete as to constitute plain error," *citing* United States v. Glover, 50 M.J. 476, 478 (C.A.A.F. 1999)). *Cf.* United States v. Verdi, 5 M.J. 330 (C.M.A. 1978); United States v. Sawyer, 4 M.J. 64 (C.M.A. 1977); United States v. Jones, 3 M.J. 279 (C.M.A. 1977); United States v. Burx, 36 C.M.R. 95 (C.M.A. 1966); United States v. Crigler, 27 C.M.R. 337, 339 (C.M.A. 1959) ("[W]e need not consider whether the law officer expounded a correct principle of law for, if there was error in giving the instruction, it was induced by the accused" and error cannot be claimed.).

[131] *See* United States v. Guthrie, 53 M.J. 103, 106 (C.A.A.F. 2000) ("Absent plain error, failure to object to instructions as given or to request additional instructions forfeits the issue on appeal."); United States v. Czekala, 42 M.J. 168, 170 (C.A.A.F. 1995) (applied waiver absent objection to theo jury instructions); United States v. Yanke, 23 M.J. 144 (C.M.A. 1987); United States v. Walk, 26 M.J. 665 (A.F.C.M.R. 1988) (improper to instruct on command drug policies).

(Rel.3—1/07 Pub.62410)

a necessary instruction may be nonprejudicial,[132] however, and thus not grounds for reversal.

§ 22-35.00 Trial by Judge Alone

Instructions are not required when trial is by judge alone.[133] Although this is common sense in one respect,[134] the absence of formal instructions often makes it difficult to determine the law applied in a bench trial. Absent an opinion or special findings[135] that make reference to law, a judge's general verdict will normally be assumed to have correctly applied the applicable law, unless the law, as determined by the appellate court, could not sustain the verdict.

Counsel seeking to establish the law to be applied by the trial judge in a bench trial might thus do well to formally move for a "clarification of the law"; that is, counsel should submit a statement of the law believed applicable and seek a judicial ruling on it. This would preserve the issue adequately for appeal.

§ 22-40.00 DELIBERATIONS

§ 22-41.00 In General

In trials with court members, the court closes for deliberations on the findings and sentence after the judge's instructions.[136] Deliberations are conducted in a closed session at which only the members are present.[137] Prior to deliberations, the judge instructs the court members that there must be full and free discussion and that superiority of rank must not be exercised in any manner to control the independence of the members.[138]

Unless otherwise directed by the military judge, members may take with them in deliberations their notes, if any, any exhibits admitted in evidence, and any

---

[132] *See* Rose v. Clark, 478 U.S. 570 (1986) (applied harmless error test when judge erroneously shifted the burden of proof); Hopper v. Evans, 456 U.S. 605, 613–14 (1982) (harmless not to instruct on lesser-included offense); United States v. Remai, 19 M.J. 229 (C.M.A. 1985). *See also* United States v. Jackson, 196 F.3d 383 (2d Cir. 1999) (court sets forth framework for analysis when applying harmless error test for failure to instruct on element); United States v. Wells, 52 M.J. 126, 130 (C.A.A.F. 1999) (test for harmless error analysis when a lesser included offense instruction is not given). *Compare* Neder v. United States, 119 S. Ct. 1827 (1999) (failure to instruct on elements subject to harmless error test) *with* United States v. Griffin, 50 M.J. 480 (C.A.A.F. 1999) (failure to instruct on a lesser included offense could not be tested for harmlessness).

[133] R.C.M. 920(a) ("judge shall give the members").

[134] There is surely no need for the judge to instruct himself or herself.

[135] *See* Section 22-52.00.

[136] R.C.M. 921(a); 1006(a). *See also* United States v. Gray, 51 M.J. 1, 47-48 (C.A.A.F. 1999) (court rejected the argument that a recess for the night by the panel constituted improper deliberation).

[137] R.C.M. 921(a); 1006(a).

[138] R.C.M. 921(b); 1006(b). *See* Dep't of Army Pam. 27-9, Military Judges' Benchbook ¶ 2-30.

written instructions. Members may request that the court-martial be reopened and that portions of the record be read to them or additional evidence introduced. The military judge may, in the exercise of discretion, grant such request.[139]

The use at trial of written transcripts of available audio recordings, especially wiretaps, has been controversial as has been permitting the transcripts to be considered during deliberations. The Court of Appeals for the Armed Forces has sustained both use at trial and consideration of such transcripts during deliberations.[140]

Normally, the members will use a findings worksheet,[141] which will set forth the possible verdicts, including applicable lesser-included offenses. The judge may examine the findings worksheet prior to announcement of findings[142] in order to ensure legality.

§ 22-42.00 Voting

Voting is by secret written ballot,[143] with the ballots counted by the junior court member.[144] Each specification and charge should be voted on

[139] R.C.M. 921(b). *See, e.g.,* United States v. Ureta, 44 M.J. 290, 299 (C.A.A.F. 1996) (harmless error to take transcript of Article 32 testimony into deliberation room); United States v. Austin, 35 M.J. 271, 275 (C.M.A. 1992) (R.C.M. 921 spells out what can be taken by members when deliberating and depositions are not included, R.C.M. 702(a) Discussion; a verbatim Article 32 transcript is close enough to a deposition to count as one and thus is not able to be taken into deliberations. At 277 n.6, the court opines that taking such a transcript into the deliberation room is not per se reversible error; it must be tested for prejudice. Crawford, J., concurring in part and in result, claims that statement refers only to harmless error analysis). *See also* United States v. Paahuli, 50 M.J. 782, 789–90 (N.M. Crim. App. 1999) (judge did not err in allowing members to take a videotaped interview of victim into deliberation room, citing cases; even if it had been error it would not have been prejudicial), *aff'd on other grounds,* 54 M.J. 181 (C.A.A.F. 2000).

[140] United States v. Craig, 60 M.J. 156 (Armed 2004) ("Appellate courts have differed over whether transcripts should be used only as demonstrative exhibits within the courtroom or should accompany the jurors to the deliberation room. We join the majority of federal courts of appeals in holding that trial judges have considerable discretion in determining whether to allow the fact finder to consider such transcripts during deliberations. That determination will not be reversed on appeal absent an abuse of discretion." 60 M.J. 162 (Armed 2004), footnotes omitted).

[141] *See* R.C.M. 921(d) Discussion.

[142] R.C.M. 921(d).

[143] R.C.M. 921(c); 1006(d). *See* United States v. Greene, 36 M.J. 1068 (A.C.M.R. 1993) (failure to instruct on secret ballot did not constitute plain error and no prejudice existed; note that the court used a theory that non-secret balloting might expose members to command influence in order to consider an affidavit that a secret ballot was actually taken).

[144] R.C.M. 921(c)(6)(B). Article 51, U.C.M.J., and R.C.M. 921(c)(6)(B) require that the junior member collect and count the ballots and that the President check the count. Absent prejudice to the accused, a judge's failure to instruct the members as to this aspect of the findings procedure is harmless. United States v. Truitt, 32 M.J. 1010 (A.C.M.R. 1991).

(Rel.3—1/07 Pub.62410)

separately.[145] Under normal circumstances, a finding of conviction requires that at least two-thirds of the members find the accused guilty beyond a reasonable doubt.[146] A conviction for spying,[147] for which the death sentence is mandatory, requires a unanimous vote. If the accused is not convicted by the requisite vote, "the members shall vote on each included offense on which they have been instructed, in order of severity beginning with the most severe."[148] If the accused is not convicted of either the charged offense or of a lesser-included offense, he or she is automatically acquitted of the applicable specification or charge;[149] a hung jury cannot take place on findings.

Under Rule for Courts-Martial 921(c)(4), when an accused is convicted but a defense of lack of mental responsibility has been raised[150] the members will vote on that defense. A "finding of not guilty by . . . reason of lack of mental responsibility results" when "a majority of the members present concur that the accused has proven lack of mental responsibility by clear and convincing evidence."[151]

§ 22-50.00 FINDINGS

§ 22-51.00 In General

In the absence of special findings made by the military judge,[152] all findings equate to a general verdict and are announced without explanation and without polling.[153] The announcement of findings is made in open court by the president

---

[145] "Each specification shall be voted on separately before the corresponding charge. The order of voting on several specifications under a charge or on several charges shall be determined by the president unless a majority of the members object." R.C.M. 921(c)(6)(A).

[146] R.C.M. 921(c)(2)(B). *Note* Dodson v. Zelez, 917 F.2d 1250, 1256–57 (10th Cir. 1990) (noting inconsistency between 2/3 vote for conviction and 3/4 vote for sentences greater than 10 years, court required 3/4 vote for mandatory life sentence verdict).

[147] U.C.M.J. art. 106.

[148] R.C.M. 921(c)(5).

[149] R.C.M. 921(c)(3). *See* United States v. Wallace, 35 M.J. 897 (A.C.M.R. 1992) (improper instructions included "similar to if [sic] candidates were running for office" and may have implied run-off voting).

[150] *See* R.C.M. 916(k)(1).

[151] R.C.M. 921(c)(4).

[152] *See* Section 22-52.00.

[153] R.C.M. 922(e). *See generally* United States v. Thomas, 39 M.J. 626 (N.M.C.M.R. 1993), *rev'd on other grounds*, 47 M.J. 322 (C.A.A.F. 1997) (plain error not to instruct to vote first on life in prison before voting on death penalty). Although the prohibition on member polling is essential in the ordinary case in order to protect the privacy of the individual members, the same argument cannot be made in a unanimous vote capital case. Given the need for each member to concur in the vote, polling ought to be permitted in order to eliminate any question, however minor, that each member has concurred.

(Rel.3—1/07 Pub.62410)

of the court.[154]

For historical reasons, the phrasing of the verdict has depended on the result. If a guilty verdict had been reached, the president would announce, "It is my duty as President of this court to inform you that two-thirds of the members present and voting find you of the offense, guilty." If an acquittal resulted, the president would use the word, *advise* rather than inform. The present form abandons this usage in favor of the simple announcement that "this court-martial finds you. . . ."[155] Given the normal use of "findings worksheets," however, the prior use can be expected to continue in many locations.

In circumstances in which the verdict is unclear, the military judge should request a clarification from the president of the court.[156]

§ 22-52.00 Special Findings[157]

Under Article 51(d) of the Uniform Code of Military Justice, when trial is by military judge alone,

> [t]he military judge . . . shall make a general finding and shall in addition on request find the facts specially. If an opinion or memorandum of decision is filed, it will be sufficient if the findings of fact appear therein.[158]

Either trial or defense counsel may request special findings;[159] the request may be a general one or may consist of requests to find specific facts. The goal is to preserve issues of law for appeal:

> Special findings are to a bench trial as instructions are to a trial before members. Such procedure is designed to preserve for appeal questions of law. . . . It is the remedy designed to rectify judicial misconceptions regarding: the significance of a particular fact, . . . the application of any presumption, . . . or the appropriate legal standard. . . .[160]

---

[154] The actual procedure may vary by armed force and location. At one time, it was common for both the accused and the defense counsel to formally "report" to the president (i.e., come to attention before the president and salute) for the verdict. This is no longer the practice in the armed forces; instead, the accused and counsel normally rise and remain at their places.

[155] Dep't of Army Pam. 27-9, Military Judges' Benchbook, ¶ 2-33 (C1 15 February 1985).

[156] *Cf.* United States v. King, 50 M.J. 686, 688 (A.F. Crim. App. 1999).

[157] Much of this section is based upon Fredric Lederer, Special Essential and Similar Findings (32d Military Judge Course, TJAGSA, 5 June 1989), which, in turn, was based on the prior writings of a similar name by Professor, then Major, David Schlueter.

[158] Article 51(d) is "patterned on" Fed. R. Crim. P. 23(c). United States v. Gerard, 11 M.J. 440, 441 (C.M.A. 1981).

[159] *See generally* Schinasi, *Special Findings: Their Use at Trial and on Appeal*, 87 Mil. R. Evid. 73 (1980).

[160] United States v. Falin, 43 C.M.R. 702 (A.C.M.R. 1971) (citations omitted).

(Rel.3—1/07 Pub.62410)

"Special findings ordinarily include findings as to the elements of the offenses of which the accused has been found guilty, and any affirmative defense relating thereto."[161] Findings are not warranted "as to matters which are irrelevant, immaterial, or so remote as to have no effect on the case."[162] There may be dispute, however, as to whether specific matter fits that description.[163] Special findings are not required on questions of law or interlocutory matters.[164]

The question is whether the judge can *require* either a detailed request or a written request. Chief Judge Everett has divided special findings requests into two categories: general requests (which require the judge to determine which findings to make) and findings on specific matters.[165] It is unclear whether counsel can be required to submit a detailed written request for findings — at least insofar as findings on specific matters are concerned. The rules for courts-martial state that "[i]f the request is for findings on specific matters, the military judge may require that the request be in writing." R.C.M. 918(b). It is unclear whether this provision complies with Article 51(d).

In *United States v. Gerard*,[166] the Court dealt with the untimely request for special findings by a defense counsel who had been promised (but not supplied with) a copy of the record before authentication in order to prepare specific written questions as directed by the trial judge. Judge Fletcher held that in light of Article 51(d)'s blanket requirement for special findings, the trial judge could not lawfully deny special findings because of untimeliness, despite the *Manual for Courts-Martial*'s timeliness requirements. Concurring, Chief Judge Everett stated that neither Article 51(d) nor Federal Rule of Criminal Procedure 23(c) had "been interpreted to require any particular form of request for special findings" and that "any requirement that an accused make his request for special findings in writing probably runs counter to Article 51(d)."[167] However, he added

---

[161] Discussion to R.C.M. 918(b). *See also* United States v. Falin, 43 C.M.R. 702, 704 (A.C.M.R. 1971) (jurisdiction). When relevant, a special finding should also be made as to mental responsibility.

[162] United States v. Burke, 4 M.J. 530, 535 (N.M.C.M.R. 1977).

[163] In United States v. Burke, 4 M.J. at 535, an assault case, the court sustained the refusal of the trial judge to "enter special findings as to the guilt of a prosecution witness in the assaults." Concurring, Judge Granger argued that it was important to know whether the witness was an accomplice and thus of suspect credibility. He found, however, that the trial judge's statement that he viewed the witness as an accomplice "obviated the necessity for" making a finding.

[164] *See, e.g.*, United States v. Curry, 15 M.J. 701 (A.C.M.R. 1983) (suppression motion); United States v. Kressin, 2 M.J. 283 (A.F.C.M.R. 1976), *reversed on other grounds*, 5 M.J. 393 (C.M.A. 1978) (suppression motion); United States v. Ericson, 13 M.J. 725 (N.M.C.M.R. 1982) (speedy-trial motion; challenge to members). Motions will likely require essential findings, however. *See* R.C.M. 905(d).

[165] United States v. Gerard, 11 M.J. 440, 443 (C.M.A. 1981) (Everett, C.J. concurring).

[166] 11 M.J. 440 (C.M.A. 1981).

[167] 11 M.J. at 442–43.

(Rel.3—1/07   Pub.62410)

that if counsel wish findings on "specific matters," the trial judge could, pursuant to the *Manual*, require a written request. Judge Cook dissented. Because of the three disparate opinions, it is unclear whether *Gerard* bars requiring a written request.

§ 22-53.00 Reconsideration

Reconsideration of findings is governed by Rule for Courts-Martial 924:

(a) *Time for reconsideration.* Members may reconsider any finding reached by them before such finding is announced in open session. Members may consider any finding of guilty reached by them at any time before announcements of the sentence.

(b) *Procedure.* Any member may propose that a finding be reconsidered. If such a proposal is made in a timely manner the question whether to reconsider shall be determined in closed session by secret written ballot. Any finding of not guilty shall be reconsidered if a majority vote for reconsideration. Any finding of guilty shall be reconsidered if more than one-third of the members vote for reconsideration. When the death penalty is mandatory, a request by any member for reconsideration of a guilty finding requires reconsideration. Any finding of not guilty only by reason of lack of mental responsibility shall be reconsidered on the issue of the finding of guilty of the elements if more than one-third of the members vote for reconsideration, and on the issue of mental responsibility if a majority vote for reconsideration.[168] If a vote to reconsider a finding succeeds, the procedures in R.C.M. 921 shall apply.

(c) *Military judge sitting alone.* In trial by military judge, the military judge may reconsider any finding of guilty at any time before announcement of sentence.

§ 22-54.00 Impeachment of Verdict

Both civilian and military law make significant efforts to protect general verdicts.[169] Impeachment of verdicts is discouraged to the greatest extent

---

[168] *See generally* United States v. Thomas, 39 M.J. 626, 630 (N.M.C.M.R. 1993) (discussion that a non-unanimous vote cannot be reconsidered to yield a unanimous capital result), *rev'd on other grounds*, 47 M.J. 322 (C.A.A.F. 1997) (plain error not to instruct to vote first on life in prison before voting on death penalty).

[169] *See, e.g.,* Tanner v. United States, 483 U.S. 107 (1987) (in a 5-4 decision, Court held that drug and alcohol consumption during a trial does not constitute an outside influence); McDonald v. Pless, 238 U.S. 264 (1915); Hyde & Schneider v. United States, 225 U.S. 347 (1912); United States v. Witherspoon, 16 M.J. 252 (C.M.A. 1983) (Court members' improper visit to scene and reliance on adverse information obtained in unauthorized view did not prejudice the accused, where information was equivalent to information known to members as a matter of common knowledge); United States v. Johnson, 23 M.J. 327 (C.M.A. 1987) (affidavit alleging that Court member had extensive training in martial arts and performed demonstration during deliberations not admissible); *but see* Mattox v. United States, 146 U.S. 140 (1892) (jurors may testify about prejudicial information brought to their attention). Arguably, this is due to the very nature of such verdicts,

(Rel.3—1/07 Pub.62410)

possible. Yet, it is apparent that, under certain circumstances,[170] particularly in cases of alleged command influence, it is critical to discover what happened during deliberations and, if necessary, to overturn the verdict. Accordingly, Military Rule of Evidence 606(b) provides:

> Upon an inquiry into the validity of the findings or sentence, a member may not testify as to any matter or statement occurring during the course of the deliberations of the members of the court-martial or, to the effect of anything upon the member's or any other member's mind or emotions as influencing the member to assent to or dissent from the findings or sentence or concerning the member's mental process in connection therewith, except that a member may testify on the question whether extraneous prejudicial information was improperly brought to the attention of the members of the court-martial, whether any outside influence was improperly brought to bear upon any member, or whether there was unlawful command influence. Nor may the member's affidavit or evidence of any statement by the member concerning a matter about which the member would be precluded from testifying be received for these purposes.

Rule for Courts-Martial 923 then provides:

> Findings which are proper on their face may be impeached only when extraneous prejudicial information was improperly brought to the attention of a member, outside influence was improperly brought to bear upon any member, or unlawful command influence was brought to bear upon any member.

> The Court of Military Appeals held that the exception for "command influence" extends to "use of rank by a court member to pervert military justice."[171]

Impropriety should be raised before the court adjourns, if possible, and will usually be suggested in this situation by a member's statement to the judge, counsel, or bailiff.[172] In addition, the problems that the rule is designed to prevent

---

particularly civilian ones. Deliberations are often characterized by emotional heat, peer pressure, and discussion of extraneous facts and issues. Further, it is by no means clear that juries always follow their instructions closely. If the circumstances of the average jury verdict were brought out, it would be hard to sustain it. Notwithstanding the peculiar nature of the deliberative process, the *results* appear to be essentially accurate, given the nature of the American criminal justice process.

[170] *See* 2 Edward J. Imwinkelried, Uncharged Misconduct Evidence § 9:79 (Rev. Ed. 1988 with 2005 Supp); 3 J. Weinstein &. M. Berger, Evidence ch. 606 (2d ed. 2005) (citing cases).

[171] United States v. Accordino, 20 M.J. 102, 104 (C.M.A. 1985). The court added: "It is only when recourse is made to rank to 'enhance' an argument — *i.e.*, to coerce a subordinate to vote in a particular manner — that the line is crossed."20 M.J. 105 (C.M.A. 1985). *See also* United States v. Martinez, 17 M.J. 916 (N.M.C.M.R. 1984).

[172] *Compare* Parker v. Gladden, 385 U.S. at 366–67 (Harlan, J., dissenting) (petitioner's wife asked individual jurors a series of questions sent to her by petitioner) *with* United States v. Stone, 26 M.J. 401 (C.M.A. 1988) (failure to raise the issue of misconduct by court members until 12 days after trial constitutes a waiver). The military judge may order a post-trial hearing on his or

"disappear in large part if such investigation . . . is made by the judge and takes place before the juror's discharge and separation."[173] After trial, affidavits may be used if their subject matter comes within a cognizable exception to the general rule prohibiting impeachment of verdicts.[174]

---

her own initiative, at the request of the parties, or at the direction of the convening authority to investigate allegations under Rule 606. United States v. Witherspoon, 16 M.J. 252 (C.M.A. 1983); United States v. Carr, 18 M.J. 297 (C.M.A. 1984). An investigation of misconduct of court members should be a judicial, rather than an administrative, inquiry. If the question of misconduct is raised before the record is authenticated, the judge should conduct an Article 39(a) session. If it is raised after authentication, the convening authority should convene a posttrial hearing pursuant to *DuBay*. United States v. Stone, 26 M.J. 401.

[173] 8 J. Wigmore, Evidence § 2350, at 691 (J. McNaughton rev. ed. 1961).

[174] *See Accordino, above* note 156, at 103, n.4.

CHAPTER 23

SENTENCING

§ 23-10.00 INTRODUCTION
   § 23-11.00 Sentencing in Brief
   § 23-12.00 Sentencing Philosophy
   § 23-13.00 Disparate Sentencing
§ 23-20.00 CONSTITUTIONAL LIMITATIONS
   § 23-21.00 In General
   § 23-22.00 Cruel and Unusual Punishment
§ 23-30.00 PERMISSIBLE SANCTIONS
   § 23-31.00 In General
   § 23-32.00 Specific Sanctions
      § 23-32.10 — The Death Penalty
      § 23-32.20 — Separation from the Armed Forces
         § 23-32.21 — — In General
         § 23-32.22 — — Dismissal
         § 23-32.23 — — Dishonorable Discharge
         § 23-32.24 — — Bad-Conduct Discharge
   § 23-33.00 Deprivation of Liberty
      § 23-33.10 — In General
      § 23-33.20 — Confinement
      § 23-33.30 — Hard Labor without Confinement
      § 23-33.40 — Confinement on Bread and Water
      § 23-33.50 — Restriction
   § 23-34.00 Financial Sanctions
      § 23-34.10 — Deprivations of Pay
      § 23-34.20 — Fines
   § 23-35.00 Reduction in Grade
   § 23-36.00 Reprimand
§ 23-40.00 SENTENCING EVIDENCE
   § 23-41.00 In General
   § 23-42.00 Evidence Admitted During Trial on the Merits
   § 23-43.00 Evidence Resulting from a Guilty Plea
      § 23-43.10 — In General
      § 23-43.20 — Providence Inquiry
      § 23-43.30 — Stipulation of Fact
   § 23-44.00 Prosecutorial Sentencing Evidence
      § 23-44.10 — In General
      § 23-44.20 — Data from the Charge Sheet

(Rel.3—1/07 Pub.62410)

§ 23-44.30 — Personnel Records

    § 23-44.31 — — In General

    § 23-44.32 — — Nonjudicial Punishment Records

    § 23-44.33 — — Written Reprimands

§ 23-44.40 — Previous Convictions

§ 23-44.50 — Evidence in Aggravation

    § 23-44.51 — — In General

    § 23-44.52 — — Impact on Victim or Family

    § 23-44.53 — — Effect and Amount of Drugs

    § 23-44.54 — — Financial Matters

    § 23-44.55 — — Impact on Discipline and Mission

    § 23-44.56 — — Future Dangerousness

§ 23-44.60 — Rehabilitative Potential

§ 23-44.70 — Capital Cases

§ 23-45.00   Defense Sentencing Evidence: Extenuation and Mitigation

§ 23-45.10 — In General

§ 23-45.20 — Extenuation and Mitigation Evidence

    § 23-45.21 — — Testimony by the Accused

        § 23-45.21(a) — — In General

        § 23-45.21(b) — — Unsworn Statements

    § 23-45.22 — — Defense Witnesses

    § 23-45.23 — — Command Influence

§ 23-45.30 — Capital Cases

§ 23-46.00   Prosecution Rebuttal

§   23-50.00 SENTENCING FACTORS

§ 23-51.00   In General

§ 23-52.00   Maximum Imposable Sentence

    § 23-52.10 — In General

    § 23-52.20 — The "Escalator Clauses"

    § 23-52.30 — Rehearings

§ 23-53.00   Sentencing Factors in Noncapital Cases

    § 23-53.10 — The Accused's Plea

    § 23-53.20 — Cooperation with the Authorities

    § 23-53.30 — The Accused's False Testimony on the Merits

    § 23-53.40 — Time Spent in Pretrial Confinement

    § 23-53.50 — The Accused's Absence from Trial

    § 23-53.60 — Administrative Consequences of a Sentence

    § 23-53.70 — Recalcitrance

    § 23-53.80 — Prior Article 15

§   23-60.00 SENTENCING ARGUMENT

§ 23-61.00   In General

§ 23-62.00   Defense Arguments *for* Serious Punishments

§   23-70.00 INSTRUCTIONS

(Rel.3—1/07 Pub.62410)

§ 23-80.00 DELIBERATIONS AND SENTENCE
   § 23-81.00   Sentence Worksheet
   § 23-82.00   Procedure
   § 23-83.00   Reconsideration of Sentence
   § 23-84.00   Defective Sentences
   § 23-85.00   Suspension of Sentence
   § 23-86.00   Vacation Proceedings

§ 23-10.00   INTRODUCTION

§ 23-11.00   Sentencing in Brief

Although civilian and military criminal trials are nearly identical insofar as trial on the merits is concerned, there are significant differences where sentencing is concerned. Unlike civilian proceedings, courts-martial are bifurcated, and sentencing takes place after findings in an adversary proceeding. Further, unlike the civilian federal courts, courts-martial do not use sentencing guidelines. Although a similar procedure has been studied, military law uses the more traditional process of selecting a sentence designed to fit the individual offender and case.

The first portion of trial by court-martial is "findings." If the accused is found not guilty and acquitted, trial ends. However, should the accused be convicted of any offense, the court-martial proceeds to adversarial sentencing,[1] a procedure normally used in most civilian jurisdictions only in death-penalty cases. During sentencing, the prosecution will present what is sometimes called the "case in aggravation," after which the defense will present a "case in extenuation and mitigation." Thereafter, counsel for both sides may present rebuttal and surrebuttal as appropriate. Finally, counsel argue their positions much as they present closing arguments on the merits.

Although the rules of evidence have historically been said to be "relaxed" during sentencing, the accused during adversary sentencing holds rights remarkably similar to those held during findings.[2]

Depending upon the case, sentencing will be by either the military judge or the court members. If the accused elected trial with members after arraignment, the members will sentence,[3] even if the accused pled guilty. If, however, the

---

[1] *See* R.C.M. 1001(a)(1) for the general procedure to be followed.

[2] This is a far cry from the usual civilian summary sentencing after a presentence report. For a civilian perspective on the rights held in civilian practice, *see* Alan C. Michaels, *Trial Rights at Sentencing*, 81 N.C. L. Rev. 1771 (2003).

[3] Jury sentencing in non-capital cases is highly unusual in the United States, but serves useful functions. It ensures that those intimately familiar with military life can meaningfully evaluate the impact of that life on an accused's behavior and can also adjudge a punishment that in addition to being just will have a beneficial aspect on military life and discipline. At the same time, member

(Rel.3—1/07 Pub.62410)

accused requested and received trial by military judge alone,[4] the judge will ordinarily sentence.[5] When court members sentence, they receive judicial instructions after arguments and before deliberations.

Potential sanctions depend upon both the offenses involved and the jurisdictional limit applicable to the type of court-martial involved. In general terms, under the Uniform Code of Military Justice, sanctions may include in an appropriate case limitations on freedom, including confinement, reduction in grade, financial penalties, punitive discharges, or death. Although only two-thirds of the members must agree on sentences as severe as ten years of confinement, longer prison terms require a three-quarters vote. Life imprisonment and death require unanimous agreement.

"Jury" sentencing is done by secret written ballot following open discussion of the topic. Voting begins with the most lenient proposed sentence and proceeds to more severe offenses until a sentence receives the requisite vote.

Although punitive separations from the armed forces and death sentences may not be ordered into effect until after the termination of the appellate process,[6] absent a decision by the convening authority to "defer" a sentence to confinement,[7] adjudged imprisonment begins immediately at the close of trial.[8]

Civilian criminal jurisprudence has been roiled by the Supreme Court's 2004 decision in *Blakely v. Washington*,[9] holding that "any fact that increases the penalty for a crime beyond the prescribed statutory maximum must be submitted to a jury, and proved beyond a reasonable doubt,"[10] and its federal analog, *United States v. Booker*.[11] *Blakely* and *Booker* are inapplicable to the armed forces if only because the right to trial by jury is inapplicable. However, it is interesting to note that in member trials, sentencing is done by the members, inherently meeting *Blakely's* forum requirement.

§ 23-12.00 Sentencing Philosophy

The traditional goals for sentencing are:

---

sentencing serves as a check on overly severe judges. For a civilian perspective *see* Jenia Iontcheva, *Jury Sentencing as Democratic Practice*, 89 Va. L. Rev. 311 (2003).

[4] This option is unavailable if the accused is charged with a capital offense, *i.e.*, an offense for which the death penalty may be adjudged.

[5] Unless the judge has been exposed to information that could impel sentencing by members.

[6] *See generally* Chapter 25.

[7] *See generally* Section 24-30.00.

[8] R.C.M. 1113(d)(2)(A).

[9] 542 U.S. 296 (2004) (state sentencing).

[10] 542 U.S. at 301 (2004).

[11] 543 U.S. 220 (2005).

(Rel.3—1/07 Pub.62410)

Rehabilitation

Specific (or special) deterrence

General deterrence

Incapacitation (or warehousing)

Retribution

Respect for law and order

Restitution[12]

Until the 1970's, rehabilitation of the offender, often accompanied by acceptance of a medical model for incarceration,[13] was the most widely expressed, single civilian goal in recent history. During the more conservative Reagan years, however, society became increasingly disenchanted with rehabilitation, which came to be generally viewed as unworkable.[14] Accordingly, the pendulum swung to retribution and incapacitation.

Although military law explicitly states that the purpose of findings is truth finding[15] (subject to the constraints of due process), specific sentencing goals

---

[12] Fredric I. Lederer, *Fundamental Criminal Procedure* § 230 (199987) (desktop unpublished draft manuscript). *See also* Albert W. Alschuler, *The Changing Purposes of Criminal Punishment: A Retrospective on the Past Century and Some Thoughts about the Next*, 70 Univ. Chi. L. Rev. 1 (2003); Vowell, *To Determine an Appropriate Sentence: Sentencing in the Military Justice System*, 114 Mil. L. Rev. 87, 91–102 (1986).

[13] Within the military, specific deterrence was also favored. General deterrence was disparaged for some years. *Compare* United States v. Lania, 9 M.J. 100 (C.M.A. 1980) *with* United States v. Mosely, 1 M.J. 350 (C.M.A. 1976) (overruled by *Lania*).

[14] In fairness, it is unclear how often rehabilitation programs received adequate support. By their very nature, rehabilitation programs are resource-heavy. Further, it is unclear how many were conducted by staffs who accepted their goals. Professor Lederer notes that, while once touring the United States Penitentiary in Leavenworth with a JAGC advanced class, the official in charge of rehabilitation programs announced that all such efforts were pointless and then warned that he would refuse to acknowledge the statement if quoted.

[15] R.C.M. 102(a). *See also*, Mil. R. Evid. 102; United States v. Tipton, 23 M.J. 338 (C.M.A. 1987); United States v. Eshalomi, 23 M.J. 12 (C.M.A. 1986); United States v. Thomas, 22 M.J. 388 (C.M.A. 1986), *cert. denied*, 479 U.S. 1085 (1987); United States v. Deland, 22 M.J. 70 (C.M.A.), *cert. denied*, 479 U.S. 856 (1986); United States v. Callara, 21 M.J. 259, 263 (C.M.A. 1986). Military law follows civilian precedent. *See generally* Frankel, *The Search for the Truth: An Umpireal View*, 123 U. Pa. L. Rev. 1031 (1975); United States v. Inadi, 475 U.S. 387, 396 (1986) (As to the admissibility of co-conspirators' declarations into evidence, the Court was concerned with the "accuracy of the truth-determining process in criminal trials."); Nix v. Whiteside, 475 U.S. 157, 166 (1986) (The Court recognized that the defense counsel's duty "is limited to legitimate, lawful conduct compatible with the very nature of a trial as a search for the truth."); United States v. Leon, 468 U.S. 897, 907 (1984) ("An objectionable collateral consequence of this interference with the criminal justice system's truth-finding function is that some guilty defendants may go free or receive reduced sentences as a result of favorable plea bargains."); Jenkins v. Anderson, 447 U.S. 231, 238 (1980) ("Attempted impeachment on cross-examination of a defendant — may enhance the reliability of the criminal process.").

(Rel.3—1/07   Pub.62410)

have not been adopted by the armed forces. Instead, Rule for Courts-Martial 1001(g) provides, in part, that in closing argument trial counsel "may also refer to generally accepted sentencing philosophies, including rehabilitation of the accused, general deterrence, specific deterrence of misconduct by the accused, and social retribution." Perhaps more importantly, the Military Judges' Benchbook, the form instruction guide used throughout the military, states:

> Our society recognizes five principal reasons for the sentence of those who violate the law. They are:
>
> 1. Rehabilitation of the wrongdoer.
>
> 2. Punishment of the wrongdoer.
>
> 3. Protection of society from the wrongdoer.
>
> 4. Preservation of good order and discipline in the military, and
>
> 5. Deterrence of the wrongdoer and those who know of his/her crime(s) and his/her sentence from committing the same or similar offenses.[16]

To the extent that these goals are stated in priority order, incapacitation and retribution appear to be stressed.

It is unfortunate that neither Congress nor the President have expressly stated sentencing goals and thus supply judges and court members with inadequate sentencing guidance. At present, in most articles of the Code, Congress has simply declared that a person "shall be punished as a court-martial may direct." Such abdication virtually ensures disparity of sentencing.[17]

§ 23-13.00 Disparate Sentencing

Disparate sentencing is an ongoing sentencing problem present in the armed forces as well as in civilian life.[18] Disparity is often due to the absence of articulated sentencing goals, leaving each judge[19] to his or her own individual sentencing philosophy. In the armed forces, sentencing is the responsibility not only of judges, but also of court members.[20] Accordingly, at least theoretically, disparity is a greater risk in the armed forces than in many civilian jurisdictions, and some commentators have proposed elimination of "jury" sentencing for this

---

[16] Dep't Army Pam. 27-9, Military Judges' Benchbook 902 (September 2002). A judge may give a general deterrence instruction so long as the instructions include other factors and emphasize the need for individualized consideration. United States v. Loving, 34 M.J. 956, 965 (A.C.M.R. 1992), citing United States v. Lania, 9 M.J. 100 (C.M.A. 1980).

[17] See also Vowell, above note 12 at 87–89.

[18] The civilian Federal Sentencing Guidelines are largely an attempt to reduce, if not eliminate, disparity.

[19] Or, court members, in the case of the armed forces.

[20] When trial on the merits is by members. See Section 23-11.00.

(Rel.3—1/07 Pub.62410)

reason.[21] Depending upon one's perspective, however, it is unlikely that disparity is a major problem in the military.

The limited number of military judges and normal assignment policies make it probable that any given military command will normally use the same military judge for a significant time period.[22] Judicial disparity at the same command is not ordinarily a problem then, although disparity within the armed force or the military generally may be. Because an accused will elect the sentencing agency more likely to be lenient, the right to choose either member or judge sentencing[23] works to check severe sentencing and thus disparity.

In *United States v. Mamaluy*,[24] the Court of Military Appeals disapproved an instruction to the court members that they could consider sentences in other cases for similar offenses.[25] However, a unique military solution exists with regard to the problem of disparity in sentencing. The Courts of Criminal Appeals[26] — appellate courts vested with fact-finding powers — often reduce sentences simply to eliminate disparity. In this regard, the Air Force Court of Military Review, the predecessor court to the Air Force Court of Criminal Appeals, opined:

> In *United States v. De Los Santos*, 3 M.J. 829 (A.F.C.M.R. 1977), and more recently, in *United States v. Kent*, 9 M.J. 836 (A.F.C.M.R. 1980), we examined the conditions requiring sentence comparison in determining sentence appropriateness. Our decision in *Kent* details the stepped process in ascertaining the applicability of the exception and the consideration required by an appropriate reviewing authority. Initially, a direct correlation

---

[21] The Military Justice Act of 1983 Advisory Commission, Vol. I, Pt. 2 (Dec. 1984).

[22] Or a small number of possible judges when a number ride circuit.

[23] Theoretically, sentencing will be by members unless the judge grants the accused's request for trial by judge alone. Sentencing by the judge is thus not a "right" in the usual sense.

[24] 27 C.M.R. 176, 178–81 (C.M.A. 1959). The trial judge also instructed the members that they could consider local conditions and the impact of inadequate sentences on the civilian community. The court held this instruction was harmless error. Comparative sentences may be part of a defense response to the post-trial recommendation, *see generally* Section 24-62.00; United States v. Mann, 22 M.J. 279 (C.M.A. 1986).

[25] The court reasoned that the appellate courts would not know what other cases the court members might have relied upon; that individualized sentences should be based on the seriousness of this offense, the character of this accused, and the objectives of sentencing; and that such an instruction would require the court to become involved in collateral issues. How the members learn of a co-accused's sentence may be important:

> Accordingly, we hold that reference before a panel to a specific sentence limitation agreed to by a convening authority in a coactor's case, absent a comprehensive limited instruction, improperly invades the panel's sentence deliberations and is prejudicial error. However, failure to object or to request a curative instruction waives the issue on appeal, absent plain error.

United States v. Schnitzer, 41 M.J. 603, 606 (A. Ct. Crim. App. 1995).

[26] *See generally* Section 25-50.00.

(Rel.3—1/07 Pub.62410)

between the offenses and offenders and the presence of highly disparate sentences must be established. Once these conditions are met, comparison of the relative culpability of the individuals and all other sentencing considerations present in the other record of trial is required to determine whether there are good and cogent reasons for the disparity in punishment. If there are no good and cogent reasons for the disparity, the resolution of sentence appropriateness in the case undergoing review, requires consideration of the lesser sentence in the companion case. *United States v. Kent, above.* However, even where all of these criteria are met and considered, neither punishment equalization nor sentence amelioration are required as a matter of law. Whether, and to what extent, any amelioration is granted is within the sound discretion of the approving or affirming authority as a part of the overall consideration of sentence appropriateness. On review, this exercise of discretion will be tested for abuse, and corrective action will result only from a finding that an abuse occurred.[27]

Sentencing must be individualized, and apparent disparity is thus not conclusive.[28]

Defense counsel have sought on occasion to raise the issue of sentence disparity solely on the basis of the court-martial promulgating orders from other related trials. In *United States v. Ballard*[29] the court upheld the lower court's refusal to admit such orders:

> From the mere fact of court-martial promulgating orders or similar documents, it is simply not possible to assess the multitude of aggravating and mitigating sentencing factors considered in the cases they represent. Further, appellant's approach cuts both ways. If the defense has a right to introduce sentences from other cases, how could the prosecutor be denied the same right?

[27] United States v. Coldiron, 9 M.J. 900, 902–03 (A.F.C.M.R. 1980), *pet. denied,* 10 M.J. 249 (C.M.A. 1981) (footnotes omitted). *See also* United States v. Wacha, 55 M.J. 266 (C.A.A.F. 2001) (reviewing responsibility of the Courts of Criminal Appeals); United States v. Durant, 55 M.J. 258 (2001) (disparate sentences were not unlawful given differences in sentencing evidence); United States v. Jones, 39 M.J. 315 (C.M.A. 1994) (sentence appropriateness generally left to the Court of Criminal Appeals; decision to leave accused's sentence unchanged following disapproval of conviction of 18 year absence without leave was not an abuse of discretion); United States v. Schnitzer, 41 M.J. 603, 605 (A. Crim. App. 1995) (dictum); United States v. Thorn, 36 M.J. 955, 959–60 (A.F.C.M.R. 1993).

[28] *See, e.g.,* United States v. Snelling, 14 M.J. 267, 268 (C.M.A. 1982) ("sentence appropriateness should be judged by individualized consideration") (citing United States v. Mamaluy, 27 C.M.R. 176, 180–81 (C.M.A. 1959): "However proper it may be for . . . the Courts of Military Review to consider sentence comparison as an *aspect* of sentence appropriateness, it is only one of many aspects of that consideration." *Snelling,* 14 M.J. at 268); United States v. Snodgrass, 37 M.J. 844, 849 (A.F.C.M.R. 1993) ("Sentence comparison, however, does not normally furnish grounds for post-trial relief . . ."); United States v. Coldiron, 9 M.J. 900 (A.F.C.M.R. 1980), *pet. denied,* 10 M.J. 249 (C.M.A. 1981).

[29] 20 M.J. 282, 285 (C.M.A. 1985). *Cf.* United States v. Brock, 46 M.J. 11 (C.A.A.F. 1997).

(Rel.3—1/07   Pub.62410)

One of the functions of the Courts of Criminal Appeals is to rectify inappropriate sentence disparity among related accused when possible. The Court of Appeals for the Armed Forces has summarized the law thusly:

> [A]n appellant bears the burden of demonstrating that any cited cases are "closely related" to his or her case and that the sentences are "highly disparate." If the appellant meets that burden, or if the court raises the issue on its own motion, then the Government must show that there is a rational basis for the disparity. Our review of a decision from a Court of Criminal Appeals is limited to three questions of law: (1) whether the cases are "closely related" (*e.g.,* coactors involved in a common crime, servicemembers involved in a common or parallel scheme, or some other direct nexus between the servicemembers whose sentences are sought to be compared); (2) whether the cases resulted in "highly disparate" sentences; and (3) if the requested relief is not granted in a closely related case involving a highly disparate sentence, whether there is a rational basis for the differences between or among the cases.[30]

§ 23-20.00 CONSTITUTIONAL LIMITATIONS

§ 23-21.00 In General

Other than due process, the constitutional limitation most likely to be raised incident to sentencing will be the prohibition on cruel and unusual punishment.[31] In civilian life, the prohibition on double jeopardy can also be of significant importance, as ordinarily it would prohibit imposition on retrial of a sentence more severe than that adjudged at a first trial. Given the strict prohibition in the *Manual for Courts-Martial* on increasing a sentence[32] in such a case, the constitutional provision is of no importance in the armed forces.

---

[30] United States v. Lacy, 50 M.J. 286, 288 (C.A.A.F. 1999). *See also* United States v. Durant, 55 M.J. 258 (2001) (disparate sentences were not unlawful given differences in sentencing evidence); United States v. Sothen, 54 M.J. 294 (C.A.A.F. 2001) (court may examine military and civilian co-actors sentences in determining whether the sentences are "highly disparate"); United States v. Simoy, 50 M.J. 1 (C.A.A.F. 1999); United States v. Noble, 50 M.J. 293 (C.A.A.F. 1999) (court did not find disparate treatment of two mess sergeants accused of fraternization where appellant was court-martialed and the other was given an honorable discharge under early release program); United States v. Fee, 50 M.J. 290, 291 (C.A.A.F. 1999) ("there was a proper basis for differentiating" sentences received by co-actors, thus the sentences were not disparate).

[31] With the exception of cases dealing with the constitutional propriety of requiring imprisonment in lieu of fines for indigents, the Supreme Court has implicitly rejected any equal protection claim based on "normal" sentencing disparity. Presumably, sentencing disparity caused by membership in any suspect classification would invalidate the sentence. Non-adversarial sentencing will not normally involve the right to confrontation. *E.g.*, United States v. Silverman, 976 F.2d 1502 (6th Cir. 1992) (en banc) (confrontation clause does not apply under federal sentencing guidelines); United States v. Wise, 976 F.2d 393 (8th Cir. 1992) (en banc) (same).

[32] R.C.M. 810(d)(1).

(Rel.3—1/07 Pub.62410)

§ 23-22.00   Cruel and Unusual Punishment[33]

The Eighth Amendment of the United States Constitution states: "Excessive bail shall not be required, nor excessive fines imposed, nor cruel and unusual punishments inflicted." Article 55 of the Uniform Code provides:

> Punishment by flogging, or by branding, marking, or tattooing on the body, or any other cruel or unusual punishment, may not be adjudged by a court-martial or inflicted upon any person subject to this chapter. The use of irons, single or double, except for the purpose of safe custody, is prohibited.[34]

At minimum, the Eighth Amendment bars "inhumane methods of punishment. . . . Indeed, during debate in the First Congress . . . one Congressman objected to adoption of the Eighth Amendment precisely because 'villains often deserve whipping, and perhaps having their ears cut off.' "[35] The Supreme Court has explained:

> The prohibitions of the Eighth Amendment are not limited, however to those practices condemned by the common law in 1789. . . . The prohibition . . . also recognizes the "evolving standards of decency that mark the progress of a maturing society." . . . In discerning those "evolving standards," we have looked to objective evidence of how our society views a particular punishment today. . . . The clearest and most reliable objective evidence of contemporary values is the legislation enacted by the country's legislatures.[36]

Insofar as sentencing is concerned, the Eighth Amendment's impact could be divided into the types of punishments prohibited and the degree to which the Amendment limits the quantum of a punishment. Because contemporary[37] military law permits only a few types of punishments,[38] the nature of which are clearly lawful, the Eighth Amendment is primarily important only to the extent that it might theoretically limit sentencing severity.[39]

---

[33] The material in this section is taken largely from Fredric Lederer, *Fundamental Criminal Procedure* § 230 (1999) (desktop published).

[34] In United States v. Valead, 32 M.J. 122, 127 (C.M.A. 1991), Judge Everett, concurring in the result noted that a violation of the constitutional provision also violates article 55. *See also* United States v. Wappler, 9 C.M.R. 23 (C.M.A. 1953).

[35] Rumell v. Estelle, 445 U.S. 263, 287 (1980) (footnote omitted). *See also* Weems v. United States, 217 U.S. 349, 358 (1910) (declaring unconstitutional the Philippine punishment "cadena temporal").

[36] Penry v. Lynaugh, 492 U.S. 302, 330-31 (1989) (citations omitted).

[37] Pre-twentieth century military history is filled with examples of barbaric punishments, such as branding, that would likely violate the Eighth Amendment.

[38] *See* Section 23-31.00.

[39] *See* United States v. Miller, 30 M.J. 703, 705–06 (C.G.C.M.R. 1990) (rejecting defense assertion that a bad-conduct discharge was cruel and unusual when given to a member of the Coast Guard for peacetime unauthorized absence or desertion).

(Rel.3—1/07 Pub.62410)

With the exception of capital cases,[40] which the Supreme Court expressly distinguished because of the penalty concerned,[41] until its 1983 decision in *Rummel v. Estelle*,[42] the Court had made it clear that it would almost never invoke the Eighth Amendment to hold a sentence unconstitutionally dispropor- tionate.[43] Although *Rummel* was interpreted by some as authorizing review of some sentences because of its language that "successful challenges to the proportionality of particular sentences [should be] exceedingly rare,"[44] the Court clearly modified that language. In *Hutto v. Davis*,[45] the Court appended to the quoted *Rummel* language the following footnote:

> We noted in *Rummel* that there could be situations in which the proportion- ality principles would come into play, such as "if a legislature made overtime parking a felony punishment by life imprisonment."[46]

Arguably, the Court changed the emphasis of the original footnote. That change, plus the strength of the Court's per curiam reversal in *Hutto v. Davis*,[47] indicated to most commentators that the Court would not interfere with sentences on the basis of excessive length in any but the most preposterous cases. This conclusion was proven erroneous in *Solem v. Helm*,[48] when a majority of the Court declared that a life sentence without the possibility for parole constituted cruel and unusual punishment when imposed as the result of a seventh nonviolent felony. Although the Court's decision could be limited to its facts, the language of the decision is far broader, stating: "In sum, we hold as a matter of principle that a criminal sentence must be proportionate to the crime for which the defendant has been convicted."[49]

---

[40] The Eighth Amendment has been used to declare the death penalty invalid in a number of cases. Roper v. Simmons, 543 U.S. 551 (2005)(juvenile offenders under the age of 18 cannot be executed); Atkins v. Virginia, 536 U.S. 304 (2002)(those sufficiently retarded cannot be executed); Edmund v. Florida, 458 U.S. 782, 787, 801 (1982) (holding the death sentence invalid in a felony murder case "for one who neither took life, attempted to take life, nor intended to take life"); Coker v. Georgia, 433 U.S. 584 (1977) (plurality held the death penalty unconstitutional for rape). *See also* Ford v. Wainwright, 477 U.S. 399 (1986) (execution of the insane was cruel and unusual punishment forbidden by the Eighth Amendment).

[41] Rummel v. Estelle, 445 U.S. 263, 271 (1980) (citing, among other cases, Furman v. Georgia, 408 U.S. 238, 306 (1972)).

[42] 445 U.S. 263, 271 (1980).

[43] Rummel v. Estelle (holding a sentence to life imprisonment following three minor theft con- victions constitutional under a Texas recidivist statute).

[44] 445 U.S. at 272.

[45] 454 U.S. 370 (1982) (holding constitutional a Virginia sentence of forty years' imprisonment for possession of approximately nine ounces of marijuana).

[46] 454 U.S. at 374 n.3 (citing 445 U.S. 263, 274 n.11).

[47] 454 U.S. at 374 n.3

[48] 463 U.S. 277 (1983).

[49] 463 U.S. at 290.

The Court supplied the following guidance for reviewing sentences:

> In sum, a court's proportionality analysis under the Eighth Amendment should be guided by objective criteria, including (i) the gravity of the offense and the harshness of the penalty; (ii) the sentences imposed on other criminals in the same jurisdiction; and (iii) the sentences imposed for commission of the same crime in other jurisdictions.[50]

Notwithstanding *Solem*, the Court held in 1984 that a state death penalty case need not be compared to all other capital cases in the same state for the sentence to stand,[51] and in 1991 in *Harmelin v. Michigan*[52] the Court upheld a mandatory life sentence for possession of 672 grams of cocaine. In *Harmelin*, although they differed on the test to be applied (with only four dissenting justices adhering fully to *Solem*) seven justices recognized the possibility that some sentences could be so disproportionately severe in quantum as to be cruel and unusual. Justice Scalia, joined by Chief Justice Rehnquist, opined, however, that disproportionately severe sentences could not violate the constitution in non-capital cases. In 2003, in *Ewing v. California,*[53] the Court sustained a sentence of twenty-five years to life for theft of about $1,200 in merchandise pursuant to California's "three strikes law."

It is apparent from the Court's zig-zag in the area that the extent to which the Eighth Amendment limits sentence magnitude in any but the most extreme cases must be considered uncertain. Even if the prohibition on cruel and unusual punishment both requires proportionality *and* applies to the armed forces, it would doubtless be true that the unique nature of military life would in some cases result in a different application of the prohibition in the armed forces than in civilian life. In *United States v. Curtis,*[54] the Court of Military Appeals mandated a limited proportionality review for death penalty cases holding that the Courts of Military Review should consider Supreme Court cases reviewing state capital cases to determine whether the death sentence before them is "*generally proportional* to those imposed by other jurisdictions in similar circumstances."[55]

---

[50] 463 U.S. at 292.

[51] Pulley v. Harris, 465 U.S. 37 (1984).

[52] 501 U.S. 957 (1991).

[53] 538 U.S. 11 (2003).

[54] 33 M.J. 101, 109 (C.M.A. 1991).

[55] 33 M.J. at 109 (C.M.A. 1991) (emphasis in original); *but see* United States v. Murphy, 36 M.J. 8, 9 (C.M.A. April, 1992) (summary disposition) (Crawford, J., dissenting, stating that the proportionality requirement is not required by the Constitution, Code, or *Manual*). *See also* United States v. Loving, 34 M.J. 956, 969 (A.C.M.R. 1992). The Navy-Marine Court of Military Review subsequently addressed the proper scope of proportionality review in United States v. Curtis, 38 M.J. 530, 541–43 (N.M.C.M.R. 1993), *rev'd on other grounds*, 46 M.J. 129 (C.A.A.F. 1997).

(Rel.3—1/07 Pub.62410)

§ 23-30.00 PERMISSIBLE SANCTIONS

§ 23-31.00 In General

The types of sanctions that a court-martial sentence can lawfully include, as well as their permissible magnitudes, are limited by the Uniform Code of Military Justice, the *Manual for Courts-Martial*, and the jurisdictional limitation of the applicable forum. A special court-martial cannot, for example, dismiss an officer, and the death sentence can only be adjudged by a general court-martial. Unlike many civilian jurisdictions that permit "creative sentencing," the armed forces are limited to the sanctions specified in the *Manual*.[56] Rule for Courts-Martial 1003(b) authorizes only the following punishments:[57]

Death

Punitive separation from the armed forces

Confinement

Hard labor without confinement

Restriction to specified limits

Reduction in pay grade[58]

Fine Forfeiture of pay and allowances

Reprimand

With the exceptions, Congress has generally delegated to the President to prescribe the types and quantum of sentences that can be adjudged.[59]

In the case of a retrial, Article 63 of the Uniform Code and Rule for Court-Martial 810(d)(1) provide that normally the maximum sentence that may be adjudged will be the lawful sentence actually adjudged at the prior trial for the same offense as ultimately approved by the convening authority.[60] Because some types of punishments may be converted to other types,[61] sentencing upon retrial

---

[56] Except that in cases involving the law of war, "a general court-martial may adjudge any punishment not prohibited by the law of war." R.C.M. 1003(b)(12).

[57] The 1995 Change to the *Manual for Courts-Martial* amended Rules 1003, 1104, 1107, 1113, 1301, 1305, and Appendix 11 to eliminate confinement on bread and water or diminished rations as a court-martial punishment.

[58] The punishment of loss of numbers, lineal position, or seniority, originally available only in cases involving Navy, Marine Corps, and Coast Guard officers no longer exists.

[59] *See* United States v. Bivins, 49 M.J. 328, 329 (C.A.A.F. 1998); United States v. Turner, 30 M.J. 1276 (N.M.C.M.R. 1990) (congressional delegation of power does not violate the Constitution).

[60] *See generally* § 23-52.30, *below. See also* R.C.M. 810(d)(1) as amended by the 1995 Change to the *Manual* (sets forth the maximum sentence on a rehearing when new charges are added to comply with earlier agreement).

[61] *See generally* § 24-74.00, *below.*

(Rel.3—1/07 Pub.62410)

is not necessarily limited to the *type* of punishment previously adjudged. In *United States v. Turner,*[62] for example, the court held that when the accused previously received an approved punitive discharge but no confinement, on retrial the judge should have instructed the members that they could have adjudged confinement instead of a discharge.

§ 23-32.00   Specific Sanctions

§ 23-32.10   The Death Penalty[63]

The death penalty in the armed forces is mandatory for spying and available for offenses such as premeditated murder. Only a unanimous general court-martial with not less than 12 members[64] can adjudge death, and then only if the convening authority has referred the case as "capital."[65]

The last soldier executed under the Uniform Code of Military Justice was PFC John Bennett, hanged in 1961 for rape and attempted murder.[66] The decisions of the Supreme Court in the early 1970s, holding virtually all state capital punishment laws unconstitutional,[67] cast doubt on the constitutionality of the military death penalty.[68] Following the 1982–1983 contradictory decisions of the Courts of Military Review,[69] the Court of Military Appeals held the military death penalty provisions unconstitutional in *United States v. Matthews.*[70] Rather

---

[62] 34 M.J. 1123 (A.F.C.M.R. 1992), *aff'd,* 39 M.J. 259 (C.A.A.F. 1994).

[63] The second, third, fourth, and seventh paragraphs of this subsection are taken in substantially verbatim form from Gaydos, *A Prosecutorial Guide to Sentencing,* 114 Mil. L. Rev. 1, 78–80 (1986). For a review of the details of the military death penalty and its comparison with elements of the civilian adjudicative process at that time, *see* United States v. Curtis, 44 M.J. 106, 166–67 (C.A.A.F. 1996), *rev'd on other grounds,* 46 M.J. 129 (C.A.A.F. 1997).

[64] National Defense Authorization Act for Fiscal Year 2002, Pub. L. No. 107-107 (Dec. 28, 2001) added Article 25a to require "not less 12" for capital case unless members are not reasonably available" for certain reasons.

[65] Absent such a referral, the death penalty cannot be adjudged, normally leaving life imprisonment as the maximum possible sentence. R.C.M. 201(f)(1)(A)(iii).

[66] English, *The Constitutionality of the Court-Martial Death Sentence,* 21 A.F. L. Rev. 552 (1979).

[67] *See, e.g.,* Jurek v. Texas, 428 U.S. 262 (1976); Proffitt v. Florida, 428 U.S. 242 (1976); Gregg v. Georgia, 428 U.S. 153 (1976); Furman v. Georgia, 408 U.S. 238 (1972).

[68] *See generally,* Pfau & Milhizer, *The Military Death Penalty and the Constitution: There Is Life After Furman,* 97 Mil. L. Rev. 35 (1982); Pavlick, *The Constitutionality of the U.C.M.J. Death Penalty Provisions,* 97 Mil. L. Rev. 81 (1982).

[69] The military death penalty provisions were upheld in United States v. Matthews, 13 M.J. 501 (A.C.M.R. 1982), *rev'd,* 16 M.J. 354 (C.M.A. 1983); United States v. Rojas, 15 M.J. 902 (N.M.C.M.R. 1983); United States v. Hutchinson, 15 M.J. 1056 (N.M.C.M.R. 1983). The military death penalty was held to be unconstitutional in United States v. Gay, 16 M.J. 586 (A.F.C.M.R. 1983).

[70] 16 M.J. 354 (C.M.A. 1983).

(Rel.3—1/07 Pub.62410)

than seeking an amendment to the Uniform Code, the President responded by promulgating new capital punishment procedures effective 25 January 1984,[71] provisions which were incorporated into the Rules for Courts-Martial.[72]

The capital punishment procedures contained in Rule for Courts-Martial 1004 are designed to ensure that a death penalty is adjudged only after an individualized evaluation of the accused's case, and only after specific aggravating factors are found to have been present. The *Manual* now contains an exclusive list of aggravating circumstances, at least one of which must be unanimously found applicable before the death penalty may be adjudged.[73] Before arraignment, the trial counsel must give the defense written notice of those aggravating circumstances that the prosecution intends to prove.[74] After the evidence supporting the case has been introduced, the military judge must instruct the court members on such aggravating circumstances as may be in issue, and must instruct the members to consider all of the defense evidence in extenuation and mitigation.[75]

Before a death penalty may be adjudged, the court members must unanimously find beyond a reasonable doubt that one or more of the aggravating circumstances existed,[76] and they must also unanimously find that any mitigating circumstances are substantially outweighed by the aggravating circumstances.[77] When the members announce their sentences, they also announce which aggravating circumstances were found by unanimous vote.[78]

The method of execution depends upon applicable service regulations.[79] At present, lethal injection is prescribed.

---

[71] Exec. Order No. 1246049, Fed. Reg. 3169 (1984).

[72] R.C.M. 1004.

[73] *See* Section 23-46.00.

[74] R.C.M. 1004(b)(1).

[75] R.C.M. 1004(b)(6).

[76] R.C.M. 1004(b)(7). Air Force Instruction 51-201, Law, Administration of Military Justice ¶ 4.5.2 (26 November 2003) provides:

In a case referred as capital, the pretrial advice must specify the aggravating circumstances relied upon and provide the convening authority with conclusions as to whether capital referral is warranted based on the analysis as set forth in R.C.M. 1004(a)(4).

[77] R.C.M. 1004(b)(4)(B). Zant v. Stephens, 462 U.S. 862 (1983) (sentence based in part on invalid aggravating circumstances could stand so long as there was one valid remaining aggravating circumstance that would establish death eligibility).

[78] R.C.M. 1004(b)(8). *See generally* Hart v. Loving, 47 M.J. 438 (C.A.A.F. 1998) (reviewing capital case requirements).

[79] R.C.M. 1113(d)(1)(A).

(Rel.3—1/07 Pub.62410)

The constitutionality of the military death sentence continues to be a controversial topic.[80] One author claims it to be unconstitutional because:

> First, the Eighth Amendment prohibits imposition of the death penalty in that no meaningful distinction exists between premeditated murder. . .and unpremeditated murder. Second, the military sentencing procedures violate the Eighth Amendment because no provision exists to ensure adequate reflection of community standards in a court-member's consideration of the death penalty. Third, the lack of guidelines to the convening authority and inadequate pretrial advice render the military scheme arbitrary and capricious and hence violative of the Fifth and Eighth Amendments. Fourth, the large potential variation in size of military court panels in capital cases violates the Fifth Amendment. Fifth, the allocation of one peremptory challenge per side and the selection procedures of court members in a death penalty case violate the Fifth and Eighth Amendments because no provision is made to ensure fact-finding panels which will generate confidence that the death penalty will be imposed in a reasoned way and because decisions reflecting the conscience of the community are not guaranteed.[81]

The Army Court of Military Review, en banc, sustained a death penalty against attacks on Rule 1004 in 1990.[82] Holding that "aggravating factors" are not elements of the offense and thus need not be legislated by Congress, the Court of Military Appeals finally upheld the facial constitutionality of the military death penalty in 1991 in *United States v. Curtis*.[83] In 1996, the Court directly decided and sustained the constitutionality of the military death penalty.[84]

§ 23-32.20   Separation from the Armed Forces

§ 23-32.21   In General

Just as a civilian employer may terminate employees, the armed forces may discharge personnel for a wide variety of reasons. Such terminations are

---

[80] *Compare* Intoccia, *Constitutionality of the Death Penalty Under the Uniform Code of Military Justice,* 32 A.F. L. Rev. 395 (1990) *with* Spradling & Murphy, *Capital Punishment, the Constitution, and the Uniform Code of Military Justice,* 32 A.F. L. Rev. 415 (1990).

[81] Intoccia, *above* note 80, at 395–96.

[82] United States v. Murphy, 30 M.J. 1040, 1054–59 (A.C.M.R. 1990) (en banc), *rev'd on other grunds,* 50 M.J. 4 (C.A.A.F. 1998).

[83] 32 M.J. 252, 260 (C.M.A. 1991) (President has a special role and powers in setting court-martial maximum sentence). In *Curtis,* the court also rejected a defense challenge to a death penalty imposed by less than 12 court-members. 32 M.J. 267–69 (C.M.A. 1991). Chief Judge Sullivan, concurring, noted his "personal view" that "in peacetime, a servicemember in a capital case should be tried by a 12-member court-martial." 32 M.J. 271 (C.M.A. 1991). The most recent development in military death penalty litigation is the defense argument that "death penalty-qualified appellate counsel" (meeting the 1989 ABA House of Delegates guidelines for such counsel) are required. *See also* United States v. Loving, 41 M.J. 213, 300 (C.M.A. 1994) (refused to require compliance with ABA guidelines), *aff'd,* 517 U.S. 748 (1996).

[84] Loving v. United States, 517 U.S. 748 (1996).

(Rel.3—1/07   Pub.62410)

accomplished by administrative discharges.[85] However, inasmuch as the armed forces traditionally constituted a separate society within the larger civilian polity, courts-martial have long had the ability in proper cases to separate offenders as a punishment. Unlike administrative discharges, which cannot be adjudged by courts-martial,[86] in serious cases offenders can be "exiled" from the armed forces[87] by their forcible return to civilian life.[88]

"There are only three types of punitive separation authorized as a punishment at courts-martial: dismissal,[89] dishonorable discharge,[90] and bad-conduct discharge.[91] Such discharges are treated within the service as extremely serious punishments.

Both a dishonorable and a bad-conduct discharge adjudged by a general court-martial automatically preclude receipt of veteran's benefits, based on the terms of service from which the accused is discharged. . .but the effect on a veteran's benefits of a bad-conduct discharge adjudged by a special court-martial must be determined on a case-by-case basis.[92]

§ 23-32.22   Dismissal

A dismissal is the only type of punitive separation that can be imposed on a commissioned officer, a commissioned warrant officer, or a cadet.[93] Only a general court-martial may adjudge a dismissal,[94] but it may award a dismissal for any Code violation.[95] Should this option be carried to extremes and a dismissal be imposed for a trivial offense, it would appear subject to attack on cruel and unusual punishment grounds.[96]

---

[85] *See* Section 3-22.00. "Administrative" discharge does not necessarily connote a "bad" discharge. Honorable discharges awarded to personnel who properly complete their agreed-upon service adequately are also administrative in nature.

[86] R.C.M. 1003(b). *See also* United States v. Phipps, 30 C.M.R. 14 (C.M.A. 1960).

[87] The now abandoned ceremony of "drumming" an offender out of the service is representative of both the stigma that was connected with such a separation and the acceptance of the philosophy of rejection and exile.

[88] It is by no means clear whether the social stigma that long accompanied such a punitive separation still exists in civilian society.

[89] R.C.M. 1003(b)(10)(A).

[90] R.C.M. 1003(b)(10)(B).

[91] R.C.M. 1003(b)(10)(C).

[92] Waller v. Swift, 30 M.J. 139, 144 (C.M.A. 1990) (citing 38 U.S.C. § 3103). Accuracy in any judicial instructions that address these collateral consequences is clearly necessary. *See* United States v. Goodwin, 30 M.J. 989, 991 (A.C.M.R. 1990); United States v. Harris, 26 M.J. 729, 734 (A.C.M.R. 1988). *See also* § 23-53.60.

[93] R.C.M. 1003(b)(10)(A).

[94] U.C.M.J. art. 19; U.C.M.J. art. 20.

[95] R.C.M. 1003(b)(10)(A).

[96] *See* Section 23-22.00. Of course, given the current state of the law, there is little certainty that mere excessiveness would be sufficient for relief.

(Rel.3—1/07   Pub.62410)

§ 23-32.23　Dishonorable Discharge

Noncommissioned warrant officers and enlisted personnel may be separated by dishonorable discharge[97] if convicted of an offense carrying a dishonorable discharge as part of the maximum punishment[98] and if tried by general court-martial.[99] Dishonorable discharges are reserved customarily for only the most serious offenses.

§ 23-32.24　Bad-Conduct Discharge

Only enlisted members may receive a bad-conduct discharge.[100] A bad-conduct discharge may be imposed for offenses authorizing a punitive discharge, if the accused is convicted at a general court-martial or at a special court-martial empowered to adjudge a bad-conduct discharge.[101]

§ 23-33.00　Deprivation of Liberty

§ 23-33.10　In General[102]

There are only four types of deprivation of liberty that may be imposed by a court-martial:[103] confinement;[104] hard labor without confinement;[105] confinement on bread and water or diminished rations;[106] and restriction to specified limits.[107]

---

[97] R.C.M. 1003(b)(10)(B). United States v. Stockman, 43 M.J. 856 (N.M. Crim. App. 1996) (court converted dismissal of warrant officer to dishonorable discharge).

[98] The maximum punishment authorized for each offense is found in MCM, 2005, part IV.

[99] U.C.M.J. art. 19; U.C.M.J. art. 20.

[100] R.C.M. 1003(b)(10)(C).

[101] Procedural prerequisites that must be met before a special court-martial may adjudge a bad-conduct discharge are outlined in U.C.M.J. art. 19 and R.C.M. 201 (f)(2)(B).

[102] Gaydos, *above* note 63, at 81.

[103] R.C.M. 1003(b). A court-martial may not impose correctional custody, extra duty, or extra training as punishment. *See, e.g.,* United States v. Miller, 17 M.J. 817 (A.C.M.R. 1984).

[104] R.C.M. 1003(b)(7). R.C.M. 1003(d) contains provisions for enhanced punishment when the accused has multiple convictions within specific periods of time. The FY 1998 Authorization Act would changed Article 56a to permit "confinement for life without eligibility for parole." This may not preclude clemency, and the members may be told of this option.

[105] R.C.M. 1003(b)(6).

[106] R.C.M. 1003(b)(9); MCM (2002 ed.).

[107] R.C.M. 1003(b)(5).

§ 23-33.20   Confinement

§ 23-33.21   In General

Traditionally, a sentence to confinement was a sentence to "confinement at hard labor." Although the *1984 Manual* eliminated the phrase "at hard labor" from this form of punishment, "confinement" may properly include hard labor.[108]

A commissioned officer may be confined only by a general court-martial.[109]

Depending upon the branch of the armed forces and the applicable regulations, an approved sentence to confinement for an enlisted member automatically reduces the offender to the lowest pay grade.[110]

A court-martial may sentence an accused to confinement but may not specify the place of confinement.[111] Although offenders, particularly serious offenders, may be placed in a civilian federal prison, ordinarily military prisoners will serve confinement sentences in either local military facilities or in the Disciplinary Barracks ("DB") at Fort Leavenworth, Kansas.[112] The length of sentence necessary to send a prisoner to the "DB" or a civilian federal prison varies and is usually determined by applicable regulation.[113]

Military prisoners remain subject to the Uniform Code of Military Justice while serving their sentences, even if they have been otherwise discharged from the armed forces.[114]

Although the Armed Forces do not have consecutive or concurrent sentences in the usual sense, a court-martial yields a unitary single sentence, when the accused is in civilian (or foreign nation) custody and the Armed Forces have only been given temporary custody for purposes of trial, the convening authority may postpone any sentence to confinement until after the accused has been permanently released to the Armed Forces.[115]

---

[108] R.C.M. 1003(b)(7) Discussion.

[109] R.C.M. 1003(c)(2)(A)(ii). United States v. Carmichael, 27 M.J. 757 (A.F.C.M.R. 1988) (when confinement has not been adjudged, it may not be substituted for nonpayment of imposed fines).

[110] U.C.M.J. art. 58a(1). This result is defended on the grounds that enlisted personnel holding pay grades greater then E-1, particularly noncommissioned officers and petty officers, ought not to hold that rank and grade if convicted of an offense sufficiently serious enough to merit a sentence to confinement. Unfortunately, automatic reduction permits a form of "blackmail" in which judges and court members are loathe to adjudge confinement of senior individuals for fear of the enormous loss of status and pay that would accompany even one day's worth of confinement.

[111] R.C.M. 1003(b)(8).

[112] The Navy tends not to use the "DB." Instead, its serious offenders are handled by the federal Bureau of Prisons.

[113] *See, e.g.*, Army Reg. No. 633-30 Military Sentences to Confinement (28 February 1989).

[114] U.C.M.J. art. 2(a)(7).

[115] The National Defense Authorization Act for Fiscal Year 1993, Pub. L. No. 102-484 § 1059(a) (October 23, 1992).

(Rel.3—1/07   Pub.62410)

§ 23-33.22 Life Without Parole Eligibility

A sentence of life without parole is now an available sentence for homicide offenses occurring after November 17, 1997, in which a sentence of confinement for life may be adjudged.[116] Although the new Article 56a of the Uniform Code of Military Justice does not explicitly require an instruction to the court members as some states do,[117] the Military Judges' Benchbook, the uniform source of judicial form instructions, includes appropriate instructions. The 2002 Benchbook[118] instructs members considering such a sentence to not rely "upon possible mitigating action by the convening authority or any higher authority," making it clear that such action is possible. It also notes that such a sentence does not "preclude clemency." and does not "preclude clemency."[119] Precedent suggests that when the prosecution argues that the accused presents a risk of future dangerousness, upon request the accused charged with a capital crime is entitled to an instruction on the ineligibility for parole when "life imprisonment" is an option.[120]

§ 23-33.30 Hard Labor Without Confinement

Up to three months of hard labor without confinement may be imposed on enlisted soldiers.[121] The accused's commanding officer designates the "hard labor," which is performed in addition to the soldier's regular duties.[122]

Hard labor without confinement is often disfavored and may be disapproved by a convening authority because it customarily requires supervision of the offender's "hard labor," usually by a noncommissioned or petty officer. The need for supervision makes the punishment extraordinarily "labor-intensive" and is likely not to be "cost-effective."[123]

Depending upon the branch of the armed forces and the then-applicable regulations, an approved sentence to hard labor without confinement for an enlisted member automatically reduces the offender to the lowest pay grade.[124]

---

[116] The National Defense Authorization Act for Fiscal Year 1998, Pub. L. No. 105-85 § 581 (November 18, 1997) adding Article 56a.

[117] *See* Simmons v. South Carolina, 512 U.S. 154, 168 n.7 (1994).

[118] Dep't of Army Pam. 27-9, Military Judges' Benchbook 968, 970 (15 September 2002).

[119] Dep't of Army Pam. 27-9, Military Judges' Benchbook 63, 92 (15 September 2002).

[120] *See, e.g.,* Kelly v. South Carolina, 534 U.S. 246 (2002); Simmons v. South Carolina, 512 U.S. 154 (1994) (Per opinions of JJ. Blackmun and O'Connor, speaking for seven justices); Shafer v. South Carolina, 532 U.S. 36 121 S.Ct. 1263 (2001) (remanded to determine if evidence or argument raised issue of future dangerousness). *See also* § 23-44.56.

[121] R.C.M. 1003(b)(7).

[122] R.C.M. 1003(b)(7) Discussion; Gaydos, *above* note 63, at 80.

[123] *But see* Major Joseph B. Berger III, *Making Little Rocks Out of Big Rocks: Implementing Sentences to Hard Labor Without Confinement,* The Army Lawyer, December, 2004, at 1 (arguing for more extensive use of the sanction and proposing implementation guidance).

[124] U.C.M.J. art. 58a(1).

(Rel.3—1/07 Pub.62410)

§ 23-33.40 Confinement on Bread and Water

Prior to the 1995 Change to the *Manual for Courts-Martial*, enlisted sailors attached to, or embarked in, a vessel[125] could be sentenced to confinement on bread and water or confinement on diminished rations for up to three days.[126] The 1995 Change to the *Manual for Courts-Martial* amended Rules for Courts-Martial 1003, 1104, 1107, 1113, 1301, 1305, and Appendix 11 to eliminate confinement on bread and water or diminished rations as a court-martial punishment.

§ 23-33.50 Restriction

When an individual is "restricted," he or she must remain within the geographical limits specified.[127] An accused may be sentenced to restriction for up to two months.[128] When a court-martial adjudges restriction, the court should specify the limits of the restriction.[129]

§ 23-34.00 Financial Sanctions

§ 23-34.10 Deprivations of Pay

The only form of deprivation of pay that may be imposed as a court-martial punishment is forfeiture of pay and allowances.[130] As it is no longer expressly authorized, detention of pay — a temporary withholding of pay — is no longer a proper court-martial sentence.

A forfeiture of pay and allowances deprives an accused of pay and allowances as they accrue.[131] It cannot be applied retroactively. If the court imposes partial forfeitures, the forfeitures apply only to basic pay,[132] and they must be adjudged as an exact amount of dollars to be forfeited each month for a specified number

---

[125] A servicemember is not "attached to or embarked in a vessel" when that ship is in port for a long-term overhaul and the servicemember is berthed in shore barracks. United States v. Edwards, 46 M.J. 41 (C.A.A.F. 1997); United States v. Lorance, 35 M.J. 382 (C.M.A. 1992); United States v. Yatchak, 35 M.J. 379, 381 (C.M.A. 1992).

[126] R.C.M. 1003(b)(9) MCM (1994 ed.).

[127] Restriction is often used as a pretrial control mechanism. Pretrial restriction is not, however, a punishment.

[128] R.C.M. 1003(b)(5).

[129] R.C.M. 1003(b)(5) Discussion. *See also* United States v. Massey, 17 M.J. 683 (A.C.M.R. 1983). *Cf.* United States v. High, 39 M.J. 82 (C.M.A. 1994).

[130] R.C.M. 1003(b)(2). Historically loss of *retirement pay* due to punitive discharge has not been viewed as punishment. United States v. Reed, 54 M.J. 37, 45 (C.A.A.F. 2000).

[131] R.C.M. 1003(b)(2) Discussion.

[132] R.C.M. 1003(b)(2); United States v. Humphrey, 14 M.J. 661 (A.C.M.R. 1982); United States v. Mahone, 14 M.J. 521 (A.F.C.M.R. 1982).

(Rel.3—1/07 Pub.62410)

of months.[133] Total forfeitures may apply to basic pay and to all allowances: "Allowances shall be subject to forfeiture only when the sentence includes forfeiture of all pay and allowances."[134]

Until April 1996,[135] it was possible for military prisoners serving even lengthy sentences to receive pay, so long as the prisoner had not been sentenced to total forfeitures and had not as yet been discharged. After a newspaper "expose" Congress amended the Uniform Code, creating a new Article 58(b).[136] Article 58b(a)(1) now provides for automatic forfeitures of all pay and allowances in a court-martial when an accused receives a sentence which includes confinement for more than six months or death, or confinement for six months or less and a dishonorable or bad-conduct discharge or dismissal.[137] In order to protect family members from total loss of income, Congress also provided, in Article 586(b), however, that:

> In any case involving an accused who has dependents, the convening authority or other person acting under. . .[article 60] may waive any or all of the forfeitures of pay and allowances required by subsection (a) for a period not to exceed six months. Any amount of pay or allowances that, except for the waiver under this subsection, would be forfeited shall be paid, as the convening authority or other person taking actions directs, to the dependents of the accused.

As phrased, the Article makes this entirely discretionary with the convening authority,[138] does not appear to require a formal application by the accused or family members, and would appear to permit an application by family members against the will of the accused.

Whether a staff judge advocate's discretionary advice to the convening authority regarding an Article 58b "deferment" request by the accused requires

---

[133] R.C.M. 1003(b)(2). If the adjudged sentence does not include the phrase "per month," the amount announced is the total amount to be forfeited. United States v. Henderson, 21 M.J. 853 (A.C.M.R. 1986) ("Forfeiture of $413 pay for three months" resulted in a one-time forfeiture of $413.00); United States v. Davis, SPCM 20417 (A.C.M.R. 23 Apr. 1984); United States v. Walker, 9 M.J. 892 (A.F.C.M.R. 1980). *Cf.* United States v. Datema, SPCM 21367 (A.C.M.R. 27 Sept. 1985) (omission of "per month" not fatal where record clearly demonstrated that forfeitures were to be applied on a monthly basis); United States v. Crandall, SPCM 20537 (A.C.M.R. 10 July 1984) (omission of word "pay" inconsequential).

[134] R.C.M. 1003(b)(2).

[135] New provisions do not apply unless some offenses occurred after this date. United States v. Beasley, 51 M.J. 103 (C.A.A.F. 1998).

[136] National Defense Authorization Act for Fiscal Year 1996, P.L. No. 104-06 § 1122(a)(1) (February 10, 1996).

[137] United States v. Pedrazoli, 45 M.J. 567, 569 (A.F. Crim. App. 1997), *remanded*, 48 M.J. 473 (C.A.A.F. 1998).

[138] United States v. Clemente, 46 M.J. 715, 720–21 (A.F. Crim. App. 1997), *aff'd*, 50 M.J. 36 (C.A.A.F. 1999).

(Rel.3—1/07 Pub.62410)

service on the accused currently seems unlikely; however, the Court of Appeals for the Armed Forces appears divided on the issue.[139]

As of April 1, 1996,[140] the effective date of the forfeitures portion of a sentence became the earlier of 14 days after sentence is adjudged or the convening authority's action.[141]

As a matter of policy, an accused who is not serving confinement and is not dismissed from the service cannot be deprived of more than two-thirds pay for any month unless specifically requested by the accused.[142]

It appeared that retired personnel could not be sentenced to forfeitures.[143] Change 7 to the *Manual for Courts-Martial*, however, amended Rule for Courts-Martial 1003(b)(2) to expressly provide that retired pay is subject to forfeiture.

A servicemember sentenced to confinement whose service obligation expires prior to the end of that confinement can find himself or herself totally deprived of all pay and allowances purely as an administrative consequence of that termination of service.[144] Resumption of pay and allowances requires administrative action outside the jurisdiction of courts-martial.

Forfeiture of pay issues have become increasingly complicated over the years, and are now problematical for the parties, counsel, and judge.[145] As Judge Effron has opined:

> The interaction between adjudged and mandatory forfeitures involves technical and complicated relationships between statutory provisions, made all the more difficult by the tension between the convening authority's broad discretion over the adjudged forfeitures and restricted discretion over mandatory forfeitures. The Executive Branch should consider the desirability of providing the services with uniform guidance, either in the Manual

---

[139] United States v. Key, 57 M.J. 246 (C.A.A.F. 2002).

[140] United States v. Beasley, 51 M.J. 103 (C.A.A.F. 1998).

[141] FY 1996 Department of Defense Authorization Act, P.L. 104-06 § 1121(a)(1) (February 10, 1996) (amending Article 57). *See also* United States v. Clemente, 46 M.J. 715 (A.F. Crim. App. 1997), *aff'd*, 50 M.J. 36 (C.A.A.F. 1999); United States v. Pedrazoli, 45 M.J. 567, 569 (A.F. Crim. App. 1997) (*ex post facto* clause not violated), *remanded*, 48 M.J. 473 (C.A.A.F. 1999).

[142] R.C.M. 1107(d)(2) Discussion. In United States v. Warner, 25 M.J. 64 (C.M.A. 1987), this language was held mandatory.

[143] *Cf.* United States v. Allen, 33 M.J. 209, 216 (C.M.A. 1991).

[144] *See, e.g.,* United States v. Albert, 30 M.J. 331 (C.M.A. 1990); United States v. Bedania, 12 M.J. 373 (C.M.A. 1982).

[145] This is especially true when administrative loss of pay eligibility is included. This is not a "forfeiture" but few accused understand or care about the technical legal distinction when plea bargaining for continued financial support of families.

(Rel.3—1/07 Pub.62410)

or through appropriate regulations, that would address differing scenarios.[146]

§ 23-34.20   Fines

As amended in 2002, Rule for Courts-Martial 1003(b)(3) provides:

> Any court-martial may adjudge a fine in lieu of or in addition to forfeitures. Special and summary courts-martial may not adjudge any fine or combination of fine and forfeitures in excess of the total amount of forfeitures that may be adjudged in that case. In order to enforce collection, a fine may be accompanied by a provision in the sentence that, in the event the fine is not paid, the person fined shall, in addition to any period of confinement adjudged, be further confined until a fixed period considered an equivalent punishment to the fine has expired. The total period of confinement so adjudged shall not exceed the jurisdictional limitations of the court-martial.

In a civilian case, a "conviction" includes any disposition following an initial judicial determination or assumption of guilt, such as when guilt has been established by guilty plea, trial, or plea of nolo contendere, regardless of the subsequent disposition, sentencing procedure, or final judgment. However, a "civilian conviction" does not include a diversion from the judicial process without a finding or admission of guilt; expunged convictions; juvenile adjudications; minor traffic violations; foreign convictions; tribal court convictions; or convictions reversed, vacated, invalidated or pardoned because of errors of law or because of subsequently discovered evidence exonerating the accused.[147]

Rule for Courts-Martial 1003(b)(3) permits the combination of a fine and forfeitures in a single summary or special court-martial so long as the combined total does not exceed the jurisdictional maximum punishment of the court.[148]

Unlike a forfeiture, a fine is due immediately upon execution regardless of the accused's ability or right to receive pay.[149] "A fine normally should not be

---

[146] United States v. Emminizer, 56 M.J. 441, 445 (C.A.A.F. 2002). *See also* United States v. LaJaunie, 60 M.J. 280 (C.A.A.F. 2004)(accused complained of convening authority's pre-*Emminizer* action in approving a waiver of automatic forfeitures for the benefit of the accused's family but without modifying the adjudged forfeitures).

[147] Exec. Order No. 13262 (April 11, 2002). In a letter to the Joint Service Committee on Military Justice dated July 27, 1998, the National Institute of Military Justice opined that this definition admitted prior "convictions" "not admissible in any other court or for any purpose."

[148] United States v. Tualla, 52 M.J. 228 (C.A.A.F. 2000) (relying on United States v. Harris, 19 M.J. 331 (C.M.A. 1985). The degree to which Article 58b, U.C.M.J., may affect this is unclear. *See* 52 M.J. at 231–232. This may be case specific. *See* United States v. Hood, 53 M.J. 214 (C.A.A.F. 2000).

[149] The Discussion to R.C.M. 1003(b)(3) states "A fine is in the nature of a judgment and, when ordered executed, makes the accused immediately liable to the United States for the entire amount of money specified in the sentence."

(Rel.3—1/07 Pub.62410)

adjudged against a member of the armed forces unless the accused was unjustly enriched as a result of the offense of which convicted."[150]

Although there is little debate over the right of courts to adjudge fines in appropriate cases, there has been great controversy over the ability of courts to enforce those fines via confinement when the fine is not paid on account of indigency.[151] Rule for Courts-Martial 1113(d)(3) provides in this regard:

> Confinement may not be executed for failure to pay a fine if the accused demonstrates that the accused has made good faith efforts to pay but cannot because of indigency, unless the authority considering imposition of confinement determines, after giving the accused notice and opportunity to be heard, that there is no other punishment adequate to meet the Government's interest in appropriate punishment.

In *United States v. Tuggle*,[152] a hearing was held by a military magistrate to determine whether the failure of the accused to pay a fine was wilful. Having held that the accused was not indigent and had not made a good-faith effort to pay, the convening authority subsequently ordered executed the military judge's alternative punishments of one year's confinement and a further reduction in grade. On appeal, the court held that the factual determinations of the magistrate and convening authority should be treated as those of a military judge for purposes of appellate review.[153] It also held that although confinement could be used to enforce a fine, and transformed into punishment when the fine was not paid, the Rules for Courts-Martial did not permit a reduction in grade as a consequence of nonpayment.[154] The Court of Appeals for the Armed Forces evinced no difficulty in *United States v. Palmer*[155] in sustaining the legality of conditional confinement for an accused who received appropriate due process and whom a hearing officer determined had not made a good faith effort to pay.[156]

The Army and Air Force Courts of Military Review differed on the legality of a conditional sentence to confinement adjudged as an alternative to an unpaid

---

[150] Discussion to R.C.M. 1003(b)(3). The Discussion continues: "Ordinarily, a fine, rather than a forfeiture, is the proper monetary penalty to be adjudged against a civilian subject to military law." As is apparent from its text, the Discussion assumes that fines may be adjudged in other circumstances than unjust enrichment; the constraint is not mandatory. *See also* United States v. Williams, 18 M.J. 186, 189 n. 6 (C.M.A. 1984).

[151] *See generally* Bearden v. Georgia, 461 U.S. 660 (1983); Wood v. Georgia, 450 U.S. 261 (1981); Tate v. Short, 401 U.S. 395 (1971); Williams v. Illinois, 399 U.S. 235 (1970).

[152] 31 M.J. 778, 780 (A.C.M.R. 1990), *rev'd in part*, 34 M.J. 89 (C.M.A. 1992).

[153] 31 M.J. at 780 (A.C.M.R. 1990).

[154] 31 M.J. at 781 (A.C.M.R. 1990).

[155] 59 M.J. 362, 365 (C.A.A.F. 2004).

[156] 59 M.J. 362, 365 (C.A.A.F. 2004).

(Rel.3—1/07 Pub.62410)

fine if the sentence does not otherwise contain confinement.[157]

The constitutionality of confinement in lieu of a fine for an indigent remains unsettled. In *Wood v. Georgia*, Justice White, dissenting, opined:

> As I see it, if an indigent cannot pay a fine, even in installments, the Equal Protection Clause does not bar the State from specifying other punishment, even a jail term, in lieu of the fine. To comply with the Equal Protection Clause, however, the State must make clear that the specified jail term in such circumstances is essentially a substitute for the fine and serves the same purpose of enforcing the particular statute that the defendant violated.[158]

If Justice White was correct, Rule 1113(d)(3) may be constitutionally deficient as it leaves the question of fine equivalency to an authority other than Congress or even the President.

In *United States v. Rascoe*,[159] the Navy-Marine Court of Military Review engaged in a lengthy review of the fine and confinement problem. Although recognizing that confinement might be lawful as an alternative to a fine, as distinguished from a tool designed to enforce a fine, it held that the Uniform Code, *Manual for Courts-Martial*, and precedent supplied inadequate guidance for an authority's decision to transform a fine into punishment. Accordingly, it adopted the civilian criteria in use in the civilian federal courts[160] and also construed Rule 1113 to refer to the officer exercising general court-martial jurisdiction over the accused at the time that action is taken under the Rule.[161] Although the court determined that it was proper for such an officer to act, given the limitations of the Rule, it had to strain greatly to reach that result.

Normally, a fine should be reserved for cases where the accused has been unjustly enriched, but this is not a mandatory limitation.[162] A fine adjudged at a general court-martial can be any amount[163] so long as the punishment is not cruel and unusual.[164]

---

[157] *Compare* United States v. Blizzard, 34 M.J. 763, 765 (A.C.M.R. 1992); United States v. Bevins, 30 M.J. 1149 (A.C.M.R. 1990) (procedure held lawful) *with* United States v. Arnold, 27 M.J. 857 (A.F.C.M.R. 1989) *and* United States v. Carmichael, 27 M.J. 757 (A.F.C.M.R. 1988) (unlawful).

[158] 450 U.S. at 285–86.

[159] 31 M.J. 544 (N.M.C.M.R. 1990).

[160] 31 M.J. at 563 (N.M.C.M.R. 1990) (citing 18 U.S.C. §§ 3572, 3614).

[161] 31 M.J. at 568.

[162] R.C.M. 1003(b)(3) Discussion; United States v. Parini, 12 M.J. 679 (A.C.M.R. 1981); United States v. Finley, 6 M.J. 727 (A.C.M.R. 1978); United States v. Combs, 15 M.J. 743 (A.F.C.M.R. 1983); United States v. Ford, 12 M.J. 636 (N.M.C.M.R. 1981).

[163] United States v. Williams, 18 M.J. 186 (C.M.A. 1984).

[164] United States v. Williams, 18 M.J. 186 (C.M.A. 1984); United States v. Parini, 12 M.J. 679, 684 (A.C.M.R. 1981) (A fine imposed by a general court-martial can be any amount unless it is so excessive and unusual, and so disproportionate to the offense committed, as to shock public

(Rel.3—1/07 Pub.62410)

In *United States v. Tuggle*,[165] the Court of Military Appeals stated that it "will not attempt to impose a duty on family members to mortgage their homes to satisfy a fine adjudged upon a servicemember. The fine in this case is one to correct an unjust enrichment by a convicted servicemember and not to impose collateral hardship on a servicemember's family." The court held that the convening authority should have considered whether voluntary pay allotments would have been sufficient to pay the fine imposed before ordering contingent confinement executed. *Tuggle* implies that it is ordinarily improper to consider assets held by other family members in determining whether a convicted servicemember can pay a fine.

§ 23-35.00 Reduction in Grade

An officer cannot be reduced in grade by a court-martial.[166]

Reduction to the lowest or any intermediate enlisted grade is an authorized punishment for enlisted personnel[167] who are not retired.[168] "In the case of enlisted members above the fourth enlisted pay grade, summary courts-martial may not adjudge confinement, hard labor without confinement, or reduction except to the next pay grade."[169]

Article 58a(a) provides:

Unless otherwise provided in regulations to be prescribed by the Secretary concerned, a court-martial sentence of an enlisted member in a pay grade above E-1, as approved by the convening authority, that includes —

(1) a dishonorable or bad-conduct discharge;

(2) confinement; or

(3) hard labor without confinement;

---

sentiment and violate the judgment of reasonable people concerning what is right and proper under the circumstances). *See, e.g.,* United States v. Smith, 44 M.J. 720, 723 (Army Crim. App. 1996). In *Smith* the Court also held that in light of the statutory provision for parole a judge could not lawfully provide that in the event that the accused had not paid his $100,000.00 fine by the date upon which he was eligible for parole he would serve either until he paid the fine, or another 50 years' imprisonment.

[165] 34 M.J. 89, 92 (C.M.A. 1992).

[166] R.C.M. 1003(c)(2)(A)(i). During time of war an officer's sentence of dismissal may be commuted to reduction to any enlisted grade.

[167] R.C.M. 1003(b)(5).

[168] United States v. Allen, 33 M.J. 209, 216 (C.M.A. 1991).

[169] R.C.M. 1301(d)(2). Under U.C.M.J. art. 58a, *below,* approved confinement or hard labor without confinement would automatically reduce an enlisted member to the lowest enlisted grade unless service regulations provided otherwise.

(Rel.3—1/07 Pub.62410)

reduces that member to pay grade E-1, effective on the date of that approval.[170]

In an extraordinary break from past tradition in 2002, the Army availed itself of the Article 58a "escape clause" by providing by regulation that automatic reduction in grade will apply only to cases that include an approved sentence of dishonorable or bad conduct discharge, whether or not suspended or confinement in excess of 180 days or six months, depending upon how the sentence is adjudged.[171]

Such a reduction is considered "administrative" in nature. Article 58a often complicates the prosecution of senior noncommissioned or petty officers in light of the fact that even a day's confinement would reduce them to the lowest enlisted grade, a fact of enormous financial consequences alone. If an enlisted member is reduced in grade and does not receive a punitive discharge, when eligible for retirement the servicemember will retire only in the grade held the day prior to retirement.[172] Retired enlisted personnel are not affected by Article 58a,[173] and personnel who serve contingency confinement sentences because they have not paid fines may not be implicated because the confinement is in lieu of a different sanction.[174]

Loss of numbers (for promotion seniority), lineal position, or seniority, a punishment originally available only in cases involving Navy, Marine Corps, and Coast Guard officers no longer exists.[175]

---

[170] For naval regulations in this area *see* JAGINST 5800.7D ¶ 0152cd(2) (15 March 2004) (subject to the convening authority's discretion, automatic reduction when the sentence includes, whether or not suspended, a punitive discharge or confinement in excess of 90 days or three months).

[171] Army Reg. 27-10, Military Justice ¶ 5-298e. (16 November 2005). Professor Lederer notes that during his active duty tenure he argued for eliminating automatic reduction in grade not only because it was sometimes overly harsh but because it often led court members to choose not to confine senior noncommissioned officers, especially those nearing retirement.

[172] National Defense Authorization Act for fiscal year 1989 § 622.. Prior to October 1, 1988, an enlisted soldier would retire at the highest grade held even though reduced by court-martial. This amendment closes the gap created by the Tower Amendment, 10 U.S.C. § 614 (1982). Comptroller Decision B-225150 (May 4, 1987) to the contrary is now moot. It is arguable that the language in the Act could be interpreted to permit the individual to retire at the highest grade held prior to October 1, 1988.

[173] United States v. Allen, 33 M.J. 209, 216 (C.M.A. 1991).

[174] *Cf.* United States v. Tuggle, 34 M.J. 89 (C.M.A. 1992) (confinement held to satisfy fine; sentence altered to impose reduction to E-4).

[175] See the Analysis of R.C.M. 1003(b), MCM, 2005 at A21-72 (the punishment was eliminated in 1999).

§ 23-36.00 Reprimand

"Any court-martial may include a reprimand as part of the adjudged sentence.[176] The convening authority determines the content of the reprimand and . . .issues it in writing."[177]

§ 23-40.00 SENTENCING EVIDENCE

§ 23-41.00 In General

Sentencing in the armed forces follows the traditional approach; an individualized sentence is to be devised that fits the offender and the offense. With a very few exceptions, the Uniform Code and the *Manual for Courts-Martial* prescribe maximum sentences rather than fixed or minimum ones. As a result, perhaps the most critical sentencing need is for adequate information for the sentencing agency, judge or court-members:

> The premise has been that the sentencing authority should receive full information concerning the accused's life and characteristics in order to arrive at a sentence which will be appropriate in light of the purpose for which a sentence is imposed.[178]

According to the National Advisory Commission Task Force on Corrections, the information furnished the sentencing authority should include at least the following:

(1) complete description of the situation surrounding the criminal activity;

(2) the offender's educational background;

(3) offender's employment background;

(4) offender's social history;

(5) residence history of the offender;

(6) offender's medical history;

---

[176] R.C.M. 1003(a), (b)(1).

[177] Gaydos, *above* note 63, at 84; R.C.M. 1003(a), (b)(1).

[178] United States v. Mack, 9 M.J. 300, 316 (C.M.A. 1980) (Everett, C.J., in majority opinion). United States v. Hughes, 26 M.J. 119, 121 (C.M.A. 1988) ("a court-martial may not have all the information available to it for sentencing that would be possessed by a federal or state judge engaged in sentencing"); United States v. Neil, 25 M.J. 798, 801 (A.C.M.R. 1988) ("military practice remains much more restrictive than its civilian counterpart"). In United States v. Slovacek, 21 M.J. 538, 541 (A.F.C.M.R. 1985), *cert. denied*, 484 U.S. 855 (1987), the court noted that the general philosophy is that "the sentencing authority should be given as much relevant information as is available." On this basis, the court admitted a juvenile adjudication because it was the functional equivalent to the conviction and would have been considered under the sentencing law of the place of trial. *See also* United States v. Cook, 10 M.J. 138, 140 (C.M.A. 1981) ("a review of the total criminal background of a defendant has always been approved") (Everett, C.J., in majority opinion).

(Rel.3—1/07 Pub.62410)

(7) information about the environment to which the offender will return;

(8) information about any resources available to assist the offender; and

(9) a full description of the offender's criminal record.[179]

Unlike the usual civilian practice, in which a presentence report is supplied to the sentencing judge by an official agency,[180] military sentencing is dependent upon the information supplied by counsel as part of an adversarial sentencing process, information which may not, in any given case, fulfill the above criteria. The information potentially available for sentencing consideration includes evidence adduced in the case-in-chief, information obtained during any guilty-plea providency inquiry, government evidence in aggravation, and defense evidence in extenuation and mitigation. To this may be added whatever may be judicially noticed[181] and whatever proper general background information is known to the sentencing agency.[182]

Because of the mandate of Military Rule of Evidence 311, unlawfully obtained evidence that is suppressed on motion of defense counsel may not be used on sentencing.[183]

§ 23-42.00   Evidence Admitted During Trial on the Merits

All evidence admitted during trial on the merits[184] and reasonable inferences that can be drawn from that evidence[185] may be considered by the sentencing

---

[179] National Advisory Commission, Task Force on Corrections 184–85 (1973).

[180] See, e.g., Fed. R. Crim. P. 32.

[181] See, e.g., United States v. Anderson, 22 M.J. 885 (A.C.M.R. 1986) (proper for trial judge to take judicial notice that there exists a comprehensive program for the treatment of child molesters at the United States Disciplinary Barracks at Fort Leavenworth; however, judge exceeded scope of his discretion when he further recognized this program as a leader in the field, a matter subject to debate).

[182] In United States v. Williams, 35 M.J. 812, 819 (A.F.C.M.R. 1992) (The court held that Rule for Courts-Martial 1001 limited sentencing evidence to those categories set forth in Rule for Courts-Martial 1001 and necessarily excluded evidence of future dangerousness of the accused.), rev'd, 41 M.J. 134 (C.M.A. 1994).

[183] The civilian federal rule may be different. See United States v. Camacho, 779 F.2d 227 (5th Cir. 1985).

[184] R.C.M. 1001(f)(2).

[185] United States v. Stevens, 21 M.J. 649 (A.C.M.R. 1985). In Stevens, the accused, stationed in Panama, was convicted of larceny of one-half pound of TNT. The accused tried to detonate the explosive by rigging it to a roadside traffic sign and stretching a trip wire across the road. As rigged, the TNT was incapable of detonating. The court held that the trial counsel could argue, and the sentencing authority could consider, that serious injury might have occurred to a passerby if the TNT had exploded as the accused intended. This argument was "illustrative of the outer limits of reasonable inferences to be drawn from the facts" of the case. The court held that it was error for the sentencing authority to consider that "members of the American community in Panama might have assumed that the explosion was the work of terrorists" and "would have been terrified

(Rel.3—1/07   Pub.62410)

authority in arriving at an appropriate sentence. This rule applies to matters that are accepted into evidence for a limited purpose.[186] This prophylactic rule eliminates what otherwise might be an impossible burden on the military judge to issue extensive limiting instructions.[187]

§ 23-43.00 Evidence Resulting from a Guilty Plea

§ 23-43.10 In General

As in civilian life, no military accused can plead guilty unless the judge ascertains, via questioning of the accused, that the plea is "provident."[188] During such an inquiry, the military judge customarily solicits a significant amount of information concerning the offense. Should the plea be pursuant to a pretrial agreement, or plea bargain, the prosecution also will likely require the accused to supply information about the offense via a stipulation of fact.

The fact that the accused pled guilty does not act as a waiver of the right against self-incrimination for the sentencing phase of the trial.[189]

§ 23-43.20 Providency Inquiry

At least to the extent that information elicited from the accused during the providency inquiry[190] is made under oath,[191] that information may be considered on sentencing.[192] Abandoning its prior position that use of such information might "have a dampening effect" on the inquiry,[193] the court noted that the "accused who testifies during a providence inquiry is warned that he waives the privilege against self-incrimination" and thus "is on notice that his answers may

---

'for weeks and maybe for months' by the fear of a mad bomber." Such a conjecture went beyond the limits of reasonable inferences to be drawn from the evidence presented at trial. 21 M.J. at 652 (A.C.M.R. 1985).

[186] R.C.M. 1001(f)(2)(A).

[187] Gaydos, *Prosecutorial Guide to Court-Martial Sentencing*, 114 Mil. L. Rev. 1 (1986) (hereinafter Gaydos).

[188] Meaning voluntarily and intelligently made. In military law, the plea must also be factually accurate. *See generally* Chapter 19.

[189] Mitchell v. United States, 526 U.S. 314 (1999).

[190] *See generally* Chapter 19; R.C.M. 910.

[191] R.C.M. 910(e) requires that the accused be placed under oath during the providency inquiry. *See also* Mil. R. Evid. 410.

[192] United States v. Holt, 27 M.J. 57 (C.M.A. 1988). *See also* Mitchell v. United States, 526 U.S. 314, 324 (1999)(Under Federal Rule of Criminal Procedure 11, a statement made during the plea inquiry may be used at sentencing but the defendant does not waive the right against self-incrimination for sentencing); United States v. Figura, 44 M.J. 308, 310 (C.A.A.F. 1996) ("Absent a prohibition in the RCM 1000 series in the *Manual* . . . information elicited from the defendant under oath during the providency inquiry may be considered during sentencing.").

[193] United States v. Simpson, 17 C.M.R. 44, 46 (C.M.A. 1967).

(Rel.3—1/07 Pub.62410)

be used adversely to him." [194] The court added that "if the sworn testimony . . . is sufficiently reliable to support findings of guilt, it would seem reliable enough to be considered in connection with sentencing." [195] Although the court appears to have emphasized the fact that the accused's statements are under oath, its rationale for their admission on sentencing was that the statements constitute admissions under the hearsay rule. [196] As admissions need not be under oath, [197] it is by no means clear that the accused's remarks need be under oath to be admissible for sentencing. [198]

Procedurally, as the court noted in *United States v. Figura*, [199] "There is no demonstrative right or wrong way to introduce evidence taken during a guilty plea . . . . The judge should permit the parties ultimately to choose a method of presentation." [200] In a trial by judge alone, it is sufficient that the judge heard the accused's statements made during the providency inquiry. [201] Trial counsel may use the information during argument without the need to have a transcript prepared of the inquiry. [202] Should trial be with members, the information may be provided "either by a properly authenticated transcript [203] or by the testimony of a court reporter or other persons [204] who heard what the accused said during the providence hearing." [205] Of course, a stipulation could also be used. [206]

---

[194] *Holt*, 27 M.J. at 59.

[195] 27 M.J. at 59.

[196] 27 M.J. at 60.

[197] *See* Mil. R. Evid. 801(d)(2).

[198] A conclusion that would be relevant only if the judge should forget to have the accused placed under oath. In such a circumstance, the defense might argue on appeal that the oath is critical for purposes of reliability, an uphill battle given the thousands of pleas accepted without oaths prior to the 1984 imposition of the oath requirement.

[199] 44 M.J. 308, 310 (C.A.A.F. 1996).

[200] 44 M.J. 308, 310 (C.A.A.F. 1996). Another possibility not adopted by the majority would be for the judge to summarize the evidence taken during providency. Judge Sullivan asserted: "judges — use your power under RCM 920 to give the jury a good, exhaustive, accurate, and fair view of the facts . . . ." 44 M.J. 308, 310 (C.A.A.F. 1996).

[201] It is unclear whether the trial judge in a bench trial may consider for sentencing the accused's providency admissions absent formal submission of the information by counsel during sentencing. If this information is so usable, the prosecution might be able to attack the accused's credibility based on that information alone.

[202] Mil. R. Evid. 801(d)(2).

[203] The accused's statement is an admission; the transcript containing the admission is a public record. Mil. R. Evid. 803(8). *Cf.* United States v. Irwin, 39 M.J. 1062, 1066 (A.C.M.R. 1994) (questioned playing tape of inquiry to court members), *aff'd*, 42 M.J. 479 (1995).

[204] Testimony by the trial counsel will generally not be a viable alternative. *See, e.g.,* Model Rules of Professional Conduct Rules 1.7; 3.7 (2004).

[205] *Holt*, 27 M.J. at 61.

[206] R.C.M. 811(c). If the accused offers to plead guilty pursuant to a pretrial agreement, the govern-

(Rel.3—1/07　Pub.62410)

There are limits, however, to the use of information gained during the providence inquiry. In *United States v. Holt*,[207] the court sustained admission of that data for sentencing on authority of Rule for Courts-Martial 1001(b)(4), which provides that "[t]he trial counsel may present evidence as to any aggravating circumstances directly relating to or resulting from the offenses of which the accused has been found guilty." Should the accused's providence inquiry statement include material "far afield" from the instant offense, it will not be evidence "directly relating to or resulting from the offenses of which the accused has been found guilty."[208] The court voiced concern over uncharged misconduct evidence and opined that even if such evidence might be admissible against the accused in a contested case, it did not seem germane to a providence inquiry and thus "upon proper defense objection, should not be received or, if it has been received, should be stricken on motion."[209]

A military judge may not as part of the providence inquiry ask whether the accused would be willing to cooperate with the government,[210] as such a request may impinge on the accused's right to remain silent.

§ 23-43.30 Stipulation of Fact[211]

As a precondition to entering into a pretrial agreement, the government may require that the accused offer into evidence a stipulation of fact.[212] This stipulation normally includes a factual summary of the accused's conduct establishing guilt, but may also properly include aggravating circumstances relating to the accused's offenses.[213]

The government can require the accused to stipulate to other aggravating facts, including the contents of relevant personnel records. Ordinarily, the mere agreement by the parties that certain facts are true does not make them admissible; the rules of evidence apply fully.[214] The parties may, however, make explicitly

---

ment could require as a condition to the pretrial agreement that the accused consent to stipulate to the admissibility of his or her future testimony as it is given at the providence inquiry. R.C.M. 705(c)(2)(A).

[207] 27 M.J. 57 C.M.A. 1988).

[208] *Holt*, 27 M.J. at 60.

[209] 27 M.J. at 60.

[210] United States v. Miller, 23 M.J. 553 (C.G.C.M.R. 1986).

[211] Gaydos, *above* note 187, at 16.

[212] R.C.M. 705(2)(c)(A). *See* ch. 12.

[213] United States v. Silva, 21 M.J. 336 (C.M.A. 1986); United States v. Martin, 20 M.J. 227 (C.M.A. 1985); United States v. Marsh, 19 M.J. 657 (A.C.M.R. 1984); United States v. Sharper, 17 M.J. 803 (A.C.M.R. 1984).

[214] R.C.M. 811(e).

admissible by stipulation evidence which would be ordinarily inadmissible.[215] Such a stipulation may be subject to challenge, however, in the event of prosecutorial overreaching.[216]

Although a stipulation of fact may not be contradicted so long as it remains valid,[217] the parties may supplement the stipulation with other evidence.[218]

§ 23-44.00   Prosecutorial Sentencing Evidence

§ 23-44.10   In General

The key to understanding presentencing evidence lies in appreciating the fact that the military relies on an adversarial presentation of evidence to the sentencing authority within specific constraints. "Although some judges[219] and commentators[220] analogize military sentencing evidence to the federal presentencing report,[221] such generalizations are not generally useful."[222]

Rule for Courts-Martial 1001(a)(1) provides "[a]fter findings of guilty have been announced, the prosecution and defense may present matter pursuant to this rule to aid the court-martial in determining an appropriate sentence." The prosecution presents its evidence first, ordinarily using the following sequence:[223]

---

[215] United States v. Glazier, 26 M.J. 268, 270 (C.M.A. 1988). "The stipulation should be unequivocal that counsel and the accused agree not only to the truth of the matters stipulated but that such matters are admissible in evidence against the accused." 26 M.J. 268, 270 (C.M.A. 1988).

[216] 26 M.J. 268, 270 (C.M.A. 1988).

[217] R.C.M. 811(e).

[218] See United States v. Terplep, 57 M.J. 344, 348 (C.A.A.F. 2002).

[219] See, e.g., United States v. Holt, 22 M.J. 553, 556 (A.C.M.R. 1986), aff'd, 27 M.J. 57 (C.M.A. 198); United States v. Hanes, 21 M.J. 647 (A.C.M.R. 1985); United States v. Harrod, 20 M.J. 777 (A.C.M.R. 1985). In Harrod, the Army Court of Military Review outlined its liberal sentencing philosophy as follows:

> [I]t is clear that in promulgating the . . . 1984 Manual . . . the President intended to
> greatly expand the types of information that could be presented to a court-martial
> during the adversarial presentencing proceeding . . . . [W]e believe that military judges
> and court members are intended to have access to substantially the same amount of
> aggravating evidence during the presentencing procedure as is available to federal
> district judges in presentencing reports.

Harrod, 20 M.J. at 779–80.

[220] See, e.g., R.C.M. 1001 Analysis (the presentencing provisions are intended to permit "the presentation of much of the same information to the court-martial as would be contained in a presentence report, but it does so within the protections of an adversarial proceeding"); United States v. Clemente, 50 M.J. 36 (C.A.A.F. 1999) ("The RCM 1001 rules permit a number of alternative means for introducing evidence both by the prosecution and the defense.").

[221] See generally Fed. R. Crim. P. 32(c). [Cf. United States v. Hughes, 26 M.J. 119, 121 (C.M.A. 1988); United States v. Neil, 25 M.J. 798, 800–01 (A.C.M.R. 1988)].

[222] Gaydos, above note 187, at 20.

[223] R.C.M. 1001(a)(1)(A).

(Rel.3—1/07 Pub.62410)

(i) service data relating to the accused taken from the charge sheet;

(ii) personal data relating to the accused and of the character of the accused's prior service as reflected in the personnel records of the accused;

(iii) evidence of prior convictions, military or civilian;

(iv) evidence of aggravation; and

(v) evidence of rehabilitative potential.[224]

This same sequence is used in either contested cases or guilty plea cases.[225] It is important to note that the prohibition on the admissibility of evidence does not prevent its admission under another rule if the evidence is "relevant and reliable."[226] Rule for Courts-Martial 1001 is exhaustive; the prosecution may not introduce evidence on sentencing that is not expressly permitted by the Rule.[227]

Except for the charge sheet, expressly referred to in Rule 1001, evidence offered under each of these categories must also be admissible under the Military Rules of Evidence.[228] "Despite some dicta in case law to the contrary,[229] the Military Rules of Evidence are *not* relaxed for the government"[230] in its initial sentencing case. Military Rule of Evidence 1101(c) provides that the rules of evidence may be relaxed pursuant to Rule for Courts-Martial 1001. In turn, Rule for Courts-Martial 1001(c)(3) provides that the "military judge may, with respect to matters in extenuation or mitigation or both, relax the rules of evidence."[231]

---

[224] R.C.M. 1001(a)(1)(A).

[225] R.C.M. 1001(a)(1) ("After findings of guilty have been announced . . ."). *See also* United States v. Vickers, 13 M.J. 403 (C.M.A. 1982) (interpreting the *1969 Manual for Courts-Martial*, the court held that "regardless of the plea, the prosecution after findings of guilty may present evidence which is directly related to the offense for which an accused is to be sentenced so that the circumstances surrounding that offense or its repercussions may be understood by the sentencing authority" 13 M.J. 406 (C.M.A. 1982) and suggested that the scope of admissible aggravation evidence is the same in both contested cases and guilty plea cases).

[226] United States v. Gogas, 58 M.J. 96 (C.A.A.F. 2003); United States v. Ariail, 48 M.J. 285, 287 (C.A.A.F. 1998). *See also* United States v. Prevatte, 40 M.J. 396, 397 n.* (C.M.A. 1994).

[227] *See* United States v. Clemente, 50 M.J. 36, 37 (C.A.A.F. 1999) ("[A]dmission of presentencing evidence is limited by R.C.M. 1001 rules and Military Rules of Evidence. . . .").

[228] Mil. R. Evid. 1101(a). Mil. R. Evid. 412 (rape-shield rule) applies, for example. *See, e.g.,* United States v. Fox, 24 M.J. 110 (C.M.A. 1987). *Cf.* § 23-45.21(b).

[229] *See, e.g.,* United States v. Martin, 20 M.J. 227 (C.M.A. 1985).

[230] Gaydos, *above* note 187, at 21 (emphasis in original). *But see* United States v. McDonald, 55 M.J. 173, 176 (C.A.A.F. 2001) (despite absence of express authority judge authorized use of telephone testimony for a government aggravation witness).

[231] In dicta in *United States v. Dimberio*, 52 M.J. 550, 560 n.5 (N.M. Crim. App. 1999), *aff'd on other grounds*, 56 M.J. 20 (C.A.A.F. 2001), the court opined, "The rules of evidence in sentencing are relaxed only with regard to the manner by which the evidence is presented to the sentencing authority. The evidence in question still must otherwise satisfy the applicable rules of admissibility." This statement appears too limiting given both the applicable procedural rule and customary practice.

Rule for Courts-Martial 1001(d) then provides that if the rules of evidence are relaxed for the defense during its case in extenuation or mitigation, the rules may be relaxed to the same degree during the prosecution case in *rebuttal.*[232]

Despite the use of an adversarial sentencing system, the Court of Appeals for the Armed Forces has held that the Sixth Amendment right of confrontation does not apply to the presentencing portion of a non-capital court-martial. The Court will apply, however, the due process clause, which requires "that the evidence introduced in sentencing meet minimum standards of reliability."[233] At the same time, the Air Force Court of Criminal Appeals has upheld the use of the doctrines of "opening the door" and curative admissibility rules apply during sentencing.[234]

§ 23-44.20　Data from the Charge Sheet

Pursuant to normal practice, not later than the beginning of the sentencing portion of trial, the trial counsel verifies the personal data on the charge sheet[235] with the defense counsel. Sentencing will customarily begin with the trial counsel providing the sentencing authority with the charge sheet data, "the pay and service of the accused and the duration and nature of any pretrial restraint."[236] Trial counsel will ordinarily read the charge sheet information out loud.[237] However, the judge, as a discretionary matter, may permit counsel to offer a summary sheet.[238] The defense counsel may object to data that is materially inaccurate or incomplete.[239] "Objections not asserted are waived."[240]

§ 23-44.30　Personnel Records

§ 23-44.31　In General

Rule 1001(a)(1)(A)(ii) permits the prosecution to offer "personal data relating to the accused and of the character of the accused's prior service as reflected

---

[232] 52 M.J. 550, 560 n.5 (N.M. Crim. App. 1999).

[233] United States v. McDonald, 55 M.J. 173, 177 (C.A.A.F. 2001)(testimony of absent aggravation witness, who had been present until deployed, via telephone was acceptable; lack of affirmative authorization of telephone testimony in lieu of deposition was not necessary).

[234] United States v. Stadler, 44 M.J. 566, 569 (A.F. Crim. App. 1996) ("Comment which is improper, standing alone, may become permissible when properly made in response to defense argument."), *aff'd on other grounds,* 47 M.J. 206 (C.A.A.F. 1997).

[235] DD Form 458; MCM, 2005, App. 4.

[236] R.C.M. 1001(b)(1). Although the Rule originally also included the accused's age, the charge sheet (DD Form 458, August 1984), contains no entries concerning the accused's age or date of birth, and "age" was deleted from the Rule in 1986. Analysis of R.C.M. 1001(b), MCM, 2005, A21-70.

[237] Dep't of Army Pam. 27-9, Military Judges' Benchbook 87 (15 September 2002).

[238] R.C.M. 1001(b)(1).

[239] R.C.M. 1001(b)(1).

[240] R.C.M. 1001(b)(1).

(Rel.3—1/07　Pub.62410)

in the personnel records of the accused." The origins of this provision can be found in the revision to the original *1969 Manual for Courts-Martial* which added ¶ 75d to supply additional sentencing information.[241]

Rule 1001(b)(2) specifies:

> Under regulations of the Secretary concerned, trial counsel may obtain and introduce from the personnel records of the accused evidence of the accused's marital status; number of dependents, if any; and character of prior service. Such evidence includes copies of reports reflecting the past military efficiency, conduct, performance, and history of the accused and evidence of any disciplinary actions including punishments under Article 15.

"Personnel records of the accused" includes all those records made or maintained in accordance with departmental regulations that reflect the past military efficiency, conduct, performance, and history of the accused. If the accused objects to a particular document as inaccurate or incomplete in a specified respect, or as containing matter that is not admissible under the Military Rules of Evidence, the matter shall be determined by the military judge. Objections not asserted are waived.

The Rule defines "Personnel records of the accused" as including "all those records made or maintained in accordance with departmental regulations." The services have implementing regulations that will normally determine what constitutes "Personnel records."[242] Admissibility thus is dependent upon the

---

[241] Optional matter presented when court-martial constituted with military judge. Under regulations of the Secretary concerned, the trial counsel may, prior to sentencing, obtain and present to the military judge any personnel records of the accused or copies or summaries thereof. Summaries of such records will be prepared and authenticated by the custodian thereof as provided in appendix 8g. Personnel records of the accused include all those records made or maintained in accordance with departmental regulations which reflect the past conduct and performance of the accused. If the accused objects to the data as being inaccurate or incomplete in a specified matter or material particular, or as containing certain specified objectionable matter, the military judge shall determine the matter. Objections not asserted will be regarded as waived. The accused may submit in rebuttal any matter which reflects on his past conduct and performance. In cases where members determine sentence, the military judge may admit for their consideration any information from these records which reflects the past conduct and performance of the accused.

MCM, 1969 (rev. ed.) ¶ 75d (substantially unchanged in MCM, 1969 (rev. ed.) ¶ 75b(2) (C5, 1 April 1982). *See also* White, *Mining the Gold in Personnel and Finance Records*, Trial Counsel Forum, Oct. 1982, at 2.

[242] Army Reg. No. 27-10 Military Justice ¶ 5-295 (16 November 2005), for example, provides in relevant part:

¶ 5-26. Personal data and character of prior service of the accused.

a. For purposes of R.C.M. 1001(b)(2) and (d), trial counsel may, in the trial counsel's discretion, present to the military judge (for use by the court-martial members or military judge sitting alone) copies of any personnel records that reflect the past conduct and performance of the accused, made or maintained according to departmental regulations. Examples of personnel records that may be presented include —

regulation that gives rise to the document or entry. **243** Should the regulation be unconstitutional or otherwise unlawful, for example, the record or entry will fall.

(1) DA Form 2, DA Form 2-2A and DA Form 2-1.

(2) Promotion, assignment, and qualification orders, if material.

(3) Award orders and other citations and commendations.

(4) Except for summarized records of proceedings under Article 15 (DA Form 2627-1); records of punishment under Article 15, from any file in which the record is properly maintained by regulation.

(5) Written reprimands or admonitions required by regulation to be maintained in the MPRJ or OMPF of the accused.

(6) Reductions for inefficiency or misconduct.

(7) Bars to reenlistment.

(8) Evidence of civilian convictions entered in official military files.

(9) Officer and enlisted evaluation reports.

(10) DA Form 3180-R (Personnel Screening and Evaluation Record).

(11) Records relating to Discipline and Adjustment Boards and other disciplinary records filed in corrections files in accordance with AR 190-47.

b. These personnel records include local nonjudicial punishment files, personnel records contained in the OMPF or located elsewhere, including but not limited to the CMIF and the correctional file, unless prohibited by law or other regulation. . . .Such records may not, however, include DA Form 2627-1 [(Summarized Record of Proceedings under Article 15, U.C.M.J.].

c. Original records may be presented in lieu of copies with permission to substitute copies in the record. (*See* MRE 901, for authentication of original copies.)

JAGINST 5800.7D ¶ 0141 (15 March 2004) now provides:

0133 Personal Data and Character of Prior Service of the Accused

If otherwise admissible, trial counsel are authorized to present, and summary court-martial officers are authorized to obtain and introduce into evidence, matters set out in R.C.M. 1001(b)(2), MCM. Records of nonjudicial punishment must relate to offenses committed prior to trial and during the current enlistment or period of service of the accused, provided such records shall not extend to offenses committed more than 2 years prior to the commission of any offense of which the accused stands convicted. In computing the 2-year period, periods of unauthorized absence as shown by the personnel records of the accused should be excluded.

See United States v. Oenning, 20 M.J. 935 (N.M.C.M.R. 1985). Under Navy regulations, an Article 15 for offenses committed more than two years prior to commission of any offense charged is not admissible. The court held in *Oenning* that an Article 15 more than two years old may be admitted to rebut the inference that the accused had good military character during that period of time.

243 *Cf.* United States v. Douglas, 57 M.J. 270, 273 (C.A.A.F. 2002) (stipulation attached to prior conviction was not admissible under R.C.M. 1001(b)(3) as prior conviction but as personnel under service regulation pursuant to R.C.M. 1001(b)(2)); United States v. Shears, 27 M.J. 509, 510 (A.C.M.R. 1988). But the Rules for Courts-Martial and the Military Rules of Evidence control admissibility rather than the administrative regulations. *See, e.g.,* United States v. Vasquez, 52 M.J. 597 (N.M. Crim. App. 1999) (request for discharge in lieu of court martial including an admission by the accused constitutes "personnel records" for sentencing purposes), *rev'd,* 54 M.J. 303 (C.A.A.F. 2001) (to encourage plea bargaining, the court prohibited the request from being

(Rel.3—1/07 Pub.62410)

Because the admissibility of documents is regulation dependent, it is easily possible to have a situation in which one type of document is admissible and a related type is not. In *United States v. Fontenot*,[244] for example, the court sustained admission of pretrial confinement records of disciplinary action against the accused,[245] maintained pursuant to regulation,[246] but disapproved the use of signed and unsworn statements of prison guards which were not.[247]

Because the Rule refers to records reflecting "*military* efficiency, conduct, performance, and history,"[248] it is unclear whether enlistment records ought to be admissible. They may well include evidence of prior misconduct that would bear on sentencing;[249] yet, should the accused's record before joining the armed forces be admissible?[250] Construing the Rule's predecessor provision, the Navy Court of Military Review held in 1978 that enlistment records did not relate to "past conduct and performance."[251] Notably, however, the Rule refers to "history" as well as to other factors. The Army Court of Military Review held that it was error for the trial judge to admit an accused's enlistment contract as a personnel record when that contract referred to civilian arrests. Reasoning that such arrests were not admissible, the court wrote, "'Bootstrapping' the impermissible information to a personnel record cannot alter this result: 'what the government cannot successfully introduce into evidence through the front door it cannot successfully introduce through the back door via an administrative record-keeping regulation.' "[252] This case seems to be implicitly overruled.[253]

The trial counsel *may* but need not present evidence from the accused's personnel records,[254] an option that, strangely enough, has given rise to one of the most significant questions concerning the use of personnel records on sentencing. If the prosecution fails to offer favorable data, the defense may offer it, but only at the risk of permitting expansive government rebuttal. Absent such

---

admitted as a personnel but did not prohibit the evidence to the underlying offenses to be admitted in aggravation).

[244] 29 M.J. 244 (C.M.A. 1989). *See also* United States v. Davis, 44 M.J. 13 (C.A.A.F. 1996) (held disciplinary records admissible under R.C.M. 1001(b)(3)).

[245] Department of Defense Form 508.

[246] *See* United States v. Perry, 20 M.J. 1026 (A.C.M.R. 1985).

[247] United States v. Fontenot, 29 M.J. 244, 248 (C.M.A. 1989).

[248] Emphasis added. It is unclear whether "military" modifies only "efficiency" or extends to "history" as well.

[249] *Cf.* United States v. Honeycutt, 6 M.J. 751, 753 (N.C.M.R. 1978).

[250] United States v. Martin, 5 M.J. 88, 889 (N.C.M.R. 1978).

[251] 5 M.J. 88, 889 (N.C.M.R. 1978).

[252] United States v. Delaney, 27 M.J. 501, 504 (A.C.M.R. 1988) (quoting from United States v. Brown, 11 M.J. 263, 266 (C.M.A. 1981)).

[253] United States v. Ariail, 48 M.J. 285 (C.A.A.F. 1998).

[254] United States v. Wingart, 27 M.J. 128, 131 (C.M.A. 1988).

a defense offer, the defense could rely on the prosecution's initial presentation and limit the government's ability to present damaging evidence.[255]

The debate began in 1983, when the Court of Military Appeals, in *United States v. Morgan*,[256] construed ¶ 75d of the *1969 Manual* and then applicable Army regulations to require application of a "rule of completeness" to the government's proffer of personal data.[257] Under *Morgan*, the defense could require the government to offer other, favorable, personal data. Viewed objectively, such a result is desirable and follows the approach taken in both the civilian and military Rule of Evidence 106:

> When a writing or recorded statement or part thereof is introduced by a party, an adverse party may require the introduction at that time of any other part or any other writing or recorded statement which ought in fairness to be considered contemporaneously with it.

Of course, there is always some risk that it may be unclear as to exactly what records "ought in fairness to be considered contemporaneously with" the government data. This is, nevertheless, something a judge can readily handle. Application of the *Morgan*/Rule 106 approach, however, apparently gave rise to unanticipated results, as counsel sought tactical advantage. Some prosecutors refrained from offering personnel data, both for fear that admission would carry with it material favorable to the defense and to compel the defense to offer it, opening the door to widespread prosecutorial rebuttal. In turn, the defense refrained from offering the evidence to avoid the rebuttal.[258] Clearly, the goal

---

[255] 27 M.J. 130–32 (C.M.A. 1988). In *Wingart*, the court noted that under Rule 1001(d) the trial counsel cannot rebut his or her own evidence. Accordingly, if the trial counsel presents evidence favorable to the accused, he or she is unable to contest it with non-Rule 1001(a)(1)(A) evidence. 27 M.J. 131 (C.M.A. 1988).

[256] 15 M.J. 128 (C.M.A. 1983).

> [W]e believe that a service member generally thinks of his 201 file as a single entity, which reflects his military record during his current enlistment. This being so, when personnel records are offered in evidence by the trial counsel pursuant to paragraph 75d, the rule of completeness should apply to all the documents contained in an accused's Military Personnel Records Jacket . . . Of course, if the shoe is on the other foot and defense counsel offers in evidence documents from an accused's Military Personnel Records Jacket for purposes of extenuation and mitigation, then the trial counsel may object if the defense has omitted portions thereof without which only an incomplete picture of the accused's conduct and behavior is provided.

15 M.J. 133–34 (C.M.A. 1983).

Judge Cook, concurring in the result in *Morgan*, indicated that the "production of the MPRJ *in toto*, if at all, is absurd." 15 M.J. at 137 (C.M.A. 1983).

> We are seeing frequent instances where it is reasonable to infer that an accused did not submit efficiency or performance report to the trial court for fear of "opening the door" to damaging rebuttal, much of it being other acts of misconduct. Our concern goes to the trial court passing sentence without the benefit of important information.

(Rel.3—1/07 Pub.62410)

of providing the judge or court members with accurate sentencing data was given short shrift.

A subsequent amendment to the *Manual* arguably mooted *Morgan*. [259] Conceding that in 1985, the court, [260] however, adhered via dictum to the *Morgan* rule on the basis of Military Rule of Evidence 106, writing that "[t]he significance of *United States v. Morgan* . . . is that it makes the entire personnel file 'a writing' in terms of the rule of completeness." [261]

The drafters of Rule for Courts-Martial 1001(b)(2) sought to moot the *Morgan* problem. [262] In its current form, [263] the Rule both makes it plain that the trial counsel need not introduce *all* of an accused's personnel records and that "[i]f the accused objects to a particular document as inaccurate or incomplete in a specified respect . . . the matter shall be determined by the military judge." Accordingly, the defense may still complain that the government's evidence is so inaccurate or incomplete that related material must be offered with it. However, the limitation to "a specific respect" suggests strongly that the defense's option is highly restrictive.

Given Rule 1001(b)(2), the defense counsel may still be placed in the position of having to give up favorable evidence or risk government rebuttal. Arguably,

---

Therefore, we implore military judges to apply the discretion vested in their position during sentence proceedings.

United States v. Smith, 16 M.J. 694, 706 (A.F.C.M.R. 1983).

[259] In relevant part, MCM, 1969 (rev. ed.), ¶ 75b(2) (C5, 1 April 1982) provided:

Personal data and character of prior service of the accused. Under regulations of the Secretary concerned, the trial counsel may obtain and introduce from the personnel records of the accused evidence of the marital status of the accused and the number of dependents, if any, of the accused, and evidence of the character of prior service of the accused.

The court in *Morgan* denominated this change as a "substantial revision." United States v. Morgan, 15 M.J. at 131 n.4., and the Army Court of Military Review held it dispositive. United States v. Abner, 17 M.J. 747, 748 (A.C.M.R. 1984); *contra*, United States v. Robbins, 16 M.J. 736, 739 (A.F.C.M.R. 1983).

[260] United States v. Salgado-Agosto, 20 M.J. 238 (C.M.A. 1985) (per curiam) (dealing with admission of a nonjudicial punishment record).

[261] Salgado-Agosoto, 20 M.J. at 239, n.2. *See also* United States v. Merrill, 25 M.J. 501, 502 (A.F.C.M.R. 1987). ("[W]hen a trial counsel introduces derogatory information from an accused's personnel record he must, if challenged by the defense, also introduce the favorable information which is included within the record").

[262] Analysis of Rule 1001(b), MCM, 2005, at A21-70. The first three sentences are unchanged from the 1981 revision of the *1969 Manual*. The fourth sentence of R.C.M. 1001(b)(2) was modified by substituting "a particular document" for "the information," a change intended to avoid the *Morgan* result.

[263] The Rule was also amended in 1986, by substituting "any records" for "all those records" to further implement the intent to do away with the *Morgan* decision. Analysis of Rule 1001, MCM, 2005 A21-70.

(Rel.3—1/07 Pub.62410)

this is an appropriate result, given the adversary system, although one must remain concerned about the scope of the permissible rebuttal. The Court of Military Appeals approved one alternative to the defense dilemma in *United States v. Wingart*, [264] holding that, when the trial judge exercises his or her power to consider evidence not offered by counsel, [265] the text of the rules compels the conclusion that the evidence is not subject to government rebuttal.

§ 23-44.32 Nonjudicial Punishment Records

Rule 1001(b)(2) expressly refers to "evidence of any disciplinary actions including punishments under Article 15." A properly-imposed [266] record of nonjudicial or mast [267] punishment under Article 15 of the Uniform Code of Military Justice [268] is thus admissible during the sentencing stage of the trial as a personnel record [269] if it is complete [270] and properly within the accused's personnel records. [271] As is always the case with personnel records, the critical issue will be whether the record has been imposed, filed, maintained, [272] and offered as evidence pursuant to applicable regulations. [273] So long as the record complies with the applicable regulation, it appears that no specific staleness rule applies. [274]

---

[264] 27 M.J. 128, 133 (C.M.A. 1988).

[265] 27 M.J. at 132 (C.M.A. 1988) (citing R.C.M. 801(c)).

[266] *See, e.g.*, United States v. Gilford, 16 M.J. 578 (A.C.M.R. 1983) (per curiam and pre-Rules for Courts-Martial). In *Gilford*, the issue was whether the officer imposing nonjudicial punishment had the authority to do so. The court held that the rear detachment commander at Fort Bragg had U.C.M.J. authority over a member of a battalion who had deployed to the Sinai, but who was AWOL at that time. The captain who commanded the detachment "assumed command of the organization and was the individual that higher authority looked to for the administration and discipline of the organization and those individuals who did not deploy with the parent battalion," even when no written attachment orders were cut.

[267] The term used in the Navy.

[268] *See generally* Section 8-20.00. Information on how to obtain Article 15 records and other documents from the Army's "restricted fiche" portion of personnel record can be found in the Army's *Trial Counsel Forum*, Sept. 1984, at 14.

[269] *Cf.* United States v. Woodworth, 24 M.J. 544 (A.C.M.R. 1987).

[270] *See, e.g.*, United States v. Hardy, 21 M.J. 198 (C.M.A. 1986); United States v. Negrone, 9 M.J. 171 (C.M.A. 1980) (rejecting waiver when form was incomplete).

[271] *See, e.g.*, United States v. Cohan, 43 C.M.R. 309 (C.M.A 1971) (construing the predecessor provision to R.C.M. 1001(b)(2)).

[272] *See, e.g.*, United States v. Yong, 17 M.J. 671 (A.C.M.R. 1983).

[273] 17 M.J. 671 (A.C.M.R. 1983). Army regulations, for example, prohibit use of summarized (less serious) records of nonjudicial punishment recorded on DA Form 2627-1. Army Reg. No. 27-10 Military Justice ¶ 5-25a(4) (24 June 1996).

[274] *Cf.* United States v. Sims, 28 M.J. 578, 583 (A.C.M.R. 1989) (dictum to effect that fact that record was over ten years old went only to weight).

(Rel.3—1/07 Pub.62410)

When offered, records of Article 15 punishment must also be authenticated under the Military Rules of Evidence.[275] Because admission of the imposition of Article 15 punishment must be made in the form of properly prepared, filed, and maintained *records*,[276] in the absence of a proper record, attempts to offer its content via oral testimony of a witness must fail.[277]

The history of military law over the past decade or so is replete with debate concerning whether — and when — records of nonjudicial punishment and summary courts-martial may be admitted against the accused at sentencing.[278] The root of the concern is simply that the accused does not have the right to counsel at either proceeding. Absent the accused being "attached to or embarked in a vessel," however, the accused may reject Article 15 punishment and demand trial by court-martial; also, the accused has an absolute right to reject trial by summary court-martial. Accordingly, military law has conditioned the use of records of Article 15 punishment and summary court-martial on adequate proof that the accused was given the right to consult with counsel prior to imposition of punishment or trial.[279] The court mandated that only "[t]hose hearings in which the accused was represented by counsel, or has executed a valid waiver of the assistance of counsel may be used."[280] Consultation with counsel was considered necessary for a valid waiver of the right to counsel.[281]

---

[275] 28 M.J. 578, 583 (A.C.M.R. 1989). In *Woodworth*, the court held the records inadmissible, including Article 15 records, because the lack of a proper attesting certificate signed by the appropriate custodian. Mil. R. Evid. 902(4a). 24 M.J. at 546.

For the Navy, the Court Memorandum, service record page 601-6R, is the appropriate personnel record . . . . Unlike the records of nonjudicial punishment used in the Army or the Marine Corps, no entry is required or even authorized in a page 601-6R to indicate whether or not a nonjudicial punishment has been appealed or the outcome of any appeal.

United States v. Yarbough, 30 M.J. 1292, 1295 (N.M.C.M.R. 1990) (en banc).

[277] *See, e.g.*, United States v. McGill, 15 M.J. 242 (C.M.A. 1983) (dictum); United States v. Yong, 17 M.J. 671, 673 (A.C.M.R. 1983) (pre-R.C.M. cases).

[278] *See* United States v. Kelly, 45 M.J. 259 (C.A.A.F. 1996); United States v. Mack, 9 M.J. 300 (C.M.A. 1980); United States v. Mathews, 6 M.J. 357 (C.M.A. 1979); United States v. Booker, 5 M.J. 238 (C.M.A. 1977), *vacated in part*, 5 M.J. 246 (C.M.A. 1978).

[279] 5 M.J. 238 (C.M.A. 1977). Under *Booker*, the individual must "be told of his right to confer with an independent counsel before he opts for disposition of the question." *Booker*, 5 M.J. at 243.

[280] *Booker*, 5 M.J. at 238 (footnotes omitted). Although *Booker* itself only applied to sentence enhancement via an "escalator" provision, it was soon applied to all sentencing use. United States v. Mathews, 6 M.J. 357, 358 (C.M.A. 1979). Subsequently, the court declared that mast or nonjudicial punishment imposed on a person "attached to or embarked in a vessel," who could thus not refuse punishment, could also be used at sentencing. *Mack*, 9 M.J. at 320. *See also* United States v. Lecolst, 4 M.J. 800, 801 (N.C.M.R. 1978); United States v. Penn, 4 M.J. 879 (N.C.M.R. 1978).

[281] *Booker*, 5 M.J. at 243. *See also* United States v. Kelly, 45 M.J. 259 (C.A.A.F. 1996) (rein-

(Rel.3—1/07 Pub.62410)

Given, however, that the armed forces have not always used adequate forms, and that personnel seem to incorrectly fill out even appropriate forms with more frequency than one might expect, the question of *proof* of the accused's notice of these rights has been difficult. In *United States v. Mack*, for example, [282] the accused's Article 15 form notified him of the availability of counsel and counsel's location, but lacked a box on the form for the accused to show that he had either consulted with counsel or waived consultation. Notwithstanding this, the court held that absent credible evidence to the contrary, this notice, coupled with the presumption of regularity, was sufficient to meet the counsel requirements; the record showed that the accused "was offered some opportunity to consult with counsel." [283] In 1984, in *United States v. Wheaton*, the court added:

> [I]f an accused is given written advice that he is entitled to consult counsel, then it can be presumed that counsel was made available to him. A subsidiary presumption is that, if the right to counsel was not exercised, the accused made an informed decision not to exercise the right. Thus, if an appellant is notified of his right to counsel, it can be presumed either that he consulted counsel or waived his right to counsel. If these presumptions are applicable to a record of conviction by summary court-martial, as we held [in *United States v.*] *Kuehl*, [284] we see no reason not to apply them to a record of nonjudicial punishment . . . .

> [I]n *Mack* we did not consider directly whether an accused must specifically indicate in writing his wishes as to the exercise of his statutory right to object to nonjudicial punishment.

> Although neither *Kuehl* nor *Mack* applies directly to the case at bar, we conclude that, under their reasoning, the military judge properly admitted the three prosecution exhibits in this case. The presumption of regularity — on which we relied in *Mack* — supports the inference that if nonjudicial punishment was imposed after the accused was advised of his right to trial by court-martial, he must have decided not to exercise that right. In sum, Wheaton's acknowledgment of his right, together with the absence of any indication of his exercise of that right, allows an inference that the right was waived. [285]

---

forced *Booker* even though in a distinguishable case the Supreme Court, in Nichols v. United States, 511 U.S. 738 (1994), that upheld admissibility of an uncounseled misdemeanor conviction not involving a prison term to enhance sentence).

[282] 9 M.J. 300, 322 (C.M.A. 1980).

[283] 9 M.J. 300, 323 (C.M.A. 1980). Judge Everett then set forth the procedure to be followed when the accused wishes to show that he was not offered the opportunity to consult counsel. 9 M.J. 300, 323 (C.M.A. 1980). Dissenting, Judge Fletcher claimed that *Mack* overruled United States v. Mathews, 6 M.J. 238 (C.M.A. 1977), insofar as "the requirements necessary for the record of an Article 15 disciplinary action to be admissible." 9 M.J. 300, 328 (C.M.A. 1980).

[284] 11 M.J. 126 (C.M.A. 1981).

[285] United States v. Wheaton, 18 M.J. 159, 160–61 (C.M.A. 1984) (footnote omitted).

(Rel.3—1/07 Pub.62410)

In light of the right against self-incrimination, the Court of Military Appeals also held that the trial judge may not question the accused concerning his or her knowledge of his or her rights when offered Article 15 punishment.[286]

Although the Rules for Courts-Martial are silent on the need for these counsel notice requirements, it appears that their continued application has been taken for granted by all concerned.[287]

Whether records of nonjudicial punishment must also be final in the sense that any appeals have concluded is unclear.[288] The Navy-Marine Court of Military Review, addressing the Navy form, which does not contain an appellate portion, viewed the question simply as one of the completeness of the form used at trial to prove the fact of the punishment.[289]

---

[286] United States v. Sauer, 15 M.J. 113, 114 (C.M.A. 1983), *overruling* United States v. Spivey, 10 M.J. 7 (C.M.A. 1980); United States v. Mathews, 6 M.J. 357 (C.M.A. 1979). *See also* United States v. Cowles, 16 M.J. 467 (C.M.A. 1983) (applying *Sauer* to guilty plea case).

[287] *See, e.g.,* United States v. Sims, 28 M.J. 578, 582–83 (A.C.M.R. 1989).

[288] *But see* United States v. Yarbough, 30 M.J. 1292, 1299 (N.M.C.M.R. 1990) (en banc) (Strickland, concurring in part and dissenting in part):

> While there are no cases precisely on point, there exists ample authority from which to conclude that the record of a nonjudicial punishment pending appeal is inadmissible in aggravation. The leading case on admissibility of records of nonjudicial punishment is *United States v. Mack*, 9 M.J. 300 (C.M.A. 1980). *Mack* was decided on the basis of completeness of the form on which the nonjudicial punishment results were recorded. However, I am convinced that the underlying rationale of this decision was the finality of these results.
>
> Cases relating to records of court-martial convictions required to be final provide valuable guidance in applying the presumption of regularity and official records exception to the hearsay rule and, thus, in deciding the admissibility of Prosecution Exhibit 1. These and other cases relating specifically to records of nonjudicial punishment draw a clear distinction between records that are required to indicate finality and those that are not. The principles we glean from them are as follows:
>
> *First.* If a prior action is provable by a document which is not required to address finality and, therefore, does not do so, the document, if otherwise in proper form, is *prima facie* admissible as evidence of the prior action. If there is a ground not appearing, nor required to appear, in the document upon which the admissibility of the underlying action is subject to attack, such as lack of finality, the burden is upon the defense to rebut the *prima facie* showing of admissibility represented by the document itself, in this case, Prosecution Exhibit 1 . . . .
>
> *Second.* If a prior conviction is proved by a document which requires an entry as to the outcome of *required* review, and the place for such entry is blank, the result is an affirmative indication on the face of the document that the review has not been completed, so that the conviction is not final. . . . Hence, the document is *prima facie* inadmissible, and the prosecution would have the burden of rebutting the inference of non-finality arising from the face of the document. The result is the same if the face of the document shows that, as a practical matter, *required* review could not have been completed in the elapsed time. . . .

(Rel.3—1/07 Pub.62410)

The Court of Military Appeals indicated that, in light of the waiver provisions of the Military Rules of Evidence, [290] ordinarily the trial judge has no *sua sponte* duty to exclude an incomplete or inadequate record of nonjudicial punishment. [291] However, should the defects in such a record be so serious as to constitute "plain error." [292] the judge must take action. [293] In 2004, the Court of Appeals for the Armed Forces expressly opined that "summary court-martial convictions and nonjudicial punishment" records are "governed by the objection and plain error provisions of" Military Rule of Evidence 103. [294] This provides an appropriate

Third. If regulations require that a record indicate *whether or not* an accused has submitted an optional, defense-initiated appeal, and the record fails to do so, no affirmative indication results either way; the record is *incomplete* and *prima facie* inadmissible, and its proponent has the burden of establishing the facts necessary for admissibility. . . .

Fourth. If a record indicates that an accused has submitted an optional defense-initiated appeal but fails to show an outcome of such appeal, the result should, if the presumption of regularity is rigorously applied, be an affirmative indication that the appeal is still pending. . . . Alternatively, the record may be regarded as incomplete . . . but, in either case, the record is *prima facie* inadmissible, and the proponent has the burden of showing that the optional appeal was denied, withdrawn, or never actually submitted.

Thus, we see that what is at stake is not the admissibility, *vel non*, of the underlying action, but simply who has the burdens of proof and, more importantly, of going forward, on the question of admissibility; and the rule seems to be that, if the document is *prima facie* admissible, the defense has the burdens of raising and proving collaterally any grounds for inadmissibility of the underlying action, whereas, if the document is *prima facie* inadmissible, the prosecution has the burden of proving collaterally the admissibility of the underlying action unless relieved of such burden by a failure to object amounting to waiver.

Although the difference may seem of little practical significance, we think that it affects the situation where, as here, no objection is made. If a record is *prima facie* inadmissible, its inadmissibility should be patent to the judge and counsel, and, if the defense counsel fails to object, either the objection is deemed waived, or else a claim of plain error may be entertained. If, however, the record is *prima facie* admissible, it is not subject to a bare objection, and, in the absence of evidence introduced, or at least offered, by the defense showing the latent inadmissibility of the underlying action, *no* error, plain or otherwise, is committed in receiving the document in evidence, and no issue of waiver arises. If the defense counsel is aware of any latent matters that would render the underlying action inadmissible and suffers the document to be received without raising them, an adequacy of counsel issue may be presented, but not plain error.

Yarbough, 30 M.J. at 1295–96 (emphasis in original).

[290] Mil. R. Evid. 103(a)(1).

[291] United States v. Dyke, 16 M.J. 426, 427 (C.M.A. 1983).

[292] *See* Mil. R. Evid. 103(d).

[293] *Dyke*, 16 M.J. at 427.

[294] United States v. Kahmann, 59 M.J. 309, 313 (C.A.A.F. 2004). As *Kahmann* only dealt with a summary court-martial conviction, the non-judicial punishment language strictly speaking is dicta.

and traditional procedural framework that absent plain error results in waiver should defense could not make an adequately and timely objection.

Vacations of punishment under Article 15 are admissible in evidence.[295] The "normal inference" that the sentencing authority may make is that the vacation was the result of misconduct by the accused.[296] Unless contrary evidence is offered, there is a presumption that the vacation was preceded by "an opportunity to appear" and "to rebut any derogatory or adverse information" when the punishment falls within Article 15(e)(1)–(7).[297] Even if the punishment does not fall within that portion of Article 15, there is a lawful presumption that the vacation was accomplished while affording the accused necessary due-process requirements.[298] The burden is on the defense counsel to make a specific objection that "the vacation of suspension was not preceded by the notice and opportunity to reply demanded."[299] At such a "vacation proceeding," the accused does not have the right to counsel.[300]

§ 23-44.33 Written Reprimands

Written reprimands or admonitions that are properly prepared and filed in accordance with the service regulations are admissible in evidence as personnel records.[301] As is always the case with personnel records, reprimands that are not made in compliance with service regulations are inadmissible. In *United States v. Boles*,[302] for example, the accused, pending civilian trial for arson, was reprimanded for the civilian arrest less than a week before his court-martial for larceny. Noting that trial counsel had explained the reprimand as having been made "for the purpose of aggravating the . . . case," the Court of Military Appeals noted that the applicable Air Force Regulation was "corrective rather than punitive in nature," and that the reprimand was not made in conformity with the regulation.[303] Accordingly, it was inadmissible. The Air Force Court of

---

[295] United States v. Covington, 10 M.J. 64 (C.M.A. 1980). *See* United States v. Stewart, 12 M.J. 143, 144 n.2 (C.M.A. 1981): "[S]ince appellant appeared in court in the uniform of a Specialist Four and testified concerning his awareness of the reduction in grade, the military judge arguably was on notice to inquire further into compliance with the required procedures." In essence, the presumption had been rebutted.

[296] United States v. Covington, 10 M.J. at 65, 68.

[297] 10 M.J. at 68 (citing MCM, 1969, para. 134).

[298] 10 M.J. at 68.

[299] 10 M.J. at 68.

[300] 10 M.J. at 66.

[301] *See, e.g.*, United States v. Dudley, 34 M.J. 603 (A.F.C.M.R. 1992); United States v. King, 29 M.J. 535 (A.F.C.M.R. 1989).

[302] 11 M.J. 195 (C.M.A. 1981). *Cf.* United States v. Beaver, 26 M.J. 991 (A.F.C.M.R. 1988) (letter of reprimand prepared six days prior to trial was admissible).

[303] *Boles*, 11 M.J. at 119.

(Rel.3—1/07 Pub.62410)

Military Review distinguished *Boles*, however, in *United States v. Hagy*,[304] and sustained the admission of a letter of reprimand for narcotics possession filed three days before the accused's trial for unrelated offenses.[305] In *Hagy*, the court reasoned that the commander's action was properly "corrective."[306]

In *United States v. Hood*,[307] the court rejected the defense claim that a letter of reprimand was not admissible because the accused did not commit the act alleged in it. The court stated:

> We agree with the ruling of the military judge that such argument constitutes an impermissible collateral attack on the LOR.[308] The defense may not litigate at trial the underlying dereliction for which the reprimand was issued, for it is a collateral issue. . . .

> An accused may mitigate or explain a LOR or similar document during sentencing . . . however, contesting the merits of whether the LOR was properly issued is not a matter in extenuation or mitigation and is not allowable.[309]

§ 23-44.40 Previous Convictions

Rule 1001(b)(3)(A) permits the prosecution to offer into evidence on sentencing "evidence of military or civilian convictions of the accused." A court-martial "conviction" is defined as a case in which a "sentence has been adjudged."[310] The Rule did not, however, define a civilian "conviction," leaving that to the law of the jurisdiction in which the conviction was adjudged.[311] The 2002

---

[304] 12 M.J. 739, 744 (A.F.C.M.R. 1981).

[305] The narcotic, a "blue pill," was found while the accused was being held in pretrial confinement.

[306] 12 M.J. at 744. *But see* United States v. Williams, 27 M.J. 529 (A.F.C.M.R. 1988) (improper to grant continuance to permit processing of reprimand written for aggravation).

[307] 16 M.J. 557 (A.F.C.M.R. 1983).

[308] Letter of reprimand.

[309] *Hood*, 16 M.J. at 559.

[310] R.C.M. 1001(b)(3)(A). The Discussion to the Rule states: "A vacation of a suspended sentence (*see* R.C.M. 1109) is not a conviction and is not admissible as such, but may be admissible under subsection (b)(2) of this rule as reflective of the character of the prior service of the accused."

[311] United States v. Hughes, 26 M.J. 119, 119–20 (C.M.A. 1988) (citing Analysis to R.C.M. 1001(b)(3)(A) and holding that an "Order Deferring Adjudication" for the accused from Texas did not constitute a "conviction"). *See also* United States v. Ariail, 48 M.J. 285 (C.A.A.F. 1998) (prior state conviction may be admissible as personnel record); United States v. White, 47 M.J. 139 (C.A.A.F. 1997) (accused waived the issue whether the plea of nolo contendere was a conviction under state law by testifying about the plea); United States v. Slovacek, 24 M.J. 140 (C.M.A.), *cert. denied*, 484 U.S. 855 (1987) (juvenile adjudications are not convictions); United States v. Evans, 26 M.J. 961 (A.C.M.R. 1988) (probationary status under Georgia First Offender Act not conviction). As to pre-R.C.M. cases *see, e.g.*, United States v. Cook, 10 M.J. 138 (C.M.A. 1981) (law of forum applies: action of Florida court in withholding adjudication of guilt and sentence accompanied by probation was a "conviction" for purposes of Air Force regulations and

(Rel.3—1/07　Pub.62410)

amendments to the *Manual for Courts-Martial* added the following to Rule for Courts-Martial 1001(b)(3)(A):

> In a civilian case, a "conviction" includes any disposition following an initial judicial determination or assumption of guilt, such as when guilt has been established by guilty plea, trial, or plea of nolo contendere, regardless of the subsequent disposition, sentencing procedure, or final judgment. However, a "civilian conviction" does not include a diversion from the judicial process without a finding or admission of guilt; expunged convictions; juvenile adjudications; minor traffic violations; foreign convictions; tribal court convictions; or convictions reversed, vacated, invalidated or pardoned because of errors of law or because of subsequently discovered evidence exonerating the accused.[312] A civilian juvenile adjudication is not a "conviction" for court-martial sentencing purposes.[313]

Although the accused may show that an appeal is pending, an appeal does not prohibit admission of the underlying conviction.[314] However, a "conviction by summary court-martial or special court-martial without a military judge may not be used for purposes of this rule until review has been completed pursuant to Article 64 or Article 66, if applicable."[315] Admission of a summary

---

admissible under MCM, 1969 (rev. ed.) ¶ 75d); United States v. Holloway, CM 443289 (A.C.M.R. 7 June 1983) (vacation of the suspension of a civilian sentence is not a "conviction" under ¶ 75d).

The difficulty in making a determination of state law is illustrated in *United States v. Browning*, 29 M.J. 174, 175 (C.M.A. 1989), in which Judges Cox and Everett differed on whether South Carolina traffic tickets constituted "convictions" under South Carolina law. *See also* United States v. White, 47 M.J. 139, 141 (C.A.A.F. 1997) ("While the *Manual* cannot anticipate every future point of contention on this issue, admissibility of major categories of prior civilian judgments is a matter that readily could be clarified through an amendment to RCM 1001(b)(3).").

[312] Exec. Order No. 13262 (April 11, 2002). In a letter to the Joint Service Committee on Military Justice dated July 27, 1998, the National Institute of Military Justice opined that this definition admitted prior "convictions" "not admissible IN ANY OTHER COURT or FOR ANY PURPOSE."

[313] United States v. Slovacek, 24 M.J. 140 (C.M.A. 1987), *cert. denied*, 484 U.S. 55 (1987) (dictum).

[314] R.C.M. 1001(b)(3)(B). Under the *1969 Manual*, the conviction had to be final in the sense that the accused had been tried for an offense within the meaning of Article 44(b): "No proceeding . . . is a trial in the sense of this article until the finding of guilty has become final after review." MCM, 1969 (rev. ed.) ¶ 75b(3)(b) (C5, 1 April 1982). Absent specific regulatory provision, an inference of finality could be drawn after sufficient time has passed since trial. *See* United States v. Heflin, 1 M.J. 131, 132 n.4 (C.M.A. 1975). *See also* United States v. Lachapelle, 10 M.J. 511 (A.F.C.M.R. 1980) (six months sufficient, plus inference that promulgating order establishes finality) (citing United States v. Graham, 1 M.J. 308 (C.M.A. 1976)); United States v. Tennent, 7 M.J. 593 (N.C.M.R. 1979) (95 days sufficient for inference).

[315] R.C.M. 1001(b)(3)(B). Note that there is no requirement that the government show notice of the right to consult with counsel. *But see* Air Force Instruction 51-201, Administration of Military Justice Guide ¶ 8.6 (26 November 2003): "Previous Convictions. R.C.M. 1001. Do not offer evidence of previous conviction by SCM [summary courts-martial], in which the accused was not represented by counsel unless the accused waived the right to counsel. . . . A conviction by SCM is not admissible until review pursuant to Article 64(a), U.C.M.J."

court-martial requires that the accused has received the opportunity to consult with counsel before deciding to proceed with it.[316]

Although Military Rule of Evidence 403 applies, no specific "staleness" rule exists.[317]

Although the text of Rule 1001(b)(3) does not refer to "prior" or "previous" convictions, the title of the subsection explicitly refers to "prior convictions of the accused." Under prior *Manuals*, courts debated the admissibility of convictions that were prior to some, but not all, of the offenses for which the accused was being sentenced.[318]

Although convictions may be proven by any evidence admissible under the Military Rules of Evidence,[319] including direct testimony by a witness with firsthand knowledge, conviction, as the Discussion to Rule 1001(b)(3)(C) notes, "[n]ormally . . . may be proved by use of the personnel records of the accused, by the record of the conviction, or by the order promulgating the result of trial." Documentary evidence, such as Department of Defense Form 493 (Extract of Military Records of Previous Convictions), Department of Army Form 2-2 (Record of Court-Martial Conviction),[320] the court-martial promulgating order,[321] or the record of trial[322] must be properly authenticated.[323] Documents

---

As to past views of the Court of Military Appeals on the admissibility of summary courts-martial, *compare* United States v. Cofield, 11 M.J. 422, 432 (C.M.A. 1981) (prior summary court-martial conviction for larceny could not be used for impeachment because of the questionable reliability of a conviction obtained without the presence of a defense counsel) *with* United States v. Alsup, 17 M.J. 166 (C.M.A. 1984) (summary court-martial conviction was admissible during sentencing).

[316] *See above* notes 278-81. *Cf.* United States v. Kelly, 45 M.J. 259 (C.A.A.F. 1996).

[317] The Analysis to R.C.M. 1001(b)(3) notes that the subsection deletes the prior *Manual*'s "exclusion of convictions more than 6 years old." Although the drafters adopted the approach followed by Mil. R. Evid. 609 in permitting use of convictions pending appeal, Rule 609(b)'s 10-year staleness rule was not adopted.

[318] *See, e.g.*, United States v. Geib, 26 C.M.R. 172, 174-75 (C.M.A. 1958) (MCM 1951, ¶ 75b(2) permitted use of a conviction so long as it was prior to any one of the instant offenses); United States v. Austin, 3 M.J. 1060 (A.F.C.M.R. 1977); United States v. Burke, 39 C.M.R. 718, 720 (A.B.R. 1968); States v. Boice, 33 C.M.R. 954 (A.F.B.R. 1963).

[319] R.C.M. 1001(b)(3)(C). *See generally* United States v. Barnes, 33 M.J. 468 (C.M.A. 1992) (discussing admissibility in the context of DOD Form 1966/3).

[320] *See, e.g.*, United States v. Lemieux, 13 M.J. 969 (A.C.M.R. 1982).

[321] *See, e.g.*, United States v. Hines, 1 M.J. 623, 626 (A.C.M.R. 1975).

[322] *See, e.g.*, United States v. Wright, 20 M.J. 518 (A.C.M.R. 1985) (record of trial can be used to prove a conviction so long as only relevant portions are considered and the probative value outweighs any prejudicial effect). *See also* United States v. Decker, CM 444320 (A.C.M.R. 5 Oct. 1984) (error for the trial judge to admit extraneous bench warrant and other offense references).

[323] *See generally* Mil. R. Evid. 901, 902. Although the document used to prove the conviction must be properly authenticated, collateral documents used to establish an evidentiary foundation do not have to be authenticated. *See* Mil. R. Evid. 104(a); United States v. Yanez, 16 M.J. 782 (A.C.M.R. 1983) (unauthenticated record of trial can be used to establish *Booker* compliance as an evidentiary foundation to admissibility of a summary court-martial conviction).

ordinarily will satisfy the hearsay rule under the exceptions for public records,[324] "business" records,[325] or former testimony.[326] Convictions already received into evidence as impeachment during the trial on the merits can be considered during sentencing without being reintroduced after findings.[327]

Admission of a prior conviction of the accused includes admission of the sentence.[328] The Navy-Marine Court of Military Review held, however, that "evidence to explain the detailed facts underlying a prior conviction is inadmissible in the prosecution's case-in-chief during sentencing."[329]

§ 23-44.50 Evidence in Aggravation

§ 23-44.51 In General

Rule for Courts-Martial 1001(b)(4) provides:

> The trial counsel may present evidence as to any aggravating circumstances directly relating to or resulting from the offenses of which the accused has been found guilty. . . . Except in capital cases a written or oral deposition taken in accordance with R.C.M. 702 is admissible in aggravation.[330]

The Discussion states in relevant part:

> Evidence in aggravation may include evidence of financial, social, psychological, and medical impact on or cost to any person or entity who was the victim of an offense committed by the accused and evidence of significant adverse impact on the mission, discipline, or efficiency of the command directly and immediately resulting from the accused's offense.

The Analysis to the Rule notes:

> Subsection (4) makes clear that aggravation may be introduced whether the accused pleaded guilty or not guilty, and whether it would be admissible on the merits. . . . This subsection does not authorize introduction in

---

[324] Mil. R. Evid. 803(8).

[325] Mil. R. Evid. 803(6).

[326] Mil. R. Evid. 804(b)(5).

[327] R.C.M. 1001(f)(2)(A). For foundational elements necessary to admit prior convictions of the accused as impeachment, *see* Mil. R. Evid. 609.

[328] United States v. Maracle, 26 M.J. 431, 433 (C.M.A. 1988).

[329] United States v. Brogan, 33 M.J. 588, 593 (N.M.C.M.R. 1991) (but also noting that evidence of the elements of the offense can be produced). *See also* United States v. Malhiot, 60 M.J. 695 (A.F. Ct. Crim. App. 2004), discussed in Major Robert Wm. Best, *Just a Little Down the Track: 2004 Developments in the Sentencing*, The Army Lawyer, May, 2005, at 87, 87–90.

[330] The language is taken from United States v. Vickers. 13 M.J. 403 (C.M.A. 1982). Evidence of uncharged misconduct which is admissible as aggravation should be offered during sentencing and not during the providency inquiry even if it has been obtained from the accused in the form of a stipulation. United States v. Ross, 34 M.J. 183, 187 (C.M.A. 1992); United States v. Goree, 34 M.J. 1027 (N.M.C.M.R. 1992).

(Rel.3—1/07 Pub.62410)

general of evidence of bad conduct or uncharged misconduct. The evidence must be of circumstances directly relating to or resulting from an offense of which the accused has been found guilty. [331]

In his well-written article, "A Prosecutorial Guide to Court-Martial Sentencing," [332] then Major Gaydos initially suggests that aggravation evidence be thought of as "two separate and distinct theories" — "evidence that is directly related to the circumstances surrounding the offense *and* evidence concerning the repercussions of the offense." He then sets forth a three-step methodology for aggravation evidence analysis:

> First, does the offered evidence involve a circumstance directly relating to the charged offense or a repercussion of the charged offense? Second, is the evidence offered in a form admissible under the Military Rules of Evidence? . . . Finally, does the offered evidence satisfy the balancing test of Mil. R. Rule 403? [333]

The Court of Military Appeals held:

> The standard for admission of evidence under this rule is not the mere relevance of the purported aggravating circumstance to the offense. . . . Instead, a higher standard is required, namely the aggravating circumstances proffered must directly relate to or result from the accused's offense. [334]

In *United States v. Gordon*, [335] a negligent homicide case in which the accused was convicted of drowning another during a rowboat ride, the brigade commander testified in aggravation to the effect that the crime "undermined his soldier's confidence in each other and compromised his transportation unit's 'paramount' concern for safety." [336] Emphasizing that the accused was convicted of only

---

[331] Analysis to Rule for Courts-Martial 1001(b)(4), MCM, 2005, A21-71 (citations omitted).

[332] 114 Mil. L. Rev. 1, 48, 49 (1986) (emphasis in original).

[333] 114 Mil. L. Rev. 1, 48-49 (1986) at 63 (footnote omitted). United States v. Gogas, 58 M.J. 96, 98–99 (C.A.A.F. 2003). *Cf.* United States v. Shupe, 36 M.J. 431, 435 (C.M.A. 1993) ("Our first inquiry is whether the evidence showed uncharged misconduct or merely misconduct included in the charged misconduct.").

[334] United States v. Gordon, 31 M.J. 30, 36 (C.M.A. 1990). *See also* United States v. Schlamer, 52 M.J. 80 (C.A.A.F. 1999) (held that in the murder case the judge did not abuse his discretion in admitting during sentencing evidence describing mutilating a woman with a knife, the same type of evidence used in the case); United States v. Schap, 49 M.J. 317 (C.A.A.F. 1998) (book on use of knives admissible in murder case involving knife); States v. Wilson, 47 M.J. 152 (C.A.A.F. 1997) (statement that formed basis for disrespect charge that former prosecutor was "bitch and out to get" accused properly admitted as directly relevant to offense); United States v. Gargaro, 45 M.J. 99 (C.A.A.F. 1996) (proper to establish that AK-47s illegally returned from Gulf War were found in the hands of drug dealers); United States v. Irwin, 42 M.J. 479, 483 (C.A.A.F. 1995) (threat made by defendant to victim admissible in sentencing even though prior to breaking into home and before rape); United States v. Rust, 41 M.J. 472 (C.A.A.F. 1995) (victim's husband's suicide note independent of accused's offenses and not relevant).

[335] Gordon, 31 M.J. at 36.

[336] 31 M.J. at 35.

(Rel.3—1/07 Pub.62410)

negligent acts, the court held the commander's testimony erroneous, as "it did not directly relate to or result *from the offense of which the accused has been found guilty.*"[337] Turning to the commander's testimony that the accused's actions undermined the command's concern for safety, the court again held the testimony inadmissible, because the "negligent acts did not occur in the course of his command's transportation duties but during an off duty frolic," and the alleged "adverse impact on the unit" was not *directly related to nor resulted from* the accused's offense.[338] It is thus apparent that the court is likely to apply a demanding test to aggravation evidence. In *United States v. Shupe,*[339] for example, the court sustained as proper aggravation evidence that the accused had introduced a greater quantity of LSD onto his base than he had admitted to via his guilty plea. The court opined that the aggravation evidence showed that the admitted introduction "was not an isolated transaction but was part of an extensive and continuing scheme to introduce and sell LSD to numerous buyers assigned to the naval base."[340] Similarly, the Court of Appeals for the Armed Forces held in *United States v. Nourse,*[341] that in the case of an accused charged with larceny it was proper to show that he committed other larcenies from the same civilian government agency as part of a "continuing scheme to steal."[342]

The accused's intent or motive as expressed in his or her own words is normally admissible.[343]

The degree of relationship between the accused's act and the alleged results needed to offer evidence of resulting harm is unclear. In *United States v. Witt,*[344] the Army Court of Military Review held that the provisions of Rule 1001(b)(4) *"only require, as a threshold, a reasonable linkage between the offense and alleged effect thereof."*[345] The court added that on appeal the question is not

---

[337] 31 M.J. at 36 (emphasis in original).

[338] 31 M.J. at 36. Cf. United States v. Gruninger, 30 M.J. 1142 (A.F.C.M.R. 1990) (improper argument).

[339] 36 M.J. 431 (C.M.A. 1993).

[340] 31 M.J. at 436.

[341] 55 M.J. 229 (C.A.A.F. 2001).

[342] 55 M.J. at 232. *Compare Nourse with* United States v. Wingart, 27 M.J. 128 (C.M.A 1988)(distinguished in *Nourse. Wingart* was a conviction for indecent acts in which the Court held "it was error to admit evidence of previous uncharged sexual misconduct with another victim . . . ." 55 M.J. at 231).

[343] *See* United States v. Ringuette, 29 M.J. 527, 529 (A.F.C.M.R. 1989) (citing United States v. Martin, 20 M.J. 227, 232 (C.M.A. 1985) (Everett, C.J. concurring)); United States v. Lynott, 28 M.J. 918 (C.G.C.M.R. 1989).

[344] 21 M.J. 637 (A.C.M.R. 1985).

[345] 21 M.J. at 641 (A.C.M.R. 1985) (emphasis added). *See also* United States v. Armon, 51 M.J. 83 (C.A.A.F. 1999) (witnesses could testify as to adverse impact of appellant falsifying his combat record).

whether the "court would have admitted this evidence in aggravation at the trial level; rather the proper test is whether the military judge has abused his discretion."[346] In *United States v. Anderson,*[347] a child pornography case, the Court considered the admissibility of data contained within a Senate report concerning the probable effects of child pornography (offered to show the impact on the victimized children in the pornography in the accused's possession). Sustaining the military judge's admission of the report, the case appears to make admissible substantial amounts of generalized opinion as to the effects of crime.

Stipulations of fact from other courts-martials involving other parties do not have enough indicia of reliability or trustworthiness to make them admissible over an assertion of the right to confrontation.[348]

§ 23-44.52   Impact on Victim or Family[349]

In their attempt to punish offenders for the full scope of their acts many jurisdictions have permitted the introduction of "victim impact statements." Such a statement sets forth the consequences of the crime to the accused, his or her family, and, perhaps, society. The use of victim impact statements in capital cases has been controversial with opponents arguing that a defendant ought not to be punished for the unforseen, fortuitous consequences of an act. Having declared the use of victim impact statements in capital cases unconstitutional in 1987 in *Booth v. Maryland*[350] on the grounds that they did not generally show "blameworthiness," in 1991 the Supreme Court in *Payne v. Tennessee*[351] overruled its prior decision and held victim impact statements fully constitutional. Justices Souter and Kennedy opined, however, that *Payne* did not justify admission of "information concerning a victim's family members' characterization of and opinions about the crime, the defendant, and the appropriate sentence."[352]

---

[346] 21 M.J. at 641-42 (A.C.M.R. 1985).

[347] 60 M.J. 548, 555–58 (A.F. Ct. Crim. App.), *pet. denied,* 60 M.J. 403 (C.A.A.F. 2004) (admission of evidence was not an abuse of the military judge's discretion), discussed in Major Robert Wm. Best, *Just a Little Down the Track: 2004 Developments in the Sentencing,* The Army Lawyer, May, 2005, at 87, 87–90.

[348] United States v. Frazier, 32 M.J. 651, 654 (A.F.C.M.R. 1991).

[349] Effective June 1, 2000, Military Rule of Evidence 615 was amended by operation of law to adopt Federal Rule of Evidence 615(4) which prohibits the exclusion of "a person authorized by statute to be present." This brings military practice into conformity with the Victim Crime Bill of Rights, 42 U.S.C. § 10606.

United States v. Spann, 51 M.J. 89 (C.A.A.F. 1999) (judge's refusal to sequester witnesses harmless error; 42 U.S.C. 10606 does not directly supersede Mil. R. Evid. 615).

[350] 482 U.S. 496 (1987).

[351] 501 U.S. 808 (1991) *overruling* South Carolina v. Gathers, 490 U.S. 805 (1989) and Booth v. Maryland, 482 U.S. 496 (1987).

[352] 501 at 835 n.1 (1991) (Justices Souter and Kennedy, concurring).

(Rel.3—1/07 Pub.62410)

Payne necessarily holds implicitly that victim impact statements are admissible in non-capital cases.

The Court of Military Appeals has sustained the use of victim impact testimony of a rape victim and her parents on the impact of the crime on the victim and family[353] and the admission of expert testimony on the impact of sodomy on an accused's minor victims.[354]

Although impact evidence may not be inadmissible per se, inflammatory evidence may be inadmissible because of its form:

> Even relevant evidence must be excluded if its tendency to inflame the passions of the court exceeds its probative value. Mil. R. Evid. 403. Emotional displays by aggrieved family members, though understandable, can quickly exceed the limits of propriety and equate to the bloody shirt being waved.[355]

The Army Court of Military Review opined, however, that it is permissible for the trial counsel to ask the court members in argument to consider the fear the victim had, and must have had, during the offense.[356]

In *United States v. Davis*,[357] the court opined that the Rules for Courts-Martial did not authorize a victim to give an opinion as to an appropriate sentence.[358]

---

[353] United States v. Fontenot, 29 M.J. 244, 255 (C.M.A. 1989). *See also* United States v. Patterson, 54 M.J. 74, 78 (C.A.A.F. 2000) (expert could testify as to the impact of grooming on the victim; expert's testimony that "persons who groom children for sexual abuse are not capable of rehabilitation" was not plain error); United States v. Kinman, NMCM 95 00006 (N.M. Crim. App. Jan. 17, 1996) (letter written by victim as part of therapy program admissible in aggravation under Mil. R. Evid. 803(4)); United States v. Hollingsworth, 44 M.J. 688 (C.G. Crim. App. 1996) (expert testimony admissible as to difficulty for victim to put offense behind her).

[354] United States v. Stark, 30 M.J. 328 (C.M.A. 1990). *See also* United States v. Patterson, 54 M.J. 74, 78 (C.A.A.F. 2000) (expert could testify as to the impact of grooming on the victim; expert's testimony that "persons who groom children for sexual abuse are not capable of rehabilitation" was not plain error); United States v. Jones, 44 M.J. 103 (C.A.A.F. 1996) (despite acquittal of accused, aggravated assault of Mrs. U. for having sex with her while HIV positive, sexual relations while HIV positive and failure to inform her of that condition was admissible when sentencing accused for adultery); United States v. Pingree, 39 M.J. 884, 885–86 (A.C.M.R. 1994) (special education teacher's testimony about change of incest victim's behavior is admissible as R.C.M. 1001(b)(4) aggravating circumstances).

[355] *Fontenot*, 29 M.J. at 252 (quoting United States v. Pearson, 17 M.J. 149, 153 (C.M.A. 1984)).

[356] United States v. Edmonds, 36 M.J. 791, 793 (A.C.M.R. 1993) (arguably dictum).

[357] 39 M.J. 281 (C.M.A. 1994) (dictum).

[358] "Just as opinion testimony as to the propriety of a specific sentence for an accused's offense is not allowed . . . we are not going to open the door for such testimony regarding no punishment." 39 M.J. at 283 (C.M.A. 1994).

§ 23-44.53   Effect and Amount of Drugs

When an accused has been convicted of a drug-related offense, the potential use and impact of any drugs in the accused's possession is potentially admissible as aggravation evidence.[359] As the Court of Military Appeals noted in 1987:

> In the instant case, appellant distributed LSD to a fellow servicemember who could have been a user or could have been a subsequent distributor to other servicemembers. Such a potential for harm is a circumstance surrounding the offense and, therefore, properly before the sentencing authority. To hold otherwise would require the trier-of-fact to operate from a vacuum and be insulated from the reality of the drug epidemic in our society.[360]

Although the information may be potentially admissible, its actual admission will be dependent upon the specific evidence proffered. Although expert testimony and learned treatises are generally admissible, some Drug Enforcement Administration publications, for example, may not be.[361]

§ 23-44.54   Financial Matters

It is permissible for the trial counsel to establish the value of the property that the accused stole, including the black-market value of these same items.[362] Trial counsel may then establish actuarially the value of the accused's retirement income and contrast the retirement income to the accused's ill-gotten gains if invested in a prudent manner.[363]

§ 23-44.55   Impact on Discipline and Mission

Direct impact on discipline, readiness, and mission accomplishment may be shown by the government.[364] Prosecutors, however, have tended to try to

---

[359] *See, e.g.*, United States v. Witt, 21 M.J. 637 (A.C.M.R. 1985) (proper to show that buyer of accused's LSD assaulted several soldiers with a knife shortly after ingesting the LSD). *See also* United States v. Shupe, 36 M.J. 431 (C.M.A. 1993) (sustaining as proper aggravation evidence that the accused had introduced a greater quantity of LSD onto his base than he had admitted to via his guilty plea); United States v. Vickers, 13 M.J. 403 (C.M.A. 1982) (court held that prosecution could introduce evidence that the amount of heroin accused transferred could have been divided into 37 to 42 usable quantities).

[360] United States v. Needham, 23 M.J. 383, 384 (C.M.A. 1987). *See also* United States v. Corl, 6 M.J. 914, 916 (N.C.M.R.), *aff'd*, 8 M.J. 47 (C.M.A. 1979).

[361] *Compare* Needham, 23 M.J. at 385 *with* United States v. Eads, 24 M.J. 919, 920 (A.F.C.M.R. 1987).

[362] United States v. Hood, 12 M.J. 890, 891 (A.C.M.R. 1982) (pre-Rules).

[363] 12 M.J. at 892 (A.C.M.R. 1982).

[364] *See, e.g.*, United States v. Thorton, 32 M.J. 112, 113 (C.M.A. 1991).

"stretch" that ability and often found that their efforts, successful at trial, are held erroneous on appeal.[365]

§ 23-44.56 Future Dangerousness

In *United States v. Williams*, three judges of the United States Court of Appeals for the Armed Forces held that evidence of future dangerousness provided by a qualified expert is permitted in sentencing.[366]

§ 23-44.60 Rehabilitative Potential

Until modified by the 1994 Change to the *Manual for Courts-Martial*, Rule 1001(b)(5) provided:

> *Evidence of rehabilitative potential.* The trial counsel may present, by testimony or oral deposition in accordance with R.C.M. 702(g)(1), evidence, in the form of opinions concerning the accused's previous performance as a servicemember and potential for rehabilitation. On cross-examination, inquiry is allowable into relevant and specific instances of conduct.[367]

The Rule permits expert testimony.[368]

---

[365] *See, e.g.,* United States v. Gordon, 31 M.J. 30, 36 (C.M.A. 1990); United States v. Gruninger, 30 M.J. 1142, 1143 (A.F.C.M.R. 1990) ("*absent evidence an accused's crime in any way affected his duty*," argument that conduct menaced the Air Force held unacceptable; cases cited) (emphasis in original); United States v. Caro, 20 M.J. 770 (A.F.C.M.R. 1985). *See also* United States v. Bartoletti, 32 M.J. 419 (C.M.A. 1991) (dictum that crime statistics are not admissible without a foundation that these crimes had an adverse impact on community and resulted from the accused's crime).

[366] 41 M.J. 134 (C.M.A. 1994). The court has in the past permitted testimony as to "'chances' of overcoming drug addiction," 41 M.J. at 138 (C.M.A. 1994), and "cited with approval a Supreme Court decision upholding admissibility of 'predictions of future dangerousness' during sentencing." 41 M.J. at 139 (C.M.A. 1994). *See also* United States v. McElhaney, 54 M.J. 120 (C.A.A.F. 2000) (The court below erred in holding that the judge's ruling on future dangerousness was appropriate even though the expert had never personally examined appellant.); United States v. George, No. 97 01969 (N.M. Crim. App., Aug. 6, 1998) (court held that a licensed social worker who treated defendant for seven months could testify that appellant's prognosis for rehabilitation was guarded and questionable and concluded he was "predatory in nature"), *aff'd on other grounds,* 52 M.J. 259 (C.A.A.F. 2000) (harmless error); United States v. Scott, No. 9502201 (A. Crim. App. May 29, 1998) (based on psychiatric examination expert concluded that the accused had the potential to re-offend), *aff'd,* 51 M.J. 326 (C.A.A.F. 1999). It is very difficult to predict future dangerousness. *See, e.g.,* Alison et all, *The Academics and Practitioner: Pragmatists' Views of Offender Profiling,* 10 Psychology, Public Policy, and Law 71 (2004); John Monahan, *Violence Risk Assessment: Scientific Validity and Evidentiary Admissibility,* 57 Wash. & Lee L. Rev. 901 (2000).

[367] *See* United States v. King, 30 M.J. 334, 336 (C.M.A. 1990) (specific instances may not be shown on direct).

[368] United States v. Stinson, 34 M.J. 233, 238 (C.M.A. 1992) (prosecution was permitted to introduce expert testimony on person's prospects for treatment (pedophile)); United States v. Plott, 35 M.J. 512, 516 (A.F.C.M.R. 1992) (dictum to same effect). *But see* United States v. King, 35 M.J. 337, 342–43 (C.M.A. 1992) (impermissible to introduce statistical evidence as to the prognosis of the child abuser).

(Rel.3—1/07 Pub.62410)

Insofar as drug offenses are concerned, the court has opined:

> In *United States v. Horner*,[369] . . . we held that a person's rehabilitative potential is based upon his entire character, morality, and determination to succeed. In forming an opinion about rehabilitative potential, knowledge of a person's success or failure in previous efforts to recover is extremely helpful. Thus, when a witness is asked for an opinion about an individual's "rehabilitative potential," the fact that the accused has failed to recover during past periods of treatment is an extremely important and rational basis upon which to form a conclusion.[370]

The government's ability to present evidence as to lack of rehabilitative potential has given rise to a significant degree of litigation.[371] This has been especially true where commanders have been called to testify.

Summarizing its earlier cases,[372] the Court of Military Appeals declared:

> The primary thrust of these decisions is that this *Manual* rule does not permit a commander to give an opinion on a servicemember's "potential for rehabilitation" if his opinion is based solely on his view of the severity of the offense. The proffered rationale for this holding was the Court's conclusion that the only opinion testimony permitted by this rule is that which is rationally based on an individual assessment of a servicemember's character and potential.

> A secondary thrust . . . concerns the scope of the opinion which a commander may present to the members for purposes of sentencing. These decisions suggest that RCM 1001(b)(5) does not authorize admission of a commander's opinion as to an appropriate punishment for the offenses for which a servicemember has been found guilty at a court-martial. . . .

---

[369] 22 M.J. 294, 295 (C.M.A. 1986). In *Horner*, the court held:

> The witness' function in this area is to impart his/her special insight into the accused's personal circumstances. It would be ironic and absurd if R.C.M. 1001(b)(5) were construed to allow the parties to call witnesses simply for the purpose of telling the court-martial what offenses, in the witnesses' estimation, require punitive discharge or lengthy confinement, etc.

[370] United States v. Wilson, 31 M.J. 91, 94 (C.M.A. 1990) (citing United States v. Gunter, 29 M.J. 140 (C.M.A. 1989)). Lack of rehabilitative potential is not the same as an opinion as to what an appropriate sentence might be. United States v. Davis, 39 M.J. 281, 283 (C.M.A. 1994) ("Just as opinion testimony as to the propriety of a specific sentence for an accused's offense is not allowed . . . we are not going to open the door for such testimony regarding no punishment") (citing *Ohrt* and *Horner*).

[371] *See, e.g.*, United States v. Clayton, 32 M.J. 159 (C.M.A. 1991) (dicta dealing with rebuttal evidence); United States v. Corraine, 31 M.J. 102 (C.M.A. 1990); United States v. Aurich, 31 M.J. 95 (C.M.A. 1990) (effect at bench trial); United States v. Wilson, 31 M.J. 91 (C.M.A. 1990); United States v. Cherry, 31 M.J. 1 (C.M.A. 1990); United States v. Kirk, 31 M.J. 84 (C.M.A. 1990); United States v. Jones, 30 M.J. 898, 901 (A.F.C.M.R. 1990). In United States v. Pompey, 32 M.J. 547, 553 (A.F.C.M.R. 1990), the court suggested that R.C.M. 1001(b)(5) is more troublesome than it is likely ever to be worth.

[372] United States v. Antonitis, 29 M.J. 217 (C.M.A. 1989); United States v. Ohrt, 28 M.J. 301 (C.M.A. 1989); United States v. Horner, 22 M.J. 294 (C.M.A. 1986).

(Rel.3—1/07 Pub.62410)

A third aspect . . . is the euphemism rule which was announced in *United States v. Ohrt*. . . . There, this Court indicated that a commander's opinion stopping short of expressly recommending a punitive discharge but which impliedly advocated separation from the service was also prohibited at court-martial.[373]

The court has also held that "a commander's statement that *he does not want an accused back in his unit* — absent a full, logical, and acceptable explanation" proves absolutely nothing and is, therefore, inadmissible.[374] "Evidence of 'rehabilitative potential' must be based upon personalized knowledge of an accused's character and potential. It cannot be based solely upon the commander's view of the severity of the offense or offenses charged."[375] Unlike the "lay" command witness dealt with in *Ohrt*, an expert witness may testify as to rehabilitative potential.[376]

Despite an alleged theory of rehabilitative potential — or aggravation — a victim may not testify to the victim's opinion of proper punishment or the victim's reaction to any given punishment.[377]

A witness may ordinarily only testify to his or her opinion of the accused's potential for rehabilitation; not the basis for that opinion.[378]

Erroneous admission of such evidence can be cured by adequate judicial instructions.[379] Failure to object may waive error,[380] but sufficiently serious error may constitute "plain error" and compel reversal.[381] Admission of the

---

[373] *Cherry*, 31 M.J. at 4–5. *Ohrt* and its progeny apply to government rebuttal as well as the government's sentencing case-in-chief. United States v. Pompey, 33 M.J. 266, 270 (C.M.A. 1991). *See also* United States v. Littlewood, 53 M.J. 349 (C.A.A.F. 2000) (error to admit commander's testimony that appellant's acts were prejudicial to good order and discipline). United States v. Ramos, 42 M.J. 392, 396 ¶ 18 (C.A.A.F. 1995) ("The mirror image [of *Ohrt*] might reasonably be that an opinion that an accused could 'continue to serve and contribute to the United States Army' simply is a euphemism for, 'I do not believe you should give him a punitive discharge.' ").

[374] United States v. Aurich, 31 M.J. 95, 96 (C.M.A. 1990) (per curiam) (emphasis in original). Note footnote * at 96 in *Aurich*, in which Judges Cox and Everett opine that, absent use in rebuttal, "we believe it to be the rare case where it is necessary for the Government to introduce such opinions."

[375] United States v. Williams, 47 M.J. 142, 144 (C.A.A.F. 1997).

[376] United States v. Mahaney, 33 M.J. 846, 848 (A.C.M.R. 1991) (social worker could testify based on ten weeks of group therapy).

[377] United States v. Davis, 39 M.J. 281, 282–83 (C.M.A. 1994) (technically dictum as no prejudice found).

[378] United States v. Rhoads, 32 M.J. 114, 116 (C.M.A. 1991) (citing United States v. Kirk, 31 M.J. 84 (C.M.A. 1990)). *See also* United States v. Oquendo, 35 M.J. 24, 26–27 (C.M.A. 1992).

[379] 35 M.J. 24, 26–27 (C.M.A. 1992). 31 M.J. at 5–6 (citing *Horner*, 22 M.J. at 296).

[380] *See* United States v. Wilson, 31 M.J. 91 (C.M.A. 1990).

[381] United States v. Kirk, 31 M.J. 84, 89 (C.M.A. 1990). *See also* United States v. Dudding, 37 M.J. 429 (C.M.A. 1993) (expert testimony by prosecution expert to effect that accused should be sentenced to lengthy confinement for treatment purposes wasn't "plain error").

(Rel.3—1/07 Pub.62410)

evidence in a trial by military judge alone is less likely to cause reversible error.[382]

The 1994 Change to the *Manual for Courts-Martial* amended Rule 1001(b)(5), greatly increasing its size, to provide:

(5) Evidence of rehabilitative potential. Rehabilitative potential refers to the accused's potential to be restored, through vocational, correctional, or therapeutic training or other corrective measures to a useful and constructive place in society.

(A) In general. The trial counsel may present, by testimony or oral deposition in accordance with R.C.M. 702(g)(1), evidence in the form of opinions concerning the accused's previous performance as a servicemember and potential for rehabilitation.

(B) Foundation for opinion. The witness or deponent providing opinion evidence regarding the accused's rehabilitative potential must possess sufficient information and knowledge about the accused to offer a rationally based opinion that is helpful to the sentencing authority. Relevant information and knowledge include, but are not limited to, information and knowledge about the accused's character, performance of duty, moral fiber, determination to be rehabilitated, and nature and severity of the offense or offenses.

(C) Bases for opinion. An opinion regarding the accused's rehabilitative potential must be based upon relevant information and knowledge possessed by the witness or deponent, and must relate to the accused's personal circumstances. The opinion of the witness or deponent regarding the severity or nature of the accused's offense or offenses may not serve as the principal basis for an opinion of the accused's rehabilitative potential.

(D) Scope of opinion. An opinion offered under this rule is limited to whether the accused has rehabilitative potential and to the magnitude or quality of any such potential. A witness may not offer an opinion regarding the appropriateness of a punitive discharge or whether the accused should be returned to the accused's unit.

(E) Cross-examination. On cross-examination, inquiry is permitted into relevant and specific instances of conduct.

(F) Redirect. Notwithstanding any other provision in this rule, the scope of opinion testimony permitted on redirect may be expanded, depending upon the nature and scope of the cross-examination.

This Change may limit what was otherwise admissible.

In an interesting post-Rule 1001(b)(5) amendment case, the Court of Appeals for the Armed Forces held the testimony of the accused's commander that she had wanted to administratively discharge the accused to be error. The Court, however, held the error to be non-prejudicial because the case was before the

---

[382] *See, e.g.*, United States v. Taylor, 38 M.J. 254, 257 (C.M.A. 1993); *Corraine*, 31 M.J. 102; *Aurich*, 31 M.J. 95 (per curiam).

(Rel.3—1/07 Pub.62410)

judge alone and other evidence "amply demonstrated appellant's abysmal disciplinary record."[383]

§ 23-44.70   Capital Cases

Assuming that the death sentence is authorized for the offense, and that the accused was convicted by a unanimous vote of "not less than twelve"[384] members,[385] unless death is mandated[386] it may not be adjudged unless the members unanimously find that one or more of the specific aggravating factors set forth in Rule 1004(c) are present.[387] Further, "[a]ll members [must] concur

---

[383] United States v. Williams, 50 M.J. 397, 400 (C.A.A.F. 1999); United States v. Duncan, 53 M.J. 494, 500 (C.A.A.F. 2000). When asked about eligibility for parole, the judge indicated that the members should not be concerned about the impact of parole in determining appropriate sentence. "In view of the sheer brutality of appellant's crimes, it is quite clear that these were not collateral matters but 'crucial sentencing concern[s] which should have been addressed by the military judge.' " In any event, any error was harmless.

[384] National Defense Authorization Act for Fiscal Year 2002, Pub. L. No. 107-107 (Dec. 28, 2001) adds Article 25a to require "not less 12" for capital case unless members are not reasonably available" for certain reasons.

[385] R.C.M. 1004(a)(1) & (2).

[386] R.C.M. 1004(d) (spying).

[387] Rule 1004(c) states:

Death may be adjudged only if the members find, beyond a reasonable doubt, one or more of the following aggravating factors:

(1) That the offense was committed before or in the presence of the enemy, except that this factor shall not apply in the case of a violation of Article 118 or 120;

(2) That in committing the offense the accused —

(A) Knowingly created a grave risk of substantial damage to the national security of the United States; or

(B) Knowingly created a grave risk of substantial damage to a mission, system, or function of the United States, provided that this subparagraph shall apply only if substantial damage to the national security of the United States would have resulted had the intended damage been effected;

(3) That the offense caused substantial damage to the national security of the United States, whether or not the accused intended such damage, except that this factor shall not apply in case of a violation of Article 118 or 120;

(4) That the offense was committed in such a way or under circumstances that the lives of persons other than the victim, if any, were unlawfully and substantially endangered, except that this factor shall not apply to a violation of Articles 104, 106a, or 120;

(5) That the accused committed the offense with the intent to avoid hazardous duty;

(6) That, only in the case of a violation of Article 118 or 120, the offense was committed in time of war and in territory in which the United States or an ally of the United States was then an occupying power or in which the armed forces of the United States were then engaged in active hostilities;

(7) That, only in the case of a violation of Article 118(1):

(Text continued on page 23–63)

(A) The accused was serving a sentence of confinement for 30 years or more or for life at the time of the murder;

(B) The murder was committed while the accused was engaged in the commission or attempted commission of any robbery, rape, aggravated arson, sodomy, burglary, kidnapping, mutiny, sedition, or piracy of an aircraft or vessel, or was engaged in flight or attempted flight after the commission or attempted commission of any such offense;

(C) The murder was committed for the purpose of receiving money or a thing of value;

(D) The accused procured another by means of compulsion, coercion, or a promise of an advantage, a service, or a thing of value to commit the murder;

(E) The murder was committed with the intent to avoid or to prevent lawful apprehension or effect an escape from custody or confinement;

(F) The victim was the President of the United States, the President-elect, the Vice President, or, if there was no Vice President, the officer in the order of succession to the office of President of the United States, the Vice President-elect, or any individual who is acting as President under the Constitution and laws of the United States, any Member of Congress (including a Delegate to, or Resident Commissioner in, the Congress) or Member of Congress elect, justice or judge of the United States, a chief of state or head of government (or the political equivalent) of a foreign nation, or a foreign official (as such term is defined in section 1116(b)(3)(A) of title 18, United States Code), if the official was on official business at the time of the offense and was in the United States or in a place described in Mil. R. Evid. 315(c)(2), 315(c)(3);

(G) The accused then knew that the victim was any of the following persons in the execution of office: a commissioned, warrant, noncommissioned, or petty officer of the armed forces of the United States; a member of any law enforcement or security activity or agency, military or civilian, including correctional custody personnel; or any firefighter.

(H) The murder was committed with intent to obstruct justice;

(I) The murder was preceded by the intentional infliction of substantial physical harm or prolonged, substantial mental or physical pain and suffering to the victim;

(J) The accused has been found guilty in the same case of another violation of Article 118;

(8) That only in the case of a violation of Article 118(4), the accused was the actual perpetrator of the killing or was a principal whose participation in the burglary, sodomy, rape, or aggravated arson was major and who manifested a reckless indifference for human life;

(9) That, only in the case of a violation of Article 120:

(A) The victim was under the age of 12; or

(B) The accused maimed or attempted to kill the victim;

(10) That, only in the case of a violation of the law of war, death is authorized under the law of war for the offense;

(11) That, only in the case of a violation of Article 104 or 106a:

(A) The accused has been convicted of another offense involving espionage or treason for which neither a sentence of death or imprisonment for life was authorized by statute; or

(B) That in committing the offense, the accused knowingly created a grave risk of death to a person other than the individual who was the victim.

For purposes of this rule, "national security" means the national defense and foreign relations of the United States and specifically includes: a military or defense advantage over any foreign

(Rel.3—1/07   Pub.62410)

that any extenuating or mitigating circumstances are substantially outweighed by any aggravating circumstances admissible."[388]

Notwithstanding Rule for Courts-Martial 922(e), Judge Cox believed that fundamental notions of fairness demand that in death sentence cases each member should be polled or sign the death sentence worksheet.[389]

As Judge Cox's concern demonstrates, there is a strong belief that in light of their severity and finality capital cases are "different." The Court of Appeals for the Armed Forces has clearly taken its review responsibilities in capital cases most seriously. Indeed Chief Judge Crawford has even opined that the Court may have lowered "an appellant's burden in ineffective assistance of counsel cases in which the death penalty has been imposed."[390]

§ 23-45.00 Defense Sentencing Evidence: Extenuation and Mitigation

§ 23-45.10 In General

Traditionally, the heart of the sentencing portion of trial by court-martial was the defense effort to achieve the most lenient sentence possible by the presentation of favorable information to the sentencing authority.[391] In light of the high guilty-plea rate,[392] "extenuation and mitigation" is frequently the most important aspect of the case for the accused.

Rule for Courts-Martial 1001(c)(1) summarizes the potential scope of the defense case:

> The defense may present matters in rebuttal of any material presented by the prosecution and may present matters in extenuation and mitigation regardless whether the defense offered evidence before findings.

> (A) *Matter in extenuation.* Matter in extenuation of an offense serves to explain the circumstances surrounding the commission of an offense,

---

nation or group of nations; a favorable foreign relations position; or a defense posture capable of successfully resisting hostile or destructive action from within or without.

The prosecution must serve timely notice on the defense of the aggravating factors it plans to prove except that failure to do so "shall not bar later notice and proof of such additional aggravating factors unless the accused demonstrates specific prejudice from such failure and that a continuance or a recess is not an adequate remedy." R.C.M. 1004(b)(1). In *United States v. Gray*, 51 M.J. 1, 46–47 (C.A.A.F. 1999), the Court held that R.C.M. 1004(c)(7)(I) was not unconstitutionally vague.

[388] R.C.M. 1004(b)(4)(C). The 1994 change to the *Manual for Courts-Martial* has added to and clarified the aggravating factors. *See* Appendix 2, *below.*

[389] United States v. Curtis, 33 M.J. 101, 110 (C.M.A. 1991) (Cox, J., concurring).

[390] United States v. Murphy, 50 M.J. 4, 35 (C.A.A.F. 1998) (Crawford, J. dissenting).

[391] Until the 1980s, the government's ability to present evidence was comparatively limited. In addition, many trial counsel tended not to oppose the defense evidence, relying instead on closing argument.

[392] Common to both civilian and military law.

(Rel.3—1/07 Pub.62410)

including those reasons for committing the offense which do not constitute a legal justification or excuse.[393]

(B) *Matter in mitigation.* Matter in mitigation of an offense is introduced to lessen the punishment to be adjudged by the court-martial, or to furnish grounds for a recommendation of clemency. It includes the fact that nonjudicial punishment under Article 15 has been imposed for an offense growing out of the same act or omission that constitutes the offense of which the accused has been found guilty, particular acts of good conduct or bravery and evidence of the reputation or record of the accused in the service for efficiency, fidelity, subordination, temperance, courage, or any other trait that is desirable in a servicemember.

Evidence of earned decorations has always been of importance. In *United States v. Demerse*,[394] the court emphasized the importance of Vietnam War awards, holding that the failure of defense counsel to present such evidence as sentencing evidence was prejudicial legal error. The right to present evidence in extenuation and mitigation does not include the right to controvert the guilty findings that led to sentencing.[395]

Critically, the *Manual for Courts-Martial* provides:

The military judge may, with respect to matters in extenuation or mitigation or both, relax the rules of evidence. This may include admitting letters, affidavits, certificates of military and civil officers, and other writings of similar authenticity and reliability.[396]

Under this authority, the defense may present evidence on sentencing that would be inadmissible on findings.

Should the accused desire to testify to present or planned cooperation with the government, the defense may ask that the courtroom be closed to protect the accused against possible reprisals.[397]

---

[393] One court has held that this does not include evidence of an acquittal of an alleged accomplice. United States v. Raines, 32 C.M.R. 550 (A.B.R. 1962). In *United States v. Loya*, 49 M.J. 104 (C.A.A.F. 1998), the Court reversed the sentence of a homicide accused who had been prevented from presenting evidence that the victim's medical treatment had contributed to his death.

[394] 37 M.J. 488, 492 (C.M.A. 1993).

[395] United States v. Teeter, 16 M.J. 68, 72–3 (C.M.A. 1983) (judge properly instructed members to disregard accused's testimony during which "he attempted to resurrect his alibi defense"). Given the right of the members or judge to reconsider a finding of guilty, it is not clear that this bar is appropriate.

[396] R.C.M. 1001(c)(3). This provision is similar to MCM, 1969 (rev. ed.) ¶ 75c(3).

[397] In United States v. Martinez, 3 M.J. 600, 602–04 (N.C.M.R. 1977), *rev'd on other grounds*, 5 M.J. 122 (C.M.A. 1978), the court held that, under the circumstances of the case, the trial judge abused his discretion in not clearing the courtroom so that the accused could respond to the questions of the judge and the court members as to his willingness to cooperate with law-enforcement officials.

(Rel.3—1/07　Pub.62410)

§ 23-45.20 Extenuation and Mitigation Evidence

§ 23-45.21 Testimony by the Accused

§ 23-45.21(a) In General

Perhaps the most important potential extenuation and mitigation evidence is the accused's testimony. The accused has the right to present either personally or through counsel an unsworn statement during which he or she is not under oath and on which he or she cannot be cross-examined.[398] The accused may also present a sworn statement that is subject to cross-examination.[399] As these are *rights* of the accused, the accused may also remain silent.

> The military judge shall personally inform the accused of the right to present matters in extenuation and mitigation, including the right to make a sworn or unsworn statement or to remain silent, and shall ask whether the accused chooses to exercise those rights.[400]

Failure to advise the accused of allocution rights will be tested for specific prejudice.[401]

The fact that the accused pled guilty does not act as a waiver of the right against self-incrimination for the sentencing phase of the trial.[402]

§ 23-45.21(b) Unsworn Statements

Rule 1001(c)(2)(A) provides:

> The accused may testify, make an unsworn statement, or both in extenuation, in mitigation or to rebut matters presented by the prosecution, or for all three purposes whether or not the accused testified prior to findings. The accused may limit such testimony or statement to any one or more of the specifications of which the accused has been found guilty. This subsection does not permit the filing of an affidavit of the accused.

---

[398] R.C.M. 1001(c)(2)(C).

[399] R.C.M. 1001(c)(2)(B). As to the scope of cross-examination see, e.g., United States v. Thomas, 16 M.J. 899, 900 (A.C.M.R. 1983); United States v. Robideau, 16 M.J. 819 (N.M.C.M.R. 1983). Technically, the Rules contemplate not a "sworn statement," but sworn *testimony*, a terminology difference that may be crucial. United States v. Martinsmith, 41 M.J. 343, 348 (C.A.A.F. 1995).

[400] R.C.M. 1001(a)(3). *See also* United States v. Hawkins, 2 M.J. 23 (C.M.A. 1976) (dictum that even if it is shown that defense counsel has fulfilled the judge's allocution advice under the predecessor provision to R.C.M. 1001(a)(3), such advice does not alleviate the requirement imposed on the military judge).

The judge should take care that his or her advice to an accused of limited education not appear threatening and thereby deprive the accused of the right to make a statement to the court members.

[401] United States v. Grady, 30 M.J. 911, 914 (A.C.M.R. 1990) (citing United States v. Williams, 23 M.J. 713 (A.C.M.R. 1986)).

[402] Mitchell v. United States, 526 U.S. 314 (1999)(defendant may not be required to testify during sentencing and no adverse inference can be drawn from the silence of the defendant).

Reasoning that the right to make an unsworn statement is a personal one, the Court of Appeals for the Armed Forces has opined via dicta that:

> Therefore, if an accused is absent without leave his right to make an unsworn statement is forfeited unless prior to his absence he authorized his counsel to make a specific statement on his behalf. Although defense counsel may refer to evidence presented at trial during his sentencing argument, he may not offer an unsworn statement containing material subject to the attorney-client privilege without waiver of the privilege by his client. [403]

The right to make an unsworn statement [404] is valuable and has been said to be "generally considered unrestricted." [405] The Court of Appeals for the Armed Forces has clarified that statement, however, by holding that an unsworn statement is constrained by Rule 1001(c)(2)(A) and must be "relevant as to extenuation, mitigation, or rebuttal." [406] At present, the law dealing with whether an accused may testify in an unsworn statement to lesser sanctions imposed on co-actors, is unclear with authority permitting such references [407] and authority approving judicial instructions to members to ignore it. [408]

The mere fact that a statement in allocution might contain matter that would be inadmissible if offered as sworn testimony does not, by itself, provide a basis for constraining the right of allocution. If, in the future, the *Manual*'s traditional, largely unfettered right of allocution should lead to a plethora of mini-trials, the

---

[403] United States v. Marcum, 60 M.J. 198, 210 Armed F. 2004) (holding that defense counsel violated the attorney-client privilege via an "unsworn statement" by disclosing notes made by the absent accused and given to counsel).

[404] United States v. Marcum, 60 M.J. 198, 210 (C.A.A.F. 2005) (holding that defense counsel violated the attorney-client privilege via an "unsworn statement" by disclosing notes made by the absent accused and given to counsel).

[405] *E.g.*, United States v. Simoy, 50 M.J. 1, 3 (C.A.A.F. 1999) (citing United States v. Grill, 48 M.J. 131 (C.A.A.F. 1998), dicta that defense could introduce the sentence of co-accused in mitigation); United States v. Rosato, 32 M.J. 93, 96 (C.M.A. 1991) (citations omitted); United States v. Grill, 48 M.J. 131 (C.A.A.F. 1998). The accused may tell panel members that the commander would administratively discharge the accused if the accused is not punitively discharged. United States v. Britt, 48 M.J. 233 (C.A.A.F. 1998) (found the error in not admitting this statement was harmless). *But see* United States v. Oaks, 2003 CCA Lexis 301 (A.F. Crim. App. December 10, 2003) (pretrial agreement may limit accused's ability to refer to sentences adjudged in other cases).

[406] United States v. Barrier, 61 M.J. 482 (C.A.A.F. 2005) (judge did not err by giving "*Friedman* Instruction" to members to not consider unsowrn unsworn statement's reference to punishment received by another accused).

[407] United States v. Grill, 48 M.J. 131 (C.A.A.F. 1998) (unsworn testimony as to disparate sanctions). *See also* United States v. Sowell, 59 M.J. 954 (N-M.C. Ct. Crim. App. 2000) (en banc) (permissible to exclude unsworn statement as to the acquittal of a co-conspirator), *reversed*, 62 M.J. 150 (C.A.A.F. 2005) (permissible to rebut prosecution argument).

[408] United States v. Barrier, 61 M.J. 482 (C.A.A.F. 2005). Note especially Judge Crawford's biting concurrence comparing the current state of the law to Alice in Wonderland.

(Rel.3—1/07 Pub.62410)

President has the authority to provide appropriate guidance in the *Manual for Courts-Martial.*[409]

An unsworn statement may be made to rebut sworn prosecution testimony,[410] or prosecution argument.[411] The services differ on their procedure for unsworn statements. The Navy does not permit the accused to make an unsworn statement from the witness box, while this is routine in the Army.[412]

The accused cannot be cross-examined on an unsworn statement whether made personally or through counsel.[413] In the past, judges occasionally have advised counsel of serious questions raised by an unsworn statement and invited a response from counsel or the accused.[414] This is clearly improper.[415] The accused cannot even make a voluntary sworn response to a member's question.[416]

The degree to which an accused may make an unsworn statement in rebuttal or in response to court member questions has sometimes proven troublesome. In *United States v. Provost,*[417] the Court had held that the accused had a right to make an unsworn statement in surrebuttal. Yet in *United States v. Satterley,* (ArmedF.),[418] the Court held the judge did not abuse his discretion in refusing to allow the accused to make an additional unsworn statement to answer a matter of interest to the court-members. Of significance to the Court were that the accused had rested, that the judge offered as an alternative a stipulation of fact, and that the judge had given a limiting instruction with respect to the court members' concern. Judge Effron, dissenting, believed that the accused had been deprived of an important right. The government may rebut an unsworn statement

---

[409] United States v. Grill, 48 M.J. 131, 133 (C.A.A.F. 1998).

[410] United States v. Provost, 32 M.J. 98, 99 (C.M.A. 1991).

[411] United States v. Sowell, 62 M.J. 150, 152 (C.A.A.F. 2005).

[412] *See, e.g.,* United States v. Welch, 1 M.J. 1201, 1202 (A.F.C.M.R. 1976) (Air Force should discontinue its practice of having the accused give an unsworn statement from the counsel statement.).

[413] *See, e.g.,* United States v. King, 30 C.M.R. 71 (C.M.A. 1960); United States v. Clark, 50 C.M.R. 350 (A.C.M.R. 1975) (remanded as to sentence); United States v. Royster, 43 C.M.R. 468 (A.C.M.R. 1970) (error but not prejudicial); United States v. Jackson, 36 C.M.R. 677 (A.B.R. 1966) (board reassessed the sentence).

[414] *See, e.g.,* United States v. Grady, 30 M.J. 911, 913–714 (A.C.M.R. 1990).

[415] *See, e.g.,* King, 30 C.M.R. 71 (C.M.A. 1960) (when court member attempted to question accused's unsworn statement, it was error not to instruct members that they must not draw adverse inferences from this method of proof; rehearing on sentence ordered based on the above and improper argument by the prosecutor).

[416] United States v. Martinsmith, 37 M.J. 665, 667 (A.C.M.R. 1993) *aff'd,* 41 M.J. 343 (C.A.A.F. 1995).

[417] 32 M.J. 98, 99 (C.M.A. 1991).

[418] 55 M.J. 168 (C.A.A.F. 2001).

(Rel.3—1/07   Pub.62410)

and the accused may reply to the rebuttal. Because trial judges ride a circuit, and it may take some time to obtain rebuttal, the Air Force Central Circuit enacted a rule that required trial defense counsel to provide notice of "arguably inadmissible, immaterial, or irrelevant matter that might be included in the accused's unsworn statement. . ." ten days prior to trial. This rule has been upheld.[419]

The judge can and should give an appropriate explanatory instruction.[420] The Air Force Court of Military Review has approved comment by trial counsel that an accused's testimony was not given under oath.[421]

§ 23-45.22 Defense Witnesses

The ability to obtain defense extenuation and mitigation witnesses is governed by Rule for Courts-Martial 1001(e)(1), which encourages the accused to use alternatives to live-witness testimony:

> During the presentence proceedings, there shall be much greater latitude than on the merits to receive information by means other than testimony presented through the personal appearance of witnesses. Whether a witness shall be produced to testify during presentence proceedings is a matter within the discretion of the military judge, subject to the limitations in subsection (e)(2) of this rule.

Rule 1001(e)(2), Limitations, places severe restrictions on the ability to obtain sentencing witnesses:

> A witness may be produced to testify during presentence proceedings through a subpoena or travel orders at Government expense only if —
>
> (A) The testimony expected to be offered by the witness is necessary to resolve an alleged inaccuracy or dispute as to a material fact;
>
> (B) The weight or credibility of the testimony is of substantial significance to the determination of an appropriate sentence;
>
> (C) The other party refuses to enter into a stipulation of fact containing the matters to which the witness is expected to testify, except in an extraordinary case when such a stipulation of fact would be an insufficient substitute for the testimony;
>
> (D) Other forms of evidence, such as oral depositions, written interrogatories, or former testimony would not be sufficient to meet the needs of the court-martial in the determination of an appropriate sentence; and
>
> (E) The significance of the personal appearance of the witness to the determination of an appropriate sentence, when balanced against the

---

[419] Armstrong v. Mahoney, Misc. No. 99-01 (A.F. Crim. App. Jan. 14, 1999), *pet. denied*, 51 M.J. 349 (C.A.A.F. 1999).

[420] *See, e.g.,* Welch, 1 M.J. at 1203.

[421] United States v. Turner, 30 M.J. 1183, 1184 (A.F.C.M.R. 1990) (citing United States v. Breese, 11 M.J. 17 (C.M.A. 1981)); United States v. Smith; 23 M.J. 744 (A.C.M.R. 1987).

(Rel.3—1/07 Pub.62410)

practical difficulties of producing the witness, favors production of the witness. Factors to be considered include the costs of producing the witness, the timing of the request for production of the witness, the potential delay in the presentencing proceeding that may be caused by the production of the witness, and the likelihood of significant interference with military operational deployment, mission accomplishment, or essential training.[422]

Although the Rule does not limit the right of the defense to present live witnesses whom it procures through its own means, it does prohibit use of either government funds or subpoena to obtain such witnesses unless they qualify under the Rule. In *United States v. Combs*,[423] the Court of Military Appeals endorsed these limitations when it held that the military judge did not abuse his discretion in denying a defense motion for production of the accused's mother as an extenuation and mitigation witness.

One solution to the clash between the defense desire for extenuation and mitigation testimony and the government's concern about limited resources is the use of high-quality video testimony. Although this could be adduced via videotape, live two-way testimony is far more useful. William & Mary's Courtroom 21 Project[424] has shown the utility of inexpensive two-way remote testimony using ISDN based video-conferencing. Given that video-conferencing is becoming commonplace in the armed forces, counsel faced with an inability to obtain the physical presence of sentencing witnesses should seek remote video appearances.[425]

§ 23-45.23 Command Influence

The sentencing phase of a court-martial presupposes the defense's ability to freely present relevant extenuation and mitigation evidence. Quite frequently, that evidence takes the form of defense witnesses who are asked to give evidence favorable to the defense — usually favorable character or rehabilitative potential evidence. This can prove frustrating to convening authorities who have referred cases to trial in the hope of sentences to confinement and punitive discharges. Unfortunately, on occasion commanders have attempted to resolve their

---

[422] As for procurement of witnesses, see generally Chapter 20. *See, e.g.*, United States v. Mitchell, 41 M.J. 512 (A. Crim. App. 1994) (denial of Chief of Chaplains, for whom the accused had served as a driver seven years before, as an E&M rehabilitation witness and use instead of a compelling stipulation of fact wasn't an abuse of discretion).

[423] 20 M.J. 441 (C.M.A. 1985). *Cf.* United States v. Loya, 49 M.J. 104 (C.A.A.F. 1998) (error not to admit evidence of poor medical treatment that may lessen punishment).

[424] Courtroom 21, "The Courtroom of the 21st Century Today," is the world's most technologically advanced courtroom. A joint project of the College of William & Mary and the National Center for State Courts, Courtroom 21 is an international demonstration and experimental project.

[425] *See* United States v. Mitchell, 41 M.J. 512, 515, n. 7 (A. Crim. App. 1994).

(Rel.3—1/07 Pub.62410)

frustration by directly or indirectly encouraging personnel not to serve as defense witnesses.[426]

In *United States v. Jameson*,[427] actual reprisals were taken against defense witnesses after their testimony. The Navy-Marine Court of Military Review wrote:

> We agree, and, like the panel that first considered this case, we view unlawful command influence directed against actual or prospective providers of favorable Article 60b(1), U.C.M.J., matters as an analog[ue] of unlawful command influence directed against actual or prospective witnesses at trial. . . .[428]

> We note the word "attempt" in the Article 37(a) phrase "attempt to coerce or, by any unauthorized means, influence . . .," from which it may be argued that unlawful command influence cannot exist unless the source thereof specifically intends, with all the requisite scienter, to exert such unlawful command influence. Although no one has made it, we reject any such argument. While specific intent and scienter may be required for a successful prosecution under Article 98 of one who violates the quoted portion of Article 37(a), an accused whose case is adversely affected by unlawful command influence, and the integrity of the military justice system in general, are just as victimized whether the source of the influence intended the adverse effects on the case or not; likewise, an accused whose case is unaffected, because the source's attempt has failed, will be denied relief, although the source may still be prosecuted for the attempt under Article 98. Consequently, whatever may be the result when an otherwise lawful command action is taken for the sole or principal purpose to influence a court-martial adversely to an accused, it is our view that, when an unlawful act of a commander or his staff proximately causes coercion or other unlawful influence upon a case, that case has been tainted by unlawful command influence, even if it is not proved that the commander or staff member concerned specifically intended to perpetrate unlawful command influence upon that case.

> We deem such a rule to be not only legally sound but also systemically beneficial in adjudicating issues of command influence. Attempting to determine people's real motives and intents is quintessentially unscientific and, therefore, risky and conductive to grave injustice and actual or feigned moral outrage. Also, people, having complex personalities, may act in a

---

[426] These efforts have traditionally taken the form of command letters or memoranda, many of which have been misinterpreted to give rise to unintended results on the part of subordinates. *See generally* § 15-90.00, *above*. In United States v. Clemons, 35 M.J. 770, 772–73 (A.C.M.R. 1992), however, the accused's commander "counselled" potential defense extenuation and mitigation witnesses, an activity the court found constituted command influence. In *Clemons* the court held that the judge's expansive corrective actions (including foreclosing prosecution aggravating testimony and allowing the accused to testify to what the expected witness testimony would have been) was adequate to redress the problem.

[427] 33 M.J. 669 (N.M.C.M.R. 1991).

[428] 33 M.J. at 673 (N.M.C.M.R. 1991).

(Rel.3—1/07 Pub.62410)

single matter out of multiple motives and intents, some benign, others not so benign; hence, the attempt could easily degenerate into a mind-boggling effort to assess the relative potency of the several motives and intents found to be present. Moreover, in this case several commanders and staff members were involved, each of whom may not have shared precisely the same motives or intents as the others. Finally, we believe that the process of litigating command influence issues will benefit if it is possible to render an adjudication of unlawful command influence without concomitantly stigmatizing the perpetrators thereof as military justice outlaws. . . .[429]

In addition to the summary reliefs of Sergeant Hilinski and Staff Sergeant Gurule following their testimony, while the post-trial review in Jameson, the trial in Jones, and several administrative discharge boards were pending, the Commanding Officer of the Fourth Recruit Training Battalion addressed the members of her battalion in response to a seemingly widespread conception, directly attributable to the adverse actions taken against Sergeant Hilinski and Staff Sergeant Gurule, that testifying for the defense could be hazardous to one's Marine Corps career. The substance of her remarks was that persons with relevant information were encouraged to testify for the defense, but that, if their testimony deviated from Marine Corps policy, they would be held accountable for it. Although her remarks were ostensibly intended as a remedy for the foregoing conception, we think that they could only have had just the opposite effect of tending to induce her listeners, if they got involved at all, to engage in fear-based self-censorship calculated to tailor the content of their testimony to Marine Corps policy.[430]

. . . Whether or not we, ourselves, would find unlawful command influence on this evidence is unimportant; but we cannot deny the reality that this record does, indeed, contain "some evidence sufficient to render reasonable a conclusion in favor of the allegation [of unlawful command influence] asserted," and that the Government has not disproved unlawful command influence by clear and positive evidence. While there is not direct evidence that the unlawful command influence affected, specifically, the convening authority's action on the appellant's case, neither is there reliable evidence that it did not. On the whole record, we are simply left with a reasonable doubt as to whether or not the convening authority's action was affected by unlawful command influence. Because of the rules relating to the allocation of burden of proof and risk of non-persuasion, this is enough to require corrective action.[431]

§ 23-45.30 Capital Cases

In *Lockett v. Ohio*,[432] and *Eddings v. Oklahoma*,[433] the Supreme Court held that, in capital cases, the sentencing authority should not be precluded from

---

[429] 33 M.J. at 673 (N.M.C.M.R. 1991).

[430] 33 M.J. at 676–77 (N.M.C.M.R. 1991).

[431] 33 M.J. at 677 (N.M.C.M.R. 1991).

[432] 438 U.S. 586 (1978).

(Rel.3—1/07 Pub.62410)

considering as a mitigating factor any aspect of the defendant's character or record that would lessen the severity of the punishment, nor may the sentencing authority refuse to consider any relevant mitigating evidence. In *Skipper v. South Carolina*,[434] the Court held that mitigation includes the behavior of the defendant in prison while awaiting trial, and that exclusion of this evidence from a capital sentencing hearing would violate the accused's rights.

The potential scope of extenuation and military evidence in the armed forces is sufficiently broad to satisfy constitutional needs. The possibility of severe limitations on live-witness testimony could be troubling. One would presume that, in a capital case, a military judge would be more likely to permit the use of governmentally funded defense witnesses than in noncapital cases.

§ 23-46.00 Prosecution Rebuttal

Rule for Courts-Martial 1001(d) provides:

> The prosecution may rebut matters presented by the defense. The defense in surrebuttal may then rebut any rebuttal offered by the prosecution. Rebuttal and surrebuttal may continue, in the discretion of the military judge. If the Military Rules of Evidence were relaxed under subsection (c)(3) of this rule, they may be relaxed during rebuttal and surrebuttal to the same degree.

As in the case-in-chief, the defense counsel must be aware of the possibilities for rebuttal after the defense presents its case during the sentencing stage of the court-martial. The witnesses, including the accused, may "open the door" for the prosecution to present evidence that would be inadmissible absent defense sentencing evidence. In *United States v. Flynn*,[435] for example, it was proper for the military judge to take judicial notice of, and instruct the members about, the existence of sexual offender rehabilitation programs at the Army's two major correctional facilities after "the defense previously introduced evidence suggesting that incarceration for child molesters at the United States Disciplinary Barracks . . . or any other penal institution was not appropriate."[436] "Door opening" permits expansive rebuttal,[437] which can include evidence of specific

---

[433] 455 U.S. 104 (1982). *See also* Sumner v. Shuman, 483 U.S. 66 (1987) (mandatory death sentence for accused who murdered fellow prisoner without consideration of evidence in mitigation violates the Eighth and Fourteenth Amendments); Hitchcock v. Dugger, 481 U.S. 393 (1987) (error for trial judge not to instruct advisory jury about mitigating factors and not to consider evidence of mitigating circumstances not specifically enumerated in state death-penalty statute).

[434] 476 U.S. 1 (1986). When the accused is tried for an offense that would have been tried by a civilian court prior to *Solorio v. United States*, 483 U.S. 435 (1987), the defense might introduce, under R.C.M. 1001(c)(1)(B), the maximum sentence, if less in the civilian jurisdiction. Note, Army Law 27 (Dec. 1987).

[435] 28 M.J. 218 (C.M.A. 1989).

[436] 28 M.J. at 221–622 (C.M.A. 1989).

[437] Although the rules for admission of past conviction evidence have changed (*see* R.C.M.

(Rel.3—1/07 Pub.62410)

past acts of misconduct by the accused,[438] otherwise inadmissible records of nonjudicial punishment,[439] and adverse duty performance.[440] As the Court of Military Appeals long ago observed with respect to rebuttal:

> As the Government here contends, were we to adopt a contrary view, an accused would occupy the unique position of being able to "parade a series of partisan witnesses before the court" — testifying at length concerning specific acts of exemplary conduct by him — without the slightest apprehension of contradiction or refutation by the opposition.[441]

In addition to cross-examining defense character witnesses, the prosecution may also introduce reputation and opinion evidence in rebuttal to the defense evidence.[442]

Rebuttal evidence must, however, "rebut." If it does not answer the defense case, it is inadmissible.[443] The courts of military review have held in pre-Rules

1001(b)(3)(A)), pre-Rules cases dealing with prior convictions are illustrative of the scope of door-opening. United States v. Hamilton, 42 C.M.R. 283 (C.M.A. 1970) (prior civilian conviction not admissible under *1951 Manual* was admissible in rebuttal); United States v. Plante, 32 C.M.R. 266 (C.M.A. 1962) (conviction more than six years old normally inadmissible under the *Manual*, but admissible in rebuttal to evidence of good character during the same period of time); United States v. Marshall, 44 C.M.R. 727 (N.C.M.R. 1971) (when accused states he has no prior convictions other than one admitted by prosecution, it is permissible for the prosecution to cross-examine and to admit other convictions). However, the mere fact that the accused may have made a statement does not *per se* open the door to rebuttal. *E.g.,* United States v. Goree, 34 M.J. 1027 (N.M.C.M.R. 1992) (unsworn statement that accused had performed well was an opinion that was not subject to rebuttal with uncharged misconduct).

[438] *See* United States v. Blau, 17 C.M.R. 232 (C.M.A. 1954) (In rebuttal to evidence of specific acts, prosecution witness could testify that the accused's character was poor with respect to trustworthiness and honesty and that he was a troublemaker; at court member's request witness could give basis for opinion); United States v. Ledezma, 4 M.J. 838 (A.F.C.M.R. 1978) (Accused made an unsworn statement as to regret for committing crime and resolved never to repeat misconduct; proper for prosecution to introduce evidence that the accused had told his supervisor that if he found who reported him he would "get a contract on him"); United States v. Jeffries, 47 C.M.R. 699 (A.F.C.M.R. 1973).

[439] United States v. Strong, 17 M.J. 263 (C.M.A. 1984).

[440] United States v. Stark, 17 M.J. 778 (A.F.C.M.R. 1983).

[441] United States v. Blau, 17 C.M.R. 232, 244 (C.M.A. 1954).

[442] United States v. Boughton, 16 M.J. 649, 649–50 (A.F.C.M.R. 1983) ("A commander is responsible for the welfare and discipline of everyone under his command and may properly testify in rebuttal during the sentencing portion of the trial, as to his knowledge of the conduct and performance of his subordinate even when the knowledge is imparted to him by others."); United States v. Evans, 20 M.J. 504 (A.F.C.M.R. 1985) (During sentencing, two defense witnesses stated that the accused could be rehabilitated, and the accused, in an unsworn statement, said that he wanted to stay in the service and would never use drugs again. The court held it permissible to call a drug rehabilitation counselor who testified that the accused's attitude toward rehabilitation was poor and that the accused believed neither that he had a drug problem nor that he needed a rehabilitation program).

[443] *See, e.g.,* United States v. Armstrong, 12 M.J. 766 (A.C.M.R. 1981); United States v. Wright,

(Rel.3—1/07 Pub.62410)

for Courts-Martial cases that the prosecution may not rebut an unsworn statement of the accused by introducing evidence as to the character of the accused for untruthfulness. [444] "The prosecution may, however, rebut *any* statements of facts therein." [445]

Rule for Court-Martial 1001(c)(2)(C) provides in part that "an accused may make an unsworn statement and may not be cross-examined by trial counsel upon it or examined upon it by the court-martial." This prevents the judge or members from questioning appellant about the unsworn statement, [446] but does not preclude the Government from rebutting the unsworn statement. [447] In *United States v. Provost*, [448] the court held that the defendant has the right to make an unsworn statement in rebuttal to the prosecution evidence.

"[R]ace is an inappropriate factor upon which generally to determine a sentence." [449]

§ 23-50.00   SENTENCING FACTORS

§ 23-51.00   In General

Rule for Courts-Martial 1002 provides:

> Subject to limitations in this *Manual*, the sentence to be adjudged is a matter within the discretion of the court-martial; except when a mandatory minimum sentence is prescribed by the code, a court-martial may adjudge any punishment authorized in this *Manual*, including the maximum punishment or any lesser punishment, or may adjudge a sentence of no punishment.

A.C.M. 23922 (A.F.C.M.R. 30 Aug. 1983) (The accused made an unsworn statement that "I would like to get my life straightened out as soon as I can get all this bad stuff behind me." The court held that the trial counsel could not rebut this by introducing evidence that the accused tried to sell drugs between the time of apprehension and the time of trial, and that he made a statement that he was always going to use marijuana). As for rebuttal of unsworn statements, Section 23-45.21(b), *see* United States v. Privette, 31 M.J. 791, 793 (A.F.C.M.R. 1990). The accused may reply to the rebuttal evidence. United States v. Provost, 32 M.J. 98 (C.M.A. 1991).

[444] *See* United States v. Shewmake, 6 M.J. 710 (N.C.M.R. 1978); United States v. McCurry, 5 M.J. 502 (A.F.C.M.R. 1978); United States v. Stroud, 44 C.M.R. 480 (A.C.M.R. 1971).

[445] R.C.M. 1001(c)(2)(C) (emphasis added).

[446] United States v. Satterley, 52 M.J. 782 (A.F. Crim. App. 1999), *aff'd*, 55 M.J. 168 (C.A.A.F. 2001).

[447] *See* United States v. Manns, 54 M.J. 164 (C.A.A.F. 2000) (unsworn statement that he "tried to obey the law" was an assertion of fact that could be rebutted by the prosecution). *But see* United States v. Cleveland, 29 M.J. 361 (C.M.A. 1990) (statement that "I feel that I have served well" was like an argument and not a statement of fact subject to rebuttal); United States v. Partyka, 30 M.J. 242, 247 (CMA 1990) (accused's efforts to blame the victim and her parents for his sexual abuse was held to not be a "statement of fact" within the meaning of R.C.M. 1001(c)(2)(C)).

[448] 32 M.J. 98, 99 (C.M.A. 1991).

[449] United States v. Green, 37 M.J. 380, 385 (C.M.A. 1993).

(Rel.3—1/07   Pub.62410)

Accordingly, determination of sentence in a given case requires knowledge of the maximum imposable sentence and of the evidence relevant to proper sentencing factors.

§ 23-52.00   Maximum Imposable Sentence

§ 23-52.10   In General

With few exceptions, the substantive punitive articles of the Uniform Code of Military Justice provide only that an offender "shall be punished as a court-martial may direct." Article 56 of the Code vests the power to prescribe maximum sentences in the President. Consequently, the maximum sentence is customarily supplied in Part IV of the *Manual for Courts-Martial*,[480] an executive order. The maximum sentence for personnel on active duty[481] will be the lesser of the maximum applicable under the *Manual* or the jurisdictional limit of the court-martial. If the accused has been convicted of offenses that are "multiplicitous," or not legally separate, "the maximum punishment for those offenses shall be the maximum authorized punishment for the offense carrying the greatest maximum punishment."[482]

In *United States v. Turner*,[483] the Navy-Marine Court heard a challenge to the constitutionality of the congressional delegation to the President of the power

---

[480] R.C.M. 1003(c)(1)(A). For the maximum punishments for offenses not specified in Part IV, see R.C.M. 1003(c)(1)(B):

(i) Included or related offenses. For an offense not listed in Part IV of this *Manual* which is included in or closely related to an offense listed therein the maximum punishment shall be that of the offense listed; however if an offense not listed is included in a listed offense, and is closely related to another or is equally closely related to two or more listed offenses, the maximum punishment shall be the same as the least severe of the listed offenses.

(ii) Not included or related offenses. An offense not listed in Part IV and not included in or closely related to any offense listed therein is punishable as authorized by the United States Code, or as authorized by the custom of the service. When the United States Code provides for confinement for a specified period of not more than a specified period the maximum punishment by court-martial shall include confinement for that period. If the period is 1 year or longer, the maximum punishment by court-martial also includes a dishonorable discharge and forfeiture of all pay and allowances; if 6 months or more, a bad-conduct discharge and forfeiture of all pay and allowances; if less than 6 months, forfeiture of two-thirds pay per month for the authorized period of confinement.

[481] For reservists, see R.C.M. 1003(c)(3).

[482] R.C.M. 1003(c)(1)(C). The Rule provides:

When the accused is found guilty of two or more offenses, the maximum authorized punishment may be imposed for each separate offense. Except as provided in paragraph 5 of Part IV, offenses are not separate if each does not require proof of an element not required to prove the other. If the offenses are not separate, the maximum punishment for those offenses shall be the maximum authorized punishment for the offense carrying the greatest maximum punishment.

[483] 30 M.J. 1276 (N.M.C.M.R. 1990).

(Rel.3—1/07 Pub.62410)

to set maximum punishments. Holding that the delegation was "not sufficiently definite,"[454] the court nevertheless sustained the constitutionality of the codal provision on the grounds of "a special long-standing, non-traditional constitutional relationship between Congress and the President as concerns the government of the military, such that the normal rules regarding separation of powers and Congressional delegation do not apply."[455]

§ 23-52.20   The "Escalator Clauses"

The *Manual for Courts-Martial* sometimes permits an increase in the ordinary maximum punishment for recidivists. Rule for Courts-Martial 1003(d) states:

(1) *Three or more convictions.* If an accused is found guilty of an offense or offenses for none of which a dishonorable discharge is otherwise authorized, proof of three or more previous convictions adjudged by a court-martial during the year next preceding the commission of any offense of which the accused stands convicted shall authorize a dishonorable discharge and forfeiture of all pay and allowances and, if the confinement otherwise authorized is less than 1 year, confinement for 1 year. In computing the 1-year period preceding the commission of any offense, periods of unauthorized absence shall be excluded. For purposes of this subsection, the court-martial convictions must be final.

(2) *Two or more convictions.* If an accused is found guilty of an offense or offenses for none of which a dishonorable or bad-conduct discharge is otherwise authorized, proof of two or more previous convictions adjudged by a court-martial during the 3 years next preceding the commission of any offense of which the accused stands convicted shall authorize a bad-conduct discharge and forfeiture of all pay and allowances and, if the confinement otherwise authorized, is less than 3 months, confinement for 3 months. In computing the 3 year period preceding the commission of any offense, periods of unauthorized absence shall be excluded. For purposes of this subsection the court-martial convictions must be final.

(3) *Two or more offenses.* If an accused is found guilty of two or more offenses for none of which a dishonorable or bad-conduct discharge is otherwise authorized, the fact that the authorized confinement for these offenses totals 6 months or more shall, in addition, authorize a bad-conduct and forfeiture of all pay and allowances.

Summary courts-martial convictions may not be used to trigger the escalator clauses.[456]

---

[454] 30 M.J. at 1281 (N.M.C.M.R. 1990).

[455] 30 M.J. at 1283 (N.M.C.M.R. 1990). *Cf.* United States v. Bivins, 49 M.J. 328, 329 (C.A.A.F. 1998).

[456] R.C.M. 1003(d) Discussion.

(Rel.3—1/07 Pub.62410)

§ 23-52.30 Rehearings

Rehearings are governed by Article 63 of the Uniform Code of Military Justice and Rule for Courts-Martial 810. Until Article 63 was amended in 1992, it limited the maximum sentence that could be adjudged at a rehearing to the sentence originally imposed by the original court-martial unless the punishment prescribed for the offense is mandatory or additional charges were involved.[487] The 1992 codal amendments altered Article 63 to adopt the position taken by Rule 810(d)(1),[488] which requires the convening authority to ensure that the sentence from the rehearing is no greater than that which was approved by the convening or higher authority in the first case. Because of the way Article 63 was originally drafted, without the change court-members at the retrial would have to be instructed that the maximum available sentence would be that actually imposed at the first trial. Under the amendment, the members may now sentence the accused normally; the convening authority, however, cannot approve a sentence in excess of that approved at the first trial. As court members are likely in many cases to adjudge a sentence less than the maximum available, the practical effect of the change may be to increase the sentences members actually adjudge on retrial, preventing a form of sentence "windfall."

§ 23-53.00 Sentencing Factors in Noncapital Cases

In light of the failure to declare a priority among the various sentencing goals, sentencing judges or court members are left vast discretion. In large measure, when sentencing, the judge or members can consider anything so long as it has come to their attention though admissible evidence or is within their common experience.[459] Some matters, however, merit special consideration.

§ 23-53.10 The Accused's Plea

The standard sentencing instruction in a guilty plea case reads:

> A plea of guilty is a matter of mitigation which must be considered along with all other facts and circumstances of the case. Time, effort, and expense to the government (usually are) (have been) saved by a plea of guilty. Such a plea may be the first step toward rehabilitation.[460]

---

[487] United States v. Lawson, 34 M.J. 38 (C.M.A. 1992). In *Lawson* Judge Cox opined that when sentencing is by members, military law ought to ensure that the members are told what the original maximum punishment was so that they can fully appreciate the societal interest represented by that punishment. 34 M.J. 38 (C.M.A. 1992) at 4243 (Cox, J., concurring in part and in the result).

[488] The National Defense Authorization Act for Fiscal Year 1993, Pub. L. No. 102-484 § 1059(a) (October 23, 1992).

[459] *See, e.g.,* Dep't of Army Pam. 27-9 Military Judges' Benchbook ch. Section IV (15 September 2002).

[460] Dep't of Army Pam. 27-9 Military Judges' Benchbook 71 (15 September 2002). *See also* R.C.M. 1001(f)(1); United States v. Simpson, 16 M.J. 506 (A.F.C.M.R. 1983); United States v.

(Rel.3—1/07 Pub.62410)

This instruction restates the law that is accepted throughout the United States. Those who plead not guilty complain that they are penalized for exercising their constitutional and statutory rights. The instruction and its underlying principle is justified by the argument that the offender who pleads guilty gets justice while the guilty-plea offender gets a less severe sentence than he or she would ordinarily receive. It should be noted by all that even if this analysis is correct, the notguilty accused pragmatically pays for the exercise of his or her rights.

The prosecution may not comment on the decision of the accused to plead not guilty by asserting that the defendant hasn't even taken the first step towards rehabilitation. He can't admit what he did. [461] The fact that the accused pled not guilty should not be considered adversely to him or her.

§ 23-53.20 Cooperation with the Authorities

In *Roberts v. United States*, [462] the Court held that absent exercise of the right against self-incrimination or adequate timely articulated explanation, it was proper for the court to consider, on sentencing, numerous refusals by the accused to cooperate with the government. Although *Roberts* permits consideration of the accused's noncooperation with the government, it seems unlikely that such consideration is pragmatically possible unless the right against self-incrimination has been extinguished. Accordingly, in the average case, the fact that the accused has cooperated is admissible in mitigation. The failure of the accused to cooperate most likely might be usable in rebuttal to evidence of future rehabilitation.

§ 23-53.30 The Accused's False Testimony on the Merits

If the court members' findings indicate that they must have disbelieved the sworn testimony of the accused on the merits, they may consider the accused's mendacity during sentencing[463] if certain prerequisites are met:[464]

McLeskey, 15 M.J. 565 (A.F.C.M.R. 1982). *Accord* United States v. Fisher, 21 M.J. 327 (C.M.A. 1986) (An instruction about the mitigating effect of a guilty plea is appropriate, but absent a defense objection or request for instruction, failure to give the instruction is not reversible error).

[461] United States v. Jones, 30 M.J. 898, 901 (A.F.C.M.R. 1990) (citing United States v. Johnson, 1 M.J. 213 (C.M.A. 1975)).

[462] 445 U.S. 552 (1980). Conversely, evidence that the accused cooperated is admissible during sentencing. *See, e.g.*, United States v. Thomas, 11 M.J. 388 (C.M.A. 1981); United States v. Shue, 766 F.2d 1122, 1129–30 (7th Cir. 1985). (When the defense alleges or creates the impression of full cooperation with the police, it is proper for the prosecutor to cross-examine the accused concerning his post-arrest silence); United States v. Frentz, 21 M.J. 813 (N.M.C.M.R. 1985) (Where the accused used invocation of his rights as a defense to establish credibility, it was proper for the government to cross-examine the accused and introduce extrinsic evidence as to invoking the right to remain silent).

[463] United States v. Grayson, 438 U.S. 41 (1978) (per Burger, C.J., in which White, Blackmun, Powell, Rehnquist, & Stevens, J.J., joined; Justice Stewart filed a dissenting opinion in which

(Rel.3—1/07 Pub.62410)

The court[465] must conclude that the accused lied;[466]

The court must conclude that the false testimony was willful and concerned a material matter;[467] and

The court may not punish the accused for lying, but may properly consider the accused's false testimony only as a factor relating to the accused's rehabilitative potential.[468]

The military judge must give a limiting instruction outlining these prerequisites if the trial counsel argues the accused's mendacity[469] and may give the limiting instruction sua sponte even if the trial counsel does not argue the matter.[470]

§ 23-53.40 Time Spent in Pretrial Confinement

The military judge must instruct, upon defense request, that time spent in pretrial confinement should be considered in deciding an appropriate sentence.[471] Since the accused receives administrative day-for-day credit for time spent in

---

Justices Brennan and Marshall joined). *See also* United States v. Mack, 9 M.J. 300, 318–19 (C.M.A. 1980); United States v. Warren, 10 M.J. 603 (A.F.C.M.R. 1980), *aff'd*, 13 M.J. 278 (C.M.A. 1982).

[464] United States v. Warren, 13 M.J. 278 (C.M.A. 1982).

[465] United States v. Beaty, 14 M.J. 155 (C.M.A. 1982). These prerequisites also apply to the military judge when acting as sentencing authority.

[466] United States v. Warren, 13 M.J. 278 (C.M.A. 1982).

[467] 13 M.J. at 286 (C.M.A. 1982). United States v. Carey, CM 441279 (20 May 1983). The appellate court may be willing to forgive the trial judge for omitting this portion of the instruction if it is clear from the facts that the court members believed the accused lied, and the lie involved material matters.

[468] 13 M.J. at 286 (C.M.A. 1982). United States v. Watkins, 17 M.J. 783 (A.F.C.M.R. 1983), *aff'd* 21 M.J. 224 (C.M.A.), *cert. denied*, 476 U.S. 1108 (1986). The trial judge must make it clear that the court members cannot punish the accused for committing perjury. *See also* United States v. Miree, SPCM 18301 (A.C.M.R. 7 Nov. 1983) (Failure to limit consideration to impact on rehabilitation is not cured by the general instruction that the accused should be "sentenced only for the offense for which he has been found guilty"). United States v. Carey, CM 441279 (A.C.M.R. 20 May 1983). *Accord* United States v. Pointer, CM 442435 (A.C.M.R. 30 Dec. 1983) (improper for trial counsel to argue "rehabilitation is not even an issue" for a drug peddler who lies to the military judge).

[469] United States v. Gore, 14 M.J. 945 (A.C.M.R. 1982); United States v. Rench, 14 M.J. 764 (A.C.M.R. 1982); United States v. Baxter, 14 M.J. 762 (A.C.M.R. 1982).

[470] United States v. Cabebe, 13 M.J. 303 (C.M.A. 1982). The *Warren* instruction can be given over the defense's objection. United States v. Fisher, 17 M.J. 768 (A.F.C.M.R. 1983), *rev'd on other grounds*, 24 M.J. 358 (C.M.A. 1987).

[471] United States v. Davidson, 14 M.J. 81 (C.M.A. 1982). Note that an accused can still receive the maximum punishment authorized, even though they were in pretrial confinement. United States v. Groshong, 14 M.J. 186 (C.M.A. 1982).

(Rel.3—1/07 Pub.62410)

pretrial confinement,[472] a complete instruction should also inform the court members about the administrative credit.[473]

§ 23-53.50   The Accused's Absence from Trial

If the accused is tried in absentia,[474] the sentencing authority may not punish the accused for the unauthorized absence, but may consider the accused's voluntary absence as an indication of the accused's rehabilitation potential.[475]

§ 23-53.60   Administrative Consequences of a Sentence

As a general rule, the court members cannot be instructed on, and cannot consider, the administrative consequences of their sentence.[476] Their duty is to

---

[472] United States v. Allen, 17 M.J. 126 (C.M.A. 1984). *Accord* R.C.M. 305(k).

[473] United States v. Stark, 19 M.J. 519 (A.C.M.R. 1984), *aff'd* 24 M.J. 381 (C.M.A. 1987), *cert. denied*, 484 U.S. 1026 (1988). The court suggests the following instruction:

> In determining an appropriate sentence in this case you should consider that the accused has spent days in pretrial confinement. In this connection, you should consider the fact that if you adjudge confinement . . . as part of your sentence, the days (he) (she) spent in pretrial confinement will be credited against any sentence to confinement you adjudge. This credit will be given by authorities at the correctional facility where the accused is sent to serve confinement and will be given on a day-for-day basis.

Stark, 19 M.J. at 527 n.3.

See also United States v. Noonan, 21 M.J. 763 (A.F.C.M.R. 1986) (The court members also should be instructed as to how many days' credit will be given if the accused receives credit for illegal pretrial confinement pursuant to R.C.M. 305(k)).

[474] *See generally* Section 16-20.00.

[475] United States v. Chapman, 20 M.J. 717 (N.M.C.M.R. 1985), *aff'd*, 23 M.J. 226 (C.M.A. 1986).

[476] United States v. Tschip, 58 M.J. 275 (C.A.A.F. 2003)(instruction that reference by the accused to an administrative discharge was a collateral matter and that the members should not speculate about it was not error); United States v. Perry, 48 M.J. 197 (C.A.A.F. 1998) (in light of lack of inadequate evidentiary foundation judge did not abuse his discretion in refusing to give instruction that punitive discharge may result in recoupment of Academy educational expenses); United States v. McElroy, 40 M.J. 368 (C.M.A. 1994) (although generally the judge should not instruct on the collateral administrative consequences of a sentence, the judge's instructions as to vested veteran's benefits were not substantially erroneous); United States v. Pollard, 34 M.J. 1008, 1014 (A.C.M.R. 1992) (evidence of child sex offender programs that required sentence of longer than six months was collateral and should not have been admitted); United States v. Wheeler, 18 M.J. 823, 823–825 (A.C.M.R. 1984), *aff'd*, 2 M.J. 76 (C.M.A.), *cert. denied*, 479 U.S. 27 (1986). *See also* United States v. Rosato, 32 M.J. 93, 96 (C.M.A. 1991) (evidence concerning details of rehabilitation programs "need not be generally admitted as a sentence concern" but not all such evidence is inadmissible). If there is a question from court members as to the collateral consequences of a particular sentence, the following instruction may be given: "There are many administrative and practical effects that may result from a conviction or a particular punishment. All effects are not predictable and it would be speculative for me to instruct you on possible collateral effects." U.S. Army, Trial Judiciary Memorandum 88-21, November 8, 1988 (resulting from United States v. Lenard, 27 M.J. 739 (A.C.M.R. 1988)); United States v. McLaren, 34 M.J. 926, 934 (A.F.C.M.R.

(Rel.3—1/07 Pub.62410)

adjudge a sentence based on the evidence presented in court without regard to outside considerations, such as the possibility of clemency action[477] or the possibility of parole.[478] Command policies and directives regarding the disposition of offenders or directives impacting on the military corrections system are not appropriate sentencing factors, and the military judge has a sua sponte duty to exclude them from consideration.[479] The court members, however, may consider that a punitive discharge is a serious punishment[480] that deprives an

---

1992) (not necessarily error to answer members' questions about collateral consequences of sentencing options; ordinarily the judge should tell the members that collateral consequences are "not germane"); United States v. Hopkins, 25 M.J. 671 (A.F.C.M.R. 1987). However, servicemembers reasonably close to retirement may introduce evidence as to the monetary loss of their potential retirement benefits. United States v. Becker, 46 M.J. 141 (C.A.A.F. 1997); United States v. Greaves, 46 M.J. 133 (C.A.A.F. 1997). *See also* United States v. Stargell, 49 M.J. 92 (C.A.A.F. 1998) (appropriate to argue unless BCD awarded accused would obtain retirement pay). The administrative consequences of convictions are potentially quite large. *See generally* Major Jeff Walker. *The Practical Consequences of a Court-Martial Conviction*, The Army Lawyer, December, 2001 at 1.

[477] Dep't Army Pam. 27-9, Military Judges' Benchbook 132-33 (15 September 2002).

[478] *See, e.g.*, United States v. Wheeler, 18 M.J. 823, 824–825 (A.C.M.R. 1984) (members should determine an appropriate sentence without regard to parole); United States v. Bates, CM 443075 (A.C.M.R. 11 Apr. 1984); United States v. Howell, 16 M.J. 1003, 1007 (A.C.M.R. 1983) (Naughton, J., concurring) (improper for trial counsel to tell court members to consider fact the accused will receive "good time").

[479] United States v. Grady, 15 M.J. 275 (C.M.A. 1983) (The mention of command policies about disposition of offenders invades the province of the court members to determine an appropriate sentence and risks improperly injecting the "commander" into the court-martial sentencing. This prohibition applies to both the trial counsel and the defense counsel.). *See also* United States v. Reitz, 17 M.J. 51 (C.M.A. 1983) (improper reference to Chief of Naval Operations' antidrug policy); United States v. Kiddo, 16 M.J. 775 (A.C.M.R. 1983) (improper for trial counsel to purport to speak for convening authority); United States v. Schoemake, 17 M.J. 858 (N.M.C.M.R. 1984) (improper reference to the Marine Corps' strong policy against drugs); United States v. Visalli, NMCM 84 1589 (N.M.C.M.R. 23 Aug. 1984) (improper reference to Chief of Naval Operations' antidrug buzz words "Not on my watch, not in my ship, and not in my Navy"); United States v. Harris, ACM S26157 (A.F.C.M.R. 25 Jan. 1984) (improper reference to Air Force drug policy). *But cf.* United States v. Colon-Rodriquez, CM 443211 (A.C.M.R. 30 June 1983) (Trial counsel argued: "Your Army needs for this individual not to remain in the service any longer." This argument was proper because it merely informed the members that they should consider the needs of the service. It did not inject command policy or the opinions of higher authorities.); United States v. Robertson, 17 M.J. 846 (N.M.C.M.R. 1984) (on the facts of the case, it was not prejudicial error for trial counsel to refer to commandant's drug policy); United States v. Barus, 16 M.J. 624 (A.F.C.M.R. 1983) (Trial counsel's argument that "we try to let everybody know what our policy is in the Air Force" was not improper because it did not refer to any specific policy and, therefore, did not suggest any particular sentence).

Argument that erroneously invokes command policy need not be "plain error." United States v. Kropf, 39 M.J. 107 (C.M.A. 1994) Judge Crawford suggests, however, "this is an area in which trial counsel are well advised to tread softly." 39 M.J. at 109 (C.M.A. 1994)).

[480] *See* United States v. Soriano, 20 M.J. 337 (C.M.A. 1985) (It was error for the trial judge to instruct that "A punitive discharge may affect an accused's future with regard to his legal rights, economic opportunities and social acceptability" instead of "will clearly affect").

(Rel.3—1/07 Pub.62410)

individual of substantially all benefits administered by the Veterans Administration.[481] The judge has a duty to instruct the members that a punitive discharge is a severe punishment, and the Court has endorsed a traditional instruction that such a discharge has an "ineradicable stigma."[482]

Although the guidelines in the area are unclear, there is some authority that suggests that a military judge may consider administrative consequences of a sentence, such as rules governing parole eligibility, when sitting as the sentencing authority.[483] The Army Court of Military Review has held, however, that it was error for a military judge "to construct a sentence specifically in reliance upon the collateral matter of what drug treatment programs may be available at the confinement center."[484]

Interestingly, in *United States v. Coder*,[485] a case of first impression, the court held that when the accused, a sentenced prisoner at the Disciplinary Barracks, had received administrative discipline for the same offense for which he was convicted and sentenced, no sentence credit is required.

In light of their importance, the impact on retirement benefits of a sentence often presents special concerns. The courts have not demonstrated a consistent approach. In *United States v. Boyd*,[486] for example, the court held the trial judge did not abuse his discretion in denying a request for an instruction on the impact of the loss of retirement benefits on the defendant who had completed 15 and 1/2 years of service. Yet, in *United States v. Greaves*,[487] the court held the judge abused his discretion in failing to give an instruction on the loss of retirement benefits when the defendant was only 9 weeks away from retirement eligibility and did not have to reenlist to reach 20 years. And in *United States v. Washington*,[488] the Court held that the judge erred in refusing the defense the opportunity

---

[481] United States v. Chasteen, 17 M.J. 580 (A.F.C.M.R. 1983); United States v. Simpson, 16 M.J. 506 (A.F.C.M.R. 1983).

[482] United States v. Rush, 54 M.J. 313, 315–16 (C.A.A.F. 2000) (error not prejudicial).

[483] *See* United States v. Hannan, 17 M.J. 115 (C.M.A. 1984):

Thus, in seeking to arrive at an appropriate sentence, Judge W. properly took into account the rules governing parole eligibility. Indeed, military judges can best perform their sentencing duties if they are aware of the directives and policies concerning good-conduct time, parole, eligibility for parole, retraining programs, and the like.

17 M.J. at 123.

[484] United States v. Grady, 30 M.J. 911, 914 (A.C.M.R. 1990) (citing United States v. Murphy, 26 M.J. 454 (C.M.A. 1988), *cert. denied*, 490 U.S. 1107 (1989)). It may be appropriate for the judge to instruct on available prison rehabilitation or therapy programs, even over defense objection. United States v. Duncan, 53 M.J. 494, 500 (C.A.A.F. 2000) (raised by a question by the members; citing at 499 United States v. Greaves, 46 M.J. 133, 139 (C.A.A.F. 1997) as controlling).

[485] 39 M.J. 1006, 1009–1010 (A.C.M.R. 1994) (accused received administrative discipline after trial but before action).

[486] 52 M.J. 758 (AF Ct. Crim. App. 2000), *aff'd*, 55 M.J. 217 (C.A.A.F. 2000).

[487] 46 M.J. 133, 139 (C.A.A.F. 1997).

[488] 55 M.J. 441 (C.A.A.F. 2001).

(Rel.3—1/07 Pub.62410)

to show the financial impact the accused would experience in the event a punitive discharge deprived her of retirement eligibility. And, in *United States v. Stargell*,[489] the court held that it was appropriate for the prosecution to argue that unless the defendant was given the punitive discharge, he would coast his way to retirement. Interestingly, in *United States v. Burt*,[490] the Court held that defense counsel's decision to reject an instruction referring to loss of retirement benefits was a legitimate tactical decision.[491]

§ 23-53.70 Recalcitrance

In *United States v. Edwards*,[492] the Court of Military Appeals opined:

> If a "proper foundation" is laid, "an accused's recalcitrance in refusing to admit his guilt after findings is, in a proper case, an appropriate factor for the members to consider in their sentencing deliberation on his rehabilitation potential." . . . As a general rule, the predicate foundation is that an accused has either testified or has made an unsworn statement and has either expressed no remorse or his expression of remorse can be arguably construed as being shallow, artificial, or contrived. . . . There may be other evidence in the record which gives rise to the inference that an accused is not remorseful.[493]

§ 23-53.80 Prior Article 15

An accused who has previously received Article 15 punishment for the same offense of which the accused has been convicted has the right to have any punishment received as a result of the non-judicial punishment to be taken into account during sentencing.[494] *United States v. Gammons*,[495] provides guidance on how credit is assessed depending on how the defense proceeds with respect to the Article 15.

> If the accused offers the record of a prior NJP during sentencing by members for the purpose of evidence in mitigation, the military judge must instruct the members on the specific credit to be given for the prior punishment under NJP. In the alternative, the accused may request that the instruction simply ask that the panel shall consider the punishment imposed in a prior NJP in adjudging the sentence. . . . In a judge-alone trial, if the accused offers the record of prior NJP for the purpose of evidence in mitigation during sentencing, the military judge will state on the record the specific credit awarded for the prior punishment.[496]

---

[489] 49 M.J. 92 (C.A.A.F. 1998).

[490] 56 M.J. 261 (C.A.A.F. 2002).

[491] Given that the instruction also referred to secretarial clemency.

[492] 35 M.J. 351 (C.M.A. 1992).

[493] 35 M.J. at 355 (C.M.A. 1992).

[494] United States v. Pierce, 27 M.J. 367 (C.M.A. 1989).

[495] 51 M.J. 169 (C.A.A.F. 1999).

[496] 51 M.J. at 184.

If the accused elects credit at an Article 39(a) session it should be "similar to adjudication of credit for illegal pretrial confinement."[497]

§ 23-60.00   SENTENCING ARGUMENT

§ 23-61.00   In General

Following rebuttal by trial counsel of any defense evidence on extenuation and mitigation,[498] counsel will argue. The sequence of argument is: trial counsel, defense counsel, and "[r]ebuttal arguments in the discretion of the military judge."[499] Rule 1001(g) provides:

> After introduction of matters relating to sentence under this rule, counsel for the prosecution and defense may argue for an appropriate sentence. Trial counsel may not in argument purport to speak for the convening authority or any higher authority, or refer to the views of such authorities or any policy directive relative to punishment or to any punishment or quantum of punishment greater than that court-martial may adjudge. Trial counsel may, however, recommend a specific lawful sentence and may also refer to generally accepted sentencing philosophies, including rehabilitation of the accused, general deterrence, specific deterrence of misconduct by the accused, and social retribution. Failure to object to improper argument before the military judge begins to instruct the members on sentencing shall constitute waiver of the objection.

Arguments that have been problematical include: placing undue emphasis on military-civilian relations that may be affected by the outcome of the case;[500] placing the court members in the place of the victim, thus inviting the court

---

[497] 51 M.J. at 184. *See also* United States v. Rock, 52 M.J. 154 (C.A.A.F. 1999).

[498] And, customarily, following any necessary conference on sentencing instructions, if members are involved.

[499] R.C.M. 1001(a)(1)(F). *See* United States v. Martin, 36 M.J. 739, 741 (A.F.C.M.R. 1993) (judge should not have given trial counsel option of arguing first or last, but no prejudice found), *aff'd*, 39 M.J. 481 (1994); United States v. Budicin, 32 M.J. 795, 797 (N.M.C.M.R. 1990) ("trial counsel should not routinely be permitted to choose whether to argue first or last on sentence" and should be limited to a "truly responsive rebuttal").

[500] Such references are not generally supported by the evidence and operate solely against the accused. United States v. Boberg, 38 C.M.R. 199 (C.M.A. 1968); United States v. Cook, 28 C.M.R. 323 (C.M.A. 1959); United States v. Hurt, 27 C.M.R. 3 (C.M.A. 1958); United States v. Childress, 33 M.J. 602, 606 (A.C.M.R. 1991) (argument that accused robbery would adversely affect United States-German relations was not supported by the evidence and was error; although such an error normally is not reversible in absence of defense objection cumulative errors in this case necessitated reversal); United States v. Poteet, 50 C.M.R. 73 (N.C.M.R. 1975). However, noting R.C.M. 1001(b)(4), the Court of Military Appeals has implied that "evidence of community impact may be introduced in an appropriate case." United States v. Sherman, 32 M.J. 449, 451–52 (C.M.A. 1991).

(Rel.3—1/07 Pub.62410)

members to set aside their impartiality;[501] appeals to religious matters;[502] and command interest or policies.[503]

In 2000, the Court of Appeals for the Armed Forces declared 'that Golden Rule arguments asking the members to put themselves in the victim's place are improper and impermissible arguments in the military justice system.'[504] But, the Court also opined that "we also recognize that an argument asking the members to imagine the victim's fear, pain, terror, and anguish is permissible, since it is simply asking the members to consider victim impact evidence."[505]

Counsel may argue, however, "matters of common knowledge within the community," including the predictable effects of refusing to deploy to a war zone in time of hostilities.[506] At least in the absence of a defense objection, the Court of Appeals for the Armed Forces has declined to reverse a sentence adjudged in a case involving importation of about 99 pounds of marijuana after trial counsel referred in part to the "war on drugs."[507]

---

[501] *See* United States v. Shamberger, 1 M.J. 377 (C.M.A. 1976) (trial counsel suggested that court members place themselves in place of helpless husband witnessing gang-rape of his wife); United States v. Wood, 40 C.M.R. 3 (C.M.A. 1969) (trial counsel urged members to consider victim to be their child). *But see* United States v. Edmonds, 36 M.J. 791, 793 (A.C.M.R. 1993) (In what is arguably dictum the court opined, however, that it is permissible for the trial counsel to ask the court members in argument to consider the fear the *victim* had, and must have had, during the offense, as distinguished from asking the members to put themselves in place of the victim); United States v. Baer, 53 M.J. 235 (C.A.A.F. 2000) (improper but non-prejudicial to ask sentencer "to imagine the helplessness and the terror. . .you're being taped and bound almost like a mummy . . .").

[502] "While no authority from our higher court that is precisely on point as to biblical argument has been cited by either party, we accept the basic premise of the appellant's citations, a premise apparently accepted by the Government *sub silentio*, that an appeal to religious impulses or beliefs as an independent source of a higher law calling for a particular result would constitute improper argument." United States v. Kirk, 41 M.J. 529, 533 (C.G. Crim. App. 1994) (dictum).

[503] R.C.M. 1001(g); United States v. Grady, 15 M.J. 275 (C.M.A. 1983); United States v. Olson, 22 C.M.R. 32 (C.M.A. 1965). *See also* United States v. Schnitzer, 44 M.J. 380 (C.A.A.F. 1996) (trial counsel preempting defense counsel about pretrial agreement does not bring the convening authority into the courtroom); United States v. Thomas, 44 M.J. 667 (N.M. Crim. App. 1996) (counsel reminded that command or departmental policies such as zero tolerance policies have no place at court-martial); United States v. Leggio, 30 C.M.R. 8 (C.M.A. 1960) (error to refer to policy message concerning removal of troublemakers from the service). *Cf.* Caldwell v. Mississippi, 472 U.S. 320 (1985) (improper to argue that the responsibility for appropriate sentence is with appellate court and not jury). Argument that erroneously invokes command policy need not be "plain error." United States v. Kropf, 39 M.J. 107 (C.M.A. 1994) Judge Crawford suggests, however, "this is an area in which trial counsel are well advised to tread softly." 39 M.J. at 109 (C.M.A. 1994)).

[504] United States v. Baer, 53 M.J. 235 (C.A.A.F. 2000) (dictum).

[505] 53 M.J. at 238, *citing* United States v. Holt, 33 M.J. 400, 408–409 (CMA 1991).

[506] United States v. Meeks, 41 M.J. 150, 158 (C.M.A. 1994) (citation omitted).

[507] United States v. Barramartinez, 58 M.J. 173 (C.A.A.F. 2003).

(Rel.3—1/07 Pub.62410)

Even unintentional racist comment is improper and will likely compel reversal.[508]

It should go without saying that, although counsel are advocates, they must be courteous although assertive. Trial counsel may not, for example, express contempt for court members who do not render a severe sentence,[509] and defense counsel should not express displeasure with the verdict.[510] Nevertheless, some degree of "puffery" is permitted advocates.[511]

The failure of defense counsel to make a timely objection to improper prosecution argument will waive the objection,[512] absent plain error.[513] It is essential that defense counsel take an active role in sentencing argument.[514]

§ 23-62.00   Defense Arguments *for* Serious Punishments

There are occasions when the accused expressly wishes counsel to seek a sentence that ought to be avoided when viewed rationally. This is particularly true of punitive discharges. On occasion, counsel whose client prefers to avoid confinement or other sanction may expressly and reasonably seek a discharge[515] in lieu of other punishment.[516] Such an argument may suggest, however, that

[508] United States v. Thompson, 37 M.J. 1023 (A.C.M.R. 1993) (en banc) (Racial remarks by trial counsel referring to *Boyz N the Hood* was plain error). *See also* United States v. Rodriguez, 60 M.J. 87 (C.A.A.F. 2004) (testing racially tinged argument for specific prejudice) (discussed 22-23.10 at note 19).

[509] United States v. Wood, 40 C.M.R. 3 (C.M.A. 1969).

[510] United States v. Richards, 47 C.M.R. 675 (A.C.M.R. 1975).

[511] United States v. Gibson, 30 M.J. 1138, 1139 (A.F.C.M.R. 1990). This does not justify exceeding the bounds of fair inference. *Cf.* United States v. White, 36 M.J. 306 (C.M.A. 1993) (but improper remarks did not substantially prejudice the accused's rights).

[512] *E.g.,* United States v. Sherman, 32 M.J. 449 (C.M.A. 1991); United States v. Martin, 36 M.J. 739, 741 (A.F.C.M.R. 1993) ("absent an error of such dimension that a miscarriage of justice would otherwise result"), *aff'd,* 39 M.J. 481 (C.M.A. 1994).

[513] United States v. Powell, 49 M.J. 460 (C.A.A.F. 1998); United States v. Kropf, 39 M.J. 107 (C.M.A. 1994); United States v. Thompson, 37 M.J. 1023 (A.C.M.R. 1993) (en banc) (plain error analysis). Plain error can result even in judge alone trials. 37 M.J. at 1028–29 (A.C.M.R. 1993). It is instructive to note the Court's observation in United States v. Robbins, 52 M.J. 455, 457 (C.A.A.F. 2000). Resolving a hearsay issue, the Court opined, "When the issue of plain error involves a judge-alone trial, an appellant faces a particularly high hurdle. A military judge is presumed to know the law and apply it correctly, is presumed capable of filtering out inadmissible evidence, and is presumed not to have relied on such evidence on the question of guilt or innocence."

[514] *See, e.g.,* United States v. Edwards, 35 M.J. 351, 354 (C.M.A. 1992) ("trial defense lawyer is 'no potted plant' ").

[515] Even if the accused desires a punitive discharge, defense counsel has an obligation to caution the accused about the serious and lasting consequences, and should attempt to dissuade the accused from such a decision.

[516] United States v. Weatherford, 42 C.M.R. 26 (C.M.A. 1970); United States v. Blunk, 37 C.M.R.

(Rel.3—1/07 Pub.62410)

counsel is arguing against the wishes of the client and, subject to self-incrimination concerns, may wish to ensure that counsel's position accords with that of the client. Generally, unless the record leaves no doubt as to the accused's desires, the defense counsel may not concede the appropriateness of a discharge.[517] When counsel does argue for a punitive discharge, it should only be for the least serious punitive discharge, the bad-conduct discharge.[518]

§ 23-70.00 INSTRUCTIONS

If there is a finding of guilty in a case with court members, the judge is required to give sentencing instructions following counsels' argument on sentence.[519] As with instructions on the findings, the judge will hold an Article 39(a) session to discuss the instructions with counsel and to receive any proposed instructions.

The judge will ordinarily address sentencing goals as well.[520] The judge, however, may not refer to command or service policy.[521]

Necessary instructions include a statement of the maximum authorized punishment (and any mandatory minimum), the procedures for deliberation and voting, and, at minimum, a statement to the effect that the members must consider all of the sentencing evidence. Rule for Courts-Martial 1005 sets forth requirements

---

26 (C.M.A. 1970); United States v. Houston, 50 C.M.R. 741 (A.C.M.R. 1975); United States v. Tinch, 43 C.M.R. 565 (A.C.M.R. 1970). *See also* United States v. Lyons, 36 M.J. 425 (C.M.A. 1993) (accused asked for discharge knowing that his pretrial agreement limited confinement to 45 days if a punitive discharge was granted).

[517] United States v. Quick, 59 M.J. 383 (C.A.A.F. 2004) (although counsel's concession of discharge and 40 year sentence was error, it was not prejudicial); United States v. Bolkan, 55 M.J. 425, 428 (C.A.A.F. 2001) ("when the accused asks the sentencing authority to be allowed to remain in the service, defense counsel errs by conceding the propriety of a punitive discharge" citing other cases); United States v. Holcomb, 43 C.M.R. 149 (C.M.A. 1971). *Cf.* United States v. Volmar, 15 M.J. 339 (C.M.A. 1983) (arguing for a bad-conduct discharge rather than a dishonorable discharge may not be error under some circumstances, even when no inquiry is made); United States v. Butts, 25 M.J. 535 (A.C.M.R. 1987)(when counsel argue for a punitive discharge and there is no inquiry by the military judge, court may find implied consent for this argument in the record).

[518] United States v. McMillan, 42 C.M.R. 601 (A.C.M.R. 1970). In an officer's case, only a dismissal is available.

[519] R.C.M. 920(b); 1005(b). The Federal Rules of Criminal Procedure permit the judge to give the instructions before or after the arguments of counsel. Fed. R. Crim. P. 30.

[520] *See* § 23-12.00, *above*.

[521] United States v. Kirkpatrick, 33 M.J. 132, 134 (C.M.A. 1991) (command policy considerations are improper, and defendant's failure to object does not constitute waiver given the importance of this matter to the military justice system); United States v. Grady, 15 M.J. 275 (C.M.A. 1983). *Compare* United States v. Kirkpatrick, *above, with* United States v. Kropf, 39 M.J. 107 (C.M.A. 1994) (finding reference to Navy's "zero tolerance policy towards drugs" not to be plain error, and distinguishing *Kirkpatrick* and *Grady*).

for the content of sentencing instructions, including a requirement that the members consider "matters in extenuation and mitigation." [522]

When the accused has been in pretrial confinement, the judge must instruct the court members on the credit the accused is entitled to for being in pretrial confinement, [523] unless the judge will administratively deduct this credit from any confinement announced by the court. Instructions are to a significant degree matters within the judge's discretion and are reviewed for abuse of discretion. [524]

At present neither the Rules for Courts-Martial nor the Military Judge's benchbook (which contains standard procedures, provide a procedure by which the members of a court-martial formally can recommend clemency to the convening authority). Instructing the members as to a procedure is not "plain error," pending adoption of a set practice. [525]

§ 23-80.00   DELIBERATIONS AND SENTENCE

§ 23-81.00   Sentence Worksheet

In a court-martial with member-sentencing, the trial counsel will ordinarily prepare a sentence worksheet tailored to reflect all sentencing alternatives. [526] The military judge and the defense counsel examine the worksheet at an Article 39(a) session. [527] During deliberations, the court members use the sentence worksheet as a guide to assist them in putting their sentence in proper form. [528] When the verdict is returned, the worksheet is marked as an appellate exhibit and attached to the record of trial. [529]

---

[522] R.C.M. 1005(e)(5). *See* United States v. Wheeler, 38 C.M.R. 72, 75 (C.M.A. 1967). How members should consider matters in an unsworn statement has sometimes been troublesome. *Cf.* United States v. Hopkins, 56 M.J. 393 (C.A.A.F. 2002) (judge's instructional reference to unsworn statement was sufficient).

[523] *See also* United States v. Groshong, 14 M.J. 186 (C.M.A. 1982).

[524] *E.g.,* United States v. Hopkins, 56 M.J. 393, 395 (C.A.A.F. 2002) (judge denied requested defense instruction as to the accused's remorse).

[525] United States v. Weatherspoon, 44 M.J. 211 (C.A.A.F. 1996).

[526] R.C.M. 1005(e)(1) Discussion. For an example, see MCM, 2005, App. 11. *But cf.* United States v. Brandolini, 13 M.J. 163 (C.M.A. 1982) (not error to omit "no punishment" from worksheet where it was not a plausible alternative).

[527] R.C.M. 1006(e) Discussion.

[528] R.C.M. 1006(e) Discussion.

[529] Benchbook 964. *See also* United States v. King, 13 M.J. 838, 842 (A.C.M.R. 1982) (error for trial judge not to allow defense counsel to examine worksheet and append it to trial record).

§ 23-82.00 Procedure[530]

After all the evidence has been presented, counsel have made their closing arguments, and the military judge has instructed on the law, the court members retire to deliberate on the sentence.[531] Deliberations must take place with all members present and without any outside intrusions.[532]

Before voting, the members should enter into full and free discussion of all available evidence.[533] The members may ask for additional evidence if it appears that they have insufficient evidence for a proper determination, or if it appears they have not received all available admissible evidence.[534]

When the court members have completed their discussions, each member may propose a complete sentence in writing.[535] The junior court member collects the proposals[536] and delivers them to the president of the court who arranges them in order of their severity.[537] The court members then votes on the proposals by secret, written ballot,[538] beginning with a vote on the least severe proposal.[539]

---

[530] Much of this subsection has been taken from Gaydos, *above* note 187, at 72–74. The footnotes have been renumbered.

[531] R.C.M. 1006(a).

[532] R.C.M. 1006(a).

[533] R.C.M. 1006(b).

[534] R.C.M. 1006(b). The military judge decides whether the additional evidence will be produced as an interlocutory, discretionary ruling. Factors the trial judge will consider include the difficulty in obtaining the witness, the materiality of the evidence, the likelihood that the evidence is subject to a claim of privilege, and the objections of the parties. United States v. Lampani, 14 M.J. 22, 26 (C.M.A. 1982). Members may question witnesses but must comply with procedural requirements. United States v. Blackmon, 39 M.J. 1091, 1093 (A.C.M.R. 1994) (failure to mark members' questions requires rehearing on sentence even though question was related to defendant's unsworn statement).

[535] R.C.M. 1006(c).

[536] R.C.M. 1006(c).

[537] R.C.M. 1006(c). The president's determination of the relative severity of the proposed sentences is subject to the objection of a majority of the other members. The trial judge may assist by providing factual statements about relative severity of different punishments, but may not make conclusory comments such as "a BCD is more severe than confinement." United States v. Holland, 19 M.J. 883 (A.C.M.R. 1985); United States v. Cavalier, 17 M.J. 573 (A.F.C.M.R. 1983).

[538] U.C.M.J. art. 51; R.C.M. 1006(d)(2). *See* United States v. Greene, 41 M.J. 57, 58 (C.M.A. 1994) (failure of judge to instruct on secret ballot wasn't plain error and given otherwise proper instructions and absent evidence of influence of superiority of rank, the accused's substantial rights were not affected). *Compare Greene with* United States v. Boland, 42 C.M.R. 275 (C.M.A. 1970).

[539] R.C.M. 1006(d)(3)(A); United States v. Simoy, 50 M.J. 1 (C.A.A.F. 1998) (plain error); United States v. Lumm, 1 M.J. 35, 36 (C.M.A. 1975); United States v. Thomas, 46 M.J. 311 (C.A.A.F. 1997) (plain error not to instruct to vote first on life in prison before voting on death penalty). Failure to instruct the members to begin voting with the lightest proposal may constitute plain error, even absent defense objection. United States v. Fisher, 21 M.J. 327 (C.M.A. 1986); United States v. Scott, 22 M.J. 646 (A.C.M.R. 1986).

(Rel.3—1/07 Pub.62410)

The members continue to vote on the proposals in the increasing order of their severity until the required number of concurring votes are obtained to select a sentence.[540]

For sentences including the death penalty, the vote must be unanimous.[541] For noncapital sentences, a two-thirds concurrence is required for sentences including confinement for ten years or less,[542] and a three-fourths concurrence is required for sentences including more than ten years' confinement.[543]

With the exception of a conviction for spying, in which the judge is to announce the death penalty "by operation of law," in those few cases in which a mandatory sentence or minimum sentence is involved,[544] the members will be instructed to return it. The Court of Military Appeals held that should the members not comply with that instruction, the sentence is unlawful and can be corrected, despite the failure of the members to return it.[545]

If none of the proposed sentences receive the required votes for concurrence, the members repeat the entire process of discussion, proposal, and balloting.[546] The court members have no duty to agree on a sentence;[547] therefore, it is possible to have a "hung jury" for purposes of sentencing.[548] The military judge may not coerce the members into reaching a compromise sentence.[549] If the

---

[540] R.C.M. 1006(d)(3)(A). Once the required number of votes is obtained on a proposed sentence, that sentence becomes the sentence of the court. Voting should be on the proposed sentence in its entirety. United States v. Dees, NMCM 84 2131 (N.M.C.M.R. 19 Oct. 1984). If the members vote in order of decreasing severity, the appropriate remedy if discovered during trial is a mistrial as to sentence. United States v. Jackson, 34 M.J. 1145 (A.C.M.R. 1992).

[541] U.C.M.J. art. 52(b)(1); R.C.M. 1006(b)(4)(A).

[542] U.C.M.J. art. 52(b)(2); R.C.M. 1006(d)(4)(B).

[543] U.C.M.J. art. 52(b)(3); R.C.M. 1006(d)(4)(C). Under current law, all aspects of a sentence that includes more than ten years confinement require a three-fourths concurrence. Garrett v. Lowe, 39 M.J. 293, 296–7 (C.M.A. 1994). Interestingly, Judge Cox suggested in *Garrett* that given the plain meaning of Article 52(b)(3) perhaps it is only the confinement portion of the sentence that requires a three-quarters vote; all other aspects may be adjudged by a two-thirds vote. 39 M.J. 293, 297–98 (C.M.A. 1994) (Cox, J., dissenting and suggesting that *Manual for Courts-Martial* requirements for three-fourths vote may be *ultra vires*).

[544] *See, e.g.,* U.C.M.J. art. 118 (Murder), requiring either death or life imprisonment.

[545] United States v. Shroeder, 27 M.J. 87, 90 (C.M.A. 1988), *cert. denied,* 489 U.S. 1012 (1989). *See also* Garrett v. Lowe, 39 M.J. 293 (C.M.A. 1994) (reaffirming *Schroeder*). In *Garrett*, despite the fact that members have no discretion under the statute, the court upheld the requirement that the members vote on a mandatory life sentence.

[546] R.C.M. 1006(d)(3)(A).

[547] Unless there is a mandatory minimum sentence. *See Shroeder*, 27 M.J. at 90.

[548] R.C.M. 1006(d)(6).

[549] United States v. Straukas, 41 C.M.R. 975 (A.F.C.M.R. 1970) ("Hung jury" instruction that members were under an obligation to reach a sentence created a fair risk of a compromise verdict requiring a rehearing on sentence).

members cannot agree on a sentence, the military judge should declare a mistrial and return the case to the convening authority who may direct a rehearing on sentence or order a sentence of "no punishment."[550]

The court must announce its sentence as soon as it is determined.[551] "Announcement" occurs when the president of the court-martial reads, in open court, the sentence that was actually reached by the court during its deliberations.[552]

Prior to announcement of the sentence, the military judge should review the sentence worksheet to ensure that the sentence is in a proper form.[553] Examination of the sentence worksheet,[554] or oral clarification of the worksheet,[555] does not constitute "announcement" of the sentence.

If the president of the court incorrectly states the sentence that was agreed upon during deliberations, this "slip of the tongue" does not constitute an announcement of the sentence.[556] A "slip of the tongue" concerning the court's sentence can be corrected anytime before the authenticated record of trial is forwarded to the convening authority[557] without resorting to formal reconsideration procedures.[558]

In announcing the sentence, the president should not disclose the specific number of votes for or against the sentence.[559] If the court's oral announcement

---

[550] R.C.M. 1006(d)(6).

[551] U.C.M.J. art. 53; R.C.M. 1007(a); United States v. Lee, 13 M.J. 181 (C.M.A. 1982) (error for military judge to seal the court's sentence pending resolution of defense petition to dismiss charges based on violation of the USAREUR 45-day rule).

[552] R.C.M. 1007(b).

[553] R.C.M. 1006(e) Discussion. *See* United States v. Jones, 34 M.J. 270 (C.M.A. 1992) (military judge may not correct unambiguous sentence two months after the trial — Query whether a different result would apply if the judge corrected an ambiguous sentence worksheet). The 1995 change to the *Manual for Courts-Martial* amended R.C.M. 1009(c)(1) to permit a judge to clarify an ambiguous sentence "as soon as practical after the ambiguity is discovered." When an ambiguous sentence is announced by members the ambiguity may be called to their attention by the judge or convening authority. R.C.M. 1009(c)(2) and (d).

[554] R.C.M. 1006(e). If the sentence to confinement is five years or more with no discharge, the judge should conduct a sidebar to ensure all sentence elements are present. United States v. Baker, 32 M.J. 290 (C.M.A. 1991). If the worksheet is not ambiguous, the sentence may not be increased at a posttrial session.

[555] R.C.M. 1006(e).

[556] R.C.M. 1007(b).

[557] R.C.M. 1007(b).

[558] R.C.M. 1009.

[559] R.C.M. 1006(e) Discussion. Since the *1984 Manual*, the court is no longer required to announce that the required "two-third's" or "three-fourths" concurrence was obtained. There is a presumption that the court members properly complied with the military judge's voting instructions. R.C.M. 1006(e) Analysis.

(Rel.3—1/07   Pub.62410)

of a sentence is legal and unambiguous, a conflicting sentence worksheet does not affect the validity of the sentence.[560]

Revision proceedings cannot be used after adjournment to increase a sentence even when it was caused by a clerical error.[561]

Military law lacks any explicit procedure by which a sentence can be "sealed" for deferred announcement, and in 1982 the Court of Military Appeals condemned such a technique as a violation of Article 53 of the Uniform Code of Military Justice.[562] Should a military judge improperly seal a sentence, the act will be tested for prejudice.[563] Any error can be waived by the accused.[564]

§ 23-83.00 Reconsideration of Sentence[565]

After a sentence proposal receives the required number of concurring votes during the balloting, that sentence becomes the final verdict,[566] and there can be no further balloting unless done pursuant to proper reconsideration procedures.[567]

The court[568] may reconsider a sentence, with a view towards decreasing it, anytime before the record of trial is authenticated.[569] A sentence can be reconsidered, with a view toward increasing it, only before that sentence is announced in open court.[570]

As a general rule, the military judge does not instruct on reconsideration procedures unless one of the court members requests the instruction or proposes reconsideration.[571] Once a timely proposal for reconsideration is made by one

---

[560] United States v. Donnelly, 12 M.J. 503 (A.F.C.M.R. 1981).

[561] United States v. Jones, 34 M.J. 270 (C.M.A. 1992), citing United States v. Baker, 32 M.J. 290 (C.M.A. 1991).

[562] United States v. Lee, 13 M.J. 181 (C.M.A. 1982).

[563] 13 M.J. 181 (C.M.A. 1982).

[564] United States v. Washington, 35 M.J. 774, 775 (A.C.M.R. 1992).

[565] This subsection has been taken from Gaydos, *above* note 187, at 72–74. The footnotes have been renumbered.

[566] R.C.M. 1009(d) Discussion.

[567] R.C.M. 1009.

[568] R.C.M. 924(c). The military judge presiding over a trial by military judge alone may reconsider a sentence in accordance with the same timing limitations applicable to reconsideration by the court members.

[569] R.C.M. 1009(a).

[570] R.C.M. 1009(b). *See generally* United States v. Morero, 41 M.J. 537 (N.M. Crim. App. 1994).

[571] Benchbook 104; United States v. Bridges, NMCM 84 1964 (N.M.C.M.R. 7 Feb. 1984) (Although the trial judge can clarify ambiguities in a sentence reached by the court members, it is improper for the trial judge to suggest to the court members that they should reconsider their verdict). *Compare Bridges, above with* United States v. Perez, 40 M.J. 373, 376 (C.M.A. 1994) (although there is no express authority to do so, the judge may direct that the members reconsider inconsistent findings. 40 M.J. 377 (C.M.A. 1994)).

(Rel.3—1/07 Pub.62410)

of the court members, the entire panel must vote on whether they wish to reballot.[572] Voting must be by secret written ballot.[573] Reconsideration to increase a sentence requires a majority of the members voting for reconsideration.[574] To decrease a sentence that includes confinement for more than ten years, requires more than one-fourth of the members voting for reconsideration.[575] A sentence that includes ten years of confinement or less may be reconsidered with a view towards decreasing the sentence if more than one-third of the members vote for reconsideration.[576]

§ 23-84.00   Defective Sentences[577]

Normally, ambiguities or illegalities in the sentence should be detected by the military judge when the sentence worksheet is examined prior to announcement of the verdict.[578] After the sentence is announced, the military judge can seek a clarification of the ambiguity or illegality any time prior to adjournment.[579] After the case is adjourned, the military judge may initiate a reconsideration proceeding, but only with a view to clarifying or decreasing the sentence.[580]

---

[572] R.C.M. 1009(d)(2).

[573] R.C.M. 1009(d)(2).

[574] R.C.M. 1009(d)(3)(A).

[575] R.C.M. 1009(d)(3)(B)(ii).

[576] R.C.M. 1009(d)(3)(B)(iii).

The following chart shows the number of votes required for sentence reconsideration by various size panels:

Number of Court members	To increase a sentence	To decrease a sentence 10 yrs. or less	To decrease a sentence more than 10 yrs.
3	2	2	1
4	3	2	2
5	3	2	2
6	4	3	2
7	4	3	2
8	5	3	3
9	5	4	3
10	6	4	3
11	6	4	3
12	7	5	4
13	7	5	4
14	8	5	4

[577] This subsection has been taken from Gaydos, *above* note 187, at 72–74. The footnotes have been renumbered.

[578] R.C.M. 1006(e) Discussion.

[579] R.C.M. 1009(c)(2)(B).

[580] R.C.M. 1009(c)(2)(B); R.C.M. 1009(b).

(Rel.3—1/07 Pub.62410)

The convening authority may also order a proceeding to seek clarification,[581] or the convening authority may approve the lowest, legal, unambiguous sentence adjudged.[582] If the announced sentence is not the one actually determined by the court-martial, the error may be corrected by a new announcement made before the record of trial is authenticated and forwarded to the convening authority."[583] The judge may clarify a sentence at any time until the convening authority's action.[584]

§ 23-85.00   Suspension of Sentence[585]

The court may not suspend a sentence;[586] that authority is reserved to the convening authority[587] who may not delegate that decision.[588] A recommendation by the court to suspend a sentence does not, standing alone, impeach the sentence.[589]

A suspension may be made conditional upon fulfillment of specified conditions so long as determination of the fulfillment of the condition doesn't amount to an improper delegation of the power to suspend.[590] "Unless otherwise stated, an action suspending a sentence includes as a condition that the probationer not violate any punitive article of the code."[591] "Suspension shall be for a stated period or until the occurrence of an anticipated future event. The period shall not be unreasonably long."[592] Vacation of a suspension is governed by Rule

---

[581] R.C.M. 1009(c)(3).

[582] R.C.M. 1009(c)(3).

[583] R.C.M. 1007(b). *See* United States v. Spaustat, 57 M.J. 256 (C.A.A.F. 2002).

[584] R.C.M. 1009(c).

[585] The first paragraph of this subsection has been taken from Gaydos, *above* note 187, at 72–74. The footnotes have been renumbered.

[586] United States v. Occhi, 2 M.J. 60 (C.M.A. 1976).

[587] U.C.M.J. art. 71(d). *See generally* R.C.M. 1108.

[588] *E.g.*, United States v. Wendlandt, 39 M.J. 810 (A.C.M.R. 1994).

[589] *See, e.g.*, United States v. Cimoli, 10 M.J. 516 (A.F.C.M.R. 1980); United States v. McLaurin, 9 M.J. 855 (A.F.C.M.R. 1980).

[590] *E.g.*, United States v. Wendlandt, 39 M.J. 810, 813 (A.C.M.R. 1994) (making suspension contingent on certification of successful completion of medical treatment for sexual offender treatment was an improper delegation).

[591] R.C.M. 1108(c).

[592] R.C.M. 1108(d). United States v. Leonard, 41 M.J. 900 (C.G. Crim. App. 1995) (in light of the *Coast Guard Military Justice Manual*, suspensions in excess of 18 months are ordinarily improper absent special circumstances in the record; however, suspensions specified in a pretrial agreement stand absent plain error); Spriggs v. United States, 40 M.J. 158 (C.M.A. 1994) (15 years too long for suspension). The maximum period of suspension, and how suspension is to be calculated may be dictated by service regulation. *See, e.g.*, United States v. Wendlandt, 39 M.J. 810, 812 (A.C.M.R. 1994) (Interpreting Army Reg. 27-10 ¶ 5-29 (22 December 1989) "one calculates the maximum allowable suspension period (two years or the unexecuted confinement, whichever is longer) from the date of the action, and then measures the actual suspension against that calculation").

(Rel.3—1/07   Pub.62410)

for Courts-Martial 1109.[593]

§ 23-86.00 Vacation Proceedings

A sentence suspension can be vacated when a servicemember violates the terms of the suspension. As the Court of Appeals for the Armed Forces opined in 1995, in *United States v. Connell*,[594]

R.C.M. 1109 sets forth in detail the procedure that must be followed if a suspended execution of a court-martial sentence is to be vacated. Without unnecessary recital of minutae, suffice it here to note that, where the sentence is of a general court-martial or where it is of a special court-martial and includes a bad-conduct discharge (as here), there are three markers along the pathway.

The first is encountered if the probationer is placed in confinement incident to his alleged violation of the conditions of suspension and a formal hearing on the alleged violation is not held within 7 days. R.C.M. 1109(c)(4). Under these conditions, a "neutral and detached . . . hearing officer" must "determine whether there is probable cause to believe that the probationer violated the conditions of the" probation. R.C.M. 1109(c)(4) and (C); . . .

The second requires "a hearing on the alleged violation of the conditions of suspension" that is to be held by the special court-martial convening authority "personally." R.C.M. 1109(d)(1)(A). This provision implements the statutory mandate of Article 72(a), U.C.M.J., 10 U.S.C. § 872(a), that, before vacation of suspension of any general court-martial sentence or of a special court-martial sentence that includes an approved bad-conduct discharge, "the officer having special court-martial jurisdiction over the probationer shall hold a hearing on the alleged violation of probation." In this connection, a probationer enjoys due process that includes notice of the hearing; of the alleged violation; of the "right to be represented at the hearing by civilian counsel provided by the probationer or, upon request," by detailed military defense counsel; and of the "opportunity to be heard," to present his own evidence, and to "cross-examine adverse witnesses." R.C.M. 1109(d)(1)(B).

The third prescribes a decision by the general court-martial convening authority as to "whether the probationer violated a condition of suspension, and, if so, whether to vacate the suspended sentence." R.C.M. 1109(d)(2)(A). That decision is based on the hearing officer's summarized record of the earlier proceeding and written recommendation concerning the vacation. R.C.M. 1109(d)(1)(D). Again, both the report and recommendation of the special court-martial convening authority and the

---

[593] When based upon a pretrial agreement, use of misconduct for purposes of vacating a suspension depends upon specific terms of the agreement and the timing of the misconduct. *See* United States v. Saylor, 40 M.J. 715, 718 (N.M.C.M.R. 1994). *See generally* United States v. Smith, 47 M.J. 263 (C.A.A.F. 1997); United States v. Connell, 42 M.J. 462 (C.A.A.F. 1995).

[594] 42 M.J. 462, 463-64 (C.A.A.F. 1995) (emphasis in original; paragraph numbers omitted).

decision-making by the general court-martial convening authority are specific creatures of statute. See Art. 72(b).[595]

The Court of Appeals for the Armed Forces held in *United States v. Mitchell*[596] that when an accused has promised to make restitution in a pretrial agreement, the failure of the accused to comply with that term permits vacation of sentence, even when indigent—at least when the accused acted in bad faith.[597]

A convicted servicemember seeking to challenge a vacation of sentence may do so via a petition for extraordinary relief[598] or on direct appeal.[599] An incomplete record may result in a remand by the appellate court for additional fact-finding.[600] With recruitment lagging and personnel resources strained by war and deployments, commanders today are more willing to suspend the execution of discharges,[601] ultimately making it more probable that there will be more efforts to vacate suspended sentences.

---

[595] *See also* United States v. Miley, 59 M.J. 300 (C.A.A.F. 2003) ("SPCMCA is required to provide an evaluation of any contested facts and a determination of whether the facts, as found, warrant vacation of the suspension. That obligation arises as a requirement under R.C.M. 1109(d)(1)." 59 M.J. at 304). *But see* 59 M.J. at 305, Baker, J. and Crawford, C.J. dissenting.

[596] 51 M.J. 490 (C.A.A.F. 1999).

[597] "The record reflects that appellant either made a bargain that he knew he could not keep, or he allowed his assets to be dissipated. . . . Either alternative constitutes bad faith." 51 M.J. at 494.

[598] Hoby v. United States, 46 M.J. 653 (N.M. Crim. App. 1997).

[599] United States v. Smith, 46 M.J. 263 (C.A.A.F. 1997); United States v. Connell, 42 M.J. 462 (C.A.A.F. 1995).

[600] *E.g.*, United States v. Miley, 51 M.J. 232 (C.A.A.F. 1999).

[601] *See also* Section 12-25.18, *above* (pretrial agreement provisions subject to cancellation upon misconduct).

(Rel.3—1/07   Pub.62410)

CHAPTER 24

POST-TRIAL RESPONSIBILITIES AND ACTIONS

§ 24-10.00 INTRODUCTION

§ 24-20.00 POST-TRIAL DEFENSE DUTIES

§ 24-21.00 In General

§ 24-22.00 The Identity of the Post-Trial Defense Counsel

§ 24-22.10 — In General

§ 24-22.20 — For Service of the Post-Trial Recommendation

§ 24-30.00 DEFERMENT OF CONFINEMENT

§ 24-31.00 — In General

§ 24-32.00 — Alternative Restraint

§ 24-33.00 — Rescission of Deferment

§ 24-40.00 DEFENSE-SUBMITTED INFORMATION UNDER RULE 1105

§ 24-41.00 — In General

§ 24-42.00 — Timing

§ 24-43.00 — Waiver

§ 24-44.00 — Special and Summary Courts-Martial

§ 24-50.00 THE RECORD OF TRIAL

§ 24-51.00 The Requirement of a Verbatim Record

§ 24-51.10 — In General

§ 24-51.20 — Recording Failure; Incomplete Record

§ 24-52.00 Authentication

§ 24-53.00 Certificate of Corrections

§ 24-54.00 Service of the Record of Trial

§ 24-60.00 THE POST-TRIAL RECOMMENDATION

§ 24-61.00 In General

§ 24-62.00 The Staff Judge Advocate

§ 24-62.10 — In General

§ 24-62.20 — Disqualification of Staff Judge Advocate

§ 24-63.00 Content of Recommendation

§ 24-64.00 Defense Response

§ 24-64.10 — In General

§ 24-64.20 — Timeliness and Waiver

§ 24-65.00 The Staff Judge Advocate's "Addendum"

§ 24-65.10 — In General

§ 24-65.20 — New Matter

§ 24-70.00 ACTION BY THE CONVENING AUTHORITY

(Rel.3—1/07 Pub.62410)

  § 24-71.00 **In General**

  § 24-72.00 **Disqualification of the Convening Authority**

  § 24-73.00 **Response to Matters Outside the Record**

    § 24-73.10 — **Postponement of Confinement — Effect of Civilian Sentence**

  § 24-74.00 **Sentence Conversions**

  § 24-75.00 **Restraint Pending Appeal**

  § 24-76.00 **Rehearings and *DuBay* Hearings**

§ **24-80.00 POST-TRIAL DELAY**

§ **24-90.00 APPELLATE REMEDIES**

§ 24-10.00 INTRODUCTION

Because of the historical origins of courts-martial,[1] the findings and sentence of a court-martial are subject to modification by the convening authority; indeed, under the Uniform Code of Military Justice as originally enacted, a court-martial result was clearly not "final" until approved by the convening authority. As initially enacted, Article 64 of the Uniform Code provided that:

> In acting on the findings and sentence of a court-martial, the convening authority shall approve only such findings of guilty, and the sentence or such part or amount of the sentence, as he finds correct in law and fact and as he in his discretion determines should be approved. Unless he indicates otherwise, approval of the sentence shall constitute approval of the findings and sentence.[2]

Although the record of trial was to be forwarded to the convening authority, both law and practice recognized that the record alone would be insufficient for a nonlegally trained officer. Consequently, two additional sources of information developed: defense-initiated claims of error (and requests for clemency) and the staff judge advocate's post-trial review.

Article 61, as initially enacted, provided in part that "[t]he convening authority shall refer the record of every general court-martial to his staff judge advocate or legal officer, who shall submit his written opinion thereon to the convening authority." This "opinion" became the post-trial review. As set forth in the *1969 Manual for Courts-Martial*, in all general courts-martial and in all special courts-martial in which the sentence included a bad conduct discharge, a staff judge advocate or legal officer was required to submit a written post-trial review:

> The review will include a summary of the evidence in the case, his opinion as to the adequacy and weight of the evidence and the effect of any error or irregularity respecting the proceedings, and a specific recommendation as to the action to be taken. Reasons for both the opinion and recommendation will be stated. The review may include matters outside the record of

---

[1] *See generally* Chapter 1.

[2] *See* Pub. L. No. 506, 81st Cong., ch. 169, § 1, art. 64, 64 Stat. 108 (1950).

(Rel.3—1/07 Pub.62410)

trial which, in the opinion of the reviewer, may have a legitimate bearing on the action of the convening authority.[3]

If no discharge was adjudged by a general court-martial, the usual practice was to undertake an abbreviated post-trial review. When an acquittal took place, the review was limited to an opinion that there was jurisdiction over the offense and the accused.

Ironically, although the Uniform Code failed to define the "opinion" requirement or attach any appellate importance to it, the "opinion"—the post-trial review—took on enormous importance in military law. As evidenced by the *1969 Manual*, the review became progressively more complicated and demanding. Imperfections in the post-trial review, as distinguished from the underlying trial, required reversal of countless cases.

As a consequence of what was perceived as needless appellate delay and workload,[4] the post-trial review procedure was substantially revised by The Military Justice Act of 1983 and the implementing *Manual for Courts-Martial*. Under revised Article 64(a) of the Code:

The judge advocate's review shall be in writing and shall contain the following:

(1) Conclusions as to whether —

(A) the court had jurisdiction over the accused and the offense;

(B) the charge and specification stated an offense; and

(C) the sentence was within the limits prescribed as a matter of law.

(2) A response to each allegation of error made in writing by the accused.

(3) If the case is sent for action under subsection (b),[5] a recommendation as to the appropriate action to be taken and an opinion as to whether corrective action is required as a matter of law.

The statutory revision served to sharply limit the requirements, and thus the possible adverse effects, of the post-trial review, which was renamed by the

---

[3] MCM, 1969 (rev. ed.) ¶ 85b.

[4] *See, e.g.*, S. Rep. No. 53, 98th Cong., 1st Sess. 20 (1983) quoted in United States v. Curry, 28 M.J. 419, 421–22 (C.M.A. 1989); United States v. Acosta, 46 C.M.R. 582 (A.C.M.R. 1972); United States v. Knoche, 46 C.M.R. 458 (A.C.M.R. 1972) (citing numerous cases).

[5] Article 64(b) of the Code states:

The record of trial and related documents in each case reviewed under subsection (a) shall be sent for action to the person exercising general court-martial jurisdiction over the accused at the time the court was convened (or to that person's successor in command) if —

(1) the judge advocate who reviewed the case recommends corrective action;

(2) the sentence approved under section 860(c) of this title (article 60(c)) extends to dismissal, a bad-conduct or dishonorable discharge, or confinement for more than six months; or

(3) such action is otherwise required by regulations of the Secretary concerned.

(Rel.3—1/07 Pub.62410)

Manual the "[r]ecommendation of the staff judge advocate or legal officer."[6] The revision accompanied amendment of Article 60 of the Uniform Code to make it clear that "[t]he authority under this section to modify the findings and sentence of a court-martial is a matter of command prerogative involving the sole discretion of the convening authority"[7] rather than a quasi-judicial function.[8]

§ 24-20.00   POST-TRIAL DEFENSE DUTIES

§ 24-21.00   In General

Absent an acquittal, the defense counsel's responsibilities do not end with trial. In *United States v. Palenius*,[9] the Court of Military Appeals noted the "minimum duties" of trial defense counsel:

> First, the trial defense counsel should advise his client concerning the appeal process. . . . Additionally, he should take action on behalf of his client as necessary during the intermediate reviews contemplated by the Uniform Code of Military Justice. This includes the reviewing of the staff judge advocate's report with his client and the presentation of pleas to the convening authority for modification or reduction of sentence if in his or his client's judgment such is appropriate or desirable. . . .

> [T]he trial defense attorney can and should remain attentive to the needs of his client by rendering him such advice and assistance as the exigencies of the particular case might require. . . .

> Finally, the prevailing practice among some trial defense attorneys of ceasing all activity on behalf of their clients and, in effect, terminating the relationship of attorney and client without the permission of their clients or of the courts can no longer be countenanced. The trial defense attorney can with honor and should maintain the attorney-client relationship with his client subsequent to the finding of guilty while performing the duties we set forth today until substitute trial counsel or appellate counsel have been properly designated and have commenced the performance of their duties, thus rendering further representation by the original trial defense attorney or those properly substituted in his place unnecessary.[10]

Although it is inherently difficult to detail potential defense responsibilities, the 1983 Military Justice Act and the *1984 Manual for Courts-Martial* and now the *2005 Manual* expressly set forth a number of potential defense actions.[11] Insofar as the convening authority is concerned, counsel may:

---

[6] R.C.M. 1106.

[7] U.C.M.J. art. 60(c)(1).

[8] *Cf.* United States v. Healy, 26 M.J. 394, 395–96 (C.M.A. 1988).

[9] 2 M.J. 86 (C.M.A. 1977).

[10] 2 M.J. at 93 (C.M.A. 1977) (footnote omitted).

[11] In large part, codifying prior practice.

(Rel.3—1/07   Pub.62410)

1. Petition for deferment of confinement;

2. Provide any written matters which may reasonably tend to affect the convening authority's decision;

3. Respond to the recommendation of the staff judge advocate;

4. Respond to any addendum to the SJA's recommendations;

5. Respond to matters outside the record not known by the accused and upon which the convening authority will rely in making a decision; or

6. Respond to service of the record of trial on counsel or the accused.[12]

In large part, the defense counsel's primary post-trial duty is to submit favorable information to the convening authority on behalf of the accused and to respond, when appropriate, to the staff judge advocate's recommendation.

Defense counsel retains the ethical duty of zealous representation of the client. When a staff judge advocate becomes aware of a potential conflict between the accused and defense counsel during the post-trial stage, the SJA should notify counsel so that counsel can determine whether counsel has been discharged or must withdraw.[13]

§ 24-22.00 The Identity of the Post-Trial Defense Counsel

§ 24-22.10 In General

Under *United States v. Palenius*,[14] absent waiver, the accused retains the services of the defense counsel after trial. As evidenced by Rule for Courts-Martial 1106(f)(2),[15] the attorney-client relationship between the accused and trial defense counsel continues "until substitute trial defense counsel or appellate counsel have been designated and commenced the performance of their duties."[16] The trial defense counsel may apply to the "judge or court then having jurisdiction of the cause to be relieved of the duty of further representation of the convicted

---

[12] R.C.M. 1106(f)(3). Terminology can be confusing and may result in mislabeling. *See, e.g.*, United States v. Thompson, 26 M.J. 512, 514 (A.C.M.R. 1988). Accordingly, it is recommended that defense counsel label their responses as "post-trial submissions." The staff judge advocates and appellate courts are required to examine the substance of the response to determine appropriate action.

[13] United States v. Carter, 40 M.J. 102, 105 (C.M.A. 1994) (complaints by client about lawyer). United States v. Brownfield, 52 M.J. 40 (C.A.A.F. 1999) (Despite the fact that clemency would be unlikely, counsel is not free to ignore the accused's request. Counsel should seek to resolve the dispute or seek substitute counsel).

[14] 2 M.J. 86 (C.M.A. 1977). *See also* United States v. Harris, 30 M.J. 580 (A.C.M.R. 1990) (defense counsel's failure to properly gather clemency materials constituted ineffectiveness of counsel and required reversal).

[15] Set forth in Section 24-22.20.

[16] United States v. Palenius, 2 M.J. 86, 93 (C.M.A. 1977).

accused."[17] Severance of the attorney-client relationship will take place at that time. If the accused alleges that the trial defense counsel was ineffective, however, the allegedly ineffective counsel cannot continue to represent the accused, and new counsel is required.[18]

The mere reassignment of trial defense counsel does not terminate the attorney-client relationship.[19] As a result, in the event of such a reassignment, unless the accused has concurred in the appointment of new defense counsel, the staff judge advocate's recommendation should be sent to the military counsel's new duty station.[20] If, however, the defense counsel is no longer on active duty, the attorney-client relationship terminates.[21] "Good cause" also justifies terminating

---

[17] 2 M.J. 86, 93 (C.M.A. 1977).

[18] United States v. Stith, 5 M.J. 879 (A.C.M.R. 1978). If the trial defense counsel is aware of the allegation before the staff judge advocate's recommendation, counsel should not accept service of the post-trial recommendation on behalf of the accused. 5 M.J. 879 (A.C.M.R. 1978); United States v. Dupas, 14 M.J. 28 (C.M.A. 1982) (allegation of ineffective counsel does not affect privileged communications except insofar as necessary for the counsel to defend against the allegation); United States v. Clark, 22 M.J. 708 (A.C.M.R. 1986); United States v. Martel, 19 M.J. 917 (A.C.M.R. 1985). See also Bittaker v. Woodford, 331 F.3d 715 (9th Cir. 2003) (claim of ineffectiveness waives privilege but only to the limited procedural stage necessary, here habeas rather than on subsequent retrial).

[19] See, e.g., United States v. Iverson, 5 M.J. 440 (C.M.A. 1978) (citing United States v. Tellier, 32 C.M.R. 323 (C.M.A. 1962)). See also United States v. Antonio, 20 M.J. 828, 830 (A.C.M.R. 1985) (citing cases).

[20] R.C.M. 1104(b)(1)(c). But see United States v. Derksen, 24 M.J. 818, 821–22 (A.C.M.R. 1987) (when the accused has been transferred from Germany to the United States, substitute service may be made under R.C.M. 1104(b)(1)(C)).

When the mail is being used, "it would appear that defense counsel should bear the responsibility of advising the legal officer as to any unusual circumstances that might delay his receipt of the post-trial review through the mails, rather than the legal officer having a duty to inquire as to the whereabouts of counsel." United States v. Kincheloe, 14 M.J. 40, 43 n.7 (C.M.A. 1982). In Kincheloe, the defense counsel was travelling between permanent duty stations for a number of days and was living at various temporary addresses that were unknown to the staff judge advocate. Thus, action in the case was taken 14 days after it was mailed to counsel. Defense counsel was certain that the post-trial review did not reach him until approximately two days after the action had been taken. His rebuttal was not sent on to the Court of Military Review nor was any issue raised until more than two years after the post-trial review.

[21] United States v. Polk, 27 M.J. 812, 816 (A.C.M.R. 1988) (counsel on terminal leave has no military duty of representation). Counsel who has left the service has the ethical obligation to complete representation on a case or to see that there is a proper transfer to another attorney. ABA Rules of Professional Conduct, Rule 1.3 (1998). Counsel who has been released from active duty may properly agree with the accused to continue representation in a civilian capacity. United States v. Andrews, 44 C.M.R. 219, 222 (C.M.A. 1972), cited in Polk, above, 27 M.J. at 815). Notwithstanding Andrews, the Navy-Marine Court of Criminal Appeals denied former military IDC the ability to continue representation after counsel became a civilian. United States v. Nguyen, 2001 CCA LEXIS 290 (N-M. Ct. Crim. App. November 16, 2001) (unpublished decision), writ petition granted, 56 M.J. 252 (C.A.A.F. 2001) (former military individual defense counsel may continue to represent defendant after counsel's separation from the service). See generally Section 5-63.00.

the relationship.[22] In *United States v. Iverson*,[23] however, the court held that substitution of defense counsel should not take place "[a]bsent a truly extraordinary circumstance rendering virtually impossible the continuation of the established relationship[.] [O]nly the accused may terminate the existing affiliation with his trial counsel prior to the case reaching the appellate level."[24]

The Court of Military Appeals held that when the accused discharges counsel after trial, failure to assign substitute counsel can be reversible error for purposes of post-trial action.[25] The court has also opined that should the SJA become aware of a potential defense conflict of interest before service of the SJA recommendation, the SJA should notify defense counsel so that counsel may determine the status of the attorney-client relationship and take appropriate action.[26]

The changing identity of defense counsel, inherent at the moment in a number of the services because of military reassignments, has raised questions concerning the impact at this stage in the process of an absent or defective attorney-client relationship. In *United States v. Hickok*,[27] defense counsel filed a clemency package and then left the service. As the accused had no counsel for purposes of service and response to the post-trial recommendation, the court ordered a new action. In *United States v. Miller*,[28] the failure of substitute counsel to establish an attorney-client relationship with the accused prior to actually accepting service and responding to the post-trial recommendation was held, in the absence of specific prejudice, to be non-prejudicial error. In *United States v. Howard*,[29] the court held that when counsel does not establish an attorney-client relationship, the test is whether there is a "colorable showing of possible prejudice." The court is torn between the right of the accused to have effective counsel at this stage and the plain fact that an absent or impaired formal relationship sometimes may not result in actual prejudice.[30]

---

[22] United States v. Iverson, 5 M.J. 440 (C.M.A. 1978) (citing United States v. Eason, 45 C.M.R. 109, 113 (C.M.A. 1962)).

[23] 5 M.J. 440 (C.M.A. 1978).

[24] 5 M.J. 442–43 (C.M.A. 1978). Judge Cook indicated in a number of cases that "when a case leaves the command level, the attorney-client relationship between the accused and military counsel at that level ends by operation of law." 5 M.J. 445 (C.M.A. 1978). In other words, when appellate defense counsel has been appointed, trial defense counsel's representation is terminated.

[25] United States v. Leaver, 36 M.J. 133 (C.M.A. 1992).

[26] United States v. Knight, 53 M.J. 340, 342 (C.A.A.F. 2000) (becoming aware of ineffectiveness claim the SJA must notify defense counsel of the complaint so the issue of further representation can be resolved); United States v. Carter, 40 M.J. 105 (C.M.A. 1994).

[27] 45 M.J. 142 (C.A.A.F. 1996).

[28] 45 M.J. 149 (C.A.A.F. 1996).

[29] 47 M.J. 104, 108 (C.A.A.F. 1997).

[30] *See, e.g.*, United States v. Wiley, 47 M.J. 158 (C.A.A.F. 1997) (although counsel's perfor-

§ 24-22.20   For Service of the Post-Trial Recommendation

The accused may have more than one counsel. Although all counsel may have continuing representational duties, the staff judge advocate is required to serve various documents, notably the post-trial recommendation, on the "defense counsel." Therefore, it is essential that one individual be clearly identified as having responsibility for service. Rule for Courts-Martial 1106(f)(2) thus provides:

> The accused may, at trial or in writing to the staff judge advocate or legal officer before the recommendation has been served under this rule, designate which counsel (detailed, individual military, or civilian) will be served with the recommendation. In the absence of such designation, the staff judge advocate or legal officer shall cause the recommendation to be served in the following order of precedence, as applicable on: (1) civilian counsel; (2) individual military counsel; or (3) detailed defense counsel. If the accused has not retained civilian counsel and the detailed defense counsel and individual military counsel, if any, have been relieved or are not reasonably available to represent the accused, substitute military counsel to represent the accused shall be detailed by an appropriate authority. Substitute counsel shall enter into an attorney-client relationship with the accused before examining the recommendation and preparing any response.

Because civilian defense counsel may not be aware of counsel's post-trial responsibilities, the Court of Military Appeals stated that "where a civilian counsel is involved, it is appropriate for the judge to discuss with him in open court the post-trial responsibilities to which he will be subject under *Goode* unless specifically released therefrom by the accused."[31] We suggest that the obligation falls on the trial counsel to ensure that the trial judge asks not only civilian counsel but individual defense counsel or detailed counsel who will perform the post-trial duties if counsel is about to permanently leave the installation.

If civilian counsel is unavailable for service of the staff judge advocate's recommendation, detailed counsel may not be served solely because of that status unless he or she formed an attorney-client relationship with the accused.[32] If

---

mance was deficient, the accused was not prejudiced by the deficiency and the deficient performance constituted harmless error). The court is thus faced with deciding whether to address the issue systemically, in order to guarantee a meaningful attorney-client relationship, or to use a results-specific test similar to the test applied to determine inadequacy of counsel.

[31] United States v. Robinson, 11 M.J. 218, 224 (C.M.A. 1981). United States v. Goode, 1 M.J. 3 (C.M.A. 1975), required service of the post-trial review on defense counsel so that the defense could respond to it. *See* Section 24-64.00 *et seq.*

[32] 11 M.J. 218, 224 (C.M.A. 1981) *Robinson* also indicated that where military counsel has participated with the civilian counsel, service may be properly made on the military counsel. "[A]bsent a clear indication to the contrary . . . [the court will assume] that this occurred with civilian counsel's consent." 11 M.J. at 223 n.2 (C.M.A. 1981) (dictum). At least this portion of the case has been superseded by R.C.M. 1106(f)(2).

(Rel.3—1/07   Pub.62410)

the other options set forth in Rule 1106(f)(2) are not feasible, substitute counsel may be appointed for the accused.[33] Substitute counsel may not, however, be appointed merely for the administrative convenience of the government.[34]

§ 24-30.00   DEFERMENT OF CONFINEMENT

§ 24-31.00   In General

A court-martial cannot defer a sentence.[35] The accused or defense counsel may request deferment,[36] however, after adjournment of the court.[37] This application must be in writing[38] and directed to the officer who convened the court or, if the accused is no longer under that person's jurisdiction, to the person exercising general court-martial jurisdiction.[39] The convening authority in "his sole discretion" may grant the application,[40] and the decision is reviewable only for "abuse of discretion."[41] Under Rule for Courts-Martial 1101(c)(3):

> The accused shall have the burden to show that the interests of the accused and the community in release outweigh the community's interests in

---

[33] R.C.M. 1106(f)(2). *See, e.g.,* United States v. Johnston, 51 M.J. 227, 229 (C.A.A.F. 1999).

[34] *See, e.g.,* United States v. Elliott, 11 M.J. 1 (C.M.A. 1981). The accused may consent, however, to substitution of counsel. United States v. Antonio, 20 M.J. 828 (A.C.M.R. 1985) (consent waives otherwise improper severance).

[35] R.C.M 1101(c)(2). *See also* MCM, 1969 (rev. ed.) ¶ 88f.

[36] "A postponement of the service and of the running of the sentence." R.C.M. 1101(c)(1).

[37] R.C.M. 1101(c)(1). A request may also be made following an appellate reversal. *Cf.* Moore v. Atkins, 30 M.J. 249 (C.M.A. 1990).

[38] R.C.M. 1101(c)(1). Article 57(d) does not provide that the application be in writing.

[39] R.C.M. 1101(c)(2); Article 57(d).

[40] R.C.M. 1101(c)(2); Article 57(d).

[41] R.C.M. 1101(c)(3). Judge Cook strongly believed that the decision is not reviewable for an abuse of that discretion. Pearson v. Cox, 10 M.J. 317, 321 (C.M.A. 1981); United States v. Brownd, 6 M.J. 338, 341 (C.M.A. 1979). Chief Judge Everett has not expressly indicated his views. In dictum in *United States v. Brownd*, 6 M.J. 338 (C.M.A. 1979), Judge Fletcher stated that he and Judge Perry "are not persuaded that 'sole discretion' is absolute and unreviewable. Rather we are impelled in our judicial responsibility to conduct a review of the convening authority's action to determine whether he has abused his discretion." 6 M.J. at 339 (C.M.A. 1979). The standard to be applied is set forth by the American Bar Association:

> (b) Release should not be granted unless the court finds that there is no substantial risk the appellant will not appear to answer the judgment following conclusion of the appellate proceedings and that the appellant is not likely to commit a serious crime, intimidate witnesses or otherwise interfere with the administration of justice. In making this determination, the court should take into account the nature of the crime and length of sentence imposed as well as the factors relevant to pretrial release. ABA Standards, Criminal Appeals § 2.5(b) (1970).

In *Moore v. Akins*, 30 M.J. 249 (C.M.A. 1990), the court held that, absent a finding of flight risk or of possible obstruction of justice, an accused's confinement must be deferred on request following reversal of his or her conviction by the Court of Military Review.

(Rel.3—1/07 Pub.62410)

confinement. Factors that the authority acting on a deferment request may consider in determining whether to grant the deferment request include: the probability of the accused's flight; the probability of the accused's commission of other offenses, intimidation of witnesses, or interference with the administration of justice; the nature of the offenses (including the effect on the victim) of which the accused was convicted; the sentence adjudged; the command's immediate need for the accused; the effect of deferment on good order and discipline in the command; and the accused's character, mental condition, family situation, and service record.[42]

Although Rule for Courts-Martial 1101(c)(3) does not expressly require the convening authority to specify the reasons for denying deferment, the Analysis states, "Because the decision to deny a request for deferment is subject to judicial review, the basis for denial should be included in the record."[43] Further, the courts have held that the absence of any justification can constitute an abuse of discretion.[44]

When a convening authority denies a deferral request without explanation, the accused should petition the court of criminal appeals for extraordinary relief. Otherwise, absent bad faith or caprice on the part of the convening authority, the accused cannot complain of prejudice.[45] Finally in *United States v. Sloan*,[46] the Court of Military Appeals declared:

> When a convening authority acts on an accused's request for deferment, . . . the action must be in writing (with a copy provided to the accused) and must include the reasons upon which the action is based.[47]

> "[A]n appellant is not entitled to appellate relief when the convening authority erroneously fails to cite reasons for denying a deferment request." Instead, appellant must seek appropriate relief at the time of the denial.[48]

It remains apparent that the time necessary to complete the military appellate process[49] often results in sentence completion before termination of "direct"

---

[42] This rule does not change *Brownd, above* note 41. Longhofer v. Hilbert, 23 M.J. 755 (A.C.M.R. 1986).

[43] Analysis of the Rules for Courts-Martial, MCM, 2005, A21-80. When the convening authority's decision not to defer confinement is attacked via a request for extraordinary relief, the Court of Military Review will consider post-trial affidavits. Sullivan v. LaBoa, 34 M.J. 593, 594 (A.C.M.R. 1992).

[44] United States v. Brownd, 6 M.J. 338 (C.M.A. 1979); Longhofer v. Hilbert, 23 M.J. 755, 757–58 (A.C.M.R. 1986) (per curiam).

[45] United States v. Dunlap, 39 M.J. 1120, 1122 (A.C.M.R. 1994).

[46] 35 M.J. 4 (C.M.A. 1992). Judges Wiss, Sullivan, and Gierke concurred on this point; Judge Cox opined that failure to include a written explanation was not an abuse of discretion; Judge Crawford took the position that the court's supervisory authority did not permit requiring a written justification.

[47] 35 M.J. at 7 (C.M.A. 1992).

[48] United States v. Robinson, 43 M.J. 501, 507 (A.F. Crim. App. 1995), citing United States v. Edwards, 39 M.J. 528 (A.F.C.M.R. 1994).

[49] Which should be more expeditious than in civilian life.

(Rel.3—1/07 Pub.62410)

appeals. Although immediate incarceration is becoming more popular in civilian life, to the extent that military personnel serve a significant part of their sentences only to have their convictions reversed or their sentences revised below the term of confinement actually served, something is terribly wrong. To correct such a problem, either appeals must be made more efficient or deferment must be granted more often.

§ 24-32.00 Alternative Restraint

When confinement is deferred, alternative restraint cannot be imposed. Rule for Courts-Martial 1101(c)(5) provides:

When deferment of confinement is granted, no form of restraint or other limitation on the accused's liberty may be ordered as a substitute form of punishment. An accused may, however, be restricted to specified limits or conditions may be placed on the accused's liberty during the period of deferment for any other proper reason, including a ground for restraint under R.C.M. 304.

It is improper for the staff judge advocate to advise the convening authority prior to decision that if a request for deferment is granted, the accused may not be restricted.[50] One wonders whether this benefits either side in close cases.

§ 24-33.00 Rescission of Deferment

Rescission of deferred confinement is governed by Rule for Courts-Martial 1101(c)(7), which states, in part:

(A) *Who may rescind.* The authority who granted the deferment or, if the accused is no longer within that authority's jurisdiction, the officer exercising general court-martial jurisdiction over the command to which the accused is assigned, may rescind the deferment.

(B) *Action.* Deferment of confinement may be rescinded when additional information is presented to a proper authority which, when considered with all other information in the case, that authority finds, in that authority's discretion, is grounds for denial of deferment under subsection (c)(3) of this rule. The accused shall promptly be informed of the basis for the rescission and of the right to submit written matters in the accused's behalf and to request that the rescission be reconsidered. However, the accused may be required to serve the sentence to confinement pending this action.

(C) *Execution.* When deferment is rescinded after the convening authority's action under R.C.M. 1107, the confinement may be ordered executed. However, no such order may be issued within 7 days of notice of the rescission to the accused under subsection (c)(7)(B) of this rule, to afford the accused an opportunity to respond. The authority rescinding the

---

[50] Pearson v. Cox, 10 M.J. 317 (C.M.A. 1981). In *Pearson,* the court held that extraordinary relief is not necessary to cure such an error; instead, the accused can submit another application to the convening authority.

(Rel.3—1/07 Pub.62410)

deferment may extend this period for good cause shown. The accused shall be credited with any confinement actually served during this period.

§ 24-40.00 DEFENSE-SUBMITTED INFORMATION UNDER RULE 1105

§ 24-41.00 In General

Because the convening authority may, as a discretionary matter, disapprove all or any part of the findings and sentence,[51] the defense is well advised to seek at least clemency from the convening authority. As a result, Article 60(b)(1) provides that "the accused may submit to the convening authority matters for consideration by the convening authority with respect to the findings and the sentence,"[52] a right implemented by Rule for Courts-Martial 1105(b), which states that the defense may submit "any matters which may reasonably tend to affect the convening authority's decision."[53]

Rule 1105 permits a post-trial defense submission even prior to the recommendation of the staff judge advocate.[54] The rules of evidence do not apply.[55] Matters that may be submitted under the Rule include:

(1) Allegations of errors affecting the legality of the findings or sentence;

(2) Portions or summaries of the record and copies of documentary evidence offered or introduced at trial;

(3) Matters in mitigation which were not available for consideration at the court-martial;[56] and

---

[51] U.C.M.J. art. 60.

[52] *See also* U.C.M.J. art. 38(c):

In any court-martial proceeding resulting in a conviction, the defense counsel —

(1) may forward for attachment to the record of proceedings a brief of such matters as he determines shall be considered in behalf of the accused on review (including any objection to the contents of the record which he considers appropriate);

(2) may assist the accused in the submission of any matter under section 860 of this title (article 60); and

(3) may take other action authorized by this chapter.

[53] R.C.M. 1105 is technically more restrictive than Article 60(b). The distinction, however, seems meaningless: matters not specified in Rule 1105 would be unlikely to affect the convening authority. As to the scope of proper matters, *see United States v. Davis*, 29 M.J. 249 (A.F.C.M.R. 1990) (error for convening authority not to consider videotape submitted by the accused; accused not limited to written matters).

[54] The former post-trial review; *see* Section 24-60.00.

[55] R.C.M. 1105.

[56] The Discussion to Rule 1105(b)(3) suggests that "post-trial conduct of the accused, such as providing restitution to the victim or exemplary behavior, might be appropriate."

(Rel.3—1/07 Pub.62410)

(4) Clemency recommendations by any member, the military judge, or any other person. The defense may ask any person for such a recommendation.[57]

In *United States v. Cox*,[58] the Air Force Court of Military Review held that, when material submitted under Rule 1105 does not allege "legal error," any response to it by the staff judge advocate need not be served on the defense.[59]

Because neither the accused nor the convening authority is limited to the record of trial when submitting or considering material favorable to the accused, defense counsel should be imaginative when submitting favorable material. Counsel might, for example, submit the results of polygraph[60] or other tests (*e.g.*, hypnosis or truth serum)[61] of the accused or witnesses. It would be a mistake, however, for the defense to retry the case before the convening authority. Counsel should exercise professional judgment on a case-by-case basis to determine which aspects of the trial or post-trial proceedings would be particularly helpful to address in seeking a sentence reduction or other corrective action.

In *United States v. Davis*,[62] the Court of Military Appeals, construing Article 60(b)(1), held that despite Rule 1105(b)'s reference to "written matters," a staff judge advocate erred in advising the convening authority that he need not consider a videotape submitted by the accused. The court advised that " 'Matters' is a

---

[57] R.C.M. 1105(b). Rather than having a number of clemency letters submitted as part of the record of trial, it may be better to use these as part of the defense submission prior to the convening authority's action. If clemency letters are not submitted either at trial or to the convening authority, they may not be admissible when presented first to a court of military review. United States v. Healy, 26 M.J. 394, 397 (C.M.A. 1988) (Court of military review "has no duty to receive information or data that purports to be relevant only to clemency."); United States v. Sylvester, 47 M.J. 390, 392 (C.A.A.F. 1998) (no requirement that clemency request be in writing but desirable to memorialize the oral presentation).

[58] 20 M.J. 945 (A.F.C.M.R. 1985).

[59] 20 M.J. at 947 (A.F.C.M.R. 1985). Allegations of legal error must be responded to in the staff judge advocate's recommendation, which must be served on the defense.

[60] United States v. Guerrero, 2001 CCA LEXIS 131 (A.F. Crim. App) (making clemency contingent on taking and passing a polygraph test does not violate due process).

The witnesses may not be required to take a polygraph examination, but the accused can certainly volunteer. Because of the limited number of polygraph examiners, the government may not be willing to perform such an examination. Under these circumstances, the accused may seek to have the examination performed by someone outside of the service. If financial circumstances make that impossible, the defense counsel could make a post-trial motion to the convening authority for such an examination to be performed. In many instances, the convening authority is willing to ask or order the investigative agency to perform the examination. The convening authority may condition the examination to require a written agreement with the accused that the polygraph results may be considered regardless of the outcome.

[61] United States v. Carr, 18 M.J. 297 (C.M.A. 1984).

[62] 33 M.J. 13 (C.M.A. 1991).

(Rel.3—1/07 Pub.62410)

broad term, which would include almost any matter."[63] Somewhat strangely, however, the court continued to construe liberally the "consideration" requirement, commenting that a convening authority need not, for example, read every word on every page of a thirty-page document: "In short, we believe that Congress intended to rely on the good faith of the convening authority in deciding how detailed his 'consideration' must be."[64] Does such an interpretation make a convening authority's consideration non-reviewable?

R.C.M. 1105(b) was amended in 1998 to clarify that a convening authority is required to consider only written matters presented by the accused but *may* consider other matters.

The defense may also want to raise legal matters. This is especially true when corrective action could be taken at the situs of the trial. The failure to raise legal issues, however, does not amount to a waiver.

Failure to submit a clemency request[65] or to advise the convening authority of a judicial recommendation for sentence suspension will likely constitute ineffectiveness of counsel.[66]

§ 24-42.00   Timing

To simplify the rule governing times for submission under Rules for Courts-Martial 1105, 1106, and 1107, the National Defense Authorization Act for fiscal year 1987 set forth a simplification of these rules by amending Article 60.[67] Under both Article 60(b) and Rule 1105(c), the accused and his defense counsel now have ten days from the service of the record of trial[68] or receipt of the recommendation of the staff judge advocate to make submissions.[69] Furthermore, if the accused shows good cause, the period may be extended for twenty additional days.[70] Rule 1105(c)(4) states: "[G]ood cause for an extension ordinarily does not include the need for securing matters which could reasonably have been presented at the court-martial."

---

[63] 33 M.J. at 15 (C.M.A. 1991).

[64] 33 M.J. at 16 (C.M.A. 1991) (dictum).

[65] United States v. Cobe, 41 M.J. 654 (N.M. Crim. App. 1995) (Failure to prepare clemency petition constituted post-trial ineffectiveness—cause and prejudice found; new recommendation and action required).

[66] United States v. Rich, 26 M.J. 518, 520–21 (A.C.M.R. 1988) (citing United States v. Davis, 20 M.J. 1015 (A.C.M.R. 1985)). *Compare* United States v. Davis, *above, with* United States v. Barnes, 3 M.J. 406 (C.M.A. 1977). *Cf.* United States v. Harris, 30 M.J. 580 (A.C.M.R. 1990) (defense failure to gather clemency materials constituted ineffectiveness of counsel).

[67] Military Justice Amendments of 1986, § 806, Pub. L. No. 99-661, 100 Stat. 3905 (1986).

[68] *See* R.C.M. 1104(b).

[69] In a summary court-martial, the accused has seven days after announcement of sentence. U.C.M.J. art. 60(b)(1).

[70] U.C.M.J. art. 60(b)(1) and (2).

(Rel.3—1/07   Pub.62410)

§ 24-43.00 Waiver

Waiver of the right to submit material under Rule 1105 is governed by Rule 1105(d), which takes the general approach that the accused waives the right to submit material that was not actually submitted.[71]

§ 24-44.00 Special and Summary Courts-Martial

Submissions under Rule for Courts-Martial 1105 are not limited to general courts-martial and those special courts-martial in which a bad-conduct discharge has been adjudged. Because the staff judge advocate or legal officer is not required to make a recommendation under Rule for Courts-Martial 1106,[72] the defense cannot rely on the SJA to summarize the pertinent aspects of the accused's service record or other key aspects of the proceeding that are important to the defense. Although this does not impose a significant burden on the defense, it will require the defense to alter slightly the nature of its presentation to the convening authority. There is no burden on the defense, however, to prepare a comprehensive post-trial review. As with the submission after a more serious case, the matters presented to the convening authority should reflect counsel's professional judgment as to the type of submission that will best serve the interests of the accused before the particular convening authority.

The absence of a requirement for a formal SJA recommendation in non-BCD special courts-martial continues prior practice. As in the past, the convening authority may refer the case to the SJA for informal advice. Although this does not invoke the formal procedures of Rule for Courts-Martial 1106, the SJA should be careful to insure that the limits of Rule for Courts-Martial 1107(b)(3) are observed with respect to matters that may be considered by the convening authority. For example, if the SJA submits "matters adverse to the accused from outside the record, with knowledge of which the accused is not chargeable," the

---

[71] R.C.M. 1105(d) provides:

(1) *Failure to submit matters.* Failure to submit matters within the time prescribed by this rule shall be deemed a waiver of the right to submit such matters.

(2) *Submission of matters.* Submission of any matters under this rule shall be deemed a waiver of the right to submit additional matters unless the right to submit additional matters within the prescribed time limits is expressly reserved in writing.

(3) *Written waiver.* The accused may expressly waive, in writing, the right to submit matters under this rule. Once filed, such waiver may not be revoked.

(4) *Absence of accused.* If, as a result of the unauthorized absence of the accused, the record cannot be served on the accused in accordance with R.C.M. 1104(b)(1) and if the accused has no counsel to receive the record, the accused shall be deemed to have waived the right to submit matters under this rule within the time limit which begins upon service on the accused of the record of trial.

[72] R.C.M. 1106(a).

(Rel.3—1/07 Pub.62410)

accused must be given an opportunity for rebuttal under Rule for Courts-Martial 1107(b)(3)(B)(iii).[73]

Rule 1105(c) sets forth the submission time for defense counsels:[74]

(1) *General and special courts-martial.* After a general or special court-martial, the accused may submit matters under this rule within the later of ten days after a copy of the authenticated record of trial or, if applicable, the recommendation of the staff judge advocate or legal officer is served on the accused. If . . . the accused shows that additional time is required for the accused to submit such matters, the convening authority may, for good cause, extend the 10-day period for not more than 20 additional days.

(2) *Other special courts-martial.* After a special court-martial in which a bad-conduct discharge was not adjudged, the accused may submit matters under this rule within 20 days after the sentence is announced or within 7 days after a copy of the record of trial is served on the accused under Rule for Courts-Martial 1104(b)(1), whichever is later. The convening authority may, for good cause, extend either period for not more than 10 additional days.

(3) *Summary courts-martial.* After a summary court-martial the accused may submit matters under this rule within 7 days after the sentence is announced. . . . [T]he convening authority may, for good cause, extend the period for up to 20 additional days.[75]

§ 24-50.00   THE RECORD OF TRIAL

§ 24-51.00   The Requirement of a Verbatim Record

§ 24-51.10   In General

The Uniform Code of Military Justice does not explicitly provide for verbatim records of trial. Rather, Article 54 requires:

A *complete* record of the proceedings and testimony shall be prepared —

(A) in each general court-martial case in which the sentence adjudged includes death, a dismissal, a discharge, or (if the sentence adjudged does not include a discharge) any other punishment which exceeds that which may otherwise be adjudged by a special court-martial; and

(B) in each special court-martial case in which the sentence adjudged includes a bad-conduct discharge.[76]

---

[73] Effron, *Post-Trial Submissions to the Convening Authority under the Military Justice Act of 1983,* Army Law, July 1984, at 65.

[74] R.C.M. 1105(c).

[75] R.C.M. 1105(c).

[76] U.C.M.J. art. 54(c)(1) (emphasis added).

The Code's legislative history, however, states: "It is intended that records of general courts-martial shall contain a verbatim transcript of the proceedings,"[77] and the *Manual for Courts-Martial* expressly adopts the requirement.[78] Special courts-martial in which a sentence other than a bad-conduct discharge is adjudged and summary courts-martial need not have a verbatim transcript prepared.[79]

The verbatim record requirement requires that the record of trial be "substantially verbatim."[80] A record may be deficient in the sense either that the transcript of the proceedings is not "substantially verbatim," or that the record omits critical elements such as exhibits, written findings, or records.[81] "Insubstantial omissions from a record of trial do not affect its completeness."[82]

---

[77] S. Rep. No. 486, 81st Cong., 1st Sess. 24 (1949); H.R. Rep. No. 491, 81st Cong., 1st Sess. 27 (1949). Special courts-martial were not empowered to adjudge bad-conduct discharges when the Uniform Code was first enacted. The Armed Forces use a variety of means to produce the record. In 2001, The Judge Advocate General of the Army announced at the Retired Army Judge Advocates annual meeting his intent for the Army to adopt voice recognition technology.

Except as otherwise provided in subsection (j) of this rule [videotape records], the record of trial shall include a verbatim written transcript of all sessions except sessions closed for deliberations and voting when:

(i) Any part of the sentence adjudged exceeds six months confinement or other punishments which may be adjudged by a special court-martial; or

(ii) A bad-conduct discharge has been adjudged.

[78] R.C.M. 1103(b)(2)(B).

[79] R.C.M. 1103(c) and (d); 1305. Because of the limited number of court reporters, verbatim records are rarely, if ever, prepared or transcribed unless mandated.

[80] United States v. Gray, 7 M.J. 296, 297 (C.M.A. 1979). *See also* United States v. Henry, 53 M.J. 108, 111 (C.A.A.F. 2000) ("Substantial omissions have included unrecorded sidebar conferences that involved the admission of evidence [and] . . . letter of dishonor in a worthless check case. . . ." Requirement for verbatim record is jurisdictional and non-waiveable); United States v. Kulathungam, 54 M.J. 386 (C.A.A.F. 2001) (lack of verbatim record and impermissible change by counsel and reporter does not require dismissal of charges); United States v. Brown Austin, 34 M.J. 578, 581–83 (A.C.M.R. 1992) (definition of verbatim record of trial; government's burden when there is a substantial omission from the record).

[81] *E.g.*, United States v. Villareal, 52 M.J. 27 (C.A.A.F. 1999) (failure to attach special findings on command influence did not make record so misleading or incomplete so as to render appellate review meaningless); United States v. Abrams, 50 M.J. 361 (C.A.A.F. 1999) (failure to attach and seal military records of key government witness required reversal to augment record); United States v. Massengill, 48 M.J. 396 (C.A.A.F. 1997) (absence of SJA's recommendation and proof of its service rendered record substantially incomplete) (summary disposition); United States v. Mark, 47 M.J. 99 (C.A.A.F. 1997) (absence from the record of SJA's recommendation and defense counsel's response required remand). *But see* United States v. Santoro, 46 M.J. 344 (C.A.A.F. 1997) (reconstructed record was adequate in light of action by the Court of Criminal Appeals in dismissing contested charge and approving only a sentence of no punishment).

[82] United States v. Henry, 53 M.J. 108, 111 (C.A.A.F. 2000) ("[i]nsubstantial omissions include the absence of photographic exhibits of stolen property . . ., a flier given to the members . . ., a court member's written question . . ., and an accused's personnel record . . . ."); United States v. McCullah, 11 M.J. 234, 236–37 (C.M.A. 1981); United States v. Joseph, 36 M.J. 846, 849

(Rel.3—1/07 Pub.62410)

Substantial omissions, on the other hand, give rise to a presumption of prejudice. . . . Moreover, substantial omissions may be qualitative as well as quantitative. . . . Sometimes the omissions are so substantial that the only remedy is a new trial. . . . At other times, the omitted material is sufficiently retrievable that a record can be salvaged and pronounced "substantially verbatim."[83]

A verbatim transcript includes: all proceedings including sidebar conferences, arguments of counsel, and rulings and instructions by the military judge; matter which the military judge orders stricken from the record or disregarded; and when a record is amended in revision proceedings . . . the part of the original record changed and the changes made, without physical alteration of the original record. Conferences under R.C.M. 802 need not be recorded, but matters agreed upon at such conferences must be included in the record.[84]

When authorized by the Secretary concerned, audiotape or videotape may be used in lieu of a traditional court recording.[85] However, absent "military exigencies," a written transcript must be made of the recording.[86] Even in such circumstances, a written version of the record must be prepared for appellate review.[87]

Civilian trials are increasingly using videotape and computer-based demonstrative evidence and materials. When used at a court-martial, such materials should be made part of the trial record. In *United States v. Seal*,[88] the court held that

---

(A.C.M.R. 1993) (citing *McCullah*, lack of flyer in record is insubstantial); United States v. Norris, 33 M.J. 635, 638 (C.G.C.M.R. 1991) (failure to include various enclosures, including Article 32 enclosures and a clemency petition, did not affect need for a complete record in light of the presumption of regularity and the nature of the appellate court's review function; however, court stated that although waiver can apply to defense actions in this area, "overreliance. . . can lead to important issues being missed . . ."). *See also* United States v. Stoffer, 53 M.J. 26 (C.A.A.F. 2000) (record not verbatim because of missing document—court's approval of no punishment was appropriate); United States v. Mark, 47 M.J. 99 (C.A.A.F. 1997) (missing SJA recommendation is structural error requiring new recommendation and action—harmless error test does not apply); United States v. Booth, 33 M.J. 939, 941 (N.M.C.M.R. 1991) (copies of diagrams used at trial ought to be attached to the record of trial so appellate court can consult them). The Court of Military Appeals granted a petition for review to determine whether the absence from the record of sealed personnel records of a witness showing that he was subject to internal investigation for tight handcuffs made the record non-verbatim. United States v. Charles, 38 M.J. 215 (C.M.A. 1993).

[83] United States v. Lashley, 14 M.J. 7, 9 (C.M.A. 1982).

[84] R.C.M. 1103(b)(2) Discussion. For a listing of the matters that must be attached to the record, *see* R.C.M. 1103(b)(2)(D); 1103(b)(3). *See also* United States v. Abrams, 50 M.J. 361, 364 (C.A.A.F. 1999) (Remanded because the judge did not seal and attach personnel records he reviewed in camera and decided were not discoverable.)

[85] R.C.M. 1103(j)(1).

[86] R.C.M. 1103(j)(2). For "military exigencies," see R.C.M. 1103(j)(3).

[87] R.C.M. 1103(j)(4).

[88] 38 M.J. 659 (A.C.M.R. 1993).

(Rel.3—1/07 Pub.62410)

failure to include media footage played at trial during sentencing deprived the court of a verbatim record and compelled reversal. In so holding, the court stated that either the judge or trial counsel "should have ensured that either the videotapes or a transcription of the verbal contents were included in the record."[89] Given the ease with which such material may be retained or otherwise preserved via videotape or, more likely today, DVD, soon, CD-ROM disk, one might argue that a written transcription would be inadequate in many cases.

Although the record of trial is prepared by the court reporter, the trial counsel is responsible for the record "[u]nder the direction of the military judge."[90] The Army Court of Criminal Appeals clearly held that before authentication the military judge exercises the authority to deal with untimely preparation of the record.[91]

There is no right to a daily transcript.[92] Therefore presumably no right to realtime transcription.

Omission from the record of trial of one or more exhibits, or other information, may be waived, depending upon its importance, by failure of the defense to timely object to the absence of such material.[93]

§ 24-51.20 Recording Failure; Incomplete Record

The armed forces tends to use voicewriting ("closed mask" recording), which is necessarily hardware-dependent. Equipment failures occur occasionally. Should the error be detected quickly, that part of the proceedings that was not recorded can often be repeated and the error mooted. However, if that is impossible, the *Manual for Courts-Martial* provides for either a rehearing or approval of a sentence that could be adjudged by a special court-martial without a verbatim record.[94]

§ 24-52.00 Authentication

It is imperative that the record of trial be accurate.[95] "A record is authenticated by the signature of a person specified in this rule who thereby declares that the

---

[89] 38 M.J. at 662 (A.C.M.R. 1993).

[90] R.C.M. 1103(b)(1)(A); 1103(c).

[91] United States v. Chisholm, 58 M.J. 733 (A. Ct. Crim. App.), aff'd, 59 M.J. 151 (C.A.A.F. 2003) (not resolving questions concerning judicial authority in this area as "premature.").

[92] United States v. Anderson, 36 M.J. 963, 973 (A.F.C.M.R. 1993).

[93] *Compare* United States v. Branoff, 38 M.J. 98, 105 (C.M.A. 1993) (failure to attach regulations did not violate due process when the defense did not request that they be made part of the record or object to their exclusion from the authenticated record of trial) *with* United States v. Seal, 38 M.J. 659 (A.C.M.R. 1993) (failure to include videotapes played during sentencing made record non-verbatim and required reversal).

[94] R.C.M. 1103(f).

[95] It is somewhat ironic that American courts place such great weight on the written transcript

(Rel.3—1/07 Pub.62410)

record accurately reports the proceedings." [96] Prior to formal authentication, the trial counsel is required to review and correct the record, [97] and "[e]xcept when unreasonable delay will result, the trial counsel shall permit the defense counsel to examine the record before authentication." [98]

> If the defense counsel discovers errors or omissions in the record, the defense counsel may suggest to the trial counsel appropriate changes to make the record accurate, forward for attachment to the record under Article 38(c) any objections to the record, or bring any suggestions for correction of the record to the attention of the person who authenticates the record. [99]

Generally, the military judge will authenticate the record of trial. [100] If the record cannot be authenticated by the military judge by reason of his death, disability or absence, substitute authentication may be made by the trial counsel, [101] a member, or the court reporter, depending on circumstances. [102]

---

when it is obvious to all that matters not preserved by the written record (*e.g.*, the judge's demeanor and tone of voice) may be of equal or greater importance. The *Manual's* authorization of video records, subject to service regulations, is an important recognition of this, even if it is of little practical use given military exigency and service disinterest.

[96] R.C.M. 1104(a)(1).

[97] R.C.M. 1103(i)(1)(A). For summary courts-martial, *see* R.C.M. 1103(i)(2).

[98] R.C.M. 1103(i)(1)(B).

[99] R.C.M. 1103(i)(1)(B) Discussion.

> [T]he military judge present at the end of the proceedings shall authenticate the record of trial, or that portion over which the military judge presided. If more than one military judge presided over the proceedings, each military judge shall authenticate the record of the proceedings over which that military judge presided.

R.C.M. 1104(a)(2)(A). *See also* Article 54.

Authentication of special court-martial records not involving a bad-conduct discharge is left to service regulations. R.C.M. 1104(a)(2)(A).

In United States v. Lawer, 41 M.J. 751, 757 (C.G. Crim. App. 1995), the court expressly wished to "validate" the trial judge's novel teleconferencing authentication procedure. The judge held a Rule 802 conference via telephone to decide how to handle unsworn statement content that was inconsistent with the providency inquiry. With defense agreement, the accused supplied written responses to the judge's clarifying questions that were then attached to the record, which was authenticated.

[101] Assistant trial counsel may, in some cases, authenticate the record of trial if he or she was present in court throughout the trial. United States v. Credit, 4 M.J. 118 (C.M.A. 1977). A good resource case is United States v. Andrade, 3 M.J. 757 (A.C.M.R. 1977). R.C.M. 1104(a)(2)(B) and R.C.M. 502(d)(5) allow the prior practice of trial counsel authenticating the record of trial. *See also* United States v. Galaviz, 46 M.J. 548 (N.M. Crim. App. 1997) (failure to attach reason for substitute authentication harmless error—no question as to veracity of record of trial).

> If the military judge cannot authenticate the record of trial because of the military judge's death, disability, or absence, the trial counsel present at the end of the proceedings shall authenticate the record of trial. If the trial counsel cannot authenticate the record of trial because of the trial counsel's death, disability, or absence, a member

(Rel.3—1/07 Pub.62410)

Trial counsel may not authenticate the record of trial unless the judge is genuinely absent for a lengthy period of time.[103] The Discussion to the Rules for Courts-Martial indicates that a two-week absence in the United States of a judge stationed in Germany does not constitute an "absence."[104] A judge's permanent change of station from Okinawa to Quantico, Virginia, however, was found to be sufficient.[105] Although the record should be prepared and authenticated as rapidly as possible, the absence at this time of an express post-trial "speedy-trial" rule[106] removes the incentive for trial counsel to use substitute authentication too readily.

Pursuant to Rule for Courts-Martial 918(b) special findings may be announced orally in open court or in writing during or after the court-martial. Under Rule for Courts-Martial 905(d) essential findings need only be stated "on the record." Accordingly, some judges wait to attach written findings to the record prior to authentication, sometimes in the form of an appellate exhibit. When these are first produced at authentication, significant notice issues are posed. Although both parties ordinarily review the record before authentication, attachment of findings at authentication could escape counsels' notice. Until such time as the Rules clarify the procedure to be followed in such a case, military judges would be wise to formally supply counsel with their written findings prior to authentication and provide counsel an opportunity to respond formally to them.

§ 24-53.00 Certificate of Corrections

It may become necessary to correct the record after authentication.[107] Prior to January 18, 1982, the trial judge could make these changes via a certificate of correction without further complication.[108] These certificates would then be

---

shall authenticate the record of trial. In a court-martial composed of a military judge alone, or as to sessions without members, the court reporter shall authenticate the record of trial when this duty would fall upon a member under this subsection. A person authorized to authenticate a record under this subsection may authenticate the record only as to those proceedings at which that person was present.

R.C.M. 1104(a)(2)(B). *See also* U.C.M.J. art. 54(a).

[103] *See* United States v. Miller, 4 M.J. 207 (C.M.A. 1978); United States v. Cruz-Rijos, 1 M.J. 429 (C.M.A. 1976).

[104] R.C.M. 1104(a)(2)(B) Discussion.

[105] United States v. Lott, 9 M.J. 70 (C.M.A. 1980). *See also* R.C.M. 1104(a)(2)(B) Discussion.

[106] *See* Section 24-80.00.

[107] Substantive error may be discovered, for example, by the staff judge advocate or appellate counsel.

[108] This procedure was set forth in ¶ 86c of the *1969 Manual*, which provided that where a record of trial "upon review has been found to be incomplete or defective in some material respect" it was permissible to submit such a certificate of correction to set forth the true facts. R.C.M. 1104(a) is based on this.

submitted as part of the record of trial and would be conclusive in the absence of a charge of deliberate falsification. In *United States v. Anderson*,[109] however, Judge Fletcher, writing for the majority,[110] indicated that "when, after authentication, it becomes necessary for the trial judge to propose substantive changes in the record of trial to accurately reflect proceedings in the case, pursuant to a Certificate of Correction, he should give notice to all parties, providing an opportunity to be heard on the issues of the proposed correction."[111] *Anderson* was codified in Rule for Courts-Martial 1104(d)(2).

Under the Rule, "notice to the parties" does not necessarily require a formal hearing. The Discussion states:

> The type of opportunity to respond depends on the nature and scope of the proposed correction. In many instances an adequate opportunity can be provided by allowing the respective parties to present affidavits and other documentary evidence to the person authenticating the certificate of correction or by a conference telephone call among the authenticating person, the parties, and the reporter. In other instances, an evidentiary hearing with witnesses may be required.[112]

As the Discussion is nonbinding, the definition of "opportunity to respond" awaits judicial clarification. Given the three opinions in *Anderson*,[113] the ultimate answer is unclear.

§ 24-54.00 Service of the Record of Trial

Article 54 of the Uniform Code and Rule for Courts-Martial 1104 require that an authenticated copy of the record of trial be served on the accused.[114] Rule 1104(b)(1)(C) provides for substitute service if it is impractical to serve the accused because of the accused's transfer to a distant place, the unauthorized absence of the accused, or military exigencies.[115] At trial, the accused may orally request that his or her copy of the record of trial be served on defense counsel,

---

[109] 12 M.J. 195 (C.M.A. 1982).

[110] Chief Judge Everett concurred in the result. Like Judge Cook, he was concerned with the mechanics of the hearing.

> [R]egardless of who proposes a correction or what it concerns, the judge must allow the defense counsel, as the representative of the accused, a reasonable opportunity to know that a correction is being considered and an opportunity to contest the correction with supporting affidavits or other appropriate evidence if the defense counsel so chooses.

12 M.J. at 199 (footnote omitted).

[111] *Anderson*, 12 M.J. at 197 (footnote omitted).

[112] R.C.M. 1104(d)(2) Discussion. *See also* United States v. Anderson, 12 M.J. 195, 198 (C.M.A. 1982).

[113] *See above* note 109.

[114] U.C.M.J. art. 54.

[115] R.C.M. 1104(b)(1)(C).

(Rel.3—1/07 Pub.62410)

or such a request may be made in writing. Service is critical because, unless the record of trial has been served upon the accused's counsel or the accused, the convening authority may not take action unless the accused is absent without authority.[116]

The convening authority is responsible for deleting from the record any classified material and attaching a certificate noting that fact and the procedure for reviewing that portion of the record.[117]

Failure to serve the record of trial is not prejudicial when the accused clearly did not plan on presenting a brief to the convening authority, and an attempt had been made to provide the accused with a copy of the record of trial.[118] The court hinted in *United States v. Diamond*[119] that it may be sufficient that the record of trial is available for inspection by individual defense counsel.

§ 24-60.00 THE POST-TRIAL RECOMMENDATION

§ 24-61.00 In General

Rule for Courts-Martial 1106(a) provides that before a convening authority may take action on a record of trial resulting in a finding of guilty, the convening authority's staff judge advocate or legal officer shall forward a recommendation to the convening authority.[120] This recommendation is distinct from a Staff Judge Advocate's post trial recommendation as to deferment of post-trial confinement or forfeitures.[121]

As previously noted,[122] the requirement is intended to supply the convening authority with information and advice to use in the convening authority's decision on the findings and sentence. The recommendation is the successor to the far more demanding and expansive post-trial review.[123]

---

[116] R.C.M. 1104(b)(1)(C).

[117] R.C.M. 1104(b)(1)(D).

[118] United States v. Diamond, 18 M.J. 305 (C.M.A. 1984).

[119] 18 M.J. 305 (C.M.A. 1984).

[120] R.C.M. 1106(a); U.C.M.J. art. 60(d). *Cf.* United States v. Sparks, 20 M.J. 985 (N.M.C.M.R. 1985) (legal officer need not be certified under Article 27(b); presumption that case was properly transferred). *See also* United States v. Finister, 51 M.J. 185 (C.A.A.F. 1999) (enlisted machinist was disqualified to prepare recommendation; doing so was plain error that did not require a showing of prejudice to the accused).

[121] *See* United States v. Brown, 54 M.J. 289 (C.A.A.F. 2000) (recommendation to convening authority need not be served on the defense under current law).

[122] Section 24-10.00.

[123] Section 24-10.00.

(Rel.3—1/07 Pub.62410)

After the record of trial is completed, a copy is sent to the action officer responsible for the draft recommendation.[124] If the convening authority does not have a staff judge advocate or a legal officer,[125] he or she may request the assignment of such, or send the record for action to any "officer exercising general court-martial jurisdiction as provided in Rule for Courts-Martial 1107(a)."[126] If the convening authority has a legal officer, that officer's duties differ from those of a staff judge advocate. Rule for Courts-Martial 1106(d)(4) states that the staff judge advocate, as compared to the legal officer, shall state whether corrective action should be taken on the findings and sentence based upon allegations of *legal errors* raised under Rule 1105.[127] Such recommendations are not required by the legal officer.[128]

After the recommendation is signed by the staff judge advocate, it is served on the accused and defense counsel.[129] The Army Court of Military Review held that a presumption of regularity exists and that no affirmative proof of

---

[124] Normally this is prior to authentication, and the recommendation cannot be put in final form until authentication. Upon authentication, the drafter must examine the errata sheet prepared by the individual who authenticated the record to see that there have been no substantive changes.

[125] "Legal officer" is a term used primarily in the Navy for an officer who is not a judge advocate and likely not a lawyer.

[126] R.C.M. 1106(c)(1)(B). *See also* U.C.M.J. art. 60(d).

[127] R.C.M. 1106(c)(4). *But see* United States v. Russett, 40 M.J. 184, 185 (C.M.A. 1994) (recommendation need not recite judge's multiplicity determinations).

[128] Should a superior competent authority require a special court-martial-convening authority without a staff judge advocate to forward the case to the officer exercising general court-martial jurisdiction over the accused, a staff judge advocate would review it. Such an approach would provide the accused with a legal review and would not violate the accused's rights, *United States v. Due*, 21 M.J. 431 (C.M.A. 1986), even though its effect is also to divest the special court-martial convening authority of the discretion inherent in Rule 1106. Of course, if the case forwarding is ordered for an improper purpose, such as prior lenient action taken on other courts-martial by the special court-martial convening authority, the defense should so note via written objection.

[129] R.C.M. 1106(f)(1) provides:

Before forwarding the recommendation and the record of trial to the convening authority for action under R.C.M. 1107&, the staff judge advocate or legal officer shall cause a copy of the recommendation to be served on counsel for the accused. A separate copy will be served on the accused. If it is impracticable to serve the recommendation on the accused for reasons including but not limited to the transfer of the accused to a distant place, the unauthorized absence of the accused, or military exigency, or if the accused so requests on the record at the court-martial or in writing, the accused's copy shall be forwarded to the accused's defense counsel. A statement shall be attached to the record explaining why the accused was not served personally.

Prior to 1 April 1990, service on the accused was not required. Exec. Order No. 12708, 55 Fed. Reg. 11353 (1990), Amendments to the *Manual for Courts-Martial* 1984. Change 7 amended R.C.M. 1105(c)(1) and 1106(f)(7), clarifying the method of service and the time element. *See also* United States v. Lowery, 37 M.J. 1038 (A.C.M.R. 1993) (if violation of service rule alleged, defense must establish the prejudice).

(Rel.3—1/07 Pub.62410)

service is ordinarily required: "In the absence of evidence to the contrary, we will presume that both the staff judge advocate and the trial defense counsel properly discharged their post-trial duties."[130]

After service of the recommendation, the defense has a limited period to make a response formerly called the "*Goode*"[131] rebuttal.[132] After receiving any defense response, the staff judge advocate may direct that an addendum be prepared to the recommendation, replying to the defense response. This may also be served on the defense.[133] These documents are given to the convening authority,[134] who should read them;[135] the staff judge advocate may orally brief the convening authority as well.

Although the Rules for Courts-Martial set forth time limits for the defense's response to the staff judge advocate's recommendation,[136] they do not specify a time by which either the record of trial must be completed and authenticated or the recommendation must be made.[137]

§ 24-62.00 The Staff Judge Advocate

§ 24-62.10 In General

The post-trial recommendation must be written by the staff judge advocate or legal officer.[138] The recommendation may be prepared by a legal officer, even if a staff judge advocate is available.[139] The officer preparing the recommendation, however, must be legally impartial.[140] In actual fact, the impartiality

---

[130] United States v. Cook, 31 M.J. 745, 746 (A.C.M.R. 1990) (citing United States v. Roland, 31 M.J. 747 (A.C.M.R. 1990)).

[131] United States v. Goode, 1 M.J. 3 (C.M.A. 1975).

[132] In addition to the *Goode* response, the defense may want to attach a petition for clemency or a request for deferment if no prior submission or request has been made.

[133] 1 M.J. 3 (C.M.A. 1975).

[134] *But see* United States v. Camacho, 25 M.J. 367 (C.M.A. 1987) (Daily Journal, Everett, C.J., dissenting from denial of review) (staff judge advocate removed 30 defense clemency attachments and summarized them).

[135] As "a convening authority is no longer required to read the record of trial," the recommendation and defense submissions are critical. United States v. Camacho, 25 M.J. 367 (C.M.A. 1987) (Daily Journal, Everett, C.J., dissenting from denial of review) (citing Military Justice Act of 1983, Pub. L. No. 98-209, 97 Stat. 1393).

[136] R.C.M. 1106(f)(5).

[137] *See generally* Section 24-80.00.

[138] It is plain error for the recommendation to be written by an enlisted person; a legal officer must at least be a commissioned officer. United States v. Smith, 34 M.J. 894, 895 (N.M.C.M.R. 1992).

[139] United States v. Curry, 28 M.J. 419, 421–22 (C.M.A. 1989).

[140] *See* Section 24-62.20.

(Rel.3—1/07 Pub.62410)

requirement seems impossible to meet in light of the staff judge advocate's function as a command's "chief prosecutor." Judge Fletcher indicated that each time he had a question as to the adequacy of the post-trial review, he found himself "engaged in a form of mental gymnastics attempting to reconcile the elevated status we have given the post-trial review."[141] He would have also recognized that for "all practical purposes," the staff judge advocate was the "chief counsel for the given command among whose various functions include the responsibilities of being the chief prosecutor."[142] The *2005 Manual* seeks to remove this conflict. It is, however, by no means clear that the creation of the "post-trial recommendation" rather than a thorough review accomplishes this.

In ordinary practice, the post-trial recommendation is rarely written personally by the staff judge advocate.[143] The first draft is written by an individual in the office other than the trial counsel,[144] normally a lawyer, but sometimes a paralegal. The draft is then sent to the staff judge advocate via the deputy staff judge advocate. The SJA will make any desired changes and then return the recommendation for any necessary changes. After final signature by the SJA, the recommendation is served on the trial defense counsel, unless other arrangements have been made.[145]

§ 24-62.20 Disqualification of Staff Judge Advocate

The Uniform Code specifically provides: "No person who has acted as member, military judge, trial counsel, assistant trial counsel, or investigating officer in any case may later act as a staff judge advocate or legal officer to any reviewing authority upon the same case."[146] The purpose of this provision

---

[141] United States v. Morrison, 3 M.J. 408, 410 (C.M.A. 1977). Chief Judge Everett, then a staff member, questioned J. Ferguson about the "split personality" of the staff judge advocate. *Hearings on S. Res. 260, Before Subcomm. of Senate Judiciary Comm.*, 87th Cong., 2d Sess. 195 (1962).

[142] 3 M.J. at 410. *But see* United States v. Hardin, 7 M.J. 399, 403 n.5, 405–07 (C.M.A. 1979) (Cook, J., dissenting). *See also* United States v. Caritativo, 37 M.J. 175, 183 (C.M.A. 1993) (asserts that this statement from *Hardin* overstates the role of the staff judge advocate).

[143] *See* United States v. Thompson, 3 M.J. 966 (N.C.M.R. 1977). An SJA in a large office may have as many as 30 lawyers working for him or her at any one time.

[144] *See, e.g.*, United States v. Hightower, 18 C.M.R. 9 (C.M.A. 1955).

[145] Service of the record on defense counsel shall constitute service on the accused. United States v. Euring, 27 M.J. 843 (A.C.M.R. 1989). *But see* United States v. Miller, 45 M.J. 148 (C.A.A.F. 1996) (harmless error for substitute counsel not to contact defendant); United States v. Hickok, 45 M.J. 142 (C.A.A.F. 1996) (prejudicial error not to serve counsel with SJA recommendation).

[146] U.C.M.J. art. 6(c); *see also* R.C.M. 1106(b); United States v. Dresen, 47 M.J. 122 (C.A.A.F. 1997) (SJA not disqualified when requesting appeal of decision requiring new SJA recommendation and action); United States v. Rice, 33 M.J. 451, 453 (C.M.A. 1991) (legal officer disqualified because of strong personal feelings or bias against appellant); United States v. Jolliff, 46 C.M.R. 95 (C.M.A. 1973); United States v. Coulter, 14 C.M.R. 75 (C.M.A. 1954); United States v. Hill, 7 M.J. 533 (A.C.M.R. 1979) (disqualification of trial counsel may not be waived by failing to

is to ensure that the accused receives a thorough and impartial review.[147] Early post-trial review cases that interpreted this provision have been factually distinguished but not overruled; accordingly, they may retain precedential effect. Such cases indicated that a staff judge advocate could be disqualified for preparing or signing a posttrial review if the staff judge advocate participated in a grant of immunity or an agreement favorable to a prosecution witness.[148]

The Code provision referring to the "same case" has been extended not only to disqualify as a staff judge advocate an individual who was the trial counsel in the accused's case,[149] but also an individual who was the trial counsel in a closely related case.[150] The disqualification goes beyond the trial to the author of the post-trial recommendation[151] and to a staff judge advocate who supervises a trial counsel who has made a promise of leniency to a prosecution witness in the accused's trial. The disqualification extends to promises to recommend Article 15 disposition, favorable action on a discharge in lieu of court-martial,[152] and trial counsel testifying on behalf of a prosecution witness at the witness' trial to obtain leniency for the witness.[153]

This disqualification also extends to the staff judge advocate and the convening authority who participated in a promise of clemency or immunity for a prosecution witness.[154] Recommending a grant of testimonial immunity to a defense

---

request it in *Goode* rebuttal). *See* United States v. Caritativo, 37 M.J. 175 (C.M.A. 1993) (disqualification because of advice to trial counsel or dissuading defense from submitting to nonjudicial punishment waived by failure to assert bias); United States v. Kemp, 7 M.J. 760 (A.C.M.R. 1979) (trial counsel's participation was harmless error because discussion of issues and opinion of staff judge advocate was drafted by another attorney). The Discussion to R.C.M. 1106(b) states that a witness may be ineligible to serve as legal officer. United States v. Rice, 33 M.J. 451, 453 (C.M.A. 1991) (legal officer's testimony was sufficient to disqualify him despite absence of defense objection; plain error exists).

[147] United States v. Coulter, 14 C.M.R. 75 (C.M.A. 1954).

[148] United States v. Kennedy, 8 M.J. 577 (A.C.M.R. 1979) (recommendation of clemency in return for testimony disqualifies the staff judge advocate); United States v. Ward, 1 M.J. 176 (C.M.A. 1975) (staff judge advocate who told witness he would recommend clemency to the convening authority was disqualified). *But see* United States v. Newman, 14 M.J. 474 (C.M.A. 1983).

[149] United States v. Coulter, 14 C.M.R. 75 (C.M.A. 1954).

[150] United States v. Hightower, 18 C.M.R. 9 (C.M.A. 1955).

[151] *See generally* United States v. McCormick, 34 M.J. 752, 755–56 (N.M.C.M.R. 1992) (who drafts is the key question, not who signed or adopted the recommendation).

[152] United States v. Levy, SPCM 13758 (A.C.M.R., July 20, 1979).

[153] United States v. Johnson, 4 M.J. 8 (C.M.A. 1977).

[154] *See* United States v. Johnson, 4 M.J. 8 (C.M.A. 1977); United States v. Chavez-Rey, 1 M.J. 34 (C.M.A. 1975). *But see* United States v. Walters, 30 M.J. 1290 (N.M.C.M.R. 1990) (grant of transactional immunity to prosecution witness did not, per se, disqualify the convening authority from taking action).

witness while the trial is ongoing does not disqualify the staff judge advocate, however.[155] The rationale for disqualifying the staff judge advocate and the convening authority was that their impartiality would be suspect in weighing the testimony of the witness who had been granted immunity or given a pretrial agreement. The factual weakness of this argument was noted by Judge Latimer in his dissent in *United States v. White*.[156] As noted earlier, the disqualification is also based on the appearance of evil.

Clarifying the earlier cases, the Court of Military Appeals held that, for the convening authority to be disqualified, "there must be some direct unattenuated causal relationship between the grant of clemency or immunity and the subsequent action."[157] When there is an absence of a quid pro quo, neither the convening authority nor staff judge advocate will be disqualified.[158]

Preparation of the post-trial recommendation also raises questions as to impartiality when that recommendation is subsequently attacked. Given a defense attack on the post-trial recommendation, the same staff judge advocate who prepared the initial recommendation will be disqualified from preparing a later one.[159]

If the staff judge advocate testifies as a witness and must evaluate his or her own testimony, he or she will be disqualified.[160] Conversely, if the staff judge advocate's testimony was objective in nature and uncontroverted, or if it related solely to a matter of formality, the staff judge advocate will not be disqualified.[161] Regardless, when the staff judge advocate has a "personal connection"

---

[155] *See* United States v. Griffin, 8 M.J. 66, 69–70 (C.M.A. 1979); United States v. Choice, 49 C.M.R. 663 (C.M.A. 1975).

[156] 27 C.M.R. 137 (C.M.A. 1958).

[157] United States v. Turcsik, 13 M.J. 442, 445 (C.M.A. 1982).

[158] United States v. Decker, 15 M.J. 416 (C.M.A. 1983).

[159] United States v. Engle, 1 M.J. 387 (C.M.A. 1976); United States v. Kemp, 7 M.J. 760 (A.C.M.R. 1979) (inconsequential inaccuracies). A challenge is not consequential where the advice is correct in every respect. United States v. Collins, 6 M.J. 256 (C.M.A. 1979) (staff judge advocate not disqualified because of frivolous motion attacking pretrial advice). *See also* United States v. Lynch, 39 M.J. 223 (C.M.A. 1994) (When there is a legitimate factual issue concerning a pretrial waiver of conflict-free counsel between the defense counsel and the staff judge advocate, the SJA is disqualified from preparing post-trial recommendation).

[160] United States v. Guiterrez, 57 M.J. 148 (C.A.A.F. 2002); United States v. Choice, 49 C.M.R. 663 (C.M.A. 1975); United States v. Gavitt, 37 M.J. 761 (A.C.M.R. 1993); United States v. Wilson, 8 M.J. 800 (N.C.M.R. 1980); United States v. Treadwell, 7 M.J. 864 (A.C.M.R. 1979) (SJA disqualified where he had to weigh his own testimony on a motion at trial). *See also* United States v. Loving, 41 M.J. 213, 288 (C.M.A. 1994) (challenging the pretrial advice because of the accused's wrong age, incorrect restraint information and the accused's awards does not disqualify the SJA from performing post-trial duties); *cf.* United States v. Bygrate, 40 M.J. 839, 845 (N.M.C.M.R. 1994) (SJA who took premature position on appropriate sentence disqualified).

[161] United States v. Choice, 49 C.M.R. 663 (C.M.A. 1975); United States v. Gray, 14 M.J. 816 (A.C.M.R. 1982).

with the case as distinguished from only "an official or disinterested" interest, he or she is disqualified.[162] Pre-recommendation remarks by a staff judge advocate to the media approving of a sentence may require preparation of the recommendation by a different officer.[163]

The disqualification of the staff judge advocate does not disqualify the successor or acting staff judge advocate.[164]

There have been a number of cases dealing with informal, and thus inappropriate, arrangements made by disqualified staff judge advocates to have other staff judge advocates prepare post-trial recommendations.[165] The Army Court of Military Review observed:

> The confusion seems to be over how to request the assignment of another staff judge advocate to prepare the recommendation. The convening authority may request another convening authority to make his staff judge advocate available or he may request the Judge Advocate General to assign a staff judge advocate for the limited purpose of preparing the post-trial recommendation. Informal coordination can be made between staff judge advocates for convening authorities and the Judge Advocate General but the actual request must be made by the convening authority.[166]

---

[162] 49 C.M.R. at 664. SJA not disqualified when he testified on speedy-trial motion concerning "removal of a file from defense counsel upon submission" of request for administrative discharge in lieu of court-martial). *See also* United States v. Calhoun, ACM 32314, 1999 C.C.A. LEXIS 166 (A.F. Crim. App. May 25, 1999) (limited pretrial advice supplied to SJA A, SPCM staff judge advocate by seeking SJA B, who was co-located and supervising GCM SJA, did not disqualify SJA B from preparing post-trial review), *aff'd*, 53 M.J. 47 (C.A.A.F. 2000); United States v. Wansley, 46 M.J. 335 (C.A.A.F. 1997) (SJA for GCM authority not disqualified by comments made by the Chief of Military Justice for the special court-martial convening authority in local post newspaper without showing approval or reliance on the remarks).

[163] United States v. Bygrave, 40 M.J. 839, 845–46 (N.M.C.M.R. 1994).

[164] An affidavit or order need not be set forth in the record of trial when the signature is that of the "acting staff judge advocate or legal officer." Even absent an affidavit, there is a rebuttable presumption of regularity that a person signing as a staff judge advocate was acting in that position. *Cf.* United States v. Gray, 14 M.J. 816 (A.C.M.R. 1982); Section 24-30.00. When the officer signs "for" the staff judge advocate, the court may seek affidavits to determine if the officer was acting as the staff judge advocate. United States v. Holbrook, ACMR 8702823 (A.C.M.R. Apr. 25, 1988). If the person was not actually signing as the acting staff judge advocate, there is error and a new recommendation may be ordered. United States v. Wilson, 16 M.J. 581 (A.C.M.R. 1983), *rev'd in part on other grounds*, 20 M.J. 300 (C.M.A. 1985); United States v. Gray, 14 M.J. 816 (A.C.M.R. 1982).

[165] United States v. Gavitt, 37 M.J. 761 (A.C.M.R. 1993) (normally a new SJA is assigned). *See also* United States v. Hall, 39 M.J. 593 (A.C.M.R. 1994).

In *Gavitt* and United States v. Wilson, 16 M.J. 581 (A.C.M.R. 1983), the court held that the error caused by these informal arrangements couldn't be waived; in *Hall*, however, the court held that the error was "consciously and deliberately waived." 39 M.J. at 595.

[166] 39 M.J. at 596.

§ 24-63.00　Content of Recommendation

Rule for Courts-Martial 1106 envisions that the recommendation of the staff judge advocate will be brief. Rule 1106(d) provides in part:

> (2) *Form.* The recommendation of the staff judge advocate or legal officer shall be a concise written communication.

> (3) *Required contents.* Except as provided in subsection (e) of this rule, the recommendation of the staff judge advocate or legal officer shall include concise information as to:

> (A) The findings and sentence adjudged by the court-martial;[167]

> (B) A summary of the accused's service record, to include length and character of service, awards and decorations received, and any records of nonjudicial punishment and previous convictions;[168]

> (C) A statement of the nature and duration of any pretrial restraint;

> (D) If there is a pretrial agreement, a statement of any action the convening authority is obligated to take under the agreement or a statement of the reasons why the convening authority is not obligated to take specific action under the agreement; and

> (E) A specific recommendation as to the action to be taken by the convening authority on the sentence.

Given the minimal demands of Rule 1106(d)(3), the staff judge advocate's recommendation *could* consist of simply filling in the blanks in the form appearing on the following page.

If the staff judge advocate is to be helpful, however, there should be some summary of the evidence in the case as well as matters in aggravation, extenuation, and mitigation. As Rule for Courts-Martial 1106(d)(1) states: "The purpose

---

[167] In United States v. Howard, 35 M.J. 763, 767 (A.C.M.R. 1992), the staff judge advocate included information about the results of a previous trial on the same charges. The court held that this did not constitute error, but the accused waived the issue by failing to object and because there was no evidence of improper motive on the part of the staff judge advocate.

[168] *See, e.g.,* United States v. Wellington, 58 M.J. 420 (C.A.A.F. 2003) (incorrect statement of two past judicial punishments constituted plain error despite absence of trial defense objection to the recommendation); United States v. Demerse, 37 M.J. 488 (C.M.A. 1993) (failure to include Vietnam awards was plain error). *See also* United States v. Santiago, 41 M.J. 377 (C.M.A. 1994) (summary disposition) (failure to object to staff judge advocate's omission of defendant's decorations and misstatement of character of service was not plain error); United States v. Hollon, 39 M.J. 38 (C.M.A. 1993) (summary disposition) (plain error not to present evidence of five years of service in the Army, two Army Achievement Medals, an Army Good Conduct Medal, Humanitarian Service Medal, Overseas Service Ribbon, Expert Field Medical Badge and Expert Qualification Badge for M-16); United States v. Lynch, 39 M.J. 37 (C.M.A. 1993) (summary disposition) (harmless not to mention Sea Service Deployment Ribbon); United States v. McKinnon, 38 M.J. 667 (A.C.M.R. 1993) (waiver of failure to include several awards and decorations); United States v. Czekala, 38 M.J. 566, 571 (A.C.M.R. 1993) (failure to raise absence of information on Joint Service commendation resulted in waiver), *aff'd,* 42 M.J. 168 (C.A.A.F. 1995).

(Rel.3—1/07　Pub.62410)

of the recommendation . . . is to assist the convening authority to decide what action to take on the sentence in the exercise of command prerogative." Generally it will be plain error for a staff judge advocate to fail to call the convening authority's attention to a sentencing judge's clemency recommendation.[169] However, there is no requirement to summarize clemency matters in the SJA recommendation.[170]

Rules 1105 and 1106 were amended to require the SJA, absent a written request to the contrary by the accused, to inform the convening authority of a recommendation for clemency by the sentencing authority, made in conjunction with the announced sentence.

STAFF JUDGE ADVOCATE RECOMMENDATION

_____

Date

_____

Accused's name

_____

_____

Length of Service   _Character of Service_

_____

_____

Awards and decorations   _Number of prior convictions_

_____

_____

Number of Article 15's   _Nature and length of pretrial restraint_

_____

_____

_____

Pretrial disposition recommendations

CHARGES

Offense	_Findings_	_Sentence_
_____	_____	_____
_____	_____	_____
_____	_____	_____
_____	_____	_____
_____	_____	_____

---

[169] United States v. Clear, 34 M.J. 129, 132 (C.M.A. 1992), citing United States v. McLemore, 30 M.J. 605, 607–08 (N.M.C.M.R. 1990). See also United States v. Beaudin, 35 M.J. 385 (C.M.A. 1992) (it was error, albeit harmless, not to mention that trial judge considered offenses multiplicitous). The _Clear_ decision, and its reasoning and implications, were criticized in Major Eugene R. Milhizer, _United States v. Clear, Good Idea—Bad Law_, Army Law, June, 1992, at 3.

[170] United States v. Curtis, 44 M.J. 106, 164 (C.A.A.F. 1996), _rev'd on other grounds_, 46 M.J. 129 (C.A.A.F. 1997). _See also_ United States v. Corcoran, 40 M.J. 478, 484 (C.M.A. 1994) (no requirement to reflect recommendations of Family Advocacy Team).

(Rel.3—1/07 Pub.62410)

Plea agreement: _____

Recommendation: _____

The staff judge advocate is not required to examine the record for legal errors, unless the defense counsel has made a prior allegation of legal error.[171] The staff judge advocate's response to this "may consist of a statement of agreement or disagreement with the matter raised by the accused" and what corrective action is needed.[172] If the staff judge advocate on his or her own finds legal errors,

[171] R.C.M 1106(d)(4). *See* United States v. Craig, 28 M.J. 321, 324 (C.M.A. 1989) (alleged "disregard" for evidence in extenuation and mitigation was not a "legal error"); United States v. Hill, 27 M.J. 293 (C.M.A. 1988).

In United States v. Williams-Oatman, 38 M.J. 602, 604 (A.C.M.R. 1993), a case in which defense counsel unartfully complained of the admission into evidence of the accused's possession of a knife, the court stated:

> The recommendation to the convening authority is not a *pro forma* act by the staff judge advocate but a meaningful evaluation of the matters submitted on behalf of an accused. If the intent of the trial defense counsel is not clear, it is incumbent on the staff judge advocate to "protect the record" and discuss all possible interpretations of the R.C.M. 1105 submissions.

Accordingly, the SJA in *Williams-Oatman* erred by merely treating the defense submission as a clemency request.

The court recently has addressed multiplicity matters in the context of clemency concerns. Referring to its prior decision in *United States v. Beaudin*, 35 M.J. 385 (C.M.A. 1992), the court observed:

> *Beaudin* does not require that every multiplicity ruling be included in the SJA recommendation to the convening authority. As a practical matter, for an SJA to mention that the offenses were considered multiplicitous for sentencing may be adverse to the interests of an accused. If a convening authority is informed that the accused has received a sentence based on the offenses being treated as multiplicitous thereby limiting the maximum punishment, that convening authority may be less inclined to grant clemency. The requirement for the SJA to comment on the multiplicity question arises when the defense counsel first raises the issue as part of the defense submission to the convening authority. In effect, in *Beaudin* the SJA overruled the judge by indicating that the judge's decision concerning multiplicity was erroneous. . . . As the concurring judges in *Beaudin* noted, the post-trial recommendation should not be encumbered with unnecessary requirements as interpreted by an intermediate appellate court.

United States v. Russen, 40 M.J. 184, 186 (C.M.A. 1994). *See also* United States v. Welker, 44 M.J. 85 (C.A.A.F. 1996) (If no legal error at trial, it is harmless error not to respond to defense allegation of legal error. However, Senior Judge Everett would require service response to allegation of error unless "*clearly without* merit".) 44 M.J. at 92 (C.A.A.F. 1996). *Cf.* United States v. Green, 44 M.J. 93, 95 (C.A.A.F. 1996) ("A staff judge advocate (SJA), although not required to examine the record for legal error, must nonetheless respond to any allegations of legal error submitted by the defense." Applied harmless error test?). *Cf.* United States v. Hamilton, 47 M.J. 32 (C.A.A.F. 1997) (applied *Welker*).

[172] R.C.M 1106(d)(4) ("An analysis or rationale for the staff judge advocate's statement, if any, concerning legal errors is not required.").

(Rel.3—1/07 Pub.62410)

there should also be a recommendation for corrective action.[173] The staff judge advocate may submit "any additional matters deemed appropriate . . . includ[ing] matters outside the record."[174] "If the proceedings resulted in an acquittal of all charges and specifications or if, after the trial began, the proceedings were terminated without findings and no further action is contemplated, a recommendation under this rule is not required."[175]

In *United States v. Heirs*,[176] the Court of Military Appeals, dealing with statements made by an accused during an unsuccessful providency inquiry, held that "[i]f inadmissible at trial, such statements cannot be considered during the posttrial review of the sufficiency of the Government's evidence."[177] Accordingly, the post-trial recommendation cannot use inadmissible evidence to sustain the findings or sentence. Otherwise, however, inadmissible evidence of uncharged misconduct may be used to rebut a judge's recommendation for sentence suspension.[178]

Distinguishing *United States v. Brannon*,[179] the court in *United States v. Green*[180] held that unexplained references to appellant's race in the SJA recommendation does not constitute legal error. "[R]ace may be a relevant factor in specific cases depending upon the particular purpose for which its consideration is offered; . . . a convening authority is not required to be race-ignorant; he or she is only required to be race-neutral." Critically, the court's holding does not mean that all racial references are either lawful or appropriate. It is incumbent on defense counsel to examine the post-trial recommendation for inappropriate comment and when necessary make a timely challenge. Absent proper objection, the defense will waive any error.[181]

§ 24-64.00 Defense Response

§ 24-64.10 In General

The staff judge advocate's recommendation must be served on the accused[182]

---

[173] R.C.M 1106(d)(4).

[174] R.C.M. 1106(d)(5).

[175] R.C.M. 1106(e).

[176] 29 M.J. 68 (C.M.A. 1989) (per curiam).

[177] 29 M.J. at 69 (C.M.A. 1989).

[178] United States v. Groves, 30 M.J. 811 (A.C.M.R. 1990) (allegation was neither "unreliable nor misleading," citing United States v. Mann, 22 M.J. 279, 280 n.2 (C.M.A. 1986)) (alternative holding of no prejudice).

[179] 33 M.J. 179 (C.M.A. 1991) (summary disposition).

[180] 37 M.J. 380 (C.M.A. 1993).

[181] 37 M.J. at 385 (C.M.A. 1993).

[182] U.C.M.J. art. 60(d). *See also* R.C.M. 1106(f)(1), which states, in part:

If it is impracticable to serve the recommendation on the accused for reasons including

and on the defense counsel,[183] who may respond to it. Rule for Courts-Martial 1106(f)(4) provides: "Counsel for the accused may submit, in writing, corrections or rebuttal to any matter in the recommendation believed to be erroneous, inadequate, or misleading, and may comment on any other matter."[184] The rule does not provide for personal appearance before the convening authority; only a written response may be made. The defense response, previously known as the "*Goode*" response,[185] is of great importance, as it is a particularly timely point at which to correct error or submit favorable data.

The defense response as well as material submitted under Rule 1105 should be attached to the recommendation. Unfortunately, the routine use of "boilerplate"

but not limited to the transfer of the accused to a distant place, the unauthorized absence of the accused, or military exigency, or if the accused so requests on the record at the court-martial or in writing, the accused's copy shall be forwarded to the accused's defense counsel. A statement shall be attached to the record explaining why the accused was not served personally.

R.C.M. 1106(f)(1) was promulgated in its present form in 1990 (Executive Order 12708 (March 23, 1990)) to parallel Article 60(d), which in turn was enacted as part of the Military Justice Act of 1983. The House Report expressly states that Article 60(d) could be satisfied by service on the defense counsel. H.R. Rep. No. 549, 98th Cong., 1st Sess. 15 (1983). R.C.M. 1106 permits such service when it is "impracticable" to serve the accused, unless the accused is proceeding *pro se* (without counsel). *See* United States v. Roland, 31 M.J. 747 (A.C.M.R. 1990); United States v. Euring, 27 M.J. 843 (A.C.M.R. 1989); United States v. Derksen, 24 M.J. 818 (A.C.M.R. 1987); *but see* United States v. Shaw, 30 M.J. 1033 (A.F.C.M.R. 1990).

The provisions of Article 54(d) and R.C.M. 1104 dealing with service of the record of trial on the accused do not apply to R.C.M. 1106. United States v. Roland, 31 M.J. 747 (A.C.M.R. 1990); United States v. Euring, 27 M.J. 843, 845 (A.C.M.R. 1989). In *United States v. Leaver*, 36 M.J. 133 (C.M.A. 1992), the court found prejudicial error when the recommendation was served on counsel who was alleged to be ineffective. The 1994 change to the *Manual for Courts-Martial* amends R.C.M. 1105(c)(1) and 1106(f)(7) to clarify the method of service and the time element.

[183] In *United States v. Moseley*, 35 M.J. 481 (C.M.A. 1992), the court held that total failure to serve the recommendation on defense counsel required automatic reversal despite the fact that the accused had personally been served. *Cf.* United States v. Miller, 45 M.J. 148 (C.A.A.F. 1996) (harmless error for substitute counsel not to contact defendant); United States v. Hickok, 45 M.J. 142 (C.A.A.F. 1996) (prejudicial error not to serve counsel with SJA recommendation).

[184] *See also* U.C.M.J. art. 60(d). Just as when counsel argues for a punitive discharge at trial, if the defense counsel as part of the post-trial submission seeks a punitive discharge "even in a tactical step to accomplish mitigation of other elements of a possible sentence—counsel must make a record that such advocacy is pursuant to the accused's wishes." United States v. Dresen, 40 M.J. 462, 465 (C.M.A. 1994).

[185] United States v. Goode, 1 M.J. 3 (C.M.A. 1975). In *Goode*, the court stated:

it is ordered that on and after May 15, 1975, a copy of the written review . . . be served on counsel for the accused with an opportunity to correct or challenge any matter he deems erroneous, inadequate or misleading, or on which he otherwise wishes to comment. Proof of such service, together with any correction, challenge or comment which counsel may make, shall be made a part of the record of proceedings.

1 M.J. at 6.

(Rel.3—1/07 Pub.62410)

language in the recommendation sometimes makes it unclear whether the defense has made such a submission, an ambiguity that can result in appellate reversal.[186]

The degree of importance placed on the response, and the Court's frustration with continuing administrative errors connected with it was perhaps best illustrated in *United States v. Johnston*[187] when the Court opined:

> Our concern is ensuring that the law is adhered to, established procedures followed, and staff judge advocates do their jobs. Obviously the supervisory responsibility for military justice advice to convening authorities lies with the Judge Advocate General of the Armed Forces . . . . Hopefully, these statutory officers are kept abreast of the numerous cases in which this Court must act on issues resulting from sloppy staff work and inattention to detail. . . . All this court can do to ensure that the law is being followed and that military members are not being prejudiced is to send these cases back for someone TO GET THEM RIGHT.[188]

Failure to serve a copy of the recommendation on the defense in a timely fashion can result in setting aside the convening authority's action with a requirement for a new recommendation and action.[189]

---

[186] Some staff judge advocates have used a recommendation form that states that "*if* the defense counsel submitted a response . . . or other matters . . . it is attached at TAB A for your consideration." (Emphasis added.) When there is no TAB A, in some cases the courts have ordered a new recommendation. United States v. Craig, 28 M.J. 321, 324–25 (C.M.A. 1989) (remanding for new action after consideration of clemency matters); United States v. Hallums, 26 M.J. 838 (A.C.M.R. 1988). *Cf.* United States v. Moody, 27 M.J. 683 (A.C.M.R. 1988) (since there were no substantial mitigating factors in defense submissions, there was harmless error). *Compare Craig, above, with* United States v. Stephens, 56 M.J. 391, 392 (C.A.A.F. 2002) (convening authority's reference to materials considered when those materials did not include clemency materials, or the SJA's recommendation, did not vitiate convening authority's action). To avoid the courts guessing whether the defense submissions were attached to the staff judge advocate recommendations, a number of methods could be employed:

> *(1) specifically list by title or description each defense submission as an enclosure to the post-trial recommendation;*
>
> *(2) have the convening authority sign a statement at the end of the addendum before taking action that he has considered the post-trial recommendation and defense submissions;*
>
> *(3) avoid using the contingent language mentioned above;*
>
> *(4) have the convening authority initial or sign each defense submission; and*
>
> *(5) when no matters are submitted by the defense, have the record contain a certificate of service on the defense counsel for the record of trial and post-trial recommendation with a statement that no matters were submitted.*

See also United States v. Garcia, 49 M.J. 21 (C.A.A.F. 1998) (summary disposition) (finding no error and distinguishing *Craig* based on "unopposed and uncontradicted affidavit of the Staff Judge Advocate establishing delivery of appellant's clemency request to the convening authority").

[187] 51 M.J. 227 (C.A.A.F. 1999).

[188] 51 M.J. at 229–230 (emphasis in original).

[189] *E.g.,* United States v. Williams, 57 M.J. 1 (C.A.A.F. 2002).

(Rel.3—1/07 Pub.62410)

§ 24-64.20   Timeliness and Waiver

The accused has ten days from receipt of the recommendation of the staff judge advocate to respond, [190] although if the accused shows good cause, the period may be extended for twenty additional days. [191] Rule for Courts-Martial 1106 does not define "good cause." Should the defense have insufficient time to respond, at the appellate level it should make an offer of proof as to the nature of the material that would have been submitted. [192] Otherwise, an untimely response will be treated as a waiver. [193] At present, what view the courts will take on waiver is unclear, [194] but, the rule may be that "If defense counsel does

---

[190] R.C.M. 1106(f)(5).

[191] R.C.M. 1106(f)(5). In *United States v. Sosebee*, 35 M.J. 892 (A.C.M.R. 1992), despite the accused's untimely submission, the court held that the "spirit" of the rule should have been followed and that a prudent staff judge advocate would accept an untimely submission, and refused to apply waiver, reversing the case for a new action. Query this result.

[192] United States v. DeGrocco, 23 M.J. 146 (C.M.A. 1987). *See also* United States v. Pearson, 15 M.J. 888 (A.C.M.R. 1983).

[193] R.C.M. 1106(f)(6). In *United States v. Mercier*, 5 M.J. 866 (A.F.C.M.R. 1978), the court held that where defense counsel submitted his rebuttal half an hour late, and the convening authority had already taken his action, errors in the review were waived. Courts may have been particularly hostile to untimeliness in the past, in part because of the tendency of some civilian counsel to delay making a response to the post-trial review until paid by the client. Note that Rule 1106 does not recognize exceptions beyond the 20-day extension for good cause.

[194] Prior to the *1984 Manual*, the courts dealt extensively with waiver. In *United States v. Barnes*, 3 M.J. 406 (C.M.A. 1977), appellate defense counsel asserted that the post-trial review was deficient in numerous respects. Because trial defense counsel had not challenged the review, however, the court found waiver. *See also* United States v. Morrison, 3 M.J. 408 (C.M.A. 1977). In *United States v. Turcsik*, 13 M.J. 442 (C.M.A. 1982), the Court of Military Appeals implied that defense counsel could waive the convening authority's disqualification for granting immunity. *See also* United States v. Smart, 21 M.J. 15, 17–18 (C.M.A. 1985) (waiver invoked despite lack of service on counsel); United States v. Hannan, 17 M.J. 115 (C.M.A. 1984) (SJA should have discussed parole eligibility in light of letter from the military judge to the convening authority—accused waived error by not seeking clarification of review); United States v. Lockhausen, 8 M.J. 262, 263 n.1 (C.M.A. 1980) (waiver of SJA's failure to mention that one prosecution witness had received promise from company commander not to prefer charges); United States v. Hairston, 15 M.J. 892, 894 (A.C.M.R. 1983) (waiver of SJA's statement concerning prior finding against the accused for possession of a controlled substance. *Compare* United States v. Veney, 6 M.J. 795 (A.C.M.R. 1978) (no waiver for failure to mention military judge's recommendation for suspension of part of sentence) *with* United States v. Ringor, 3 M.J. 1104 (N.C.M.R. 1977).

Rejecting a paternalistic, limited approach to waiver places the responsibility where it belongs —on the individual defense counsel familiar with the facts of the case. Given the presence of independent defense counsel in most services, there is no reason to believe that defense counsel will be anything less than zealous in their representation. In *United States v. Demerse*, 37 M.J. 488, 494 (C.M.A. 1993), Judge Crawford, dissenting, opined that in light of the Congressional change from the post-trial review to the new recommendation, any errors in the recommendation should be viewed against a waiver framework.

not make a timely comment on an omission in the SJA's recommendation, the error is waived unless it is prejudicial under a plain error analysis."[195]

However, the appellate courts may take corrective action on their own. In *United States v. Thompson*,[196] the court, dealing with the staff judge advocate's failure to reply to the defense response, held that "[w]hen an SJA fails to comment on a legal issue raised by defense counsel in the post-trial submission, both the failure to comment and the issue raised will be reviewed for prejudice in accordance with Article 59(a)."[197]

If the trial defense counsel does not request an extension, the convening authority has no obligation to grant one.[198] If a response is received late but before the convening authority takes action, the response should be forwarded to the convening authority,[199] unless time-consuming comment would be required from the staff judge advocate.

A defense failure to submit a response can constitute ineffectiveness of counsel if the accused can show both deficiency on the part of counsel and prejudice.[200]

§ 24-65.00 The Staff Judge Advocate's "Addendum"

§ 24-65.10 In General

If defense counsel advises the staff judge advocate or legal officer of perceived errors in the post-trial recommendation, that officer "may supplement the recommendation"[201] via an "addendum" to the recommendation. Ideally, the addendum is used to correct errors in the initial recommendation to ensure that

---

[195] United States v. Scalo, 60 M.J. 435, 436 (C.A.A.F. 2005) citing R.C.M. 1106(f); United States v. Kho, 54 M.J. 63, 65 (C.A.A.F. 2000). On appeal, the Court reviews the issue de novo. —To prevail under a plain error analysis, Appellant must persuade this Court that: "(1) there was an error; (2) it was plain or obvious; and (3) the error materially prejudiced a substantial right." *Id* quoting United States v. Kho, 54 M.J. at 65.

[196] 26 M.J. 512 (A.C.M.R. 1988).

[197] 26 M.J. at 514 (A.C.M.R. 1988) (discussing "the ambiguous dictates of R.C.M. 1105 and 1106."). *See also* United States v. Spurlin, 33 M.J. 443 (C.M.A. 1991) (failure to include clemency submission tested for prejudice); United States v. Siders, 15 M.J. 272 (C.M.A. 1983) (same); *but see* United States v. Moseley, 35 M.J. 481 (C.M.A. 1992) (automatic reversal for failure to serve SJA recommendation on defense counsel). *See also* § 24-90.00.

[198] United States v. Angelo, 25 M.J. 834, 836 (A.C.M.R. 1988) (found waiver after 13-day delay in making submission).

[199] 25 M.J. 834, 836 (A.C.M.R. 1988).

[200] United States v. Robertson, 39 M.J. 211, 218 (C.M.A. 1994) (no prejudice found). *See also* United States v. Sylvester, 47 M.J. 390, 393 (C.A.A.F. 1998) (accused has burden to indicate what additional information he would have submitted).

[201] R.C.M. 1106(f)(7).

(Rel.3—1/07 Pub.62410)

the convening authority is properly advised.[202] A response is not required to a defense request for clemency.[203]

In *United States v. Boston*,[204] the Air Force Court of Military Review applied a broader approach to a pre-Rules defense response to a post-trial review and required "that when the defense counsel submits comments or challenges to the review . . . the staff judge advocate must, at a minimum, indicate his concurrence or disagreement with those comments prior to submitting them to the officer exercising general court-martial authority." This appears more demanding than the present Rule 1106 obligation, but may signal the future direction of judicial interpretation. Indeed, the Court of Military Appeals has indicated in dicta that the staff judge advocate's failure to respond to legal errors raised by the defense will result in prejudice "in most instances" and requires that the record of trial be returned to the convening authority for a new recommendation.[205]

§ 24-65.20 New Matter

If "new matter" is contained in the addendum, the addendum must be served on the accused in the same manner as the original recommendation.[206] "[T]he dividing line between what is and is not 'matter from outside the record of trial' can be wafer thin."[207] The Discussion to Rule 1106(f)(7) states:

> "New matter" includes discussion of the effect of new decisions on issues in the case, matter from outside the record of trial, and issues not previously

---

[202] *Cf.* United States v. Redding, 6 M.J. 660 (A.F.C.M.R. 1978) (recommends that errors raised by defense be corrected in addendum to post-trial review).

[203] United States v. Harrison, 26 M.J. 553 (A.C.M.R. 1988). When the trial counsel attaches derogatory information to a clemency petition prior to the action of the convening authority, however, the derogatory information must be served on the defense counsel. United States v. Torres, 25 M.J. 555 (A.C.M.R. 1987). *See also* United States v. Anderson, 53 M.J. 374 (C.A.A.F. 2000) (note by the Chief of Staff was erroneously attached to appellant's clemency submission and did not involve supplement to SJA recommendation under R.C.M. 1106(f)(7)); United States v. Harris, 53 M.J. 86, 88 (C.A.A.F. 2000).

[204] 7 M.J. 953, 955 (A.F.C.M.R. 1979). *Cf.* R.C.M. 1106(d)(4). United States v. Moore, 27 M.J. 656 (A.C.M.R. 1988) (failed to respond to seven legal errors); United States v. Coder, 27 M.J. 650 (A.C.M.R. 1988) (mention of sentence disparity did not amount to an allegation of legal error); United States v. Ghiglieri, 25 M.J. 687 (A.C.M.R. 1987) (failure of the SJA to respond to an allegation of legal error is not prejudicial when there was no error).

[205] United States v. Hill, 27 M.J. 293, 296 (C.M.A. 1988). *See also* United States v. Goodes, 33 M.J. 888 (C.G.C.M.R. 1991) (affected portions of sentence set aside to teach a lesson); *but see* United States v. Williams-Oatman, 38 M.J. 602 (A.C.M.R. 1993) (no need to return record if allegations of legal error lacked merit).

[206] R.C.M. 1106(f). *See also* United States v. Narine, 14 M.J. 55, 57 (C.M.A. 1982).

[207] United States v. Haynes, 28 M.J. 881, 882 (A.F.C.M.R. 1989). *See also* United States v. Norment, 34 M.J. 224 (C.M.A. 1992) (staff judge advocate's addendum reporting his personal investigation into the accused's allegations should have been served on the accused for response under R.C.M. 1106(f)(7).

(Rel.3—1/07 Pub.62410)

discussed. "New matter" does not ordinarily include any discussion by the staff judge advocate or legal officer of the correctness of the initial defense comments on the recommendation.[208]

In *United States v. Buller,*[209] the court stated:

The essence of the RCM 1106(f)(7) is fair play—providing the accused with notice of the new issues or new information raised by the SJA and an opportunity to respond. In general, we have presumed prejudice when the defense has not been provided with notice of new matter and an opportunity to respond, . . . but we have not engaged in such a

---

[208] *See also* United States v. Thompson, 25 M.J. 662, 664–65 (A.F.C.M.R. 1987) (recommending a change in the location of confinement constitutes "new matter" when it amounts to denying the accused a chance at rehabilitation). *See also* United States v. Gilbreath, 57 M.J. 57 (C.A.A.F. 2002) (in trial by judge alone, staff judge advocate's addendum response that referred to the sentence as having been imposed by a "jury" was incorrect and suggested improper reliance on nonexistent members; failure to serve the addendum on the defense required reversal).

The accused must have a "*meaningful* opportunity to comment," and if the addendum is based on information unknown to the accused it should reflect that information so that the accused can respond to it. United States v. Cassell, 33 M.J. 448, 450 (C.M.A. 1991) (emphasis in original) (despite literal compliance with Rule 1106(d), given unique facts of the case, too much occurred "off the record"; matter made known to the SJA required disclosure in interests of fundamental fairness and "the need for the appearance of an open and proper military legal system"). *See also* United States v. Carnley, 46 M.J. 401 (C.A.A.F. 1997) (SJA's response with material from Article 32 investigation that defendant was impaired at the time of the offenses was new matter); United States v. Chatman, 46 M.J. 321 (C.A.A.F. 1997) (charge dismissed based on recommendation of Article 32 investigating officer is "new matter" because it is not part of the record of trial); United States v. Jones, 44 M.J. 242 (C.A.A.F. 1996) (Staff judge advocate's response on accused's ineligibility for return to duty noted to be new matter. Judge Crawford disagreed, concurring only in the result.); United States v. Jones, 36 M.J. 438 (C.M.A. 1993) (after accused's response, yeoman contradicted accused's statement as to length of service, which information was not communicated to the accused and was thus new matter). *Compare Jones with* United States v. Godfrey, 36 M.J. 629 (A.C.M.R. 1992) (when accused mentioned the sentence of one co-conspirator, it was not new matter to mention sentences of other co-conspirators).

Justice Crawford's dissent in *United States v. Leal,* 44 M.J. 235, 237 (C.A.A.F. 1996) (Crawford, J., dissenting), criticizes the majority opinion for holding that "when the defense seeks to distort the truth and this distortion is corrected by the Staff Judge Advocate (SJA) with reliable evidence that is known to the defense, this correction is new matter that must be served on the defense." In the future, while SJAs may cite in their recommendation inadmissible evidence, *e.g.,* reprimands and convictions, such inadmissible evidence will be considered new matter (that impacts on performance). Citing its own precedent, the Air Force Court of Criminal Appeals has held that the mention of new matter in the SJA addendum is "presumptively prejudicial." United States v. Gonyea, 44 M.J. 811 (A.F. Crim. App. 1996).

United States v. Cornwell, 49 M.J. 491, 492 (C.A.A.F. 1998) ("In our view RCM 1106(f)(7) does not apply to the types of oral conversation between the convening authority and his staff judge advocate (SJA) that took place in this case.").

[209] 46 M.J. 467 (C.A.A.F. 1997).

(Rel.3—1/07 Pub.62410)

presumption when the information is neutral and 'trivial.' " . . . Neither the rule nor our precedents require otherwise.[210]

If the staff judge advocate or legal officer fails to comply with the service requirement, the appellate court must determine if the matter was erroneous, inadequate, or misleading. If so, the appellate court may take corrective action without returning the record of trial to the convening authority.[211]

§ 24-70.00   ACTION BY THE CONVENING AUTHORITY

§ 24-71.00   In General

Both the authenticated record of trial[212] and the post-trial recommendation, together with any defense submissions and addenda, are forwarded to the convening authority,[213] who must consider them.[214]

The convening authority shall take action on the sentence and, in the discretion of the convening authority, the findings, unless it is impracticable. If it is impracticable for the convening authority to act, the convening authority shall, in accordance with such regulations as the Secretary concerned may prescribe,

---

[210] 46 M.J. at 469; *see* United States v. Ferguson, No. 9801572 (A. Crim. App. Aug. 7, 2000) (When accused makes a second request for discharge in lieu of court-martial, including commander's recommendation from first request for such discharge in SJA addendum was not new matter in the addendum), *pet. denied*, 55 M.J. 237 (C.A.A.F. 2001).

[211] R.C.M. 1106(d)(6). *See* United States v. Wheelus, 49 M.J. 283 (C.A.A.F. 1998); United States v. Haynes, 28 M.J. 881, 882 (A.F.C.M.R. 1989); United States v. Blodgett, 20 M.J. 756 (A.F.C.M.R. 1985). *Cf.* United States v. Smart, 21 M.J. 15 (C.M.A. 1985). *See also* § 24-90.00.

[212] R.C.M. 1104(e). *See generally* Section 24-50.00.

[213] Given command disruptions and reorganizations due to both the "drawdown" and urgent deployments, convening authority action has become problematical in some cases. This has been especially true when the accused has been left behind at an installation incident to deployment and action is taken by arrangement with an officer who is not the *de jure* convening authority. *See* United States v. Watson, 37 M.J. 166 (C.M.A. 1993) (When Marine 1st Division deployed, memorandum of understanding between CG of deploying forces and CG of Camp Pendleton made Camp Pendleton CG *de facto* commander of 1st Division elements left on the base.). Query whether the *de facto* commander rule employed in *Watson* comports with the Code requirement.

[214] U.C.M.J. Art. 60(c)(2); R.C.M. 1107(b)(3)(A)(iii). The difficulty is that sometimes it is unclear whether the convening authority actually reviewed materials such as clemency petitions. In such a case, the Air Force Court of Military Review has established a presumption of regularity pursuant to which the court will assume that the convening authority considered the servicemember's petition if set procedures are followed. United States v. Foy, 30 M.J. 664 (A.F.C.M.R. 1990) (en banc). *See also* United States v. Crawford, 34 M.J. 758, 761 (A.F.C.M.R. 1992). In *United States v. Kimble*, 35 M.J. 904, 905 (A.C.M.R. 1992), the court opined:

> Where the recommendation or addendum clearly describes the matters submitted by an accused and clearly indicate[s] that those documents are attached, we hold that there is no requirement for an affirmative statement or indication by the convening authority that he has reviewed those matters.

(Rel.3—1/07   Pub.62410)

forward the case to an officer exercising general court-martial jurisdiction who may take action under this rule.[215]

The Discussion to Rule 1107(a) states in part:

> The convening authority may not delegate the function of taking action on the findings or sentence. The convening authority who convened the court-martial may take action on the case regardless [of] whether the accused is a member of or present in the convening authority's command.

Although the convening authority should consider the staff judge advocate or legal officer's recommendation, particularly a recommendation to take corrective action in order to cure error arising at trial,[216] the convening authority has the absolute power to take any action he or she sees fit so long as an acquittal is not effected or the sentence increased.[217] The convening authority has, for example, the sole authority to suspend sentences. This power is expansive, and the convening authority may make a suspension contingent on the accused agreeing to conditions which could not be imposed by the court-martial[218] so

---

[215] R.C.M. 1107(a). The Discussion adds:

> It would be impracticable for the convening authority to take initial action when, for example, a command has been decommissioned or inactivated before the convening authority's action: when a command has been alerted for immediate overseas movement; or when the convening authority is disqualified because the convening authority has other than an official interest in the case or because a member of the court-martial which tried the accused later became the convening authority.

Even though the 1983 legislation that created the present post-trial action intended it to be a "clemency" device, the courts have not yet decided that the action is "not part of the criminal trial process." United States v. Vith, 34 M.J. 277, 279 n.4 (C.M.A. 1992). The convening authority who approves the sentence without mentioning findings "impliedly acts in reliance on the statutorily required recommendation of the SJA . . . and thus effectively purports to [approve] implicitly the findings as reported to the convening authority by the SJA." United States v. Diaz, 40 M.J. 335, 337, 342 (C.M.A. 1994).

[216] See United States v. Bashaw, 6 M.J. 179 (C.M.A. 1979). Corrective action may be taken while the case is on appeal as long as it is not designed to usurp the power of the appellate court. United States v. Kraffa, 11 M.J. 453 (C.M.A. 1981).

If the convening authority wishes to moot trial error by disapproving some findings, the staff judge advocate must advise how to adjust the sentence. United States v. Reed, 33 M.J. 98, 99 (C.M.A. 1991) ("[i]f appellate authorities confidently can discern the extent of the error's effect on the sentencing authority's decision, then the decision can be adjusted accordingly. If, however, the extent of the error's effect is more ambiguous, the sentencing proceeding must be conducted again." 33 M.J. 98, 99 (C.M.A. 1991), citing United States v. Sales, 22 M.J. 305, 308 (C.M.A. 1986)). See also United States v. Davis, 47 M.J. 484 (C.A.A.F. 1998) (citing Jones, permissible to reduce assault with intent to commit rape to indecent assault and affirm sentence of BCD and six months' confinement); United States v. Carroll, 45 M.J. 604 (Army Ct. Crim. 1997) (When convening authority on his own dismisses charge, he may reassess sentence without ordering a rehearing.).

[217] R.C.M. 1107(b)(1); 1107(c). See United States v. Josey, 58 M.J. 105 (C.A.A.F. 2003).

[218] United States v. Schneider, 38 M.J. 387 (C.M.A. 1993) (convening authority did not exceed

long as the power to suspend is not improperly delegated in some fashion. [219] Approval of sentence does not prohibit suspension of all or part of the approved sentence. [220] The permissible period of suspension may be limited by secretarial regulation. [221]

The convening authority will generally accept the advice of the staff judge advocate or legal officer rather than guess whether the advice in the post-trial recommendation is correct. Prior to the *1984 Manual*, when the convening authority took action that differed from the staff judge advocate's post-trial review recommendations, the Court of Military Appeals, [222] contrary to the *1969 Manual*, [223] required justification for such action:

> Requiring the government officials to justify their actions is a healthy procedure which encourages more effective government and enhances the integrity of any criminal justice system. With this in mind, we reaffirm our previous decisions which have construed the justification provision as mandatory rather than discretionary. [224]

The justification would be examined to determine if it was "minimally sufficient." [225] The Military Justice Act of 1983 nullified the case law giving rise to this requirement by making the convening authority's action on the findings and sentence a matter of command prerogative rather than a command determination of the legality of the proceedings. [226]

Many would relieve the convening authority of even the present role. Their feeling is that the convening authority's review and action are merely "eyewash,"

---

authority by conditioning suspension of forfeitures for the support of appellant's ex-wife and children even though conditions more demanding than a state court's); United States v. Cowan, 34 M.J. 258, 260 (C.M.A. 1992) (suspension could be made conditional on initiation and maintenance of allotment to sister for benefit of minor child; power to impose "reasonable and lawful conditions" as a condition for suspension is inherent in convening authority's powers).

[219] United States v. Wendlandt, 39 M.J. 810 (A.C.M.R. 1994) (suspension may not be based on the successful completion of sexual therapy program because "successful completion" required a subjective judgment to be made by the director of the therapy program rather than the convening authority).

[220] *E.g.*, United States v. Wright, 35 M.J. 899 (A.C.M.R. 1992) (approval of total forfeiture of pay and allowances did not prohibit suspension of part of forfeited pay, while maintaining the otherwise total forfeiture of pay and allowances).

[221] R.C.M. 1108(d). *See* United States v. Cabble, 38 M.J. 654 (A.C.M.R. 1993) (interpreting Army Reg. 27-10).

[222] United States v. Keller, 1 M.J. 159 (C.M.A. 1975).

[223] MCM, 1969 (rev. ed) ¶ 85c.

[224] United States v. Keller, 1 M.J. 159, 160 (C.M.A. 1975).

[225] United States v. Harris, 10 M.J. 276 (C.M.A. 1981).

[226] U.C.M.J. art. 60(c). *See also* R.C.M. 1106(d) Analysis; R.C.M. 1107(b)(1). *See* United States v. McKnight, 30 M.J. 205 (C.M.A. 1990) (convening authority could disregard without explanation staff judge advocate's opinion that the evidence was insufficient).

(Rel.3—1/07 Pub.62410)

noting that the convening authority rarely takes any action favorable to the accused not necessary to moot possible appellate error. Other critics would leave the convening authority only the power to exercise clemency on sentencing, with the rationale being that legal issues are actually determined by the staff judge advocate.

To take action:

The convening authority shall state in writing and insert in the record of trial the convening authority's decision as to the sentence, whether any findings of guilt are disapproved, and orders as to further disposition. The action shall be signed personally by the convening authority. The convening authority's authority to sign shall appear below the signature.[227]

The convening authority must expressly provide in the action any confinement credit that may be necessary to compensate for unlawful pretrial confinement.[228]

Unfortunately, administrative errors in post-trial actions are commonplace. In one case in which both a pretrial agreement quantum and the post-trial action were problematical, Senior Judge Crean complained:

My concern is not with the legal requirements of the system, which is done professionally, but with the administration of the system. Too many cases before this Court are so replete with senseless administrative errors that someone viewing the military justice system from the outside could conclude that it was being administered by a group of bumbling idiots out of a "Looney Tunes" cartoon rather than what is actually a professionally administered system. Incidents of poor administration reflect adversely on the United States Army and may harm the soldiers who make up this Army.[229]

Defense counsel sometimes submit belated clemency requests and materials. In some circumstances, a convening authority may recall an action in order to consider and act on these materials.[230] However, a convening authority who has taken action "cannot arbitrarily change his earlier action in some *substantive* way in order to correct a mistake."[231]

---

[227] R.C.M. 1107(f)(1). *See also* United States v. Cox, 50 M.J. 802, 804 (A.F. Crim. App. 1999) (although convening authority didn't personally sign the court-martial's findings and sentence as required, given the personal judgment of the convening authority, the error did not void the action).

[228] R.C.M. 1107(f)(4)(F). *See also* United States v. Stanford, 37 M.J. 388 (C.M.A. 1993) (failure of action to note credit for pretrial confinement non-prejudicial, but record returned for correction of the post-trial action).

[229] United States v. Yarbrough, 36 M.J. 1071, 1075 (A.C.M.R. 1993).

[230] United States v. Maners, 37 M.J. 966, 967–68 (A.C.M.R. 1993) (if action is not yet published, or the accused hasn't been officially notified, or if the record of trial hasn't been forwarded), citing United States v. Jackson, 36 M.J. 844 (A.C.M.R. 1993); R.C.M. 1107(f)(2).

[231] United States v. Diaz, 40 M.J. 335, 337, 345 (C.M.A. 1994) (emphasis added). *Cf.* United States v. Harris, 53 M.J. 86 (C.A.A.F. 2000) (convening authority can reassess the sentence).

(Rel.3—1/07 Pub.62410)

§ 24-72.00 Disqualification of the Convening Authority

The convening authority must be impartial. Otherwise he or she is disqualified from taking action.[232] What constitutes disqualification is undergoing reexamination by the courts.[233] The courts are in particular examining when the staff judge advocate to a convening or reviewing authority must be disqualified.[234]

In *United States v. Newman*,[235] the Court of Military Appeals held that "a grant of testimonial immunity—whether to a government or defense witness—does not affect the impartiality of the convening authority or his right to review the record of trial." The court recognized that two types of immunity exist and that it "need not consider under what circumstances, if any, a grant of transactional immunity or a sentence reduction may disqualify a convening authority from performing appellate review."[236] Whether disqualification is required depends upon the "key inquiry,"[237] that is, whether the actions of the convening authority "before or during the trial create, or appear to create, a risk that he will be unable to evaluate objectively and impartially all the evidence in the record of trial—including the testimony of any witness who has been immunized, granted a sentence reduction, or given other concessions."[238] The court indicated

---

[232] *E.g.*, United States v. Davis, 58 M.J. 100 (C.A.A.F. 2003) (convening authority who expresses inelastic attitude toward drug abusers requesting clemency is disqualified); United States v. Gutierrez, 57 M.J. 148, 150 (C.A.A.F. 2002) (Acting SJA disqualified because as Chief of Criminal Law she helped marshal case against defendant, "orchestrate[d] the timing of the Article 32 investigation to force the defense to assume responsibility for the delay" and had to evaluate her own testimony on speedy trial issue).

[233] *See, e.g.*, United States v. Dresen, 47 M.J. 122 (C.A.A.F. 1997) (SJA not disqualified requesting appeal of decision requiring new SJA recommendation and action); United States v. Fisher, 45 M.J. 159 (C.A.A.F. 1996) (mid-trial statements about defense counsel's suppression motion did not invalidate pretrial actions, but required new action); United States v. Fisher, 45 M.J. 159, 160 (C.A.A.F. 1996) (convening authority disqualified for action because of his comment that he thought "that any lawyer that would try to get the results of the urinalysis suppressed was unethical"); United States v. Edwards, 45 M.J. 114 (1996) (did not apply waiver because defense counsel allegedly did not know about convening authority's pretrial action); United States v. Fernandez, 24 M.J. 77 (C.M.A. 1987) (convening authority not disqualified based on a policy letter revealing "his serious concern about preventing the illegal distribution of drugs").

[234] *See, e.g.* United States v. Taylor, 60 M.J. 190 (C.A.A.F. 2004)(SJA disqualified by publication of an article in the base newspaper that concerned the accused's case and which could have been imputed to the SJA); United States v. Stirewalt, 60 M.J. 297 (C.A.A.F. 2004)(former Article 32 investigating officer acted subsequently as acting SJA and performed other case-related functions; actions did not give rise to specific prejudice). *See also* notes 232-33.

[235] 14 M.J. 474, 482 (C.M.A. 1983). *See also* United States v. Vith, 34 M.J. 277 (C.M.A. 1992); United States v. Decker, 15 M.J. 416 (C.M.A. 1983).

[236] 14 M.J. at 482. *See also* United States v. Walters, 30 M.J. 1290 (N.M.C.M.R. 1990) (dicta that grant of transactional immunity would not affect convening authority).

[237] 14 M.J. at 482.

[238] 14 M.J. at 482.

that the staff judge advocate "should" refer to any grant of immunity in the post-trial re-view to "facilitate appellate review."[239] In reaching its conclusion the court cited *United States v. White*,[240] in which the court observed:

> While the staff judge advocate merely presents his opinion to the convening authority . . . it is the convening authority who is by law empowered to act on the record. . . . Whether the fact is that the convening authority actively sought out the witness or the staff judge advocate did so with his concurrence, the grant of immunity was given by the convening authority. This involves him in the prosecution of the case to an extent where there is at least some doubt of his ability to impartially perform his statutory duty. He must weigh the evidence, pass on the credibility of witnesses and satisfy himself from the evidence that the accused is guilty beyond a reasonable doubt. It is asking too much of him to determine the weight to be given this witness' testimony since he granted the witness immunity in order to obtain his testimony. This action precludes his being the impartial judge he must be to properly perform his judicial functions.

Judge Everett was more persuaded by the dissent of Judge Latimer to the effect that "to grant immunity is purely an official act that falls upon a convening authority by virtue of his assignment."[241]

§ 24-73.00   Response to Matters Outside the Record

"[I]f the convening authority considers matters adverse to the accused from outside the record, with knowledge of which the accused is not chargeable, the accused shall be notified and given an opportunity to rebut."[242]

---

[239] 14 M.J. at 482 n.7.

[240] 27 C.M.R. 137, 138 (C.M.A. 1958).

[241] United States v. Newman, 14 M.J. 474, 480 (C.M.A. 1983) (citing United States v. White, 27 C.M.R. 137, 140 (C.M.A. 1958)). He continued:

> His position is substantially similar to that of judges in civilian courts who, in many jurisdictions, must approve or consent to grants of immunity before they become valid. The purpose of the grant is merely to remove the bar of self-incrimination which closes the mouth of one who is known to have some information relating to the offense. The interest of the law is to ascertain the truth. It is not necessary that a convening authority, to make those objectives attainable, have a fixed opinion on the veracity of a witness. On the contrary, he could not possibly make that determination until the person who received the grant had testified under oath, been cross-examined, and subjected to the tests of credibility and balanced against any witnesses testifying in opposite vein. It should be obvious that the witness starts under a cloud of unreliability, for he is himself a party to the crime and there is a natural tendency to reject the testimony of an admitted criminal. About all this case accomplishes is to discourage a commander from performing administrative duties which are calculated to permit the court-martial to ascertain all of the facts.

27 C.M.R. 137, 140 (C.M.A. 1958).

[242] R.C.M. 1107(b)(3)(B)(iii). United States v. Harris, 56 M.J. 480, 482 (C.A.A.F. 2002) (accused was on notice that service record matters could be considered by the convening authority);

The convening authority may consider items not admissible in evidence, such as the results of polygraph examinations or the use of truth serums,[243] but cannot go outside the record of trial to sustain a finding of guilty.[244] Two members of the Court of Military Appeals indicated that the convening authority may not consider unfavorable evidence over the objection of defense counsel; nor can the convening authority be presented with information known to be unreliable or misleading.[245] In *United States v. Moles*,[246] Judge Cook, dissenting, stated that the convening authority should be able to consider all available evidence, provided the accused is given the opportunity to rebut adverse evidence.

A staff judge advocate may not provide a reviewing authority with post-trial information taken from an obviously misinformed convicted servicemember or solicited from him in clear violation of service regulations.[247] The Court of Military Appeals also held it reversible error to include, in a post-trial review, matters that were elicited from the accused during a post-trial interview held in the absence of counsel.[248]

§ 24-73.10 Postponement of Confinement—Effect of Civilian Sentence

Article 57(e)(1), added to the Uniform Code in 1992,[249] provides that when a convicted servicemember is in the custody of a state, the District of Columbia, or a foreign country, and has been temporarily returned for trial by court-martial,

---

United States v. Anderson, 53 M.J. 374 (C.A.A.F. 2000) (note by the Chief of Staff was erroneously attached to appellant's clemency submission was adverse matter required to be served on the accused under R.C.M. 1107(b)).

[243] United States v. Carr, 18 M.J. 297 (C.M.A. 1984). *See also* United States v. Wynn, 26 M.J. 232 (C.M.A. 1988) (summary disposition) (error to advise convening authority not to consider statistics related to other punishments imposed on officers of the convening authority's command); United States v. Kirk, 24 M.J. 453 (C.M.A. 1987) (Despite *United States v. Gipson*, 24 M.J. 246 (C.M.A. 1987) holding that it was an abuse of discretion for the judge not to allow the defense to seek to lay a foundation for the admission of the testimony of a polygraph examiner testifying for the accused, it was not error for the staff judge advocate to advise the convening authority that in the SJA's view the polygrapher's conclusions have little weight.). *See generally* Section 20-33.33(c).

[244] United States v. Mann, 22 M.J. 279 (C.M.A. 1986). In *United States v. Drayton*, 40 M.J. 447, 451 (C.M.A. 1994), the court, emphasizing that under UCMJ art. 60(c)(3) the staff judge advocate no longer must weigh the factual sufficiency of the evidence of guilt, opined that when such a weighing is conducted voluntarily, evidence not presented at trial cannot be used to sustain a guilty finding.

[245] 22 M.J. at 280 n.2.

[246] 10 M.J. 154, 159 (C.M.A. 1981).

[247] 10 M.J. at 158 (C.M.A. 1981).

[248] United States v. Hill, 4 M.J. 33 (C.M.A. 1977).

[249] The National Defense Authorization Act for Fiscal Year 1993, Pub. L. No. 102-484 § 1059(a) (October 23, 1992).

service of any military sentence to confinement may be postponed by the convening authority until the permanent return of that person to military custody.

§ 24-74.00 Sentence Conversions

The Uniform Code provides that the convening authority may "approve, commute, or suspend the sentence in whole or in part."[250] Using this Code authority as justification, convening authorities have in the past "mitigated" or "commuted" sentences,[251] in particular converting punitive discharges to confinement. Accordingly, an accused sentenced only to a discharge occasionally has been shocked to have the discharge disapproved and sentences of confinement for six months or so substituted,[252] all on the grounds of clemency.

Because the convening authority may not increase the severity of a sentence,[253] the legality of such a conversion is suspect. In the past, conversion of a punitive discharge to confinement has been sustained because it "lessens the severity of the punishment."[254] The Discussion to Rule for Courts-Martial 1107(d)(1) thus states:

> One form of punishment may be changed to a less severe punishment of a different nature, as long as the changed punishment is one which the court-martial could have adjudged. For example, a bad-conduct discharge adjudged by a special court-martial could be changed to confinement for up to one year (but not vice versa).[255]

In *Waller v. Swift,*[256] the Court of Military Appeals appears to have held that

---

[250] U.C.M.J. art. 60(c)(2). This action may be taken *sua sponte*. More often the convening authority will be responding to the staff judge advocate's recommendation or a defense submission.

[251] *See, e.g.,* United States v. Petty, 30 M.J. 1237, 1238 (A.C.M.R. 1990) (convening authority converted partial forfeitures to period of forfeiture of all pay and allowances).

[252] *See, e.g.,* United States v. Coleman, 31 M.J. 653, 659 (C.G.C.M.R. 1990) (conversion of dishonorable discharge to 18 months' suspended confinement approved, even though accused would receive a bad-conduct discharge from an earlier court-martial).

[253] *See, e.g.,* R.C.M. 1107(d)(1); Waller v. Swift, 30 M.J. 139, 143 (C.M.A. 1990); United States v. Petty, 30 M.J. 1237, 1238 (A.C.M.R. 1990) (the *effect* of the conversion was to increase the severity of the sentence).

[254] United States v. Prow, 32 C.M.R. 64 (C.M.A. 1962) (Board of Review conversion of bad conduct discharge to three months' confinement with forfeitures sustained). *See also* United States v. Brown, 32 C.M.R. 333 (C.M.A. 1962) (conversion of bad-conduct discharge to six months' confinement and forfeitures).

[255] Six months' confinement was the jurisdictional limit of a special court-martial. It may well be that a punitive discharge adjudged by a general court-martial is subject to conversion to a greater term. *Cf.* Waller v. Swift, 30 M.J. 139, 144 (C.M.A. 1990) ("it seems to follow that a bad-conduct discharge imposed by a general court-martial could properly be commuted into substantially more than 6 months' confinement"); United States v. Darusin, 43 C.M.R. 194, 196 (seven months).

[256] 30 M.J. 139 (C.M.A. 1990). *See also* United States v. Carter, 45 M.J. 168 (C.A.A.F. 1996) (approved conversion of punitive discharge to two years at the request of the defendant); Frazier v. McGowan, 48 M.J. 828 (C.G. Crim. App. 1998) (BCD, two months' restriction, and three months at hard labor converted to 12 months' confinement), *aff'd,* 52 M.J. 384 (C.A.A.F. 1999).

"commutation" depends to some degree upon the sentencing agency's specific intent unless the accused consents to the commutation:

> However appropriate this rationale [permitting conversion of punitive discharges] might be under some circumstances—especially where the bad-conduct discharge was changed with the accused's consent or, at least, without his well founded objection—we do not believe that it applies here. Obviously Waller and his lawyer did not view the 12 months' confinement as being a "lesser" punishment than the bad-conduct discharge. Moreover, from our examination of the record of trial, it seems clear that the members of the court-martial were of the same opinion. [257]

The court held, however, that although Waller's discharge could not be converted to twelve months' confinement, in effect it could be converted to the time the accused had spent in confinement pending the action of the court. Dissenting, Judge Cox opined:

> A sentence to confinement for one year is either less than, equal to, or greater than being awarded a bad conduct discharge. Because I am of the opinion that a punitive discharge is a serious and strong punishment, I believe the one-year sentence to be a commutation. [258]

Although military law has long recognized punitive discharges as severe sentences, as Judge Cox noted in *Waller*, it is distinctly possible that contemporary society would now reject the argument that a punitive discharge is more severe than confinement. If so, just as changing social norms have altered the effect of the constitutional prohibition on cruel and unusual punishments, it may no longer be appropriate to substitute confinement for a punitive discharge.

§ 24-75.00   Restraint Pending Appeal

When an accused is sentenced to confinement, confinement ordinarily begins immediately. Rule 1107(f)(4) provides:

> (D) *Custody or confinement pending appellate review; capital cases.* When a record of trial involves an approved sentence to death, the convening authority shall, unless any approved sentence of confinement has been ordered into execution and a place of confinement designated, provide in the action for the temporary custody or confinement of the accused pending final disposition of the case on appellate review.

> (E) *Deferment of service of sentence to confinement.* Whenever the service of the sentence to confinement is deferred by the convening authority under R.C.M. 1101(c) before or concurrently with the initial action in the case, the action shall include the date on which the deferment became effective. The reason for the deferment need not be stated in the action.

---

[257] 30 M.J. at 144.

[258] 30 M.J. at 145 (citing United States v. Ohrt, 28 M.J. 301, 306 (C.M.A. 1989)).

(Rel.3—1/07 Pub.62410)

§ 24-76.00 Rehearings and *DuBay* Hearings [259]

Just as the military judge may order a post-trial hearing, [260] the convening authority may do this on his or her own pursuant to R.C.M. 1102. [261] For example, if the convening authority determines that sufficient error has occurred to make approval of a conviction inappropriate or legally pointless, a rehearing may be ordered. [262] When additional information is needed to determine whether prejudicial error occurred, a limited evidentiary hearing—a *DuBay* hearing—may be ordered by the convening authority. If a post-trial recommendation is prepared after such a hearing, it should be served on defense counsel. [263] Prior to the *1984 Manual*, the failure to serve the SJA's recommendation on the defense counsel would result in the action being set aside and the record returned to the convening authority for such action. [264] Rule for Courts-Martial 1106(d)(6) sought to eliminate this burdensome requirement. [265]

§ 24-80.00 POST-TRIAL DELAY

Post-trial delay has long been a problem in the armed forces. In *United States v. Dunbar*, [266] for example, the court dealt with a forty-three-minute absence without leave trial in which over two and one-half years passed between the convening authority's action and receipt of the record in Washington for review. The Court of Military Appeals characterized the situation thus: "The events in the several months preceding receipt of the record conjure mental images resembling the bumbling and bungling of a 'Three Stooges' episode." [267]

The applicable law has varied. Until 20 July 1974, the military courts applied the rule that

> before ordering a dismissal of the charges because of post-trial delay there must be some error in the proceedings which requires that a rehearing be held and that because of the delay appellant would be either prejudiced in the presentation of his case at a new hearing or that no useful purpose would otherwise be served by continuing the proceedings. [268]

---

[259] *See also* § 25-12.20, *below.*

[260] *See* § 14-64.10.

[261] McKinney v. Ivany, 48 M.J. 908 (Army Ct. Crim. App. 1998).

[262] R.C.M. 1107(f)(3).

[263] *Cf.* United States v. Robinson, 1 M.J. 914 (N.C.M.R. 1976). Whether review will be required will depend on the court order, not on the Code or the *Manual.*

[264] United States v. Johnson, 5 M.J. 664 (A.C.M.R. 1978).

[265] R.C.M. 1106(d)(6); United States v. Blodgett, 20 M.J. 756 (A.F.C.M.R. 1985).

[266] 31 M.J. 70 (C.M.A. 1990).

[267] 31 M.J. at 71 (C.M.A. 1990).

[268] United States v. Gray, 47 C.M.R. 484, 486 (C.M.A. 1973).

In 1974, however, the Court of Military Appeals announced, in *Dunlap v. Convening Authority*,[269] the *"Dunlap"* rule, a quasi-post-trial "speedy-trial" rule:

> 30 days after [June 21, 1974] . . . a presumption of denial of speedy disposition of the case will arise when the accused is continuously under restraint after trial and the convening authority does not promulgate his formal and final action within 90 days of the date of such restraint after completion of trial. In the language of *Burton*, "this presumption will place a heavy burden on the government to show diligence, and in the absence of such a showing the charges should be dismissed."[270]

The court adopted *Dunlap*, stating that "[d]elay by the convening authority in acting on the record of conviction by a court-martial has been the subject of critical comment for a number of years."[271] However, *Dunlap* had its detractors, who complained of its "inflexibility."[272] In 1979, the court abandoned *Dunlap* in *United States v. Banks*.[273] Rather than accepting the service's complaints as valid, the court gave as its rationale that "convicted service persons now enjoy protections which had not been developed when *Dunlap* was decided."[274] After *Banks*, delay was to be tested for prejudice,[275] and the pre-*Dunlap* rule[276] was revived. Before the defense will be entitled to relief because of post-trial delay, it would seem that the delay must be shown to be both unreasonable and prejudicial to the accused. Absent some error in the proceedings at trial, a post-trial delay, standing alone—even if excessive or unreasonable—does not warrant appellate relief.[277]

In *United States v. Clevidence*,[278] however, the Court of Military Appeals was faced with a delay of 200 days until authentication, causing a 313-day delay until

---

[269] 48 C.M.R. 751 (C.M.A. 1974).

[270] 48 C.M.R. at 754 (C.M.A. 1974).

[271] 48 C.M.R. at 753 (C.M.A. 1974).

[272] United States v. Banks, 7 M.J. 92, 94 (C.M.A. 1979). Real and perceived resource limitations, including lack of court reporters and overworked defense counsel, were alleged. In their haste, trial counsel in lieu of judges sometimes unnecessarily authenticated records of trial. Simple inefficiency or service unwillingness to allocate adequate resources were often at fault.

[273] 7 M.J. 92, 94 (C.M.A. 1979).

[274] 7 M.J. at 93 (C.M.A. 1979).

[275] United States v. Williams, 55 M.J. 302, 305 (C.A.A.F. 2001) (absent establishing prejudice, 753 day delay does not entitle appellant to relief); United States v. Hudson, 46 M.J. 226 (C.A.A.F. 1997) (839-day delay reinforced rule that defendant must demonstrate prejudice to obtain relief on post-trial delay, as the court refused to abandon *Banks*). *See also* United States v. Bell, 46 M.J. 351 (C.A.A.F. 1997) (737-day delay from trial to action); United States v. Santoro, 46 M.J. 344 (C.A.A.F. 1997) (more than seven-year delay from action to receipt of record by convening authority).

[276] *See* text *above* note 268; United States v. Dunbar, 31 M.J. 70 (C.M.A. 1990).

[277] *See, e.g.*, United States v. Gray, 47 C.M.A. 484 (C.M.A 1973) (readopted in *Banks*); United States v. Clevidence, 14 M.J. 17, 20 (C.M.A. 1982) (Cook, J., dissenting)).

[278] 14 M.J. 17 (C.M.A. 1982).

supervisory approval.[279] The Coast Guard Court of Military Review had branded the case as "another deplorable example of official indifference toward the timely posttrial review of Coast Guard courts-martial which has formerly been condemned by the Chief Counsel and by this Court."[280] The Court of Military Appeals then decided to exercise its "supervisory authority" and set aside the findings and sentence.[281] Judge Cook dissented, claiming that the court had created in place of *Dunlap* "a rule totally without definition."[282]

In *United States v. Shely*,[283] the court held that the accused had demonstrated prejudice for a 439-day delay between the sentence and the action by the confining authority. For nearly one year after serving his sentence to confinement, the accused was held in a barracks for personnel awaiting court-martial or other disciplinary proceedings instead of in the transient barracks that normally held personnel in post-trial status awaiting a transfer.

He reveals that the conditions under which he lived and worked differed substantially from those to which he was entitled—including less satisfactory duty assignments; thrice-daily muster requirements, close supervision, and loss of his identification card during the work-day; denial of leave during the first six months because he was in a disciplinary status; and denial of promotion and the corresponding pay increase because of his disciplinary status.[284]

Denial of medical benefits or adverse impact on civilian employment prospects[285] may constitute "prejudice."[286] The Air Force Court of Military Review held, however, that "in order for us to consider evidence of employment prejudice, an appellant must identify the organization or individual who denied employment and the time frame in which it occurred."[287]

In 1990, the Court of Military Appeals attempted to refine further its "prejudice" test:[288]

It would seem that delay in finalizing a court-martial conviction reviewable under Articles 66 and 67 . . . respectively, might occur at any of three stages:

---

[279] 14 M.J. 17 (C.M.A. 1982)

[280] 14 M.J. at 18 (C.M.A. 1982) (quoting 11 M.J. 661, 666).

[281] 14 M.J. at 19 (C.M.A. 1982).

[282] 14 M.J. at 19 (C.M.A. 1982).

[283] 16 M.J. 431 (C.M.A. 1983).

[284] 16 M.J. 433 (C.M.A. 1983).

[285] *E.g.*, United States v. Jones, 61 M.J. 80,82 (C.A.A.F. 2005). An accused may be on "excess leave" while awaiting final action.

[286] United States v. Bourgette, 27 M.J. 904 (A.F.C.M.R. 1989) (en banc).

[287] 27 M.J. 906 (A.F.C.M.R. 1989), *overruling in part* United States v. King, 18 M.J. 535 (A.F.C.M.R. 1984).

[288] United States v. Dunbar, 31 M.J. 70, 72–73 (C.M.A. 1990).

(Rel.3—1/07 Pub.62410)

first, between completion of the trial and action by the convening authority; second, while pending resolution in an appellate court—either a Court of Military Review or this Court; and, finally, in the administrative handling and transportation of the record and critical documents either to the Court of Military Review or to this Court as a predicate for review. Logically, each of these three possibilities is quite different from the others.

The first—delay at the convening authority stage—was at issue in *United States v. Clevidence*, 14 M.J. 17 (C.M.A. 1982). We set aside the findings and sentence and dismissed the charges because Clevidence had demonstrated that he had been specifically prejudiced in his pursuit of civilian employment by the lack of speedy review of his case by the convening authority. We took that action "in the exercise of our supervisory authority over military justice" in order to "halt the erosion in prompt posttrial review of courts-martial" by "register[ing] our emphatic disapproval of such 'inordinate and unexplained' delay in a case like this." 14 M.J. 19 (C.M.A. 1982). . . .

The second possibility—delay in disposition of an appeal by an appellate court—would involve special considerations unlike any that come into play at the other two stages. In an appropriate case, it would be necessary to weigh those peculiar factors—such as deference to the uniqueness of judicial decisionmaking and hesitancy to pierce the shroud of that decisionmaking—against the need to resolve an appeal without extreme and unnecessary delay.

The third—delay in the administrative handling and forwarding of the record of trial and related documents to an appellate court—is the least defensible of all and worthy of the least patience. Unlike action by the convening authority, this stage involves no discretion or judgment; and, unlike an appellate court's consideration of an appeal, this stage involves no complex legal or factual issues or weighing of policy considerations. Gross negligence—pure and simple—is all that can account for mishandling like that involved in *Green* and for the bungling or indifference reflected in this case.

At least where—as in *Clevidence*—the case involves relatively nonserious offenses, we would have little hesitancy to respond appropriately where an accused could demonstrate that such inexcusable delay in ministerial handling of a record caused him personal suffering apart and distinct from that flowing from the fact of a conviction. Such an accused has been punished for his misdeed through his sentence; he need not suffer added harm from reprehensible indifference to administrative responsibility. . . .

Dunbar's claim of prejudice is not based on any error in his trial. Rather, according to his affidavit filed in the court below, it focuses on three aspects of his personal life that he contends were adversely affected by this untoward delay.

(Rel.3—1/07 Pub.62410)

We agree with the Court of Military Review and with the Government's position in this Court that relief may not be predicated upon claims of prejudice that are unverified and unverifiable. This burden rests with appellant.

Concurring in the result, however, Judge Cox succinctly rejected most claims of prejudice based on delay in the post-trial process:

> On appeal, an appellant is stripped of his presumption of innocence. A record has been made, and there is no possibility of loss of evidence or witnesses due to delay. . . .

> The delay in this case was unexplained and unjustified. Although such mismanagement of a case is fortunately the exception rather than the standard practice, an inexcusable delay has at one time or another permeated all of the services. . . . Military justice deserves better.

> The appropriate remedy, the only remedy available to appellant, however, is to have his case heard on appeal. The United States Navy-Marine Corps Court of Military Review and this Court have afforded him that relief. He is entitled to nothing further.[289]

Dismissal is not the only possible remedy.[290] The Court of Appeals for the Armed Forces has made it clear that an accused does not need to request "speedy post-trial processing" and that "unreasonable, unexplained, and dilatory post-trial processing" must be considered in determining whether an accused merits relief.[291]

The Navy-Marine Corps Court of Military Review, in *United States v. Hobbs,*[292] relied on the statement by the Court of Military Appeals in *Clevidence*[293] that it would have hesitated to dismiss charges for post-trial delay if

---

[289] 31 M.J. 74-6 (C.M.A. 1990). *See also* United States v. Jenkins, 38 M.J. 287 (C.M.A. 1993) (no prejudice established from action 479 days after trial).

[290] *E.g.,* United States v. Collazo, 53 M.J. 721 (A. Crim. App. 2000) (granted six months reduction of eight year sentence for post-trial delay, an approach affirmed in *United States v. Tardif,* 57 M.J. 219 (C.A.A.F. 2002)). *See also* United States v. Bodkins, 60 M.J. 322 (C.A.A.F. 2004) (under *United States v. Tardif, above,* the court of criminal appeals has broad discretion to grant or deny relief for unreasonable or unexplained post-trial delay, and a finding of specific prejudice is not required; the court has discretion to take into account the impact—or lack thereof—of any delay on the accused; in so doing, the court may consider the absence of a defense request for action as one factor among other considerations in assessing the impact of delay in a particular case, but it may not elevate that factor into the conclusive basis for denying relief by using the mere absence of a request to find waiver)

[291] United States v. Bodkins, 60 M.J. 3, 22 (C.A.A.F. 2004). In *Bodkins,* the Court held that the absence of a request for "speedy" process 22 2004) did not constitute waiver; however, it did not define the scope of any potential waiver theory that might be applicable from lack of defense action. It did note that continuing eligibility for limited military benefits could be considered as a factor in assessing the impact of post-trial delay.

[292] 30 M.J. 1095 (N.M.C.M.R. 1989).

[293] 14 M.J. 17; *see above* note 268.

(Rel.3—1/07 Pub.62410)

the offenses had been more serious.[294] In *Hobbs*, which involved an accused convicted of distributing 5.02 grams of marijuana, the court decided to cure a 412-day delay before the convening authority's approval[295] by disapproving the accused's bad-conduct discharge but sustaining the remainder of the accused's sentence.[296]

As previously noted, the Coast Guard has at times had a significant delay problem,[297] one large enough that the Coast Guard Court of Military Review felt it necessary to grant an unconditional release from a sentence of confinement.[298] The Air Force Court of Military Review, however, determined that a 432-day delay between trial and action was not shown to be unreasonable or prejudicial in light of the complexity of the (murder) case.[299]

In 1993, the Navy-Marine Corps Court of Military Review held that, in the absence of specific prejudice, delay occasioned by a one-year loss of record with subsequent reconstitution did not require dismissal.[300] In 1994, the same court held that an eight-year delay in the convening authority's approval of the record of trial, following loss of the original, did not justify *per se* setting aside the findings and sentence.[301] Troubled by a significant delay, the Navy-Marine Corps Court of Criminal Appeals, in 1995, subsequently compensated for the delay by eliminating a punitive discharge.[302]

To assist in addressing post-trial timeliness issues, the Air Force Court of Criminal Appeals has held that a military judge may hold hearings and grant relief on such issues before authentication of the record of trial.[303] In 2004 the United States Court of Appeals for the Armed Forces acted to remedy an apparent unwarranted delay. In a case involving a delay of 2,150 days without a first level appellate resolution, the Court directed:

> the Navy-Marine Corps Court of Criminal Appeals to use its best efforts to render a decision on Petitioner's appeal without delay. In deciding Petitioner's case, the Navy-Marine Corps Court will determine whether

---

[294] 14 M.J. at 19.

[295] Complicated by failure to serve the recommendation on the defense before action.

[296] *See also* United States v. Jones, 61 M.J. 80, 82 (C.A.A.F. 2005) (disapproving bad conduct discharge but otherwise sustaining findings and sentence).

[297] *E.g.*, United States v. Olivari, 33 M.J. 933, 935 (C.G.C.M.R. 1991).

[298] Collazo v. Welling, 34 M.J. 793 (C.G.C.M.R. 1992) (more than five months without convening authority's action on the record or on clemency request justifies extraordinary relief; petitioner's prior conditional release from confinement was altered to an unconditional one).

[299] United States v. Mansfield, 33 M.J. 972, 996–97 (A.F.C.M.R. 1991).

[300] United States v. Dupree, 37 M.J. 1089 (N.M.C.M.R. 1993).

[301] United States v. Henry, 40 M.J. 722 (N.M.C.M.R. 1994).

[302] United States v. Thomas, 41 M.J. 873, 877 (N.M. Crim. App. 1995).

[303] United States v. Nelson, 46 M.J. 764 (A.F. Crim. App. 1997).

(Rel.3—1/07 Pub.62410)

the lengthy delay in this case violated Petitioner's Fifth Amendment right to due process. The court will also determine whether the lengthy delay in this case warrants some form of relief.[304]

In doing so, the Court invited petitioner to seek further relief if the Court of Criminal Appeals had not ruled within 90 days.

It is apparent that, although the demise of the *Dunlap* automatic-dismissal rule may have pleased the armed forces, it has, at least occasionally, left us with significant post-trial delays. Given sufficient recurrences, *Dunlap* may live again.

§ 24-90.00 APPELLATE REMEDIES

The Court of Appeals for the Armed Forces is split on how to address errors in the post-trial process. Some judges would draw fine distinctions without examining earlier decisions or considering the theory of inaction. The Court of Appeals has, at least once,[305] seemed to reject the notion that inaction may be a legitimate defense strategy.[306] However, counsel are not required to undertake a futile act.

Because of the concern over the number of cases involving post-trial matters and inconsistency at least as to new matters, the court will require the defense, who is in the best position to demonstrate prejudice, to do so.[307] But "the threshold should be low, and if an appellant makes some colorable showing of possible prejudice, we will give that appellant the benefit of the doubt."[308] This standard is not new but recognizes, *sub silentio*, prior decisions.[309]

Judge Sullivan suggested that the new matters issue could be solved if all addenda were served on defense counsel.[310] The court has upheld the courts

---

[304] Toohey v. United States, 60 M.J. 100, 104 (C.A.A.F. 2004).

[305] United States v. Ellis, 47 M.J. 20 (1997).

[306] Siverson v. O'Leary, 764 F.2d 1208, 1216 (7th Cir. 1985); Warner v. Ford, 752 F.2d 622, 625 (11th Cir. 1985).

[307] United States v. Lee, 52 M.J. 51 (C.A.A.F. 1999) (accused failed to establish prejudice in claim of post-trial ineffectiveness of counsel); United States v. Chatman, 46 M.J. 321 (C.A.A.F. 1997). *Cf.* United States v. Robertson, 39 M.J. 211 (C.M.A. 1994). *See also* United States v. Hood, 47 M.J. 95 (C.A.A.F. 1997) (failure to consult defendant about submitting rough draft of unsworn statement and mother's letter with both positive and negative comments was not of such significant nature as to prejudice the ability of the convening authority to meet its post-trial responsibility).

[308] United States v. Chatman, 46 M.J. 321, 323–24 (C.A.A.F. 1997). *See also* United States v. Gilbreath, 57 M.J. 57 (C.A.A.F. 2002) (only "colorable showing of prejudice" needed); United States v. Mark, 47 M.J. 99 (C.A.A.F. 1997) (refused to apply harmless standard when no SJA recommendation); United States v. Buller, 46 M.J. 467, 469 n.3 (C.A.A.F. 1997) (appellant in best position to tell court whether comments on his financial status were erroneous).

[309] *See also* United States v. Wansley, 46 M.J. 335, 337 (C.A.A.F. 1997) ("Subsequent to the convening authority's action, the defense had ample opportunity to obtain and submit information that would demonstrate such approval or reliance [on articles by the Chief of Military Justice].").

[310] United States v. Buller, 46 M.J. 467, 469 (C.A.A.F. 1997) (Sullivan, J., concurring).

(Rel.3—1/07 Pub.62410)

below in disapproving a discharge as a signal to SJAs to devote proper attention to posttrial matters.[311] This action was termed a proper exercise of the court's supervisory authority.[312] Notwithstanding this, it is unclear that Judge Sullivan's solution would yield significant sentence results.

A review of the cases remanded under the rationales of *United States v. Carter*[313] and *United States v. Demerse,*[314] for example, reveals that none of the cases returned to the lower courts or the convening authorities resulted in a reduction of the sentence.

The most recent pronouncement, in *United States v. Wheelus,*[315] set forth the following process for resolving claims of error connected with a convening authority's post-trial review:

> First, an appellant must allege the error at the Court of Criminal Appeals. Second, an appellant must allege prejudice as a result of the error. Third, an appellant must show what he would do to resolve the error if given such an opportunity.

If an appellant meets this threshold, then it is incumbent upon the Courts of Criminal Appeals . . . to remedy the error and provide meaningful relief. . . . If the appellant makes such a showing, the Court of Criminal Appeals must either provide meaningful relief or return the case to the . . . convening authority for a new post-trial recommendation and action.

Lastly, there are those cases where an appellant has not been prejudiced, even though there is clearly error in the post-trial proceedings. If that be the case, then the Courts . . . preferably should say so and articulate reasons why there is no prejudice.[316]

---

[311] United States v. Cook, 46 M.J. 37 (C.A.A.F. 1997).

[312] 46 M.J. 37 (C.A.A.F. 1997).

[313] 40 M.J. 102 (C.M.A. 1994).

[314] 37 M.J. 488 (C.M.A. 1993).

[315] 49 M.J. 283, 288–89 (C.A.A.F. 1998).

[316] *See* United States v. Hartfield, 53 M.J. 719 (A. Crim. App. 2000) (combined Wheelus and Powell tests); United States v. Mark, 47 M.J. 99 (C.A.A.F. 1997) (missing SJA recommendation is structural error requiring new recommendation and action—harmless error test does not apply).

CHAPTER 25

APPEALS, EXTRAORDINARY RELIEF, AND EXECUTION OF SENTENCE

§ 25-10.00   INTRODUCTION
   § 25-11.00   In General
   § 25-12.00   The Appellate Process in Brief
      § 25-12.10 — In General
      § 25-12.20 — *DuBay* Hearings
   § 25-13.00   Deferral of Confinement Pending Appeal; "Excess Leave"
      § 25-13.10 — Release Pending Appeal; Deferral
      § 25-13.20 — Confinement Completion Prior to Appellate Completion; Excess Leave
§ 25-20.00   JURISDICTIONAL PREREQUISITES FOR JUDICIAL APPEAL; INFERIOR TRIBUNALS AND SENTENCES
§ 25-30.00   AUTOMATIC APPEAL AND ITS WAIVER
§ 25-40.00   THE RIGHT TO COUNSEL ON APPEAL
   § 25-41.00   In General
   § 25-42.00   Frivolous Appeals
§ 25-50.00   THE COURTS OF CRIMINAL APPEALS (THE COURTS OF MILITARY REVIEW)
   § 25-51.00   In General
   § 25-52.00   Jurisdiction
   § 25-53.00   Scope of Review
      § 25-53.10 — In General
      § 25-53.20 — Fact-Finding Powers
      § 25-53.30 — Sentencing
   § 25-54.00   Reconsideration
   § 25-55.00   Effect of Reversal of Conviction
§ 25-60.00   THE COURT OF APPEALS FOR THE ARMED FORCES
   § 25-61.00   In General
   § 25-62.00   Jurisdiction
   § 25-63.00   Issues Not Asserted Below
   § 25-64.00   Abatement Due to Death of the Accused
§ 25-70.00   REVIEW BY THE SUPREME COURT
§ 25-80.00   INTERLOCUTORY GOVERNMENT APPEALS
   § 25-81.00   In General
   § 25-82.00   Appealable Orders
      § 25-82.10 — In General

(Rel.3—1/07 Pub.62410)

§ 25-82.20 — **Specific Types of Orders**
§ 25-83.00   **Scope of Review**
§ 25-84.00   **Procedure**
§ 25-90.00   **EXTRAORDINARY WRITS**
  § 25-91.00   **In General**
  § 25-92.00   **Relief in Aid of Jurisdiction**
  § 25-93.00   **"Agreeable to the Usages and Principles of Law"**
  § 25-94.00   **Legislative Review Appropriate**
§ 25-100.00   **EXECUTION OF SENTENCE**
§ 25-110.00   **RESTORATION; NEW TRIAL**
§ 25-120.00   **UNLAWFUL POST-TRIAL CONFINEMENT**

§ 25-10.00   INTRODUCTION

§ 25-11.00   In General

Although the enactment of the Uniform Code of Military Justice was the largest change in military criminal law in the 20th century,[1] the single most important and innovative change within the Code was its establishment of the present appellate system in general, and the United States Court of Military Appeals now the Court of Appeals for the Armed Forces in particular.[2]

As then Captain Willis has pointed out,[3] prior to the Code, the armed forces lacked a binding appellate structure. Instead, from 1920 until 1948, military law was command-centered,[4] with the Army, for example, using advisory boards of review located in the office of The Judge Advocate General of the Army.[5] The lack of a proper appellate system was thus a natural focus of the post-World War II reform efforts. Rejecting proposals for either an all-military court or a "civilian board responsible only to the Secretary of Defense,"[6] Professor Morgan, primary drafter of the Uniform Code,[7] proposed a "civilian Judicial Council to

---

[1] *See generally* Chapter 1.

[2] *See, e.g.,* H. R. Rep. No. 491, 81st Cong., 1st Sess. 6 (1949). U.S. Court of Military Appeals Committee Report (Jan. 27, 1989); Draft, Reform of the Court of Military Appeals, App. B (May 7, 1979); Mundy v. Weinberger, 554 F. Supp. 811 (D.D.C. 1982).

[3] Willis, *The United States Court of Military Appeals: Its Origin, Operation and Future,* 55 Mil. L. Rev. 39 (1972) [hereinafter Willis].

[4] *See generally* Chapter 1. *See also* Willis, *above* note 3, at 41 (citing the report to Hon. Wilbur M. Brucker, Secretary of the Army, by the Committee on the Uniform Code of Military Justice, Good Order and Discipline in the Army at 251 (January 18, 1960)).

[5] 55 Mil. L. Rev. 52–3 (1972). In 1948, a complex Judicial Council was created. *See generally* Fratcher, *Appellate Review in American Military Law,* 14 Mil. L. Rev. 111 (1963).

[6] Willis, *above* note 3, at 59.

[7] Professor Morgan had served under General Samuel Ansell, Acting Judge Advocate General of the Army from 1917 until the end of World War I and perhaps the single best known military law "reformer" in American history. Although General Ansell was largely unsuccessful and

be located in the Office of the Secretary of Defense."[8]

The concept of a centralized civilian appellate tribunal was controversial from the beginning,[9] and as a compromise, the members of the "Judicial Council" were initially to be appointed by the secretaries of the armed forces.[10] As enacted, however, the Uniform Code of Military Justice prescribed a three-judge Court of Military Appeals with the judges to hold fifteen-year terms.[11] As Congress created the court without Article III guarantees, such as life-tenure,[12] it is considered a Congressional, Article I court.[13] Although Congress did not require that judges of the court have military experience,[14] the three initial appointees all had prior service as officers, and most judges subsequently appointed have had similar backgrounds.

Supporters of a supreme military appellate court wished for the incorporation of civilian influences as an antidote to improper command control over the military criminal legal system.[15] The creation of the civilian Court of Military Appeals, the "Supreme Court of the military,"[16] at the pragmatic apex of the

---

resigned from the Army, Professor Morgan successfully incorporated many of General Ansell's reforms into the Uniform Code. *See generally* Sections 1-43.10, 1-44.00, and 1-45.00.

[8] Willis, *above* note 3, at 59.

[9] *See, e.g.,* W. Generous, Swords and Scales, The Development of the Uniform Code of Military Justice 40, 44–49 (1973) [hereinafter Generous]; Willis, *above*, note 3, at 59–69.

Although decisions of the court have continued to be controversial, the comments of United States District Judge Wayne Alley (BG, U.S. Army, JAGC, ret.) seem appropriate:

> Despite grumbling about particular decisions within the military, there never was an effective or organized mutiny against the Court. Its dominant position is so well embedded that it is simply an accepted fact of institutional life.

United States Court of Military Appeals Report, January 27, 1989 at 3.

[10] Generous, *above* note 9, at 44. Strangely, power to appoint the judges was given to the President only after what was then the Bureau of the Budget intervened. Generous, *above* note 9, at 44.

[11] Initial appointments were staggered.

[12] The President also may appoint the Chief Judge and, for cause, remove judges, all factors that seem inconsistent with Article III status. The National Defense Authorization Act for Fiscal Year 1993 provides for rotation of the Chief Judge every five years. 10 U.S.C. § 143(a).

[13] *See generally*, Note, *Military Justice and Article III*, 103 Harv. L. Rev. 1909 (1990); Fallon, *Of Legislative Courts, Administrative Agencies, and Article III*, 101 Harv. L. Rev. 916 (1988). Difficulties linked with the absence of Article III status (*e.g.*, the judges' terms, retirement rights, and judicial status) long led to personnel difficulties on the court. *See generally* United States Court of Military Appeals Committee Report (1989); Office of General Counsel, Department of Defense, Department of Defense Study Group on the United States Court of Military Appeals (1988). Thus far, the court has been expanded to five judges, and the retirement program has been improved, but efforts to give the judges life tenure and constitutional Article III status have been unsuccessful.

[14] *See* Generous, *above* note 9, at 49.

[15] *See, e.g.,* 95 Cong. Rec. 5726 (1949) (remarks of Rep. Philbin).

[16] Willis, *above* note 3, at 49; Nufer, American Servicemembers' Supreme Court, Impact of the U.S. Court of Military Appeals on Military Justice (1981).

(Rel.3—1/07 Pub.62410)

military criminal legal system[17] first led to the concept of "military due process,"[18] then to judicial adoption of most of the Bill of Rights for servicemembers,[19] and finally to the "civilianization" of military justice and massive insertion of civilian due process standards.[20]

Although one may reasonably argue with aspects of the court's jurisprudence, viewed as an institution the Court of Military Appeals (now the Court of Appeals for the Armed Forces) is clearly a success. It has fulfilled its congressional mandate by taking control of military criminal decisional law and modernizing it. Although reasonable people might differ, we would also conclude that, with rare exception, the Court of Appeals has also kept the unique nature of the armed forces in mind. If the new appellate structure has failed at all,[21] it is almost certainly in its duty to speedily resolve its cases. In a jurisdiction in which rapidity of case disposition is especially desirable,[22] the military appellate courts have been particularly tardy in their processing time.[23] One must note, however, that this has not improved dramatically in recent years.

§ 25-12.00   The Appellate Process in Brief

§ 25-12.10   In General

After conviction, the convening authority reviews the case and may approve, as "a matter of command prerogative" at his or her "sole discretion," only that portion of the findings and sentence he or she finds appropriate.[24] Upon initial

---

[17] No direct route to the Supreme Court existed until 1983. *See generally* Sections 25-70.00 and 26-10.00.

[18] United States v. Clay, 1 C.M.R. 74 (C.M.A. 1951).

[19] United States v. Jacoby, 29 C.M.R. 244 (C.M.A. 1960) (the Bill of Rights is applicable to courts-martial except when "expressly or by necessary implication inapplicable"). *See also* Section 1-52.00.

[20] *See generally* Cooke, *The United States Court of Military Appeals, 1975-1977: Judicializing the Military Justice System*, 76 Mil. L. Rev. 43 (1977); *see also* Section 1-47.00. A review of the role of the Court of Military Appeals as the arbiter of military justice is outside the scope of this treatise. However, even the most minimal study of the topic will reflect the court's ever-increasing influence, both directly through its decisions, and indirectly through its creation of legal "mindset." The impact of the court's judges and staff in law-reform efforts as part of the Code Committee, Joint Service Committee on Military Justice, and the Joint Committee's Working Group cannot be ignored, either. *See* Lederer, *The Military Rules of Evidence: Origins and Interpretation*, 130 Mil. L. Rev. 5, 9–12, 26 (1990).

[21] Whether the Courts of Criminal Appeals or the Court of Appeals.

[22] One could argue that it is only a speedy trial that is essential in order to return personnel to duty as soon as possible. *See, e.g.,* U.C.M.J. art. 10. However, speedy appeal is desirable as well, not only to protect an erroneously convicted accused, but also to permit the earliest return to productive duty of a properly convicted accused.

[23] *See, e.g.,* Section 25-51.00; *below* note 54.

[24] U.C.M.J. art. 60(c)(1). *See generally* Chapter 24.

approval, the convening authority may order "executed"[25] any part of the sentence that does not include death, dismissal, or a bad-conduct or dishonorable discharge.[26] The punitive discharges[27] may be executed if the accused has waived appeal.[28] Otherwise, appellate review and secretarial approval[29] are required. As a result, any sentence to confinement may be executed, even though appeal is pending.[30] Indeed, under the Code, "[a]ny period of confinement included in a sentence of a court-martial begins to run from the date the sentence is adjudged by the court-martial."[31]

If the conviction is approved in whole or part, the appellate-review process automatically begins,[32] unless the accused has waived appeal.[33]

Following final action by the convening authority, a copy of the record[34] and post-trial documents are forwarded to the appropriate Judge Advocate General.[35]

---

[25] "An order executing the sentence directs that the sentence be carried out." R.C.M. 1113(a) Discussion.

[26] R.C.M. 1113(c). Pending final action, the effective date of the forfeitures and reduction in grade portion of a sentence is now the earlier of 14 days after sentence is adjudged or the convening authority's action. FY 1996 Department of Defense Authorization Act, P.L. 104-106 § 1121(a)(1) (February 10, 1996) (amending Article 57).

[27] Dismissals require approval by the Secretary or Assistant Secretary concerned. R.C.M. 1113(c)(2).

[28] See Section 25-30.00.

[29] Death requires approval of the President. See Section 25-100.00.

[30] See also R.C.M. 1113(d)(2).

[31] U.C.M.J. art. 57(b).

[32] Minor cases involving summary and special courts-martial not involving a bad-conduct discharge or confinement for one year or more are not subject to the full appellate process that follows. Automatic appeal has always been somewhat controversial. In 2004, Major Lippert suggested in a well written article that automatic appeal for special courts-martial should be abandoned in favor of Article 69 review in the office of The Judge Advocate General. Major Jeffery D. Lippert, *Automatic Appeal Under UCMJ Article 66: Time for a Change*, 182 Mil. L. Rev. 1 (2004). Professor Lederer differs. Although there may be a case for modification of the Article 66 process, Professor Lederer suggests that at most substitution of the current system most frequently applicable to appeals before the Court of Appeals for the Armed Forces (whereby the accused petitions for review) might be warranted. In his view, the flaw in Major Lippert's proposal is that it is largely driven by problems with court-reporting in the military that causes delays due to problems in production of the record of trial. In light of his experience as Director of William & Mary Law School's Courtroom 21 Project, Professor Lederer is confident that current technology could resolve the current court reporting problems if properly utilized.

[33] R.C.M. 1110. United States v. Doeinck, 51 M.J. 121 (C.A.A.F. 1998) (summary disposition) (Waiver before Court of Appeals can be made based on assurance that accused knows consequences and agrees with waiver. No requirement for written waiver signed by the accused.).

[34] When a record is sent to the Court of Military Review on appeal, and the accused was convicted of some but not all of the charged offenses, the entire record must be transcribed and forwarded. Otherwise, the record will not be "verbatim." United States v. Alston, 30 M.J. 969, 971 (N.M.C.M.R. 1990) (en banc) (citing R.C.M. 1103(c)(1); 1103(b)(2)(B)(ii)&).

[35] U.C.M.J. art. 65(a).

(Rel.3—1/07 Pub.62410)

If the case's sentence includes death, a dismissal, bad-conduct discharge, or confinement for one year or more,[36] the case must be referred to a Court of Criminal Appeals. If the case fails to satisfy these jurisdictional requirements, the Judge Advocate General must evaluate the case and determine whether he or she will vacate or modify the findings or sentence[37] or exercise his or her discretionary authority to forward the case to a Court of Criminal Appeals.[38]

Appeal from a Court of Criminal Appeals is potentially available to the Court of Appeals for the Armed Forces — a five-judge civilian court expected to enforce the procedural safeguards that Congress conferred upon members of the armed forces[39] as well as their constitutional rights. Review by writ of certiorari may lie to the Supreme Court.

Like their civilian counterparts, both the Courts of Criminal Appeals and the Court of Appeals hear appeals from legal errors that allegedly occurred in the lower courts. Ordinarily, absent "plain error," the defense waives or forfeits any claim of error when trial defense counsel fails to make a timely objection or offer of proof. What constitutes "plain error" and whether it necessitates or permits remedial action is an ongoing question.[40]

At least in theory, no special rules exist for review of capital cases:[41] the scope of review is identical for all cases. In practice, however, one might reasonably infer that the judges give greater scrutiny to such cases.

---

[36] U.C.M.J. art 66(b). As enacted, the Uniform Code also provided automatic appeal in the event the accused was a general or flag officer. This provision subsequently was deleted as unnecessary.

[37] U.C.M.J. art 66(b). See generally Everett, *Some Comments on the Role of Discretion in Military Justice*, 37 Law & Contemp. Prob. 173 (1972). Insofar as the Army is concerned, both Colonel Gilligan and Professor Lederer's experience is that this responsibility is taken quite seriously and that cases routinely receive multiple reviews before the Judge Advocate General takes action.

[38] U.C.M.J. art. 69.

[39] *See* Chaparro v. Resor, 298 F. Supp. 1164, 1167 (D.S.C. 1969) (quoting Burns v. Wilson, 346 U.S. 137, 141 (1953), *reh'g denied*, 346 U.S. 844 (1953)), *vacated on other grounds*, 412 F.2d 443 (4th Cir. 1969).

[40] *See, e.g.*, United States v. Powell, 49 M.J. 460 (C.A.A.F. 1998); United States v. Toro, 37 M.J. 313 (C.M.A. 1993). *See also* United States v. Jones, 37 M.J. 322, 323 (C.M.A. 1993). In *United States v. Robbins*, 52 M.J. 455, 457 (C.A.A.F. 2000) the Court opined, "When the issue of plain error involves a judge-alone trial, an appellant faces a particularly high hurdle. A military judge is presumed to know the law and apply it correctly, is presumed capable of filtering out inadmissible evidence, and is presumed not to have relied on such evidence on the question of guilt or innocence."

[41] United States v. Loving, 41 M.J. 213, 266 (C.A.A.F. 1994), *aff'd*, 517 U.S. 748 (1996). Of course, the nature of death penalty review may require unique concerns such as a proportionality review. 41 M.J. at 290 (C.A.A.F. 1994).

(Rel.3—1/07   Pub.62410)

As in civilian courts, decisions of the Courts of Criminal Appeals and the Court of Appeals for the Armed Forces are made by majority vote. An evenly divided vote affirms the decision below.[42]

§ 25-12.20   *DuBay* Hearings

The appellate courts are sometimes faced with factual disputes. When an appeal cannot be resolved without factual clarification a *"DuBay"* hearing may be ordered.[43] Such a hearing is conducted by a military (trial) judge and is limited to the questions set forth by the appellate court in its order. The Air Force Court of Military Review set forth the elements that should be examined before a *DuBay* hearing will be held:

> First, there must be some issue presented to us by the record or by the appellant. Second, the issue must be one for which the scope of review permits resort to matters outside the record under review, if necessary. Third, the issue must be justiciable: if it is moot, if the appellant lacks standing to assert the rights involved, or if the issue is not yet ripe then a remand would be wasteful. Fourth, the issue must be presented in such a way that resolution depends at least in part upon facts. Fifth, those facts must not yet be clear in the record. Sixth, the needed facts must be such that resort to affidavits would be unsatisfactory. Seventh, the movant must establish that a fact-finding hearing is likely to be effective, that the facts can be found, or that the likely ineffectiveness of the hearing is itself conclusive.[44]

§ 25-13.00   Deferral of Confinement Pending Appeal; "Excess Leave"

§ 25-13.10   Release Pending Appeal; Deferral

As previously noted,[45] despite a pending appeal, a sentence to confinement ordinarily goes into effect immediately after trial.[46] The Uniform Code permits the convening authority, as a discretionary matter,[47] to "defer" a sentence to

---

[42] United States v. Acevedo, 50 M.J. 169, 174 (C.A.A.F. 1999). *See also* Dew v. United States, 48 M.J. 639 (Army Crim. App. 1998) (evenly divided en banc court decision denies request for extraordinary relief).

[43] United States v. DuBay, 37 C.M.R. 411 (C.M.A. 1967).

[44] United States v. Tripp, 38 M.J. 554, 556–57 (A.F.C.M.R. 1993).

[45] Section 25-12.00.

[46] U.C.M.J. art. 57(b).

The authority acting on the deferment request may, in that authority's discretion, defer service of a sentence to confinement. The accused shall have the burden to show that the interests of the accused and the community in release outweigh the community's interests in confinement. Factors that the authority acting on a deferment request may consider in determining whether to grant the deferment request include: the probability of the accused's flight; the probability of the accused's commission of other offenses, intimidation of witnesses, or interference with the administration of justice; the

(Rel.3—1/07   Pub.62410)

confinement[48] on request of the accused until execution of sentence.[49] "The deferment may be rescinded at any time by the officer who granted it or, if the accused is no longer under his jurisdiction, by the officer exercising general court-martial jurisdiction over the command to which the accused is currently assigned."[50]

Although deferral "is to provide a procedure similar to release on bail pending appeal in civilian courts,"[51] and it is thus possible for a convening authority to choose not to begin an offender's sentence to confinement until after appeal, this is seldom done by a convening authority.[52] When deferral is authorized, it is normally used to defer confinement until the convening authority's initial action on the case.[53] As a practical matter at least, the armed forces lack any equivalent to "bail pending appeal."

§ 25-13.20   Confinement Completion Prior to Appellate Completion; Excess Leave

Military procedure thus results in convicted offenders serving their prison sentences while their appeals are heard. Given the inordinate delay often

---

nature of the offenses (including the effect on the victim) of which the accused was convicted; the sentence adjudged; the command's immediate need for the accused; the effect of deferment on good order and discipline in the command; and the accused's character, mental condition, family situation, and service record. The decision of the authority acting on the deferment shall be subject to judicial review only for abuse of discretion. The action of the convening authority shall be written and a copy shall be provided to the accused.

R.C.M. 1101(c)(3)

[48] U.C.M.J. art 57(c); R.C.M.1101(c).

[49] U.C.M.J. art 57(c); R.C.M.1101(c). See also U.C.M.J. art. 71; *see generally* Section 25-100.00.

[50] U.C.M.J. art 57a(a). *See also* R.C.M. 1101(c)(7)(B):

Deferment of confinement, forfeitures, or reduction in grade may be rescinded when additional information is presented to a proper authority which, when considered with all other information in the case, that authority finds, in that authority's discretion, is grounds for denial of deferment under subsection (c)(3) of this rule. The accused shall promptly be informed of the basis for the rescission and of the right to submit written matters in the accused's behalf and to request that the rescission be reconsidered. However, the accused may be required to serve the sentence to confinement, forfeitures, or reduction in grade pending this action.

[51] Longhofer v. Hilbert, 23 M.J. 755, 757 (A.C.M.R. 1986), *pet. denied*, 24 M.J. 62 (C.M.A. 1987) (new convening authority erroneously "rescinded" deferral pending appeal of convicted colonel's confinement) (citing S. Rep. No. 1601, 90th Cong., 2d Sess. 3 (1968)).

[52] When permitted, which is rare, deferral of confinement usually lasts only until the convening authority takes post-trial action on the case.

[53] *See* R.C.M. 1101(c)(6)(A): "[Deferment of a sentence to confinement ends when] [t]he convening authority takes action under R.C.M. 1107, unless the convening authority specifies in the action that service of confinement after the action is deferred."

(Rel.3—1/07   Pub.62410)

apparently inherent in the appellate system,[54] it is not surprising that a number of convicted servicemembers complete their sentences before their appeals are resolved. During most of the history of the Uniform Code, such a person would be returned to duty pending completion of the appellate process. Many servicemembers in this position proved to be discipline problems, however, if only because most had unexecuted punitive discharges pending and lacked incentive to perform properly. The Army coped with this situation by permitting a servicemember whose appeal was still undecided, but whose confinement had been served, to take "excess leave" — leave without pay.

This voluntary option proved unsatisfactory because, at least in the Army, a person who took this option at the close of his or her prison sentence was denied government funds for transportation home from prison, while a person insisting on a return to duty was reassigned at government expense to the installation nearest his or her home. When a large number of problem offenders wound up at Fort Bragg, North Carolina, the commanding general there brought great pressure to bear on the Army to modify the Uniform Code by providing for mandatory excess leave. Professor Lederer notes that a number of Army officials apparently believed it was easier to have Congress change the Code than to alter personnel assignment or finance policies. Ultimately, supporters of the change succeeded, and Article 76a of the Code now permits the armed forces to compel an accused to take excess leave pending completion of an appeal if the approved sentences includes "an unsuspended dismissal or an unsuspended dishonorable or badconduct discharge." Such an offender is faced with obtaining civilian employment with the ever-present risk of recall to active military service.

§ 25-20.00   JURISDICTIONAL PREREQUISITES FOR JUDICIAL APPEAL; INFERIOR TRIBUNALS AND SENTENCES

Although the right to an appeal from a court-martial is extraordinarily broad and protective, access to that right is a function of the sentence adjudged and initially approved by the convening authority. Under Article 66(b) of the Uniform Code of Military Justice, a Court of Criminal Appeals may only review cases in "which the sentence, as approved, extends to death, dismissal of a commissioned officer, cadet, or midshipman, dishonorable or bad-conduct discharge, or confinement for one year or more." Cases in which the sentence is not severe enough to permit review by a Court of Criminal Appeals "shall be reviewed by a judge advocate under regulations of the Secretary concerned."[55] Implementing Article 69 of the Code, however, the Rules for Courts-Martial require that all

---

[54] U. S. Court of Military Appeals Committee Report (Jan. 27, 1989). If the government wishes to continue confinement after the reversal of a conviction, it must comply with R.C.M. 305. United States v. Dombrowski, 46 M.J. 209 (C.A.A.F. 1997).

[55] U.C.M.J. art. 64(a).

(Rel.3—1/07   Pub.62410)

general court-martial records "be sent directly to the Judge Advocate General concerned if the approved sentence includes death or if the accused has not waived review under R.C.M. 1110."[56] Accuseds who have a general court-martial conviction, but who are not entitled to review by a Court of Criminal Appeals, thus have their records sent to the Judge Advocate General where, in any event, they will be examined.[57] Under the *Manual*:[58]

> The judge advocate's review shall be in writing and shall contain the following:
>
> (1) Conclusions as to whether —
>
> (A) The court had jurisdiction over the accused and each offense . . .;
>
> (B) Each specification . . . stated an offense; and
>
> (C) The sentence was legal;
>
> (2) A response to each allegation of error made in writing by accused. . . .[59]

> The record of trial [and related documents in each case reviewed] shall be sent for action to the officer exercising general court-martial jurisdiction over the accused at the time the court was held (or to that person's successor in command) when:
>
> (1) The judge advocate who reviewed the case recommends corrective action;
>
> (2) The sentence approved under . . . (article 60(c)) includes to dismissal, a bad-conduct or dishonorable discharge, or confinement for more than 6 months; or
>
> (3) Such action is otherwise required by regulations of the Secretary concerned.[60]

When the record is sent to the general court-martial convening authority, the reviewing judge advocate must include a recommendation as to the appropriate action to be taken.[61] Under the Rules for Courts-Martial:

> If the judge advocate who reviews the case under this rule states that corrective action is required as a matter of law, and the officer exercising general court-martial jurisdiction does not take action that is at least as favorable to the accused as that recommended by the judge advocate, the record of trial and the action thereon shall be forwarded to the Judge Advocate General concerned for review under R.C.M. 1201(b)(2).[62]

---

[56] R.C.M. 1111(a)(1). *See also* R.C.M. 1111(a)(2).

[57] U.C.M.J. art. 69(a). In the Army, such records would be examined in the Examination and New Trials Division. *See* text *below* note 64.

[58] *See also* R.C.M. 1112(d).

[59] R.C.M. 1112(d).

[60] R.C.M. 1112(e).

[61] U.C.M.J. art. 60(d).

[62] R.C.M. 1112(g)(1).

(Rel.3—1/07　Pub.62410)

If trial is by general court-martial and the sentence does not permit judicial review,

> [t]he record of trial . . . shall be examined in the office of the Judge Advocate General. . . . If any part of the findings or sentence is found to be unsupported in law or if reassessment of the sentence is appropriate, the Judge Advocate General may modify or set aside the findings or sentence or both.[63]

Under Article 69(b), when a court-martial conviction is not referred to a Court of Criminal Appeals or automatically reviewed in the office of the Judge Advocate General under Article 69(a):

> The findings or sentence, or both . . . may be modified or set aside, in whole or in part, by the Judge Advocate General on the ground of newly discovered evidence, fraud on the court, lack of jurisdiction over the accused or the offense, error prejudicial to the substantial rights of the accused, or the appropriateness of the sentence. If such a case is considered upon application of the accused, the application must be filed in the office of the Judge Advocate General by the accused on or before the last day of the two-year period beginning on the date the sentence is approved under . . . (article 60(c)), unless the accused establishes good cause for failure to file within that time.[64]

Accordingly, at the very least, all general courts-martial will be reviewed in the office of the Judge Advocate General concerned,[65] and should the Judge Advocate General direct, the case may be reviewed by a Court of Criminal Appeals, even though it would not ordinarily be subject to judicial review.[66]

---

[63] U.C.M.J. art. 69(a).

[64] U.C.M.J. art. 69(b). *See also* Section 25-11.00. Modification by the Judge Advocate General is ancillary to the direct appeals process and may be accomplished pursuant to abbreviated procedures. Curci v. United States, 577 F.2d 815, 818 (2d Cir. 1978). Although legal principles control the decisions of the Judge Advocate General, (McPhail v. United States, 1 M.J. 457 (C.M.A. 1976)), a lengthy statement of reasons supporting an exercise of this discretionary power is not necessary. *Curci,* 577 F.2d at 818. Note that requests for new trials in cases subject to appellate review, or in which review is pending or completed, are covered by U.C.M.J. art. 73.

As originally enacted, Article 69 did not have a time limit. Accordingly, the Army was forced to review cases dating from the beginning of the Nation.

[65] Under U.C.M.J. art. 69(c):

If the Judge Advocate General sets aside the findings or sentence, he may, except when the setting aside is based on lack of sufficient evidence in the record to support the findings, order a rehearing. If he sets aside the findings and sentence and does not order a rehearing, he shall order that the charges be dismissed. If the Judge Advocate General orders a rehearing but the convening authority finds a rehearing impractical, the convening authority shall dismiss the charges.

[66] U.C.M.J. art. 69(d). A number of cases have been reviewed under this provision. *See, e.g.,* The Army Court of Criminal Appeals has held that Article 76 "does not preclude our examination of petitioner's court-martial to determine whether the issues she has raised received full and fair consideration at trial and during review in the Office of The Judge Advocate General." Dew v.

Summary courts-martial and special courts-martial in which the approved sentence does not include a bad-conduct discharge cannot directly[67] reach the appellate courts.

Mandatory appellate review of summary and most special courts-martial, therefore, consists only of review by a judge advocate, with the accused granted the opportunity to appeal to the Judge Advocate General concerned. The utility of this review of "inferior" courts-martial is hard to predict. In the authors' experience, judge advocates take their legal review responsibilities seriously, and the Judge Advocate General[68] and his staff routinely perform multiple, painstaking Article 69 appeal reviews. All this must be viewed, however, against the nature of the records involved. Summary courts-martial have virtually no records, and, depending upon the military service and its practice, special courts may have severely truncated summarized records. Appeal may thus be difficult, and may often consist of allegations not substantiated by the all-too-limited record.

At first blush, limited appellate review of inferior courts-martial might suggest due process problems. Yet, even if appeals were constitutionally required,[69] the scope of review must be evaluated against the sanctions involved and the fact that summary courts-martial, at least, are voluntary; the accused may reject one and risk trial by special or general court-martial. Pragmatically, military review may be more useful than that accorded many civilian defendants adjudged guilty of offenses with similar punishments.[70]

Civilian federal appellate courts have supervisory power over their subordinate courts. Whether the Court of Appeals and the Courts of Criminal Appeals have similar jurisdiction is a highly controversial topic of great significance.[71] If the Court of Appeals has supervisory power over the military criminal legal system,

United States, 48 M.J. 639, 647 (Army Crim. App. 1998) (en banc). "Under the criteria for mandamus relief, the question is whether The Judge Advocate General's decision affirming the legal sufficiency of the trial was more than gross error—that it amounted to a judicial usurpation of power." 48 M.J. at 652.

[67] As for extraordinary relief, see Section 25-90.00.

[68] In the Army, at least.

[69] At least theoretically, however, appeals are not constitutionally required. McKane v. Durston, 153 U.S. 684 (1894) (oft-cited dictum).

[70] When viewed solely in terms of sentence, every summary and special court-martial can be said to deal only with a "misdemeanor," because of the limited sanctions available to the court-martial. "Review in misdemeanor cases also is discretionary in some jurisdictions." Y. Kamisar, W. LaFave, J. Israel, Modern Criminal Procedure 1467 (7th ed. 1990).

[71] See generally § 25-91.00, below. Compare McPhail v. United States, 1 M.J. 457, 460–63 (C.M.A. 1976) ("jurisdiction to require compliance with applicable law from all courts and persons purporting to act under its authority," 1 M.J. 463 (C.M.A. 1976)) with Dukes v. Smith, 34 M.J. 803 (N.M.C.M.R. 1992) (en banc) (no supervisory power over Article 15 punishment).

(Rel.3—1/07   Pub.62410)

in general its potential jurisdiction would be far broader than that specifically accorded it by statute.[72]

§ 25-30.00   AUTOMATIC APPEAL AND ITS WAIVER

When the Uniform Code was first enacted, both post-trial review and appeal to the then Board of Review[73] were automatic. The right to automatic appeal of serious convictions was viewed as one of the accused's protections against possible military overreaching. Over the years, however, it became apparent that there were some accused who did not wish an appeal; indeed, some wished their sentences to be executed (ordered into effect) as rapidly as possible.[74] As a consequence, in 1983,[75] Article 61 was amended to permit a convicted accused to "opt out" of the automatic system by waiving the right to appeal. Article 61(a) now provides:

> In each case subject to appellate review under . . . (article 66 or 69(a)), except a case in which the sentence as approved under . . . (article 60(c)) includes death, the accused may file with the convening authority a statement expressly waiving the right of the accused to such review. Such a waiver shall be signed by both the accused and by defense counsel and must be filed within 10 days after the action under . . . (article 60(c)) is served on the accused or on defense counsel. The convening authority or other person taking such action, for good cause, may extend the period for such filing by not more than 30 days.[76]

The Article further permits an appeal to be withdrawn at any time unless the death sentence is involved.[77] Waiver of the right to appeal, or withdrawal of an appeal, bars appellate review by the Court of Criminal Appeals.[78]

---

[72] Dukes v. Smith, 34 M.J. 803 (N.M.C.M.R. 1992) (en banc) (no jurisdiction or supervisory power over Article 15 related matters).

[73] When jurisdictionally appropriate.

[74] There are those who so wish to have their military connection and responsibility severed that they prefer to have a punitive discharge executed rather than risk the possibility of it being nullified on appeal.

[75] The Military Justice Act of 1983, Pub. L. No. 98-209, § 5(b)(1), 97 Stat. 1397 (1983). *See also* United State v. Smith, 44 M.J. 387 (C.A.A.F. 1996) (R.C.M. 1110(f) does not establish an outside limit on deadline for waiver of appeal).

[76] Note that appellate rights cannot be waived until *after* the convening authority has acted and the action has been served on defense counsel; an earlier waiver is invalid. United States v. Miller 62 M.J. 471 (C.A.A.F. 2006); United States v. Hernandez, 33 M.J. 145, 148–49 (A.C.M.R. 1991). *See also* United States v. Smith, 44 M.J. 387 (C.A.A.F. 1996) (waiver of right to appeal after consultation with counsel but before action by convening authority was invalid); Chapel v. United States, 21 M.J. 687 (A.C.M.R. 1985).

[77] U.C.M.J. art. 61(b). However, once a Court of Criminal Appeals receives the record of trial for appeal, it is "within the sound discretion of that court to decide whether the record should be withdrawn" at the accused's request. United States v. Ross, 32 M.J. 715, 716 (C.G.C.M.R. 1991).

[78] U.C.M.J. art. 61(c).

(Rel.3—1/07   Pub.62410)

Although an accused may waive "appeal,"[79] he or she may not waive automatic review by a judge advocate.[80]

§ 25-40.00   THE RIGHT TO COUNSEL ON APPEAL

§ 25-41.00   In General

Under prevailing constitutional law, an indigent defendant has the right to the assistance of counsel on an appeal;[81] this right does not extend, however, to discretionary appeals, including review by writ of certiorari.[82] Compared to civilian defendants, military accused have a far greater right to counsel.

Regardless of his or her financial status, any accused whose case is appealed to the Court of Criminal Appeals, or beyond,[83] has a right to free military appellate counsel, as well as to retain at his or her own expense civilian counsel.[84] In order to ensure appellate counsel, each of the armed forces maintains in Washington, D.C., separate offices of appellate counsel to represent the defense and government.[85] Recently, in a number of capital cases, attempts have been made to obtain "death penalty qualified counsel," those whose qualifications meet ABA recommendations. Thus far, all such attempts have failed,[86] in part on the grounds that military counsel are sufficiently competent to handle such cases. In one such case,[87] the Navy-Marine Court of Military Review observed that

---

[79] Except in a capital case. As in all cases of waiver, a waiver may be legally invalid. *E.g.,* United States v. Gomez-Perez, 215 F.3d 315, 319 (2d Cir. 2000) ("In some cases, a defendant may have a valid claim that the waiver of appellate rights is unenforceable, such as when the waiver was not made knowingly, voluntarily, competently, . . . when the government breached the agreement. . . .").

[80] R.C.M. 1112(a).

[81] Douglas v. California, 372 U.S. 353 (1963). Counsel must render "effective assistance." Evitts v. Lucey, 469 U.S. 387 (1985). Appellate defense counsel are held to the same standard of competency as trial advocates. United States v. Loving, 34 M.J. 1065, 1067 (A.C.M.R. 1992), citing United States v. Hullum, 15 M.J. 261, 267 (C.M.A. 1983). There is no constitutional right, however, to pro se representation on appeal. United States v. Forrest, 2000 CAAF LEXIS 411 (C.A.A.F. April 12, 2000), *citing* Martinez v. Court of Appeal of California, 120 S. Ct. 684 (2000).

[82] Ross v. Moffitt, 417 U.S. 600 (1974). *See also* Pennsylvania v. Finley, 481 U.S. 551 (1987) (no right to counsel for indigents at postconviction proceedings).

[83] Including discretionary appeals to the Court of Appeals or the Supreme Court.

[84] U.C.M.J. art. 70; R.C.M. 1202.

[85] Due to size, the Coast Guard may assign appellate representation as an additional duty to law specialists normally assigned other duties. Lack of uniformity among the services in rank or status (civilian v. military) of appellate counsel does not violate equal protection. United States v. Loving, 34 M.J. 1065, 1069 (A.C.M.R. 1992), *aff'd,* 41 M.J. 213 (C.A.A.F. 1995).

[86] *See generally* § 5-31.00, *above.*

[87] United States v. Thomas, 33 M.J. 768 (N.M.C.M.R. 1991) (request in the nature of extraordinary relief for death penalty qualified appellate counsel denied).

(Rel.3—1/07   Pub.62410)

the procedurally simple and more protective military system is significantly different from the more difficult civilian one.[88] Certainly, the very structure of the defense appellate agencies with their large number of counsel and potential additional resources may be sufficient to distinguish military practice from the usual civilian one.

Because appellate counsel is detailed from the defense appellate office of the service involved, it is highly unusual for an accused to be represented on appeal by the same lawyer who defended the accused at trial. This practice, which differs from the ordinary civilian process by which the convicted defendant is frequently represented on appeal by the same lawyer who initially tried the case, has logical but surprising consequences. Military appellate defense counsel, who must zealously represent their clients on appeal, are quite prepared to assert that trial defense counsel was ineffective. In civilian practice, it is rare for appellate lawyers to assert ineffectiveness on direct appeal.[89] As a result, it often seems from the appellate reports that military counsel at trial are more likely to have been ineffective than civilian lawyers. Such is surely not the case. The apparent disparity, certainly of such allegations brought on appeal, stems directly from the usual identity of the military appellate defense counsel. Coordination between trial and appellate defense counsel can sometimes be problematical,[90] especially given the possibility that appellate counsel will assert that trial defense counsel were ineffective.

Funding for civilian expert assistance to appellate defense counsel is at least theoretically possible.[91]

The practice of appellate counsel before the Courts of Criminal Appeals is governed by the Courts' Rules of Practice and Procedure.[92] Consistent with Article 70 of the Uniform Code and Rule 1202 of the Rules for Courts-Martial, Rules 10 and 11 provide that, absent waiver, the accused will be represented by military or civilian counsel. The court may also request counsel for a case before the court when counsel has not been assigned.[93]

---

[88] 33 M.J. 771 (N.M.C.M.R. 1991).

[89] As this would normally assert that the appellate lawyer was inadequate at trial, ineffectiveness of counsel claims are more likely to be made during postconviction collateral attacks.

[90] E.g., United States v. Dorman, 58 M.J. 295, 298 (C.A.A.F. 2003) ("Pursuant to trial defense counsel's continuing obligation to the client and the corresponding duty of confidentiality, we hold that trial defense counsel must, upon request, supply appellate defense counsel with the case file, but only after receiving the client's written release") (note omitted).

[91] United States v. Tharpe, 38 M.J. 8, 14–16 (C.M.A. 1993); United States v. Curtis, 31 M.J. 395 (Daily Journal, C.M.A. 1990); United States v. Thomas, 33 M.J. 644, 648 (N.M.C.M.R. 1991).

[92] Courts of Criminal Appeals Rules of Practice and Procedure, 44 M.J. 1xiii (1996) [hereinafter cited as C.C.A. Rules] (Rules 8 through 16 deal with counsel). Note that Rule 26 provides that the chief judge of an individual court has the power to promulgate internal rules for that court.

[93] C.C.A. Rule 11(b)(1).

(Rel.3—1/07 Pub.62410)

In light of the amount of time necessary to prepare and argue some appellate cases, and in light of reassignments, resignations, and retirements, any given case may experience a substantial turnover in appellate counsel. At the least this causes appellate delay.[94] Appellate delay has been a vexatious problem, and the Court of Appeals for the Armed Forces has expressed its deep concern and disapproval.[95]

If the accused wishes appellate counsel, a request should be made within ten days of receipt of notice of the action by the convening or reviewing authority.[96] The request should be forwarded to the convening or reviewing authority, or to the Judge Advocate General's office, and may be accompanied by a statement of the alleged errors and grounds for relief.[97] Although untimely compliance with this requirement could be argued to constitute waiver, the general standard for waiver requires a knowing and intelligent relinquishment of the right to appellate counsel,[98] and that standard, plus Article 61's specific procedure for waiver of appeal,[99] makes waiver unlikely.

Should the accused choose to exercise his right to employ civilian counsel pursuant to Article 70(d),[100] notice of such action must be forwarded to the convening or reviewing authority within ten days of service of the action.[101] Following a timely notice of intent to retain civilian counsel, appellate defense counsel will be appointed to represent the defendant until the civilian counsel's appearance.[102] The appointed counsel will remain to assist civilian counsel unless excused by the defendant.[103]

---

[94] United States v. Loving, 41 M.J. 213, 326–30 (1994) (Wiss, J., dissenting).

[95] United States v. Brunson et al, 59 M.J. 41 (C.A.A.F. 2003); Diaz v. The Judge Advocate General of the Navy, 59 M.J. 34 (C.A.A.F. 2003); United States v. May, 47 M.J. 478 (C.A.A.F. 1998).

[96] C.C.A. Rule 10.

[97] C.C.A. Rule 10.

[98] E.g., United States v. Butler, 26 C.M.R. 398 (C.M.A. 1958); United States v. Jones, 26 C.M.R. 489 (C.M.A. 1958).

[99] See Section 25-30.00.

[100] "The accused has the right to be represented before the Court of Criminal Appeals, the Court of Appeals for the Armed Forces or the Supreme Court by civilian counsel if provided by him." U.C.M.J. art. 70(d).

[101] C.C.A. Rule 10.

[102] C.C.A. Rule 11(a)(2).

[103] C.C.A. Rule 1(a)(2). The Court of Military Appeals has recently indicated its concern with the adequacy of the continuity of defense representation. United States v. Gray, 39 M.J. 351, 437 (C.M.A. 1994) (interlocutory order).

(Rel.3—1/07 Pub.62410)

§ 25-42.00   Frivolous Appeals

Appellate defense counsel must zealously represent their clients, but they need not ordinarily assert frivolous appeals.[104] Given the nature of the military appellate courts, however, the Court of Military Appeals held:

[W]e will require that when the accused specifies error in his request for appellate representation or in some other form, the appellate defense counsel will, at a minimum, invite the attention of the Court of Military Review to those issues and, in its decision, the Court of Military Review will, at a minimum, acknowledge that it has considered those issues enumerated by the accused and its disposition of them.[105]

"*Grostefon*" practice, as it might be termed, has often proven troublesome for the courts. Many appellate counsel have apparently simply passed on to the court their client's documents with their allegations of error. Frustrated, members of the Air Force Court of Military Review, suggesting ways in which to handle *Grostefon* cases, suggested that there is no reason why defense appellate counsel cannot summarize for the court the accused's submitted materials rather than

---

[104] *See, e.g.*, Anders v. California, 386 U.S. 738 (1967).

[105] United States v. Grostefon, 12 M.J. 431, 436 (C.M.A. 1982). If further appeal is necessary, the accused may have appellate defense counsel identify the issues in the petition for review by the Court of Military Appeals. 12 M.J. 437 (C.M.A. 1982). In United States v. Healy, 26 M.J. 394, 397 (C.M.A. 1988), the court commented:

Grostefon did not expand the scope of review under Article 66 or require that all the personal desires of the accused be accommodated. . . .

Instead, the purpose of our holding in *Grostefon* was to assure that an accused had the opportunity to bring to the attention of the appellate court any issue he wished to have considered with respect to the findings and sentence, as finally approved by the convening authority. Thus, we require appellate defense counsel to invite the attention of the Court of Military Review or of this Court to issues specified by an accused. Thereby, we have sought to guarantee that no accused would be left with the belief that his lawyer had not raised an issue which he wished to have considered. Imposition of this requirement was viewed as especially important in military justice, because the defense counsel at both the trial and appellate levels usually are military officers, and an accused whose issues have not been raised on appeal might conclude that the omission was the result of command influence.

In applying *Grostefon*, we have allowed appellate defense counsel simply to identify issues which the accused wished to have raised, rather than requiring counsel to brief those issues fully. In turn, if the issue has been identified as possibly meritorious, the Court may require briefs thereon. . . . However, *Grostefon* did not signal abolition of basic rules of appellate practice and procedure. Thus, in *United States v. Sumpter*, 22 M.J. 33 (C.M.A. 1986); and *United States v. Mitchell*, [20 M.J. 350 (C.M.A.1985)] *supra* at 351, we noted that *Grostefon* did not excuse the filing of untimely motions in the Court of Military Review or late petitions for grant of review in this Court.

See also United States v. Peel, 29 M.J. 235, 243 (C.M.A. 1989) (considering "substance rather than form" errors asserted by accused's mother were adopted by accused and were covered by *Grostefon*) (dictum).

(Rel.3—1/07 Pub.62410)

submitting those materials directly. [106] Although endorsing a requirement that appellate counsel summarize the matters raised by the appellant, the Court of Appeals has disapproved an Army Court of Military Review order prohibiting the submission of handwritten correspondence from the appellant. [107] *Grostefon* might be reexamined in light of *Austin v. United States,* [108] in which the Court stated:

> [T]hough indigent defendants pursuing appeals as of right have a constitutional right to a brief filed on their behalf by an attorney, *Anders* . . ., that right does not extend to forums for discretionary review.

§ 25-50.00   THE COURTS OF CRIMINAL APPEALS (THE COURTS OF MILITARY REVIEW)

§ 25-51.00   In General

The Courts of Criminal Appeals are the first true appellate tribunal in the military criminal legal system. In terms of their overall goals and purposes, the Courts of Criminal Appeals are functionally identical with their civilian counterparts. Underlying both are the goals of protecting procedural due process and other fundamental rights, as well as ensuring that the verdict is supported by the evidence. [109] Originally entitled "boards of review" by the Uniform Code of Military Justice, Congress changed "boards" to "courts" in 1968 [110] "to improve and enhance the stature and independent status of these appellate bodies," [111] and further changed the name to the Court of Criminal Appeals.

The Courts of Criminal Appeals are designed "to provide a single appellate body for the review of court-martial cases within each service." [112] The Army, Navy, Air Force, and Coast Guard have Court of Criminal Appeals panels composed of at least three judges each. [113] Under the Uniform Code, judges of

---

[106] United States v. Bell, 34 M.J. 937, 943–44 (A.F.C.M.R. 1992) (en banc). Although conceding that the instant case was exceptional, the dissent in *Bell* argues that in addition to other factors the perception of appellants is important and that their submissions ought normally to be considered. 34 M.J. 955 (A.F.C.M.R. 1992).

[107] United States v. Gunter, 34 M.J. 181 (C.M.A. 1992) (per curiam).

[108] 513 U.S. 5, 8 (1994) (dealing with collateral attacks).

[109] Sweet v. Taylor, 178 F. Supp. 456, 459 (D. Kan. 1959).

[110] Act of Oct. 24, 1968, Pub. L. No. 90-632, 82 Stat. 1341.

[111] S. Rep. No. 1601, 90th Cong., 1st. Sess. (1968), *reprinted in* 1968 U.S. Code Cong. & Admin. News 4501, 4515.

[112] S. Rep. No. 1601, 90th Cong., 1st. Sess. (1968), *reprinted in* 1968 U.S. Code Cong. & Admin. News 4501, 4515.

[113] *See* C.C.A. Rule 1. All of the appellate courts except the Coast Guard use only full-time judges. Four of the five Coast Guard appellate judges are "part-time judges" having other principal duties. United States v. Kovac, 36 M.J. 521, 527 (C.G.C.M.R. 1992). *See also* United States v. Carpenter, 37 M.J. 291 (C.M.A. 1993) (collateral duties did not disqualify Coast Guard Court of Military Review judges).

(Rel.3—1/07   Pub.62410)

the Courts of Criminal Appeals may be either commissioned officers or civilians[114] so long as they are members of a bar of a federal court or the highest court of a state.[115]

The Judge Advocate General of each armed force is responsible for establishing a Court of Criminal Appeals and designating a chief judge from among those selected to serve on the court.[116] The chief judge then has the duty to assign judges to panels, and to determine which of the three judges on each panel will serve as senior judge.[117] Neither party to an appeal may *voir dire* an appellate judge in preparation for a challenge; counsel are restricted to filing a motion for judicial disqualification, the results of which will be reviewed on an abuse of discretion basis.[118]

Despite provisions designed to prohibit both command influence[119]

---

[114] 37 M.J. 291 (C.M.A. 1993). Generally, the judges are senior military attorneys. The Coast Guard and the Navy have employed civilians on their panels, however. Willis, *The United States Court of Military Appeals — "Born Again,"* 52 Ind. L.J. 151, 154 n. 16 (1976). In 1992 the Coast Guard used two retired Coast Guard officers as judges. Although they initially considered themselves "civilians," after consideration of statutory changes to the Uniform Code, the court concluded that they served as commissioned officers. United States v. Kovac, 36 M.J. 521, 525 (C.G.C.M.R. 1992). In Ryder v. United States, 515 U.S. 177 (1995), the Court held that at least when viewed as "civilians," the Coast Guard's judges' appointments had violated the Constitution's Appointments Clause. *See also* United States v. Ryder, 44 M.J. 9 (C.A.A.F. 1996) (on remand held that Secretary of Transportation could appoint civilians as appellate military judges).

[115] U.C.M.J. art. 66(a). Insofar as potential disqualification of appellate judges is concerned, *see* United States v. Morgan, 47 M.J. 27 (C.A.A.F. 1997). *See also* United States v. Lynn, 54 M.J. 202 (C.A.A.F. 2000). United States v. Hamilton, 41 M.J. 32 (C.M.A. 1994) (judges on Court of Military Review did not err in not permitting voir dire).

[116] U.C.M.J. art. 66(a).

[117] U.C.M.J. art. 66(a). Two of three panel judges constitute a quorum. United States v. Lee, 54 M.J. 285 (C.A.A.F. 2000). As for the duties of the chief judge and the ability of The Judge Advocate General to appoint an acting chief judge for a specific case when the chief judge is recused or otherwise disqualified, See Walker v. United States, 60 M.J. 354 (C.A.A.F. 2004) (permitting such appointment).

[118] United States v. Hamilton, 41 M.J. 32, 38–39 (C.M.A. 1994). Judges ordinarily recuse themselves from cases in which they were involved as counsel. Supervisory lawyers such as United States Attorneys can find themselves "conflicted out" of a substantial number of cases for a significant period if the jurisdiction applies a per se disqualification test rather than one of actual involvement. In the military context, this issue more often arises at the appellate level where a new judge of a court of criminal appeals acted in the former assignment as a senior member of an appellate defense or government office. The Court of Appeals for the Armed Forces has not as yet developed a generally applicable rule for this scenario. United States v. Jones, 55 M.J. 317 (C.A.A.F. 2001).

[119] No member of a Court of Criminal Appeals shall be required, or on his own initiative be permitted to prepare, approve, disapprove, review, or submit, with respect to any other member of the same or another Court of Criminal Appeals, an effectiveness, fitness, or efficiency report, or any other report documents used in whole or in part for the purpose of determining whether

U.C.M.J. art. 66(g). and bias, [120]

U.C.M.J. art. 66(h). the Code and the Rules for Courts-Martial are both silent on assignment criteria for appellate judges. Accordingly, each branch of the armed forces may assign individuals to its Court of Criminal Appeals as it sees fit, a process that has led to difficulties in the past. Although the Courts of Criminal Appeals have had a large number of first rate, highly competent [121] judges, they also have had far less qualified individuals appointed. Unlike civilian jurisdictions in which this may result from the political process, this has occurred on occasion because the Courts of Criminal Appeals have not always been viewed as desirable military assignments. [122] Indeed, sometimes they have been used either as "dumping grounds" for officers considered otherwise unassignable, or as interim assignments for highly competent officers awaiting their next assignment. Most suggestions for some form of judicial tenure are intended to protect judges against command influence. [123] Ironically, some form of improved rank or status might well be desirable to attract the most capable officers. [124] At the very least, it would be desirable to decrease "personnel turbulence." [125]

---

a member of the armed forces is qualified to be advanced in grade, or in determining the assignment or transfer of a member of the armed forces, or in determining whether a member of the armed forces is qualified to be advanced in grade, or in determining the assignment or transfer of a member of the armed forces, or in determining whether a member of the armed forces shall be retained on active duty.

[120] Command influence of the traditional sort does not appear to have been a problem at the appellate level. The line between the Courts of Criminal Appeals and the armed forces' normal ability to inquire into allegations of wrongdoing has proven troublesome, however. *See* United States Navy-Marine Corps Court of Military Review v. Carlucci, 26 M.J. 328 (C.M.A. 1988).

No member of a Court of Criminal Appeals shall be eligible to review the record of any trial if such member served as investigating officer in the case or served as a member of the court-martial before which such trial was conducted, or served as military judge, trial or defense counsel, or reviewing officer of such trial.

[121] If not scholarly.

[122] The armed forces value "command time," which in the legal branches translates to duty as staff judge advocates or commanders of legal services offices. Further, criminal law occupies an increasingly small amount of legal time, thus decreasing promotion opportunities for true criminal-law specialists.

[123] There has been at least one situation in which a department planned to investigate appellate judges as if they were only commissioned officers. *See* United States Navy-Marine Corps Court of Military Review v. Carlucci, 26 M.J. 328 (C.M.A. 1988).

[124] *See, e.g.,* Note, *Military Justice and Article III,* 103 Harv. L. Rev. 1909 (1990). Although officers are assigned by order of superior authority, senior-officer assignments often take into account both the perceived "desirability" of an assignment and the officer's own wishes. Politics is far from absent in the legal branches; as a result, it is possible to make assignment to a Court of Criminal Appeals more attractive.

[125] "Although four of the current eleven judges are serving a second tour of duty with the court, from Spring 1989 to Fall 1990, some fourteen losses and fourteen gains occurred." Clerk of Court Notes, Army Law, January, 1991 at 41 (suggesting a possible explanation for the increase from 79 days to about 100 days in decision time of the Army Court of Military Review).

(Rel.3—1/07 Pub.62410)

Although the Courts of Criminal Appeals ordinarily sit in Washington, D.C., the Uniform Code additionally provides that "[t]he Secretary concerned may direct the Judge Advocate General to establish a branch office with any command."[126]

This provision allows the appellate system to be "exported" to a war zone to expedite appeals.

The Courts of Criminal Appeals function under the Courts of Criminal Appeals Rules of Practice and Procedure,[127] a set of uniform rules promulgated and periodically reviewed by the Judge Advocate General pursuant to Article 66(f) of the Code. Cases are ordinarily heard by three-judge panels, a majority of which constitutes a quorum.[128] The court may also sit en banc,[129] at which time a majority of the entire court constitutes a quorum, and the matter shall be decided by a majority of the judges sitting on the case.[130] In the absence of a quorum, "any judge present for duty may issue all necessary orders concerning any proceedings pending" preparatory to a hearing or decision[131] and in normal cases "provided such action does not finally dispose of a petition, applied, or case before the Court."[132]

Appellate arguments before the Courts of Criminal Appeals are ordinarily open to the public.[133]

Decisions of the Courts of Criminal Appeals are published in West's *Military Justice Reporter*. However, the courts routinely issue large numbers of unpublished decisions. The use of unpublished opinions can be troublesome, and one judge of the Army Court of Military Review has complained that one such use "amounts to judicial censorship."[134]

---

[126] U.C.M.J. art. 68.

[127] *See above* note 92. *See also* United States v. Gilley, 59 M.J. 245 (C.A.A.F. 2004) (Court of Criminal Appeals is not able to create its own filing deadlines).

[128] C.C.A. Rule 4(a). *E.g.,* United States v. Lee, 54 M.J. 285 (C.A.A.F. 2000).

[129] C.C.A. Rule 17(a) provides that a majority of the Court's judges may order en banc consideration. The Rule adds that "Such [a hearing] ordinarily will not be ordered except" (1) when . . . necessary to secure or maintain uniformity of its decisions, or (2) when the proceeding involves a question of exceptional importance, or (3) when the sentence . . . extends to death." A party may request en banc consideration "within 7 days after the government files its reply [brief] "C.C.A. Rule 17(b). For a brief discussion of when en banc consideration is merited, see United States v. Felix, 40 M.J. 356, 358, n. 2 (C.M.A. 1994).

[130] C.C.A. Rule (4)(b).

[131] C.C.A. Rule 4(a) & (b).

[132] C.C.A. Rule 4(a).

[133] *See* United States v. Schneider, 38 M.J. 387, 397 (C.M.A. 1993) (prejudicial error when well-intentioned plan excluded some spectators from hearing argument before Court of Military Review).

[134] United States v. Whitt, 31 M.J. 443, 444 (C.M.A. 1990) (summary disposition) (Everett, C.J. concurring). (citing unpublished opinion).

(Rel.3—1/07 Pub.62410)

§ 25-52.00   Jurisdiction

The Code mandates appellate review in three categories of cases, even if that portion of sentence is suspended:

     1) cases involving a death sentence;

     2) cases involving the dismissal of a commissioned officer, cadet, or midshipman, a dishonorable or bad-conduct discharge; and

     3) cases involving a sentence of confinement at hard labor for one year or more.[135]

In addition, as a discretionary matter The Judge Advocate General may send to the Court of Criminal Appeals a court-martial case not otherwise subject to review by that court.[136]

In *Dew v. United States*,[137] the Army Court of Criminal Appeals, sitting en banc, held that Article 76 "does not preclude our examination of petitioner's court-martial to determine whether the issues she has raised received full and fair consideration at trial and during review in the Office of The Judge Advocate General."[138] "Under the criteria for mandamus relief, the question is whether The Judge Advocate General's decision affirming the legal sufficiency of the trial was more than gross error—that it amounted to a judicial usurpation of power."[139] Agreeing that the court had jurisdiction to issue a writ of mandamus to The Judge Advocate General directing that TJAG send a case to the Court of Criminal Appeals under Article 66 of the Code, the court divided, however, on the standard to be used.[140]

Once the Court of Criminal Appeals acquires jurisdiction, it retains jurisdiction even if the defendant is released from active service.[141] Jurisdiction to reconsider the case[142] is also retained until a petition or certificate for review by the Court

---

[135] U.C.M.J. art. 66(b); § 866(b) (1986); *see also* C.C.A. Rule 2.

[136] U.C.M.J. art. 69(a); U.C.M.J. art. 69(d).

[137] 48 M.J. 639 (Army Crim. App. 1998).

[138] 48 M.J. at 647.

[139] 48 M.J. at 652.

[140] *Compare* 48 M.J. at 653, n.21 with the dissent at 660–661.

[141] *E.g.*, United States v. Woods, 26 M.J. 372 (C.M.A. 1988); United States v. Ballard, 37 C.M.R. 103 (C.M.A. 1967); United States v. Speller, 24 C.M.R. 173 (C.M.A. 1957). *See also* Steele v. Van Riper, 50 M.J. 89 (C.A.A.F. 1999) (per curiam) (issuance of administrative discharge after trial does not deprive the court of jurisdiction to review the case but it does effectively remit that part of the sentence, including a punitive discharge, affected by the discharge). *Compare* United States v. Woods, above (Secretary's approval of an offer to resign for the good of the service vacated convening authority's action), *with* United States v. Hargrove, 50 M.J. 665 (A. Crim. App. 1999) (distinguishing *Woods*, refused to set aside convening authority's action in part because of approval of resignation in lieu of court-martial was speculative).

[142] *See generally* Section 25-56.00; C.C.A. Rule 19, *above* note 92.

(Rel.3—1/07   Pub.62410)

of Appeals is filed, or until the time provided for filing has expired.[143] Indeed, a petition for reconsideration by the Court of Criminal Appeals renders a petition for review by the Court of Appeals moot because the Court of Criminal Appeals decision then lacks finality.[144]

In 2003, a number of observers noted with some concern the fact that some court of criminal appeals opinions replicated large portions of counsels' pleadings.[145] In *United States v. Jenkins*,[146] the lower court opinion "consists of 45 paragraphs, not including record excerpts. Thirty-one of these paragraphs are taken virtually or wholly verbatim from 29 of the 33 paragraphs in the Government's 19-page Answer before the CCA. This is done without attribution. These paragraphs include the statement of facts, legal analysis, and conclusions of law." The Court of Appeals for the Armed Forces set aside the opinion below because it could not "determine that Appellant received the "awesome, plenary, and de novo" review to which he was entitled by law.

§ 25-53.00   Scope of Review

§ 25-53.10   In General

The Uniform Code of Military Justice prescribes in Article 59(a) that "A finding or sentence of court-martial may not be held incorrect on the ground of an error of law unless the error materially prejudices the substantial rights of the accused."[147] Under Article 66(c), the Court of Criminal Appeals "may affirm only such findings of guilty and the sentence or such part or amount of the sentence, as it finds correct in law and fact and determines, on the basis of the entire record, should be approved."[148]

---

[143] United States v. Smith, 18 C.M.R. 84 (C.M.A. 1955); *see also* United States v. Kraffa, 11 M.J. 453 (C.M.A. 1981); § 25-55.00.

[144] United States v. Weeden, 12 C.M.R. 161 (C.M.A. 1953).

[145] As to ethical issues see generally Jaime S. Dursht, Judicial Plagiarism: *It May Be Fair Use But Is It Ethical?* 18 Cardozo L. Rev. 1253 (1996).

[146] United States v. Jenkins, 60 M.J. 27, 28 (C.A.A.F. 2004).

[147] U.C.M.J. art. 59(b) permits approval of legally correct lesser-included offenses. In United States v. Brown, 45 M.J. 389 (C.A.A.F. 1996), four judges held that in a contested case they could approve a "closely related" offense.

In United States v. McCoy, 31 M.J. 323, 327 (C.M.A. 1990), the defense asserted that prosecutorial misconduct required automatic reversal. The court held that in light of Article 59(a), unless actual prejudice is present, reversal cannot be ordered absent a "presumption of prejudice." The court then determined that the proceedings were not "so fundamentally unfair that the search for specific prejudice may be foregone." 31 M.J. at 328 (C.M.A. 1990) (distinguishing the constitutional automatic-reversal rule for coerced confessions that existed at the time).

[148] "Courts of Military Review are not required to address specifically in writing all assigned errors so long as the written opinion notes the errors and finds them without merit." United States v. Curtis, 44 M.J. 106, 126 (C.A.A.F. 1996), *rev'd on other grounds*, 46 M.J. 129 (C.A.A.F. 1997).

(Rel.3—1/07 Pub.62410)

Unlike the Court of Appeals, or, for that matter, any other American appellate court, the Courts of Criminal Appeals have extensive fact-finding power,[149] a power that significantly affects the scope of review. In 1990, for example, the Court of Military Appeals was faced with a case[150] in which the trial judge had permitted cross-examination without, in the opinion of the Court of Military Review, balancing its prejudicial impact against its probative value.[151] On appeal, the government asserted that the Court of Military Review had erred, as it had "substituted its own judgment for that of the military judge rather than determining whether his ruling was an abuse of discretion."[152] The Court of Military Appeals declared:

> This argument misunderstands the role Congress intended a Court of Military Review to play in the military justice system.
>
> Article 66(c) establishes the standard of review. . . .
>
> This awesome, plenary, *de novo* power of review grants unto the Court of Military Review authority to, indeed, "substitute its judgment" for that of the military judge. It also allows a "substitution of judgment" for that of the court members. In point of fact, Article 66 requires the Court of Military Review to use its judgment to "determine[,] on the basis of the whole record" which findings and sentence should be approved. This mandate neither stops the Court of Military Review from applying an "abuse of discretion" test, nor requires such a test.[153]

It may be that this language permits the Courts of Criminal Appeals to depart from the "abuse of discretion standard" normally applicable[154] to appellate courts in such areas as causal challenges of court members,[155] continuances[156] and

---

See also United States v. Matias, 25 M.J. 356, 363 (C.M.A. 1987) ("we are aware of no requirement of law that appellate courts in general or a court of military review in particular, must articulate its reasoning on every issue raised by counsel").

[149] *See* Section 25-53.20.

[150] United States v. Cole, 31 M.J. 270 (C.M.A. 1990).

[151] Mil. R. Evid. 403.

[152] *Cole*, 31 M.J. at 272.

[153] 31 M.J. at 272. The Court of Military Appeals noted that as *it* lacks fact-finding powers, it would be required to use an "abuse of discretion" test.

[154] Certainly, the Court of Military Appeals has made it clear that the mere claim of "judicial discretion" will not shield the actions of a trial judge:

> It is clear that the mantle of judicial discretion will not protect a decision based on the judge's arbitrary opinions as to what constitutes a fair court-martial. Since such a motion may raise issues of crucial importance of the integrity of the military justice system, the military judge may not be satisfied with mere perfunctory conclusions in determining whether a military accused is receiving a fair trial. In addition, the application of law to the facts by the military judge must be reasonable in some objective sense to be upheld by this Court.

United States v. Rosser, 6 M.J. 267, 271 (C.M.A. 1979).

[155] *See, e.g.,* United States v. Tippit, 7 M.J. 908 (A.F.C.M.R. 1979), *aff'd*, 9 M.J. 106 (1980); United States v. Findlay, 7 M.J. 931 (A.C.M.R. 1979). *See also* Section 15-54.00.

(Rel.3—1/07 Pub.62410)

other interlocutory determinations,[157] and mistrial declarations.[158] If so, it would ordinarily expand the protections granted to appellant.[159] Given its nature, it seems unlikely that the courts' fact-finding powers would create a test more favorable to the government than the "abuse of discretion test."

When reviewing a case, the Courts of Appeals must ensure that the evidence is sufficient to support the conviction, and this determination is also affected by the courts' fact-finding power:

> We will address the assignment dealing with legal sufficiency of the evidence first because only after finding legal sufficiency, must we determine factual sufficiency, *i.e.*, are we convinced beyond a reasonable doubt of appellant's guilt. . . . "The test for [legal sufficiency] is whether, considering the evidence in the light most favorable to the prosecution, a reasonable fact-finder could have found all the essential elements beyond a reasonable doubt."[160]

Because of its protective function, a Court of Criminal Appeals may examine issues and take notice of errors that are not assigned by counsel.[161] Inconsistent verdicts, however, are legally permissible,[162] as they may result from leniency rather than error.

Once the Court of Criminal Appeals has determined that error occurred at trial, it must test for prejudice. A distinction is drawn between nonconstitutional errors,

---

[156] *See, e.g.*, United States v. Thomson, 3 M.J. 271 (C.M.A. 1977); United States v. Henry, 1 M.J. 533 (A.F.C.M.R. 1975).

[157] *See, e.g.*, United States v. Otero, 5 M.J. 781, 784 (A.C.M.R. 1978).

[158] *See, e.g.*, United States v. Rosser, 6 M.J. 267, 270–71 (C.M.A. 1979); United States v. Thompson, 5 M.J. 28, 30 (C.M.A. 1978); *see* Arizona v. Washington, 434 U.S. 497, 506 n.18 (1978).

[159] The ability of the courts of criminal appeals to expansively find facts post-trial has troubled some. *See* Jividen, *USAF, Will the Dike Burst? Plugging the Unconstitutional Hole in Article 66(c), UCMJ*, 38 A.F. L. Rev. 63 (1994).

[160] United States v. Elmore, 31 M.J. 678, 683 (N.M.C.M.R. 1990) (quoting United States v. Turner, 25 M.J. 324 (C.M.A. 1987) (citing in turn Jackson v. Virginia, 443 U.S. 307, 319 (1979). *See also* United States v. Sills, 56 M.J. 239 (C.A.A.F. 2002) (court must find guilt beyond a reasonable doubt); United States v. Pacheco, 56 M.J. 1 (C.A.A.F. 2001) (applying Jackson v. Virginia); United States v. Gordon, 31 M.J. 30, 34 (C.M.A. 1990) (citing United States v. Hart, 25 M.J. 143, 146 (C.M.A. 1987), *cert. denied*, 488 U.S. 830 (1988)) (whether "any rationale trier of fact could have found the essential elements of the crime beyond a reasonable doubt." 31 M.J. 34 (C.M.A. 1990)).

[161] United States v. Cain, 5 M.J. 698 (N.C.M.R. 1978). The Court of Appeals has specified issues that have not been raised by counsel. *E.g.*, United States v. Sims, 33 M.J. 684 (A.C.M.R. 1991) (despite lack of any errors raised by counsel, the court determined that the accused's pleas were improvident and that the trial judge erred by failing to order a mental evaluation of the accused). *Compare* Fidell & Greenhouse, *A Roving Commission: Specified Issue and the Function of the United States Court of Military Appeals*, 122 Mil. L. Rev. 117 (1988) *with* Everett, *Specified Issues in the United States Court of Military Appeals: A Rationale*, 123 Mil. L. Rev. 1 (1989); Early, *Longstreet & Richardson, and the Specified Issue: The Current Practice*, 123 Mil. L. Rev. 9 (1989).

[162] United States v. Emmons, 31 M.J. 108, 112 (C.M.A. 1990).

(Rel.3—1/07   Pub.62410)

which must be tested for prejudice under Article 59(a) of the Code, and constitutional errors. Errors of a nonconstitutional dimension are harmless only when the trier of fact was not influenced by them, or when they had only a minimal effect on the resolution of the case.[163] Before a constitutional error may be declared harmless, however, the appellate court must be convinced that the error was harmless beyond a reasonable doubt.[164]

If prejudicial error is found, a Court of Criminal Appeals may order a rehearing[165] or, in a rare case, dismiss the charges against the accused.

§ 25-53.20   Fact-Finding Powers

As noted above, the Court of Criminal Appeals is unique among appellate tribunals in that it possesses general fact-finding power as well as the usual ability to review questions of law. The Court of Military Appeals observed:

> Essentially, the Court of Military Review provides a de novo trial on the record at appellate level, with full authority to disbelieve the witnesses, determine issues of fact, approve or disapprove the findings of guilty, and within the limits set by the sentence approved below, to judge the appropriateness of the accused's punishment. We believe such a court's exercise of its fact-finding powers in determining the degree of guilt to be found on the record is more apposite to the action of a trial court than to that of an appellate body.[166]

In 1953, the Air Force Board of Review stated that when considering witness credibility, "The court . . . must arrive at a candid, honest and dispassionate finding, and is not at liberty to reject the testimony of any witness on the basis of mere caprice."[167] Although the court may reach a different conclusion than

---

[163] United States v. Barnes, 8 M.J. 115, 116 (C.M.A. 1979), *on further review*, 9 M.J. 921 (A.C.M.R. 1980). The test is that of U.C.M.J. art. 59(a).

[164] *See, e.g.*, United States v. Simmons, 59 M.J. 485 (C.A.A.F. 2004) (applied *Chapman* to fourth amendment issue); United States v. Ward, 1 M.J. 176, 180 (C.M.A. 1975) (citing Chapman v. California, 386 U.S. 18 (1967)). The Supreme Court had applied an automatic reversal rule to coerced confessions, *see* Payne v. Arkansas, 356 U.S. 560 (1958). However, in *Arizona v. Fulminante*, 499 U.S. 279 (1991), the Court (in what is technically dicta) abrogated that rule in favor of the more usual harmless error test for constitutional error. Although the Court of Military Appeals could continue the automatic reversal rule, it is unlikely to do so.

[165] *See generally* R.C.M. 810 for the procedures and limitations applicable to new trials.

[166] United States v. Crider, 46 C.M.R. 108, 111 (C.M.A. 1973). *See also* United States v. Parker, 36 M.J. 269, 271 (C.M.A. 1993) (given its fact-finding power the court was termed the "800 pound gorilla"); United States v. Givens, 30 M.J. 294, 299 (C.M.A. 1990). Of course, the Court of Criminal Appeals cannot increase a sentence or substitute a finding of guilty more severe than that adjudged. *See also* U.C.M.J. art. 66(c); United States v. Taliau, 7 M.J. 845 (A.C.M.R. 1979). The Courts of Criminal Appeals also use post-trial affidavits to supplement the record. *E.g.* United States v. Williams, 60 M.J. 360 (C.A.A.F. 2004) .

[167] United States v. Harris, 9 C.M.R. 814, 818 (A.F.B.R. 1953) (also observing that "[i]t is a general

(Rel.3—1/07 Pub.62410)

the trial court, considerable weight must be given to the trial court's determination.[168] This deference is justified by the trial court's opportunity actually to see and hear the witness' testimony and demeanor.[169] Notwithstanding this deference, the Court of Criminal Appeals must be convinced of the appellant's guilt beyond a reasonable doubt.[170]

The Court of Appeals for the Armed Forces explained the duties of the courts of criminal appeal thusly:

> [T]he Court of Criminal Appeals applies neither a presumption of innocence nor a presumption of guilt. The court must assess the evidence in the entire record without regard to the findings reached by the trial court, and it must make its own independent determination as to whether the evidence constitutes proof of each required element beyond a reasonable doubt. In contrast to the lay members who serve on courts-martial, the mature and experienced judges who serve on the Courts of Criminal Appeals are resumed to know and apply the law correctly without the necessity of a rhetorical reminder of the "presumption of innocence."[171]

The Court of Criminal Appeals' fact-finding ability is significantly limited in that it may act only with respect to the findings and sentence as approved by the convening authority's action[172] and in reviewing the case, the court is limited to the record.[173] Accordingly, ordinarily only evidence which was admitted at trial may be considered on appeal,[174] although the record may be corrected on

---

rule that when a witness who is unimpeached testifies to facts within his knowledge, which are not improbable, or in conflict with other evidence, the witness is to be believed. This rule has been applied to the uncontradicted testimony of an accused or an interested witness." 9 C.M.R. 814, 818 (A.F.B.R. 1953)).

[168] United States v. Beazley, 1 C.M.R. 231, 239–40 (A.B.R. 1951), *petition denied*, 1 C.M.R. 99 (C.M.A. 1951). The courts of criminal appeals are generally reluctant to overturn the verdict of court members, but the same difference does not apply to the verdicts of military judges. One of the most significant cases in the last thirty years was the overturning of the conviction of Dr. Billig by court members. United States v. Billig, 26 M.J. 744 (N.M.C.M.R. 1988).

[169] *Beazley*, 1 C.M.R. at 239–40; *accord* United States v. Frierson, 43 C.M.R. 292 (C.M.A. 1971); United States v. Michaud, 2 M.J. 428 (A.C.M.R. 1975). Article 66(c) expressly states that re-evaluation of witness credibility must be made "recognizing that the trial court saw and heard the witnesses."

[170] United States v. Taliau, 7 M.J. 845, 848 (A.C.M.R. 1979). *See also* United States v. Martinez, 50 M.J. 344 (C.A.A.F. 1998) (summary disposition) (court must independently evaluate the sufficiency of the evidence based upon an independent determination of credibility and the weight to be accorded the evidence of record).

[171] United States v. Washington, 57 M.J. 394, 399–400 (C.A.A.F. 2002).

[172] U.C.M.J. art. 66(c). *See also* United States v. Smith, 39 M.J. 448, 451 (C.M.A. 1994) (court may not find as facts allegations of which the fact-finder has found the accused not guilty).

[173] 39 M.J. 448, 451 (C.M.A. 1994). This is not so when determining possible sentence disparity. *See, e.g.*, United States v. Lacy, 50 M.J. 286 (C.A.A.F. 1999). *See generally* § 25-53.30 *below*.

[174] United States v. Starr, 1 M.J. 186 (C.M.A. 1975); United States v. Lanford, 20 C.M.R. 87

(Rel.3—1/07 Pub.62410)

appeal to reflect accurately what transpired at trial.[175] In addition, evidence introduced for one purpose at trial may not be used by an appellate court "as though admitted for another purpose, unavowed and unsuspected."[176]

With regard to other factual determinations, the Court of Criminal Appeals has greater flexibility. According to the Coast Guard Court of Military Review, for instance, the power of independent evaluation under the Code extends to a determination of the voluntariness of an admission.[177] The court also has the general ability to take judicial notice,[178] and is not bound by concessions of counsel.[179]

(C.M.A. 1955); United States v. DeLeon, 19 C.M.R. 43 (C.M.A. 1955); United States v. Pierce, 2 M.J. 654 (A.F.C.M.R. 1976). *But see* Mil. R. Evid. 201(f) (judicial notice may be taken at any stage in the proceedings).

In determining a convening authority's intent, the court may use other aspects of the record, including the staff judge advocate's post-trial review. United States v. Panikowski, 8 M.J. 781, 782 n.1. (A.C.M.R. 1980).

In resolving an issue of mental responsibility, the Court of Military Review even has the power and authority to consider evidence occurring after trial. United States v. Burns, 9 C.M.R. 30 (C.M.A. 1953); United States v. Sudler, 2 M.J. 558 (A.C.M.R. 1976); *see also* United States v. Thomas, 32 C.M.R. 163 (C.M.A. 1962). In United States v. Parker, 36 M.J. 269, 271 (C.M.A 1993), the court sustained the refusal of the Court of Military Review to receive a third-party witness affidavit. However, in doing so, it made clear that it was ruling on the legality of what the court below *had* done, not what it *could* do.

[175] United States v. McLaughlin, 39 C.M.R. 61, 62 (C.M.A. 1968); United States v. Vintress, 38 C.M.R. 56 (C.M.A. 1967); United States v. Roberts, 22 C.M.R. 112 (C.M.A. 1956). Unsworn statements by counsel have been accepted as evidence of extra-record events. United States v. Hilow, 32 M.J. 439, 445, n. 2 (C.M.A. 1991) (Cox, J., complains that unsworn assertions of fact by defense counsel were considered rather than requiring a statement from the appellant).

[176] United States v. Rener, 37 C.M.R. 329, 334 (C.M.A. 1967) ("Such, at all events, is the result when the purpose in reserve is so obscure and artificial that it would be unlikely to occur to the minds of uninstructed court members; and even if it did, would be swallowed up and lost in the one that was disallowed"). *See, e.g.*, United States v. Pastor, 8 M.J. 280 (C.M.A. 1980), in which the accused was convicted of committing indecent sexual acts with his stepdaughter. At trial, the government unsuccessfully attempted to introduce testimony from the victim's mother as evidence of fresh complaint without advancing any other ground for admissibility. On appeal however, government counsel argued that the evidence was admissible to explain how the victim's mother became aware of the alleged indecent acts. Because this was not the justification for admission asserted at trial, on appeal the admissibility of the evidence was evaluated solely on the basis of whether it was properly excluded as evidence of fresh complaint.

[177] *E.g.*, United States v. Whipple, 4 M.J. 773 (C.G.C.M.R. 1978).

[178] *See* United States v. Nelson, 1 C.M.R. 169 (C.M.A. 1951); *see, e.g.*, United States v. Strawbridge, 21 C.M.R. 482 (A.B.R. 1956) (taking judicial notice of the trial record of another court-martial); United States v. Roberson, 12 C.M.R. 768 (A.F.B.R. 1953), *petition denied*, 13 C.M.R. 142 (C.M.A. 1953) (taking judicial notice of Army regulations).

[179] *Cf.* United States v. Emmons, 31 M.J. 108, 110 (C.M.A. 1990) (CMA may reject concessions, citing United States v. McNamara, 23 C.M.R. 39, 42 (C.M.A. 1957)).

(Rel.3—1/07 Pub.62410)

The actual limits of the fact-finding powers of the Courts of Criminal Appeals — and their powers to grant relief to an accused — are unclear. Judge Cox has opined:

> Moreover, Courts of Military Review are something like the proverbial 800-pound gorilla when it comes to their ability to protect an accused. Frequently, we have acknowledged their "awesome, plenary, *de novo* power of review" under Article 66(c). . . . "A clearer carte blanche to do justice would be difficult to express." . . .[180]

§ 25-53.30 Sentencing

The Courts of Criminal Appeals may review sentences and may decrease them if appropriate, a power frequently exercised, particularly in cases of disparate sentences among co-actors. Article 66(c) of the Uniform Code of Military Justice states that the Court of Criminal Appeals can approve "the sentence or such part or amount of the sentence, as it finds correct in law and fact and determines, on the basis of the entire record, should be approved."[181] In 1957, the United States Supreme Court determined that Article 66 clearly gives the Court of Criminal Appeals power to modify a sentence without remanding the record to the court-martial for resentencing.[182]

The Court of Appeals for the Armed Forces has Defined the Sentencing Responsibility of the Court of Criminal Appeals:

> A Court of Criminal Appeals must determine whether it finds the sentence to be appropriate. It may not affirm a sentence that the court finds inappropriate, but not "so disproportionate as to cry out" for reduction. As the Army Court has recognized, Article 66(c)'s sentence appropriateness provision is "a sweeping Congressional mandate to ensure 'a fair and just punishment for every accused.' "Article 66(c) "requires that the members of [the Courts of Criminal Appeals] independently determine, in every case within [their] limited Article 66, UCMJ, jurisdiction, the sentence appropriateness of each case [they] affirm.[183]

The Courts of Criminal Appeals may not "impose" a sentence for the first time on appeal.[184] However, the use in the armed forces of a single unified

---

[180] United States v. Parker, 36 M.J. 269, 271 (C.M.A. 1993) (Cox, J.) (citations omitted). *Cf.* United States v. Powell, 49 M.J. 460 (C.A.A.F. 1998).

[181] U.C.M.J. 66(c). *But see* United States v. Hutchison, 57 M.J. 231, 234 (C.A.A.F. 2002) ("In the present case, the lower court discussed a wide variety of subjects in a manner that raises the possibility that the court acted because it viewed the state court proceedings as inappropriate and sought to lessen the punishment from those proceedings. Under Article 66(c), however, although the court may take into account factors in the record such as the conviction and punishment by state authorities for the same act, it is limited to considering whether the military sentence is inappropriate.").

[182] Jackson v. Taylor, 353 U.S. 569 (1957); Fowler v. Wilkinson, 353 U.S. 583 (1957).

[183] United States v. Baier, 60 M.J. 382, 384-85 (C.A.A.F. 2005) (notes and citations omitted).

[184] *See* DeCoster v. Madigan, 223 F.2d 906 (7th Cir. 1955); United States v. Lynch, 26 C.M.R. 303 (C.M.A. 1958).

(Rel.3—1/07 Pub.62410)

sentence that is not quantified by the court-martial by offense (*i.e.*, a "gross sentence") effectively precludes a challenge to a sentence on this basis. In *Jackson v. Taylor*,[185] for example, the accused, convicted of premeditated murder and attempted rape, was sentenced to life imprisonment. On appeal, the Army Board of Review held the murder conviction incorrect in law and fact,[186] but upheld the attempted rape conviction, modifying the sentence to twenty years of confinement. Via a civilian federal habeas corpus petition, the accused argued that the military appellate court was without authority to impose such a sentence, claiming that the life-imprisonment sentence resulted from the murder conviction and that, consequently, the twenty-year sentence imposed on appeal was not a "part or amount" of the original court-martial sentence. The Supreme Court rejected this argument, characterizing the life sentence as a gross sentence intended to cover both convictions and reasoning that the modified sentence simply represented an exercise of the appellate court's statutory prerogative to affirm part of the sentence imposed by the court-martial.[187]

Given the unitary sentence rule, when a Court of Criminal Appeals sustains an accused's conviction for some, but not all, of the offenses of which he or she was convicted, sentence reassessment is ordinarily appropriate.[188] The court should evaluate the probable impact on sentencing of the disproved offenses and determine whether the sentence is unconscionably disproportionate to the affirmed charges.[189]

The Courts of Criminal Appeals have plenary power to reduce sentences and may order sentence rehearings.[190] Although they may modify a sentence to correct prejudicial errors[191] or to decrease sentence disparity among co-accused or co-actors, they may also reduce sentences in the interests of justice as a discretionary matter.[192] In modifying sentences, the court may alter the type of

---

[185] 353 U.S. 569 (1957).

[186] United States v. Fowler, 2 C.M.R. 336 (A.B.R. 1952).

[187] *Jackson*, 353 U.S. at 577.

[188] The Court of Criminal Appeals may determine, however, that erroneous conviction of one or more offenses played no significant part in sentencing.

[189] United States v. Davis, 48 M.J. 494 (C.A.A.F. 1998); United States v. Cook, 48 M.J. 434 (C.A.A.F. 1998); United States v. Cruz, 49 C.M.R. 291 (C.M.A. 1974); United States v. Stene, 22 C.M.R. 67 (C.M.A. 1956); United States v. Fisher, 6 M.J. 592 (A.F.C.M.R. 1978); United States v. Joslin, 2 M.J. 629 (A.F.C.M.R. 1976). *See also* United States v. Reed, 33 M.J. 98, 99 (C.M.A. 1991), citing United States v. Sales, 22 M.J. 305, 308 (C.M.A. 1986) ("[I]f appellate authorities confidently can discern the extent of the error's effect on the sentencing authority's decision, then the decision can be adjusted accordingly. If, however, the extent of the error's effect is more ambiguous, the sentencing proceeding must be conducted again").

[190] United States v. Sills, 56 M.J. 239 (C.A.A.F. 2002).

[191] United States v. Malia, 6 M.J. 65, 68 (C.M.A. 1978); *e.g.*, United States v. Jenkins, 7 M.J. 504 (A.F.C.M.R. 1979).

[192] *E.g.*, United States v. Schumacher, 11 M.J. 612 (A.C.M.R. 1981).

(Rel.3—1/07 Pub.62410)

punishment adjudged so long as the new sentence is less severe than the prior one. The court may, for example, convert a death sentence to a dishonorable discharge and confinement.[193] In determining whether to reduce a sentence, however, the Court of Criminal Appeals is limited to matters included in the entire record — the court-martial transcript, any allied papers, and appellate briefs[194] — plus, in the case of co-actors, the court's own records, which it may judicially notice.

Although the Court of Criminal Appeals has the power to remit or disapprove a sentence, it lacks the authority to suspend one,[195] an anomaly based on the historic notion that the judiciary lacks the constitutional authority to suspend a sentence without express authority. Under the constitution, the powers of suspension and probation are believed to be entrusted exclusively to the legislative and executive branches of government.[196]

§ 25-54.00   Reconsideration

Under Rule 19,[197] a Court of Criminal Appeals has the *sua sponte* discretion to enter a reconsideration order not later than thirty days after service of its decision upon the accused.[198] In addition, the court may entertain a motion for reconsideration by "defense counsel within 30 days after receipt of a decision or order by counsel, or by the appellant."[199] The government must submit a request for reconsideration "within 30 days after the decision or order is received by counsel."[200]

If a petition or certificate of review under Article 67(b) has been delivered to the Court of Appeals, however, the jurisdiction of the Court of Criminal Appeals is deemed to have lapsed, and reconsideration orders no longer may be entertained.[201] Once the Court of Criminal Appeals' jurisdiction has lapsed, the court can obtain jurisdiction only on remand.[202] The Court of Criminal

---

[193] *See* United States v. Russo, 29 C.M.R. 168 (C.M.A. 1960).

[194] United States v. Fagnan, 30 C.M.R. 192, 195 (C.M.A. 1961). *In Fagnan*, the military appellate court properly refused to consider a psychiatric report and letter regarding the accused's good conduct in post-trial confinement when assessing the appropriateness of a court-martial sentence.

[195] United States v. Darville, 5 M.J. 1 (C.M.A. 1978); United States v. Woods, 30 C.M.R. 61 (C.M.A. 1960); United States v. Cavallaro, 14 C.M.R. 71 (C.M.A. 1954); United States v. Simmons, 6 C.M.R. 105 (C.M.A. 1952).

[196] United States v. Darville, 5 M.J. 1, 2 (C.M.A. 1978) (citing *Ex parte* United States, 242 U.S. 27 (1916)); *see* U.C.M.J. art. 71.

[197] *above* note 92.

[198] C.C.A. Rule 19(a).

[199] C.C.A. Rule 19(b)(1).

[200] C.C.A. Rule 19(b)(2).

[201] C.C.A. Rule 19(a).

[202] *See* U.C.M.J. art. 67(f).

(Rel.3—1/07   Pub.62410)

Appeals can direct the Judge Advocate General to return the record of a case before the court to the Court of Criminal Appeals for reconsideration in light of the Court of Appeals' opinion. [203]

§ 25-55.00   Effect of Reversal of Conviction

If the Court of Criminal Appeals reverses a conviction, it may order a rehearing [204] or a dismissal of charges. The Government may, of course, attempt to appeal the decision [205] to the Court of Appeals.

If the servicemember whose conviction is reversed is in confinement, "the servicemember must be released from confinement, unless and until the Government shows reasons, such as risk of flight or obstruction of justice, that warrant keeping him in confinement." [206]

Unless a new trial or hearing is ordered and a previously executed sentence is reimposed, a reversed conviction requires the restoration of "all rights, privileges, and property affected by an executed court-martial sentence [other than an executed dismissal or discharge] which has been set aside or disapproved." [207]

In *United States v. Miller* [208] the court clarified the rules when the Court of Criminal Appeals reverses a conviction while the accused is still in post-trial confinement.

> If the Judge Advocate General immediately decides not to pursue the case any further, there must be immediate notice to the convening authority of the opinion of the Court of Criminal Appeals and immediate direction to release the accused or conduct a hearing under RCM . . . on pretrial confinement. . . . If there is not such an immediate decision, there will be a 30-day period during which the Judge Advocate General is considering whether to accept the lower court's opinion or to pursue it further by way of a motion for reconsideration or certification to this Court. During such period, the accused remains in confinement because the opinion below is inchoate. . . .
>
> After considering the matter, if the Judge Advocate General decides to certify the case to this Court, the accused's interest in the favorable decision

---

[203] U.C.M.J. art. 67(f).

[204] *See* R.C.M. 810. *See also* Section 25-110.00. *See generally* Gibson, *Conducting Courts-Martial Rehearings*, Army Law., December 1991, at 9.

[205] If the Judge Advocate General certifies the case, it must be heard.

[206] Moore v. Akins, 30 M.J. 249 (C.M.A. 1990).

[207] U.C.M.J. art. 75(a). *See* Groves v. United States, 47 F.3d 1140 (Fed. Cir. 1995). In the case of a dismissal, ordinarily an administrative discharge is substituted for the disapproved dismissal. U.C.M.J. art. 75(c). A similar result follows in the event of a punitive discharge "unless the accused is to serve out the remainder of his enlistment." U.C.M.J. art. 75(b).

[208] 47 M.J. 352, 361–62 (C.A.A.F. 1997).

of the court below (even if inchoate) requires either that the accused be released in accordance with that decision or a hearing on continued confinement be conducted under R.C.M. 305.

§ 25-60.00 THE COURT OF APPEALS FOR THE ARMED FORCES

§ 25-61.00 In General[209]

Articles 141–46 of the Uniform Code of Military Justice[210] establish and define the structure and organization of the Court of Appeals for the Armed Forces[211] as well as its powers. The court was established pursuant to the power "to make Rules for the Government and Regulation of the land and naval Forces"[212] and, absent life-tenure for its judges, is considered an "Article I" federal court. It is composed of five civilian members appointed by the President with the advice and consent of the Senate for a term of fifteen years.[213] No military experience or affiliation is required for service on the court.[214] Instead, political affiliation is of statutory concern as not more than two members of the court may be appointed from the same political party.[215]

For most purposes, judges of the Court of Appeals rank as judges of the United States Courts of Appeal and Article III judges may sit on the court on an interim basis.[216]

---

[209] See also Section 25-11.00.

[210] U.C.M.J. art. 141–46. Originally the code dealt with the court in Article 67.

[211] Often known as "COMA." Now the United States Court of Appeals for the Armed Forces.

[212] U.S. Const. art. I, § 8; see Gallagher v. Quinn, 363 F.2d 301 (D.C. Cir.), cert. denied, 385 U.S. 881 (1966) (upholding the constitutionality of the Uniform Code of Military Justice). The court was intended from the start to be a specialized court. In 1994, in the process of noting that it was not bound by a legal conclusion reached by a circuit court of appeals, the court even suggested that "to the extent that an issue involves interpretation and application of the [UCMJ] and the [MCM] in the sometimes unique context of the military environment, this Court may be better suited to the task [than a civilian United States Court of Military Appeals]." Garrett v. Lowe, 39 M.J. 293, 296 (C.M.A. 1994).

[213] U.C.M.J. art. 142(a); (b).

[214] As a historical note, the first panel of judges were all reserve officers — one from each branch of the service. These selections simply represented a political maneuver by President Truman. See Willis, above note 3, at 71–72. The precedent of appointing judges with military experience was reversed in 1956 when President Eisenhower nominated Homer Ferguson to the Court. Ferguson was a former Republican senator with no military connection. W. Generous, above note 9, at 97. In 1991, Congress prohibited the appointment to the court of retired officers who retired from active duty. For a historical review of the appointment of judges to the court see Jonathan Lurie, Presidential Preferences and Aspiring Appointees: Selections to the U.S. Court of Military Appeals 1951-1968, 29 Wake Forest L. Rev. 521 (1994).

[215] U.C.M.J. art. 142(b)(3).

[216] See, e.g., United States v. Rushatz, 31 M.J. 450, 451 (C.M.A. 1990) (D.C. Circuit judge sat by appointment). Prior to the amendment, Article 67(a)(3) of the Code provided:

(Rel.3—1/07 Pub.62410)

Once appointed, a Court of Appeals judge may be removed only by the President after proper notice and hearing for "neglect of duty; or misconduct; or mental or physical disability."[217] The Court of Appeals for the Armed Forces has adopted The Code of Conduct for United States Judges.[218]

The Court of Appeals sits in Washington, D.C., and is associated with the Department of Defense for administrative purposes only.[219] The Uniform Code of Military Justice[220] grants the Court of Appeals authority to promulgate its own rules of practice and procedure, which it has done.[221] The court now uses a term of court that extends from October 1st until September 30th.[222]

In general theoretical terms, the Court of Appeals is similar to any other American appellate court. Lacking the unique fact-finding powers of the Courts of Criminal Appeals,[223] the court reviews cases for legal error. Its jurisdiction is normally exercised by petition, a discretionary procedure similar to writ of certiorari. What is apparently unique to the court is its extensive practice of

---

If a judge of the United States Court of Military Appeals is temporarily unable to perform his duties because of illness or other disability, the President may designate a judge of the United States Court of Appeals for the District of Columbia Circuit to fill the office for the period of disability.

Article 142(f), Service of article III judges, now reads:

(1) The Chief Justice of the United States, upon the request of the chief judge of the court, may designate a judge of the United States court of appeals or of a United States district court to perform the duties of judge of the United States Court of Military Appeals —

(A) during a period a judge of the court is unable to perform his duties because of illness or other disability; or

(B) in any case in which a judge of the court recuses himself.

(2) A designation under paragraph (1) may be made only with the consent of the designated judge and the concurrence of the chief judge of the court of appeals or district court concerned.

The court has taken advantage of the statutory ability to use Article III judges. In United States v. Schneider, 36 M.J. 353, 364 (C.M.A. 1993), due to recusals, Judge Sporkin sat with a member of the Sixth Circuit and a member of the Federal Circuit, in addition to two Court of Military Appeals judges. National Institute of Military Justice, Military Justice Gazette (June 1993) at 2.

[217] U.C.M.J. art. 67(a)(2).

[218] United States v. Butcher, 56 M.J 87, 91 (C.A.A.F. 2001).

[219] The Court was designed to retain an independence befitting a supreme appellate tribunal, and its ever-troublesome administrative connection with the Department of Defense is not intended to affect it in a meaningful fashion. U.S. Court of Military Appeals Committee Report 22–23 (Jan. 27, 1989); Report of the Dept. of Defense Study Group on the United States Court of Military Appeals A-5, F-5 (July 25, 1988).

[220] U.C.M.J. art. 144.

[221] 40 M.J. LXVII at www.armfor.uscourts.gov/Rules.doc.

[222] 27 M.J. 412 (1988).

[223] *See* Section 25-53.20.

"specifying issues." Rather than relying solely on assignments of error by counsel, the court has institutionalized, via its centralized civil service staff, the practice of searching records for potential issues and specifying those issues by court order for briefing and argument.[224] Although specifying issues may be particularly appropriate for a court intended to protect the rights of servicemembers, it appears likely that the Court of Appeals has done so too extensively.[225]

Like any other American appellate court, the Court of Appeals has the power within its jurisdiction to interpret regulations, executive orders (including the *Manual for Courts-Martial*), statutes, and applicable constitutional provisions.[226] The court may also invalidate, for purposes of military criminal law, any regulation, executive order,[227] or statute that conflicts with higher legal authority. The court has consistently struck down provisions that violate the accused's constitutional rights.[228] The Court has specifically held that it has jurisdiction " 'to determine on direct appeal if the adjudged and approved sentence is being executed in a manner that offends the Eighth Amendment or Article 55.' "[229]

---

[224] *See* Early, *Longstreet & Richardson, USCMA and the Specified Issue: The Current Practice,* 123 Mil. L. Rev. 9 (1989); Everett, *Specified Issues in the United States Court of Military Appeals: A Rationale,* 123 Mil. L. Rev. 1 (1989); Fidell & Greenhouse, *A Roving Commission: Specified Issues and the Function of the United States Court of Military Appeals,* 122 Mil. L. Rev. 117 (1988).

[225] *See, e.g.,* United States Court of Military Appeals Committee Report, January 27, 1989, at 4.

[226] The court's power to make constitutional determinations as an Article I court is analogous to the ability of the tax courts, also Article I tribunals, to make constitutional determinations. *See, e.g.,* Pennsylvania Mut. Indem. Co. v. Commissioner, 32 T.C. 653 (1959), *aff'd,* 277 F.2d 16 (3d Cir. 1960).

[227] *See, e.g.,* United States v. Ware, 1 M.J. 282, 285 n.11 (C.M.A. 1976) (*Manual* provision must yield to the Uniform Code of Military Justice); United States v. McCormick, 30 C.M.R. 26, 28 (C.M.A. 1960) (President has authority to prescribe in the *Manual* rules of evidence and procedure and maximum punishments for particular offenses, but may not create offenses under the Code); United States v. Armbruster, 29 C.M.R. 412, 414 (C.M.A. 1960) (construing *Manual* provisions for compliance and conformity with the Code is the court's responsibility).

[228] *E.g.,* United States v. Booker, 5 M.J. 238 (C.M.A. 1977); United States v. Alderman, 46 C.M.R. 298 (C.M.A. 1973); United States v. Jacoby, 29 C.M.R. 244 (C.M.A. 1960). Of course, the Court will interpret the Code so that it accords with the Constitution, if such a construction is possible. United States v. Jacoby, 29 C.M.R. 244, 248 (C.M.A. 1960).

Although the United States Supreme Court's policy is to independently review the entire record when constitutional rights are at issue (*see* Bachellar v. Maryland, 397 U.S. 564 (1970)), albeit showing great deference to the lower court's findings of fact (*see, e.g.,* Ker v. California, 374 U.S. 23 (1963); Haynes v. Washington, 373 U.S. 503 (1963)), the Court of Military Appeals refuses to extend its inquiry to questions of fact, even under these circumstances. United States v. Lowry, 2 M.J. 55, 58 (C.M.A. 1976).

[229] United States v. Erby, 54 M.J. 476, 478 (C.A.A.F. 2001), *quoting* United States v. White, 54 M.J. 469 (C.A.A.F. 2001). The Court opined that the same powers are held by the Courts of Criminal Appeal. 54 M.J. at 478.

(Rel.3—1/07 Pub.62410)

In short, it can review the conditions of confinement. In interpreting the Constitution, the court is bound, of course, by the decisions of the Supreme Court.

Since its inception, the court has been troubled by its status as an Article I institution[230] tied to the Department of Defense, and by "personnel turbulence" among its judges. Article III status would deprive the President of the limited power he has over the court's membership. Judicial terms would be for life rather than fixed fifteen-year terms, and the President would not have the right to pick the chief judge. The Department of Defense clearly believes that this highly limited control over the court is important and valuable. Expressing numerous concerns, including the possibility that Article III status would expand the court's jurisdiction, a Department of Defense Study Group concluded:

> Retaining COMA as an Article I court will allow continued, special deference to be given to the military and will allow Congress to fully exercise its Article I powers over the military as the Supreme Court has interpreted them and as the framers of the Constitution envisioned them. [231]

Quite frankly, the Department of Defense position seems overstated, particularly with a five-member court. Given the input DOD already has in the appointment of judges by the President, its fear is almost certainly unfounded. The necessity for Article III status is unclear, but should it be granted by Congress, it is improbable that it would adversely affect the court or the armed forces. Given the surface impression of potential DOD influence on the court through budget and personnel matters,[232] distancing the court from DOD is desirable. Whether that would resolve the personnel problems the court has experienced would be another matter.

The court has long suffered from unusual turnover. Although this has been due to a number of different reasons, it is noteworthy that Judge Duncan left the court for an appointment as a United States district judge, surely one of few Circuit Court of Appeals-level judges to accept such a seat. "Personnel turbulence" appears to stem primarily from past defects in the court's retirement plan, perhaps now adequately fixed by statutory amendment, and lack of prestige. The simple fact of the matter is that the Court of Appeals is *not* a Circuit Court of Appeals. Article III status might be the solution to this, but it is by no means certain that an appellate court, the jurisdiction of which pertains only to criminal cases, and military criminal cases at that, would have prestige equal to a

---

[230] The court is responsible to Congress through the committees on armed services rather than judiciary. *See* Note, *Military Justice and Article III*, 103 Harv. L. Rev. 1909 (1990). *See generally* Schleuter, *The Twentieth Annual Kenneth J. Hodson Lecture: Military Justice for the 1990's — A Legal System Looking for Respect*, 133 Mil. L. Rev. 1, 25-7 (1991).

[231] Office of the General Counsel, Department of Defense, Report of the Department of Defense Study Group on the Unites States Court of Military Appeals 39 (1988).

[232] On occasion, there may have been substance to such concerns. *See* Mundy v. Weinberger, 554 F. Supp. 811 (D.D.C. 1982).

(Rel.3—1/07 Pub.62410)

traditional Article III federal circuit.[233] Other than improving the court's retirement plan, the only major change made to the court to resolve the turnover problem was the increase in the court's membership in 1990 to five judges. Unfortunately, as of June 1991, it appeared that the President would not readily fill the two additional positions.[234] Certainly his delay in filling them must make one ponder, particularly given the number of interested and qualified candidates. Finally, Judge Susan J. Crawford was sworn in on November 19, 1991, Judge H. F. "Sparky" Gierke on November 20, 1991, and Judge Robert Wiss on January 2, 1992. Judge Gierke is a prior Army military judge and Judge Wiss retired as a Rear Admiral in the Navy Reserve. Judge Crawford served for six years as the General Counsel for the Army and nearly two years as the DOD Inspector General. Seniority is determined by the date on which they took the oath of office. Judge Wiss died on October 23, 1995.

Andrew S. Effron was sworn in on August 1, 1996 with a formal investiture on September 25, 1996. Judge Gierke's term was extended for a full 15 years.[235] Chief Judge Cox retired in 1999, with Judge Crawford succeeding him as Chief Judge on October 1, 1999.

Judge James E. Baker was sworn in September 19, 2000, with a formal investiture on December 1, 2000. With the retirement of Judge Sullivan, Charles E. "Chip" Erdmann was confirmed by the Senate on September 2, 2002 and sworn in on Oct. 15, 2002 with a formal investiture on January, 8, 2003. On December 9, 2006 the Senate confirmed Scott W. Stucky and Margaret A. Ryan.

§ 25-62.00   Jurisdiction

Although the Court of Appeals is the highest court in the military system, its jurisdiction is limited to appeals from court-martial convictions; it lacks any express authority over administrative matters.[236] Direct review by the Court of

---

[233] There is, of course, no logical reason for this. Unfortunately, we suspect that the American bar and bench do not give criminal jurisprudence its due, and lack of understanding of military law and life simply complicates the problem.

[234] After months of delay, on 13 February 1991, the President nominated Susan Crawford, leaving two vacancies.

[235] National Defense Authorization Act for Fiscal Year 1997, Pub. L. No. 104-201 § 1066 (Sept. 23, 1996).

[236] Parisi v. Davidson, 405 U.S. 34, 44 (1972); *see also* Mueller v. Brown, 40 C.M.R. 246 (C.M.A. 1969) (no jurisdiction to review administrative action absent court-martial proceedings). The court might reach such matters, however, by extraordinary writ incident to its role in supervising military criminal law. *See generally* Section 25-90.00. A study completed January 13, 1998 in accordance with section 551 of the National Defense Authorization Act for Fiscal Year 1996 did not recommend expanding the Court of Appeal's jurisdiction. *Cf.* Clinton v. Goldsmith, 526 U.S. 529 (1999). The Court also has held that it has jurisdiction to review sentence conditions such as the manner in which confinement is served, at least to the degree that they might violate the Uniform Code of Military Justice or the Constitution. United States v. Erby, 54 M.J. 476, 478 (C.A.A.F. 2001)

(Rel.3—1/07 Pub.62410)

Appeals cannot occur until a Court of Criminal Appeals has taken final action on both the findings and the sentence in a case.[237] Once the Court of Appeals obtains jurisdiction, the court does not lose it despite change in the accused's military status.[238]

Under Article 67 of the Uniform Code of Military Justice, the Court of Appeals for the Armed Forces exercises mandatory review in two types of cases:

1) all cases in which the sentence, as affirmed by a Court of Criminal Appeals extends to death; and

2) all cases reviewed by a Court of Criminal Appeals which the Judge Advocate General concerned orders sent to the Court of Appeals for the Armed Forces for review.[239]

---

[237] United States v. Best, 16 C.M.R. 155, 158 (C.M.A. 1954).

[238] United States v. Sanchez, 53 M.J. 393, 397 (C.A.A.F. 2000) (Court has jurisdiction over allegations of Article 55 and eighth amendment violations concerning sentences on direct appeal. J. Sullivan dissented on jurisdiction issue citing *Goldsmith.*); Steele v. Van Riper, 50 M.J. 89 (C.A.A.F. 1999) (per curiam) (issuance of administrative discharge after trial does not deprive the court of jurisdiction to review the case but it does effectively remit that part of the sentence, including a punitive discharge, affected by the discharge); United States v. Jackson, 3 M.J. 153 (C.M.A. 1977). Similarly, insanity on the part of the accused arising during the appellate process does not divest the court of its jurisdiction. United States v. Bell, 20 C.M.R. 108, 111 (C.M.A. 1955). The court also retains jurisdiction to grant an accused's petition and review the record, even after the sentence has been reduced by a Court of Military Review to a level that originally would not have required the Court of Military Appeals to grant the petition had the case been referred to the Court of Military Review by the Judge Advocate General. United States v. Reid, 31 C.M.R. 83, 86–87 (C.M.A. 1961).

[239] U.C.M.J. art. 67(a)(1)–(2). Whether review of those cases that the Judge Advocate General orders sent to the court under Article 67(b)(2) is truly mandatory is arguable. The court has recognized its obligation to review the record in these cases. United States v. Engle, 11 C.M.R. 41 (C.M.A. 1953). However, the court has refused to review issues certified by the Judge Advocate General when the resolution in the court would not materially alter the situation for the accused or the government (*see, e.g.*, United States v. Britton, 26 M.J. 24 (C.M.A. 1988); United States v. McAnally, 10 M.J. 270 (C.M.A. 1981); United States v. Clay, 10 M.J. 269 (C.M.A. 1981) (collecting cases)), and when the certified issues are questions of fact. United States v. Moreno, 20 C.M.R. 104 (C.M.A. 1955). It is unclear whether the government's sole right to certify cases for review implicates the equal protection clause. An accused who wishes to raise the issue must meet applicable standing requirements. United States v. Schoof, 37 M.J. 96, 98 (C.M.A. 1993) ("Having not requested certification of any question of law by the Judge Advocate General, Schoof lacks standing to challenge application of Article 67(a)(2) on the grounds that it denies him equal opportunity with the Government to reach this Court. Additionally, since this Court granted review on the only issue raised by Schoof in his petition, any challenge to his inability to bring that issue to this Court via certification is moot;" as certified cases are mandatory appeals, the court should answer the certified question). *But see* United States v. Hickok, 45 M.J. 142 (C.A.A.F. 1996) (court did not answer the certified questions).

Probably in answer to *Schoof*, the Navy TJAG certified cases for defense, United States v. Sweet, 42 M.J. 183 (1995); United States v. Booker, 42 M.J. 267 (1995).

(Rel.3—1/07 Pub.62410)

In addition, the Court of Appeals exercises discretionary review over all cases reviewed by a Court of Criminal Appeals. It may grant review upon petition of the accused for good cause shown.[240] When a case is remanded, appellate jurisdiction is based on original sentence and not the consequences of any new sentence based upon a rehearing.[241] Virtually all of the court's cases are heard pursuant to this discretionary review.

The accused has sixty days to petition the Court of Appeals for a review of a Court of Criminal Appeals decision,[242] beginning on the earlier of either the date on which the accused is notified of the Court of Criminal Appeals decision or the date on which a copy of the Court of Criminal Appeals decision, after being served on appellate counsel of record for the accused, is deposited in the mail.[243] The Court of Appeals must act promptly in accordance with the rules of the Court once a petition is received.[244]

The court may not review questions of fact; rather, review in all cases is limited to questions of law[245] or mixed questions of law and fact.[246] The distinction between questions of law and of fact is nebulous, and questions that appear factual have been addressed by the court.[247] Moreover, the characterization of an issue as one of fact by a lower court does not preclude the Court of Appeals from determining whether issues of law actually are presented.[248]

The court may act only upon "the findings and sentence as approved by the convening authority and as affirmed or set aside" by a Court of Criminal Appeals.[249] The Court of Appeals ordinarily limits review to issues raised in

---

[240] U.C.M.J. art. 67(a)(3). If the Judge Advocate General directs a Court of Criminal Appeals to review an otherwise unreviewable case pursuant to his authority under Article 69, there may be no further review in the Court of Appeals. U.C.M.J. art. 69. Moreover, the court may review such cases if the Judge Advocate General so orders. U.C.M.J. art. 69.

[241] United States v. Johnson, 45 M.J. 88, 90 (C.A.A.F. 1996).

[242] U.C.M.J. art. 67(b). United States v. Byrd, 53 M.J. 35 (C.A.A.F. 2000). The accused is not entitled to petition the court while he is voluntarily absent without leave, nor may counsel do so on his or her behalf. United States v. Smith, 46 C.M.R. 247, 249 (C.M.A. 1973).

[243] U.C.M.J. art. 67(b).

[244] U.C.M.J. art. 67(b).

[245] U.C.M.J. art. 67(c); United States v. Nargi, 2 M.J. 96, 98 (C.M.A. 1977); see also United States v. Morris, 49 M.J. 227 (C.A.A.F. 1998) (distinguishing Nargi); S. Rep. No. 486, 81st Cong., 2d Sess. 29, reprinted in 1950 U.S. Code Cong. & Admin. News 2222, 2225.

[246] United States v. Lowry, 2 M.J. 55, 58 (C.M.A. 1976); see also United States v. Flagg, 29 C.M.R. 452, 456 (C.M.A. 1960).

[247] See, e.g., United States v. Brown, 3 M.J. 402 (C.M.A. 1977) (factual evidence was insufficient as a matter of law to support a finding of guilt beyond a reasonable doubt).

[248] United States v. Lowry, 2 M.J. 55 (C.M.A. 1976); United States v. Bunting, 19 C.M.R. 296 (C.M.A. 1955).

[249] U.C.M.J. art. 67(c). Rule 4 of the U.S. Court of Appeals Rules of Practice and Procedure

(Rel.3—1/07 Pub.62410)

the accused's petition for review[250] or assignment of errors,[251] the Judge Advocate General's certificate of review,[252] or the court's order granting review.[253]

The court cannot render advisory opinions or declaratory judgments, but must decide only those issues raised in the cases before it.[254]

Given reversible error, the Court of Appeals may set aside either the findings or sentence or both.[255] The court may not reassess a sentence, however.[256] Assuming that the court does not remand a case to the Court of Criminal Appeals for further consideration,[257] unless the evidence is insufficient to support the findings, the court must either set aside the lower court's decision and order a rehearing[258] or order that the charges be dismissed.[259] Even if the court either directs or permits a rehearing, the applicable convening authority may determine that a rehearing is impractical and dismiss the charges.[260]

§ 25-63.00   Issues Not Asserted Below

The Court of Appeals for the Armed Forces has not as yet fully resolved how to treat issues not addressed earlier in the appellate process and thus raised for the first time before the court.[261] In particular, the court has not decided whether

---

incorporates the scope of review detailed in Article 67(d), but expands the scope insofar as the court "may take action to grant extraordinary relief in aid." U.S. Court of Appeals Rules of Practice and Procedure; www.armfor.uscourts.gov/Rules.doc>.

[250] *See* U.S. Court of Appeals Rules of Practice and Procedure, 19(a), 21.

[251] *See* U.S. Court of Appeals Rules of Practice and Procedure, 19(c), 20 & 21.

[252] *See* U.S. Court of Appeals Rules of Practice and Procedure, 19(b) & 22.

[253] U.C.M.J. art. 67(c).

[254] *See* United States v. Thompson, 9 C.M.R. 90, 92 (C.M.A. 1953). The Judge Advocate General's ability to compel review in the Court of Military Appeals under Article 67(b)(2), however, may obligate the court to decide a raised or certified issue regardless of whether it is moot. United States v. Engle, 11 C.M.R. 41, 47–48 (C.M.A. 1953) (Brosman, J., concurring). 11 C.M.R. 47 (C.M.A. 1953) (Quinn, J., concurring) (indicating that the challenged issue was not moot because it actually was raised by the record).

[255] *See* U.C.M.J. art. 67(d).

[256] *See* United States v. Darville, 5 M.J. 1 (C.M.A. 1978). Although *Darville* addressed the sentencing authority of a Court of Military Review, the reasoning is equally applicable to the Court of Military Appeals.

[257] U.C.M.J. art. 67(d).

[258] U.C.M.J. art. 67(e).

[259] U.C.M.J. art. 67(e).

[260] U.C.M.J. art. 67(e).

[261] United States v. Washington, 43 M.J. 180 (C.A.A.F. 1996) (summary disposition) (denied motion to raise issue for first time); United States v. Smith, 41 M.J. 385 (C.A.A.F. 1995); United States v. Johnson, 42 M.J. 443 (C.A.A.F. 1995).

(Rel.3—1/07   Pub.62410)

such a situation should be viewed as waiver of the issue. Judge Crawford has observed:

> We have not addressed the question of waiver of an issue raised for the first time before this Court. . . . Absent a showing of good cause for failure to raise an issue or manifest injustice, this Court should not exercise its discretion to entertain an issue raised for the first time before this Court. . . .

The failure to invoke waiver absent such a showing prevents finality, taxes scarce resources, and encourages withholding of objections.[262]

§ 25-64.00   Abatement Due to Death of the Accused

From 1953 until Jul 1, 2003, the Court of Appeals for the Armed Forces followed a judicially created policy of "abatement ab initio" when the accused died after conviction but prior to completion of the right to direct appeal. Upon proof of death, the appellate court would enter an order in effect nullifying the entire trial. In *United States v. Rorie,*[263] however, the Court overruled its prior precedents and repudiated its doctrine. In its place, the Court declared:

> We therefore adopt the rule established by the U.S. Supreme Court in *Dove* [v. United States, 423 U.S. 325 (1976)] . . . When an appellant dies pending an Article 67(a)(3) appellate review by this Court, we will dismiss or deny the petition but will not abate the action ab initio. . . . In view of our conclusion that an appeal to the Courts of Criminal Appeals is an appeal of right, we leave to those courts or the Judge Advocates General to establish the parameters of a policy of abatement in the event that an appellant dies pending review at a Court of Criminal Appeals.[264]

§ 25-70.00   REVIEW BY THE SUPREME COURT

In 1983, Congress provided for the first time a direct route from the Court of Appeals to the Supreme Court.[265] Pursuant to Article 67a(a) of the Uniform Code, "Decisions of the Court of Appeals for the Armed Forces are subject to review by the Supreme Court by writ of certiorari."[266] The Supreme Court may not review, however, "any action of the Court of Appeals for the Armed Forces in refusing to grant a petition for review."[267] Accordingly, access to the Supreme

---

[262] Johnson, 42 M.J. at 447-48 (Crawford, J., concurring).

[263] 58 M.J. 399 (C.A.A.F. 2003).

[264] 58 M.J. at 407. The Court reserved comment on capital cases and appeals certified by the Judge Advocate Generals. As for a civilian perspective see State v. Korsen, 111 P.3d 130 (Idaho 2005) (abatement not required).

[265] *See generally* Section 26-11.00.

[266] "as provided in section 1259 of title 28."

[267] U.C.M.J. art. 67a(a). On cases granted and remanded, the court has adopted a grant and affirm policy to allow appeal to the Supreme Court. United States v. Wynn, 26 M.J. 405 (C.M.A. 1988).

(Rel.3—1/07   Pub.62410)

Court is still tightly controlled. Indeed, "in 1981, only seven percent of the cases filed with the Court of Military Appeals would have been authorized for potential review by the Supreme Court."[268]

Under the Code, a military accused may petition the Court without costs or fees[269] and is entitled to receive free military counsel.[270] When the Supreme Court takes a military case, the government would ordinarily be represented by the Solicitor General. However, military appellate counsel may represent the government "when requested to do so by the Attorney General."[271]

The first military case decided by the Supreme Court was *Solorio v. United States*,[272] which the Court used to overrule its prior jurisdictional decision in *O'Callahan v. Parker*.[273] *Solorio*, a watershed decision, is likely to be indicative of the Court's approach to military cases. As of the end of the 1998 Term of the Supreme Court, it has accepted eight cases.[274] Two of these ratified the foundations of the system and affirmed the process.[275] Two were brought by the Solicitor General who probably believed the opinions were unprecedented and too creative. His suspicions were confirmed without the Court deciding whether less stringent constitutional standards should apply to the military.[276]

It should be noted that because the Supreme Court's certiorari jurisdiction is limited only to cases actually decided by the Court of Military Appeals, cases not resolved by that court can receive civilian federal review only via collateral attack.[277]

---

[268] Matias v. United States, 19 Cl. Ct. 635, 641 (1990) (quoting Hearings on the Military Justice Act of 1982 (ultimately the Military Justice Act of 1983)).

[269] U.C.M.J. art. 67a(b).

[270] U.C.M.J. art. 70(c). Civilian counsel may be employed at no cost to the government. U.C.M.J. art. 70(d).

[271] U.C.M.J. art. 70(b).

[272] 483 U.S. 435 (1987).

[273] 395 U.S. 258 (1969).

[274] Clinton v. Goldsmith, 526 U.S. 529 (1999); United States v. Scheffer, 523 U.S. 303 (1998) (upholding per se rule of evidence excluding exculpatory polygraphs); Edmond v. United States, 520 U.S. 651 (1997) (held Secretary of Transportation could appoint civilian judges to Court of Criminal Appeals but found them inferior officers); Loving v. United States, 517 U.S. 748 (1996) (upheld first federal capital system death penalty); Ryder v. United States, 515 U.S. 177 (1995) (civilian judges of Coast Guard Court of Criminal Appeals not properly appointed); Davis v. United States, 512 U.S. 452 (1994) (*Edwards* not triggered unless unequivocal request for counsel — § 5-11.10); Weiss v. United States, 510 U.S. 163 (1994); Solorio v. United States, 483 U.S. 435 (1987).

[275] Weiss v. United States, 510 U.S. 163 (1994); Solorio v. United States, 483 U.S. 435 (1987).

[276] *See* § 1-52.00.

[277] *See generally* Chapter 26.

(Rel.3—1/07 Pub.62410)

§ 25-80.00   INTERLOCUTORY GOVERNMENT APPEALS

§ 25-81.00   In General

In the absence of statute, the prosecution lacks the right to appeal.[278] As the Supreme Court noted in *United States v. Sanges*, it was "settled by an overwhelming weight of American authority, that the State has no right to sue out a writ of error upon a judgment in favor of the defendant in a criminal case, except under and in accordance with express statutes."[279] When the Uniform Code was first enacted, Congress included Article 62(a):

> If a specification before a court-martial has been dismissed on motion and the ruling does not amount to a finding of not guilty, the convening authority may return the record to the court for reconsideration of the ruling and any further appropriate action.

The reference to "reconsideration" proved troublesome, but was ultimately interpreted literally; the court had to reconsider, but could adhere to the earlier ruling.[280] Accordingly, no government appeal was possible absent the unlikely possibility of extraordinary relief.[281]

Via the Military Justice Act of 1983, Congress amended Article 62[282] to parallel 18 U.S.C. § 3731[283] and permit some government appeals:

---

[278] United States v. Schloz, 19 M.J. 837, 840 (N.M.C.M.R. 1984) (citing United States v. Sisson, 399 U.S. 267 (1970)).

[279] 144 U.S. 310, 312 (1892) (the rationale being that the defendant was harassed with the same charge unless there was statutory authorization). *See also* Arizona v. Manypenny, 451 U.S. 232 (1981). Nor should the accused be faced with the anxiety, cost of civilian litigation, or loss freedom because of pretrial confinement, as the *Manual* contains no bail provision or separate release procedure.

United States v. Mosley, 42 M.J. 300 (C.A.A.F. 1995) (When judge granted right to expert even though not applying correct test, the court seemed to hold judge's ruling could not be reversed even though there had been no compliance with the discovery rules.). Some would argue that United States v. Manuel, 43 M.J. 282 (C.A.A.F. 1995), shows deference to the Court of Criminal Appeals, but this viewpoint overlooks two cases at the end of the 1994 Term, United States v. Sztuka, 43 M.J. 261 (C.A.A.F. 1995) and United States v. Fisiorek, 43 M.J. 244 (C.A.A.F. 1995), and maybe United States v. Mosley, 42 M.J. 300 (C.A.A.F. 1995).

[280] United States v. Ware, 1 M.J. 282 (C.M.A. 1976).

[281] R.C.M. 908 Analysis.

[282] Military Justice Act of 1983, Pub. L. No. 98-209, § 5(c)(1), 97 Stat. 1393, 1398 (1983).

[283] Section 3731, Title 18, of the United States Code provides for appeals from a "judgment, or order of a district court dismissing an indictment or information as to any one or more counts." It also permits appeal from an "order . . . suppressing or excluding evidence. . . ." Section 3731 has been read as intending "to remove all statutory barriers to Government appeals whenever the Constitution would permit." United States v. Wilson, 420 U.S. 332, 337 (1975). Section 3731 was not adopted verbatim; the amendment attempts to resolve some matters left open by the civilian statute.

(Rel.3—1/07 Pub.62410)

In a trial by court-martial in which a military judge presides and in which a punitive discharge may be adjudged, the United States may appeal an order or ruling of the military judge which terminates the proceedings with respect to a charge or specification [or] . . . which excludes evidence that is substantial proof of a fact material in the proceeding. [However, the United States may not appeal an order or ruling that is, or] that amounts to, a finding of not guilty with respect to the charge or specification. [284]

Article 62 does not require the government to appeal every permissible ruling. That would "disrupt trial dockets and could interfere with military operations and other activities, and would impose a heavy burden on" the appellate system. [285]

Although § 3731 provides that "no appeal shall lie where the double jeopardy clause" [286] prohibits further prosecution, Article 62 prohibits an appeal from a ruling that is the equivalent of a finding of not guilty, [287] a test less demanding for the government. Thus, under Article 62 the empaneling of the court and presentation of evidence would not bar a government appeal. [288] It is critical to note that the mere fact that jeopardy has attached to a proceeding does not prohibit government appeal of a ruling; it merely prohibits a new trial on those issues following "termination" of the first trial. If the judge's ruling at trial does not terminate the proceedings in a fashion constitutionally analogous to an acquittal, appeal is constitutionally permissible.

§ 25-82.00   Appealable Orders

§ 25-82.10   In General

Assuming that a case is serious enough to potentially permit a government appeal, [289] appeal requires a ruling that terminates the proceeding as to a specification [290] or that excludes evidence [291] "that is substantial proof of a fact

---

[284] U.C.M.J. art. 62(a)(1). *See also* R.C.M. 908. Note that a ruling of the president of a court-martial without a military judge is not appealable. R.C.M. 908(d).

[285] R.C.M. 908 Analysis, MCM, 2005, A21-57.

[286] 18 U.S.C. § 3731.

[287] *See* United States v. McShane, 28 M.J. 1036 (A.F.C.M.R. 1989) (dismissal of charge by judge prior to plea, assembly of members, and presentation of evidence was not equivalent to a finding of not guilty). The trial judge's characterization of his own action is not determinative for Article 62 jurisdiction purposes. United States v. Brooks, 41 M.J. 792, 795 (A. Crim. App. 1995) (judge's "acquittal" following conviction by members did not function as a finding of not guilty for Article purposes), *rev'd*, 42 M.J. 484 (C.A.A.F. 1995).

[288] United States v. Poduszczak, 20 M.J. 627 (A.C.M.R. 1985).

[289] *I.e.*, there is a possibility of a punitive discharge being adjudged. U.C.M.J. art. 62(a); United States v. Wilson, 20 M.J. 335 (C.M.A. 1985).

[290] Or the "functional equivalent" of a ruling that terminates the proceedings. United States v. True, 28 M.J. 1, 2 (C.M.A. 1989) (abatement order). *See also* United States v. Eiland, 39 M.J. 566

(Rel.3—1/07 Pub.62410)

material in the proceeding."[292]

Although dismissal motions[293] are clearly appealable, there is no hard and fast rule for determining what constitutes "substantial proof" of a "material fact." Initially, "material" is normally used in two alternative meanings: either "important" or "critical" to proof of a case or related to that case.[294] If "material" is used in this latter meaning, the government's threshold is far less demanding than it would be in the case of the former. Perhaps more important is the degree to which the appellate court must determine whether evidence constitutes "substantial proof of a fact material in the proceeding."

In 1987, the Navy-Marine Corps Court of Military Review opined:

> We are not persuaded by the Respondent's argument that the evidence was cumulative. In an interlocutory appeal, it is beyond the scope of this Court to speculate as to what weight or importance a particular piece of evidence might have at trial. It is sufficient that the petitioner believes that the evidence is significant enough to seek reversal of a military judge's exclusionary ruling rather than continue at trial with whatever other evidence that might be available.[295]

Taken literally, the court has assumed too much. Although it is surely appropriate for the Court of Military Review to give deference to the party whose case is affected, the statute creates a standard that the court must implement. At the very least, the evidence ought to be such that a reasonable person could consider it "substantial proof."

(N.M.C.M.R. 1993) (same); United States v. Brooks, 42 M.J. 484 (C.A.A.F. 1995) (found judge's ruling to be appealable).

[291] A ruling that affects the burden of proof rather than excluding evidence is not appealable under Article 62. United States v. Mahoney, 24 M.J. 911, 913 (A.F.C.M.R. 1987).

[292] R.C.M. 908. United States v. True, 28 M.J. 1 (C.M.A. 1989) (judge's order abating the proceeding because the government would not fund expert investigator; conditional nature of order did not prevent appeal); United States v. Hamilton, 36 M.J. 927, 928 (A.F.C.M.R. 1993) (granted in limine motion to deny admission of key witness deposition subject to Article 62 appeal); United States v. Mahoney, 24 M.J. 911 (A.F.C.M.R. 1987) (judge's holding that switching the burden of proof was ex post facto was not appealable); United States v. Harrison, 23 M.J. 907 (N.M.C.M.R. 1987) (ruling that pretrial advice did not state legal conclusion was appealable). *See also* United States v. LeCompte, 131 F.3d 767 (8th Cir. 1997) (government successfully appealed decision by trial judge to exclude under Fed. R. Evid. 403 evidence offered by the government under Fed. R. Evid. 414); United States v. Gibson, 39 M.J. 319, 323, n. 4 (C.M.A. 1994) (dictum that trial judge's ruling that inconsistent statement was inadmissible was appealable).

[293] *See generally* Section 18-20.00.

[294] "[T]hat is of consequence to the determination of the action." Fed. R. Evid. 401; Mil. R. Evid. 401. To be potentially admissible, evidence must not only be logically relevant (i.e., tend to prove or disprove the fact the evidence concerns) but that *fact* must be related to the case; in common-law terminology, the fact must be *material*.

[295] United States v. Scholz, 19 M.J. 837, 841 (N.M.C.M.R. 1984).

(Rel.3—1/07 Pub.62410)

§ 25-82.20   Specific Types of Orders

When a party fails to comply with an applicable disclosure or discovery provision,[296] the trial judge has wide discretion to remedy the dereliction. The Court of Military Appeals has observed, for example, in the related area of destruction or loss of apparently exculpatory evidence that:

> Some suggested remedial actions include exclusion of inculpatory evidence; requiring the Government to stipulate as to the facts and circumstances surrounding the loss or destruction . . . or the condition of the evidence; or even dismissal of charges or specifications.[297]

Under normal circumstances, a judge's action *vis-à-vis* a discovery or disclosure matter will not be appealable under Article 62. However, it is clear that a judge could take action explicitly dismissing a charge or specification or which would have the same pragmatic effect. In such a case, appeal should lie as it should for a suppression order excluding evidence that would be "substantial proof" of a material fact.

A decision to suppress evidence that has the consequence of making prosecution of a given specification impossible, as by suppressing all relevant evidence, is clearly appealable, as would be an order suppressing "evidence that is substantial proof of a fact material in the proceeding,"[298] a far more permissive test, as the usual suppression motion does not terminate a prosecution. There is no requirement that the prosecution certify that the suppression order will eliminate a reasonable possibility of a successful prosecution.

Similarly, a granted defense motion in limine may be appealed if the evidence is "substantial proof" of a "material" fact.

Failure to grant a continuance,[299] review of release from confinement, ordering a new Article 32 investigation,[300] or exclusion of parties or witnesses are generally not appealable under Article 62.

§ 25-83.00   Scope of Review

In Article 62 cases, the Courts of Criminal Appeals act as ordinary appellate courts without their unique fact-finding powers.[301] Consequently, they must

---

[296] *See generally* Chapter 11.

[297] United States v. Kern, 22 M.J. 49, 52 (C.M.A. 1986).

[298] United States v. Poduszczak, 20 M.J. 627 (A.C.M.R. 1985) (judge erred in ruling that the accused's confession was sufficiently corroborated); United States v. Scholz, 19 M.J. 837 (N.M.C.M.R. 1984) (excluding urinalysis test was appealable under R.C.M. 908).

[299] United States v. Browers, 20 M.J. 356, 359 (C.M.A. 1985).

[300] United States v. Penn, 21 M.J. 907 (N.M.C.M.R. 1986).

[301] U.C.M.J. art. 62(b).

(Rel.3—1/07   Pub.62410)

review cases solely for legal error below[302] and are ordinarily bound by the trial judge's findings of fact unless they are clearly erroneous.[303] "Nonetheless, in entering a finding of fact, the military judge must rely on evidence of record which fairly supports that finding; in the absence of *any* such evidence, the finding is error as a matter of law."[304] The courts may make a *de novo* ad hoc judgment on the meaning of relevant facts when dealing with constitutional issues.[305] Similarly, the appellate courts normally should have the power to reverse when the trial judge misunderstood the legal significance of a fact found by the judge when that misunderstanding causes an error as to the court's ultimate finding.[306]

§ 25-84.00   Procedure

Procedurally:

An appeal of an order or ruling may not be taken unless the trial counsel provides the military judge with written notice of appeal from the order or ruling within 72 hours of the order or ruling. Such notice shall include a certification by the trial counsel that the appeal is not taken for the purpose of delay and (if the order or ruling appealed is one which excludes evidence) that the evidence excluded is substantial proof of a fact material in the proceeding.[307]

---

[302] Of course, at some point factual error becomes legal error, and the line between the two may be hard to define. *See* Bose Corp. v. Consumers Union of the United States, Inc., 466 U.S. 485, 501 (1984).

[303] *See, e.g.*, United States v. Gore, 60 M.J. 178, 185 (C.A.A.F. 2004); United States v. Pollard, 27 M.J. 376 (C.M.A. 1989) (affirming the Court of Military Review's reversal of the trial judge's ruling and remanding the case to determine if the technical violations rendered accused's urinalysis unreliable as a matter of fact); United States v. Horton, 25 M.J. 388 (C.M.A. 1987) (affirming the Army Court of Military Review and the trial judge in excluding evidence based essentially on the fact the urinalysis test was not directly observed); United States v. Wood, 25 M.J. 46 (C.M.A. 1987) (probable cause is legal, not factual, conclusion); United States v. Wilson, 23 M.J. 899 (A.C.M.R. 1987) (judge was clearly erroneous when he ruled, as a matter of law, that the contemplation of disciplinary procedure by the commander ordering the testing converted the examination into an illegal inspection); United States v. Burris, 21 M.J. 140. (C.M.A. 1985) and the cases cited therein.

[304] United States v. Bradford, 25 M.J. 181, 184 (C.M.A. 1987) (emphasis in original) (citing United States v. Burris, 21 M.J. 140, 144 (C.M.A. 1985)). *But see* United States v. Sztuka, 43 M.J. 261 (C.A.A.F. 1995) (Crawford, J., dissenting) ("Without any explanation, the majority rejects the findings of fact by the trial judge and the court below and casts aside the standard or review enunciated and followed by this court for years.").

[305] United States v. Abell, 23 M.J. 99, 102–03 (C.M.A. 1986). *Cf.* United States v. Payne, 47 M.J. 37 (C.A.A.F. 1997).

[306] United States v. Shakur, 817 F.2d 189 (2d Cir. 1987).

[307] U.C.M.J. art. 62(a)(2).

Absent a request for a delay, failure to file within seventy-two hours constitutes waiver.[308] The trial counsel, however, may request a delay for no more than seventy-two hours to determine whether to make an appeal under Article 62 and Rule for Courts-Martial 908.[309] This delay applies to matters affected by the ruling when the trial counsel provides the military judge with notice of intent to appeal,[310] which identifies the issue to be appealed and certifies that the appeal is not taken for the purpose of delay.[311]

Pursuant to Rule 21(d)(1) of the Courts of Criminal Appeals Rules of Practice and Procedure, implementing Rule for Courts-Martial 908(b)(6), the appealing trial counsel "shall have 20 days from the date written notice to appeal is filed . . . to forward [the appeal]. . . ." to the government's representative. That requirement has been construed as requiring forwarding within twenty days; not *receipt* in twenty days;[312] otherwise, the appeal is untimely and absent good cause for delay the appeal will be dismissed.[313] Once the government's representative has received the appeal, however, that person "shall promptly decide whether to file the appeal. . . ."[314] Under Court Rule 21, the representative must promptly file the record of trial with the Court of Criminal Appeals, and the appeal must be filed within twenty days from the filing of the record of trial unless a delay is authorized for good cause. In *United States v. Pearson*,[315] the court held that Court Rule 21(d) requires that the original record of trial be filed with the Court of Military Review promptly and that "promptly" normally means "within 1 working day of receipt by the representative, unless circumstances make it impracticable in which case the record must be filed as soon thereafter as is practical." The court further held "that the delay in filing of the trial record is not justified by the representative's evaluation process, a matter relevant only to the decision to file or abort an appeal."[316]

Unless the appeal is frivolous, the "time involved in processing an interlocutory government appeal of a ruling by the military judge" is not included in determining the government's speedy-trial accountability.[317]

---

[308] United States v. Mayer, 21 M.J. 504 (A.F.C.M.R. 1985) (failure to file in 72 hours fatal). United States v. Flores-Galarza, 40 M.J. 900, 905 (N.M.C.M.R. 1994) (The 72-hour limit for serving written notice of an Article 62/R.C.M. 908 appeal cannot be extended by the trial judge and is jurisdictional).

[309] R.C.M. 908(b)(1).

[310] R.C.M. 908(b)(3).

[311] R.C.M. 908(b)(3).

[312] United States v. Bolado, 34 M.J. 732, 735 (N.M.C.M.R. 1991).

[313] United States v. Combs, 38 M.J. 741, 743 (A.F.C.M.R. 1993).

[314] R.C.M. 908(b)(6).

[315] 33 M.J. 777, 780 (N.M.C.M.R. 1991).

[316] 33 M.J. 777, 780 (N.M.C.M.R. 1991).

[317] R.C.M. 707(c)(1)(D)&(E); United States v. Ramsey, 28 M.J. 370, 371, 373 (C.M.A. 1989).

Once written notice of appeal is served, the court-martial may not proceed on the affected charges or specifications, pending disposition by the Court of Criminal Appeals.[318] As to unaffected specifications:

(A) Motions may be litigated, in the discretion of the military judge, at any point in the proceedings;

(B) When trial on the merits has not begun.

(i) a severance may be granted upon request of all the parties;

(ii) a severance may be granted upon request of the accused and when appropriate under R.C.M. 906(b)(10); or

(C) When trial on the merits has begun but has not been completed, a party may, on that party's request and in the discretion of the military judge, present further evidence on the merits.[319]

Once an appeal has been noticed, the record must be transcribed in a verbatim fashion[320] and forwarded to a government representative of the Judge Advocate General who "shall promptly decide whether to file the appeal with the Court of Criminal Appeals and notify the trial counsel of that decision."[321]

On appeal the parties are customarily represented by appellate military counsel,[322] although any civilian attorney retained by the accused may appear. An Article 62 appeal must be prosecuted expeditiously and is afforded priority in the Courts of Criminal Appeals.[323] When a case is appealed to the Court of Criminal Appeals, the ruling or order which is the subject of the appeal is automatically stayed.[324] In hearing a government appeal under the Article, the Court of Military Review "may act only with respect to matters of law";[325] the court does not have its usual power to find facts. Further appeal to the Court of Appeals is possible on petition of the accused or by certification by the Judge Advocate General.[326]

---

[318] R.C.M. 908(b)(4).

[319] R.C.M. 908(b)(4).

[320] R.C.M. 908(b)(5).

[321] R.C.M. 908(b)(6). "The matter forwarded shall include: a statement of the issues appealed; the record of the proceedings or, if preparation of the record has not been completed, a summary of the evidence; and such other matters as the Secretary concerned may prescribe." R.C.M. 908(b)(6).

[322] R.C.M. 908(c)(1).

[323] U.C.M.J. art. 62(a)(3), (b).

[324] R.C.M. 908(b)(4).

[325] U.C.M.J. art. 62(b).

[326] After the Court of Criminal Appeals has decided any appeal under Article 62, the accused may petition for review by the Court of Appeals for the Armed Forces, or the Judge Advocate General may certify a question to the Court of Appeals for the Armed Forces. The parties shall be notified of the decision of the Court of Criminal Appeals promptly. If the decision is adverse

(Rel.3—1/07 Pub.62410)

§ 25-90.00   EXTRAORDINARY WRITS

§ 25-91.00   In General

In the most general terms it can be said that, among their other powers, courts hold the power to compel subordinate courts and officers to comply with the law, to safeguard their jurisdiction, and to ensure that persons held in custody in the jurisdiction are held lawfully. [327] Because courts ordinarily do not reach beyond their ordinary function of case-disposition, court orders in these areas are known as *extraordinary writs*. Perhaps the best-known extraordinary writ is the "great writ" — the writ of *habeas corpus* — by which an imprisoned individual may test the legality of his or her custody and thence the legality of an underlying conviction. [328] An order that prohibits the commission of an act is a writ of *prohibition*, while an order to an inferior court or officer to comply with the law is a writ of *mandamus*:

> The writ of mandamus is a command issued from a court of competent jurisdiction to an inferior court or officer, requiring the performance of a specified act which the court or officer has a legal duty to do. Mandamus is an extraordinary writ, issuable only where there is no other complete and adequate remedy. The writ is available to compel both the performance of a ministerial duty and the exercise of judicial discretion. The office of

---

to the accused, the accused shall be notified of the decision and of the right to petition the Court of Appeals for the Armed Forces for review within 60 days orally on the record at the court-martial or in accordance with R.C.M. 1203(d). If the accused is notified orally on the record, trial counsel shall forward by expeditious means a certificate that the accused was so notified to the Judge Advocate General, who shall forward by expeditious means a certificate that the accused was so notified to the Judge Advocate General, who shall forward a copy to the clerk of the Court of Appeals for the Armed Forces when required by the Court. If the decision by the Court of Criminal Appeals permits it, the court-martial may proceed as to the affected charges and specifications pending further review by the Court of Appeals for the Armed Forces or the Supreme Court, unless either court orders the proceedings stayed. Unless the case is reviewed by the Court of Appeals for the Armed Forces, it shall be returned to the military judge or the convening authority for appropriate action in accordance with the decision of the Court of Criminal Appeals. If the case is reviewed by the Court of Appeals for the Armed Forces, R.C.M. 1204 and 1205 shall apply. R.C.M. 908(c)(3).

While there is an automatic stay while the case is on appeal to the Court of Criminal Appeals, there is no automatic stay while a decision is appealed to the Court of Appeals. R.C.M. 908(a)(4).

[327] Courts hold other powers as well. At common law, the writ of coram nobis, for example, allowed a court to review a conviction it had adjudged when the defendant asserted a unknown factual error that affected the conviction. In Tillman v. United States, 32 M.J. 962 (A.C.M.R. 1991), the court granted post-appeal *coram nobis* to an accused who asserted that ineffective assistance of appellate counsel had "deprived him of a proper review . . . of a fine-enforcement provision improperly approved by the convening authority." 32 M.J. at 963 (A.C.M.R. 1991). *See also* Garrett v. Lowe, 39 M.J. 293 (C.M.A. 1994) (scope of *coram nobis*).

[328] *See generally* Section 26-30.00.

(Rel.3—1/07   Pub.62410)

mandamus is not to establish a right, but to enforce a clear and complete right already established.

The use of mandamus in aid of appellate jurisdiction has primarily been to confine an inferior court to a lawful exercise of its prescribed jurisdiction, or to compel it to act when it has a duty to act.[329]

Mandamus is not to be used as a substitute for an appeal, whether interlocutory or "ordinary."[330]

Civilian courts ordinarily hold the authority to issue extraordinary writs, either via inherent authority by virtue of their very existence or by statute, or by both. In addition to any common-law authority they may have, the civilian federal courts have been granted extraordinary-writ authority by the All-Writs Act:

The Supreme Court and all courts established by an act of Congress may issue all writs necessary or appropriate in aid of their respective jurisdictions and agreeable to the usages and principles of law.[331]

The authority of military courts to issue extraordinary writs has long been controversial. Unlike most civilian courts, military courts are not common-law courts, have extremely limited jurisdiction, and, insofar as federal courts are concerned, are not Article III courts. Accordingly, it is unlikely that they can be said to have "inherent power" to issue extraordinary relief.[332] Insofar as the All-Writs Act is concerned, although the Courts of Criminal Appeals and Court of Appeals are literally "courts established by an act of Congress," courts-martial proper may not be. Notwithstanding that Congress has established the legal framework by which courts-martial are called into existence and dispose of cases, they are not courts of continuing jurisdiction and were not individually created

---

[329] Rankin, *The All Writs Act and the Military Judicial System*, 53 Mil. L. Rev. 103, 105–06 (1971) (footnotes omitted). Relief, however named, lies if a jurisdiction defect is shown. Nkosi v. Loew, 38 M.J. 552, 553 (A.F.C.M.R. 1993) (denying relief).

[330] Kerr v. United States District Court, 426 U.S. 394 (1976); Will v. United States, 389 U.S. 90 (1967). However, prior to the 1983 amendment to Article 62 (*see* Section 25-81.00), the government used the All-Writs Act as a means of interim government appeals. *See, e.g.*, Dettinger v. United States, 7 M.J. 216 (C.M.A. 1979). *See also* Coffey v. Commanding Officer, USS Charleston 33 M.J. 938, 939 (N.M.C.M.R. 1991) (extraordinary relief denied to accused seeking to prohibit vacation of prior punishment suspension; Article 69 provides sufficient relief). In Pascascio v. Fischer, 34 M.J. 996, 1000–02 (A.C.M.R. 1992), the court held that a writ of mandamus, the functional military equivalent to an interlocutory appeal, doesn't apply ordinarily for a speedy trial motion denial; extraordinary relief may be proper for cases involving a motion denial that "constitutes a usurpation of judicial power or amounts to a recurring legal error. . . ."

[331] 18 U.S.C. § 1651(a).

[332] *Cf.* United States v. Murphy, 50 M.J. 4, 5 (C.A.A.F. 1998) ("Unlike the practice in the United States Courts of Appeal and District Courts, neither the UCMJ nor the Manual for Courts-Martial . . . provides procedures for collateral, post-conviction attacks on guilty verdicts. . . . Nevertheless, we have relied upon a variety of [non-extraordinary writ] procedures to ensure that a military accused's rights are fully protected.")

(Rel.3—1/07   Pub.62410)

by Congress. Although courts-martial fit the "plain meaning" of the All-Writs Act, if one leaves the text at all for interpretative purposes, the determinative fact may be that the Senate does not advise and consent in the appointment of military judges. Such an approach would be difficult, however, as Congress also has no voice in the appointment of the judges of the Courts of Criminal Appeals. One may be left with the conclusion that either both courts-martial military judges and the Courts of Criminal Appeals have all-writs authority or neither.

The ability of military courts to issue extraordinary writs is not an academic matter; rather, it is a fundamental question of power. Adherents of command control of the military judicial system reject the power of military courts, most especially local military judges, to issue orders to general and flag officers, the Secretary of Defense and the President.[333] Additionally, there are those who fear that extraordinary writs would be the tool used by the military courts to extend their jurisdiction into areas not expressly authorized by Congress,[334] most notably administrative personnel matters. This is not an unrealistic concern. In *United States v. Biagase*,[335] in what may be an unprecedented action the *military judge*, faced with a command influence concern, removed the unit's "first sergeant from the rating chain of any witness who testified, requiring justification for any downward movement in the witnesses' ratings . . . ."[336]

The Supreme Court,[337] the Court of Appeals for the Armed Forces,[338] and the *Manual for Courts-Martial*[339] recognize the authority of the military *appellate* courts to issue extraordinary writs under the All-Writs Act. Analysis of the power of military courts to issue extraordinary relief requires, at a minimum, analysis of the All-Writs Act's requirements that courts issue writs only when "necessary or appropriate in aid of their respective jurisdictions and agreeable to the usages and principles of law."

---

[333] Clinton v. Goldsmith, 526 U.S. 529 (1999) (Court of Appeals lacked jurisdiction under All Writs act to enjoin executive branch officials from dropping convicted servicemember from the rolls).

[334] *See, e.g.*, Keys v. Cole, 31 M.J. 228 (C.M.A. 1990) (preferring not to exercise jurisdiction even if it has it, court, in declining to grant relief in back-pay matter, discusses (at 234) extent to which courts might reach the issue as incident to confinement). *But see* United States v. Ouimette, 52 M.J. 691 (C.G. Crim. App. 2000) (dictum that court has jurisdiction as to the conditions of post-trial confinement).

[335] 50 M.J. 143 (C.A.A.F. 1999).

[336] 50 M.J. at 152. The Court noted the trial judge's actions with apparent approval.

[337] Clinton v. Goldsmith, 526 U.S. 529 (1999); Noyd v. Bond, 395 U.S. 683 (1969).

[338] United States v. Frischolz, 36 C.M.R. 306 (C.M.A. 1966).

[339] R.C.M. 1204(a) Discussion.

(Rel.3—1/07 Pub.62410)

§ 25-92.00   Relief in Aid of Jurisdiction

The actual jurisdiction of the military appellate courts are set forth in Articles 66, 67, and 69 of the Uniform Code.[340] Grant of extraordinary relief is not limited to actual jurisdiction, but extends at least to the potential jurisdictions of the courts.[341] A case is potentially within the jurisdiction of the appellate courts when the Uniform Code permits the Court of Criminal Appeals to hear the case. Because appellate jurisdiction depends upon both the trial forum and the offense with which an accused is charged, until a case is actually referred to a court-martial, it is unclear whether a case is within the potential jurisdiction of the appellate courts, even if an accused has been charged with a serious offense for which conviction ordinarily would merit appellate review.

The role of the Court of Appeals in supervising military justice in the armed forces has been a matter of considerable interest and great controversy. If the court has supervisory power, as it has claimed, it may greatly extend its reach via extraordinary relief. Potentially every act connected with a criminal offense under the Uniform Code would be under the court's hand.[342] It is, for example, unclear whether nonjudicial punishment ought to be subject to the court's

---

[340] See Section 25-52.00 above.

[341] United States v. Snyder, 40 C.M.R. 192 (C.M.A. 1969). What constitutes "relief in aid of jurisdiction" may be subject to debate. Compare United States v. Lemoine, 34 M.J. 1120 (A.F.C.M.R. 1992) (dictum that mandamus would not be in aid of jurisdiction where convicted Air National Guard officer requested relief from excess leave status, see § 25-13.20) with Lemoine v. Baker, 36 M.J. 86 (C.M.A. 1992) (granting relief in same case). See also Parker v. United States, 60 M.J. 446 (C.A.A.F.) (Crawford, J. concurring in part and dissenting in part: request for appointment of an expert to determine whether the accused is mentally retarded for purposes of the death penalty while case is pending before the Court of Criminal Appeals is "in aid of jurisdiction" but not "agreeable to the usages and principles of law."), order granted, 61 M.J. 63 (C.A.A.F. 2005).

[342] Virtually every aspect of military life is governed by the Uniform Code. Should the Court of Military Appeals have power to ensure that every act incidental to punitive discipline is done correctly, the court's power would be great indeed. Cf. Clinton v. Goldsmith, 526 U.S. 529, 534 n.6 (1999) (Court seemed to chastise the Court of Appeals. "One judge was even more emphatic [as to extensive jurisdiction of the Court of Appeals]: We should use our broad jurisdiction under the [UCMJ] to correct injustices like this and we need not wait for another court to perhaps act. . . . Our Court has the responsibility of protecting the rights of all servicemembers in court-martial matters."). As to the Court's view of its jurisdictional ambit, see United States v. White, 54 M.J. 469, 472 (C.A.A.F. 2001) (court has jurisdiction "to determine if certain punishments violate the Eighth Amendment or Article 55"); United States v. King, 53 M.J. 425 (C.A.A.F. 2000) (notwithstanding Goldsmith court took jurisdiction when total failure of right to counsel at Article 32 investigation could not be remedied by appellate review except for ordering a new trial); United States v. Ouimette, 52 M.J. 691 (C.G. Crim. App. 2000) (court has jurisdiction as to the conditions of post-trial confinement that is being served—distinguishing dropping from the roles as in Goldsmith).

(Rel.3—1/07 Pub.62410)

supervision.[343] By definition, offenses subject to nonjudicial punishment under Article 15 should be "minor." Yet, they may be sufficiently serious enough to permit trial by court-martial and a punitive discharge. Further, the Navy, on at least two occasions, has used nonjudicial punishment ("mast") to punish individuals who could not be successfully prosecuted by court-martial because of the exclusionary rule.[344] Surely, such behavior ought to be subject to supervisory power if the Court of Appeals has any.[345]

In the 1970s, the court sought to exercise its power indirectly to supervise nonjudicial punishment and summary courts-martial. In *McPhail v. United States*,[346] the court granted extraordinary relief in a case that was subject to review only by the service Judge Advocate General[347] and not directly reviewable by the appellate courts. Although the court recognized that there were limits to its authority, it held that "as to matters reasonably comprehended within the provisions of the Uniform Code of Military Justice, we have jurisdiction to require compliance with applicable law from all courts and persons purporting to act under its authority."[348] Although its author has since "recanted" and disavowed this language,[349] the court has indicated that *McPhail* retains its vitality.[350] Dealing with the trial by special court-martial[351] of an officer, the court noted that *McPhail* had never been overruled and that "on no occasion has Congress indicated any dissatisfaction with the scope of our All-Writs-Act supervisory jurisdiction, as we had explained it in *McPhail*."[352] The court then concluded that it had jurisdiction to grant extraordinary relief if the petitioner's trial "violates her constitutional rights," stating: "Congress never intended that this Court sit by helplessly while courts-martial are misused in disregard of an accused servicemember's rights under the Constitution or the Uniform Code."[353]

---

[343] *Contra* United States v. Edwards, 46 M.J. 41, 43 (C.A.A.F. 1997) ("The jurisdiction of our Court does not extend to direct review of nonjudicial punishment proceedings."); Dukes v. Smith, 34 M.J. 803 (N.M.C.M.R. 1992) (en banc) (no supervisory power over Article 15 punishment).

[344] Jones v. Commander, 18 M.J. 198 (C.M.A. 1984); Dobzynski v. Green, 16 M.J. 84 (C.M.A. 1983).

[345] Fletcher v. Covington, 42 M.J. 116 (C.A.A.F. 1995).

[346] 1 M.J. 457 (C.M.A. 1976).

[347] McPhail v. United States, 1 M.J. 457 (C.M.A. 1976).

[348] 1 M.J. at 463 (C.M.A. 1976).

[349] Stewart v. Stevens, 5 M.J. 220, 221 (C.M.A. 1978) (Cook, J., concurring).

[350] Unger v. Ziemniak, 27 M.J. 349 (C.M.A. 1989).

[351] A case not reviewable by the appellate courts. 27 M.J. at 351 (C.M.A. 1989).

[352] 27 M.J. at 353 (C.M.A. 1989).

[353] 27 M.J. at 355 (C.M.A. 1989). As the court then chose not to grant relief technically its decision is dictum.

(Rel.3—1/07   Pub.62410)

That language, and more,[354] indicates that the court is prepared to adopt a very substantial supervisory jurisdiction.[355]

> We are convinced that, from the outset, Congress has never intended to allow evasion of the safeguards provided to servicemembers by the Constitution and the Uniform Code. If, however, this Court lacked jurisdiction to grant extraordinary relief in cases like this, it would be easy to bypass those safeguards. Instead of separating servicemembers pursuant to punitive discharges adjudged by courts-martial — in which event, the accused might seek judicial review by the Court of Military Review, this Court, and the Supreme Court — a two-step process could be used which avoided judicial review within the military justice system. The servicemember could initially be tried and convicted by court-martial in a proceeding in which no discharge was adjudged or, if adjudged, was not "approved." Thus, no review under Articles 66(b) and 67(b) would be available. In turn, the court-martial conviction could be the basis for some type of administrative separation.
>
> For example, if Lieutenant Unger is convicted by special court-martial, it seems probable that her career as a commissioned officer in the Navy will soon end — even though the special court-martial has not sentenced her, and could . . . not sentence her, to a dismissal. Admittedly, her naval service would not end under the same conditions of stigma as if she were sentenced to dismissal. However, as a foreseeable result of the court-martial conviction, she would lose many of the benefits of her training at the Naval Academy and her 8 years of military service.
>
> If, as Lieutenant Unger claims, her trial by court-martial violates her constitutional rights, we are convinced that we have jurisdiction to grant extraordinary relief. Congress never intended that this Court sit by helplessly while courts-martial are misused in disregard of an accused servicemember's rights under the Constitution or the Uniform Code. Accordingly, under the circumstances of this case, we are convinced that we have jurisdiction to grant extraordinary relief.

27 M.J. at 355 (C.M.A. 1989).

[355] Goldsmith v. Clinton, 48 M.J. 84 (C.A.A.F. 1998) (jurisdiction over whether servicemember may be dropped from the roles), rev'd, 526 U.S. 529 (1999); United States v. Miller, 46 M.J. 248 (C.A.A.F. 1997) (court suggested that person may seek extraordinary relief for violation of religious rights while in jail); United States v. Curtin, 44 M.J. 439 (C.A.A.F. 1996) (third party may challenge subpoena under the Right to Financial Privacy Act, 12 U.S.C. § 3410); Carlson & Ryan-Jones v. Smith, 43 M.J. 402 (C.A.A.F. 1995) (ordered in camera inspection of records pertaining to victims in on-going special court-martial of officer); Gray v. Mahoney, 39 M.J. 299 (C.M.A. 1994) (court granted extraordinary relief as to disposition of evidence which involved report to service ethics committee because of defense counsel conduct); e.g., Cunningham v. Gilevich, 36 M.J. 94 (C.M.A. 1992) (although de facto immunity was not present, command actions were in violation of Article 31 and required prohibiting prosecution as then constituted); Lemoine v. Baker, 36 M.J. 86 (C.M.A. 1992) (release from active duty to appellate leave status ordered for convicted reservist not sentenced to confinement). But see McKinney v. Jarvis, 46 M.J. 870 (Army Crim. App. 1997) (denied writ seeking temporary restraining order to stop Article 32 investigation and to disqualify convening authority from continuing investigation because he was the accuser); Barnard v. Marsh, 43 M.J. 180 (C.A.A.F. 1995) (refused to hear issue of illegal pretrial confinement of individual who had completed sentence and was released even though others may be similarly situated); United States v. Mulloy, 40 M.J. 297 (C.M.A. 1994) (court refused to grant hearing on whether there should be review of Court of Military Review writ asking court to review disposition under Article 69); United States v. Butcher, 40 M.J. 296 (C.M.A. 1994) (same); Paterson

(Rel.3—1/07 Pub.62410)

In 1994, the court even implied that it could intervene to prohibit cruel and unusual post-trial prison conditions at the Army's Disciplinary Barracks — at least during the period in which the accused's appeals are not yet final.[356]

In 1995, in what could reasonably be termed an extraordinary event, despite the absence of jurisdiction over Article 15 non-judicial punishment, three judges

v. Phillips, 32 M.J. 30 (C.M.A. 1990) (summary disposition) (refused to enjoin transfer of claimed conscientious objection to Saudi Arabia despite *Unger* rationale assertion.) *See also* Dukes v. Smith, 34 M.J. 803 (N.M.C.M.R. 1992) (en banc) (no supervisory power over Article 15 punishment); United States Navy-Marine Corps Court of Military Review v. Carlucci, 26 M.J. 328 (C.M.A. 1988). *Carlucci* was a unique case dealing with the attempt by the Navy Inspector General to inquire into alleged judicial misconduct by judges of the Navy-Marine Court of Military review. The court cited as one of its reasons for taking jurisdiction its *potential* jurisdiction based on hypothetical disciplinary proceedings, despite the fact that no action had yet been taken on which disciplinary proceedings could even be based. Despite the fact that the Court of Military Appeals does not have any original jurisdiction, let alone jurisdiction over a civilian in a noncriminal proceeding (*see* Parisi v. Davidson, 405 U.S. 34, 44 (1972) (jurisdiction of Court of Military Appeals limited by Uniform Code of Military Justice to considering appeals from court-martial proceedings); *cf.* Marbury v. Madison, 1 Cranch 137, 175 (1803) (issuance of mandamus to a nonjudicial federal officer would be exercise of original, not appellate, jurisdiction)), it took original jurisdiction over the matter and enjoined investigation by the Department of Defense Inspector General.

In United States v. Smith, 34 M.J. 247 (C.M.A. 1992), the court in dictum refused to "exercise its supervisory authority to mandate the appointment of appellate defense counsel in every case to be reviewed by a service Court of Military Review." 34 M.J. at 248 (C.M.A. 1992). Obviously, members of the court continue to believe that it does indeed have supervisory authority of some type.

The fact that the court can issue extraordinary writs does not mean that it will grant them. Most petitions are unsuccessful. *See, e.g.*, Wroten v. United States, 37 M.J. 205 (C.M.A. 1992) (recusal of trial judge requested); Curtis v. Gordon, 36 M.J. 207 (C.M.A. 1992) (temporary restraining order for time to file extraordinary writ requiring the appointment of expert to help defense on proportionality review denied); Guitard v. United States, 36 M.J. 92 (C.M.A. 1992) (court refused to restrain discharge when case remanded to convening authority who dismissed charges and ordered convening of separation board which voted for separation); Hamilton v. DeGuilio, 35 M.J. 829 (A.C.M.R. 1992) (court refused to consider affidavit submitted one week before brief was due — error was raised without affidavit); United States v. Mahoney, 36 M.J. 679, 686 (A.F.C.M.R. 1992) (court refused to prevent judge from holding post-trial session to determine if there was a blatant disregard of judicial order); Sands v. Colby, 35 M.J. 620 (A.C.M.R. 1992) (dismissed writ based on lack of jurisdiction and speedy trial violation).

The court has consistently refused to intervene in service academy cheating scandals. Steve v. Dalton, 39 M.J. 403 (C.M.A. 1994) (Annapolis)); Hall v. Hoffman, 2 M.J. 170 (C.M.A. 1976) (West Point).

In numerous cases, the Court of Appeals has held it would not grant extraordinary relief before the Article 69 process is completed. Wilson v. United States, 15 M.J. 91 (C.M.A. 1983); Trainer v. Commanding Officer, 15 M.J. 75 (C.M.A. 1982); Vorbeck v. Convening Authority, 11 M.J. 91 (C.M.A. 1981).

[356] United States v. Coffey, 38 M.J. 290, 291 (C.M.A. 1993) (allegations of post-conviction prison conditions amounting to cruel and unusual punishment during are not subject to potential extraordinary relief absent exhaustion of administrative remedies).

(Rel.3—1/07 Pub.62410)

voted to stay Article 15 proceedings pending government response.[357] The accused had moved for extraordinary relief after court-martial charges for drug use were dismissed in favor of non-judicial punishment. Curiously, the disposition change followed the accused's discovery request for a report detailing misconduct at the forensic laboratory that had tested his urine.[358] What the court would ultimately have done will remain unknown, as petitioner withdrew his petition.

Some have argued that in the past the court has undertaken a role far beyond its jurisdiction.[359] In 1989, the United States Court of Military Appeals Court Committee reported: "It is important . . . that the Court exercise 'inherent or supervisory' power only to preserve and protect the jurisdiction that Congress has conferred upon it and that such power not be used to expand jurisdiction by decision."[360]

The scope of the Court's power in this area was decided by the Supreme Court in 1999. In *Goldsmith v. Clinton*,[361] petitioner, a convicted Air Force major incarcerated at the Disciplinary Barracks sought from the Air Force Court of Criminal Appeals, a writ of mandamus to ensure continuation of HIV medication. After the Court denied the writ, he filed a similar petition before the Court of Appeals for the Armed Forces. In the latter petition he also asked that the Air Force be prohibited from dropping him from the rolls as a consequence of a recent statutory change that mandates administrative elimination from the service of officers who serve more that 6 months' confinement after completion of appellate review.

Surprisingly, the Court determined that it had jurisdiction and reached the merits of the petition. The Court observed:

> [W]e conclude that, if this Court is empowered to grant extraordinary relief in a case that it cannot possibly review directly, it is also empowered by the All Writs Act to grant extraordinary relief in a case in which the court-martial rendered a sentence that constituted an adequate basis for direct review in this Court after review in the intermediate court. Moreover,

---

[357] Fletcher v. Covington, 42 M.J. 116 (C.A.A.F. 1995).

[358] 42 M.J. 116 (C.A.A.F. 1995).

[359] U.S. Court of Military Appeals Committee Report 5 (Jan. 27, 1989).

[360] U.S. Court of Military Appeals Committee Report 5 (Jan. 27, 1989). In 1989, Congress clarified the potential jurisdiction of the court by expressly extending jurisdiction to special courts-martial and summary courts-martial via an expansion of the Judge Advocates General's certification authority. U.C.M.J. art. 69(d).

See also Conference Report 103-357, National Defense Authorization Act for Fiscal Year 1994, Cong. Rec. H9473 (daily ed. Nov. 10, 1993) (requiring the Secretary of Defense to report on the relationship between Articles 66 and 69).

[361] 48 M.J. 84 (C.A.A.F. 1998), *rev'd*, 526 U.S. 529 (1999). Petitioner's original conviction had been affirmed by the United States Air Force Court of Criminal Appeals. He did not further appeal to the United States Court of Appeals for the Armed Forces.

(Rel.3—1/07 Pub.62410)

in our view, Goldsmith's failure to petition this Court for discretionary review pursuant to Article 67 did not waive or otherwise affect our extraordinary-writ jurisdiction in connection with this case.[362]

In *Clinton v. Goldsmith*[363] the Supreme Court reversed, noting that "the express terms of the [All Writs] Act confine the power of the CAAF to issuing process 'in aid of' its existing statutory jurisdiction; the Act does not enlarge that jurisdiction" to enjoin the executive branch from dropping a convicted servicemember from the roles. It seemed to indicate that it will strictly limit the jurisdiction of the Court of Appeals. *Goldsmith* does not of course clearly delimit the constraints applicable to the military appellant courts. In *United States v. King*,[364] decided after *Goldsmith*, the Navy-Marine Corps Court of Criminal Appeals held that it did not have jurisdiction to grant relief to an accused defendant charged with espionage who claimed that the government was interfering with his attorney-client relationship by requiring a security officer to be present during all communications. Citing the accused's right to counsel, the Court of Appeals for the Armed Forces implicitly reversed the Court of Criminal Appeals by staying the Article 32 and issuing an order to await issuance of an appropriate security clearance to defense counsel, a less restrictive security device considered acceptable by the government.[365]

§ 25-93.00 "Agreeable to the Usages and Principles of Law"

This aspect of the All-Writs Act requires that, before an extraordinary writ may issue, the court must be faced with extraordinary circumstances.[366] Ordinarily, the accused must have exhausted all other adequate remedies,[367] and the

---

[362] 48 M.J. at 89.

[363] 526 U.S. at 534-35 (1999).

[364] 53 M.J. 425 (C.A.A.F. 2000). *See also* United States v. Salahuddin, 54 M.J. 918 (A.F. Crim. App. 2001) (assuming it had jurisdiction under *Goldsmith* to grant hearing prior commitment to the Attorney General for treatment, the court denied relief), *pet. denied*, 54 M.J. 456 (C.A.A.F. 2001).

[365] The actual order provides:

That the stay of proceedings issued by this Court be continued, to be lifted upon a showing that:

(1) Defense counsel have been granted clearances and the ISO [Information Security Officer] monitoring requirements have been rescinded; or

(2) The Government demonstrates that defense counsel have not promptly provided all information necessary to initiate processing for the required security clearances; or

(3) Lifting the stay is warranted for other good cause shown.

[366] *See, e.g.*, Font v. Seaman, 43 C.M.R. 227, 230 (C.M.A. 1971). *Cf.* Woodrick v. Divich, 24 M.J. 147 (C.M.A. 1987) (ROTC student granted injunction of court-martial to exhaust relief in Article III courts).

[367] *See, e.g.*, United States v. White, 54 M.J. 469, 472 (C.A.A.F. 2001) (court has jurisdiction "to determine if certain punishments violate the Eighth Amendment or Article 55" — but prisoner

exercise of jurisdiction must be consistent with judicial economy.[368] The courts will often[369] grant extraordinary relief, for example, to correct illegal confinement[370] or to prevent trial of the accused when it is clear that jurisdiction is lacking[371] or some other bar to prosecution exists.[372] Exhaustion, including trial and ordinary appeal, may not be required when the issues are "recurrent" with "broad ramifications" and have been "thoroughly briefed and argued" by counsel.[373] "Recognizing the traumatic effect of confinement, this Court has also sought to assure that an accused will be promptly released from unlawful confinement — either before or after trial."[374]

The Court of Appeals was reminded in *Goldsmith*:

> Even if the CAAF had some seriously arguable basis for jurisdiction in these circumstances, resort to the All Writs Act would still be out of bounds, being unjustifiable either as "necessary" or as "appropriate" in light of alternative remedies available to a servicemember demanding to be kept on the rolls.[375]

Sometimes exhaustion of remedies and judicial economy go hand in hand. On occasion the appellate courts will not grant extraordinary relief, but will order

---

must exhaust administrative remedies); United States v. King, 53 M.J. 425 (C.A.A.F. 2000) (court took jurisdiction when total failure of right to counsel could not be remedied by appellate review except for ordering a new trial); United States v. Coffey, 38 M.J. 290, 291 (C.M.A. 1993) (allegations of postconviction prison conditions amounting to cruel and unusual punishment are not subject to potential extraordinary relief absent exhaustion of administrative remedies); Dale v. United States, 41 C.M.R. 254 (C.M.A. 1970) (seek relief under Article 138); Font v. Seaman, 43 C.M.R. 227, 231 (C.M.A. 1971) (seek relief from trial judge).

[368] *See, e.g.,* Murray v. Haldeman, 16 M.J. 74 (C.M.A. 1983).

[369] But not always.

[370] *See, e.g.,* Berta v. United States, 9 M.J. 390 (C.M.A. 1980) (show cause why release from illegal pretrial confinement should not be granted); Collier v. United States, 42 C.M.R. 113 (C.M.A. 1970) (illegal post-trial confinement).

[371] *See, e.g.,* Flenier v. Koch, 19 C.M.A. 630 (1970) (no jurisdiction over the person — civilian offense victim of off-post offense); Zamora v. Woodson, 42 C.M.R. 5 (C.M.A. 1970) (no jurisdiction over the person — civilian in Vietnam).

[372] *See, e.g.,* Burtt v. Schick, 23 M.J. 140 (C.M.A. 1986) (double jeopardy).

[373] Murray v. Haldeman, 16 M.J. 74, 76–77 (C.M.A. 1983) (quoting in part Shepardson v. Roberts, 14 M.J. 354 (C.M.A. 1983)). *See also* United States v. Curtin, 44 M.J. 439 (C.A.A.F. 1996) (because of broad-ranging implications and recurrent problems, the court held that a subpoena by a trial counsel under R.C.M. 703 was a "judicial subpoena"); Grady v. Darley, 44 M.J. 48 (C.A.A.F. 1996) (to prevent chilling effect on defense counsel in the military, the court directed judge to determine whether defendant and his counsel were raising directly or indirectly the advice of former military counsel as a defense to obstruction of justice — implicit in order was belief that, if so, it would be a waiver of attorney-client privilege).

[374] Waller v. Swift, 30 M.J. 139, 142-43 (C.M.A. 1990) (extraordinary relief in the nature of a petition for habeas corpus granted to prohibit "commutation" of a bad-conduct discharge to 12-month confinement). *See also* Moore v. Akins, 30 M.J. 249 (C.M.A. 1990).

[375] 526 U.S. 529, 537 (1999).

(Rel.3—1/07 Pub.62410)

or encourage the trial judge to hold an Article 39(a) session to litigate the subject matter of the petition.[376]

The impact of *Goldsmith* on the Court's willingness to extend its reach beyond customary limits remains unclear. In *United States v. King*,[377] an espionage case, the Court heard petitioner accused's complaint that he was being forced to communicate with counsel in the presence of a security officer. In *United States v. Nguyen*,[378] the court granted a stay to determine whether civilian counsel, who the Navy ruled was disqualified because of prior active duty representation, should be allowed to represent the accused. Some would argue that these cases required that the Court implicitly distinguish *Goldsmith*. Others would maintain that protection of the right to counsel, even at the Article 32 stage is a core component of the military criminal legal system and within the Court's ambit. Certainly the right to counsel in the pretrial stage of probable serious criminal prosecution is a far cry from petitioner Goldsmith's request to have the government barred from administratively dropping him from the roles. At the same time, it is at least arguable that the Court is being far more cautious in its use of extraordinary relief. In *United States v. Beck*,[379] for example, the Court refused to stay court-martial proceedings while a United States District Court considered petitioner's claim that he had been fraudulently induced into the armed forces.[380] In 2004, however, the Court granted a mandamus request and ordered the removal of a prisoner from deathrow of a person not then subject to a death sentence.[381] Subsequently, the Court acted after a petitioner had not yet received initial appellate review after over five years by directing the Court of Criminal Appeals to promptly act on the case and inviting petitioner to seek further relief if the lower court had not yet done so within 90 days.[382] However laudable, the Court's inmate relief case may be as a matter of policy and justice, it is hard to see how it complied with the Court's jurisdictional constraints. Its post-trial delay decision, although arguable, appears more in accordance with the Court's normal jurisdiction, but is clearly an act of supervisory authority.

---

[376] *See, e.g.,* Phillippy v. McLucas, 50 C.M.R. 915 (C.M.A. 1975); Catlow v. Cooksey, 44 C.M.R. 160, 162 (C.M.A. 1971).

[377] 53 M.J. 425 (C.A.A.F. 2000).

[378] 56 M.J. 233 (C.A.A.F. 2001).

[379] 56 M.J. 426 (C.A.A.F. 2002) (per curiam).

[380] The Court opined:

Issuance of an extraordinary writ staying court-martial proceedings requires the careful exercise of discretion. When a writ petition asks us to stay a court-martial in deference to proceedings in a court outside the military justice system, it would be inappropriate to issue a stay absent a persuasive ruling from such a court or similar prudential considerations.

56 M.J. at 427.

[381] Kreutzer v. Harrison, 60 M.J. 453 (C.A.A.F. 2005).

[382] Toohey v. United States, 60 M.J. 100, 104 (C.A.A.F. 2004).

(Rel.3—1/07 Pub.62410)

The *Manual for Courts-Martial*[383] encourages and the Court of Appeals requires the petitioners to seek their initial relief from the Court of Criminal Appeals before seeking relief from the Court of Appeals.[384]

§ 25-94.00   Legislative Review Appropriate

Although the authority of the military appellate courts to grant extraordinary relief now appears to be settled, it would be desirable to have legislative review and Uniform Code amendment in this area. Most particularly, the authority of military judges at the trial level to grant relief should be clarified. If military justice is to be equated with civilian due process, extraordinary relief powers are unavoidable. Should advocates of command control fear judicial interference, Congress could, however unnecessarily, limit extraordinary-relief jurisdiction until after a case has been referred to trial. Command action violating the Uniform Code of Military Justice, whether by unlawful confinement,[385] abuse of procedural protections,[386] or otherwise is sufficiently frequent that relatively easy and local legal remedy ought to be available to provide petitioners with meaningful relief. Although military charges may be subordinate in grade to the convening authorities their orders would affect, they remain *judges*. Further, the present method of appointment of military judges and the lack of any form of judicial tenure hardly suggests a significant risk of judicial "loose canons."

§ 25-100.00   EXECUTION OF SENTENCE

Under the Uniform Code of Military Justice, that part of a sentence that provides for a punitive discharge, including an officer's dismissal, or death may not be finally approved ("executed") until after completion of the appellate process.[387]

The Court of Appeals for the Armed Forces may entertain petitions for extraordinary relief and may issue all writs necessary or appropriate in aid of its jurisdiction and agreeable to the usages and principles of law. Any party may petition the Court of Appeals for the Armed Forces for extraordinary relief. However, in the interest of judicial economy, such petitions usually should be filed with and adjudicated before the appropriate Court of Criminal Appeals prior to submission to the Court of Appeals for the Armed Forces.

R.C.M. 1204(a) Discussion.

[384] Armed F. R. 4(b) <www.armfor.uscourts.gov/Rules.doc>

[385] *See, e.g.*, Longhofer v. Hilbert, 23 M.J. 755 (A.C.M.R. 1986) (unlawful rescission of posttrial deferral of confinement).

[386] *See, e.g.*, Jones v. Commander, 18 M.J. 198 (C.M.A. 1984); Dobzynski v. Green, 16 M.J. 84 (C.M.A. 1983).

[387] U.C.M.J. art 71(c); *see also* R.C.M. 1113(c). Except for death cases, the accused may withdraw or waive appeal and thus permit execution of sentence. Lesser punishment such as confinement may be approved, which makes it exceedingly difficult to make an accused whole should his or her conviction be reversed on appeal.

Completion of the appellate process for these purposes is defined by U.C.M.J. 71(c)(1).

(Rel.3—1/07   Pub.62410)

In the case of commissioned officers, cadets, and midshipmen, even if sustained on appeal, a dismissal "may not be executed until approved by the Secretary concerned or such Under Secretary or Assistant Secretary as may be designated by the Secretary concerned"[388] who also has the power to commute or suspend the sentence.[389] Under the Rules for Courts-Martial, "The Secretary concerned may, for good cause, substitute an administrative discharge for a discharge or dismissal executed in accordance with the sentence of a court-martial."[390]

A death sentence requires the approval of the President.[391]

The convening authority may suspend execution of all sentences other than death.[392] Should the probationer violate one or more of the conditions of suspension, the suspension may be vacated.[393] Should the suspended sentence include "a bad-conduct discharge, or of any general court-martial sentence, the officer having special court-martial jurisdiction over the probationer shall hold a hearing on the alleged violation of probation."[394]

Should he or she wish to exercise clemency, the service Secretary concerned "may, for good cause, substitute an administrative form of discharge for a discharge or dismissal executed in accordance with the sentence of a court-martial."[395]

§ 25-110.00   RESTORATION; NEW TRIAL

Under Article 75(a) of the Uniform Code of Military Justice:

> Under such regulations as the President may prescribe, all rights, privileges, and property affected by an executed part of a court-martial sentence which has been set aside or disapproved, except an executed dismissal or discharge, shall be restored unless a new trial or rehearing is ordered and

---

[388] U.C.M.J. art. 71(b); R.C.M. 1206(a). "In time of war or national emergency he may commute a sentence of dismissal to reduction to any enlisted grade. A person so reduced may be required to serve for the duration of the war or emergency and six months thereafter." U.C.M.J. art. 71(b).

[389] U.C.M.J. art. 71(b).

[390] R.C.M. 1206(b)(2).

[391] U.C.M.J. 71(a). Death may not be suspended.

[392] U.C.M.J. art. 71(d).

[393] U.C.M.J. art. 72.

[394] U.C.M.J. art. 72(a).

[395] U.C.M.J. art. 74(b). *See also* United States v. Byrd, 53 M.J. 35 (C.A.A.F. 2000) (premature execution of a punitive discharge does not deprive the appellate courts of jurisdiction); Steele v. Van Riper, 50 M.J. 89 (C.A.A.F. 1999) (per curiam) (issuance of administrative discharge after trial does not deprive an appellate court of jurisdiction to review the case but it does effectively remit that part of the sentence, including a punitive discharge, affected by the discharge).

such executed part is included in a sentence imposed upon the new trial or rehearing.[396]

New trials are governed by Article 73, which provides:

At any time within two years after approval by the convening authority of a court-martial sentence, the accused may petition the Judge Advocate General for a new trial on the grounds of newly discovered evidence or fraud on the court. If the accused's case is pending before a Court of Criminal Appeals or before the Court of Appeals for the Armed Forces, the Judge Advocate General shall refer the petition to the appropriate court for action. Otherwise the Judge Advocate General shall act upon the petition.[397]

The Rules for Courts-Martial amplify the Uniform Code by stating:

A new trial shall not be granted on the grounds of newly discovered evidence unless the petition shows that:

(A) The evidence was discovered after the trial;

(B) The evidence is not such that it would have been discovered by the petitioner at the time of trial in the exercise of due diligence;[398] and

---

[396] U.C.M.J. art. 75(a). As for the financial implications of a reversed conviction, see Dock v. United States, 46 F.3d 1083, 1086 (Fed. Cir. 1995) (if a retrial sentence includes forfeitures imposed at the original trial, the forfeitures are effective from the first trial's effective date; the accused is not entitled to pay and allowances until the second conviction despite the fact that the first conviction was set aside). See also Groves v. United States, 47 F.3d 1140 (Fed. Cir. 1995) (reversal of conviction and restoration of all rights and privileges entitles defendant to back pay and special pays absent other executive action).

[397] "No fraud on the court-martial warrants a new trial unless it had a substantial contributing effect on a finding of guilty or the sentence adjudged." R.C.M. 1210(f)(3). The Discussion to R.C.M. 1210(f)(3) adds:

Examples of fraud on a court-martial which may warrant granting a new trial are: confessed or proved perjury in testimony or forgery of documentary evidence which clearly had a substantial contributing effect on a finding of guilty and without which there probably would not have been a finding of guilty of the offense; willful concealment by the prosecution from the defense of evidence favorable to the defense which, if presented to the court-martial, would probably have resulted in a finding of not guilty; and willful concealment of a material ground for challenge of the military judge or any member or of the disqualification of counsel or the convening authority, when the basis for challenge or disqualification was not known to the defense at the time of trial (see R.C.M. 912).

See, e.g., United States v. Giambra, 33 M.J. 331, 335 (C.M.A. 1991) (where attempted rape and indecent assault complainant admitted committing perjury on stand, case remanded for a DuBay hearing on the perjury issue).

[398] E.g., United States v. Good, 39 M.J. 615, 617 (A.C.M.R. 1994) (holding that the results of a post-trial sanity board finding the accused's co-conspirator and chief government witness to lack ability to appreciate the wrongfulness of his actions dealt with matter unknown at trial that would not have been discovered through due diligence of counsel).

(Rel.3—1/07 Pub.62410)

(C) The newly discovered evidence, if considered by a court-martial in the light of all other pertinent evidence, would probably produce a substantially more favorable result for the accused.[399]

Under Article 73, a petition for new trial must be made within two years after the convening authority's approval of sentence. In its 1998 decision in *United States v. Murphy*,[400] the Court of Appeals for the Armed Forces arguably used a "work-around" to avoid the two year rule when on direct appeal the Court applied the substance of Rule 1210(f)(2) after appellant complained that his death sentence was unjustified in light of medical and sociological information obtained five years after his conviction.

"Petitions for a new trial based upon a witness' change in testimony are not viewed favorably in the law."[401] Insofar as such a change of testimony is concerned, the Army Court of Review has stated, "In exercising our discretion on petitions for a new trial we have the prerogative of weighing the testimony at trial against the post-trial evidence to determine which is credible."[402]

The mere "submission of a petition[403] for a new trial does not stay the

---

[399] R.C.M. 1210(f)(2). As for the standard to be used when determining whether the Court of Military Review properly rejected a request for a new trial — and the degree to which it can resolve disputed facts in the process, *see* Fidell, *Going on Fifty: Evolution and Devolution in Military Justice*, 32 Wake Forest L. Rev. 1213 (1997); United States v. VanTasell, 38 M.J. 91, 97 (C.M.A. 1993) (Gierke, J., concurring) (court has not sorted out whether R.C.M. 1210(f) supersedes the "legitimate dispute" test in United States v. Lilly, 25 M.J. 403 (C.M.A. 1988)). *See also* United States v. Singleton, 41 M.J. 200, 204–06 (C.M.A. 1994). Although apparently attempting to limit its holding to the specific facts of the case, the Court of Appeals for the Armed Forces appears to have created a more favorable rule for the situation in which the prosecutrix in a child molestation case has recanted her testimony. United States v. Cuento, 60 M.J. 106, 113 (C.A.A.F. 2004)("When the alleged perjurer is the prosecutrix herself," we remain "disinclined" to burden Appellant with mechanical application of a rigorous standard. Under the unique circumstances of this case, . . . we find that the weight of J's recantation cannot adequately be measured without a *DuBay* hearing before a military judge at which J would testify under oath and be subject to cross-examination.) (citation omitted).

[400] 50 M.J. 4, 14–16 (C.A.A.F. 1998) (ordering a *DuBay* hearing to test the evidence).

[401] United States v. Hanson, 39 M.J. 610, 612 (A.C.M.R. 1994), citing United States v. Bacon, 12 M.J. 489 (C.M.A. 1982).

[402] Hanson, 39 M.J. at 612, finding trial testimony of victim more credible than post-trial statements).

A petition for a new trial shall be written and shall be signed under oath or affirmation by the accused, by a person possessing the power of attorney of the accused for that purpose, or by a person with the authorization of an appropriate court to sign the petition as the representative of the accused. The petition shall contain the following information, or an explanation why such matters are not included:

(1) The name, service number, and current address of the accused;

(2) The date and location of the trial;

(3) The type of court-martial and the title or position of the convening authority;

(4) The request for the new trial;

(Rel.3—1/07 Pub.62410)

execution of a sentence."[404]

Once a new trial is granted, the case is forwarded to a convening authority.[405] "At a new trial, the accused may not be tried for any offense of which the accused was found not guilty or upon which the accused was not tried at the earlier court-martial."[406]

If a previously executed sentence of dishonorable or bad-conduct discharge is not imposed on a new trial, the Secretary concerned shall substitute therefor a form of discharge authorized for administrative issuance unless the accused is to serve out the remainder of his enlistment.[407]

As Article 73 indicates, new trial requests ordinarily are made to the Judge Advocate General. In *United States v. Williams*,[408] however, the request was made to the trial judge during a post-trial Article 39(a) session. It is unclear that this procedure was ever contemplated by the Rules for Courts-Martial. Notwithstanding this, in *Williams*, the Court of Military Appeals accepted the procedure stating that such a request should be governed by the "criteria delineated in Article 73 . . . and R.C.M. 1210(f)."[409]

In *United States v. Fisiorek*[410] the court seemed to adopt a new standard when new evidence is presented prior to sentencing. "It is now beyond doubt in military jurisprudence that a military judge is empowered to reopen a case even after findings have been announced."[411] In such a case the court seems to have endorsed a more liberal application of the newly discovered evidence rule.

> Let there be no doubt that a party should not be allowed to profit from his or her lack of due diligence in investigating the case, nor should a party

---

(5) The sentence or a description thereof as approved or affirmed, with any later reduction thereof by clemency or otherwise;

(6) A brief description of any finding or sentence believed to be unjust;

(7) A full statement of the newly discovered evidence or fraud on the court-martial which is relied upon for the remedy sought;

(8) Affidavits pertinent to the matters in subsection (c)(6) of this rule; and

(9) The affidavit of each person whom the accused expects to present as a witness in the event of a new trial. Each such affidavit should set forth briefly the relevant facts within the personal knowledge of the witness.

R.C.M. 1210(c).

[404] R.C.M. 1210(d).

[405] R.C.M. 1210(h)(1).

[406] R.C.M. 1210(h)(2).

[407] U.C.M.J. art. 75(b). For officer dismissal, *see* U.C.M.J. art. 75(c).

[408] 37 M.J. 352 (C.M.A. 1993).

[409] 37 M.J. at 355–56 (C.M.A. 1993) (footnote omitted).

[410] 43 M.J. 244 (C.A.A.F. 1995).

[411] 43 M.J. at 247 ¶ 13 (C.A.A.F. 1995).

(Rel.3—1/07 Pub.62410)

be allowed to play games with the court and " 'hide' evidence, awaiting the verdict before springing the evidence upon opponents. . . . But the same policy considerations for granting new trials long after the completion of a trial do not necessarily apply to motions to reopen a case. . . . If the trial is still on-going, the parties are only marginally inconvenienced; all decision-makers are in place. . . ."[412]

The majority "decline[d] . . . to fashion a particular rule to guide military judges. . . ."[413] The "primary consideration should be whether the discovery of the new evidence is bona fide. . . ."[414] What is clear is that "the military judge [has the authority] to convene a post-trial session to consider newly discovered evidence and to take whatever remedial action is appropriate."[415]

Upon retrial, the "law of the case" will apply. At minimum, that will likely require application of the holding of the appellate court in reversing the initial conviction both on retrial[416] and on any subsequent further appeal.[417]

It should be noted that the Analysis of Rule for Court-Martial 1210(a), as amended in 1998, declares that the rule:

was amended to clarify its application consistent with interpretations of Fed. R. Crim. P. 33 that newly discovered evidence is never a basis for a new trial of the facts when the accused has pled guilty." . . . Article 73 authorizes a petition for a new trial of the facts when there has been a trial. When there is a guilty plea, there is no trial. See R.C.M. 910(j). The amendment is made in recognition of the fact that it is difficult, if not impossible, to determine whether newly discovered evidence would have an impact on the trier of fact when there has been no trier of fact and no previous trial of the facts at which other pertinent evidence has been adduced. Additionally, a new trial may not be granted on the basis of newly discovered evidence unless "the newly discovered evidence, if considered by a court-martial in the light of all other pertinent evidence, would probably produce a substantially more favorable result for the accused." R.C.M. 1210(f)(2)(C).[418]

§ 25-120.00　UNLAWFUL POST-TRIAL CONFINEMENT

An accused who is held unlawfully past the expiration of his confinement sentence is entitled to meaningful relief, relief that can be granted by the Court of Criminal Appeals.[419]

---

[412] 43 M.J. at 247 ¶ 15 (C.A.A.F. 1995).

[413] 43 M.J. at 248 ¶ 17 (C.A.A.F. 1995).

[414] 43 M.J. at 248 ¶ 17 (C.A.A.F. 1995)

[415] United States v. Meghdadi, 60 M.J. 438, 441 (C.A.A.F. 2005) (quoting United States v. Scaff, 29 M.J. 60 (C.M.A. 1989).

[416] See Jones v. Cassens Transp., 982 F.2d 983, 987 (6th Cir. 1993).

[417] See United States v. Jordan, 38 M.J. 346, 350 (C.M.A. 1993) (Wiss, J., dissenting).

[418] Appendix 21, MCM, 2002.

[419] United States v. Keith, 36 M.J. 518 (A.C.M.R. 1992) (issue raised during appeal).

(Rel.3—1/07　Pub.62410)

Should a convicted member of the armed forces claim that his or her confinement is cruel and unusual in violation of Article 55 or the Constitution, the Court of Military Appeals has held that the intermediate appellate courts have power to consider such an issue if the defendant has exhausted his administrative remedies.[420] It is unclear whether a military trial judge has jurisdiction to entertain such a claim in the first instance.

In *United States v. White*[421] the Court of Appeals for the Armed Forces held that it had jurisdiction to determine whether the court-martial sentence was executed in a manner that offends the Eight Amendment or Article 55. To succeed petitioner must show that he or she "has exhausted the prisoner-grievance system . . .and. . .has petitioned for relief under Article 138. . ."[422] In addition, petitioner "must establish 'a clear record' of . . .'the legal deficiency in administration of the prison'."[423]

---

[420] United States v. Coffey, 38 M.J. 290 (C.M.A. 1993). *See also* United States v. Haymaker, 46 M.J. 757 (A.F. Crim. App. 1997) (discussing whether the court had or should exercise jurisdiction to consider the claim that the prisoner was deprived of proper medical care); United States v. Miller, 46 M.J. 248, 250 (C.A.A.F. 1997) ("Appellant has not demonstrated that he exhausted either the applicable prisoner-grievance system or remedies pursuant to Article 138, and he has not demonstrated unusual or egregious circumstances that would justify his failure to do so."); United States v. Dew, 48 M.J. 639 (Army Crim. App. 1998) (court has jurisdiction to determine if TJAG should be required to order review under Article 69).

[421] 54 M.J. 469, 472 (C.A.A.F. 2001).

[422] In addition, petitioner "must establish 'a clear record&requo 54 M.J. at 472, *quoting Miller*, 46 M.J. at 250.

[423] 54 M.J. at 472, *quoting Miller*, 46 M.J. at 250.

CHAPTER 26

CIVILIAN COLLATERAL RELIEF

§ 26-10.00 INTRODUCTION
  § 26-11.00 In General
  § 26-12.00 The Historical Evolution of Civilian Collateral Attack
§ 26-20.00 THE CLAIMS COURT
§ 26-30.00 HABEAS CORPUS
  § 26-31.00 In General
  § 26-32.00 Custody
      § 26-32.10 — Generally
      § 26-32.20 — What Constitutes Custody
      § 26-32.30 — Who Is a Custodian
      § 26-32.40 — Prematurity
      § 26-32.50 — Concurrent-Sentence Doctrine
      § 26-32.60 — Mootness
  § 26-33.00 Exhaustion of Military Remedies
      § 26-33.10 — Generally
      § 26-33.20 — Meeting the Exhaustion Requirement
      § 26-33.30 — Presentation of Claims
      § 26-33.31 — Fair Identification of Claims
      § 26-33.32 — Fair Presentation of Claims
  § 26-34.00 Waiver
  § 26-35.00 "New" Rules

§ 26-10.00 INTRODUCTION

§ 26-11.00 In General

Although the military criminal legal system evolved as a legal entity separate and distinct from the civilian system,[1] and despite the Uniform Code of Military Justice's provision for finality,[2] courts-martial are not immune from civilian

---

[1] *See generally* Chapter 1.

[2] U.C.M.J. art. 76 provides:

The appellate review of records of trial provided by this chapter, the proceedings, findings, and sentences of courts-martial as approved, reviewed, or affirmed as required by this chapter, and all dismissals and discharges carried into execution under sentences by courts-martial following approval, review, or affirmation as required by this chapter, are final and conclusive. Orders publishing the proceedings of courts-martial and all action taken pursuant to those proceedings are binding upon all departments, courts, agencies, and officers of the United States, subject only to action upon a petition for a

(Rel.3—1/07 Pub.62410)

judicial oversight.[3] As in any civilian conviction, the last direct appeal does not necessarily end a military defendant's litigation. Instead, collateral relief is available. In light of the thoroughness of appellate review,[4] however, meaningful collateral relief is available only from the civilian federal courts.[5]

---

new trial as provided in section 873 of this title (article 73) and to action by the Secretary concerned as provided in section 874 of this title (article 74), and the authority of the President.

[3] Schlesinger v. Councilman, 420 U.S. 738, 745, 749 (1975) (Article 76 prescribes point at which finality attaches and does not prohibit collateral relief); Gusik v. Schilder, 340 U.S. 128, 132 (1950) (interpreting predecessor Articles of War). *See also* Cooper v. United States, 20 Cl. Ct. 770 (1990). Of course, the United States Court of Military Appeals is a "civilian" court. However, as it is the apex of the "military" criminal legal system, we distinguish it from the civilian federal district courts and the circuit courts of appeal.

[4] *See generally* Chapter 25.

[5] Other than the improbable event of a grant of habeas corpus by either a Court of Military Review or the United States Court of Military Appeals (*see* Moore v. Akins, 30 M.J. 249 (C.M.A. 1990) (habeas granted); Unger v. Ziemniak, 27 M.J. 349 (C.M.A. 1989); Levy v. Resor, 37 C.M.R. 399 (C.M.A. 1967) (habeas corpus and mandamus); United States v. Frischolz, 36 C.M.R. 306 (C.M.A. 1966) (coram nobis) (*see above* Chapter 25, note 320), the only potential collateral relief within the armed forces is the civilian Board for Correction of Military Records contained within each military department. In relevant part, 10 U.S.C. § 1552(a) provides:

(1) The Secretary of a military department may correct any military record of the Secretary's department when the Secretary considers it necessary to correct an error or remove an injustice. Except as provided in paragraph (2), such corrections shall be made by the Secretary acting through boards of civilians of the executive part of that military department. The Secretary of Transportation may in the same manner correct any military record of the Coast Guard. . . .

(4) Except when procured by fraud, a correction under this section is final and conclusive on all officers of the United States. . . . (b) No correction may be made under subsection (a)(1) unless the claimant or his heir or legal representative files a request for the correction within three years after he discovers the error or injustice. However, a board established under subsection (a)(1) may excuse a failure to file within three years after discovery if it finds it to be in the interest of justice.

Insofar as courts-martial convictions are concerned, however, the Boards for Correction of Military Records are severely limited:

With respect to records of courts-martial and related administrative records pertaining to court-martial cases tried or reviewed under chapter 47 of this title [the Uniform Code of Military Justice], action under subsection (a) may extend only to —

(1) correction of a record to reflect actions taken by reviewing authorities under chapter 47 of this title [the Uniform Code of Military Justice]; or

(2) action on the sentence of a court-martial for purposes of clemency.

10 U.S.C. § 1552(f).

Accordingly, though a convicted accused may petition a departmental Board for the Correction of Military Records, the board's jurisdiction will be limited to the exercise of clemency; the findings may not be disturbed. The authors believe that even this limited form of relief is exercised infrequently.

(Rel.3—1/07 Pub.62410)

A military accused may seek collateral relief in the form of a suit for back pay in the United States Claims Court or via a petition for habeas corpus from a federal district court. In general terms, the Claims Court has jurisdiction "when the conviction has monetary consequences,"[6] and federal habeas lies when the accused is in "custody." In addition to these "usual" routes for collateral attack, some civilian federal courts have held that they have jurisdiction to issue writs of mandamus directing military officials to nullify courts-martial convictions,[7] and some have indicated a readiness to enter declaratory judgements concerning the legality of such convictions.[8]

Because courts-martial are not within the purview of the Administrative Procedure Act, 5 U.S.C. § 551(F), (G) (*see* McDaniel, *The Availability and Scope of Judicial Review of Disretionary Military Administrative Decisions*, 108 Mil. L. Rev. 135, 137 (1985)), except for public agency information aspects, judicial review is foreclosed even from that unlikely route.

The parole boards operated by the military departments are not ordinarily thought of as providing collateral relief. They may take actions, however, that may to some degree yield similar relief. *E.g.*, United States v. Olinger, 45 M.J. 644, 649 (N.M. Crim. App. 1997). Navy Clemency and Parole Board has binding clemency powers which permit it to remit an unexecuted punitive discharge).

[6] Refre v. United States, 11 Cl. Ct. 81, 83 (1986), *aff'd*, 833 F.2d 1022 (Fed. Cir. 1987), *cert. denied*, 486 U.S. 1011 (1988). Federal district courts have jurisdiction over "back pay" claims when the amount of the claim is under the jurisdictional floor of the Claims Court. 28 U.S.C. §§ 1346(a)(2), 1491.

[7] *See, e.g.*, Hatheway v. Secretary of the Army, 641 F.2d 1376, 1379 (9th Cir.), *cert. denied*, 454 U.S. 864 (1981) ("The district court had equitable jurisdiction under 28 U.S.C. § 1331 and mandamus jurisdiction under § 1361" (citing Kauffman v. Secretary of the Air Force, 415 F.2d 991, 994–96 (D.C. Cir.), *cert. denied*, 396 U.S. 1013 (1970)); Baker v. Schlesinger, 523 F.2d 1031, 1034-35 (6th Cir. 1975), *cert. denied*, 424 U.S. 972 (1976)). In discussing the scope of the district court's jurisdiction in *Hatheway*, the court, ultimately denying Hatheway's claims as not meeting the necessary burden of proof, added:

> The district court could not, however, directly review the determination of the military courts. "The valid, final judgments of military courts, like those of any court of competent jurisdiction not subject to direct review for errors of fact or law, have res judicata effect and preclude further litigation of the merits." Schlesinger v. Councilman, 420 U.S. at 746.

> The district court's authority to order the Army to upgrade Hatheway's discharge could be exercised only upon a determination that the court-martial judgment was void, *i.e.*, "because of lack of jurisdiction or some other equally fundamental defect, the judgment neither justifie[d] nor bar[red] relief from its consequences." 420 U.S. at 747.

See also Melvin v. Laird, 365 F. Supp. 511 (E.D.N.Y. 1973) (citing cases). *See generally Review by Federal Civil Courts of Court-Martial Convictions — Modern Cases*, 95 A.L.R. Fed. 472 § 7 (1989). Note that mandamus may require prior exhaustion of remedies. *See* Williams v. Secretary of Navy, 77 F.2d 552 (Fed. Cir. 1986); Section 26-33.00.

[8] *See, e.g.*, Davis v. Marsh, 876 F.2d 1446, n.4 (9th Cir. 1989) (citing Hatheway v. Secretary of the Army, 641 F.2d 1376 (9th Cir. 1981)); Hatheway v. Secretary of the Army, 641 F.2d 1376, 1379 (9th Cir.), *cert. denied*, 454 U.S. 864 (1981), *above* note 7; Melvin v. Laird, 365 F. Supp. 511 (E.D.N.Y. 1973).

Until 1983, civilian collateral relief was of extraordinary systemic importance, as it provided the only procedural route for civilian review of courts-martial.[9] Absent any direct route to the Supreme Court, only those few cases that zigzagged their way into and through the federal district courts or the Court of Claims[10] provided a vehicle for the Supreme Court's review of military criminal law. Not only was this grossly inefficient, it was one-sided, as it deprived the government of the ability to challenge adverse decisions of the Court of Military Appeals. Instead, the government could only respond to those cases launched into the civilian courts by the accused. In 1983, however, Congress authorized the Supreme Court to review decisions of the Court of Military Appeals via writ of certiorari.[11] As a consequence, collateral relief is no longer of great importance in ensuring an appellate route to the Supreme Court[12] although it may be of significance in individual cases. What is unclear is the effect, if any, of the availability of the certiorari petition on the scope of collateral review. In 1990, the Claims Court, in *Matias v. United States*,[13] citing the legislative history of the certiorari provision,[14] held that the expanded "direct" route of appeal did not "eliminate all collateral attacks."[15] Although that holding seems clearly correct, whether the *scope* of collateral review will ultimately be affected remains unanswered.

The scope of civilian collateral relief to the convicted military servicemember primarily depends on the scope and application of applicable federal statute.[16]

It is important to note that military defense counsel may be prohibited from seeking civilian collateral relief for their clients.[17]

---

[9] *See, e.g.*, O'Callahan v. Parker, 395 U.S. 258 (1969).

[10] Now the United States Claims Court. *See above* note 33.

[11] U.C.M.J. art. 67a(a); 28 U.S.C. § 1259; Military Justice Act of 1983, Pub. L. No. 98-209, 97 Stat. 1393, 1406. *See generally* Chapter 25.

[12] Limitations on the Supreme Court's certiorari power under Article 67 are such, however, that significant categories of cases may reach the Court only via civilian collateral relief. Notwithstanding this, it seems unlikely that the collateral attack route will be necessary as a route for important legal issues. One would assume that most, if not all, issues can be presented by cases in which certiorari may lie.

[13] 19 Cl. Ct. 635 (1990).

[14] S. Rep. No. 53, 98th Cong., 1st Sess. (1983); H.R. Rep. NO. 549, 98th Cong., 1st Sess. (1983); *The Military Justice Act of 1982: Hearings on S. 2521 Before the Subcomm. on Manpower and Personnel of the Senate Comm. on Armed Services*, 97th Cong., 2d Sess. (1982).

[15] *Mathias*, 19 Cl. Ct. at 641.

[16] Although the Constitution prohibits suspension of the "Privilege of the Writ of Habeas Corpus" except in cases of "Rebellion or Invasion" (U.S. Const. art. I, § 9), it fails to supply further details of its implementation.

[17] *See* Section 5-14.00.

(Rel.3—1/07　Pub.62410)

§ 26-12.00   The Historical Evolution of Civilian Collateral Attack

In his thorough and well written article, *Civilian Courts and the Military Justice System: Collateral Review of Courts-Martial*,[18] Major Richard Rosen reviewed and analyzed the history of civilian review of courts-martial. In 1879, in *Ex parte Reed*,[19] the Supreme Court held that so long as a court-martial "had jurisdiction over the person and the case, its proceedings cannot be collaterally impeached for any mere error or irregularity."[20] During the post-Civil War period[21] The Supreme Court extended the limited review principles articulated in *Reed* to bank pay claims in the Court of Claims.[22] Similarly, in 1886, relying on *Grant v. Gould*,[23] the Court held that writs of prohibition to enjoin the proceedings of courts-martial were "never to be issued unless it clearly appear[ed] that the . . . court [was] about to exceed its jurisdiction."[24] Convicted servicemembers could attack subject-matter jurisdiction, in-personam jurisdiction, compliance with the statutory requirements for creating a court-martial, and the legality of the adjudged and approved sentence. "With the onset of World War II, some lower federal courts began broadening the issues cognizable in collateral challenges to include constitutional claims."[25]

In 1953, a plurality of the Supreme Court decided the "watershed"[26] case of *Burns v. Wilson*,[27] announcing that "it is not the duty of the civil courts to simply

---

[18] 108 Mil. L. Rev. 5 (1985) [hereinafter cited as Rosen]. Virtually the entirety of this subsection is taken from Major Rosen's article, and the authors gratefully acknowledge the kind permission of Major Rosen to quote and paraphrase his article so extensively.

Older articles addressing collateral relief include: Strassburg, *Civilian Judicial Review of Military Criminal Justice*, 66 Mil. L. Rev. 1 (1974); Case note, *Judicial Review — Abstention — Federal Court Abstains from Pre-trial Jurisdictional Attack on Military Courts-Martial — Sedivy v. Richardson, 485 F.2d 1135 (3d Cir. 1973)*, 7 Creighton L. Rev. 386 (1974); Weckstein, *Federal Court Review of Courts-Martial Proceedings: A Delicate Balance of Individual Rights and Military Responsibilities*, 54 Mil. L. Rev. 1 (1971); Burris & Jones, *Civilian Courts and Courts-Martial — The Civilian Attorney's Perspective*, 10 AM. Crim. L. Rev. 139 (1971); Sherman, *Judicial Review of Military Determinations and the Exhaustion of Remedies Requirement*, 55 Va. L. Rev. 483 (1969); Note, *Civilian Court Review of Court-Martial Adjudications*, 69 Colum. L. Rev. 1259 (1969).

[19] 100 U.S. 13 (1879).

[20] 100 U.S. 23 (1879).

[21] Rosen, *above* note 18, at 30.

[22] Keyes v. United States, 109 U.S. 336, 340 (1883), *aff'g* 15 Ct. Cl. 532 (1879).

[23] 126 Eng. Rep. 434 (C.P. 1792).

[24] Smith v. Whitney, 116 U.S. 167, 176 (1886).

[25] Rosen, *above* note 18, at 37–38 (footnote omitted). "This expansion, although influenced by such factors as the rapid increase in the number of courts-martial during the war and a concomitant growth in dissatisfaction with the military justice system, was principally in response to the parallel enlargement of collateral review in the civilian sector." Rosen, *above* note 18, at 37–38. (footnotes omitted).

[26] Rosen, *above* note 18, at 50.

[27] 346 U.S. 137 (1953).

(Rel.3—1/07 Pub.62410)

repeat that process. . . . . It is the limited function of the civil courts to determine whether the military has given fair consideration to each of these claims."[28] Given the votes of justices who would have supported an even more permissive test, the literal language of the Court in *Burns* gave rise to the "full and fair consideration" test. Absent full and fair consideration, a civilian federal court could review the conviction; otherwise, collateral review would be barred. Major Rosen writes:

> *Burns* was greeted with confusion. While most courts had little difficulty in applying the "full and fair" consideration test to the factual determination of military courts, many chafed at having to acquiesce in the military's resolution of legal issues. . . . In essence, the courts could not agree on what their responsibilities were under the *Burns* standard of review. The result was a divergence in the approaches taken by the various lower federal courts; this division has yet to be rectified by the Supreme Court. Except for [the] Court's decision in *United States v. Augenblick*,[29] in which it held that collateral review of courts-martial is limited to issues of constitutional dimension, the Supreme Court has given little guidance in this area. . . .[30]

> [S]ince *Burns*, the federal courts have been unable to agree on a uniform scope of collateral review of military convictions. Indeed, it is sometimes difficult to reconcile the various standards applied within individual courts. Although generalizations are dangerous, the approaches taken by the federal courts roughly fall into four broad categories.

> First, several early courts, finding no apparent constitutional infirmities, expressly avoided reaching the issue of the proper scope of review under *Burns*. Second, in what was the prevailing view until about 1970, many federal courts strictly applied the apparent meaning of the *Burns* test and refused to review either the factual or legal merits of constitutional claims litigated in the military courts. . . .

> Third, some courts, notably the Court of Claims, and now the Court of Appeals for the Federal Circuit, use a fact-law dichotomy in applying *Burns*. The courts will not review factual issues "fully and fairly" considered by the military, but will review legal determinations de novo. . . .

---

[28] 346 U.S. at 144 (1953).

[29] 393 U.S. 348 (1969).

[30] *See* Rosen, *above* note 18, at 56 (footnote omitted). Major Rosen adds:

It is somewhat puzzling why the federal courts should have experienced so much confusion over the meaning of *Burns*. The *Burns* standard of "full and fair" consideration was not a new concept. It did not appreciably differ from the standard applied by the federal courts in state habeas proceedings from the time of the Supreme Court's decisions in *Frank* and *Moore* to its decision in *Brown v. Allen*. Thus, for nearly 40 years the federal courts had applied a similar standard of review in civilian habeas cases.

See Rosen, *above* note 18, at 56.

(Rel.3—1/07 Pub.62410)

Finally, most courts now have either developed their own standards for collateral review of constitutional claims or simply review such claims without any apparent qualification. In these cases, the courts either cite and distinguish Burns or, increasingly, ignore it all together. . . .

Generally, most courts will now conduct a de novo review of constitutional claims in collateral proceedings without considering the prior determinations of the military courts. Some structure their constitutional analysis to the unique requirements of the military or, on occasion, give deference to constitutional standards developed by the military courts. Other courts apply their own constitutional views to the cases. Moreover, while many courts limit their review to legal, as opposed to factual, issues involving constitutional questions, an increasing number reweigh the evidence adduced in the court-martial proceedings, or conduct their own hearings, and second-guess the military tribunals in their factual determinations. Finally, few, if any, of these courts have acknowledged any continued validity in the *Burns* decision.[31]

Major Rosen concluded that, as of 1985, "[t]here exists a relative state of anarchy in the relations between the federal civilian and military judiciary."[32] That state of "anarchy" continues.

§ 26-20.00   THE CLAIMS COURT

Jurisdiction is vested in the United States Claims Court[33] "to render judgment upon any claim against the United States founded either upon the Constitution, or any Act of Congress or any regulation of an executive department."

(a)(1) The United States Claims Court shall have jurisdiction to render judgment upon any claim against the United States founded either upon the Constitution, or any Act of Congress or any regulation of an executive department, or upon any express or implied contract with the United States, or for liquidated or unliquidated damages in cases not sounding in tort. . . . (2) To provide an entire remedy and to complete the relief afforded by the judgment, the court may, as an incident of and collateral to any such judgment, issue orders directing restoration to office or position, placement in appropriate duty or retirement status, and correction of applicable records, and such orders may be issued to any appropriate official of the United States. In any case within its jurisdiction, the court shall have the power to remand appropriate matters to any administrative or executive body or official with such direction as it may deem proper and just. The "claim" must be for money owed by the government.[34]

---

[31] *See* Rosen, *above* at 59–60 (footnotes omitted).

[32] *See* Rosen, *above* at 88.

[33] Formerly the Court of Claims. *See* The Federal Courts Improvement Act of 1982, Pub. L. No. 97-164, 96 Stat. 25.

[34] 28 U.S.C. § 1491.

(Rel.3—1/07   Pub.62410)

In order to attack a conviction in the Claims Court, an accused will sue for the pay and allowances to which he or she would have been entitled absent the conviction. If the court has jurisdiction, it may invalidate a conviction.

In *United States v. Augenblick*,[35] the Supreme Court, applying its *Burns v. Wilson* "full and fair consideration" test,[36] reversed a decision by the Court of Claims granting relief to a convicted servicemember, stating:

> But apart from trials conducted in violation of express constitutional mandates, a constitutionally unfair trial takes place only where the barriers and safeguards are so relaxed or forgotten . . . that the proceeding is more a spectacle . . . or trial by ordeal . . . than a disciplined contest.

Subsequently, in 1983 the United States Court of Appeals for the Federal Circuit,[37] in *Bowling v. United States*,[38] stated that the lower court had

> correctly held that judgments by courts-martial, although not subject to direct review by federal civil courts, may nevertheless be subject to narrow collateral attack in such courts on constitutional grounds if the action is otherwise within a court's jurisdiction. . . . However, the constitutional claims made must be serious ones to support an exception to the rule of finality. They must demonstrate convincingly that in the court-martial proceedings there has been such a deprivation of fundamental fairness as to impair due process. . . . Our own precedents hold that questions of fact resolved by military courts cannot be collaterally attacked. . . . This court will not reweigh the evidence presented at plaintiff's court-martial in order that it might substitute its judgment for that of the military trial court.[39]

Accordingly, the Claims Court will entertain collateral attacks on courts-martial convictions alleging "significant" or "serious" constitutional errors, even if there has been "full and fair consideration" of those matters in the military courts.[40]

---

[35] 393 U.S. 348 (1969).

[36] *See above* note 27 and accompanying text.

[37] The appellate court for the Claims Court.

[38] 713 F.2d 1558 (Fed. Cir. 1983) (affirming the decision of the Claims Court dismissing Bowling's suit for back pay and reinstatement).

[39] 713 F.2d at 1561 (Fed. Cir. 1983).

[40] *See also* Cooper v. United States, 20 Cl. Ct. 770 (1990); Matias v. United States, 19 Cl. Ct. 635, 639 (1990); Refre v. United States, 11 Cl. Ct. 81 (1986), *aff'd*, 833 F.2d 1022 (Fed. Cir. 1987), *cert. denied*, 486 U.S. 1011 (1988). In *Cooper*, however, the court wrote:

> Even when properly hearing a collateral attack on a court-martial conviction, the scope of renew for the Claims Court is exceedingly narrow. Military tribunals must be accorded reasonable scope for the exercise of judgment. . . . Finally, this court notes that in its review, it must accord a particularly high level of deference to the military judicial system. As the Supreme Court noted in *Burns*, "[m]ilitary law . . . is a jurisprudence which exists separate and apart from the law which governs in our federal judicial establishment." Congress, and not the judiciary, is charged with the responsibility of striking the correct balance between the rights of service members and the "overriding demands of discipline and duty" required in the armed services.

20 Cl. Ct. at 774.

§ 26-30.00 HABEAS CORPUS

§ 26-31.00 In General

The statutory authority for habeas corpus relief for military accused is 28 U.S.C. § 2241, which provides in relevant part:

(a) Writs of habeas corpus may be granted by the Supreme Court, any justice thereof, the district courts and any circuit judge within their respective jurisdictions. . . .

(c) The writ of habeas corpus shall not extend to a prisoner unless —

(1) He is in custody under or by color of the authority of the United States or is committed for trial before some court thereof; or

(2) He is in custody for an act done or omitted in pursuance of an Act of Congress, or an order, process, judgment or decree of a court or judge of the United States; or

(3) He is in custody in violation of the Constitution or laws or treaties of the United States.

Because a servicemember convicted by court-martial is clearly convicted pursuant to an "Act of Congress," the Uniform Code of Military Justice, the primary jurisdictional requirement for habeas relief[41] is that the servicemember be in "custody." If custody exists, the petitioner may also have to exhaust all applicable military remedies[42] and must not have "waived" the error he or she asserts.[43]

§ 26-32.00 Custody

§ 26-32.10 Generally

An applicant for federal habeas relief must be "in custody" when the petition for habeas relief is filed or the court will lack jurisdiction to hear the petition.[44]

---

[41] For comprehensive treatment of the law of habeas corpus, *see, e.g.*, J. Liebman, Federal Habeas Corpus Practice and Procedure (1988); D. Wilkes, Federal and State Post Conviction Remedies and Relief (1987); L. Yackle, Postconviction Remedies (1981). *See also* Y. Kamisar, W. Lafave & J. Israel, Modern Criminal Procedure ch. 28 (7th ed. 1990).

[42] *See* Section 26-33.00.

[43] *See* Section 26-34.00.

[44] 28 U.S.C. § 2241(c). *See, e.g.*, Escobedo v. Estelle, 655 F.2d 613, 615 n.5 (5th Cir. 1981) (custody is statutory prerequisite for subject-matter jurisdiction in federal habeas corpus); Bowman v. Wilson, 514 F. Supp. 403 (E.D. Pa. 1981) (custody goes to subject-matter jurisdiction), *rev'd on other grounds*, 672 F.2d 1145 (3d Cir. 1982). Even if there were no statutory requirement of custody, the historical requirement thereof probably would be in effect. L. Yackle, Postconviction Remedies 181–82 (1980) [hereinafter cited as Yackle].

Once the district court has jurisdiction, that jurisdiction is not defeated by the unconditional release of the petitioner prior to completion of the habeas proceedings. Carafas v. LaVallee, 391 U.S. 234, 238 (1968).

(Rel.3—1/07 Pub.62410)

The prerequisite not only identifies persons who may need postconviction relief, it also balances the competing individual and societal interests present in collateral proceedings.[45] The burdens imposed on the individual must be sufficiently great to outweigh considerations of comity and finality of judgments[46] and to warrant extraordinary relief.

§ 26-32.20 What Constitutes Custody

Custody encompasses a variety of restraints. The paradigmatic custodial situation is that of a petitioner who is incarcerated when the habeas petition is filed. Beyond this textbook scenario, some problems exist in defining custody. The Supreme Court has made clear that the use of habeas relief is not restricted to situations in which the applicant is in actual, physical custody.[47] A habeas applicant must show, however, "something more than moral restraint," although generalizations referring to "restraints not shared by the public generally"[48] should not be taken literally.[49] Such phrases simply reflect the notion that custody includes more than mere physical detention in jail or prison.

It is clear that a habeas petitioner is in custody when he or she is subject to restraints incident to bail or personal recognizance,[50] a suspended sentence,[51] probation,[52] parole,[53] or consecutive sentences.[54] While there is some division among lower courts, the weight of authority holds that a petitioner subject only to the payment of a fine is not in custody.[55] The petitioner in this instance may

---

[45] Yackle, *above* note 41, at 177.

[46] Thus, habeas relief is invariably denied when the petitioner complains only of a fine with no possibility of detention. *See* Section 26-22.20.

[47] Justices of Boston Municipal Court v. Lydon, 466 U.S. 294, 300 (1984) (quoting Jones v. Cunningham, 371 U.S. 236, 239 (1963)). Wales v. Whitney, 114 U.S. 564, 571 (1885) (naval officer ordered to remain in District of Columbia pending court-martial was not in custody so as to invoke federal habeas jurisdiction). *See* Note, *Developments in the Law — Federal Habeas Corpus*, 83 Harv. L. Rev. 1038, 1073 n.8 (1970) [hereinafter cited as *Developments*].

[48] Jones v. Cunningham, 371 U.S. 236, 240 (1963).

[49] *Developments, above* note 47, at 1076–77.

[50] Justices of Boston Municipal Court v. Lydon, 466 U.S. at 301. *See also* Hensley v. Municipal Court, 411 U.S. 345 (1973). This includes pretrial release (Oliphant v. Schlie, 544 F.2d 1007 (9th Cir. 1976), *rev'd other grounds*, 435 U.S. 191 (1978)) and release pending appeal. United States *ex rel.* Wojtycha v. Hopkins, 517 F.2d 420 (3d Cir. 1975)).

[51] Walker v. North Carolina, 372 F.2d 129 (4th Cir. 1967) (per curiam). *See* Katz v. King, 627 F.2d 568 (1st Cir. 1980).

[52] Cervantes v. Walker, 589 F.2d 424 (9th Cir. 1978); Drollinger v. Milligan, 552 F.2d 1220 (7th Cir. 1977).

[53] Jones v. Cunningham, 371 U.S. 236 (1963). *See* Martineau v. Perrin, 601 F.2d 1201 (1st Cir. 1979) (suggesting paroled prisoner is in custody even if none of usual parole conditions are imposed).

[54] Peyton v. Rowe, 391 U.S. 54 (1968).

[55] *Compare* Thistlethwaite v. New York, 497 F.2d 339 (2d Cir. 1974) (in custody) (dictum) *with*

suffer no present burden severe enough to outweigh the considerations of comity and finality of criminal judgments that habeas review contemplates.[56] Similarly, a habeas petitioner is not in custody if, at the time the petition is filed, he has completed his sentence and is not restrained by parole conditions.[57] Habeas applicants who die[58] or escape[59] are not in custody.

Custody situations involving military personnel tend to follow the general principles established for collateral attack of civilian criminal convictions. Personnel who are absent without leave and detained by civilian authorities pending transfer to military authorities are in custody.[60] A military person being held for transfer to a foreign nation for trial pursuant to an executive agreement or treaty is in custody.[61] Someone awaiting court-martial[62] or released on probation[63] is also in custody. Though the petitioner must be in custody when the petition for habeas relief is filed,[64] the petitioner's transfer from the district in which the habeas petition was properly filed does not defeat jurisdiction.[65]

Hanson v. Circuit Court, 591 F.2d 404 (7th Cir. 1979) (collecting cases; not in custody) *and* Wright v. Bailey, 544 F.2d 737 (4th Cir. 1976) (same). Custody exists, however, if the petitioner could be imprisoned for failing to pay the fine. *Cf.* Spring v. Caldwell, 692 F.2d 994 (5th Cir. 1982) (arrest warrant issued to enforce payment of fine insufficient to yield custody); *Wright, above* (no custody where sentence did not allow for incarceration for refusal to pay fine).

[56] Yackle, *above* note 44, at 187. *See* Pueschel v. Leuba, 383 F. Supp. 576 (D. Conn. 1974).

[57] Yackle, *above* note 44, at 187. *See Developments, above* note 47, at 1076–78.

[58] Dove v. United States, 423 U.S. 325 (1976). *See In re* Kravitz, 504 F. Supp. 43 (M.D. Pa. 1980) (mootness).

[59] Gonzales v. Stover, 575 F.2d 827 (10th Cir. 1978). *See also* Lewis v. Delaware State Hosp., 490 F. Supp. 177 (D. Del. 1980) (escapee remains in custody because of threat of confinement on recapture; petition may be dismissed at end of 30-day stay if petitioner still at large). The courts appear to be implicitly using the equitable doctrine of "clean hands." Estelle v. Dorrough, 420 U.S. 534 (1975), *on remand*, 512 F.2d 1061 (5th Cir. 1975) (direct appellate review of conviction); Molinaro v. New Jersey, 396 U.S. 365, 366 (1970) (per curiam) (violation of bail resulting in flight from jurisdiction).

[60] United States *ex rel.* Crane v. Laird, 315 F. Supp. 837 (D. Ore. 1970). However, a person who is absent without leave is, by analogy to an escaped prisoner, not in custody. United States *ex rel.* Rudick v. Laird, 412 F.2d 16 (2d Cir. 1969).

[61] Williams v. Rogers, 449 F.2d 513 (8th Cir. 1971) (trial in foreign country represents likelihood of future confinement; petitioner being held for transfer is subject to more than normal restraints incident to military life).

[62] McCahill v. Eason, 361 F. Supp. 588 (N.D. Fla. 1973), *vacated and remanded without opinion*, 498 F.2d 910 (5th Cir. 1974).

[63] Lebron v. Secretary of the Air Force, 392 F. Supp. 219 (S.D.N.Y.), *aff'd mem.*, 535 F.2d 1242 (2d Cir. 1975).

[64] *See* Wishmeyer v. Bolton, 361 F. Supp. 629 (N.D. Fla. 1973), *vacated without opinion on other grounds*, 498 F.2d 911 (5th Cir. 1974), *rev'd without opinion on other grounds*, 514 F.2d 1071 (5th Cir. 1975).

[65] Taylor v. Chaffee, 327 F. Supp. 1131 (C.D. Cal. 1971); Gregory v. Laird, 326 F. Supp. 704 (S.D. Cal. 1971).

(Rel.3—1/07 Pub.62410)

As in civilian cases, a military prisoner who has escaped is not in custody.[66] Finally, a person convicted by court-martial and discharged from the service but not imprisoned is not in custody and cannot petition for habeas relief.[67]

§ 26-32.30   Who Is a Custodian

Traditionally, the habeas jurisdiction of federal courts was limited to prisoners who were physically within the territorial jurisdiction of the court.[68] Such approach emphasized the risk and inconvenience of transporting a prisoner to a distant forum.[69] This rule presented no problem in the vast majority of cases. Prisoners challenged convictions by filing applications for habeas relief in the federal judicial district in which they were confined.

As to persons confined overseas, and therefore beyond the jurisdiction of any federal court, the Supreme Court implicitly held in a series of cases that such a person could seek habeas relief in the federal courts in the District of Columbia.[70] But as to persons confined in one state and challenging a conviction rendered in another, the law was confused.[71] The Supreme Court, faced with a situation where no federal court would hear the prisoner's habeas claims, reinterpreted the jurisdictional requirement of the habeas statutes. In *Braden v. 30th Judicial Circuit Court*,[72] the Court determined that a writ of habeas corpus acts not upon the prisoner, but upon the person holding the prisoner in allegedly unlawful custody.[73] The habeas statutes thus require jurisdiction over the custodian, not the habeas petitioner. As long as the custodian can be reached by service of process, the district court has jurisdiction. After *Braden*, jurisdiction

---

[66] United States *ex rel.* Bailey v. Commanding Officer, Office of Provost Marshall, 496 F.2d 324 (1st Cir. 1974); United States *ex rel.* Clapper v. Veth, 320 F. Supp. 1398 (E.D. Pa. 1970).

[67] United States v. Augenblick, 393 U.S. 348 (1969). A servicemember in transit to a new duty station is not in custody in a federal judicial district through which he or she is passing and in which he or she is on leave. Piland v. Eidson, 477 F.2d 1148 (9th Cir. 1973); Carney v. Secretary of Defense, 462 F.2d 606 (1st Cir. 1972); Jarrett v. Resor, 426 F.2d 213 (9th Cir. 1970); Perez Jimenez v. Laird, 325 F. Supp. 457 (D.P.R. 1971) (reserve member); Morales Crespo v. Perrin, 309 F. Supp. 203 (D.P.R. 1970). *See* Morales v. Obarski, 337 F. Supp. 368 (D.P.R. 1971). *But see* United States *ex rel.* Lohmeyer v. Laird, 318 F. Supp. 94 (D. Md. 1970).

[68] Ahrens v. Clark, 335 U.S. 188 (1948). *See* 28 U.S.C. § 2241(a) (1988).

[69] *Ahrens,* 335 U.S. at 191.

[70] *Ex parte* Hayes, 414 U.S. 1327 (1973) (Douglas, J.) (opinion in chambers) (soldier in Germany invoking Court's original habeas jurisdiction); Burns v. Wilson, 346 U.S. 137, *reh'g denied,* 346 U.S. 844, 851–52 (1953) (Frankfurter, J., dissenting). *Cf.* United States *ex rel.* Toth v. Quarles, 350 U.S. 11 (1955); Hirota v. MacArthur, 338 U.S. 197, 199 (1948) (Douglas, J., concurring); Johnson v. Eisentrager, 339 U.S. 763 (1950).

[71] Yackle, *above* note 41, at 196–97.

[72] 410 U.S. 484 (1973).

[73] 410 U.S. at 494–95 (1973).

lies in the district where the petitioner is physically located or in the district where "a custodian responsible for the confinement is present."[74]

In the usual situation involving military prisoners, the custodian will be the commanding officer of the correctional facility. Not all military cases are so easily resolved. More problematic are those involving prisoners held overseas, personnel in transit, or personnel surrendering after being absent without leave. The general rule is that established in *Schlanger v. Seamans*:[75] the proper respondent to a habeas petition (*i.e.*, the petitioner's custodian) is a military officer in the petitioner's chain of command.[76] The custodian need not be the person with ultimate administrative authority over the petitioner.[77] In accord with the rationale of *Braden*, only the custodian must be within the federal court's jurisdiction.[78]

§ 26-32.40 Prematurity

Traditionally, habeas relief would be denied in a challenge to a future sentence if awarding the relief would not bring about the petitioner's prompt release. In *Peyton v. Rowe*,[79] the Supreme Court ended the prematurity doctrine. The Court reasoned that a prisoner serving the first of two or more consecutive sentences imposed by the same sovereign was, in effect, under an aggregate term encompassing the future and present sentences. *Braden v. 30th Judicial Circuit Court*[80]

---

[74] McCoy v. United States Bd. of Parole, 537 F.2d 962, 964 (8th Cir. 1976). *See* Shelton v. Taylor, 550 F.2d 98 (2d Cir. 1977). The petition may be transferred to a more convenient forum (i.e., where the records and witnesses are located). *See* 28 U.S.C. § 1404(a); Meyer & Yackle, *Collateral Challenges to Criminal Conviction*, 1 Kan. L. Rev. 259, 337 (1973).

[75] 401 U.S. 487 (1971). The petitioner's official duty station was an air force base in Georgia. However, he had been given temporary leave to attend school in Arizona at his own expense. The habeas petition named as respondents the service Secretary, the commander of the base in Georgia, and the Air Force ROTC commander at the school.

[76] *Ex parte* Hayes, 414 U.S. 1327 (1973) (Douglas, J.) (opinion in chambers); Dillon v. Chandler, 452 F.2d 1081 (9th Cir. 1971); Meck v. Commanding Officer, Valley Forge Gen. Hosp., 452 F.2d 758 (3d Cir. 1971); Kinnell v. Warner, 356 F. Supp. 779 (D. Hawaii 1973). *See also* Miller v. Laird, 352 F. Supp. 1037 (W.D. Tex. 1972), *aff'd*, 474 F.2d 999 (5th Cir. 1973); Schmidt v. Laird, 328 F. Supp. 1009 (E.D.N.C. 1971).

[77] *Kinnell*, 356 F. Supp. at 782.

[78] 356 F. Supp. at 782. *See Ex parte* Hayes, 414 U.S. 1327 (1973) (Douglas, J.) (opinion in chambers); Schlanger v. Seamans, 401 U.S. 487 (1971). *But see* Smith v. Campbell, 450 F.2d 829, 831 (9th Cir. 1971); Meck v. Commanding Officer, Valley Forge Gen. Hosp., 452 F.2d 758, 761 (3d Cir. 1971) (court relies on Ahrens v. Clark, 335 U.S. 188 (1948); analysis is questionable after Braden v. 30th Judicial Circuit Court, 410 U.S. 484 (1973)). Venue follows jurisdiction in the context of habeas corpus, venue lying where the custodian is located. The venue provision usually governing suits against federal officials (28 U.S.C. § 1391(e)) is inapplicable to habeas corpus. Schlanger v. Seamans, 401 U.S. 487, 490 n.4 (1971). *Cf.* Jarrett v. Resor, 426 F.2d 213 (9th Cir. 1970); United States *ex rel.* Rudick v. Laird, 412 F.2d 16 (2d Cir. 1969).

[79] 391 U.S. 54 (1968). *See* Walker v. Wainwright, 390 U.S. 335 (1968).

[80] 410 U.S. 484 (1973).

(Rel.3—1/07 Pub.62410)

resolved the question of what happens when a petitioner serving a sentence in one jurisdiction faces a future sentence, as evidenced by a detainer, in another jurisdiction. The Court held that the warden of the state with physical custody of the petitioner was the agent of the state that had issued the detainer. *Peyton*, then, was equally applicable.[81]

Peyton and *Braden* are easily justified on policy grounds. Postponing a collateral challenge creates the risk of prejudice to the petitioner because of failing memories, death of key witnesses, and other problems caused by stale proceedings. In addition, delay robs the applicant of the opportunity to vacate the sentence or conviction before actually serving it.[82]

§ 26-32.50   Concurrent-Sentence Doctrine

Related to prematurity is the concurrent-sentence doctrine. Under this theory, a challenge to one of several sentences being served concurrently need not be heard on the merits. The doctrine can be traced to English[83] and early American sources.[84] Its initial use was confined to direct appellate review of criminal convictions. The rule was once seen both as one of convenience and judicial economy,[85] and as one mandated by the case and controversy requirement of Article III of the Constitution.[86] The Supreme Court, in *Benton v. Maryland*,[87] though, rejected the constitutional justification for the rule, determining that the collateral consequences of a conviction met the Article III demand for a case or controversy. Thus, to the extent that the doctrine survives, it is only a device of judicial economy to be applied at the court's discretion.[88]

Applying the concurrent-sentence doctrine to collateral attack is natural. Just as under the prematurity doctrine,[89] the merits of the case need not be reached

---

[81] 410 U.S. at 489 n.4 (1973). The Court reserved the question whether the result would be different if no detainer had been filed. Must the custodian have some nexus with the second jurisdiction? Arguably, the presence of a detainer should not be important. Yackle, *above* note 41, at 190.

[82] Yackle, *above* note 41, at 188–89. Since consecutive sentences, as such, are not available in the military, the prematurity doctrine is of limited application. However, there are some instances in which consecutive sentences are possible. *See* U.C.M.J., art. 14, 10 U.S.C. § 814; MCM, 1969 (rev. ed.) ¶¶ 97*b*, 131*d*, 215*c*.

[83] Grant v. Astle, 99 Eng. Rep. 459 (K.B. 1781); Peake v. Oldham, 98 Eng. Rep. 1083 (K.B. 1775).

[84] Locke v. United States, 11 U.S. (7 Cranch) 339 (1813).

[85] Hirabayashi v. United States, 320 U.S. 81 (1943). *See* Roviaro v. United States, 353 U.S. 53, 59 n.6 (1957); Putnam v. United States, 162 U.S. 687 (1896).

[86] If the petitioner was left serving a concurrent sentence of equal length, there was no case or controversy. *See* Barenblatt v. United States, 360 U.S. 109, 115 (1959).

[87] 395 U.S. 784 (1969).

[88] 395 U.S. at 791 (1969). *See* Andresen v. Maryland, 427 U.S. 463, 469 n.4 (1976); Barnes v. United States, 412 U.S. 837, 841 (1973); United States v. Grimes, 641 F.2d 96, 97 n.2 (3d Cir. 1981); United States v. Gray, 626 F.2d 494, 501–05 (5th Cir. 1980).

[89] Section 26-22.40.

because a favorable judgment would not entitle the petitioner to release.[90] The result here is easier to defend than the analogous situation under the prematurity doctrine: no further detention is possible, in the present or future, because of the sentence under attack. The Court in *Benton* seemed to recognize that distinction by suggesting that the argument for using the doctrine in habeas corpus might be stronger.[91] Lower courts have interpreted *Benton* as endorsing the doctrine's use in habeas corpus, and challenges to one of several concurrent sentences are routinely dismissed.[92]

Yet, most decisions state the rule in flexible terms, leaving its application to the court's discretion.[93] Dismissal of a petition on doctrinal grounds is reviewable only for abuse of discretion, the decision turning on the degree of prejudice to the petitioner because of the conviction being attacked.[94] Clearly, if one sentence is longer than another one being served concurrently, it can be challenged.[95] A petitioner who can show that the challenged conviction contributes to the severity of punishment can usually obtain review of the merits of his petition.[96] It is not enough, however, to claim that the other sentences may be overturned, leaving the petitioner restrained only by the challenged sentence. Such allegation is speculative and fails to meet the requisite standard of prejudice.[97]

Because courts-martial do not adjudge concurrent sentences, the concurrent-sentence doctrine, as such, would be inapplicable to military petitioners unless the petitioner was in custody as a result of multiple convictions resulting from military and civilian trials. A court-martial sentence is an aggregate result of all the specifications of which the accused was convicted. It is difficult to see how,

---

[90] Yackle, *above* note 41, at 191.

[91] Benton v. Maryland, 395 U.S. at 793 n.11.

[92] Vanetzian v. Hall, 562 F.2d 88 (1st Cir. 1977); Van Geldern v. Field, 498 F.2d 400 (9th Cir. 1974); United States *ex rel.* Weems v. Follette, 414 F.2d 417 (2d Cir. 1969). *See* United States v. Rapp, 642 F.2d 1120 (8th Cir. 1981); Calhoun v. Bordenkircher, 510 F. Supp. 1181 (N.D. W. Va. 1981). *But see* United States *ex rel.* Guy v. McCauley, 385 F. Supp. 193 (E.D. Wis. 1974). As with the prematurity doctrine, the concurrent-sentence doctrine has little application in the military. However, a prisoner remanded to the custody of civilian authorities under Article 14 for trial on civilian charges may be faced with a sentence running concurrent with the sentence imposed by a court-martial.

[93] *Weems*, 414 F.2d at 419.

[94] *Van Geldern*, 498 F.2d at 403. *See also* Dennis v. Hopper, 548 F.2d 589 (5th Cir. 1977) (inquiry is specific detriment to petitioner).

[95] Stepp v. Beto, 398 F.2d 814 (5th Cir. 1968).

[96] *See Van Geldern*, 498 F.2d at 403. *See generally* Note, *Habeas Corpus Relief and the Concurrent Sentence Doctrine*, 25 U. Miami L. Rev. 354 (1971). For example, the sentence can affect parole eligibility, custody status, and furlough privileges.

[97] *Van Geldern*, 498 F.2d at 403.

(Rel.3—1/07 Pub.62410)

in the average case, a court could find an error to have had no effect on the sentence even though it applied only to a single specification.[98]

§ 26-32.60   Mootness

The habeas applicant must present a case or controversy within the terms of Article III of the Constitution. Thus, when the petitioner is unconditionally released after the habeas petition is filed, but before the proceedings on the petition are completed, the court must determine if the case is moot under Article III.[99] In the context of habeas corpus, the current standard of mootness is governed by *Carafas v. LaVallee*:[100] when a prisoner files a habeas petition while in custody, his subsequent release is immaterial. The federal habeas court can exercise its power under Article III and grant relief as long as some legal consequences of the conviction exist after release, ensuring the prisoner's stake in the petition's outcome.[101]

Carafas does not mean that the collateral consequences of a conviction satisfy the custody requirement for federal habeas jurisdiction.[102] Carafas only means that federal habeas jurisdiction, once properly invoked, cannot be defeated by the prisoner's release prior to completion of the proceedings on the habeas petition.[103]

---

[98] It is possible, of course, to determine that conviction of one offense had no impact on sentence and was thus harmless. Conviction of spying (U.C.M.J. art. 106), for example, carries a mandatory sentence of death regardless of whether the accused has been convicted of other offenses. *See also* U.C.M.J. art. 118(1) & (4) (death or life imprisonment for murder). So long as such a conviction is lawful, concurrent conviction of another offense would appear irrelevant. More problematical is conviction of a serious offense coupled with a lesser offense such as absence without leave (unlawful absence), although the Courts of Military Review have often held errors associated with some, but not all, specifications to be harmless insofar as the resulting general sentence.

[99] The custody prerequisite is related to, but distinct from, mootness. *See* Escobedo v. Estelle, 655 F.2d 613, 615 n.5 (5th Cir. 1981). The custody requirement is imposed by history and statute while mootness stems from the Article III requirement that an actual controversy exists at all stages of review. In addition, custody is a stricter requirement than mootness, going initially to the issue of subject-matter jurisdiction. Yackle, *above* note 41, at 214–15.

[100] 391 U.S. 234 (1968). *See* Levy v. Parker, 396 U.S. 1204 (1969) (Douglas. J.).

[101] While *Carafas* limits the collateral consequences only to legal consequences, in light of the substantial restrictions existing after conviction, this limitation presents no problem. *See* Note, *The Collateral Consequences of a Criminal Conviction*, 23 Vand. L. Rev. 929 (1970). Social consequences stemming from a conviction do not meet the *Carafas* standard. Yackle, *above* note 41, at 220.

[102] Martineau v. Perrin, 601 F.2d 1201 (1st Cir. 1979); Harrison v. Indiana, 597 F.2d 115 (7th Cir. 1979). *See* Kravitz v. Pennsylvania, 546 F.2d 1100 (3d Cir. 1977); Harvey v. South Dakota, 526 F.2d 840 (8th Cir. 1975); *Developments, above* note 47, at 1077–78.

[103] *Carafas*, 391 U.S. at 238. *See* Gosa v. Mayden, 413 U.S. 665, 670 n.3 (1973). *Carafas* ensures that the usual delays in habeas proceedings do not frustrate the availability of habeas relief when challenging convictions the sentences for which have been served. *See* Kravitz v. Pennsylvania,

(Rel.3—1/07   Pub.62410)

Carafas, on its face, applies only to challenges to convictions. There is some indication that a different standard exists when only the sentence is being attacked. The Court noted first, in *Pollard v. United States*,[104] that collateral consequences follow convictions, and an attack only upon the sentence may have minimal effect.[105] Reaching the issue again in *North Carolina v. Rice*,[106] the Court wondered whether the same collateral consequences that prevent mootness in the usual habeas situation would come into play if the petitioner were successful in obtaining a retroactive change in his sentence.[107] Though *Rice* is rarely used in habeas cases, an unwary litigant may easily run afoul of it.

§ 26-33.00 Exhaustion of Military Remedies

§ 26-33.10 Generally

If habeas petitioners meet the initial prerequisite of custody, "they must next deal with a kaleidoscopic system of procedural rules known as the 'exhaustion doctrine.'"[108] The exhaustion rule concerns only "the appropriate exercise of power."[109] It is not a jurisdictional prerequisite to federal habeas review.[110] But like custody, exhaustion helps strike the balance between finality of criminal judgments and the preservation of federal constitutional rights. Similarly, exhaustion parallels other limits on federal equitable relief[111] and other policies of federal judicial economy.[112]

---

546 F.2d 1100 (3d Cir. 1977). A pardon, however, may moot the case. *Compare* Tornello v. Hudspeth, 318 U.S. 792 (1943) (denial of certiorari) (moot) *and* Bjerkan v. United States, 529 F.2d 125 (7th Cir. 1975) (motion under 28 U.S.C. § 2255 moot) *with* Watkins v. Thomas, 623 F.2d 387 (5th Cir. 1980) (not moot) *and* Robson v. United States, 526 F.2d 1145 (1st Cir. 1975) (not moot).

[104] 352 U.S. 354 (1957).

[105] 352 U.S. at 358 (1957).

[106] 404 U.S. at 244 (1971).

[107] 404 U.S. at 248 (1971). The decision is criticized by Yackle, *above* note 41, at 222.

[108] Yackle, *above* note 41, at 231.

[109] Bowen v. Johnston, 306 U.S. 19, 27 (1939). *See also* Granberry v. Greer, 481 U.S. 129, 134 (1987) ("In *Ex parte* Hawk, 321 U.S. 114, 117 (1944), this Court reiterated that country was the basis for the exhaustion doctrine. . . . In 1948, Congress codified the exhaustion doctrine in 28 U.S.C. § 2254, citing *Ex parte Hawk* as correctly stating the principle of exhaustion." (citation omitted)).

[110] Fay v. Noia, 372 U.S. 391, 419–20 (1963). Thus, the exhaustion requirement may be waived by the government. *E.g.*, Middendorf v. Henry, 425 U.S. 25, 29 n.6 (1976); Granberry v. Greer, 481 U.S. at 131. ("failure to exhaust state remedies does not deprive an appellate court of juries to consider the merits of a habeas corpus application" (citation omitted)).

[111] *See, e.g.*, Schlesinger v. Councilman, 420 U.S. 738 (1975); Parisi v. Davidson, 405 U.S. 34, 40 n.6 (1972).

[112] *See* Noyd v. Bond, 395 U.S. 683 (1969).

(Rel.3—1/07 Pub.62410)

Several rationales have been advanced for exhaustion. While usually placed in the context of federal habeas relief for state prisoners,[113] these justifications are equally applicable to federal habeas relief for military prisoners.[114] First, there are relative advantages to having military judges determine federal issues in a procedural context familiar only to military judges.[115] Such an arrangement also reduces the caseload in the federal courts, since resort to military remedies might render federal habeas relief unnecessary.[116] Prior adjudication may persuade a habeas petitioner that his claims are without merit or, at least, clarify the facts and issues (both legal and uniquely military issues) for more effective federal habeas review.[117]

By further analogy to federal habeas relief for state prisoners, exhaustion can be seen as preventing an insensitivity to federal constitutional law on the part of military judges preserving the orderly administration of military justice.[118] Most important in the military context is Congress' confidence that the military justice system "generally is adequate to and responsibly will perform its assigned task. . . . [I]t must be assumed that the military court system will vindicate servicemen's constitutional rights."[119] Thus, exhaustion of military remedies is arguably even more appropriate than exhaustion of state remedies.

§ 26-33.20　Meeting the Exhaustion Requirement

The issue of exhaustion of military remedies was not directly decided until the Supreme Court's decision in *Gusik v. Schilder.*[120] In *Gusik*, the Court held that a habeas petitioner must exhaust his military remedies, including a petition for a new trial,[121] before seeking federal habeas relief. Reasoning that exhaustion of military remedies serves the same purposes as exhaustion of state remedies, the Court expressly applied the exhaustion rules used for state prisoners.[122]

---

[113] 28 U.S.C. § 2254.

[114] *Development, above* note 47, at 1232.

[115] *Development, above* note 47, at 1232. *See* Rose v. Dickson, 327 F.2d 27, 28 (9th Cir. 1964); Comment, *Habeas Corpus — Effect of Supreme Court Change in Law on Exhaustion of State Remedies Requisite to Federal Habeas Corpus*, 113 U. Pa. L. Rev. 1303, 1304 (1965).

[116] *Developments, above* note 47, at 1232. *See* Goodloe v. Parratt, 605 F.2d 1041, 1048 (8th Cir. 1979); Kelman, *Federal Habeas Corpus as a Source of New Constitutional Requirements for State Criminal Procedure*, 28 OHIO ST. L.J. 46, 53 (1967).

[117] *Developments, above* note 47, at 1232. *See* Laubach, *Exhaustion of State Remedies as a Prerequisite to Federal Habeas Corpus: A Summary*, 1966-1971, 7 Gonzaga L. Rev. 34, 35 (1971).

[118] Yackle, *above* note 41, at 232.

[119] Schlesinger v. Councilman, 420 U.S. 738, 758 (1975). *See* Noyd v. Bond, 395 U.S. 683, 694 (1969).

[120] 340 U.S. 128 (1950).

[121] U.C.M.J. art. 73, 10 U.S.C. § 873.

[122] *Ex parte* Hawk, 321 U.S. 114, 116 (1944); Mooney v. Holohan, 294 U.S. 103, 115 (1935); 28 U.S.C. § 2254.

(Rel.3—1/07　Pub.62410)

Present case law mandates that all direct review available in the military be exhausted before federal habeas relief is sought.[123]

The availability of postconviction relief from the Court of Military Appeals[124] raises the issue of whether such relief must be sought in order to satisfy the exhaustion requirement. In the analogous situation involving state prisoners, state postconviction remedies must usually be exhausted if the highest state court to which the claim can be presented has not had an opportunity to reach the merits of the claim.[125] Thus, if the Court of Military Appeals has not ruled on the issue,

---

[123] Noyd v. Bond, 395 U.S. at 693 (dictum). Scott v. Schlesinger, 498 F.2d 1093 (5th Cir. 1974) (U.C.M.J. art. 66); United States ex rel. Berry v. Commanding General, Third Corps, 411 F.2d 822 (5th Cir. 1969) (U.C.M.J. art. 67); Gorko v. Commanding Officer, 314 F.2d 858 (10th Cir. 1963) (U.C.M.J. art. 67). Review under Article 69 is required when no other remedy is available. Compare Smith v. Secretary of the Navy, 392 F. Supp. 428 (W.D. Mo. 1974) (conviction not reviewed by Court of Military Review) with Betonie v. Sizemore, 369 F. Supp. 340 (M.D. Fla. 1973), aff'd in part, rev'd in part on other grounds, 496 F.2d 1001 (5th Cir. 1974) and Brown v. United States, 365 F. Supp. 328 (E.D. Pa. 1973), aff'd in part and remanded in part on other grounds, 508 F.2d 618 (3d Cir. 1974) (Article 69 review not required when Court of Military Review had reviewed conviction). Contra Cole v. Laird, 468 F.2d 829 (5th Cir. 1972). The defendant must also petition for a new trial under Article 73, even if the chances of the petition being granted are minimal. Gusik v. Schilder, 340 U.S. 128 (1950); Osborne v. Swope, 226 F.2d 908 (9th Cir. 1955). A new trial is available under Article 73 only for new evidence or fraud on the court-martial. E.g., United States v. Thomas, 11 M.J. 135 (C.M.A. 1981); United States v. Jophlin, 3 M.J. 858 (A.C.M.R. 1977). Federal habeas relief before trial is generally disfavored. E.g., Sedivy v. Richardson, 485 F.2d 1115 (3d Cir. 1973). See Schlesinger v. Councilman, 420 U.S. 738 (1975) (federal injunctive relief improper before court-martial when issue is whether offense is service-connected). But see Noyd, 396 U.S. at 696 n.8 (exhaustion is not required when personal jurisdiction is challenged; no special military expertise is needed and it is unfair to force petitioner to military trial when military jurisdiction is contested).

A habeas petition containing exhausted and unexhausted claims must be dismissed. Rose v. Lundy, 455 U.S. 509 (1982). The petitioner then has the option of either proceeding simultaneously with a new federal habeas petition containing the exhausted claims, exhausting his state remedies on the unexhausted claims, and filing a second habeas petition when the unexhausted claims are exhausted; or waiting until all claims are exhausted before refiling a federal habeas petition. If the first option is chosen, the subsequent federal habeas petition risks dismissal. 455 U.S. 519–22 (1982) (plurality opinion) (applying Rule 9(b) of Rules Governing Section 2254 cases). While Rose deals with a federal habeas petition by a state prisoner, it is probably applicable to military prisoners. See Rule 1(b) of Rules Governing Section 2254 Cases, Adv. Comm. Notes.

[124] E.g., Moore v. Akins, 30 M.J. 249 (C.M.A. 1990) (habeas granted); Unger v. Ziemniak, 27 M.J. 349 (C.M.A. 1989) (relief possible even when case could not be reviewed by military appellate courts); Levy v. Resor, 37 C.M.R. 399 (C.M.A. 1967) (habeas corpus and mandamus); United States v. Frischolz, 36 C.M.R. 306 (C.M.A. 1966) (coram nobis). Cases indicate that Courts of Military Review have similar powers. E.g., Dettinger v. United States, 7 M.J. 216 (C.M.A. 1979); Gragg v. United States, 10 M.J. 732 (N.C.M.R. 1980).

[125] Postconviction remedies must be exhausted if a prisoner fails to appeal or to raise federal claims on appeal. Goodloe v. Parratt, 605 F.2d 1041 (8th Cir. 1979); Callahan v. LeFevre, 605 F.2d 70 (2d Cir. 1979); Ralph v. Blackburn, 590 F.2d 1335 (5th Cir. 1979); Staten v. Alabama, 576 F.2d 654 (5th Cir. 1978). Similarly, exhaustion demands that postconviction relief be sought

(Rel.3—1/07 Pub.62410)

postconviction relief should be sought there.[126]

On the other hand, exhaustion of military postconviction remedies is not appropriate in all cases. In *Noyd v. Bond*,[127] the Supreme Court held that the petitioner had to seek the requested relief from the Court of Military Appeals before applying for federal habeas relief. The situation in *Noyd* was one ultimately subject to direct review by the Court of Military Appeals. In requiring exhaustion of military remedies, the Supreme Court noted that the Court of Military Appeals had jurisdiction to issue any necessary writ in the case, but suggested that the result might be different if the Court of Military Appeals could not have reviewed the case.[128] The implication of the Court's suggestion is clear: the Court of Military Appeals cannot grant postconviction relief in cases over which it has no review authority.[129] Such situations would include those in which the time for appeal has run, even though the case was originally reviewable,[130] and those in which review of factual findings is required.[131] Thus, exhaustion should not be required until it is clear that the Court of Military Appeals can grant the necessary relief in the case.[132]

---

if material facts were inadvertently omitted on direct review and those facts can now be presented. Picard v. Connor, 404 U.S. 270, 276 (1971). *See* Needel v. Scafati, 412 F.2d 761 (1st Cir. 1969). In the more common case, prisoners make claims that rest on allegations never made earlier and certainly not in the record on direct review, and consideration of the new issues in a postconviction proceeding is required. Zicarelli v. Gray, 543 F.2d 466 (3d Cir. 1976); Daniels v. Nelson, 453 F.2d 340 (9th Cir. 1972); Brown v. Crouse, 395 F.2d 755 (10th Cir. 1968). The effect of a change in law, occurring between the military courts' denial of relief and final judgment by a federal habeas court, may result in the petitioner being sent back to the military justice system for re-exhaustion. *See* YACKLE, *above* note 44, at 281–86 (describing the possible scenarios and the results). *But cf.* Owsley v. Peyton, 352 F.2d 804, 805 (4th Cir. 1965) (re-exhaustion not required when intervening federal court decision is by a lower court, since only Supreme Court decisions are binding on states). Appellate review of any postconviction proceeding is generally required (obviously, only if the initial results are unfavorable to the prisoner). YACKLE, *above* note 41, at 273–74.

[126] *Developments, above* note 47, at 1235. *See* Noyd v. Bond, 395 U.S. 683, 696 (1969).

[127] 395 U.S. 683 (1969).

[128] 395 U.S. at 695 n.7. (1969).

[129] *E.g.,* Hendrix v. Warden, 49 C.M.R. 146 (C.M.A. 1974); United States v. Bevilacqua, 39 C.M.R. 10 (C.M.A. 1968). *See* Robison v. Abbott, 49 C.M.R. 8 (C.M.A. 1974); U.C.M.J. arts. 66(b), 67(b), 10 U.S.C. §§ 866(b), 867(b).

[130] The Court of Military Appeals has asserted the power to grant relief in such cases. *See above* note 124.

[131] Article 67(d) restricts the Court's review to matters of law. The Court, however, has construed its jurisdiction to include matters of mixed law and fact, mislabeled questions of fact, factual determinations unsupported by substantial evidence, and factual findings when fundamental rights are involved. Note, *Civilian Court Review of Court-Martial Adjudications*, 69 Colum. L. Rev. 1259, 1264 (1969). *See also* Jackson v. Virginia, 443 U.S. 307 (1979).

[132] *Developments, above* note 47, at 1235 & n.136. *See* Yackle, *above* note 41, at 274–81. The Court of Military Appeals, though, is usually petitioned for relief before federal habeas relief is

(Rel.3—1/07 Pub.62410)

§ 26-33.30 Presentation of Claims

§ 26-33.31 Fair Identification of Claims

If exhaustion has any meaning, a prisoner must not only pursue military remedies, but must also present to the military courts essentially the same claims that would be presented to a federal habeas court.[133] A prisoner must present the substance of his claims in order to give the military courts a fair opportunity to consider them.[134] What constitutes a fair identification of a claim, though, is less than clear.[135] Arguably, close cases should be resolved in favor of the habeas petitioner.[136] At a minimum, each situation should be viewed in light of the purposes of the exhaustion doctrine.[137]

Exhaustion only requires that substantially equivalent claims be fairly raised. A decision on the merits is not required.[138] Where a court has not considered the claim[139] or has disposed of it on procedural grounds,[140] the exhaustion requirement is satisfied.

§ 26-33.32 Fair Presentation of Claims

Exhaustion requires that claims be presented in a posture allowing the military courts a fair opportunity to reach the merits.[141] If the issue is presented in a

---

sought. *Developments, above* note 47, at 1236 & nn. 189–93. Similarly, exhaustion of administrative remedies, specifically, review by a Board of Correction under 10 U.S.C. § 1552, should not be required. *See* Cole v. Laird, 468 F.2d 829 (5th Cir. 1972). The Board's review is analogous to an act of clemency and does not affect the validity of a court-martial. *Developments, above* note 47, at 1237 & n.197. In addition, the availability and effectiveness of relief is questionable. *Developments, above* note 47, at 1237 n.202.

[133] *See* Picard v. Connor, 404 U.S. 270, 276 (1971).

[134] *See* 404 U.S. at 276–78 (1971). The best source to determine if a claim was raised is the petitioner's appeal brief. If a fair reading of the brief reveals that the claim was identified so that the military courts could have reached the merits, the federal court may proceed. *See, e.g.,* Smith v. Digmon, 434 U.S. 332 (1978); Harkins v. Wyrick, 589 F.2d 387 (8th Cir. 1979); Rachel v. Bordenkircher, 590 F.2d 200 (6th Cir. 1978); Houston v. Estelle, 569 F.2d 372 (5th Cir. 1978); Blankenship v. Estelle, 545 F.2d 510 (5th Cir. 1977).

[135] Yackle, *above* note 41, at 252–56.

[136] Yackle, *above* note 41, at 256. *But see* Ray v. Howard, 486 F. Supp. 638 (E.D. Pa. 1980); Rivers v. Martin, 484 F. Supp. 162 (W.D. Va. 1980).

[137] Yackle, *above* note 41, at 256. *See* Section 26-31.00.

[138] DeCoster v. Madigan, 223 F.2d 906 (7th Cir. 1955). *See* Smith v. Digmon, 434 U.S. 332 (1978).

[139] Cronnon v. Alabama, 557 F.2d 472 (5th Cir. 1977), *later appeal,* 587 F.2d 246 (5th Cir.), *cert. denied,* 440 U.S. 974 (1979).

[140] Anders v. Turner, 379 F.2d 46 (4th Cir. 1967). Disposition on procedural grounds then raises the problem of waiver or procedural bypass. *See* Section 26-34.00.

[141] *See* Yackle, *above* note 41, at 258.

(Rel.3—1/07 Pub.62410)

procedural manner such that the court is justified in refusing to consider the issue, the prisoner may be required to pursue alternative avenues of relief that are still open.[142]

§ 26-34.00 Waiver

During the last forty years, the Supreme Court has sharply changed its definition of waiver. In 1963 the Court held that absent a "deliberate bypass," failure of a defendant to raise an issue at trial as required by applicable procedural rules did not waive the issue for habeas purposes.[143] However, in a series of cases beginning in 1973, the Court created the "cause and actual prejudice" standard.[144] Under this approach, a petitioner who failed to raise an issue at trial must demonstrate both adequate cause for the waiver *and* that actual prejudice resulted from the alleged error. The Court has been extraordinarily demanding in its application of adequate "cause" for failing to raise an issue at trial,[145] although it has recognized that an issue "so novel that its legal basis is not reasonably available to counsel" escapes the cause requirement.[146]

A defendant's "actual innocence" will excuse waiver. In *Sawyer v. Whitley*,[147] the Court held that before a petitioner in a capital case who is challenging the death penalty may bring "a successive, abusive, or defaulted federal habeas claim" on the grounds that he or she is "actually innocent," he or she "must show by clear and convincing evidence that but for a constitutional error, no reasonable

[142] *See, e.g.*, Pitchess v. Davis, 421 U.S. 482 (1975); Fay v. Noia, 372 U.S. 391, 434–35 (1963) (by implication); *Ex parte* Hawk, 321 U.S. 114 (1944); Smith v. Secretary of Navy, 392 F. Supp. 428 (W.D. Mo. 1974). *See generally* Yackle, *above* note 41, at 259–60.

[143] Fay v. Noia, 372 U.S. 391 (1963). The Court has abandoned the "deliberate bypass" standard in state cases. Overruling Townsend v. Sain, 372 U.S. 293 (1963), the Court held in *Keeney v. Tamayo-Reyes*, 504 U.S. 1 (1992), that a state prisoner's failure to develop material facts in state court waives any right to a further federal evidentiary (factual) hearing unless petitioner can demonstrate cause and prejudice. 372 U.S. at 328–29 (1963). In so doing, the Court justified its new requirement by claiming that it bolsters state factual determinations and is in accord with the policies furthered by the requirement for exhaustion of state remedies. Dissenting, Justice O'Connor claimed that *Keeney* changes "the law of habeas corpus in a fundamental way . . . ." 372 U.S. at 331 (1963). She sharply distinguished between whether a federal court will consider a habeas claim and whether an evidentiary hearing will be held once the court has decided to consider the claim.

[144] Smith v. Murray, 477 U.S. 527 (1986); Murray v. Carrier, 477 U.S. 478 (1986); Reed v. Ross, 468 U.S. 1 (1984); United States v. Frady, 456 U.S. 152 (1982); Engle v. Isaac, 456 U.S. 107 (1982); Wainwright v. Sykes, 433 U.S. 72 (1977); Francis v. Henderson, 425 U.S. 536 (1976); Davis v. United States, 411 U.S. 233 (1973).

[145] *See* Engle v. Isaac, 456 U.S. 107 (1982).

[146] Reed v. Ross, 468 U.S. 1, 16 (1984).

[147] 505 U.S. 333 (1992). Dissenting, Justices Stevens, Blackmun and O'Connor argued for a clearly erroneous standard.

juror would have found the petitioner eligible for the death penalty under the applicable state law."

Insofar as military cases are concerned, Major Rosen[148] has written:

[T]he federal courts should apply the stricter "cause and actual prejudice" test to issues petitioners fail to preserve in the military justice system. This assumption is compelled by the special deference the Supreme Court has shown the military courts in past decisions. . . . Indeed, the Tenth Circuit, in *Wolff v. United States*,[149] applied the "cause and prejudice" standard to a habeas petition challenging for the first time the form of immunity given a key prosecution witness at a court-martial.[150]

Both the Tenth[151] and Ninth[152] Circuits have applied the "cause and prejudice" requirements to an attempt to collaterally attack a court-martial conviction. The Ninth Circuit reasoned that the same reasons justifying application of the prerequisites to civilian state defendants apply to servicemembers, adding that "adoption of a waiver rule *more* strict than that enunciated in *Sykes* would erode to the vanishing point the limited jurisdiction federal courts do have to review courtsmartial for constitutional error."[153]

§ 26-35.00   "New" Rules

Just as the Supreme Court has narrowed habeas corpus via the "cause and prejudice" standard,[154] it has also limited the use of habeas petitions to apply "new" rules to cases already decided.[155] In *Saffle v. Parks*,[156] the Court wrote:

In *Teague*, we defined a new rule as a rule that "breaks new ground," "imposes a new obligation on the States or the Federal Government," or was not "*dictated*" by precedent existing at the time the defendant's conviction became final."[157]

If a "new" rule is involved, it will not be retroactive unless it comes within either of two exceptions:

[I]f the rule places a class of primary, private individual contact beyond the power of the criminal law-making authority to proscribe . . . or would

---

[148] *See* Rosen, *above* note 8.

[149] 737 F.2d 877 (10th Cir. 1984).

[150] Rosen, *above* note 8, at 79.

[151] Wolff v. United States, 737 F.2d 877, 879 (10th Cir.), *cert. denied*, 469 U.S. 1076 (1984).

[152] Davis v. Marsh, 876 F.2d 1446 (9th Cir. 1989) (suit for declaratory judgment, damages and order prohibiting sexual harassment).

[153] 876 F.2d at 1449 (emphasis in the original).

[154] *See* Section 26-34.00.

[155] Teague v. Lane, 489 U.S. 288 (1989) (plurality).

[156] 494 U.S. 484 (1990).

[157] 494 U.S. at 488 (1990) (quoting Teague v. Lane, 489 U.S. 288 (1989) (emphasis in original)).

(Rel.3—1/07   Pub.62410)

be a "watershed rule[s] of criminal procedure" implicating the fundamental fairness and accuracy of the criminal proceeding.[158]

[158] 494 U.S. at 494-95.